REFORMED
DOGMATICS

REFORMED DOGMATICS

ABRIDGED IN ONE VOLUME

HERMAN BAVINCK
JOHN BOLT, EDITOR

B
Baker Academic
a division of Baker Publishing Group
Grand Rapids, Michigan

Published by Baker Academic
a division of Baker Publishing Group
P.O. Box 6287, Grand Rapids, MI 49516-6287
www.bakeracademic.com

Printed in the United States of America

Library of Congress Cataloging-in-Publication Data
Bavinck, Herman, 1854–1921.
    [Gereformeerde dogmatiek. English]
    Reformed dogmatics / Herman Bavinck ; John Bolt, editor.
        p.   cm.
    "Abridged in one volume."
    Includes bibliographical references and index.
    ISBN 978-0-8010-3648-4
    1. Christelijke Gereformeerde Kerk (Netherlands)—Doctrines. 2. Reformed Church—Doctrines.
3. Theology, Doctrinal. I. Bolt, John, 1947– II. Title.
BX9474.3.B38 2011
230′.42—dc22   2010052237

Unless otherwise indicated, all Scripture quotations are from the New Revised Standard Version of the Bible, copyright © 1989, by the Division of Christian Education of the National Council of the Churches of Christ in the United States of America. Used by permission. All rights reserved.

To Eugene P. Heideman and Jan Veenhof,
pioneers in the Bavinck renaissance

Contents

EDITOR'S PREFACE

Herman Bavinck's *Reformed Dogmatics* is a classic. Taking on the project of preparing a one-volume "outline" of a four-volume magisterial work like Bavinck's is not something to be done lightly. Nearly three decades of close involvement with Bavinck's theology has given me a great respect for the man and his achievement, and this volume is intended to honor that respect fully. I accepted the publisher's request because Baker Academic had not only been a major and enthusiastic supporter of publishing *Reformed Dogmatics* in English but also demonstrated the utmost respect to the Bavinck legacy by producing a first-rate publication, an achievement for the ages. Confidence in my ability to do the job was enhanced by many who told me that the précis I prepared for each chapter of the English translation of *Reformed Dogmatics* were very helpful. Professor Roger Nicole kindly suggested that taken together, they would make a nice one-volume summary of Bavinck's theology.

So here it is. Although I have made generous use of the aforementioned précis, this volume is something different. In my abridgment I worked hard to preserve Bavinck's own voice, even his own words, keeping my transitions and paraphrases to a minimum. Careful readers should be able to recognize whole sentences and sections taken straight from *Reformed Dogmatics*, and it is my hope that even the most attentive readers will hear only Bavinck's voice throughout. At the same time, it is well to think of this volume via the metaphor of a large symphony orchestra; the composer and conductor is Bavinck. My own role here—I truly hope unnoticeable!—is to have served as Bavinck's editorial assistant, helping to select where *his* score could be shortened and reconfigured for the sake of this one performance. The score is his and he will conduct the orchestra, not me. Where my own part is noticeable, it is a part that will be heard by a discriminating listener but always with the same tune. On occasion, in places where I have self-consciously

xi

"intruded" into the text, I will indicate this with an appropriate footnote.[1] Most of the "ed. notes" consist of additional historical comments when reductions in the text make them necessary, illustrative references to contemporary thinkers and issues under discussion in the text, and updated bibliographic material. I have not amended the text by removing elements that might be bothersome to ecumenical spirits (e.g., some of his comments on Roman Catholicism) or where I might disagree with his judgments (e.g., on the cessation of the extraordinary gifts of the Holy Spirit after the apostolic age; the office of evangelist). In other words, I have worked hard to remove my own subjectivity from decisions about what to throw onto the cutting room floor. On the few occasions that I dissent from one or more of Bavinck's judgments, I do so on the basis of more objective, historical developments (e.g., Vatican II), or more recent scholarship (e.g., on infant baptism in the early church), and clearly indicate so in my note.[2] What continues to amaze me, even after all these years, is how rarely such correction is needed. Footnotes not so marked are either consistent with Bavinck's own notes or instances of my putting into footnotes material originally in the body of the text.

Here are the guidelines I have followed in preparing this volume. I have significantly reduced the amount of detail, especially on historical theology, for which Bavinck is rightly famous. I have been selective in what exposition and critique of particular thinkers are included and in the supporting literature that is cited in the notes, with regular reference only to classic works—Augustine, Thomas Aquinas, John Calvin, major ecclesiastical documents, and so forth. My goal here was to reduce the amount of detail without sacrificing the important concreteness of Bavinck's discussion. In reducing fifty-eight chapters to twenty-five, I have obviously combined many chapters and tried to reduce as much redundancy as possible. The major structural change involved moving the chapter on providence (vol. 2, chap. 14, ##301–6) from its placement as a separate chapter following the material on anthropology to the concluding section in chapter 10, "Creator of Heaven and Earth." In this way, the two loci of theology proper and anthropology are kept whole and distinct and maintained in the classic order of Protestant Orthodoxy.[3] A minor change involved removing the first three sections of *Reformed Dogmatics*, vol. 2, chapter 3 (##178–80) from the fuller discussion of God's names (chap. 8) and adding them to chapter 7. They were enfolded into the broader discussion of "Knowing God," leaving a single chapter for the more systematic discussion, "The Living, Acting God," which classifies God's attributes. The other noticeable structural difference between this abridgment and the original four volumes of *Reformed Dogmatics* is the clear division of the book into seven sections—prolegomena plus the six classic loci—which highlights the traditional order present in the full work but, because of the division within the loci of soteriology at the

---

1. Such as in chapter 16, note 1.
2. Such as in chapter 22, notes 46, 51, 91.
3. See chapter 10, note 104.

break between vols. 3 and 4, was not as immediately transparent. The greatest reductions occurred in volume 1 (chaps. 1–6), the least in the eschatology section (chaps. 23–25). The eschatology section in volume 4 was the shortest and most compact of Bavinck's treatment of each loci and consequently much more difficult to reduce.

The language of this volume, down to specific phrasing and key citations, was directly taken from the full work. Occasionally I have taken whole sentences and even paragraphs directly from the larger work but rearranged them to fit a new, abridged, narrative structure. At the same time, some repetition of key ideas remains. Especially in matters of prolegomena, Bavinck's case for a Reformed understanding of revelation, religion, and the task of theology in the church is cumulative, and I have tried to preserve that feature in the first part as well. To facilitate easy reference to *Reformed Dogmatics*—especially for those dedicated souls who desire more—this volume retains the section numbers in square brackets [ ] that go back to the original Dutch second edition. Finally, in preparing this volume I have not written a new and distinct biographical and theological introduction; readers are encouraged to attend to the introductions in any one of the four full volumes.

The labor on this volume took place from July 2008 through September 2009. I want to express my gratitude here to the administration and Board of Trustees of Calvin Theological Seminary for the partial sabbatical granted to me during the school year 2008–9, which liberated me from all faculty responsibilities save teaching one course per quarter. My thanks also to my faculty colleagues who went through a lengthy year of fine-tuning a wholly revised and reshaped curriculum without any assistance or hindrance from me. My colleagues have also been uniformly supportive of my preoccupation with Bavinck, for which I am grateful. In the fall quarter of 2008, I was privileged to lead a group of a dozen or so CTS students in a seminar focusing on the first volume of *Reformed Dogmatics*. Half the members of this class continued to meet weekly over the course of the second and third quarters on an informal basis to discuss volume 2. Since I was in the midst of my abridgment work on precisely those two volumes during those months, I was not only encouraged by their high level of interest but also learned from their responses where they saw the key points of each chapter; both were significant contributions to my progress. CTS students David Salverda (vols. 1 and 2) and Gayle Doornbos (vols. 3 and 4) provided both savvy computer support (especially for entering Hebrew and Greek words) and prudential editorial advice. During the summer months of 2009 and into September, as I was bringing the work to a conclusion, I relied heavily on Gayle's solid theological and editorial judgments and exemplary work ethic. I could not have completed my work when I did without her assistance, for which I am profoundly grateful.

As from the very beginning of my editorial work on *Reformed Dogmatics*, I remain gratefully indebted to my friends and colleagues on the Board of the Dutch Reformed Translation Society who consented to and supported the preparation of this volume. And finally to the Baker Academic editorial staff: Thank you for your professional, courteous, and warmly encouraging support. Thank you, Jim Kinney, for coming up with the idea for this volume and shepherding it to its publication; to Wells Turner: you are an editor extraordinaire in text and people skills; you improve my work, remain unfailingly patient with my foibles and flaws, and never intrude yourself into the process. It is a privilege to be part of the team that brought this project to its completion. Thank you all.

Canadian Thanksgiving 2009

ABBREVIATIONS

General and Bibliographic

ANF   *The Ante-Nicene Fathers.* Edited by Alexander Roberts and James Donaldson. 10 vols. New York: Christian Literature, 1885–96. Reprinted, Grand Rapids: Eerdmans, 1950–51.

CR   Corpus reformatorum. Edited by C. G. Bretschneider, H. E. Bindseil, et al. 101 vols. Halle a. Salle and Brunsvigae: Schwetschke, 1834–1959.

DB   *Dictionary of the Bible.* Edited by James Hastings. 5 vols. New York: C. Scribner Sons, 1898–1904.

DC   *A Dictionary of Christ and the Gospels.* Edited by James Hastings. 2 vols. New York: C. Scribner Sons, 1906–8.

Eng.   English versification, where this differs from the MT or LXX

ET   English translation

f./ff.   and the verse/verses following

KJV   King James Version

LXX   Septuagint (Greek translation of the Old Testament)

marg.   marginal reading; alternate translation

MT   Masoretic (Hebrew) Text of the Old Testament

NIV   New International Version

NPNF (1)   *A Select Library of Nicene and Post-Nicene Fathers of the Christian Church.* Edited by Philip Schaff. 1st series. 14 vols. New York: Christian Literature, 1887–1900. Reprinted, Grand Rapids: Eerdmans, 1956.

NPNF (2)   *A Select Library of Nicene and Post-Nicene Fathers of the Christian Church.* Edited by Philip Schaff and Henry Wace. 2nd series. 14 vols. New York: Christian Literature, 1890–1900. Reprinted, Grand Rapids: Eerdmans, 1952.

NRSV   New Revised Standard Version

PG   Patrologiae cursus completus: Series graeca. Edited by J.-P. Migne. 161 vols. Paris: Migne, 1857–66.

PL   Patrologiae cursus completus: Series latina. Edited by J.-P. Migne. 221 vols. Paris: Migne, 1844–65.

pl.   plural

PRE[1]   *Realencyklopädie für protestantische Theologie und Kirche.* Edited by J. J. Herzog. 1st ed. 22 vols. Hamburg: R. Besser, 1854–68.

PRE[2]   *Realencyklopädie für protestantische Theologie und Kirche.* Edited by J. J. Herzog and G. L. Plitt. 2nd rev. ed. 18 vols. Leipzig: J. C. Hinrichs, 1877–88.

PRE[3]   *Realencyklopädie für protestantische Theologie und Kirche.* Edited by Albert Hauck. 3rd rev. ed. 24 vols. Leipzig: J. C. Hinrichs, 1896–1913.

RSV   Revised Standard Version

sing.   singular

v./vv.	verse/verses	1–4 Macc.	1–4 Maccabees
Vulg.	Vulgate (Latin translation of the Bible)	Sir.	Sirach
		Tob.	Tobit
		Wis.	Wisdom of Solomon

Old Testament

Gen.	Genesis
Exod.	Exodus
Lev.	Leviticus
Num.	Numbers
Deut.	Deuteronomy
Josh.	Joshua
Judg.	Judges
Ruth	Ruth
1–2 Sam.	1–2 Samuel
1–2 Kings	1–2 Kings
1–2 Chron.	1–2 Chronicles
Ezra	Ezra
Neh.	Nehemiah
Esther	Esther
Job	Job
Ps(s).	Psalms
Prov.	Proverbs
Eccles.	Ecclesiastes
Song of Sol.	Song of Solomon
Isa.	Isaiah
Jer.	Jeremiah
Lam.	Lamentations
Ezek.	Ezekiel
Dan.	Daniel
Hosea	Hosea
Joel	Joel
Amos	Amos
Obad.	Obadiah
Jon.	Jonah
Mic.	Micah
Nah.	Nahum
Hab.	Habakkuk
Zeph.	Zephaniah
Hag.	Haggai
Zech.	Zechariah
Mal.	Malachi

Old Testament Apocrypha

Bar.	Baruch
1–2 Esd.	1–2 Esdras

New Testament

Matt.	Matthew
Mark	Mark
Luke	Luke
John	John
Acts	Acts
Rom.	Romans
1–2 Cor.	1–2 Corinthians
Gal.	Galatians
Eph.	Ephesians
Phil.	Philippians
Col.	Colossians
1–2 Thess.	1–2 Thessalonians
1–2 Tim.	1–2 Timothy
Titus	Titus
Philem.	Philemon
Heb.	Hebrews
James	James
1–2 Pet.	1–2 Peter
1–3 John	1–3 John
Jude	Jude
Rev.	Revelation

Other Ancient Writings

2 Bar.	*2 (Apocalypse of) Baruch*
Barn.	*Barnabas*
1–2 Clem.	*1–2 Clement*
Did.	*Didache*
Diogn.	*Diognetus*
Herm. *Mand.*	Shepherd of Hermas, *Mandate*
Herm. *Sim.*	Shepherd of Hermas, *Similitude*
Herm. *Vis.*	Shepherd of Hermas, *Vision*
Ign. *Eph.*	Ignatius, *To the Ephesians*
Ign. *Magn.*	Ignatius, *To the Magnesians*
Ign. *Phld.*	Ignatius, *To the Philadelphians*
Ign. *Rom.*	Ignatius, *To the Romans*
Ign. *Smyrn.*	Ignatius, *To the Smyrnaeans*
Ign. *Trall.*	Ignatius, *To the Trallians*
Pol. *Phil.*	Polycarp, *To the Philippians*

PART I

PROLEGOMENA
INTRODUCTION TO DOGMATIC THEOLOGY

1

DOGMATIC THEOLOGY
AS A SCIENCE

TERMINOLOGY

[1] Throughout the history of the church, theologians have used different terms to describe the orderly study of the Christian faith and the summary of its truth content.[1] Many Protestant theologians of the immediate post-Reformation period began to follow the Lutheran Philipp Melanchthon's *Loci Communes* ("Common Places") in designating the various topics of theology as *loci*.[2] This term, a translation of the Greek τοποι, comes from classical writers such as Cicero who used the term for the general rules or places where a rhetorician could find the arguments needed when treating any given topic. *Loci*, in other words, were the data bases, the proof-text barrels used by debaters as sources of material to bolster their arguments. For theologians seeking to serve the church, the *loci* were the places one could look for Scripture's own statements about a particular topic.

---

1. A sample: *On First Principles* (Origen); *The Divine Institutes* (Lactantius); *Enchiridion* or *Little Handbook* (Augustine); *Sentences* (Peter Lombard); *Summa Theologiae* (Thomas Aquinas); *Loci Communes* or *Common Places* (Philipp Melanchthon); *Institutes of the Christian Religion* (John Calvin).

2. Ed. note: Thus a traditional Reformed work of theology such as Louis Berkhof's *Systematic Theology*, new one-volume edition (Grand Rapids: Eerdmans, 1996 [1932; 1938]), 74, divides the material into six loci: doctrine of God (theology), doctrine of humanity (anthropology), doctrine of Christ (Christology), doctrine of applied salvation (soteriology), doctrine of the church (ecclesiology), and doctrine of the last things (eschatology).

When Melanchthon wrote his *Loci Communes*, the first major work in Reformation evangelical theology, he was commenting on the *Sentences* of Peter Lombard and Paul's Epistle to the Romans. The end result was an outline of the principal truths of the Christian faith as taught in Scripture, treated under a number of basic rubrics or categories such as God, creation, sin, law, grace, faith, hope, love, and predestination. The purpose was to instruct the faithful in the teachings of the Bible.

Over time, as subsequent generations of theologians desired a more systematic treatment of the truths of the faith, the looser term *loci* passed into disfavor and a preference grew for the word *theologia*. However, *theologia* by itself did not do justice to the different kinds of literature that served the church, and qualifiers such as "didactic," "systematic," "theoretical," or "positive" were added to distinguish these *summary* overviews of biblical teaching from biblical ethics or "moral" theology as well as from "practical" or pastoral theology. Eventually, the term "dogmatics" was added to describe this specific kind of *theologia*.[3] "Dogmatics" has the advantage of anchoring such study in the normative teachings or dogmas of the church. Dogmas are truths properly set forth in Scripture as things to be believed. Although a truth confessed by the church is not a dogma *because* the church recognizes it but solely because it rests on God's authority, religious dogma is always a combination of divine authority and churchly confession. Dogmas are truths *acknowledged* by a particular group, though church teaching must never be identified with divine truth itself.

[2] The word *dogma*, from the Greek *dokein* ("to be of the opinion"), denotes that which is definite—that which has been decided—and is therefore fixed. Thus the church fathers speak of the Christian religion or doctrine as the *divine dogma*, of Christ's incarnation as the *dogma of theology*, of the truths of the faith that are authoritative in and for the church as the *dogmata of the church*, and so forth. Included are doctrinal truths and rules for Christian living that are established and not subject to doubt. There are varieties of *dogma* based on different authorities. Political dogma rests on the authority of the civil government, while philosophical dogmas derive their power from self-evidence or argumentation. By contrast, religious or theological dogmas owe their authority solely to a divine testimony, whether this is perceived, as among pagans, from an oracle, or, among Protestant Christians, from Scripture or, among Roman Catholics, from the magisterium of the church. The Reformation tradition recognizes no truth other than that which is given on the authority of vGod in Holy Scripture. "The Word of God grounds the articles of faith and beyond that no one, not even an angel."[4] Dogmas, articles of faith, are only those truths "which are properly set forth in Scripture

3. One of the first was L. Reinhart, *Synopsis theologiae dogmaticae* (1659).
4. *The Smalcald Articles*, II.2, in vol. 3 of *The Creeds of Christendom*, ed. Philip Schaff and rev. David S. Schaff, 6th ed., 3 vols. (New York: Harper & Row: 1931; repr., Grand Rapids: Baker Academic, 1990).

as things to be believed."[5] Among Reformed theologians, therefore, the principle into which all theological dogmas are distilled is: *Deus dixit*—God has said it.

The concept of dogma also contains a social element. Truth always seeks to be honored as truth, and the authority of dogma depends on its ability to command recognition and thus to maintain itself. Though a given proposition is true in and of itself if it rests on the authority of God quite apart from any human recognition, it is intended, and has an inherent tendency, to be recognized by us as such. Dogma can never be at peace with error and deception. It is, therefore, of the greatest importance for every believer, and particularly for theologians, to know which scriptural truths, under the guidance of the Holy Spirit, have been brought to universal recognition in the church of Christ. By this process, after all, the church is kept from immediately mistaking a private opinion for the truth of God.

The church of Christ therefore has a responsibility with respect to dogma. To preserve, explain, understand, and defend the truth of God entrusted to her, the church is called to appropriate it mentally, to assimilate it internally, and to profess it in the midst of the world as the truth of God. The power of the church to lay down dogmas is not sovereign and legislative; it is a power of service to and for the Word of God. Still, this authority has been granted by God to his church; it enables and authorizes her to confess the truth of God and to formulate it in speech and writing. The dogmatic theologian's task is to examine how the church's dogma arose genetically from Scripture and how, in accordance with that same Scripture, it ought to be expanded and enriched. The dogmatic theologian searches for the inner coherence of Scripture's teaching and its full expression. In this the theologian is guided by the confessions of the church but is not restricted to their historical and particular limitations.

A tension thus is apparent in that religious or theological dogma combines divine authority and churchly confession, presenting the dogmatic theologian with the challenge of determining the relation between divine truth and the church's confession. Church dogma is never identical with the absolute truth of God itself since the guidance of the Holy Spirit promised to the church does not exclude the possibility of human error. At the same time, it is a mistake to devalue dogma itself as a temporary aberration from the pure essence of a non-dogmatic gospel as many modern theologians do.[6] Opposition to dogma is not a general objection to dogma as such but a rejection of *specific* dogmas judged unacceptable *by some*. Adolf von Harnack in his *History of Dogma*, for example, developed the thought that Christian dogma was a product of the

5. A. Hyperius, *Methodi theologiae, sive praecipuorum Christianae religionis* (Basel: Oporiniana, 1574), 34–35.
6. Ed. note: To this should also be added "postmodern theologians" who substitute Christian discipleship for firm doctrinal content in attacks on "propositional truth" which they regard as a form of cultural imperialism; see, e.g., Carl Raschke, *The Next Reformation: Why Evangelicals Must Embrace Postmodernism* (Grand Rapids: Baker Academic, 2005); for critique see, *inter alia*, Andreas Köstenberger, ed., *Whatever Happened to Truth* (Wheaton: Crossway, 2006).

Greek spirit working on the substratum of the gospel[7] and, with many others, sought the *essence* of Christianity in a general moral conviction wrought in the human soul that God is our Father, that we are all brothers and sisters, and that this kingdom of God exists in an individual's soul.[8] Harnack did not repudiate all dogma but simply substituted a new dogma for the old dogmas of historic Christianity. Dogma cannot be avoided in religion; one who clings to the truth of religion cannot do without dogma and will always recognize unchanging and permanent elements in it. A religion without dogma, however vague and general it may be, does not exist, and a non-dogmatic Christianity, in the strict sense of the word, is an illusion and devoid of meaning. Without faith in the existence, the revelation, and the knowability of God, no religion is possible. Those who claim to be non-dogmatic simply indicate their disagreement with *specific* dogmas; rejection of orthodox Christian dogma is itself most dogmatic. The disagreement, then, is not about *whether* religion requires dogma; it is about *which* dogmas one affirms and rejects.

Finally, the word "dogma" is sometimes employed in a broader, and then again in a more restricted, sense. Sometimes it denotes the Christian religion as a whole, including the articles of faith drawn from Scripture and the rites and ceremonies of the church. As a rule, however, the word is used in a more restricted sense for the *doctrines* of the church, for the articles of faith that are based on the Word of God and therefore obligate everyone to faith. Dogmatic theology, then, is the system of the articles of faith.

[4] This formal understanding of dogmatics, however, is limited. We need to move on to the material content of dogmas. Is dogmatic theology about "doctrine of God, primarily, and of creatures according to the respect in which they are related to God as to their source and end," as Thomas Aquinas, for example, defined it?[9] Concerned about the "practical" application of theology, some are inclined to shift the emphasis to the human person in need of salvation or to the Christian life of discipleship as a focal point.

The move toward a more subjective, practical notion of theology received a great boost by the philosophy of Immanuel Kant (1724–1804). Denying that we could *know* anything about God, since he defined "knowledge" strictly in terms of sensory experience of phenomena in this world, Kant sought to rescue faith by positing as *moral* truths the existence of God, the soul and its immortality. Dogma thus has the status of personal conviction of faith grounded in moral motives. Nineteenth-century theologians who followed Kant shared his basic metaphysical

7. Adolf von Harnack, *History of Dogma*, trans. N. Buchanan, J. Millar, E. B. Speirs, and W. McGilchrist, and ed. A. B. Bruce, 7 vols. (London: Williams & Norgate, 1896–99), I, 17.

8. A. von Harnack, *What Is Christianity?* trans. Thomas Bailey Saunders (New York: Harper, 1957); ed. note: for a more complete summary and critique of this position, see H. Bavinck, "The Essence of Christianity," in *Essays on Religion, Science and Society*, ed. John Bolt, trans. Harry Boonstra and Gerrit Sheeres (Grand Rapids: Baker Academic, 2008), 33–47.

9. T. Aquinas, *Summa Theol.*, I, Q.1 art. 3, 7.

conviction that God cannot be *known* but only *believed*.[10] For Friedrich Schleiermacher (1768–1834), the content of the Christian faith is nothing more than the piety and faith of Christian believers at a given time. In his own words: "Christian doctrines are accounts of the Christian religious affections set forth in speech," and "Dogmatic Theology is the science which systematizes the doctrine prevalent in a Christian Church at a given time."[11] Others, such as Albrecht Ritschl (1822–89), followed Kant more directly in construing the content of the Christian faith in strictly moral-ethical terms, while Ernst Troeltsch (1865–1923) made the historical, psychological, and comparative scientific study of religions the object of theological inquiry and summary. When dogmatic theology becomes nothing more than a description of the historical phenomenon that is called the Christian faith, it ceases to be theology and simply becomes the study of religion.[12]

The historical, social, and psychological study of concrete religion, including the Christian religion, is a valid and appropriate discipline. What is problematic is the claim that such study is *all* that can legitimately be done; that we cannot *know* what we *believe*. Whether the reasons are philosophical or apologetic, to turn theology into religious studies is to evade the question of truth. The strain that this places on theological practitioners is intolerable; the human soul rebels at ignoring or denying in the academy what one confesses in church. The human mind is not amenable to such double-entry bookkeeping, to a dual conception of truth. What in effect often happens is that the Christian confession yields to a science of religion that claims to be without bias. The academy arrogates unto itself the mantle of knowledge and science by studying religion *scientifically*, and relegates dogmatic theology to a church seminary concerned about faith-experience and the practice of ministry. To the degree that a study of the Christian religion is "scientific," it can only be descriptive.

[5] But science aims at *truth* and if dogmatic theology aims to be real science, it cannot be satisfied with description of what *is* but must demonstrate what *necessarily* has to be considered truth. Christian theology must resist those who turn their backs on all metaphysics, dogma, and dogmatic theology and think of religion in terms of subjective moods of the mind. Religion is then reduced to a matter of feeling and mood and not one of ideas that are true or false. It is a mistake to oppose dry intellectualism in theology with a radical turn to feeling. The Christian religion stands or falls on the truth of our *knowledge* of God; if God cannot be known, if God is not known, then religion itself collapses. Thus, Christian theology depends for its very existence on the assured conviction that God *can* be known, that he *has* revealed himself to humanity and that we *can*

---

10. Ed. note: See Claude Welch, *Protestant Thought in the Nineteenth Century*, 2 vols. (New Haven: Yale University Press, 1972, 1985).

11. F. Schleiermacher, *The Christian Faith*, ed. and trans. H. R. McIntosh and J. S. Steward (Edinburgh: T&T Clark, 1928), §§15, 19.

12. Ed. note: For further discussion of this point, see H. Bavinck, *Essays on Religion, Science and Society*, chaps. 1, 3.

speak about that knowledge in an orderly manner. Dogmatic theology is, and can only exist as, the scientific system of the knowledge of God. More precisely and from a Christian viewpoint, dogmatic theology is the knowledge that God has revealed in his Word to the church concerning himself and all creatures as they stand in relation to him.

[6] Not everyone is happy with such an understanding of theology. Objections are raised against the idea that God can be *known* as well as to the claim that a systematic, scientific examination of this knowledge is possible or should be attempted. The objectors insist that the Christian faith is not about head knowledge but about a *personal* relationship to God in Christ resulting in a godly life. If we must speak of knowledge, so they insist, it is of a quite different sort; call it *faith-knowledge*.[13] The objection to a speculative and rationalistic theology that loses sight of faith and the place of the heart is understandable and right. However, to *substitute* feeling or moral conduct for knowledge confuses categories and creates grave difficulties of its own. When we speak of "faith knowledge" we must ask: Is there a real object to our faith? If we say we *believe* in God, does God truly, i.e., objectively, exist or is God only a matter of our *subjective* consciousness? As much as we should appreciate the concerns of those who insist that the *way* we come to the knowledge of God is different from the means by which we gain knowledge of this world and its objects, we cannot avoid the question of truth. It is true that we do not believe that God exists, in the first place, *because* someone has marshaled an abundance of data and evidence that convinces our reason. We come to know through faith and not through external sense perception of things. But we cannot bracket our intellect from our faith-knowledge; faith is the faculty by which we come to know, it is not the *source* of faith. It is quite true that God cannot, like the phenomena of nature and the facts of history, be made the object of empirical investigation. For God to be knowable he must have revealed himself not only in deeds but also in words. The objective knowledge we need for dogmatic theology comes from divine revelation. To say that dogmatic theology is the system of the knowledge of God serves to cut off all autonomous speculation; it is to say that God cannot be known by us apart from his revelation and that the knowledge of God we aim at in theology can only be a transcript of the knowledge God has revealed concerning himself in his Word.

THEOLOGY AS THE SCIENCE OF GOD

[7] Our task today is to frame the whole of Christian knowledge in accordance with the manner in which it develops out of the evangelical faith. The knowledge of God we examine and summarize must always remain the knowledge of faith.

---

13. E.g., Julius Kaftan, *The Truth of the Christian Religion*, trans. George Ferries, 2 vols. (Edinburgh: T&T Clark, 1894).

At the same time, we insist that God has revealed himself in such a way that from this revelation we can learn to *know* him by faith. Furthermore, if God's revelation contains real *knowledge* of God, it can also be thought through scientifically and gathered up in a system. Theologians are bound to God's revelation from beginning to end and cannot bring forth new truth; they can only as thinkers reproduce the truth God has granted. Since revelation is of such a nature that it can only be truly accepted and appropriated by a saving faith, it is absolutely imperative that a dogmatic theologian be active as believer at the beginning, the continuation, and the conclusion of the work. A Christian theologian can never arrive at knowledge that is higher than the Christian faith. Precisely because a true faith-knowledge of God exists, dogmatic theology has the knowledge of God as part of its content and can rightly claim to be a science.

This seems strange to many Christians today because by "science" they have in mind the *natural* sciences such as physics, chemistry, biology, and geology. It is exactly here that we have our problem—a tyranny of empiricism and naturalism.[14] It is a mistake to concede to the materialism of either of these philosophical positions since it is becoming increasingly clear that even the "hardest" of the physical sciences such as physics incorporate, as sciences, some measure of subjectivity. What one accepts as "facts" is often determined by a priori religious and philosophical commitments. What we believe we see and how we interpret what we think we have seen are, of course, not subject to arbitrary whim; skepticism is as unwarranted as credulity. At the same time, fully detached scientific objectivity is a myth. It is totally futile to silence all subjectivity in a scientist, to deny to faith, religious and moral convictions, metaphysics and philosophy their influence on scientific study. One may attempt it but will never succeed because the scholar can never be separated from the human being.

[8] With this in mind, we can speak with complete justice of dogmatic theology as a science about God, and there is no objection whatever to gathering this knowledge of God in a system.[15] We understand by "system" nothing more than the ordinary scientific project of gathering a particular discipline's body of knowledge into an intelligible, coherent, meaningful, ordered whole. Objections arise to the idea of "system" from a number of quarters, notably from poets and literary critics who resist the abstraction needed to do systematic or dogmatic theology. A typical comment: "The Bible wasn't written as systematic theology . . . [but as a narrative] . . . in images and stories."[16]

---

14. Ed. note: "Empiricism" combined with "naturalism" (or "materialism") is the conviction that natural, material reality is all that can be known and that it is knowable only through the senses.

15. Ed. note: At a very simple level, the scientific character of dogmatic theology can be defended by noting that "theologians use footnotes too." "Scientific," like the also much-maligned term "Scholasticism," refers to a *formal* method of proceeding with the content of a discipline; it does not determine the content. See note 19 below.

16. Ed note: Luci Shaw, "Reversing Entropy," *Image: A Journal of the Arts* 41, no. 4 (Winter 2003–4): 96.

We must acknowledge that the complaint sometimes is valid; theology can be poorly presented and appear abstract, lifeless, intellectually arid. At the same time, misuse or abuse does not invalidate all use. There is no room in dogmatic theology for a system that attempts to deduce the truths of faith from an a priori principle, say, from the essence of religion, from the essence of Christianity, from the fact of regeneration, or from the experience of the devout. This is speculation and must be resisted. Dogmatic theology is a positive science that gathers its material from revelation and does not have the right to modify or expand that content by speculation apart from that revelation. When because of limitations or weakness a theologian is faced with the choice either of simply letting the truths of faith stand alongside each other or, in the interest of maintaining the systematic form, fail to do justice to one of them, we must let the system go.[17] Theologians must resist the temptation to let a system rule. But such dilemmas occur because we theologians are finite and limited. There is no conflict in God; God's thoughts cannot be opposed to one another; they are necessarily an organic unity. The imperative task of the theologian is to think God's thoughts after him, to trace their unity, mentally absorb it, and set it forth in a work of theology. The theologian's sole responsibility is to think God's thoughts after him and to reproduce the unity that is objectively present in the thoughts of God and has been recorded for the eye of faith in Scripture.

The theologian's task is that of a servant and, as is the case for all scientific work, calls for modesty. A theologian's confidence comes from the conviction: God has spoken. Thus, a theologian takes his or her place within the community of faith and acknowledges what a rich privilege and honor it is to work with God's revelation *in submission* to Holy Scripture. The knowledge of God, laid down in his Word, *is given to the church*. It is the church's task to proclaim it to the world and, for that reason too, it is a part of the calling of every believer to learn to know the love of Christ that surpasses all knowledge, to deepen faith through knowledge, in order that the final end of theology, as of all things, may be that the name of the Lord is glorified. Theology exists for the Lord's sake.

[11–12] The truth of theology needs to be defended against the opponents of the faith (apologetics) as well as applied to the life of Christian discipleship (ethics). Theological ethics may not be separated from dogmatic theology; who we are as human beings restored in Christ must govern our conduct. Utterly dependent on God for life and for salvation, we remain responsible agents. While dogmatic theology describes the deeds of God done for us and in us, theological ethics spells out what those for whom and in whom God has acted, in love and grace, must now do. Dogmatic theology thus relates closely to the creed—confessing

17. Ed. note: Dutch Reformed theologian Hendrikus Berkhof captures the limits of "system" nicely when he includes as an epigraph to his *Christian Faith: An Introduction to the Study of the Faith*, trans. Sierd Woudstra (Grand Rapids: Eerdmans, 1979), the following lines from Alfred Tennyson: "Our little systems have their day; / They have their day and cease to be: / They are but broken lights of Thee, / And Thou, O Lord, art more than they."

what God has done; theological ethics deals with God's precepts and command-ments. Dogmatic theology is the system of the knowledge of God; ethics is that of the service of God.

[13] The material for constructing a dogmatic theology comes from Holy Scripture, church teaching, and Christian experience. From the beginning, Scripture served as the rule of faith and the foundation of all theology. Both the Old Testament and the apostolic writings held authority in the churches of Christ and were viewed as sources of knowledge. Dogma was that which Christ and the apostles had taught; Scripture was the rule of faith (*regula fidei*) to which the church's confession and dogma were subordinate. From ancient times on, the most important proof for the church's dogma was the proof from Scripture. The apostles' witness and teaching, orally and in writing, were the standard by which the truth about Jesus Christ was measured; it shaped and became the *canon* of the Christian church.

As subsequent generations developed baptismal liturgies, statements of faith, and pastoral guidance for conduct, a growing body of post-apostolic writings became an important part of the church's rule of faith.[18] As the church spread into and engaged the broader world, it became necessary to clarify and firm up the rule of faith against false teaching. The church needed strong leadership over against a wide range of sects and heresies, and by necessity bishops increasingly took on a role as the defenders of apostolic teaching. With this, the idea surfaced that the bishops were the lawful successors of the apostles and the bearers of Christian truth who, in virtue of the "grace of truth" given them, were entitled to decide what was the pure, apostolic Christian truth. Through this process, the teaching of the bishops became the "rule of truth," and the authority of Scripture receded into the shadows.

[14] Protests against the devaluation of Scripture in the church rose in the Middle Ages and flowered during the time of the Reformation. Protestantism repeatedly resists attempts to elevate tradition above Scripture and tries to renew the church's moorings in Scripture. Many times in the history of Christian theology appeals are made for a simple, practical, biblical Christianity that avoids so-called "Scholastic" theology.[19] While such efforts are to be praised for their intention, we also cannot overlook the fact that in the post-Reformation period, under the influence of pietism and rationalism, this passion for "biblical theology" was also a

---

18. Including texts such as the *Didache, Shepherd of Hermas, Letter to Diognetus*, and the writings of apostolic fathers such as Ignatius (ca. AD 35–107), Justin Martyr (AD 110–165), and Irenaeus (AD 120–202).

19. Ed. note: "Scholasticism" is often used as a term of reproach; it is said to signal an arid intel-lectualism and a "dead orthodoxy"; for a summary and critique of this view, see Richard A. Muller, "Scholasticism and Orthodoxy in the Reformed Tradition: An Attempt at Definition," Inaugural Ad-dress, Calvin Theological Seminary, September 7, 1995. Published by Calvin Theological Seminary. Properly understood, "Scholasticism" refers to a *method*; the method of the schools. Cf. Richard A. Muller, *Post-Reformation Reformed Dogmatics*, vol. 1, *Prolegomena to Theology*, 2nd ed. (Grand Rapids: Baker Academic, 2003), 34–37.

rallying cry against the church's confession. It is an error to elevate tradition above Scripture; it is also an error to use Scripture to denigrate or dismiss the church's tradition. Good church tradition is nothing other than the church's understanding of Scripture, the basis of its self-understanding as the body of Christ created by the Holy Spirit and the apostolic witness and teaching. To set Scripture over against church teaching is as wrong as separating heart and mind, feeling and knowing. The sole aim of dogmatic theology is to set forth the thoughts of God that he has laid down in Holy Scripture

[15–17] Not everything that describes itself as "biblical" is necessarily faithful to the apostolic tradition and theologically helpful. A pietism that turns to Christian subjective experience as a replacement for a concern about Christian truth in dogma paves the way for a modern philosophical turn to the subject and away from objective reality. For philosophers such as René Descartes (1596–1650), Immanuel Kant (1724–1804), and Georg Wilhelm Friedrich Hegel (1770–1831), and theologians such as Friedrich Schleiermacher (1768–1834) and Albrecht Ritschl (1822–89), subjective experience replaced knowledge as the foundation of theology, which was itself separated from science and metaphysics. Taking the starting point in Christian consciousness, attempts were made to ground theology in morality (Kant and Ritschl), in the feeling of absolute dependence (Schleiermacher), or in the unfolding of the universal Spirit (Hegel). In order to maintain objectivity in the theological disciplines, a shift in orientation led to an emphasis on the scientific study of religion, its history, and psychology. Christianity was to be examined historically and critically, just as one studies the other religions of the world.[20] If one comes to a conclusion that Christianity, let us say, is superior to other religions, the reasons must be empirical and historical; no appeal to divine revelation is permitted.

[18] This approach is not without its serious difficulties. There should be no objection as such to empirical studies of religious traditions, including Christianity. There is much to be gained by looking at the historical, social, and psychological dimensions of the faith, even for a Christian dogmatic theology. It is fascinating, not to mention fruitful, to look at religious phenomena such as conversion, faith, prayer, devotion, ecstasy, contemplation, and so forth from a psychological angle.[21] Furthermore, it is a mistake to overlook or deny the importance of confessional and cultural factors in dogmatic treatises. No one is free from the biases of church

---

20. A key figure here is the German theologian and philosopher Ernst Troeltsch (1865–1923). Ed. note: For a fuller discussion of the issues see Herman Bavinck, *Essays on Religion, Science and Society*, especially chaps. 1 and 3.

21. Ed. note: See Herman Bavinck, *The Philosophy of Revelation* (New York: Longmans, Green, 1909; repr., Grand Rapids: Eerdmans, 1953; Grand Rapids: Baker Academic, 1979), 209. Here Bavinck suggests that Christian dogmatic theology, "especially in the doctrine of the *ordo salutis*, must become more psychological." He follows through on his own suggestion with a remarkable analysis of conversion in relation to the psychosexual development of adolescents in H. Bavinck, *Reformed Dogmatics*, ed. John Bolt (Grand Rapids: Baker Academic, 2003–8), III, 556–64 (##426–27a).

upbringing and particular environmental contexts. We are always products of our background, including our ecclesiastical upbringing. Yet, it is also a significant error to exaggerate these factors and to reduce theology to a descriptive work using scientific methods ("history of religions" or "psychology of religion") as *the* proper method for dogmatic theology.

Pure objectivity, a science without any presuppositions, is impossible for all research, even in the physical or natural sciences. It is especially true for studies that deal with the deepest longings and expressions of the human soul. A researcher who personally lacks religious sensibilities and conviction is as handicapped in studying religion as someone who is tone-deaf is in being a music critic. These personal convictions will intrude. How does one determine the standard for "true" or "good" religion? It is frankly impossible for human beings to do so on their own; to do it responsibly requires divine revelation. No one approaches the world's religions without some idea what religion is, what a good religion looks like, and what is a deformation of religion. No one can adopt an attitude of complete neutrality to the study of religion and treat all religions equivocally. At some point, the investigator's own religious commitments will become obvious.

It is time for those who attempt to create an authoritative theology from the empirical data of the Christian religion alone to acknowledge the impossibility of their task. It is a laudable goal in science to strive to be empirical, to try to arrive at a dogmatic theology that flows from the concreteness of the Christian community as it is experienced and lived, as it is based not on abstract ideas but on facts. Well and good. But the path chosen by the scientific historical and psychological study of religion does not and cannot lead to this goal. Suppose that scholars could show historically and psychologically how religion originates, grows, develops, and falls into decay—something they are not now and probably will never be able to do. Let them also, if need be, prove statistically that religion is a cultural power of the first rank and will probably remain so in the future. How can they ever deduce from all this that religion is based on *truth*, that an invisible reality underlies it? In other words, let them show that a belief in God is universal; that atheism is rare and counterintuitive. But, then, the question is unavoidable: Is God real? Or is belief in God like belief in the tooth fairy—useful mythology for children that one ought to and usually does outgrow? The answer to that question cannot be obtained from empirical study alone. Anyone who has not acquired this conviction by another route will certainly not get it by way of the history-of-religions and psychological methods. One arrives at metaphysics, at a philosophy of religion, only if from another source one has gained the certainty that religion is not just an interesting phenomenon—comparable to belief in witches and ghosts—but truth, the truth that God exists, reveals himself, and is knowable. Religion and faith must precede theological reflection; the theologian must be a person of faith, and the first *theological* step for a person of faith is to acknowledge revelation.

THE PROBLEM OF CERTAINTY: CHURCH AND SCRIPTURE

[19] From what has been said so far, it should be apparent that the method of dogmatic theology is determined by whether in religion, and specifically in Christianity, there is a way to arrive at certainty other than that which is usually taken in science, especially the natural sciences. Does theology possess a certain degree of independence from other sciences? Even though it may exhibit parallels with general human certainty, is religious certainty nonetheless unique, following its own path?[22] We will deal with this at greater length later when we consider revelation and faith.[23] But a few remarks may be helpful here.

It is clear that there are varying kinds and degrees of certainty in the broader range of human sensing and knowing. There is a certainty that is acquired by *personal observation*; we are absolutely certain of that which we see with our eyes and hear with our ears and touch with our hands. There is an *intuitive* kind of certainty, moreover, which, in virtue of the peculiar organization of our mind, arises automatically and spontaneously without any compulsion and prior to all rational reflection. For example, we intuitively and without proof accept that a straight line is the shortest distance between two points, that sense perception does not deceive us, that the world outside us really exists, that the laws of logic are reliable, that there is a difference between true and false, good and evil, right and wrong, beautiful and ugly, and so forth. Beyond this there is a certainty that is based on the *witness of credible persons*, a certainty that is of the greatest significance and substantially expands our knowledge in daily living and in the study of history. Finally, there is still another form of certainty that is acquired by *reasoning and supported by proofs*. In different arenas of human knowledge, including the distinct sciences, we will be compelled by different proofs and have varying levels of certainty. A lover does not seek *mathematical* certainty before plighting his troth; one does not ordinarily require *chemical* certainty that the food about to be eaten is free of poison. There is no single kind of certainty that is equally strong in all the sciences; the certainty obtainable in mathematical science differs from that in natural science, and the latter again differs from that in history, morality, law, philosophy, and so forth.

Now, what about religion? It seems clear that religious certainty is not to be reduced to that which comes from our senses or is mathematically and logically deduced from our sensory experience. If God exists and he is truly God he cannot, *by definition*, be contained by our senses and reasoning. An accessible God, called up by our will and under our control, cannot be said to be God. Religion has a character of its own and must have a certainty of its own available to the simple and unsophisticated as well as to the philosophically literate.

---

22. Ed. note: For an illuminating and accessible discussion of faith's certainty in relation to other kinds of certainty, see Herman Bavinck, *The Certainty of Faith*, trans. H. der Nederlanden (Jordan Station, ON: Paideia, 1980).

23. Ed. note: See chaps. 4 and 6 below.

Our aptitude for God cannot vary in accord with our intellectual capacity for abstraction and speculation. If religion is to be what it is said to be, namely the service of God, the love of God with all one's mind, heart, and strength, then it must be grounded in *revelation*, in a word from God that comes with his authority. Divine authority is the foundation of religion and therefore the source and basis of theology as well. All this is naturally implied in the concept and essence of religion.

Christianity meets these criteria. Objectively, it claims that God reveals himself in nature and history and particularly and centrally in Christ, a general and a special revelation. Christianity makes universal claims and nevertheless claims a distinct place for itself. Subjectively, it makes an appeal to and connects with a humanity created in the image of God that, although it is fallen, cannot forget or erase its divine origin, nature, and destiny. At the same time, Christianity says that we cannot naturally understand the things of the Spirit of God (1 Cor. 2:14) but must be born again and renewed to understand God's revelation and submit to the authority of his Word. Either one believes that Christianity is no different from other human religions, that there are a variety of paths to religious truth, *or* one believes that God in Christ is the highest revelation and makes universal claims. In the former case one is no longer qualified or able to write a Christian work of theology; a dogmatic theologian can only take a stand within the circle of faith if the work is to be true.

[20–21] For a theologian to work with the reality of God, God must speak first. If theology is to deal with real knowledge, God must be knowable and have made himself known, and we human creatures must have the capacity to know God. For a theology to be true, the religion on which the theologian's faith is based must be true, and the theologian's faith must be genuine. A true religion has its own distinct path to knowledge and certainty. Christian theologians must place themselves within the circle of faith and, while using church tradition and personal experience, take their stand in the reality of revelation. Bound by revelation, taking seriously the confessions of the church, a theologian must appropriate the Christian faith personally. This is a liberating reality; it made it possible for heroic figures such as Martin Luther to stand up to false teaching and misconduct in the church. We must obey God rather than men.

If the Christian theologian is to take a stand in faith based on revelation, where is revelation to be found? At most, three factors come up for consideration—Scripture, the church, and the Christian consciousness—and all three in turn, successively or in conjunction, have been used as sources for Christian theology. The Reformation returned to Holy Scripture and, along with the ancient Christian church, acknowledged it as the sole foundation of theology. Rome has a tendency to elevate tradition next to Scripture, while rationalists and mystics alike draw the content of their theology from the religious subject. Since Schleiermacher, much of theology has changed, among orthodox as well as modern theologians, into a theology of consciousness. This is reflected in the concern among many evangelical Christians for a "personal relationship to Jesus," a call that is sometimes set over against "head knowledge," doctrine and theology.

This is at best a half-truth. The idea that good theology is, has always been, and must be, personal is so self-evident that it should not have to be expressly mentioned or demanded. The knowledge of God given in revelation is not abstract and impersonal but the vital and personal knowledge of faith. The objective revelation in Scripture must be completed in subjective illumination, which is the gift of the Holy Spirit. Furthermore, all works of scholarship, including dogmatic theology, bear the stamp of their authors. Precisely because a work of dogmatic theology is not a mere historical account but sets forth what we *ought* to believe, it cannot escape the influence of individuality. But this is something very different from the notion that the theologian is free from all objective constraints. The expectation that doctrinal theology be personal may not lead to caprice or arbitrariness as though the content of faith does not matter. It is God's will that we should love him also with the mind and think of him in a manner worthy of him. To that end he gave his revelation, the revelation to which dogmatic theology is absolutely bound, just as every other science is bound to the object it studies. If a work of theology turns out to be only the subjective and hence individual knowledge of someone's personal Christian faith, it can no longer be considered a work of Christian dogmatic theology. Dogmatics can exist only if there is a divine revelation on whose authority it rests and whose content it unfolds.

How we come to know the content of Christian theology parallels the way we come to know anything. We are products of our environment also in the area of religion. We receive our religious ideas and impressions from those who raise and nurture us, and we remain at all times bound to the circle in which we live. In no domain of life are the intellect and the heart, reason and conscience, feeling and imagination, the epistemic *source* of truth but only organs by which we perceive truth and make it our own. We are receptors of truth that is outside us and greater than us; we are not our own creators, not the makers of our own worlds. Just as physically we are bound to nature and must receive food and drink, shelter and clothing from it, so psychically—in the arts, sciences, religion, and morality—we are dependent on the world outside us. In short, we are not autonomous.

To claim radical autonomy for ourselves places us in the camps of either deism or pantheism. Deism makes human beings independent of God and the world, teaches the all-sufficiency of reason, and leads to rationalism. Pantheism, on the other hand, teaches that God discloses himself and comes to self-consciousness in human beings and fosters mysticism. Both destroy objective truth, leave reason and feeling, the intellect and the heart, to themselves, and end up in unbelief or superstition. Reason criticizes all revelation to death, and feeling gives us the right to imagine the world as we wish and to claim as dogma what seems right to us. It is therefore noteworthy that Holy Scripture never refers human beings to themselves as the epistemic source and standard of religious truth. Indeed, how could it? We are by nature blind and corrupt in the imaginings of our hearts. For the knowledge of truth, Scripture always refers us to objective revelation, to the word and instruction that proceeded from God (Deut. 4:1; Isa. 8:20; John 5:39; 2 Tim. 3:15; 2 Pet. 1:19; etc.). Where the objective truth is personally appropriated by us by faith, that faith still is never like a fountain that from itself brings forth the living water but like a channel that conducts the water to us from another source.

[22] From the preceding it might seem that the correct method in theology is followed by developing a "biblical theology." There are works of theology that claim to do nothing more than summarize the teachings of Scripture.[24] This definition, however, lacks methodological self-awareness. No one is completely unbiased in relating to Scripture and reproduces its content accurately and objectively. Every believer and every theologian first of all receives his or her religious convictions from a faith community, brings along from that background a certain under-standing of the content of revelation, and looks at Scripture with the aid of the glasses that their churches have put on them. All theologians stand consciously or unconsciously in the tradition of the Christian faith in which they were born and nurtured and come to Scripture as Reformed, or Lutheran, or Roman Catholic Christians. In this respect as well, we cannot simply divest ourselves of our en-vironment; we are always children of our time, the products of our background. Theological textbooks tend to reflect the personal and ecclesiastical viewpoint of their authors. This is unavoidable. When theologians attempt to transcend Christian tradition in order to be more purely "biblical," they often create "new" traditions of their own that are no more objective (or "biblical") than those who honestly acknowledge their ecclesiastical traditions. These new traditions do not prove to be as durable as the traditions they reject. Ironically, when ecclesiastical tradition speaks *for* the Bible it is usually more true *to* the Bible.

It is a mistake to treat the Bible as a legal document that should be consulted when we have specific questions. It is composed of many books written by various authors, dating back to different times and divergent in content. It is a living whole, not abstract but organic. It is not given to us simply to parrot its exact words and phrases but so that we, drawing from the entire organism of Scripture, as free and thoughtful children, think God's thoughts after him. This is a demanding task that no person can possibly do alone. The church was appointed this task and given the promise of the Spirit's guidance into all truth, a task which has taken centuries. Isolating oneself from the church, i.e., from Christianity as a whole, from the history of dogma in its entirety, is to lose the truth of the Christian faith. Such a person becomes a branch that is torn from the tree and shrivels, an organ that is separated from the body and therefore doomed to die. Only within the communion of the saints can the length and the breadth, the depth and the height, of the love of Christ be comprehended (Eph. 3:18). We must not separate

---

24. Ed. note: This could be said to be the position of Charles Hodge, who defined the task of the theologian thus: "to collect, authenticate, arrange, and exhibit [the truths of Scripture] in their internal relation to each other." C. Hodge, *Systematic Theology*, 3 vols. (New York: Charles Scribner's Sons, 1888), I, 1; see further, note 27 below.

biblical theology and dogmatic theology, as though one reproduced the content of Scripture while the other restated the dogmas of the church. The sole aim of dogmatic theology is to set forth the thoughts of God that he has laid down in Holy Scripture.

Dogmatic theology does this, in a scholarly fashion, in a scholarly form, and in accordance with a scholarly method. In that sense, Reformed scholars in earlier centuries defended the validity of so-called Scholastic theology in distinction from a more basic church catechesis. In this way they maintained the unity and bond between faith and theology, church and school *and* held high the scientific character of theology. However high and wonderful the thoughts of God might be, they were not aphorisms but constituted an organic unity, a systematic whole, that could also be thought through and cast in a scientific form. Scripture itself prompts this theological labor when everywhere it lays the strongest emphasis, not on abstract cognition, but on doctrine and truth, knowledge and wisdom.

[23] A good dogmatic method, therefore, needs to take into account Scripture, church, and Christian experience (consciousness) to keep a theologian from one-sidedness. As a rule we receive our religious convictions from our environment. That is true in all religions, including Christianity. When, as often happens, doubt arises about the teachings of one's church, we may find ourselves drawn to the doctrines of another historical Christian church; Baptists do become Pentecostals; Lutherans do become Reformed. In such cases, though change is significant, there is no loss of religion itself or of Christian identity. A dogma remains that is established and supplies comfort and support in life. On this basis, then, a dogmatic theology that describes the truth of God as it is recognized in a particular church remains possible.

But when doubt makes much deeper inroads in the religious life so that one loses all faith and falls into skepticism and agnosticism, then faith, confession, and dogmatic theology are impossible; mere negation is incapable of creating fellowship. Since human beings seek fellowship in their convictions, some move away from the fellowship of the church into a school of philosophy or a social movement. In such cases it is important to note that religious faith remains; it has only transferred its object and found certainty in a new dogma.

[24] Accordingly, Christian theology is possible only for one who lives in the fellowship of faith with one Christian church or another. This is implicit in the very nature of religious faith, which is distinguishable from scientific concepts, among others, in that the former is not rooted in one's own insight, in the authority of some human being, but only in the authority of an external object of devotion, i.e., God. This authority is *acknowledged*; its ideas have found credence and recognition in a religious circle, i.e., a church. Dogma does not traffic in human opinion but with divine truth. A church does not believe its confession because of scientific proof but because it believes God has spoken. To seek religious conviction in a school of philosophy confuses religion with science and gains nothing but a learned judgment or opinion that is eminently disputable.

A church is the natural soil for religion and theology, and in this present age there is a plurality of churches and a similar plurality of theologies. This will be the case until in Christ the church has attained its full maturity and all have come to the unity of faith and the knowledge of the Son of God. It is an obligation for every church and every theologian to seek this unity of truth by thinking through the faith of one's own church and presenting it faithfully. Christ promised his church the Holy Spirit, who would guide her into all truth. This promise sheds a glorious light on the history of dogma as the explication of Scripture, the exposition that the Holy Spirit has given, in the church, of the treasures of the Word. A theologian should not restrict his work to his own fellowship but view it in the total context of the unique faith and life of his church, and then again in the context of the history of the whole church of Christ. We stand on the shoulders of previous generations; we know we are surrounded by a cloud of witnesses and are called to let our witness merge with the voice of these many waters. Every work of theology ought to be in full accord with and a part of the doxology sung to God by the church of all ages.

Virtually every work of dogmatic theology begins with the doctrine of Scripture as the sole foundation of theology. The best-equipped theologian carries out the task by living in full communion of faith with the church of Christ. Of course, there is a difference between the way in which a theologian is shaped and the primary principle from which a work of theology receives its material. In all sciences, practitioners gain initial acquaintance with the field from an authority and must know the history of the field and the present state of knowledge before moving on to independent work and new areas of research. In other words, pedagogically, the tradition precedes the scientific work. But the tradition is never confused with the discipline itself or considered to be the source of knowledge for the discipline. Knowing that astrology and alchemy are part of the tradition of modern astronomy and chemistry respectively does not lead one to search in either for true knowledge about those fields. It is similar for theology. Pedagogically, the church is prior to Scripture. But in the logical order, Scripture is the sole foundation of church and theology. In case of conflict between them, the church and confession must yield to Scripture. Only Scripture is self-authenticating (αὐτόπιστος) and its own interpreter, and nothing may be put on a level with Scripture. All Christian churches are united in the confession that Holy Scripture is the foundation of theology, as the Belgic Confession states in its fifth article.[25]

Admittedly, article 2 of the Belgic Confession states that God is known by two means—nature and Scripture—and all Reformed theologians uphold natural theology in its truth and value. Calvin incorporated natural theology into the

25. "We receive all these books and these only as holy and canonical, for the regulating, founding, and establishing of our faith. And we believe without a doubt all things contained in them—not so much because the church receives and approves them as such but above all because the Holy Spirit testifies in our hearts that they are from God, and also because they prove themselves to be from God. For even the blind themselves are able to see that the things predicted in them do happen."

body of Christian theology, saying that Scripture was the spectacles by which believers see God more distinctly also in the works of nature.[26] Natural theology was accepted by the Reformed but never as an independent source of saving truth apart from faith. Reformed theology took its stand in faith and then, with Christian eyes, armed by Holy Scripture, also discovered in nature the footprints of the God whom it had come to know—in Christ and by Scripture—as Father. Nature did not stand on its own as an independent principle alongside Holy Scripture, each of them supplying a set of truths of its own. Rather, nature was viewed in the light of Scripture, and Scripture was needed to see nature rightly as the gift of the Creator.

So, though we do acknowledge a knowledge of God derived from nature, dogmatic theology still has but one external foundation (*principium externum*), i.e., Holy Scripture. Important as the church's traditions and confessions are, they are not an additional epistemic source for theology *alongside* Holy Scripture. Today there is no "pure tradition" of Christianity apart from Scripture; we no longer have any knowledge of Christian truth except that which comes to us from Holy Scripture. All dogmatic theologians assert that clear and complete knowledge of God can only be obtained from Scripture and that it is the sole foundation of theology. The attributes of authority, sufficiency, and perfection, which Protestants in their struggle with Rome attributed to Holy Scripture, demonstrate the same thing. The term "foundation" (*principium*) here is much to be preferred over "source" (*fons*). The latter describes the relation between Scripture and theology as a mechanical one, as though dogmas could be drawn from Holy Scripture like water from a well.[27] But "foundation" or "first principle" suggests an organic connection. In a formal sense, there are no dogmas in Scripture, but the material for them is all to be found in it. Hence dogmatic theology can be defined as the truth of Scripture, absorbed and reproduced by the thinking consciousness of the Christian theologian.

FAITH AND METHOD: THE ORGANIZATION OF THEOLOGY

[25] This, however, is not to deny the personal character of doctrinal theology, which seeks to describe not merely what was historically the case but rather what

26. John Calvin, *Institutes of the Christian Religion*, I.vi.1 (ed. John T. McNeill and trans. Ford Lewis Battles, 2 vols. [Philadelphia: Westminster, 1960], 1:69–71).

27. Ed. note: This theological method distances itself at this point from the Princeton tradition represented by Charles Hodge, who advocates an empirical-inductive method that sees the Bible as a "storehouse of facts." The task of the theologian is then "to ascertain, collect, and combine all the facts" in an orderly system, guided by the same rules as the man of Science" (C. Hodge, *Systematic Theology*, I, 10–11). Bavinck insists here that it is also inappropriate to use the language of "experiment" and "hypothesis" with respect to theology. When God speaks in his word there is no longer any room for "experiment." On Hodge, see further A. Kuyper, *Principles of Sacred Theology*, trans. J. H. De Vries (Grand Rapids: Eerdmans, 1965 [1898]), 318–19; Robert McCheyne Edgar, "Christianity and the Experimental Method," *Presbyterian and Reformed Review* 6, no. 22 (April 1895): 201–23.

in religion ought to count as truth. Dogmatic theology must be free from arbitrariness and caprice; it is bound to a real object that must exist in the real world. Furthermore, this object must be knowable and the theologian must be strictly bound to that object. To say that theology must be personal may not be used as a reason to deny the reality of its knowable object. The tendency to set the personal character of theology over against its objectivity is a mistake. Theology can be personal only if its object is real. This is true of all human knowledge and science. Every science is bound to its object, and that object, with its authority and normative power, remains prior to and greater than the corresponding science.

We also need to acknowledge the differences between theology and many other sciences. Personal assent matters more in theology than in most other sciences; human sympathies and antipathies are heavily invested in it. In dogmatic theology, personality plays an important role, not because it is unfortunately unavoidable, but because it ought to play an important role. The revelation in which God communicates knowledge of himself intends to foster religion; it is *designed* to generate faith in our hearts, to place us in a proper relation to God. Revelation is designed to give us knowledge—not merely abstract theoretical knowledge, as in the other sciences, but vital personal knowledge: in a word, the knowledge of faith. Hence for dogmatic work, personal faith is imperative.

Personal faith, however, is not the source of true religious knowledge for in that case the inner self of human beings would have to be considered as the object and source of theology. This is to confuse the reality of God with our subjective sense of God. Human subjective response to God is crucial; Scripture teaches that objective revelation should be completed in subjective illumination. The Reformed doctrine of Scripture is most intimately tied in with that of the testimony of the Holy Spirit. The external word does not remain outside us but, through faith, becomes an internal word. The Holy Spirit who gave us Scripture also bears witness to that Scripture in the hearts of believers. Scripture itself attends to its own acceptance in the consciousness of the church of Christ. Believers, in consequence, feel that with their whole souls they are bound to Scripture. They are inducted into it by the Holy Spirit, the church's supreme Teacher (*Doctor ecclesiae*). And the whole intent of believers is to take the thoughts of God laid down in Scripture into their consciousness and to understand them rationally. But in all this they remain human beings with disposition, upbringing, and insights all their own. Faith itself does not originate in the same way in every person, nor does it have the same strength in all. Individual powers of reasoning differ in sharpness, depth, and clarity since the influence of sin also remains operative in the human consciousness and intellect. As a result of all these influences, doctrinal theology continues to bear a personal character and is diverse.

As in every other science, so it is the case here. Even prophets and apostles saw the same truth from different perspectives. Unity of faith has no more been realized than unity of knowledge. But precisely through this diversity, God leads his church toward unity. Once that unity of faith and knowledge has been reached, dogmatic theology too will have accomplished its task. Until then, however, it is entrusted with the calling, in the domain of science, to interpret the thoughts that God has laid down for us in Holy Scripture.

[26] A theologian will be most fully equipped to carry out this task by living in communion of faith with the church of Christ and confessing Scripture as the only and sufficient basis (*principium*) of the knowledge of God. Accordingly, theologians receive the content of their faith from the hands of the church; pedagogically, we come to Scripture through the church. But no more than any other believer can this be the stopping-off place. We are called to analyze the very fiber of the dogmas we have come to know from the church and to examine how they are rooted in Holy Scripture. Thus the task is sometimes said to consist in, first, objectively reproducing the dogmas and then tracing them back to Holy Scripture—a method called *historical-analytical*. In this way one begins with the church's teaching and summarizes it. For a few dogmas as such this method may be highly commendable, and it may be true that theologians undervalue it. Nonetheless, the objection to it is that by using this method one cannot achieve a unified scientific system—the theologian will be overwhelmed by the disparate dogmas under review. The dogmatic theologian therefore will do better taking a different road. Instead of proceeding from the river back to the source (historical-analytic method), it is preferable to travel from the source to the river. Without shortchanging the truth that in a pedagogical sense the church precedes Scripture, a theologian can nevertheless be positioned in Scripture itself as the foundation of theology (*principium theologiae*) and from there develop dogmas. What a theologian does in that case is to replicate, as it were, the intellectual labor of the church. We are shown how dogmas have arisen organically from Scripture—that the firm and broad foundation on which the edifice of dogmatics rises is not a single text in its isolation but Scripture as a whole. This is properly called the *synthetic-genetic* method.

This synthetic-genetic method brings word and historical fact together, acknowledging that the Bible does not merely convey facts that we have to explain but itself clearly illumines those facts. Scripture is not a collection of facts or sayings but the living Word of God, the witness of the Holy Spirit. Scripture not only calls for assent; it demands faith. God speaks; we must believe, trust, and obey. Scripture's message, furthermore, is a unity that displays an organic wholeness and order. The different dogmas are not isolated propositions but constitute a unity. The dogmatic theologian is called to a critical task of genetically and systematically unfolding the dogmatic truths of Scripture, a task already implied in the systematic nature of the work one does on the dogmatic material. In this genetic and systematic unfolding of the dogmas, the theologian is to point out possible deviations, to fill possible gaps, and so to work at the development of dogmas in the future. In that way dogmatic theology attempts to furnish an exposition of the treasures of wisdom and knowledge that are hidden in Christ and exhibited in Scripture.

[27–28] How should such a dogmatic work then be organized and structured? What is its logical order? Early works in theology were simple and lacked systematic order. Origen's work *On First Principles* (*Peri Archon*) introduces some order in the material and is divided into four major parts: God, the world, freedom, and revelation. Augustine's *Enchiridion* treats subjects of dogmatic theology and ethics under the headings of the three Christian virtues: faith, hope, and love. Peter Lombard in the Middle Ages divided his *Sentences* into four books. The first three deal with things (*res*), the last with signs (*signa*). The entire content of revelation, to his mind, consists of these two: *things* and *signs*. In accordance with this order, the first book of the *Sentences* deals with the mystery of the Trinity and the second with the creation and formation of physical and spiritual things: creation, angels, the six-day period of creation, humanity, fall, sin. The third book deals with the incarnation of the Word: the person and work of Christ; faith, hope, and love; the four principal virtues; and other ethical topics. Finally, the fourth book, concerning the sacraments, contains the doctrine of the seven sacraments, the resurrection, the judgment, heaven, and hell.

There is discernible progress here. There is better grouping and delimitation of the topics; the whole is divided into four parts, each with its own distinct object, and the ethical material is incorporated in the dogmatics itself. The sacraments, formerly only touched upon, are treated at length. On the other hand, the order still leaves much to be desired, and several subjects, such as Scripture, the church, and particularly soteriology, are left virtually undiscussed. A place of honor, especially from a formal viewpoint, needs to be given to Bonaventure's *Breviloquium*. We find here a firmly methodical approach, complete mastery of the material, a clean delimitation of the topics, and a purposefully chosen principle of division. This is apparent when in part I, chapter 1, Bonaventure states that though theology comprises all seven topics it is nevertheless a single science, for "God is not only the efficient and exemplary Cause of things through creation, but also their refective [or renewing; *refectivum*] Principle through redemption, and their perfective Principle through remuneration [restoration]."[28]

Thomas's division in his *Summa* is quite different and inferior. This work contains three parts; the parts are divided into questions, and these again into articles. Part I deals with God and his creation before and apart from sin: God as first principle and exemplary cause of all things. Part II speaks of man as his image and again is divided into a *prima* and a *secunda*. The third part describes the way by which we human beings can attain to the blessedness of eternal life, i.e., Christ and the sacraments. An appendix composed of three questions discusses purgatory. Thomas frames every tenet of faith in the form of a question and raises all the objections advanced against it by opponents. Then, with an appeal to authority (Scripture, church fathers, or Aristotle), he demonstrates the truth of the thing

---

28. Cited from *The Works of Bonaventure*, vol. 2, *The Breviloquium*, trans. Jose De Vinck (Paterson, NJ: St. Anthony Guild Press, 1963), 33.

questioned and draws the conclusion. This is then further explained and finally defended against the objections raised.

[30–31] Reformation theology was originally characterized by an anti-Scholastic attitude and initially presented in a very simple and practical form. Melanchthon's *Loci Communes*, published in 1521, have their roots in lectures on Paul's Epistle to the Romans. They are practical through and through in that they treat only anthropological and soteriological topics, especially those of sin and grace and law and gospel, while leaving undiscussed the objective dogmas of God, Trinity, creation, incarnation, and satisfaction. Subsequent editions, however, expanded the number of *loci* and their content, and successive editions exhibit an ever-growing approximation to the synthetic division, which begins with God and from there descends to his works in nature and grace. Zwingli's *Commentary on True and False Religion*, as well as his *Exposition of the Christian Faith*, while also treating a number of dogmatic *loci*, were soon overshadowed by Calvin's *Institutes of the Christian Religion*. Its final (1559) edition contained four books, covering the knowledge of God as Creator, God as Redeemer in Christ, and the work of the Holy Spirit (internal = book 3; external = book 4). The division is not strictly trinitarian but derived from the Apostles' Creed. The starting point of the *Institutes* is theological; however, Calvin does not proceed from an abstract concept of God but from God as he is known by humanity from nature and Scripture.

In the course of the seventeenth century, the treatment of the separate *loci* became increasingly more Scholastic, and their connectedness with the life of faith became less apparent as it was experienced less. A reaction followed: theology became increasingly *analytic*; that is to say, it was seen as a *practical* science whose concern was human salvation and well-being.[29] Theology was viewed less as the science of God and more about human wisdom needed for arriving at salvation. There appear to be advantages in focusing on those concerns that are important to all believers such as the question: "What must I do to be saved?" The Heidelberg Catechism also repeatedly asks us, "What does it benefit you to know this?" Nonetheless, this method is inadequate *theologically* since it diverts us from the objective reality of God to anthropological concerns. The covenant theologian Johannes Coccius similarly exchanged the theological for an anthropological viewpoint. In his *Doctrine of the Covenant and Testament of God* (1648) he divided all the material of dogmatics in terms of the covenant idea in the hope of offering a more biblical-theological and anti-Scholastic dogmatics. But Coccius' arrangement of the different covenant dispensations so sharply distinguished them, treating the history of the covenant of grace as a series of *abrogations*, an abolition of the covenant of works, that the unity of God's covenant promise was lost. The major objection to this approach is that its theological starting point is not God but the covenant between God and humanity. Here, doctrines of God and humanity

---

29. Ed. note: The word "analytic" here refers not to the Anglo-Saxon tradition of "analytic philosophy" but to the method of beginning with a stated goal and working back to the means.

function only in an introductory way as presupposition for the work of salvation. Any boundary between the history of revelation and the content of dogmatics is lost in this approach, and the distinctive work of dogmatic theology is subsumed under a specious "biblical theology" which undermines it.

[32] The shape of dogmatic theology was changed significantly under the influence of modern philosophy, which diminished its content and enlarged the formal discussion about method. Questions about methodology and epistemology became primary, trumping metaphysical ones. Since Kant declared God to be unknowable, reason and natural theology were substituted for divine revelation. Morality and religious feeling became the starting point and subject matter of theology; the prolegomena of religious philosophy grew in size and influence in comparison with the content of theology. This is a major change from the Reformation era and earlier where Scripture's truth and authority were simply assumed and the battles took place over particular dogmas. Now, reason and historical criticism of Scripture together served as challenges to the church's dogmas. The conviction took hold that human reason, even apart from faith, could of itself produce all the truths of natural theology. Reason not only received its own domain alongside revelation but eventually extended its powers over that of revelation itself. Reason was given the prerogative of investigating the truth of revelation. Natural theology was believed to provide a solid ground on which to stand, a purely scientific foundation, and revelation too was examined this way. Reason was no longer content with the modest role of servant and demanded a controlling voice. The prolegomena to theology consistently grew in scope and shaped the content.

[33] Rationalist foundations for theology, however, could not withstand the philosophical challenge initiated by Kant. Schleiermacher, among others, attempted to save faith and the doctrine of faith by restricting them to feelings and the description of feeling, specifically the "feeling of absolute dependence."[30] Yet, the actual organization of dogmatic theology does not change dramatically in the nineteenth century. Attacks on the Christian religion in the nineteenth century were primarily directed against the foundations themselves. The philosophical underpinnings of dogmatics came under fire; not isolated doctrines but the very possibility of doctrine and dogmatic theology were questioned. When, in addition, Holy Scripture is robbed of its divine authority by historical criticism, it should not surprise us that religious life loses its vitality. Faith is no longer sure of itself; the childlike and simultaneously heroic statement "I believe" is heard less and less as criticism, doubt, and uncertainty gain the upper hand. Even the warrant for and value of religion was seriously disputed. Consequently, and partly caused by all this, religious life in the late nineteenth and early twentieth centuries is dramatically less vigorous than before. There may be movement in the domain of religion and the study of religion, but there is little

30. F. Schleiermacher, *The Christian Faith*, §4.

genuinely religious life. People perhaps still believe their confessions, but they no longer confess their faith.[31]

[34] The irony here is that in the attempt to liberate theology from past errors, including the error of metaphysics, theologians such as Schleiermacher only made it even more dependent on philosophy. When questions of theological method and/or apologetics dominate a theologian's work we generally see a weaker tie to the truth of Scripture and tradition and an increasing dependence on the philosophy *du jour*. Even when Reformed theologians begin their work with the natural knowledge of God and the rational and historical proofs of the Christian religion, all as a *preamble* to the content of theology proper, they forsake the starting point in faith. Giving reasons for believing ought to arise out of faith itself and not serve as the preamble to theology.[32] Still, dealing with the foundations of theology before the content is a useful and good thing. Care must be taken to ensure that this prolegomena material does not lose its theological character and make dogmatic theology subservient to philosophy. The foundations of faith (*principia fidei*) are themselves articles of faith (*articuli fidei*), based not on human arguments and proofs but on divine authority. The recognition of revelation, of Scripture as the Word of God, is an act of faith as well as its fruit. Dogmatic theology is from start to finish the work of a believer who is confessing and giving an account of the ground and content of his faith. The foundations of faith are twofold: the external and internal, the objective and the formal, revelation and faith. These two topics are the proper subject matter of theological prolegomena.

When we move to the *content* of dogmatic theology, different organizing principles have been suggested, including the creedal trinitarian structure, Father and Creation, Son and Redemption, Holy Spirit and Sanctification.[33] Although not objectionable as such, this scheme is not altogether satisfactory for a number of reasons. First, it cannot accommodate the treatment of the Trinity itself because it does not naturally fit in any of the three economies and so has to be discussed by way of hypothesis in a prior chapter. Furthermore, in following this division one runs the risk that the outward or external works of God (*opera Dei ad extra*) are conceived too much as the individual works of the three Persons (*opera Dei personalia*) and not enough as essential works of the one God (*opera Dei essentialia*), i.e., the common works of the divine person. Although this structure preserves unity, the Trinity is viewed only economically and its ontological character not recognized. In addition, the *loci* on creation, angels, humanity, sin, church, etc., cannot come into their own. Organizing the content of dogmatic theology on a christological

31. A. Schweizer, *Die christliche Glaubenslehre nach protestantischen Grundsatzen dargestellt*, 2 vols. in 3 (Leipzig: S. Hirzel, 1863–72).

32. Ed. note: This position thus differs significantly from that of Benjamin Warfield; see his reviews of Francis R. Beattie, *Apologetics, or, the Rational Vindication of Christianity* (1903), and H. Bavinck, *De Zekerheid de Geloofs* (1901), in *Selected Shorter Writings of Benjamin B. Warfield*, ed. John E. Meeter, 2 vols. (Phillipsburg, NJ: P&R, 1973 [1907]), II, 93–123.

33. See *Heidelberg Catechism*, Lord's Day 8.

basis is even less satisfying because it often rests on the false assumption that rather than Scripture the person of Christ specifically is the foundation and epistemic source of dogmatics. However, we know Christ only from and through Scripture. In addition, though Christ is quite certainly the central focus and main content of Holy Scripture, he cannot be its starting point. Christ presupposes the existence of God and humanity. He did not make his historical appearance immediately at the time of the promise (in Eden) but many centuries later. Furthermore, God's revelation through the Son does not nullify the many and varied ways he spoke through the prophets. Scripture *as a whole* is God's Word to us and not the New Testament alone nor the words of Jesus alone.

Other organizations of dogmatic theology, such as those modeled on the three virtues (faith, hope, and love); on the scheme of faith, prayer, and commandment; on the final end and destiny of humanity; on the covenant or the fellowship between God and man; on the kingdom of God; on the concepts of life, love, spirit, etc., are also inadequate. Although they may have many practical advantages and be perfectly appropriate in a catechism, these systems are unsuitable for a work of theology, which is a system of the knowledge of God; they are not central and comprehensive enough. Either they have been introduced from the outside and do not govern the system, or they are strictly adhered to as principles of organization but fail to do justice to the various *loci*.

[35] The content of dogmatic theology is the knowledge of God as he has revealed it in Christ through his Word. The knowledge of believers is unique in that they view the whole of life religiously and theologically and see everything in God's light, from the perspective of eternity (*sub specie aeternitatis*). That is the difference between their worldview and a philosophical or scientific worldview. In dogmatic theology it is always Christian believers who are speaking. They do not speculate about God or proceed from an abstract philosophical concept of God, but only describe the knowledge of God that has been revealed to them in Christ. In every dogma, therefore, throbs the heartbeat of religion. Theologians explicate the content of their faith as it is objectively exhibited by God himself before their believing eyes in revelation. They are not governed by the believing subject but by the object of faith and derive the principle of organization and the arrangement of the material from the selfsame object that it is their task to describe.

If this starting point is correct, then the method of organization that commends itself is the *historic-genetic* or *synthetic* method. It takes its point of departure in God and views all creatures only in relation to him. Proceeding from God, it descends to his works, in order through them again to ascend to and end in him. So in this method God is beginning, middle, and end. From him, through him, and to him are all things (Rom. 11:36). The content of the Christian faith is the knowledge of God in his being and in his works.

God and his works are, however, clearly distinguished. God is Creator, Redeemer, and Perfecter. He is "the efficient and exemplary Cause of things through creation, their renewing Principle through redemption, and their perfective Principle in restoration" (Bonaventure). Dogmatic theology is the system of the knowledge of God as he has revealed himself in Christ; it is the system of the Christian religion. And the essence of the Christian religion consists in the reality that what the Father has created, ruined by sin, is restored in the death of the Son of God and re-created by the grace of the Holy Spirit into a kingdom of God. Dogmatic theology shows us how God, who is all-sufficient in himself, nevertheless glorifies himself in his creation, which, even when it is torn apart by sin, is gathered up again in Christ (Eph. 1:10). It describes for us God, always God, from beginning to end—God in his being, God in his creation, God against sin, God in Christ, God breaking down all resistance through the Holy Spirit and guiding the whole of creation back to the objective he decreed for it: the glory of his name. Dogmatic theology, therefore, is not a dull and arid science. It is a theodicy, a doxology to all God's virtues and perfections, a hymn of adoration and thanksgiving, a "glory to God in the highest" (Luke 2:14). Theology is about God and should reflect a doxological tone that glorifies him.

2

THE HISTORY AND LITERATURE
OF DOGMATIC THEOLOGY

THE FORMATION OF DOGMA

[36] The Bible is not a textbook of theology; its language is the fresh and immediate expression of concrete life. Dogmatic theology arises from sustained reflection on the truth of Scripture and is the task and fruit of the whole church, not just of individuals. Scripture is a gold mine; it is the church that extracts the gold, puts its stamp on it, and converts it to general currency. It is possible to err on the side of either overestimating or disparaging the church's tradition of dogma formation and theology. Protests against the church's teaching are often made by appealing to the original and "authentic" teaching of or example of Jesus.

This critical posture is taken by influential church historian Adolf von Harnack, who saw the doctrinal development of the early church as a mingling of Christian religion and pagan Hellenic philosophy and culture.[1] As we read in the previous chapter, he saw this infusion of the Greek spirit into Christianity as a grand error, a progressive corruption of the simple gospel of Jesus, a false interpretation of the original essence of Christianity. This essence can be reduced to a formula: the fatherhood of God, the brotherhood of man, and the infinite worth of the human soul.[2] The kingdom of God is a moral reality brought into being by those in whom

---

1. "Dogma in its conception and development is a work of the Greek spirit on the soil of the Gospel" (Adolf von Harnack, *History of Dogma*, trans. N. Buchanan, J. Millar, E. B. Speirs, and W. McGilchrist, and ed. A. B. Bruce, 7 vols. [London: Williams & Norgate, 1896–99], I, 17).

2. Adolf von Harnack, *What Is Christianity?* trans. Thomas Bailey Saunders (New York: Harper & Brothers, 1957).

the image of Jesus lives. Christian theology ought to get rid of its whole history of dogma and to return, decisively and radically, to the original gospel of Jesus found primarily in the Sermon on the Mount. This is, of course, only Harnack's personal dissenting and equally dogmatic point of view; it is an alternative to the church's self-understanding, but it is no less a dogma for all that. Harnack simply replaces the church's dogma with his own.

[37] Diametrically opposed to this is the overestimation that the history of dogma is accorded from the side of Roman Catholicism. Christian truth is not completely embodied in Scripture and tradition, but official church teaching (*ex cathedra* by the pope) is also crowned with infallible authority. At the same time, the Roman Catholic Church does not equate ecclesiastical interpretation with divine truth but insists that the church receives no new revelations. The pope possesses only interpretive power; he may proclaim as dogma only that which was, at all times, materially implicit in Scripture and tradition. The pope, furthermore, is not inspired (like prophets and apostles) but only receives the special *assistance* of the Holy Spirit. Rome continues to face the dilemma of whether to subordinate Scripture to dogma or dogma to Scripture.

From the beginning the Reformation was on its guard against both the underestimation and overestimation of history. The Reformation was not opposed to all tradition but only to a false and corrupted tradition. It accepted the Apostles' Creed and the creedal statements of the first four councils, and took advantage of the theology of the church fathers, especially Augustine. However, the Reformation returned to Holy Scripture and recognized no tradition except that which flowed from Scripture and was subject to its norms. The material for dogmatic theology is given in Holy Scripture; under the guidance of the Holy Spirit the church interpreted Scripture, formulated key dogmas, and provided summaries of Christian truth. The history of dogma formation and dogmatic reflection has experienced both forward and backward movement but does reflect an overall advance. The Holy Spirit's leading is the guarantee that it will; he does not rest until he has caused the fullness of Christ—which includes the fullness of his truth and wisdom—to dwell in the church and has filled that church with all the fullness of God (Eph. 3:19). On key doctrines we see growing clarity in the church's understanding; there is a history of doctrinal development as well as a history of scientific theological development. These two histories—dogma and dogmatic theology—are related but do need to be distinguished.

DOGMA IN THE EARLY CHURCH

[38] The earliest period of dogma formation, from the second through fourth centuries—the era of the Apostolic Fathers—operated with the basic oral and written teaching of the apostles. The church articulated its dogmas in epistolary writings and simple creeds. Analytic reflection on the fundamentals of the Christian gos-

pel—the person and work of Christ, the Holy Spirit, faith, repentance, church, baptism, communion—was secondary to the practical questions of discipleship. The concern was more to convert Christian truth into the practice of a life lived under the sway of the gospel. The accent, thus, was not on *gnosis* but on a holy life, on the practice of the Christian virtues of love, meekness, humility, obedience, chastity, peace, unity, etc. Generally speaking, the real essence of Christianity, in distinction from Judaism and paganism, was not yet clearly recognized and in any case was better understood ethically than dogmatically.

However, the Christian church could not stop at this simple repetition and practical application of the truth of Scripture because it faced open opposition from the side of a pagan culture that forced Christians into reflection and defense. Initially content with persecution, hatred, and mockery,[3] the pagan world took account of Christianity and began to attack it scientifically, in a manner not unlike present-day opposition to Christianity.[4] All the arguments later advanced against Christianity can already be found in writers such as Celsus and Julian (the "Apostate").[5] These writers included in their arsenal arguments against the authenticity and truth of many Bible books (the Pentateuch, Daniel, and the Gospels) and against revelation and miracles in general; against an assortment of dogmas such as the incarnation, satisfaction, forgiveness, the resurrection, and eternal punishment; arguments also against norms of morality such as asceticism, contempt of the world, and lack of refinement; and, finally, slanderous accusations of worshiping an ass's head and of committing child murder, adultery, and all sorts of immorality.

This scientific polemic, however, did not succeed in overcoming Christianity either. Consequently, pagans saw themselves forced either to revive the old religion, as Neopythagoreanism and Neoplatonism attempted and especially the Mithras religion[6] aspired to do, or to combine Christianity with paganism as in gnosticism and Manichaeism. Gnosticism was a particularly powerful attempt to

3. See Tacitus, *Annals*, xv.44; Lucian, *Peregrinus Proteus*.

4. K. A. Kellner, *Hellenismus und Christenthum* (Köln: M. DuMont-Schauberg, 1866), 431ff. Ed. note: Twenty-first-century examples include Richard Dawkins, *The God Delusion* (New York: Houghton-Mifflin, 2006); Sam Harris, *Letter to a Christian Nation* (New York: Knopf, 2006); Christopher Hitchens, *God Is Not Great: How Religion Poisons Everything* (New York: Warner Books, 2007).

5. See Origen, *Contra Celsum*, trans. H. Chadwick (Cambridge: Cambridge University Press, 1953; repr., 1965). Ed. note: The Emperor Julian (332–363) attempted to re-paganize the empire and wrote a three-volume attack against Christianity, *Against the Galileans*, in 363. This work is known only through Cyril of Alexandria's apologetic work, *For the Holy Religion of the Christians against the Books of the Impious Julian* (see Johannes Quasten, *Patrology*, 4 vols. [Utrecht: Spectrum, 1950–], III, 129–30).

6. Franz Cumont, *Die Mysterien des Mithra: Ein Beitrag zur Religionsgeschichte der römischen Kaiserzeit* (Leipzig: Teubner, 1903); Julius Grill, *Die persische Mysterienreligion im römischen Reiche und das Christentum* (Tübingen: Mohr, 1903); ed. note: More recent literature includes: David Ulansey, *The Origins of the Mithraic Mysteries: Cosmology and Salvation in the Ancient World* (New York: Oxford University Press, 1989); Manfred Claus, *The Roman Cult of Mithras: The God and His Mysteries*, trans. Richard Gordon (New York: Routledge, 2001); Roger Beck, *The Religion of the Mithras Cult: Mysteries of the Unconquered Sun* (Oxford: Oxford University Press, 2006).

absorb Christianity (and so deprive it of its absolute character) in its combination and fusion of a range of pagan elements: Neoplatonic philosophy, Syrian and Phoenician mythology, Chaldean astrology, Persian dualism, etc. In this connection the main question was how the human spirit had fallen into the bonds of matter and could now be delivered from these bonds. Matter, the cause of evil, cannot be explained as coming from God but is derived from a lower deity, the demiurge, who stands between the supreme God and the world of the senses and is equated with the God of the Old Testament. Proceeding from God—for the purpose of liberating spirits in bondage to matter—are various aeons, which represent the different religions and culminate in the aeon Christ. What saves a person is *gnosis* combined with *ascesis*. *Pistis* (faith; theology) may be fine for the unlearned, but *gnosis* (knowledge; philosophy) is supreme and the possession of the truly spiritual (πνευματικοι). These ideas were harmonized with Scripture by allegorical exegesis and presented in forms and images derived from mythology and adorned by fanciful imagination. They changed Christianity from a history to an idea, into a speculative philosophy, which has exerted its influence throughout the centuries, right down to the systems of Hegel and Schelling.

To counter these various attacks Christians were forced to reflect on the content of revelation and to posit a true Christian *gnosis* against the false. Accordingly, revealed truth now became the object of methodical scientific thought. Theology arose, not from within and for the church and for the purpose of training its ministers, but prompted by and in opposition to the attacks aimed at Christianity. Naturally, knowledge of pagan philosophy was needed for such rational activity. Actually, theology originated with the help of and in alliance with philosophy. This had already been attempted by the gnostics as well, but there was an essential difference in the way the gnostics and the apologists sought such synthesis. For the gnostics the use of philosophy was material and shaped the content of the notion of sin and deliverance, while for the apologists it was mainly formal. While the gnostics presented the different philosophies as a religious process in which Christianity was included, the apologists tried to show that the Christian religion, which they recognized and accepted as the supreme truth, is the true philosophy that unites within itself all elements of truth that come from without.

The fundamental idea of the apologists is this: God is one, inexpressible, spiritual, etc., but through the Logos he is also the Creator of the world, the final cause of all that is, and the first principle of everything that is morally good. Gnostic dualism is overcome here since the world everywhere bears the stamp of the divine Logos, and matter is good and created by God. Humanity was originally created good, received reason and freedom, and was destined for immortality (ἀθανασια); this it had to and could attain in the way of free obedience. But seduced by demons, humanity came under the sway of sensuality and fell into error and death. At this point as well, dualism is avoided and the cause of sin is located in the human will. New means are therefore required to bring human beings back from the way of deception and death and to lead them to immortality. From the most ancient times, God revealed himself by the Logos, imparting the knowledge of the truth even to some pagans but especially to the prophets of Israel and finally in his Son Jesus Christ. In him all earlier truth is confirmed and perfected. Through Christ, as the teacher of truth, humanity is again brought to its destination. Accordingly, though the apologists are guilty of some intellectualism as well as moralism, still there is present, as for example in Justin Martyr, an effort to understand Christ also as Reconciler and Redeemer by whose blood we receive the forgiveness of sin.[7]

[39] The beginnings of theology in the apologists were not only weak but also marred in many respects by one-sidedness and error. The problems that presented themselves were numerous and immense, much too deep for rapid and correct resolution. Differences in understanding were frequent, while divergence in trends and schools arose as well. Soon, two dogmatic trends became distinguishable. The one is represented by Tertullian, Cyprian, Lactantius, as well as Irenaeus, which is sharply opposed to philosophy and warns against it. Here we also include Irenaeus's pupil Hippolytus of Rome, the likely author of *Refutation of All Heresies*, initially attributed to Origen.[8] All these men are sharply opposed to philosophy. Irenaeus issued strong warnings against it, and Tertullian banished it totally and in the sharpest possible terms in his familiar saying: "What fellowship is there between Athens and Jerusalem, the academy and the church, Christians and heretics?"[9] Still, they all make the most naïve use of it. Tertullian's great importance for theology lies in the fact that he introduced a number of terms crucial to later trinitarian and christological dogma, such as *trias, trinitas, satisfacere, meritum, sacramentum, una substantia* and *tres personae, duae substantiae in una persona,* etc., none of which occurs in Scripture. But as these men do this, they nevertheless position themselves in the faith of the church; they are historical, positive, and realistic, and do not make a qualitative—at most a quantitative—distinction between faith and theology, *pistis* and *gnōsis.*[10]

It must be granted that in the case of these men we cannot yet speak of a dogmatic system. In their work the various dogmas stand, unconnected, side by side; one looks in vain for a specific organizing principle. Even more, Tertullian and Hippolytus have not yet succeeded in completely overcoming gnosticism in Christology. Still, their theology, particularly that of Irenaeus, shaped that of succeeding centuries. All the later dogmas can be found in his work. The unity of God, the essential unity of Father and Son, the unity of the God of creation and redemption, the unity of the God of the Old Testament and the God of the New Testament, the creation of the world out of nothing, the unity of the human race, the origin of sin in the freedom

---

7. Ed. note: English translations of the apologists include the *Ante-Nicene Fathers*, ed. Alexander Roberts and James Donaldson, 10 vols. (New York: Christian Literature, 1885–96; repr., Grand Rapids: Eerdmans, 1950–51).

8. Ed. note: See "Introduction to Hippolytus's *The Refutation of all Heresies*," *ANF*, V, 3–7.

9. Irenaeus, *Against Heresies*, II, 25–28, *ANF*, I, 350–53; Tertullian, *The Prescription against Heretics*, chap. 7, *ANF*, III, 246.

10. Irenaeus, *Against Heresies*, II, 25–28, *ANF*, I, 350–53.

of the will, the two natures of Christ, the absolute revelation of God in Christ, the resurrection of all human beings, etc., are all clearly stated and maintained by Irenaeus over against gnosticism. In the work of Irenaeus, Christianity for the first time unfolded its own independent theological science.[11]

The attitude adopted toward philosophy and gnosticism by the Alexandrian theologians was quite different. Toward the end of the second century and the beginning of the third, at various places, but especially in Alexandria, the ambition arose to articulate the truth of Christianity scientifically and thus to convey it to contemporary consciousness. The origin and establishment of the Catechetical School in Alexandria are not known to us, but it existed already about AD 190 and rapidly rose in status and influence. The first teacher who is known to us from writings that survive is Clement of Alexandria. But he is overshadowed by Origen, the most influential theologian of the early centuries. It was their aim to convert the church's doctrine into a speculative science. They did, to be sure, uphold the faith and, by contrast with the gnostics, based themselves on the positive doctrine of the church. Clement even called the faith a γνωσις συντομοος (concise science) and valued it more highly than pagan wisdom. Christianity is a way to salvation for all human beings and can be appropriated only by faith. The content of that faith has been summarized by the church in its creed, and the sole epistemic source of truth is revelation, Holy Scripture. All this is held as firmly by Clement and Origen as by Irenaeus and Tertullian.

The difference begins with the fact that the Alexandrians assumed a qualitative distinction between faith and science. Faith may be wholesome and necessary for the unlearned; for the learned it is not enough. Theology must aim to develop the content of faith into a science that does not rest on authority but finds its certainty and validity within itself. *Pistis* (faith) must be raised to the level of *gnosis* (knowledge). Here *gnosis* is no longer a means with which a theologian resists and fights against heresy but becomes its own goal. *Pistis* merely produces a fleshly or "somatic" Christianity, but the task of theology is to develop from Scripture a spiritual or "pneumatic" Christianity. What Philo attempted to do for the Jews, Clement and Origen undertook for Christians. Familiar with the whole of Greek philosophy from Socrates on, especially that of Plato and the Stoa, Origen produced a system that risked collapsing theology into philosophy, including the subordination of the Son, the eternity of creation, the preexistence of souls, a dualism of spirit and matter, earthly purification, and the restoration of all things. A pneumatic, allegorical exegesis served to harmonize it all with Scripture, but in fact, the Christian religion was dissolved into ideas and created a compromise between the foolishness of the cross and the wisdom of the world. Origen's is the most impressive and richest specimen of the mediating theology that surfaces in the church again and again.[12]

11. A. Harnack, *History of Dogma*, II, 230–318.
12. Charles Bigg, *The Christian Platonists of Alexandria* (Oxford: Clarendon; New York: Macmillan, 1886).

By the beginning of the third century, the foundations of Christian theology had been laid. Against paganism and Judaism, gnosticism and Ebionitism, the church had deliberately assumed a firm position and rescued the independence of Christianity. In the third century, however, a variety of internal disputes arose concerning the relation of the Logos (and the Spirit) to the Father. Combating the heresy of Unitarian Monarchianism in both its dynamic and modalistic forms, the church formulated at the Councils of Nicea (AD 325) and Constantinople (381) the dogma that Jesus Christ was God and distinct from the Father (and the Spirit). That three hypostases, Father, Son, and Spirit, existed in the divine being was accepted doctrine both in the East and in the West by the end of the fourth century. Related topics having to do with the person of Christ engaged theological thought in the following century, but the foundation had been laid, and the boundaries within which Christian speculation was to test its strength had been marked off.

The dogmatic writers of this early period served the cause of apologetics and polemics and generally restricted themselves to an explanation of points of doctrine in dispute. Although a large number of treatises were published that dealt with particular dogmatic and ethical subjects—the unity of God, the reality of Christ's incarnation—only Origen's *On First Principles* and Lactantius's *Divine Institutions* can be considered specimens of a dogmatic system.

FROM CONSTANTINE TO AUGUSTINE TO THE MIDDLE AGES

[40–41] With the coming of the Christian Emperor Constantine and the Edict of Toleration (AD 313), external pressure was replaced by the internal pressure of heresy in the church. The major dogmatic developments, especially in Christology, took place in the East. The Councils of Ephesus (431) and Chalcedon (451) set christological boundaries with the formulation "one person, two natures, without separation and division, without mixture and change." Debates, however, continued about one nature or two ("Monophysitism") as well as one will or two ("Monotheletism"). Although christological debates dominated the fourth to the eighth centuries, the demands of catechesis led to numerous treatises on a broad range of topics—God, cosmology, anthropology, and moral issues such as virginity. Important dogmatic works during this period include those of the three Cappadocians, Gregory of Nyssa (ca. 330–ca. 395; *On Not Three Gods*; *On the Making of Man*; *On the Holy Trinity*; *The Great Catechism*), Gregory of Nazianzus (329/30–389/90; *Orations*); Basil (330–379; *On the Holy Spirit*). To this trio of Eastern theologians must be added John Chrysostom (ca. 347–407; *On the Priesthood*). Of greater dogmatic importance were the writings of Pseudo-Dionysius (*The Divine Names*; *The Celestial Hierarchy: The Ecclesiastical Hierarchy*) along with the orthodox summary works of John of Damascus (ca. 665–ca. 750; *Exposition of the Orthodox Faith*; *Source of Knowledge*). The Damascene was also a strong defender of the veneration of images, a key and controversial element of Eastern Orthodox Christianity. Thus began the great period of Byzantium, lasting from the ninth century until the capture of Constantinople by the Turks in 1453. At that time Eastern Orthodoxy survived in large part because of its influence and support in Russia.

[42] From the beginning, the church and theology in the West bore a character of their own. In the East, the dominant theme in theology was enthrallment of humanity to corruption (φθορά) and its liberation by Christ that makes us partakers of life, immortality, the divine nature. In the West, on the other hand, the human relationship to God is thought of in legal and political categories, that of a guilty being before a just God whose commandments have been violated. Christ by his work obtains the grace of God, the forgiveness of sins, and the power to obey the law, and directs those who are new creatures toward an active life of obedience and submission. In the East, people resonate especially with the apostle John; in the West, with Paul.[13] In the former the point of gravity lies in Christ's incarnation; for the latter his death. In the former the person of Christ is primary; in the latter the work of Christ. In the East the primary focus is the divine-human nature, the unity of the two natures in Christ. In the West, on the other hand, what counts is the distinction between the two natures, the mediatorial place occupied by Christ between God and humanity. Mystical and liturgical emphases dominate in the East; political and juridical ones in the West. Since this difference was present from the beginning, the coming of the schism was only a matter of time. With the rise of Constantinople, the Eastern church sought a unity in two parts with two emperors, two capitals, and two bishops of equal rank. Rome, however, asserted itself, not as a political city alongside Constantinople, but as apostolic seat (*sedes apostolica*) on a level much higher than Constantinople. Rome represented and defended a religious interest, basing its claims and rights on Matthew 16:18 and demanding a universal (or *catholic*) place. There is, thus, in the Western church an aggressive, world-conquering impulse. This dual tendency combined with differences in usages, rites, and especially with respect to the *filioque*, led to the final schism of 1054.

Nonetheless, in many respects the West was dependent on the East. It appropriated the fruits of the Apostolic Fathers and the apologists as well as the conciliar theological and christological dogmas. The major councils, from Nicea (325) to Constantinople IV (869–70) were held in the East, in Asia Minor or Constantinople, and were recognized by the West as well. The objective foundations of the doctrine of the church are the same in the East and the West. Eastern thought also moved westward through the efforts of Hilary of Poitiers (d. 368), Ambrose (d. 397), Jerome (d. 420), Rufinus of Aquileia (d. 410), and John Cassian (360–430). Old Testament allegorical exegesis, trinitarian and christological

13. Ed. note: See Krister Stendahl, "The Apostle Paul and the Introspective Conscience of the West," *Harvard Theological Review* 55 (July 1963): 199–215.

discussion, Platonic theology, monasticism, asceticism and the ideal of virginity, infiltrated the Western church as well and became part of its patrimony.

[43] This entire dogmatic development in East and West culminates in Augustine. The doctrine of the Trinity and Christology of the Eastern theologians—the doctrine of humanity, sin, grace, faith, satisfaction, and merit in the work of Tertullian and Ambrose; Neoplatonism; Cyprian's doctrine of church and sacrament; Jerome and Hilary's monastic ideal—all this was absorbed and, over a lifetime of rich experience, internally appropriated by Augustine. Though he did not produce a theological dogmatic system—the closest is his *Enchiridion*: *Handbook on Faith, Hope, and Love*, an interpretation of the principal truths of faith that follows the Apostles' Creed—no church father entered into all the problems of theology more deeply than Augustine. He was the first person who attempted clearly to account for all the theological issues that would later be treated in the prolegomena of dogmatic theology and who penetrated the ultimate psychological problems of the human person seeking to know God.

Augustine's point of departure was the human being, human self-consciousness, human ineradicable yearning and need for truth, happiness, and goodness, all of which are one. The knowledge of self and the knowledge of God are the two poles between which all human thought oscillates. Knowledge of nature is not despised, it is made subordinate. "I desire to know God and the soul! O that I may know myself! O that I may know You!"[14] Consumed by the burning love of truth, Augustine found his thought inevitably converging in God who is the supreme truth, the only good, eternal reason, the origin of all things. Therefore, because God is himself the whole truth, being itself, the good and the beautiful, there can only be rest for human beings when they think and strive in him alone.[15] However, it is not reason that leads us to God and truth, it is faith. All of Augustine's thought is religious, theological; he views everything in the light of God, including the world. On the one hand, it is nonbeing, an image, and therefore perishable. On the other, as God's creation, it is a work of art created in accordance with the ideas in the mind of God, little by little, step by step, realizing those ideas and forming a universe that contains the richest diversity within itself. Creation is a cosmos, based on idea, number, order, and measure, and held together by one divine will, one intellect. Creation is a most spacious, immeasurable commonwealth in which sin is a privation compensated for by punishment and an ultimate co-contributor to the beauty and harmony of the whole. Augustine did take sin seriously: "You have not yet considered what a great burden sin is."[16] Sin is, above all, haughtiness—pride (*superbia*) in the soul and lust (*concupiscentia*) in the body. In Adam we all sinned, and thus sin became the fate of us all. It is a lack of God (*carentia dei*), a privation of the good (*privatio boni*), not just an act but a condition; it

14. Augustine, *Soliloquies*, II, 2.
15. Augustine, *Confessions*, I, 1.
16. Ed. note: This specific slogan is also found in Anselm, *Cur Deus Homo*, chap. 21.

is vitiated nature, a defect, a lack, a corruption, an inability not to sin. Salvation from this condition exists only by grace, which has its origin in predestination and is objectively revealed in the person and work of Christ. Objective grace is the sure and proper foundation of the Catholic faith but must also come into us subjectively as internal grace to infuse faith and love.

But in Augustine that grace only works within the boundaries of the visible church and its sacraments. The church is an institution of salvation, a dispenser of grace, the seat of authority, the guarantor of Scripture, the dwelling place of love, a creation of the Spirit, indeed, the very kingdom of God. Augustine sensed deeply the importance of community to religion; the church is the mother of believers. It is difficult to harmonize Augustine's doctrines of predestination and grace with this concept of church and sacrament. "Many who seem to be outside are inside, and many who are inside seem to be outside."[17] There are sheep outside the sheepfold and wolves inside it. Both Roman Catholics and Protestants, with some justification, appeal to Augustine. Rome appeals to him for its doctrine of the church, the sacraments, and authority, while the Reformation felt kinship with him in the doctrine of predestination and grace. He is the theologian of the greatest importance for all theological work that comes after him. Every reformation returns to him and to Paul. For every dogma he found a formula that was taken over and repeated by everyone else. His influence extends to all churches, schools of theology, and sects. Augustine, therefore, does not belong to one church but to all churches together. He is the universal teacher (*Doctor universalis*). Even philosophy neglects him to its own detriment. And because of his elegant and fascinating style, his refined, precise, highly individual, and nevertheless universally human way of expressing himself, more than any other church father, he can still be appreciated today. He is the most Christian as well as the most modern of all the fathers; of all of them he is closest to us. He replaced the aesthetic worldview with an ethical one, the classical with the Christian. In dogmatic theology we owe our best, our deepest, our richest thoughts to him. Augustine has been and is *the* dogmatician of the Christian church.

[44] For more than a century, Augustinianism was the object of an intense struggle about the doctrine of grace. In addition to genuine Pelagians such as the British monk himself, Celestius,[18] and Julian of Eclanum,[19] he was also opposed by some critics within the monastic tradition including John Cassian and Vincent of Lerins (who in his *Commonitorium* not only lists the marks of tradition but also, at the end, registers his opposition to a rigorous Augustinianism). In this struggle the Synod of Orange (529) took some decisions favoring Augustine but did not prevent the spread of semi-Pelagian ideas. It accepted prevenient grace but did

---

17. Multi qui foris videntur intus sunt et multi qui intus videntur foris sunt.

18. Ed. note: Like Pelagius, Celestius was a native of Britain who denied original sin and the efficacy of baptism in the remission of sins. He was condemned by the Council of Carthage in AD 411.

19. Ed. note: Julian of Eclanum (ca. 386–454) was one of Augustine's most able and fiercest opponents, accusing the Bishop of Hippo of retaining vestiges of Manichaeanism in his doctrine of total depravity.

not decisively adopt irresistible grace and particular predestination. In the years following, not much Augustinianism was left intact. Pope Gregory the Great (d. 604; *The Book of Pastoral Rule*), sometimes called the fourth great teacher of the church (alongside Augustine, Jerome, and Ambrose), produced nothing new but appropriated and in various ways applied the ideas of earlier church teachers to life. His bent was both practical and mystical-allegorical. He sanctioned the external legal religion of the Roman Catholic Church and conferred on medieval Catholicism its actual character. He is the capstone of the ancient world, the foundation stone of the new. Through his liturgical writings and his church music, he introduced the Roman Catholic form of worship to the Germanic peoples of the north. By popularizing the dogmas of the church fathers, he made church doctrine of practical usefulness for uncivilized pagan Germanic peoples and promoted superstition, asceticism, and works righteousness. Along with Boethius (ca. 480–ca. 524; *The Consolation of Philosophy*) and Cassiodorus, he exerted great influence on education and the rise of science among the Germanic peoples. Cassiodorus (d. ca. 565) wrote *The Liberal Arts and Disciplines*, discussing the seven liberal arts, and furnished a methodology for theological study. Boethius introduced the knowledge and use of Greek philosophy to the Germanic nations. And in the church Gregory brought them theology.

Among the Germanic peoples who were Christianized by the seventh and eighth centuries, one of the first theologians was Isidore of Seville (ca. 560–636; *Sentences*). His writings, which encompass everything there was to be known at the time, are grammatical, historical, archaeological, dogmatic, moral, and ascetic in nature. He brought classical and patristic learning to his people, offering extracts from pagan and Christian works but nothing original. Isidore's work is a compendium that delivered the theological capital of previous centuries to the Germanic people. But an independent treatment of this legacy was not achieved. Although Charlemagne attempted to introduce by force the culture of antiquity into the kingdom of France, and there was no lack of men of great learning in the Carolingian period, the characteristic feature of this period is diligent gathering and slavish reproduction. *The* authorities were Augustine and Gregory. Among Carolingian theologians the most important was Alcuin (d. 804), who was familiar with the works of the church fathers, rebutting adoptionist errors with the same arguments that were advanced against Nestorianism in an earlier age. In the ninth century, the study of Augustine led Gottschalk to confess double predestination. The *filioque* formula entered France from Spain and was incorporated in the Apostles' Creed. Already at the Synod of Gentilly (767), people were convinced that it was creedal, and the Synod of Aachen (809) officially included it in the creed. The Seventh Ecumenical Council (Nicea II, 787), which called for the cult (*servitium*) and adoration (*adoratio*) of images, was not recognized in the Carolingian world; but after the ninth century, the opposition gradually grew silent. The Carolingian period saw further development of the Mass, especially by Radbert Paschasius (*De corpore et sanguine domini,* 831). Also deserving of mention in this period is John Scotus Eriugena (ca. 810–ca. 877), although he belongs to philosophy more than theology. He is the father of speculative theology, linking himself up with the gnosis of Origen and the mysticism of Pseudo-Dionysius. His fundamental principle is the Neoplatonic doctrine of emanation. In his work *De divisione naturae*, he first states that theology and philosophy are really one. Right reason (*recta ratio*) and true authority (*vera auctoritas*) are not in conflict. Faith locates its truth as *affirmative* theology in Scripture and tradition, but reason, as *negative* theology, strips this truth of its wrappings and seeks out the idea of it. Thus he changes dogmatic truth into the philosophical doctrine of a cosmic and theogonic process. He subsumes all that exists under one heading, viz., *nature*, which—in four stages of being—manifests itself through the Logos in the world of phenomena and then returns to God.

ROMAN CATHOLIC DOGMATIC THEOLOGY

[45–46] It is inappropriate to speak of Roman Catholic theology until after the Great Schism with the East. After the tenth century, new life stirred the Western church, thanks in good measure to the monastic reforms begun at Cluny as well as the expansion of horizons as a result of the crusades. The birth of the universities led to a scientific theology using the Scholastic method. Scholastic theology, in distinction from positive theology, which presents dogmas in a simple propositional form, means that the material of dogmas is processed in accordance with a scientific method, the method followed in the schools. Scholasticism simply begins where positive theology leaves off. The latter is content when it has stated and proven the dogmas. But Scholastic theology proceeds from these dogmas as its first principles and tries by reasoning to trace their interconnectedness, to penetrate more deeply into the knowledge of revealed truth, and to defend them against all opposition.

This method brought great gains to the study of theology but also contributed to significant losses. Lacking solid knowledge of Greek and Hebrew, theologians neglected the study of Scripture and other original sources; Aristotle's philosophic methodology took center stage. By losing its connection to Scripture and the living faith of the church, dogmatic theology became more like a system of philosophy. In the work of Anselm of Canterbury (ca. 1033–1109; *Monologion*; *Proslogion*; *Cur Deus Homo*) we still see a sincere desire to deepen the understanding given in faith, and a form of writing that resembles Plato's Dialogues more than Aristotle. In the work of Peter Lombard and Alexander of Hales, theology moved beyond individual treatises to systematic handbooks on dogmatic theology and ethics. In the hands of Albertus Magnus, Thomas Aquinas, and Bonaventure, the Aristotelian method became the accepted manner of defending church doctrine. Scholasticism did not maintain this high level, but in the work of Duns Scotus (ca. 1265–1308) and especially in the nominalism of William of Ockham (ca. 1285–1347) and Gabriel Biel (ca. 1420–95), theology lost its certainty. Nominalists denied the existence of universals and, consequently, the possibility of a science of theology. Reality is an arbitrary act of the divine will. As a result skepticism, as well as the mysticism of Eriugena, Eckhart, and Böhme, flourished in spite of ecclesiastical condemnation.

It is now clear, contrary to judgments of earlier scholarship, that the mysticism of the Middle Ages was not hostile to Scholasticism. Mystically oriented men such as Hugo and Richard of St. Victor treated various parts of theology with the same method as Lombard had done. Conversely, Scholastics including Alexander of Hales, Albertus Magnus, Aquinas, and Bonaventure left behind a legacy of mystical writings as well. Aquinas even incorporated mysticism in Scholastic theology.[20] So there is no question of inherent conflict and antagonism between them. What is essential is to distinguish healthy from unhealthy mysticism, true from false mysticism. Neoplatonism, gnosticism, Erigena, Amalric, Eckhart, Molinos, Böhme, etc., were consistently condemned, but the writings of Pseudo-Dionysius, Albert, Bonaventure, etc., have always been praised and approved by the Roman Catholic Church. The purpose of mystical theology is not, however, to increase faith's knowledge of God through scientific exercise, but through spiritual exercises including contemplation of Scripture, prayer, fasting, and asceticism, to have communion with God. Augustine and Pseudo-Dionysius were the primary inspiration for sound mysticism in the Middle Ages.

[47–48] The Middle Ages also gave birth to significant protest movements, including the Cathars, the Waldensians, and Protestant precursors such as John Wycliffe and John Huss. Even though the conciliar movement in the church, notably at the Council of Constance (1414), was motivated by concern for reform, little reform was achieved. The Roman Catholic Church resisted then as it did at the Council of Trent (1545–63) against the sixteenth-century Protestant Reformation. The post-Tridentine Roman Catholic Church was again shaped by Thomas Aquinas and was marked by sharp polemic against the Reformation. A neoscholastic theology that included diligent study of Scripture and tradition arose and flourished in Spain thanks to (primarily Dominican) scholars such as Francisco de Vitoria, Melchior Canus, and Peter de Soto. But it was especially the Jesuits, such as Bellarmine, Peter Canisius, and Fr. Suárez, who contributed to its revival and fluorescence. This Jesuit theology was Pelagian and diverged from Thomas in the doctrine of sin, free will, and grace. The anti-Jesuit work of Dominican Augustinians such as Baius of Louvain and, later, Cornelius Jansen, bishop of Ypres, finally was condemned, by the often-reaffirmed bull Unigenitus (1713). Pelagianism triumphed in dogmatics, probabilism in ethics, and papal curialism in the church.

[49] Roman Catholicism has come under severe attack by the modern rationalism of, among others, Bacon, Descartes, Leibniz, and Wolff. Historical and critical studies pushed theology to the side, and Scholasticism withdrew into the schools. Deism and naturalism rose up and influenced or sidelined Roman Catholic theology. In 1773 the Jesuit order was suppressed by Pope Clement XIV himself.

---

20. T. Aquinas, *Summa Theol.*, II, 2 qu., 179ff.

Conflicts with Protestant theologians were pushed into the background, and a struggle was joined against freethinkers and unbelievers. With philosophers such as Jacobi, Schelling, and Hegel revisioning Christian doctrine and theology in the terms of speculative philosophy, some were led to a conciliatory and mediating position, bringing the two together, but this was condemned by the church. Rome entered a period of condemnation of modern thought, actively placing thinkers and writers on the Index of proscribed books.

However, these efforts failed to satisfy, and the nineteenth century witnessed a rebirth of neoscholasticism. The Jesuit order was restored in 1814, and papal authority was enhanced by the 1854 proclamation of the dogma concerning the immaculate conception of Mary, the publication of the Syllabus of Errors in 1864, and finally by Vatican I's approval of papal infallibility in 1870. In 1879 Pope Leo XIII, in his encyclical *Aeterni Patris*, acclaimed Thomas as the teaching doctor of the church, and Thomism regained momentum in Roman Catholic theology. Restricted as it is to scholarly life, Thomism does not have the capacity to nurture or renew Roman Catholic piety. It is more likely that Reform Catholicism or Roman Catholic Americanism, with its acceptance of much that is good in modern life, will lead the Roman church to serious self-evaluation.[21]

LUTHERAN DOGMATICS

[50] Martin Luther was not really the first Lutheran dogmatician; that honor belongs to Philipp Melanchthon and his *Loci Communes* (1521). Still, Luther's rediscovery of the gospel of grace was profoundly important for theology, giving it a new life. Controversy arose rather quickly in the Lutheran camp. Melanchthon's dissent from Luther on predestination and the Lord's Supper initiated a division between his followers (Philippists) and "strict" Lutherans known as Gnesio-Lutherans who considered their opponents crypto-Calvinists. Lutheran orthodoxy achieved its definitive form in the Formula of Concord (1577–80) and was defended by seventeenth-century Lutheran Scholastics such as Joh. Gerhard (d. 1637; *Loci communes theologici*), Joh. Quenstedt (1617–88; *Theologia didactico-polemica sive systema theologicum*), and D. Hollaz (d. 1713; *Examen theologicum acroamaticum*).

[51] In the eighteenth century, the human subject asserted itself in different forms. The pietism of Spener (1635–1705; *Pia desideria*) and Francke (d. 1727) challenged orthodoxy with its biblical realism and, in some cases, apocalyptic expectation. Nicholas von Zinzendorf (1700–1760), patron of the Moravian

21. Ed note: The truth of this judgment made at the beginning of the twentieth century can be seen in the changes adopted by the Roman Catholic Church at the Second Vatican Council, especially *Gaudium et spes*, "Pastoral Constitution on the Church in the Modern World," December 7, 1965. Cf. Pope John Paul II's encyclical, *Centesimus Annus* of 1991, a centenary commemoration of Pope Leo XIII's *Rerum Novarum*.

Brethren, moved beyond the penitential pietism of Spener to a proclamation of a sweet Savior. In Lutheran lands, orthodoxy was undermined by shifting the center of gravity to the human subject. Enlightenment rationalism ran along parallel lines and also undermined the authority of orthodox doctrine and theology by enthroning autonomous reason to a place of dominance over the objective truth of Scripture. Philosophy triumphed over theology. The content of religion and theology as Immanuel Kant develops it in his *Religion within the Limits of Reason Alone*,[22] is rationalistic and oriented toward morality; religion has become a means of achieving virtue.

In reaction, the Romanticism of Johann Georg Hamann (1730–88), Friedrich H. Jacobi (1743–1819), and Johann Gottfried Herder (1744–1804) celebrated the immediate experience of human feeling, the locus of the divine in each person. This trend found its culmination in the theology of Schleiermacher who considered religion as the enjoyment of God in feeling, a feeling that leads to the desire for community. Religious consciousness is the foundation for all theological reflection. The turn to the subject also found expression in Hegel's idealism. Unlike Schleiermacher who shared Kant's agnosticism, Hegel embraced a theory of the knowability of the Absolute. Combining the notion that thinking (or *Geist*/Spirit) produces being with that of evolutionary becoming, Hegel saw history, including the history of religion, as the history of ideas made incarnate. The Christian conviction of the incarnation is thus important because it expresses the idea of the union of God and man. By divorcing Christianity from its particular historical base, the Hegelian emphasis repudiated orthodox Christianity. When thinkers such as Friedrich W. J. Schelling (1775–1854) recognized certain difficulties with the Hegelian system of merging theology and philosophy into a single idea, they began to emphasize human freedom and action over necessity. Instead of logical necessity, the emphasis shifted to a theosophic opposition of contraries, chaos opposed by order, matter opposed by spirit, all as a cosmic, theogonic process.

[52–53] Dissatisfaction with these trends gave rise to a revival of interest in classic Lutheran theology in the late nineteenth century. Theologians such as Kaftan and Seeberg attempted a "mediating theology" that sought to join orthodoxy and modernism in some kind of synthesis. At the same time a resistance to the mingling of theology and philosophy led to a "return to Kant" movement. Theology, according to Ritschl, is thus about value judgments; the kingdom of God is a moral community. Ritschlian social gospel theology had a profound influence beyond Germany itself, especially in America.[23] Though Ritschl separated theology and philosophy, science and religion, into two distinct domains, objections arose against his a prioristic commitment to the isolation of Christianity

22. I. Kant, *Religion within the Limits of Reason Alone*, trans. Theodore M. Greene and Hoyt H. Hudson (La Salle, IL: Open Court, 1934; repr., New York: Harper & Brothers, 1960).

23. Ed. note: Especially in the writings of Walter Rauschenbusch, *A Theology for the Social Gospel* (New York: Abingdon, 1945); idem, *Christianizing the Social Order* (New York: Macmillan, 1912); idem, *Christianity and the Social Crisis* (New York: Macmillan, 1907).

from all scientific inquiry. As the nineteenth century came to a conclusion, the a priori superiority of Christianity was set aside by many scholars and Christian theology was abandoned for a universal history of religions that includes the Christian faith. In this way, so it was believed, the entire theological enterprise could be made scientific, objective. While religion is personal, subjective, and mystical, it is possible scientifically to discern the essence of religion and to study the various social forms it takes. This history-of-religions approach (German: *Religionsgeschichte*; Dutch: *Godsdienstwetenschap*), of which Ernst Troeltsch[24] is the best example, means the end of Christian dogmatics. It is impossible for the Christian theologian, or anyone else for that matter, to set aside a commitment to the faith and treat all religions objectively and neutrally as equals.

REFORMED DOGMATICS

[54] It is much more difficult to describe the history of Reformed theology than that of Lutheran theology. The Reformed church is not limited to one country and nation but has expanded into various countries and nations, and its distinctive expression is not laid down in a single confession but in numerous creeds. Although agreeing in many areas, Lutherans and Calvinists from the outset had important differences—geographically as well as theologically. At the heart of the theological difference was a difference in ultimate emphasis. The primary question asked by Lutherans was anthropological: "How can I be saved?" Works-righteousness was seen as the great departure from gospel truth. The Reformed, by contrast, sought to explore the foundations of salvation in the electing counsel of God and asked the theological question: "How is the glory of God advanced?" Avoiding idolatry is the major concern for the Reformed. While doctrines such as election, justification, regeneration, and sacraments were richer and more multifaceted among the various Reformed churches than in the Lutheran, the history of Reformed theology was for a long time less well studied.[25]

Reformed theology begins with Ulrich Zwingli (1484–1531), whose starting point in the radical dependence of humanity on a sovereign and gracious God was marred by vestiges of humanistic philosophical ideas. John Calvin (1509–64) was a more systematic thinker, as well as a thoroughly biblical and practical theologian; his *Institutes of the Christian Religion* were studied throughout the Protestant

---

24. Ed. note: Ernst Troeltsch, *Writings on Theology and Religion*, trans. and ed. Robert Morgan and Michael Pye (Atlanta: John Knox, 1977); further discussion of this point in Herman Bavinck, *Essays on Religion, Science and Society*, ed. John Bolt, trans. Harry Boonstra and Gerrit Sheeres (Grand Rapids: Baker Academic, 2008), chaps. 1–3.

25. Ed. note: This changed in the twentieth century as scholarship on Calvin and Reformed Orthodoxy flourished. See the annual "Calvin Bibliography" that appears in the *Calvin Theological Journal*; and Richard A. Muller, *Post-Reformation Reformed Dogmatics: The Rise and Development of Reformed Orthodoxy, ca. 1520–ca. 1725*, 2nd ed., 4 vols. (Grand Rapids: Baker Academic, 2003).

world. Calvin's successor in Geneva, Theodore Beza (1519–1605; *Tractationes theologicae*), was an influential theologian as well as biblical scholar who produced his own Greek text of the New Testament. Another Swiss reformer, Heinrich Bullinger (1504–75), played a leading role in consolidating the Reformed faith and participating in the formulation of the First and Second Helvetic Confessions (1536 and 1566) as well as the *Consensus Tigurinus* (1549). Thanks to Calvin's influence, the Reformed faith, often carried by refugees fleeing religious persecution, spread from Switzerland to France, Germany, the Low Countries, and the British Isles. Although the English Reformation initially had a strong Reformed tone that lasted into the seventeenth century, Anglican lukewarmness led to the Puritan movement. It was in Scotland under the leadership of John Knox that Calvinism flourished. Although the (German) Reformed theology of the Palatinate (Heidelberg) did develop somewhat independently of Calvin, building on the covenantal emphasis of Bullinger, it is a mistake to accent theological differences with the Swiss Reformation.

[55–56] In the seventeenth century, Reformed theologians moved away from Calvin's "biblical theology" to a more Scholastic one, paralleling the developments of the Middle Ages. Theologians such as Jerome Zanchius (1516–90) and Polanus (d. 1619) demonstrated solid acquaintance with the church fathers and the medieval Scholastics. Constructive Reformed theology of this sort reached a zenith and a terminus in such confessional statements as the Canons of Dordt (1618–19), the Westminster Confession of Faith and Larger and Shorter Catechisms (1646), and the Helvetic Consensus (1675). However, direct challenges to the Reformed faith also developed. Rationalism, mysticism, subjectivism, Anabaptism, Socinianism, Cartesianism, and especially Arminianism reared their heads. In the Netherlands the federalist theology of Johannes Cocceius (1603–69) was allied with Cartesianism and opposed by men such as G. Voetius (1589–1676; *Disputationes Theologicae Selectae*; *Politica Ecclesiastica*). Eventually the Scholastic theology of Voetius et. al. was eclipsed by Cartesian and Cocceian theology. Departures from the Reformed faith were particularly striking at the French Academy at Saumur, where Moise Amyraut introduced rationalist universalism (*Amyraldiansm*) into the church. In seventeenth-century England in particular, Arminian strains gained influence not only in the Anglican church but also among dissenters. Under the influence of Armininism and Amyraldianism, English theology became embroiled in bitter struggles over justification. A "neonomian" view, held by Richard Baxter (1615–91; *Justifying Righteousness*), among others, considered faith as the *ground* of justification. Their opponents insisted that this ground could only be found in the imputed righteousness of Christ.[26]

---

26. Ed. note: This debate has resurfaced among North American evangelicals in the twenty-first century. See, *inter alia*, Guy Prentiss Waters, *Justification and the New Perspectives on Paul: A Review and Response* (Phillipsburg, NJ: P&R, 2004); idem, *The Federal Vision and Covenant Theology: A Comparative Analysis* (Phillipsburg, NJ: P&R, 2006); R. Scott Clark, ed., *Covenant, Justification and Pastoral Ministry* (Phillipsburg, NJ: P&R, 2007); Gary L. W. Johnson and Guy P. Waters, eds., *By Faith Alone:*

In the midst of such controversy, nonconformist, dissenting, and Baptist groups grew as did deism, especially during the confusing time of the Puritan Revolt. An independent or congregational ecclesiology received confessional grounding in the Savoy Declaration (1659) and had as its most prominent theologian the great divine John Owen (1616–83), of whose works an edition was published in London (1826) in twenty-one volumes. English theology was more absorbed by biblical, historical, pastoral, and practical studies than in dogmatics as such. By comparison, dogmatic theology was vigorous in Scotland, most notably in the work of Samuel Rutherford (ca. 1600–1661; *Exertationes Apologeticae pro Divina Gratia*). In seventeenth-century England, the popular realism of the people combined with the political and ecclesiastical confusions of the day and the intellectual currents arising from Occam's nominalism and Francis Bacon's empiricism yielded a longing for a religious vision that sought commonality. Deism provided that vision as it reduced the essence of all religions, including Christianity, to five truths: God exists; he ought to be worshiped; worship must lead to virtue; people need to repent of their sins; their deeds will be rewarded and punished in the future (Lord Herbert of Cherbury, 1593–1648; *De Veritate*). The program of the deists involved a frontal attack on revelation. John Locke (1632–1704; *The Reasonableness of Christianity* [1695]) assigned to reason the decision concerning revelation. John Toland (1670–1722; *Christianity Not Mysterious* [1696]) stated that Christianity not only contained nothing *against* reason but also nothing *above* reason. Anthony Collins (1676–1729; *Discourse on Freethinking* [1713]) recommended *free* thinking, i.e., unbelieving. Matthew Tindal (1657–1733; *Christianity as Old as Creation* [1730]) set aside all revelation with a claim that natural theology was sufficient. Deism ended in skepticism in Henry Dodwell (1641–1711; *Christianity Not Founded on Argument* [1742]), a skepticism perfected by David Hume (1711–76; *Philosophical Essays* [1748], *Natural History of Religion* [1757], *Dialogue on Natural Religion* [1776]). Responses to this drift away from the faith was provided by important, if rationalist, apologetic works such as those of William Paley (1743–1805; *Evidences of Christianity* [1794], *Natural Theology* [1802]).

[57] During the middle of the eighteenth century, Reformed theology everywhere declined as deism and rationalism, in Remonstrant as well as Socinian dress, gained ground, often in the name of a more "biblical" theology. In the Netherlands the traditional Scholastic theology looked weary; while impressive multivolume works such as Bernhardus De Moor's *Commentarius perpetuus in Marcki Compendium* (6 vols, 1761–71) and Campegius Vitringa's posthumously published *Doctrina Christiane Religiones per aphorismos summatim descripta* (9 volumes, 1761) saw the light of day; they were primarily historical and descrip-

Answering the Challenges to the Doctrine of Justification (Wheaton: Crossway, 2007); Cornelis P. Venema, *The Gospel of Free Acceptance in Christ: An Assessment of the Reformation and New Perspectives on Paul* (Edinburgh: Banner of Truth, 2006).

tive works. One notable exception is Alexander Comrie (1706–74; *The ABC of Faith*; *Exposition of the Catechism*; and with Nic. Holtius, *Examination of the Tolerance Project*, 10 volumes), whose dedicated defense of the Reformed faith was devout and vigorous. The theologians of the English church, in response to deism, were occupied with apologetic questions concerning predictive prophecy, miracles, and revelation. Important Scottish theologians included Thomas Boston (d. 1732; *A Complete Body of Divinity*, 3 vols. [1773]) and the pair of Seceder brother preachers Ebenezer (1680–1754) and Ralph (1685–1752) Erskine. The Scottish church, after the English church confronted it, had its own neonomian conflict over the doctrine of justification, the so-called "Marrow Controversy" prompted by Edward Fisher's *The Marrow of Modern Divinity* (1646; republished in 1700, 1718).[27]

[58] As we move into the nineteenth century, when Reformed theology was at a nadir, an international evangelical renewal movement (the *Réveil*) competed with modernist theology as taught by C. W. Opzoomer (1821–92; *De Godsdienst*) and J. H. Scholten (1811–85; *Doctrine of the Reformed Church*) for the soul of Dutch Reformed churches. With roots in Scotland and carried over to France and Switzerland, the *Réveil* was a powerful spiritual movement with Christian roots but distinguished by its individualistic, aristocratic, methodistic, and philanthropic character. Reactive against rationalistic deism and dogmatic confessionalism alike, the *Réveil* took different shapes in different places, picking up and advancing the varieties of pietism that preceded it, including the Methodism of the Wesleys and Whitefield and the Moravian Brethren. The importance of the Wesleys and Methodism for English church life and theology cannot be overestimated. The preaching of John Wesley (1703–91) and George Whitefield (1714–71) individualized the gospel and made it into a question of life and death for everyone. Methodism did not depart from one or the other of the Anglican Church's Thirty-nine Articles but concentrated the entire truth of the Christian religion around two points: a personal conversion; a new life characterized by Christian perfection that emphasized personal evangelism and moral rigor on matters such as abstaining from tobacco and alcohol. As a result, certain dogmas were opposed, modified, or deemed of secondary importance. Methodism's influence on the English-speaking church (and beyond) is incalculable; Wesley has been the reshaper of English and American Protestantism, the mediate producer of revivals that have been recurrent in Protestant churches ever since his emergence on the scene.

[59] Methodism was, in the main, a phenomenon of the "common people." The circles of [Anglican] influential leaders in church and theology became embroiled in controversies between the High Church party and the Oxford Movement with its strong affinity to Rome and the Broad Church party that sought a more

27. Ed. note: The strongly Calvinistic views of Edward Fisher generated a protracted controversy in the Church of Scotland when its General Assembly (in 1720) condemned his republished *Marrow of Modern Divinity* for allegedly favoring antinomianism.

latitudinarian church and a reconciliation between Christianity and culture. For the latter, the doctrine of the incarnation was central; the church is to be incarnate in the world in leading efforts of social reform. In the late days of the nineteenth century, evolutionism, idealism, and even Buddhism and spiritism competed for the religious affection of the English peoples.

[60] Reformed theology was introduced to North America from many directions, including England, Scotland, France, Holland, and Germany. A distinction needs to be made here between the Puritan Calvinism that took root in New England and the Scottish Presbyterian Calvinism that was imported into the southern and central states. The first and most important theologian of New England was Jonathan Edwards (1703–58), who combined profound metaphysical mental ability with deep piety. In the first half of the nineteenth century the theology of Edwards was modified in a Pelagian direction by Timothy Dwight (1752–1817) and Nathaniel W. Taylor (1786–1858) and given the label "New School." "Old School" Presbyterianism, found especially at Princeton Theological Seminary, is in the main a reproduction of the Calvinism of the seventeenth century as it was laid down in the Westminster Confession and the Helvetic Consensus and elaborated especially by F. Turretin in his *Theologia Elenctica*. The same system is represented as well by the Southern theologians James H. Thornwell (1812–62), Robert J. Breckinridge (1800–1871), and Robert L. Dabney (1820–98). Another, more recent representative of the Old School is W. G. T. Shedd, emeritus professor since 1890 at Union Seminary, New York, and author of the two-volume *Dogmatic Theology*. The American church also includes a strong revivalist stream, continuing the spirit of the Great Awakening, and a modernist trend as well in such theologians as Union Seminary Professor Charles Briggs (1841–1913), who was tried for heresy, and Arthur C. Mc Giffert (1861–1933), also of Union Seminary. At the beginning of the twentieth century, Reformed Christianity seemed in crisis in America and a rosy future unlikely for Calvinism in America.[28]

28. Ed. note: Further examination of Reformed theology in America through the twentieth century can be found in David F. Wells, ed., *Reformed Theology in America: A History of Its Modern Development* (Grand Rapids: Baker Academic, 1997). Included is an entire section on Dutch Reformed Theology.

3

FOUNDATIONS
OF DOGMATIC THEOLOGY

SCIENCE AND THOUGHT (*PRINCIPIA*)

[61–63] If we consider theology a science, we must inquire into the scientific foundations of its structure. In the modern era this is a task usually given to philosophy, an illusory starting point since then dogmatic theology has no independent scientific status of its own. Other approaches, such as Troeltsch's, that begin with the comparative study of religions in order to derive the essence of Christianity, are also doomed to failure. Theology is a science about God, not about religion or faith. The aim of theology is nothing other than that the rational creature know God and, knowing him, glorify him (Prov. 16:4; Rom. 11:36; 1 Cor. 8:6; Col. 3:17). It is God's good pleasure (εὐδοκια) to be known by human beings (Matt. 11:25–26). Normatively, theology is an independent discipline of study and should begin with revelation, proceed from faith, and articulate its own first principles (principia)[1] rather than deriving them from other disciplines.

By *principia* is usually meant the basic causes and ground of reality as well as the means by which we come to know them. Thus Aristotle, for instance, distinguished principles of *being* (*essendi*), of *existence* (*existendi*), and of *knowing* (*cognoscendi*). Theologians also adopted this terminology. By way of revelation God makes

---

1. Ed. note: For a full discussion of the classical use and meaning of *principia* language in theology, see Richard A. Muller, *Dictionary of Latin and Greek Theological Terms* (Grand Rapids: Baker Academic, 1985), 245–46, s.v. "principia theologiae." In what follows, the word *principia* will be variously translated as "fundamental principles," "foundations," or "sources."

himself known to us as the primary efficient cause of all things. Holy Scripture is the external instrumental efficient cause of theology, and divine revelation also requires the internal illumination of the Holy Spirit. We thus identify three fundamental principles for theology: God is the essential foundation (*principium essendi*); Scripture is the external cognitive foundation (*principium cognoscendi externum*); and the Holy Spirit is the internal principle of knowing (*principium cognoscendi internum*). The foundations of theology are thus trinitarian: The Father, through the Son as Logos, imparts himself to his creatures in the Spirit. Theologians also distinguish God's own trinitarian self-knowledge (*archetypal*) from the revealed knowledge accommodated to human understanding (*ectypal*).

[64–65] Historically, there are two basic schools of scientific thought that relate subject and object in different ways: rationalism (subject oriented) and empiricism (object oriented). This division was evident in Greek thought and has endured into modern times. Rationalism (Parmenides, Plato, Descartes, Spinoza, Leibniz) is the not unreasonable attempt to impose mental order on the changing world of perceptions and representations. On the other hand, if we claim to have access only to representations and not the things themselves, a form of idealism gains the upper hand in which only thought is judged to be real. Idealism turns the faculty by which we order and analyze our perceptions into the very source of knowledge itself, as it were making the eye into the source of light. The consequence of this move is the conclusion that our senses always deceive us and give us a false impression of reality. Idealism yields the remarkable conclusion that the only reality for us is that about which we are conscious; my thought is therefore about my thought and not the thing itself. That which is not my thought is inconceivable, unknowable to me; it does not exist for me. This conviction that there is no reality outside me to which I am accountable in any sense violates the natural realism of our ordinary experience in the world. By nature we are realists, not dualists who separate thinking from being as Plato, Descartes, Kant, and even Spinoza, Fichte, Schelling, and Hegel end up doing. As Schelling remarkably acknowledged: "It is hard to get to reality [from here]."

[66] On the other hand, empiricism proceeds from the diametrically opposite view that sense perceptions alone are the source of our knowledge. Precursors of modern empiricism (Francis Bacon, Locke, Hume, A. Comte, J. Stuart Mill) can be found in the Greek atomists and the medieval nominalists. For empiricism, the mind is a passive blank slate; human consciousness is completely subjected to the world outside us. In the pursuit of knowledge, the faculty of perception is all that there is for us. All intellectual activity has its beginning and source in this faculty. This view fails to take into account the active role of the human mind, the role of unproven presuppositions in all scientific observation. In addition to its flawed starting point, empiricism denies the term "science" for all but the "exact sciences." The entire range of the "human sciences," including theology, is excluded; the fundamental religious and metaphysical questions faced by all people must be ignored. Taken strictly, this leads to materialism, because even

human consciousness itself, including our faculty of knowing, finally has to be reduced to explainable causes in the material, sensory world. Mind is only matter, the matter of the physiological brain. It is especially here that modern philosophy and science are most disappointing and need fundamental revision so that we are protected from both materialism and idealism. This reductionism does a terrible injustice to the world of nonmaterial things, the world of values, of good and evil, law and custom, religion and morality, all those things that inspire love and hatred in our hearts, lift us up and comfort us or crush and grieve us. This world of the human "spirit," that whole magnificent invisible world, is as much a reality to us as the "real world" that we perceive with our senses.

Realism and Universals (*Logos*)

[67–68] The proper starting point for any theory of knowledge is the universal and natural certainty we find spontaneously in our ordinary experience. Reality exists outside us quite apart from our reflection on it. In Tertullian's words: "First there was man, then the philosopher or the poet."[2] One must first live, then philosophize (*Primum vivere, deinde philosophari*). We trust our senses, which lead us to believe in an objective world external to us, and our mental representations of that world point back to that reality. From this we conclude that scientific demonstrative certainty is neither the basic nor the only kind of human certainty; there is also a universal, metaphysical, intuitive, immediate kind of certainty that is self-evident and which we call the "certainty of faith." Christian thinkers from Augustine on rejected rationalism and innate ideas in favor of a "realism" that acknowledges the primacy of the senses and the constraints placed by reality on the human mind.

Sense perception is the starting point of all human knowledge. "The mind does not know things apart from sense perception."[3] "All intellectual knowledge proceeds from the senses."[4] "Our intellect understands nothing apart from sense images."[5] Here the doctrine of creation is important. The intellect is bound to the body and thus to the cosmos and therefore cannot become active except by and on the basis of the senses. All Christian theologians believed this. However, in distinction from empiricist thought, Christian theology also insists that the mind has its own nature, operates in its own way, and possesses the freedom to soar beyond the senses to the world of ideas and the ideal. The human mind is not a blank page on which the external world merely writes what it pleases, nor a mirror in which objects are simply reflected. While it can form the representations of the real world external to it that are faithful interpretations of that world, forming such

2. Tertullian, *De testimonio animae*, chap. 5; see *The Soul's Testimony*, *ANF*, III, 178.
3. Aristotle, *De sensu*, c. 6.
4. T. Aquinas, *Summa Theol.*, I, qu. 84, art. 1 and 7.
5. T. Aquinas, *Summa contra gentiles*, III, 41.

representations is an act of consciousness in which the intellect is active and not merely passive. The very perception by the senses is an act of consciousness. The mind that sees the object is the same mind that forms the representation. The human intellect also has the capacity to abstract general and universal judgments from particular events; it is therefore the organ of science. Thomas Aquinas succinctly and lucidly expressed this as follows: "Science is not concerned with individual cases; the intellect concerns itself with universal matters."[6] The object of science is the universal and necessary, so science can only be produced by the intellect. Contrary to all forms of nominalism, which by denying the reality of universals in effect makes all science impossible, realism correctly assumes their reality in the thing itself (*in re*) and therefore also in the human mind subsequent to the thing itself (*in mente hominis post rem*).

[69] There is a good theological explanation for this: the same *Logos* created both the reality outside us (John 1:3; Col. 1:15) and the laws of thought within us. The world is created in such a way that an organic connection and correspondence is possible between our minds and the reality external to us. The world is an embodiment of the thoughts of God. Only in this way is science possible. In the words of the Belgic Confession (art. 2), the creation is "a beautiful book in which all creatures, great and small, are as letters to make us ponder the invisible things of God." The created world is the external foundation of human knowledge (*principium cognoscendi externum*). However, we need eyes in order to see the world as God's creation. The Logos, who shines in the world, must also let his light shine in our consciousness. That is the light of reason, the intellect, which, itself originating in the Logos, discovers and recognizes the Logos in things. This is the internal foundation of knowledge (*principium cognoscendi internum*), which can only be a gift of God's mind. Christian thinkers such as Augustine often borrow Plato's imagery of the sun to explain this. Just as the sun objectively illumines the object and subjectively the human eye, so God, or the idea of the good, is the light by which the truth or essence of things becomes visible and by which at the same time our mind is able to see and recognize that truth.[7] Augustine adopted this image and said, "God is the sun of minds." In the unchangeable light of truth, our minds see and make judgments about all things ("in the unchanging truth itself the rational and intellectual mind perceives all things and in the same light it judges all these things").[8] Just as with the physical eye we cannot see anything unless the sun sheds its rays over it, so neither can we see any truth except in the light of God, which is the sun of our knowledge.[9] God is the light of reason in which, by which, and through which all things that shine so as to be intelligible, shine. Thomas repeatedly speaks in the same way and uses the same metaphor, being careful to point out that this did not mean

---

6. T. Aquinas, *Summa Theol.*, Ia, qu. 1, art. 2; idem, *Summa contra gentiles*, I, 44.

7. Hermann Siebeck, *Geschichte der Psychologie*, 2 vols. (Gotha: F. A. Perthes, 1880–84), I, 226; II, 70.

8. Augustine, *The Literal Meaning of Genesis*, VIII, 25.

9. Augustine, *Soliloquies*, I, 8, 13; idem, *The Trinity*, 12, 15.

that human reason is itself divine.[10] Reason is not itself the divine Logos; rather, it participates in it.[11]

So, in the final analysis, it is God alone who from his divine consciousness and by way of his creatures conveys the knowledge of truth to our minds—the Father who by the Son and in the Spirit reveals himself to us. "There are many who say, 'O that we might see some good!' Let the light of your face shine on us, O Lord!" (Ps. 4:6).

RELIGIOUS FOUNDATIONS

[70] Just like science, so religion too has its fundamental principles or foundations (*principia*). To know them we need to determine the essence of religion, especially as it differs from science, morality, and art. The meaning of the Christian religion cannot be determined from the disputed etymology of the word "religion." A common explanation is that of Lactantius who linked it to the verb *religare* and considered religion the bond that unites human beings to God.[12] This Christianizing of the word has been generally accepted and is found in the Vulgate in Acts 26:5 and James 1:27. The word has passed into all European languages and, alongside piety and godliness, has found and retained acceptance in English as well.

The Bible provides no general idea of religion but covenantally presents God's revelation as its objective side and the fear of the Lord as the subjective side. Covenant (ברית) is the basic term for the divine establishment (διαθηκη; Exod. 20:1ff.; 34:10ff.; 34:27ff.; Isa. 54:10; etc.) that grounds Israel's religion. This covenant embodies divine ordinances that Israel must keep (תורה; instruction, teaching, law, the book of the law of the Lord). These are called דברים, words (Num. 12:6; Ps. 33:4; etc.); מצוות, commandments (Gen. 26:5; Exod. 15:26; etc.); פקודים, precepts (Ps. 119:4, 5, 15; etc.); חקים, statutes, decrees (Exod. 15:26; Lev. 25:18; Job 28:26; Ps. 89:32, MT [89:31 Eng.]; etc.); משפטים, legal cases and verdicts (Num. 36:13; Ps. 19:10 MT [19:9 Eng.]; etc.); ארחות, דרכים, ways, paths (Deut. 5:33; Job 21:14; Ps. 25:4; etc.); משמרות, laws to be kept (Gen. 26:5; Lev. 18:30; etc.). The many expressions indicate how in Israel's religion the objective side of religion—the ordinances of God—is in the foreground.

The commandments must be internalized; God is to be revered and his revelation is to be believed and obeyed. The יראת יהוה, the fear of the Lord, expresses the inner disposition of the devout Israelite toward the holy laws that the Lord has instructed him to keep. Biblical religion is in the first place a matter of the heart; it is never exhausted by external observance. The Lord's claims do not remain outside and above the Israelites as the object of their terror and fear but become

10. T. Aquinas, *Summa Theol.*, I, qu. 12, art. 2, ad 3; qu. 79, art. 4; qu. 88, art. 3, ad 1; II, 1, qu. 109, art. 1 and 2; idem, *Summa contra gentiles*, III, 47.

11. T. Aquinas, *Summa Theol.*, I, qu. 79, art. 4.

12. Lactantius, *Divine Institutes*, N, 28.

the object of their love. They ponder them with their intellect and observe them with their will. They are their delight all day long.

In the New Testament, we encounter essentially the same view. Only now God gives his (objective) revelation, not in a series of laws, but in the person of Christ. He is the *way* and the *truth* (John 14:6). The *way of the Lord* (Acts 18:25; 19:9, 23; 22:4), the *teaching* (Matt. 7:28; 22:33; John 7:16–17; Acts 2:42; Rom. 6:17; 1 Tim. 1:10; 4:6, 16; 6:1, 3; 2 Tim. 4:2–3; Titus 1:9; 2:1, 7, 10), the *gospel* (Mark 1:1, 14–15; etc.), and the *Word of God* (Matt. 13:19; Mark 2:2; 4:14f.; 2 Cor. 5:19; etc.) are all concentrated in Christ and are nothing other than an explication of his person and work. The subjective side of New Testament religion is given primarily through two Greek words: εὐσέβεια and πιστις. Εὐσέβεια indicates holy reverence toward God; its meaning is related to that of the Latin *pietas* and hence expresses an attitude such as is present in children toward their parents. The word repeatedly occurs in the New Testament, especially in the Pastoral Letters. But what εὐσέβεια really is and ought to be was first revealed only in the gospel (1 Tim. 3:16).

The usual word for subjective religion in the New Testament is faith (πιστις). Corresponding to the good news of forgiveness and salvation in Christ on the human side is faith, which is a childlike trust in God's grace and hence immediately produces love in our hearts. Πιστις and ἀγαπη are the basic attitudes inherent in Christian piety. The words λατρεια (Rom. 9:4; 12:1; Heb. 9:1, 6) and θρησκεια (Acts 26:5; Col. 2:18; James 1:27) refer to the worship and adoration offered to God from the principle of faith.

[71] In keeping with this teaching of Scripture we distinguish between objective and subjective religion, recognizing that these two aspects are inseparable. True godliness is never merely objective or external, and faith cannot be only personal or subjective; it requires an external ground. True religion claims the whole person, soul and body, the mind, the heart, and full strength; it requires that human beings serve God with a sincere faith, firm hope, and ardent love, with worship in spirit and in truth, with the sacrifices of a broken spirit and a contrite heart. Religion is a matter of knowing, loving, and serving God from the heart. Hence it is first of all a duty with which God confronts us human beings in the first table of his law, a duty to which subjective religion in human beings must correspond. It is the inner disposition and motivation to know and serve God in the way he has revealed in his Word. Thus, according to Thomas Aquinas, religion is not a matter of theological virtues (faith, hope, love), which have God as their direct object, but of the moral virtues (prudence, justice, fortitude, and temperance), in which God is the end. The actual object in religion here is the devotion dutifully offered to God. Religion belongs to the virtue of justice; it is the virtue by which human beings offer to God the devotion and worship that is due him.

[72] The Reformation theologians distinguished more clearly piety as the principle and worship as the act of religion. Piety is first of all a state of being, a habit and disposition leading human beings to worship God. Second, faith, hope, and love are not placed alongside religion as separate theological virtues

but incorporated into religion itself as the primary acts of internal religion. Religion, says Zwingli, embraces the total piety of Christians—faith, life, laws, rites, and sacraments. It consists in "that linkage by which a human has a firm trust in God—as one might expect—as the highest good and enjoys him in the place of a parent." Finally, "it is the marriage between the soul and God."[13] In Calvin we encounter three key concepts. The first is the knowledge of God, the sense of his attributes. This knowledge, secondly, is the appropriate teacher of piety, which Calvin defines as "reverence joined with love of God which the knowledge of his benefits induces." Finally, religion, in the sense of worship or devotion, is also born from piety.[14] Schleiermacher even defined religion in terms of piety, as the "absolute feeling of dependence."[15] While this definition is inadequate, it contains elements of truth. We human creatures *are* radically dependent on God. Subjectively, this is known as faith, faith that leads to service, acts of obedience, and love. True religion consists of absolute trust in God and a sincere desire to live in obedience to him.

Our relationship with God is so deep and tender, so rich and many-dimensional, that it is difficult to express it in a single concept. However, the concept of *dependence* is a good starting point since it describes what is basic to our creatureliness. We are created, contingent, self-conscious, rational and moral creatures who are related to and mutually dependent on other created, contingent, self-conscious, rational and moral creatures. Common to us all is our absolute dependence on our Creator. Of course, stones, plants, and animals are also dependent on the Creator who upholds all things by his power. We humans are dependent in a wholly different way; we are *aware* of our dependence and because we are rational and moral creatures we also have a freedom that no other creatures or created entities enjoy. We are, in this manner, akin to God; we are his offspring and his image. We are absolutely dependent in such a manner that the denial of this dependence never makes us free, while the acknowledgment of it never reduces us to the status of a slave. On the contrary: in the conscious and voluntary acceptance of this dependence, we human beings arrive at our greatest freedom. We become human to the degree that we are children of God. Our dependence on God is not to be thought of in terms of sovereign power alone; the sovereign and holy God is our Father in heaven, the gracious, merciful, just, and holy One.

The predisposition to religion is present in every human; "the seed of religion has been implanted in all humans."[16] But in fallen humanity this predisposition is corrupted and, thanks to false objective revelation, produces worship that is "idolatry" or "will-worship" (ἐθελοθρησκεια). Two things are, therefore, necessary

---

13. Ulrich Zwingli, *Opera*, ed. J. M. Schulthess, 8 vols. (Turici: F. Schulthess, 1842), III, 155, 175, 180.

14. J. Calvin, *Institutes of the Christian Religion*, I.ii.1 (ed. John T. McNeill and trans. Ford Lewis Battles, 2 vols. [Philadelphia: Westminster, 1960], 1:39–41).

15. F. Schleiermacher, *The Christian Faith*, ed. H. R. MacIntosh and J. S. Steward (Edinburgh: T&T Clark, 1928), §4.2, p. 15.

16. J. Calvin, *Institutes*, I.iv.1.

for a religion to be true: first, that the objective revelation that comes to us from without again makes God known to us as he really is; second, that the corrupted religious predisposition in human beings be regenerated and renewed. What is needed is exactly what the Christian gospel gives: a Holy Spirit-inspired Scripture that bears fruit in the fertile soil of Holy Spirit-regenerated human hearts. The latter results in a religious disposition—the Christian's subjective response to God and his revelation—that the Bible calls *faith*, along with an active desire to live according to all God's commandments and glorify him.[17] Hence, no more beautiful description of religion is conceivable than that offered in the Heidelberg Catechism's commentary on the First Commandment (Lord's Day 34, answer 94): "That I, not wanting to endanger my salvation, avoid and shun all idolatry, magic, superstitious rites, and prayer to saints or to other creatures. That I sincerely acknowledge the only true God, trust him alone, look to him for every good thing humbly and patiently, love him, fear him, and honor him with all my heart. In short, that I give up anything rather than go against his will in any way."

[73–75] The modern age has given rise to a scientific, historical, or psychological comparative study of all religions. While all religions do have formal similarities (revelation, cult, dogma), no generic religion exists, only concrete ones, all with conflicting claims. Efforts to arrive at the essence of religion in general have led to meager results with vague proposals, and the search must be judged a dead end. It is impossible to take a stance in a truly objective vantage point external to all religions from which to judge them. Furthermore, while it is possible and appropriate to do historical comparative studies of religious phenomena, practices, and sacred texts, there is no way of objectively and neutrally examining the attitudes and dispositions that underlie religious phenomena and practice. Only a religious person is able to study and evaluate religious phenomena in their actual significance. A tone-deaf person is ill suited to be a music critic. A student of the science of religion has to do more than simply observe and describe; he or she must introduce order into the chaos of phenomena, determine the place and value of the different religions, trace the life and growth and hence also the degeneration and adulteration of religion, and indicate where religion displays itself in its purest form and richest development. This requires a standard of measurement that must be applied to the various religious phenomena. Judgment cannot be avoided or evaded, including judgments about whether a particular religion is "true" or "false." All religions make claims that call for decision: believe its founding stories and doctrines or not; honor its cultic practices and obey its moral commandments or not. Judgments of faith, doctrine, ritual, and moral practice are inevitable. The "truth question" is unavoidable. No universal science of all religions that satisfies us with its objectivity and accuracy is possible. Most attempts to reduce the varied and rich reality of human religions founder on the shoals of oversimplification; here, as elsewhere, life is abundantly richer than theory.

17. Heidelberg Catechism, Q&A 114.

[76] None of this should discourage us from all scientific examination of human religious life. Let us begin, anthropologically, by considering the place of religion in the human psyche. Is religion primarily knowledge, morality, or feeling? Gnosticism already said that gnosis was redemptive, that knowledge was "the redemption of the inner man."[18] This gnosticism has at all times found its defenders in the Christian church, but it emerged again especially in modern philosophy. Much modern thought, notably idealism, has a gnostic, intellectualistic view of religion. For Hegel, the entire world is an unfolding of mind. Religion is a form of knowledge superseded only by philosophy. "Man only knows of God insofar as God has knowledge of himself in man; this knowledge is the self-consciousness of God but also a knowledge of the same by man, and this knowledge of God by man is the knowledge of man by God. The mind of man in coming to know God, is just the mind of God itself."[19]

[77] The Kantian tradition, however, defines religion voluntaristically as moral conduct and locates its seat in the human will. There is a Pelagian impulse at work here in that faith is seen as a "new obedience" achievable by human striving. The ethical emphasis does deserve our appreciation by reminding us of the ethical bond between human beings in religion and the link between faith and works; faith is dead without works, without love. We must, however, also take care to distinguish religion and morality, faith and works. The former precedes and is the basis for the latter and has to do with our duties toward God; the latter has to do with our duties toward our neighbor. In the final analysis religion is at the core of all true morality; only God can compel the conscience. Freedom of conscience is an inexorable demand and inalienable right for all human beings because they are created in the image of God

[78] Others, such as Schleiermacher, influenced by Romanticism, consider religion as primarily aesthetic and locate it in human feeling. The history of mysticism and Pietism paved the way for this development; Schleiermacher considered himself a "Moravian of a higher order." In the second lecture of his *Speeches on Religion* (1799), he describes religion as the immediate consciousness of the essence of all that is finite in and through the infinite. Religion is neither thinking nor acting, neither metaphysics nor morality, but feeling for the infinite. The object of that feeling is not a personal God with whom we live in fellowship but the universe, the world as a whole, conceived as a unity. And the faculty for the perception of that infinite is not the intellect, reason, or will but feeling, the focus of the mind on and capacity for intuiting the infinite. In *The Christian Faith* (1821–22) piety is also feeling, a feeling of absolute dependence. Still, there is a difference between the two works. In *Speeches*, God is the [cosmic] whole and feeling intuition of the infinite; in *The Christian Faith*, he is the absolute causality

---

18. Irenaeus, *Against Heresies*, I, chap. 21.

19. G. W. F. Hegel, *Sämtliche Werke*, ed. H. Glockner, "Jubilee" ed., 22 vols. (Stuttgart, 1927–30), XVI, 428 ("*Vorlesungen über die Philosophie der Religion*," in *Werke*, XII, 428).

of the world, and feeling is immediate self-consciousness and absolute dependence. In this way God tends more to acquire an existence of his own, one that
is distinct from the world, and religion therefore also acquires its own content,
one that is distinct from the intuition of the world. The later Schleiermacher is
thus preferable to the earlier; nonetheless, the reduction of religion to aesthetic
feeling remains an error.

Religion is central to all human cultural acts and products: science, morality,
and art. It is as much a mistake to confuse religious and aesthetic feeling as it is to
confuse faith with gnosis or morality, all frequent errors of modernity. The two
are essentially distinct. Religion is life, reality; art is ideal, appearance. Although
our imaginations may for a moment lift us above reality and induce us to live in
the realm of the transcendent and ideal, art cannot close the gap between the ideal
and reality. Indeed, reality itself does not change on account of it. Although art
gives us distant glimpses of the realm of glory, it does not induct us into that realm
and make us citizens of it. Art does not atone for our guilt, or wipe away our tears,
or comfort us in life and death. It never turns the beyond into the here and now.
Only religion can do that.

Here too it must be said that the affections, feelings, are an important part of
religion. A personal relation to God does not leave people cold and indifferent
but moves them in the depths of their hearts. It arouses in them a strong feeling
of delight or displeasure and generates a long series of affections: sense of guilt,
sorrow, contrition, regret, sadness, joy, trust, peace, rest, etc. Religion awakens
the deepest and most tender affections in the human heart. Affections give one's
religion warmth, inwardness, life and power, feelings that sharply contrast with
the deadness of intellectualism and the coldness of moralism. The heart is the
center of religion. But feeling is not the only religious function nor the only seat
and source of religion. Feeling, here taken not as a separate faculty, which it is not,
but as the whole of our passions and affections, is, in the nature of the case, passive. It reacts only to what is brought into contact with it by the consciousness and
then turns into a feeling of delight or displeasure. It possesses nothing of itself and
does not produce anything from within itself. By itself every feeling and affection
is neither good nor bad, neither true nor untrue. These are the categories of faith,
a faith that then also impacts the feeling. But when feeling is detached from faith
and made into an independent and exclusive source and seat of religion, it loses its
own quality and becomes completely independent of the categories of truth and
untruth, good and evil. Then every individual feeling is already as such religious,
true, good, and beautiful. And that was Romanticism's great fault as a whole.

[79] While intellect, morality, and feeling do play significant roles in true religion, it is a mistake to reduce religion to a single faculty. True religion embraces
the whole person in relation to God and includes knowledge, willing, and feeling.
We must love God with our whole mind, soul, and strength. Precisely because
God is God he claims us totally, in soul and body, with all our capacities and in
all our relations. Admittedly, there is order in this relation of a human being to

God. Knowledge is primary. There can be no true service of God without true knowledge: "I do not desire anything I do not know" (*Ignoti nulla cupido*). To be unknown is to be unloved. "Whoever would approach God must believe that he exists and that he rewards those who seek him" (Heb. 11:6). But that knowledge of God penetrates the heart and arouses there an assortment of affections—fear and hope, sadness and joy, guilt feelings and forgiveness, misery and redemption—as the Scriptures, especially the Psalms, bear ample testimony.

[80] What then is the origin of religion in human experience? A satisfactory answer to this question is as unlikely as that concerning the origin of language. Strictly speaking, societies without any religion are as abundant as societies without language; that is to say, there are none. Accounting for this by historical, sociological, or psychological reasons alone always fails. Neither fear, priestly deception, human weakness, the search for happiness, nor ignorance offers a satisfactory explanation. Thinking in evolutionistic terms, Darwin thought the germ of religion existed embryonically in animals, for example, in the love that a dog displays toward its owner and that is accompanied by a feeling of subordination and fear.[20] But this analogy fails because we do not know the psychic life of dogs, and the ritual acts accompanying all religion—sacrifice, prayer—are unknown in the animal world. Religion is one of the distinctive features of our humanity in contrast with other animals. In the words of Lactantius: "Religion is virtually the only thing which distinguishes man from the beasts."[21]

Some attempt to locate religion's roots in the human quest for self-preservation from the many threatening hostile forces that surround us. Religion is a psychological and negative coping mechanism directly arising from the human need to alleviate fear. Others, thinking more positively, find those origins in the human desire for happiness and see in religion a means to gain benefits. Yet others find it in the human spirit's striving for mastery over nature's necessity; religion arises from the human longing for moral freedom. This longing is regarded in some circles as the quest of the human spirit for its proper divinity. When the human spirit recognizes, believes in, and trusts the power of religion, then it possesses infinite life as the most intimate dimension of our own being. Hence, according to Rudolf Eucken, religion is rooted in "the presence of divine life in human beings; it develops in apprehending this life as the life of their own being; hence it consists in the fact that human beings, in the innermost ground of their being, are lifted up into the divine life and thereby become participants in its divinity."[22]

These explanations run contrary to the way human beings experience their own religious journeys. The explanations offered above are abstractions; they afford no way out of their own circularity. If people attribute divinity to anything—forces of nature, their own spirit—we are no closer to answering the question of where

---

20. Charles Darwin, *The Descent of Man*, rev. ed. (New York: Appleton, 1896).

21. Lactantius, *Divine Institutes*, VII, 9.

22. Rudolf Eucken, *Der Wahrheitsgehalt der Religion*, 2nd ed. (Leipzig: Veit & Co., 1905), 149ff.

the inclination to make such an attribution comes from. A certain sense of the deity must be present before human beings can make anything the object of religious devotion. In fact, we enter into religious communities by upbringing and education, receive the concept of deity, accept it inasmuch as it comports with our own experience, and make it our own. Religion is not a general plea for help or benefits but a targeted call to a power greater than ourselves on whom we sense our dependence. Religion always assumes a certain distinction between God and the world, between the power of a being above nature and subordinate forces in nature. True, that divine power can then be conceived as inhabiting the natural phenomena, but it is never the power of nature itself that is the object of religious veneration but the divine being that manifests itself and works in it.

The most important objection against all efforts to find the origin of religion on strictly scientific, historical, psychological, or sociological terms is that the God who is thus "discovered" is not really God at all. Rather, God is conceived as in some way or other, if not humanity's creation then at least humanity's servant. God becomes nothing but a helper-in-need, a being whose existence is invented to provide human beings with some kind of benefit. Religion becomes a means to satisfy the fleshly or moral but always selfish needs of human beings. *Egoism* was the source and origin of religion.[23] This would suggest that as humanity's capacity for satisfying basic needs increases that religion would gradually disappear, that modernity would become increasingly "secular."[24] The assumption behind many of the attempts to find the origin of religion in natural human desiring and willing is that God does not create human beings; human beings create God. Subjective religion is the source of objective religion. Human beings determine whether and how they will serve God. But this understanding is fundamentally at war with the essence of religion and destroys the very phenomena it has to explain. If "God" were indeed a human projection or creation, a human effort to explain reality now known to us via science, or a means of providing security, comfort, and benefits now available to us through technological mastery, then indeed religion would wither away. But if God is real and religion is inevitable for us as human beings, then religion remains. It has, and it will.

[81] The scientific, historical study of religions is unable to find the answer to the origin of religion. It is not possible to explain the universality of religion from factors present in human beings that are not themselves religious but that

23. Eduard von Hartmann, *Religionsphilosophie* (Leipzig: Friedrich, 1888), I, 27.
24. Ed. note: The argument that the modern industrial state would increasingly become "secular" was a staple of sociological literature in the second half of the twentieth century. See Bryan R. Wilson, *Religion in a Secular Society* (London: Watts, 1966); idem, *Religion in Sociological Perspective* (Oxford: Oxford University Press, 1982). The events of the late twentieth and early twenty-first centuries provide a serious challenge to the secularization thesis; vital religious life persists in our modern industrial world. See Steve Bruce, ed., *Religion and Modernization: Sociologists and Historians Debate the Secularization Thesis* (Oxford: Clarendon; Oxford: Oxford University Press, 1992); David Martin, *On Secularization: Towards a Revised General Theory* (Aldershot, England: Ashgate, 2005).

by somehow combining under the impact of natural influences from without cause religion to spring up. Religion cannot be understood without God, and to know him he must reveal himself to us. God is the great supposition of religion; his existence and revelation are the foundation on which all human religion rests. Revelation is religion's external principle of knowing. At the same time, there must exist in human beings a certain faculty or natural aptitude for religion. God does not do half a job. He creates not only the light but also the eye to see it. Corresponding to the external reality there is an internal organ of perception. The ear is designed for the world of sounds. The "logos" implicit in creatures corresponds to the "logos" in human beings and makes science possible. Beauty in nature finds a response in the human sense of beauty. Similarly, God's revelation finds a response in the human expression of religious devotion and practice. One always finally encounters in humans a certain religious propensity that is called by various names: "the seed of religion," "a sense of divinity" (Calvin), religious feeling (Schleiermacher, Opzoomer), belief (Hartmann), a feeling for infinity (Tiele), etc. There is always in humans a certain capacity for perceiving the divine to which scientific inquiry into religion has to return and in which it must end.

Religion is distinguished from all the forces of culture and maintains its independence from them all. Religion is central; science, morality, and art are partial. While religion embraces the whole person, science, morality, and art are respectively rooted in the intellect, the will, and the emotions. Religion aims at nothing less than eternal blessedness in fellowship with God; science, morality, and art are limited to creatures and seek to enrich this life with the true, the good, and the beautiful. Religion, accordingly, cannot be equated with anything else. In the life and history of humankind, it occupies an independent place of its own, playing a unique and all-controlling role. Its indispensability can even be demonstrated from the fact that at the very moment people reject religion as an illusion they again turn some creature into their god, thus seeking to compensate for their religious need in some other way. Revelation and religion are, therefore, not alien to human nature. Rather, as God's image bearers, human beings are by nature religious; religion is a universal reality; we are created for God. Religion exists because God is God and wants to be honored. To that end he reveals himself to us and makes us subjectively fit to know him. This means that, as Scripture teaches, human beings from the first moment of their existence were religious beings, created in God's image. Religion was not something added later by a separate creation or a long process of evolution. The fall does not alter this though the forms of our religious life differ in the distinct states of integrity, sin, and, finally, grace and glory. The three realities—God, revelation, religion—abide and are rooted in the very trinitarian being of God. It is the Father who reveals himself in the Son and by the Spirit. No one knows the Father except the Son and anyone to whom the Son, by the Spirit, chooses to reveal him (Matt. 11:27; John 16:13–14; 1 Cor. 2:10).

4

REVELATION

THE IDEA OF REVELATION

[82] The concept of revelation is a necessary correlate of all religion; belief in revelation can be found in all religions. In so-called "nature religions," knowledge of the gods is obtained through signs and oracles given in extraordinary natural events. The Indian Vedas, the call of Zarathushtra to be a prophet, the prophet Muhammad's revelations described in the Qur'an—all illustrate the general belief in revelation universally found in religions. Revelation and religion stand or fall together; without revelation there is no religion.[1] The reason for this is directly tied to the nature of religion itself. In the previous chapter we saw that religion is essentially distinct from science, art, and morality, and is so because it puts human beings in relation, not to the world or to fellow human beings, but to a supernatural, invisible, external power, however they may then conceive that power. This remains true even when thinkers remove from religion this relation to a supernatural power and conceive it as a relation of a human to him- or herself (Feuerbach), to humanity as a whole (Comte), to the universe as a whole (Strauss), to the true, the good, and the beautiful (Haeckel), to the spirits of the dead (spiritism), etc. The religious impulse remains, though the character of religion changes; religion is converted into superstition or dissolved in illusion. "Belief in one or more supernatural powers, in a God or a divine world, is

---

1. "The idea of revelation is common to all religions, however differently the term may be interpreted" (C. P. Tiele, *Elements of the Science of Religion*, 2 vols. [Edinburgh and London: William Blackwood & Sons, 1897–99], I, 131).

the foundation on which all religion rests. There is no religion without a god."[2] Nor is Buddhism an exception, for when it first made its appearance, Buddha was its god.[3]

From this it follows that in religion the deity must exist to the mind of the believer, must reveal himself, and hence to some extent must be knowable. Religion is either an illusion or it must be based on belief in the existence, revelation, and knowability of God. For God to be God he cannot be accessible to ordinary human investigation; if we are to know him he must come forward out of his hiddenness, in some way make himself perceivable, and hence reveal himself. All religion is supernaturalistic in the sense that it is based on the belief in a divine power that is distinct from and elevated above the world and nevertheless somehow descends into it and has communion with it. However God chooses to do this, by nature or history, in the intellect or in the heart, by theophany or prophecy, this much is certain: all religion rests on revelation, on belief in a conscious, voluntary, intentional disclosure of God to human beings.

This is further confirmed when we ask what it is we look for in religion and what is at stake in religion. In general, it is safe to say that in religion we seek deliverance from evil and the acquisition of what we consider the highest good; in other words, redemption. All religions are religions of redemption; all religious doctrine is a doctrine of salvation.[4] Disagreements exist concerning the *what* and *how* of religion, but the question remains: "What must I do to be saved?" The answer to the three major concerns of religion—God, humanity, salvation—require revelation. We need revelation to know God and to understand ourselves and our situation before God in his world. To know ourselves truly it is not enough to attempt by scientific research to gain knowledge about our "humanness" which can be obtained by scientific research—anatomy, physiology, and psychology. We need more, we need answers to questions about human origin and destiny, our relation to God, our misery because of sin, our need for redemption, our memories of paradise, and our hopes for the future.[5] These questions are beyond the scope of science; they can be uncovered only by revelation. This is especially true with respect to the question of salvation. A belief in saviors is also universal[6] and can rest only on revelation. Revelation and grace are closely connected, as are grace and faith.

[83] The universality of religion is rooted in the reality of God's general or natural revelation to all people, which we will discuss later in this chapter. What is of interest to us here is the question about the relation between believing and knowing, theology and philosophy. If God can only be known by God, and if the general human knowledge of God available to all people is insufficient and

---

2. Ibid., II, 73.

3. Ibid., I, 128; II, 74; G. T. Ladd, *Philosophy of Religion*, 2 vols. (New York: Scribner, 1905), I, 107ff.

4. C. P. Tiele, *Elements*, I, 62ff.; II, 75, 117.

5. Ibid., II, 75ff., 109ff.

6. Ibid., I, 130, 166; II, 124ff.

cannot provide us with satisfying answers to our deepest questions, then our knowing is intimately joined to our faith in the God who reveals. We need faith to understand revelation. Depending on philosophy to provide categories for understanding revelation often leads to abstraction and intellectualism. Deism in particular subordinated revelation to reason, making scriptural revelation unnecessary. The important truths of Christianity could be known by reason alone. By giving reason the weight it did, deism legitimated the right of human beings to pronounce judgment on revelation; no truth of Christianity could add to what was known through reason, and human reason determined whether or not the content of revelation was true. Special or biblical revelation was rendered superfluous. Since this rationalism was cold and spiritually as well as intellectually unsatisfying, others began to understand revelation as the spark of divinity evidenced in artistic genius (Romanticism, Hamann, Herder, Jacobi) and moral perfection (Kant, Ritschl). Since Jesus embodies this genius and moral perfection supremely, he becomes the great Revealer, who somehow communicates his divinity and holiness to those in communion with him. A good example is the German idealist philosopher Johann Gottlieb Fichte (1762–1814). According to Fichte, humanity's destiny is moral perfection, an ethical kingdom of God. However, since humanity may for a time fall into a deep moral decay, it then becomes necessary for God to take extraordinary measures by raising up a person who with divine authority and power again reminds humankind of its moral destiny, lifts it up out of its decay, and again persuades it to go forward on the road of virtue. Revelation is some "manifestation" that makes such a strong impression on people that they are compelled to learn to understand this manifestation's moral purpose. Revelation is God's extraordinary way of grabbing our attention. In that way the person of Christ was raised up by God in an extraordinary manner to proclaim with authority the content of natural religion and morality and to instill it in the hearts of human beings. Here revelation is a stratagem in the divine nurture of the human race, and the Christian faith is understood as a historical process of moral amelioration, building the kingdom of God on earth.

The theology of Schleiermacher was a variation on the same theme. Revelation is centered in the person of Christ and not in doctrine or what we believe about him. In his *Speeches on Religion* he conceived revelation in a personal way as "every original and new communication of the universe and of that person's inmost life."[7] Similarly, in the *Christian Faith* he spoke of "newness and originality in history," of "the originality of a fact which underlies a religious community." In Christianity the person of Christ has such original significance; since he fully and uninterruptedly participated in communion with God, he is in a special sense the revelation of God, even though we do not know how he became that revelation. Furthermore, by the spiritual energies that proceed from Christ, we too are incorporated in the

---

7. F. Schleiermacher, *On Religion, Speeches to Its Cultured Despisers* (New York: Harper & Brothers, 1950), 89.

communion of God and participate in a new and holy life that is freed from sin. So while revelation is typically marked by its own inherent originality, its effect and aim consist in the new life it imparts. By these assertions Schleiermacher paved the way for the view of revelation that defined it in terms of the communication not of doctrine but of life.

This changed view of revelation gained ground in all the nineteenth-century schools of theology. The so-called mediating theology (*Vermittelungstheologie*)[8] emphasized history more than Schleiermacher did, doing greater justice to the historical continuity of God's revelation in Christ with that revelation in Israel, especially in the prophets. It also returned to the confession of his deity and, in clearer terms than we find in Schleiermacher, attributed the working of Christ in his church to the Spirit of God. Nonetheless, this new view of revelation, centered in the God-consciousness of Jesus which is communicated to Christians, found ready acceptance.[9] Here even Ritschl showed affinity with Schleiermacher when, while rejecting mysticism, he still returned to the person of Christ and called Christ—specifically in his professional life as founder of the kingdom of God—the revealer of God's love, grace, and faithfulness.[10]

When we compare this newer concept of revelation with what was generally accepted before that time, we find that it is distinguished by the following features: (1) Special revelation, which is the basis of Christianity, is more organically conceived and more intimately connected in heart and conscience with general revelation in nature and history; (2) scholars adhering to this newer concept attempt to understand special revelation itself as a historical process, not only in word but also in deed, both in prophecy and miracle, which then culminate in the person of Christ; (3) they view its content as existing exclusively or predominantly in religious-ethical truth, which aims primarily not at teaching, but at moral amelioration, redemption from sin; and (4) they make a sharp distinction between the revelation that gradually took place in history and its documentation or description in Holy Scripture; the latter is not itself the revelation but only a more or less accurate record of it. Properly nuanced, these features are an enrichment of our understanding of revelation.

The nineteenth century also produced philosophical understandings of revelation in which God's self-consciousness in humanity is identical to humanity

8. Ed. note: *Vermittelungstheologie* ("mediating theology") was a specific school of nineteenth-century German theology that, influenced by Schleiermacher, sought to synthesize Christianity and modern idealistic philosophy into a rationally and morally defensible religion. Representatives include I. A. Dorner, J. Neander, H. Martensen, K. Nitzsch, and J. Müller.

9. C. E. Nitzsch, *System of Christian Doctrines* (Edinburgh: T&T Clark, 1849), §22; I. A. Dorner, *A System of Christian Doctrine*, trans. Alfred Cave and J. S. Banks, rev. ed., 4 vols. (Edinburgh: T&T Clark, 1888), II, 133ff.; H. L. Martensen, *Christian Dogmatics*, trans. William Urwick (Edinburgh: T&T Clark, 1871), §§11, 12.

10. A. Ritschl, *Unterricht in der Christlichen Religion*, 6th ed. (Bonn: A. Marcus, 1903), §§20ff.; idem, *Die Christliche Lehre von der Rechtfertigung und Versohnung*, 3rd ed., 3 vols. (Bonn: A. Marcus, 1895–1903), III, 190ff., 599ff.

gaining consciousness of God (Schelling, Hegel). This consciousness is expressed first symbolically in art, then visually in religion, and finally in its highest form conceptually in philosophy. The history of religions is the history of the Absolute coming to himself in human consciousness and achieves its zenith in Christianity, which brings to light the essential unity of God and humanity. This evolutionary pantheism found favor among a number of nineteenth-century theologians such as David Friedrich Strauss (1810–74).[11] Revelation coincides with course of nature, the true revelation of rational knowledge. All notions of supernatural revelation have vanished here. The content of biblical revelation is given the same status as other ancient religious texts: the Bible and Babel dwell on the same plain.[12]

The Christian doctrine of revelation cannot survive this turn. If God's revelation coincides with the course of nature, with immanent cosmic evolution; if the revelations on which the religions base themselves are merely the creations of human fantasy; if the truth that the believer finds in revelation is a human invention, and childlike faith in it is superstition; if nature alone is the true revelation, i.e., the true source of rational knowledge,[13] then we are, as the apostle Paul said in a similar context, "to be pitied more than all people" (1 Cor. 15:19).

[84] The theological discussion of revelation in our day remains confused and inherently contradictory, in large measure because many theologians continue to speak of "revelation" when on the basis of their stated convictions they have forfeited the right.[14] On a naturalistic level there cannot be such a reality as revelation; there is no personal communication from God to humanity. If God does not exist and if, as Feuerbach has it, "anthropology is the secret of theology," then by that token religion and revelation are automatically condemned and are nothing but the reactions of human fantasy. However, the term "revelation" remains in use even among naturalist philosophers and theologians. The reality of religion depends on some form of revelation, and the very possibility of revelation as a communication from a personal God requires a theistic, supernaturalist worldview. A materialist worldview is diametrically opposed to all ideas of such revelation. A supernaturalistic worldview affirms both creation and providence; since God created the world and by his providence still maintains and governs it, he is absolutely elevated above the world and can use it in the manner it pleases

11. David Friedrich Strauss, *Die christliche Glaubenslehre in ihrer geschichtlichen Entwicklung und im Kampfe mit der modern Wissenschaft*, 2 vols. (Tübingen: C. F. Osiander, 1840–41), §19; idem, *The Old Faith and the New, a Confession by David Friedrich Strauss*; authorized translation from the 6th ed. by Mathilde Blind (New York, Holt, 1873).

12. Friedrich Delitzsch, *Babel and Bible*, trans. W. H. Corruth (Chicago: Open Court, 1903); German original: *Babel und Bibel: Ein Rückblick und Ausblick* (Stuttgart: Deutsche Verlags-Anstalt, 1904).

13. E. Haeckel, *The Riddle of the Universe at the Close of the Nineteenth Century*, trans. Joseph McCabe (New York: Harper & Brothers, 1900), 306–7; German original: *Die Welträthsel* (Stuttgart: E. Strauss, 1899), 354.

14. Ed. note: For a twentieth-century argument against the very notion of revelation as theologically important, see Gerald Downing, *Has Christianity a Revelation?* (London: SCM Press; Philadelphia: Westminster, 1964).

him. Thus, both creation and providence are proof that God can, and wants to, reveal himself.

Still, the question persists: assuming that God reveals himself, where do we go to find out the truth about revelation in the midst of competing revelatory claims? All religions, after all, appeal to revelation. The various sciences of religion as usually conducted are of little help here. Their chief error here is a commitment to a religiously neutral scientific method; an attempt to find a value-free, unprejudiced, objective standpoint, an impossible goal. A true concept of revelation can be derived only from revelation itself. If no revelation ever took place, all reflection on the concept is futile. This does not make our quest for truth any easier. It is indeed a perplexing fact that all religions base themselves on revelation and on that basis present themselves as the true religion. It is, therefore, understandable that many theorists retreat to the position of indifferentism and try to console themselves with the idea that it does not matter what one believes provided one lives a good life. But this consolation soon evaporates. The world's concrete religions will not allow such neutral indifferentism; divisions exist and the scientific investigator cannot avoid making judgments. No science, especially not the science that deals with the most intimate dimension of human experience, is without presupposition or bias. The sciences of religion cannot and do not take positions outside the stream of human history and experience; they are imbedded in it. Science cannot create unity in the most basic convictions of the heart. If there is ever to be unity, it will have to be achieved in the way of mission; only religious unity will be able to bring about the spiritual and intellectual unity of humankind. And only revelation can give us the answer to revelation.

This apparent circularity must not lead us to a counsel of despair about the possibility of truth and a subsequent turn to relativism. The fact that all religions appeal to a revelation cannot be an argument for Christians to relinquish their conviction about the truth of the Christian religion any more than logically thinking or ethical or aesthetic persons will relinquish their convictions concerning the laws of thought, morality, or beauty because there are thousands of people who say that truth, virtue, and beauty are merely relative concepts and find their criterion in the individual human beings themselves. There are fundamental divisions in the human race on these important matters, and it is true that Muslims, Buddhists, and others will reason from their revelation in the same way and proceed from their beliefs much as Christians do. In this respect everyone had best be fully convinced in his or her own mind. Christians can only bear witness to the truth, trusting that the God who has revealed himself to us as Creator and Redeemer is the same who provides his followers with wisdom to understand his revelation. We therefore believe that a science—driven by free convictions, of course, and not by coercion—that allies itself with the Christian faith will be able to do more and labor more energetically for the spiritual and intellectual unity of humankind than a naturalistic one. Such unity is guaranteed in the unity of God and is the hope of all religion. Scientific investigation rooted in Christian revelation will also yield results that serve God and are a blessing to the world. Christians can proceed to do their work positively, not speculatively, and do it with confidence and joy. They do not dictate to God whether and how he may reveal himself but listen to what God himself has to say on that matter. We will now continue by listening to what Holy Scripture teaches concerning revelation: its subject and object, its essence and content, its manner and intent.

GENERAL REVELATION

[85] Instructed by Holy Scripture, early Christian theology was led to make a distinction between "natural" revelation (religion, theology) and "supernatural" revelation. Christianity accounted for those elements she held in common with other religions by confessing that God makes himself known to all people through his creation. Justin Martyr, for example, speaks of a "human teaching" obtained from "the seed of reason (σπερμα του λογου) that is innate in the whole human race." He distinguishes this from "a [spiritual] knowledge (γνωσις) and vision (θεωρια)" that comes to us only through Christ.[15] What is unique and distinctive about Christianity is based on God's special revelation in Scripture. The great theological debates in the church concerned the nature of the relationship between these two, especially the boundaries between the two kinds of revelation.

Although some theologians tried after the fact to prove key Christian dogmas from nature and reason,[16] the distinction between natural and supernatural, or scriptural, theology was progressively made more rigorous and turned into an absolute contrast. Supernatural, scriptural revelation began to refer to another order of knowledge that surpassed even the intellect of sinless human beings and angels. When notions of merit were mixed into this discussion the lines between faith and reason were blurred and the understanding of sin's impact on our knowledge of God obscured. Rationalism and supernaturalism often joined hands in unseemly marriage.

The Reformation did not dispute the distinction between natural and supernatural revelation but in principle assigned it a very different meaning. "Supernatural" was taken primarily to refer to revelation that far exceeded the thoughts and wishes of *sinful* fallen human beings. Natural theology was affirmed but incorporated in the doctrine of the Christian faith.[17] The Reformers believed

---

15. Justin Martyr, *2 Apology*, 8, 10, 13.

16. E.g., Augustine (the Trinity in *The Trinity*); Anselm (the doctrines of the incarnation and satisfaction in *Cur deus homo*). The most radical in this respect was Raymond of Sabunde, who in his *Liber naturalis sive creaturarum*, attempted to construct the whole Christian doctrine of faith from human nature without help from Scripture and tradition and without using the Scholastic method.

17. U. Zwingli, *Commentary on True and False Religion*, ed. S. M. Jackson and C. N. Heller (Durham, NC: Labyrinth, 1981), §3, "God"; J. Calvin, *Institutes of the Christian Religion*, I.i–v (ed. John T. McNeill and trans. Ford Lewis Battles, 2 vols. [Philadelphia: Westminster, 1960], 1:35–69).

that the human mind was so darkened by sin that it could not rightly know and understand natural revelation either. God, therefore, needed to provide the glasses (Calvin) of Scripture to aid our "reading" of natural revelation. Human beings also needed eyes of faith, provided by the illumination of the Holy Spirit, to see God in the works of his hands. The extreme wing of the Anabaptist tradition went farther, rejecting the natural order and attempting in revolutionary fashion to establish a kingdom of heaven on earth. Socinianism also rejected natural theology and inferred all knowledge of God from special revelation. Even Luther was not free from a dualistic view that separated the spiritual and temporal realms. As a result, a sound theological understanding of revelation failed to gain ground in the divided Protestant world, with tragic consequences. In Anabaptism and Socinianism, excessive supernaturalism turned into rationalism; among Lutherans and some Calvinists, reason came to have a degree of authority alongside faith. Eventually an expanding natural theology was judged by German naturalists and English deists to make revelation unnecessary. By contrast the influence of Immanuel Kant's philosophy led theologians to search for nonrational means of affirming the reality of God. In addition, the history of religions demonstrated that a purely natural religion did not exist anywhere and that all religions were positive (concrete). Finally, historical-biblical criticism undermined supernatural revelation and erased the boundaries between it and natural revelation.

[86] The Scriptures do not distinguish between "natural" and "supernatural" revelation. Creation revelation is no less supernatural than Scripture; in both, God himself is at work, and his providential creating, sustaining, and governing form a single mighty ongoing revelation. In its origin all revelation is supernatural. God is always working (John 5:17). That work of God outward began with the creation that is the first revelation of God, the beginning and foundation of all subsequent revelation. In creating the world by his Word and making it come alive by his Spirit, God already delineated the basic contours of all subsequent revelation. Even before the fall into sin God speaks a special word to humanity: the covenant of works with its probationary command and promise (Gen. 2:16). "Thou shalt not eat . . ." could never have been inferred from nature alone. We are left with a simple and stark choice: revelation or naturalism; belief in a higher supernatural power or the conviction that nature is all that there is. As image bearers of God, human beings are intrinsically supernaturalists.

Supernatural revelation is not the same as immediate revelation. All revelation is mediate; God always makes himself known by means, by theophanies, by word and deed. Sin does not alter matters. Even dreams and visions occur organically and thus mediately. The distance between the Creator and creature is much too great for human beings to perceive God directly. The finite is not capable of containing the infinite (*finitum non est capax infiniti*). What this means for the *visio dei* in state of glory, when "we will be like Him, because we will see Him just as He is" (1 John 3:2), is a matter we shall discuss later. We do know, however, that even then the Creator-creature difference will remain. No creature can see or understand God as he is and as he speaks in himself. Revelation therefore is always an act of grace; in it God condescends to meet his creature, a creature made in his image. All revelation is anthropomorphic, a kind of humanization of God. It always occurs in certain forms, in specific modes. In natural revelation his divine and eternal thoughts have been deposited in creatures in a creaturely way so that they could be understood by human thought processes.

The entrance of sin did not alter the fact of revelation. God does not withdraw himself; he continues to reveal himself in the maintenance and governance of all things. God's general revelation still holds for all people at all times; he displays in creation his eternal power and divinity, and in blessings and judgments alternately shows this goodness and wrath (Job 36; 37; Ps. 29; 33:5; 65; 67:7; 90; 104; 107; 145; 147; Isa. 59:17–19; Matt. 5:45; Acts 14:16–17; Rom. 1:18). He reveals himself in the history of nations and persons (Deut. 32:8; Ps. 33:10; 67:4; 115:16; Prov. 8:15–16; Acts 17:26; Rom. 13:1). He also discloses himself in the heart and conscience of every individual (Job 32:8; 33:4; Prov. 20:27; John 1:3–5, 9–10; Rom. 2:14–15; 8:16). God also speaks in a special way through creation signs accompanied by revelation as in the rainbow sign to Noah (Gen. 9:12–17), the seven years of plenty followed by seven of famine in Egypt (Gen. 41ff.), and the plagues accompanying the exodus (Exod. 6ff.). For these and other reasons, the distinction between natural and supernatural revelation should not be identified with the distinction between general and special revelation. The latter contrast is preferable to the former.

[87] It is the unanimous conviction of Christian theologians that general revelation is inadequate. Augustine is convinced that there is some truth among the pagans that Christians can use profitably,[18] but for him philosophy cannot save. It knows the goal but not the road that leads to it[19] and often leads us astray, suppressing the truth in unrighteousness and exalting in its own pride,[20] lacking the piety and love necessary to the knowledge of the truth.[21] There is no disagreement between Roman Catholic and Protestant theologians on the insufficiency of general revelation. Thomas asserts the necessity of revelation even for the mixed articles of faith also known to reason[22] and the catechisms and councils of the Roman church follow suit.[23] The reasons are clear: general revelation fails to point us to sin, divine wrath, and grace; what knowledge of God is given in general

---

18. Augustine, *On Christian Doctrine*, II, 60.

19. Idem, *Confessions*, V, 5; VII, 26; idem, *City of God*, X, 29.

20. Idem, *The Trinity*, XIII, 12, 13, 24.

21. Idem, *Confessions*, V, 4; idem, *City of God*, IX, 20.

22. T. Aquinas, *Summa Theol.*, I, qu. (1) art. 1; idem, *Summa contra gentiles*, I, 4.

23. "It is true that the invisible things of God from the creation of the world are, as the Apostle teaches, clearly seen, being understood by the things that are made: his eternal power also, and divinity. But the mystery which hath been hidden from ages and generations so far transcends the reach of man's understanding, that were it not made manifest by God to His Saints, to whom He willed to make known by the gift of faith, the riches of the glory of this mystery among the Gentiles, which is Christ, man could by no effort attain to such wisdom" ("Preface" to the Roman Catechism [Council of Trent]).

revelation is uncertain, inconsistent, mixed with error, and unattainable for most people; and, finally, no concrete religion has ever existed that matches what deists and history-of-religions scholars contend is the essential core of natural, rational religion in general. There is no temple dedicated to deism, no cultic ritual that nourishes the faith of naturalists and materialists. Religions are living realities; while eighteenth-century thinkers were able to find pleasure in the abstractions of reason, the nineteenth century with its sense of history soon saw that such a natural religion neither existed nor can exist anywhere. Today it is generally agreed that all religions are concrete and rest on revelation.[24]

[88] General revelation is of great significance, nonetheless, for the world of paganism. It is the stable and permanent foundation of all pagan religions. According to Scripture, the character of pagan religions consists in idolatry. Heathen gods are idols; they do not exist; they are lies and vanity (Isa. 41:29; 42:17; 46:1f.; Jer. 2:28; Ps. 106:28; Acts 14:15; 19:26; 1 Cor. 8:5; Gal. 4:8). At work in those religions is a demonic power (Deut. 32:17; Ps. 106:28; 1 Cor. 10:20ff.; Rev. 9:20). The condition in which the pagan world finds itself outside of the revelation to Israel and outside of Christ is described as darkness (Isa. 9:1; 60:2; Luke 1:79; John 1:5; Eph. 4:18), ignorance (Acts 17:30; Rom. 1:10ff.; 1 Pet. 1:14), imaginary and vain wisdom (1 Cor. 1:18f.; 2:6; 3:19f.), and sin and unrighteousness (Rom. 1:24ff.; 3:9f.). Attempts fail us to account for both the elements of continuity and the great diversity among religions by tracing them to a common origin and a movement from an animal state without religion to primitive religions (animism, fetishism) to more spiritual and ethical religions. Among other things, they ignore the possibility of retrogression in religion. Certain nineteenth-century scholars even claimed that an original monotheism or henotheism was basic to all pagan religions.[25]

This seems reasonable because we are left to conclude that though the origins of religion elude us as a scientific question, the idea of God is foundational at the very beginning. When we pass judgment on a religion, distinguishing healthy from pathological expressions, acknowledging both advance and decline over time, then it is logical to posit what a religion's essence must have been in the earliest beginning as its leading idea and dynamic. Certainly the least one then has to acknowledge is that one must judge the essence of a religion, not by its most primitive beginnings, but by its later times of flourishing, just as one can only know the child from the mature adult and an acorn from the oak that grows from it.[26] But then, by analogy, one is forced, whether one wants to or not, to posit the idea of God as the foundation of all religion; a foundation universally

24. F. Schleiermacher, *The Christian Faith*, ed. H. R. MacIntosh and J. S. Steward (Edinburgh: T&T Clark, 1928), §10.

25. Among others, F. W. J. Schelling, Max Müller, L. W. E. Rauwenhoff, S. Hoekstra, O. Pfleiderer, A. Jeremias, H. Winckler.

26. Pfleiderer, *Religion und Religionen*, 5; C. P. Tiele, *Elements*, II, 141–42; G. T. Ladd, *Philosophy of Religion*, I, 34, 103, 144.

present at the origins of all religions. Without God, without the acknowledgment of his existence, his revelation, and his knowability, one cannot satisfactorily explain the origin and essence of religion.

This also leads us to recognize that there are elements of truth, even in the pagan religions. Previous examinations of non-Christian religions that pursued a strictly dogmatic, apologetic, and polemical approach often treated the founders of [non-Christian] religions, such as Muhammad, simply as impostors, enemies of God, accomplices of the devil. But ever since those religions have become more precisely known, this interpretation has proven to be untenable; it clashed both with history and psychology. Also among pagans, says Scripture, there is a revelation of God, an illumination by the Logos, a working of God's Spirit (Gen. 6:17; 7:15; Pss. 33:6; 104:30; Job 32:8; Eccles. 3:19; Prov. 8:22f.; Mal. 1:11, 14; John 1:9; Rom. 2:14; Gal. 4:1–3; Acts 14:16–17; 17:22–30). Many church fathers (Justin Martyr, Clement of Alexandria, Augustine, and others) assumed an operation of the Logos in the pagan world. In Augustine's words, "Still, since God's image has not been so completely erased in the soul of man by the stain of earthly affections, as to have left remaining there not even the merest lineaments of it, whence it might be justly said that man, even in the ungodliness of his life, does or appreciates some things contained in the law."[27] Also, many impure people recognize much that is true.[28]

In the Middle Ages Thomas said the same, even citing Augustine (and Bede) as authority: "There is no false doctrine which does not at some time mix some truth with falsehoods."[29] The Reformed theologians acknowledge this by their doctrine of common grace. By it they repudiated the Pelagian error which taught the sufficiency of natural theology while at the same time recognized the truth, beauty, and goodness that is present also in the pagan world.[30] As a rule this operation of common grace was acknowledged in the life of morality and intellect, society and state, but less frequently recognized in the religions of pagans. The religions were usually traced to deception or demonic influences. However, an operation of God's Spirit and of his common grace is discernible also in the religions. Calvin rightly spoke of a "seed of religion," a "sense of divinity."[31] The various religions, however mixed with error they may have been, to some extent met people's religious needs and brought consolation amid the pain and sorrow of life. All the elements and forms that are essential to religion (a concept of God, a sense of guilt, a desire for redemption, sacrifice, priesthood, temple, cult, prayer, etc.), though corrupted, nevertheless do also occur in pagan religions. Christianity is the true religion, the truth of all religions; the pagan religions are caricatures. Christ is the Promised One to Israel and the desire of all the gentiles. Israel and the church are elect for the benefit of humankind. In Abraham's seed all the nations of the earth will be blessed.

27. Augustine, *On the Spirit and the Letter*, chap. 48.
28. Augustine, *Retractions*, I, chap. 4.
29. T. Aquinas, *Summa Theol.*, I 2 qu. 109 art. 1; II 2 qu. 172 art. 6.
30. J. Calvin, *Institutes*, II.ii.13.
31. Ibid., I.iii.1–3; I.iv.1; II.ii.18.

[89] Yet general revelation has meaning not only for the pagan world but also in and for the Christian religion. The Scriptures themselves value general revelation; the Bible bears ample testimony to the glory of God in creation (Pss. 8; 19; 29), directs us to the Spirit of God as the source of all creation's life (Gen. 2:7; Job 33:4; Ps. 104:29–30; Isa. 32:15), and credits the Spirit of God with artistic and leadership gifts (Exod. 31:2–5; 35:30–35; Num. 27:18; Judg. 3:10; 6:34; 11:24; 13:25; 14:6; Job 32:8). Biblical faith is positioned to look out upon nature and history and discover there the traces of the God who is known through Christ as Father. Christians, equipped with the spectacles of Scripture,[32] see God in everything and everything in God. As a result Christians feel at home in the world as God's creation; it is God's fatherly hand from which they receive all things also in the context of nature.

Here, too, Christians have a firm foundation on which they can meet all non-Christians. They have a common basis with non-Christians in their humanity as religious beings created in God's image. Religion belongs to the essence of a human. The idea and existence of God, the spiritual independence and eternal destiny of the world, the moral world order and its ultimate triumph—all these are problems that never cease to engage the human mind. Metaphysical need cannot be suppressed; general revelation keeps human desiring and questing alive and philosophers perennially employed. We cannot escape the reality that we have been created in God's image and can only find rest in God; the gospel of Christ offers the fulfillment of that longing. General revelation preserves humankind in order that it can be found and healed by Christ and until it is.

All revelation—general and special—finally finds its fulfillment and meaning in Christ. God's revelation in Scripture and in Christ provides the spectacles of faith that enable us to understand general revelation better, as well as a basis for encounters with non-Christians. In no way should the Christian faith be represented as otherworldly or anti-creation. Rather, grace and nature are united in the Christian faith, and general revelation links the kingdom of heaven and the kingdom of earth—it joins creation and redemption together in one great eschatological cantata of praise. A religious life is woven into the very fabric of ordinary human experience. God is one and the same loving God in creation and redemption; grace restores nature.

SPECIAL, SCRIPTURAL REVELATION

[90] Christianity, like all religions, cannot survive on general revelation alone; a special divine disclosure or manifestation is needed. All religion can be reduced to three basic needs. First, religious belief desires a God *who is near*, so that in

---

32. Raymond of Sabunde, *Theologia Naturalis* (*Prologus*) (Artentinae: Martinus Flach, 1496); J. Calvin, *Institutes*, I.vi.1.

almost every religion there are holy places, holy times, and holy images. Second, in all religions one can find the belief that the gods in some way *reveal their will* to human beings. Finally, there is a universal belief in the special *assistance* of the gods in times of distress. Belief in manifestation, prediction, and miracle are thus necessary elements in all religions. Nearness and approachability, communication of the divine will, help in trouble—these are the great religious concerns. In addition to these concerns, biblical religion may also share some forms with other religions (sacrifices, temples, priests), but its substance is still categorically different. In Holy Scripture, God takes the initiative; the Messiah came forth only from Israel.

The key words and terms by which the Bible expresses the concept of revelation are mainly these: גלה, to uncover (niphal: be uncovered, display, appear, be revealed; Gen. 35:7; 1 Sam. 2:27; 3:21; Isa. 53:1; 56:1; Hosea 7:1; etc.); ראה, to see (niphal: be seen, show oneself, appear; Gen. 12:7; 17:1; 18:1; etc.); ידע, to know (niphal, piel, hiphal, hithpael: make known, teach; Num. 12:6); ἐπιφανειν, to appear (Luke 1:79; Titus 2:11); subst. ἐπιφανεια, appearance, especially of Christ's return (2 Thess. 2:8; 1 Tim. 6:14; 2 Tim. 4:1; Titus 2:13; 2 Tim. 1:10 of Christ's first coming); ἐμφανιζειν, to manifest oneself, make oneself visible; passive, show oneself, appear (Matt. 27:53; John 14:21–22); γνωριζειν, to make known (Luke 2:15; Rom. 9:22; Eph. 3:3, 5, 10); δηλουν, to make known, disclose, reveal (1 Pet. 1:11; 2 Pet. 1:14); δεικνυναι, to show (John 5:20); λαλειν, to speak (Heb. 1:1; 2:2; 5:5); and especially ἀποκαλυπτειν and φανερουν. New Testament usage of these terms is not entirely clear or consistent; etymologically, however, ἀποκαλυπτειν indicates the removal of a cover by which a given object was hidden, and φανερουν denotes making known a matter that was hidden or unknown before. Ἀποκαλυψις takes away the cause by which something was hidden and is now revealed; φανερωσις publicly makes known the matter itself. Both verbs are in turn distinguished from γνωριζειν and δηλουν by the fact that the former bring things to light while the latter two now also bring what is revealed into the content of our thinking consciousness.[33]

Human beings universally find revelational significance in perceived appearances of the divine (theophany), oracular divination through sacred words and formulas (magic), and the mediation of designated spokespersons who are believed to know the divine will (prophecy). When we encounter contemporary phenomena such as spiritism, theosophy, telepathy, voodoo, and witchcraft, as well as unspeakable acts of human cruelty and evil that suggest demonic influence, we need to acknowledge with the Scriptures that the so-called "dark side" of human nature includes supersensory forces that are beyond our ability to explain on broad scientific grounds. "There are more things in heaven and earth than are dreamt of

---

33. Cf. Hermann Cremer, *Biblisch-theologisches Wörterbuch der neutestamentlichen Gräcität* (Gotha: F. A. Perthes, 1880); in English, *Biblico-Theological Lexicon of New Testament Greek*, trans. William Urwick, 4th ed. (Edinburgh: T&T Clark; New York: Scribner, 1892).

in your philosophy" (Shakespeare). The worldview of Scripture affirms the reality of such phenomena (Gen. 41:8; Exod. 7:8–12; Deut. 13:1–2; Matt. 7:22; 24:24; 2 Thess. 2:9; 2 Tim. 3:8; Rev. 13:13–15). At the same time it is fundamentally opposed to them; it neither recognizes nor tolerates them, but categorically forbids them (Lev. 19:26, 31; 20:27; Num. 23:23; Deut. 18:10–11; Acts 8:9; 13:6; 16:16; 19:13f.; Gal. 5:20; Rev. 21:8; 22:15). Whatever correspondence there might be in form, the substance is different. The difference between scriptural religion and that of the pagans does not consist in the uniqueness of covenant, circumcision, sacrifice, tabernacle, priesthood, prophecy; etc., as *forms*. Even the Christian religion has its sacrifice (Eph. 5:2), its priest (Heb. 7), and its temple (1 Cor. 3:16f.; etc.). What occurs in paganism in the form of caricature has become shadow and image in Israel and authentic spiritual reality in Christianity thanks to God's full revelation in Jesus Christ. What makes Christianity different is its faith that the Messiah has come.

[91] The human religious quest, we have said, comes down to three basic desires: a longing for a God who is near, a God who communicates to us, and a God who is strong enough to deliver. Biblical revelation indicates several distinct modes of revelation by which these human needs are met. The biblical revelation of nearness can be found in the perceptible manifestation of divine presence (theophanies; Gen. 12:7; 17:1, 22; 26:24; 35:9; Exod. 6:2; also cf. Gen. 11:5; Exod. 4:24; 12:12, 23; 17:6; Num. 23:4, 16; 1 Sam. 3:21; 2 Sam. 5:24). These manifestations do not presuppose God's corporeality nor are they emanations of the divine Being; they can be impersonal presence (wind, fire)[34] or via personal beings (angels), in the Old Testament,[35] and even more so in the New.[36] In all these signs we see a manifestation of the divine glory (כבוד, δοξα; Exod. 16:10; 24:17; Lev. 9:6, 23–24; Num. 14:10; 16:19; 20:6), a glory described as a consuming fire (Exod. 24:17; Lev. 9:23–24) as well as a cloud (1 Kings 8:10–11; Isa. 6:4).

Among God's envoys who speak for him, the Messenger of God (מלאך יהוה) occupies a special place. He appears to Hagar (Gen. 16:6–13; 21:17–20); to Abraham (Gen. 18; 19; 22; 24:7; 40); to Jacob (Gen. 28:13–17; 31:11–13; 32:24–30; cf. Hosea 12:4; Gen. 48:15–16); to Moses (Exod. 3:2f.; 13:21; 14:19; 23:20–23; 32:34; 33:2f.; Josh. 5:13–14; Judg. 6:11–24; 13:2–23). This מלאך יהוה is to be

---

34. Thus to Abraham (Gen. 15:17f.), to Moses (Exod. 3:2; 33:18f.), on Sinai (Exod. 19:9, 16f.; 24:16, cf. vv. 9–11; Deut. 5:23; 9:15; Heb. 12:18), to the people (Exod. 13:21f.; 14:19–24; 40:38; Num. 9:21; 14:14; Deut. 1:33; Neh. 9:12, 19; Ps. 78:14), above the tabernacle (Exod. 33:9; 40:34f.; Lev. 9:23; Num. 9:15–23; 11:17, 25; 12:5; 17:7; 20:6; Deut. 31:15; Ps. 99:7; Isa. 4:5), and in the holy of holies (Exod. 25:8, 22; 29:45–46; Lev. 16:2; 26:11–12; Num. 7:89); cf. also to Elijah (1 Kings 19:11f.).

35. Thus Gen. 18; 19; 28:12; 32:1–2; Deut. 33:2; Job 33:23; 1 Kings 13:18; Dan. 8:13; 9:21; 10:5; Zech. 1:7–6:5.

36. Angels are present at the birth of Jesus (Matt. 1:20; 2:13, 19; Luke 1:11; 2:9), repeatedly in his life (John 1:51; Matt. 4:6), at the time of his suffering (Matt. 26:53; Luke 22:43), and at the resurrection and ascension (Matt. 28:2, 5; Luke 24:23; John 20:12; Acts 1:10). In the history of the apostles, they repeatedly make appearances (Acts 5:19; 8:26; 10:3; 11:13; 12:7; 23:9; 27:23; Rev. 22:6, 16). Finally, at his return Christ will be accompanied by the angels (Matt. 16:27; 25:31; Mark 8:38; Luke 9:26; 1 Thess. 3:13; etc.).

regarded as a true personal revelation and appearance of God, distinct from him (Exod. 23:20–23; 33:14f.; Isa. 63:8–9), and still one with him in name (Gen. 16:13; 31:13; 32:28, 30; 48:15–16; Exod. 3:2f.; 23:20–23; Judg. 13:3), in power (Gen. 16:10–11; 21:18; 18:14, 18; Exod. 14:19; Judg. 6:21), in redemption and blessing (Gen. 48:16; Exod. 3:8; 23:20; Isa. 63:8–9), in adoration and honor (Gen. 18:3; 22:12; Exod. 23:21). Later in Israel's history the tabernacle and temple as God's dwelling place (1 Kings 8:10f.; 2 Chron. 7:1f.; Pss. 68:17; 74:2; 132:13f.; 135:21) becomes the location to which the longings of Israel's devout are directed (Pss. 27:4; 42; 43; 48; 50; 63:2; 65; 84; 122; 137). But all Old Testament theophany is incomplete; God does not dwell in a house made by human hands (1 Kings 8:27; Jer. 7:4; Mic. 3:11; Acts 7:48; 17:24); the high priest enters the holy of holies only once every year; the prophets point to an even more glorious coming of God in judgment and redemption (Pss. 50:3; 96:13; Isa. 2:21; 30:27, 40f., passim; Mic. 1:3; 4:7; Zeph. 3:8; Joel 3:17; Zech. 2:10f.; 14:9). Theophany reaches its climax in Christ who is the ἄγγελος, δόξα, εἰκων, λογος, υἱός του θεου in whom God is fully revealed and fully given (Matt. 11:27; John 1:14; 14:9; Col. 1:15; 2:19; etc.). By him and by the Spirit whom he sends forth, God's dwelling among his people becomes a true spiritual reality (John 14:23; Rom. 8:9, 11; 2 Cor. 6:16). The believing community is (now) the house of God, the temple of the Holy Spirit (Matt. 18:20; 1 Cor. 3:16; 6:19; Eph. 2:21), though it attains its full realization only in the New Jerusalem. Then the tabernacle of God will be with his people; he will dwell among them; they will be his people, and God himself will be with them and be their God. They will see his face, and his name will be on their foreheads (Matt. 5:8; 1 Cor. 15:28; 1 John 3:2; Rev. 21:3; 22:4).

[92] Prophecy, or "inspiration," is another mode of revelation; in it God communicates his thoughts to human beings. This address can be an audible voice (Gen. 2:16; 3:8–19; 4:6–16; 6:13; 9:1, 8f.; 32:26f.; Exod. 19:9f.; Num. 7:89; Deut. 5:4; 1 Sam. 3:3f.; Matt. 3:17; 17:5; John 12:28–29), dreams (Num. 12:6; Deut. 13:1–6; 1 Sam. 28:6, 15; Joel 2:28f.),[37] visions (Gen. 15:1, 11; 20:7, 46:2; Num. 12:6; 22:8–13; 24:3; 1 Kings 22:17–23; Isa. 6; 21:6; Jer. 1:11–14; 24:1; Ezek. 1–3; 8–11; 40; Dan. 1:17; 2:19; 7; 8; 10; Amos 7–9; Zech. 1–6; Matt. 2:13, 19; Luke 1:22; 24:23; Acts 7:55; 9:3; 10:3, 10; 16:9; 22:17; 26:19; 1 Cor. 12–14; 2 Cor. 12:1; Rev. 1:10; etc.), or a communication by casting lots (Urim and Thummim).[38] Again, in form these are similar to their function in nonbiblical religions, though significant differences remain. Unlike the Greek seers, the

---

37. In Scripture revelatory dreams also occur among non-Israelites (Gen. 20; 31; 40; 41; Judg. 7; Dan. 2 and 4), and convey either a word, a communication from God (Gen. 20:3; 31:9, 24; Matt. 1:20; 2:12, 19, 22; 27:19), or a representation of the imagination, which then often requires explanation (Gen. 28; 37:5; 40:5; 41:15; Judg. 7:13; Dan. 2 and 4).

38. The lot was used on many occasions: on the great Day of Atonement (Lev. 16:8); in dividing the land (Josh. 13:6; 14:2; etc.; Neh. 11:1), the cities of the Levites (Josh. 21:4), the booty (Joel 3:3; Nah. 3:10; Obad. 11), and garments (Matt. 27:35; John 19:23); in deciding difficult cases (Josh. 7:1ff.; 1 Sam. 14:42; Prov. 16:33; 18:18; Jonah 1:7); in elections to office (1 Sam. 10:19; Acts 1:26; 1 Chron. 24:5; Luke 1:9; etc.); the trial by ordeal (Num. 5:11–31) can also be counted in this category.

biblical recipients of revelation did not experience a suppression of consciousness; even in prophetic ecstasy they remained conscious of themselves, saw, heard, thought, spoke, raised questions, and gave answers (Exod. 4–6; 32:7f.; Isa. 6; Jer. 1; Ezek. 4–6; etc.). God reveals his counsel, especially concerning the future (Num. 23f.; 1 Kings 22:17; 2 Kings 5:26; 8:11f.; Jer. 1:13f.; 4:23f.; 14:18; 24:1f.; Ezek. 8; Amos 7–9; Zech. 1–6; Revelation; etc.), in images and visions; prophets hear voices and sounds (1 Kings 18:41; 2 Kings 6:32; Isa. 6:3, 8; Jer. 21:10; 49:14; Ezek. 1:24, 28; 2:2; 3:12; Rev. 7:4; 9:16; 14:2; 19:1; 21:3; 22:8; etc), and are even taken up in the spirit and translocated (Ezek. 3:12f.; 8:3; 43:1; Dan. 8:2; Matt. 4:5, 8; Acts 9:10–11; 22:17; 23:11; 27:23; 2 Cor. 12:2; Rev. 1:9; 12; 14:1; 21:10).

Still, most revelations to prophets occurred apart from visionary experience and through the inward illumination of the Holy Spirit. In the Old Testament, most revelations to the prophets occurred without any vision;[39] often even when the word "vision" is used it is simply a synecdoche for divine prophecy more broadly, occurring where nothing has been seen (Isa. 1:1; 2:1; Amos 1:1; Hab. 1:1; 2:1; 1 Sam. 3:15). The more important point here is that genuine prophecy comes from the outside; from God. His Spirit comes upon the prophet, suddenly, powerfully, and momentarily (Num. 24:2; Judg. 6:34; 14:19; 15:14; 1 Sam. 10:6; 19:20, 23; 1 Chron. 12:18; 2 Chron. 15:1; 20:14; Isa. 8:11; Ezek.1:3; 3:22; 8:1; 11:5; 37:1; 40:1). This is confirmed by the New Testament's testimony concerning the Old Testament prophets, that they spoke from and by the Spirit of God (Acts 28:25; 1 Pet. 1:11; 2 Pet. 1:21).

While the Holy Spirit in the Old Testament comes upon a person momentarily, it is not until the New Testament that the supreme and definitive prophet makes his appearance. As Logos, he is the full and complete revelation of God (John 1:1, 18; 14:9; 17:6; Col. 2:9). The Holy Spirit does not come upon him but indwells him without measure (John 3:34). From his conception through his ministry to his death and resurrection he lives, he speaks, he acts in the power of the Holy Spirit (Matt. 3:16; 12:28; Luke 1:17; 2:27; 4:1, 14, 18; Rom. 1:4; Heb. 9:14). He bestows that same Spirit upon his disciples, not only as the Spirit of regeneration and sanctification, but also as the Spirit of revelation and illumination (Mark 13:11; Luke 12:12; John 14:17; 15:26; 16:13; 20:22; Acts 2:4; 6:10; 8:29; 10:19; 11:12; 13:2; 18:5; 21:4; 1 Cor. 2:12f.; 12:7–11). While some individual believers are still equipped by the Holy Spirit for the office of prophet, it is more important to underscore the universal anointing and prophetic task of all believers (Matt. 11:25–27; John 6:45; Acts 2:17f.; 1 Pet. 2:9; 1 John 2:20). Prophecy as a special gift is destined to pass away in the New Jerusalem (1 Cor. 13:8; Rev. 21:27; 22:4, 15).[40]

39. E.g., in the case of Isaiah, Haggai, Malachi, Obadiah, Nahum, Habakkuk, Jeremiah, Ezekiel.
40. For further reading on prophecy, see A. B. Davidson, *Old Testament Prophecy* (Edinburgh: T&T Clark, 1903).

[93] In miracles God reveals himself by his works. Word and deed go together; God's word is an act (Ps. 33:9), and his activity is speech (Pss. 19:2; 29:3; Isa. 28:26). God's works are first to be observed in creation and providence, which are an ongoing work and a miracle (Ps. 33:6, 9; John 5:17). A distinction must be maintained, however, between the ordinary order of nature and extraordinary deeds of divine power. Miracles are a בריאה, a creation, something new that has never been seen otherwise (Exod. 34:10; Num. 16:30). Miracles are signs אותות, σημεια (Exod. 3:12; 12:13; John 2:11; 4:54; 6:14; 9:16; 11:47) that display the power and glory of God (Isa. 35:1–2; Joel 3:18; Amos 9:13; John 1:14). This power and freedom of God is proclaimed by nature (Jer. 5:22; 10:12; 14:22; 27:5; Isa. 40:12; 50:2–3; Pss. 33:13–17; 104; Job 5:9f.; 9:4f.; etc.) but emerges especially in the history of his people (Deut. 10:21; 11:3; 26:8; 29:2; 32:12f.; Pss. 66:5f.; 74:13f.; 77:15f.; 78:4f.; 135:8f.; Isa. 51:2, 9; Jer. 32:20f.; Acts 7:2f.). Thus the history of salvation is replete with miracles until the consummation.

The miracles described in the Old Testament did not, however, bring about a full or permanent renewal of creation itself. As the memory of them faded, their effect diminished; life resumed its normal course and nature seemed to triumph. God's revelation then came through prophets who proclaimed a coming Day of the Lord (יום יהוה) on which he will reveal his glory and display his miraculous power through miraculous signs in the heavens (Amos 8:8f.; Joel 2:30), judging the nations (Isa. 24:16f.), and saving his people (Isa. 9:3; 10:24f.; 11:15f.; 43:16–21; 52:10; 62:8). God's people will be forgiven, made holy and embraced in a new covenant (Isa. 44:21–23; 43:25; Ezek. 36:25–28; Jer. 31:31f.; Zech. 14:20–21). Peace, security, and prosperity will be the watchword as nature itself becomes a paradise (Hosea 2:17f.; Joel 3:18; Jer. 31:6, 12–14; Isa. 11:6–8; 65:25; Ezek. 34:29; 36:29f.; Zech. 8:12). A new heaven and a new earth are on the way, and the former things will no longer be remembered (Isa. 65:17; 66:22).

All this is fulfilled in Christ. His incarnation is the greatest of all miracles, God himself descending and taking on our full humanity. His miracles are the signs (σημεια) of the presence of God, a demonstration of divine power, proof of the messianic era (Matt. 11:3–5; 12:28; Luke 13:16). The anticipation of final glory can be seen especially in Jesus's powerful acts of healing and restoring creation. In Jesus, miracle becomes history; his history is itself a miracle. The person and work of Christ are the central revelation of God; all other revelation is grouped around this center. With the establishment of Christianity, God now manifests his power and glory especially in spiritual miracles, in the new birth and new life bestowed on those who were dead (Eph. 2:1–10). Scripture does describe a new aeon when "miracle" will become "nature," when what ought to be is reconciled with what is; when the fullness of Christ's kingdom comes in all its glory and a new heaven and a new earth are established in which righteousness dwells definitively (Rev. 21–22).

[94–95] God's self-revelation to us does not come in bits and pieces; it is an organic whole, a grand narrative from creation to consummation. All nature and history testify to God the Creator; all things return to him. This revelation that is outside us is matched by the active revelation of God within human beings in intellect and reason, conscience and heart. God's Spirit dwells in all his image bearers, an indwelling that is even stronger a revelation than in nature and history, though it is not a saving presence. It is very important to distinguish the saving work of the Holy Spirit in applying the benefits of Christ from what John Calvin referred to as "those most excellent blessings which the Divine Spirit dispenses to whom he will for the common benefit of mankind."[41] Fallen humanity sees this revelation only in part and with blinded eyes, even suppressing its truth in willful sin (Rom. 1:18–23), and needs gracious illumination to see correctly. This is provided in Scripture where we are shown nature's significance as a witness to God's power and majesty (Job 28:25f.; Pss. 19:1; 90:2; Prov. 8:24f.; Isa. 40:26; Matt. 5:45; Rom. 1:18–20).

The purpose of all revelation—in creation, via prophets and apostles, in Scripture—is that human beings should know, serve, and honor God. Since, after the fall, revelation in nature and history is inadequate to that end, a gracious and transforming special revelation is needed. Special revelation is *salvific* revelation and is different from natural revelation in form and content. Certainly it is the same God who makes himself known to human beings, both in general and in special revelation, but whereas in general revelation God's deity (θειοτης) comes to the fore, in special revelation it is the Triune God who ever more clearly makes himself known in his personal distinctions. Of course, all God's outward works (*opera ad extra*) are the essential works of God, the works performed by the triune Godhead in its oneness. In the works of nature it is at most only the Father as Creator who speaks to us by the Word (Logos) and the Spirit. But in the works of grace, God comes to us as Father in the entirely unique sense of the Son, and as Father reveals himself to us by that Son who became incarnate in Christ and by the Spirit of that Christ. Special revelation is the *saving* revelation of God.

In this revelation God makes himself known to us as the Triune God, Father, Son, and Holy Spirit. This revelation is historical and progresses over the course of many centuries, reaching its culmination in Jesus Christ, the mediator of creation and redemption. He is the Logos who made and sustains all things (John 1:3; Col. 1:15; Heb. 1:3) and may be considered the angel of YHWH who led Israel (Exod. 14:19; 23:20; 32:34; 33:2; Isa. 63:8–9), and the content of prophecy (John 5:39; 1 Pet. 1:11; Rev. 19:10). In the fullness of time he became flesh and dwelt among us (John 1:14). Thus Christ is the mediator of both creation and re-creation. "It was his part and his alone, whose ordering

---

41. Ed. note: J. Calvin, *Institutes*, II.ii.16. Calvin even forestalls a likely objection: "Nor is there any ground for asking what concourse the Spirit can have with the ungodly, who are altogether alienated from God? For what is said as to the Spirit dwelling in believers only, is to be understood of the Spirit of holiness by which we are consecrated to God as temples. Notwithstanding of this, He fills, moves, and invigorates all things by the virtue of the Spirit, and that according to the peculiar nature which each class of beings has received by the Law of Creation."

of the universe reveals the Father, to renew the same teaching."[42] Seeing the
soteric significance and power of revelation, especially in Christ, it is clear why
it is a mistake to reduce the fullness of revelation to any one or more of its rich
aspects. In revelation God himself comes to us and imparts himself, granting to
us not only truth but also righteousness and life. Revelation is not exclusively
addressed to the human intellect nor does it consist only of prophecy or inner
illumination. Revelation includes events and words that explain events; above
all God's revelation comes in *saving power*, it opens the eyes of the blind, it sets
prisoners free. At the same time we must not be so taken by the transformative
power of revelation that we ignore the full scope of human sin. Revelation is also
needed to set our minds free from error, lies, deception of our intellects. Revelation is not only a communication of life but also an announcement of truth;
revelation yields doctrine. Revelatory word and deed belong together in God's
plan and acts of salvation.

[96] Finally, then, the purpose and goal of special revelation is God's own trinitarian glory, his delight in himself. The aim of revelation is to re-create humanity
after the image of God, to establish the kingdom of God on earth, to redeem
the world from the power of sin, and thus to glorify the name of the Lord in all
his creatures. With the completion of Christ's work, his Word is also completed
(Heb. 1:1–4); strictly speaking, we look for no further revelation. The question
of whether the gift of prophecy (prediction) and of miracles has continued after
the apostolic age and still continues is, therefore, of secondary importance. The
testimonies of the church fathers are so numerous and powerful that for the most
ancient times this question can hardly be answered in the negative.[43] But even
if those extraordinary gifts and powers have in part remained in the Christian
church, the content of this special revelation, which is concentrated in Christ
and recorded in Scripture, is not enriched by them. On the other hand, if we
agree with Augustine that they have diminished or ceased, special revelation
is not impoverished by this fact.[44] Scripture clearly teaches that God's full revelation has been given in Christ and that the Holy Spirit who was poured out in
the church has come only to glorify Christ and take all things from Christ (John
16:14). This does mean that in addition to the objective work of Christ in revelation and redemption, the work of the Spirit is needed to enable human beings
to acknowledge and accept the divine revelation and thereby become the image
of the Son. As our Lord said to Peter when Peter confessed him to be the Son
of God: "Flesh and blood has not revealed this to you, but my Father who is in
heaven" (Matt. 16:17; cf. Gal. 1:15–16).

42. Athanasius, *On the Incarnation*, chap. 14; Irenaeus, *Against Heresies*, I, IV, 6.
43. T. Aquinas, *Summa Theol.*, II, 2 qu. 178; Gisbert Voetius, *Selectae disputationes theologicae*, 5
vols. (Utrecht, 1648–69), II, 1002ff.
44. According to H. J. A. M. Schaepman, *Menschen en Boeken* (Utrecht: Wed. J. R. van Rossumn,
1893–1903): "Now that the miracle of Christianity has become constitutive of humanity, the few miracles
which occur are no longer an urgent necessity for the maintenance of the Christian faith" (18).

[97] God redeems and reveals; we know, understand, and believe. Revelation and religion are distinct but not separable. Revelation is possible only if God has a personal existence distinct from the world and possesses the will and power to reveal himself in deeds and words. God addresses with his speech, he communicates his thoughts to us analogous to the communication of one human to another, a father to his child, a teacher to his or her pupil. Revelation thus places us under obligation to listen, to accept it and respond to it with a life consisting in knowing, serving, and loving God with all our minds and hearts. Revelation is a conscious and free act of a gracious and loving God who makes himself known to us so that we may accept the grace of God by faith in Christ or, in case of impenitence, receive a more severe judgment. He speaks to us to take us up into fellowship with him and make us partakers of his divine nature (2 Pet. 1:4). God still speaks today; while special revelation in a sense belongs to the past, from day to day God continues in a special way to reveal himself to all who live under the gospel. The witness of the Spirit continues until in the final manifestation of Christ the full effect of revelation in the history of humankind will be completed. The time of sowing will then be concluded in the time of harvest.

"Natural" and "Supernatural"

[98–99] In the remainder of this chapter we will explore further the doctrine of revelation contained in Scripture in its relation to the natural revelation in creation. We begin with calling attention to two ways in which the doctrine of revelation has been misconstrued in the Christian church: by supernaturalism as well as by naturalism (rationalism). We first consider supernaturalism, which arose primarily in Roman Catholicism and then influenced various schools of thought within Protestantism. The distinction between "natural" and "supernatural" is foreign to the Scriptures; nature is God's creation, and the natural arises from and depends on the supernatural. Yet, arising first in the writings of the church fathers, this distinction has validity in reminding us that God's grace in Christ, the miracle of rebirth by the Holy Spirit, and so forth, cannot come forth from the normal, ordinary, natural course of events. As acts of God they point to a reality that is "beyond" nature, a supersensible world. Taken in this sense the term "supernatural" is essentially a synonym for "theistic"; it reminds us that this world is not all that there is. "Supernatural," thus, is all that surpasses created things and does not have its cause in creatures but in the omnipotence of God. Picking up our discussion from the preceding section of this chapter, all revelation is therefore supernatural; special revelation in the forms of miracle, theophany, prophecy, and illumination is supernatural.

The difficulties with the term "supernatural" arise from the history of its use. The term has been identified with the notion of miracle—which is a mistake since not all supernatural events are miraculous, though all miracles are supernatural. In reaction, modern thinkers use the term for immanent realities that defy simple empirical description or analysis. Supernatural or "spiritual" in these contexts refers to the "extra" in humans, the extra that is beyond the material and physical. In addition, in Roman Catholicism, human destiny was divided into a natural and supernatural end. Redemption then restores humanity to its original, natural, created state of wholeness while the supernatural end points to the higher destiny of the *visio dei*, the mystical union with God, to θεωσις or divinization. While the seeds of this doctrine had already been planted in some pronouncements of the church fathers, it was actually first developed by Scholasticism, especially by Hales, Bonaventure, and Thomas.[45] This doctrine of man's supernatural end was made church dogma by the First Vatican Council when it decreed that "revelation must . . . be called absolutely necessary . . . because God, in his infinite goodness, has destined man for a supernatural goal, namely, to share divine benefits that completely surpass human understanding."[46] The sharpness of this contrast between natural and supernatural runs the grave risk of dualistically separating (supernatural) revelation from creation and nature. Special revelation should never be separated from its organic connection to history, the world, and humanity. Stated theologically, the religious antithesis should be between grace and sin and not between grace and nature.

Joined with a sacramental understanding of the church as the necessary channel of grace, the dualism of nature and grace leads to a hierarchically structured worldview in which the (supernatural) church is sacred and the (natural) world profane. For Catholicism, reality becomes holy only when it is ecclesiastically consecrated and pressed into the service of the church.[47] What is distinctively Christian is thus identified with and restricted to the ecclesiastical; for the world to be influenced in a Christian direction it needs to submit to the domination of the church.[48] The nature/grace dualism also fuels the opposite of world domination: world contempt leading to asceticism and monasticism. When gracious special revelation is understood in this way it comes altogether to stand by itself, without any organic connection to nature and history. Special revelation is not seen as entering into the fabric of the world and humanity but as floating outside and above it. This was all the more the case when special revelation was treated as a doctrine, the proclamation of uncomprehended and incomprehensible mysteries whose truth was confirmed by miracles.

45. Alexander of Hales, *Summa universae theologiae*, II qu. 91 m. 1 a. 3; Bonaventure, *Breviloquium*, V, 1; T. Aquinas, *Disputed Questions on Truth*, qu. 27; idem, *Summa Theol.*, I, 2 qu. 62, art. 1.

46. H. J. D. Denzinger, *Enchiridion symbolorum et definitionum* (Wirceburgi, 1856), n. 882f.; Vatican Council I, sess. III. c. 2; cf. can. II, 3.

47. Joseph Deharbe, *Verklaring der Katholieke Geloofs- en Zedeleer*, ed. B. Dankelman, 3rd ed., 4 vols. (Utrecht: J. R. Van Rossum, 1880–88), I, 170; III, 588f.; IV, 598f.

48. Ed. note: Roman Catholicism after the Second Vatican Council repudiates all political notions of dominion for the church. See *Lumen Gentium: Dogmatic Constitution on the Church*: *Gaudium et Spes: Dogmatic Constitution on the Church in the Modern World*; and *Dignitatis Humanae: Declaration on Human Dignity*.

The Reformation revolted against this worldview and converted the quantitative antithesis between revelation and nature into a qualitative, ethical one. Grace was not opposed to nature but to sin. The reality of the incarnation militates against any nature/grace dualism; the gospel is not hostile to the world as creation but to the world under dominion of sin, the alien element that has insinuated itself into the world. Revelation and creation are not opposed to each other, for creation itself is a revelation. The revelation given in Christ proclaims to us that God loved the world, and that Christ came not to condemn but to save the world (John 3:16–17), to destroy not the works of the Father but only the works of the devil (1 John 3:8). And just as Christ himself assumed a full human nature, denied the natural life in an ethical sense but did not mutilate and mortify it physically, and in the end raised his body from the dead, so his disciples, while indeed called to cross-bearing and self-denial and following their Master, are not called to asceticism and world flight. On the contrary, Jesus prayed to the Father that his disciples would not be taken out of the world but kept in the world from the evil one (John 17:15). The Reformation sought a Christianity that was hostile, not to nature but only to sin, and had a reforming and sanctifying effect upon natural life as a whole, including the world of culture, society, and politics. In the Reformation the adage came again into its own: nature commends grace; grace emends nature.

[100] If supernaturalism undervalues nature, naturalism exalts it at the expense of revelation. Rationalists and deists accept the idea of revelation only insofar as it satisfies the bar of reason. The arguments against revelation arise from the conviction that all revelation is at odds with reason and science, which do not need the hypothesis of God or the supernatural. Revelation is unnecessary.[49] In addition, even if revelation occurred, we would not be able to recognize it; there are no universal criteria to help us determine the truth of a revelational claim. This is not the end of the matter, however, since rationalism must still account for the universality of religion and the accompanying conviction among people that their religion is based on revelation. Rationalism grossly oversimplifies the matter; revelation cannot be so easily dismissed from our reflection on religion. Explanations for the persistence of revelation in religion are explained in terms of various theories of accommodation,[50] allegory,[51] mythology,[52] or symbolism, or it is given a broad "religious-historical"[53] interpretation.

---

49. Included in the list of thinkers who on naturalist and rationalist grounds challenge revelation are, among others, Leibniz, Spinoza, Lessing, Fichte, Kant, Voltaire, Rousseau.

50. K. G. Bretschneider, *Systematische Entwickelung aller in der Dogmatik vorkommenden Begriffe* (Leipzig: J. A. Barth, 1841), 135ff.

51. Thomas Woolston, *Six Discourses on the Miracles of Our Saviour and Defences of His Discourses* (1727; repr., New York: Garland, 1979).

52. D. F. Strauss, *Das Leben Jesu*, 2 vols. (Tübingen: C. F. Osiander, 1835–36), 27; ET: *The Life of Jesus, Critically Examined*, trans. Marian Evans, 2 vols. (New York: Calvin Blanchard, 1860; repr., St. Clair Shores, MI: Scholarly Press, 1970).

53. See H. Bavinck, *Reformed Dogmatics*, ed. John Bolt (Grand Rapids: Baker Academic, 2003–8), I, 70–76, 170–74 (##17–18, 53).

These various attempts to give naturalistic and rationalist explanations of revelation have made their contributions to a better understanding of Scripture in its organic connection with nature and history. However, shifting and conflicting interpretations indicate the elusiveness of a satisfactory purely scientific explanation. Scriptural revelation and biblical religion remain riddles to those who fail to begin from a position of faith. Scripture resists all naturalistic and rationalist explanations of its origins as revelation and attributes it solely to an extraordinary operative presence of God the Holy Spirit. Prophecy in earlier times never came by the will of human beings, but the Holy Spirit moved the prophets (2 Pet. 1:21; 1 Cor. 2:11–12). Scripture does not give us data to interpret; it is itself the interpretation of reality, the shaper of a distinct worldview, a worldview that is theistic, supernaturalistic. Our acceptance of any revelation is determined by our worldview; what is decisive here is not historical criticism but self-criticism, not science but faith. Intellectual and philosophical obstacles to accepting revelation are not insignificant but they are not ultimately the decisive factor. What is decisive is whether the religion that is based on the revelation is received in faith; Christ who is at the center of the scriptural narrative is the real stone of stumbling for unbelief. Religion itself is interconnected with, and dependent on, revelation. Those who abandon revelation also lose the religion based on it. The revelation of Scripture and the religion of Scripture, the Bible, and the Christian faith, stand or fall together.

[101] This theistic worldview is sharply opposed by all monisms that reduce reality to a single substance, either matter (materialism) or mind (pantheism). The worldview of theism, by contrast, honors the distinction between God and the world and the distinct physical, psychological, social, and ethical realities of the world. Instead of monistic uniformity, theism aims at unity in diversity, honoring the multiformity of creation itself. While materialism stumbles into psychological phenomena, pantheism cannot find a bridge between thought and existence and does not know what to do with multiplicity. Existence itself is a mystery and a miracle. That anything exists at all compels astonishment in the thinking mind, and this astonishment, accordingly, has rightly been called the beginning of philosophy. The more deeply human beings penetrate this existence intellectually, the more astonished they become, for within the sphere of existence, of the cosmos, we see various forces in action: in the mechanical, vegetative, animal, and psychological world, but also in religious and ethical, aesthetic and logical phenomena. Each of these forces operates according to its own nature, its own law, and in its own way. All these elements and forces with their inherent laws, according to the theistic worldview, are from moment to moment upheld by God, who is the final, supreme, intelligent, and free causality of all things. As creatures, they have no stability or durability in themselves. It is God's omnipresent and eternal power that upholds and governs all things. In him, in his plan and also in his rule, originates the unity or harmony that holds together and unites all things over the entire range of their diversity and leads them to a single goal. God is present in all things. In him all things live and move and have their being. Nature and history

are his work; he works always (John 5:17). All things reveal God to us. Although his finger may be more clearly observable to us in one event than in another, the pure in heart see God in all his works.

This worldview is fully compatible with the reality of revelation and miracles. Nature is not a machine, as deists claim, nor a finished product, but in the process of becoming. Revelation and miracles are not contrary to nature but part of a nature caught up in an ongoing teleological development toward its divine destiny. Thomas already observed: "When God does anything contrary to the course of nature, the whole order of the universe is not subverted, but the course resulting from the relation between one particular thing and another."[54] Miracles do not bring about a change in the forces inherent in nature nor in the laws according to which they operate. The only thing that happens in a miracle is that the operation of the forces of nature is suspended at a given point as the result of the appearance of another force which works according to a law of its own and produces an effect of its own. Miracles are not alien intruders in a fallen creation but are incorporated in the divine design of the world itself and serve God's work of redeeming and perfecting fallen nature.

MIRACLES, LANGUAGE, AND HISTORY

[102] Still, revelation and miracles constitute an order of reality that is essentially distinct from the ordinary order of nature. They are not simply the product of a heightened natural capacity of inspired human beings. Nor should they be linked to such esoteric phenomena as spiritism, hypnotism, and telepathy. The miracles of Scripture are a unique and an indispensable component of a Christian worldview. God's presence and activity is neither restricted to the natural order nor excluded from it. Revelation and miracle are at the same time closely bound to the natural and distinct from it. We should avoid apologetic approaches that find new scientific insights serving as easy explanations of biblical miracles.[55] Nor should we be held hostage to what science declares to be possible or impossible in the natural world. Theologians and natural scientists should respect each other and acknowledge the respective limits of their work. We must repudiate all attempts to retain some value for biblical miracles by separating what is scientific or historical "fact" in it from some putative remaining religious, ethical, spiritual, or "mythical" value.[56] Miracles cannot be so easily dispensed with. Indeed, miracle is

54. Thomas Aquinas, *On the Power of God*, trans. Lawrence Shapcote (Westminster, MD: Newman, 1952), qu. 6, art. 1, as cited by Eugen Müller, *Natur und Wunder, ihr Gegensatz und ihre Harmonie* (Freiburg i.B. and St. Louis: Herder, 1892), 133.

55. Ed. note: Such as, for example, taking the shift from Newton's "closed" mechanical physics to Einstein and company's more "open" quantum physics as paving the way for scientifically accepting miracles such as Jesus's sudden postresurrection appearance to the disciples in the upper room.

56. Ed. note: A good example of this is the "demythologizing" program of New Testament scholar Rudolf Bultmann and its antecedents in nineteenth-century thinkers such as David Friedrich Strauss.

as indispensable to religion as revelation. "A faith without miracles is a crippled faith" ("Ein Glaube ohne Wunder ist ein wunder Glaube"—Jos. Muller). If we deny miracles, we call into question the entire biblical revelation and Christian gospel. Revelation and miracles are not simply individual acts of God but follow a divinely planned order in a progressive history. The question of revelation is whether we believe or not. Faith in revelation is a matter of hope for deliverance, for another and better world in which sin and death are overcome. In revelation God comes to us to bring us to him to dwell with us forever.

[103] Not only is there a close bond between religion and revelation but also one between revelation and a religion's "scripture." Almost all religions have some texts that include myths, ceremonial rules, liturgical texts, priestly documents, and so forth. Many also have a sacred book or collection of books serving as sacred scripture. These scriptures contain the content of religion—its ideas, doctrine, dogma—which it owes to revelation, expresses in words, passes from one generation to another, and finally renders permanent in scripture. This should not surprise us—it is a very ordinary and fully human process in language. Integral to human self-consciousness is our ability and desire to self-expression; we think and we speak; we speak and commit to writing. The written word of Christian Scripture is the incarnation of the spoken word and renders revelation permanent, universal, everlasting. Thus words create peoples and nations. Language is the soul of a nation, the custodian of the goods and treasures of humankind, the bond that unites human beings, peoples, and generations, the one great tradition that unites in consciousness the world of humankind, which is one by nature. The same is true for those who live by the revelation given in Holy Scripture; the word of revelation created a new people, a holy nation, called out of darkness into light (1 Pet. 2:9–10). Biblical revelation is a history and creates a history. The great deeds and events of salvation history do belong to the past but they continue to have a powerful effect to this day. History too is the bearer of the thoughts of God, the revelation of God's intent, which over and over filled the apostle Paul with wonder and adoration, the revelation of mystery, without which human beings grope around in the dark. Biblical revelation participates in the ebb and flow of history but it also encompasses eternal thoughts, which not only had meaning for the moment in which their disclosure occurred and for the persons to whom it came, but which are of value for all times and all human beings.

[104] In the Christian tradition truth is incarnational, based on the history of the incarnate Son of God in our space and time. It is a truth both historical and universal and is borne through history incarnationally, through the tradition of the church universal. For divine revelation to fully enter the life of humankind, it assumed the servant form of written language. In this sense Scripture too is an incarnation of God, the product of God's incarnation in Christ. Scripture has an instrumental significance; it does not call forth devotion to itself but to the Christ it proclaims. Twin errors are to be rejected. The first is to equate scriptural revelation with inspiration itself, thus separating Scripture from the history of redemption

and revelation that stands behind it. All restrictions of revelation to the inspired word of Scripture ignore the fact that not all inspiration and revelation given by God is recorded in Scripture (John 21:25). What has been recorded is that which was handed down by the apostles for the church's benefit. Revelation in its origin and in its continuing effect is thus bound to tradition. This too is "natural"; in his revelation God follows the basic lines he has drawn for the coexistence of human beings. Humanity is not an aggregate of individuals but an organic whole in which all people live interdependently. Revelation follows this law; re-creation is adapted to creation. Just as in every domain of life we participate in the goods of humankind by means of tradition, so also in religion. That, too, belongs to the idea of the incarnation. It is itself an event, which at one time happened in time but which through the tradition becomes the possession and blessing of all human beings. The fact is that we inherit all things from previous generations. We bring nothing into the world (1 Tim. 6:7). Physically and psychologically, intellectually and ethically, we are dependent on the world around us. Religiously, things are no different. The revelation that consists in history can come to us only in the way of tradition, tradition understood in the broadest possible sense.

The second error is to distinguish Scripture and revelation to the point of separation. This theme comes in many variations: "Not the letter but the Spirit"; "not Scripture but the person of Christ"; "not the word but the fact is the fundamental principle of Scripture." Lessing managed to produce the familiar petition: "O Luther, you great and holy man! You have delivered us from the yoke of the pope but who will deliver us from the yoke of the letter, the paper pope?" This view is no less wrong but even more dangerous than the other for in many cases revelation and divine inspiration (θεοπνευστια) do coincide. Those who deny divine inspiration and despise Scripture will also in large part lose the revelation; they will have left nothing but human writings. In addition the revelation, even where in fact or word it preceded its recording, is known to us solely from Holy Scripture. We literally know nothing of the revelations of God in the time of Israel and in Christ except from Holy Scripture. There is no other primary principle. With the fall of Holy Scripture, therefore, all of revelation falls as well, as does the person of Christ. Precisely because revelation is history there is no way to learn something about it other than the ordinary way that applies to all of history, and that is human attestation. To our mind attestation decides about the reality of a fact. We have no fellowship with Christ except through fellowship in the word of the apostles (John 17:20–21; 1 John 1:3). For us, for the church of all the ages, revelation exists only in the form of Holy Scripture. Finally, divine inspiration, as will be evident later, is an attribute of the Scriptures, a unique and distinct activity of God in connection with the production of Scripture and therefore also itself to be acknowledged and honored to that extent as an act of revelation. Hence contempt for and the rejection of Scripture is not a harmless act with regard to human testimonies concerning revelation but denial of a special revelational act of God. We may not fail to do justice to revelation for the sake of Scripture nor fail to do justice to Scripture for the sake of revelation. We may not neglect history for the sake of the Word; we may not show contempt for the Word in our embrace of history. Both orthodox intellectualism and Anabaptistic spiritualism fail to honor scriptural revelation as the last act in God's divine pedagogy proclaiming Christ and his salvation. In that sense, Scripture is the end, the crown, the making permanent, and the publication of revelation, the means by which immediate revelation is made mediate and recounted in books. Scripture alone is the one certain revelation we have from God.

[105] Revelation as a whole is not complete until the parousia of Christ. It is divided into two dispensations, the objective revelation of God in Christ (including the Old Testament time of preparation) and the dispensation of the Spirit, in which the objective salvation in Christ is subjectively appropriated by the believer. The entire economy of the Old Testament can be regarded as a coming of God to his people, a search for a "tabernacle" for Christ. Christ is the content; the Logos who shines in the darkness comes to his own and becomes flesh in Jesus. As yet the Holy Spirit had not been given because Christ had not yet been glorified (cf. John 7:39). The dispensation of the Son then makes way for the dispensation of the Spirit. The Holy Spirit takes everything from Christ, adding nothing new to the now-complete revelation. The Holy Spirit applies the finished work of Christ, God's full gift and revelation to humanity. Christ is the Logos, full of grace and truth; his work is completed; the Father himself rests in the Son's labor. His work cannot be augmented or increased; in Christ God both fully revealed and fully gave himself. Consequently Scripture is also complete; it is the perfected Word of God. There is no new objective revelation in the dispensation of the Spirit.

But though the revelation has been completed, its effect does not for that reason cease but now enters into the whole spectrum of the life and history of humankind. The effect of Christ's work continues as history continues to be unfolded according to God's purpose, until God is dwelling with humanity; that is the ultimate goal of all revelation. By means of Scripture, God himself now bears revelation into the world and realizes its content in the life and thought of humankind. By his Spirit he indwells the church of Christ and is in its midst wherever two or three are gathered in Christ's name. He ever continues to perform miracles, for he renews the church of Christ by regeneration, sanctification, and glorification; the spiritual miracles do not cease, for God works always. The Spirit regenerates individual believers, gathers and indwells the church, and affects the consciousness of humanity. The Holy Spirit not only regenerates but also illumines. Word and deed go hand in hand, also in the economy of the Holy Spirit. Now too revelation is not just doctrine that illumines the mind but at the same time a life that renews the heart. We must avoid both the one-sidedness of intellectualism and that of mysticism, for they are both a denial of the riches of revelation. Since both head and heart, the whole person in being and consciousness, must be renewed, revelation in this dispensation is continued jointly in Scripture and in the church. In this context the two are most intimately connected. Scripture is the light of the church, the church the life of Scripture. The life of the church is a mystery without the light of Scripture, while apart from the church Scripture is an enigma and offense. Until the consummation when revelation ends and Scripture is no longer necessary, church and Scripture are inseparably joined by God the Holy Spirit.

Scripture is not a book of times long past, an ancient chronicle which only links us with persons and events of the past. Holy Scripture is the ever-living, eternally youthful Word, which God, now and always, issues to his people. It is the eternally ongoing speech of God to us. Divine inspiration, accordingly, is a permanent attribute of Holy Scripture. It was not only "God-breathed" at the time it was written; it *is* "God-breathing." "It was divinely inspired, not merely while it was written, God breathing through the writers; but also, whilst it is being read, God breathing through the Scripture, and the Scripture breathing Him [He being their very breath]."[57] Scripture does not intend first of all to give us historical information; Scripture is tendentious: whatever was written in former days was written for our instruction, that by steadfastness and by the encouragement of the Scriptures we might have hope (Rom. 15:4). Scripture was written by the Holy Spirit that it might serve him in guiding the church, in the perfecting of the saints, in building up the body of Christ. In it God daily comes to his people. Some day when being and consciousness are completely renewed, revelation will end and Scripture will no longer be necessary. Divine inspiration (θεοπνευστια) will then be the portion of all God's children. They will all be taught by the Lord and serve him in his temple. Prophecy and miracle have then become "nature," for God dwells among his people.

---

57. J. A. Bengel, *Gnomon of the New Testament*, rev. and ed. Andrew R. Fausset, 5 vols. (Edinburgh: T&T Clark, 1877), IV, 319 (commentary on 2 Tim. 3:16).

5

HOLY SCRIPTURE

[106] In this chapter, we examine in greater detail Scripture's testimony about itself, particularly its inspiration and attributes. Evidence for the doctrine that Scripture is inspired by God is found already in the Old Testament. The prophets were conscious of being called by God, standing before his face, and having a message that was not their own word but God's (Exod. 3; 4:12; Num. 11:29; 22:38; 23:5; Deut. 18:15–18; 1 Sam. 3; 1 Kings 17:1; 2 Kings 3:14; 5:16; 2 Chron. 36:15; Jer. 1; 26:5; 27:15; 29:15; Ezek. 1–3; Amos 3:7–8; 7:15). A much-used formula is: "thus says the Lord," or "the word of the Lord came to me," or word, oracle, נאם (pass. part.), the "utterance" of YHWH. The prophets clearly distinguish themselves from YHWH; he speaks to them (Isa. 8:1; 51:16; 59:21; Jer. 1:9; 3:6; 5:14; Ezek. 3:26; etc.); they listen with their ears and see with their eyes (Isa. 5:9; 6:8; 21:3, 10; 22:14; 28:22; Jer. 23:18; 49:14; Ezek. 2:8; 3:10, 17; 33:7; 40:4; 44:5; Hab. 3:2, 16; 2 Sam. 7:27; Job 33:16; 36:10), and ingest the words of YHWH (Jer. 15:16; Ezek. 3:1–3). They thus make a sharp distinction between what God has revealed to them and what arises from within their own hearts (Num. 16:28; 24:13; 1 Kings 12:33; Neh. 6:8; Ps. 41:6–7). Their complaint against the false prophets is precisely that they speak from within their own hearts (Ezek. 13:2–3, 17; Jer. 14:14; 23:16, 26; Isa. 59:13), without being sent (Jer. 14:14; 29:9; Ezek. 13:6).

The same is true for the written prophetic word. The texts where a command to write is given are few in number (Exod. 17:14; 24:3–4; 34:27; Num. 33:2; Deut. 4:2; 12:32; 31:19; Isa. 8:1; 30:8; Jer. 25:13; 30:2; 36:2, 24, 27–32; Ezek. 24:2; Dan. 12:4; Hab. 2:2) and apply to only a small part of Old Testament Scripture.

Written prophecy is a later but necessary stage in the history of revelation, a way for the divinely inspired prophetic word to address future generations. God's word was not revealed to the prophets for their own sakes but for God's people. Prophets began to write because they wished to address people other than those who could hear them. Speaking or writing in YHWH's name, they are under solemn obligation to pass on what they have received—no more and no less (Deut. 4:2; 12:32; Jer. 1:7, 17; 26:2; 42:4; Ezek. 3:10). Many of the written prophecies may never have been communicated orally; the majority show careful, artful craftsmanship as intentional writings. From a salvation-historical perspective, the commitment of God's word to writing suggests that henceforth the service of YHWH would have to find acceptance by word and reasoned persuasion.[1] The written prophetic word was to be received with the same authority as an oral word from the Lord (Jer. 36:10, 11; 25:3; Isa. 34:16).

The Old Testament prophets did not, as is claimed by critical scholars, "invent" ethical monotheism. Prophecy presumes the Torah, though it is not simply inferred from it; prophecy is a covenant-renewing new revelation. Prophecy assumes a covenant made by God with Israel, a gracious election of Israel (Hosea 1:1–3; 6:7; 8:3; Jer. 11:6f.; 14:21; 22:9; 31:31f.; Ezek. 16:8f.; Isa. 54:10; 56:4, 6; 59:21). The Torah had authority from the beginning of Israel's existence as a people. The covenant made at Mount Sinai was foundational and the place of Moses as a prophet and mediator of the Old Testament is unique (Exod. 33:11; Num. 12:6–8; Deut. 18:18; Pss. 103:7; 106:23; Isa. 63:11; Jer. 15:1; etc.). The Torah everywhere ascribes to itself a divine origin. It is YHWH who by Moses gave the Torah to Israel.

The historical books of the Old Testament are properly *prophetic* history, a commentary on the divine acts of salvation history (1 Chron. 29:29; 2 Chron. 9:29; 20:34; etc.). These books are not intended as precise historiography (at least, not by modern standards). Their purpose is to describe Israel's history from the vantage point of covenant and Torah (Judg. 2:6–3:6; 2 Kings 17:7–23, 34–41). Israel's history is written to disclose the mind and ways of God, in the past, the present, and the future; Israel's historians and chroniclers are prophetic messengers of the word of YHWH. The poetic books, too, presuppose an earlier, objective revelation from the covenant God and apply it to the religious-ethical aspects of Israel's life. Ecclesiastes sketches the vanity of the world without, and in opposition to, the fear of the Lord. Job is preoccupied with the problem of the justice of God vis-à-vis the sufferings of the pious. Proverbs depicts to us true wisdom in its application to the many aspects of human life. The Song of Solomon celebrates the intimacy and power of love. And, in the mirror of the experiences of God's devout people, the Psalms display the manifold grace of God. David, the sweet psalmist of Israel, spoke by the Spirit of the Lord, whose

---

1. A. Kuenen, *The Prophets and Prophecy in Israel*, trans. Adam Milroy (London, 1877; repr., Amsterdam: Philo, 1969); ed. note: pagination in the Dutch edition, *De Profeten en de Profetie onder Israël* (Leiden: P. Engels, 1875), I, 74; II, 345f.

word was on his tongue (2 Sam. 23:1–3). Eventually, these writings were all received in an authoritative canon.

This recognition and reception took place as the various writings of the Old Testament were formed and became known. The laws of YHWH were deposited in the sanctuary (Exod. 25:22; 38:21; 40:20; Deut. 31:9, 26; Josh. 24:25f.; 1 Sam. 10:25). The poetic products were preserved (Deut. 31:19; Josh. 10:13; 2 Sam. 1:18); at an early stage the Psalms were collected for use in the cult (Ps. 72:20); the men of Hezekiah made a second collection of the Proverbs (Prov. 25:1). The prophecies were widely read: later prophets based themselves on earlier ones (Dan. 9:2). The LXX contains several apocryphal writings, but these themselves witness to the authority of the canonical books (1 Macc. 2:50; 2 Macc. 6:23; Wis. 11:1; 18:4; Bar. 2:28; Tob. 1:6; 14:7; Sir. 1:5 [marg.]; 17:12; 24:23; 39:1; 46:15; etc.). Philo cites only the canonical books. The fourth book of Ezra ([= 2 Esd.] 14:18–47) knows of the division into twenty-four books. Josephus counts twenty-two books divided into three parts. In the opinion of most scholars, the Old Testament canon of Philo and Josephus was identical with ours.[2]

[107] For Jesus and the apostles, the books of the Old Testament canon had divine authority. This is reflected in the way they refer to the Old Testament as authoritative ("it is written": Matt. 4:4ff.; 11:10; Luke 10:26; John 6:45; 8:47; "Scripture says": Matt. 21:42; Luke 4:21; John 7:38; 10:35) as well as in explicit teaching (Matt. 5:17; Luke 16:17, 29; John 10:35; Rom. 15:4; 1 Pet. 1:10–12; 2 Pet. 1:19, 21; 2 Tim. 3:16). Our Lord even speaks directly of God or the Holy Spirit as the primary author (Matt. 15:4; 22:43; Mark 12:26, 36) and the writer to the Hebrews does the same: (1:5f.; 3:7; 4:3, 5; 5:6–7; 7:21; 8:5, 8; 10:16, 30; 12:26; 13:5). Not only is the Old Testament frequently cited in the New Testament—commonly in the Greek translation of the LXX—but it is also always acknowledged as authoritative. Over and over Jesus and the apostles justify their conduct and prove their teaching by an appeal to the Old Testament (Matt. 12:3; 22:32; John 10:34; Rom. 4; Gal. 3; 1 Cor. 15; etc.). To their minds, this divine authority of Scripture is extended so far that a single word, even an iota or a dot, is covered by it (Matt. 5:18; 22:45; Luke 16:17; John 10:35; Gal. 3:16). This is not challenged by the various and diverse manners in which the New Testament authors cite the Old Testament or the surprising meaning that they find in the text of the Old Testament. In the case of Jesus and the apostles, this exegesis of the Old Testament assumes the understanding that a word or sentence can have a much deeper meaning and a much farther reaching thrust than the original author suspected or put into it. The New Testament ultimately, also in its use of the Old Testament, seeks in the power of the Holy Spirit to bear witness to the Christ. It is this apostolic testimony that led to the church accepting these

---

2. G. Wildeboer, *Het ontstaan van den kanon des Oude Verbond* (Groningen: Wolters, 1891), 126ff., 134; ET: *The Origin of the Canon of the Old Testament*, trans. Benjamin Wisner Bacon (London: Luzac, 1895); H. L. Strack, "Kanon des Alten Testaments," *PRE*[3], IX, 741–68.

writings as canonical. It is Christ himself who is the "Word" to whom Scripture bears testimony.

Two key passages in which Holy Scripture provides self-testimony affirming the divine authorship of the Old Testament are 2 Timothy 3:16 and 2 Peter 1:19, 21. In the former, the translation "every scripture inspired by God is also profitable" suffers from the fact that after ὠφελιμος the predicate ἐστιν would need to be present. The translation "every scripture (in general) is inspired by God and profitable" is self-evidently excluded. What remains, therefore, is a choice between only two translations: "all Scripture" or "every Scripture," included, that is, in the sacred writings (v. 15), "is inspired by God" (cf. "whatever was written in former days," Rom. 15:4). Materially this does not yield any difference.

[108] Scripture's self-testimony about the divine origin of its message is inseparably linked to the One who came to earth to make known the Father and to accomplish his work. Jesus Christ is the Logos who makes known the Father (John 1:1, 18; 17:6), the one in whom the fullness of God dwells (Col. 1:19; 2:9), the faithful and true witness (Rev. 1:5; 3:14; cf. Isa. 55:4), the Amen in whom all the promises of God are "yes" and "amen" (Rev. 3:14; 2 Cor. 1:20). He was sent by God (John 8:42) and bears witness only to what he has seen and heard (John 3:32); he speaks the words of God (John 3:34; 17:8) and only bears witness to the truth (John 5:32ff.; 18:37); his witness is true (John 8:14; 14:6), confirmed by the witness of God himself (John 5:32ff.; 8:18). The doctrine of the divine authority of Holy Scripture constitutes an important component in the words of God that Jesus preached, and if he was mistaken on this point he was wrong at a point that is most closely tied in with the religious life and he can no longer be recognized as our highest prophet. We cannot take Jesus seriously as a teacher and reject his own teaching concerning Holy Scripture.

Jesus has not left to us anything in writing, however, and he himself is gone away. To ensure that his true witness was passed on pure and unalloyed to humankind he chose the apostles who were specifically given him by the Father (John 17:6), chosen by himself (John 6:70; 13:18; 15:16, 19), and in various ways prepared and equipped by him for their future task. The apostles had been the ear- and eyewitnesses of Jesus's words and works (1 John 1:1) and were now called to bring this witness to Israel and to the whole world (Matt. 28:19; Luke 24:48; John 15:27; 17:20; Acts 1:8). To equip them to do the task faithfully they were given the Holy Spirit, the Spirit of truth (Matt. 10:20; John 14:26; 15:26–27; 16:7; 20:22). The Holy Spirit takes the disciples into his service *with* their personalities and gifts, their memories and judgment; he adds nothing materially new to the revelation. The Spirit takes everything from Christ and only to that extent brings everything to the apostles' remembrance (John 16:13–14), thus glorifying Jesus just as Jesus's witness was a glorification of the Father (John 17:4).

After the day of Pentecost, equipped with that Spirit in a special sense (John 20:22; Acts 1:8; Eph. 3:5), the apostles now also openly acted as witnesses (Acts 1:8, 21, 22; 2:14, 32; 3:15; 4:8, 20, 33; 5:32; 10:39, 41; 13:31). From the beginning and in their own right the apostles supervised the church (Acts 8:14; 9:32; 11:22), made decisions in the Holy Spirit (Acts 15:22, 28), and enjoyed generally recognized authority in the name of Christ. Although Jesus nowhere left an express command to record his words and deeds (only in Revelation is there a repeated command to write: 1:11, 19; etc.), the apostles in their writing speak with the same authority of their Lord, writing being a special form of witness that is faithful and true (Luke 1:2; John 1:14; 19:35; 20:31; 21:24; 1 John 1:1–4; 1 Pet. 1:12; 5:1; 2 Pet. 1:16; Heb. 2:3; 3 John 12; Rev. 1:3; 22:18–19).

Among the apostles, Paul again stands by himself. He maintains that he was set apart before he was born (Gal. 1:15), called to be an apostle by Jesus himself (Gal. 1:1), had personally seen Jesus (1 Cor. 9:1; 15:8), was granted revelations and visions (2 Cor. 12; Acts 26:16), had received his gospel from Jesus (Gal. 1:12; 1 Tim. 1:12; Eph. 3:2–8), and saw himself called to defend his apostolate against the Judaizers (Gal. 1–2; 1 Cor. 1:10–4:21; 2 Cor. 10:13). He was therefore convinced that there was no other gospel than the one he preached (Gal. 1:7), that he was trustworthy (1 Cor. 7:25), that he had the Spirit of God (1 Cor. 7:40), that Christ spoke through him (2 Cor. 13:3; 1 Cor. 2:10, 16; 2 Cor. 2:17; 5:20), that he preached the Word of God (2 Cor. 2:17; 1 Thess. 2:13), right down to the phraseology and words (1 Cor. 2:4, 10–13), not only when he spoke but also when he wrote (1 Thess. 5:27; Col. 4:16; 2 Thess. 2:15; 3:14). Like the other apostles, Paul repeatedly acted with full apostolic power (1 Cor. 5; 2 Cor. 2:9), and issued binding commands (1 Cor. 7:40; 1 Thess. 4:2, 11; 2 Thess. 3:6–14). Although he occasionally appealed to the judgment of the church (1 Cor. 10:15), it was only for vindication, not for approval. Paul was so far from making himself dependent on the judgment of the church that he said (1 Cor. 14:37) that if anyone thought he was a prophet or spiritual, this would come out in the acknowledgment that what Paul was writing was a command of the Lord.

From the very beginning these apostolic writings had authority in the churches where they were known. They were soon circulated and, as a result, gained ever more extensive authority (Acts 15:22f.; Col. 4:16). Jude was known to Peter, and 2 Peter 3:16 implies familiarity with many letters of Paul and puts them on the same level with the other Scriptures. Gradually, translations of New Testament writings appeared for the purpose of being read in the church. These translations must already have existed in the first half of the second century.[3] Dogmatic use was already made of them by Athenagoras, Theophilus, Irenaeus, Tertullian, and others. The Peshitta and the fragment of Muratori all establish beyond doubt that in the second half of the second century most New Testament writings had canonical authority and enjoyed equal status with the books of the Old Testament. Differences continued to exist about some books: James, Jude, 2 Peter, 2 and 3 John, but in the third century the objections against these disputed works

---

3. Papias, according to Eusebius, *Ecclesiastical History*, III, 39; Justin Martyr, *1 Apology*, 66–67.

(ἀντιλεγομενα) increasingly diminished. The Synods of Laodicea (366), Hippo Regius (393), and Carthage (397) included them and closed the canon.

We should see these decisions of the church as simply the codification and registration of precedents that had long been operating in the churches with respect to these writings. The canon was not created by the church; it was only recognized. "The Canon has not been produced, as some say, by a single act of human beings, but little by little by God, the director of minds and times."[4] Long before the formal establishment of the dogma of New Testament Scripture in the second half of the second century, the New Testament writings had achieved generally recognized authority as a result of the authority of the apostles and public reading in the churches.[5] The guiding principles that led the church to recognize the canonicity of the Old Testament and New Testament writings cannot be determined with certainty. Apostolic origin cannot have been the deciding factor, for Mark, Luke, and the Letter to the Hebrews were also included. Neither is the recognition of canonicity grounded in the exclusivity of the Gospels as writings about Jesus Christ; Luke 1:1 makes mention of many others and, according to Irenaeus,[6] there was this "immense mass of apocryphal and spurious writings." What we can say is that the recognition must have been immediate and rooted in the books themselves. They were accepted without doubt or protest as holy, divine writings. They have authority of themselves, by their own right, because they exist. It is the Spirit of the Lord who guided the authors in writing them and the church in acknowledging them. To sum it up: Scripture considers itself, and makes itself known as, the Word of God.

The expression "word of God" or "word of the Lord" has various meanings in Scripture. Often it denotes the power of God by which he creates and upholds all things (Gen. 1:3; Pss. 33:6; 147:17–18; 148:8; Rom. 4:17; Heb. 1:3; 11:3). The term further describes the special revelation by which God makes something known to the prophets: "the word of the Lord came. . . ." In the New Testament the word does not "come" anymore; it does not come now and then from above and without to the prophets but *has come* in Christ and remains. The "word of God" also denotes the content of revelation, the ordinances, laws, commandments, statutes which have been given to Israel (Exod. 9:20–21; Judg. 3:20; Pss. 33:4; 119:9, 16–17; etc.; Isa. 40:8; Rom. 3:2; etc.). In the New Testament it is the name for the gospel, which has been disclosed by God in Christ and proclaimed by the

---

4. Ed. note: Bavinck's original note read simply "Loescher cited in *PRE*² VII, 424." The reference is to Valentin Loescher, *De Causa Linguae Ebraeae* (1706), and appears in the article "Kanon des alten Testaments," by Herman L. Strack, *PRE*², VII, 412–51.

5. This subject was the source of an important debate between the historian of dogma, Adolf von Harnack, and New Testament scholar Theodor Zahn. On this debate, see W. Koeppel, "Die Zahn-Harnacksche Streit über die Geschichte des neutestamentlichen Kanons," *Theologische Studien und Kritiken* 64 (1891): 102–57; F. Barth, "Die Streit zwischen Zahn und Harnack über der Ursprung des N. T. Kanons," *Neue Jahrbuch für deutsche Theologie* (1893): 56–80.

6. Irenaeus, *Against Heresies*, I, 20.

apostles (Luke 5:1; John 3:34; 5:24; 6:63; 17:8, 14, 17; Acts 8:25; 13:7; 1 Thess. 2:13; etc.). Finally, the designation "Word of God" is used for Christ himself. He is the Logos in an utterly unique sense: Revealer and revelation at the same time. All the revelations and words of God, in nature and history, in creation and re-creation, both in the Old and the New Testaments, have their ground, unity, and center in him. He is the sun; the individual words of God are his rays. The word of God in nature, in Israel, in the New Testament, in Scripture may never even for a moment be separated and abstracted from him. God's revelation exists only because he is the Logos. He is the First Principle of cognition, in a general sense of all knowledge, in a special sense, as the Logos incarnate, of all knowledge of God, of religion, and theology (Matt. 11:27).

[109] From its very beginning, the Christian church has always accepted Holy Scripture as the Word of God, beginning with the Old Testament. In Israel, from the most ancient times on the authority of YHWH's commandments and statutes, i.e., of the Torah and of the prophets, it is established. In Israel, Moses and the prophets have always been men of divine authority, and their writings were immediately recognized as authoritative. Over time, however, that author-ity was undermined by a gradually emerging reliance on oral tradition that was also believed to have been passed down from Moses. Jesus and the early church shared the Jewish honoring of the Old Testament, though they did not accept the broader claims of Jewish rabbinic tradition. The church, therefore, was never without a Bible, even at Pentecost. The church fathers say little about the dogma of Scripture; for them its authority was a given. This was understood to mean an infallible Bible and the image of "dictation by the Holy Spirit" is even used. God is the author of Holy Scripture and its [human] writers were simply the hands of the Holy Spirit. The Scripture is "a letter of an omnipotent God to his creature."[7] Scripture's authority is plenary; nothing is indifferent and superfluous, but every-thing is full of divine wisdom; "for nothing is without meaning or without the seal that belongs to God."[8] Origen in particular beat this drum and stated that there was nothing in Scripture "which did not come down from the fullness of the divine majesty." Similarly, Jerome said: "Each and every speech, all syllables, marks and periods in the divine scriptures are full of meanings and breathe heav-enly sacraments." Hence Holy Scripture was without any defect or error, even in chronological, historical matters.[9] Augustine, in his letter to Jerome, writes that he firmly believed that none of the canonical writers "erred in anything they wrote." Hence when there is mistake, "one is not allowed to say: the author of this book did not hold to the truth but either the copy of a book is faulty, or the interpreter erred, or you do not understand it."[10]

7. Cf. Irenaeus, Augustine, Isidore, etc., in P. Dausch, *Die Schriftinspiration: Eine biblisch-geschicht-liche Studie* (Freiburg i.B.: Herder, 1891), 87.

8. Irenaeus, *Against Heresies*, IV, 21, 3.

9. Theophilus, *To Autolychus*, 21; Irenaeus, *Against Heresies*, III, 5.

10. Augustine, *Against Faustus*, XI, 5.

At the same time, especially in the context of Montanist and other forms of spiritual "enthusiasm," defenders of Scripture's necessity such as Irenaeus, Origen, Eusebius, Augustine, and Jerome began to emphasize strongly the self-consciousness of the biblical writers in the event of inspiration, acknowledging the presence of prior investigation, differences in intellectual development, the use of sources and of memory, as well as differences in language and style among them. But none of this detracted from their belief in the divine origin and authority of Holy Scripture. This conviction was universally accepted and is demonstrated more powerfully in the practical use of Scripture in preaching, in argumentation, in the exegetical treatment of Scripture than in any isolated dogmatic statements. In this first period the church was preoccupied more with the establishment of the canon than with the concept of inspiration but understood by canonical writings the "divine scriptures" (especially of the Old Testament) and ascribed authority to them alone.[11]

[110] As this recognition was extended to include the apostolic writings of the New Testament, the conviction that these were "divine writings" was the church's universal belief. Formally speaking, the acknowledgment of Scripture as divine and authoritative revelation enjoyed undisputed sway in the medieval church. The Council of Trent affirmed this trust in the Scriptures, though it also extended inspiration to the church's tradition. In the post-Tridentine era, Roman Catholic theologians developed a variety of views on scriptural inspiration, including differing convictions about the nature and extent of inspiration. Some (Augustinians, Dominicans, Jansenists) maintained the more rigorous view that the Spirit of God exerted a positive influence on the authors, extending even to individual words. A less rigorous view (Jesuits at Louvain) rejected the verbal inspiration of Scripture and extended the notion of general inspiration to other writings as well, provided they contained no falsehoods. Yet others held to the view that the Spirit's guidance was only passive or negative, preserving the authors from error. Finally, yet others limited inspiration to the so-called religious-ethical teachings, allowing for varying degrees of fallibility for the rest.

Modern Roman Catholic thought tends toward a middle way between the rigorous notion of verbal inspiration and ideas of limited inspiration. The First Vatican Council (1870) declared that the church regards the books of Holy Scripture "holy and canonical not because they were composed by human industry alone and later approved by [the church's] authority; nor because they contain revelation without error; but because, written under the inspiration of the Holy Spirit, they have God as their author; and because they have been entrusted as such to the Church." In canon 2.4 the council once more calls the

---

11. H. Denzinger, *Enchiridion symbolorum et definitionum* (Wirceburgi: Stahelianis, 1856), n. 49, 125; K. R. Hagenbach, *Lehrbuch der Dogmengeschichte*, 3 vols. in 2 (Leipzig: Weidmann, 1840–41), I, §§31ff.; ET: *A Textbook of the History of Doctrines*, trans. C. W. Buch and rev. Henry B. Smith, 2 vols. (New York: Sheldon, 1867); Wilhelm Kölling, *Die Lehre von der Theopneustie* (Breslau: C. Dülfer, 1891), 84ff.; W. Sanday, *Inspiration: Eight Lectures on the Early History and Origin of the Doctrine of Biblical Inspiration; Being the Bampton Lectures for 1893* (London and New York: Longmans, Green, 1893).

books of Holy Scripture "divinely inspired," and in chapter 3, "On Faith," declares that "the divine and catholic faith believes all those matters that are contained in the word of God, whether in Scripture or tradition. . . ."[12] This decree is perfectly clear in that it views inspiration as a positive activity of God, on the one hand, and on the other regards the infallibility of Scripture as a consequence of that inspiration. Nonetheless, a growing trend among Roman Catholic theologians is "concessionism," an attempt to affirm biblical inspiration in a general sense while also accepting many of the most radical conclusions of historical criticism. Here, a crucial difference emerges. Protestants have no choice but to hold a strict theory of inspiration, for if it should collapse, everything else would collapse for them as well. But Roman Catholics can in all sorts of ways accommodate modern scholarship, inasmuch as for them the dogma remains firm on the basis of the church's authority.

[111] By contrast, the Reformers fully accepted the God-breathed character of Scripture. They accepted inspiration in its full positive sense and extended it to Scripture in all its parts. Luther now and then, from his soteriological position,[13] expressed an unfavorable opinion about some books of the Bible (Esther, Ezra, Nehemiah, James, Jude, Revelation) and admitted some minor discrepancies, but on the other hand he clung to the inspiration of Scripture in the strictest sense, even extending it to the very letters.[14] Lutheran confessions assume the divine origin and authority of Scripture everywhere.[15] Lutheran dogmaticians followed suit as did Reformed scholars. Calvin, for example, regards Scripture in the full and literal sense as the Word of God.[16] The Reformed confessions almost all have an article on Scripture and clearly express its divine authority;[17] and all the

12. H. Denzinger, *The Sources of Catholic Dogma*, trans. Roy J. Defaerrari, 30th ed. (Fitzwilliam, NH: Loreto, 2002), ##1787, 1809, 1792. Leo XIII adopted the same position in his encyclical *On the Study of Holy Scripture*, November 18, 1893; in his letter of September 8, 1899, to the French clergy; and in his letter of November 25, 1899, to the Order of the Friars Minor (Franciscan). In the encyclical, inspiration is defined as follows: "For, by supernatural power, He [the Holy Spirit] so moved and impelled them [the sacred authors] to write—He was so present to them—that the things which He ordered, and those only, they, first, rightly understood, then willed faithfully to write down, and finally expressed in apt words and with infallible truth. Otherwise, it could not be said that He was the Author of the entire Scripture" (Denzinger, *Sources,* #1952).

13. Ed. note: Using the hermeneutical principle "Is Christ preached?" as a criterion for canonicity.

14. J. Köstlin, *The Theology of Luther in Its Historical Development and Inner Harmony*, trans. Charles E. Hay, 2 vols. (Philadelphia: Lutheran Publication Society, 1897), II, 521ff.; Fr. Pieper, "Luther's Doctrine of Inspiration," *Presbyterian and Reformed Review* 4 (April 1893): 249–66.

15. Augsburg Confession, preface 8, art. 7; Smalcald Articles, in vol. 3 of *The Creeds of Christendom*, ed. Philip Schaff and rev. David S. Shaff, 6th ed., 3 vols. (New York: Harper & Row: 1931; repr., Grand Rapids: Baker Academic, 1990), II, art. 2, 15; Formula of Concord, "Epitome."

16. J. Calvin, *Institutes of the Christian Religion*, I.vii–viii (ed. John T. McNeill and trans. Ford Lewis Battles, 2 vols. [Philadelphia: Westminster, 1960], 1:74–92); idem, *Commentary*, on 2 Tim. 3:16 and 2 Pet. 1:20.

17. First Helvetic Confession, 1–3; Second Helvetic Confession, 1, 2, 13, 18; Gallican Confession, 5; Belgic Confession, 3; Ang., 6; Scots Confession, 18, etc.

Reformed theologians take the same position.[18] However, a fully organic view of inspiration that acknowledges the full participation of the human authors of Scripture was only feebly developed. The desire to defend the full divine authority of Scripture, not to concede anything to detractors, led to excessive claims. Biblical writers were not authors but scribes, amanuenses, notaries, the hands and pens of God. Inspiration was always positive, an "impulse to write" and "the suggestion of matters and words." Inspiration extended to all chronological, historical, and geographic matters, indeed to the words, even the vowels and the diacritical marks.[19] Barbarisms and solecisms were not accepted in Holy Scripture; differences in style were explained in terms of the will of the Holy Spirit, who wanted to write now in one way and now in another.[20] The ultimate excess? In 1714, according to Tholuck,[21] Nitzsche in Gotha wrote a dissertation on the question of whether Holy Scripture itself was God.

This zeal to defend Scripture by extreme conclusions regarding its inspiration was understandable given the long history of human rebellion against God and critical opposition to his revelation. The rationalist Scripture criticism that arose in the eighteenth century has an ancient pedigree. Ignoring the simple fact that God's word always comes to pass, King Jehoiakim in a futile act of defiance burned the scroll of Baruch (Jer. 36). Marcion and others separated the God of the Old Testament from the God of the New, and even in the New Testament used the Pauline law/gospel, flesh/spirit contrast as a critical hermeneutical tool to drive a wedge between Scripture and Scripture. Enemies of the faith such as Celsus, Porphyry, and Julian the Apostate slandered the God and the people of the book. After a long period of almost universal and undisputed dominance for Scripture in the West, modern rationalist criticism in the eighteenth and nineteenth centuries again called into question the authenticity of the biblical writings. A great deal of attention is paid to the doctrine of biblical inspiration in the modern era while critical hostility to the Bible seems to have increased. Whether it be Celsus or Porphyry, Voltaire or Renan, Strauss or Baur, the result is consistently the same: Scripture is considered a book full of error and lies.

18. Zacharius Ursinus, *Volumen tractationum theologicarum* (Neustadt: Mathes Harnisch, 1584), 1–33; Jerome Zanchi, *De operum theologicorum*, 8 vols. ([Geneva]: Samuelis Crispini, 1617), VIII, col. 319–451; Franciscus Junius, *Theses Theologicae*, in vol. 1 of idem, *Opuscula theological selecta*, ed. Abraham Kuyper (Amsterdam: F. Muller, 1882), chap. 2; Amandus Polanus, *Syntagma theologiae christianae*, I, 15; H. Bavink, ed., *Synopsis Purioris theologiae* (Leiden: D. Donner, 1881), disp. 2.

19. J. Buxtorf, *Tractatus de punctorum origine, antiquitate et auctoritate* (1648); idem, *Anticritica* (1653); Johann Heinrich Alsted, *Praecognita theologiae, I–II*, books I and II of *Methodus sacrosanctae theologiae octo libris tradita* (Hanover: C. Eifrid, 1619), 276; Polanus, *Syn. Theol.*, I, 75; G. Voetius, *Selectae disputations theologicae*, 5 vols. (Utrecht, 1648–69), I, 34; Consensus Helvetica, art. 2.

20. J. Quenstedt and Hollaz, according to Rohnert, *Inspiratione*, 205, 208; G. Voetius, *Select. Disp.*, I, 34; Gomarus, *Opera omnia theologica*, 601.

21. A. Tholuck, *Vermischte Schriften grösstentheils apologetischen Inhalts*, 2 vols. (Hamburg: F. Perthes, 1862), II, 86.

Wanting to hold on to some form of scriptural value, theologians modified their view of inspiration. One approach reduced its inspired character to religious-ethical matters only and allowed for all kinds of historical, geographical, and other error. The Word of God was to be distinguished from Scripture. Only doctrine is immediately inspired; in the rest error was easily possible.[22] A split was created between "that which is needed for salvation" and "the incidentally historical." This distinction is impossible; in Scripture, doctrine and history are completely intertwined. It is also at variance with the way Jesus, the apostles, and the whole Christian church used Scripture. Consequently, this dualistic view made way for another, the dynamic conception of Schleiermacher who transferred inspiration from a quality or property of Scripture to the personality and aptitude of the authors.[23] The difference between the inspiration of biblical writers and all believers is now only a matter of degree. Not all parts of Scripture, however, share in this inspiration, this Word of God, to the same degree. Rather, the closer a thing is to the center of revelation, the more it breathes the Spirit of God. Scripture, accordingly, is simultaneously a divine and a human book containing the highest truth on the one hand and at the same time weak, fallible, and imperfect. Scripture is not the revelation itself but only the record of revelation; not the Word of God itself but only an account of that Word.

At the theological heart of this revision of the doctrine of inspiration, shifting from the text of Scripture to the person(ality) of the authors, is a profound commitment to the person of Christ. He is the First Principle of theology. In a strange way, the Bible remains because though it is judged in many ways to be fallible and deficient, it is still believed in some way to reveal Christ and the genius of his teaching and example. Modern theologians, for all their criticism, continue to acknowledge the religious value of Holy Scripture, and not only regard it as a source for knowledge of Israel and early Christianity but continue to maintain it as a means for nurturing the religious-ethical life.

This is an unstable and finally untenable position. Thankfully, the situation in the church is better than in the academy. There are still many Christians in whom remains the consciousness of Scripture as God-breathed and authoritative for teaching and practice. We need not overlook the valuable insights gained from historical research of the biblical world, textual-critical advances, and the like, to recognize that separating the "religious" value of Scripture from its historical and lingual objectivity is a fatal flaw. Even scientifically oriented theologians such as Albrecht Ritschl and Julius Kaftan, in different and yet not satisfactory ways, should be appreciated for their insistence on the objectivity of revelation in Christ as foundational to the Christian religion.[24] They recognize rightly that,

22. Otto Fock, *Der Socinianismus* (Kiel: C. Schröder, 1847), 326ff.

23. F. Schleiermacher, *The Christian Faith*, ed. and trans. H. R. MacIntosh and J. S. Steward (Edinburgh: T&T Clark, 1928), §§128–32.

24. Albrecht Ritschl, *Die christliche Lehre von der Rechfertigung und Versohnung*, 4th ed., 3 vols. (Bonn: A. Marcus, 1895–1903), II, 9ff.; W. Herrmann, *Die Bedeutung der inspirationslehre für die evan-*

according to the Christian faith, revelation is not first of all to be found in human beings but lies outside them in history. Hence the external historical revelation of God is the cognitive source of the Christian faith and consequently the authority principle, the natural and necessary first principle of dogmatics.[25] Though Kaftan undermines his own position by seeing Scripture solely as a *record* of revelation, and filtering his use of Scripture through the two predetermined hermeneutical "practical" lenses of "the kingdom of God" and "reconciliation," rejecting everything that does not agree with these two themes, he is correct in asserting that the authority of revelation is the indispensable foundation of dogmatics and that Scripture and the confessions are *the* authorities that decide what is truly Christian.

Scripture's Self-Testimony: Organic Inspiration

[112] Holy Scripture nowhere offers a clearly formulated dogma on inspiration but confronts us with the witness of its God-breathed character, and it furnishes us all the components needed for construction of the dogma. It contains and teaches the God-breathed character of Scripture in the same sense and in the same way—just as firmly and clearly but just as little formulated in abstract concepts—as the dogma of the Trinity, the incarnation, vicarious atonement, etc. We do have, as we have discussed earlier in this chapter, the example of our Lord's own attitude and that of his apostles to the Old Testament. This more inductive and broad approach to the question of inspiration is taken by some to mean that we must incorporate what we learn about Scripture's genesis and history, its content and form, in our doctrine of inspiration. If our statements about Scripture's self-testimony regarding inspiration are to be judged true and good they must accord with the phenomena of Scripture and be deduced from them. "Let Scripture speak for itself and bear witness of itself," they say. Their opposition is to all theories and systems that force Scripture into what they judge to be a straitjacket of conformity to orthodox and Scholastic thought. The latter, so they accuse, lacks respect for Scripture and does violence to the text, to the facts of Scripture.[26]

We need to honor the concern that the church not force a predetermined notion of inspiration and authority on the biblical text rather than letting the text itself speak. The question before us is whether inspiration is indeed a fact taught by Holy Scripture and whether we are willing to believe it. If Scripture does teach it we must also believe what it says just as much as we are bound by Scripture's pronouncements about God, Christ, salvation, etc. The so-called phenomena of

---

gelischen kirche (Halle: Niemeyer, 1882); J. Kaftan, *Wesen der christelichen Religion* (Basel: Bahnmaier's Verlag, 1881), 307ff.; Carl Emmanuel Nitzsch, *System of Christian Doctrines* (Edinburgh: T&T Clark, 1849), 212–52; E. Haupt, *Die Bedeutung der Heiligen Schrift für den evangelischen Christen* (Bielefeld and Leipzig: Velhagen & Klasing, 1891).

25. J. Kaftan, *Zur Dogmatik* (Tübingen: Mohr [Siebeck], 1904), 21ff., 109ff.

26. G. Wildeboer, *De Letterkunde des Ouden Verbonds* (Groningen: Wolters, 1893), V.

Scripture cannot undo this self-testimony of Scripture and may not be summoned against it as a party in the discussion. Human scientific research cannot become an independent third-party arbitrator deciding what parts of Scripture, if any, are reliable and to be accepted. Those who make their doctrine of Scripture dependent on historical research into its origination and structure have already begun to reject Scripture's self-testimony and therefore no longer believe that Scripture. They think it is better to build up the doctrine of Scripture on the foundation of their own research than by believingly deriving it from Scripture itself. In this way, they substitute their own thoughts for, or elevate them above, those of Scripture. Historical-critical study may yield a clear insight into the origination, history, and structure of Scripture but never leads to a doctrine, a dogma of Holy Scripture. This can, in the nature of the case, be built only on Scripture's own witness concerning itself. No one would dream of calling a history of the origin and components of the Iliad a doctrine. Therefore, it is not just some inspiration theory that (stands or) falls with this method but inspiration itself as a fact and testimony of Scripture.

Scripture says about itself that it is "divinely inspired" or "God-breathed" (θεοπνευστος). This verbal, which in Scripture occurs only in 2 Timothy 3:16, can be taken either actively or passively and can mean both "God-breathing" and "God-breathed." But the latter meaning (contra Cremer's New Testament lexicon) undoubtedly deserves preference, for (1) objective verbals compounded with θεος most frequently—though not always—have a passive meaning as in the case of θεογνωστος, θεοδοτος, θεοδιδακτος, θεοκινητος, θεοπεμπτος, etc.; (2) the passive meaning is supported by 2 Peter 1:21, where it is said that holy men spoke "borne by the Holy Spirit" (φερομενοι); (3) where the word occurs outside the New Testament it always has a passive meaning; and (4) it is unanimously understood in that sense by all the Greek and Latin church fathers and authors.[27] In the Vulgate it is accordingly translated by "*divinitus inspirata*" as well. It is of course undeniable that the Bible is "inspiring"; the quarrel is with those who *reduce* the meaning of 2 Timothy 3:16 to the active sense and fail to acknowledge that it is "inspired" before it can be said to be inspiring. Biblical inspiration may not be equated with heroic, poetic, or other religious inspiration. Cicero's comment, "No one ever became a great man without divine inspiration," does not do justice to Holy Scripture; neither to primary or secondary authors.

At the same time, however, we should not forget that biblical inspiration is possible because the Spirit of God is immanent in creation. The inspiration of poets, artists, seers, and others can indeed serve *by analogy* to illumine the inspiration of which Holy Scripture speaks. The immanence of God is the basis of all inspiration, including divine inspiration (Pss. 104:30; 139:7; Job 33:4). Existence and life are conferred on every creature from moment to moment by the inspiration

27. Cf. the thorough argumentation of Prof. B. B. Warfield, "God-Inspired Scripture," *Presbyterian and Reformed Review* 11 (January 1900): 89–130; ed. note: this essay is reprinted in *Revelation and Inspiration*, vol. 1 of *The Works of Benjamin B. Warfield* (New York: Oxford University Press, 1927; repr., Grand Rapids: Baker Academic, 1991), 229–82.

("breath") of the Spirit. More particularly, that Spirit of the Lord is the principle of all intelligence and wisdom (Job 32:8; Isa. 11:2); all knowledge and skill, all talent and genius, proceed from him. The Spirit in creation precedes and prepares the way for the Spirit in re-creation. Scriptural revelation, too, participates in the gracious, redemptive renewing of creation that comes through the work of Christ the Son. While inspiration is, properly speaking, a pneumatological category, a work of the Holy Spirit, it is fully part of the creating and providential work of the Father and the redemptive work of the Son.

To clarify matters under discussion, biblical inspiration must nonetheless not be considered a work of God's general providence but of his *saving* purpose in special revelation. The operations of God's Spirit in nature, in humankind, in the church, in the prophets, and in the biblical authors, though related and analogous, are not identical. The Spirit's special work of inspiring the biblical authors to commit to writing the revelation given to them includes aids to memory (John 14:26), new insights into past events from the light of the resurrection and ascension (John 16:12–14), and even sanctified judgment on issues contemporaneous to the writer for which he has no express divine commandment (1 Cor. 7:24, 40). The Holy Spirit does not set aside the human author but uses him with all his own unique gifts, experience, and ability.

[113] What we described in the previous paragraphs is best defined by the term "organic inspiration." We begin by affirming that in Scripture when a prophet or spokesman for God speaks, the Lord himself is speaking. We read, for example, "that which was spoken by the Lord through the prophet, saying..." [cf. Greek text of Matt. 1:22]. For God's speaking, the Greek preposition ὑπό is used; God is the subject, he speaks. The prophets, however—speaking or writing—are God's instruments; in reference to them the preposition διά with genitive is used, never ὑπό (Matt. 1:22; 2:15, 17, 23; 3:3; 4:14; etc.; Luke 1:70; Acts 1:16; 3:18; 4:25; 28:25). God, or the Holy Spirit, is the actual speaker, the informant, the primary author, and the writers are the instruments by whom God speaks, the secondary authors, the scribes. Inspiration should not be reduced to mere preservation from error, nor should it be taken in a "dynamic" way as the inspiration of persons. It is a mistake to begin from a presupposition of "without error" and infer back to the inspired character of the text. The Christian church, both the Roman Catholic and the Protestant, do not regard the books of the Bible holy and canonical "because they contain revelation without error, but because, written under the inspiration of the Holy Spirit, they have God as their author, and because they have been entrusted as such to the church."[28]

The "dynamic" view that inspiration consists only in actively arousing religious affections in the biblical authors, which were then committed to writing, confuses inspiration with regeneration, puts Scripture on a par with devotional literature,

---

28. Ed. note: Bavinck provides no reference for this originally Latin citation. It is likely from Christian Pesch, *De Inspiratione Sacra Scriptura* (Friburgi Brisgoviae: Herder, 1906), 412 (see note 30, below).

and denies in principle that God revealed himself to human beings by speaking, by thoughts, and by words. Divine inspiration is above all God speaking to us by the mouth of prophets and apostles, so that their word is the Word of God. What has been written is "that which has been spoken by God"; the Holy Spirit will speak (λαλησαι) whatever he hears and will declare (ἀναγγελει) the things that are to come (John 16:13). The words of God (λογια θεου, Acts 7:38; Rom. 3:2; Heb. 5:12; 1 Pet. 4:11) are always "oracular utterances, divinely authoritative communications."[29] In 2 Timothy 3:16 Scripture is called "God-breathed," not primarily with a view to its content but in virtue of its origin. It is not "inspirited because and insofar as it inspires" but, conversely, "it breathes God and inspires because it has been inspired by God."[30]

At the same time a "mechanical" view of inspiration fails to do justice to the role of the biblical writers as secondary authors. A one-sided emphasis on the divine, supernatural element in inspiration disregards its connection with the author's gifts, personality, and historical context. God treats human beings, including the biblical writers, not as blocks of wood but as intelligent and moral beings. For this accent on the human and historical side of Scripture we can thank the probing and pushing of modern thinkers who have helped us see this more clearly. Neither a "dynamic" nor a "mechanical" view suffices. The proper view of biblical inspiration is the organic one, which underscores the servant form of Scripture. This is the only way to honor the divine pedagogy apparent in Scripture whereby God in the course of the centuries progressively, step by step from lower to higher, from lesser to greater, from shadow into light, makes himself known to his people. The biblical writers should not be detached from their individual personalities and lifted above the history of their own time.

[114] We observe God's own pattern in creating a world as an "other," a dependent but distinct reality in which his human image bearers have their appropriate freedom, rationality, and will. God never coerces; he seeks to *persuade*. The Logos, in becoming flesh, does not take some unsuspecting person by surprise, but enters into human nature and prepares and shapes it by the Spirit into his own appropriate medium. In regeneration and conversion he does not suppress and destroy the powers and gifts of human persons but restores and strengthens them by cleansing them from sin. The Spirit of the Lord entered into the prophets and apostles themselves and so employed and led them that they themselves examined and reflected, spoke and wrote as they did. It is God who speaks through them; at the same time it is they themselves who speak and write. Driven by the Spirit, they themselves yet spoke (ἐλαλησαν, 2 Pet. 1:21). Their native disposition and bent, their character and inclination, their intellect and development, their emotions and willpower are not undone by

29. B. Warfield, "The Oracles of God," *Presbyterian and Reformed Review* 11 (April 1900): 217–60; ed. note: this essay is reprinted in *Revelation and Inspiration*, vol. 1 of *The Works of Benjamin B. Warfield* (New York: Oxford University Press, 1927; repr., Grand Rapids: Baker Academic, 1991), 335–94.

30. C. Pesch, *De Inspiratione*, 412.

the calling that later comes to them but, as they had been already shaped by the Holy Spirit in advance, so they are now summoned into service and used by that same Spirit. Their whole personality with all their gifts and powers are made serviceable to the calling to which they are summoned. The prophets and apostles, as they proceed to write, completely remain themselves. They retain their powers of reflection and deliberation, their emotional states and freedom of the will. Research (Luke 1:1), reflection, and memory (John 14:26), the use of sources, and all the ordinary means that an author employs in the process of writing a book are used. In several cases the personal experience and life history of the prophets and apostles (as in the Psalter) even yielded the material they needed for their writing. Hence there is room in Scripture for every literary genre, for prose and poetry, ode and hymn, epic and drama, lyrical and didactic poems, psalms and letters, history and prophecy, vision and apocalyptic, parable and fable (Judg. 9:7f.); and every genre retains its own character and must be judged in terms of its own inherent logic.

The Bible is God's Word in human language. As Christ the Word (λογος) became flesh (σαρξ) and dwelled among the human race (John 1:14), so analogously the Word became Scripture, the means by which God speaks universally to all people. Organic inspiration is the working out and application of the central fact of revelation: the incarnation of the Word. The Word became Scripture, and as Scripture subjected itself to the fate of all Scripture. All this took place in order that the excellency of the power, also of the power of Scripture, may be God's and not humanity's. Scripture is totally the product of the Spirit of God, who speaks through the prophets and apostles, and at the same time totally the product of the activity of the authors.[31]

[115] Organic inspiration is "graphic" inspiration, and it is foolish to distinguish inspired thoughts from words and words from letters. While it is important to emphasize the intensely personal character of Scripture and its claims on us, the "personal" may never be misued to weaken the actual text of Scripture. For us, the person of Christ, the Word incarnate, cannot be separated from the text of the written gospel. If the apostolic witness concerning Christ is not reliable, no knowledge of Christ is possible. Add to this that if Christ is authoritative he is authoritative also in the teaching concerning Scripture. In that case inspiration has to be accepted above all on his authority. The "personal" theory conflicts with the authority of Christ himself. We cannot separate knowing and believing as the so-called "mediating theology" (*Vermittelungstheologie*) does when its proponents deny inspiration from their university lecterns but actually confess it from their pulpits. Head and heart cannot be divided in this way without serious spiritual pathology being the result.

---

31. Ed. note: It is very important here to note that Bavinck is making a *pneumatological* point and not a christological one. It is not appropriate to apply the christological categories of Chalcedon to the Scriptures—the Bible is not "truly God and truly human." Rather, the work of the Holy Spirit is *in* the human person in such a way that the human nature is not ontologically divinized but retains its full humanity.

Taking the text of Scripture seriously as the Word of God does mean that we do not read it atomistically, as though each word or letter by itself has its own divine meaning. Words are included in thoughts and vowels in words. The full humanity of human language is taken seriously in the notion of organic inspiration. The history of the doctrine of inspiration shows progressive expansion of the notion even to the vowels and the punctuation (*inspiratio punctualis*). This was followed by a progressive shrinking, from the punctuation to the words (verbal inspiration), from the individual words to the word, the idea (word in place of verbal inspiration), from the word as idea to the subject matter of the word (*inspiratio realis*), then from the subject matter to Scripture's religious-ethical content, to the special object of saving faith (*inspiratio fundamentalis, religiosa*), from these matters to the persons (*inspiratio personalis*), and finally from this to the denial of all inspiration as supernatural gift. Traveling down this path leads nowhere but to a rejection of the Christian faith itself. It is true enough that there is a "center" and a "periphery" in Scripture; not every text or passage or book is equally close to the circle of faith's center. Not all the books of the Bible are of equal value. However, the periphery is not excluded from the circle of divine thoughts but a part of it. Scripture's inspiration is plenary.

[116] Critical opposition to this view of inspiration remains strong. While objections—e.g., from historical criticism—should not be ignored, we must not overlook the spiritual-ethical hostility to Scripture from the forces of unbelief. If Scripture is the account of the revelation of God in Christ, it is bound to arouse the same opposition as Christ himself who came into the world for judgment (κρισις) and is "set for the fall and rising of many" (Luke 2:34). He brings separation between light and darkness and reveals the thoughts of many hearts. Similarly, Scripture is a living and active word, a "discerner" of the thoughts and intentions of the heart (cf. Heb. 4:12). By itself, therefore, it need not surprise us in the least that Scripture has at all times encountered contradiction and opposition. Christ bore a cross, and the servant (Scripture) is not greater than its master. Scripture is the handmaiden of Christ. It shares in his defamation and arouses the hostility of sinful humanity.

While not all questioning of Scripture reveals hostile unbelief, it is important to underscore the duty of every person to be humble before Scripture. Holy Scripture must judge us, not the reverse. The Holy Spirit opens our heart to trust, believe, and obey God's Word in Scripture. Submission remains a struggle, even an intellectual one. We must acknowledge our limitations, the reality of mystery, and our weakness of faith, without despairing of all knowledge and truth. Our hope is in Christ, the true man in whom human nature is restored. That is the purpose of Scripture: to make us wise unto salvation (2 Tim. 3:15). The battle against the Bible is, in the first place, a revelation of the hostility of the human heart. But we need to remind ourselves that hostility does not come to expression only—and perhaps not even most forcefully—in the criticism to which Scripture has been subjected in our time. Scripture as the Word of God encounters opposition and unbelief in every "unspiritual" person. In the days of dead orthodoxy, an unbelieving attitude toward Scripture was in principle as powerful as in our historically oriented and critical century. The forms change, but the essence remains the same. Whether hostility against Scripture is expressed in criticism like that of Celsus and Porphyry or whether it is manifest in a dead faith, that hostility in principle is the same. We are blessed when we *do* the Word (James 1:22). Knowing the master's will and refusing to do it results in a more severe beating (Luke 12:47).

It remains the duty of every person, therefore, first of all to put aside his or her hostility against the Word of God and "to take every thought captive to obey Christ" (2 Cor. 10:5). Only the pure of heart will see God. Self-denial is the condition for being a disciple of Jesus; humility the condition for learning. Augustine said, "When a certain rhetorician was asked what was the chief rule in eloquence, he replied, 'Delivery'; what was the second rule, 'Delivery'; what was the third rule, 'Delivery'; so if you ask me concerning the precepts of the Christian religion, first, second, third, and always I would answer, 'Humility.'" Calvin cites this statement with approval, along with "a saying of Chrysostom's . . . that the foundation of our philosophy is humility."[32] And Pascal cries out to humanity: "Humble yourself, powerless reason! Be silent, stupid nature! . . . Listen to God!"

This does not mean that the believer is delivered from all questions about Scripture. Believers are not freed from all doubt, and in Scripture too there is much that raises doubt. All believers know from experience that this is true. There is not a single Christian who has not in his or her own way learned to know the antithesis between "the wisdom of the world" and "the foolishness of God." It is one and the same battle, an ever-continuing war that has to be waged by all Christians, learned or unlearned, to "take every thought captive to the obedience of Christ" (2 Cor. 10:5). Here on earth no one ever rises above that battle. There is no faith without struggle. To believe is to struggle, to struggle against the appearance of things. Easy concessions to intellectual challenges weaken believers but do not liberate them. We need not disguise the intellectual problems in Scripture nor ignore them, even if many will probably never be resolved. We should comfort ourselves with the knowledge that these difficulties, which Scripture itself presents against its own inspiration, are in large part not recent discoveries of our century but have been known at all times. Nevertheless, Jesus and the apostles, Athanasius and Augustine, Thomas and Bonaventure, Luther and Calvin, and Christians of all churches have down the centuries confessed and recognized Scripture as the Word of God. Those who want to delay belief in Scripture till all the objections have been cleared up and all the contradictions have been resolved will never ar-

---

32. J. Calvin, *Institutes*, II.ii.11. Ed. note: The citation from Augustine is *Letters*, cxiii, 3, 22 (PL 33:442; cf. Fathers of the Church, 18:282). The reference to Chrysostom is from *De profectu evangelii* 2 (PG 51:312), which reads "Θεμέλιος γάρ ἐστι τῆς καθ' ἡμᾶς φιλοσοφίας ἡ ταπεινοφροσύνη" (http://www .documentacatholicaomnia.eu/02g/0345-0407,_Iohannes_Chrysostomus,_De_profectu_evangelii,_ MGR.pdf).

rive at faith. "For who hopes for what he sees?" (Rom. 8:24). Jesus calls blessed those who have not seen and yet believe (John 20:29).

To put this in perspective, there are objections and conundrums in every science. Those who do not want to start in faith will never arrive at knowledge. Epistemology, the theory of knowledge, is the first principle of philosophy, but it is riddled with mystery from start to finish. Those who do not want to embark on scientific investigation until they see the road by which we arrive at knowledge fully cleared will never start. Those who do not want to eat before they understand the entire process by which food arrives at their table will starve to death. And those who do not want to believe the Word of God before they see all problems resolved will die of spiritual starvation. Nature contains so many enigmas that it can often make us doubt that there exists a wise and just God. We could then, also with respect to Scripture, simply throw ourselves into the arms of agnosticism and pessimism. But despair is a death leap also in the area of science. The mysteries of existence do not decrease but increase with the adoption of unbelief. And the unease of the heart grows larger.

[117] Nonetheless, there are appropriate responses to some of the objections raised against the doctrine of inspiration. The organic view of inspiration affirms the idea that the Holy Spirit, through the process of inscripturation, did not spurn anything human to serve as an organ of the divine. God's revelation is not abstractly supernatural but concrete, historical, flesh and blood; it is not high above us but descends into our situation. Divine revelation is now an ineradicable constituent of this cosmos in which we live and, effecting renewal and restoration, continues its operation. The human has become an instrument of the divine; the natural has become a revelation of the supernatural; the visible has become a sign and seal of the invisible. In the process of inspiration and inscripturation, use has been made of all the gifts and forces resident in human nature. This helps account for such matters as differences in language and style, in character and individuality, that are discernible in the books of the Bible. Similarly, the use of sources, the authors' familiarity with earlier writings, their own inquiries, memory, reflection, and life experience are all included by the organic view. The Holy Spirit did not suddenly descend on them from above but employed their whole personality as his instrument. Here too the saying "grace does not cancel out nature but perfects it" is applicable. The personality of the authors is not erased but maintained and sanctified.

The organic view of revelation and inspiration also brings with it the notion that ordinary human life and natural life are made serviceable to the thoughts of God. Although Christ did not sin, he counted nothing human as alien to himself, and Scripture portrays his human limitations, his weariness, his tears. Scripture does not overlook even the most minor concerns of daily life (2 Tim. 4:13). Christianity is not antithetically opposed to that which is human but is its restoration and renewal. Scripture speaks to all of life but it does so *theologically*. Its intent is integrally given with its content: "Whatever was written in former times was given for our instruction" (Rom. 15:4). It is "useful for teaching, for reproof, for correction, and for training in righteousness, so that everyone who belongs to God may be proficient, equipped for every good work" (2 Tim. 3:16–17). It serves to make us wise unto salvation (2 Tim. 3:15). Scripture is not a manual for science; it is not written to furnish us with a history of Israel or a biography of Jesus, or to provide us geographical awareness of the land of Palestine. Its true purpose is to "make us wise unto salvation."

This does not mean that the Scriptures are irrelevant for science and human knowledge of the world. Much misuse has been made of Baronius's saying: "Scripture does not tell us how the heavens move but how we move to heaven."[33] But Scripture is a light on our path and a lamp for our feet, also with respect to science and art. It claims authority in all areas of life. Christ has [been given] all power in heaven and on earth. Inspiration extends to all parts of Scripture, and religion is a matter of the whole person. A great deal of what is related in Scripture is of fundamental significance also for the other sciences. The creation and fall of humankind, the unity of the human race, the flood, the rise of peoples and languages, etc., are facts of the highest significance also for the other sciences. At every moment science and art come into contact with Scripture; the primary principles for all of life are given us in Scripture. This truth may in no way be discounted.

On the other hand, there is also a large truth in the saying of Cardinal Baronius. Scripture's historical and other "facts" are not communicated in isolation and for their own sake but with a theological aim, namely, that we should know God unto salvation. Scripture never intentionally concerns itself with science as such. Christ himself, though free from all error and sin, was never, strictly speaking, active in the field of science and art, commerce and industry, law and politics. He was our Savior who came, full of grace and truth, to reveal the Father's glory and to redeem his people. However, since sin's corruption touches all dimensions of our lives, the grace of Christ also extends as far into the uttermost reaches of our existence. So too, Scripture address our whole being, our life in family and society, in science and art. Of course, Scripture is not a scientific text in any strict sense; it does not speak the exact language of science and the academy but the language of observation and daily life. It is probable that the authors of Scripture knew no more than all their contemporaries about the sciences of astronomy, geology, zoology, physiology, medicine, etc. Nor was it necessary. For Holy Scripture uses the language of everyday experience, which is and remains always true, and addresses us in the core of our being as religious creatures who long for fellowship with God. The Bible is a book for humanity, for concrete life; it speaks in ordinary human language, language that is intelligible to the most simple person, clear to the learned and unlearned alike. It employs the language

33. Augustine already said, "We do not read in the gospel how our Lord said: 'I will send you the Paraclete who will teach you about the course of the sun and the moon.' For he wanted to make Christians, not mathematicians" (*Acts or Disputation against Fortunatus the Manichaean*, I, 10).

of observation and wisdom which will always continue to exist alongside that of science and the academy.

We are not to take refuge in the true claim that Holy Scripture has its own intentional historiography, one that is not like the modern quest for factual precision, in order to circumvent the actual historicity of its narratives. Of course, it is not the purpose of these histories to tell us precisely all that has happened in times past with the human race and with Israel but to relate to us the history of God's revelation. Scripture only tells us what is associated with that history and aims by it to reveal God to us in his search for and coming to humanity. Sacred history is religious history; but it is *history*, not legend or imaginative fable. All the historiography in Holy Scripture bears witness to the fact that it follows a direction of its own and aims at a goal of its own. While we are not given the degree of exactness we might frequently wish, especially as modern people, we should be satisfied with what we have been given. It is sufficient.

We need to acknowledge that the doctrine of Scripture is far from being fully developed; there is plenty of work for biblical scholars yet to do. We have learned much about the truly human character of Scripture; the variety of literary genres— prose and poetry, history and prophecy, parable and fable, wisdom literature—but even then we are not always sure. Whether the rich man and the poor Lazarus are fictitious characters or historical persons is an open question. Similarly, what historical weight do we give the books of Job, Ecclesiastes, and Song of Solomon? In terms of prophecy, we note that the Old Testament prophets picture the future in colors derived from their own environment, and therefore in each case confront the question of whether what they write is intended realistically or symbolically.

God is infinite, all-knowing, and holy; all our talking about him, also in the Bible, is *human* speech. The Bible always speaks of the highest and holiest things, of eternal and invisible matters, in a human way. Like Christ, it does not consider anything human alien to itself. But for that reason it is a book for humanity and lasts till the end of time. It is old without ever becoming obsolete. It always remains young and fresh; it is the word of life. The Word of God endures forever.

6

FAITH

[130] Corresponding to the external principle (revelation) discussed in the previous chapter, there has to be an internal principle in human beings to receive revelation. Revelation must be received as well as given. Human beings are intimately connected to the rest of creation. A human body has been taken from the dust of the earth, is composed of the same basic elements as other bodies, and is therefore akin to the physical world. Its vegetative life is nourished from the earth. But we are also sentient creatures who perceive the external world and are capable through our reason (λογος) to discern the order and design (λογος) in intelligible things. In the same way that human beings are designed for and connected to their external world by many relationships, so too they have a faculty for perceiving the divine. As we have noted earlier in this volume, Scripture tells us that this religious disposition, the innate *sensus divinitatis*, arises from our being created in God's image. Religion presupposes revelation and the human capacity to receive it.

This religious capacity always occurs in the concrete and is instilled in us by our parents and religious caretakers in community. As with language, so it is with religion. The faculty of speech is something we possess at birth, but the language in which we will later express our thoughts is given us by our environment. The [general] rule is that people die in the religion in which they were born; a change of religion is the exception, not the rule. Conversion is usually the result of a crisis of faith; most people who are satisfied with their religion do not challenge its grounds. In the same way that a hungry man does not question the preparation

111

or ingredients of the bread placed before him, religious faith does not arise from reflection; we live first, then we philosophize. Excessive religious self-critique is a sign of spiritual poverty.

Nonetheless, critical reflection on faith does have a positive side, though it cannot compensate for lost faith. The nature of religion requires of theology its own epistemology. A theologian is not a philosopher, and philosophical theories about knowledge are not needed as a prerequisite for doing theology. Philosophical training is useful to a theologian but no particular philosophical system should frame theological work. Religion is more deeply rooted in human nature than any other power; only religion breeds martyrs. When it comes to our religious life, our sensory knowledge and our reason run up against boundaries; the depths of the human soul are mysterious and elude our analysis. Can we fully explain why we believe what we do? We struggle to explain, to communicate reasons for our faith. Often, we can do nothing else but to assert faith's independent reason: "Here I stand; I can do no other, God help me!"

[131] While the riddle of faith and the variety of grounds for faith must be respected, we can explore the means by which faith comes to fruition. The organ by which we obtain religious knowledge—be it intellect, heart, or conscience—receives content from the outside. People who claim to have arrived at religious knowledge and certainty simply by intellect, reason, heart, and/or conscience evidence a lack of psychological and epistemological sophistication. These functions cannot be the source of religious faith because they are only formal; they include no material content. Religion presupposes and demands the existence, self-revelation, and knowability of God. Revelation comes to us from without; it seeks our response but does not ask for our approval. Rather, it insists that we believe and obey. Fundamental to all our questions in this area is the matter of authority. Do we accept an authority beyond ourselves and external to us or do we insist on *autonomy*? And if we choose autonomy, do we locate its source in our minds, our hearts, or our consciences? The way we construe the theological enterprise varies significantly with the answers given to this question.

Human beings are by nature religious, and our religious capacity is always expressed concretely, awakened by and accommodated to a historical religion. But we must also add: this capacity is corrupted by sin and itself needs redemption. Scripture expressly states that the unspiritual cannot understand the things of the Spirit, that they are folly to them, that they reject and deny them in a spirit of hostility (1 Cor. 2:14). It is the confession of the Christian church that God's redemption and revelation in Christ is subjectively applied to believers by the Holy Spirit. God's objective revelation in Christ, recorded in Scripture, is the prior external source of religious knowledge (*principium cognoscendi externum*); the Holy Spirit is the internal source of knowledge (*principium cognoscendi internum*). No one knows the Father except the Son and anyone to whom the Son chooses to reveal him (Matt. 11:27), and no one can say "Jesus is Lord" except by the Holy Spirit (1 Cor. 12:3). While Rome teaches that the institutional church is the dwelling place of the Spirit, according to the Reformation this temple is the church as organism, the community of the faithful. The testimony of the Holy Spirit is the property of all believers.

As we explore faith and its various grounds, the different authorities to which we appeal, we need to acknowledge both the validity and the limitation of each one. Intellect, the heart, and human conscience each provides us with elements of faith's grounds, but taken by themselves each yields distortion. An exclusively intellectual understanding of faith leads to speculation and ignores the important affective and moral dimensions of faith. Similarly, an exclusive focus of religious feeling ignores questions about truth and about right and wrong. To do justice to faith we need to consider each one in turn, noting important features that are essential and those that obscure the heart of religion as a unique phenomenon, including but still distinct from science, art, and morality. We shall now consider key dimensions of faith, its relation to theology, and the key question about authority, taking separate looks at the intellect, feelings, and morality. These three correspond to three distinct theological methods that can be called, respectively, the historical-apologetic, the religious-empirical, and the ethical-psychological. We begin with the intellect and the historical-apologetic approach.

FAITH, INTELLECT, AND THEOLOGY: HISTORICAL-APOLOGETIC METHOD

[132] The first theological activity in the church arose from an apologetic need to defend the gospel against Jews and Greeks. From its earliest beginning the church had to endure all sorts of attack and so continually saw itself called to self-defense. Apologetics is nothing new but as old as revelation itself; we need only think of the Old Testament prophets who were forced to authenticate their message. Christian apologists compared their faith with the intellectual and practical content of paganism and judged the former to be vastly superior. Christianity was seen to be a blessing to the state, conducive to the prosperity of the empire, and a benefaction to all humanity. Christianity was a liberation, a deliverance from the futile spirits of pagan darkness, including the futility of pagan thought. "Christianity is a divine revelation, but it is at the same time pure reason; it is the true philosophy."[1] Christian apologists thus started with a firm, unshakable conviction about the truth of the gospel, a conviction that even on occasion resulted in martyrdom.[2]

1. A. von Harnack, *The Mission and Expansion of Christianity in the First Three Centuries*, trans. James Moffatt (London: Williams and Northgate, 1908; repr., New York: Harper Torchbooks, 1961), 225–26.

2. Ed. note: The most notable example was Justin Martyr (ca. 100–ca. 165), arguably the greatest of the second-century apologists and author of *Dialogue with Trypho the Jew, The First Apology, The Second Apology* (in *ANF*, I, 159–270).

An important feature of this faith was the belief that in the pagan world there was also much that is true and good and beautiful. Whatever "seeds of truth" present there are traceable to the Logos, who created the world, enlightens every human being coming into the world, and in Christ became flesh. Or, it was believed, they originate in special revelation that from ancient times on was given by God to humankind and preserved to some degree among the gentiles. The Christian religion was, in this view, as old as the world itself, germinally present from the beginning in divine revelation. Christianity receives testimony from all that is true and good in the religions and philosophical systems of paganism and, indeed, in every human soul. "The soul is naturally Christian."

The apologists did not, however, gloss over the key differences. The holy character of Christ and the prophets is superior to that of founders of other religions. The self-sacrificial death of Christ and the historical apostolic witness to his resurrection are given only in the Christian gospel; its message of redemption and hope for eternal life are unique. The antiquity and unity of the Scriptures, their sublimity and simplicity, the riches and many-sidedness evidence in Scripture, the predictions of the prophets and their fulfillment, the miracles—all these elevate the Christian truth above other claims and beyond all doubt. The conduct of Christians stood in marked contrast to the idolatry, superstition, magic, practice of adultery and abortion, and the like among the pagans, and was simultaneously marked by singular brotherly love, hospitality, generosity, and the care of widows and orphans, the poor and sick, prisoners and slaves, the persecuted and the dead. Christianity was a blessing to the empire, an argument that had compelling cogency because Christians were firm in their belief and lived in practice.

[133] Medieval Scholastic theology, though based on faith, in time turned the truth of faith into the content of reason and created a division between natural and supernatural truth, between scientific reason and faith. In response to the Reformation, Roman Catholic thought turned to the church itself as the most compelling ground for belief in Scripture and revelation. Though Vatican I affirmed the internal help of the Holy Spirit, it also anathematized those who reject the church as a necessary external sign.[3] External proofs are, for Rome, "preambles of faith," the necessary foundation for supernatural infused grace. Historical apologetics and reason serve as "motivations toward belief" (*motiva credibilitatis*); these natural human actions serve as preparation for the sacramentally infused

3. The Vatican Council [I] session III, chap. 3, "On Faith," declared: "For, to the Catholic Church alone belong all those many and marvelous things which have been divinely arranged for the evident credibility of the Christian faith. But, even the Church itself by itself, because of its marvelous propagation, its exceptional holiness, and inexhaustible fruitfulness in all good works; because of its catholic unity and invincible stability, is a very great and perpetual motive of credibility, and an incontestable witness of its own divine mission" (H. Denzinger, *The Sources of Catholic Dogma [Enchiridion Symbolorum]*, trans. from the 30th ed. by Roy J. Deferrari [London and St. Louis: Herder, 1955], #1794). The anathema reads as follows: "If anyone shall have said that divine revelation cannot be made credible by external signs, and for this reason men ought to be moved to faith by the internal experience alone of each one, or by private interpretation: let him be anathema" (ibid., #1812).

supernatural grace that leads ultimately to the vision of God. Human beings proceed upward to the vision in degrees as on a ladder.

The Reformation, in principle, opposed this hierarchical system of Rome and affirmed faith's sole dependence on divine authority and the work of the Holy Spirit. Yet Protestant theologians too returned to notions of natural theology and sought historical proofs for the truth of revelation. Even Calvin says that he would find it easy to prove the divinity of Holy Scripture and cites various grounds for it,[4] and many other theologians followed suit.[5] Unwittingly, the conviction that these proofs are sufficient to bring about at least a "human faith" contributed to the emancipation of reason from faith and placed the dogmas of natural theology and of Holy Scripture outside saving faith. Rationalism, in the form of Socinianism, Arminianism, Cartesianism, and deism followed this drift and infiltrated Protestant theology. Natural theology was moved to a place of independence alongside revealed theology, and eventually replaced it. Deism judged that natural theology was perfectly adequate to meet humanity's fundamental religious needs. The desire for a truly scientific approach to religion led to the history-of-religions method by Troeltsch and others. Theology is radically emancipated from the church and faith and treated in an objective, neutral, historical-critical manner. In response, some adopted a supernaturalist posture that affirmed the divine authority of revelation but fatally also yielded to the radical divorce between piety and reason. This is a far cry from the effective apologetic greatness of the second century.

[134] While subjected to serious critique by such thinkers as Rousseau, Kant, Lessing, and Schleiermacher, we must not forget the truth inherent in this intellectual defense of faith, this historical-apologetic stance. All believers have a duty, with gentleness and fear, to give an account of the hope that is in them and to confute those who contradict the gospel (1 Pet. 3:15; Titus 1:9). Good apologetics is a blessing to the church and to the world; the early church proved this. A valid apologetic, however, *follows* faith and does not attempt to argue the truth of revelation in an a priori fashion. Christians need not hide from their opponents in embarrassed silence; the Christian faith is the only worldview that fits the reality of life. Apologetic intellectual labor should not lead to exaggerated expectations nor deny the genuine subjectivity of Christian truth. Relying on reason to convert or ground the faith on intellectual grounds alone will always disappoint. Submitting to the validation of revelation by an intellectual priesthood provides feeble

4. John Calvin, *Institutes of the Christian Religion*, I.vii.4–viii.13 (ed. John T. McNeill and trans. Ford Lewis Battles, 2 vols. [Philadelphia: Westminster, 1960], 1:78–92).

5. Zacharias Ursinus, *Volumen Tractationum Theologicarum* (Neustadtii Palatinorum: Mathes Harnisch, 1584), 1–33; Jerome Zanchi, *Operum Theologicorum*, 8 vols. ([Geneva]: Sumptibus Samuelis Crispini, 1617), col. 335ff.; Amandus Polanus, *Syntagma Theologiae Christianae*, 5th ed. (Hanover: Aubry, 1624), I, 17ff., 27–28. H. Bavinck, ed., *Synopsis purioris theologiae* (Leiden: Donner, 1881), disp. 2, 10ff.; cf. Heinrich Heppe, *Dogmatik der evangelischen-reformierten Kirche* (Elberfeld: R. L. Friedrich, 1861), 20–22. Ed. note: ET: *Reformed Dogmatics*, trans. Ernst Bizer (London: Allen & Unwin, 1950); H. E. F. Schmid, *The Doctrinal Theology of the Evangelical Lutheran Church*, trans. Charles A. Hay and Henry Jacobs, 5th ed. (Philadelphia: United Lutheran Publication House, 1899), 57ff.

certainty. It is a mistake to base faith's assurance on the need to travel a long and tortuous road of rational and historical verification for no other reason than that such a journey is never done. Faith's questions and challenges always remain with us as long as we remain pilgrims. Furthermore, as we face life's trials and troubles and seek faith's consolation we do not have the scholar's leisure to engage in calm, extensive investigation and reflection. If this were to become our model, most of us would become dependent on a new clerical priesthood; our salvation would rest on the conclusions of intellectuals. This is intolerable; eternity cannot hang from a spider web. To live and die in the comfort and blessing of salvation we need more than fallible human intellectual conclusions; we need a word from God. Faith that we have heard such a word rests on the testimony of the Holy Spirit, which provides a sure certainty. Faith and reason belong together; neither a subjection of faith to reason nor a divorce of faith and reason serve the church and the cause of truth.

[135] In reaction and response to the divorce of revelation and reason, European intellectual thought of the nineteenth century yielded to Romanticism, to the dominance and autonomy of the subject. Idealism sought objectivity from within the subject; in thinkers such as Fichte the world (non-ego) was seen as the product of the human subjects' mind (ego). The philosophic prophet of this restoration of idealism was Hegel, for whom the universe itself became a process of becoming, the evolution of the logical idea. From the theological rationalism of God, virtue, and morality, Hegel turned classic Christian dogma such as the Trinity and incarnation into speculative philosophic truths. Since religion in this view cloaks itself in forms and symbols (myths), all dogmas must be stripped of their historical symbolic forms to uncover their underlying idea. History is but the shell, the wrapping; the core itself is deep and true philosophy. Reason is the way to the final truth of all symbolic forms and representations. In this way theology and philosophy were reconciled, but the historical Christian faith was radically transformed. A personal God is exchanged for the absolute idea. Athough it was part of a reaction against a deistic as well as supranaturalist rationalism, Hegel represents the ultimate triumph of reason.

[136] Whereas rationalism falsified the whole Christian religion, Hegel and Schleiermacher are to be commended for returning to the church and its dogma and for pointing to the harmony of subject and object, thinking and being. People of culture had turned away with contempt from revelation and religion, from church and faith. Schleiermacher and Hegel courageously turned back to the church and its dogmas and discovered there, be it only in a certain sense, deep religious truth. Rationalism falsified the whole Christian religion. It was a manifestation of moral strength to break with the rationalistic demand for lucidity, to take up the cudgels for the despised religion of the church, and again to assert the validity and value of the Christian faith. Both insisted that thinking and being are most intimately related and correspond to each other. Rationalism attempted to justify religion before the unqualified court of common sense. But Hegel and Schleiermacher both understood that religion occupies a place of its own in human life, that it is

a unique phenomenon and therefore also requires a uniquely appropriate organ in human nature.

They were also guilty of the same error; not content with the thesis that thinking and being correspond to each other; they equated the two. Ideas are the real world; created reality is an emanation of thought. This equation of thinking and being is the basic error of all speculative philosophy beginning with Plato and given new currency in modernity by Descartes, Spinoza, and Fichte. The error here is transparent: however much resemblance there may be between thought and existence, the difference between them is no less real. From thought one cannot conclude to existence because the existence of all creatures is not an emanation of thought but arises from an act of power. The Christian teaching, by contrast, affirms that the essence of all things is because of the thought of God but the existence is because of his will, to his exercise of creating power. Human thought, accordingly, presupposes existence. It arises only upon the basis of the created world. We can only reflect (*re*-flect) on that which has been *pre*-conceived and comes to our consciousness through the world. But if with modern philosophy one rejects all matter that has come to us from without and adopts as one's starting point pure reason or abstract feeling, one retains nothing, or at most a principle so general, so devoid of content and vague that nothing—let alone the entire universe or all of Christian revelation and religion—can be deduced from it. This speculative theology was therefore not innocent. Theology became anthropology, "pisteology," or ecclesiology, rather than the knowledge of God; in short, a new form of gnosticism.

The history of thought since Hegel and Schleiermacher demonstrates this last point to a fault. Abandoning the historical realism of Christian orthodoxy and taking refuge in speculative thought, much modern theology became functionally gnostic. Schleiermacher started from a position of faith but the mediating theology that followed him found proof of truth in cognitive necessity. Desirous of reaching religions "cultured despisers" (Schleiermacher), it did not succed in changing the folly of the cross into worldly wisdom, nor, in spite of its sagacious insights, did it win back the children of this age for Christ. No religion is reducible to a logically ordered system of truth; Christianity in particular is a *history*, a history of [divine] grace, and grace is something other and more than a logical conclusion. In the Christian religion, accordingly, even the most profound thinker can never rise above a childlike position of authority and faith. Since religious rationalism moves in a tiny circle of intellectual arguments and abstract ideas no one cares about and no soul can live by, it dooms itself to sterility. The currents of life flow past it undisturbed.

FAITH, FEELING, AND THEOLOGY: RELIGIOUS-EMPIRICAL METHOD

[137] When historical and speculative argumentation failed to bear fruit, many theologians turned to religious experience to derive grounds for the certain truth

of Christianity. The influence of Schleiermacher is crucial for this development, notably his insistence that religion is not a matter of knowing or doing but of a certain state of feeling and, in keeping with this, that dogmatic theology is a description of pious states of mind. With a waning faith in biblical authority, thanks to historical criticism, Christian experience became the ground of certainty and opened the door to a scientific, religious-empirical approach to theology. Here too Christian certainty is not sought in external historical or rational proofs but in believing consciousness. After Kant's metaphysical refusal, it was hoped that in this way Christian theology could regain its honorable status in the eyes of secular science. What it needed to do was become thoroughly empirical and build a scientific construction on the facts of religious experience. Repudiating all metaphysics, theology now took its starting point in the believing subject. The most thorough systematic formulation of a dogmatic theology in this vein was produced by the Erlangen theologian F. H. R. Frank (1827–94).[6]

According to Frank, neither external proofs nor the authority of Scripture, church, and tradition are able to provide religious certainty, only the experience of rebirth. From the new life in Christ, believers are able to immediately posit the entire content of the truths of the Christian faith. His dogmatic system focuses on the question of religious certainty.[7] Frank first attempts to describe systematically the psychological path by which a believer comes to certainty[8] and then, in a separate treatment,[9] he summarizes the truth-*content* of the Christian faith. To be fair to him, Frank does not deny the prior and external reality of faith's objects. Nor does he deny that Christian certainty is produced by the Word,[10] and he does not want to derive objective truths strictly from the born-again subject.[11] They have independent significance. Frank clearly intends that we take his two treatments (*System of Christian Certainty* and *System of Christian Truth*) together; a reciprocity exists between religious consciousness of rebirth, certainty, and the truths of the faith. After completing his *System of Certainty*, Frank speaks of a "reversal" taking place whereby the certainty obtained by religious experience

6. Ed. note: The Erlangen School refers to a group of Lutheran theologians who, since ca. 1840, taught in the theology faculty at the University of Erlangen (Bavaria). Among its influential members are the biblical theologian J. Chr. K. von Hofmann (1810–77), New Testament scholar Theodor Zahn (1838–1933), and dogmatic theologians G. Thomasius (1802–75) and Franz Herrmann Reinhold Frank (1827–94). Though less bound to Lutheran confessional orthodoxy than many other Lutherans, the Erlangen School did contribute to a nineteenth-century revival of Lutheran confessional and theological interest.

7. Ed. note: Franz Herman Reinhold Frank wrote two major systematic works on "certainty": *System der Christlichen Gewissheit* [*System of Christian Certainty*], 2 vols. (Erlangen: A. Deichert, 1870–73); and *System der Christlichen Wahrheit* [*System of Christian Truth*]. *System der Christlichen Wahrheit* was published as two volumes in 1878–80 by A. Deichert, Erlangen; 2nd ed., 1885–86; 3rd ed., 1894.

8. Ed. note: In his *System of Christian Certainty*.

9. Ed. note: In his *System of Christian Truth*.

10. Franz Herman Reinhold Frank, *Dogmatische Studien* (Erlangen: A. Deichert, 1892), 56.

11. Ibid., 68–69.

about the truth content of the faith now generates its own truth claims. From within the experience of rebirth, Christians now spontaneously and immediately posit the entire content of the truths of the Christian faith.[12] Thus, the ground and authority for faith and theology comes from religious experience.

[138] According to Frank, Christian truth groups itself around the experience of rebirth in three circles: (1) that which is immediately given with the fact of rebirth, viz., the reality of sin, righteousness, and future perfection; (2) believers' explanation of their new state by necessary reference to the reality of a personal God, the existence of God as the triune being, and the atonement secured by the God-man;[13] (3) the transient, temporal means that effect the redemptive experience in the life of the Christian, including the church, the Word of God, Scripture, the sacrament, miracles, revelation, and inspiration. Frank's system contains an important truth: rebirth is necessary to see the kingdom of God. Had he restricted his insight to the epistemological issue—how does a believer arrive at certainty?—no objection would be raised. However, to infer content from experience and epistemology confuses being and knowing, objective truth and subjective certainty. Here again we see the characteristic confusion typical of modern thought in both its empiricist and idealist forms. The organization of dogmatic theology into a twofold system of certainty and a system of truth cannot be maintained since Christian certainty cannot be described apart from the metaphysical and historical truth to which it pertains. Frank, too, is a subjectivist.

[139–40] Other efforts to ground theological certainty in experience have not succeeded either. Certainty with respect to the truth of Christianity is not grounded in the Christian person but in the Word of God attested by the Holy Spirit. Part of the problem is the ambiguity of the word "experience." Experience is crucial to all religion, but in Christianity it must be prompted by the Word of God, accompany and follow faith, not precede it, and always be subject to correction by Scripture. Scripture, not experience, is the norm for our faith. In the articles of the Apostles' Creed, for example, we cannot simply exchange "I experience" for "I believe." The *effect* of belief must not be confused with its *content* and *ground*. The truth of historical Christianity cannot rest on experience as its ultimate ground.

It would be wrong, of course, to discount the importance of religious experience. Religious experience is inseparable from godliness and finds its classic expression in the Bible as a whole, especially in the Psalms. Appeals to experience call for caution since—as the great spiritual writers knew well—they are subject to all sorts of pathology, they lift us up emotionally and they drop us low. Experience by itself is not sufficient; it consistently needs the corrective of the Word of God. Scripture is the norm also for our emotional life and tells us what we ought to experience. And there is more. If for once I may also appeal to experience—experience

12. F. H. R. Frank, *Gewissheit*, I, 193.
13. These three truths jointly form the group of transcendent truths and indicate the factors that have brought about this moral change of rebirth in Christ.

teaches us that no individual believer ever arrived at knowledge and acceptance of the historical facts and truths of Christianity by this method. Experience cannot bear the burden laid on it; the truth of historic Christianity cannot rest on experience as its ultimate ground. The historical facts of Christianity—incarnation, crucifixion, resurrection, ascension, Pentecost—cannot be inferred directly from immediate religious consciousness in the same way, while a general sense of God and the conviction of conscience can. Furthermore, religious experience is such a subjective and individualistic principle that it opens the door to all sorts of arbitrariness in religion and actually enthrones anarchism: religion as a private thing. But Scripture says: "to the teaching and to the testimony! Surely for this word which they speak there is no dawn" (Isa. 8:20).

FAITH, MORALITY, AND THEOLOGY: ETHICAL-PSYCHOLOGICAL METHOD

[141] Closely linked to the immediately preceding religious-empirical (feeling-based) method associated with Schleiermacher and Frank is the ethical-psychological method, which is closer to Kant and accents moral self-assertion rather than emotional experience. Here, Christianity is not a feeling, or a doctrine, or historical fact but a religious-ethical power addressed to the human conscience. It is possible, in this view, by practical reason, to infer rationally the existence of God, freedom, and immortality. Assumed here is an understanding of the human person as possessing an antecedent moral state, a predisposition toward the good, a need for redemption, a feeling of dissatisfaction, etc. When Christianity comes in contact with such persons, it commends itself without argument and proof to their consciences as divine truth. For it satisfies their religious-ethical needs, accords with their noble and higher aspirations, reconciles them to themselves, liberates them from the guilt and burden of sin, gives them peace, comfort, blessedness, and in all these things proves itself to be the power and wisdom of God.

This posture, which argues for the agreement with or superiority of the Christian faith for human morality, goes back to the Apologists; we see it in Tertullian, who appeals to the witness that the soul involuntarily bears to Christ.[14] Others use this argument when pointing to the "good" they see in the pagans. They regard Christianity as the true philosophy. "Whatever things are well spoken of by all are ours as Christians."[15] Duns Scotus, in the prologue to his *Sentences*, similarly points to the rationality of the content of revelation, to its moral influence, and to its sufficiency for human beings seeking to attain their destiny. Even Rousseau in his *Emile* could not refrain from praising the life and teaching of Jesus:

14. Tertullian, *The Soul's Testimony*, 1; cf. idem, *Apology*, 17.
15. Justin Martyr, *2 Apology*, 13; cf. Adolf von Harnack, *History of Dogma*, trans, N. Buchanan, J. Millar, E. B. Speirs, and W. McGilchrist, and ed. A. B. Bruce, 7 vols. (London: Williams & Norgate, 1896–99), II, 129ff., 144ff.

"Indeed, if the life and death of Socrates are those of a sage, the life and death of Jesus are those of a God." In the modern era the moral argument has increased in importance largely thanks to philosopher Immanuel Kant.

According to Kant's system of philosophy, there are two sources of human knowledge, the senses for the matter and the intellect for the form of our knowledge. Above them stands reason, pure reason, whose a priori synthetic principle is that it rises from the conditioned to the unconditioned.[16] In virtue of this characteristic, theoretical reason forms principles or ideas that are absolute, unconditioned, transcendent. These ideas, produced by reason in keeping with its very nature, are, in the main, the trio of God, freedom, and immortality. The objects of these ideas are not perceptible and therefore not knowable. We arrive at them only by necessary rational inference.[17] All three of them are theoretically unprovable; they do not increase our knowledge but merely regulate and order it.[18] Theoretical reason cannot teach us that these ideas have reality or what they are.

Reason, however, is not only theoretical but also practical; it carries within itself a moral law, a categorical imperative, and confronts us with our duty. By demanding that we perform our duty unconditionally, without ulterior motives, solely out of respect for that duty as such, practical reason points us to an order above nature, a *moral* world order. We become aware of a supreme good, which far transcends the material goods of this world and consists in nothing other than the union of virtue and happiness. If this imperative of duty is not an illusion but realizable, in other words, if the moral world order within and outside us will triumph over the order of nature—then freedom, and with it God and immortality, have to exist as well. These three, accordingly, are the postulates of practical reason; their reality is required by the moral law. Practical reason demands that they exist.[19]

This famous theory of Kant is not beyond criticism. When Kant speaks of practical reason postulating the idea of God and freedom, who exactly does the inferring? But Kant distinguishes two "agents": one that holds up the duty of the moral imperative and another that by reasoning infers from it the existence of the ideas. In the case of the second, practical reason itself then engages in logical reasoning and becomes theoretical.[20] Of greater weight even is another objection: what could be the ground on the basis of which the theoretical or practical reason infers the existence of these ideas? Kant argues that it is unavoidable for every rational being to draw these conclusions. In other words, the assumptions of the existence of freedom, God, and immortality are equally as necessary as the moral

16. I. Kant, *Critique of Pure Reason*, trans. N. K. Smith (1929; repr., New York: St. Martin's Press, 1965), 327–67, 386–93.

17. Ibid., 333–41.

18. Ibid., 386, 554, 576, 586, 589, 593ff.

19. I. Kant, *Critique of Practical Reason*, trans. Mary Gregor (Cambridge: Cambridge University Press, 1997), 92–122.

20. L. W. E. Rauwenhoff, *Wijsbegeerte van den Godsdienst* (Leiden: Brill & Van Doesburgh, 1887), 325, 328.

law itself,[21] and Kant argues above all that the moral law, to be realizable, has to assume these three ideas as existent. But if this is Kant's opinion, we are dealing not with psychologically mediated but with objectively *logical* postulates, and the question arises: Why then is such a logical postulate not a matter of knowledge, not an element of theoretical reason? Why does Kant call this knowing only practical? Elsewhere,[22] Kant declares that moral faith is held to be true on the basis of psychological-moral grounds. This moral faith, therefore, does not say, "It is certain," but "I am morally certain." It therefore rests on the presupposition of moral convictions.[23]

In line with this view, he writes in his *Critique of Practical Reason*: "The person of integrity may say: 'I will that there be a God; I will let no one deprive me of this faith. My moral interest demands the existence of God. Moral faith is not a commandment; a faith that is commanded is an absurdity. The sense of duty is objective; so also is the capacity to act morally and to be happy.' But whether that connection between virtue and happiness is forged by a personal God or by the nexus of nature is something we do not know. Moral interest is decisive here. It is within our power of choice, but practical reason decides in favor of belief in a wise creator of the world."[24] In Kant, in fact, one discerns a double aim: on the one hand he aims to maintain the rationality of faith, on the other, the freedom of faith. Belief in freedom, God, and immortality is objective insofar as it is postulated by the practical reason that belongs to all; yet it nevertheless also depends on the moral disposition of the individual person.[25]

[142] Kant's divide between the world of pure (senses and facts of science) and practical (supersensible values) reason has had a profound influence on theology. If the supersensible (noumenal) world is unknowable, theology as knowledge of God is impossible and becomes an examination of human moral conduct, a form of religious moral idealism. Ethical modernists go further; abstaining from attempts at fashioning a philosophical system, they separate faith and science as sharply as possible, and restrict religion to the realm of morality. Religion here is moral idealism, devotion to a moral ideal, belief in the power of goodness, a power that may have objective existence but may also be nothing more than a conception of the human mind.[26] This understanding of religion and theology came to a high point in the cultural Protestantism (theological liberalism) of Albrecht Ritschl. For Ritschl, religion and theology are not part of the world of nature and law but of the spirit and freedom. Christianity is an ethical religion, an ellipse with

21. I. Kant, *Practical Reason*, 119 note.
22. Ibid., 92–122.
23. I. Kant, *Pure Reason*, 640–66.
24. I. Kant, *Practical Reason*, 119–21.
25. On the practical reason as a theoretical postulate of Kant, see, *inter alia*, Arthur Schopenhauer, *Die Welt als Wille und Vorstellung*, 6th ed., 2 vols. (Leipzig: Brockhaus, 1887), I, 610–25; ed. note: ET available: *The World as Will and Representation*, 2 vols. (New York: Dover, 1969).
26. L. W. E. Rauwenhoff, *Wijsbegeerte*, 116ff., 366ff.

two foci: redemption and the kingdom of God, the absolutely spiritual and the absolutely moral religion.

[143–44] This theory of knowledge (epistemology), which Ritschl substitutes for the Platonic or metaphysical view, is of the greatest significance for his theology. It would be rather harmless if it only meant that we could never learn to know things apart from perception, solely by speculative thinking and reasoning. Where it goes astray is the strong impression—never adequately repudiated by Ritschl—that in his view a thing completely coincides with and is exhaustively present in its appearance. If no substance or bearer exists behind the phenomena, if there really exist only effects, not things, if the existence of things is no more than "subsistence in relationships," then all objects would depend, in their "being" and their "being thus," on the observing subject and all science would run aground on the reef of illusionism and solipsism. The very premise of efforts to postulate religion from practical moral experience is flawed since it turns the order of our experience upside down. Religion does not follow but is prior to morality; there is no morality without metaphysics, no sense of duty apart from an absolute power that binds the conscience.

To be appreciated in Ritschl is his insistence that to get to know religion a person must himself or herself take a position in religion. It is wrong to first construct a natural theology apart from the Christian faith and to make it the preamble to one's theology. Religion is in a class of its own and never the fruit of a scientific study of nature. Furthermore, it is always positive (concrete), has its own source, and is the product of revelation. It can only be known, therefore, if one takes one's position within its circle, the circle of revelation. It is very important to acknowledge the role of (even subjective) faith in the process of acquiring theological knowledge. We note this emphasis in Ritschl with appreciation; it is one we have also made frequently in the preceding pages. Our appreciation notwithstanding, we also need to mention several fatal errors.

Ritschl ties the Christian religion to the person of Christ, but Christ is now understood not in terms of church doctrine but as a person who reveals God through the believer's experience of his person. And here is how a person comes to faith; here is the locus of authority for Ritschl. It is the individual with a strong moral consciousness, one who feels a moral need, who thirsts for the moral ideal and thus seeks after God—such a person encounters the Gospels' portrait of Jesus and is unable to resist. The impression that the person of Christ makes on us, the power that flows from the gospel into our hearts, the moral experience of mortification and joy, the correspondence between the idea of the kingdom of God and our needs and demands—these appear to be, for Ritschl and his followers, the final grounds for the truth of revelation in the person and life of Christ. Religion is life: subjective religion is primary and central and constitutes the heart of objective religion.

But who is the "person of Christ" in view here, the one who is the ground of our faith, of crucial importance to us as our moral teacher and guide? It turns out that he is not the one confessed by the church but the one whose portrait is painted by the experts in historical-critical inquiry into the Gospels. Here, as they set up a tension between the "Jesus of history" and the "Christ of faith," Ritschl's successors run into unsolvable conflicts as they debate about exactly what it was in the image of Jesus that produced faith and how this took place. Was it his "inner life," his "moral energy," or was it, perhaps, as Harnack suggested, solely the relation between God the Father and the human soul that gave human beings value as moral partners in the kingdom of God? In that case, only the Father and not the Son belong in the gospel as Jesus proclaimed it. However understood, it is clear that in the school of Ritschl the content of faith is restricted to the religious-ethical dimension. The Ritschlians do affirm the importance of the historical dimensions of salvation in Christ; though their Christology is impoverished, virtually all of them still insist that should historical-critical research deprive us of the lordship of Christ, the Christian faith would rise up in protest. For that we must be thankful. But we must also protest against a method that derives the *content* of faith from one's own moral grasp of Jesus's ethical teaching as the Ritschlians do. We cannot do this faithfully apart from the faith of the church, the body on earth he himself founded.

[145] This ethical-practical method of vindicating religion and Christianity does have much to commend it. The correspondence between a religion and the moral needs of human beings are of great significance. The satisfaction of the human heart and conscience are the seal and crown of religion. A religion that has no consolation to offer in time of mourning and sorrow, in life and in death, that has nothing to say at sickbeds and deathbeds, that cannot fortify the doubting ones, nor raise up those who are bowed down, is not worthy of the name. The contrast often made between truth and consolation does not belong in religion. A truth that contains no comfort, which does not connect with the religious-ethical life of human beings, ceases by that token to be a religious truth. Just as medical science in all its specialties is oriented to the healing of the sick, so in religion people have a right to look for peace and salvation.

This is the strength of the ethical-psychological method. Here religion is judged by its ability to satisfy the human heart, to provide consolation and comfort for guilty consciences and troubled souls. We grant that to be true a religion must provide consolation. However, conversely, this provision does not prove a religion's truth. After all, some comfort and satisfaction can be found in all religions. The experiences of misery and guilt, of doubt and confidence, of endurance and hope, are present not only among Christians but also in varying degrees among Muslims and Buddhists. When Ritschl and others separate theology from all metaphysics and rootedness in salvation-historical facts, they reduce religion to its subjective practical moral usefulness "for us." But religious-ethical experience and appraisal cannot guarantee the truth of their object. "Value" is not identical with "truth." I may well regard something that is "false" to be *valuable for me*. When value judgments are detached from all metaphysics, they cannot be the foundation and content of dogmatics. Religion implies the conviction of the reality of its object. Religious and ethical appraisal assumes the truth of the person or matter to which it relates. Value judgments, accordingly, depend on factual judgments; they stand or fall together. If the assessment of an object is not grounded in its reality, it is nothing but illusion, a creation of the imagination, or the formation of an ideal. It is not enough to seek and to meet people's perceived needs. Efforts to postulate the reality of God, freedom, and immortality from practical, moral reason demonstrate nothing more than the "good" within us. In the end what is produced was already contained in the subjective point of departure itself. Religious knowledge is found in the moral value of personal religious affirmation.

We must also be careful not to oversell the religious readiness of people to receive the gospel. It is true that we are, to paraphrase Augustine, created for God with a restlessness in our hearts for him. Yet, in the real world one finds almost no sign of an unconscious aspiration of the soul toward *Christianity*. The gospel is often received with joy as a liberation from bondage but the history of missions teaches us almost nothing about a ripeness of people for the gospel as such. The gospel is not naturally to the liking of human beings, not a *ready match for the needs of people* as they themselves picture those needs. Outside of revelation, human beings do not even know themselves and their real needs. The often-repeated claim that Christianity corresponds to human needs, while true, brings with it the very real danger that the truth is tailored to suit human nature. The thesis that the truth is authentically human because it is so intensely divine very easily turns into its opposite, viz., that it is only divine because it is human. The preaching that, rather than speaking to the heart of Jerusalem, flatters it is not uncommon even on Christian pulpits. Religious experience, taken as the articulation of felt human needs, cannot serve as adequate proof for the truth of Christianity. And those who elevate it to the status of a source or standard of the truth of the Christian faith gradually rob the latter of its historical character and permit it to be reduced to a number of vague religious-ethical propositions. This, however, is nothing but a new form of the frequently but futilely attempted split between "idea" and "fact" in Christianity. Cut down the tree, and its fruit can no longer be picked. Stop up the spring, and fresh clear water will no longer flow from it.

[146] The most serious objection here is that this approach always proceeds from and ends in a radical dualism between faith and knowledge. While we acknowledge a distinction here, faith does have its own certainty that is not the certainty of scientific proof. But the dualism that has come to prevail in modern philosophy permits the entire created world to fall apart in two totally separate sections and is consequently in conflict with the unity of the human spirit, the unity of science and of truth, the unity of the world, the unity of the divine Being himself. For that reason it is also unable to reconcile believing and knowing with each other; in fact, it rather intensifies the conflict. This is intolerable and unnecessary. In its domain the heart is as good an organ for the perception of truth as the head. Faith with its grounds has as much validity as science with its proofs.

The unity of the human spirit rebels against such a separation, and the variety of forms such separation takes demonstrates its arbitrariness. In particular the historical content of the Christian has an objectivity that is not reducible to religious experience. Redemption includes liberation from falsehood and discovery of the truth. Objective religion is not the product of subjective religion but is given in divine revelation; dogma is not a symbolic interpretation of spiritual experience but an expression of truth given by God in his Word.

FAITH AND ITS GROUND

[147] We are searching, it should be recalled, for the means by which divine revelation is appropriated; for the best way of understanding how we receive the Word of God within. We have attempted thus far in this chapter to show that this "internal principle" of the Christian religion and theology cannot be located in the intellect or reason, in the heart or the will of the "natural" (unspiritual) person. No proofs and arguments, no religious experience or ethical satisfaction, after all, constitute the deepest ground of faith; they all presuppose a sturdier foundation on which they are built and from which they themselves derive their value. Nonetheless, it is true that Christian theology as an area of scientific inquiry must begin with the human subject. This is not subjectivism; all science begins here. Light presupposes the eye, and sound is perceptible only by the ear. All that is objective exists for us only by means of a subjective consciousness; without consciousness the whole world is dead for us. Always in human beings an internal principle has to correspond to the external principle (revelation) if there is to be a relation between object and subject.

So, too, one finds the internal principle corresponding to divine revelation here. Christian theology has always taken its position in the believing subject, in faith, in the believing community. The slogan that guides and controls Christian theology is: *per fidem ad intellectum* ("through faith to understanding"). Scripture itself directs us to this, to the inner illumination of the Holy Spirit. After God spoke to us by the Son, the Holy Spirit came to lead us into the truth. God not only gave us the Scriptures but also founded and maintains a church, which by faith accepts and confesses the Word of God.[27] The truth of God can be known only in faith. Though terms such as "rebirth," "purity of heart," "the Spirit of God," among others, are used in Scripture for the internal principle, the means by which revelation is appropriated, the preferred term is "faith." Since all knowledge is mediated through human consciousness, revelation too is known as an act of human consciousness, namely faith. The revelation of God is a system of words and deeds of God, which exist outside and independently of us. How could

27. See H. Bavinck, *Reformed Dogmatics*, ed. John Bolt (Grand Rapids: Baker Academic, 2003–8), I, 504–7 (#131).

they ever become our knowledge apart from our consciousness? The revelation of God is gospel, promise, the promise of forgiveness and salvation; but on our part nothing can match a promise except believing it: faith. Only by faith does a promise become our possession. Faith, accordingly, is the internal principle of knowledge (*principium internum cognoscendi*) of revelation and thus of religion and theology.

Both objectively and subjectively, revelation connects with nature, re-creation with creation. In all areas of life we start by believing. Our natural inclination is to believe. It is only acquired knowledge and experience that teach us skepticism. Faith is the foundation of society and the basis of science. Ultimately all certainty is rooted in faith. The universality of faith points to the importance of immediate, intuitive grasp of truth; our sure knowledge of reality is not limited to that which we obtain through our senses. It is immediate certainty rather than demonstrable certainty that makes possible life in community, in society. Augustine understood this. Those who do not believe, he says, never arrive at knowledge: "Unless you have believed you will not understand."[28] If people accepted the proposition, "I ought not to believe what I do not see," all the ties of family, friendship, and love would be ruptured. "If, then, it is the case that, when we do not believe what we cannot see, human society, itself, suffering the collapse of concord, will not stand, how much more should faith be applied to divine things, although they cannot be seen."[29] Arriving at certainty by a method other than mathematical and logical proofs, therefore, is not at all foreign to human nature; it is basic to our human living. Without believing as such, without faith, there cannot be normal people and a normal science.

[148] Nonetheless, general immediate certainty is not identical to religious faith. Saving faith has as its object not simply God's words and deeds as such, but the *grace* of God in Jesus Christ. Faith is also a matter of knowledge and truth, but above all it is trust and surrender to God, a religious relationship between a human being and God. The road to the human heart taken by the Spirit of God runs through the human head and human consciousness. Though revelation took place in space and time and the Christ was a historical flesh-and-blood human person, the object of Christian faith is invisible and not susceptible to observation. If a thing can be immediately observed by us, faith is superfluous; faith is opposed to sight (Rom. 8:24; 2 Cor. 5:7), a conviction and hope about things "unseen" (Heb. 11:1). Many people saw Jesus and still did not believe in him; only his disciples saw in him "a glory as of the only begotten of the Father" (John 1:14). The categories of truth and falsehood are inadequate here; faith includes a heartfelt *trust* in a total surrender to God, who has revealed himself in Christ, and a personal appropriation of the promises extended in the gospel.

28. Augustine, *The Trinity*, XV, 2, and passim.
29. Augustine, *Concerning Faith of Things Not Seen*, chap. 3; idem, *On the Profit of Believing*, chap. 10ff.; idem, *Confessions*, VI, 5.

Saving faith in the promises of God, in the grace of Christ, also differs from
faith in general in that our knowledge of it comes to us through the testimony
of others (e.g., the apostles). That is why knowledge of saving faith is bound to
Scripture; its true object, as Calvin puts it, is Christ "clothed with his gospel."[30]
Faith, consequently, reaches out in a single act to the person of Christ as well
as to Scripture. It embraces Christ as Savior and Scripture as the Word of God.
Therefore both approaches are true: by Christ to Scripture and by Scripture to
Christ; Scripture leads us to Christ and directs the thought and affections of
human beings to him who now dwells in heaven. Conversely, faith in Christ in
turn affects our belief in Scripture. It binds and fastens us securely to Scripture
and causes us to trust it in times of distress and death. Our soul, accordingly, may
be inseparably bound to Christ, the living Lord in the heavens, by the mystical
union forged by the Holy Spirit; still, to our consciousness, Christ, in fact the
whole realm of "things hoped for," exists only through the witness of God in his
Word. For that reason, saving faith always includes a cognitive component as well.
Our faith is bound to Holy Scripture; it rests upon the witness of the apostles
and prophets as the Word of God.

When faith is understood primarily as intellectual assent, as it is in Roman
Catholicism, it becomes objectified as "historical faith." The Vatican Council [I]
described faith as "a supernatural virtue by which, with the inspiration and help of
God's grace, we believe that what he has revealed is true, not because its intrinsic
truth is perceived by the natural light of reason, but because of the authority of
God himself who reveals, and who can neither deceive nor be deceived."[31] Faith,
in Roman Catholic thought, is a firm and certain assent to the truths of revelation
on the basis of the authority of God in Scripture and the church.[32] Understandably, this faith was considered insufficient for salvation and had to be augmented.
The addition by which this "unformed" faith becomes "formed" (*fides formata*) is
through another virtue in the will, namely love. Faith is hereby degraded to one of
the seven "preparations" for the "infused grace" of "justification," and the point of
gravity then shifts to love, i.e., good works. In this way the Reformation's *sola fide*
was denied in favor of the meritoriousness of intellectual assent as preparation
for the infused grace of justification.

While faith for Rome was only preparatory, in Reformation thought faith was
an act of the person newly regenerated by the special grace of the Holy Spirit.
Faith was religious through and through and had its own kind of certainty. The
Reformation made a fundamental distinction between "historical faith" and "saving
faith." In some cases historical faith might indeed precede saving faith and be of

30. J. Calvin, *Institutes*, III.ii.6; cf. Luther in J. Köstlin, *The Theology of Luther in Its Historical Development and Inner Harmony*, trans. Charles E. Hay, 2 vols. (Philadelphia: Lutheran Publication Society, 1897), II, 434ff.

31. *Documents of Vatican Council I, 1869–1870*, sel. and trans. John F. Broderick (Collegeville, MN: Liturgical Press, 1971), session III, "On Faith," chap. 3; H. Denzinger, *Sources*, #1789.

32. T. Aquinas, *Summa Theol.*, II, 2, qu. 2, art. 1, qu. 4, art. 2.

great value as such, but it was and remained essentially different from saving faith. For the Reformers, saving faith could not be reduced to knowledge but certainly included it. The Reformation was unanimous in confessing that saving faith is a gift of God. It was not the product of natural human powers, nor of common grace, but of the special grace of the Holy Spirit; it was an activity of the newly born-again person and therefore also sufficient for salvation. Here faith regains the central place it has in the New Testament; it does not have to be augmented by love; it is sufficient to obtain a share in all the benefits of salvation. Those who believe in that way are not in the vestibule but in the very sanctuary of Christian truth. They are incorporated into Christ, participants in all his benefits, heirs of eternal life.

With this deep view of faith, Reformation theologians struggled to correctly describe its nature. Divergent definitions were given: "knowing," "agreeing," "trusting," "taking refuge in," etc. What was important is the conviction in Reformation theology that faith was not a matter of knowing a number of doctrinal truths but consisted in the soul's union with the person of Christ according to the Scriptures and with Scripture as the Word of Christ. The object of saving faith was the grace of God in Christ; its foundation the witness of God in his Word; its author the Holy Spirit. In every respect it was religiously determined. Knowledge (*notitia*) and assent are included along with trust (*fiducia*), and it is the mistake of fideism along with pietism to be indifferent to knowledge and thus to doctrine and theology.

[149] Saving faith is accompanied by its own certainty that rests on the testimony and promises of God himself. Scripture speaks of the confidence (παρρησια, Heb. 4:16), the confidence of access (πεποιθησις, Eph. 3:12), the full assurance (πληροφορια, Heb. 6:11–12; 10:22) of faith; attributed to it are such qualities as courage (θαρσος, Matt. 9:2), rejoicing (καυχησις, Rom. 5:11), and joy (χαρα, 1 Pet. 1:8; etc.). It contrasts with doubt, anxiety, fear, distrust (Matt. 6:31; 8:26; 10:31; 14:31; 21:21; Mark 4:40; Luke 8:25; John 14:1; Rom. 4:20; James 1:6). Certainty is a characteristic of faith throughout Scripture. Even in the midst of the most severe trials, when everything is opposed to them, hoping against hope, believers stand firm as seeing the Invisible (Job 19:25; Pss. 23; 32; 51; Rom. 4:20–21; 5:1; 8:38; Heb. 11; etc.). They will sooner give up everything than renounce their faith. Nothing is more precious to them than faith, not their money, their goods, their honor, or even their lives. Faith is "the victory that overcomes the world" (1 John 5:4).

This certainty surpassed that known by Greek philosophy, both the "opinion" (δοξα) obtained by the senses and the "knowledge" (ἐπιστημη) gained by reflection. Aristotle made a further distinction between the knowledge that is based on proofs and that which rests on evidence. So in science there were three ways to obtain certainty: perception, argumentation, and evidence. This neatly opened the door for interminable debates between empiricists and rationalists but, instead of settling this, Christianity posited yet another certainty: the certainty of faith. Concretely and practically, this certainty was displayed to a skeptical world in the believing community, especially in its martyrs. Theoretically it was asserted and unfolded in Christian theology.

It is here, in the matter of certainty, that we see the real difference between Rome and the Reformation. The key question is whether the certainty of faith also includes the assurance of salvation, absolute certainty of one's own salvation. From Augustine on, this assurance of salvation has been denied and combated by the Roman Catholic Church and Catholic theology. Roman Catholic theologians do, however, recognize the certainty of faith with respect to the objective truths of revelation. "I would more easily doubt that I lived," wrote Augustine, "than doubt that there truth existed, which is 'clearly seen, being understood by the things that are made' (Rom. 1:20)."[33] Protestant theologians generally concur with this and no one has articulated this certainty of faith more sharply and vigorously than Calvin. In his thinking faith is "certain," "firm," "full and fixed," more "certainty" than "apprehension," "heartfelt confidence and assurance."[34] In the thinking of Lutheran as well as Reformed theologians, faith is "firm assent," a "certain knowledge," which excludes all doubt and uncertainty.[35]

By contrast, the moral certainty, for which Kant argued as the foundation of practical reason, divorces practical and theoretical reason and thus cannot sustain the truth of Christian revelation. Whereas, on Kant's terms, believing is a weaker form of knowing, in the Christian religion believing is certainty itself. Kant for the most part accepted three kinds of certainty—empirical, logical, and his own contribution, moral certainty. Because God is supersensible and thus unknowable, we are left with the moral certainty that arises from the moral truths we need for our life together. On practical and psychological grounds, human beings believe in the existence of God, the soul, and immortality. This is moral faith. The certainty secured by this faith is not theoretical in nature but practical and moral.

Kant's theory of moral certainty has exerted great influence on theology. After the authority of Scripture and the church had been undermined, people sought the foundation of religion and theology in moral certainty. The familiar text John 7:17,[36] already cited by Kant himself,[37] became the starting point of this school of thought. Again, though we can appreciate the profound truth in this notion of moral certainty, it is not advisable for us to exchange the religious certainty of Holy Scripture, the church, and Christian theology for Kant's brand of moral certainty.

To begin with, it needs saying that certainty is a state of mind and that it is the normal state of the human mind, just as health is of the body. Doubt, uncertainty,

---

33. Augustine, *Confessions*, VII, 10.

34. J. Calvin, *Institutes*, I.vii.5; II.ii.8; III.ii.14ff.; III.xiv.8; III.xiv.24.

35. H. Schmid, *Doctrinal Theology of the Evangelical Lutheran Church*, 412ff.; Heidelberg Catechism, Q&A 21; H. Heppe, *Dogmatik der evangelischen reformierten Kirche*, 384ff.

36. "If anyone chooses to do God's will, he will find out whether my teaching comes from God or whether I speak on my own" (NIV).

37. I. Kant, *Religion within the Limits of Reason Alone*, trans. Theodore M. Greene and Hoyt H. Hudson (New York: Harper & Row, 1934), 104.

by contrast, is unrest, unease, wretchedness. Strictly speaking, therefore, certainty as such cannot be said to be "moral." There is a moral certainty with respect to *moral* truths; there is also, however, a certainty that the intellect experiences when its pursuit of knowledge and truth is satisfied. When it finds truth, it is satisfied; it rests in it; it feels safe and secure. Certainty is rest, peace, joy, bliss; there is rest and relaxation in truth (*in veritate requies*). It is a mistake to set scientific (truth) certainty over against moral (practical) certainty; in reality no such dualism exists. The head and the heart, subjectively speaking, and objectively speaking, visible and invisible things, cannot be split in two in that way. Scientific "truth" can be held as established or certain on either moral or immoral grounds and it is the mind that must weigh the grounds for moral truths. The heart also has its say in our scientific explorations. For all these reasons, the moral certainty of Kant cannot replace the Christian's assurance of faith.

THE TESTIMONY OF THE HOLY SPIRIT

[150] Why then do we believe what we do? How can we be sure of what we believe? Believing itself is no proof for the truth of that which is believed. There is a huge difference between subjective certainty and objective truth. In the case of faith or belief, everything depends on the grounds on which it rests. From the beginning, as Christian theology wrestled with these questions, it has believed that intellectual and historical proof cannot provide the final ground of faith. While revelation may be made credible by proofs, it is and remains a truth of faith, a gift of grace. Only the Spirit of God can make a person inwardly certain of the truth of divine revelation. God's revelation can be believed only in a religious sense, on God's own authority. The ground for faith is the internal testimony of the Holy Spirit. Once again, Augustine is our guide: It is all grace. "God works our faith, acting in a marvelous way in our heart in order that we may believe."[38] Believing, after all, is always voluntary: "No one believes except willingly." To that end God by his grace bends the will and prompts us to believe with the intellect.[39]

Even Rome acknowledges this. The Jesuit Suarez[40] held the view that not only the object but also the ground of faith itself was a matter of faith. We do not only believe that Scripture is true *since* God has revealed himself there, but we also believe *that* God revealed himself there because God himself witnesses to that fact

38. Augustine, *Predestination of the Saints*, 2, 6.

39. Augustine, *Confessions*, XIII, 1; idem, *To Simplician—On Various Questions* (*De diversis quaestionibus ad Simplicianum*), 1, qu. 2, n. 21. Ed. note: available in J. H. S. Burleigh, *Augustine: Earlier Writings* (Philadelphia: Westminster, 1953), 404–5; idem, *On the Predestination of the Saints*, 19; idem, *On the Gift of Perserverance*, 16.

40. Ed. note: Francisco Suárez (1548–1617), Spanish Jesuit, is the founder of a "new" Thomism that conceived of the individual person as the object of divine grace; he proposed a system of "congruism," in which he used a notion of middle knowledge to teach that God only "foresaw" acts of human beings.

in Scripture. Revelation is simultaneously the "by which" (*quo*) it is believed and the "what" (*quod*) that is believed. "For it is one and the same act that believes God and believes by God." Just as the eye perceives the colors as well as the light by which those colors become visible, and as reason knows the derivative truths as well as the first principles by which the secondary truths become knowable, so faith knows both the revealed truths and the witness on which they rest, as divine. And the Vatican Council (I) decreed "no one can consent to the gospel preaching, as he must to obtain salvation, without the illumination and inspiration of the Holy Spirit."[41] Rome, therefore, finally adopts the same subjective standpoint as the churches of the Reformation. It is the Spirit of God alone who can make a person inwardly certain of the truth of divine revelation.

We must now address the problem that this position seems circular and leads to infinite regress: We believe Scripture is God's revelation because the Bible tells us so. Such circularity can be broken only by the inner conviction that God has spoken. This witness of God is the final ground of faith; our will to believe is, by God's grace, the final cause of our faith. Is this not pure fideism? Our answer is twofold: Our first and immediate response to the question "Why do you believe" must be "Because God has spoken" (*Deus dixit*). There is no other, deeper ground. But there is more to be said. God has left himself with faithful witnesses to his Word. The testimony of the prophets and apostles is the vehicle by which God speaks to us. Thomas uses the image of an ambassador in this regard.[42] An ambassador authenticates himself by the content of his message, e.g., by secrets that only the one who commissioned him can know. Thus the fulfillment of prophecy authenticates the prophet's message. In the case of the Gospels' teaching about our Lord we rely on the faithfulness of the apostolic witness to his life, death, and resurrection (e.g., 1 Cor. 15).

[151] We conclude from this that the Holy Spirit's testimony concerning the truth of Scripture is a witness confirmed in the body of Christ's believers on earth. The apostolic witness, the proclamation of the gospel, through the work of the Holy Spirit, created the church. In this way, speaking loosely but truthfully, Scripture (i.e. the gospel concerning Jesus Christ) created the church. Scripture's authority thus arises from its own content; it is not granted by the church's decision. This is what the Reformation teachers such as Calvin meant when they spoke of Scripture, through the work of the Holy Spirit, as self-authenticating (αὐτόπιστος). The entire church originates and exists by the Spirit's work alone. The entire application of salvation is a work of the Holy Spirit, and the witness to Scripture is but one of many of his activities in the community of believers. This testimony is not a private inner illumination but the experience of all Christians. It is also not, contrary to the rationalism of the Socinians, Remonstrants, and even some Reformed theologians such as Amyrald, an illumination of the

41. *Documents of Vatican Council I*, session 3, "De fide," chap. 3.
42. T. Aquinas, *Summa Theol.*, III, qu. 43, art. 1.

intellect. The Spirit leads us to accept in trusting faith the promises of God. These are communicated to us in Holy Writ. Scripture is recognized by its own truth through the testimony of the Spirit in the hearts of believers as members of the body of Christ. Although proofs and reasonings are of great value, this testimony surpasses them by far; it is more excellent than all reason or practical-moral intuition. Here is the only place that faith and theology can stand: Protestant and Roman Catholic theologians alike have to admit that the final and deepest ground of faith cannot lie outside us in proofs and arguments, in church and tradition, but can be found only in human beings themselves, in the religious subject as a member of the church of Jesus Christ.

[152] Taking this stance in the religious subject and the faith of the church is troubling to some theologians who desire more definitive historical-apologetic grounds. We need to remind ourselves that in fact all truth, all science, has a subjective starting point; objective reality can be approached only from the vantage point of the subject; the thing in itself is unknowable and does not exist for us. The obligation of Christian theologians is to think about this religiously and theistically. God who created all things placed human beings in a meaningful relationship to other created things. Here arises the conviction that the agreement between subject and object, which is foundational to all knowledge, originates from the divine mind of the Creator. It is the one selfsame Logos who made all things in and outside human beings. He is before all things, and they still continue jointly to exist through him (John 1:3; Col. 1:15–17). And it is the Spirit of God who is the source and agent of all life in humanity and in the world (Gen. 1:2; Pss. 33:6; 104:30; 139:7; Job 26:13; 33:4), especially of the intellectual, ethical, and religious life (Job 32:8; Isa. 11:2). All cognition of truth is a witness of the Spirit of God to the Word, by whom all things are made. All human knowledge is itself a witness of the human spirit to the corresponding phenomena outside itself. Our spirit does nothing but continually bear witness to the truth that comes to us from without. That spirit does not, by thinking and reasoning, bring forth that truth from within itself; it does not create or produce it; it only *re*-produces it and *re*-flects on it. The truth is antecedent to and independent of the human spirit; it rests within itself, in the Logos, in which all things have their existence. As human beings we do not create truth; we grasp it, absorb it, and bear witness to it.

By analogy, what is true in general about human knowledge is also true about the truth of the gospel. Jesus witnessed to what he had seen and heard (John 3:32). He bore witness to the truth (John 18:37); similarly, the apostles were witnesses of the Word of Life they had seen and touched in Christ (John 15:27; 1 John 1:3). We do not discover this truth on our own; rather, it has found us. Having been found by the truth, we become its witnesses. All truth turns those who know it into witnesses, proclaimers, prophets. Entering into our spirits, it brings its own witness along with it; it engenders that witness in us by itself. This witness of the human spirit to truth is the presupposition and foundation, as well as an analogy, of the testimony of the Holy Spirit.[43] But analogy is not identity. The external foundation (*principium externum*) of the Christian religion is not the general revelation of God in nature but a special revelation of God in Christ. The internal principle (*principium internum*) must correspond to that external principle. Because the "natural" (unspiritual) person is not equipped to discern the things of the Spirit, a rebirth and special illumination of the Holy Spirit must take place. Promised by the prophets of the Old Testament (Jer. 31:34; Ezek. 36:25f.; Joel 2:28f.), the Spirit, the Paraclete (John 15:26; 16:14) was poured out on the day of Pentecost (Acts 2). It is the Spirit that creates the new humanity where God's dwelling will be forever.

The truth of the gospel is compelling in much the same way that all "first principles" are. The moral law is also αὐτόπιστος; that stealing is wrong cannot be proven to someone who rejects the moral law. It is powerful because it exists, posits, and maintains itself. It compels because it is categorical and suffers no excuses or exceptions. The same situation prevails in theology. Proofs here are possible only with respect to inferred propositions. The deity of Christ can be proven to the person who recognizes the authority of Scripture. But the authority of Scripture rests in itself and cannot be proven. Holy Scripture is self-attested (αὐτόπιστος) and therefore the final ground of faith. No deeper ground can be advanced. While it is possible for a Christian to respond to the question "Why do you believe the Bible?" by pointing to marks and criteria of Scripture, the majesty of its style, the fulfillment of prophecy, the sublimity of its content, the depth of its ideas, the abundant fruit it has borne, etc., are not the grounds for a believer's faith. The soul's bond to Scripture as the Word of God lies behind the [believer's] consciousness and underneath the proofs. It is mystical in nature—like the belief in the first principles of the various sciences. "God said it" (*Deus dixit*) is the foundational principle (*primum principium*) to which all dogmas, including the dogma of Scripture, can be traced.

[153] This conclusion sounds arbitrary to many. After all, do not Muslims appeal to the same logic in defending their faith in the Qur'an? Do believers have anything more than their subjectivity as a response to opponents of the faith? In response, we note that unbelief too is rooted in the human heart. Proofs and arguments affect both faith and unbelief but are conclusive in neither. The believer is not disadvantaged here. In addition, God is known universally even to those who deny it (Rom. 1:18ff.); he is sufficiently knowable to those who seek him and also sufficiently hidden to those who run away from him. "There is enough light for those who only desire to see and enough darkness for those of a contrary disposition. There is enough clarity to illumine the elect and enough darkness to humble them. There is enough darkness to render the reprobate sightless and enough clarity to condemn them and to render them inexcusable."[44] In addition,

43. J. Calvin, *Institutes*, II.viii.1.
44. B. Pascal, *Oeuvres*, 3 vols. (Paris: Hachette, 1869), I, 345.

the inner testimony of the Spirit is not private but universal. The church of all ages bears witness to Scripture as the Word of God. Nurtured in community, faith does not come into being by the insight of our intellect or a decision of our will but by the gracious and overpowering illumination of God's Spirit. That is why most people stay in the faith communities in which they were born and nurtured; their Scriptures confirm what they experience in community.

Conversions do, of course take place; the history of Christian missions depends on it and is proof of it. Such conversions are always of a religious-ethical, a spiritual nature. What really causes us to believe, or change our beliefs, is not only the insight of our intellect, nor primarily a decision of our will, but a power that is superior to us, bends our will, illumines our mind, and without compulsion still effectively takes our thoughts and reflections captive to the obedience of Christ (2 Cor. 10:5). Believing is an immediate (i.e., unmediated by proofs) linkage of the human consciousness to divine revelation. It is also a transformation of our will that is made willingly: "No one believes except willingly" (*Nemo credit nisi volens*). Because our wills are transformed and renewed, our believing is a free act of self-denial. True knowledge of God is compelling but never coerced. The *Letter to Diognetus* states beautifully: "It is not like God to use compulsion."[45] Believing is not arbitrary, but neither is it blind. Just as the human eye, seeing the sun, is immediately convinced of its reality, so the regenerate person "sees" the truth of God's revelation. Believers cannot relinquish this faith any more than they can relinquish themselves.

Opposition to faith also comes from within. Sins of the heart and errors of the mind gang up on faith as believers continue to experience the conflict within between "spirit" and "flesh," the "old" and the "new." As long as believers are on earth, this kind of spiritual dualism remains in them. This should not destroy faith but confirm it; what better proof do we have that our faith is not native to our soul, or the product of a syllogism, or an act of our own will? Yet, we believe! Our struggles with the old sinful flesh demonstrate that our own spirit does not by nature impel us to call God our Father and to count ourselves among his children. Only the Holy Spirit can testify to our soul, "I am your salvation," and we easily recognize how different that testimony is from the temptation of Satan, when he whispers, "Peace, peace, and no danger." "Can a person, impelled by the devil, possibly call God Abba! Father! in faith?"[46] That is the first assurance of the Holy Spirit: we are God's children.

[154] It is important that we not restrict this witness of the Holy Spirit to Holy Scripture alone. Jesus promised the Holy Spirit as the Comforter, the Spirit of truth, who leads first the apostles, then, by their word, also all other believers, into the truth. He witnesses of Christ to them and glorifies him (John 14:17;

---

45. *Diogn.*, chap. 7.

46. Johann Heinrich Heidegger, *Corpus Theologicae Christianae*, 2 vols. (Zürich: J. H. Bodmer, 1700), XXIV, 78.

15:26; 16:14). To that end he convicts people of sin (John 16:8–11), regenerates them (John 3:3), and prompts them to confess Christ as Lord (1 Cor. 12:3). He further assures them of their adoption as children of God and of their heavenly inheritance (Rom. 8:14f.; 2 Cor. 1:22; 5:5; Eph. 1:13; 4:30), makes known all the things believers have received from God (1 Cor. 2:12; 1 John 2:20; 3:24; 4:6–13), and in the church is the author of all Christian virtues and all spiritual gifts (Gal. 5:22; 1 Cor. 12:8–11). From this it is evident that the Spirit is intimately bound up with the full faith life of believers. The Holy Spirit communicates in, with, and through our own spirit in faith. Faith itself is the work of the Holy Spirit (1 Cor. 12:3) and receives its seal and confirmation in the Spirit of adoption. Believing itself is a witness of the Holy Spirit in our hearts and through our spirit.

Since our sinful spirits are often at odds with the Spirit of God and we must be guided toward greater obedience, an important work of the Holy Spirit is to assure us that we are God's children. The illumination of the Holy Spirit is not the cognitive source of Christian truth; it only seals in our hearts the truth of Scripture and salvation history. Faith is concentrated on the historical realities of redemption, and results in trust that these historical acts are God's saving acts for us. It is the same Spirit that inspired the apostolic witness that now seals the truth of that witness in believers' hearts. Christians submit to Scripture because they believe it is a divine Word, a Word from God. In this connection it is not the authenticity, nor the canonicity, nor even the inspiration, but the *divinity* of Scripture, its divine authority, which is the true object of the testimony of the Holy Spirit. All criticism of Scripture that detracts from this divinity of Holy Scripture is profoundly disturbing because it undermines Scripture's witness concerning our adoption as children, the hope of glory, and the assurance of salvation. Hence the doctrine of Scripture entails a profound religious interest. Its God-breathed and God-breathing character and authority is not an indifferent matter, borrowed from non-Christian sources, but is confessed by that community on the basis of God's Word and is integrally connected with its own existence. Because Christ is the heart of Scripture, our faith in Scripture increases and decreases along with our trust in Christ. What is at stake with the authority of Scripture is the truth of Christianity itself and the testimony of the Holy Spirit, who illumines our intellect, opens our hearts, and assures us that "the Spirit is the truth" (1 John 5:6). This testimony is provided in Scripture itself, is embodied in the blessings the church has experienced through the ages in obedience to that word and testimony, and is implied in the bond that individual believers have to Scripture, a bond that comes to expression in the personal conviction that the Word of God is the truth.

[155] This testimony of the Holy Spirit is not nullified by the variable responses to it among believers. There are differences in confession and they are significant, not the least in the selectivity with which they approach Scripture. Still, when it comes to convictions concerning Scripture itself, there is remarkable unity among different church groups. The unity of the Christian church with respect

to Scripture is much greater than in any other dogma, not even excepting that of the Trinity and the deity of Christ. Scripture has been given to the whole church, and the Spirit's testimony concerning Scripture is a cornerstone of the church's very existence. Take away the testimony of the Holy Spirit, not only in relation to Scripture, but to all the truths of redemption, and there is no more church. For the witness the Holy Spirit bears to Scripture as the Word of God is but a single tone in the song he has put on the lips of the believing community. It is but a small part of that splendid divine work assigned to the Holy Spirit: to cause the fullness of Christ to dwell in his community.

We must never underestimate the power of the Holy Spirit and the Scriptures even and especially against its foes. As the witness rendered by the Holy Spirit in the hearts of all the children of God concerning the truth as it is in Christ Jesus our Lord, it does not fail to impress even the most stubborn adversary. In much the same way that the human conscience is not rendered powerless by immoral people who oppose its witness, and science is not rendered mute by vestiges of superstition and skepticism, so Scripture is not ineffectual because its truth falls on deaf ears in unspiritual people. The power of all these moral forces lies precisely in the fact that they do not offer rational proof for themselves but with sublime majesty confront the consciousness of every human being. They are powerful as a result of the authority with which they assert themselves. Scripture has maintained its authority in the church of Christ to this day. It has prompted all believers— including the greatest minds and noblest spirits—to yield to its authority. What power in the world is comparable to that of Scripture? The testimony of the Holy Spirit is the triumph of the foolishness of the cross over the wisdom of the world, the victory of the thoughts of God over the deliberations of human beings. In this sense the apologetic value of the testimony of the Holy Spirit is second to none. Surely this is the victory that overcomes the world: our faith! (1 John 5:4).

FAITH AND THEOLOGY

[156] Is this resting in the testimony of the Holy Spirit for certainty of faith enough? A Christian believer does not need more; he or she does not *need* a scientific theology. Yet, the Christian church, not content to limit itself to faith, almost from the beginning pursued knowledge of religious truth and gave birth to a special branch of science: theology. Not all believers fully approved; some Christians challenged and continue to challenge the validity and value of theology. In the words of Tertullian: "As far as we are concerned, there is no need for curiosity after Jesus Christ, nor for inquiry after the gospel. When we believe, we desire nothing beyond believing."[47] God, it was also said, does not desire anything from Christians other than good works, and it is better "with a

---

47. Tertullian, *The Prescription against Heretics*, 8.

simple unfettered mind-set to pursue one's own course than to devote a lot of care to the study of decrees and learned opinions."[48] There is a long-standing tradition of hostility to theology in the Christian church, preferring a simpler and more practical Christianity; "heart and hands over head" is not a new slogan.

Following Renaissance humanism's repudiation of medieval Scholasticism, Reformation thinkers initially concentrated also on the practical benefits of faith. Luther's assessment of Aristotle, Scholasticism, and reason is well known. Melanchthon, in the first edition of his *Loci*, wrote: "This is what it is to know Christ: to know his benefits, not what you (Scholastics) teach, to gaze upon his natures and the modes of this incarnation." Zwingli said that being a Christian "did not consist in prattling about Christ but to walk as he walked." Calvin puts an equally strong emphasis on this practical side of the faith.[49] But many went beyond this and rejected all theology, especially within the Anabaptist tradition and later in Pietist circles. In the seventeenth century when in Protestant churches the Scholastic treatment of theology began to make headway, there was reaction on all sides. Calixtus and Cocceius, Spener and Zinzendorf, Fox and Wesley, etc., were all driven by a desire for more simplicity and truth in the doctrine of faith. The trend toward a practical, nondogmatic Christianity intensified as the nineteenth century unfolded, thanks, among other things, to historical criticism and Schleiermacher's theology of feeling. Over time, antipathy to dogmatics became more general. Theology became regarded as the offspring of an ill-starred marriage between original Christian faith and Greek philosophy in which the pure, simple gospel of Jesus had been falsified.[50] The life of Christian love was said to have been turned into cold and arid orthodoxy, a "knowledge" that conflicts with modern science and thus alienates the educated classes from the Christian faith.[51]

Some of these complaints against theology are valid. It has sometimes lacked appropriate humility and degenerated into hairsplitting. All too often it has forgotten that our knowing on earth is a knowing in part and looking into a mirror dimly. Sometimes it seemed to proceed from the idea that it could answer all questions and resolve all issues. It has often been lacking in modesty, tenderness, and simplicity. Theology especially ought to take to heart the admonition "not to think of itself more highly than it ought to think" (cf. Rom. 12:3) and avoid speculation. It is better to honestly admit that a thing is not clear than to make a wild guess. However, abuse does not cancel out use (*abusus non tollit usum*), and ignoring theology reduces the Christian religion to feeling or morality. Not

48. John of Damascus, "De haeresibus," *Opera Omnia* (Basel, 1575), 585.

49. J. Köstlin, *Theology of Luther*, I, 137ff.; P. Melanchthon, *Loci Comm.*, ed. Augusti (1821), 9; H. Bavinck, *De Ethiek. van Ulrich Zwingli* (Kampen: Zalsman, 1880), 119; J. Calvin, *Institutes*, I.ii.2; I.v.9; I.xii.1; idem, *Commentary*, on Rom. 1:19.

50. A. von Harnack, *History of Dogma*, I, 17; E. Hatch, *The Influence of Greek Ideas and Usages upon the Christian Church* (London, 1890); cf. also J. Kaftan, *The Truth of the Christian Religion*, trans. George Ferries, 2 vols. (Edinburgh: T&T Clark, 1894).

51. Cf., e.g., J. Kaftan, *Glaube und Dogma*, 3rd ed. (Bielefeld: Velhagen & Klasing, 1889).

only is theology important for the sake of clarity; it is also important to avoid the one-sided interpretations of the gospel that arise from a split between faith and metaphysics. The gospel is based in reality; if God and the history of salvation are not real but only states of our souls' desires and moral longing, all religion is a delusion. Religion that consists only of moral practice is of little comfort; all our efforts at self-help have not been able to save us. Efforts to locate a "pure" gospel behind the dogmas of the Christian church lead to a canon within the canon and break fellowship with the universal church of all ages. Invalidating the history of dogma also forfeits the opportunity to influence the culture and science of our own day. The Christian life slips into the pathologies of mysticism and separatism, and scientific thought is not freed from error by the truth of Christ. What the essence of Christianity is, in what things the revelation or Word of God consists, who the person of Christ is—all these questions are not decided by the apostles; everyone settles these matters in accordance with his or her own insights. There is no apostolically defined church left, only individual cults.

Once this principle of criticism was introduced into the catholic consensual tradition of Christianity there was no stopping. Close scrutiny of the history of dogma reveals that the doctrines of the Logos, the Trinity, the first and second Adam (etc.), all of them dogmas that are said to prove the admixture of Greek philosophy, are found, perhaps not in so many words but certainly in substance, already in Scripture. In their view the promise of the Spirit who would lead God's people into all truth proves to have been empty. The church in faith did not overcome the world; the reverse is true. If so, then the apostolic witness itself, the New Testament writings included, must also come under the sharp knife of critical surgery. Apparently, to such minds, the apostles, particularly Paul and John, already falsified the gospel. As early as 1893 Ernst von Bunsen asserted that Paul changed the gospel of Jesus into a speculative theology, and many people concur with him.[52] Although it is hard to excise a gospel fact such as the resurrection of Christ, nonetheless people do try to rob it of its religious value.[53] The result is that the history of dogma becomes completely suspect; it becomes one enormous aberration of the human, i.e., of the Christian, spirit. In a word: the history of dogmas is (as in Strauss) the history of their criticism.[54]

The validity and justification of theology arises from the essence of the Christian faith itself as divine revelation addresses humanity in its totality and in all its life relationships. Revelation has the whole world as its object. In all areas of life it joins the battle against deception. It offers material for the profoundest thought processes, and in the field of science plants the knowledge of God alongside and

---

52. Ernst Bunsen, *Die Reconstruction der Kirchlichen Autorität* (Leipzig: Brockhaus, 1893); see also H. Bavinck, *Reformed Dogmatics*, I, 117–18 (#36).

53. A. von Harnack, *History of Dogma*, V, 83ff.

54. Even Auguste Sabatier says, "The history of a dogma is its true criticism." *Les religions d'autorité et la religion de l'esprit* (Paris: Librairie Fischbacher, 1904), xi; cf. idem, *Esquisse* (Paris: Fischbacher, 1898), 208ff.

in organic connection with that of humanity and the world. This is also the reason
for theology's close relationship with philosophy.

[157] From the beginning, Christian theology has used the insights of the
philosophic tradition to understand and explain the faith. Christian theology did
not simply adopt one philosophic system wholesale but borrowed from many,
though always testing philosophies by revelation. Theology thus arises from the
church as believers think through the precepts of the faith, making selective use
of philosophy as its servant. The early church only utilized the philosophy that
was most suited for thinking through and defending the truth of God. They
went to work eclectically and did not take over any single philosophical system,
be it either from Plato or from Aristotle, but with the aid of Greek philosophy
produced a Christian philosophy of their own. The church was at all times alert
against the misuse of philosophy; it not only rejected gnosticism but also condemned Origenism. After initially being wary of Scholasticism and philosophy,
the Reformers soon realized that if they were to avoid becoming a sect, their
theological work needed philosophy. Even Luther and Melanchthon, therefore,
resumed the use of philosophy and recognized its usefulness.[55] Calvin assumed this
high position from the start, saw in philosophy an "outstanding gift of God," and
was followed in this assessment by all Reformed theologians. Theology only works
with philosophy in a proper manner when it brings along its own criteria, tests
all philosophy by them, and takes over what it deems true and useful. No single
philosophical system serves here; what theology needs is philosophy in general.

[158–59] Although theology moves "from faith to understanding" (Augustine), it is nevertheless distinct from faith and is a fruit of the church as organism
rather than institute. The distinction between faith and theology is clear from
efforts in the church to distinguish the basic truths that must be affirmed to be
a Christian from the larger body of truths discussed by theologians. The Roman
Catholic notion of "implicit faith," as well as the Protestant distinction between
"infused theology" (all believers) and "acquired theology" (scientific theologians
only), or later between "fundamental" and "non-fundamental" articles of faith,[56]
all reflect the distinction between faith and theology both in content and scope.
What they led to, unfortunately, was the unhelpful question about the minimum
amount of knowledge required in order to be saved. Protestant theologians who
wrestled with this issue were aware of the juxtaposition—employed in the description of faith—of a certain knowledge "by which I hold as true all that God has
revealed in his Word" and the "confidence that all my sins have been forgiven me

55. Cf. H. Schmid, *Doctrinal Theology of the Evangelical Church*, §5.
56. Thus John Calvin: "For not all the articles of true doctrine are of the same sort. Some are so
necessary to know that they should be certain and unquestioned by all men as the proper principles of
religion. Such are: God is one; Christ is God and the Son of God; our salvation rests in God's mercy;
and the like. Among the churches there are other articles of doctrine disputed, which still do not break
the unity of faith" (*Institutes*, IV.i.12; IV.ii.1).

for Christ's sake."[57] This could give rise to locating the point of gravity either in the "general" faith or in the "special" faith; emphasizing "knowledge" or "confidence." Once again, these discussions led in some quarters to divisions among believers along the lines of head and heart, doctrine and life, and rationalism versus pietism.

Although the distinction between essential and nonessential articles of faith was important for ecumenical relations between Protestant groups, it had the potential for reducing the faith to quantitative measurement. Such an arithmetic of belief obscured the qualitative, gracious, personal, organic relation to Christ so important in the Reformation protest against Roman Catholic sacramentalism and its doctrine of implicit faith. For the Reformers, faith is trust in the grace of God and not calculable; it is a personal relation to Christ and not subject to quantifiable addition. The content of faith is not reducible to an arithmetic addition of articles. All believers, in principle, share the same knowledge and trust in the grace of God. There is a difference between faith and theology, not in essence but in degree. Theology is a source of faith; its "object" is accessible only through faith, it reflects on the content of faith, and it is to be done in faith. Theology itself bears a religious character that also belongs to the knowledge of faith. "A theology of the unregenerate" is possible in the same sense as a "historical faith," but it corresponds equally as little or as much to true theology as "historical faith" does to "saving faith." True Christian theology deepens and broadens faith-knowledge but remains inextricably connected to it. Faith and theology both need each other. Faith preserves theology from secularization; theology preserves faith from separatism. Thus the church and theological schools ought to be in solidarity with each other; good theology must be situated in the life of the believing community of faith. Faith and theology have in common the principle, the Word of God; the object, the knowledge of God; the goal, the glory of God. The distorted relation that everywhere exists today between the church and theology is a disaster for both.

Since theology is believing reflection on faith, we must also consider the role of reason in theology. Reason and faith must not be dualistically separated by placing faith above (*supra*) or even opposed (*contra*) to reason. Threatening on the one hand is rationalism and on the other supernaturalism. Faith is, after all, not an organ or faculty next to or above reason but a disposition or habit of reason itself. Faith is a voluntary act of the human consciousness—animals do not believe—and as a habit becomes the natural breath of the children of God. Believing is a *free* act: Christians do not believe on command, out of fear, or in response to violence. Their submission to the Word of God is not slavery but freedom. In that sense faith is not a sacrifice of the intellect but mental health (*sanitas mentis*). Faith does not relieve Christians of the desire and need to study and reflect on faith; it spurs them on to that end. Theology requires disciplined preparation in the arts more broadly. There is no admission to the temple of theology except by way of

57. Ed. note: Bavinck takes this from the Heidelberg Catechism, Lord's Day 7, Q&A 21.

the study of the arts. Indispensable to the practitioner of the science of theology is philosophical, historical, and linguistic preparatory training. This equips one for the task of building a theological system organically from the whole of Scripture in its literary diversity. Then follows the task of intellectually mining the material gathered from Scripture and recapitulating it into a meaningful system of thought in the language of the day.

It is good to emphasize the importance of utilizing the whole of Scripture in the theological task. Dogma has to be built, not on a few isolated texts, but on Scripture in its entirety. It must arise organically from the principles that are everywhere present for that purpose in Scripture. The doctrines of God, of humanity, of sin, of Christ, etc., after all, are not to be found in a few pronouncements but are spread throughout Scripture and are contained, not only in a few proof texts, but also in a wide range of images and parables, ceremonies and histories. No part of Scripture may be neglected. Failure to be true to this principle has led to arbitrary selectiveness in using Scripture, to one-sidedness and error in theology and to pathology in the religious life. The Marcionite error of rejecting the Old Testament has repeatedly reemerged in the Christian church and plays a large role in modern theology as well.

The whole of Scripture led the church to its dogmatic conclusions; the doctrines of the Trinity, the two natures of Christ, vicarious atonement, the sacraments, etc., are not based on single scriptural proof texts but are constructed from many givens distributed throughout the Bible. Dogmas are concise summaries in our own language of everything Scripture teaches about the subject in question. In this task it is often necessary to use language that is not literally taken from Scripture. Catholic as well as Protestant theologians defended the right to do this, not because they wanted to be less but more scriptural. To their mind, Scripture above all came into its own in all its splendor not when a single text was cited, but when the whole truth contained in many texts was condensed and reproduced in a dogma. God has not called us to repeat but to *re*-flect on what he has thought and laid out in his revelation. It is the task of the thinking theological mind to gather up and recapitulate all truth in one system.[58] System is the supreme *desideratum* in all science. Also, theology does not rest until it has discovered the unity underlying revelation. It may not impose that system from without, nor press the truth into a philosophical system that is foreign to its nature. But it keeps searching until the system that is present in the object itself has been reproduced in the human mind. Faith and reason do not clash; the Christian religion is a "reasonable form of worship" (λογικη λατρεια, Rom. 12:1).

[160] The theological task also calls for humility. Christian theology always has to do with mysteries that it knows and marvels at but does not fully comprehend and fathom. These must not be identified with the New Testament notion of mystery. The New Testament term μυστηριον does not denote an intellectually

---

58. See H. Bavinck, *Reformed Dogmatics*, I, 38–46 (##6–8).

uncomprehended and incomprehensible truth of faith, but a matter that was formerly hidden in God, was then made known in the history of salvation culminating in Christ, and is now understood by believers.[59] Neither is it a secret gnosis available only to an elite, nor is it unknown because of the great divide between the natural and the supernatural. The divide is not so much metaphysical as it is spiritual—*sin* is the barrier. Sin, not ignorance or stupidity, is the barrier to the full vision of God. The wonder of God's love may not be fully comprehended by believers in this age, but what is known in part and seen in part *is* known and seen. In faithful wonder, the believer is not conscious of living in the face of mystery that surpasses reason and thus it is not an intellectual burden. Rather, in the joy of God's grace there is intellectual liberation. Faith turns to wonder; knowledge terminates in adoration; and confession becomes a song of praise and thanksgiving. Faith is the knowledge that is life, "eternal life" (John 17:3).

59. Hermann Cremer, *Biblico-Theological Lexicon of New Testament Greek*, trans. D. W. Simon and William Urwick (Edinburgh: T&T Clark, 1872), s.v. "προνοια"; Johann Caspar Suicerus, *Thesaurus ecclesiasticus* (Amsterdam: J. H. Wetsten, 1682), s.v. "μυστηριον." Ed. note: Bavinck cites the following Scripture passages on μυστηριον: on the hiddenness of the kingdom of God: Matt. 13:11; Mark 4:11; Luke 8:10; Rev. 1:20; 17:5, 7; on the universal decree of God concerning redemption in Christ: Rom. 16:25; Eph. 1:9; 3:3; 6:19; Col. 1:26–27; 2:2; 4:3; on the manner in which it is carried out: Rom. 11:25; 1 Cor. 15:51; 2 Thess. 2:7; Rev. 10:7; on the mystery now being made public by the apostles as the stewards of the mystery of God: Rom. 16:25–26; Col. 1:26; Matt. 13:11; 1 Cor. 4:1; on its becoming increasingly manifest in history: 1 Cor. 15:51–52; 2 Thess. 2:7; on its being made known to believers: Matt. 11:25; 13:11; 16:17; Rom. 11:33; 1 Cor. 1:30; on walking by faith because walking by faith, we know in part, and now see in a mirror dimly: Rom. 11:34; 1 Cor. 13:12; 2 Cor. 5:7.

PART II

THE TRIUNE GOD AND CREATION

7

KNOWING GOD

DIVINE MYSTERY AND INCOMPREHENSIBILITY

[161] The knowledge of God is the exclusive content of theology. All the doctrines treated in dogmatic theology—whether they concern the universe, humanity, Christ, and so forth—are but the explication of the one central dogma of the knowledge of God. All things are considered in light of God, subsumed under him, traced back to him as the starting point. This knowledge is inseparable from our self-knowledge. Augustine desired to know nothing other and more than God and himself. "I desire to know God and the soul. Nothing more? No: nothing at all."[1] For that reason, too, Calvin began his *Institutes* with the knowledge of God and the knowledge of ourselves, and for that reason the Genevan catechism, answering the first question, "What is the chief end of human life?" stated, "That human beings may know the God by whom they were created."[2]

Mystery is the lifeblood of theological reflection. From the start of its labors, dogmatic theology is shrouded in mystery; it stands before God the incomprehensible One. This knowledge leads to adoration and worship; to know God is to live. Knowing God is possible for us because God is personal, exalted above the earth and yet in fellowship with human beings on earth. Good theology puts this

---

1. Augustine, *Soliloquies*, bk. I, ch. 2.
2. Cf. Westminster Shorter Catechism, Q&A 1, in *Creeds of Christendom*, ed. P. Schaff and rev. D. S. Schaff, 6th ed. (New York: Harper & Row, 1931; repr., Grand Rapids: Baker Academic, 1990), III, 676. Ed. note: On the Genevan Catechism, including a translation of it, see I. John Hesselink, *Calvin's First Catechism: A Commentary*, Columbian Studies in Reformed Theology (Louisville: Westminster John Knox, 1997). A translation of the catechism is also available online: http://www.ondoctrine.com/2cal0504.htm.

knowledge of God on public display. It resists allowing theology to degenerate into rhetoric, a theology merely of *words*; it seeks the heart of the matter, knowing God in order to worship him, love him, and serve him. Such theology is never a dry and academic exercise; it is eminently practical and superlatively fruitful for life. The knowledge of God in Christ, after all, is life itself (Ps. 89:16; Isa. 11:9; Jer. 31:34; John 17:3).

We need to pause here to note how audacious is our claim to know God and speak for him. How dare we? How can we? We are human and he is the Lord our God. Between him and us there seems to be no such kinship or communion as would enable us to name him truthfully. Can we really and truly *know* God? Scripture leaves us in no doubt here, not for a moment. In Scripture, therefore, the knowability of God is never an issue. The fool may say in his heart, "There is no God," but those who open their eyes perceive from all directions the witness of his existence, of his eternal power and deity (Isa. 40:26; Acts 14:17; Rom. 1:19–20). We dare speak of God for only one reason: he has revealed himself. Our knowledge of God does not arise from our own investigation and reflection, but because God on his part revealed himself to us in nature and history, in prophecy and miracle, by ordinary and by extraordinary means. The purpose of God's revelation, according to Scripture, is precisely that human beings may know God and so receive eternal life (John 20:31).

Thanks to that revelation, it is certain, first of all, that God is a person, a conscious and freely willing being, not confined to the world but exalted high above it. The pantheistic understanding that equates God and the world is absolutely foreign to Scripture. Although exalted above the earth, God is also fully immanent and actively relates to a particular people. God's special relationship with his people Israel, with Zion as his dwelling place, suggests not confinement or limitation but election. God chose a people for himself. Evolutionist accounts of Israel's religion do not do justice to the biblical account. Israel's religion did not evolve from henotheism to ethical monotheism but is rooted in the divine call of Abraham/Israel and God's initiative in establishing a covenant with Israel. Revelation is the foundation of Israel's religion, though it must be granted that her actual religious practice often failed to live up to the revealed divine call and will. Though the Old Testament refers to "other gods," it never takes their reality seriously. Israel's God is God alone, the Lord of heaven and earth. He is the Creator of heaven and earth, who manifests himself in various ways to specific people at particular times.

This Old Testament revelation is never exhaustive of God's being but partial and preparatory to the supreme and permanent revelation in Jesus Christ. It is, however, a *true* revelation. Old Testament events such as Jacob's dream at Bethel, Moses and the burning bush, the pillar of fire leading the people of Israel, the thunder on Mount Sinai, etc., do not encompass and confine God but are genuine signs and pledges of God's presence. This personal God who comes near, who in his revelation limits himself, as it were, to specific places, times, and persons, is at the same time infinitely exalted above the whole realm of nature and every creature. Throughout the Old Testament these two elements occur hand in hand: God is with those who are of a contrite and humble spirit and nevertheless is the high and lofty One who inhabits eternity (Isa. 57:15). The New Testament teaches us the same thing: God dwells in inaccessible light. No one has seen him or can see him (John 1:18; 6:46; 1 Tim. 6:16). He is above all change (James 1:17), time (Rev. 1:8; 22:13), space (Acts 17:27–28), and creatures (Acts 17:24). No one knows him except the Son and the Spirit (Matt. 11:27; 1 Cor. 2:11). But God has caused his fullness to dwell in Christ bodily (Col. 2:9), resides in the church as in his temple (1 Cor. 3:16), and makes his home in those who love Jesus and keep his Word (John 14:23). Or to put it in modern theological language, in Scripture the personality and the absoluteness of God go hand in hand.

[162] This unity of God's personality and absoluteness is not maintained outside the revelation given in Scripture. Philosophers, notably in the Platonist tradition, see God (the Good) as the distant One, the unknowable One, transcending even Being itself. In Plotinus only negative theology remains; we can only say what God is not. Gnosticism went even further, considering God as absolutely unknowable and ineffable, the eternal silent abyss. Christian theology agrees that human knowledge of God is not exhaustive; we cannot know God in his essence. Since no description or naming of God can be adequate, human language struggles even to say what God is not. The *Letter of Barnabas* already poses the question: "If the Son of God had not become incarnate, then how could human beings have beheld him and lived?" Justin Martyr calls God inexpressible, immobile, nameless. Even words such as "Father," "God," and "Lord" are not real names but "appellations derived from [his] beneficence and works." If we nevertheless call him "one," "good," "Father," "Creator," "Lord," and so forth, we do not thereby express his true essence but only his power. He even transcends oneness. As Athanasius puts it, he "transcends all being and human comprehension."[3] Origen, Eusebius, and many other theologians of the early centuries expressed themselves similarly, as did Augustine.[4]

In his description of God, Augustine proceeds from the concept of "being." He is the One who is, as the name YHWH indicates. This is his true name, the name that indicates what he is in himself; all other names indicate what he is toward us (*Serm.* 6 n. 4; *Serm.* 7 n. 7). Therefore, when we want to say what he

3. *Barn.*, chap. 5; Justin Martyr, *1 Apology*, 61; idem, *2 Apology*, 6; idem, *Dialogue with Trypho*, 127; Irenaeus, *Against Heresies*, IV, 20; Clement of Alexandria, *Stromateis*, V, 11–12; idem, *Paedagogus*, I, 8; Athanasius, *Against the Pagans*, 2.

4. Origen, *On First Principles*, I, 1, 5ff.; idem, *Against Celsus*, VI, 65; Eusebius, *Preparation for the Gospel*, V, 1; Theophilus, *To Autolycus*, I, 3; Tatian, *Oratio ad Graecos* (Leipzig: Heinrichs, 1888), 5; Minucius Felix, *The Octavius of Marcus Minucius Felix*, trans. G. W. Clarke (New York: Newman, 1974); Novatian, *Novatiani Romanae urbis Presbytery de trinitate liber* (Cambridge: Cambridge University Press, 1909), 2; Cyprian, *On the Vanity of Idols*, 5; Lucius C. Lactantius, *Divine Institutes*, trans. Sister Mary Francis McDonald (Washington, DC: Catholic University of American Press, 1964), I, 6.

is, we are only saying what, by comparison with all finite beings, he is not. He is "inexpressible. It is easier for us to say what he is not than what he is." He is not earth, sea, heaven, angel, and so on, nothing creaturely. All we can say is what he is not (*Expositions on the Psalms*, Ps. 85 n. 12; *On Christian Doctrine*, I, 6; *On Order*, II, 47). "By thinking, we try to reach a nature than which nothing is better or more sublime" (*On Christian Doctrine*, I, 7). "Who is there whose conception of God truly corresponds to how he is?" (*Isa.* VI, 29). He is incomprehensible and has to be so, "for if you comprehend him it is not God you comprehend" (*Serm.* 117 n. 5). If, then, we finally want to say what we think of him, we struggle with language. "For what is thought of God is truer than what is said, and his being is truer than what is thought" (*The Trinity*, VII, 4). If we nevertheless insist on saying something about him, our language is not "adequate" but only serves to enable us to say something, and to think of a being who surpasses all else (*On Christian Doctrine*, I, 6). "Just as no intellect is able properly to conceive of God, so no definition is able properly to define or describe him" (*De cogn. verae vitae* 7). "God is known better by not knowing" (*On Order*, II, 44).

[163] This incomprehensibility of God's essence was most vigorously affirmed by Pseudo-Dionysius and John Scotus Eriugena, for whom God transcends even being and knowing. It is only because he is the cause and origin of all things that we, like Scripture, can name him in terms of his effects. Hence, on the one hand, he is "nameless" (anonymous), and on the other, he "has many names." But even the positive names we assign to God by virtue of his works do not reveal God's essence to us, for they fit him in a totally different and infinitely more perfect way than they do creatures. Consequently, negative theology is more excellent than positive theology: it makes God known to us as transcending all creatures. Nevertheless, even negative theology fails to furnish us any knowledge of God's being, for in the final analysis God surpasses both all negation and all affirmation, all assertion and all denial. We only know that God is, not who he is.[5]

Scholastic theology was more cautious and positive but affirmed God's essential unknowability. Thomas Aquinas distinguished the immediate vision of God, or knowledge by faith, from knowledge by reason. The former is ordinarily reserved for heaven; on earth all knowledge is mediate. God is knowable only in his works, notably in the perfections of his creatures. God is knowable only "insofar as he is represented in the perfections of his creatures."[6] In the subsequent development of Scholasticism, however, thanks to the elaborate dialectical treatment accorded

---

5. Pseudo-Dionysius, *The Divine Names*, I, 1 (588B), in *Pseudo-Dionysius: The Complete Works*, trans. Colin Luibheid, Classics of Western Spirituality (New York and Mahwah, NJ: Paulist Press, 1987), 49–50. Pseudo-Dionysius, *The Divine Names and Mystical Theology*, trans. John D. Jones (Milwaukee: Marquette University Press, 1980), c. 1 §1ff., §2; c. 5. Erigena, *The Divine Nature*, I, 7ff.; II, 23ff.; III, 19ff.; A. Stöckl, *Geschichte der Philosophie des Mittelalters*, 3 vols. (Mainz: Kirchheim, 1864–66), I, 45ff.; F. C. Baur, *Die christlichen Lehre von der Dreieinigkeit und Menschwerdung Gottes*, 3 vols. (Tübingen: C. F. Oslander, 1841–43), II, 274; J. I. Doedes, *Inleiding tot de Leer van God* (Utrecht: Kemink, 1876), 133ff.

6. T. Aquinas, *Summa Theol.*, I, qu. 12–13.

all the divine attributes, this truth of the incomprehensibility of God was pushed into the background. God's existence, names, essence, persons, and attributes were so minutely and precisely developed that no room was left for his incomprehensibility. Nominalism and mysticism were the two responses to this development.

Nominalism registered its protests against even the mild affirmation by Scotus that there was some quidditive, albeit imperfect knowledge of God,[7] and became more or less skeptical. Thus Occam declared: "Neither the divine essence, nor divine quiddity, nor anything that pertains to the nature of God, nor anything that is truly God, can be known by us here so that there is nothing else that comes to us from God in the way of an object."[8] Mystics such as Nicholas of Cusa, in his work *On Learned Ignorance* (1440), asserted that no truth could be obtained by reason but only by faith—faith conceived mystically as a new organ in humans. After the Reformation, Roman Catholic theology returned to Scholasticism and again adopted the doctrine of the unknowability of God's essence in the way Thomas understood it.[9] At the Lateran Council, convened by Pope Innocent III, this doctrine was even ecclesiastically defined and proclaimed: "God is ineffable."

The theology of the Reformation did not modify this view. Luther distinguished a "hidden" and a "revealed," in other words, God himself and the Word of God. Even when he concentrated on the God who has revealed himself in the incarnate Christ, Luther did not acknowledge the revelation of a fullness of God's being; on the contrary, there remained in God a dark and hidden background: "God as he is in his own nature and majesty, God in his absoluteness." And he, according to Luther, is "plainly unknowable, incomprehensible, and inaccessible."[10] Later Lutheran theologians, though they did not make such a sharp distinction between God's essence and his revelation, nevertheless all affirmed that there is no possibility of adequately naming and defining God.[11]

Although not necessarily following Luther's "hidden God," Reformed theology in its aversion to all idolatry has insisted that God infinitely surpasses our understanding, imagination, and language. Calvin writes that we are toy-

7. Duns Scotus, *Sentences*, I, dist. 3, qu. 2.

8. According to A. Stöckl, *Geschichte der Philosophie des Mittelalters*, 3 vols. (Mainz: Kirchheim, 1864–66), II, 1009.

9. Cf., e.g., Franciscus Sylvius, *Commentarii in totam primam partem S. Thomae Aquinatis*, 4th ed., 4 vols. (Antwerp, 1693), I, 96ff. Ed. note: An English edition of 1726 (Venice: Typographia Balleoniana) is also available in microform (Pius XII Memorial Library, St. Louis University, St. Louis, MO). C. R. Billuart, *Cursus theologiae*, 9 vols. (1769–70), I, 228ff.; Dionysius Petavius, *De theologicis dogmatibus*, 8 vos. (Paris: Vivès, 1865–67), I, chap. 5; VIII, c. 6; G. M. Jansen, *Praelectiones theologiae fundamentalis* (Utrecht, 1875–77), II, 78ff.; *Theologia Wirceburgensi*, 3rd ed., 10 vols. in 5 (Paris: Berche et Tralin, 1880), II, 73ff.; Christian Pesch, *Praelectiones dogmaticae* (1895), II, 46ff.

10. J. Köstlin, *The Theology of Luther in Its Historical Development and Inner Harmony*, trans. Charles E. Hay, 2 vols. (Philadelphia: Lutheran Publication Society, 1897), I, 99ff., 428ff.

11. Johann Gerhard, *Loci theologici*, ed. E. Preuss, 9 vols. (Berlin: G. Schlawitz, 1863–75), II, c. 5; cf. Heinrich F. F. Schmid, *Die Dogmatik der evangelische-lutherischen Kirche*, 9th ed. (Gütersloh: Gütersloher Verlagshaus Mohn, 1979), §17; Karl Bretschneider, *Handbuch der Dogmatik der evangelisch-lutherischen Kirche*, 4th ed., 2 vols. (Leipzig: J. A. Barth, 1838), I, 443.

ing with idle speculations when we pose the question: What is God? For us it is
enough to inquire: "What is his nature and what is consistent with his nature?"[12]
Reformed theologians unanimously affirm that God infinitely surpasses our understanding, imagination, and language. However, in Reformed theology, too,
the significance of God's incomprehensibility was increasingly lost from view.
While it was still taught, it existed in the abstract and exerted no influence. By
contrast, though with similar results, the breakaways from Reformed thought,
namely, Socinianism and Arminianism, were quite indifferent to the question
itself. All talk of *knowing* God was judged to be idle metaphysical speculation
and to be discarded in favor of simplicity and obedience to God's will. It is as
if people had lost all sense of the majesty and grandeur of God. Disregarding
all so-called metaphysical questions, people rushed on to the will of God in
order to know and to do it. Eternal life, they maintained, does not consist in
knowing God but in doing his will.

[164] As the Reformation tradition's consciousness of divine incomprehensibility waned, philosophers, notably Kant, reaffirmed it. According to the
Königsberg philosopher, the three transcendental ideas—the soul, the world,
and God—cannot be objectively demonstrated; they can only be postulated
as the necessary conditions for knowledge. That they are "known" by practical
reason does not add to our volume of real, meaning scientific, knowledge; all
these ideas do is regulate our knowledge. The concept of God does not belong
in metaphysics (which is nonexistent) but in ethics.[13] This commitment to
philosophical agnosticism and divine unknowability was shared by Fichte[14]
and Schleiermacher. In his *Christian Faith*, Schleiermacher stated that God is
the "whence" of our existence; and as such an absolute causality, he cannot be
the object of our knowing but only the content of the feeling of absolute dependence.[15] With the exception of Hegel, the doctrine of divine unknowability
has penetrated modern consciousness. All predicates about God are seen to be
statements about humanity writ large. God is a human projection (Feuerbach);
religion is the deification of humanity itself. For others, however, this sort of
atheism claimed too much. Human limitations and the finiteness of human
knowledge should lead us to abstain from such judgments. Knowledge is limited
to the observable (Auguste Comte; positivism), and beyond that we confess our
ignorance (agnosticism). The result is similar: Speculation is eschewed because
all metaphysics is distrusted.

    12. J. Calvin, *Institutes of the Christian Religion*, I.ii.2; I.v.9 (ed. John T. McNeill and trans. Ford
Lewis Battles, 2 vols. [1559; Philadelphia: Westminster, 1960], 1:41–43, 61–62); idem, *Commentary*,
on Rom. 1:19.
    13. I. Kant, *Critique of Practical Reason*, trans. Mary Gregor (Cambridge: Cambridge University
Press, 1997), 103ff.
    14. J. G. Fichte, *Attempt at a Critique of All Revelation*, trans. Garrett Green (Cambridge and New
York: Cambridge University Press, 1978), 152ff.
    15. F. Schleiermacher, *The Christian Faith* (Edinburgh: T&T Clark, 1989), §4.4.

In response, theology fell victim to the dread of agnosticism and muted its voice, hardly daring any longer to speak of a *knowledge* of God.[16] It tried as much as possible to exclude all metaphysics and to restrict itself to the realm of the "religious," however this was conceived. Theology become ashamed of its own name and allowed itself to be rebaptized into a science of religion. For although agnosticism is in fact the death of theology, many theologians have nevertheless maintained it in another form, attempting what amounts to rescue missions for theology. Kant regained by practical reason what he had lost by theoretical reason. The Englishman Herbert Spencer, who vigorously combated God's knowability with an array of arguments,[17] nonetheless left room for a religious veneration of the Unknowable. In the same way others searched for compensation in humanism, moral idealism, the formation of ideals, spiritism, theosophy, Buddhism, etc., in exchange for what science had stolen from them in Christian theology.

[165] Agnosticism does have weighty arguments on its side. As humans we are limited in our finiteness. As sophists and skeptics of all have known and proclaimed: all human knowledge is subjective and relative. Nothing in the universe stands by itself: object and subject are interdependent. We can therefore never say what a thing essentially is aside from our observation of that thing. We can only say that at a given moment something appears to us to be such and such. In that respect: "Man is the measure of all things." This is indeed a weighty argument; it proves too much, as we have shown in our treatment of idealism.[18] Excessive appeals to the subjectivity of our thought renders the entire external world meaningless to us; it discredits all knowledge. Nonetheless, what is true about agnosticism with respect to our knowledge in general is particularly true about our knowledge of God. We must add to our *epistemological* quandaries the fact that God-knowledge is anthropomorphic; it is accommodated to our necessary creaturely limitation. Kant's arguments that the transcendent ideas of God, the world, and the soul regulate our conduct but are not capable of scientific demonstration must be addressed. Modern thought, after Fichte, goes further and argues that divine absoluteness and personality are forever incompatible. To conceive of God in personal terms is to make him finite. For God to relate to us, he must be somehow limited. Those who desire such a God are still in the power of eudaemonism.[19] Consequently, all

16. Ed. note: This posture of epistemological humility and daring not to speak about the knowledge of God can also be found in contemporary so-called postmodern theology. See, e.g., Brian J. Walsh and J. Richard Middleton, *Truth Is Stranger Than It Used to Be: Biblical Faith in a Postmodern Age* (Downers Grove, IL: InterVarsity, 1995). The critique is usually directed at what is labeled "propositional truth." For a constructive response, see Andreas Köstenberger, ed., *Whatever Happened to Truth* (Wheaton, IL: Crossway, 2006).

17. H. Spencer, *First Principles*, 5th ed. (London: Williams & Norgate, 1887), 68–97.

18. See H. Bavinck, *Reformed Dogmatics*, ed. John Bolt (Grand Rapids: Baker Academic, 2003–8), I, 214–17 (#64).

19. J. G. Fichte, "Über den Grund unseres Glaubens an eine göttliche Weltregierung," in idem, *Gesamtausgabe*, 15 vols. (Stuttgart: Bad Cannstatt, 1977), V, 318–57; cf. Kuno Fischer, *Geschichte der neueren Philosophie*, 2nd ed., 11 vols. (Heidelberg: Winter, 1924), V, 628ff.

that is reasonably left is some version of an impersonal moral world order. This line of argument is widespread in the modern world.

Now, Christian theology has always acknowledged the tension between our view of God as personal and absolute. We are limited to the knowledge obtained by sense perception; we affirm the unsearchable majesty and sovereign highness of God. But though God is thus beyond our full comprehension and description, we do confess to having the knowledge of God. This knowledge is analogical and the gift of revelation. We know God through his works and in his relation to us, his creatures. This truth is beyond our comprehension; it is a mystery but not self-contradictory. Rather, it reflects the classic distinction Christian theology has always made between negative (*apophatic*) and positive (*cataphatic*) theology. Then, we do acknowledge that in strict terms speaking of "knowing the absolute" is a contradiction. For us to know is to make distinctions, to abstract, to restrict and limit. If this is how thought is structured, then we invariably either lower the Absolute to the level of the finite and make God into a personal, limited, human-like being; or attempt to transcend all the limitations of space and time, strip our idea of God of all likeness to a finite creature, and end up with an empty abstract idea devoid of value for religion. Via thought, the Absolute has been reduced to nothing. We are caught up in an insoluble antinomy. It is as if we are only left with the choice between gross realism and vacuous idealism, between a God who is nothing but an enlarged version of a human person and a cold abstraction that freezes and destroys the religion of the heart.

[166] To a considerable extent we can assent to and wholeheartedly affirm this doctrine of the unknowability of God. There is no name that fully expresses his being, no definition that captures him. He infinitely transcends our picture of him, our ideas of him, our language concerning him. He is not comparable to any creature. Christian theology has always opposed in the strongest terms all forms of shallow rationalism that consider a fully adequate knowledge of God a possibility.[20] Augustine articulated the profound religious importance of this when he said: "We are speaking of God. Is it any wonder if you do not comprehend? *For if you comprehend, it is not God you comprehend.* Let it be a pious confession of ignorance rather than a rash profession of knowledge. To attain some slight knowledge of God is a great blessing; to comprehend him, however, is totally impossible."[21] God is the sole object of all our love, precisely because he is the infinite and incomprehensible One. Although Scripture and the church, thus as it were, accept the premises of agnosticism and are even more deeply convinced of human limitations and the incomparable grandeur of God than Kant and Spencer, they draw from these realities a very different conclusion. Hilary put it as follows: "The perfection of learning is to know God in such a way that, though

20. Basil, *Hexaemeron*, hom. 1; Gregory of Nazianzus, *Orat.* 28; cf. Joseph Schwane, *Dogmengeschichte*, 2nd ed. of vols. I–II, 1st ed. of vols. III–IV (Freiburg i.B.: Herder, 1882–95), II, 27ff.

21. Augustine, *Lectures on the Gospel of John*, tract. 38, *NPNF¹*, VII, 217–21.

you realize he is not unknowable, yet you know him as indescribable."[22] Christian theology teaches that our knowledge of God is *analogical*. It is a knowledge of a being who is unknowable in himself, yet able to make something of himself known in the being he created. What agnosticism regards as irresolvable contradiction, Christian theology regards as an adorable mystery. It is completely incomprehensible to us how God can reveal himself and to some extent make himself known in created beings: eternity in time, immensity in space, infinity in the finite, immutability in change, being in becoming, the all, as it were, in that which is nothing. This mystery cannot be comprehended; it can only be gratefully acknowledged and received in faith.

If we cannot speak of God analogically, then we cannot speak of him at all. If God cannot be known, nor can he be felt or experienced in any way, we have no choice but to be silent. All religion then implodes, it is empty. It is true that certain terms such as "personality," when applied to God, mean something different than what we mean in applying them to human persons. To apply this strictly to God in the sense that modern people speak of "selves" would make us guilty of the heresy of tritheism. At the same time to avoid the important analogies between human persons and the "personal" God inevitably leads to reducing God to an abstract idea or empty symbol. In doing this, modern philosophical agnosticism makes the same error as ancient gnosticism. By reducing God to "inexpressible depth" and "eternal silence," they make the universe godless, in the most absolute sense of the word. What it all comes down to is whether God has willed and found a way to reveal himself in the domain of creatures. This, the Christian church and Christian theology affirm, has indeed occurred. Thanks to revelation, we have true knowledge of God, knowledge that is relative and finite rather than comprehensive. Incomprehensibility does not imply agnosticism but an ingredient of the Christian claim to have received by revelation a specific, limited, yet well-defined and true knowledge of God. In the words of Basil, "The knowledge of God consists in the perception of his incomprehensibility."

The Problem of Atheism

[167] From the preceding we conclude that the knowledge of God, given in revelation, is so rich and profound that it can never be fully comprehended by any human being. God's knowledge and power are not confined to the world nor exhaustively displayed there; a full revelation to creatures is not even possible inasmuch as the finite cannot grasp the infinite. "No one knows the Father except the Son" (Matt. 11:27; cf. Deut. 29:29). In affirming this we are certainly not nullifying God's knowability. God's incomprehensibility, so far from canceling out God's knowability, rather presupposes and affirms it. Though we can never

22. Hilary of Poitiers, *On the Trinity*, II, 7.

know God in the full richness of his being, he is known to all people through his revelation in creation, the theater of his glory. According to Scripture the whole universe is a creation and hence also a revelation of God (Acts 17:23–24; Rom. 1:19–20). The world is never godless. Taken in an absolute sense, as the denial of an absolute power, atheism is almost unthinkable. In the final analysis, all people recognize a power that they venerate as God. Even agnosticism itself is proof of this point: like skepticism, it cannot maintain itself except with the aid of what it opposes. And precisely because the world cannot be conceived as godless, there are no atheistic and a-religious peoples. In the end there are no atheists; there is only argument about the nature of God. Thus pagans even accused Christians of being "atheists" because they did not worship the national deities,[23] and more recently, employing it in a broad sense, Voetius applied it also to Descartes.[24]

Admittedly, there exists a practical atheism, living without God in the world (Pss. 14:1; 53:2; Eph. 2:12). But a conscious theoretical atheism in an absolute sense, if it ever occurs, is rare. Atheistic naturalism and similar forms of thought are philosophical rather than religious trends and owe their existence to criticism of the religious views of others. They never arise spontaneously or give rise to communities of believers existing over time. Even philosophers acknowledge this when they grant religious representations as necessary for people who are incapable of rising to the heights of pure conceptuality. Belief in a personal God is both natural and normal; it arises in human consciousness spontaneously and universally. Unbelief requires enormous effort. There is no proof available to it. To prove that there is no God one would have to be omniscient and omnipresent, that is, to be God![25] Human beings cannot resist the recognition of a Supreme Power; at the very moment they deny the true God, they fashion for themselves a false God. Thus, philosophical atheism, naturalism, and materialism again and again change into pantheism.[26] The religious impulse is universal.

23. Johann Caspar Suicerus, *Thesaurus ecclesiasticus* (Amsterdam: J. H. Wetsten, 1682), s.v. "θεος"; Adolf von Harnack, *Der Vorwurf des Atheismus in den drei ersten Jahrhundert* (Leipzig: J. C. Hinrichs, 1905).

24. Johann Franz Buddeus, *Theses theologicae de atheismo et superstitione*, ed. J. Lulofs (1747), 116; on Voetius, see A. C. Duker, *G. Voetius*, 4 vols. (Leiden: Brill, 1897–1915), II, 151ff.

25. G. Voetius, "De atheismo," *Select. disp.*, I, 114–225; G. J. Vossius, "De origine ac progressu idololatriae," *Opera omnia*, I, chap. 3; Leydecker, *Fax veritas*, III, controv. 3; F. Turretin, *Institutes of Elenctic Theology*, trans. G. M. Giger and ed. J. T. Dennison, 3 vols. (Phillipsburg, NJ: Presbyterian and Reformed, 1992), III, qu. 2.; S. Maresius, *Syst. theol.* (1673), 44; Buddeus, *Theses theol.*; C. Hodge, *Systematic Theology*, 3 vols. (New York: Charles Scribner's Sons, 1888), I, 198, 242; R. Flint, *Antitheistic Theories: Being the Baird Lectures for 1877* (Edinburgh and London: W. Blackwood, 1879), lecture 1; S. Hoekstra, *Das Christens Godsvrucht* (Amsterdam: Gebroders Kraay, 1866), 6; J. I. Doedes, *Inleiding tot de Leer van God* (Utrecht: Kemink, 1870), 57ff.; J. B. Heinrich and C. Gutberlet, *Dogmatische Theologie*, 2nd ed., 10 vols. (Mainz: Kirchheim, 1881–1900), III, 23ff.; P. B. Adlhoch, "Zur wissenschaftlichen Erklärung des Atheismos," *Philosophisches Jahrbuch* 18/3–4 (1905); A. Sabatier, *Outlines of a Philosophy of Religion*, trans. T. A. Seed (New York: James Pott, 1902), 66ff.

26. Ludwig Büchner, *Force and Matter*, 4th ed., trans. from the 15th German ed. (New York: P. Eckler, 1891), 370ff.; E. Haeckel, *Naturale Schöpfungsgeschichte* (Berlin: G. Reimer, 1889), 20, 32, 64; ed. note: ET: *The History of Creation*, trans. E. R. Lankester, 2 vols. (New York: D. Appleton, 1883);

[168] Explanations for this universal religious impulse vary. Already in ancient times it was suggested that religion is something innate in human beings. This is a reasonable notion. From our earliest youth we are all aware of psychic, spiritual, and moral realities such as faith, hope, and love that are just as, if not more, real to us as purely material forces such as gravity and temperature. The marvel of self-consciousness is proof of this; we think and are aware that we are thinking. Augustine was right when he wrote that the truth of spiritual things is much more certain than that of visible things. "Nothing can be more absurd than to say that the objects we see with our eyes have being while the things we discern with our intellect do not, since only a fool would doubt the fact that the intellect is of incomparably higher rank than the eyes."[27] In pursuing the question how we learn anything at all, Greek philosophy spoke of universal ideas. Plato believed learning was a matter of memory, the embodied soul recalling the pure forms or ideas it witnessed in its preexistent state;[28] Aristotle began with sense perception but nevertheless judged that inherent in reason as such are a number of very general principles that are axiomatic, underlie all arguments, and are acknowledged by everyone;[29] the Stoics spoke of "common" or "natural" ideas, "implanted preconceptions," concepts that everyone derives from sense perception by virtue of the structure of human thinking.[30] Strictly speaking, it was Cicero who first developed the notion of "innate ideas" or "inborn principles of the virtues," implanted in the soul by God, and judged that "By nature we believe the gods exist."[31]

In modern philosophy, the trajectory of thought beginning with Descartes, while judging all knowledge to be triggered by the senses, did consider it finally to arise from the inner mental capacity for representation. Kant modified this with his teaching about innate forms of perception, categories of mind, and forms of reason. Idealism, notably that of Fichte and Hegel, extended this by considering all knowledge, indeed all being itself, to arise out of the thinking process. The notion of innate ideas rests on the premise that all learning presupposes some kind of antecedent knowledge. Reasoning and proofs are based on principles that are axiomatic, a priori, certain. Experience merely furnishes "opinions," contingent truths. Universal and necessary truths can only originate in the human mind. The fact that such universal and necessary truths exist is established by universal agreement. The opposition between soul and body is especially of such a nature that mental representations and concepts cannot have their origin in sense percep-

idem, *Der Monismus als Band zwischen Religion und Wissenschaft*, 6th ed. (Bonn: Emil Strauss, 1893); idem, *The Riddle of the Universe at the Close of the Nineteenth Century*, trans. Joseph McCabe (New York: Harper & Brothers, 1900), 288ff.

27. Augustine, *The Immortality of the Soul*, 10 n. 17; idem, *City of God*, xix, 18.

28. Eduard Zeller, *Die Philosophie der Griechen in ihrer geschichtlichen Entwicklung*, 4th ed., 3 vols in 6. (Leipzig: O. R. Reisland, 1879–1920), II, 639, 643f., 829.

29. Ibid., III, 188ff.

30. Ibid., IV, 74ff., 389ff.

31. Cicero, *Tusculan Disputations*, I, 16, 36; III, 1, 2; idem, *De finibus*, V, 21, 59; idem, *The Nature of the Gods*, I, 1, 2; cf. E. Zeller, *Philosophie der Griechen*, IV, 659ff.

tion. They must be explained either in terms of the human mind or of the Spirit of God, in whom humans view all ideas.

The notion of innate ideas was criticized by Socinianism, which rejected all natural theology, and by empiricists such as Locke and Hobbes, who insisted that all knowledge stems from sense perception. "There is nothing in the mind which was not previously in the senses." For them the theory of innate ideas was superfluous inasmuch as the origination of these ideas can very well be explained in another way. History teaches that there is great diversity in human representation and concept formation across peoples and cultures. Even moral principles are different among people and thus cannot be innate. The greatest possible divergence of opinion exists with respect to good and evil. And, so believed Herbert Spencer and many after him, the theory of evolution has a perfectly reasonable explanation that potentially resolves the ancient conflict between empiricism and nativism. Applying the law of evolution to the human mind led to the conclusion that it did not come into existence all at once, nor was it endowed from the beginning with an immutable set of capabilities, but gradually became what it is now. In this view, empiricism was correct with respect to the very earliest beginnings of human history; originally the human mind was a blank. But the experience of countless generations had gradually so shaped the mind that it can now be deemed to possess an array of forms and ideas by which it is naturally adapted to its entire environment. That is the truth of nativism.[32]

[169] What does Christian theology think of the notion of innate ideas? It would seem, at first glance, to be a formulation amenable to the universal Christian theological assumption that there are truths known by nature and not by revelation, truths obtained spontaneously, as it were, and not by intentional study and reflection. Furthermore, this would serve as a significant rejoinder to the challenge of atheism if an idea of God is innate in all of us. However, that is not the position taken by Christian theology. It did assume that some natural truth was universally known apart from special revelation, but it uniformly rejected the notion of innate ideas. It is in mystical experience that some, such as Augustine and Bonaventure, taught a knowledge of God that is immediate, apart from the senses. Yet, even then, both placed limits on this knowledge; it was a gift of grace and thus not a strictly innate idea. All we can say is that as created beings we have a God-given disposition or capacity to know him. Scholastic theology rejected the notion of innate ideas and taught instead that the essence of things is the real object of intellectual knowledge; that all knowledge begins with sense perception; and that the intellect has the capacity to create ideas by abstracting from particular things that which is common and universal in them. These ideas are not innate, do not come ready-made with the intellect but, in keeping with

---

32. Charles Darwin, *The Descent of Man* (New York: D. Appleton and Co., 1871), chaps. 3–4; Spencer, according to Spruyt, *Proeve van eene geschiedenis van de leer der aangeboren begrippen* (Leiden: Brill, 1879), 342; L. Büchner, *Force and Matter*, 344ff.

its nature, are abstracted from the observation of *sensory* things. This is also true of the idea of God. God is not the substance but the *cause* of things. Accordingly, his existence and perfections can to a certain extent be known by perception and reflection from his works. We can speak of innate knowledge only in the sense that there has been created in our understanding a natural disposition (*habitus*) to proceed from the finite to the infinite, from the particular to the universal.[33] This is what we mean by "natural theology": the affirmation that such a *natural* disposition or capacity for knowing God exists in every created human person.

NATURAL THEOLOGY

It is this capacity that Calvin called a *sensus divinitatis* and a *semen religionis*.[34] Although Luther and the Lutheran confessions are very negative on all natural theology,[35] the Reformed confessions and theologians consistently affirmed it.[36] Calvin distinguished general from special grace and explained all the good remaining even in sinful humanity in terms of common grace.[37] "God himself implanted in all humans an understanding of his divine majesty, persistently renewing its memory and constantly instilling fresh drops" (*Inst.* I.iii.1). This seed of religion can never be eradicated (*Inst.* I.iii.3). Added to "this seed of religion" comes the revelation of God in his works; hence, now "people cannot open their eyes without being compelled to see him" (*Inst.* I.v.1). "There is no spot in the universe in which you cannot discern at least some sparks of his glory" (*Inst.* I.v.1). First of all, as microcosm, a human being as such is an excellent workshop for

33. Cf. H. Bavinck, *Reformed Dogmatics*, I, 223 (#67); T. Aquinas, *Summa Theol.*, I, qu. 2, art. 1; idem, *Summa contra gentiles*, I, 10–11; *Theologia Wirceburgensi*, 3rd ed., 10 vols. in 5 (Paris: Berche et Tralin, 1880), III, 5ff.; C. Pesch, *Compendium theologiae dogmaticae*, 5th ed., 4 vols. (Freiburg im Breisgau: Herder, 1935), II, 10–13; Joseph Kleutgen, *Die Philosophie der Vorzeit vertheidigt*, 2 vols. (Münster: Theissing, 1863; 2nd ed. 1878), I, 67ff., 587ff.; H. Denzinger, *Vier Bücher von der religiösen Erkenntnis*, 2 vols. (Frankfurt am Main: Minerva-Verlag, 1856; repr., Würzburg: Stahel, 1967), II, 28ff.

34. J. Calvin, *Institutes*, I.iii.1.

35. Luther believed that the image of God in fallen humanity was totally lost. "Apart from the Holy Spirit [human] reason is simply devoid of the knowledge of God. When it comes to divine matters, humans are totally in the dark." All that is left is "passive capacity," the capacity to be saved. J. Köstlin, *Theology of Luther*, II, 344ff., 455ff.

36. Ed. note: It is worth highlighting Bavinck's claim here since, thanks to the magisterial role that Karl Barth has played in Reformed and all theology during the twentieth century, the affirmation of natural theology truly fell on dark days. See Emil Brunner, *Natural Theology: Comprising "Nature and Grace," and the reply "No!" by Karl Barth*, trans. Peter Fraenkel, introd. by John Baillie (London: G. Bles, Centenary, 1946); cf. John W. Hart, *Karl Barth vs. Emil Brunner: The Formation and Dissolution of a Theological Alliance, 1916–1936* (New York: Peter Lang, 2001); James Barr, *Biblical Faith and Natural Theology* (Oxford: Clarendon, 1991); Ned Wisnefske, *Our Natural Knowledge of God* (New York: Lang, 1990); Stephen J. Grabill, *Rediscovering the Natural Law in Reformed Theological Ethics*, Emory University Studies in Law and Religion (Grand Rapids: Eerdmans, 2006).

37. Cf. H. Bavinck, "Common Grace," trans. R. Van Leeuwen, *Calvin Theological Journal* 24 (1989): 50–55.

the innumerable works of God (I.v.3–4), but this is also true of the entire realm of nature, which, speaking reverently, we may even call God.[38] All the Reformed symbols and theologians say the same. Voetius, for example, at the same time vigorously defended natural theology *and* resolutely repudiated Descartes's notion of innate ideas. For Voetius the term "implanted theology" (*theologia insita*) is "a capacity or power or aptitude belonging to the rational faculties; or a natural light in the sense that the intellect is able to grasp the truth of principles apart from any effort, previous study, or reasoning." Furthermore, there is something compelling or necessary about this grasp of the intellect; a person is led "to assent to it from a kind of natural necessity and by the force of its own inherent weight." It is as compelling as the opened eye is necessarily led to see visible things. Thus, the familiar saying, "There is nothing in the intellect that was not previously in the senses," accordingly, is recognized as true in the sense that in some fashion, as direct object or as product, or as component, or by way of contrast, the world around us is necessary to bring us to conscious knowledge.[39]

[170] It should be clear now why Christian theology affirms natural theology while at the same time rejecting the notion of "innate ideas." The danger of this theory is twofold: rationalism and mysticism. If human beings at birth came fully endowed with clear and distinct knowledge of God (Descartes), being, or all ideas (Plato), they would be completely autonomous and self-sufficient, needing neither God, the world, nor revelation. Dispensing with God's revelation, they could more efficiently find perfect knowledge in their own minds than in nature or Scripture. Furthermore, the theory of innate ideas creates an unbridgeable chasm between mind and matter, soul and body. The visible is not seen as a creation, an embodiment of God's thoughts; all knowledge of the divine comes by way of self-reflection on the divine within. The cosmos becomes the self and the self becomes the cosmos.

This is indeed what happened. Under the sway of Neoplatonism's notion of innate ideas, forms of mysticism increasingly turned to contemplative patterns that dispensed with external aids and were content with the internal word, the spiritual light, the vision of God, and communion with God in the innermost recesses of the soul. Then, dualism, linked with the theory of the innate idea of God introduced into modern philosophy by Descartes, led Leibniz, Wolff, and later Kant, Fichte, and Hegel to a rationalism that constructs the entire universe of being itself from the immanent thought processes of the human mind. This human autarchy (self-sufficiency) and contempt for the body and the material universe is completely foreign to Scripture which teaches that we are image bearers of God, soul and body. The bonds by which we are tied to the material world are not chains of slavery but means to draw us closer to God the Creator. In the

38. J. Calvin, *Institutes*, I.i–v; cf. II.ii.18; idem, *Commentary*, on Pss. 8; 19; Acts 17; 27; 28; Rom. 1:19; Heb. 11:3.

39. Gisbert Voetius, *Selectae disputations theologicae*, 5 vols. (Utrecht, 1648–69), I, 141; V, 477ff., 516, 525.

splendid language of Calvin, "there is no spot in the universe in which you cannot discern at least some sparks of his glory."[40]

Christian theology shares empiricism's polemic against mysticism and rationalism, a polemic that raises psychological and historical objections to the notion of innate ideas. While the mystics and rationalists are correct in maintaining that the essence of things cannot be grasped through sense perception but apprehended only in God (Malebranche), in the soul by recollection (Plato), or by thought processes from the human mind (Descartes, Hegel), they erred in three ways: in discounting the primacy of the senses; in exalting our immediate awareness beyond its real role; and above all in confusing the order of human knowing with the order of being itself. The sentiments of rationalists and mystics are thus pantheistic, confusing God and the order of being with the human order of knowing. They confuse the light of reason with the light of God, the universal truths in us with the ideas in the mind of God, our "logos" with "the Logos of God."

By contrast, Christian theology begins with the world as God's creation, a revelation to humans. We do not know God immediately; all our knowledge of God is obtained indirectly and bears an *analogical* character. Like all knowledge, knowledge of God is mediated to us through our senses, through speech and symbol, mediated to us by parents and others. If this were not the case, we would be unable to account for the great diversity of representations of God. If knowledge of God, of the moral order, of the beautiful—if these were all innate, they would be universally identical and acknowledged as such. We know how far this is from the truth. Although we are created with a built-in radar that senses God, it does not provide us with specific content or concrete religious belief. The parallel, rather, is with human language. It is human to have the ability to speak, an essential part of the image of God in us. Nonetheless, concrete language, which exists in countless forms, is not native but acquired; it is learned. Similarly, the natural religious ability with which we are created comes to expression in a great diversity of forms. Therefore, though we have spoken of "natural theology" in a general manner, strictly speaking, *natural religion* or *natural theology* never exists in concrete form any more than do "natural rights" and "natural morality."

[171–72] Our rejection of the doctrine of innate ideas and insistence on the primacy of sense perception for all knowledge, including the knowledge of God, must not lead us to the opposite error of undervaluing that which is basic and common to our universal experience as God's image bearers. In that respect it is appropriate to speak of "implanted knowledge of God" in some sense. From the entire realm of nature, both exterior and interior to us humans, we receive impressions and gain perceptions that foster in us the sense of God. It is God himself who does not leave us without witness. Here it is important to distinguish between *implanted* and *acquired* knowledge of God. In the former, God's revelation acts

40. J. Calvin, *Institutes*, I.v.1.

on human consciousness, creating impressions and intuitions. In the case of the acquired knowledge of God, human beings *reflect* on that revelation of God and seek by reasoning and proof to rise above impressions and intuitions to clearer ideas. This is what we call "theology," and it is part of a broader natural human desire *scientifically* to explain the how and why of our knowledge. The distinction between implanted and acquired must not be restricted to so-called natural theology in opposition to revealed or biblical theology. God reveals himself to us in his handiwork of creation, but even Christian believers depend on Scripture and the illumination of the Holy Spirit to truly know God the Creator.

What we say here about the knowledge of God is true in all spheres of life: in religion, art, morality, jurisprudence, science, and so on. The "seeds of the sciences" are naturally inherent in humans. Every science is grounded in general, self-evident principles. All knowledge rests in faith. All proof, finally, presupposes "a principle of demonstration" and these are universal. The laws of thought are the same for all; the theory of numbers is everywhere the same; the difference between good and evil is known by all. These do not come ready-made at birth. We are not born into the world as adults but as helpless infants needing care. Yet, each child comes into the world concealing within the full-grown potential adult of the future. It is when our eyes see and we are old enough to be self-conscious that we pursue knowledge and science; we take the data of our impressions and work with them. We humans are not content with impressions of things and mere consciousness in any area of knowledge. We want to know and to know that we know. We desire to explain the *how* and the *why* of our knowledge. That is why common everyday empirical knowledge is driven to achieve true, scientific knowledge. The same is true for theology and our knowledge of God. All humans possess in their minds a *capacity* to see God in his works and have the requirement of the law written in their heart (Gen. 1:26; Acts 17:27; Rom. 1:19; 2:15). We are not born with a true knowledge of God ready-made but acquire it through nurture and education. This is not, however, external to us; it is not coerced but it is natural. As seeing eyes lead one to pursue knowledge of what is visible, so our souls thirst for knowledge of the One whose presence is manifest to us. What we come into the world with is the *capacity* (aptitude, faculty) and the *inclination* (*habitus*, disposition) to arrive at some firm, certain, and unfailing knowledge of God. When we use words such as "implanted," "natural," and "innate" we thereby reject the idea that human beings are blank pages of paper to be written on by external forces that introduce God to us for the first time. We wish to affirm, rather, that human awareness of God arises spontaneously, without coercion, without scientific argumentation and proof, simply because we are created with a native *capacity* for knowing him and live in a world that speaks of God. We are created in God's image; we live in God's world. God does not leave any person without a witness (cf. Acts 14:17). Whether God speaks to us in the realm of nature or in that of grace, in creation or in re-creation, through the Logos or in Christ, in the Spirit of God or in the Spirit of Christ, it is always the same God we hear speaking to us. Nature and grace are not opposites: we have one God from whom, through whom, and to whom both exist.

"PROOFS" FOR GOD'S EXISTENCE

[173] This insight helps us to consider aright the so-called proofs for God's existence, neither overestimating nor disdaining them. It is true that Scripture makes no attempt to prove the existence of God.[41] It proceeds from it and assumes that humans know and acknowledge God. "Lift up your eyes on high and see: Who created these?" (Isa. 40:26). Scripture does not set before us an argument for God and leave it to us to decide whether we think the argument compelling or not. Instead, it speaks with authority. Christian theology does, however, accept the support given to its convictions about God by pagan philosophy, still judging these proofs within the doctrine of faith, not as preambles to it. Christian conviction about what can be known about God apart from special revelation is a valid natural theology. However, when this natural theology stands on its own, and in a self-sufficient and rationalistic fashion sets aside the need for special revelation, it is an invalid and impious activity. Under the critique of modern thought, notably Kant and Darwin, the ontological and teleological proofs have had a difficult time. The moral argument continues to have some persuasiveness in certain circles. We shall conclude this chapter with a brief look at the main arguments or, as they are often mistakenly called, "proofs" for God's existence.

[174] Although the proofs may be given different names and stated in a variety of forms, they usually come down to the same thing. Two of the proofs (the cosmological and the teleological argument) respectively deduce the existence of God from the world's origin and purpose. Two others are based, respectively, on the rational and the moral nature of humans (the ontological and the moral argument). The remaining two are based especially on history and deduce the existence of God, respectively, from the universal consent and history of humankind (the argument from consensus and the historical-theological argument).[42]

The Cosmological Argument

The cosmological argument attempts to deduce the existence of a cause from the demonstrable existence of an effect. The world is here; it must have a cause. Now by itself this conclusion is perfectly legitimate, the criticism of Hume and

41. A. B. Davidson, *The Theology of the Old Testament*, ed. S. D. F. Salmond (Edinburgh: T&T Clark, 1904), 73ff.

42. Alexander Balmain Bruce, *Apologetics* (Edinburgh: T&T Clark, 1892), 159ff.; R. Flint, *Antitheistic Theories*; J. McCosh, *The Method of Divine Government* (New York: R. Carter, 1860); Samuel Harris, *God the Creator and Lord of All*, 2 vols. (Edinburgh: T&T Clark, 1897); J. Morris, *A New Natural Theology: Based on the Doctrine of Evolution* (London: Rivington, Percival, 1896).

Kant notwithstanding. If we may no longer apply the law of causality, all science is impossible. The argument depends on the truth of the assumption that an infinite chain of causes is inconceivable, and that the law of causality also applies to the universe as a whole. An infinite series of causes is in fact inconceivable and impossible. No one accepts such an infinite series. We are led, therefore, to the notion of a self-existent, hence infinite, eternal, and absolute Cause of the world, an absolute Ground. However this is described and however it is named—a primary being, God, the Absolute, Substance, Power, Matter, or Will—this is an important conclusion. But note how short is the distance that this takes us; we know nothing about the nature or character of the cosmic cause. Is it transcendent or immanent, personal or impersonal, conscious or unconscious? Efforts to deduce answers to such questions from the cosmological argument itself attempt the impossible. So we are left with the conclusion that, granting the impossibility of an infinite series of causes, the cosmological argument at best yields a self-existent, first, and absolute World-cause. It is something, but we are still a very long way from Scripture's teaching about God.

The Teleological Argument

The teleological argument, proceeding from the world's order, harmony, beauty, and purpose, takes us one step further to infer an intelligent cause that must be conscious. Kant objected to this argument that it at most leads to a World-shaper, not to a World-creator.[43] Materialism objects that there is no purpose and that all apparent teleology in nature can be explained by immanent systems. Pantheism, on the other hand, affirms purpose but insists that it is impersonal and unconscious and that there is no warrant for asserting an intelligent cause. Both, of course, are themselves claims of faith rather than science. The same must be said for efforts to acknowledge some teleology and explain it by way of impersonal, evolutionary forces such as natural selection or even vitalism. Against these objections we can say that Scripture clearly teaches that there is purpose in creation (Gen. 1; Prov. 8; 1 Cor. 3:21–23; Rom. 8:28; etc.), that almost all philosophers affirm it, and that our ordinary experience impresses it upon us. Our experience of climate and seasons, our knowledge of blood circulation, fertilization of plants, and larger ecosystems, not to mention such complex bodily structures as the hand and eye, do not strike us as products of chance. They evidence intelligent design.[44] We understand instinctively that the universe can no more be interpreted by chance than Homer's Iliad by an arbitrary throw of the letters of the alphabet. Again, we come to a modest conclusion: If we can

---

43. I. Kant, *Critique of Pure Reason*, trans. Norman Kemp Smith (1929; repr., New York: St. Martin's Press, 1965), 522ff.

44. Ed. note: The term "intelligent design" is not Bavinck's but the editor's and should not be taken as a statement about the raging debate taking place in the early twenty-first century about evolution and intelligent design. I inserted it here deliberately to signal that the issue Bavinck is engaging here continues to the present.

establish the presence of purpose in the world, the existence and consciousness of a Supreme Being are implied.[45]

The Ontological Argument

[175] The ontological argument, in its various forms, attempts to infer existence from thought. Its classic expressions can be found in Anselm's *Monologion* and *Proslogion*. Our common sense recognizes that this argument is not true when it comes to creatures. Nonexistent beings can be conceived. With God, matters are slightly different. Although we cannot convincingly demonstrate the reality of God from our ideas about God, it is true that whenever we do think about God we *necessarily* think of God existing. *If* God exists, then of course he exists necessarily; existence and essence coincide. But this is precisely what needs to be demonstrated. Strictly speaking, the ontological argument is not a "proof." All we can conclude is that believing that God exists is not arbitrary; the moment we think about God we must conclude that God exists. The benefit of this argument is that human beings are confronted with the choice of either trusting this necessary witness of their consciousness or else despairing of their own consciousness.

The Moral Argument

The moral argument infers the existence of a supreme and sovereign Lawgiver from moral phenomena such as human conscience, fear of death and judgment, repentance, and reward and punishment. While these phenomena are powerful witness to the enduring moral nature of even fallen humanity, they are less than a proof for the existence of a righteous and holy God. Here especially, modern proponents of an evolutionary understanding of the cosmos and humanity believe that they have a satisfactory alternative explanation. Morality is a survival mechanism; over time humans recognized that certain behaviors improved survivability while others did not. Morality is thus a human construct, developed over a long period of time; it is a product of circumstances. Furthermore, the persistence of immoral and evil conduct, not to mention "natural evil," seems to contradict the notion of a Supreme and Good Lawgiver. Virtue is not always rewarded and evil is not always punished. The wicked often even enjoy prosperity and peace, while the righteous are persecuted and oppressed; and nature is apparently indifferent to good and evil so that with its disasters and catastrophes it time and again strikes those who cannot possibly be other than innocent. We have no guarantee that good will finally triumph over evil.

Once again, we do not have here a "proof" in any sense of the word; but we do have a powerful witness to the effect that in this world the brute force of nature will not have the last word. Our consciences will not leave us altogether; moral order will reassert itself even in the midst of the most egregious immorality and lawlessness. Even though the entire world should rise up in opposition and the intellect

---

45. J. Mayer, *Der teleologische Gottesbeweis und der Darwinismus* (Mainz: I. Kirchheim, 1901).

should lodge ever so many objections to this order, humans will continue to assert themselves as moral agents; they will persevere in their belief in the existence and supremacy of the moral world order, and this conviction will instinctively lead them to the recognition of a righteous and holy God, who rules supreme over all things.[46]

The Argument from Universal Consent

[176] The same is true for the argument that proceeds from the universal reality of religion. Recognized long ago by writers such as Cicero, this has been reinforced by modern studies in the history and psychology of religion. It is now practically unanimously agreed by scientists of religion that religion is the common possession of all humankind. Furthermore, nonreligious explanations of this phenomenon always fall short; the only conclusion that seems plausible is to affirm the fundamentally religious character of all human beings. This fact bears powerful witness to the existence, revelation, and knowability of God but cannot as such disprove the claim that it reflects a universal pathology of the human mind, a passing fancy, or delusion. Nothing can be indubitably inferred about the future of religion nor about the existence of God. Nonetheless, we face here the choice of trusting or doubting the universal consent; if we choose to deny it, we challenge the credibility of humanity's consent altogether and must resign ourselves to a more radical skepticism.

The Historical-Theological Argument

Finally, arguments based on the purposefulness of history presuppose what they claim to demonstrate. Claims that history's unfolding points to a wise and omnipotent World Ruler face weighty arguments at every turn, arguments so strong they could easily shake one's faith in God's providence if it had no other foundations. History confronts us at every moment with insoluble riddles. We get no answers to the "why?" that comes out of our mouth at every turn. Even when we acknowledge that there has been progress in intellectual development and material culture, we face vast differences of opinion when it comes to the question whether the human race is making religious and moral progress, and there is no statistical science that can settle it. What is worth noting is how important it is to humanity to maintain some hope for a better future; the human mind is restless until at the end of history it finds some satisfaction.[47] Thus, as belief in

---

46. Discussion about the cosmic moral order can be found, *inter alia*, in E. Zeller, *Vorträge und Abhandlungen geschichtlichen Inhalts*, 3 vols. (Leipzig: Fues [L. W. Reisland], 1865–84), III, 189ff.; M. Carrière, *De Zedelijke Wereldorde* (Leipzig: F. A. Brockhaus, 1880); E. von Hartmann, *Das sittlichen Bewusstsein* (Leipzig: W. Friedrich, 1886), 570ff.; P. Christ, *Die sittliche Weltordnung* (Leipzig: Brill, 1894); F. Traub, *Die sittliche Weltordnung* (Freiburg i.B.: Mohr [Siebeck], 1892); A. B. Bruce, *The Moral Order of the World in Ancient and Modern Thought* (London: Hodder & Stoughton, 1900).

47. Ed. note: The persistence of hope as a universal human constant has been theologically addressed by, *inter alia*, Jürgen Moltmann, *The Theology of Hope: On the Ground and the Implications of a Christian Eschatology*, trans. Margaret Kohl (London: SCM; New York: Harper & Row, 1967).

providence waned, modern people began to warm up to a faith in evolutionary progress. Logic and science can neither prove nor disprove such beliefs. History is susceptible to different interpretations that are, in the final analysis, a matter of faith, not proof. The heart rather than the intellect is the final arbiter. But it is noteworthy that belief in guidance and purpose in history is ineradicably implanted in the human heart and an indispensable component in the philosophy of history. Here again we face the dilemma: is this illusion or reality; and, ultimately, do we choose theism or atheism?

[177] Finally, that must also be our judgment concerning these "proofs" in general. Even the term "proofs" is infelicitous. The cosmological, teleological, and moral testimony to God is not a matter of logical, mathematical proof but belongs to the category of moral and religious truth. The proofs may augment and strengthen our faith, they often help to clarify it, but they do not serve as its grounds. They are, rather, the consequences, the products of faith's observation of the world. The proofs do not induce faith, and objections against them do not wreck it. They are, instead, testimonies by which God is able to strengthen already given faith. As testimonies, proclaimed as the revelation of the God of whose existence every human is by nature—and prior to any reasoning or study—assured in the very depths of his or her soul, they are of no small value. They are part of God's own revelation to humanity; they are evidence that God addresses all human beings. Together they make him known to us as the divine being who must be conceived by us as necessary and necessarily as existing; who is the sole, first, and absolute Cause of all creatures; who consciously and purposefully governs all things, and who above all reveals himself as the Holy One in the conscience of everyone who believes.

NAMING GOD: ACCOMMODATION AND ANTHROPOMORPHISM

[178] As we now move on to consider the knowledge of God that is given to us in Scripture, we need to consider some additional formal matters, specifically the nature of that knowledge: If God is truly incomprehensible, how do we describe our own efforts to name God? How true to God's own self-knowledge is our knowledge of him? How true to God himself are the names we give to him even if they are based on revelation? In Scripture, God's name is his self-revelation. Only God can name himself; his name is identical with the perfections he exhibits in and to the world. Names are the characteristic features by which things are known; for people they are personal identifiers. Although our modern age does not make of names what the ancients did when they linked names directly to a person's character, they remain important markers of our individuality, our identity, our honor and worth. We are offended when our name is misspelled or mispronounced; our dignity is affronted. How much more is this true of God. We do not name God; he names himself. He reveals his proper name to his people;

to Israel as YHWH, to the Christian church as Father. The name is God himself as he reveals himself in one relationship or another (Lev. 24:11, 16; Deut. 28:58).

The first point to be made is that God's revealed names do not reveal his being as such, but God in his revelation and multiple relations to his creatures. These names are not arbitrary, however; God reveals himself in the way he does because he is who he is. Noteworthy, nonetheless, is the fact that biblical revelation is specifically addressed to humanity and uses human language. God speaks to us in human words and even manifests himself in human forms. We must therefore speak of divine accommodation. Scripture is accommodated language; accommodated to our human language and condition, it is anthropomorphic through and through. God is described in human terms via human faculties, body parts, emotions, sensations, and actions. In Scripture all creation, the theater of God's glory, is mined for the description of the knowledge of God because God is immanent in all creation. Therefore, Christian theology opposes all dualisms, including those of modernity, that empty created reality of God, for then theology could not speak of God at all. To deny that we can see God in his works and name him in accordance with his self-revelation in his works is to deny the possibility of knowing God at all.

All the names by which God calls himself and allows us to call him are anthropomorphic—derived from earthly and human relations. When God is called El, the strong One; El Shaddai, the mighty One; YHWH, the One who is there; or Father, Son, Spirit, good, merciful, gracious, just, holy, etc., these are all expressions that first of all apply to creatures and are then transferred to God by way of eminence. Even the so-called incommunicable attributes of God—immutability, independence, simplicity, eternity, and omnipresence—are derived from the finite world and stated negatively. Eternity cannot be defined except as a negation of time. In addition, all that is attributed in Scripture to humans is also attributed to God. God is said to have a soul (Lev. 26:11) and a Spirit (Gen. 1:2; Matt. 12:28; etc.); among other things, Scripture speaks of God's face (Exod. 33:20, 23; Isa. 63:9; Ps. 16:11; Matt. 18:10; Rev. 22:4), his eyes (Ps. 11:4; Heb. 4:13), his ears (Ps. 55:3), his nose (Deut. 33:10), his mouth (Deut. 8:3), his lips (Job 11:5), his tongue (Isa. 30:27), his neck (Jer. 18:17), his arm (Exod. 15:16), his hand (Num. 11:23), his right hand (Exod. 15:12); his finger (Exod. 8:19), his heart (Gen. 6:6), his intestines (Isa. 63:15; Jer. 31:20; Luke 1:78); his bosom (Ps. 74:11; John 1:18), and his feet (Isa. 66:1). Human emotions such as joy (Isa. 62:5; 65:19), sorrow (Ps. 78:40; Isa. 63:10), grief (Ps. 95:10), fear (Deut. 32:27), zeal and jealousy (Deut. 32:21), repentance (Gen. 6:6), hatred (Deut. 16:22), wrath (Ps. 2:5), and vengeance (Deut. 32:35) are not excluded. Human actions include: investigating (Gen. 18:21), forgetting (1 Sam. 1:11), remembering (Gen. 8:1; Exod. 2:24), rebuking (Pss. 18:15; 104:7), resting (Gen. 2:2), working (John 5:17), sitting (Ps. 9:7), arising (Ps. 68:1), walking (Lev. 26:12), visiting (Gen. 21:1), writing (Exod. 34:1), killing (Gen. 38:7), inflicting (Gen. 12:17), judging (Ps. 58:11), condemning (Job 10:2), engraving

(Isa. 49:16), washing (Ps. 51:2), anointing (Ps. 2:2), adorning (Ezek. 16:11), clothing (Ps. 132:16), and crowning (Ps. 8:5). God is also frequently described with names that denote a certain occupation, office, position, or relationship among people: bridegroom (Isa. 61:10), father (Deut. 32:6), judge, king, lawgiver (Isa. 33:22), warrior (Exod. 15:3), architect and builder (Heb. 11:10), gardener (John 15:1), shepherd (Ps. 23:1), physician (Exod. 15:26), and so on. In connection with these occupational descriptions there is mention of his seat, throne, footstool, rod, scepter, weapons, bow, arrow, shield, chariot, banner, book, seal, treasure, inheritance, and so on. Finally, God's relation to his own is described in images derived from the organic and inorganic creation: God is compared to a lion (Isa. 31:4), an eagle (Deut. 32:11), a lamb (Isa. 53:7), a hen (Matt. 23:37), the sun (Ps. 84:11), the morning star (Rev. 22:16), a light (Ps. 27:1), a lamp (Rev. 21:23), a fire (Heb. 12:29), a spring or fountain (Ps. 36:9; Jer. 2:13), food, bread, drink, water, ointment (Isa. 55:1; John 4:10; 6:35, 55), a rock (Deut. 32:4), a refuge (Ps. 119:114), a tower (Prov. 18:10), a stronghold (Ps. 9:9), a shadow (Pss. 91:1; 121:5), a shield (Ps. 84:11), a road (John 14:6), a temple (Rev. 21:22), and so on.

[179] We see, therefore, that the entire creation is mined in Scripture for the description of the knowledge of God. Almost no limit is set to the use of anthropomorphic language. All creatures, animate and inanimate, organic and inorganic, furnish names with which to somewhat bring home to us the greatness of God. Although nameless within himself, in his revelation God possesses many names. "All things can be said of God," writes Augustine, "but nothing can be said worthily of him. Nothing is more widespread than this poverty [of expression]. You are looking for a fitting name for him? You will not find it. You try to speak of him in some way? You find that he is everything." To clarify this, Augustine refers to the human body and its many needs and uses, many and distinct sources; fountains provide water, the sun provides light. But when it comes to our spirits things are different; provision for our soul does not come from multiform sources but always the one selfsame divine being.

> [To meet our physical needs we go to diverse sources]: what bread is, water is not; what a garment is, a house is not; and what these things are, God is not, for they are visible things. God is all of these things to you: if you are hungry, he is bread to you; if you are thirsty, he is water to you; if you live in darkness, he is light to you, for he remains incorruptible. If you are naked, he is a garment of immortality to you when this corruptible shall put on incorruption and this mortal shall put on immortality.[48]

Bonaventure says it even better when he talks about transferring "to the divine that which pertains to the creature." This is necessary for us that we might glorify God with greater understanding. But there is more:

---

48. Augustine, *Lectures on the Gospel of John*, tract. 13.5 (on John 3:22–29).

God's glory requires this transference. For, since God is greatly to be praised, lest he should ever lack praise because of the scarcity of words, Holy Scripture has taught us that the names of creatures—indefinite in number—should be transferred to God, in order that just as every *creature* glorifies God, so also every *name* that is ascribed to creatures might glorify him, and in order that he who is so glorious that not one single name can do justice to him—for he surpasses, as it were, every name—might be glorified by all the names.[49]

Calvin concurs, speaking in words that come dangerously close to pantheism, as he himself acknowledges. "There is not an atom of the world in which one cannot discern at least some bright sparks of his glory." God is immanent in the whole of creation; the pure of heart see God everywhere. Adds Calvin: "I confess, of course, that it can be said reverently—provided it proceeds from a reverent mind—that nature is God."[50]

This affirmation does not ignore the inequality and hierarchy in creation. All creatures reflect some aspect of God's being but only human beings have the honor of being called "image, son, child of God"; they alone are called "God's offspring." This glorious reality does not permit us to detach ourselves from the realm of nature. Neither may we posit anything in creation on a par with or in opposition to God as such dualistic schemes as do gnosticism, Manichaeism, and Neoplatonism. When the cosmos is no longer seen as an integral part of God's revelation to humans, theology drifts away to a privatized existence in the human heart, conscience or will. The broader realms of nature and culture are considered neutral areas existing apart from God. Nature and the world no longer have anything to say to believers and revelation loses all influence in public life. Religion, confined to the inner recesses of the heart and the privacy of one's home, forfeits all claim to serious engagement with our public and civic life. Theology shrinks daily because it is no longer able to speak of God because it no longer speaks from him and through him. It no longer has any names with which to name God. God becomes the great Unknown; the world first becomes a domain without God (ἄθεος), then a domain that is anti-God (ἀντίθεος).

[180] Our task of naming God is truly challenging. Earlier in this chapter we learned that God is incomprehensible and far superior to all finite creatures. In his names, however, he descends to the level of the finite and becomes like his creatures. What we encounter here is an antinomy that seems insoluble. On the one hand, God is without a name; on the other, he possesses many names. After first banishing all anthropomorphism, we are now reintroducing it. What right do we have to apply these names to God? On what grounds do we ascribe them to God, who is infinitely superior to all his creatures and cannot be contained by the finite? Philosophers regularly raise this objection. They (e.g., Plato, Hegel)

49. Bonaventure, *Disputata S. Bonaventurae in libros sententiarum* (Lugduni, 1510), I, dist. 34, art. 1, qu. 4.
50. J. Calvin, *Institutes*, I.v.1, 5.

then try to find a solution by rejecting concrete representations of God in favor of abstractions such as the Absolute, the One, Life, or Reason. But, we must insist, these too are anthropomorphisms; they are attempts, via negation, to move from the finite to the infinite. Rejecting concrete anthropomorphisms in favor of abstract ones is no solution. We simply must acknowledge that even though our finite understanding of God is limited, it is no less true! We possess exhaustive knowledge of very little; all reality, including the visible and physical, remains something of a mystery to us. Our talk of spiritual matters, including those of our own souls, is necessarily metaphorical, figurative, poetic. But this does not mean that what we say is untrue and incorrect. On the contrary, real poetry is truth, for it is based on the resemblance, similarity, and kinship that exist between different groups of phenomena. All language participates in this rich interpenetration of visible and invisible. If speaking figuratively were untrue, all our thought and knowledge would be an illusion and speech itself impossible.

Of course, all our knowledge of God is *ectypal* or derived from Scripture. Only God's self-knowledge is adequate, underived, or *archetypal*. Yet our finite, inadequate knowledge is still true, pure, and sufficient. Ectypal knowledge must not be seen as merely symbolic, a product of poetic imagination. God then becomes mere projection and religion mere subjective art. Here the words we choose to describe our knowledge of God are important. For many modern theologians, the preference for "symbolic" represents a rejection of the notion of *analogical* and *ectypal*, both of which are used to affirm the full propositional truth of our knowledge of God. "Symbol" suggests an aesthetic claim instead of a truth claim; it is not a "true or false" assertion about *knowledge* but a subjective *judgment* about something we value. Christian theology teaches the opposite. It makes full use of the term "symbol" as, for example, when C. Vitringa uses it to refer to the theology whose object is to explain the sacred symbols that occur in Scripture and in the church, a branch that can be called *theologia symbolica* (1726).[51] But religious people do not regard representations of God as products of their own imagination; they regard them as objectively true, and their religion languishes and dies the moment they begin to doubt this fact. While works of art are products of our imagination, the moment we turn religion into art we lose any of its claim on us religiously and ethically. We are God's creation; he is not ours. While our knowledge of him is accommodated and limited, it is no less real, true, and trustworthy. As God reveals himself, so he truly is. His revealed attributes truly reveal his nature. If we turn the names of God into nothing more than a reflex of our own inner life, we lose all ground for faith's certainty. We cannot turn to God for surety, and humanity itself then becomes the standard of religion: as humans are, so is their God.

---

51. Ed. note: The term *theologia symbolica* is also used to describe the branch of theology that deals with the creeds and confessions, i.e., "symbols" of the Christian church. Thus Abraham Kuyper, in his magisterial *Principles of Sacred Theology*, places "Symbolics" as the first part of what he calls the "Dogmatological Group" in an encyclopedia of theology. See Abraham Kuyper, *Encyclopaedie der Heilige Godgeleerdheid*, 2nd ed., 3 vols. (Kampen: Kok, 1909), II, 366–75.

This is, of course, an impossible burden to bear. Scripture liberates us from it by declaring that God is the Creator of heaven and earth, that all things that exist existed and exist eternally as ideas in the mind of God. They derive their origin from God, are to a greater or lesser extent related to him, and so also have the capacity to display his perfections before the eyes of his creatures. Because the universe is God's creation, it is also his revelation and self-manifestation. There is not an atom of the world that does not reflect his deity. Among all creatures, furthermore, human beings occupy a unique position. Whereas creatures in general display only vestiges of God's perfections, we humans are his image and likeness. From this fact flows our right to call God by names that are derived from the realm of creatures, particularly that of humanity. We know God because we are known by him: "I understand because I am understood" (von Baader). We have the right to anthropomorphize God because he himself theomorphized when he created human beings (Jacobi). In all this, notwithstanding, Scripture continually confronts us with God's absolute transcendence over all creatures. Implied in creation is both God's transcendence and God's immanence, the essential difference as well as the close kinship between God and his creatures. He lives in a high and holy place, yes, but also with those who are contrite and lowly in spirit—that is the theme which comes to our ears from every page of Scripture (Isa. 57:15).[52] For these reasons Christian theology must be called *ectypal* or *analogical*, not *symbolic*. Implied in this is the following:

1. All our knowledge of God is from and through God, grounded in his revelation, that is, in objective reason.
2. In order to convey the knowledge of him to his creatures, God accommodates himself to their powers of comprehension.
3. Our knowledge of God is always only analogical in character and, therefore, only a finite image, a faint likeness and creaturely impression of the perfect knowledge that God has of himself.
4. Finally, our knowledge of God is nevertheless true, pure, and trustworthy because it is founded in God's own self-consciousness, its archetype, and his self-revelation in the cosmos.

---

52. See H. Bavinck, *Reformed Dogmatics*, II, 33–34 (#161).

8

THE LIVING, ACTING GOD

THE NAMES OF GOD

[181] Scripture provides us with a variety of names for God. These names are always concrete and never abstract, and the Bible is careful never to highlight one attribute of God at the expense of others but to let all of God's perfections come fully and equally into their own. The names of God are designations of his excellences, mighty deeds, praises (ἀρεται, 1 Pet. 2:9). The church's calling is to proclaim God's "virtues," that is, to honor him for the glory (δοξα) manifested in all his works. Scripture knows nothing of God's being aside from his attributes. It is important to stress the fact that God has a nature of his own, that he is an independent being whose essence is distinct from that of the universe. Yet, one must also keep in mind that Scripture knows nothing of a divine essence that can be discovered and known by the powers of the human intellect apart from revelation. It posits no split, much less a contrast, between God's ontological existence and his "economic" self-revelation. As God reveals himself, so is he; in his names he becomes knowable to us. Although our knowledge of God is never exhaustive, each of his attributes, made known to us in revelation, discloses to us the fullness of his being.

Christian theology has always acknowledged this. In speaking of God's names, theologians included everything they had to say about God, the attributes and the triune persons as well as the proper names. All were incorporated in the idea of God.[1] Over time, they began to make distinctions among the names as they

---

1. E.g., in Irenaeus, *Against Heresies*, I, 14; II, 13, 35.

searched for a particular attribute that would at once differentiate God from all creatures, one that most fundamentally described God's very being and hence from which the other attributes could, so to speak, be derived. Influenced by Platonism, the Jew Philo had connected it with the name YHWH, the only name that denoted not an effect or a power, but God's being itself. He therefore often called God "he who is" or "that which is" (ὁ ὤν or τὸ ὄν).[2] This description of God's being was then taken over by Christian theology. There were alternatives to starting with "being" as foundational; Duns Scotus, for example, considered "essence" to be equally and univocally attributed to God and humanity, and simply distinguished between finite and infinite being.[3] Others made similar kinds of distinctions while starting from a consistent position of God as absolute being.

[182] Reformed theology remained true to this theological tradition, including its diversity. As the seventeenth and eighteenth centuries unfolded, Socinians, Arminians, and deists rejected metaphysical questions and placed all emphasis on the will of God. To know God is to know his will, nothing more. The effect was to make God remote and increasingly distant from the world and humanity. A reaction set in against the cold, moralist concept of God. Philosophers came to speak of the Supreme Being or Nature and of the divine essence as Infinite Being or even Intelligent Being. Spinoza, for example, viewed God "as the [absolute], unique, infinite, necessarily existing substance, . . . the immanent first cause," and spoke again of "the intellectual love of God," which is the source of supreme bliss.[4] The great minds of the day—Goethe, Lessing, and Herder—were attracted to this along with the philosopher Hegel and the theologian Schleiermacher. In their hands this sort of speculation easily deteriorated into pantheism. Although pantheism was resisted by theistic thinkers such as Jacobi, Rothe, Lotze, Schelling, Fichte, and Dorner, their defense of theism made a fateful concession: the absolute personality of God was thought of in terms of becoming rather than being; theogonic process was introduced into the idea of God.

From our vantage point these last attempts look like a futile rearguard action. The separation of theology and philosophy, religion and metaphysics, is the dominant pattern today. Theology was removed from the mansion of science (*Wissenschaft*) and banished to the servants' quarters of private seminary instruction. Its place in the academy was taken by the exact and positive religion sciences, by the history and psychology of religion. In turn, religion increasingly sought to free itself from science and to banish all metaphysics and philosophy from its purview. As nineteenth-century theology turned away from metaphysics it reduced religion to morality. For the doctrine of God this meant that the essence

2. Eduard Zeller, *Die Philosophie der Griechen*, 3rd ed., 5 vols. (Leipzig: O. R. Reisland [L. W. Reisland], 1895), V, 356.

3. John Duns Scotus, *Quaestiones in libros sententiarum* (Frankfurt: Minerva, 1967), I, dist. 3, qu. 1; I, dist. 8, qu. 3.

4. B. Spinoza, *Ethics*, ed. and trans. James Gutman (New York: Hafner, 1949), I, prop. 7ff.; V, prop. 15ff.

of God was exclusively identified with ethical goodness. Thus Albrecht Ritschl looked to the moral structure of the family as the norm for our thinking about God.[5] In Christian understanding, he believed, God must be seen not as Lord or King or Master but as Father; God is the fountain of goodness and love; he is not Absolute Being but Love.[6] Consequently, Christian theology must proceed from the concept of love, and try to infer everything (creation, providence, reconciliation, justification) from that concept.[7] Up to the present, many theologians follow the path laid out by Ritschl. There is much of value in this response, but it too is one-sided. The challenge of theology is to do justice to all the attributes of God revealed in Scripture.

DIVINE SIMPLICITY; ESSENCE AND ATTRIBUTES

[183] It is this conviction that lies behind the teaching of Christian theology that God is "simple," that is, free from composition. God is identical with each of his attributes; he is what he possesses. In God "to be" is the same as to be wise, to be good, or to be powerful. All God's attributes are identical with his essence. In all his attributes he is pure being, absolute reality. To deny this, to assert a divine essence that is distinct from God's qualities, is to open the door to polytheism.[8] But a similar error occurs in philosophy and theology, such as when Plato posits the ideas as archetypes of existing things and ascribes to them an independent existence alongside God, or when Philo represents the divine energies as hypostases (substances).[9] Even Christian theologians have fallen into this error. In the Middle Ages, for example, Gilbert Porretan made a distinction between God's essence or nature (divinity) and God himself. Divinity, he claimed, is the form by virtue of which God is God, but not itself God. "God exists by virtue of divinity, but divinity as such is not God."[10] All these separations of God's being from his attributes must be rejected. One cannot make a distinction between determinations that are given with the idea of God and others that have been added. To do so impoverishes our understanding of God; it gives the impression that key attributes such as the love of God are not in the same absolute sense present in God as, for example, his infinity or power. God's full majesty, power and love, are diminished. It is true that the impression

---

5. A. Ritschl, *Die christliche Lehre von der Rechtfertigung und Versöhnung*, 2nd ed., 3 vols. (Bonn: A. Marcus, 1882–83), III, 223–29.

6. Ibid., 255.

7. Ibid.

8. Ed. note: The thought here is that of conceptually defining an essence of deity or godness that a number of entities have in common. Theoretically, then, Zeus, Hermes, and Baal share an essential "godness" but one has the attribute of being the head of the gods, another is the messenger of the gods, and the third controls fertility.

9. E. Zeller, *Philosophie der Griechen*, V, 358ff.

10. Cf. Dionysius Petavius, "De Deo," in *De theologicis dogmatibus*, 8 vols. (Paris: Vivès, 1865–67), I, chap. 8.

has been given that theology, proceeding from the description of God as the Supreme Being, has gone down the same path as philosophy, which views God as the Absolute and confines itself to this abstraction. Yet, convinced that we cannot refrain from speaking of God's being, Christian theology has prudently avoided the pitfalls we have just described through its doctrine of the simplicity of God.

[184] When Christian theology rejected the distinction between God's essence and attributes, this was not to deny that God has "being," nor to forbid the use of the word "being" in the doctrine of God. The distinction held at bay from God all that is nonreal, and expressed as strongly as possible that in all his attributes he is pure being, absolute reality. Because God is pure being—the absolute, perfect, unique, and simple being—we cannot define him; there is no genus to which he belongs as a member, no specific marks of distinction whereby we can distinguish him from other beings in this genus. Even the being God shares with all creatures is not to be understood univocally as identical but analogically and proportionally. Yet name him we must; we cannot refrain from speaking about his "being" and distinguishing him from all that is not God. But here we face the problem that God, on the one hand, has no name (is anonymous) and, on the other hand, has many names (is polyonymous). The number of attributes he has revealed of himself is so great that one cannot possibly sum them up completely. So we must either totally refrain from any description whatsoever or else make a selection from among them. Different schools of theology are born from the variety of such attempts to order and classify the names and attributes of God.[11] When a single attribute is chosen as foundational it affects the total portrait of God; a wrong choice here points us to a different God than the one revealed in Scripture. Choosing love, for example, exposes us to the danger of regarding other attributes of God, such as righteousness and holiness, as less real.[12]

Christian theology has sought to avoid this one-sidedness in its description of God's essence by placing God's aseity in the foreground as the primary attribute traditionally associated with the name YHWH as given in Exodus 3:14. It does not yield to philosophy exclusive use and determination of the word "absolute." In fact, there is much to be said for the thesis that the word "absolute," even when used by philosophers, actually has a religious character because it arises from a basic human metaphysical or religious need.[13] For religion and theology, God must always be God, distinct from and above all things, the Creator and Ruler of all that exists, on whom believers can rely in times of distress and death, or else God can no longer be God to them. As such God is the strictly independent and only absolute being. The notion of "absoluteness" was not obtained by abstraction, deprived of all content, and considered as the most general kind of being, but arises from religious

11. See H. Bavinck, *Reformed Dogmatics*, ed. John Bolt (Grand Rapids: Baker Academic, 2003–8), I, 287–95 (#83).
12. Friedrich A. B. Nitzsch, *Lehrbuch der evangelischen Dogmatik*, 3rd ed., ed. Horst Stephan (Tübingen: J. C. B. Mohr, 1902), 352ff.
13. Ibid., 356.

conviction that God is the One who exists of and through himself, the perfect being who is absolute in wisdom and goodness, righteousness and holiness, power and blessedness. God is absolute, that is, independent being, existing only to himself. "Absolute is that which is not dependent on anything else."[14] This conviction is the clear teaching of Holy Scripture. From everlasting to everlasting he is God, the First and the Last, from whom, through whom, and to whom are all things (Gen. 1:1ff.; Pss. 33:6, 9; 90:2; Isa. 41:4; 43:10–13; 44:6; 48:12; John 5:26; Acts 17:24ff.; Rom. 11:36; Eph. 4:6; Heb. 2:10; Rev. 1:4, 8; 4:8, 11; 10:6; 11:17; etc.).

[185] If God is God, the only, eternal, and absolute Being, this implies that he possesses all the perfections, a faint analogy of which can be discerned in his creatures. If God is the absolutely existing being, he is also absolute in wisdom and goodness, in righteousness and holiness, in power and blessedness. As the One who exists of and through and unto himself, he is the fullness of being, the independent and supremely perfect Being. Although we cannot distinguish God's essence from his attributes, it is permissible to make distinctions among the attributes. Each attribute expresses something special about God. God himself reveals his many perfections to us; we name him with the names Scripture itself provides. No one perfection fully expresses God's being. This diversity does not clash with God's simplicity. God reveals himself to finite creatures by many names because the divine essence is so infinitely and profusely rich that we cannot grasp it all at once, and God relates to us in many ways, now in one relationship, then in another.[15] God remains eternally and immutably the same, but our relation to him varies in the same way that the light that breaks up into many colors remains the same (Augustine), and fire does not change whether it warms us, illumines us, or consumes us (Moses Maimonides). God is called by different names on account of the varying effects he produces in his creatures by his ever-constant being. Although it is always the same being that confronts us in these names, each name by itself gives us a succinct statement of what that being truly is in its infinite fullness. In God, holiness and mercy may be the same in essence, yet our understanding of these two attributes, formed from God's self-revelation, differs. There is no one name capable of expressing God's being with full adequacy. Given that reality, many names serve to give us an impression of his all-transcending grandeur.

[186–87] In the past, theologians have distinguished three ways of obtaining the names of God, in the way of *negation*, or of *eminence*, or of *causality*, in relation to creatures. The first way begins with statements about what God is *not* but is then led, in some defective and inadequate fashion, to predicate something *positive* about him as well. Pseudo-Dionysius, John of Damascus, and Erigena,

14. J. Alsted, *Encyclopaedia* (Herbornae Nassovorium, 1630), 596; cf. Rudolf Eisler, *Wörterbuch der philosophischen Begriffe*, 2 vols. (Berlin: E. S. Mittler, 1904), s.v. "absolutum."

15. Augustine, *Lectures on the Gospel of John*, tract. 13; Peter Martyr Vermigli, *Petri Martyris Vermilii ... Loci Communes* (London: Kyngston, 1576), 39; Bernhard de Moor, *Commentarius perpetuus in Johannis Marckii compendium theologiae christianae didactico-elencticum*, 7 vols. in 6 (Leiden: J. Hasebroek, 1761–71), I, 582.

proceeding from this idea, worked it into a formal division, a twofold theology, namely, "apophatic" and "kataphatic."[16] Pseudo-Dionysius describes the three ways explicitly when he says that we arrive at the knowledge of God "by way of the denial and the transcendence of all things and by way of the cause of all things."[17] Scholasticism formally adopted the threefold distinction, and Roman Catholic, Lutheran, and Reformed theologians alike continue to make it. Modern thinkers from Kant to Schleiermacher, however, repudiate some or all of the ways, often by rejecting all analogical thinking *from below* to God and insisting that we can only descend to the world from a position in God.[18]

We, of course, also insist that our speaking about God must begin with revelation. The knowledge of God's attributes existed long before these three ways were conceived; they arose from reflection on attributes already well known and described. Furthermore, since the way of eminence and the way of causality are actually one, they may together be posited as the way of affirmation over against the way of negation. Finally, there is no doubt that the mode of knowing should not be confused with the mode of being. In reality God, not the creature, is primary. He is the archetype (the original); the creature is the ectype (the likeness). In him everything is original, absolute, and perfect; in creatures everything is derived, relative, and limited. God, therefore, is not really named after things present in creatures, but creatures are named after that which exists in an absolute sense in God. Conversely, because we have no knowledge of God other than from his revelation in the creaturely world we walk by faith and not by sight; we have only an analogous and proportional knowledge of God, an indirect kind of knowledge, a concept derived from the creaturely world. Although not exhaustive, this knowledge is not untrue since all creatures are God's and display something of his perfections. Therefore both the way of negation and affirmation can be taken with safety. Precisely because everything comes from God, everything points back to God and we can also ascend from earth to heaven. All thought and speech about God—whether by way of affirmation or negation—uses forms and images taken from the world.

Confessing that creaturely limitations and imperfections are not found in God, while God in an absolute sense has all the perfections we observe in creatures, we conclude that the ways of negation and affirmation are complementary. Together they form the one pure knowledge of God; what we deny in God we can state positively; what we affirm in a supereminent sense in God, we deny that they are present in creatures in the same manner. We confess God is incomprehensible and therefore knowable; he is holy, good, and righteous, but in manner unlike that of his creatures. That is the reason we can say that all attributes are simultaneously

16. Pseudo-Dionysius, *The Divine Names and Mystical Theology*, I, 2, 4; John of Damascus, *Exposition of the Orthodox Faith*, NPNF[2], I, 2, 4; Erigena, *On the Divine Nature*, I, 78.

17. Pseudo-Dionysius, *On the Divine Names*, 7, §3.

18. On the three ways, see I. A. Dorner, *A System of Christian Doctrine*, trans. Alfred Cave and J. S. Banks, rev. ed., 4 vols. (Edinburgh: T&T Clark, 1888–91), I, 201ff.; C. Hodge, *Systematic Theology*, 3 vols. (New York: Charles Scribner's Sons, 1888), I, 339.

ascribed and denied to him. Mysticism loves to speak about God in this seemingly paradoxical manner. God is simultaneously panonymous (the possessor of all names) and anonymous (the possessor of no name). Those know him best who do not know him—who think he transcends the conceivable. The most brilliant light dwells in deepest darkness (Exod. 20:21). Pseudo-Dionysius, accordingly, calls God "the affirmation of all things and the negation of all things: the Cause beyond all affirmation and denial."[19]

Of all the ways to classify God's attributes, among Reformed theologians the distinction between incommunicable and communicable properties became the favored distinction. This distinction affirms, on the one hand, that all creatures are related to God, and especially that human beings are his image and likeness, and on the other that God is essentially distinct from his creation. "Incommunicable" accents the distinctness of God, especially over against all forms of pantheism, while "communicable" underscores God's relatedness to all creatures. In the former were included oneness, simplicity, immutability, eternity; the second group was usually divided further into attributes of intellect (knowledge, wisdom, veracity), will (goodness, righteousness, holiness), and power. Incommunicable attributes accent God's transcendence; communicable attributes God's immanence. Reformed theology uses the terms "incommunicable" and "communicable" here to underscore the strong opposition of Christian theism to the twin errors of *pantheism* and *deism*.[20]

Distinguishing God's attributes, in whatever way, must never be taken as a division of God into two halves, a separation of God's absoluteness from his relatedness to creation or his being from his perfections. Our knowledge of God is indeed ectypal and analogical and based on his self-revelation. But it is true knowledge, and because God's attributes are identical with his being, we can speak truly about God as he really is. Since in his perfections God is both absolutely superior to us and in fellowship with his creatures, each of his attributes can be said, in different senses, to be both incommunicable and communicable. Relative terms, such as "Lord," "Creator," "Sustainer," "Savior," and so on, belong to God only on account of, and upon the coming into being of, the creation. No one can be called "master" unless he has servants. Human beings, the servants of God, were created in time, so in time God became our Lord.[21] The same is

19. Pseudo-Dionysius, *The Divine Names and Mystical Theology*, chap. 2; cf. M. J. Scheeben, *Handbuch der katholischen Dogmatik*, 4 vols. (1873–1903; repr., Freiburg i.B.: Herder, 1933), I, 483; ed. note: ET: *A Manual of Catholic Theology: Based on Scheeben's "Dogmatik,"* by Joseph Wilhelm and Thomas B. Scannell, 4th ed., 2 vols. (London: Kegan Paul, Trench, Trübner; New York: Benziger Brothers, 1909); J. B. Heinrich and C. Gutberlet, *Dogmatische Theologie*, 2nd ed., 10 vols. (Mainz: Kirchheim, 1881–1900), III, 309.

20. Ed. note: cf. notes 31 and 51 below.

21. Augustine, *The Trinity*, V, 16; cf. idem, *On Order*, II, 7; T. Aquinas, *Summa Theol.*, 1, qu. 13, art. 7; Anselm, *Monologion*, 15; P. Lombard, *Sententiae in IV liberis distinctae*, 3rd ed., 2 vols. (Grottaferrata: Colleggi S. Bonaventurae ad Claras Aquas, 1971–81), I, dist. 30; Bonaventure, *Disputata S. Bonaventurae in libros sententiarum* (Lugduni, 1510), I, dist. 30, art. 1; Jerome Zanchi, *Operum theologicorum*, 8 vols.

true for all metaphorical names, including the anthropomorphisms. In the same way the positive names—such as "good," "holy," "wise"—have some meaning to our mind, because we observe examples (ectypes) of them in creatures.[22] But all these names, though relative, metaphorical, and positive, nevertheless definitely denote something in God that exists in him absolutely, "properly," and hence also "negatively," that is, in another sense than it exists in creatures. The same is true for the so-called negative or incommunicable attributes. For although they deny to God some quality that pertains to creatures, they are all in a sense also positive, communicable, transferable, and relative. If not, we could neither know them nor name them. The negative terms also have a positive content. Even though we cannot understand eternity in a positive sense, it means a lot to know that God is exalted above all the conditions of time. By means of that knowledge we, as it were, continually correct our notions concerning God. We speak of him in human terms and attribute to him a range of human qualities, but as we are doing this we are ever acutely conscious of the fact that all these properties pertain to God in a sense quite different from that in which we find them in creatures. We can only name God in terms of what is revealed of him in his creatures, but in so doing we are still naming him who is infinitely exalted above all his creatures. In all creatures but especially in humanity there is something analogous to the divine being. But all the perfections found in creatures exist in God in a wholly unique and original way. Discernible in every one of God's perfections is both his absolute superiority over, and his kinship with, his creatures. Hence, in one sense each of his attributes is incommunicable and in another communicable. Scripture thus simultaneously maintains both God's transcendence over, and his orientation to, the world.

GOD'S PROPER NAMES

[188] Holy Scripture not only describes God's perfections but also reveals to us God's personal names. If we speak of God's names in distinction from his attributes and hence in a restricted sense, we understand by them the names by which we refer to or address God as an independent personal being. Such names for the divine being exist in every language. Words used for God, such as the Greek θεος, often have disputed etymologies; what is common is a connection with "heaven" which is often used interchangeably with "God" as in the Chinese word *Thian* and the Tatar and Turkish word *Taengri*. A similar move is made in Scripture when "kingdom of heaven" is used as equivalent to "kingdom of God." Derivations of the word "God" (Ger. *Gott*) are uncertain. Notions that may be present are: "the hidden One," "the One called upon," "the Good (Pure)," or "the

---

([Geneva]: Samuelis Crispini, 1617), II, 24–26; Amandus Polanus, *Syntagma theologiae christianae*, 5th ed. (Hanover: Aubry, 1624), 192.

    22. T. Aquinas, *Summa Theol.*, I, qu. 12, art. 12.

[One who] orders, arranges." The name *Asura*, used among the East Indians, and *Ahura*, a Persian name, refer to God as the Living One.[23] Neither etymology nor terminology is as important here as the *fact* of naming which is universal among the peoples of the world in all religions. Although in himself God has no name, *we* have a need to refer to him, and for this we have no other means than a name.

El, Elohim, El Shaddai

The simplest name for God in the Old Testament is *El* (אֵל); its plural construction *Elohim* אֱלֹהִים) is from the same root. This name emphasizes God's power and might; he is the high and strong One. The plural, however, must not be interpreted as a plural of majesty, which is never used in Scripture of God, nor viewed as a reference to the Trinity, as has been done by many. Since the word occurs in contexts outside of Israel as the name of one single God,[24] it is better to view it as a plural of abstraction (Ewald), or as a plural of quantity, which, as in the case of מִים and שׁמִים, is used to refer to an unbounded entity (Oehler), or as an intensive plural that serves to express fullness of power (Delitzsch). "The name Elohim describes the divine being in his original relation and constant causal relation to the universe. It is a designation of relationship, not of immediate inner being. In fact, it expresses the idea of absolute transcendence with respect to the entire universe."[25]

The name *'Elyôn* (עֶלְיוֹן; LXX: ὕψιστος) refers to God as the One who is exalted high above everything. The name is used by Melchizedek (Gen. 14:18), Balaam (Num. 24:16), and the king of Babylon (Isa. 14:14; cf. Mark 5:7; Luke 1:32, 35; Acts 16:17) and further occurs especially in poetry. The name *'Adonai* (אדני), further intensified in "Lord of lords" (אֲדֹן אֲדֹנִים) or "Lord of all the earth" (אֲדֹן כָּל-הָאָרֶץ), refers to God as the Ruler to whom all things are subject and to whom humans are related as servants (Gen. 18:27). In an earlier period the name Baal (בַּעַל) was used of God with the same meaning (Hosea 2:16 [2:18 MT]), but later this use was discontinued because of its idolatrous connotations.[26] Now these names are not proper names in the restricted sense. They are used as well of idols, people (Gen. 33:10; Exod. 7:1; 4:16), and authorities (Exod. 12:12; 21:5–6; 22:7; Lev. 19:32; Num. 33:4; Judg. 5:8; 1 Sam. 2:25; Pss. 58:1 [58:2 MT]; 82:1)

23. H. Cremer, *Biblisch-theologisches Wörterbuch der neutestamentlichen Gräcität* (Gotha: F. A. Perthes, 1880), s.v. "θεος"; J. Köstlin, "Gott," *PRE³*, VI, 779ff.; cf. F. Kluge, *Etymologisches Wörterbuch der deutschen Sprache* (Strassburg: K. J. Trübner, 1883), s.v. "Gott."

24. M. Noordtzij, *Oostersche Lichtstralen over Westersche Schriftbeschouwing* (Kampen: J. H. Bos, 1897), 41ff.

25. J. T. Beck, *Vorlesungen über christliche Glaubenslehre*, 2 vols. (Gütersloh: C. Bertelsmann, 1886–87), II, 22; cf. further, G. F. Oehler, *Theology of the Old Testament*, trans. Ellen D. Smith and Sophia Taylor (Edinburgh: T&T Clark, 1892–93), §36; A. B. Davidson, *The Theology of the Old Testament*, ed. S. D. F. Salmond (Edinburgh: T&T Clark, 1904), 41, 99; R. Kittel, "Elohim," *PRE³*, V, 316–19.

26. J. Robertson, *Israel's oude godsdienst* (Culemborg: Blom en Olivierse, 1896), 200ff.; ed. note: Eng. edition: *The Early Religion of Israel*, 2nd ed. (New York: Westminster [Thomas Wittaker], 1903).

but are nevertheless the usual names by which God is called and addressed. They are, moreover, common Semitic names referring to God in his transcendence over all creatures. Feeling deeply dependent on God as his servants, the Semites loved to call God "Lord" or "king." These names are not used to give expression to philosophical theories about God's essence but to give prominence to his relation to his creatures, especially to human beings.[27]

[189] Although high and exalted, this God also stoops down to the level of his creatures. Beyond his general revelation through creation to all peoples he makes himself known in a special sense also to Israel. Now the first name by which God appears in his special revelation is *Shaddai* (שַׁדָּי) or *'El Shaddai* (אֵל שַׁדָּי), given to Abraham when he makes him a father of many peoples and seals his covenant with him by the rite of circumcision (Gen. 17:1). Accordingly, in the period of the patriarchs this name occurs repeatedly (Gen. 28:3; 35:11; 43:14; 48:3; 49:25; Exod. 6:3; Num. 24:4). It is further found in Job, in a number of psalms, and a few times in the prophets. The New Testament equivalent is the Lord Almighty (παντοκρατωρ, 2 Cor. 6:18; Rev. 4:8; etc.). The origin of *'El Shaddai* is not certain but wherever it appears, it highlights the idea of power and invincible strength. It reveals to us God the One who possesses all power, can overcome all resistance and make all things subservient to his will. Whereas "Elohim" is the God of creation and nature, "El Shaddai" is the God who makes all the powers of nature subject and subservient to the work of grace.[28] In this name God's deity (θειοτης) and eternal power (ἀϊδιος δυναμις) are no longer an object of dread but a source of well-being and comfort. From this point on, therefore, he is over and over called the God of Abraham (Gen. 24:12), of Isaac (Gen. 28:13), of Jacob (Exod. 3:6), the God of the Fathers (Exod. 3:13, 15), the God of the Hebrews (Exod. 3:18), the God of Israel (Gen. 33:20), and in Isaiah the Holy One of Israel (Isa. 1:4; 5:19, 24; et al.). God is the Exalted One, Creator of heaven and earth, the Almighty, but at the same time he stands in a special and most beneficent relation to his people.

YHWH

As the God of grace, Scripture reveals God to us as YHWH (the LORD). YHWH is the covenant God of promise, the faithful one who saves his people. YHWH is the highest revelation of God in the Old Testament; YHWH is God's real name. The Jews called it the preeminent name, the name that describes God's essence, God's proper name, the glorious, the four-letter name (the tetragramma-

---

27. W. Robertson Smith, *Die Religion der Semiten* (Freiburg i.B.: Mohr, 1899), 48.

28. Commentary of the *Statenvertaling* on Gen. 17:1. Ed. note: The *Statenvertaling* is the annotated Dutch Scripture translation officially sanctioned by the Synod of Dordrecht, 1618–19. J. Zanchi, *Op. theol.*, II, 43; Campegius Vitringa, *Doctrina christianae religionis*, 8 vols. (Leiden: Joannis le Mair, 1761–86), I, 132; B. de Moor, *Comm. in Marckii Comp.*, I, 522ff.; G. F. Oehler, *Theology of the Old Testament*, §37; F. Delitzsch, *A New Commentary on Genesis*, trans. Sophia Taylor (Edinburgh: T&T Clark, 1899), on Gen. 17:1.

ton), and concluded from Leviticus 24:16 and Exodus 3:15 (where they read the word for "forever" as the word for "to conceal it," לְעַלֵּם) that they were forbidden to pronounce it. Thus, the LXX reads *'Adonai* for YHWH and translates it by κυριος, and the New Testament follows suit.

There is much debate and disagreement about the etymology of YHWH as well as about its meaning. Even when we turn to Exodus 3 we still run into disagreement, but it is here that we get the clearest indication. The key phrase in verses 13–15 reads: "I AM WHO I AM" (אֶהְיֶה אֲשֶׁר אֶהְיֶה); by it the Lord says that he who now calls Moses and wants to save his people is the same [God] as he who appeared to their fathers. He is who he is, the same yesterday, today, and forever. This meaning is further explained in verse 15: YHWH—the God of your fathers, the God of Abraham, Isaac, and Jacob—sends Moses, and that is his name forever. God does not simply call himself "the One who is" and offer no explanation of his aseity, but states expressly what and how he is; then how and what will he be? Unable to summarize in a single word or phrase, we are given "he will be what he will be." That sums up everything. This addition is still general and indefinite, but for that reason also rich and full of deep meaning. He will be what he was for the patriarchs, what he is now and will remain: he will be everything to and for his people. It is not a new and strange God who comes to them by Moses, but the God of the fathers, the Unchangeable One, the Faithful One, the eternally Self-consistent One, who never leaves or forsakes his people but always again seeks out and saves his own. He is unchangeable in his grace, in his love, in his assistance, who will be what he is because he is always himself. So in Isaiah he calls himself: "I am he, the first and the last" (אֲנִי הוּא, 41:4; 43:10, 13, 25; 44:6; 48:12). And indeed, his aseity underlies this view of God, but it is not in the foreground nor directly expressed in the name.

We must not understand this to mean that the name YHWH was unknown before the revelation to Moses at the burning bush and God's explanation in Exodus 6:3. Certainly it existed before this time, had already been used repeatedly by the Lord himself (Gen. 15:7; 28:13), and was current as a name of address (Gen. 14:22; 15:2, 8; 24:3; 28:16; 32:9). Exodus 6:3 records the first time the Lord made known the meaning of this name, the time when the Lord tells Moses how he wants people to understand it. From this point on the name YHWH is the description and guarantee of the fact that God is and remains the God of his people, unchanging in his grace and faithfulness. Now, after a long time from the patriarchs to the Egyptian slavery, a period when God proved that he is unchanging and faithful to his promises, *now* God says, "This is how I want you to know me and speak of me": "I am who I am, YHWH, the unchangingly faithful One, the God of the fathers, your God even now and forever." At this point God injects a totally fresh meaning into an old name, one that could only now be understood by the people. For that reason YHWH is Israel's God "from the land of Egypt" (Hosea 12:9; 13:4).

YHWH Sabaoth

[190] In the Old Testament the name YHWH is the highest revelation of God. No new names are added. YHWH is God's real name (Exod. 15:3; Ps. 83:18; Hosea 12:5; Isa. 42:8), and this name is given to no other. It occurs in abbreviated form (*-yah*), especially in combinations with names and ascriptions of praise (*hallelu-yah*; הַלְלוּ־יָהּ), and also independently (Exod. 15:2; Pss. 68:4 [68:5 MT]; 89:8 [89:9 MT]; 94:7, 12; 118:14; Isa. 12:2; 38:11), sometimes in connection with YHWH (Isa. 26:4). The combination Adonai YHWH (e.g., Ezek. 22:12) is also common. The name YHWH receives added force when combined with *Sabaoth* (יהוה צבאות; 1 Sam. 1:3; 4:4; Pss. 69:6 [69:7 MT]; 80:4 [80:5 MT]; 84:1; 84:8 [84:9 MT]; Isa. 1:24; Amos 9:5; Hag. 2:7–9). It is hard to say, however, what precisely is meant by the word "Sabaoth." Interpretations associating it with war or armies or, alternatively, with the stars of heaven, including the powers and elements of the entire cosmos (with an appeal to Gen. 2:1; Ps. 103:21; Isa. 34:1–2), are implausible since they cannot account for all uses or even changing uses in different circumstances.

Perhaps the old interpretation which, in reading "hosts," thought of angels, is the best since it finds abundant support in Scripture. The name "Lord of hosts" is repeatedly used with reference to angels (1 Sam. 4:4; 2 Sam. 6:2; Isa. 37:16; Hosea 12:5–6; Pss. 80:1 [80:2 MT], 4f.; 89:5–8 [89:6–9 MT]), and the angels are frequently pictured as a "host" surrounding the throne of God (Gen. 28:12–13; 32:1–2; Josh. 5:14; 1 Kings 22:19; Job 1:6; Pss. 68:17 [68:18 MT]; 89:8 [89:9 MT]; 103:21; 148:2; Isa. 6:2). Scripture usually speaks of a host (sing.) of angels but also repeatedly mentions many hosts of angels (Gen. 32:2; Deut. 33:2; Pss. 68:17; 148:2). This fits the meaning of the name, which has absolutely no warlike or martial character (this cannot even be inferred from 1 Sam. 4:4; 17:45; 2 Sam. 6:2), but everywhere expresses the glory of God as king (Deut. 33:2; 1 Kings 22:19; Ps. 24:10; Isa. 6:2; 24:23; Zech. 1:14; 14:16). The angels belong to the glory (δόξα) of God or of Christ: they heighten and expand it (Matt. 25:31; Mark 8:38; 2 Thess. 1:7; Rev. 7:11). Throughout the Scriptures "YHWH Sabaoth" is the solemn royal name of God, full of majesty and glory. The name *Elohim* denotes God as Creator and Sustainer of all things; *'El Shaddai* represents him as the mighty One who makes nature subservient to grace; YHWH describes him as the One who in his grace remains forever faithful; *YHWH Sabaoth* characterizes him as king in the fullness of his glory who, surrounded by regimented hosts of angels, governs throughout the world as the Almighty, and in his temple receives the honor and acclamation of all his creatures.[29]

[191] In the New Testament all these names have been retained. El and Elohim are rendered by God (θεος), Elyon is translated by "the Most High" (ὑψιστος θεος, Mark 5:7; Luke 1:32, 35, 76; 8:28; Acts 7:48; 16:17; Heb. 7:1; cf. Luke 2:14,

---

29. Cf. further concerning "JHWH Sabaoth," G. F. Oehler, *Theology of the Old Testament*, §§195ff.; R. E. Raubsch, "Zebaoth," *PRE²*, XVIII, 720.

"God in the highest," (ἐν ὑψίστοις θεῷ). Although the appellation of God as the
"God of Abraham, Isaac, and Jacob" or as "the God of Israel" passes into the New
Testament (Matt. 15:31; 22:32; Mark 12:26; Luke 1:68; 20:37; Acts 3:13; 7:32,
46; 22:14; 24:14; Heb. 11:16), generally these appositions are replaced by the
genitives "my," "your," "our," "your" (pl.), for in Christ God has become the God
and Father of his people and of each of his children (Heb. 8:10; Rev. 7:12; 19:5;
21:3). The name YHWH is explicated a few times as "the Alpha and the Omega,"
"him who is and who was and who is to come," "the beginning and the end," "the
first and the last" (Rev. 1:4, 8, 11 [KJV], 17; 2:8; 21:6; 22:13). For the rest, following the example of the LXX, which already read Adonai, the name YHWH is
translated by Lord (Κυριος, derived from κυρος, strength). Κυριος points to Mighty
One, the Lord, Owner, and Ruler who *legally* exercises power and authority (in
distinction from the δεσποτης, referring to one who *actually* exercises power),
and in the New Testament Lord is variably used both of God and of Christ. Also
the combinations "YHWH Elohim" and "YHWH Elohim Sabaoth" are found
again in the New Testament, as "Lord God" (Luke 1:16; Acts 7:37; 1 Pet. 3:15;
Rev. 1:8; 22:5) and "Lord God Almighty" (Rev. 4:8; 11:17; 15:3; 16:7; 21:22),
while in Romans 9:29 and James 5:4 "Sabaoth (hosts)" remains untranslated.

Father

The one new name, added by our Lord Jesus Christ, is the personal name
"Father" (Πατηρ), indicating God's special familial relationship with his people.
However, this name for the Deity also occurs in pagan religions[30] and is already
used several times of God in the Old Testament (Deut. 32:6; Ps. 103:13; Isa. 63:16;
64:8; Jer. 3:4, 19; 31:9; Mal. 1:6; 2:10), just as Israel is also repeatedly called his
Son (Exod. 4:22; Deut. 14:1; 32:19; Isa. 1:2; Jer. 31:20; Hosea 1:10; 11:1). In the
Old Testament the name "Father" expresses the special theocratic relation that
God sustains to his people Israel whom he graciously formed out of Abraham.
In the more general sense of Origin and Creator the name "Father" is used in
1 Corinthians 8:6; Ephesians 3:14–15; Hebrews 12:9; and James 1:17 (cf. Luke
3:38; Acts 17:28). But above all the name expresses the ethical relation in which
God, through Christ, now stands to all his children. Old Testament Israel, in its
relation to God, is the type and model of this. But now, in Christ, that relation has
been deepened and expanded, made personal, ethical, individual. The theocratic
kingdom known in Israel passes into a kingdom of the Father who is in heaven, a
kingdom made possible by the true, only begotten, and beloved Son of the Father.
Here we find perfect kingship, for here is a king who is simultaneously a Father
who does not subdue his subjects by force but who himself creates and preserves
his subjects. Here believers who are citizens obtain adoption as children and
also become conscious of it by the agency of the Holy Spirit (John 3:5, 8; Rom.
8:15f.). "Father" is thus the supreme revelation of God, and since the Father is

30. W. Robertson Smith, *Die Religion der Semiten*, 27ff.

made known to us by Jesus through the Spirit, the full, abundant revelation of God's name is trinitarian: Father, Son, and Holy Spirit. The fullness that from the beginning inhered in the name Elohim has gradually unfolded and become most fully and splendidly manifest in the trinitarian name of God.

GOD'S INCOMMUNICABLE ATTRIBUTES[31]

[192] We now move beyond God's proper names to consider broader teaching about God's nature and activity. Although some theologians (John of Damascus; Bonaventure) treat the Trinity before the general attributes of God's nature, we follow Scripture in which we find a prior and more clear revelation of the latter. The Trinity is not clearly revealed until we get to the New Testament. The names YHWH and Elohim precede those of Father, Son, and Spirit. God is independent, all-sufficient in himself, and the only source of all existence and life. YHWH is the name that describes this essence and identity most clearly: "I will be what I will be." It is in this aseity of God, conceived not only as having being from himself but also as the fullness of being, that all other divine perfections are included.

Aseity/Independence

We begin our discussion of God's attributes, therefore, with *aseity* or independence, a fact more or less recognized by all humans in the very definition of "God." If God is to be truly God, he must be sufficient unto himself. He is dependent on nothing, he needs nothing; rather, all that exists depends on him. He is the only source of all existence and life, of all light and love, the overflowing fountain of all good (Ps. 36:10; Acts 17:25), the Alpha and the Omega who is and who was and who is to come (Isa. 41:4; 44:6; 48:12; Rev. 1:8). He is the perfect, highest, the most excellent being, "than whom nothing better can exist or be thought." All being is contained in him. He is a boundless ocean of being. "If you have said of God that he is good, great, blessed, wise or any other such quality, it is summed up in a single word: *he is (Est)*. Indeed, for him to *be* is to be all these things. Even if you add a hundred such qualities, you have not gone outside the boundaries of his being. Having said them all, you have added nothing; having said none of them, you have subtracted nothing."[32]

Roman Catholic and Reformation theologians follow this Scholastic affirmation, with the Reformed eventually coming to prefer the term "independence" over

---

31. Ed. note: We are retaining the traditional distinction between incommunicable and communicable attributes, though it should be noted that Bavinck himself finds them inadequate because communicability and incommunicability are true of all the divine attributes. The terms became popular among the Reformed because they were useful in controversies with Lutherans about the "communication of properties" (*comunicatio idiomatum*).

32. Bernard de Clairvaux, *De consideratione* (Utrecht: Nicolaus Ketelaer and Gerhardus Leempt, 1473), I, 5, chap. 6.

"aseity." While aseity only expresses God's self-sufficiency in his existence, independence has a broader sense and implies that God is independent in everything: in his existence, in his perfections, in his decrees, and in his works. Accordingly, while in the past theologians mostly used the name YHWH as their starting point, in later years God's independence occurs most often as the first of the incommunicable attributes.[33] We must conceive of God's independence not only as God having being from himself but also as the fullness of being, the inclusion of other perfections. They are given with the aseity itself and are the rich and multifaceted development of it. It is this attribute that vividly and plainly marks the immeasurable distinction between the Creator and creature. There is, nevertheless, a weak analogy in all creatures also of this perfection of God. Pantheism, indeed, cannot acknowledge this, but theism stands for the fact that a creature, though absolutely dependent, nevertheless also has a distinct existence of its own. Implanted in this existence there is "a drive toward self-preservation." Every creature, to the extent that it shares in existence, fears death, and even the tiniest atom offers resistance to all attempts at annihilating it. Again: it is a shadow of the independent, immutable being of our God.

Immutability

[193] *Immutability* is a natural implication of God's aseity. While everything changes, God is and remains the same. If God were not immutable, he would not be God. To God alone belongs true being, and that which truly is remains. At first blush this immutability seems to have little support in Scripture since it portrays God as standing in the most vital association with the world. As Creator of heaven and earth he comes and goes, reveals and conceals himself, averting his face (in wrath) and turning it back in grace. God even repents (Gen. 6:6; 1 Sam. 15:11; Amos 7:3, 6; Joel 2:13; Jon. 3:9; 4:2). In the fullness of time he even becomes human in Christ and proceeds to dwell in the church through the Holy Spirit. He rejects Israel and accepts the gentiles. And in the life of the children of God there is a consistent alternation of feelings of guilt and the consciousness of forgiveness, of experiences of God's wrath and of his love, of his abandonment and his presence.

At the same time the Scriptures testify that amid all this alternation God is and remains the same. Everything changes, but God remains who he is (Ps. 102:26–28). He is YHWH, he who is and ever remains himself; with the first and with the last he is still the same God (Isa. 41:4; 43:10; 46:4; 48:12). He is who he is (Deut. 32:39; cf. John 8:58; Heb. 13:8), he alone has immortality, and remains the same (Rom. 1:23; 1 Tim. 1:17; 6:16; Heb. 1:11–12). What is true of his existence and being is also true of his thought and will. He is not a human that he should lie or repent. What he says, he will do (Num. 15:28; 1 Sam. 15:29). His gifts (charismata) and calling are irrevocable (Rom. 11:29); he does not reject

33. A. Hyperius, *Methodi theologiae, sive praecipuorum Christianae religionis* (Basel: Oporiniana, 1574), 87, 135; Peter van Mastricht, *Theoretico-practica theologia* (Utrecht: Appels, 1714), II, 3.

his people (Rom. 11:1). He completes what he has begun (Ps. 138:8; Phil. 1:6). He, YHWH, does not change (Mal. 3:6). In him there is "no variation or shadow due to change" (James 1:17).

On this foundation Christian theology constructed its doctrine of divine immutability. Contrary to both deism and pantheism, God who is cannot change, for every change would diminish his being. This doctrine of God's immutability is important; the very distinction between Creator and creature hinges on the contrast between being and becoming. Our reliance on God depends on his immutability. Philosophic notions of absolute becoming have no place in Christian theology, nor should immutability be understood in static philosophic terms. Speaking of God's immutability should never be confused with monotonous sameness or rigid immobility. The unchanging God is a living God who is related to his creatures in manifold ways and participates in their lives. God is transcendent *and* immanent. Without losing himself he can give himself and, while absolutely maintaining his immutability, he can enter into an infinite number of relations to his creatures. If God were not immutable, he would not be God.[34] It is a mark of God's greatness that he can condescend to the level of his creatures and that, though transcendent, he can dwell immanently in all created beings. Without losing himself, God can give himself, and, while absolutely maintaining his immutability, he can enter into an infinite number of relations to his creatures.

To illustrate this point Augustine spoke of the sun, which does not change whether it scorches or warms, hurts or animates, and of a coin that remains a coin whether called a price or a pledge. A pillar remains unchanged whether a person sees it on her right or on her left (Thomas). An artist does not change when he gives shape to his inner vision in words or in tone, in voice or in color, nor does a scholar when he puts down his ideas in a book. None of these comparisons is perfect, but they do suggest how a thing may change in its relations while remaining the same in essence. This is especially true of God since he, the immutable One, is himself the sole cause of all that changes. We should not picture God as *putting* himself in any relation to any creature as though it could exist apart from him. Rather, he causes them to be and by that very act, at that very time, they *are* in relation. There is absolutely no "before" or "after" in God; these words apply only to things that did not exist before, but do exist afterward.[35] It is God's immutable being itself that calls into being and onto the stage before him the mutable beings who possess an order and law that is uniquely their own.

Infinity

[194] When applied to time, God's immutability (or infinity) is called eternity; when applied to space it is called omnipresence. From time to time the two

---

34. Augustine, *On Grace and Free Will*, II, 6; idem, *On Christian Doctrine*, I, 9; idem, *Confessions*, VII, 4.

35. Augustine, *City of God*, XII, 17.

have been included under the umbrella term of "divine infinity," though the term "infinity" is ambiguous, especially when philosophers by way of negation take its meaning to be "endless." Neoplatonism, the Jewish Kabbalah, Spinoza, and Hegel all utilize variations of this theme. Properly understood, however, God's infinity is not a philosophical notion obtained negatively by abstraction from finite things. God is positively infinite in his characteristic essence, absolutely perfect, infinite in an intensive, qualitative sense. God's infinity suggests, negatively, that, unlike his creatures, there is in him no limitation. But it also suggests, positively, that God is unlimited in his virtues, that in him every virtue is present in an absolute degree; in other words, God's infinity amounts to perfection.[36] This must not, however, be understood as an infinity of magnitude—in the sense in which people sometimes speak of the infinite or boundless dimensions of the spatial universe—for God is incorporeal and has no extension. Neither is it an infinity of number—as in mathematics we speak of something being infinitesimally small or infinitely large—for this would conflict with God's oneness and simplicity. Rather, it is an "infinity of essence"; God is infinite in his characteristic essence, absolutely perfect, infinite in an intensive, qualitative, and positive sense. Understood in this way, God's infinity is synonymous with perfection and does not have to be treated as a distinct attribute.

Eternity

Infinity in the sense of not being determined by time is the eternity of God. Scripture nowhere speaks of a beginning or an end to God's existence; he enters into time but still transcends it. He is the first and the last (Isa. 41:4; Rev. 1:8), who existed before the world was (Gen. 1:1; John 1:1; 17:5, 24) and who continues despite all change (Ps. 102:27–28). He is God from eternity to eternity (Pss. 90:2; 93:2). The number of his years is unsearchable (Job 36:26). A thousand years in his sight are as brief as yesterday is to our mind (Ps. 90:4; 2 Pet. 3:8). He is the everlasting God (Isa. 40:28; Rom. 16:26), who inhabits eternity (Isa. 57:15), lives forever and ever (Deut. 32:40; Rev. 10:6; 15:7), swears by his life (Num. 14:21, 28), is called "the living and enduring God" (1 Pet. 1:23), the immortal God (Rom. 1:23; 1 Tim. 6:16), who is and who was and who is to come (Exod. 3:14; Rev. 1:4, 8). While Scripture speaks of God here in human fashion and of eternity in the forms of time, at the same time it clearly indicates that God transcends time and cannot be measured or defined by the standards of time.

Contrary to deism, God's eternity is qualitative and not merely quantitatively an infinite extension of time. Christian theology must also avoid the error of pantheism, which simply considers eternity as the substance or essence of time itself. Eternity excludes a beginning, an end, and succession of moments. Between eternity and time there is a distinction not only in quantity and degree but also in quality and essence. God is unbegotten, incorruptible, and immutable. Time

36. T. Aquinas, *Summa Theol.*, I, qu. 7.

is the mode of existence of all finite creatures. God, on the other hand, is the eternal I AM, who is without beginning or end and not subject to measuring or counting in his duration. God's eternity, however, is not static or immobile but fullness of being, present and immanent in every moment of time. God pervades time and every moment of time with his eternity; he maintains a definite relation to time, entering into it with his eternity. Between eternity and time there is a distinction not only in quantity and degree but also in quality and essence. Augustine captured the mysterious elusiveness of time by noting that time exists only where the present becomes past and the future becomes present. "What, then, is time? If no one asks me, I know; if I want to explain it to someone who asks me, I do not know. I can state with confidence, however, that this much I do know: if nothing passed away, there would be no past time; if there was nothing still on its way, there would be no future time; and if nothing existed, there would be no present time" (Augustine, *Confessions*, XI, 14).

Time is not a separate substance, a real something, but a mode of existence. If there were no creatures, there would be no time. Although time is objectively real, not merely a subjective form of observation, as Kant thought,[37] a thinking mind is needed to measure time. We recollect the past, experience the present, and hope for the future. Here a distinction between extrinsic and intrinsic time is needed. By extrinsic time we mean the accidental and arbitrary standard by which we measure motion. We derive it from the motion of the heavenly bodies, which is constant and universally known (Gen. 1:14ff.). Time in this sense will one day cease (Rev. 10:6; 21:23ff.). But intrinsic time is the mode of existence by virtue of which things have a past, present, and future. Accordingly, the essential nature of time is not that it is finite or endless but that it encompasses a succession of moments, that there is in it a period that is past, a period that is present, and a period that comes later. Thus, it follows that time—intrinsic time—is the mode of existence that characterizes all created and finite beings. One who says "time" says motion, change, measurability, computability, limitation, finiteness, creatureliness. Time is the duration of creaturely existence. Hence, there can be no time in God. From eternity to eternity he is who he is. There is in him "no variation or shadow due to change" (James 1:17). God is not a process of becoming but an eternal being. He is without beginning and end, but also knows no earlier and later. He can neither be subjected to measuring or counting in his duration. A thousand years are to him as a day. He is the eternal I AM (John 8:58). God's eternity, accordingly, should be thought rather as an eternal present without past or future. "To God all things are present. Your today is eternity. Eternity itself is the substance of God, which has in it nothing that is changeable."[38]

---

37. I. Kant, *Critique of Pure Reason*, trans. Norman Kemp Smith (New York: St. Martin's; Toronto: Macmillan, 1965 [1929]), 76 ("Time").

38. Augustine, *Confessions*, XI, 10–13; idem, *True Religion*, c. 49.

Nevertheless, God's eternity should not for that reason be conceived as an eternally static, immobile moment of time. On the contrary: it is identical with God's being and hence with his fullness of being. Not only is God eternal; he is his own eternity.[39] A true analogy of it is not the contentless existence of a person for whom, as a result of idleness or boredom, grief or fear, the minutes seem like hours and the days do not go but creep. The analogy lies rather in the abundant and exuberant life of the cheerful laborer, for whom time barely exists and days fly by. Hence, God's eternity does not stand, abstract and transcendent, above time, but is present and immanent in every moment of time. There is indeed an essential difference between eternity and time, but there is also an analogy and kinship between them so that the former can indwell and work in the latter. Time cannot exist in and by itself. God by his eternal power sustains time, both in its entirety and in each separate moment of it. God pervades time and every moment of time with his eternity. In every second throbs the heartbeat of eternity. God remains eternal and inhabits eternity, but uses time with a view to manifesting his eternal thoughts and perfections. He makes time subservient to eternity and thus proves himself to be the King of the ages (1 Tim. 1:17).

Omnipresence

[195] Infinity in the sense of not being confined by space is synonymous with God's omnipresence. While heaven and earth cannot contain God (1 Kings 8:27; 2 Chron. 2:6; Isa. 66:1; Acts 7:48), neither can he be excluded from space. Rather, he fills heaven and earth with his presence. This omnipresence includes God's being as well as his power. God is not "somewhere," yet he fills heaven and earth; he is uniquely a place of his own to himself. All of Scripture assumes that heaven, though also created, has in a special sense been God's dwelling and throne from the first moment of its existence (Deut. 26:15; 2 Sam. 22:7; 1 Kings 8:32; Pss. 11:4; 33:13; 115:3, 16; Isa. 63:15; Matt. 5:34; 6:9; John 14:2; Eph. 1:20; Heb. 1:3; Rev. 4:1ff.; etc.). But he also comes down to earth, visits his people, dwells among his people (Exod. 19:6; 25:8; Deut. 7:6; 14:2; 26:19; Jer. 11:4; Ezek. 11:20; 37:27), and is present especially in Jerusalem (Exod. 20:24; Deut. 12:11; 14:23; etc.; 2 Kings 21:7; 1 Chron. 23:25; 2 Chron. 6:6; Ezra 1:3; 5:16; 7:15; Ps. 135:21; Isa. 24:23; Jer. 3:17; Joel 3:16; etc.; Matt. 5:34; Rev. 21:10), in the tabernacle, and in the temple on Zion, his house (Exod. 40:34–35; 1 Kings 8:10; 2 Kings 11:10, 13; 2 Chron. 5:14; Ps. 9:11; Isa. 8:18; Matt. 23:21), and above the ark between the cherubim (1 Sam. 4:4; 2 Sam. 6:2; 2 Kings 19:15; 1 Chron. 13:6; Pss. 80:1; 99:1; Isa. 37:16). Noteworthy is Scripture's use of spatial imagery to signify profound religious-moral presence: God is far from the wicked (Pss. 11:5; 37:9f.; 50:16f.; 145:20) but the upright will behold his face (Ps. 11:7) along with those of a contrite and humble spirit (Isa. 57:15; Ps. 51:17–19). In Christ, and through the Spirit whom he sends, he dwells in the church as his temple (John

---

39. T. Aquinas, *Summa Theol.*, I, qu.10, art. 2.

14:23; Rom. 8:9, 11; 1 Cor. 3:16; 6:19; Eph. 2:21; 3:17), until one day he will dwell with his people and be everything to everyone (1 Cor. 15:28; Rev. 21:3).

Here again, we need to remind ourselves that in each attribute we speak of God in human terms. We always think in terms of "somewhere." But God transcends all space and location; he is not "somewhere," yet he fills heaven and earth. When Scripture uses language of infinite space with respect to God (Isa. 66:1; Ps. 139:7; Amos 9:2; Acts 17:24), we confess that God relates to space as the infinite One who, existing within himself, also fills to repletion every point of space and sustains it by his immensity. We must insist that space is not a form of external perception (Kant), which would reduce it to the physical world and leave time to the internal spiritual and intellectual world. Like time, space is the mode of existence of all created beings and can be viewed externally and internally alike.

Christian theology seeks to avoid both deism and pantheism and insists against the latter that God transcends space (and time), and against the former that he is wholly immanent in both. Augustine used the analogy of soul and body to explain this: Just as the soul in its entirety is present in the body as a whole and in every part of it, and just as one and the same truth is acknowledged everywhere, so also, by way of analogy, God is in all things and all things are in God.[40] These thoughts of Augustine surface again later in the church in Roman Catholic and Protestant theologians alike.[41] Augustine's analogy also reminds us that God is present in his creatures in different ways. There is a difference between his physical and his ethical immanence. To suggest an analogy: people, too, may be physically very close to each other, yet miles apart in spirit and outlook (Matt. 24:40–41). The soul is present throughout the body and in all its parts, yet in each of them in a unique way, one way in the head and another in the heart, in the hands differently from in the feet. Thus, to put forth the most stark example, God is present in hell as well as heaven. Less dramatically, we simply acknowledge that there is a difference among creatures as determined by the manner in which God indwells them. In created beings God dwells according to the measure of their *being:* in some in terms of nature, in others in terms of justice, in still others in terms of grace or of glory. There is endless diversity in order that all of them together might reveal the glory of God. There is also religious-moral difference: Only humans are responsible moral agents. And then this important difference: "With the pure you show yourself pure; and with the wicked you show yourself perverse" (Ps. 18:26).

This reminds us that we cannot hide from God; there is no "place" he is not (Ps. 139). There is no advantage to denying God's omnipresence. He makes it felt in our heart and conscience and is never far from any of us. Only sin separates us from

40. Idem, *Expositions on the Psalms*, VIII, 342–50 (on Ps. 74).

41. Anselm, *Monologion*, c. 20–23; T. Aquinas, *Summa Theol.*, I, qu. 8; idem, *Summa contra gentiles*, III, 68; Bonaventure, *Sent.*, I, dist. 37; Johann Gerhard, *Loci theologici*, ed. E. Preuss, 9 vols. (Berlin: G. Schlawitz, 1863–75), I, c. 8, sect. 8; A. Polanus, *Syn. theol.*, II, c. 12; J. Zanchi, *Op. theol.*, II, cols. 90–138.

God; not locally but spiritually (Isa. 59:2). To abandon God, to flee from him, as Cain did, is not a matter of local separation but of spiritual incompatibility. "It is not by location but by incongruity that a person is far from God."[42] Conversely, going to God and seeking his face does not consist in making a pilgrimage but in self-abasement and repentance. Those who seek him, find him—not far away, but in their immediate presence. For in him we live and move and have our being. "To draw near to him is to become like him; to move away from him is to become unlike him."[43] In Augustine's words:

> Do not think, then, that God is present in certain places. With you he is such as you have been. . . . He is good, if you have been good; and he seems evil to you if you have been evil; a helper if you have been good, an avenger if you have been bad. . . . you have a judge in your own heart. When you want to do something bad, you withdraw . . . hide from the public . . . , from those parts of the house that are open and visible you remove yourself to go into your own private room. But even in our private chamber you fear guilt from some other direction [and] withdraw into your heart and there you meditate. But he is even more deeply inward than your heart. Hence, no matter where you flee, he is there. . . . There is absolutely no place for you to flee to. Do you want to flee from him? Rather flee to him.[44]

Unity

[196] The last of God's incommunicable attributes, his oneness, is differentiated into the unity of singularity and the unity of simplicity. By the first we mean that there is but one divine being, that in virtue of the nature of that being God cannot be more than one being and, consequently, that all other beings exist only from him, through him, and to him. Hence, this attribute teaches God's absolute oneness and uniqueness, his exclusive numerical oneness, in distinction from his simplicity, which denotes his inner or qualitative oneness. God is numerically and quantitatively one, absolutely and exclusively. Evolutionist views of a development in the Old Testament from polytheism to monotheism are untenable. Scripture is monotheistic from beginning to end. Even though there is certainly a kind of progression in revelation and development in its ideas, the Old Testament, with its teaching of the unity of the world and of the human race, the election of, and covenant with, Israel, and its teaching of the religion and morality described in the law, is based from beginning to end on the oneness of God. YHWH is the Creator of the world (Gen. 1 and 2), the Owner and Judge of the whole earth (Gen. 14:19, 22; 18:25), the only Lord (Deut. 6:4), who will tolerate no other gods before him (Exod. 20:3). In the New Testament this singularity of God becomes even clearer in the person of Christ (John 17:3; Acts 17:24; Rom. 3:30; 1 Cor. 8:5–6; Eph. 4:5–6; 1 Tim. 2:5).

42. Augustine, *Expositions on the Psalms*, on Ps. 94.
43. Ibid., on Ps. 34.
44. Ibid., on Ps. 74.

With this confession of the only true God, the Christian church made its debut in the gentile world and confronted especially the popular polytheism of the Roman world. Feeling strong in their confessional position, Christian thinkers proved the uniqueness of God not only by appealing to Scripture but also by deriving arguments for the truth they proclaimed from every domain of human knowledge. They appealed to the witness of the human soul, to pronouncements made by many gentile philosophers and poets, to the unity of the world and the human race, to the unitary nature of truth and morality, to the nature of the divine being, which tolerates no equals. Along with polytheism they attacked all things directly or indirectly connected with it: demonism and superstition, mantic and magic, the deification of humans and emperor worship, the theaters and the games.[45] In this mighty, centuries-long struggle, polytheism was overcome and deprived both religiously and scientifically of all its power. Polytheism fails to satisfy the human spirit; only confession about the one true God sustains religion, truth, and morality.

Still, various forms of polytheistic belief and practice remain, even in the modern world. When the confession of the one true God weakens and is denied, and the unity sought in pantheism eventually satisfies neither the intellect nor the heart, then the unity of the world and of humankind, of religion, morality, and truth can no longer be maintained. Nature and history fall apart in fragments, and along with consciously or unconsciously fostered polytheistic tendencies, every form of superstition and idolatry makes a comeback. Modernity offers abundant proof for this state of affairs, and for that reason the confession of the oneness of God is of even greater significance today than it was in earlier times.[46]

Simplicity

[197] The unity of simplicity insists that God is not only truthful and righteous, loving and wise, but *the* truth, righteousness, love, and wisdom (Jer. 10:10; 23:6; John 1:4–5, 9; 14:6; 1 Cor. 1:30; 1 John 1:5; 4:8). On account of its absolute perfection, every attribute of God is identical with his essence. Although sometimes opposed on philosophical grounds, the doctrine of divine simplicity is of great importance for our understanding of God. If God is in any sense composite, then it is impossible to maintain the perfection of his oneness, independence, and immutability. Simplicity is not a philosophic abstraction but the end result of ascribing to God all the perfections of creatures to the ultimate divine degree. It is necessary as a way of affirming that God has a distinct and infinite life of his own within himself. To oppose the doctrine of divine simplicity on the grounds

---

45. A. von Harnack, *Mission and Expansion of Christianity in the First 300 Years* (New York: Harper, 1962), 125–46, 206–18, 234–39, 290–311.

46. Cf. on the unity of God: T. Aquinas, *Summa Theol.*, I, qu. 11; idem, *Summa contra gentiles*, I, c. 42; F. Turretin, *Institutes of Elenctic Theology*, trans. G. M. Giger and ed. J. T. Dennison, 3 vols. (Phillipsburg, NJ: Presbyterian and Reformed, 1992), III, qu. 3; O. Zöckler, "Polytheismus," *PRE*³, XV, 538ff.

that it is a metaphysical abstraction and inconsistent with the doctrine of the Trinity[47] is to misunderstand the doctrine and the intention behind its affirmation. The term "simple" is not an antonym of "twofold" or "threefold" but of "composite." God is not composed of three persons, nor is each person composed of the being and personal attributes of that person, but the one uncompounded (simple) being of God exists in three persons. It is, furthermore, to deny to God such categorical distinctions as genus and species, substance and accidents, matter and form, potentiality and actuality, essence and existence. If we did make such distinctions in God, he would not be the One "than whom nothing better can be thought," or the perfection of love, justice, and holiness itself. But God *is* uniquely his own, having nothing above him. Accordingly, he is completely identical with the attributes of wisdom, grace, and love, and so on. He is absolutely perfect, the One "than whom nothing higher can be thought."[48]

Here creatures are, of course, different since in them there is a distinction between existing, being, living, knowing, willing, acting, and so on. "All that is compounded is created." No creature can be completely simple, for every creature is finite. God, however, is infinite and all that is in him is infinite. All his attributes are divine, hence infinite and one with his being. For that reason he is and can only be all-sufficient, fully blessed, and glorious within himself.[49] God is therefore simple in his multiplicity and manifold in his simplicity (Augustine). Hence, every qualification, every name, used with reference to God, so far from being a negation, is an enrichment of our knowledge of his being. "The divine essence is self-determined and is distinct from everything else in that nothing can be added to it."[50]

God's Communicable Attributes[51]

Spirituality

[198] From our discussion of God's simplicity we move naturally (since all that is corporeal is composite) to the treatment of God's *spiritual* nature. That God is Spirit is the presupposition of the Old Testament and explicitly taught in the New Testament. While it is true that, speaking in human fashion, Scripture ascribes to God an array of human organs and activities—heart, intestines, seeing, hearing,

47. I. Dorner, *System of Christian Doctrine*, I, 234ff.; Albrecht Ritschl, *Theologie und Metaphysik* (Bonn: A. Marcus, 1881), 12ff.; idem, *Rechtfertigung und Versuchung*, 2nd ed., III, 2ff.; W. G. T. Shedd, *Dogmatic Theology*, 3rd ed., 3 vols. (New York: Scribner, 1891–94), I, 338; A. Kuyper, *Ex ungue leonem* (Amsterdam: Kruyt, 1882).

48. Augustine, *The Trinity*, V, 10; VI, 1; Hugo of St. Victor, *The Trinity*, I, 12.

49. D. Petavius, "De Deo," in *Theol. dogm.*, II, chap. 2.

50. T. Aquinas, *Sent.*, I, dist. 8, qu. 4, art. 1, ad. 1; Joseph Kleutgen, *Die Theologie der Vorzeit vertheidigt*, 2nd ed., 5 vols. (Münster: Theissing, 1867–74), I, 204ff.

51. Ed. note: For a reminder of important qualifications in using the terms "communicable" and "incommunicable," see note 31 above.

smelling—there are limits; organs of food intake, digestion, and reproduction, tasting and touching are not. Nowhere is a body assigned to him. Although the Old Testament also at no point explicitly states that God is Spirit, yet this view is basic to its entire description of God. He is self-existent (Exod. 3:13–14; Isa. 41:4; 44:6), eternal (Deut. 32:40; Pss. 90:1ff.; 102:27), omnipresent (Deut. 10:14; Ps. 139:1ff.; Jer. 23:23–24), incomparable (Isa. 40:18, 25; 46:5; Ps. 89:7, 9), invisible (Exod. 33:20, 23), "unpicturable" (Exod. 20:4; Deut. 5:8) since he is without form (Deut. 4:12, 15). He relates to humanity as "spirit" to "flesh" (Isa. 31:3), and it is by his Spirit that he is present in his creation and creates and sustains all things (Gen. 2:7; Job 33:4; Pss. 33:6; 104:30; 139:7; etc.).[52] In the New Testament this is more apparent. We learn that God is eternal (Rom. 16:26; 1 Tim. 6:16; 1 Pet. 1:23; Rev. 1:8; 10:6; 15:7), omnipresent (Acts 17:27–28; Rom. 1:22–23), and Jesus explicitly calls God "Spirit" (πνευμα), the reason to worship God in spirit and in truth (John 4:24). The apostles teach the same when they call God invisible (John 1:18; cf. 6:46; Rom. 1:20; Col. 1:15; 1 Tim. 1:17; 6:16; 1 John 4:12, 20).

Despite efforts by theosophists, pantheists, Socinians, and certain philosophers to ascribe a body to God, the Christian church and Christian theology have steadfastly maintained God's spirituality. The term "spirit" is used to mean that God is a unique substance, distinct from the universe, immaterial, imperceptible to the human senses, without composition or extension. Christian theology cannot be satisfied with philosophic attempts such as that of Hegel who, though he uses the word "spirit" (or "mind"; *Geist*), means by it the final and highest stage of the Idea in its development through nature. It is in humanity, especially in philosophy, that the Idea reaches this highest form. "The logical becomes nature and nature becomes Spirit (Mind)."[53] Hegel still seeks the essence of Spirit (Mind) in ideality, in "simple being-in-itself," in "I-ness,"[54] but God *becomes* Spirit (Mind) only through a lengthy process in and through humans. There can be no identification of this pantheistic vision with the Christian confession that "God is Spirit." God's spirituality is unlike any "spiritual" reality of the creation; it is unique.

Still, we can and must speak of analogues with the human spirit. God who is Spirit is also "the Father of spirits" (Heb. 12:9), and as the Creator and Father of all things—visible and invisible—the source and origin of spirits, heavenly and earthly (Heb. 11:3). Thus we can form faint impressions of divine spirituality from our own spirits, but inasmuch as our own souls are mysteries to us we are clearly at the outer boundaries of our understanding. God's spirituality is unique, and when we use the term "spirit" we must be careful that we do not apply it to God,

52. G. F. Oehler, *Theology of the Old Testament*, §46; H. Schultz, *Alttestamentliche Theologie*, 4th ed., 2 vols. (Göttingen: Vandenhoeck & Ruprecht, 1889), 496–504; A. B. Davidson, *The Theology of the Old Testament*, 106ff.
53. G. F. Hegel, *System der Philosophie*, part 3: *Die Philosophie des Geistes*, in *Sämtliche Werke*, X (1958), 474 (*Werke* VII/2, 468).
54. Idem, *Werke*, 14ff., 18ff.

angels, and souls univocally and synonymously but analogically. The spirituality
of God refers to that perfection of God that describes him, negatively, as being
immaterial and invisible, analogously to the spirit of angels and the soul of humans;
and positively, as the hidden, simple (uncompounded), absolute ground of all
creatural, somatic, and pneumatic being. Maintaining our confession that God's
nature is spiritual in a unique way is very important because the whole character
of our worship and service of God rests on it. Worship in spirit and in truth is
based on the spirituality of God. It alone—in principle and forever—spells the
elimination of all image worship.

Invisibility

[199] Implied in God's spirituality is his invisibility, an attribute clearly taught
by Scripture.[55] What then does Scripture mean when it speaks of "seeing God"?
As the church fathers wrestled with the biblical givens, they pointed out that God
could and had made himself visible by special acts of grace, and then only for a
moment; to Moses (Exod. 34), to Isaiah (Isa. 6), and to Paul (2 Cor. 12).[56] "It is not
in our power to see him, but it is in his power to appear to us."[57] Most, however,
denied a vision of God with respect to his essence[58] though this changed under the
influence of Neoplatonism, particularly as mediated through the mystical writings
of Pseudo-Dionysius. Now it was believed that the soul, elevated by supernatural
grace, could be divinized and have a clear essential vision of God. Prosper spoke
of the blessed in heaven "contemplating within their hearts the substance of their
own creator."[59] Bernard says that God will be seen in all his creatures, but that
the Trinity will also be seen in itself.[60] And the Council of Florence declared
that souls, "immediately upon their entrance into heaven, would obtain a clear
vision of the one and triune God as he really is—nevertheless in proportion to
the diversity of their merits, the one more perfectly than the other."[61] Speculation
on this point flourished in medieval Scholasticism also to justify the practice of
invoking the angels and the blessed in heaven, who on this view behold in God
everything that is going to happen and hence know the needs of believers on earth.
Even though the caution was added that the vision of God does not amount to
comprehension and differs in believers in proportion to their merits, this doctrine
nevertheless resulted in the deification of humans. The human creature, having

55. Cf. H. Bavinck, *Reformed Dogmatics*, II, 182–83 (#198).

56. Augustine, *Epist.* 112; idem, *Literal Meaning of Genesis*, XII, 27; Basil of Caesarea, *On the Hexaëmeron*, hom. 1; Hilary of Poitiers, *On the Trinity*, V.

57. Ambrose, in D. Petavius, "De Deo," in *Theol. dogm.*, VII, chap. 7.

58. Thus, e.g., Chrysostom, Gregory of Nyssa, Cyril of Jerusalem, Theodoret, Jerome, and Isidore.

59. Prosper of Aquitaine, *De vita contemplativa* (Speyer: Peter Drach, 1486), chap. 4.

60. Bernardus Zane, Sermon 4, in *Oratio in festo omnium sanctorum* (Rome: Johann Besicken, 1500–1599?).

61. Cf. H. Denzinger, *Enchiridion symbolorum* (Wirceburgi, 1856), ##430, 456, 588, 870, 875; ET: *The Sources of Catholic Dogma*, trans. from the 30th ed. by Roy J. Deferrari (St. Louis: Herder, 1955).

received a supernatural gift, by his own merits raises himself to a higher level and becomes like God.[62]

Reformation theologians were divided on this question; some Lutheran and Reformed thinkers judged that an essential vision of God was not impossible.[63] Most Reformed theologians were more modest, rejecting the idea altogether or brushing aside these speculations of Scholasticism.[64] This modesty is certainly in keeping with Scripture. The Bible indeed teaches that the blessed in heaven behold God, but does not go into any detail, and elsewhere expressly calls God invisible. What awaits us is "knowing as we are known" (1 Cor. 13:12). God, moreover, is infinite, and since human beings are finite and remain so also in the state of glory, we can never have more than a finite human vision of God. The representation of the infinite God in our finite human consciousness is and forever remains finite. Therefore the vision of God cannot be "with respect to his essence"; every vision of God always requires an act of divine condescension (συγκατάβασις), a revelation by which God on his part comes down to us and makes himself knowable. Matthew 11:27[65] remains in force also in heaven. A corollary of a vision of God in his essence would be the deification of humanity and the erasure of the boundary between the Creator and the creature. Humanity's blessedness indeed lies in the "beatific vision of God," but this vision will always be one appropriate to our finite and limited human nature. A divinization (θέωσις) such as is found in the system of the Pseudo-Dionysian hierarchy has no support in Scripture.[66]

Knowledge, Foreknowledge, Middle Knowledge

[200] Scripture presupposes God's consciousness and knowledge, speaking figuratively of this as "light" (1 John 1:5; 1 Tim. 6:16; Pss. 4:6; 27:1; 36:9; 43:3; John 1:4, 9; 8:12; James 1:17; etc.). There are other connotations of "light"—purity, holiness, joy, blessedness—but what stands out in the figurative use of the word "light" is its intellectual meaning. Knowledge, however, moves quickly to a moral call. God shines in our hearts and gives the light of the knowledge of the glory of God in the face of Jesus Christ (2 Cor. 4:6), so that we who walk in darkness (John 1:5; 3:19) learn to love the light, and again walk in it (Matt. 5:14, 16; John 3:21; Rom. 13:12; Eph. 5:8; Phil. 2:15; 1 Thess. 5:5; 1 John 1:7; etc.).

---

62. P. Lombard, *Sent.*, IV, dist. 49; T. Aquinas, *Summa Theol.*, I, qu. 12.; I, 2, qu. 3, esp. art. 12; I, qu. 4, art. 2; idem, *Summa contra gentiles*, III, chaps. 38–63; idem, *Sent.*, IV, dist. 49, qu. 1–2; Bonaventure, *The Breviloquium*, vol. 2 of *The Works of Bonaventure*, trans. Jose De Vinck (Paterson, NJ: St. Anthony Guild Press, 1963), VII, chap. 7; M. J. Scheeben, *Handbuch der katholischen Dogmatik*, I, 562ff.; II, 294ff.

63. Heinrich Bullinger, on John 1:18, *In divinum Jesu Christi . . . Evangelium secundum Ioannem* (Tigvri: Froschouer, 1561); Polyander et al., *Synopsis purioris theologiae*, ed. H. Bavinck, 6th ed. (Leiden: D. Donner, 1881), LII, 11–24; A. Polanus, *Syn. theol.*, 9, 518; John Forbes, *De visione beatifica*, in *Opera omni*, 2 vols. (Amsterdam: H. Wetstenium & R. and G. Wetstenios, 1702–3), I, 282–89.

64. J. Calvin, *Institutes*, III.xxv.11; F. Turretin, *Institutes of Elenctic Theology*, XX, qu. 8.

65. "All things have been handed over to me by my Father; and no one knows the Son except the Father, and no one knows the Father except the Son and anyone to whom the Son chooses to reveal him."

66. Cf. H. Bavinck, *Reformed Dogmatics*, II, 511–88 (##279–300), the locus on the image of God.

In God there is no darkness at all. He is light through and through. He lives in the light and is himself the source of all light. Also, the trinitarian life of God is a completely conscious one (Matt. 11:27; John 1:17–18; 10:15; 1 Cor. 2:10).

Nothing is outside the scope of God's knowledge. Pantheistic thought, however, denies this when it conceives of the Unconscious as the unity of all things. The Absolute is then incapable of consciousness. In critique, anyone who argues for a teleological worldview must have a self-conscious and intelligent God. Thus, observing purpose in the world leads necessarily to acknowledging a divine, intelligent Being. The reality of human consciousness points in the same direction: one cannot explain the rise of consciousness from that which is unconscious. Surely the effect cannot have in it more than the cause. "Would he who plants the ear not hear, and would he who forms the eye not see?" (Ps. 95:9). God's self-consciousness differs but is inseparable from his world-consciousness. Out of the infinite fullness of his own ideas God created the world to best reveal his perfections in his creatures. God's *archetypal* perfections are revealed *ectypically* in the universe. Thus, while God's knowledge and world-consciousness are communicable to humanity, they still differ qualitatively from human knowledge of the world. Unlike finite human consciousness, divine self-consciousness has no limitation; God knows everything (1 John 3:20). The content of God's self knowledge is no less than his being; being and knowing coincide in God. Before him no creature is hidden, but all are open and laid bare to his eyes (Heb. 4:13). Unlike human knowledge, God's is not based on observation (a posteriori); it is a priori, present from eternity (Rom. 8:29; 1 Cor. 2:7; Eph. 1:4–5; 2 Tim. 1:9). All things are eternally present to him; his knowledge is not susceptible of increase (Isa. 40:13f.; Rom. 11:34).[67]

[201] Consequently, strictly speaking, it is a mistake to speak of divine foreknowledge; there is only one knowledge of God. With him there are no "distinctions of time." "For what is foreknowledge if not knowledge of future events? But can anything be future to God, who surpasses all times? For if God's knowledge includes these very things themselves, they are not future to him but present; and for this reason we should no longer speak of God's foreknowledge but simply of God's knowledge."[68] "Whatever is past and future to us is immediately present in his sight."[69] "However the times roll on, with him it is always present."[70] Making distinctions in God's knowledge is a thoroughly human conception and at odds with the teaching of Scripture, yet it is raised again and again in the church. The reason God's knowledge—understood now especially as foreknowledge—is questioned is that many consider this divine omniscience as irreconcilable with

67. Irenaeus, *Against Heresies*, 1, 12; Augustine, *The Trinity*, XI, 10; XII, 18; XV, 7, 13–14; T. Aquinas, *Summa Theol.*, I, qu. 14; idem, *Summa contra gentiles*, I, chaps. 44ff.

68. Augustine, *To Simplician—On Various Questions* (*De diversis quaestionibus ad Simplicianum*), II, 2.

69. Gregory the Great, *Moralia in Iobum*, 1, 20, chap. 23. Ed. note: See H. Bavinck, *Reformed Dogmatics*, II, 188n40 (#199).

70. Marius Victor, in D. Petavius, "De Deo," in *Theol. dogm.*, IV, chap. 4.

human free will. If God indeed knows all things in advance, so it is said, everything is set in concrete from eternity, and there is no longer any room for free and contingent acts. Attempts to square omniscience and free will take one of two forms: God only knows what free human agents will do (Origen), or God knows what will happen because he has decreed that it will happen and it must (Augustine). In the latter case, we affirm both free will and omniscience as an article of faith without professing fully to understand it. Our wills have as much freedom as God wants us to have.

After the Reformation a new notion of "middle knowledge" gained ascendancy, a divine knowledge of contingent events logically antecedent to God's decrees. Promoted by Molina and Suárez, among others, it gained acceptance among Roman Catholic Jesuit theologians but was rejected by Reformed thinkers. The theory of middle knowledge attempts to harmonize the Pelagian notion of an indifferent free will with God's omniscience and thus is incompatible with a decree of God. God is seen to derive his knowledge of free human actions not from his own being but from the will of creatures and thus becomes dependent on the world for his own knowledge. Creatures gain independence, and God becomes the chief executive of a world in which he is the slave of his subordinates. This view differs from the teaching of Augustine and Thomas Aquinas who insisted that future contingent events from the vantage point of human beings are not at all contingent with respect to God. God does not sit around and wait for our acts before he knows what we do. If we leave future contingent acts of human beings completely open, we have no sure confidence of God's promises. What are we to think of a God who forever awaits all those decisions and keeps in readiness a store of all possible plans for all possibilities? What then remains of even a sketch of the world plan when it depends on humans to accomplish it? And of what value is a government whose chief executive is the slave of his own subordinates? This is exactly how God is portrayed in the theory of middle knowledge. God looks on, while humans decide. Grace is then dispensed, according to merit; predestination depends on good works. Scripture resists these inferences. While Scripture teaches conditional connections between events it never denies divine determination in those cases. In fact, the theory of middle knowledge cannot bring freedom of an indifferent human will into harmony with any notion of divine foreknowledge. The solution cannot be found in "indifference" but in "rational delight." This rational delight, rather than being in conflict with the foreknowledge of God, is implied in and upheld by it. The human will, along with its nature, antecedents and motives, its decisions and consequences, is integrated into "the order of causes that is certain to God and embraced by his foreknowledge."[71] In keeping with their divinely known and ordained nature, contingent events and free actions are links in the order of causes that, little by little, are revealed to us in the history of the world.

71. Augustine, *City of God*, V, 9.

Wisdom

[202] Viewed from another angle, God's knowledge is called "wisdom." While knowledge suggests a discursive, theoretical Greek philosophical model, wisdom is more Oriental, contemplative, intuitive, practical, goal-oriented. This Oriental characteristic is found to a high degree in Israel but now as the handmaiden of revelation. True wisdom is rooted in the fear of the Lord and consists in the moral discipline of conforming to God's law (Deut. 4:6–8; Pss. 19:7; 111:10; Job 28:28; Prov. 1:7; 9:10). Both the constitution of the world and revelation to Israel are attributed to God's wisdom (Job 9:4; 12:13, 17; 37:24–38:38; Isa. 40:28; Pss. 19:7; 104:24; Deut. 4:6–8; Jer. 10:12). In the New Testament this Wisdom is identified as the Word (Rom. 16:27; 1 Tim. 1:17; Jude 25; Rev. 5:12; 7:12). In addition, God's wisdom is especially revealed in the foolishness of the cross (1 Cor. 1:18), in Christ (1 Cor. 1:24), in the church (Eph. 3:10), in all of God's providential guidance of Israel and the gentiles (Rom. 11:33).[72]

Philo, and after him Augustine, linked this cluster of terms to Plato's Ideas, though with modification. The Ideas are now not seen as autonomous powers but subject to God's will. Augustine remains faithful to the Creator-creature distinction, insisting that these ideas in God's mind are not identical with his self-knowledge, nor with the Logos or the Son. For Augustine creation is the *product* of divine thought, the realization of the ideas of God. "Thus the wisdom of God, by which all things have been made, contains all things according to a design before it makes them."[73] "All things were created by reason, for he made nothing unwittingly. Knowing them, he made them; he did not learn to know them after they had been made."[74] Understood in this way, the notion of "ideas" found its way to other authors, including some Reformed theologians.[75] As we enter the modern world we see far less use of this notion among theologians, in large measure because "ideas" are now understood differently.

In modern philosophy ideas no longer refer to the pattern in the divine mind but to concepts, and not to concepts derived from sense perception but as products of pure thought itself. Yet fragments of the former usage remain, especially in the realm of art, where reference is made to paradigmatic patterns, to ideal

72. Cf. G. F. Oehler, *Theology of the Old Testament*, §§235ff.; Hermann Cremer, *Biblico-Theological Lexicon of New Testament Greek*, trans. D. W. Simon and William Urwick (Edinburgh: T&T Clark; New York: Charles Scribner's Sons, 1895), s.v. "σοφος"; F. Schleiermacher, *The Christian Faith* (Edinburgh: T&T Clark, 1989), §§168–69.

73. Augustine, *Lectures on the Gospel of John*, tract. 1, *NPNF¹*, VII, 131–37.

74. Augustine, *Eighty-Three Different Questions*, qu. 46, n. 2; idem, *Literal Meaning of Genesis*, V, 8; idem, *The Trinity*, XV, 13; idem, *City of God*, XI, 10.

75. Clement of Alexandria, *Stromateis*, IV, chap. 25; V, chap. 3; Tertullian, *The Soul's Testimony*, 18; Eusebius, *Preparation for the Gospel*, 1, 14, chap. 44; Origen, on John 1:1; Pseudo-Dionysius, *On the Divine Names*, chap. 5; Anselm, *Monologion*, chaps. 8ff.; P. Lombard, *Sent.*, I, dist. 35; T. Aquinas, *Summa Theol.*, I, qu. 15, qu. 44, art. 3; idem, *Summa contra gentiles*, 54; idem, *Sent.*, I, dist. 36; Bonaventure, *Sent.*, I, dist. 35; A. Polanus, *Syn. theol.*, 267–68; J. Zanchi, *Op. theol.*, II, 201; G. Voetius, *Select. disp.*, 258ff.

forms. Accordingly, we speak of an idea of God, of freedom, of art, of science, of the true, the good, and the beautiful, etc. Applied to God, the idea means that God has made all things with wisdom, that wisdom is "the firstborn of his ways" (Prov. 8:22; Col. 1:15; Rev. 3:14). God is the supreme artist. Just as a human artist realizes his idea in a work of art, so God creates all things in accordance with the ideas he has formed. The world is God's work of art. He is the architect and builder of the entire universe. God does not work without thinking, but is guided in all his works by wisdom, by his ideas. These ideas, of course, are not outside God but original, coming from his very being. It is in this sense alone that we can speak of creatures participating in God's being. The nature of this participation is not such that creatures are modifications of the divine being or that they have in some realistic sense received this divine being into themselves. Rather, they participate through the divine wisdom displayed in the multiplicity of beings God has created. All that is displays the divine wisdom in which it participates.

From this it is clear that sin has no "being" of its own; it is not a realization of the divine wisdom; it is diminution of being, privation, deformation. Although it is an object of God's knowledge and is made subservient to his glory by his wisdom, yet in itself it is not an idea of his wisdom, nor a ray of his light. Evil is known in light of the idea of the good of which it is the privation.[76] By contrast, Wisdom is and remains the "master worker" (Prov. 8:30), the "fashioner of all things" (Wis. 7:22), which creates and governs all things, leading them onward to their destination, which is the glorification of God's name.

Trustworthiness

[203] The last of God's intellectual attributes is his trustworthiness. God is true and trustworthy; he can be counted on. He is the only God, and he cannot lie or be in error. He is truth in its absolute fullness, the source and ground of all truth, all reality. He is the light by which alone we can know truth. The Hebrew word אֱמֶת derives from the verb אמן (to make firm, to build, to undergird; intransitive: to be firm; Hiphil: to hang onto, to trust in, to be sure of). It denotes, subjectively, the act of hanging onto something, faith (Greek: πιστις), and, objectively, the firmness, trustworthiness, and truth of the person or cause in which a person has put his or her trust. English translations, accordingly, have "true," "faithful," and "faithfulness." That is why the trustworthiness of God is an attribute of the will as well as the intellect. Veracity and truth, trustworthiness and faithfulness, are so closely associated that they cannot be split apart. The name YHWH as such already expresses that he remains who he is, a God of faithfulness and without deceit (Deut. 32:4; Jer. 10:10; Ps. 31:6; 2 Chron. 15:3). It implies (1) that he is the real, the true God in contrast to false gods, the idols, which are "vanities" (Deut. 32:21; etc.); and (2) that as such he will always stand by his words and promises and prove them true, so that he will be seen as completely trustworthy. He is not

76. T. Aquinas, *Summa Theol.*, I, qu. 15, art. 3.

a human that he should lie or change his mind (Num. 23:19; 1 Sam. 15:29). All that proceeds from him bears the stamp of truthfulness.

Over and over Scripture mentions God's kindness (חֶסֶד) and faithfulness (cf. Gen. 24:49; 47:29; Josh. 2:14; 2 Sam. 2:6; 15:20; Ps. 40:11), his steadfast love (חֶסֶד) and truth (Gen. 24:27; Exod. 34:6; Pss. 57:3; 61:7; 89:14; etc.).[77] God repeatedly confirms his word by swearing an oath by himself (Gen. 22:16; etc.; Heb. 6:13). As such a God of truth and faithfulness, he keeps covenant (Deut. 4:31; 7:9; Ps. 40:11; Hosea 11:1; etc.) and is a completely trustworthy refuge for all his people (Pss. 31:5–6; 36:5ff.; 43:2; 54:7; 57:3; 71:22; 96:13; 143:1; 146:6; etc.). Similarly, in the New Testament he is called the true God; that is, only he is the real and true God who revealed himself in Christ (John 17:3; 1 John 5:20). His Word is the truth, his gospel is truth, Christ is the truth (John 14:6; 17:17; Eph. 1:13). The New Testament is the fulfillment and confirmation of the promises he made in the days of the Old Testament, his holy covenant and the oath he swore to Abraham (Luke 1:68–73). God cannot deny himself (2 Tim. 2:13). In Christ all his promises are "Yes" and "Amen" (2 Cor. 1:18, 20).

Scripture, accordingly, uses the word "truth" in several senses. Metaphysical or ontological truth consists of truth or veracity in essence; gold that is gold not only in appearance but also in reality is true gold. In this sense truth is a property of all being; it is identical with substance. God is called true in distinction from all idols that are no gods at all. Ethical truth consists of truth or veracity in expression (in words); a correspondence between a person's being and self-revelation; lying is the sin against ethical truth. In God's case, there is complete correspondence between his being and his revelation (Num. 23:19; 1 Sam. 15:29; Titus 1:2; Heb. 6:18). It is impossible for God to lie or deny himself. Finally, there is logical truth which consists in correspondence between thought and reality, the conformity or adequation of the intellect to the (real) thing. Our concepts are true when they bear the exact imprint of reality; here truth is opposed to error. Now God is the truth in that he knows all things as they really are, truly, adequately. Indeed, in his knowing he is the truth itself, just as in his being he is the ontological truth. God's Word, law, and gospel, accordingly, are pure truth. They are all as they should be. Now though these three meanings of the term "truth" are distinct, they are also one; in all three senses there is correspondence between thought and being, between the ideal and the real. God is truth in a metaphysical sense, for he is the unity of thought and being. God is truth in an ethical sense, for he reveals himself, speaks, acts, and appears as he truly is and thinks. And he is the truth in a logical sense, for he conceives things as they are; rather, things are as he conceives them to be. He is the truth in its absolute fullness. He, therefore, is the primary, the original truth, the source

77. Ed. note: The English translation of חֶסֶד as "kindness" and "steadfast love" reflects the Dutch distinction between *weldadigheid* and *goedertierenheid*.

of all truth, the truth in all truth. "You I invoke, O God, the truth in, by, and through whom all truths are true."[78]

Goodness

[204] The first of God's moral attributes is his goodness. This is not to be understood in a relative or utilitarian sense but absolutely. God's goodness is perfection, the sum of all goodness. "No one is good but God alone" (Mark 10:18; Luke 18:19). He is perfect (τελειος, Matt. 5:48). His goodness, accordingly, is one with his absolute perfection. In him "idea" and "reality" are one. He has no goal outside himself but is self-sufficient, all-sufficient (Ps. 50:8ff.; Isa. 40:28ff.; Hab. 2:20). It is fitting to use the term "blessedness" here. Blessedness, in the tradition of Aristotle, involves a unity of thinking and thought as well as not being subject to striving and craving. God is the Blessed One because he is at rest in the plenitude of his perfections. When God loves others, he loves himself in them; he is blessed in himself as the sum of all goodness, of all perfection. It is important to stress this in order to avoid thinking of the divine goodness in terms of a primacy of will as Duns Scotus and others after him did. Bonaventure had a much sounder view when he saw the intellect and the will as being conjointly the seat of blessedness.[79] Just as in the case of humans, beatitude embraces body and soul and all our faculties, so in the case of God it consists not only in perfect knowledge but equally in perfect power, goodness, holiness, and so on. "Beatitude is the perfect state of all goods in their aggregation."[80]

Blessedness is a good also for God's creatures. God himself is the supreme good of all creatures, the object of every creature's desire. As the overflowing fountain of all good,[81] God manifests his goodness to his creatures as steadfast love, as mercy, as forbearance, and most wonderfully as grace. Steadfast love (חֶסֶד) denotes God's special favor to his people, his chosen (Num. 14:19; 2 Sam. 7:15; 22:50; 1 Chron. 17:13; Pss. 5:7; 18:51). In the New Testament it is manifest in the full riches of God in Christ (Rom. 2:4; 2 Cor. 10:1; Eph. 2:7; Col. 3:12; Titus 3:4). The goodness of God, when shown to those in misery, is called mercy (רַחֲמִים, σπλαγχνα, viscera, misericordia; New Testament: ἐλεος, οἰκτιρμος), and it is tender (Ps. 103:13), great and abundant (Exod. 20:6; 2 Sam. 24:14; Neh. 9:19; Pss. 51:12; 119:156). In the New Testament God, the father of mercies (2 Cor. 1:3), reveals his mercy in Christ (Luke 1:50ff.), who is a merciful high priest (Matt.

78. Augustine, *Soliloquies*, I, 1; cf., T. Aquinas, *Summa Theol.*, I, qu. 16, 17; I, 2, qu. 3, art. 7; idem, *Summa contra gentiles*, I, chaps. 59–62; III, chap. 51; Bonaventure, *Sent.*, I, dist. 8, art. 1; J. Gerhard, *Loci theol.*, II, c. 8, sect. 16; A. Polanus, *Syn. theol.*, II, chap. 27; J. Zanchi, *Op. theol.*, II, cols. 226–42; L. Meijer, *Verhandelingen over de goddelyke eigenschappen*, 4 vols. (Groningen: Jacob Bolt, 1783), IV, 1–88.
79. Bonaventure, *Sent.*, IV, dist. 49, pt. 1, art. 1, qu. 4–5.
80. Boethius, *The Consolation of Philosophy*, 4. On the blessedness of God: Augustine, *City of God*, XII, 1; T. Aquinas, *Summa Theol.*, I, qu. 26; J. Gerhard, *Loci theol.*, II, c. 8, sect. 19; J. Zanchi, *Op. theol.*, II, 155ff.; A. Polanus, *Syn. theol.*, II, chap. 17.
81. Belgic Confession, art. 1.

18:27; 20:34; etc.; Heb. 2:17). The goodness of God, which spares those who are deserving of punishment, is called forbearance or patience (רוח or אֶרֶךְ אַפַּיִם, μακροθυμια, ἀνοχη, χρητοτης), an attribute frequently mentioned in Scripture (Exod. 34:6; Num. 14:18; Neh. 9:17; Pss. 86:15; 103:8; 145:8; Joel 2:13; Jon. 4:2; Nah. 1:3). God's forbearance remains operative in the New Testament age and is tied to the proclamation of Christ (1 Tim. 1:16; 2 Pet. 3:15). Above all, God's goodness is manifested in his grace, his demonstration of voluntary, unmerited favor shown to undeserving sinners.

The full doctrine of grace was first developed in the Christian church by Augustine. When God's goodness conveys not only benefits but God himself, it appears as love. Portrayed as covenantal, marital love in the Old Testament (Deut. 4:37; 7:8, 13; 10:15; 23:5; 2 Chron. 2:11; Isa. 43:4; 48:14; 63:9; Jer. 31:3; Hosea 11:1, 4; 14:4; Zeph. 3:17; Mal. 1:2), it is supremely revealed as ἀγαπη in the New Testament, the love the Father gives to and through the Son. The relation between Father and Son is portrayed as a life of love (John 3:35; 5:20; 10:17; 14:31; 15:19; 17:24, 26). But in Christ, who himself loves and proved his love in his self-offering (John 15:13), that love is bestowed not only on the world and the church in general (John 3:16; Rom. 5:8; 8:37; 1 John 4:9), but also individually and personally (John 14:23; 16:27; 17:23; Rom. 9:13; Gal. 2:20). Indeed, God not only loves but is himself love (1 John 4:8), and his love is the foundation, source, and model of our love (1 John 4:10–11). We need to exercise caution here not to take the confession "God is love" in an exclusive sense as though all the divine attributes radiate from the core essence of divine love. It is also true to say, "God is holy; God is just," and so forth.

Holiness

[205] God is holy as well as good, morally perfect. People and things only become sanctified in relation to God by being chosen and set apart. The stem קדשׁ, related to חדשׁ, is usually traced to the root קד, meaning "to cut, separate," and hence it expresses the idea of being cut off and isolated. The word "holy" is used first of all with reference to an array of persons and things that have been set apart from general use and placed in a special relation to God and his service. Because YHWH is holy, he wants a holy people for himself, a holy priesthood, a holy dwelling (Exod. 19:6; 29:43; Lev. 11:44–45; 19:2; 20:26; 21:8; Deut. 28:9–10). Included, among other things, in the call for separation and holiness are a "holy people" (Exod. 19:6), a "holy place" (Exod. 29:31), a "holy year of jubilee" (Lev. 25:12), a "holy sabbath" (Exod. 16:23), "holy vessels" (Num. 16:37), "holy water" (Num. 5:17), and the sanctuary (Exod. 15:17), with its "holy place" and "holy of holies" (Exod. 26:33–34). This does not mean that creation is intrinsically evil; it is good but it is *profane* (חל), not in communion with God and unfit for his service. God the Holy One alone can sanctify and make the unclean holy: "I am the Lord, who sanctifies you" (Exod. 31:13; Lev. 20:8; 21:8, 15, 23; 22:9, 16, 32; Ezek. 20:12; 37:28). God does this, negatively, by choosing a people, person, place,

day, or object and setting it apart from all others; and positively, by consecrating these persons or things and causing them to live in accordance with specific rules. He sanctified the whole people of Israel by choosing her from among all the peoples of the earth, by incorporating her in his covenant, and making his laws known to her (Exod. 19:4–6). Sanctification is something more than merely being set apart; it is, by means of washing, anointing, sacrifice, and the sprinkling with blood (etc.), to divest a thing of the character it has in common with all other things, and to impress upon it another stamp, a stamp uniquely its own, which it must bear and display everywhere (Lev. 8:15; 16:15–16; Job 1:5; etc.). As the Holy One, God is the creator, redeemer, and king of Israel (Isa. 43:14–15; 49:7; 54:5; 62:12). Accordingly, his redeemed people thank and praise him as the Holy One (Pss. 30:4; 71:22; 97:12; 1 Chron. 16:10, 35).

For Israel, God's holiness means deliverance (Pss. 22:3–4; 89:18; 98:1; 103:1; 105:3; 145:21), answer to prayer (Pss. 3:4; 20:6; 28:2), and comfort (Isa. 5:16; Hab. 1:12), but also punishment and chastisement when Israel breaks the covenant with God, desecrates his name, violates his laws, and becomes unholy. But even in chastisement God does not forget his people, and his holiness remains the cause of their redemption (Isa. 6:13; 10:20; 27:13; 29:23–24; 43:15; 49:7; 52:10; Jer. 51:5; Hosea 11:8–9; etc.). In the end God's holiness will vindicate itself by making known to the gentiles that he is the Lord (Jer. 50:29; Ezek. 36:23; 39:7) and will redeem Israel and cleanse it from all its iniquities (Ezek. 36:25ff.; 39:7). This brings us to the New Testament where God's holiness is finally supremely manifest in Christ, in whom God gives himself to the church, which he redeems and cleanses from all its iniquities. Here, when the Holy One of God appears (Mark 1:24; Luke 4:34; Acts 3:14; 4:27), the One who forms the sharpest contrast with the world (John 15:18) and in an absolute sense consecrates himself to God (John 17:19), the holiness of God ceases to be primarily the principle of punishment and chastisement, and the Holy Spirit (rarely so called in the Old Testament [Ps. 51:11; Isa. 63:10–11] but regularly in the New) becomes the principle of the sanctification of the church. From now on the church is the "holy nation" (1 Pet. 2:5, 9; Eph. 2:19; 5:27), composed of the elect, the holy and blameless (Eph. 1:1, 4; Col. 1:2, 22; 3:12; 1 Cor. 7:14), completely freed and cleansed from sin and eternally consecrated with soul and body to God.

Righteousness (Justice)

[206] Closely related to holiness is God's righteousness, by which he equitably and justly vindicates the righteous and condemns the wicked. The words צַדִּיק, צֶדֶק, and צְדָקָה describe the state of a law-abiding person, and the first meaning of "righteousness" seems to be forensic: one who is proved right before a trial judge and therefore has to be acquitted is considered צַדִּיק. God is the Judge of all the earth (Gen. 18:25) who manifests his righteousness in history, in his government of the world, and in his providential guidance of Israel. God is righteous and all

his judgments are righteous (Pss. 119:137; 129:4). God's wrath is terrible[82] and must be taken seriously (Job 21:17; Pss. 2:5; 6:1; 38:1; 76:7; 90:7; 102:10; Jer. 10:24; 42:18). He judges the wicked (Ezek. 7:4, 9, 27; 8:18; 9:10), including and even especially his own covenant people (Isa. 42:24–25; Jer. 7:20; 21:5; 32:31; etc.; Lam. 2:2ff.; 3:43; Ezek. 5:13ff.; 7:3; 13:1; etc.; Zech. 7:12ff.). Still, in Scripture, while God's retributive justice is real, his remunerative justice is far more prominent. Here God's righteousness is viewed favorably as the attribute by virtue of which God vindicates the righteous and raises them to a position of honor and well-being. This is the pattern for earthly justice as well—for kings, judges, and every Israelite. YHWH is the true judge, and the manifestation of his righteousness is simultaneously the manifestation of his grace.

Therefore, though Israel is a sinful people and has therefore been severely punished (Isa. 43:26; 48:1; 53:11; 57:12; 59:4; 64:5), yet over against the gentiles, Israel is in the right. Despite all its transgressions Israel's cause is righteous, and when she has been sufficiently chastised, God's righteousness will reawaken and recognize that right, and he will deliver his people from all their misery (Isa. 40:1ff.; 54:5, 7ff.; 57:15ff.; 61:1ff.). The salvation Israel awaits is more than restoration of outward blessings of prosperity and peace, it is above all his forgiveness, the Spirit he will pour out on them to give them new hearts. Salvation consists in God's being fully their God and in their being completely his people (Isa. 43:25; Jer. 31:33–34; 32:39–40; 33:8; Ezek. 11:19; 36:25; Joel 2:28ff.). This righteousness is not for Israel alone but for gentile peoples as well (Isa. 2:2ff.; 45:22). The Lord will give *his* justice to his people by the Messiah, who will bring forth justice to the gentiles (Isa. 42:1), and the Lord will create a new heaven and a new earth, in which righteousness dwells (Isa. 65:17ff.).

This is the meaning of "righteousness" in the New Testament. The righteousness of God (δικαιοσυνη θεου) consists in the fact that through and by the Messiah it brings righteousness to his people: in Christ it offers a means of atonement, which proves God to be righteous; able to justify the believer and grant forgiveness to (1 John 1:9), and bestow salvation on his own (John 17:25; 2 Tim. 4:8). Although God's wrath rests on the wicked already (John 3:36; Eph. 2:3; 1 Thess. 2:16), the manifestation of that wrath in all its terror is reserved for the future (Matt. 3:7; Luke 3:7; 21:23; Rom. 5:9; 1 Thess. 1:10; 5:9; Eph. 5:6; Col. 3:6; Rev. 6:16–17; 11:18; 14:10; 16:19; 19:15).[83]

In dogmatic *theology* the term "righteousness" has a broader meaning as the sum of all divine virtue. The advantage of this use is to afford opportunity to defend God's justice against assailants such as the Gnostics, Marcion, and modern

---

82. Cf. on the wrath of God: L. Lactantius, *De ira Dei*; Tertullian, *De ira Dei*; Lange, "Zorn Gottes," *PRE¹*, XVIII, 657–71; R. Kübel, "Zorn Gottes," *PRE²*, XVIII, 556–68; G. F. Oehler, *Theology of the Old Testament*, §48; H. Cremer, *Lexicon*, s.v. "ὀργη."

83. On the righteousness of God in Scripture, H. Cremer, *Lexicon*, s.v. "δικαιοσυνη"; J. Köstlin, "Gott," *PRE²*, V, 311; idem, G. F. Oehler, *Theology of the Old Testament*, §47; A. B. Davidson, *Theology of the Old Testament*, 129ff.; also see the literature in the later chapter on justification.

theologians who only see God as love and draw sharp divisions between law and gospel, the God of wrath and the God of grace. Speaking of God's justice does bring us before additional questions. In the case of God one cannot conceive of a law that is above him and to which he would have to conform, for his will is the supreme law. Furthermore, before God creatures do not have rights or claims; he is their Creator and there is no law apart from him to which appeal can be made. It is true that God is not under external obligation but his righteousness and justice do rest on a moral foundation. God does not act arbitrarily or capriciously with his creatures but covenantally in grace with his people; he binds himself by his holiness and grace. By giving each creature its distinct nature and governing creation by his laws and ordinances, God grants "rights" that are structured into the very existence and nature of all existing beings. These are especially accorded to rational creatures and among them again for all the areas of life. All laws and rights, whatever they may be, have their ultimate ground, not in a social contract, nor in self-existent natural law or in history, but in the will of God, viewed not as "absolute dominion" but as a will of goodness and grace. God's grace is the fountainhead of all laws and rights. God is the supreme Lawgiver, and the entire order of justice undergirding every domain of life is rooted in him.

God's Sovereign Will

[207] The attributes that belong to God's sovereignty are ultimately grounded in his will as Creator and Lord of all. Everything derives from God's will: creation and preservation (Rev. 4:11), government (Prov. 21:1; Dan. 4:35; Eph. 1:11), Christ's suffering (Luke 22:42), election and reprobation (Rom. 9:15ff.), regeneration (James 1:18), sanctification (Phil. 2:13), the suffering of believers (1 Pet. 3:17), our life and lot (James 4:15; Acts 18:21; Rom. 15:32), even the most minute details of life (Matt. 10:29; etc.). Philosophy has never been satisfied with this and continues to look for a deeper explanation, for realities beyond God as ultimate grounds. But, contrary to attempts by rationalistic philosophers, nothing can be considered beyond God's will. To consider pure thought itself as absolute, as Hegel does, removing all content from it and trading *being* for *becoming* and *actuality* for *potentiality*, is metaphysical sleight-of-hand, skilful playing with concepts. Existence cannot be derived from absolute thought without a will. Philosophers such as Schelling who turned to the primacy of the will made the opposite mistake. "Ultimately," he said, "there is no other being than volition. Volition is archetypal being, and to it alone all the predicates of such being apply: groundlessness, eternity, freedom from dependence on time, self-affirmation. All philosophy is solely aimed at finding this supreme expression."[84] Will is ultimate

84. F. W. J. Schelling, "Philosophische Untersuchungen über das Wesen der menschlichen Freiheit und die damit zusammenhängenden Gegenstände," in *Ausgewählte Werke*, 4 vols. (Darmstadt: Wissenschaftliche Buchgesellschaft, 1968), IV, 294; ET: *Schelling: Of Human Freedom*, trans. James Gutmann (Chicago: Open Court, 1936).

being and anterior to the intellect. "Things have their ground in that which in God is not God himself, that is, in that which is the ground of his existence." Things have their ground in this dark nature, in the unconscious will of God. Here the will is not a will in the true sense of the word, but simply an unconscious desire, a blind urge, a dark force of nature. Although the world as we know exhibits order, regularity, and form, the threat of chaos is ever present. The entire cosmic process is inferred by Schelling from the antithesis between nature and spirit, darkness and light, the real and the ideal, which have been coexistent in God himself from all eternity. An assumption here is the notion that the will is ungoverned by the intellect and that all willing is a kind of primal desiring, striving, restlessness, longing for what is not yet. The consequence: If the will is as primary as striving, no rest or blessedness is possible for creatures except by annihilation of the will, the loss of the soul.

This is the teaching of Buddhism (Nirvana) and varieties of pantheistic mysticism, but it is most decidedly not the teaching of Scripture or Christian theology. Christianity does not seek the annihilation of the soul or the elimination of the will. Instead, true blessedness raises the soul to the highest level of love. A will that finds rest and enjoyment in what it has acquired is present in creatures. It is simply the love that embraces its object and is blessed in so doing. Here our convictions about God's will are instructive. God's willing does not arise out of lack; it is not a craving for what God does not yet possess. God is all-sufficient and blessed in himself; his love is divine self-love. God is himself the object of his will, not in the sense of being his own cause but in the full sense of willing his own delight and good pleasure. God's will is not a force or energy inside him, distinct from him; it is rather coexistent with his own divine being, his own divine love. The triune God eternally loves himself with divine love and is completely blessed within himself. This *necessary* will within God is to be distinguished from God's free will toward his creatures, which is the final ground of all things created. As the Blessed One, God is himself the supreme good, for his creatures and for himself. All things are created by and for his willing good pleasure, his glory.

[208] Although God's will is one, we must distinguish God's will in relation to himself—"propensity toward himself as goal"—from his will with respect to his creatures—"propensity toward his creatures as means." God eternally and *necessarily* delights in himself. Here freedom and necessity coincide. With respect to creatures things are very different. Here God is free to do whatever he pleases (Ps. 115:3; Prov. 21:1; Dan. 4:35); owes no one an accounting and justifies none of his deeds (Job 33:13). Humans are to him like clay in the hands of a potter (Job 10:9; 33:6; Isa. 29:16; 30:14; 64:8; Jer. 18:1ff.). "Even the nations are like a drop from a bucket, and are accounted as the dust on the scales" (Isa. 40:15ff.). It is as foolish for humans to magnify themselves against God as it would be for an axe to magnify itself against him who hews with it or for a saw to boast against him who wields it (Isa. 10:15)! No human can assert his "rights" before God or ask him: "What are you doing?" (Job 9:2ff., 12; 11:10). "Does the clay say to him

who fashions it: what are you making?" (Isa. 45:9). Before God we must be silent, lay our hand on our mouth (Job 40:4). So also the New Testament teaches. Can God not do what he wants to do with what belongs to him (Matt. 20:15)? All things depend solely on God's will for their being—that they are and what they are (Rev. 4:11). God's will is the ultimate ground of all things. Both mercy and hardening originate there (Rom. 9:15–18). In the church the Holy Spirit apportions to each one individually as he wills (1 Cor. 12:11). Humans have no right whatever to object to God's free dispositions (Matt. 20:13ff.; Rom. 9:20–21). For all these reasons, Christian theology speaks of God's will in relation to his creatures as *free*. Thus, Augustine asserted that the will of God is the final ground of all things;[85] there is nothing deeper. To the question: Why did God create the world? the answer is: Because he so willed. Those who then proceed to ask about the cause of that will "demand something that is greater than the will of God; but none such thing can be found."[86]

Proceeding from God's absolute freedom, many theologians began to think along the lines of medieval nominalism. It was Duns Scotus who consistently applied to God the Pelagian notion of the freedom of the will as absolute indifference. Here is the fundamental assertion: "The will of God wills this"; nothing takes precedence over the antecedent reason of the will.[87] Creation is radically contingent; God created the world in absolute freedom, granted that the decree to do so was made from eternity.[88] From God's absolute free will Scotus also inferred human freedom of will as absolutely as possible. The human will is free, he says, "with respect to opposite actions and opposite objects."[89] It is itself alone the complete cause of all its actions, not an external good. "Nor is it any goodness of the object that necessarily prompts the assent of the will, but the will assents freely to any good whatever and thus assents freely to a greater or to a lesser good."[90] "Nothing other than the will is the complete cause of volition in the will."[91] The will is even antecedent to the intellect, for though it is the case that the intellect offers to the will the object of its striving, it nevertheless is the will that fixes the intellect's attention upon the object. And, formally, the will, not the intellect, is the seat of blessedness.[92] There are radical consequence to this nominalism. For Scotus, the will is the seat of blessedness, the second table of the law could have been different, the Logos could have assumed a nature other than human, and the incarnation would probably have occurred apart from sin. God could have redeemed humanity some other way, even apart from Christ's merits. Scotus

85. Augustine, *City of God*, XXI, 8; idem, *The Trinity*, III, 7, 19.
86. Augustine, *On Genesis, against the Manicheans*, I, 2; idem, *City of God*, V, 9.
87. Duns Scotus, *Sent.*, I, dist. 8, qu. 5, n. 24.
88. Ibid., II, dist. 1, qu. 2, n. 5.
89. Ibid., I, dist. 39, qu. 5, nn. 15ff.
90. Ibid., I, dist. 1, qu. 4, n. 16.
91. Ibid., II, dist. 25, qu. 1, n. 22.
92. Ibid., IV, dist. 49, qu. 4.

raised God's freedom and omnipotence to such a height that at least the means that must lead to the goal become completely arbitrary.[93] Others—Occam, the Jesuits, the Socinians, the Remonstrants, Descartes—followed the same path, severing God's will from his nature and his perfections. This is the road of formal arbitrariness; everything including creation, incarnation, the moral law, truth and untruth, could have been different. Against both pantheism and deism, Christian theology maintains that the world was brought into being by an act of God's free and sovereign will, and that God had his own wise reasons for his will.

Nominalism put Christian theology on guard; its task was to continue to affirm God's will as the ground of all things while taking care not to divest this will of all its natural specificity and let it degenerate into pure arbitrariness. In response, Christian theology, in its doctrine of God, took its point of departure in God's nature, not his will. The *existence* of things depends on God's will, but their nature or *essence* depends on his mind. God creates and preserves the world by the Logos; it therefore rests on God's thoughts. God does not act arbitrarily and "accidentally" but with supreme wisdom. To avoid charges of arbitrariness in God while maintaining his original free will as the ground of creation, theologians looked for the divine motives guiding the will. Theologians who pondered the "why" of God's free act of creation spoke of God's goodness, his love, or his glory. Scientific theology that looks for "causes" cannot avoid raising such questions, never forgetting that the first duty of every practitioner of science, and particularly of any theologian, is to be humble and modest. For theology this means being strictly tethered to the facts and evidences that God discloses in nature and Scripture. Theology must refuse the seductions of pantheism, which make the world necessary, and those of deism, which make the world a product of chance. Against both, Christian theology stoutly maintains that the world was brought into being by an act of God's free and sovereign will, and that God had his own wise reasons for that will. To us a thing is good for the sole reason that God wills it. God himself can never have willed anything unless it is either good in itself or for some other reason.[94] God freely created a world that is radically contingent for his good pleasure. God's will is one with his being, wisdom, goodness, and all his other perfections.[95] For that reason the human heart and head can rest in God's will, for it is the will of an almighty God and a gracious father, not that of a blind fate, incalculable chance, or dark force of nature. His sovereignty is one of unlimited power, but also of wisdom and grace. He is both king and father at one and the same time.

The Problem of Evil: Revealed and Hidden Will

[209] Additional difficulties for the doctrine of the will of God remain. Just as God and the world are distinct, leading us to distinguish God's "propensity

93. Cf. ibid., IV, 388ff.
94. G. Voetius, *Select. disp.*, I, 387.
95. T. Aquinas, *Summa Theol.*, I, qu. 19, art. 5.

toward himself" from his "propensity toward his creatures," so also in the world of creatures, God's willing is diverse. We can make as many distinctions in the will of God (as it relates to his creatures) as there are creatures; the free will of God is as richly variegated as that whole world is. Most important is the fact that God is father to all his creatures but not in the same way. In our world there is one thing that creates a special difficulty for the doctrine of God's will, and that is the problem of evil, both ethical and physical. Although evil is under God's control, it cannot in the same sense and in the same way be the object of his will as is the good. There is a big difference between the will of God that prescribes what we must do (Matt. 7:21; 12:50; John 4:34; 7:17; Rom. 12:2) and the will of God that tells us what he does and will do (Ps. 115:3; Dan. 4:17, 25, 32, 35; Rom. 9:18–19; Eph. 1:5, 9, 11; Rev. 4:11). The petition that God's will may be done (Matt. 6:10) is very different in tenor from the childlike and resigned prayer: "Your will be done" (Matt. 26:42; Acts 21:14). That the actual will of God is the will of his good pleasure, that this will is identical with God's being and efficacious, is most consistently taught in Reformed theology. God's "hidden"—or, better, "the will of God's good pleasure"—and revealed wills are not incompatible; his decree is his ultimate will, and his revealed will indicates what he wills that we do. Failure to grant this distinction or some variation of it runs the risk of making God the author of sin and fails to accord to human beings rational, moral responsibility before God. Furthermore, it creates an insoluble dualism between God's intent and the actual result of world history. This outcome then will be an eternal disappointment for God: his plan for the world has failed, and in the end Satan triumphs. But God's revealed (preceptive) will is not really his (ultimate) will but only the command he issues as the rule for our conduct. In his preceptive will he does not say what *he* will do; it is not the rule for *his* conduct; it does not prescribe what *God* must do, but tells us what *we* must do. It is the rule for *our* conduct (Deut. 29:29). It is only in a metaphorical sense, therefore, that it is called the will of God. The revealed will is the way the hidden will is brought to realization. It is in the way of admonitions and warnings, prohibitions and threats, conditions and demands that God carries out his counsel, while God's secret will only ensures that human beings violating God's commandment do not for a moment become independent of God, but in the very moment of violating it serve the counsel of God and become, however unwillingly, instruments of his glory. Those who deny God's revealed will fail to take sin seriously; denying the hidden will undermines faith in God's sovereignty. In the former case, the spiritual risk is shallow optimism that closes its eyes to painful realities; in the latter, dark cynicism that curses life on earth and despairs of the world and human destiny. Christian theism acknowledges the reality of the world's darkness but refuses to deny either the revealed, preceptive will of God or the conviction that God's hidden purposes will come to glorious fruition. Furthermore, we also in faith often witness God's sovereignty at its most brilliant when he magnifies his wisdom in human folly, his strength in human weakness, and his grace and righteousness in human sin.

Omnipotence

[210] God is omnipotent in his sovereignty. Names such as El, Elohim, El Shaddai, and Adonai indicate his power: he is the mighty king and lord over all. All his works proclaim his omnipotent power. He is further called "great and terrible" (אֵל גָּדוֹל וְנוֹרָא, Deut. 7:21ff.); "the Mighty One of Israel" (אֲבִיר יִשְׂרָאֵל, Isa. 1:24); "the great and mighty God (הָאֵל הַגָּדוֹל הַגִּבּוֹר) whose name is YHWH of hosts" (Jer. 32:18); "strong and mighty" (עִזּוּז וְגִבּוֹר, Ps. 24:8), "the Lord" (אָדוֹן, κυριος, Matt. 11:25; Rev. 1:8; 22:5). Similarly, in the New Testament he is called "the great king" (μεγας βασιλευς, Matt. 5:35; 1 Tim. 1:17), "the King of kings and Lord of lords" (βασιλευς των βασιλευοντων και κυριος των κυριευοντων, 1 Tim. 6:15; cf. Rev. 19:16); "the Lord Almighty" (παντοκρατωρ, 2 Cor. 6:18; Rev. 1:8; 4:8; 11:17); "the only Sovereign" (μονος δυναστης, 1 Tim. 6:15), who possesses both the power (ἐξουσια ἀρχη) and the authority (δυναμις, κρατος) to act (Matt. 28:18; Rom. 9:21) and the ability, fitness, and power to act (Matt. 6:13; Rom. 1:20). God's omnipotence is further evident from all his works. Creation, providence, Israel's deliverance from Egypt, nature with its laws, the history of Israel with its marvels—all loudly and clearly proclaim the omnipotence of God. Nothing is too hard for God; for him all things are possible (Gen. 18:14; Zech. 8:6; Jer. 32:27; Matt. 19:26; Luke 1:37; 18:27). Out of stones he can raise up children to Abraham (Matt. 3:9). His power is, above all, evident in the works of redemption: in the resurrection of Christ (Rom. 1:4; Eph. 1:20). From him derives the dominion of humankind (Gen. 1:26; Ps. 8), the authority of governments (Prov. 8:15; Rom. 13:1–6), the strength of his people (Deut. 8:17–18; Ps. 68:35; Isa. 40:26ff.), the might of a horse (Job 39:19ff.), the mighty voice of thunder (Pss. 29:3; 68:33; etc.). His is the power to dispense grace above all we ask or think (2 Cor. 9:8; Eph. 3:20; 2 Pet. 1:3), to raise the dead in the last day (John 5:25ff.). Power belongs to God (Ps. 62:11), and his is the glory and the strength (Ps. 96:7; Rev. 4:11; 5:12; 7:12; 19:1).

Entirely in keeping with their doctrine of the will and freedom of God, the nominalists defined the omnipotence of God not only as his power to do whatever he wills, but also as his power to will anything. In accord with his "absolute" power (distinguished from his "ordained" power) they judged God could also sin, err, suffer, die, become a stone or an animal, change bread into the body of Christ, do contradictory things, undo the past, make false what was true and true what was false, and so forth. According to his absolute power, therefore, God is pure arbitrariness, absolute potency without any content, which is nothing but can become anything. On the other hand, Plato, among others, said that the real world we know is the only possible world. Scripture and Christian orthodoxy, by contrast, while stating that God cannot deny himself,[96] and that his will and being coincide, also insist that the possible is greater than that which exists. What

96. He cannot lie, he cannot repent, he cannot change, he cannot be tempted (Num. 23:19; 1 Sam. 15:29; Heb. 6:18; James 1:13, 17), and he cannot deny himself (2 Tim. 2:13).

the Reformed tradition denied was a notion of "absolute power" that was not bound to God's own nature. Thus, Calvin, fighting back, rejected as profane this "fiction of absolute power."[97] God's existence is not exhausted by the existence of the world; so too his omnipotence infinitely transcends even the boundless power manifested in the world. The actual does not completely cover the possible. God's existence is not exhausted by the existence of the world; eternity does not fully empty itself in time; infinity is not identical with the sum total of finite beings; omniscience does not coincide with the intellectual content embodied in creatures. So also, God's omnipotence infinitely transcends even the boundless power manifested in the world.[98]

Perfection, Blessedness, and Glory

[211] God is the sum total of all his perfections, the One than whom no greater, higher, or better can exist either in thought or reality. God, in other words, fully answers to the idea of God. He also has perfect knowledge of himself and has instilled in our hearts an impression of himself. Our idea of God comes from him; we cannot avoid God's reality in the world and in our lives, even though our hearts' sense of God is darkened. When we are instructed by Scripture, our sense of God is clarified, we learn anew to know God as he truly is, and say Amen! to all his perfections. Every attribute of God is precious to believers.

Because God is perfect, Scripture also speaks of him as the "Blessed One." In Scripture the words אַשְׁרֵי and μακαριος, "blessed," usually have a religious meaning. They refer to the person who lives in communion with God and is the recipient of God's special benefits, above all the benefit of the forgiveness of sins (Ps. 32:1; Rom. 4:8). In the New Testament, God himself is twice called "blessed" (1 Tim. 1:11; 6:15). In the New Testament the Hebrew word root אַשְׁרֵי is rendered by μακαριος (according to Cremer, more emphatic and ideal than εὐδαιμων) and is in turn translated *beatus* in Latin, *blessed* in English, and *zalig* in Dutch. God's blessedness has three components: First it expresses the fullness of God's absolute perfection; he is the sum total of all virtues, the supreme being, the supreme good, the supreme truth (etc.); in other words, because God is absolute life, the fountainhead of all life, he is also the absolutely blessed God. Second, implied in the words "the blessed God" is that God knows and delights in his absolute perfection. God knows his own perfection; God knows himself absolutely and loves himself absolutely. Knowledge without love and love without knowledge are both inconceivable, and neither has priority over the other. Finally, God absolutely delights in himself, absolutely rests in himself, and is absolutely self-sufficient. His life is not a process of becoming, not an evolution, not a process of desiring and

97. J. Calvin, *Institutes*, III.xxiii.1, 5; cf. I.xvi.3; II.vii.5; IV.xvii.24; idem, *Commentary*, on Isa. 23:9 and Luke 1:18.
98. Cf. I. A. Dorner, *A System of Christian Doctrine*, I, 458ff.; C. Hodge, *Systematic Theology*, I, 406ff.; W. G. T. Shedd, *Dogmatic Theology*, I, 358ff.

striving, as in the pantheistic life, but an uninterrupted rest, eternal peace. God's delight in his creatures is part and parcel of his delight in himself. "God is his own blessedness. Blessedness and God are the same. Through his intellect God is fully aware of his own perfection, and through his will he supremely loves it, that is, reposes peacefully in it, and from this repose springs joy, the joy with which God delights in himself as the supreme good."[99]

[212] The perfection of God, which is inwardly the ground of his blessedness, outwardly as it were carries his glory with it. The biblical words for glory are כָּבוֹד and δόξα; the Old Testament word כָּבוֹד, from the verb כָּבֵד, to be heavy, weighty, significant, refers to the person who is weighty, important. Also in use is the word הוֹד, which denotes the splendid appearance of one whose name is known far and wide, while הָדָר describes the splendor and beauty of that appearance.[100] The Greek equivalent used in the Septuagint and the New Testament is the word δόξα, subjectively the recognition a person receives or is entitled to receive, the fame or honor that person enjoys (synonyms: τιμη and εὐλογια, Rev. 5:12; antonym: ἀτιμια, 2 Cor. 6:8). Objectively, δόξα is the appearance, form, prestige, splendor, luster, or glory of a person or matter manifest in the public domain, or these themselves in their splendor, and in that case related to εἶδος (appearance), εἰκων (image), μορφη (form) (Isa. 53:2; 1 Cor. 11:7). The "glory of the Lord" is the splendor and brilliance that is inseparably associated with all of God's attributes and his self-revelation in nature and grace, the glorious form in which he everywhere appears to his creatures. This glory and majesty in which God is clothed and which characterizes all his activities (1 Chron. 16:27; Pss. 29:4; 96:6; 104:1; 111:3; 113:4; etc.), though manifest throughout his creation (Ps. 8; Isa. 6:3), is nevertheless especially visible in the realm of grace. It appeared to Israel (Exod. 16:7, 10; 24:16; 33:18ff.; Lev. 9:6, 23; Num. 14:10; 16:19; Deut. 5:24; etc.). It filled the tabernacle and the temple (Exod. 40:34; 1 Kings 8:11), and was communicated to all the people (Exod. 29:43; Ezek. 16:14; etc.). This glory is above all manifested in Christ, the only begotten Son (John 1:14), and through him in the church (Rom. 15:7; 2 Cor. 3:18), which is looking for "the blessed hope and the manifestation of the glory of our great God and Savior, Jesus Christ" (Titus 2:13). God's glory is often associated with

99. Pseudo-Dionysius, *The Divine Names and Mystical Theology*, chap. 11; T. Aquinas, *Summa Theol.*, I, qu. 26; idem, *Summa contra gentiles*, I, chaps. 100–102; M. J. Scheeben, *Handbuch der katholischen Dogmatik*, I, §5; J. Heinrich and C. Gutberlet, *Dogmatische Theologie*, III, 856; J. Gerhard, *Loci theol.*, II, §306; David Hollaz, *Examen theologicum acroamaticum* (Rostock and Leipzig: Russworm, 1718), I, 1, 37; Karl Gottlieb Bretschneider, *Systematische Entwicklung aller in der Dogmatik verkommenden Begriffe*, 4th ed. (Leipzig: J. A. Barth, 1841), §37; B. de Moor, *Comm. in Marckii Comp.*, I, 583; Hans Martensen, *Christian Dogmatics*, trans. William Urwick (Edinburgh: T&T Clark, 1871), §51; Friedrich A. Philippi, *Kirchliche Glaubenslehre*, 3rd ed., 7 vols. in 10 (Gütersloh: Bertelsmann, 1870–90), II, 109; Alexander von Oettingen, *Lutherische Dogmatik*, 2 vols. (Munich: C. H. Beck, 1897–1902), II, 185; M. Kähler, "Seligkeit," *PRE*[3], XVIII, 179–84.

100. Franz Delitzsch, *Biblical Commentary on the Psalms*, trans. F. Bolton, 3 vols. (Edinburgh: T&T Clark, 1871), on Ps. 8:6; cf. also A. Freiherr von Gall, *Die Herrlichkeit Gottes* (Giessen: J. Ricker [A. Töpelmann], 1900).

his holiness (Exod. 29:43; Isa. 6:3) and hence also described as a fire (Exod. 24:17; Lev. 9:24) and as a cloud (1 Kings 8:10–11; Isa. 6:4).

Undoubtedly, in referring to that fire and that cloud, Scripture had in mind the visible creaturely forms through which God manifested his presence.[101] The case is different with the light with which the glory of God is often compared and in terms of which it is often represented. Light in Scripture is the image of truth, holiness, and blessedness (Pss. 43:3; 97:11; Isa. 10:17). What light is in the natural world—the source of knowledge, purity, and joy—God is in the world of the spirit. He is the "light" of believers (Ps. 27:1); his face and his word shed light (Pss. 44:3; 89:15; 119:105); in his light they see light (Ps. 36:9). He himself is pure light, and in him is no darkness; he is the father of lights (1 John 1:5; 1 Tim. 6:16; James 1:17), and according to the promise (Isa. 9:1; 60:1, 19–20; Mic. 7:8), appeared in Christ as light (Matt. 4:16; Luke 2:32; John 1:4; 3:19; 8:12; 1 John 2:8–11), so that now his church is light in him (Matt. 5:14; Eph. 5:8; 1 Thess. 5:5) and goes out to meet the fullness of light (Rev. 21:23ff.; 22:5; Col. 1:12).

When Scripture speaks of God's face, glory, and majesty, it uses figurative language. Like all God's perfections, so also that of God's glory is reflected in his creatures. It is communicable. In the created world there is a faint reflection of the inexpressible glory and majesty that God possesses. Just as the contemplation of God's creatures directs our attention upward and prompts us to speak of God's eternity and omnipresence, his righteousness and grace, so it also gives us a glimpse of God's glory. What we have here, however, is analogy, not identity. That is why the word "glory" is to be preferred over "beauty"; "glory" is Scripture's special word for God's beauty. Augustine was fond of the notion of "God's beauty," in part a vestige of his Neoplatonist background.[102] Although he was followed in this by numerous Scholastic and Catholic theologians,[103] Protestant theologians preferred to speak of God's majesty and glory.[104] Manifest in God's glory is his sublime greatness, as it is frequently portrayed in the book of Psalms and in the Prophets (Ps. 104; Isa. 40; Hab. 3). It is called "greatness" and "sublimeness" insofar as it elicits in creatures their worshipful admiration and adoration. It is called "glorious" insofar as it elicits gratitude, praise, and honor. It is called "majesty" insofar as it is bound up with his absolute dignity and demands submission from all creatures.

---

101. Cf. H. Bavinck, *Reformed Dogmatics*, I, 341 (#94).

102. Augustine, *On Genesis, against the Manicheans*, I, 21; idem, *Sermon* 241; idem, *Literal Meaning of Genesis*, III, 14; idem, *On Order*, I, 26; II, 51; idem, *De beata vita*, 34; idem, *Against the Academics*, II, 9.

103. Pseudo-Dionysius, *The Divine Names and Mystical Theology*, chap. 4, §7; Bonaventure, *Breviloquium*, I, chap. 6; D. Petavius, *Theol. dogm.*, VI, chap. 8; M. J. Scheeben, *Handbuch der katholischen Dogmatik*, I, 589ff.; J. B. Heinrich and C. Gutberlet, *Dogmatische Theologie*, III, 852; cf. also Heinrich Krug, *De pulchritudine divina libri tres* (Freiburg i.B.: Herder, 1902).

104. J. Gerhard, *Loci theologici*, I, c. 8, sect. 18; A. Polanus, *Syn. theol.*, II, chap. 31; P. van Mastricht, *Theoretico-practica Theologia*, II, chap. 22; H. Bavinck, ed., *Synopsis purioris theologiae*, VI, 43.

9

THE TRIUNE GOD AND HIS COUNSEL

THE HOLY TRINITY IN SCRIPTURE

[213] The seeds that developed into the full flower of New Testament trinitarian revelation are already planted in the Old Testament. Elohim, the living God, creates by speaking his word and sending his spirit. The world comes into being by a threefold cause: the word of God (Gen. 1:3; Pss. 33:6, 9; 147:18; 148:8; Joel 2:11); the Word hypostatized as Wisdom (Job 28:20–28; Prov. 8:22ff.; cf. Prov. 3:19; Jer. 10:12; 51:15); and the Spirit of God (Gen. 1:2 NIV; Pss. 33:6; 104:30; 139:7; Job 26:13; 27:3; 32:8; 33:4; Isa. 40:7, 13; 59:19). Whereas God calls all things into being by his word as mediating agent, it is through his Spirit that he is immanent in the creation and vivifies and beautifies it all. The world was first conceived by God and thereupon came into being by his omnipotent speech; after receiving its existence, it does not exist apart from him or in opposition to him, but continues to rest in his Spirit. The spirit of God is the principle of all life and well-being as well as of holiness and renewal. A threefold divine principle underlies creation as well as re-creation and sustains the entire economy of Old Testament revelation.

In the Old Testament this threefold cause is even more clearly evident in special revelation, in the work of re-creation. YHWH, the covenant God, reveals himself to, saves, and preserves his people by his word and spirit. In the angel of the Lord, whether created angel or the Logos, God, specifically his Word, was uniquely and powerfully present (Gen. 16:6–13; 18; 21:17–20; 22:11–19; 24:7,

40; 28:13–17; 31:11–13; 32:24–30 [cf. Hosea 12:4]; 48:15–16; Exod. 3:2ff.; 13:21; 14:19; 23:20–23; 32:34; and 33:2ff. [cf. Num. 20:16; Isa. 63:8–9; Zech. 1:8–12; chap. 3; Mal. 3:1]). The church fathers before Augustine unanimously explained the Old Testament "angel of the Lord" as a theophany of the Logos though Augustine himself believed that these theophanies were mediated by created angels.[1] Luther and Calvin interpreted the angel of YHWH sometimes as a created angel, in other verses as the uncreated angel.[2] Later Protestant interpreters, however, understood these verses to refer mostly to the Logos, especially to define their position over against the Socinians, Remonstrants, and Rationalists, who read them only as referring to angelophanies. This difference should not be exaggerated since Augustine and those who follow him grant that in that created angel the Logos revealed himself in an utterly unique way.[3] Realizing that references to the angel of YHWH cannot all be construed the same sense, this much is clear: in the angel of YHWH, who is the preeminent bearer of that name, God, specifically his Word, was uniquely present. The angel of YHWH bears the same name, exercises the same power, brings about the same deliverance, dispenses the same blessings, and receives the same adoration and honor as YHWH.[4]

And now, just as YHWH in his work of re-creation reveals himself objectively by his Word, in the angel of YHWH, he does this subjectively in and by his spirit. The spirit of God is the principle of all life and well-being, of all the gifts and powers in the sphere of revelation: of courage (Judg. 3:10; 6:34; 11:29; 13:25; 1 Sam. 11:6), of physical strength (Judg. 14:6; 15:14), of artistic skill (Exod. 28:3; 31:3–5; 35:31–35; 1 Chron. 28:12–19), of the ability to govern (Num. 11:17, 25; 1 Sam. 16:13), of intellect and wisdom (Job 32:8; Isa. 11:2), of holiness and renewal (Ps. 51:12; Isa. 63:10; cf. Gen. 6:3; Neh. 9:20; 1 Sam. 10:6, 9), and of prophecy and prediction (Num. 11:25, 29; 24:2–3; Mic. 3:8; etc.). The Spirit will rest in an unusual measure on the Messiah (Isa. 11:2; 42:1; 61:1), but afterward be poured out on all flesh (Joel 2:28–29; Isa. 32:15; 44:3; Ezek. 36:26–27; 39:29; Zech. 12:10) and give to all a new heart and a new spirit (Ezek. 36:26–27).[5] The threefold principle that undergirds the entire economy of Old Testament revelation can be seen in the high priestly benediction (Num. 6:24–26) which refers back to a threefold revelation of God and as such is the Old Testament example of the apostolic benediction (2 Cor. 13:13); a similar threefold differentiation can be seen in Psalm 33:6; Isaiah 61:1; 63:9–12; and Haggai 2:5–6. In addition,

1. Augustine, *The Trinity*, III, 11; idem, *City of God*, XVI, chap. 29.
2. Christian J. Trip, *Die Theophanien in den Geschichtsbüchern des Alten Testaments* (Leiden: D. Noothoven van Goor, 1858), 49–58.
3. A. Rivetus according to Chr. J. Trip, *Theophanien*, 65.
4. Cf. H. Bavinck, *Reformed Dogmatics*, ed. John Bolt (Grand Rapids: Baker Academic, 2003–8), I, 329 (#91); Chr. J. Trip, *Theophanien*, 100ff.; A. Kuyper, *De Engelen Gods* (Amsterdam: Höveker & Wormser, 1902), 189.
5. Cf. on the Holy Spirit in the Old Testament also B. B. Warfield, "The Spirit of God in the Old Testament," *Presbyterian and Reformed Review* 6 (October 1895): 665–87; H. Cremer, "Geist," *PRE³*, VI, 450.

passages such as Genesis 19:24; Psalms 45:7; 110:1; and Hosea 1:7 point to self-differentiation in the divine being.

[214] These Old Testament ideas were further developed in intertestamental Judaism where Wisdom is hypostatized as divine (Sir. 1:1–30; 24; also cf. Bar. 3:9–4:4; Wis. 1:4–7; 6:12–25; 7:25–26; 8:3–4; 9:1–2, 5–9, 17; 12:1; 16:12; 18:15–16). Under Greek philosophical influence, Philo fused Plato's doctrine of the ideas, Stoic logos-doctrine, and the Old Testament doctrine of wisdom into a single system. However, keeping God and world separate in a metaphysical dualism, Philo regards the Logos as a necessary intermediary being between God and the world, a hypostasis located between God and the world and participating in both. Not uncreated in the sense in which God is uncreated, nor created as finite things are, Philo calls him a "second God." In Jewish theology this developed into a complex angelology that increasingly diverged from the Old Testament. From Jewish convictions about God's utter transcendence arose a sense that God needed a variety of intermediate beings to act in creation. Angels are used to guide the powers in nature and humanity, but in order to create or re-create, God uses *hypostases* which, though creatures, possess divine attributes because they are representatives of God. Such hypostases are *metratons*, those who share God's throne; *memra*, the Word of God; *shekinah*, the presence of God's glory; *bath kol*, the oracular voice of God, which grants revelations; and the *ruach hakkodesh,* the spirit that proceeds from God and imparts a higher knowledge.[6]

These developments clearly diverge from Old Testament teaching. The Old Testament is not dualistic; "the word" and "wisdom" are not intermediaries between God and the world but stand wholly on God's side as the first principles of the created world. Philo's intermediaries erase the boundary between Creator and creature, paving the way for gnosticism and Kabbalism. In addition, whereas "logos" in Philo is primarily God's reason and thought, in the Old Testament the "word" is not first of all reason and thought, "an intelligible world" (κοσμος νοηος), but the *spoken* word by which God creates and preserves all things. Finally, these intermediate beings have no soteriological significance, no connection with the Messiah; the Spirit of the Lord is virtually neglected. Sharing language with the New Testament, its world of ideas is quite different. To Philo, a human incarnation of the Logos (Reason) would have been an absurdity. But in the New Testament the incarnation of the Word is the supreme revelation of God. There is agreement of form here but the content differs. Philo and John only have the word "logos" in common.

[215] The true development of Old Testament trinitarian ideas is found in the New. In the incarnation of the Son and the outpouring of the Holy Spirit, the one true God is revealed as Father, Son, and Holy Spirit. The Father, who bears

---

6. J. A. Eisenmenger, *Entdecktes Judenthum*, 2 vols. (Königsberg in Preussen, 1711), I, 265ff.; II, 393ff.; F. W. Weber, *System der altsynagogalen palästinischen Theologie: Aus Targum, Midrasch und Talmud* (Leipzig: Dörffling & Franke, 1880), 172–89.

this name in relation to the Son and to his children, he who can be called Father, is also the Creator of all things (Matt. 7:11; Luke 3:38; John 4:21; Acts 17:28; 1 Cor. 8:6; Heb. 12:9). The Son, who bears this name especially because of his utterly unique relation to God, is identical with the Logos, through whom the Father created all things (John 1:3; 1 Cor. 8:6; Col. 1:15–17; Heb. 1:3). And the Holy Spirit, who received his name especially with a view to his work in the church, is the same Spirit who jointly with the Father and the Son beautifies and completes all things in the creation (Matt. 1:18; 4:1; Mark 1:12; Luke 1:35; 4:1, 14; Rom. 1:4). There is continuity here with the word and deed, prophecy and miracle revealed to Old Testament saints, but the threefold principle in creation and salvation is much clearer in the New Testament. The New Testament revelation is trinitarian through and through, from Jesus's birth (Matt. 1:18ff.; Luke 1:35) and baptism (Matt. 3:16–17; Mark 1:10–11; Luke 3:21–22) to his teaching. Distinguishing himself from the Father, he is nevertheless his only begotten and much-beloved Son (Matt. 11:27; 21:37–39; John 3:16; etc.), one who is with him in life, glory, and power (John 1:14; 5:26; 10:30), and the one who sends the Holy Spirit from the Father (John 15:26) as the Paraclete who guides and comforts Jesus's followers and remains with them forever (John 14:16). Jesus summarizes his teaching in the baptismal formula "in the name of the Father and of the Son and of the Holy Spirit" (Matt. 28:19), that is, in the one divine name (το όνομα, in singular) in which three distinct subjects (the Father, the Son, and the Spirit) reveal themselves. Just as Jesus sums up his instruction in the name of the Father, of the Son, and of the Holy Spirit, so also the apostles again and again put these names side by side and on the same level (1 Cor. 8:6; 12:4–6; 2 Cor. 13:13; 2 Thess. 2:13–14; Eph. 4:4–6; 1 Pet. 1:2; 1 John 5:4–6; Rev. 1:4–6).[7]

[216] Scripture also gives us insight to the relations among the three distinct persons of the Trinity. In the most general sense, God the Father is the Creator of all things, especially human beings (Num. 16:22; Matt. 7:11; Luke 3:38; John 4:21; Acts 17:28; 1 Cor. 8:6; Eph. 3:15; Heb. 12:9). More particularly, with theocratic significance, God is the father of his people Israel inasmuch as he created and preserved his people by his marvelous power (Deut. 32:6; Isa. 63:16; 64:8; Mal. 1:6; 2:10; Jer. 3:19; 31:9; Ps. 103:13; Rom. 9:4). He is also the father of his Son, the "Father of our Lord Jesus Christ" (Rom. 15:6; 1 Cor. 15:24; 2 Cor. 1:3; Gal. 1:1; Eph. 1:3; etc.). This sonship is metaphysical; by nature and from eternity (John 1:14; 8:38; 17:5, 24) he is the "firstborn" and "only begotten," the full image of God, who bears a unique relation to the Father. He is not a creature, but is and was and remains God, who is over all, blessed forever. The Spirit is God as the immanent principle of life throughout creation; he is both divine and personal; he is holy because he is God. Finally, as Christ is related to the Father, so the Spirit

---

7. On the doctrine of the Trinity in the New Testament, one can also consult, inter alia, I. A. Dorner, *A System of Christian Doctrine*, trans. Alfred Cave and J. S. Banks, rev. ed., 4 vols. (Edinburgh: T&T Clark, 1888–91), I, 344ff. Ed. note: Omitted is a large paragraph in which Bavinck deals with the authenticity of 1 John 5:7 as a proof text for the Trinity. He judges it "doubtful" on text-critical grounds.

is related to Christ; as the Son witnesses to and glorifies the Father, so the Spirit witnesses to and glorifies the Son. By the Spirit we have communion with no one less than the Son and the Father themselves. The Father is, thus, preeminent in creation and redemption, the first in the divine economy. It is the Father to whom we as a matter of course give the name "God." He is the one true God (μονος ἀληθινος θεος, John 17:3), the one God (εἰς θεος, 1 Cor. 8:6; 1 Tim. 2:5), who is mentioned as God and Father alongside the Lord Jesus Christ and the Holy Spirit (1 Cor. 12:6; 2 Cor. 13:13; 1 Thess. 1:3; Rev. 1:6). Even Christ calls him not only his Father but also his God (Matt. 27:46; John 20:17; Heb. 1:9; 2:17; 5:1; 10:7, 9) and is himself called "the Christ of God" (Luke 9:20; 1 Cor. 3:23; Rev. 12:10).

From this the Arians wrongly infer that the Father *alone* is God, contrary to Scripture. In fact, the names given to Christ reveal the immanent relations of the triune God. The premise underlying the name Logos is the consistent teaching of Scripture that in creation and re-creation alike God reveals himself by the Word. Thus, Logos points to the one who is able to fully reveal God because from all eternity God communicated himself in all his fullness to him. For that reason, too, the gospel is called "the Word of God" (λογος του θεου). Christ is also called "Son of God." In the Old Testament this has theocratic significance when Israel is called God's son (Exod. 4:22; 19:5–6; Deut. 1:31; 8:5; 14:1; 32:6, 18; Isa. 63:8; Jer. 31:9, 20; Hosea 11:1; Mal. 1:6; 2:10). "Son of God" has decided royal connotation as in Psalm 2:7 where YHWH says to Zion's anointed king: "You are my son; today I have begotten you." When cited in the New Testament it harkens back to God's decree in 2 Samuel 7 and to the messianic promise associated with David's throne. The writer to Hebrews (1:5; 5:5; cf. 1:2–3) links the citation from Psalm 2 to the eternity in which Christ as the Son is generated by the Father, that is, in which he is brought forth as the effulgence of God's glory and the express image of his nature. In addition, according to Acts 13:33 and Romans 1:4, Jesus Christ was proved to be God's Son with power by the resurrection from the dead.

The third name we must consider is "image of God." By analogy it applies to humans but in an absolute sense it belongs to Christ. Before his incarnation he existed in the form of God (ἐν μορφη θεου, Phil. 2:6), was rich (2 Cor. 8:9), and was clothed with glory (John 17:5). Having returned to that state by his resurrection and ascension, we can say that he was then and is now "the image of the invisible God" (εἰκων του θεου του ἀορατου, Col. 1:15; 2 Cor. 4:4), the reflection of his glory and the "very stamp of his nature" (ἀπαυγασμα της δοξης και χαρακτηρ της ὑποστασεως αὐτου, Heb. 1:3), i.e., the exact imprint of the Father's nature. As the "firstborn of all creation" (πρωτοτοκος πασης κτισεως, Col. 1:15; Rev. 1:16–18)— in the sense of existing before every creature (i.e., as firstborn [πρωτοτοκος] and not just created first [πρωτοκτιστος] or made first [πρωτοπλαστος])—he is the one in whom all things were created (ἐκτισθη, Col. 1:16). The expression "firstborn" (πρωτοτοκος) does not include Christ in the category of creatures but excludes him from it; along with "only begotten," it designates the Son, and as Logos, the full image of God, as the one who has an eternal and utterly unique relation to the Father. As mediator, Christ is represented as dependent on and subject to the Father, a servant sent to do the Father's work, obedient even to death, and one day delivering up his kingdom to the Father. These references do not in any way detract from his essential unity with the Father. Rather, though in his position and *office* as mediator he is subordinate to the Father, in his *essence* and *nature* he is equal. He is not a creature, but is and was and remains God, who is over all, blessed forever (John 1:1; 20:28; Rom. 9:5; Heb. 1:8–9; 2 Pet. 3:18; 1 John 5:20; Rev. 1:8, 17–18).

[217] Scripture—finally—also sheds light on the immanent relations of God by the name of "the Holy Spirit." As Christ is related to the Father, so the Spirit is related to Christ; as the Son witnesses to and glorifies the Father, so the Spirit witnesses to and glorifies the Son. By the Spirit we have communion with no one less than the Son and the Father themselves. And although the divine being we call God is "Spirit" (John 4:24) and "holy" (Isa. 6:3), in Scripture the term "Holy Spirit" is still a reference to a special person in the divine being distinct from the Father and the Son. The name derives from his special mode of subsistence: "spirit" means "wind," "breath." The Holy Spirit is the breath of the Almighty (Job 33:4), the breath of his mouth (Ps. 33:6). Jesus compares him to the wind (John 3:8) and "breathes" him upon his disciples (John 20:22; cf. 2 Thess. 2:8). The Spirit is God as the immanent principle of life throughout creation making all living things alive and thus putting all things in relation to God. He is not the spirit of humans or of creatures but the Spirit of God, the Holy Spirit (Ps. 51:11–12; Isa. 63:10–11). That is why he is called "holy" and the Spirit of God, the Spirit of the Lord, the Spirit of the Father (Gen. 1:2; Isa. 11:2; Matt. 10:20), as well as the Spirit of Christ, the Spirit of the Son (Rom. 8:2, 9; 1 Cor. 2:4–16; 2 Cor. 3:17–18; Phil. 1:19; Gal. 3:2; 4:6; 1 Pet. 1:11). There is no essential difference between old and new covenant teaching on this point. It is the same Spirit who at one time spoke through the prophets (Matt. 22:43; Mark 12:36; Acts 1:16; 28:25; Heb. 3:7; 10:15; 1 Pet. 1:10–11; 2 Pet. 1:21), testified in the days of Noah (1 Pet. 3:19–20), was resisted by Israel (Acts 7:51), and produced faith (2 Cor. 4:13), who would descend on the Messiah and dwell in the church (Matt. 12:18; Luke 4:18–19; Acts 2:16–18).

We speak of the Spirit "proceeding," and Scripture uses various terms for this: the Spirit is *given* by God or by Christ (Num. 11:29; Neh. 9:20; Isa. 42:1; Ezek. 36:27; John 3:34; 1 John 3:24; 4:13), *sent* or *sent forth* (Ps. 104:30; John 14:26; 15:26; 16:7; Gal. 4:6; Rev. 5:6), *poured out* (Isa. 32:15; 44:3; Joel 2:28–29; Zech. 12:10; Acts 2:17–18), *came down* from God (Matt. 3:16), *was put* in the midst of Israel (Isa. 63:11; Hag. 2:5), or *put* on someone (Matt. 12:18), or *breathed upon* persons (John 20:22), and so on. In John 15:26, where Jesus tells us that the Spirit (Paraclete) proceeds from the Father (ἐκπορεύεται παρα του πατρος), he points to Pentecost and clearly marks the *personal* existence, or personality, of the Holy Spirit. All kinds of personal capacities and activities are attributed to him: searching (1 Cor. 2:10–11), judging (Acts 15:28), hearing (John 16:13), speaking (Acts 13:2; Rev. 2:7, 11, 17, 29; 3:6, 13, 22; 14:13; 22:17), willing (1 Cor. 12:11), teaching (John 14:26), interceding (Rom. 8:27), witnessing (John 15:26), and so on. He is coordinated with the Father and the Son (Matt. 28:19; 1 Cor. 12:4–6; 2 Cor. 13:13; Rev. 1:4). None of this is possible unless the Spirit, too, is truly God. Furthermore, an array of divine attributes are ascribed equally to God's Spirit and to God himself—eternity (Heb. 9:14), omnipresence (Ps. 139:7), omniscience (1 Cor. 2:10–11), and omnipotence (1 Cor. 12:4–6)—a fact that again presupposes the essential unity of the Spirit with God himself. The same is true of the divine works of creation (Gen. 1:2; Pss. 33:6; 104:30; Job 33:4) and of re-creation. The Spirit anoints and equips Christ for his office (Isa. 11:2; 61:1 and Luke 4:18; Isa. 42:1 and Matt. 12:18; Luke 1:35; Matt. 3:16; 4:1; John 3:34; Matt. 12:28; Heb. 9:14; Rom. 1:4), equips the apostles for their tasks (Matt. 10:20; Luke 12:12; 21:15; 24:49; John 14:16ff.; 15:26; 16:13ff.; etc.), distributes gifts and powers to believers (1 Cor. 12:4–11), and causes the fullness of Christ to dwell in the church. Just as no one can come to the Father but by the Son (Matt. 11:27; John 14:6), so no one can say "Jesus is Lord" except by the Spirit (1 Cor. 12:3). No communion with God is possible except by the Spirit. The same Spirit grants to believers Christ's benefits: regeneration (John 3:3), conviction of sin (John 16:8–11), the gift of child status (Rom. 8:15), renewal (Titus 3:5), the love of God (Rom. 5:5), a wide assortment of spiritual fruits (Gal. 5:22–23), the sealing (Rom. 8:23; 2 Cor. 1:22; 5:5; Eph. 1:13; 4:30), and resurrection (Rom. 8:10–11). The Holy Spirit is God himself (or Christ) living in us (John 14:23ff.; 1 Cor. 3:16; 6:19; 2 Cor. 6:16; Gal. 2:20; Col. 3:11; Eph. 3:17; Phil. 1:8, 21). The Spirit exists alongside the Father and the Son as the cause of all blessing and well-being (Matt. 28:19; 1 Cor. 12:4–6; 2 Cor. 13:13; Rev. 1:4). To him, accordingly, full divine honor is due; to blaspheme him, says Christ, is unpardonable (Matt. 12:31–32).[8]

In all of this, of course, Scripture does not provide us with a fully developed trinitarian dogma. It teaches that the one name of God is only fully unfolded in that of the Father, the Son, and the Spirit. It plainly declares that all God's outgoing works (*ad extra*), both in creation and re-creation, have a threefold divine cause. Furthermore, this threefold cause constitutes three distinct subjects who relate to each other as persons. Scripture thus contains all the data from which theology constructed trinitarian dogma. Philosophy did not contribute anything essential; even the Logos doctrine is part of the New Testament. It was only a matter of time before the power of Christian reason was sufficiently developed to enter into the holy mystery that presents itself here.

---

8. Significant literature on the Holy Spirit includes John Owen, *Pneumatologia, or, A Discourse concerning the Holy Spirit* (London: J. Darby, 1674); idem, *The Holy Spirit* and *The Work of the Holy Spirit*, in *The Works of John Owen*, 16 vols. (London: Banner of Truth, 1966), vols. 3 and 4; A. Kuyper, *The Work of the Holy Spirit*, trans. H. De Vries (New York: Funk & Wagnalls, 1905); G. Smeaton, *The Doctrine of the Holy Spirit* (Edinburgh: T&T Clark, 1882); K. H. Cremer, "Geist, heiliger," *PRE*[3], VI, 450.

THE CONSTRUCTION OF TRINITARIAN DOGMA

[218] With Scripture providing the essential ingredients, the Apostolic Fathers do little more than cite it, though they exalt the Son and avoid both the Docetic and Ebionite heresy. He is called the Son, the only begotten Son of God (*1 Clem.* 36; Ign. *Rom.* 1; Ign. *Eph.* 20; Ign. *Smyrn.* 1; *Diogn.* 9–10; *Barn.* 7.12); the efful-gence and scepter of God's majesty (*1 Clem.* 16, 36); the Lord of earth, to whom all things are subject, the creator of all things, the judge of the living and the dead (*Barn.* 7.12; *Diogn.* 7; *Did.* 16; Pol. *Phil.* 1, 2, 6, 12); the holy and incom-prehensible Logos, who was sent to earth "as God" (*Diogn.* 7) and may properly be called "God" (*2 Clem.* 1; Ign. *Rom.* 3; Ign. *Smyrn.* 1, 10; Ign. *Eph.* 1.18–19). Faced with the challenge of gnosticism, apologists such as Justin Martyr teach the divinity of the Son, though he does not clearly express the immanent relations between Father and Son. Justin repeatedly calls Christ "God," even "God" with the definite article, "the God" (*Dialogue with Trypho*, 34, 56, 58, 113, 126; etc.), and ascribes to him preexistence, not only as a force but as a person (*Dialogue with Trypho*, 128). However, certain influences of Greek philosophic thought also find their way into Justin's formulations including subordination: the Son is "the first power after the Father" (ἡ πρωτη δυναμος μετα τον πατερα, *1 Apology*, 32); occupies "second place" (δευτερα χωρα, *1 Apology*, 13), and is "subordinate to the Father and Lord" (ὑπο τω πατρι και κυριω τεταγμενος, *Dialogue with Trypho*, 126). Although elements in Justin's thought are defective, it is a mistake to think of him as an Arian. Not only is this anachronistic, but he clearly understands the importance of the deity of Christ for the entire work of salvation and for the truth of the Christian religion. For that reason, too, he repeatedly refers to the Father, the Son, and the Spirit together as the object of our worship (*1 Apology*, 6, 13, 60, 61, 65, 67).

We owe the immediately following development of the doctrine of the Trin-ity—consisting mainly in the exclusion of philosophical elements—to three men, each of whom made a specific contribution to the Christian dogma: Ire-naeus, Tertullian, and Origen. Opposition to Greek philosophic influences is particularly strong in Irenaeus, the great opponent of gnosticism, with its idea of God as "cosmic depth" (βυθος), the emanation of the aeons, and the Logos as the immanent principle of the cosmos. For him the Logos is not a creature but a hypostatic word (*Against Heresies*, III, 8), preexistent (II, 6; IV, 12), true God (IV, 10, 14; etc.). God is simple—all spirit, all intellect, all thought, all logos (II, 16, 48)—so that both the Son and the Father are true God. The generation of the Son did not occur in time; the Son existed eternally with God (II, 18; III, 22; IV, 37). Irenaeus very clearly enunciates the unity of the Father, the Son, and the Spirit, emphatically maintaining their full divinity (IV, 6, 20, 33). Where he falls short is in showing how the Trinity exists in that unity; that is, how the Father, Son, and Spirit, though partaking in one and the same divine nature, are still personally distinct.

Here Tertullian complements and corrects Irenaeus. He was the first to deduce the Trinity of persons from the very being of God rather than from the person of the Father, thus clearly distinguishing *and* maintaining unity. The three persons are "of one substance, of one condition, and of one power: together they constitute one God." They are distinct as to their order and economy; they are three, "not in status, but in degree"; yet one God, "defined under the name of the Father, the Son, and the Holy Spirit." As a sun ray is also sun, so there are various aspects, forms, images, and units in the one undivided substance. The three persons, accordingly, are one but not identical. The Son is distinct from the Father and the Spirit is distinct from both, but they have the name "God" and "Lord" in common. Together they are one God and inseparable. Just as the trunk and the branch, the spring and the stream, the sun and the sunray are inseparable, so also are the Father and the Son. It is "a unity that derives the Trinity from within its own self" (*Against Praxeas*, 2ff.). It is Tertullian who furnished the concepts and terms that the dogma of the Trinity needed to articulate its true meaning. He replaced Logos speculation with the doctrine of filiation, thereby permanently disentangling the ontological Trinity from cosmological speculation. And he was the first who deduced the Trinity of persons, not from the person of the Father, but from the very being of God.[9]

Origen took it the next step by conceiving the immanent Trinity totally as an eternal process within the divine being itself, though he subordinates the Son to the Father by deriving the Trinity from the person of the Father. The generation [of the Son] is eternal generation (αἰώνιος γεννησις, *On First Principles*, I, 2, 4). Just as it is the very nature of light to shine so that it cannot exist without shining, so the Father cannot exist without the Son (*On First Principles*, I, 2, 2, 4, 7, 10; *Against Celsus*, IV, 14, 16). There was no time when the Son did not exist (*On First Principles*, I, 2, 2, 4; *Against Celsus*, VIII, 12); the Father is not Father before the existence of the Son but through the existence of the Son (*On First Principles*, I, 2, 10). The Father and the Son have all the divine attributes in common: the Son and the Father are one. But now, in order to maintain the distinction of persons while affirming this unity and equality, Origen calls into play the aid of subordinationism, and reaching back behind Tertullian, he again derives the Trinity from the person of the Father, instead of God's being. He thus represents the Father as *the* God (ὁ θεος), as being of himself God (αὐτοθεος), the fountain or root of deity (ῥιζα θεοτητος), the greatest God over all things (μεγιστος ἐπι πασι θεος), superior (κρειττων) to the Son, the one complete Godhead, exalted above all being, invisible, incomprehensible, and the Son as God (θεος, without the article), as "other than the Father in substance" (ἑτερος του πατρος κατ᾽ οὐσιαν).[10]

9. B. B. Warfield, "Tertullian and the Beginnings of the Doctrine of the Trinity," *Princeton Theological Review* 16 (October 1905); (January 1906); (April 1906); also published in *The Works of Benjamin B. Warfield*, 10 vols. (New York: Oxford University Press, 1930; repr., Baker Academic, 1991), IV, 3–112.

10. I. A. Dorner, *History of the Development of the Doctrine of the Person of Christ*, trans. Patrick Fairbairn, 3 vols. (Edinburgh: T&T Clark, 1868), II, 118ff.

[219] At Nicaea (AD 325), the church did not follow Origen but repudiated subordinationism and affirmed the full deity of the Son. This changed the character of the ecclesiastical and theological discussion, turning the challenge into maintaining the true unity of the Godhead. *Before* Nicaea the main difficulty was to derive a threesome from the oneness of God; *after* Nicaea the reverse is true. Elaborating, developing, and completing trinitarian doctrine fell to Athanasius, the three Cappadocians, and Augustine. Athanasius understood better than any of his contemporaries that Christianity stands or falls with the confession of the deity of Christ and the Trinity; it is the heart and center of Christianity, different in principle from Judaism, which denies distinctions, and paganism, which rejects the oneness of God (*Letters to Serapion*, I, 28). Athanasius rejects the philosophically inspired gnostic and Arian dualism between God and the world together with its array of intermediate beings (*Against the Arians*, II, 26).

For Athanasius, Father, Son, and Holy Spirit are three from eternity but with one essence and the same attributes. God does not *become* anything; he is what he is eternally. As the Trinity always was, so it is and remains; and in it the Father, the Son, and the Spirit (*Letters to Serapion*, III, 7; *Against the Arians*, I, 18). The Father was always Father; fatherhood belongs to his very nature (*Defense of the Nicene Definition*, 12). Just as one cannot conceive of the sun apart from its light, nor of a spring apart from its water, so one cannot conceive of the Father apart from the Son. God is not "without offspring" (ἄγονος); on the contrary, he is always speaking (*Against the Arians*, II, 2; *Letters to Serapion*, II, 2). Neither for the Father, nor for the Son was there a time when he did not exist (*Against the Arians*, I). This Son is not a creature and was not begotten by the will of God but is generated from within his being (*Against the Arians*, I, 25). Although Athanasius speaks more sparingly of the Spirit, the same thing is true (*Letters to Serapion*, I, 20–21; etc.). These three persons are truly distinct; they are not three parts of a single whole, or three names for one and the same being. The Father alone is Father; the Son alone is Son; the Spirit alone is Spirit (*Against the Arians*, III, 4; IV, 1; *Letters to Serapion*, IV, 4, 6–7). Athanasius maintains the unity by affirming that all three are the same in essence (ὁμοούσιοι) and one substance (ὑπόστασις), that the three persons exist in each other (*Letters to Serapion*, I, 14; III, 6; *Against the Arians*, III, 6) and are united in their working (*Letters to Serapion*, I, 28). Athanasius also teaches that the Father is the first principle and fountainhead of the Trinity (*Against the Arians*, IV, 1).

In the main, this teaching of Athanasius is affirmed by Basil and the two Gregories and clarified with more names, illustrations, and analogies. In the West, it was Hilary and especially Augustine in their respective treatises *De trinitate* who vigorously defended the doctrine. The entire Greek (Orthodox) church accepted this doctrine as defined by the ecumenical councils (of which it recognizes the first seven), diverging from the West only with reference to *filioque* (the phrase "and of the Son"). Augustine of Hippo's 15 books on *The Trinity* contain the most profound exposition of this dogma ever written, summing up what earlier fathers had said but also treating it independently and introducing important modifications. Augustine's starting point is not the person of the Father but the one, simple, uncompounded essence of God. From this absolute unity he affirms that each person is as great as the entire Trinity (*The Trinity*, VIII, 1, 2). Present in each person is the entire self-same divine being, so that there are not three Gods, three Almighties, and so forth, but only one God, one Almighty, and so on (*The Trinity*, V, 8). Hence the distinction among the persons cannot arise from attributes or accidents that one person has in distinction from another but stems from the interpersonal relations of the members of the Trinity.

The first person is, and is called, the Father because he stands in a unique relation to the Son and the Spirit, etc. (*The Trinity*, V, 5), just as the appellatives "Lord," "Creator," etc., denote God's relation to his creatures but do not introduce any change in his being (*The Trinity*, V, 16–17). Augustine goes even farther than Athanasius (cf. *Against the Arians*, I, 59) and banishes all subordinationism. The Father can be called Father only because it is as *person*, not as God, that he is the Father of the Son. Augustine also reads the Nicaean phrase "very God of very God (*The Trinity*, VII, 2–3) in that same sense. Finally, more than any church father before him, Augustine looked for images, analogies, and vestiges of the Trinity and so brought out the connections between the doctrine of God and that of the cosmos as a whole (*The Trinity*, IX–XV). Thus Augustine completed what Tertullian had begun.

In the West there is, despite all the agreement between them, another view of the doctrine of the Trinity than that which prevails in the East. The Eastern church confessed that, though both the Son and the Spirit proceed from the Father, they otherwise have no relation to one another. But it was felt in the West that the consubstantiality of the three persons and their interrelations fully come to expression only in the "*filioque*" (and of the Son). The West aligned itself with Augustine and, while it developed his trinitarian views on some points, did not introduce any changes in them nor add anything new to them. The Athanasian Creed, which is mistakenly attributed to Athanasius and certainly did not originate before AD 400, breathes the spirit of Augustine and was therefore welcomed in the West but not in the East,[11] and the Reformers, too, attested their agreement with it.[12]

THE OPPOSITION: ARIANISM AND SABELLIANISM

[220] Opposition to the dogma of the Trinity comes from outside (Jews and Muslims) and from within Christianity itself. The confession of the Trinity is the heartbeat of the Christian religion. The great challenge facing us with this dogma is to see to it that the unity of the divine essence does not cancel out the Trinity of

11. A. von Harnack, *History of Dogma*, trans. N. Buchanan, J. Millar, E. B. Speirs, and W. McGilchrist, and ed. A. B. Bruce, 7 vols. (London: Williams & Norgate, 1896–99), IV, 129ff.

12. In the Belgic Confession (art. 9), the Athanasian Creed is mentioned by name.

the persons or, conversely, that the Trinity of persons does not abolish the unity of the divine essence. All error is traceable to a departure from this doctrine: to a denial of the unity in order to preserve threeness (Arianism) or to a formulation of unity that fails to maintain threeness (Sabellianism). An important precursor of the Arians in the second and third centuries AD was Paul of Samosata, who regarded Christ as a human being whose birth was supernatural, who was anointed at his baptism with the Holy Spirit, qualified for his task, and exalted as Lord. The Samosatan, however, firmly denied Christ's preexistence and deity; his was an *adoptionist* Christology.[13] Arianism was subordinationist and adoptionist. Arius taught that inasmuch as God is "unbegotten" (ἀγέννητος) and without beginning, he is absolutely unique; before God proceeded to create the world, he brought into being, as a kind of intermediary, an independent entity (ὑπόστασις, οὐσία) through whom or through which he created all things. In Scripture this entity is called "Wisdom," "Son," "Logos," "image of God," and so on. God similarly further called into being a third and lower ὑπόστασις, namely, the Holy Spirit. Accordingly, "there was a time when he did not exist" even though he was created "before the times and ages," that is, before the existence of the world. This Logos, therefore, is not consubstantial (ὁμο οὐσιος) with the Father but totally separate from him, mutable, able to choose evil as well as the good. In fact he was "a perfect creature" who chose the good and became immutable. This Logos also became human, preached the truth, and effected our redemption, for which he is worthy of honor but not our worship. He cannot be God, for that would entail the existence of two gods. The Logos, therefore, was a created but a perfect creature who became, as it were, a God.

The Arian objection had to be taken seriously; not only did it gain many adherents especially after the conversion of Constantine, but they could and did appeal to the many passages in Scripture that enunciated the unity of God (Deut. 6:4; 32:39; John 17:3; 1 Cor. 8:6), the birth or genesis of the Son (Prov. 8:22; Col. 1:15), his subordination to the Father (John 14:28; 1 Cor. 15:28; Heb. 3:2), his limited knowledge (Mark 13:32; John 11:34), his power (Matt. 28:18) and goodness (Luke 18:19), his increase in wisdom (Luke 2:52), his suffering (John 12:27; 13:21; Matt. 26:39; 27:46), his elevation to the position of Lord and Christ (Acts 2:36; Phil. 2:9; Heb. 1:3–4; etc.). They also made use of Aristotelian philosophy to prove the uniqueness and ἀγεννησια of God.

The opposite view, that Father, Son, and Holy Spirit are only different names or modes of the one God, came to expression as monarchianism, patripassionism, and modalism. Starting out from the conviction that there was only one *monarchia*, adherents of this view were led to conclude that the Father himself had been born, suffered, and died, and that "Father" and "Son" were names for the same person in different relations, namely before and after the incarnation. In the third century this view was promulgated and further developed by Sabellius.

---

13. A. von Harnack, *History of Dogma*, I, 191; III, 14–50.

The Father, Son, and Spirit are the same God; they are three names for one and the same being. Calling this being *Huiopatōr* (υἱοπατωρ), he applied the name to its three successive energies or stages. God consisted first of all in the person (προσωπον), the appearance or mode of the Father as Creator and Lawgiver; next, in the προσωπον of the Son as Redeemer, and finally in the προσωπον of the Holy Spirit as the Vivifier. Sabellius posited a process of becoming in God: a historical succession in the revelation of his being.[14] Like Arianism, Sabellianism also appealed to Scripture and made use of Greek philosophy to advance its arguments.

[221] Both schools of thought—Arianism and Sabellianism—the one to the right and the other to the left of the church's trinitarian dogma—have persisted in the Christian church throughout the centuries. Arianism has appeared in various forms of subordinationism, in Socinianism and in full-blown Unitarianism, all of whom either deny that the Son is consubstantial with the Father or say that he is inferior to the Father. Subordinationists insist that the Father alone is God (ὁ θεος); the Son is God (θεος) derivatively, received his nature from the Father by communication. This was the view of Tertullian, Clement, Origen, Eusebius of Nicomedia, who gave the Son a place "outside of the Father" and called him "like the Father in essence" (ὁμοιουσιος). In later times this was the position of the Remonstrants,[15] and many theologians in modern times.[16] Arianism, identical to that of Arius himself, arose in the post-Reformation period, especially in England. John Milton, for example, held that the Son and the Spirit were created by the free will of the Father before the creation of the world, and were only called "God" by virtue of their office, like the judges and magistrates in the Old Testament.[17]

A third form in which Arianism reappeared is *Socinianism*, which held that the Father is the one true God and the Son is a wholly created human being with no preexistence before his immediate supernatural conception. He was created for no other purpose than to proclaim a new law and, after completing this task, was elevated to a position in heaven, where he became a partaker of divine grace. He remains for us the supreme example, nothing more. The Spirit is no more than a divine power.[18] Neither the Holy Spirit nor grace is necessary for salvation. While Arianism, also in Socinian form, seeks to affirm the oneness of the divine by placing the Son and the Spirit outside the divine being, Sabellianism in its

14. A. von Harnack, *History of Dogma*, III, 51–73; idem, "Monarchianismus," *PRE*³, XIII, 303.

15. Remonstrant Confession, art. 3; J. Arminius, *Opera theologica* (Leiden: Godefridum Basson, 1629), 232ff.; Simon Episcopius, *Institutiones theologicae*, IV, sect. 2, chap. 32, in vol. 1 of *Opera theologica*, 2 vols. (Amsterdam: Johan Blaeu, 1650–65); Philippus van Limborch, *Theologia christiana ad praxin pietatis ac promotionem pacis christianae unice directa* (Amsterdam: Arnhold, 1735), II, 17, 25.

16. J. J. van Oosterzee, *Christian Dogmatics*, trans. J. Watson and M. Evans, 2 vols. (New York: Scribner, Armstrong, 1874), II, §52.

17. J. Milton, *De doctrina christiana*, ed. Charles Sumner (Brunsvigae: F. Vieweg, 1827), I, chaps. 5–6; ET: *A Treatise on Christian Doctrine: Compiled from Scripture Alone*, trans. Charles R. Sumner (Cambridge: J. Smith for Charles Knight, 1825).

18. *The Racovian Catechism*, trans. Thomas Rees (London, 1609; repr. London, 1818), qu. 94–190.

various forms does this by absorbing them in the one divine being so that proper distinctions between them disappear. Father, Son, and Holy Spirit are one and the same person or being, three modes of activity or revelation of the one divine being. The work of the triune God was seen, as in Joachim of Fiore and David Joris, as taking place in three successive periods, each one associated with one person of the Trinity. It was, however, especially Michael Servetus who devoted his intellectual powers to repudiate the church's doctrine of the Trinity. Gnostic and theosophical speculations can be found in the trinitarian thought of Jakob Böhme, Zinzendorf, and Swedenborg. Such theosophical thinking paved the way for radically philosophical interpretations of the Trinity in Kant, Spinoza, Schelling, Hegel, and Strauss.

TRINITARIAN LANGUAGE

[222] For the Christian church, the doctrine of the Trinity was the dogma and hence the mystery par excellence. The essence of Christianity—the absolute self-revelation of God in the person of Christ and the absolute self-communication of God in the Holy Spirit—could only be maintained, the church believed, if it was grounded in the ontological Trinity. To defend Scripture's teaching, the church found it necessary to use language that went beyond Scripture, a practice condemned by Arians and their post-Reformation and modern counterparts but always defended by Christian theology.[19] Christian theological reflection on Scripture has every right to move freely beyond the exact language of Scripture to draw warranted inferences from it. These too are authoritative.[20] In fact, theological reflection on Scripture is not even possible without the freedom to use extrabiblical terminology. Their use is not designed to introduce new—extrabiblical or antibiblical—dogmas but, on the contrary, to defend the truth of Scripture against all heresy. They exercise a primarily negative function, marking the boundary lines within which Christian thought must proceed in order to preserve the truth of revelation. Those who demand a "biblical theology" are most often not as close to biblical teaching as is ecclesiastical orthodoxy with its extrabiblical terminology. This is also true for Christian doctrines other than the Trinity.

Thus also in the doctrine of the Trinity we see the gradual rise of unusual terms such as ὁμοούσιος, οὐσία, ὕπαρξις, ὑπόστασις, πρόσωπον, γεννᾶν, τριάς, *unitas, trinitas, substantia, personae, nomina, gradus, species, formae, proprietates,* and so forth. Initially the meaning of these terms was far from precise and clear. The term οὐσία (being) was employed as a rule to refer to the one being of God,

---

19. Augustine, *The Trinity*, VI, 10; T. Aquinas, *Summa Theol.*, I, qu. 29, art. 3; J. Calvin, *Institutes of the Christian Religion*, I.xiii.5 (ed. John T. McNeill and trans. Ford Lewis Battles, 2 vols [1559; Philadelphia: Westminster, 1960], 1:125–28).

20. Cf. H. Bavinck, *Reformed Dogmatics*, I, 617–18 (#159).

yet Athanasius in his polemic against Sabellianism defended himself by saying that the Son is not μονοούσιος (of one substance) but ὁμοούσιος (of the same substance) with the Father.[21] The term ὑπόστασις (subsistence; subsistent) was sometimes used to indicate the one being, then again to denote the three persons so that people sometimes spoke of the one "hypostasis" in God and then again of the three "hypostases." Basil in his letter *Concerning Ousia and Hypostasis* brought about greater uniformity in the use of these terms by employing οὐσία for God's being or essence and ὑπόστασις or πρόσωπον for the three persons, a practice that became standard in the East.[22]

In the West, terminology was more established. Tertullian had established the use of the terms *essentia* and *substantia* for God's being or essence, and the term *persona* or *subsistentia* for the persons,[23] a usage adopted by the great teachers of the church and in the creeds. Terminological confusion between Greek-speaking and Latin-speaking churches for both the being (unity) of God and the diversity of persons (threeness) reflected the different challenges faced by orthodox Christianity in East and West. Augustine disapproved of rendering the Greek word ὑπόστασις by [the Latin] *substantia*. The Latin words *substantia* and *essentia* are not strictly parallel to the Greek words ὑπόστασις and οὐσία; *substantia*, rather than *essentia*, is the Latin equivalent of the Greek word οὐσία, and *essentia* still sounded strange and unusual to Latin ears. As a result, though the expressions *una substantia* (one substance) and *tres personae* (three persons) were retained in Latin, Augustine sought to avoid *substantia* altogether because it suggests a division between essence and accidents or properties. Because this is not true of God in whom essence and attributes coincide, Augustine deemed it better to describe the divine being as *essentia*.[24] Furthermore, in the face of Arianism, it was necessary to maintain that the three persons were not three *substantiae* but three *personae*. This is the language that was developed further in medieval Scholasticism and also adopted by the Reformation theologians. According to that scheme, there is in God but one being, one essence, one nature (*unitas naturae*) and a Trinity of persons. Within that being these three persons are one, consubstantial, coessential, and they reciprocally exist in each other (ἐμπεριχώρησις, *circumincessio personarum*). But the persons are distinct; in God there are "two emanations, one through nature and another through the will; three hypostases: Father, Son, and

21. Athanasius, *Statement of Faith*, NPNF², IV, 83–85.

22. I. A. Dorner, *Doctrine of the Person of Christ*, II, 313ff.; A. von Harnack, *History of Dogma*, IV, 83; E. Hatch, *The Influence of the Greek Ideas on Christianity* (repr., New York: Harper & Brothers, 1957), 275–82.

23. A. von Harnack in his *History of Dogma*, IV, 89n2, contends that for Tertullian the meaning of *substantia* and *persona* is borrowed from "juristic and political notions," and that *substantia* then had the significance of an economy or ability (*vermögen*), which the three persons share. This opinion has been credibly refuted though others claim that the distinction is merely stylistic. Against this we note that both in the East and in the West there was a *logical* and *theological* (and not merely a *stylistic*) need to distinguish the "essence" and the "persons."

24. Augustine, *The Trinity*, V, 8; VII, 4.

Holy Spirit; . . . and three personal properties, the Father who is unbegotten, the Son who is begotten, the Holy Spirit who is spirated."[25]

Terminological disputes have been frequent in the church, particularly concerning the notion of "person." Boethius provided the influential definition of person as an individual rational being, potentially leading to tritheism and a loss of divine unity. In the modern era "personality" is attributed to heroic human qualities and often denied to God. There are analogies with human personhood but we must exercise great caution here lest we are led into tritheism. While the legitimacy of analogy allows us to speak of "nature" also with respect to God, even here there is a difference. Human nature refers to that which distinct individuals have in common; human nature does not exist in the abstract but only *in* concrete individual persons. In God, all three persons fully participate in the same divine being; it is one and the same divine nature that exists in each person individually and in all of them collectively. Consequently, there is in God but one eternal, omnipotent, and omniscient being, having one mind, one will, and one power.[26] We must not lose sight of this important point: In the dogma of the Trinity the word "person" simply means that the three persons in the divine being are not "modes" but have a distinct existence of their own. The divine being is tripersonal. Thus, settled Christian dogma teaches that in the one being of God there exist three persons, Father, Son, and Holy Spirit, who each fully share the divine essence yet differ in personal attributes. The Father is unbegotten, the Son is begotten or generated, and the Spirit proceeds from the Father (and the Son).

[223] The glory of the confession of the Trinity consists above all in the fact that that unity, however absolute, does not exclude but includes diversity. God's being is not an abstract unity or concept, but a fullness of being, an infinite abundance of life, whose diversity, so far from diminishing the unity, unfolds it to its fullest extent. In theology the distinctions within the divine being—which Scripture refers to by the names of Father, Son, and Spirit—are called "persons." In the East theologians initially used the word πρόσωπον for person, a word that corresponded to the Hebrew פָּנִים, meaning face, external appearance, role. But this word was open to misunderstanding as Sabellius taught that the one divine οὐσία or ὑπόστασις assumed different πρόσωπα or faces. Against this, the church fathers contended that the three πρόσωπα in the divine being were not simply appearances or modes of revelation, but "enhypostatic πρόσωπα," that they consisted in *hypostases*. Thus πρόσωπον was replaced by ὑπόστασις, a word that points to that which is real, not just in appearance, or that which exists independently in distinction from "accidents"

25. Bonaventure, *The Breviloquium*, in vol. 2 of *The Works of Bonaventure* (Paterson, NJ: St. Anthony Guild Press, 1963), I, chap. 3, 4; cf. Anselm, *Monologion*, chaps. 29ff.; T. Aquinas, *Summa Theol.*, I, qu. 27–32.

26. Athanasian Creed, 9–18.

that inhere in something else.[27] Difference in terminology repeatedly occasioned misunderstanding between the East and the West, though in fact both parties taught the same thing, namely, that the three divine persons are not "modes" but "subsistences." Thus, in the language of the church the word προσοπον or *persona* acquired as an essential feature the quality of self-existence, ὑποστασις, subsistence. Later, in the christological controversy, theologians were forced, in the face of Nestorianism and Monophysitism, to devise a more exact definition of the words "nature" and "person." The word "persona" now expresses two things: self-existence and rationality (or self-consciousness). This is its meaning in Scholasticism as well as in the works of the earlier Roman Catholic, Lutheran, and Reformed theologians.

In modern philosophy and psychology, however, a very different conception of personality has surfaced. In the first place, as scholars began increasingly to believe that personality can only be the mode of existence of finite beings, neither personality nor self-consciousness and self-determination could be attributed to God. If God exists, he can only be conceived as the all-powerful, everywhere-present, unconscious force and drive that is present in all things. Second, in psychology, the idea arose that even human personality in no way implies independent existence. "I-ness," the soul, is not a substance but merely the nominalistic sum of psychical phenomena, and what is called personality is but the passing mode of existence of the individual being, called a human. Thus, personality, seen as the highest stage in human development, becomes the final goal of human life, "the highest happiness attainable by earthlings" (Goethe). This naturally led to hero worship and deification of those individuals of great personality and genius. Quite inadequate with respect to humans—individual identity and personality is far more than simply the sum of psychical phenomena—this understanding is even less applicable in the doctrine of the Trinity. Here the term "person" has a meaning of its own. Calvin defined "person" simply as "subsistence in God's essence."[28] Augustine said: We speak of persons "not to express what that is but only not to be silent."[29] In the dogma of the Trinity the word "person" simply means that the three persons in the divine being are not "modes" but have a distinct existence of their own; the unity of the divine being opens itself up in a threefold existence. Human nature, which is far too rich to be embodied in a single individual, provides only a faint analogy here; the fullness of human personality can only be present in humanity as a whole. The divine nature does develop its fullness in three persons, but in God these three persons are not three individuals but a threefold self-differentiation within the divine being. This self-differentiation results from the self-unfolding

27. Cf. also the use of the word ὑποστασις in the New Testament (2 Cor. 9:4; 11:17; Heb. 1:3; 3:14; 11:1); and see Hermann Cremer, *Biblico-Theological Lexicon of New Testament Greek*, trans. D. W. Simon and William Urwick (Edinburgh: T&T Clark; New York: Charles Scribner's Sons, 1895), s.v. "ὑποστασις."

28. J. Calvin, *Institutes*, I.xiii.6.

29. Augustine, *The Trinity*, V, 9; VI, 10; cf. Anselm, *Monologion*, chap. 37, 38; J. Calvin, *Institutes*, I.xiii.2–4.

of the divine nature into personality, thus making it tri-personal. Whereas human nature unfolds in a twofold manner, in the individual and in the race as a whole, there is only one unfolding in God: the unfolding of his being into personality coincides with that of his being unfolding into three persons. The three persons are the one divine personality brought to complete self-unfolding, a self-unfolding arising out of, by the agency of, and within the divine being. In Augustine's words, "For to God it is not one thing to be and another to be a person, but it is altogether the same thing" (*The Trinity*, VII, 6).

DISTINCTIONS AMONG THE THREE PERSONS

[224] The distinction between "being" and "person," and among the persons themselves, becomes clearer when we consider the relations that produce this differentiation in the divine being. Although Scripture is rigorously monotheistic, it does ascribe a divine nature and divine perfections also to the Son and the Spirit and puts them on a par with the Father. Not only are the Father, the Son, and the Spirit distinct subjects in the one divine essence, they also always appear in a certain order. Their so-called "personal properties," as mentioned before, are: paternity (ἀγεννησια, "unbegottenness"); filiation or sonship (γεννησις, begottenness); sanctification (ἐκπορευσις, procession). The persons differ individually only in that one is Father, the other Son, and the third Spirit. These characteristics are eternal. Fatherhood is only an incidental attribute of being human; some men never become fathers, were not fathers before becoming one; our humanity as men is not exhausted by our being fathers or sons. But in God, being God and personhood coincide. In each of the three persons, we might say, the divine being is completely coextensive with being Father, Son, and Spirit. Paternity, filiation, and procession are not accidental properties but the eternal modes of existence of, and the eternal immanent relations within, that being. While our human nature unfolds over time and in space, the unfolding of God's being immediately, absolutely, and completely coincides with, and includes, the unfolding of his being into persons, as well as that of the immanent relations expressed in the names "Father," "Son," and "Spirit." The processions in his being simultaneously bring about in God his absolute personality, his trinitarian character, and his immanent relations. They are the absolute archetypes of all those processions by which human nature achieves its full development in the individual, in the family, and in humanity as a whole. The "threeness" in God derives from, exists in, and serves the "oneness." Furthermore, although the three persons do not differ in essence, they are distinct subjects, hypostases, or subsistences, related to each other in an absolute manner; their personal distinctness as subjects completely coincides with their immanent interpersonal relationships. The Father is only and eternally Father; the Son is only and eternally Son; the Spirit is only and eternally Spirit. The Father is God as Father; the Son is God as Son; the Holy

Spirit is God as Holy Spirit. Inasmuch as all three are God, they all partake of one single divine nature. Hence, there is but one God, Father, Son, and Holy Spirit. May he be praised forever!

[225–27] The name "Father" is the preferred description of the First Person; his personal attribute is fatherhood or "nonbegottenness" (ἀγεννησια). "Father" is not a metaphor derived from the earth and attributed to God; "unbegotten" is not in contrast to creatures but is an inner trinitarian relation. In Greek there are two words: γεννητος, derived from the verb γενναν, to beget, bring forth; and γενητος, a derivative of γινεσθαι, to come into being, be born. The latter, broader term denotes all that has been brought forth and has a beginning, whether it is by creation, generation, or procreation. Initially not always clearly distinguished from each other, gradually it became customary to make a distinction between the two words. In contrast to created beings, all three persons could be called ἀγενητος (unbegotten); since none had a beginning in time; ἀγενητος is an attribute of the divine being that is common to all three persons. But to the Father alone is to be attributed the word ἀγεννησια. The Son could be called γεννητος (begotten), not because he was brought forth in time, but because he was generated out of the being of the Father from eternity.[30] The church fathers pointed out that the attribute ἀγεννησια pertains to the person, not the being. God's being is the same in all three persons, but ἀγεννησια is a relation within the being. Note that being ἀγεννητον and being Father is not at all the same thing.[31] The name "Father," accordingly, is to be preferred over the term ἀγεννητος.[32] The Father is eternally Father; the Son was generated out of the being of the Father from eternity. The scriptural name "Father" is, therefore, a much better description of the personal property of the First Person and even more appropriate than the word "God." The latter is a general name signifying transcendent dignity, but the name "Father," like that of YHWH in the Old Testament, is a proper name, an attribute describing a personal property of God. Those who deny to God the name "Father" dishonor him even more than those who deny his creation; it leaves us with an abstract, deistic view of God. God is our Father, and all fatherhood on earth is but a distant and vague reflection of the fatherhood of God (Eph. 3:14–15). God is Father in the true and complete sense of the term.

Addressing God as Father, one by implication also addresses the Son. The eternity of the Father carries with it the eternity of the Son;[33] generation of

---

30. Cf. Athanasius, *On the Incarnation*, VIII, 55; Basil, *On the Holy Spirit*, V, 9; VI, 15 (ed. note: Bavinck erroneously cites Basil, *Against Eunomius*); John of Damascus, *The Orthodox Faith*, I, 8; Augustine, *The Trinity*, V, 3; Johann Caspar Suicerus, *Thesaurus ecclesiasticus* (Amsterdam: J. H. Wetsten, 1682), s.v. "ἀγεννησια."

31. Basil, *On the Holy Spirit*, VIII, 19 (ed. note: Bavinck erroneously cites Basil, *Against Eunomius*, I, 9, 15); Gregory of Nazianzus, *Theological Orations*, III; Augustine, *The Trinity*, V, 5.

32. Basil, *On the Holy Spirit*, XV, 36 (ed. note: Bavinck erroneously cites Basil, *Against Eunomius*, I, 5).

33. Athanasius, *Against the Arians*, I, 23, 28; Gregory of Nazianzus, *Theological Orations*, III, 5, 17; John of Damascus, *The Orthodox Faith*, I, 8; Hilary of Poitiers, *De trinitate contra Arianos*, XII, 24.

the Son has to be eternal, for if the Son were not eternal, the Father could not be either. The doctrine of "eternal generation" (αἰωνος γεννησις), so called for the first time by Origen, arose from scriptural names that denote the Son's relation to the Father: Word, Wisdom, Logos, Son, the Firstborn, Only Begotten and only Son, the image of God, image (εἰκων), substance (ὑποστασις), stamp (χαρακτηρ) [cf. Heb. 1:3]. Caution must be observed here;[34] "generation" points to a human analogy but we must remove all associations here with imperfection and sensuality. God's fecundity is unique to his being; it is a beautiful theme, one frequently found in the church fathers. It reminds us that God is no abstract, fixed, monadic, solitary substance, but a plenitude of life. It is his nature (οὐσια) to be generative (γεννητικη) and fruitful (καρπογονος); God is capable of communication. Those who deny this fecund productivity fail to take seriously the fact that God is an infinite fullness of blessed life; they are left with an abstract, deistic concept of God. Alternatively, to compensate for this sterility, in pantheistic fashion they include the life of the world in the divine being. Apart from the Trinity even the act of creation becomes inconceivable; if God cannot communicate himself, he is unable to exert himself outward to communicate himself to creatures.[35]

The generation of the Son is spiritual; it does not create division and separation. Therefore, the most striking human analogy is thought and speech; Scripture suggests this when it calls the Son "Logos" [Speech, Word, Reason]. Just as the human mind objectivizes itself in words, so God expresses his entire being in the Logos. For God to beget is to speak, and his speaking is eternal. Here it differs from limited and sense-related human speech which has no life in itself; when God speaks he totally expresses himself in the one person of the Logos, whom he also "granted to have life in himself" (1 John 5:26 NIV). The Son is begotten out of the very being of the Father; from eternity the Son is "God of God, Light of Light, very God of very God; begotten, not made, being of one substance with the Father," as the Nicene symbol has it. Contra the Arians, the Son is not a creature but "God over all, forever praised!" (Rom. 9:5 NIV). Not brought forth by the will of the Father out of nothing and in time, he is generated out of the being of the Father in eternity. "Generation," therefore, should not be seen as an actual work, a performance (ἐνεργεια), of the Father; rather, we should ascribe to the Father "a generative nature" (φυσις γεννητικη). Therefore, contrary to the Arians who said there was a time when the Son did not exist (ἠν ποτε ὁτε οὐκ ἠν), the generation of the Son is eternal. To reject the eternal generation of the Son fails to do justice not only to the deity of the Son, but also to that of the Father. It deprives him of the eternity of his fatherhood, and leaves unexplained how God can truly and

34. Irenaeus, *Against Heresies*, II, 28, 6; Athanasius, *Against the Arians*, II, 36; Basil, *Against Eunomius*, II, 22, 24; Gregory of Nazianzus, *Theological Orations*, XX.

35. Athanasius, *Against the Arians*, II, 2; John of Damascus, *Exposition of the Orthodox Faith*, NPNF², I, 8. Ed. note: cf. H. Bavinck, *Reformed Dogmatics*, II, 420n50 (#254).

properly be called "Father."[36] The Father is not and never was ungenerative; he begets everlastingly. "The Father did not by a single act beget the Son and then release him from his 'genesis,' but generates him perpetually."[37] For God to beget is to speak, and his speaking is eternal.[38] God's offspring is eternal.

The personal property of the Holy Spirit is "procession" (ἐκπόρευσις) or "spiration" (πνοή). Both the deity and personality of the Spirit have been contested; the crux of controversy about the Second Person was almost always his deity while for the Third Person it was his personality. It is true that these do not confront us as forcefully in Scripture as do the deity and personality of the Father and the Son. Yet the profound religious significance of making the same confession about the Spirit did become increasingly clear to the church. Over time, as the church sought to understand better the subjective dimensions of salvation—regeneration, faith, conversion, repentance, sanctification, and so on—it had to state clearly that there is no communion with the Father and the Son except in and through the Holy Spirit. Scripture establishes beyond any doubt that the Holy Spirit is the subjective principle of all salvation. The choice is clear: either the Holy Spirit is a creature—whether a power, gift, or person—or he is truly God. Only if the Holy Spirit is truly God can he impart to us the Father and the Son. He who gives us God himself must himself be truly God. Those who deny the deity of the Holy Spirit cannot maintain that of the Son. The Trinity completes itself in the divine person of the Holy Spirit.

There is, therefore, an additional theological reason for insisting on the personality and deity of the Holy Spirit. Without the personality and deity of the Spirit there can be no true unity between the Father and the Son. The entire dogma of the Trinity, the mystery of Christianity, the heart of religion, the true and genuine communion of our souls with God—they all stand or fall with the deity of the Holy Spirit. The church fathers, understanding this interconnectedness, defended the deity of the Spirit along with that of the Son.[39] In the Niceno-Constantinopolitan Creed the church confesses its faith "in the Holy Spirit, the Lord and giver of life, who proceeds from the Father and the Son; who together with the Father and Son is worshiped and glorified; and who spoke

36. Athanasius, *Defense of the Nicene Definition*, 26ff.; idem, *On the Opinion of Dionysius*, 14ff.; idem, *Against the Arians*, I, 12ff.; Basil, *Against Eunomius*, II, 14ff.; idem, *On the Spirit*, 14ff.; Gregory of Nazianzus, *Theological Orations*, III, 3ff.

37. Origen, *S. P. N. Cyrilli archiepiscopi Alexandrini Homiliae XIX. in Ieremiam prophetam*, IX, 4; idem, *On First Principles*, I, 2, 2.

38. Athanasius, *Against the Arians*, I, 14, 20; IV, 12; idem, *On the Opinion of Dionysius*, 15–16; John of Damascus, *The Orthodox Faith*, I, 8; Augustine, *The Trinity*, VI, 1; T. Aquinas, *Summa Theol.*, I, qu. 42, art. 2; Johannes Polyander à Kerckhoven, André Rivet, Antonius Walaeus, and Antoine Thysius, *Synopsis purioris theologiae*, ed. H. Bavinck, 6th ed. (Leiden: Donner, 1881), VIII, 11.

39. Cf. Athanasius in his *Letters to Serapion*; ed. note: ET: *The Letters of Saint Athanasius concerning the Holy Spirit*, trans. C. R. B. Shapland (London: Epworth, 1951); Gregory of Nazianzus in his *Theological Orations*, *On the Holy Spirit*; Basil in his third book, *Against Eunomius*, and in his *On the Spirit*; Gregory of Nyssa, especially in his writing *Against Ablabius*; Hilary of Poitiers, *On the Trinity*, XII.

by the prophets." Since that time Christians everywhere confess their faith in "a consubstantial Trinity."[40]

In describing the relation between the Holy Spirit and the Father and the Son, relations suggested by verbal forms such as "given," "sent," "poured out," "breathed out," "proceeded," and "descended," Christian theology spoke of projection, procession, outgoing, spiration, emission, outpouring. Because Scripture calls the Holy Spirit רוּחַ (wind, spirit) and πνευμα, and repeatedly associates the Spirit with breath and wind (Job 33:4; Ps. 33:6; John 3:8; 20:22; Acts 2:2; etc.), the preferred term became "spiration." Further definition was characterized by modesty, especially in distinguishing spiration from generation, inasmuch as generation gave to the Son, and spiration gave to the Spirit, the possession of "life in himself."[41] Augustine said: "Speaking of that superlatively excellent nature, who can explain the difference between 'being born' and 'proceeding'? Not everything that proceeds is born, although everything that is born proceeds, just as not every creature with two feet is a human, though every human is a biped. This much I know. But I do not know, nor do I have the skill to say, what the difference is between 'generation' on the one hand and 'procession' on the other."[42] As theologians searched for some kind of distinction they found (1) that the Son proceeds only from the Father, but the Holy Spirit from both the Father and the Son;[43] or (2) that the Spirit proceeds from the Father and the Son, as *given* by both, not as *born* from both (*ut datus, non ut natus*).[44] Especially Thomas and his followers, finally, describe the difference between generation and spiration by saying that generation occurred "in the manner of the intellect," while spiration took place "in the manner of the will." This distinction had its background in the tradition of comparing "generation" with thought and utterance and speaking of the Holy Spirit as the love that unites the Father and the Son and became virtually universal in medieval Catholicism.[45] Protestant theologians, though they did assume a distinction between "generation" and "spiration," were more reluctant to speak with this degree of certainty.

[228] Gradually, however, an important difference developed between the East and the West. The East teaches that the Spirit proceeds from the Father through the Son, but not that the Spirit is also from the Son and receives his existence from him. In the West, Tertullian wrote: "I think the Spirit proceeds from no

40. Basil, in A. Hahn, G. L. Hahn, and A. von Harnack, *Bibliothek der Symbole und Glaubensregeln der alten Kirche*, 3rd ed. (Breslau: E. Morgenstern, 1897), 70.

41. Athanasius, *Letters to Serapion*, I, 15ff.; Gregory of Nazianzus, *Theological Orations*, V, 7ff.; Basil, *The Holy Spirit*, 46ff.; John of Damascus, *The Orthodox Faith*, I, 8.

42. Augustine, *Contra Maximinum Arianorum episcopum*, III, 14 (PL 42:743); idem, *The Trinity*, XV, 17, 20; idem, *Lectures on the Gospel of John*, tract. 99, NPNF[1], VII, 131–37.

43. Augustine, *The Trinity*, XV, 26.

44. Ibid., V, 14.

45. T. Aquinas, *Summa Theol.*, I, qu. 27; idem, *Summa contra gentiles*, IV, 13, 15ff.; Bonaventure, *Breviloquium*, I, chap. 3.

other source than the Father through the Son,"[46] and after him especially Augustine views the three persons as relations in the one simple Godhead and puts the Spirit in relation not only to the Father but also to the Son. After Augustine the affirmation of the Spirit's procession from the Son as well as the Father became the standard position of the West, culminating in the insertion of the phrase "and of the Son" (*filioque*) into the text of the Nicene Creed.[47] The East, by contrast, did not go beyond the church fathers who sought the unity in the person of the Father. John of Damascus states that the Spirit is also the Spirit of the Son, since he is revealed and communicated by the Son, and goes on to say that the Spirit proceeds *from* the Father *through the Son*. But he expressly rejects the idea that he is from the Son and receives his existence from him. The Son and the Spirit are traceable to one single cause.[48] And this has remained the doctrine of the Greek Orthodox Church ever since. Orthodox opposition to the *filioque* is a last lingering remnant of subordinationism. However much the three persons are considered to be completely one and equal, that unity and equality accrue to the Son and the Spirit from the being of the Father. The Father is the fountain and origin of the Godhead and reveals himself in both: the Son imparts the knowledge of God, the Spirit the enjoyment of God. The Son does not reveal the Father in and through the Spirit; the Spirit does not lead believers to the Father through the Son. The two are more or less independent of each other: they both open their own way to the Father. Thus orthodoxy and mysticism, the intellect and the will, exist dualistically side by side, a hallmark of Greek piety.

THE TRINITARIAN ECONOMY, ANALOGIES, AND ARGUMENTS

[229] The immanent relations of the three persons in the divine being also manifest themselves outwardly (*ad extra*). All God's outward works (*opera ad extra*) are common to the three persons and indivisible. There is, however, an *appropriation* of properties and works to each person. Although they have a single author, all things proceed *from* the Father, are accomplished *by* the Son, and completed *in* the Spirit. Since the "ontological" Trinity is mirrored in the "economic" Trinity, special tasks are attributed to each of the three persons—though not exclusively, as Abelard believed[49]—in such a way that the order present between the persons in the ontological Trinity is revealed. In an economic sense, the work of creation is more specifically assigned to the Father, redemption to the Son, and sanctification to the Holy Spirit. The Father works of himself through the Son in the Spirit. Scripture marks these distinctions very clearly in

46. Tertullian, *Against Praxeas*, 4, 25.
47. H. Denzinger, *Enchiridion symbolorum* (Wirceburgi, 1856), 98, 113, 136; ET: *The Sources of Catholic Dogma*, trans. from the 30th ed. by Roy J. Deferrari (London and St. Louis: Herder, 1955).
48. John of Damascus, *The Orthodox Faith*, I, 8, 12.
49. P. Abelard, *Introductio ad theologiam*, I, chaps. 7–14 (PL 178).

the so-called differentiating prepositions: ἐκ (out of), διά (through), and ἐν (in; 1 Cor. 8:6; John 1:3, 14).

These distinctions were noted early in the church's life.[50] Athanasius repeatedly appeals to Ephesians 4:6, saying that as Father, God is *above* us all, as Son he is *through* all, and as Spirit he is *in* all, and that the Father creates and re-creates all things *through* the Son *in* the Spirit.[51] Basil was charged with error because in his prayers he would sometimes give thanks to the Father "in common with (μετά) the Son along with (σύν) the Holy Spirit" and at other times "through the Son in the Holy Spirit." In his work on the Holy Spirit Basil speaks at length about the distinctions between the prepositions, arguing against any ranking that would deny the equality of the persons.[52] The point of the prepositions, he says, is not to demonstrate a hierarchy but to indicate a specific *order* in their existence and activity. The Father is "the initiating cause"; the Son "the operating cause"; the Spirit "the perfecting cause."[53] Later theologians repeat the same distinctions.[54] All the works of God *ad extra* have one single Author (*principium*), but come into being through the cooperation of the three persons, each of whom plays a special role and fulfills a special task, both in the works of creation and in those of redemption and sanctification. All things proceed from the Father, are accomplished by the Son, and are completed in the Holy Spirit.

In the history of revelation, the economy of the Father was especially that of the Old Testament, that of the Son began with the incarnation, and that of the Holy Spirit began at Pentecost. It is a serious error to turn this economy and salvation history into a metaphysical principle by following the pantheistic tendency from Montanus through Joachim to Hegel and consider the three persons as three successive periods in God's own "history" of becoming. The economic trinity here becomes the ontological trinity and turns cosmogony into theogony. This turns trinitarian truth upside-down; it denies that the works of the triune God *ad extra* are distinct from the triune God himself and come from the one God. We come to know that God through his works of creation, revelation, and redemption; in them, guided by biblical revelation, we come to see that the work of creation is more specifically assigned to the Father, the work of redemption to the Son, the work of sanctification to the Holy Spirit. The whole series of all times is timelessly contained in God's eternal Wisdom; it is a work of the Father, the Son, and the Spirit that the Son should appear in the flesh; it is a work of the Father and the

---

50. Irenaeus, *Against Heresies*, V, 18.

51. Athanasius, *Letters to Serapion*, I, 14, 28; II, 6–7.

52. Basil, *On the Spirit*, 3ff.

53. Ibid., 21, 22, 38.

54. Cf. also F. W. J. Schelling, *Sämmtliche Werke* (Stuttgart and Augsburg: J. G. Cotta'scher, 1856–61), II/3, 341ff. Ed. note: The Schelling citations here and in later notes are to his *Philosophie der Offenbarung*. A more recent two-volume edition of this work was published in 1954 by the Wissenschaftliche Buchgesellschaft (Darmstadt). ET: *Schelling's Philosophy of Mythology and Revelation*, trans. Victor C. Hayes (Armindale, NSW: Australian Association for the Study of Religions, 1995).

Son that the Spirit be poured out on the church and made into a temple of God (1 Cor. 3:16). There has been an eternal procession of the Son and the Spirit from the Father in order that, through and in them, he himself should come to his people and finally be "all in all."

[230] The doctrine of the Trinity is so far above human understanding that from the beginning of the church's reflection, attempts have been made to elucidate it by illustrations and prove it by arguments. The number three plays an important role in Scripture[55] and in the polytheistic lore of nonbiblical peoples. Analogies for the Trinity were discovered not only in the intermediate beings that gradually emerged in Jewish theology,[56] and in the three Sephiroth ("Crown," "Wisdom," and "Understanding") mentioned in the Kabbalah,[57] but traces of the Trinity were also found in the Trimurti of the Southeast Asian Indians: Brahman, Vishnu, and Siva; in the three forms of the Chinese Tao; in the chief Germanic [Norse] gods: Odin, Thor, and Loki; and in various Chaldean, Egyptian, and Greek conceptions of the gods.[58] Another favorite was Plato's three cosmological principles: the supreme mind (νοῦς), identified with being and goodness; the world of ideas; and matter (ὕλη).[59]

More useful than such polytheistic analogies are those from nature: Justin Martyr, following Philo, employed the image of a flame which, though igniting another, nevertheless remains the same. Tertullian said that God produced the Logos as a root produces a fruit and a spring produces a river and the sun produces sun rays; he also spoke of a spring, a flood, and a stream; a root, a trunk, and a crown; etc. The following were also used as analogies of the Christian Trinity:[60] the three dimensions of space; the three components of time; the three natural kingdoms of mineral, vegetable, and animal; bodies in their solid, fluid, and gaseous state; the three functions of the human soul: reasoning, feeling, desiring; the three human capacities: head, heart, and hand; the three constituents that

55. E.g., the three years of Christ's public ministry; the three offices of Christ (prophet, priest, and king); his three days in the grave before the resurrection; the three crosses on Golgotha; the three languages in the superscription over the cross; the three beloved disciples; the three witnesses (1 John 5:8); the three prime Christian virtues (faith, hope, and love); the three kinds of lust (1 John 2:16); the three woes (Rev. 8:13; etc.); a threefold benediction; and so on.

56. F. W. Weber, *System der altsynagogalen palästinischen Theologie*, 172ff.

57. A. Franck, *The Kabbalah* (New York: Arno, 1973); Agrippa of Nettesheim, according to A. Stöckl, *Geschichte der Philosophie des Mittelalters*, 3 vols. (Mainz: Kirchheim, 1864–66), III, 413; II, 236.

58. Cf. H. Zimmern, *Vater, Sohn und Fürsprecher in der babylonischen Gottesvorstellung* (Leipzig: J. C. Hinrichs, 1896).

59. A. Tholuck, *Die speculative Trinitätslehre des späteren Orients* (Berlin: F. Dümmler, 1826); Johann Peter Lange, *Christliche Dogmatik*, 3 vols. (Heidelberg: K. Winter, 1852), II, 143ff.; F. C. Baur, *Die christliche Lehre von der Dreieinigkeit und Menschwerdung Gottes*, 3 vols. (Tübingen: C. F. Oslander, 1841–43), I, 10ff., 18ff., 33ff.; F. Delitzsch, *System der christlichen Apologetik* (Leipzig: Dörffling & Franke, 1870), 286; Otto Zöckler, *Theologia naturalis* (Frankfurt a.M.: Heyder & Zimmer, 1860), 689; cf. also F. W. J. Schelling, *Werke*, II/2, 78; II/3, 312ff.

60. Franz Delitzsch, *System der christlichen Apologetik* (Leipzig: Dörffling & Franke, 1870), 282ff.; O. Zöckler, *Theologia naturalis*, 672ff.

make up a family: man, woman, child;[61] the three transcendentals: the true, the good, and the beautiful; triadic harmony in music; the three basic colors: yellow, red, and blue; and so forth.

Augustine and especially medieval thinkers also developed logical analogies. Augustine repeatedly points out that everything must first of all have being, unity, and measure. Matter, form (or beauty), and harmony or love between the two are the fundamental components of all existence.[62] "All that is, requires a threefold cause: that by which it exists, that by which it is this particular thing, and that by which it is internally consistent."[63] Triplicity is also found in the work of Pseudo-Dionysius the Areopagite and Dante; the former divided his *Celestial Hierarchies* and the latter his *Divine Comedy* into three parts. In modern philosophy triplicity even achieved formal dominance in the work of Kant and the dialectical method of Fichte, Schelling, and Hegel. Since Idealism understands all things as products of human consciousness, as the development of an idea, it is led to hold that these are generated in a process of contradiction and becoming. Thus the Idea, unfolding and developing, proceeds through affirmation and negation to limitation, through thesis and antithesis to synthesis. The whole world develops in terms of this "order of trinities." Thus we find absolute mind coming into being as the thinking mind in and for itself, in its returning to itself, and its becoming conscious of itself.[64] As a result of philosophy's influence, this abstract triplicity became foundational for countless philosophical and theological systems.

Some sought to go beyond analogy to positive arguments for the Trinity from the nature of thought or of love. Augustine found clear imprints of the Trinity in human consciousness and reason, and especially in the self-knowledge of the human soul as memory, intelligence, and will, but he still considered these only a posteriori evidence, not a priori proof. He insists that self-knowledge and self-contemplation are generative by nature: "It begets this understanding and knowledge of itself." Now these two are united by the will or by love: "These two, begetter and begotten, are coupled together by love as the third, and this is nothing but the will seeking or holding something to be enjoyed" (*The Trinity*, XIV, 6).[65] All this is rooted in Augustine's deep conviction that it is in human beings as God's image bearers that we find the most profound analogy of the Holy Trinity (*The Trinity*, VI, 10; XV, 2; *City of God*, XI, 26). Augustine never fails to remind us of the great difference between us and our God. In human beings, for example,

61. Cf. especially Augustine, *The Trinity*, XI, 5ff.

62. Augustine, *The Trinity*, VI, 10; idem, *On True Religion*, chap. 7; idem, *De vita beata*, 34; cf. T. Gangauf, *Des heiligen Augustinus speculative Lehre von Gott dem Dreieinigen* (Augsburg: Schmidt, 1883), 209ff.

63. Augustine, *Eighty-Three Different Questions*, qu. 18.

64. Wilhelm Windelband, *A History of Philosophy*, trans. James H. Tufts, 2 vols. (New York: Harper & Row, 1958 [1901]), II, 529–623, esp. 540–96.

65. Ed. note: Translation taken from St. Augustine, *The Trinity*, trans. Edmund Hill (Brooklyn, NY: New City, 1990), 374–75.

the trinity is not the persons themselves but something in or about the persons, whereas in God the Trinity is God himself, and the three persons are the one God. In humans, memory, intelligence, and love are merely human capacities, but in the divine being the three persons are three subjects. In humans these three capacities are frequently unequal and are designed to complement each other, but in the divine being there is complete unity and equality of persons (*The Trinity*, XV, 7, 17, 20ff.). He concludes *The Trinity* with a vision of a time when we become fully God's image, when we see him face to face and our many words cease, "And we shall say one thing without end, in praising Thee in One, ourselves also made in Thee" (*The Trinity*, XIV, 12ff; XV, 28).[66] "There our being will know no death; our knowing will be untouched by error, our loving will be free from stumbling blocks" (*City of God*, XI, 28). Many theologians, philosophers, and thinkers took over this type of argumentation for the Trinity.[67]

Augustine's favorite analogy comes from love itself. Starting from the scriptural assertion that "God is love," he demonstrates that there is always a trinity present in love: "one who loves, that which is loved, and love itself." In love there is always a subject, an object, and a bond between the two. "Oh, but you do see a trinity if you see charity" (*The Trinity*, VIII, 8; IX 1, 2). This speculation, too, has been followed by many, especially by Richard of St. Victor,[68] Bonaventure,[69] and many moderns.[70] Although speculative, this analogy has clear biblical resonance. The same cannot be said of theosophical readings of the Trinity in such figures as Jakob Böhme and Schelling. Under the combined influences of Neoplatonism, gnosticism, and the Kabbalah, theosophy resurfaced shortly before the Reformation in the persons of Pico Mirandola, Reuchlin, Nettesheim, and Paracelsus. Böhme in the sixteenth and seventeenth centuries and Schelling along with Baader in the nineteenth were the true philosophers of theosophy. Schelling did not believe that being could be explained from pure thought and, rejecting both deism and

---

66. Ed. note: Translation taken from *NPNF¹*, III, 228.

67. E.g., Johannes Scotus Erigena, *The Division of Nature*, trans. Myra L. Uhlfelder (1681; repr., Indianapolis: Bobbs-Merrill, 1976), II, 113ff.; Anselm, *Monologion*, chaps. 29–67; T. Aquinas, *Summa Theol.*, I, qu. 45, art. 7; idem, *Summa contra gentiles*, IV, 26; idem, *Sent.*, I, dist. 3, qu. 2, art. 3; Bonaventure, *Breviloquium*, II, chap. 12; idem, *The Journey of the Mind to God*, chaps. 2–4; Luther, according to J. Köstlin, *Theology of Luther in Its Historical Development and Inner Harmony*, trans. C. E. Hay, 2 vols. (Philadelphia: Lutheran Publication Society, 1897), I, 99ff.; G. W. von Leibniz, *A System of Theology*, trans. Charles William Russell (London: Burns & Lambert, 1850); G. E. Lessing, *Erziehung des Menschengeschlechts und andere Schriften*, ed. Louis Ferdinand Helbig (Bern and Las Vegas: Peter Lang, 1980), §73; Schelling, *Werke*, II/3, 315; J. P. Lange, *Christliche Dogmatik*, II, 141; A. Kuyper, *De Schrift, het Woord Gods* (Tiel: H. C. A. Campagne, 1870); W. G. T. Shedd, *Dogmatic Theology*, 3rd ed., 3 vols. (New York: Scribner, 1891–94), I, 183.

68. Richard of St. Victor, *De trinitate*, III, chaps. 2ff.

69. Bonaventure, *Disputata S. Bonaventurae in libros sententiarum* (Lugdini, 1510), I, dist. 2, art. 1, qu. 2.

70. E.g., J. Müller, *The Christian Doctrine of Sin*, trans. W. Urwick, 5th ed., 2 vols. (Edinburgh: T&T Clark, 1868), II, 181ff.; A. Peip, "Trinität," *PRE¹*, XVI, 465ff.; I. A. Dorner, *A System of Christian Doctrine*, I, 432ff.

pantheism, posited a plural All-Oneness that unites the oneness of deism and the allness of pantheism. God is subject (will), object (idea), and the identity of both subject and object. Here theogony and cosmogony join: in God's self-revelation to his creatures he at the same time becomes manifest to himself. "God" is primally Spirit, the Absolute Spirit who carries in concealment all that will be; a free Spirit who is able to reveal himself outwardly. The three destinies that the Spirit carries within himself are the potencies of extradivine being,[71] enter history freely, and eventually become their own destiny, not realizing themselves fully until the end. In the historical course of revelation the absolute Spirit becomes Father, Son, and Spirit. God—the entire deity, the absolute personality, not a special figure in the Godhead—can be called Father, though only at the end of the process. The Son's generation is not eternal but relates to the Son's existence outside the Father and therefore begins at the moment of creation. The Son is not fully the Son until the end of the process.[72] The same is true of the third potency.[73] At the end, the entire deity is realized in three distinct persons who are neither three distinct gods nor merely three different names.[74]

[231] Although modern philosophy with its speculation again brought the trinitarian dogma into favor, the church and theology generally assumed a reserved attitude toward these philosophical construals of the Trinity. Many claim an ability to penetrate the mystery of the Trinity in ways that go beyond biblical modesty. A posteriori analogies and arguments were permitted, vestiges of the Trinity in creation were acknowledged, but believers were warned against relying on reason and analogies; Scripture was considered the only legitimate "proof" and humility the appropriate posture. Even Thomas warned against trying to prove the Trinity of the persons by natural reason; it derogates from the dignity of faith and may keep others from the faith when they receive the impression that faith rests on weak grounds.[75] Analogies have some value in reminding us that the creation itself shows imprints of the triune God; arguments help demonstrate that belief in the Trinity is not irrational. Scripture itself gives us freedom to explore such analogies and arguments since it teaches clearly that the entire creation and especially humankind is a work of the triune God. The thinking mind situates the doctrine of the Trinity squarely in the full-orbed life of nature and humanity. The Christian mind remains unsatisfied until all of existence is referred back to the triune God, and until the confession of God's Trinity functions at the center of our thought and life. Accordingly, though the analogies and proofs advanced for the Trinity do not demonstrate the truth of the dogma, they serve mainly

71. F. W. J. Schelling, *Werke*, II/3, 240ff., 251ff., 261, 272.

72. Ibid., *Werke*, II/3, 312, 318, 321ff., 330ff.

73. Ibid., *Werke*, II/3, 333ff.

74. Ibid., *Werke*, II/3, 335, 337.

75. T. Aquinas, *Summa Theol.*, I, qu. 32, art. 1; cf. also P. Lombard, *Sententiae in IV libris distinctae*, 3rd ed., 2 vols. (Grottaferrata: Colleggi S. Bonaventurae ad Claras Aquas), I, dist. 3, n. 6 and the commentaries there.

to make clear the many-sided usefulness and rich significance of this confession for the life and thought of God's rational creatures. In the final analysis they owe their existence to a profound religious need, not to a craving for empty speculation or to immodest curiosity. If God is indeed triune, this has to be supremely important, for all things, according to the apostle, are from him and through him and to him (Rom. 11:36).

The doctrine of the Trinity makes God known to us as the truly living God, over against the cold abstractions of Deism and the confusions of pantheism. God makes himself known as essentially distinct from the world, yet having a blessed life of his own, a plenitude of life, an "ocean of being." He is the absolute Being, the eternal One, who is and was and is to come, and in that way the ever-living and ever-productive One. It is as the triune God—Father, Son, and Holy Spirit—that we know God as love, as holy, as good, as blessed. The Trinity reveals God to us as the fullness of being, the true life, perfect holiness, eternal beauty and glory. In God, too, there is unity in diversity, diversity in unity; this order and this harmony are present in him absolutely. A doctrine of creation—God related to but not identified with the cosmos—can only be maintained on a trinitarian basis. God is distinct from the world and its process of becoming, but not distant and removed. The creation cannot be conceived as mere happenstance, nor as the outcome of divine self-development. It must have its foundation in God, yet not be a phase in the process of his inner life. The confession of a triune God points to the rich fecundity of the divine life: there is an eternal generation of the Son and a procession of the Spirit. Both of these are immanent relations within the Godhead while creation is work *ad extra*. Creation is not necessary but a freely created contingent reality. The God whose inner life is rich and communicative chose to create and in so doing he communicates himself to a reality that is truly an "other." For this reason, the entire Christian belief system stands or falls with the confession of God's Trinity. It is the core of the Christian faith, the root of all its dogmas, the basic content of the new covenant. The development of trinitarian dogma was never primarily a metaphysical question but a religious one. It is in the doctrine of the Trinity that we feel the heartbeat of God's entire revelation for the redemption of humanity. We are baptized in the name of the triune God, and in that name we find rest for our souls and peace for our consciences. Our God is above us, before us, and within us. Our salvation is bound up in the doctrine of the Trinity; we cannot of course fully plumb the mystery of this knowledge; we are given all we need to call forth a true and sincere faith.

THE COUNSEL OF THE TRIUNE GOD

[232] We now move from discussion of God's being as such—only as revealed!—to God's works. God's decrees and works in time do not exhaust the possibilities of his wisdom and knowledge, for his works are from everlasting to everlasting. The

Father eternally gives to the Son, and with him to the Spirit, to have life in himself (John 5:26). The community of being that exists among the three persons is a life of absolute activity. The Father knows and loves the Son eternally—from before the foundation of the world (Matt. 11:27; John 17:24)—and the Spirit searches the deep things of God (1 Cor. 2:10). All these works of God are immanent. With respect to his creatures God's works are classified into two groups: works *ad intra* or the decrees that are part of his counsel, and works *ad extra* such as creation and redemption. These are an exercise of his free and absolute sovereign will and are realized in God's own time. All God's decrees, even election and reprobation, are made visible to us in the progress of history. They are, however, rooted in God's eternal foreknowledge and foreordination, which stands forever and will come to pass.

Scripture does not speak abstractly about God's decrees but in terms of their realization in history. From the beginning, the human race was split into two groupings: the God-fearing, holy line of Seth (Gen. 4:25–26; 5:1–32) and the line of Cain, which increasingly alienated itself from God (Gen. 4:17–24). In a wicked world to be destroyed by the flood, God chose Noah and after him his son Shem (Gen. 6; 9:25–27). From Shem's descendants Abraham is chosen (Gen. 12); his son Isaac, not Ishmael, is the child of promise (Gen. 17:19–21; 21:12–13); of Isaac's sons, Jacob was loved and Esau hated (Gen. 25:23; Mal. 1:2; Rom. 9:11–12). When the sons of Jacob are blessed, Judah is given primacy (Gen. 49). The "promise" is to Israel (Rom. 2:28–29; 9–11); she was to be God's holy people (Exod. 19:5; Deut. 7:6; 14:2; 26:18; Ps. 135:4; Mal. 3:17); from her is the Messiah, the servant of YHWH (Isa. 41:8; 42:1; 44:1; 45:4; etc.). Here God's purpose of election is antecedent to the facts of history; history serves to affirm that preexisting purpose. The Old Testament teaches that God creates, preserves, and rules all things by his word and wisdom (Job 38; Pss. 33:6; 104:24; Prov. 8; etc.); everything has its foundation in the mind of God. But it also expressly states that God knows and declares the future in advance (Isa. 41:21–23; 42:9; 43:9–12; 44:7; 46:10; 48:3ff.; Amos 3:7). In prophecy he makes things known beforehand, both the events and the manner in which they will occur (Gen. 3:14ff.; 6:13; 9:25ff.; 12:2ff.; 15:13ff.; 25:23; 49:8ff.; etc.). With him is wisdom and power, counsel and understanding (Job 12:13; Prov. 8:14; Isa. 9:6; 11:2; 28:29; Jer. 32:19). God's counsel is his determinate thought and fixed decree pertaining to all things (Isa. 14:24–27; Dan. 4:24). All things happen in accordance with that counsel; it stands forever, and no one can withstand it (Isa. 14:24–27; 46:10; Ps. 33:11; Prov. 19:21). On the other hand, the counsel of the enemies will be nullified (Neh. 4:15; Ps. 33:10; Prov. 21:30; Jer. 19:7).

[233] The New Testament speaks in even more clear language about God's counsel. Not only are all God's works known to him from eternity (Acts 15:18; cf. the various readings), but all things happen according to "the determinate counsel and foreknowledge of God" (Acts 2:23 KJV). The New Testament word βουλη denotes the will of God as based on counsel and deliberation, and differs in that respect from θελημα, which is the divine will per se (cf. Eph. 1:11: "the

counsel of his will," βουλη του θελημα αὐτος). This counsel of God antecedes all things. It is all encompassing (Eph. 1:11), including the sinful deeds of humans (Acts 2:23; 4:28; cf. Luke 22:22), and the "objects of wrath made for destruction" (Rom. 9:22; cf. Luke 2:34; John 3:19–21; 17:12; Rom. 1:24; 1 Thess. 5:9; 1 Pet. 2:7–8; Jude 4). But the counsel of God (βουλη του θεου) has reference mainly to the work of redemption (Luke 7:30; Acts 13:36; 20:27; Heb. 6:17). The New Testament possesses a wealth of words to further describe the counsel of God: God's good pleasure (εὐδοκια: Matt. 11:26; Luke 2:14; 10:21; Eph. 1:5, 9; Phil. 2:13; 2 Thess. 1:11); his purpose (προθεσις: Rom. 8:28; 9:11; Eph. 1:11; 3:11; 2 Tim. 1:9); his foreknowledge (προγνωσις: Rom. 8:29; 11:2; 1 Pet. 1:2); his election (ἐκλογη: Mark 13:20; Acts 9:15; 13:17; 15:7; Rom. 9:11; 11:5, 28; 1 Cor. 1:27–28; Eph. 1:4; 1 Thess. 1:4; 2 Pet. 1:10; James 2:5); his predestination (προορισμος: Rom. 8:29; 1 Cor. 2:7; Eph. 1:5, 11). Consider also Acts 13:48 (cf. KJV), where we read that "as many as were ordained [τεταγμενοι] to eternal life became believers." Ephesians 2:10 says that God had "prepared" (προητοιμασεν) believers for good works.

The point of these passages is to say that in the work of salvation God does not act arbitrarily but according to a fixed plan, an unalterable purpose. Furthermore, God's purposive acting is elective; not all are saved. Romans 9 is sometimes cited in opposition to this as proof that God's acting has both its cause and operation *in time*.[76] While Romans 9 most certainly speaks of God's action in time, the ground for the action lies outside time, in the will and good pleasure of God alone. That the ground of election is found exclusively in God's grace, love, and good pleasure is also taught in other Scriptures (Matt. 11:25; Luke 12:32; Eph. 1:5, 9, 11; 2 Tim. 1:9–10). Paul makes no attempt to demonstrate the fairness or justice of election in Romans 9–11 but simply silences the objectors with an appeal to the absolute sovereignty of God. We have no "right" to quarrel with God's mercy (Rom. 9:15ff.). The New Testament more clearly affirms this mercy of God to individual persons. This is evident from the Book of Life, in which are recorded the names of the heirs of eternal life (Luke 10:20; Heb. 12:23; Phil. 4:3; Rev. 3:5; 13:8; 20:12; 21:27; 22:19; cf. Matt. 24:31; Luke 18:7; Acts 13:48; Rom. 8:33; Eph. 1:4; Titus 1:1–2; 2 Tim. 2:10; 1 Pet. 1:1, 2, 9; etc.). Another contrast with the Old Testament is a certain "spiritualization" of the promised goal of God's election: not the land of Canaan, but an eternal, blessed, heavenly "inheritance" (1 Pet. 1:4); election proper has as its purpose holiness (Eph. 1:4), adoption as children (Eph. 1:5), salvation (2 Thess. 2:13), eternal life (Acts 13:48), conformity to Christ (Rom. 8:29; John 17:24), the glorification of God (Eph. 1:6, 12).

76. W. Beyschlag, *Die paulinische Theodicee Römer IX–XI: Ein Beitrag zur biblischen Theologie*, 2nd ed. (Halle: Strien, 1896; 2nd ed. 1905); cf. multiauthor discussion "Der Gedankengang von Röm. 9–11," *Theologische Studien und Kritiken* 59 (1887): 295–320; ed. note: a more contemporary version of this objection can be found in James Daane, *The Freedom of God: A Study of Election and Pulpit* (Grand Rapids: Eerdmans, 1973).

THE PELAGIAN CHALLENGE

[234] When affirming the determining counsel of God, the major theological issue facing Christian theology concerns human freedom. Discussions within Christian theology parallel those in philosophy and other religions, notably Islam. Against all deterministic thinking, the church maintained the moral free will and responsibility of human beings. It was the teaching and influence of Pelagius that led the church under Augustine's leadership to clarify the doctrine of predestination. For Pelagians and semi-Pelagians, human nature was not absolutely corrupted by the fall. The human will is free in a libertarian sense and remains so, even since the fall; it can freely choose between two options: good or evil. Sin is never a *condition* of human nature; all sin is a free *act* of the will. There is no original sin, only bad example. Fallen human nature can and must cooperate with the grace of God; predestination is only a matter of foreknowledge. "[Salvation] is for us to will, for God to complete."[77]

By contrast, Augustine insisted that the elect "are not chosen *because* they believed but in order that they might believe" (*Predestination of the Saints*, 17). God's absolutely sovereign will is the only ground of predestination, which includes both election and reprobation. He came to his position by studying Romans[78] and sought only to pass on the teaching of Scripture (*Gift of Perseverance*, 19). Augustine's doctrine of predestination was first presented in *To Simplicianus* (AD 397), and further developed in *On Admonition and Grace* (AD 427), *On the Predestination of the Saints*, and *On the Gift of Perseverance* (AD 428 or 429). Augustine did insist that God does not foreordain to destruction and the means that lead to it—namely, sins—in the same sense in which he foreordains to salvation and to the means that lead to it. He was, however, willing to speak of reprobation; it is an act of divine justice, as election is an act of grace. God has included in the membership of the church some people who are not elect and do not persevere, in order that the predestined should not be proud and seek out a false peace (*Admonition and Grace*, 13). Why God should save only some and let others perish is a mystery. It is not unjust, for he owes no one anything. We only confess that God's virtue is manifested in both election and reprobation (*City of God*, XIV, 26).

[235] Pelagianism was condemned at the Council of Ephesus (431) and later at the Synod of Orange (529). The latter, however, was indecisive on the full extent of human corruption and thus opened the door to semi-Pelagianism. During the Middle Ages, though the crucial passage, 1 Timothy 2:4 ("who desires everyone to be saved"), continued to be read restrictively as Augustine did to avoid notions of universal salvation, the church gradually distanced itself from Paul and Augustine. Influenced by nominalism and sensing a need to counter the

---

77. G. J. Vossius, *Historiae de controversiis, quas Pelagius eiusque religuiae moverunt* (Leiden: Patius, 1618; 2nd, emended ed., Amsterdam: Elzevir, 1655); A. von Harnack, *History of Dogma*, V, 172ff.; A. Souter, *The Commentary of Pelagius on the Epistles of Paul: The Problem of Its Restoration* (London: Oxford University Press, 1907).

78. Hermann Reuter, *Augustinische Studien* (Gotha: F. A. Perthes, 1887), 5ff.

Reformation, the Roman Catholic Church hardened its stance at the Council of Trent. Among the dogmas established are: Human free will is not totally lost and can do truly good deeds (Trent, session VI, chap. 1, can. 5, 7); humans need the gracious prevenient inspiration of the Holy Spirit to do "saving good" (ibid, can. 1–3); in children of believers this grace is given in baptism; in adults in God's calling (ibid., chap. 5); infused grace is not irresistible; accepting it enables us to do good works and by a "merit of condignity" earn eternal life (ibid., chaps. 6, 8; can. 4; 9–16).

Trent is cautious; on the one hand it seems to teach a kind of election and the need for revelatory grace. Apart from a special revelation it cannot be known "whom God has chosen for himself" (Session VI, chap. 12; and can. 15–16). Trent also condemns the teaching that "the grace of justification is only attained by those who are predestined to life, but that all others who are called are indeed called but do not receive grace as being, by the divine power, predestined to evil" (ibid., can. 17)—as if anyone really taught what is contained in this canon! To reconcile the universal desire of God with the fact that not all are saved, Scholastic theologians made numerous distinctions such as antecedent and consequent will, predestination "in a full sense" and "in a limited sense," predestination to grace but not to glory, and so forth. While all those opposed to Pelagius agree that that initial grace is predestined, whenever distinctions are introduced that involve merit and reduce grace to *enabling, prevenient* grace, Paul and Augustine have been set aside. The absolutely gratuitous predestinating activity of God is reduced to, and made dependent on, a form of foreknowledge. This trend reaches its climax in the thought of Molina, who believed that God, by a mediate knowledge, saw in advance that some humans would make good use of preparatory grace and for that reason decided to bestow it. Reprobation is then only a decree of God to punish eternally those whose sin and unbelief he has foreseen.

[236] The Reformation returned to Augustine and Paul. Still, Luther's anthropological orientation and Melanchthon's synergism meant that predestination was set aside in Lutheranism, and eventually seventeenth-century Lutheran theologians approximated the Remonstrant confession. First they taught an *antecedent* will of God, by virtue of which Christ died for all, God wills the salvation of all, and the gospel is offered to all. Second, they taught a *consequent* will, by virtue of which God decides to effectively grant salvation to "those whose ultimate faith in Christ he has foreseen" and to prepare perdition for those who in the end resist grace.[79] In 1724 Mosheim declared that the Five Articles of the Remonstrants contain the pure Lutheran doctrine.[80] Here, with the departure of the

79. H. F. F. Schmid, *The Doctrinal Theology of the Evangelical Lutheran Church*, trans. Charles A. Hay and Henry Jacobs, 5th ed. (Philadelphia: United Lutheran Publication House, 1899), 279–92; cf. Luther, *Bondage of the Will*; Philipp Melanchthon, *Loci communes* (Berlin: G. Schlawitz, 1856), chapter "De hominis viribus adeoque de libeto arbitrio."

80. Alexander Schweizer, *Die protestantischen Centraldogmen in ihrer Entwicklung innerhalb der reformirten Kirche*, 2 vols. (Zürich: Orell & Füssli, 1854–56), II, 210.

Lutheran tradition itself from Luther, is also a parting of ways with the Reformed tradition, which maintained the positions of Zwingli and Calvin.

[237] It is largely thanks to Calvin that the doctrine of predestination was included in the confessions of all the Reformed churches. Calvin ably defended the doctrine against Albertus Pighius of Kampen, the Netherlands, in *A Defense of the Sound and Orthodox Doctrine of the Bondage and Liberation of the Human Will* (1543). Against Jerome Bolsec he wrote *De aeterna Dei praedestinatione* (1552), and against Rome his *Acta Synodi Tridentinae cum antidoto* (1547). Confessional and theological differences, nonetheless, remained. The Heidelberg Catechism (Q&A 52, 54), the Anglican Articles (art. 7), and the Second Helvetic Confession (art. 8) speak in restrained terms about predestination. The most rigorously Calvinistic statements on the subject are found in the Consensus of Geneva, the Canons of Dort, the Lambeth Articles[81] drawn up by Dr. Whitgift (1595),[82] the Irish Articles of 1615, and the Westminster Confession.[83]

Differences were also found among theologians about such questions as where and how the doctrine of predestination was to be treated in the body of Christian doctrine. The synthetic method, beginning with the source and foundation of all blessings, eventually prevailed over the analytic method, which considered the effects first. These differences should not be exaggerated; they were seen as permissible because the doctrine deserved sober and cautious treatment. In either case, God's gracious initiative was emphasized. In the words of Musculus, who followed the lesser preferred analytic or a posteriori method: "We treat election after faith, not because we think it follows faith, but in order that from this vantage point (namely, faith) we would look up from the stream to the source itself."[84] Systematic order and theological interest demanded that predestination be treated under the doctrine of God, and this became the regular order for all Reformed theologians. The reason for the difference with non-Reformed theologians is not that the latter seek only to reproduce Scripture while Reformed theology abstractly and speculatively deduces predestination from an a priori, philosophically deterministic concept of God. The most rigorous Calvinist seeks only to reproduce the teaching of Scripture; the real difference is that for the Reformed the primary concern in predestination is not anthropological or even soteriological but theological—the *glory of God*. The synthetic method best safeguards the religious interest of the honor of God.[85]

81. In P. Schaff, *The Creeds of Christendom*, 6th ed., 3 vols. (New York: Harper & Row, 1931; repr., Grand Rapids: Baker Academic, 1983), III, 523.

82. In P. Schaff, *Creeds of Christendom*, III, 526; ed. note: John Whitgift (1532–1604), archbishop of Canterbury under Elizabeth I, was a determined advocate of episcopacy (anti-Presbyterian) and a strong Calvinist in doctrine.

83. In Ernst Friedrich Karl Müller, *Die Bekenntnisschriften der reformierten Kirche* (Leipzig: Deichert, 1903), 542.

84. Wolfgang Musculus, *Loci communes theologiae sacrae* (Basel: Heruagiana, 1567), 534.

85. Cf. H. Bavinck, *Reformed Dogmatics*, I, 93 (#26).

Supra- and Infralapsarianism; Remonstrance

[238] The major difference within the Reformed theological camp itself had to do with the logical order of the divine decrees, the debate between supra- and infralapsarianism. The key issue here is whether to consider the decree to elect and to reprobate logically before (supra-) or after (infra-) the decree to create and to permit the fall. The differences must not be exaggerated. All followers of Augustine, including many Thomists, teach a form of double predestination that in some sense considers the fall into sin and reprobation within the counsel of God and not merely subject to his permission or foreknowledge. God's sovereignty is at stake here. The language of "permission," as Augustine well knew, must be considered positively: "And he of course permits it not against his will but with it."[86] Thus, though original sin is sufficient ground for reprobation, in the thought of Augustine it is not the final and deepest ground; that can only be given in the will and sovereign good pleasure of God. He has mercy on whom he wills and hardens the heart of whom he wills.[87] While Adam's fall and human sin may be the proximate cause of reprobation, it is not the ultimate cause. Even if unknown to us, there has to be a higher plan of God, which existed before the fall. Although Calvin, reasoning in an infralapsarian manner, often intentionally confines himself to the immediate cause of salvation and perdition, his concern is pastoral. The elect and reprobate are equally guilty but God is merciful to the former and just to the latter.[88] The elect cannot take credit; the reprobate cannot blame God. To imagine that God decided to create humanity without any preexisting plan and then waited and watched to see what humans would do is untenable. The ideas of "permission" and "foreknowledge" do not solve the difficulty; foreseeing the fall, God could have prevented it. He freely permitted it to happen since doing so seemed good to him.[89] Calvin alternates between supralapsarian and infralapsarian emphases as do later theologians who embraced supralapsarianism. They regard their own view as legitimate but do not for a moment dream of condemning the infralapsarian view or of insisting that their view be marked in the confession as the only valid one. All they plead for is the right of their position to exist alongside, not in the place of, the infralapsarian position.[90] The Synod of Dort's judgments were infralapsarian in character, emphasizing the fall of the human race "by its own fault," but it did not condemn supralapsarianism. A difficulty with the supralapsarian view is that it separates the election of the church from that of

86. Augustine, *Enchiridion*, 95, 100.

87. Augustine, *Enchiridion*, 95; idem, *On the Predestination of the Saints*, 8–9; idem, *On Rebuke and Grace*, IV, 8.

88. J. Calvin, *Institutes*, III.xxiii.9, 11.

89. J. Calvin, *Institutes*, I.xviii.1; II.iv.3; III.xxiii.68; idem, *Concerning the Eternal Predestination of God*, trans. J. K. S. Reid (London: James Clarke, 1961), 176.

90. Among the great defenders of supralapsarianism are Th. Beza, J. Piscator, A. Polanus, W. Whitaker, W. Perkins, W. Twisse, J. H. Alsted, F. Gomarus, J. Maccovius, G. Voetius.

Christ by the two decrees of creation and fall. While the Reformed confessions lean to the infralapsarian position, both views have a right to be called Reformed.

[239] Even the milder predestinarianism of infralapsarianism encountered resistance. Socinians rejected it altogether, and the Arminians' emphasis on the universality of saving grace made human beings the final arbiters of their own destiny and paved the way for rationalism. In the Reformed churches this Arminian trend gained ground in the eighteenth and nineteenth centuries. Only a few scattered theologians managed to stand firm, such as Comrie, Holtius, and Brahé in the Netherlands; Boston and the Erskines in Scotland; and especially Jonathan Edwards (1703–58) in North America.[91] When, in the nineteenth century, a deeper study of nature, history, and humanity demonstrated the untenability of deistic Pelagianism, a pantheistic or materialistic determinism came in its place. Although there is a fundamental difference between such determinism and the biblical doctrine of predestination, many, including Schleiermacher, interpret the church's doctrine in this deterministic sense. Others reduce predestination to God's immanent action in time and identify the decree with the facts of history. In this way, the distinction between eternity and time, God and the world, is erased and theism is exchanged for pantheism. Most modern theology has no doctrine of election,[92] and yet vital churches along with solid theologians[93] yielded remarkable results—strange bedfellows as well as unexpected distance among those sharing a confessional heritage. In America the Missouri Synod of the Lutheran church took a position that approximates Calvinism,[94] whereas the Cumberland Presbyterian Church modified the Westminster Confession along Arminian lines.[95] During the revision of the Westminster Confession in Scotland and America, many raised objections to the doctrine of election and reprobation, the belief in the perdition of pagans and of children who die in infancy, and in general against what they saw as the confession's tendency to proceed one-sidedly from the sovereignty of God while disregarding his universal love.[96]

[240] The counsel of God is to be understood as his eternal plan for all that exists or will happen in time. Scripture everywhere assumes that all that is and comes to pass is the realization of God's thought and will and has its model and foundation in God's eternal counsel (Gen. 1; Job 28:27; Prov. 3:19; 8:22; 19:21; Pss. 33:11; 104:24; Jer. 10:12; 51:15; Heb. 11:3; Isa. 14:24–27; 46:10;

---

91. Cf. J. Ridderbos, *De Theologie van Jonathan Edwards* (The Hague: J. A. Nederbragt, 1907).

92. Ed note: This is taken from Bavinck's citation of Julius Kaftan: "Modern German theology does not have a doctrine of election" (Julius Kaftan, *Dogmatik*, [Tübingen: Mohr, 1897; 4th ed. 1901], 475).

93. Cf., e.g., Eduard Böhl, *Dogmatik* (Amsterdam: Scheffer, 1887), 124ff., 527ff.; Charles Hodge, *Systematic Theology*, 3 vols. (New York: Charles Scribner's Sons, 1888), I, 535ff.; W. G. T. Shedd, *Dogmatic Theology*, I, 393ff.

94. A. W. Dieckhoff, *Der missourische Prädestianismus und die Concordienformel* (Rostock: E. Kahl, 1885); A. Späth, "Lutherische Kirche in America," *PRE³*, XIV, 184–213.

95. P. Schaff, *The Creeds of Christendom*, 6th ed., 3 vols. (New York: Harper & Row, 1931; repr., Grand Rapids: Baker Academic, 1990), III, 771.

96. E. F. K. Müller, *Bekenntnisschriften*, 941ff.

Acts 2:23; 4:28; Eph. 1:11; etc.). If in the case of rational creatures, idea and purpose precede action, how much more true and sublime this is for the Lord our God, apart from whose knowledge and will nothing comes into being. Rationality in the world presupposes rationality in God. There could be no rationality in creation had it not been created with intelligence and wisdom. In addition, we cannot conceive of any plan of God—in whom intelligence and will coincide—being frustrated from realization. What God wills, he does; God speaks and it comes to be; he commands and it stands firm (Ps. 33:9). The counsel of God is efficacious (Isa. 14:27; Pss. 115:3; 135:6), unchanging (Isa. 46:10; Ps. 33:11; Heb. 6:17; James 1:17), and independent (Matt. 11:26; Eph. 1:9; Rom. 9:11, 20–21).

This decree (*ad intra*) must be distinguished from its execution in time (*ad extra*) as well as from God himself. God is not identical with his decree; his self-knowledge is not exhausted in creation, providence, and redemption. God's counsel is both the "efficient" and "exemplary" cause of all that is. It is the efficient cause: all creaturely beings can come into existence only by the decree and will of God. The decree is the "womb" of all reality (Zeph. 2:2 MT, KJV). All that exists is ultimately grounded in God's good pleasure (εὐδοκια του θεου). Beyond that we cannot go. But God's counsel is also the "exemplary" cause of all that is and comes to pass. Our concepts depend on the prior existence of creation; they must conform to what is. With God, however, the idea of a thing is first; then it comes into being as he has conceived it. Taking our cue from what Scripture says about the tabernacle on earth being patterned on the heavenly one (Heb. 8:5), and fatherhood (πατρια) in heaven and earth being named after the Father (Eph. 3:15), we conclude that all things temporal are an image of the eternal, all existing things are a reproduction of the plan of God, and ultimately all that is and comes to pass is a reflection of the divine being. Although Thomas's statement has been criticized because God's world plan does not coincide with God's being, rightly interpreted, it is not untrue: "God in his essence is the likeness of all things."[97]

God's counsel is also a single and simple decree, the world plan of a single "artistic" vision, though creatures can only see it unfolding in space and time as a multiplicity. After much debate at the Westminster Assembly (1643–46), the confession writers opted for the singular: "decree," not "decrees." It is true that we creatures experience God's love and all his other perfections in the [spatial and temporal] dimensions of length, breadth, depth, and height (Eph. 3:18–19). Because God's purpose and purposes are unsearchably rich and many-sided, unfolding before us in vast multiplicity, we are led, humanly speaking, to think and speak of many divine decrees. This kind of language should not be condemned

---

97. T. Aquinas, *Summa Theol.*, I, qu. 15, art. 1; I, qu. 44, art. 3; W. Ames, *Marrow of Theology*, trans. J. D. Eusden (1968; repr., Grand Rapids: Baker Academic, 1997), I, 7, 13ff.; F. Turretin, *Institutes of Elenctic Theology*, trans. G. M. Giger and ed. J. T. Dennison, 3 vols. (Phillipsburg, NJ: Presbyterian and Reformed, 1992), IV, 1.7.

as long as the unity of the decree in God and the inseparable connectedness of all the special decrees is maintained and recognized.

PROVIDENCE AND THE OBJECTIONS TO PREDESTINATION

[241] God's counsel in reference to the physical world is called "providence" and includes preservation and governance. That things exist and the way they exist are grounded solely in God's good pleasure. If this is granted, then it must be acknowledged that the counsel of God also extends to the moral world and to human conduct. Here is where the objectors become vocal. Humanity, they argue, is characterized by moral free will; we are the creators and masters of our own destiny. Predestination robs us of our freedom; we are then simply subject to divine determinism. This way of thinking is wrong in a number of ways. Dualistically splitting the natural and moral world and limiting God's governance to the former is impossible; such a split banishes God from his world, leaving it to chance and caprice. The world, by its very design, is one organic whole. The two spheres, nature (φυσις) and morality (ἐθος), are most closely interconnected and interpenetrate each other at all times. One cannot, as all forms of Pelagianism attempt to do, designate a point in creation where the counsel and governance of God ends and the independent will and action of humans begins. This position is firmly contradicted by Scripture, religious experience, and theological reflection. Furthermore, setting matters up so that God's sovereignty and human freedom are in competition, if one can only be free at the expense of the other, then God can no longer be God; he must be banished from the world altogether. But the Christian church believes that God—because he is God and the universe is his creation—by the infinitely majestic activity of his knowing and willing, does not destroy but instead creates and maintains the freedom and independence of his creatures.

[242] Scripture rejects all such competition and teaches that faith is a gift of God's grace, a work of God. Scripture clearly teaches that faith and unbelief, salvation and perdition, are not just the objects of God's "bare foreknowledge" but especially also of his will and decree. God's foreknowledge (προγνωσις: Rom. 8:29; 11:2; 1 Pet. 1:2; cf. Acts 2:23) is not a passive form of precognition, not a state of consciousness, but—like the Hebrew ידע (Hosea 13:5 MT, NRSV note; Amos 3:2; etc.)—God's own self-determination, prior to its realization in history, to relate to the objects of his foreknowledge. It is most closely related to God's purpose (προθεσις), foreordination (προορισμος), and election (ἐκλογη), and is an act of his good pleasure (εὐδοκια). Faith is not our own accomplishment (1 Cor. 2:14); it is a gift of God (Eph. 2:8; Phil. 1:29; 1 Cor. 4:7), the fruit of election (Rom. 8:29; Eph. 1:4–5; Acts 13:48). This is the experience of every true believer. Although in theory a person may be Pelagian, in the practice of the Christian life, above all in prayer, every Christian is an Augustinian. Self-glorying is excluded, and

God alone is given the honor. Augustine was right when he said that the church's faith in God's grace expressed itself in prayers rather than in its "little works."[98] This election is sure and immutable as Scripture clearly teaches (Dan. 12:1; Matt. 24:24; 25:34; John 10:28; Rom. 8:29–30; 1 Pet. 1:2–4). Even foreknowledge, by definition, includes predestination. Either God knows the elect with certainty or not at all. If he does, foreknowledge is redundant. If not, even foreknowledge has to go. The doctrine of predestination, therefore, is a dogma of the entire Christian church. Modern attempts to impose a divine self-limitation of knowledge in God in the interest of maintaining human freedom have, for good reason, been decisively repudiated by the church.[99] Once again we concur with Augustine: "There was never a time when the church of Christ did not hold the truth of this belief in predestination, which is now being defended with fresh concern against new heretics."[100] Furthermore, Pelagianism fails to satisfy the human mind; at every point of life and of the history of humankind it conflicts with reality, the awesome reality that history unfolds according to the purpose of God.[101] Pelagianism is a veneer that, though highly deceptive, in no way changes this reality.

[243–44] Although proven untenable in general, Pelagianism has had remarkable staying power and repeatedly comes back to attack every point in the doctrine of predestination. Appealing especially to such Scriptures as 1 Timothy 2:4 and 1 Peter 3:9, Pelagians assert the existence of an *antecedent conditional* decree of God to offer to all fallen humanity grace sufficient for salvation. The reality of history, in which grace is particular and not universal, is impossible to square with this assertion. Even in the beginning, opportunity is not equal; being born in a Christian home or later becoming acquainted with the gospel is undeserved and unconditional, a gift. Furthermore, not all who hear the gospel believe it. Pelagians cannot answer the important question: If God has done his part in providing sufficient grace why is it efficacious only for some? To whom and why is "full, efficacious, grace" given? Here the Pelagian position becomes confused and introduces notions of merit, a view with no support in Scripture.[102] Finally, Pelagianism's notion of "predestination to glory," a third decree granting salvation to those who persevere (as God foresaw) makes God's decree completely conditional. There is no real decree, only a wish whose fulfillment is uncertain.

98. Augustine, *On the Gift of Perseverance*, 23; cf. C. Hodge, *Systematic Theology*, I, 16.

99. Ed. note: There is a revival of this view in early twenty-first-century North American evangelical theology under the rubric of "open theism." Important titles include: Gregory A. Boyd, *God of the Possible: A Biblical Introduction to the Open View of God* (Grand Rapids: Baker Books, 2000); Clark H. Pinnock et al., *The Openness of God: A Biblical Challenge to the Traditional Understanding of God* (Downers Grove, IL: InterVarsity, 1994); John Sanders, *The God Who Risks: A Theology of Providence* (Downers Grove, IL: InterVarsity, 1998); for a critique, see Bruce A. Ware, *God's Greater Glory: The Exalted God of Scripture and the Christian Faith* (Wheaton: Crossway, 2004).

100. Augustine, *On the Gift of Perseverance*, chap. 23.

101. C. Hodge, *Systematic Theology*, II, 349.

102. Ed. note: Bavinck's introduction here of notions of merit refers specifically to Roman Catholic ideas of a "merit of condignity," merit obtained through works empowered by the Holy Spirit.

God does not know his own. Even where churches hold the doctrine of predestination impurely, with semi-Pelagian admixtures, they still confess it. Essentially and materially, though the word used in many different ways in Christian theology, "predestination" (προορισμος) is a dogma accepted throughout Christianity and Pelagianism the subversion of the Christian religion.

PREDESTINATION AND REPROBATION

Both the supralapsarian and infralapsarian positions seek to be true to Scripture, and the difference between them cannot be resolved by an appeal to Scripture. Each group appeals to a different set of texts. Infralapsarians point to those passages in which election and reprobation have reference to a fallen world and are represented as acts of mercy and of justice (Deut. 7:6–9; Matt. 12:25–26; John 15:19; Rom. 9:15–16; Eph. 1:4–12; 2 Tim. 1:9). Supralapsarians emphasize all the texts that declare God's absolute sovereignty, especially in relation to sin (Ps. 115:3; Prov. 16:4; Isa. 10:15; 45:9; Jer. 18:6; Matt. 20:15; Rom. 9:17, 19–21). The simple fact that each of these views rests on a specific group of texts and fails to do full justice to the other group already suggests the one-sidedness of both groups. Neither party denies that the fall into sin is included in God's plan and decree; both insist that God is not the author of sin. Both parties ultimately rest their case in the sovereign good pleasure of God. They also agree on the content of the decrees. The only difference is that infralapsarians adhere to a historical, causal order of the decrees, while supralapsarians prefer the ideal, teleological order. Both positions have strengths and are also one-sided. Infralapsarianism seems more modest, less harsh, but does not finally satisfy the mind. Words like "permission" and "foreknowledge" solve nothing; all difficulties remain. Why did God, knowing everything in advance, create humans with the capacity to fall, and why did he not prevent the fall? Why did he allow all humans to fall in the fall of one person? Why does he not have the gospel preached to all humans, and why does he not bestow faith on all? In short, if God foreknows a thing and permits it, he does that either willingly or unwillingly. The latter is impossible; God's permission is efficacious, an act of his will. The notion of permission is also of no value or force against the charge that God is the author of sin; for one who permits someone to sin and to perish when able to prevent it is as guilty as he who incites someone to sin.

Supralapsarianism has in its favor that it refrains from all useless attempts to justify God and simply attributes both election and reprobation to God's sovereign good pleasure. Yet it risks making the objects of election and reprobation "possible" human beings rather than actual ones and making sin a means of reprobation in the same manner that Christ's redemptive work is the means of election. Facing the charge that their view makes God the author of sin, supralapsarians deny this vigorously and introduce important distinctions between various "causes" of both sin and reprobation. While Reformed theologians may assume a "predestination to death," no Reformed theologian has dared speak of a "predestination to sin." All insist that God is not the author of sin, that humans were not created for perdition, that in reprobation also the severity of God's justice is manifested, that reprobation is not the "primary cause" but only the "accidental cause" of sin, that sin is not the "efficient" but the "sufficient" cause of reprobation, and so forth. Since sin is not outside of God's will and yet contrary to it, with happy inconsistency supralapsarians too need to introduce notions such as "permission," "foreknowledge," "dereliction," and "preterition" with respect to sin; no one is able to come up with better ones.

[245] Neither the supralapsarian nor the infralapsarian view of predestination is capable of incorporating within its perspective the fullness and riches of the truth of Scripture and of satisfying our theological thinking. It is a mistake to posit as the ultimate end of all things the revelation of God's mercy to the elect and his justice to the lost. Nor can one regard the wretched state of the lost as the goal of predestination in parallel with predestination to glory. The debate between supra- and infralapsarians all too often focuses on individuals and fails to accent the real object of election, namely the human race reconstituted under a new head: Christ. In addition, both parties tend to place all things that are subordinate to the final goal of God's glory themselves in subordination to each other. But creation is not just a means for the attainment of the fall, nor is the fall only a means for the attainment of grace and perseverance, and these components are not just a means for the attainment of blessedness and eternal wretchedness. When we concentrate on the details and various components of God's decree and attempt logically to describe exactly how they relate to each other, we run the risk of losing sight of the fact that the decrees are as abundantly rich in content as the entire history of the world, for the latter is the total unfolding of the former. To that end we look for a new heaven and a new earth, a new humanity, a restored creation, an ever-progressing development never again disturbed by sin. That is the ultimate goal of God's plan and counsel as Scripture reveals it: the honor and glory of the triune God.

Nonetheless, the truth inherent in supralapsarianism is that all the decrees together form a unity; that there is an ultimate goal to which all things are subordinated and serviceable; that the entrance of sin to the world did not take God by surprise but was willed by him; that creation was designed to make re-creation possible; and that in the creation of Adam, things were structured with a view to Christ. The truth of infralapsarianism is that the decrees can be differentiated with a view to their teleological and causal order; that creation and fall were not merely means to an end; that sin is a catastrophe which of and by itself could never have been willed by God. Full unity of conception here is only known to God and is a teleologically and causally interconnected pattern so rich that it cannot be reproduced in a single word such as "supralapsarian" or "infralapsarian." Just as in any organism all the parts are interconnected and reciprocally determine

each other, so the world as a whole is a masterpiece of divine art, in which all
the parts are organically connected. And of that world, in all its dimensions, the
counsel of God is the eternal design. In terms of definition the counsel of God is
the comprehensive master concept; predestination concerns the eternal state of
rational creatures and the steps or means leading to it; double predestination refers
to God's active willing in both election to eternal life and reprobation to perdition.

[246] We cannot avoid the notion of "double predestination." While Scripture
seldom speaks of reprobation as an eternal decree, it does recognize even in the
negative events of history–suffering, hardening, inexplicable disasters—the active
sovereign will of God. God rejects Cain (Gen. 4:5), curses Canaan (Gen. 9:25),
expels Ishmael (Gen. 21:12; Rom. 9:7; Gal. 4:30), hates Esau (Gen. 25:23–26;
Mal. 1:2–3; Rom. 9:13; Heb. 12:17), and permits the gentiles to walk in their own
ways (Acts 14:16). On occasion the Lord rejects his own people and particular
persons (Deut. 29:28; 1 Sam. 15:23, 26; 16:1; 2 Kings 17:20; 23:27; Pss. 53:5;
78:67; 89:38; Jer. 6:30; 14:19; 31:37; Hosea 4:6; 9:17). God's rejection is more
than divine response to sin; at times there is a positive action of God, consisting
in hatred (Mal. 1:2–3; Rom. 9:13), cursing (Gen. 9:25), hardening (Exod. 4:21;
7:3; 9:12; 10:20, 27; 11:10; 14:4; Deut. 2:30; Josh. 11:20; 1 Sam. 2:25; Ps. 105:25;
John 12:40; Rom. 9:18), blinding and stupefaction (Isa. 6:9; Matt. 13:13; Mark
4:12; Luke 8:10; John 12:40; Acts 28:26; Rom. 11:8). God's reign covers all things,
and he even has a hand in people's sins. He sends a lying spirit (1 Kings 22:23;
2 Chron. 18:22), through Satan stirs up David (2 Sam. 24:1; 1 Chron. 21:1), tests
Job (ch.1), calls Nebuchadnezzar and Cyrus his servants (2 Chron. 36:22; Ezra
1:1; Isa. 44:28; 45:1; Jer. 27:6; 28:14; etc.) and Assyria the rod of his anger (Isa.
10:5ff.). He delivers up Christ into the hands of his enemies (Acts 2:23; 4:28),
sets him for the fall of many, and makes him a fragrance from death to death, a
stone of stumbling, and a rock of offense (Luke 2:34; John 3:19; 9:39; 2 Cor. 2:16;
1 Pet. 2:8). Certainly in all these works of God one must not overlook people's
own sinfulness. In the process of divine hardening humans harden themselves
(Exod. 7:13, 22; 8:15; 9:35; 13:15; 2 Chron. 36:13; Job 9:4; Ps. 95:8; Prov. 28:14;
Heb. 3:8; 4:7). Jesus speaks in parables not only in order that people will fail to
understand but also because people refuse to see or hear (Matt. 13:13). God gives
people up to sin and delusion because they have made themselves deserving of it
(Rom. 1:32; 2 Thess. 2:11). And it is ex posteriori that believers see God's governing
hand in the wicked deeds of enemies (2 Sam. 16:10; Ps. 39:9–10). Nevertheless,
in all these things God's will and power become manifest and reveal his absolute
sovereignty. He makes weal and creates woe; he forms the light and creates the
darkness (Isa. 45:7; Amos 3:6); he creates the wicked for the day of evil (Prov.
16:4), does whatever he pleases (Ps. 115:3), inclines the heart of all humans as he
wills (Prov. 16:9; 21:1), and orders their steps (Prov. 20:24; Jer. 10:23). Out of
the same lump of clay he makes one vessel for beauty and another for menial use
(Jer. 18; Rom. 9:20–24), has compassion on whomever he wills and hardens the
heart of whomever he wills (Rom. 9:18). He destines some people to disobedi-

ence (1 Pet. 2:8), designates some for condemnation (Jude 4), and refrains from recording the names of some in the Book of Life.

Believers do not claim to comprehend all this; they do believe that the alternative—pessimism as the fruit of acknowledging the blind will of a chaotic deity—is impossible. Believers are willing to look at the disturbing reality of life; they do not scatter flowers over graves, turn death into an angel, regard sin as mere weakness, or consider this the best of possible worlds. Calvinism has no use for such drivel. It refuses to be hoodwinked and is willing to speak of the "dreadful decree" (Calvin).[103] Of course it is not the decree that is dreadful, but dreadful indeed is the reality that is the revelation of that decree of God, a reality that comes through both in Scripture and in history. Since nothing can undo this, least of all illusory notions of it, Calvinism seeks to take full account of the seriousness of life, champions the rights of the Lord of lords, and humbly bows in adoration before the inexplicable sovereign will of God. This almighty God is also, we believe, our merciful Father. This is not a "solution" but an invitation to rest in him who lives in unapproachable light, whose judgments are unsearchable, and whose paths are beyond tracing out. Therein lies our only comfort in life and in death until we see our God face to face and our questions about these riddles cease.

[247] Reprobation is, however, not a part of predestination in the same sense and manner as election.[104] We may not consider God's power as "absolute" in the sense of capricious, separated from his justice. We must therefore exercise great caution in "defending" God from accusations of injustice. Augustine, for example, once commented that God would not be unjust even if he damned an innocent person: "If the human race, which exists as originally created out of nothing, had not been born under the guilt of death and with original sin, and the omnipotent Creator had wanted to condemn some to eternal perdition, who could say to the omnipotent Creator: Why have you done this?"[105] Anyone who realizes something of the incomparable greatness of God and the insignificance of humans, and considers how we frequently contemplate with complete indifference the most severe suffering of humans and animals—especially when such suffering is in our own interest or for the benefit of art or science—will think twice before condemning Augustine or others for such a statement, not to mention calling God to account. Dare we speak of our "rights" over against him who formed us out of nothing and to whom we owe everything we have and are? Still, though one

103. J. Calvin, *Institutes*, III.xxiii.7.
104. Ed. note: Bavinck's language here is similar to that found in "Conclusion: Rejection of False Accusations" in the *Canons of Dort*, where the confession repudiates the notion "that in the same manner [*eodem modo*] in which election is the source and cause of faith and good works, reprobation is the cause of unbelief and ungodliness...."
105. *Admonitio de libro de Praedestione et Gratia, et subsequente epistola Ferrandi ad Egyppium*, PL 65:843A. Ed note: Bavinck cites this as Augustine, *De praed. et gratia*, 16. Migne indicates that the author is uncertain but places it in the oeuvre of Fulgensius, North African bishop (462–527) and devotee of Augustine's theology.

may for a moment speak in this fashion to someone who believes he or she has a right to accuse God of injustice, Calvin and almost all later Reformed theologians have in the end firmly, and with indignation, rejected such "absolute rule."[106] After first insisting that God's honor and sovereignty must always be acknowledged, all Reformed theologians recommended the most cautious and tender treatment of the doctrine of predestination and warned against all vain and curious approaches to the subject. "Hence it is not appropriate for us to be too severe. If only we do not in the meantime either deny the truth of what Scripture clearly teaches and experience confirms, or venture to carp at it as if it were unbecoming to God."[107] Although God knows those who are his and the number of the elect is said to be small, "nevertheless, we should cherish a good hope for everyone and not rashly count anyone among the reprobate."[108]

Though sin is not outside the scope of God's will, it is definitely against it. The decree of reprobation, grounded in God's will, must be distinguished from its execution. God's *act* of reprobation does take account of human sin; the decree of reprobation is realized through human culpability.[109] It is a mistake to consider the decree of reprobation by itself, alongside other decrees; God's decree is as broad as reality itself, and in a single conception encompasses the goal of his glory and the means to reach it. In real life, sin and grace, punishment and blessing, justice and mercy, do not exist side by side but are the common experience of all people. Here we need to remember that the reprobate in this life also share with the elect the common blessings of God. They receive many natural gifts—life, health, strength, food, drink, good cheer, and so forth (Matt. 5:45; Acts 14:17; 17:27; Rom.1:19; James 1:17)—for God does not leave himself without a witness. He endures them with much patience (Rom. 9:22). He has the gospel of his grace proclaimed to them and takes no pleasure in their deaths (Ezek. 18:23; 33:11; Matt. 23:27; Luke 19:41; 24:47; John 3:16; Acts 17:30; Rom. 11:32; 1 Thess. 5:9; 1 Tim. 2:4; 2 Pet. 3:9). From this we conclude it is God's will that we use all the means of grace available to call even reprobates to salvation. Now, these means do not as such flow from the decree of reprobation. They can be abused to that end; they may serve to render humans inexcusable, to harden them, and to make their condemnation all the heavier—like the sun, which may warm but also scorch a person. Yet in and by themselves they are not means of reprobation but means of grace with a view to salvation.[110] Thus, whereas election and reprobation may culminate in final and total separation, on earth they continually crisscross each other. Neither is the final goal or cause; both are means to the attainment of God's glory. But whereas God is removed from all wickedness and does not will sin and

---

106. See H. Bavinck, *Reformed Dogmatics*, II, 237–40 (#208).

107. J. Calvin, *Concerning the Eternal Predestination of God*, 184; Canons of Dort, I, 12, 14.

108. Helvetic Confession, according to E. F. K. Müller, *Bekenntnisschriften*, 181.

109. F. Turretin, *Institutes of Elenctic Theology*, IV, 14; H. Bavinck, ed., *Synopsis purioris theologiae*, XXIV, 50.

110. H. Bavinck, ed., *Synopsis purioris theologiae*, XXIV, 54ff.

punishment as such and for its own sake nor delight as such in reprobation, he does delight in the election and redemption of his own.

[248–49] Predestination finally culminates, therefore, in election. Chosenness exists everywhere in life; the world is not ordered according to the Pharisaic law of work and reward. Inequality and injustice are pervasive and enduring. The rule "many are called but few are chosen" seems valid everywhere; Darwin's doctrine of the survival of the fittest has universal validity and is in force throughout God's creation. Thousands of blossoms fall to the ground so that a few may ripen and bear fruit. Millions of living beings have been born, yet only a relative few lived and those that did live end up with noticeably different life spans. Thousands of people labor with the sweat of their faces in order that a few persons may swim in wealth. Riches, art, science, all that is high and noble, are built on a foundation of poverty, deprivation, and ignorance. While Scripture and Reformed theology recognize the significance of secondary causes in all these matters, these are not the final and most fundamental causes. It is our human lot to ask these deeper "why?" questions. Why is every creature what it is? Why is there such endless diversity among creatures in kind, nature, gender, species, power, intelligence, riches, honor, and so forth? Why are some angels destined for eternal glory, while the fall and perdition of others are both foreseen and preordained? Why was the human nature that Christ assumed dignified to this honor? Why is one person born within, and another outside, the precincts of Christianity? Why does the one child die in infancy, and as a child of the covenant is taken into heaven, while another dies outside the covenant and without grace? Why does the one become a believer and another not? All of these are questions that no mortal can answer. Science can register the *that* of things but never the *why*. We can only rest in God's sovereign good pleasure.

God's sovereign will is not conditional but absolute. Although God established a causal connection between sin and punishment, and though he maintains that connection in everyone's conscience, the decree of reprobation has its ultimate ground, not in sin and unbelief, but in the will of God (Prov. 16:4; Matt. 11:25–26; Rom. 9:11–22; 1 Pet. 2:8; Rev. 13:8). Similarly, there is a causal connection between faith and salvation, but the decree of election is not prompted by foreseen faith; on the contrary, election is the cause of faith (Acts 13:48; 1 Cor. 4:7; Eph. 1:4–5; 2:8; Phil. 1:29). Even in election, it is not correct, strictly speaking, to speak of Christ as its "cause." With his church Christ is better seen as the object of the Father's electing love. He is a gift of the Father's love, which precedes the sending of the Son (John 3:16; Rom. 5:8; 8:29; 2 Tim. 1:9; 1 John 4:9). The Son did not move the Father to love; electing love arose from the Father himself. Scripture, accordingly, everywhere teaches that the cause of all the decrees does not lie in any creature but only in God himself, in his will and good pleasure (Matt. 11:26; Rom. 9:11ff.; Eph. 1:4ff.). Election is thus a source of inexpressibly great comfort for believers and unbelievers alike. If it were based on justice and merit, all would be lost. But now that election operates according to grace, there is hope even for the most wretched. The salvation of human beings is firmly established in the gracious and omnipotent good pleasure of God.

The glory of election is especially seen in its object: the people of God in Christ. To be elect "in Christ" is to be organically united to his body, the church. Christ was foreordained to be head of the church. This communal emphasis has sometimes been taken as reason to avoid speaking about personal election for individual children of God. Such a restriction is a pure abstraction since humanity, people, family, and church always consist of particular persons. It is also contrary to Scripture, for Scripture teaches a personal election (Mal. 1:2; Rom. 9:10–12 [Jacob]; Acts 13:48 [as many as]; Rom. 8:29 [whom]; Eph. 1:4 [us]; Gal. 1:15 [Paul]) and speaks of the names of the elect that are written in the Book of Life (Isa. 4:3; Dan. 12:1; Luke 10:20; Phil. 4:3; Rev. 3:5; etc.). Nonetheless, a full biblical understanding of God's election must include Christ as the elect One along with his church. Scripture teaches this in connection with the Messiah (Isa. 42:1; 43:10; Ps. 89:3, 19; Matt. 12:18; Luke 23:35; 24:26; Acts 2:23; 4:28; 1 Pet. 1:20; 2:4). This act was rightly called "election" because from all eternity the Father designated the Son to be mediator, and above all because Christ's human nature was foreordained—by grace alone and aside from any merit—to union with the Logos and to the office of mediator. Scripture states with equal emphasis that the church is elect in and for Christ, to be conformed to his image, and to see his glory (John 17:22–24; Rom. 8:29). Christ was foreordained not only to be the mediator but also to be head of the church. All things were created through him and for him (1 Cor. 3:23; Eph. 1:22; Col. 1:16ff.). Election is the very first benefit bestowed on the church, a benefit received in union with Christ. Election is the divine "idea," the blueprint of the temple that God builds in the course of the ages and of which he is the supreme builder and architect. Creation and fall, preservation and governance, sin and grace, Adam and Christ—all contribute to the construction of this divine edifice, and this building itself is built to the honor and glorification of God. "All [things] are yours, and you are Christ's, and Christ is God's" (1 Cor. 3:21–23 KJV).

10

CREATOR OF HEAVEN
AND EARTH

CREATION AND ITS RELIGIOUS RIVALS

[250] The realization of God's counsel begins with creation. Affirming the distinction between the Creator and his creature is the starting point of true religion. There is no existence apart from and independent of God, who can only be known truly through revelation. God is the sole, unique, and absolute cause of all that exists (Gen. 1:2–3; Pss. 33:6; 104:29–30; 148:5; Job 26:13; 33:4; Isa. 40:13; 48:13; Zech. 12:1; John 1:3; Col. 1:16; Heb. 1:2; etc.). He speaks and things spring into being (Gen. 1:3; Ps. 33:9; Rom. 4:17). "From him and through him and to him are all things" (Rom. 11:36; 1 Cor. 8:6; Heb. 11:3). The world is the product of his will (Ps. 33:6; Rev. 4:11), the revelation of his perfections (Prov. 8:22f.; Job 28:23f.; Pss. 104:1; 136:5f.; Jer. 10:12). It finds its goal in his glory (Isa. 43:16ff.; Prov. 16:4; Rom. 11:36; 1 Cor. 8:6).

Scripture's teaching of creation is not presented as a philosophical explanation of the problem of existence. While it does give an answer to the question of the origins, its true significance is religious and ethical. Positioning us properly before God (Exod. 20:11; Deut. 10:12–14; 2 Kings 19:15; Neh. 9:6), the doctrine of creation points us to the majesty, goodness, wisdom, and love of God (Ps. 19; Job 37; Isa. 40), inspires praise and thanksgiving (Pss. 136:3ff.; 148:5; Rev. 14:7), induces humility and meekness before God (Job 38:4f.; Isa. 29:16; 45:9; Jer. 18:6; Rom. 9:20), and provides consolation in time of suffering (Pss. 33:6f.; 65:5ff.;

89:11; 121:2; 134:3; Isa. 37:16; 40:28f.; 42:5; etc.). The teaching of creation strengthens people's faith and confirms their trust in God.

[251] Scripture yields a distinct doctrine of creation. Alternative creation stories and myths from the ancient world are not true *creation* stories. Pagan cosmogonies, which are at the same time theogonies, are all polytheistic and assume the existence of a primordial stuff of some kind. Emanationism, evolutionism, and dualism are key features; either the world emanates from God, becomes more like God, or is the product of two conflicting primordial forces.[1] In spite of striking parallels to Genesis, the Chaldean Genesis (*Enuma Elish*) is a theogony where Bel fashions the world from Tiamat, who chaotically stores all things within herself.[2] Greek philosophy fared not much better, seeking the origin of things in a material element (Ionian school; Atomists), or pantheistically in the one eternal immutable being (Eleatic school), or in eternal becoming (Heraclitus, Stoa). The Greeks knew of a φυσις (nature), and a κοσμος (world), but not of a κτισις (creation). God is at best the world's fashioner (δημιουργος) in this dualism of matter and spirit. In its controversy with gnosticism, Christianity gained a victory over pagan theogony and cosmogony. Explanations of sin that posited the existence of an inferior god alongside the supreme deity, or an eternal ὑλη (matter), however, kept surfacing also in Christian centuries.

Pantheism also had its advocates. Influenced by Neoplatonism, Pseudo-Dionysius taught an eternal existence of ideas and archetypes in God, whose superabundant goodness moved him to confer reality on them by emanation of himself to his creatures.[3] Erigena expressly teaches creation out of nothing,[4] but speaks of "four natures" in pantheistic relation. It is God himself who first, in the ideas, creates himself, then flows down into his creatures and becomes all in all in order, finally, to return to himself in the fourth nature, which does not create and is not created. The cause of this process is God's goodness, his drive to become all things.[5] Outside the Christian world pantheism was propagated by the philosophers Avicenna (1036) and Averroes (1198); among Muslims by Sufism; and among Jews by the Kabbalah.[6] All these pantheistic, dualistic, emanationistic ideas freely crisscrossed among mystics, theosophists, and Anabaptists such as [Joachim of] Fiore, the Brethren of the Free Spirit, the Libertines, Meister Eckhart, Tauler, Servetus, Frank, Schwenkfeld, Paracelsus, and Böhme. Pantheism was restored to

---

1. O. Zöckler, "Schöpfung und Erhaltung der Welt," *PRE³*, XVII, 681–704.

2. H. H. Kuyper, *Evolutie of Revelatie* (Amsterdam: Höveker & Wormser, 1903), 37–38, 117f.; cf. also H. Bavinck, *Reformed Dogmatics*, ed. John Bolt (Grand Rapids: Baker Academic, 2003–8), II, 473–507 (##268–78).

3. Pseudo-Dionysius, *The Divine Names*, chap. 4, 10.

4. Johannes Scotus Erigena, *On the Division of Nature*, trans. Myra L. Uhlfelder (1681; Indianapolis: Bobbs-Merrill, 1976), bk. III, 5, 24, 33.

5. Ibid., III, 4, 20; III, 2, 4, 9; I, 12.

6. A. Stöckl, *Geschichte der Philosophie des Mittelalters* (Mainz: Kirchheim, 1864–66), II, 28, 92, 181, 237.

a position of honor in modern philosophy by Spinoza and elevated by Schelling and Hegel to *the* system of the nineteenth century.

Here the doctrine of creation is totally rejected. Fichte wrote: "The assumption of a creation is the basic error of all false metaphysics and religious teaching. . . ."[7] Schelling called creation out of nothing a "cross to the intellect"[8] and joined theogony to cosmogony, seeking the world's ground in the dark nature of God (*Urgrund, Ungrund,* darkness). This is the principle of blind confusion, the chaotic dimension of the world, the demonic.[9] But also at work is the potency of the divine intellect, which introduces light, order, and regularity to the world. God manifests himself as Spirit in the spirit of mankind, where he achieves full personality.[10] Schleiermacher rejected the distinction between creation and providence and considered the question whether the world was temporal or eternal a matter of indifference, provided one upheld the absolute dependence of all things on God.[11] For many theologians, too, God is no more than the eternal immanent cause and ground of the world.

[252] Alongside these developments, we see emerging a materialism that sought to ground all things in notions of eternal being and indestructible material atoms, explaining all natural phenomena in terms of atomic processes of mechanical and chemical separation and union in accordance with fixed laws.[12] Like pantheism and dualism, materialism is not in any sense scientific but a religious worldview masquerading as science. The origin and end of things lie outside the boundaries of human observation and research. Science presupposes existence and rests on the foundation of what has been created. Pantheism and materialism are thus in the same position as theism, which acknowledges the mysterious origin of things. When subjected to careful scrutiny, theism is intellectually more satisfying than its rivals.

7. J. G. Fichte, *Die Anweisung zum seligen Leben* (London: Trübner, 1873), 160. Ed. note: A new German edition of this work was published in 1970 by Meiner in Hamburg. The essay is also found in J. G. Fichte, *Characteristics of the Present Age: The Way towards the Blessed Life: Or, the Doctrine of Religion* (Washington, DC: University Publications of America, 1977). For a discussion of Fichte's essay, see H. Berkhof, *Two Hundred Years of Theology* (Grand Rapids: Eerdmans, 1989), 26–28.

8. F. W. J. Schelling, *Sämmtliche Werke,* I/2, 44f.; I/8, 62f. Ed. note: Bavinck's references to Schelling concerning works incorporated in the new, unrevised, but abridged and repaginated *Ausgewählte Werke,* 4 vols. (Darmstadt: Wissenschaftliche Buchgesellschaft, 1968) will be cited with the full title of the work as well as Bavinck's original reference. Since this is not a complete edition of Schelling's original *Sämmtliche Werke* (Stuttgart & Augsburg: J. G. Cotta'scher, 1856–61), writings not included in the new edition will be cited as *Sämmtliche Werke,* using Bavinck's original reference.

9. Schelling's philosophy was given fresh theological legs in the twentieth century by Paul Tillich, *Systematic Theology,* 3 vols. (Chicago: University of Chicago Press, 1951–63).

10. F. W. J. Schelling, *Ausgewählte Werke,* IV, 303f. ("Philosophische Untersuchungen über das Wesen der menslichen Freiheit und die damit zusammenhängenden Gegenstände," *Sämmtliche Werke,* I/7, 359f.); idem, *Sämmtliche Werke,* II/2, 103f.; II/3, 262f.

11. F. Schleiermacher, *The Christian Faith,* ed. H. R. MacIntosh and J. S. Steward (Edinburgh: T&T Clark, 1928), §§36, 41.

12. F. A. Lange, *Geschichte des Materialismus und Kritik seiner Bedeutung in der Gegenwart,* 8th ed. (Leipzig: Baedekker, 1908).

Pantheism cannot overcome its fundamental problem: trying to explain how *being* emerges from *thought* or *matter* from *mind*, and how *unity* can diverge into *mulitiplicity*. Pantheism is remarkably adept with *words* that provide a semblance of solution as the following characteristic phrases illustrate: The idea assumes form, incarnates itself, objectivizes itself, passes into another mode of being; it splits off and differentiates itself; it freely decides to release and to realize itself, to turn into its opposite.[13] Make sense of that who can! Word games answer neither deep metaphysical nor religious questions. Recognizing the pantheist identity of thought and being as an error, Schopenhauer and von Hartmann gave primacy to the will and conceived the Absolute as nature, will, and drive. "Substance," the "Idea," the "All," or however pantheism may designate the Absolute, is not a fullness of being but pure potentiality, an abstraction without content, a mere nothing. And this is supposed to be the explanation of the riches of the world, the multiplicity of the existent! These sophisticated philosophical systems fail to satisfy human religious need and are riddled with internal contradictions. To them all the Christian church confesses simply, "I Believe in God the Father, Almighty, Creator of heaven and earth."

Materialism also fails to explain the origin of things. Where pantheistic monism[14] pictures the universe as proceeding from one ultimate principle, materialism assumes a multiplicity of "principles," which are only indivisible particles of matter. This worldview too lacks coherence. How can one attribute any transcendent or metaphysical significance to finite phenomena described in terms of cause and effect? How does a materialist make the metaphysical leap and speak of matter being eternal? By their own criteria, when scientists try to penetrate to what lies behind the phenomenal world they cease to act as scientists and become philosophers and metaphysicians, or, perhaps, theologians. Materialism denies its own presuppositions; it is a philosophy built upon the denial of all philosophy; it is inherently self-contradictory; it rejects all absolutes and makes atoms absolute; it denies God's existence and deifies matter. Furthermore, the essence and nature of matter remain profoundly mysterious and elude our cognitive grasp. Conceiving and imagining the nature of spirit is easier. Matter is a word, a name, but we do not really know what we mean by it. If we did understand matter, we remain stuck explaining its origin. Materialists must also declare motion, change, or even this

13. F. W. J. Schelling, *Ausgewählte Werke*, I, 386f. ("Ideen zu einer Philosophie der Natur, Einleitung," *Sämmtliche Werke*, I/2, 62f.); idem, *Ausgewählte Werke*, III, 119f., 153f. ("Bruno oder über das göttliche und natürliche Princip der Dinge," *Sämmtliche Werke*, I/4, 223f., 257f.); G. W. F. Hegel, *The Encyclopaedia of Logic (with the Zusätze)*, trans. T. F. Geraets et al. (Indianapolis and Cambridge: Hackett, 1991), 306–7; idem, *Hegel's Philosophy of Nature*, trans. M. J. Petry (London: Allen Unwin; New York: Humanities Press, 1970). Ed. note: Bavinck's references are to Hegel, *Werke*, VI, 413ff.; VII, 23ff., which comprises §§243ff. (likely through §252) of Hegel's *System der Philosophie*, found in vols. 8–10 of Hegel's *Sämtliche Werke* (Stuttgart: F. Frommann, 1958).

14. On pantheism, see H. Ulrici, "Pantheismus," *PRE¹*, 64–77; M. Heinze, "Pantheismus," *PRE³*, XIV, 627–41; A. Kuyper, "Pantheism's Destruction of Boundaries," in *Abraham Kuyper: A Centennial Reader*, ed. James D. Bratt (Grand Rapids: Eerdmans, 1998).

existing world to be absolute and eternal (like the atom). Granting metaphysical status to physical reality still fails to offer explanations for consciousness and self-consciousness, so essential to our humanity. By definition, materialism cannot solve this conundrum; it is not surprising that many materialists return to pantheism and mysticism. Such a movement can be found in Haeckel's work, for example, as he speaks of a "spirit in all things," of a "divine force," a "moving spirit," a "world soul" that indwells all things.

Creatio ex nihilo by the Triune God

[253] Christians believe that the Triune God, by his sovereign will, brought the entire world out of nonbeing into a being distinct from his own being. *Creatio ex nihilo*, "out of nothing," preserves the essential distinction between the Creator and the world and the contingency of the world in dependence on God. Proof for this cannot be given simply by appeal to the Hebrew word ברא or the Greek word κτιζειν, which is also used for human "creating." The expression "to create out of nothing" is not literally in Scripture but occurs in 2 Maccabees 7:28, where God is said to have made heaven and earth and everything in them out of nonbeing (ἐξ οὐκ ὄντων ἐποιησεν; Vulg.: *fecit ex nihilo*). The teaching is, nonetheless, clear in Scripture. Some do translate Genesis 1:1–3 as "In the beginning *when* God created heaven and earth—now the earth was a formless void . . .—then God spoke and said: 'Let there be light.'" Verse 2 would then presuppose the existence of a formless and vacuous earth in God's act of creating. Not only is this translation unacceptable,[15] but the overall view it suggests militates against the whole spirit of the creation narrative. Elohim is not presented in Genesis 1 as a cosmic sculptor who uses preexisting material to produce a work of art, but as One who merely by speaking, by uttering a word of power, calls all things into being. The whole of Scripture concurs.

God the Almighty is the infinite and sovereign owner, the קֹנֵה of heaven and earth (Gen. 14:19, 22). He speaks and it comes to be, he commands and it stands forth (Gen. 1:3; Ps. 33:9; Isa. 48:13; Rom. 4:17). All things are created by him (Col. 1:16–17), dependent on him (Exod. 20:11; Neh. 9:6; etc.), exist only by his will (Rev. 4:11), and are of him, through him, and unto him (Rom. 11:36). God alone is the Eternal and Imperishable One; there is no hint of an eternal formless matter. God is beyond time and change; present before the mountains were brought forth, his years never come to an end (Ps. 90:2; Prov. 8:25–26); his love and election are from the foundation of the world (Eph. 1:4; John 17:24; cf. Matt. 13:35; 25:34; Luke 11:50; John 17:5; Heb. 4:3; 9:26; 1 Pet. 1:20; Rev. 13:8; 17:8). Romans 4:17 teaches that God calls and summons τα μη ὄντα, the things that possibly do not yet exist, as if they did exist, ὡς ὄντα. Hebrews 11:3 announces

15. Ed. note: This is the translation adopted by the NRSV, but see its note.

that God has made the world so that what is seen is not made ἐκ φαινομενων, from that which appears before our eyes. The visible world did not proceed from what is visible but rests in God, who called all things into existence by his word.

[254] Christian theology from the beginning has taught this doctrine.[16] *Ex nihilo* does not mean that the finite world of being came forth from nonbeing, now taken as a substantive (*nihil, nothingness*).[17] Erigena, for example, described God as *nihilum* insofar as he transcends all categories and limitations, all existence and being; if he brings forth everything out of nothing, this means that he "produces essence from his own—as it were—'superessentiality,' [and] lives from his own 'supervitality.'"[18] Even odder was the way Hegel in his *Wissenschaft der Logik* defined "nothingness" as "nonbeing that is simultaneously a kind of being, and a being that is simultaneously nonbeing," a nothingness that is at the same time everything, namely, in potentiality, and nothing specific concretely.[19] Wordplay aside, "*ex*" in *ex nihilo* does not designate the cause but only excludes a material cause; the world has its cause only in God.[20] Its being is not its own but given by God who alone is the Eternal and Imperishable One.

The expression *ex nihilo* is useful because it is admirably suited for cutting off all sorts of errors at the root; notions of eternal matter, pagan ideas of formless matter (ἀμορφος ὑλη), all forms of ontological emanation. When the Scholastics spoke of an emanation or procession of all existence from a universal cause, not to mention of the creature's participation in the being and life of God, they did not mean "emanation" in the strict ontological sense of God's own being flowing out into his creatures. Their point, rather, was to say that God is a self-subsistent necessary being (*ens per essentiam*) while the creature is existent by participation (*ens per participationem*). Creatures have their own being only in God, who is their efficient and exemplary cause.[21] Christian theology therefore rejects the philosophical confusion of both gnosticism and Arianism, pantheism and deism, while affirming both emanation and creation. Knowing no creation and only emanation, gnosticism deifies the world; Arianism, knowing only creation and no emanation, makes the Son into a creature and the world mundane. But Christian theology knows both emanation and creation, a twofold communication of God—one to the Son who was in the beginning with God and was himself God, and another to creatures who originated in time. The former is called

16. Herm. *Vis.* 1.1; *Theophilus to Autolycus*, II, 4; Tertullian, *The Prescription against Heretics*, 13; Irenaeus, *Against Heresies*, II, 10.

17. Ed. note: In twentieth-century theology, the issue of "God and Nothingness" received new attention from Karl Barth; see *Church Dogmatics*, vol. III, *The Doctrine of Creation*, ed. G. W. Bromiley and T. F. Torrance (Edinburgh: T&T Clark, 1961), III/3, §§50, 289–368.

18. J. S. Erigena, *On the Division of Nature*, III, 19–20.

19. G. W. F. Hegel, *The Encyclopedia of Logic*, 139–45 (*Wissenschaft der Logik*, in *Sämtliche Werke*, IV, 87–118.

20. Irenaeus, *Against Heresies*, II, 14; Augustine, *Confessions*, XI, 5; XII, 7; idem, *Literal Meaning of Genesis*, I, 1; Anselm, *Monologion*, chap. 8; T. Aquinas, *Summa Theol.*, I, qu. 45., art. 1; and so forth.

21. T. Aquinas, *Summa Theol.*, I, qu. 45, art. 1.

generation; the latter, creation. By generation, from all eternity, the full image of God is communicated to the Son; by creation only a weak and pale image of God is communicated to the creature. Still, the two are connected. Without generation, creation would not be possible. If, in an absolute sense, God could not communicate himself to the Son, he would be even less able, in a relative sense, to communicate himself to his creature. If God were not triune, creation would not be possible.[22]

[255] The triune God, not any intermediary, is the author of creation. Irenaeus already pointed out that in creating, God needed no alien instruments, including angels.[23] Augustine puts it even more strongly: "By this supremely, equally, and immutably good Trinity all things are created" so that the entire creation bears "the stamp of the Trinity" (*vestigium trinitatis*).[24] Scripture is clear. God created all things through the Son (Ps. 33:6; Prov. 8:22; John 1:3; 5:17; 1 Cor. 8:6; Col. 1:15–17; Heb. 1:3) and through the Spirit (Gen. 1:2; Pss. 33:6; 104:30; Job 26:13; 33:4; Isa. 40:13; Luke 1:35). The outgoing works of God are indivisible, though it is appropriate to distinguish an economy of tasks in the Godhead. The initiative for creation proceeds from the Father; in an administrative sense, creation is specifically attributed to him. The Son is not an instrument but the personal wisdom, the Logos, by whom everything is created; everything rests and coheres in him (Col. 1:17) and is created for him (Col. 1:16) as the head and master of all creatures (Eph. 1:10). The Holy Spirit is the personal immanent cause by which all things live and move and have their being, receive their own form and configuration, and are led to their destination, in God.[25] Finally, just as God is one in essence and distinct in persons, so also the work of creation is one and undivided; in its unity it is still rich in diversity. The world is a unity because God is one, and its unity demonstrates the unity of God.

[256] Scripture does relate the creation in a special way to the Son through the categories of Wisdom and Logos. The Old Testament repeatedly states that God created all things by his Word (Gen. 1:3; Pss. 33:6; 148:5; Isa. 48:13), that he established the earth by Wisdom, and by his understanding spread out the heavens (Ps. 104:24; Prov. 3:19; Jer. 10:12; 51:15). This teaching is further elaborated in the New Testament where we read that God created all things by the Son (John 1:3; 1 Cor. 8:6; Col. 1:15–17), and Christ is called "the firstborn of all creation" (πρωτοτοκος πασης κτισεως, Col. 1:15), "the origin of God's creation" (ἀρχη της κτισεως του θεου, Rev. 3:14), the Alpha and Omega (Rev. 1:17; 21:6; 22:6), for whom all things have been created (Col. 1:16). Christ thus is the mediator not only of re-creation but also of creation, the Logos by whom the Father creates all

22. Athanasius, *Against the Arians*, I, 12; II, 56, 78.

23. Irenaeus, *Against Heresies*, IV, 20.

24. Augustine, *Enchiridion*, 10; idem, *On the Trinity*, VI, 10; idem, *City of God*, XI, 24; idem, *Confessions*, XIII, 11.

25. A. Kuyper, *The Work of the Holy Spirit*, trans. H. De Vries (Grand Rapids: Eerdmans, 1941 [1900]), 21; see H. Bavinck, *Reformed Dogmatics*, II, 318–22 (#229).

things. The creation proceeds from the Father through the Son and in the Spirit, so that, in the Spirit and through the Son, it may return to the Father.

This clear teaching of Scripture has, nonetheless, been turned into its contradiction by dualistic views positing a more or less sharp opposition between spirit and matter, between God and the world. Biblical language is used, especially New Testament Logos statements, but the doctrine of creation is set on its head. God is considered invisible, inaccessible, hidden; the world, if not anti-God, is nevertheless "ungodly," "godless," devoid of deity. An intermediate being—the Logos—is needed to bridge the opposition. The world as such is profane; it is not from the hand of God but from a cosmic idea, the possibility that a world is in the making. The world is willed in Christ and the incarnation is necessary even apart from sin. Found among certain Anabaptists and various nineteenth-century mediating theologians, this Christology ends in redemption swallowing up creation and grace nullifying nature. When it "belongs to the very being of the Son to have his life not only in the Father but also in the world; [so that] as the heart of the Father he is simultaneously the eternal heart of the world, the eternal World-logos,"[26] creation itself becomes necessary for God. God as such is nature, the Ur-ground, the depth-dimension and primal silence of the world (βυθος and σιγη); he needs the creation to become personality and spirit. Creation is God's own history; cosmogony is theogony.[27] The profane world acquires positive value as it becomes ensouled by the Logos or spiritualized and divinized. The end result of this worldview is a restored paganism with its enchanted world.[28]

By contrast, Christians who affirm creation do not regard nature as profane, subordinate to grace, and needing an inferior, secondary being to create it. The Son does play his own role in creation, the Logos is the one Word through whom the Father expresses all his thoughts and his entire being. The Son is, therefore, appropriately called the beginning (ἀρχη), the firstborn (πρωτοτοκος), the origin of the creation (ἀρχη της κτισεως), who causes and sustains the creation. God's word is forceful and living, effective, performative. Furthermore, the Son in a sense is also the final cause (*causa finalis*) of the world; it is created for him (Col. 1:16; Heb. 1:2). In him as head all creatures again return to the Father from whom all things came. Thus the world finds its idea, its principle (ἀρχη), and its final goal (τελος) in the triune being of God. The word that the Father pronounces in the Son is the full expression of the divine being and of all that will exist by that

---

26. Hans Martensen, *Christian Dogmatics*, trans. William Urwick (Edinburgh: T&T Clark, 1871), §125; H. A. W. Meyer, *Critical and Exegetical Handbook to the Epistles to the Philippians and Colossians*, trans. John C. Moore, rev. and ed. William P. Dickson (Edinburgh: T&T Clark, 1875), 281–87 (on Col. 1:16).

27. F. W. J. Schelling, *Sämmtliche Werke*, II, 2, 109.

28. Ed. note: The phenomenon Bavinck describes here is clearly evident in the cultural idea-world of the early twenty-first century. In response to an Enlightenment and deist understanding of a world that is purely material, even mechanical, a new spirituality has been birthed with a clear intention to "re-enchant" the world. See, e.g., Morris Berman, *The Re-enchantment of the World* (Ithaca, NY: Cornell University Press, 1981).

word as creature outside the divine being. The procession (*spiratio*) by which the Father and the Son are the "active basis" (*principium*) of the Spirit also contains within itself the willing of that world, the idea of which is comprehended within the divine wisdom.[29] The creation thus proceeds from the Father through the Son in the Spirit in order that, in the Spirit and through the Son, it may return to the Father.

CREATION'S TIME AND GOAL: A CHRISTIAN WORLDVIEW

[257] This also gives us some insight into the difficult problem of creation and time. Scripture tells us in simple human language that all things had a beginning. It speaks of a time before the birth of mountains, before the foundation of the world, before the aeons began (Gen. 1:1; Ps. 90:2; Prov. 8:22; Matt. 13:35; 25:34; John 1:1; 17:24; Eph. 1:4; 2 Tim. 1:9; Heb. 4:3; 1 Pet. 1:20; Rev. 13:8). When we as inescapably temporal creatures reflect on the mystery of time we cannot avoid thinking about that first moment when it all began, and a multitude of questions arises. How can creation, the transition to the act of creating, be squared with the immutability of God? Why did God create when he did; how is there to be found, in all that time-transcending eternity, a moment in which God passed from not-creating to creating? Why did he not begin creating aeons earlier?

Answers to these questions have not been very satisfying. Pantheism teaches that in God, being and acting are one; that God did not become a Creator, but that creation itself is God's eternal self-revelation. God only *logically* precedes the world; nature bringing forth (*natura naturans*) is inconceivable apart from nature brought forth (*natura naturata*); substance is inconceivable apart from modes and attributes, or idea apart from manifestation.[30] Origen rejected eternal matter but introduced the idea of God creating forever; countless worlds preceded ours and many will follow.[31] This view was condemned by the Council of Nicaea but has made numerous comebacks.[32] However, because only God is eternal, all speculation about pretemporal or extratemporal reality is useless. Because eternity and time differ essentially, as Kant rightly saw, the world must have had a beginning; an infinitely past time is inconceivable. Even if we extend time endlessly and grant that millions of worlds preceded ours, time remains time and never becomes eternity. The world is inconceivable apart from time; existence in time is the necessary

29. J. Kleutgen, *Die Philosophie der Vorzeit vertheidigt*, 2 vols. (Münster: Theissing, 1863; 2nd ed. 1878), II, 870.

30. J. Erigena, *On the Divine Nature*, I, 73–74; III, 8–9, 17; B. Spinoza, *The Principles of Descartes' Philosophy* (*Cogitata Metaphysica*), trans. Halbert Haine Briton (Chicago: Open Court, 1905), II, chap. 10; G. W. F. Hegel, *Werke*, VII, 25.

31. Origen, *On First Principles*, I, 2; II, 1; III, 5.

32. H. Martensen, *Christian Dogmatics*, §§65–66; I. A. Dorner, *History of the Development of the Doctrine of the Person of Christ*, trans. Patrick Fairbairn, 3 vols. (Edinburgh: T&T Clark, 1868), III, 229–48.

form of all that is finite and created. Eternity can never be predicated of anything finite and temporal. Similarly, because in eternity there is no "earlier" or "later," an "eternal creation" is impossible. These "solutions" to the question of time and eternity are failures; they extend the problem but solve nothing.

Questions about God's activity before creation are even more baseless. Augustine, Luther, and Calvin answered in the spirit of Proverbs 26:5 ("Answer fools according to their folly").[33] The query assumes that God exists in time, that his labor is strenuous and requires sabbatical leisure for renewal. But the One who dwells in eternity is pure actuality (*actus purissimus*), an infinite fullness of life, blessed in himself; even without the creation he is not idle, and involvement in it does not exhaust him. "In [God's] leisure, therefore, is no laziness, indolence, inactivity; as in His work is no labour, effort, industry. He can act while He reposes, and repose while He acts."[34] God's act of creating did not change him; creation did not emanate from him and is no part of his being. He is unchangeably the same eternal God. The world, on the other hand, was created, not *in* time, but *with* time, as all Christian theologians since Augustine have affirmed.[35]

Time makes finite things subject to change. Eternity and time are not two lines, the shorter of which for a time runs parallel to the infinitely extended one; rather, eternity is the immutable center that sends out its rays to the entire circumference of time. We confess only that God's eternal willing can and does, without ceasing to be eternal, produce effects in time, just as his eternal thought can have temporal objects as its content. The power of God's will, which is eternally one, caused things to come into being that did not exist before, yet without bringing about any change in him.[36] God eternally wills things that only take place after centuries or took place centuries before. When they happen there is change in things but not in God. Creation demonstrates "to those who have eyes for such things, how independent [God] is of what he makes, and how it is of his own gratuitous goodness that he creates, since from eternity he dwelt without creatures in less perfect a blessedness."[37] To say that creation is an act of God's will does not mean arbitrary volition as Islam, Nominalism, Socinianism, and Cartesianism teach. God's will is not capricious; we must avoid notions that provide any suggestion that it is. Christian theology teaches that God's will, free of any coercion

---

33. Augustine, *Confessions*, XI, 2; John Calvin, *Institutes of the Christian Religion*, I.xiv.1 (ed. John T. McNeill and trans. Ford Lewis Battles, 2 vols. [1559; Philadelphia: Westminster, 1960], 1:159–61); ed. note: Augustine and Calvin's answer was that "God had been building hell for the curious."

34. Augustine, *City of God*, XII, 17, trans. Marcus Dods (New York: Modern Library, 1950), 400.

35. Augustine, *Confessions*, XI, 10–13; idem, *City of God*, VII, 30; XI, 4–6; XII, 15–17; cf. Tertullian, *Against Marcion*, II, 3.

36. Ed. note: It is worth recalling here Bavinck's discussion of God's communicable and incommunicable attributes; the major point there was not to quibble about the classification but to note that in relation to his creatures we can speak of analogues in God and vice versa; God can genuinely communicate without being altered.

37. Augustine, *City of God*, XII, 17, trans. Marcus Dods, 400.

or necessity, does have its motives, and God, in performing his external works, has his high and holy purposes.[38]

[258] The question persists, however: "What moved God to call this world into existence?" The Scriptures continually trace all such matters back to God's will (Pss. 33:6; 115:3; 135:6; Isa. 46:10; Dan. 4:35; Matt. 11:25; Rom. 9:15ff.; Eph. 1:4, 9, 11; Rev. 4:11). Unlike emanationist notions that begin with a plenitude of divine actuality or being that just overflows, or their opposite, a God who is pure empty potentiality and needs the world to *become* God, Scripture states that God's will and glory are the only reasons for and goals of creation. This rejects notions of human autonomy, making humanity the end goal and all creation existing for us. God did not *need* to create, and the universe does not exist for our sake. Scripture tells us that creation reveals God's attributes and proclaims his praise (Pss. 8; 19:1; Rom. 1:19); humanity is made after God's image and for his glory (Gen. 1:26; Isa. 43:7); of him, through him, and to him are all things (Rom. 11:36). Thus, Tertullian says that God created the world "for the embellishment of his majesty."[39] This emphasis on the "glory of God" increasingly came into its own, especially in the medieval theology of Anselm,[40] and particularly in Reformed theology[41] where the honor and glory of God was made the fundamental principle of all doctrine and conduct.

Two objections have been raised against this emphasis on the glory of God as the final goal of creation. Some suggest that this makes God self-centered, self-seeking, and guilty of devaluing his creatures. This overlooks the obvious: if as humans we justly ask for honor that is our due, how much more is this true for God; he can do no other than seek the honor and glory due him; to expect less diminishes him as God. In the end, voluntarily or involuntarily, every creature will bow the knee before him (Phil. 2:9). Furthermore, God's honor does not diminish human honor and value but enhances it; God's good is our highest good. In the words of Irenaeus: "The glory of God is man alive."[42] It has also been claimed that creation meets a need in God, contributing to his perfection.[43] Here the contrast between necessary work and artistic activity that flows from the free impulse of creative imagination and genius is helpful. Devout people do not serve God out of coercion or expectation of reward, but out of free-flowing delight and love. Multiply what is true for us infinitely in order to understand God's delight, good pleasure, glory, and honor. God did not create because he *needed* the world

---

38. Cf. H. Bavinck, *Reformed Dogmatics*, II, 237–45 (##208–9) [= H. Bavinck, *The Doctrine of God*, trans. W. Hendriksen, Twin Brooks Series (1951; repr., Grand Rapids: Baker, 1985), 232–41].

39. Tertullian, *Apology*, 17.

40. Anselm, *Cur Deus homo*, 11.

41. For example, Jonathan Edwards, "Dissertation concerning the End for Which God Created the World," in *Ethical Writings*, ed. Paul Ramsey, vol. 8 of *The Works of Jonathan Edwards* (New Haven, CT: Yale University Press, 1989), 399–536.

42. Ed. note: Irenaeus, *Against Heresies*, IV, 20, 7.

43. D. F. Strauss, *Christian Faith*, I, 633.

but because he *delighted* in his own will to create and in his act of creating. The category of "artist" thus "fits" the Creator God supremely.

[259] A doctrine of creation is foundational for a biblical and Christian worldview. When creation is pantheistically deified as a living organism or materialistically reduced to blind mechanical, physical forces, we fail to appreciate the richness and diversity of the world, dissolve all distinctions in a bath of deadly conformity, and deny conscious purpose or destiny to the world. The biblical doctrine of creation recognizes profuse diversity in creation along with a profound unity in the God who created all things in accordance with his unsearchable wisdom. The scriptural words עוֹלָם and αἰῶνες assume the idea that the world has duration, or age, and that its history is important and culminates in a clear goal. The Greek word κοσμος and the Latin *mundus*, on the other hand, stress the beauty and harmony of the world. The world is both. Just as Paul simultaneously compares the church to a body and a building and speaks of a growing temple (Eph. 2:21), and Peter calls believers living stones (1 Pet. 2:5), so also the world is both a history and a work of art. It is a body that grows and a building that is erected.

Augustine understood this well. In the *City of God* he sketches the origin, essence, development, goal, and end of the heavenly city (*civitas coelestis*) in relation to the earthly city (*civitas terrena*). But at the same time he includes in it an account of the universe as a splendid harmony; the universe derives its name from the word "unity."[44] This unity is not uniformity but an infinitely varied diversity;[45] "To some things he gave more of being and to others less and in this way arranged an order of natures in a hierarchy of being."[46] God alone makes this distribution; there is no merit here:[47] "There is no nature even among the least and lowest of beasts that he did not fashion . . . the properties without which nothing can either be or be conceived."[48] This is *the* Christian worldview. The world is one created body with many members, and all point to their maker. "There is no spot in the universe," says Calvin, "wherein you cannot discern at least some sparks of his glory."[49] "Nothing in the whole world is more excellent, more noble, more beautiful, more useful, and more divine than the diversity of its many elements, the distinction and that order in which one is more noble than another and one depends on another, one is subject to another, and one receives obedience from another. Hence comes the adornment, beauty, and excellence of the whole world. Thence arise its many uses, usefulness, and benefits for us. Hence, the very goodness, glory, wisdom, and power of God shines forth and is

---

44. Augustine, *On Genesis, against the Manicheans*, I, 21.
45. Augustine, *City of God*, XI, 10.
46. Ibid., XII, 2.
47. Augustine, *Eighty-Three Different Questions*, qu. 41; idem, *Divine Providence and the Problem of Evil*, I, 19; idem, *Literal Meaning of Genesis*, I, 9; II, 13; idem, *Confessions*, XII, 9; idem, *City of God*, XI, 33.
48. Augustine, *City of God*, XI, 15.
49. J. Calvin, *Institutes*, I.v.1.

revealed more brilliantly."[50] For all of them the world is a theater, a "splendidly clear mirror of his divine glory."

Christianity thus neither holds nature in contempt nor deifies it. Sinful humanity swings between extremes of arrogant mastery over nature and desperate moments of deep and dark alienation thanks to its mysterious forces and powers. Intellectualism and mysticism alternate; unbelief makes way for superstition, and materialism turns into occultism. But confessing God as the Creator rules out egoistic arrogance as well as false optimism. Much in nature and history is unfathomable; God's ways are often unsearchable; but we do not despair since we believe all things are subject to the government of an omnipotent God and a gracious Father and will therefore work together for our good. Rightly ordered to God, we can truly appreciate the natural world as fully contingent; it *is* and it is *this way* not out of necessity but because God willed it so. Lactantius, accordingly, spoke truly when he said: "The world was made for this reason that we should be born. We are born, therefore, that we should know the Maker of the world and our God. We know Him that we may worship Him. We worship Him that we may gain immortality, . . . serve the Father and Lord Most High forever and be an everlasting kingdom for God. This is the sum of everything; this the secret of God; this the mystery of the world."[51]

HEAVEN: THE SPIRITUAL WORLD

[260] According to Holy Scripture, creation is divided into a spiritual and a material realm, "things in heaven and [things] on earth, things visible and invisible" (Col. 1:16). All religions recognize such a spiritual realm. In addition to the actual gods, a variety of demigods or heroes, demons, genii, spirits, souls, and so on have been the objects of religious veneration. Over the last few centuries belief in angels, demons, and a spiritual realm has declined. Immanuel Kant did not rule out their existence,[52] but as the nineteenth century erased the boundary between humans and animals, the eighteenth did the same for angels and humans. Swedenborg, for example, learned from angels themselves that they were really humans and that our destiny is to become angels.[53] Modern theology leaves little room for angels; Schleiermacher regarded them as accommodation to popular imagination akin

50. Jerome Zanchi, *Operum theologicorum*, 8 vols. ([Geneva]: Samuelis Crispini, 1617), III, 45.

51. Lucius C. Lactantius, *The Divine Institutes*, VII, 6, trans. Mary Francis McDonald (Washington, DC: Catholic University Press, 1964), 488.

52. Otto Zöckler, *Geschichte der Beziehungen zwischen Theologie und Naturwissenschaft*, 2 vols. (Gütersloh: C. Bertelsmann, 1877–79), II, 69, 249.

53. Emanuel Swedenborg, *The True Christian Religion Containing the Universal Theology of the New Church* (New York: Swedenborg Foundation, 1952), 29n20, 176n115, 179n118, 183n121; ed. note: the Mormon faith also tends to erase the boundary between humanity and the angelic/divine realm; cf. the Bible dictionary entry "Angels" on the official website of the Church of Jesus Christ of Latter-Day Saints, http://scriptures.lds.org/en/bd/a/84.

to fairies and elves and of no theological or religious significance.[54] Nonetheless, in opposition to materialism, around the middle of the nineteenth century there arose a spiritualist reaction which not only acknowledges the existence of deceased spirits but also the possibility of communion between them and earthly human beings.[55]

[261] Belief in a spiritual world is rooted in and profoundly expresses the truth of revelation; only God can make it known to us, and he has done so in Scripture. Attempts to "prove" the necessary existence of angels as "boundary-mediators" between Creator and creature are unacceptable because they implicitly erase that boundary and lead to gnostic pantheism. We can say this: no science or philosophy can advance any argument *against* the possibility of such spiritual beings. Humans are psychic beings and cannot explain the life of the soul from material metabolism but have to predicate some spiritual substance for that life. This continues even after death and, therefore, the reality of the spiritual world is not inconsistent with any argument of reason or fact of experience. It is inadequate reductionism to say that angels and devils are only imaginative symbolic projections created by human beings who are situated between and wrestle with the conflict between good and evil.[56]

Belief in a spiritual world is not philosophical but religious in nature. Religion needs revelation and revelation presumes a spiritual world above and behind this visible world from which we receive communication. Believing in angels expresses conviction about a world beyond our senses, about transcendence, miracle, and revelation. Not satisfied with the world present to our senses, we human beings thirst for another world no less rich than this one; dissatisfaction with materialism and naturalism always evokes spiritualism. But the spiritualism of the modern world is only a new form of superstition. Its claims are impossible to verify and its history is rife with all sorts of deceptions and unmasking. Some of the appeals to strange and marvelous phenomena may be explained in terms of psychology, while others remain mysterious. Do we attribute them to the workings of deceased humans, to demonic spirits, or to hidden powers of nature?[57] In numerous instances spiritism has seriously injured its practitioners' psychic and physical health; Scripture prohibits it (Deut. 18:11ff.). We cannot bridge the gap between this world and the beyond, and when we try we lapse into superstition and become prey to the spirits that are conjured up. While some deny the existence of angels and a spiritual realm, excessive, unhealthy interest in spirits or speculation about them is a greater problem.

---

54. F. Schleiermacher, *The Christian Faith*, ed. H. R. MacIntosh and J. S. Steward (Edinburgh: T&T Clark, 1928), §42.

55. H. N. De Fremery, *Handleiding tot de Kennis van het Spiritisme* (Bussum, 1904); idem, *Een Spiritistische Levensbeschouwing* (Bussum, 1907).

56. I. A. Dorner, *A System of Christian Doctrine*, trans. A. Cave and J. S. Banks (Edinburgh: T&T Clark, 1891), II, 98.

57. O. Zöckler, "Spiritismus," *PRE*³, XVIII, 654–66.

As we must respect the boundary between this world and the other side, so too we must plead ignorance about what takes place on other planets. Belief in the existence of animate rational beings on planets other than the earth is pure speculation and seems contradicted rather than confirmed by present-day science.[58] This conclusion is important for our doctrine of angels. There are no good philosophical arguments against the doctrine; on the basis of analogy with the human spirit, the idea has much to commend it; the world's religions affirm it; and, most importantly, Scripture teaches it. Furthermore, unlike various religions and spiritisms, Scripture tells us about angels in a way that does not detract from God's honor and leaves the purity of religion untouched. It is Scripture alone and not our experience that grounds our belief in angels. Jesus and the apostles openly and repeatedly expressed their belief in angels (e.g., Matt. 11:10 [ἄγγελος, messenger]; 13:39; 16:27; 18:10; 24:36; 26:53; Luke 20:36; 1 Cor. 6:3; Heb. 12:22; 1 Pet. 1:12; etc.). When we speak of elves and fairies, everybody knows this is meant figuratively; but in Jesus's time belief in angels was universal and his statements indicate he believed in them. Of course, true faith is about the grace of God in Christ and not about angels. In the Protestant confessions there is very little mention of angels,[59] a sin of defect rather than excess. Though not a factor or an object in our religion, in the history of revelation angels are nevertheless of great importance. We may not ignore Scripture's testimony concerning them.

THE ANGELS IN SCRIPTURE

[262] The name "angel" does not derive from their *nature* but from their *office*. The Hebrew מַלְאָךְ simply means "messenger" or "envoy," and includes human messengers sent by other humans (Job 1:14; 1 Sam. 11:3; etc.) or by God (Hag. 1:13; Mal. 2:7; 3:1). The same is true of ἄγγελος, which also denotes humans (Matt. 11:10; Mark 1:2; Luke 7:24, 27; 9:52; Gal. 4:14; James 2:25). In Scripture there is no common distinguishing name for the entire class of spiritual beings, though they are frequently called "sons of God" ([KJV, NRSV note] Job 1:6; 2:1; 38:7; Pss. 29:1; 89:6); "spirits" (1 Kings 22:19ff.; Heb. 1:14); "holy ones" (Deut. 33:2–3; Ps. 89:5, 7; Zech. 14:5; Job 5:1; 15:15; Dan. 8:13); "watchers" (Dan. 4:13, 17, 23).

The world of angels is as richly varied as is the material world, and Scripture teaches that among angels there are distinctions of rank and status, of dignity and ministry, of office and honor. First mentioned are the *cherubim* (כְּרֻבִים), who guard the Garden of Eden (Gen. 3:24), and are later depicted in the tabernacle and temple with faces turned toward the mercy seat and wings that cover it (Exod. 25:18ff.; 37:8–9; 1 Chron. 28:18; 2 Chron. 3:13; Heb. 9:5). The Lord sits

---

58. See Alfred R. Wallace, *Man's Place in the Universe: A Study of the Results of Scientific Research in Relation to the Unity or Plurality of Worlds* (New York: McClure, Phillips, 1903).

59. Belgic Confession, art. 12; Heidelberg Catechism, Lord's Day 49.

enthroned between them (Pss. 80:1; 99:1; Isa. 37:16); when God comes down to earth he is represented as riding the cherubim (2 Sam. 22:11; Pss. 18:10; 104:3; Isa. 66:15; Heb. 1:7). Revelation 4:6f. depicts them as four living creatures (ζωα), each with one face (plus eyes behind) and six wings, who surround the throne of God and sing the "thrice-holy" night and day. The cherubim are not, as some have suggested, mythical, symbolic, or divine forces in nature, but animate personal beings (Gen. 3:24; Ezek. 1; Rev. 4). It is true that their extraordinary power and majesty are expressed in symbolic form including the power of an ox, the majesty of a lion, the speed of an eagle, and the intelligence of a human. The wings with which they fly, and the sword with which they guard the garden point to the same attributes of power and glory. The cherubim are highly positioned spiritual beings who more than any other creatures reveal the power, majesty, and glory of God; they are therefore charged with the task of guarding the holiness of God in the Garden of Eden, in the tabernacle and temple, and also in God's descent to earth.

In Isaiah 6, there is mention of the *seraphim* (שְׂרָפִים) who are symbolically represented in human form but with six wings, two to cover the face, two to cover the feet, and two for the swift execution of God's commands. In distinction from the cherubim, they stand as servants around the king, who is seated on his throne; they acclaim his glory and await his commands. Seraphim are the noble ones among the angels, cherubim the powerful. The former guard the holiness of God, the latter serve at the altar and effect atonement. Finally, in Daniel we encounter two angels with proper names: Gabriel (8:16; 9:21 [cf. 10:5–6]) and Michael (10:13, 21; 12:1). Gabriel (Luke 1:17, 26) and Michael (Jude 9; Rev. 12:7; and 1 Thess. 4:6 [unnamed]) appear in the New Testament, but there is also mention of principalities and powers (Eph. 3:10; [6:12;] Col. 2:10); dominions (Eph. 1:21; Col. 1:16), thrones (Col. 1:16), and powers (Eph. 1:21; [Rom. 8:38–39;] 1 Pet. 3:22). This, along with the repeated references in John's Apocalypse to seven angels (Rev. 8:2, 6; 15:1; etc.), suggests distinctions in rank and dignity among the angels, a conclusion also prompted by the large numbers of angels spoken of in Scripture using words such as "hosts" (צְבָאוֹת), "camps" (מַחֲנַיִם; Gen. 32:1–2), legions (Matt. 26:53), and the myriads or thousand times thousand (Deut. 33:2; Ps. 68:17; Dan. 7:10; Jude 14; Rev. 5:11; 19:14).

It is appropriate to search for order in this rich testimony concerning angels. The elaborate hierarchical classification of Pseudo-Dionysius (*The Celestial Hierarchies*; *The Ecclesiastical Hierarchies*), however, far exceeds what revelation teaches. According to this revered teacher of the Roman Catholic Church, creation is seen as emanating from the unity of God down to a multiplicity of beings in hierarchical order. The *Celestial Hierarchies* consists of three classes in order—seraphim and cherubim who exclusively serve God; dominions, powers, and authorities who serve the invisible and visible creation; and principalities, archangels, and angels who serve individuals and peoples on earth. The *Celestial Hierarchies* are mirrored in the *Ecclesiastical Hierarchies*: the church's mysteries (baptism, the Eucharist, ordination), its functionaries (bishop, priest, deacon), and its laity (catechumens,

Christians, monks). The goal of both hierarchies is deification and the entire scheme found fertile soil and was generally accepted in Roman Catholicism.[60] But Scripture offers only scant information, if any, about the number of angels or the time of their creation. It does teach us what we need to know: angels all have a spiritual nature, they are all called "ministering spirits," and they all find their primary activity in the glorification of God. There is unity in their creation as spiritual, rational, and moral beings.

[263] We know that angels are all created beings (Col. 1:16; implied in Gen. 1:1–2:4; Ps. 33:6; Neh. 9:6; John 1:3; Rom. 11:36; Eph. 3:9; Heb. 1:2) but we know nothing about the *time* of their creation. Nothing is anterior to the creation of heaven and earth, but it is certain that the angels were created before the seventh day, when heaven and earth and all the host of them were finished, and God rested from his labor (Gen. 1:31; 2:1–2). The word "heaven" in verse 1 is proleptic; only later in the history of revelation do its implications become evident. Scripture sometimes speaks of heaven as the sky with its clouds (Gen. 1:8, 20; 7:11; Matt. 6:26 [ET: "air"]); then as the stellar heavens (Deut. 4:19; Ps. 8:3; Matt. 24:29); and finally as the abode of God and his angels (Pss. 115:16; 2:4; 1 Kings 8:27; 2 Chron. 6:18; Matt. 6:19–21; Heb. 4:14; 7:26; 8:1–2; 9:2ff.; etc.). Now, just as the heavens of the clouds and of the stars came into being in the course of six days, it is possible "heaven" with its angelic inhabitants was formed in stages. We just don't know.

As created beings, angels can be said to have a certain unity, at least a spiritual unity. This still leaves many questions unanswered. Details aside, Scripture does indicate that, unlike God himself, angels are not simple, omnipresent, or eternal. This has led some to conclude that angels—in their own ethereal way—are corporeal, bounded in time and space. But though angels always appear to humans in visible corporeal form and are symbolically represented in this way, it is best not to ascribe corporeality to angels in order to avoid all forms of pantheistic identity philosophy that mixes heaven and earth, matter and spirit, and erases the distinction between them. The Fourth Lateran Council in 1215 called the nature of angels "spiritual,"[61] and most Catholic and Protestant theologians concur. Some, however, occasionally restate convictions about the corporeality of angels *in some sense* because the concept of a purely incorporeal nature is metaphysically inconceivable. Like God, angels are spirits; but quite unlike God who is unbounded by time and space, angels are bounded, finite, because they are *creatures*.

Scripture is clear that angels are spirits (πνεύματα; Matt. 8:16; 12:45; Luke 7:21; 8:2; 11:26; Acts 19:12; [23:8;] Eph. 6:12; Heb. 1:14), who do not marry (Matt. 22:30), are immortal (Luke 20:35–36) and invisible (Col. 1:16), may be "legion" in a restricted space (Luke 8:30), and have no flesh and bones (Luke 24:39). The

60. John of Damascus, *Exposition of the Orthodox Faith*, II, 3; T. Aquinas, *Summa Theol.*, I, qu. 108; J. H. Oswald, *Angelologie* (Paderborn: F. Schöningh, 1883), 57f.
61. H. J. D. Denzinger, *Enchiridion symbolorum et definitionum* (Wirceburgi, 1856), 355.

view that the "sons of God" (בְּנֵי־הָאֱלֹהִים) in Genesis 6:2 are angels and not men is untenable. The punishment of the sin is imposed only on guilty humans; angels are not mentioned (Gen. 6:3, 5–7). Scripture nowhere suggests the corporeality of angels. Psalm 104:4 (cf. Heb. 1:7) only says that God uses his angels as ministers, just as wind and fire serve to carry out his commands, but absolutely not that the angels are changed into wind or fire. Angel appearances do take place in visible corporeal form, and symbolic representations of angels are always in visible form, but this proves nothing. God, too, is spirit and is nevertheless envisioned by Isaiah (chap. 6) as a King sitting on his throne. Christ appeared in the flesh and is still truly God. We conclude that it is impermissible to ascribe bodies to angels. Scripture always maintains the distinction between heaven and earth, angels and humans, the spiritual and the material, invisible and visible things (Luke 24:39; Col. 1:16). It is a form of pantheistic identity philosophy to mix the two and erase the distinction between them. Although finite creatures, angels do relate more freely to time and space than humans do. Ability to move at lightning speed and not be obstructed by material objects in immediate translocation while at the same time not being atemporally eternal as only God is, all this is quite inconceivable to us. But Scripture clearly refers to it; and in the speed of thought and imagination, of light and electricity, we have analogies not to be despised.

[264] Angels—both good and evil ones—are all rational beings, endowed with intellect and will (Job 1:6ff.; Zech. 3:1ff.; Matt. 8:28ff.; 18:10; 24:36; 2 Cor. 11:3; Eph. 6:11; etc.). They are self-conscious and speak (Luke 1:19f.), desire (1 Pet. 1:12), rejoice (Luke 15:10), worship (Heb. 1:6), believe (James 2:19), lie (John 8:44), sin (1 John 3:8; etc.). Great power is ascribed to them (Ps. 103:20; Luke 11:15ff.; Col. 1:16; Eph. 1:21; 3:10; 2 Thess. 1:7; Acts 5:19; Heb. 1:14). Roman Catholic Scholastic theology regarded angelic knowledge as intuitive and intellectual, given by their very creation via innate ideas and not by way of sense perception. Elevated to the supernatural order, they know God by immediate vision.[62] Some even taught—in the interest of defending prayer addressed to angels and saints—that angels, who see God who sees all things, saw all things in him and therefore knew all our afflictions and needs.[63] Protestants were more cautious. There is much mystery in our coming to know; how much more so for angels! (Matt. 18:10; 24:36). They acquire knowledge from their own nature (John 8:44), from the contemplation of God's works (Eph. 3:10; 1 Tim. 3:16; 1 Pet. 1:12), and from revelations imparted to them by God (Dan. 8:15ff.; Rev. 1:1). Nevertheless, they do not know either the secret thoughts of our hearts or those of each other (1 Kings 8:39; Ps. 139:2, 4; Acts 1:24 [yet cf. 2 Sam. 14:20]), so that even among themselves they need a language for communicating (1 Cor. 13:1) and to glorify God in speech and song. They do not know the future, nor

62. T. Aquinas, *Summa Theol.*, I, qu. 54–58; idem, *Summa contra gentiles*, II, 96–101; II, 49.
63. Gregory the Great, *Moralia in Iob*, 12–13; T. Aquinas, *Summa Theol.*, II, 2, qu. 83, art. 4; III, qu. 10, art. 2.

future contingencies, including the day of judgment (Mark 13:32), but can only conjecture (Isa. 41:22–23). Their knowledge is limited and capable of expansion (Eph. 3:10).

Finally, the angels are all moral beings; there are good angels, who serve God night and day, and evil angels, who did not remain in the truth. Scripture says very little about their original state except for the testimony at the end of the work of creation: "God saw everything . . . and, behold, it was very good" (Gen. 1:31 KJV). John 8:44, Jude 6, and 2 Peter 2:4 assume the original state of integrity of all angels, a crucial point that utterly rules out all Manichaeism. Where Scripture is silent, imagination and reasoning had ample play. Augustine believed that some angels fell at the very moment of creation and that God in grace definitively preserves those who did not. Protestant theology maintained this position against Origen[64] and against the Remonstrants, who considered the good angels as still capable of sinning. Holy Scripture always presents the good angels to us as a faithful company that invariably does the will of the Lord. They are called "angels of the LORD" (Pss. 103:20; 104:4), "elect" (1 Tim. 5:21), "holy ones" (Deut. 33:2–3; Matt. 25:31), "holy" or "of light" (Luke 9:26; Acts 10:22; 2 Cor. 11:14; Rev. 14:10). They daily behold God's face (Matt. 18:10) and are held up to us as examples (Matt. 6:10); some day believers will become like them (Luke 20:36).

THE MINISTRY OF ANGELS

[265] From this we conclude that angels, like humans, are a unity of created, spiritual, rational, moral beings; both were originally created in knowledge, righteousness, and holiness; both were given dominion, immortality, and blessedness; both are called the sons of God (Job 1:6; Luke 3:38). This must not lead us to overlook important differences. Only human beings bear God's image. We must reject the notion that because angels are exclusively spiritual, in a hierarchy of creatures they are closer to God. Augustine had it right: "God gave to no other creature than man the privilege of being after his own image."[65] Our image resides not only in what we have in common with angels but also in what distinguishes us. We are embodied creatures, sensuous as well as rational; to us was given dominion over the earth (Gen. 1:26), an essential part of the image restored by Christ the King who makes us kings as well as prophets and priests. Angels are not kings, only servants (Heb. 1:14). There is no consanguinity among angels, no ties of blood; we cannot speak of an "angelity" in the way we speak of a common "humanity." Angels do not share our organic unity in Adam's fall; they cannot be incorporated into a new redeemed body of Christ. A Second Adam was necessary and possible; there is no Second Lucifer. The earth is the stage of God's miraculous acts

---

64. Origen, *On First Principles*, I, 5, 3, 4.
65. Cited by T. Aquinas, *Summa Theol.*, I, qu. 93, art. 3.

where the victory of God's kingdom is won; angels turn their faces to the earth, longing to look into the mysteries of salvation (Eph. 3:10; 1 Pet. 1:12). While angels may be mightier *spirits*—greater in intellect and power—humans are far richer in relationships; the full image of God in all its richness is unfolded only in *humanity*. While all things stand in relation to Christ as Creator and as Lord and Head (Ps. 33:6; Prov. 8:22ff.; John 1:3; 1 Cor. 8:6; Eph. 1:10; 3:9–11; Col. 1:19–20; Heb. 1:2), including the angels (Col. 1:16), he is not the Reconciler and Savior of the angels. Humans alone constitute the church of Christ; she alone is his bride, the temple of the Holy Spirit, the dwelling place of God.

[266] Scripture describes the ministry of angels as *ordinary* and *extraordinary*. Their extraordinary ministry is to accompany the history of redemption at its cardinal points; the ordinary ministry is to praise God day and night. Angels guard Eden (Gen. 3:24) and convey revelations—in blessing as well as judgment—to Abraham (Gen. 18), to Lot (Gen. 19), to Jacob (Gen. 28:12; 32:1); at the giving of the law (Heb. 2:2; Gal. 3:19; Acts 7:53); in Israel's wars (2 Kings 19:35; Dan. 10:13, 20); to the prophets Elijah and Elisha, to Ezekiel, Daniel, and Zechariah. They are present at the birth of Jesus (Luke 1:13, 26–38; 2:10ff.) and his temptation (Matt. 4:11); they accompany him throughout his earthly life (John 1:51), especially in his suffering (Luke 22:43), resurrection (Matt. 28), and ascension (Acts 1:10). Subsequently they reappear from time to time in the history of the apostles (Acts 5:19; 8:26; 12:7ff., 23; 27:23; Rev. 1:1); then they cease their extraordinary ministry and will only resume a public role at the return of Christ (Matt. 16:27; 25:31; Mark 8:38; Luke 9:26; 2 Thess. 1:7; Jude 14; Rev. 5:2; etc.), when they will do battle against God's enemies (Rev. 12:7; 1 Thess. 4:16; [2 Thess. 1:7–8;] Jude 9), gather the elect (Matt. 24:31), and cast the ungodly into the fire (Matt. 13:41, 49). Angels themselves do not accomplish salvation; they participate in its history by transmitting revelations, protecting God's people, opposing his enemies, and performing an array of services in the kingdom of God. They are ministering spirits in the service of those who will inherit salvation. With Christ's coming and the full revelation of God's Word, this extraordinary ministry has ceased. What could the angels still give us now that God himself gave us his own Son?

Angels also have an ordinary ministry praising God day and night (Job 38:7; Isa. 6; Pss. 103:20; 148:2; Rev. 5:11). They rejoice over the conversion of a sinner (Luke 15:10), watch over believers (Pss. 34:7; 91:11), protect little ones (Matt. 18:10), and carry believers into Abraham's bosom (Luke 16:22). Not content with this general description, some developed the doctrine of guardian angels who watch over cities, countries, peoples of the earth, sea, world, and so on. Christian writers such as the Pastor (Shepherd) of Hermas[66] and especially Origen followed Jewish thought in ascribing special angels for special needs. Raphael, the angel of healing; Gabriel, the angel of war; Michael, the angel of prayer;

---

66. Herm. *Mand.* 6.2; Herm. *Vis.* 3.4.

and so on.[67] The church fathers and later Roman Catholic theology and the Roman Catechism (IV, chap. 9, qu. 4 and 5) recognized guardian angels. Calvin and most Reformed theologians rejected the idea of guardian angels,[68] though a few did not.[69] Lutheran confessional writings affirm an active intercession by angels in heaven,[70] though this idea is unanimously rejected by the Reformed.

Of course, Scripture does speak of angelic protection and intercession (see Deut. 32:8; Dan. 10:13, 20; Matt. 18:10; Acts 12:15; Heb. 1:14; Rev. 1:20; 2:1; 18:1ff.; Job 33:23; Zech. 1:12; Luke 15:7). But in speaking of angelic protection and intercession we must be as circumspect as Scripture itself. Consider the important text Daniel 10:13, 20, where we read about Michael, "one of the chief princes" (v. 13), the "great prince," and "protector" of the children of Israel (12:1; 10:21). Calvin and Reformed exegetes after him usually identified that prince of Persia with the Persian kings but it seems to refer to someone else, namely, the guardian spirit of Persia. In Daniel there is a war between the kingdom of God (Israel) and the kingdoms of the world (Persia) taking place on two planes: here on earth and in the realm of spirits between angels. Angels take part on both sides of the colossal spiritual struggle between God's kingdom and those of this world. That is all we may infer from it. There is absolutely no claim here that every country and people has its own angel. Similarly, we may not deduce from Revelation 1:20, etc., that every church has its angel; the "angels" (ἄγγελοι, messengers) of the seven churches are their ministers, the representatives of the churches. It is their works that are praised or blamed; the letters are addressed to them.

Best support for the doctrine of guardian angels comes from Matthew 18:10, a text undoubtedly implying that a certain class of angels is given the task of protecting "the little ones." But what does this mean? Can we go beyond the general affirmation that some angels are charged with the promotion of certain interests on earth? The apocryphal book of Tobit is the source for the idea of guardian angels and angelic intercession (Tob. 12:6–22). While Luke 15:7, 10 teaches that the angels rejoice over the repentance of one sinner, this is not intercession in the strict sense of the word. Even in Revelation 8:3, where an angel's action with a censer purifies the prayers of the saints, the text does not breathe a word about intercession. The angel is simply a servant and the ministry he performs is like

---

67. Origen, *On First Principles*, I, 8; III, 3; idem, *Against Celsus*, V, 29; VIII, 31.

68. J. Calvin, *Institutes*, I.xiv.7; *Commentary*, on Ps. 91 and Matt. 18:10.

69. J. Zanchi, *Op. theol.*, III, 142; Guillaume Bucanus, *Institutiones theologicae* (Bern: Johannes & Isaias Le Preux, 1605), VI, 28; Johannes Maccovius, *Loci communes theologici* (Amsterdam: n.p., 1658), 394; Andreas Rivetus, *Operum theologicorum*, 3 vols. (Rotterdam: Leers, 1651–60), II, 250; cf. H. Heppe, *Reformed Dogmatics*, rev. and ed. Ernst Bizer, trans. G. T. Thomson (London: George Allen & Unwin, 1950; repr., Grand Rapids: Baker Academic, 1978), 212–13; Campegius Vitringa, *Doctrina christianae religionis*, 8 vols. (Leiden: Joannis le Mair, 1761–86), II, 117.

70. Apology of the Augsburg Confession, art. 21; ed. note: ET in *The Book of Concord: The Confessions of the Evangelical Lutheran Church*, ed. Robert Kolb and Timothy Wengert (Minneapolis: Fortress, 2000), 107–294; Smalcald Articles, II/2.

that of the seraphim in Isaiah 6:6–7. Again, there is no ground here for believing in individual or national guardian angels.

[267] The problem with the doctrine of guardian angels and their intercession is that it leads to veneration and worship, a practice apparently referred to in Colossians 2:18 (θρησκεια των ἀγγελων). Many church fathers cautioned against the veneration and adoration of angels.[71] In the Old Testament dispensation, Joshua worshiped the angel (Josh. 5:14), but in the New Testament, the angel rejected John's worship (Rev. 19:10; 22:9) because angels are "fellow servants." These warnings remind us that in practice the boundaries between the worship of God and the respect due to angels is in danger of being erased. The invocation of angels was first clearly mentioned by Ambrose: "We to whom the angels have been given for assistance and protection ought to entreat them."[72] The church dealt with the issue by distinguishing "veneration" (τιμαω) that is fitting for us to offer to angels, and the "worship" (σεβαω) to which only God is entitled.[73] But the practice of invoking angels was sanctioned by the [Second] Council of Nicaea (787), and the Council of Trent later called such invocation "good and profitable" (sess. 25). The Roman Catechism (III, chap. 2, qu. 4, no. 3) justifies this because angels who behold God's face have taken upon themselves "the sponsorship of our salvation." The Roman Breviary incorporated prayers addressed to angels in the Feast of the Angels, and Roman Catholic dogmaticians unanimously defend it and treat it under "the veneration of saints."

Lutheran and Reformed people and virtually all Protestants reject the religious veneration of angels along with that of the saints[74] because Scripture clearly prohibits it (Deut. 6:13; 10:20; Matt. 4:10; Col. 2:18–19; Rev. 19:10; 22:9). Only God may be worshiped; *religious* honor may not be accorded to any creature. The Roman Catholic distinction between worship (λατρεια) and homage (δουλεια) fails to convince. Though a distinction between religious and civil honor would be reasonable, the δουλευειν accorded to angels and saints is *religious* in character and as such stands condemned by Scripture and practice. Scripture knows no twofold religious veneration, one of a lower kind and the other of a higher kind. Repeatedly δουλευειν is used with reference to God [or Christ] (Matt. 6:24; Rom. 7:6; 14:18; 16:18; Gal. 4:9; Eph. 6:7; Col. 3:24; 1 Thess. 1:9); and λατρευειν is also used of service rendered to humans. The entire distinction is arbitrary, sup-

71. Irenaeus, *Against Heresies*, II, 32; Origen, *Against Celsus*, V, 4–5; VIII, 13; Athanasius, *Against the Arians*, II, 23; Augustine, *True Religion*, 55; idem, *Confessions*, X, 42; idem, *City of God*, VIII, 25.

72. Ambrose, *De viduis*, chap. 9, §55.

73. Eusebius, *Preparation for the Gospel*; Origen, *Against Celsus*, VIII, 13, 57.

74. Luther, according to J. Köstlin, *The Theology of Luther in Its Historical Development and Inner Harmony*, trans. Charles E. Hay (Philadelphia: Lutheran Publication Society, 1897), II, 23ff.; Ulirch Zwingli, *Opera*, I, 268f., 280f.; III, 135; J. Calvin, *Institutes*, I.xiv.10–12; cf. III.xx.20–24; Johann Gerhard, *Loci theologici*, ed. E. Preuss, 9 vols. (Berlin: G. Schlawitz, 1863–75), XXXVI, §§370–480 (on angels, esp. §427); Johann Andreas Quenstedt, *Theologia didactico-polemica sive systema theologicum* (1685), I, 486; Francis Turretin, *Institutes of Elenctic Theology*, trans. George Musgrove Giger, ed. James T. Dennison, 3 vols. (Phillipsburg, NJ: Presbyterian and Reformed, 1992), VII, qu. 9.

ported neither by etymology or Scripture. By rejecting the religious veneration of angels, Protestantism acknowledges that angels are not an indispensable element in the religious life of Christians. They remain significant, however, because God chooses to use them in ways that obviously affect us even if we don't know exactly how; because their work is invisible to us it must simply be affirmed by faith. We owe them a civil honor and, were an angel to appear to us, it would be entirely fitting for us to welcome him with the deeply reverent homage we give to envoys of earthly kings and presidents. But, because God's revelation is completed in Jesus Christ, these appearances no longer occur and if they did we could not offer the kind of homage that the patriarchs, prophets, and apostles accorded the angels who appeared to them. What honor we owe them at all is simply that of a civil nature. We ought to feel ourselves one with them, live in the expectation of joining them (Heb. 12:22) and in forming with them and all other creatures a choir for the glorification of the Lord's name (Ps. 103:20–21). This is the only true veneration of angels. Understood thus, the doctrine of angels consoles and encourages us. We are not alone in our spiritual struggle but joined to a great cloud of witnesses present all around us. There is still another better world where God is served in perfection. Just as in revelation the world of angels has come down to us, so in Christ the church rises up to greet that world. We shall be like the angels and daily see the face of our Father, who is in heaven.

EARTH: THE MATERIAL WORLD

[268] We now go on to consider the material world. Unlike the spiritual realm, considered by theology only on the basis of revelation, the material physical world is accessible to all and open to legitimate philosophic and scientific inquiry. Our concern here, of course, is with a *theological* perspective on the material world; we do not propose to do physical or biological science. Stated in this way we immediately encounter difficulties. How does a theological science relate to other, particularly natural, physical sciences? Are the two complementary or contradictory? Are conflicts real or only apparent? We affirm that a theological perspective on the material world differs from but should not be isolated from a philosophic/scientific one. Theology deals with creatures only insofar as they are the works of God and reveal something of his attributes. Hence also, where it deals with creatures, it is and always remains theology. Theologians, philosophers, and natural scientists are dealing with the same world.

For that reason we cannot divide the labor of scientists and theologians in such a way that science deals with objective, material reality and religion/theology addresses only matters of subjective value and ethics. Such a division is both theoretically and practically impossible. Every scientific system is rooted in religious convictions, and all religions bring with them a certain view of the created world. All religions have their cosmogonies based on tradition, and even the creation story in Genesis 1 presents itself as a historical narrative based on tradition, sharing some aspects with the cosmogonies of other religions but in many ways exhibiting striking divergence. Many have attempted to exploit certain parallels between biblical and other ancient Near Eastern stories such as *Enuma Elish* and the *Gilgamesh Epic* in order to propose a pan-Babylonianism that sought the origins of Israel's religion in the myths and narratives of its influential neighbors.[75] With respect to Genesis 1, it is especially the portrayal of chaos under the ancient terms of תְּהוֹם [the deep] and תֹהוּ וָבֹהוּ [formless and void] that is used to underscore parallels with and even dependence on the Babylonian *Enuma Elish*. Now, the תְּהוֹם in Genesis 1:2 does correspond to the Babylonian *Tiamat*, and in the Old Testament we do encounter the idea of God waging a struggle against a natural power. In some texts there is mention of Rahab (רַהַב; Job 9:13; 26:12; Pss. 40:4 [40:5 MT, רְהָבִים; ET: "the proud"]; 87:4; 89:10f.; Isa. 30:7; 51:9f.); Leviathan (לִוְיָתָן; Job 3:8; 41:1ff.; Pss. 74:12ff.; 104:26; Isa. 27:1); the dragon (תַּנִּין; Job 7:12; Isa. 27:1; 51:9; Ezek. 29:3; 32:2); the serpent (נָחָשׁ; Job 26:13; Isa. 27:1; Amos 9:3)—powers opposed to and overcome by God. Still, a careful reading yields no ground for claiming that Israel's belief in creation bears a borrowed mythological character. The terms "Rahab," "Leviathan," and so on are used in such varied ways in the Old Testament that there is no reason to identify them with the Babylonian Tiamat.

In addition, these references point to powers vanquished by God in the course of salvation history—e.g., deliverance from Egypt (Pss. 74:13–14; 89:10; Isa. 51:9–10)—rather than to some intrinsic natural power opposed to God. That Israel's poets and prophets use mythological figures and images to depict such salvation-historical events in no way credentials pagan mythology. The Babylonian creation myth is miles apart from Genesis. Tiamat exists as chaos *before* the gods are created and subsequently rebels against them. By contrast, the תְּהוֹם in Genesis 1:2 is simply the designation of the original, *created* formless state of earth just as the phrase תֹהוּ וָבֹהוּ serves this purpose without any mythological associations. The creation narrative in Genesis is devoid of any trace of a theogony; rigorously monotheistic, it teaches a creation out of nothing, and knows nothing of primary matter. That the Jews, in exile or even earlier in Canaan, borrowed this story from the Babylonians is unbelievable. The polytheistic pagan cosmogonies would have repelled the Israelites and thus were totally unsuited to easy transformation into a suitable and beautiful monotheistic narrative like that of Genesis 1. Efforts to base the biblical story of creation on foreign sources such as Babylonian myths do not stand up under close scrutiny.

THE CREATION "WEEK" AND SCIENCE

[269] The interpretation of Genesis 1–2 has a rich and diverse history. The first verse of Genesis 1 needs to be read as the account of an independent fact. In

75. T. Aquinas, *Summa contra gentiles*, II, 2ff.

verse 2 the earth already exists, though in a disordered and vacuous state. Verse 1 reports the origin of that earth; from the very start it was created by God as *earth*, not ὕλη (matter) in an Aristotelian sense, not prime matter, not chaos in the sense of the pagan cosmogonies. "A created chaos is an absurdity" (Dillmann). The terms תֹהוּ וָבֹהוּ and תְּהוֹם mean something very different from what is usually understood by chaos. The state of the earth in Genesis 1:2 is not that of positive destruction (or opposition to God) but of not yet having been shaped; it was a תְּהוֹם, a seething watery mass that is wrapped in darkness. In Scripture's own commentary, the earth was formed "out of water and by means of water" (2 Pet. 3:5; Ps. 104:5–9). The exact time and duration of God's work of creation are much debated. It appears from the text of Genesis 1 that the references to "heaven and earth" in verse 1 and the unformed state of the earth in verse 2 are anterior to the six days of creation. The first day's work did not consist in the creation of heaven and earth but in the creation of light and the separation of light and darkness.

To understand the "week" and the "days" of creation, it is important to distinguish the first act of creation—as immediate bringing forth of heaven and earth out of nothing—from the secondary separation and formation of the six days. The two are separated by the unformed state of Genesis 1:2. The second creation takes place "in time" (*in tempore*), that is, in six days, and anticipates the works of preservation and government. The very moment when heaven and earth were created by God, they immediately and instantly passed into his preservation and government. But it definitely remains *God's* act of creation; matter does not have its own immanent developmental power to "bring forth." From the elementary matter of Genesis 1:1, God by speaking and creating brought forth the entire cosmos. While linking up with what already existed, in every new act of formation a creating word of God's omnipotence was spoken.

[270] Some have divided the creation week into two ternaries with days 1–3 corresponding to days 4–6. This holds for the first and fourth days but not for the second and the fifth or the third and sixth days. On the fifth day, though the birds of the firmament neatly fit with the second day, the fish and aquatic animals fit better with the work of the third day. There is a clear progression from a lower to a higher level, from the general conditions for organic life to organic life itself in its various forms. This suggests a preference for the old division of the week into three parts: *creation* (Gen. 1:1–2); *separation* on the first three days (light and darkness, heaven and earth, land and sea); and *adornment* on the fourth to the sixth days, the population of the prepared earth with all kinds of living entities.[76] Still, even this division is not intended as a sharp demarcation either since the plants, created on the third day, also serve as ornamentation. The *separation* and *adornment* mark the cancellation of the תֹהוּ condition of the earth. The use of the verb רָחַף ("to hover over"; cf. Deut. 32:11) suggests that in the case of רוּחַ

76. T. Aquinas, *Summa Theol.*, I, qu. 74.

אֱלֹהִים we must not think of wind only but of the Spirit of God (cf. Pss. 33:6; 104:30). The Spirit of God, as the principle of creaturely being and life, impacts the watery mass of the earth in a formative, vivifying way and so anticipates the creative words of God that in six days, acting on already existent conditions, called into being the various orders of creatures.

The first day's work consists in the creation of light, in the separation of light and darkness, in the alternation of day and night, and hence also in movement, change, becoming. It is to be distinguished from and thus precedes the emitters of light: sun, moon, and stars. Light is the most general prerequisite for all life and development, including plants, and also gives form, shape, and color to all things. On the second day a separation is made between the firmament—the sky and the clouds, which appears to our eyes as a tent (Ps. 104:2), a curtain (Isa. 40:22), a roof or dome extended over the earth (Gen. 7:11; Deut. 11:17; 28:12; Ps. 78:23; [Mal. 3:10;] etc.)—and the earth with its waters (Pss. 24:2; 136:6). The work of separation and demarcation continues as the distinction between light and darkness is now made subservient to the separation of heaven and earth: the air and the clouds above; the earth and the water beneath. At the end of the second day we do not read that God saw that it was good. The reason is likely that the work of the second day is intimately bound up with that of the third day and divine approval follows at the end of the third day when earth becomes a cosmos with continents and seas, mountains and valleys, fields and streams. Mechanical, chemical, and organic processes shape the world and clothe it in green with vegetation.

This world of vegetation could do without the sun but not without light. But animals and humans do need the sun, and before they are created, the sun, moon, and stars are readied. The fourth day recounts the appearance of the starry heavens in relation to the earth. Together they regulate night and day and the seasons, and mark time in hours, days, months, and years, governing agriculture, shipping seasons, and annual feast days. Now the earth is ready for animal and human life. On the fifth day, by a divine word of power, the waters bring forth all aquatic animals, and the sky is filled with an assortment of bird species. On the sixth day follows the creation of land animals—specifically in three kinds: wild animals, cattle, and creeping things—and, finally, also the creation of humankind, who after a specific counsel of God was formed bodily from the earth with a soul directly created by God. The whole creation was complete: "God saw everything that he had made, and indeed, it was very good" (Gen. 1:31). And on the seventh day, God rested. This rest is a consequence of God's satisfaction with, and delight in, his works. At the same time it is a positive act of blessing and sanctifying the seventh day. The creation, in its continued existence on the seventh day, having been blessed with all kinds of forces and consecrated by God to his service and honor, would henceforth develop under the providential care of the Lord and answer to its destiny.

[271] Christian theology has always treated this six-day period with special fondness, and the literature on the subject is astonishingly rich.[77] Genesis 1 is a fundamental resource for a Christian worldview. For well over a millennium, Christian writing on Genesis 1 was framed by an Aristotelian-Ptolemaic worldview where the earth sits motionless at the center of the universe; all the stars and the whole expanse of the heavens rotate around it. This Ptolemaic worldview also influenced the exegesis of the six-day period and gave rise to two distinct schools of thought. The one rejects the temporal character of the six days, for the most part ascribes visionary significance to them, sees the entire world as being created simultaneously at a single stroke, and frequently arrives at a variety of allegorical interpretations.[78] The other school adheres to the literal sense of the creation narrative, including that of the six days.[79] Roman Catholic Scholasticism and Protestant theology followed the second approach although the alternative exegesis of Augustine was consistently discussed with respect and never branded heretical.[80]

The Christian church is not confessionally tied to a specific scientific worldview. Resistance to the new Copernican cosmology did not chiefly come from the church and orthodoxy as such, in spite of claims so often made by critics of the faith.[81] Instead, it was Aristotelianism, which in the domains of science and religion, art and the church sought to maintain itself in the face of modernity.[82] Christianity and its worldview do not stand or fall with either Ptolemy or Copernicus. When Scripture speaks, as it indeed does, geocentrically and also explains the origin of things from a geocentric viewpoint, it uses the same language of ordinary daily experience spoken today even though our understanding of the movement of the heavenly bodies is different from biblical times. We can readily admit that the Bible writers shared the worldview universally assumed in their day but their normative teaching is not tied to it; presumed cosmologies are not normative. For example, from the perspective of this language employed by Scripture we can explain what is involved in the miracles narrated in Joshua 10:12–13; 2 Kings 20:9–11; and Isaiah 38:8. These are not intended as scientific accounts of an objective "standing

77. This literature has been exhaustively processed by O. Zöckler, *Geschichte der Beziehungen zwischen Theologie und Naturwissenschaft*, 2 vols. (Gütersloh: C. Bertelsmann, 1877–79); cf. idem, "Schöpfung und Erhaltung der Welt," *PRE³*, XVII, 681–704.

78. Included here are Philo, Clement, Origen, Athanasius, Augustine, Erigena, Abelard, Cajetan, Canus, Gonzales, and others, as well as Moses Maimonides.

79. This approach was followed by Tertullian, Basil, Gregory of Nyssa, Ephraem, and John of Damascus, among others.

80. Peter Lombard, *Sententiae in IV liberis distinctae*, 3rd ed., 2 vols. (Grottaferrata: Coleggi S. Bonaventurae et Claras Aquas, 1971–81), II, dist. 15, 5; T. Aquinas, *Summa Theol.*, I, qu. 74, art. 2.

81. Cf., e.g., J. W. Draper, *History of the Conflict between Religion and Science* (New York: D. Appleton, 1897).

82. E. Dennert, *Die Religion der Naturforscher*, 4th ed. (Berlin: Berliner Stadtmission, 1901), 13; R. Schmid, *Das naturwissenschaftliche Glaubensbekenntnis eines Theologen*, 2nd ed. (Stuttgart: Kielmann, 1906), 38–42 (ET: *The Scientific Creed of a Theologian*, trans. J. W. Stoughton from the 2nd German ed. [New York: A. C. Armstrong, 1906]).

still" of the sun and a "turning back" of its shadow. Even today we would describe the same phenomena in the same manner: Scripture reports the miracle as a fact; it does not tell us *how* it came about.

There is an important point here that must not be overlooked. Even if, in an astronomic sense, the earth is no longer central to us, it is definitely still central in a religious and an ethical sense.[83] Although human beings are, in many respects, the weakest of all creatures, they are still royally masters of the universe, the crown of creation. The earth may be a thousand times smaller than many other planets; in an ethical sense it is and remains the center. It is the only planet fit to be the dwelling place for higher beings.[84] Here the kingdom of God has been established; here the struggle between light and darkness is being waged; here, in the church, God is preparing for himself an eternal dwelling. To affirm this religious truth is not to make claims of physical cosmology or astronomy. Scientific information about the universe does not displace God. Some have said that they searched the heavens and did not see God. The universe with its measureless spaces remains a vast mystery to us, and those who do not find God in their immediate presence, in their heart and conscience, in the Word and the Christian community, will not find him in the universe either, even though they are equipped with the best telescopes that money can buy.

[272] The issue for Christian theology, then, is not the Copernican worldview. Theologians must take honest scientific data about the universe seriously, and are not restricted by particular cosmologies. It is on the question of origins, beginning with the genesis of the solar system and the earth, that there seems to be a major conflict between a certain scientific consensus and biblical revelation. Scientific theories attempt to explain the origin of the universe, of motion, and of organic beings from within the cosmos itself through its immanent forces. But this will not do: either one must acknowledge (in deistic fashion) that the original state of creation depends wholly on God's act, *or* one will have to view that chaotic state not only as the beginning of the present world system but also as the end and the destruction of a preceding world, and so on ad infinitum and thus *eternalize* matter and motion.[85] Even this view does not explain how matter turned into motion or how spiritual phenomena such as consciousness and thought come from matter alone. How could an unconscious, purposeless movement of atoms result in the formation of the universe? The chance of such an ordered whole originating

---

83. Ed. note: There is a remarkable irony of history here. The same "enlightened" scientific mind that no longer considered the earth as the center of the universe also unleashed the Enlightenment with its emphasis on the autonomous rational human person as the center of the universe.

84. Cf. A. R. Wallace, *Man's Place in the Universe*.

85. F. A. Lange, *Geschichte des Materialismus*, II, 522; D. F. Strauss, *Der alte und der neue Glaube* (Leipzig: Hirzel, 1872), 225; Ludwig Büchner, *Kraft und Stoff*, 133 (ET: *Force and Matter; or Principles of the Natural Order of the Universe*, 4th ed., trans. from the 15th German ed. [New York: P. Eckler, 1891]); Ernst Haeckel, *The Riddle of the Universe at the Close of the Nineteenth Century*, trans. Joseph McCabe (New York: Harper & Brothers, 1900), 249–50.

from such a chaotic state is highly improbable and actually quite impossible. "It is just as simple to regard the creation as a playful vagary of chance as to explain a Beethoven symphony from marks and dots that have accidentally appeared on a piece of paper."[86]

Even if such a hypothesis explained the phenomena—which it does not—it remains a hypothesis that cannot be proven; constructs may have some use but this does not yet make them into actual explanations of existing reality—they remain constructs. For what conclusion can be drawn for reality from a possibility? Here we must turn to revelation to give us what no natural science can teach us, revelation that is confirmed by the tradition of all peoples. It teaches us that it has pleased God, in forming the world, to proceed from the imperfect to the perfect, from the simple to the complex, from the lower to the higher. That is the element of truth in the theory of evolution recognized in Scripture, as Genesis 1:2 clearly shows. Scripture is not an alternative scientific theory into which current natural science hypotheses need to be fit. Apologists who attempt this err in failing to see the Genesis account as the only way in which we are able to speak with conviction and certainty about the world's origins. Genesis 1 gives us what science is incapable of producing: an answer to the question, "How did the world begin?" As Christian theologians wrestle with these matters, they must take the data of natural science seriously as general revelation, but realize that only special, biblical revelation can describe the true state of the world.

THE BIBLE AND GEOLOGY

[273] When we consider the history of the earth's development we encounter similar difficulties as we did with questions about the formation of the solar system. Geology, basing itself on the strata of the earth's crust and the fossils of plants, animals, and humans found in those strata, has formed hypotheses about the different periods of the earth's development that also raise questions about Scripture's teaching. Since geological theory is based on data yielded by the study of the strata of the earth's crust, any conflict between revelation and science is serious. Two areas in particular require our attention: the matter of *time* and the *order* (sequence) in which the various creatures originated. As to the *time,* the difference is very striking. Even allowing for differences between the Hebrew text of the Old Testament and the Septuagint (LXX), the biblical chronology suggests a young earth of roughly six thousand years. Geological time, by contrast, is measured in millions and even billions of years.[87] In terms of *order*, the geological order is simply irreconcilable with the order of Genesis 1.

---

86. Oswald Heer, according to Eberhard Dennert, *Moses oder Darwin?* 2nd ed. (Stuttgart: Kielman, 1907), 50.

87. Ed. note: Bavinck speaks of 20 million years as his maximum; one hundred years later the figure has gone to 14–15 billion years.

[274] Attempts at reconciling the biblical and geological accounts have met with mixed success. The *ideal* theory views Genesis 1 not as a historical account but as a literary, poetic, even allegorical description of the creating acts of God. The six days are not chronology but different lens angles on the one created world that give the limited human eye a better overview of the whole. This approach is not new and only a response to the modern geological challenge; its noteworthy early church proponents were Origen and Augustine.[88] Traveling down this road, modern philosophy and theology regards Genesis 1 as a *myth* with, at best, a religious core. A second approach is the so-called *restitution* theory that separates Genesis 1:2 and 1:3 and inserts all the events and phenomena that geology teaches us into the period before the chaos mentioned in verse 2. It views the תֹהוּ וָבֹהוּ as the term describing a destruction caused by the preceding great catastrophes. The six-day unit that begins with verse 3 then recounts the *restoration* from that state of destruction and the preparation of the earth as a dwelling place for humanity. This view was held by the Remonstrants Episcopius and Limborch, who posited the fall of the angels between Genesis 1:1 and 2,[89] and by nineteenth-century theosophists such as Schelling, Keerl, Delitzsch, and others. A third theory, *concordism*, tries to harmonize Scripture and science by viewing the days of creation as long periods of time. This view also goes back to the early church and has been revived in the modern era.[90] Some scholars combine concordism with the restitution theory and content themselves simply with agreement on essentials.[91] Finally, there is a fourth theory, sometimes called the *antigeological* theory, which continues to hold the literal and historical view of Genesis 1 and gives great geological significance to the Noahic flood as a catastrophic event that fundamentally altered the earth's axis.[92] Debates then follow about whether the Genesis flood was truly universal or only local.

[275] These four attempts to harmonize Scripture and science are not all mutually exclusive. Everyone agrees that Scripture does not speak the language of science but that of daily experience; that in telling the story of creation it assumes

88. Ed. note: See Augustine, *On Genesis*, vol. I/13 (*The Works of Saint Augustine: A Translation for the 21st Century*, trans. and ed. Edmund Hill, OP, Matthew O'Connell, John E. Rotelle, OSA [Hyde Park, NY: New City, 2002]); cf. idem, *Confessions*, bks. 11–13.

89. Simon Episcopius, *Institutiones theologicae*, in vol. 1 of *Opera theologica*, 2 vols. (Amsterdam: Johan Blaeu, 1650–65), IV, sect. 3, 3; Phillip van Limborch, *Theologica christiana ad praxin pietatis ac promotionem pacis christianae unice directa* (Amsterdam: Wetstein, 1735), II, 19–21.

90. Ed. note: Important recent volumes articulating forms of concordism are Hugh J. Ross, *Genesis One: A Scientific Perspective* (Sierra Madre, CA: Wiseman Productions, 1983); Davis A. Young, *Christianity and the Age of the Earth* (Grand Rapids: Zondervan, 1982), chaps. 3 and 4, for a history of concordism and critique; idem, *Creation and the Flood: An Alternative to Flood Geology and Theistic Evolution* (Grand Rapids: Baker Books, 1977), 81–134.

91. O. Zöckler, *Geschichte der Beziehungen zwischen Theologie und Naturwissenschaft*, II, 544.

92. This view gained credence after Newton and was set forth by Thomas Burnet in his *Theoria sacra telluri* (1682), followed in 1696 by William Whiston, *A New Theory of the Earth* (New York: Arno, 1978 [reprint of 1696 edition by R. Roberts for B. Tooke, London]).

a geocentric or anthropocentric viewpoint; and that in this connection it is not providing a lesson in geology or any other science but remains the book of religion, revelation, and the knowledge of God. "We do not read in the Gospel that the Lord said: 'I will send to you a Paraclete who will teach you about the course of the sun and the moon!' For he wanted to make Christians, not mathematicians."[93] At the same time, we must insist on the historical rather than merely mythical, poetic, or visionary character of the Genesis creation story. It is remarkable, nonetheless, that church confessions do not make fixed pronouncements about Genesis 1; Christian theology permits a variety of interpretations to exist side by side. With Augustine, whose warning was all too often ignored, we urge modesty here; avoid quick judgments about seeming conflict, enter the discussion only after serious study, and do not make yourself ridiculous in the eyes of unbelieving science by your ignorance.[94] We can, therefore, learn much from the relatively young sciences of geology and paleontology and have nothing to fear from the *facts* they bring to light. The world, too, is a book whose pages have been inscribed by God's almighty hand. Conflict arises only because both the book of Scripture and the book of nature are often so badly read and poorly understood. Theologians are to blame when they condemn science, not in the name of Scripture but of their own incorrect views; natural scientists are to blame when they interpret the facts and phenomena they discovered in a manner, and in support of a worldview, that is justified neither by Scripture nor by science. All are called to modesty, patience, and tentativeness in making pronouncements.

With these provisional remarks in place, I will venture a few suggested interpretations. It is probable, in the first place, that the creation of heaven and earth in Genesis 1:1 preceded the work of the six days in verses 3ff. by a shorter or longer period. This is not to support the *restitution* theory since the text does not say that the earth *became* waste and void, but that it was so and was so created. A day in Genesis begins and ends with the morning; thus days of morning and evening exist only after the creation of light on day one. Augustine, Thomas, and many others rightly judged therefore that the creation of heaven and earth, and the תֹהוּ וָבֹהוּ state of the earth, occurred before any day existed.[95] We are not told in how much time and in what manner God created heaven and earth, or how long the unformed state of the earth lasted. Only when the six-day work begins are we told that also the unformed earth is maintained and made fruitful by the Spirit of God (Gen. 1:2), and that all things on and in that earth have been brought into being by the Word of God (Gen. 1:3ff.).

[276] We must also proceed with caution in considering the remaining days in which the earth was formed and made into an abode for humans. Differing opinions are permitted on matters not essential to the faith. Whether one takes

93. Augustine, *Proceedings against Felix the Manichee*, I, 10.
94. Augustine, *Literal Meaning of Genesis*, I, 18–21; cf. T. Aquinas, *Summa Theol.*, I, qu. 68, art. 1.
95. Augustine, *Confessions*, XII, 8; T. Aquinas, *Summa Theol.*, I, qu. 74, art. 2; W. G. T. Shedd, *Dogmatic Theology*, 2 vols. (New York: Charles Scribner's Sons, 1888–89), I, 474.

Joshua 10:12–13 as an argument against the Copernican worldview or uses concordist arguments to reconcile science and Scripture, we sin against Augustine's wise counsel not to become fixated on obscure matters in Scripture so that, when a clearer light should dawn over a passage, we would rather shine in defending our own opinion than fight for the meaning of Holy Scripture.[96] Not only does concordism run up against the deadly shoals of shifting geological science and fail to meet its goal of harmonizing Scripture with it, the days of Genesis refer to periods in which there is but one alteration of night and day, not numerous instances. This is sufficient reason for most scholars to abandon concordism and move on to the ideal, poetic, visionary, or even mystical theory.[97] In itself this is not objectionable; we acknowledge that revelation can make use of a variety of genres, including parable and fable. However, this must not be determined arbitrarily but be clear from the text itself. The first chapter of Genesis does not give us grounds for considering it as poetry, vision, or myth; it clearly bears a historical character and forms the introduction to a book that presents itself from beginning to end as history. In addition, if we deny the historical character of the "days" then the entire order in which the creation came into being collapses, and we have removed the foundation for the institution of the week and the Sabbath, which according to Exodus 20:11 is grounded in the six-day period of creation and the subsequent Sabbath of God.

For these reasons we judge that the days of Genesis 1 are not to be identified with the periods of geology but as days, albeit extraordinary days. So much happens on each of the days that it is not likely that all these things took place within the span of a few hours. The biblical story, which is both sublime and simple, portrays the many and wonderful works of God of each day with a single brushstroke. Each day's work of creation must certainly have been much grander and more richly textured than Genesis summarily reports in its sublime narrative. For all these reasons "day," in the first chapter of the Bible, denotes the time in which God was at work creating. With every morning he brought into being a new world; evening began when he finished it. The creation days are the workdays of God. By a labor, resumed and renewed six times, he prepared the whole earth

96. Augustine, *Literal Meaning of Genesis*, bk. 1, chap. 18 (trans. John Hammand Taylor [New York: Newman, 1982], 41): "In matters that are obscure and far beyond our vision, even in such as we may find treated in Holy Scripture, different interpretations are sometimes possible without prejudice to the faith we have received. In such a case, we should not rush in headlong and so firmly take our stand on one side that, if further progress in the search of truth justly undermines this position, we too fall with it. That would be to battle not for the teaching of Holy Scripture but for our own, wishing its teaching to conform to ours, whereas we ought to wish ours to conform to that of Sacred Scripture." Cf. T. Aquinas, *Summa Theol.*, I, qu. 68, art. 1.

97. E.g., O. Zöckler, "Schöpfung," *PRE*³; J. Reinke, *Die Welt als That: Umrisse einer Weltansicht auf naturwissenschaftlicher Grundlage*, 4 vols. (Berlin: Gebruder Paetel, 1905), 481ff.; C. Holzhey, *Schöpfung, Bibel und Inspiration* (Mergentheim: Carl Ohlinger, 1902); Franz Hümmelauer, *Nochmals der biblische Schöpfungsbegriff* (Freiburg i.B.: Herder, 1898); M. Gander, *Naturwissenschaft und Glaube* (New York: Benziger Bros., 1905), 117.

and transformed the chaos into a cosmos. In the Sabbath command this pattern is prescribed to us as well; as for God, so also for man six days of labor are followed by a day of rest. In Israel the divisions of the liturgical calendar were all based on that time of creation. For the whole world it remains a symbol of the eons of this dispensation that will in God's own time culminate in the "day" of eternal rest, the cosmic Sabbath (Heb. 4).

[277] As we reflect more on the data of sciences such as geology, we need to remember that these facts are just as much words of God as those of Holy Scripture and to be accepted as such. But facts must be rigorously distinguished from their interpretation and so we do raise questions about this very young science, especially with respect to the length and duration of geological ages. Since geology can only describe conditions on earth at a given time, and nothing about their cause, origin, and duration, reconstructing the history of the earth from its phenomena is a precarious undertaking. Geology is very useful as an auxiliary science giving us important data, but it is not and cannot produce a history of creation; only conjecture remains. All birth, said Schelling, is from darkness into light; all origins are wrapped in obscurity. If no one tells us who our parents and grandparents are or were, we do not know it. Absent a creation story, the history of the earth is and remains unknown to us; geology can never rise to the level of the creation story. As the geologist Ritter von Holger very correctly and beautifully observes: "We have to contend with the unpleasant fact that we arrived at the theater only after the curtain had already fallen. We must attempt to guess the play that was presented from the decorations, set pieces, weapons, and so forth, that have been left behind on the stage (they are the paleontological discoveries or fossilizations); hence, it is entirely excusable if we make mistakes."[98]

Reading the geological record is fraught with uncertainty, in good measure because it is so fragmentary and consistency is hard to find. So much remains to be explored; so much is unknown. The assumption that current conditions are identical to those existing millions of years ago is plausible but unproven. In the words of one level-headed natural scientist: "We lack any precise standard for the calculation of prehistoric events or processes."[99] Using the fossil record is also not a sure thing. It is easy to fall into a pattern of circular reasoning especially for those who accept the theory of evolution as an a priori. It then becomes easy to overlook inconsistencies in geological layering[100] and ignore the evidence of rich realms of organic life differentiated in kinds but not augmented by transitional forms.[101] Thanks to the great distribution over the earth's surface of fossil records

98. In A. Trissl, *Das biblische Sechstagewerk vom Standpunkte der katholischen Exegese und vom Standpunkte der Naturwissenschaften*, 2nd ed. (Regensburg: G. J. Manz, 1894), 73.

99. A. Zittel, *Aus der Urzeit: Bilder aus der Schöpfungsgeschichte* (Munich: R. Oldenburg, 1875), 556.

100. Friedrich Pfaff, *Schöpfungsgeschichte* (Frankfurt a.M.: Heyder & Zimmer, 1877), 5.

101. F. Pfaff, *Schöpfungsgeschichte*, 667–709. According to *Glauben und Wissen* (March 1906): 104–5, G. H. Darwin in his South African lecture also stated the following: "We can compare the facts on which

of significant varieties of plant and animal life, all we can conclude is that they represent not so much the *time* in which these organic beings originated, but the higher or deeper *zones* in which they lived. If plants and animals now living throughout the world were suddenly buried in earth layers and had petrified we could only say something about their distribution; we could conclude absolutely nothing about the time of their origin either from the various kinds of fossils that emerged or from the different layers in which they occurred. Uncertainty pervades the evidence for distinguishing the geological periods, much less the causes of major changes from one to another and the cause of the diluvial formations and their distribution over the globe. Scientists are uncertain about the cause and the time of the formation of mountains and glaciers. The science of geology is still young and faces many unanswered questions.

[278] Then there is "the flood" (Gen. 6–9)—a story tradition found among virtually all peoples—to complicate matters even more. This flood is cataclysmic, bringing immense changes in the world. According to Scripture, before the flood, humankind was distinguished by great intellect, a vigorous enterprising spirit, titanic courage, greatly extended life expectancy, strong physiques, and appalling wickedness. But in the flood almost all people perished, numerous plant and animal species became extinct, nature was curbed, and a gentler dispensation was inaugurated, the one in which we live. It is only by and after the diluvium that the earth acquired its present form. None of this scriptural testimony is contradicted by geology, and the only difficult areas left are those of time: it is difficult to square the Noahic flood with what geology teaches about the diluvium; geological time requires a lot more than Scripture seems to permit. Over against this objection, however, we enlist the argument of Voetius: "No exact computation can be derived from Holy Scripture."[102] Dogmatism about biblical chronology and geological calculations alike should be avoided.

In summary: From the moment of creation in Genesis 1:1 to the flood, Scripture offers a time span that can readily accommodate all the facts and phenomena that geology and paleontology have brought to light in (the nineteenth) century. That is all theology needs to be concerned about; it should neither fear the sure results of science nor, in immoderate anxiety, make premature concessions to opinions of the day. Concordism is not a prudent strategy; what *is* consistent with Scripture is the scientific assumption of hierarchical order and progression in created reality: First, there was the inorganic creation; then came the organic creation, beginning with the plant kingdom; next followed the animal kingdom, and this again in the same order, first the aquatic, then the land animals, and among them

---

theories of evolution are based with a mixed and colorful heap of glass beads from which an astute person in search of truth picks out a few that he then arranges on a string, incidentally noticing that these beads look somewhat alike, . . . but the problem of introducing order in that pile of beads will probably always put the astuteness of the researcher to shame. . . . The immeasurable magnitude of the undiscovered will be forever there to humble the pride of humans."

102. Gisbert Voetius, *Selectae disputationes theologicae*, 5 vols. (Utrecht, 1648–69), V, 153.

especially the mammals.[103] Theology is the science of divine and eternal things; when wrestling with questions of natural science it should uphold its confessional convictions with dignity and honor and in patience.

FROM CREATION TO PRESERVATION: PROVIDENCE[104]

[301] When on the seventh day God completed his work that he had done, he rested (Gen. 2:2; Exod. 20:11; 31:17). God's resting was not occasioned by fatigue, nor did it consist of idleness. For God, creation is not "work"; preservation is not "rest." God's "resting" only indicates that he stopped producing new kinds of things (Eccles. 1:9–10); that the work of creation, in the true and narrow sense as producing things out of nothing, was over, and that he delighted in this completed work with divine pleasure (Gen. 1:31; Exod. 31:17; Ps. 104:31).[105] Creation now passes into preservation. These two are fundamentally distinct and yet so intimately connected that preservation itself can be called "creating" (Pss. 104:30; 148:5; Isa. 45:7; Amos 4:13). Preservation is no less a divine work than creation; God is not indolent but works always (John 5:17). All creation, from the beginning, exists only through and unto God (Neh. 9:6; Ps. 104:30; Acts 17:28; Rom. 11:36; Col. 1:15ff.; Heb. 1:3; Rev. 4:11). Creatures have no independent existence—which would, in fact, be an oxymoron, even nonexistence!—everything that is and occurs is subject to divine government. God cares for all his creatures, sees them all (Job 34:21; Ps. 33:13–14; Prov. 15:3), determines the boundaries of their habitation (Deut. 32:8; Acts 17:26), turns the hearts of all (Prov. 21:1), directs the steps of all (Prov. 5:21; 16:9; 19:21; Jer. 10:23; etc.), and deals with the host of heaven and the inhabitants of the earth according to his will (Dan. 4:35). They are in his hands as clay in the hands of a potter and as a saw in the hand of one who pulls it (Isa. 29:16; 45:9; Jer. 18:5; Rom. 9:20–21).

God's providential government extends particularly to his people. The history of God's people demonstrates that what other people meant for evil against them, God turned to their good (Gen. 50:20). When Scripture tells us that even the hairs on our heads are all numbered (Matt. 10:30) and that all things work together for our good (Rom. 8:28), we know that there is no such thing as chance or fate (Exod. 21:13; Prov. 16:33) but that God works all things according to the counsel of his will (Eph. 1:11). Scripture beautifully sums up all this in repeatedly speaking of

---

103. F. Pfaff, *Schöpfungsgeschichte*, 742.

104. Ed. note: The material that follows on providence (##301–6) is out of sequence from *Reformed Dogmatics*, volume II, where it is the brief concluding chapter of the volume. Placing it here in the chapter on creation makes it possible to have a chapter in this volume that provides a clearer demarcation between the two loci of theology proper and anthropology and also makes this chapter similar in length to others taken from volume II.

105. Augustine, *City of God*, XI, 8; XII, 17; idem, *Literal Meaning of Genesis*, IV, 8ff.; T. Aquinas, *Summa Theol.*, I, qu. 73; John Calvin, *Commentary on Genesis*, trans. J. King (Grand Rapids: Baker Academic, 1979), 103–5 (on Gen. 2:2).

God as a king who governs all things (Pss. 10:16; 24:7–8; 29:10; 44:4; 47:6–7; 74:12; 115:3; Isa. 33:22; etc.). God is King: the King of kings and the Lord of lords; a King who in Christ is a Father to his subjects, and a Father who is at the same time a King over his children; he is the true object of our faith in providence. Although this particularity is known only to believers, the general doctrine of providence is a "mixed article," known in part to all humans from God's revelation in nature and present in every—even in the most corrupt—religion. To deny this is to undermine religion; without it there is no room for prayer and sacrifice, faith and hope, trust and love. Why serve God, asks Cicero,[106] if he does not at all care about us? Even philosophy recognized and defended this providence of God.[107]

Nevertheless, the doctrine of providence as it comes to expression in pagan religion and philosophy is not Christian. The Christian posture toward creation's order is never fatalism; astrology is appalling superstition. Although providence in some form is known to all people, it is not seen as the gracious care of a loving heavenly Father. Philosophical reasoning does not comfort in times of distress and death, especially when the "god of the philosophers" (e.g., Aristotle's νοησις νοησεως; "thought thinking itself") exists in solitary self-contemplation outside the world, devoid of both will and action. There is not much help here! Stoic teaching identified foreknowledge (προνοια) with destiny (ειμαρμενη) and nature (φυσις), and Epicurus regarded providence as inconsistent with the blessedness of the gods.[108] Chance and fate ruled these kingdoms; fate always took a position behind and above the deity, whereas chance crept in to the lower creatures and minor events from below. "The big things the gods take care of; the little ones they ignore" (*magna Dei curant, parva negligunt*).[109]

[302] Christian belief in God's providence is not of that sort. Based on God's covenant promises, compassion and grace, it is a source of consolation and hope, of trust and courage, of humility and resignation (Pss. 23; 33:10ff.; 44:4ff.; 127:1–2; 146:2ff.; etc.). Providence is not a tenet of natural theology but an article of the Christian faith, arising from God's special providence at work in the cross of Christ and experienced in the forgiving and regenerating grace of God in one's own heart. Faith in Christ enables believers—in spite of all the riddles that perplex them—to cling to the conviction that the God who rules the world is the same loving and compassionate Father who in Christ forgave them all their sins, accepted them as his children, and will bequeath to them eternal blessedness. In

106. M. T. Cicero, *On the Nature of the Gods*, I, 2.

107. E.g., Socrates, in Xenophon, *Memorabilia*, I, 4; IV, 3; idem, *Oeconomicus*; Plato, *Leg.*, X, 901; idem, *Rep.*, X, 613A; Aristotle, *Eth. nic.*, X, 9; M. T. Cicero, "De Stoa," in *On the Nature of the Gods*, II; also see I, 2; III, 26; L. A. Seneca, *De providentia*; idem, *De beneficiis*; Plutarch, *De fortuna*; Plotinus, "On Fate" (*Enneads*, III, 1) and "On Providence" (*Enneads*, III, 2); Philo, *On Providence*; cf. Emil Schürer, *The History of the Jewish People in the Age of Jesus Christ (175 B.C.–A.D. 135)*, rev. and ed. Geza Vermes, Fergus Miller, and Matthew Black (Edinburgh: T&T Clark, 1979 [orig. ed., 1885]), III, 531ff.

108. E. Zeller, *Outlines of the History of Greek Philosophy*, trans. L. R. Palmer, 13th ed. (New York: Humanities, 1969), 217, 237.

109. M. T. Cicero, *On the Nature of the Gods*, II, 167.

all their suffering and tears Christians look forward with joy to the future with faith in God's fatherly hand.

In this connection it is noteworthy that Scripture does not use the abstract word "providence." Instead, it depicts the activity itself in salvation history; Scripture in its totality *is* the book of God's providence and it uses a variety of terms: creating (Pss. 104:30; 148:5); making alive (Job 33:4; Neh. 9:6); renewing (Ps. 104:30); seeing, observing, letting (Job 28:24; Ps. 33:14ff.); saving, protecting, preserving (Num. 6:24ff.; Pss. 36:6; 121:7–8); leading, teaching, ruling (Pss. 9:19–20; 25:5, 9; etc.); working (John 5:17); upholding (Heb. 1:3); caring (1 Pet. 5:7). Originating in philosophy, the word "providence" was taken over by the church fathers for use in Christian theology,[110] but they significantly changed its meaning. Originally, "providence" meant the act of foreseeing (*providentia*) or foreknowing (προνοια) what was to happen in the future. "Providence is that through which some future event is seen."[111] But the Christian faith does not understand the providence of God to mean a mere foreknowledge (*nuda praescientia*); it confesses that all things are not only known by God in advance but also determined and ordained in advance. Providence does not only involve God's mind but also his will. The origin and preservation of all things is not only a matter of foreknowledge, nor even the divine decree, but specifically in an omnipotent act of God. Hence, according to Scripture and the church's confession, providence is that act of God by which from moment to moment he preserves and governs all things.

The doctrine of providence has had a rocky road in the history of the Christian church and theology. Sometimes it was counted among God's attributes, then among the decrees (*opera Dei ad intra*), then to the outgoing works of God (*opera ad extra*). In the theology of the Reformation, providence was sometimes viewed as a "counsel" (*consilium*) according to which God governs all things,[112] then again as an external work of God.[113] Materially, such distinctions are not that important. Theologically, however, emphasizing the distinction between God's internal act (foreknowledge, purpose, and plan) and the *execution ad extra* is a significant modification. What is lost here is the true sense of *providentia*, the notion of "an order of things foreordained toward an end"; instead the focus is on the execution. From this flows the further distinction into preservation (*conservatio*) and government (*gubernatio*).[114]

110. J. C. Suicerus, "Pronoia," *Thesaurus ecclesiasticus* (Amsterdam: J. H. Wetsten, 1682).

111. "Povidentia est, per quam futurum aliquid videtur" (M. T. Cicero, *De inventione rhetorica*, II, 53).

112. Second Helvetic Confession, art. 6; Z. Ursinus, *Commentary on the Heidelberg Catechism*, trans. G. W. Willard (Grand Rapids: Eerdmans, 1954), qu. 27.

113. J. Calvin, *Institutes*, I.xvi.3–4; Johannes Polyander à Kerckhoven, André Rivet, Antonius Walaeus, and Antoine Thysius, *Synopsis purioris theologiae*, ed. H. Bavinck, 6th ed. (Leiden: Didericum Donner, 1881), XI, 3.

114. T. Aquinas, *Summa Theol.*, I, qu. 103–4; Bonaventure, *The Breviloquium*, trans. Jose De Vinck, in vol. 2 of *The Works of Bonaventure* (Paterson, NJ: St. Anthony Guilde Press, 1963), pt. II; Belgic Confession, art. 13; Heidelberg Catechism, Lord's Day 10, Q&A 27–28.

Later, to ward off pantheism and deism, concurrence or cooperation was inserted between the two. These additional nuances are helpful in countering an abstract use of "Providence" as a substitute for God himself. We should use the word with caution, in the way Scripture treats the matter.

[303] Providence is not merely foreknowledge but involves God's active will ruling all things, and includes preservation, concurrence, and government. The notion of concurrence was developed to ward off pantheism on the one side and deism on the other. In the former, providence coincides with the course of nature as blind necessity; in the latter, providence is replaced by pure chance, and God is removed from the world. Over against pantheism it was especially important to distinguish preservation from creation. Creation brings forth existence; preservation is persistence in existence. Failure to make this distinction results in the idea that providence coincides with the course of nature. Nature's laws are identical with God's decrees, and God's rule is simply "the fixed and immutable order of nature" or "the concatenation of natural things."[115] On that view there is no room for miracle, the self-activity of secondary causes, personality, freedom, prayer, sin, and religion as a whole. Nature is all that there is; its ironclad law is fixed and unchangeable; nature is our "fate." In this scenario, human hope is killed; we are bound to an irresistible blind force having neither consciousness nor will. Nothing can be farther from the Christian doctrine of God's wise, omnipotent, loving Fatherly care. God's will is the ground of our very being; our choices and actions fall within the nexus of causes and consequences of God's ordered creation.

On the other side of this spectrum stands deism, which separates God and the world and leaves the world simply to the independent insight and judgment of humans. The cosmos, once created, runs on its own power. This deistic worldview thus revives the pagan theory of chance; God is restricted to responding to what humans do; they act in complete freedom so that God neither knows nor governs what they do. The relation between God and the world is like that between a mechanical engineer and a machine. After making it and starting it, he leaves it to its own devices and only intervenes if something has to be repaired.[116] The Remonstrants shared this notion of nature's independence, considering preservation as a negative act of God only and rejecting the idea of concurrence.[117] From the middle of the seventeenth century onward a powerful emancipatory impulse gained ground and sought to free nature, world, humanity, science, and so forth, from God and to make them self-reliant in relation to him, to Christianity, church, and theology. This is the best of all possible worlds; endowed with intellect and

---

115. B. Spinoza, *Tractatus Theologico-Politicus*, trans. S. Shirley (Leiden: Brill, 1991), c. 3; F. Schleiermacher, *The Christian Faith* (1928), §46.

116. J. Volkel, *De vera religione libri quinque* (Racoviae, 1630), II, c. 7; Johann Crell, *Liber de Deo ejusque attributis*, vol. 4 of *Opera omnia* (Amsterdam: Irenicus Philalethes, 1656), c. 2–6; Otto Fock, *Der Socinianismus nach seiner Stellung in der Gesammtentwicklung des christlichen Geistes* (Kiel: C. Schröder, 1847), 496ff.

117. *Remonstrant Confession*, chap. 6; S. Episcopius, *Inst. Theol.* IV, sect. 4.

will, a self-sufficient humanity has more than adequate resources to manage on its own. Revelation, prophecy, miracles, and grace are totally redundant. Deism did not deny the existence of God, creation, or providence; on the contrary, it loved to refer to the "Supreme Being" and discoursed at length on providence. But it was not a vital faith. Acknowledging only a weak version of preservation—a kind of cooperative venture between humanity and the Creator—deism was from the outset anti-supranaturalistic. God is not truly involved in the world.

With the explosion of scientific knowledge in the nineteenth century, many more felt free to separate its pitiless and unchanging stability from God altogether; religion was relegated to the private sphere of values and morality. Because this private realm of the "spirit" was understood as the sphere of autonomy and freedom, notions of concurrence were superfluous. Others, such as the "ethical modernists" in the Netherlands,[118] set natural power and ethical power over against each other as though they were two warring Manichaean deities. This is a most serious error; not only is God removed from the world, but divine providential power is conceived as being in competition with human freedom. In this manner an attempt was made to exalt human autonomy; for humanity to have freedom God must be absent or powerless. God's sovereignty is viewed as a threat to humanity. An irreligious posture is the consequence; salvation for the Deist consists not in communion with God but in separation from him. The Deist's mind is at ease only in detachment from God, that is, in practical atheism. A Deist is a person who in a short life has not found the time to become an atheist. Deists get into trouble because they become conflicted with themselves; the area taken away from God's control then falls under the sway of another power, be it chance or fate. Pure subjectivism then must reign; nothing is or can be objectively "fortuitous." All things have a cause, and that cause is ultimately a component in the almighty and all-wise will of God.[119]

PRESERVATION, CONCURRENCE, GOVERNMENT

[304] The providence of God, thus distinguished from God's knowledge and decree and maintained against pantheism and Deism, is—in the beautiful words of the Heidelberg Catechism—"the almighty and ever present power of God by which he upholds, as with his hand, heaven and earth and all creatures and so rules them that . . . all things, in fact, come to us, not by chance but from his fatherly hand" (Lord's Day 10, Q&A 27). The doctrine of providence has enormous scope encompassing everything that exists and occurs in time. Although

---

118. Ed. note: Bavinck's reference here is to a mediating school of Dutch theology known as the *Ethischen*. See H. Bavinck, *Reformed Dogmatics*, I, 127 (#39), 171 (#53), 290–92 (#83), 372 (#102), 436 (#115), 471–72 (#123), 519–20 (#135); idem, *De Theologie van Prof. Daniel Chantepie de la Saussaye* (Leiden: D. Donner, 1884).

119. Cf. J. Calvin, *Institutes*, I.xvi.2, 9.

the doctrine of God's providence logically covers the entire scope of all God's decrees, extending to all topics covered in dogmatics, it is preferable to restrict the discussion to God's relation to his creation and creatures. Here we can speak of three aspects: "preservation," "concurrence," and "government." These do not divide the work of providence into materially and temporally distinct and successive parts for they are always integrally connected. From the very beginning, preservation is also government, and government is concurrence, and concurrence is preservation. Preservation tells us that nothing exists, not only no substance, but also no power, no activity, no idea, unless it exists totally from, through, and to God. "Concurrence" speaks of the same providence as an activity that affirms and maintains the distinct existence of creatures, and "government" describes the other two as guiding all things in such a way that the final goal determined by God will be reached. And always, from beginning to end, providence is one simple, almighty, and omnipresent power.

Unlike pantheism which denies creation, or deism which denies providence, theism maintains both and attempts for theoretical as well as practical reasons to elucidate both the unity and the distinction between the two. To acknowledge that, to see God's counsel and hand and work in all things and *also* to seek to develop creation's energies and gifts to the highest level of activity—*that* is the glory of the Christian faith and the secret of the Christian life. Scripture itself, on the one hand, describes providence as an activity of creation (Ps. 104:30), of speaking (Pss. 33:9; 105:31, 34; 107:25; Job 37:6), of sending out his Word and Spirit (Pss. 104:30; 107:25), of upholding (Heb. 1:3), so that all things exist from, through, and to God (Acts 17:28; Rom. 11:36; Col. 1:17). God is never idle. With divine potency he is always active in both nature and grace. Providence, therefore, is a positive act, not a giving of permission to exist but a causing to exist and working from moment to moment. Just as providence is a power and an act, so it is also an almighty and everywhere present power. God is immanently present with his being in all creatures; his providence extends to all creatures and nothing, however insignificant, falls outside God's providence. Providence is an activity of God as great, all-powerful, and omnipresent as creation; it is a continuous or continued creation. The two are one single act and differ only in structure.[120]

The language of "continued creation" is not meant to erase the distinction that exists between creation and providence. At the same time, we must honor Scripture's testimony that providence is a resting from the work of creation (Gen. 2:2; Exod. 20:11; 31:17). Considering providence as a seeing (Pss. 14:2; 33:13) or observing (Pss. 33:15; 103:3) presupposes the existence, the self-activity, and the freedom of the creature. Creation and providence are not identical; providence does not mean a moment by moment *creation ex nihilo.* This would destroy all continuity and the created causal order; creation then has only an "appearance

120. Augustine, *Literal Meaning of Genesis,* IV, 15; idem, *Confessions,* IV, 12; idem, *City of God,* XII, 17; T. Aquinas, *Summa Theol.,* I, qu. 104, art. 2; Z. Ursinus, *Commentary on the Heidelberg Catechism,* qu. 27.

of existence." Here creaturely independence, freedom, and responsibility disappear and historical development is impossible; God becomes the cause of sin. If providence is ever to be called a "creation," it must always be seen as a "continuous creation," not the original creation *ex nihilo*. Never to be forgotten: God is the same and it is his same omnipotent and omnipresent power that is at work both in creation and in providence. The difference between creation and preservation does not lie in God's being as such but in the relation that God assumes toward his creatures. Creation calls into being the things that are not; in preservation God summons those things that have received an existence distinct from his being to be used for his purposes. Creation yields existence, while preservation is persistence in existence. All this is a mystery far surpassing our understanding. The Christian believes that all things receive their existence from God and that, as existent creatures, increase in reality, freedom, and authenticity to the extent that their dependence on God increases. Our perfection increases as God more and more indwells us. In this sense preservation is greater than creation since it is the progressive and ever-increasing self-communication of God to his creatures.

[305] The providence of God does not cancel out secondary causes or human responsibility, a doctrine usually referred to as "concurrence." Here we consider "development," which can only proceed from a ready-made world, a cosmos, rather than a state of chaos or pure potency. Human beings were placed in creation not as helpless toddlers but as adults. Creation was formed as a diversity in unity with each creature receiving its own nature including the laws and principles by which it could develop. God conferred an order on all creatures, a law they cannot violate (Ps. 148:6), rooted in the counsel of God, a design that emerges in things great and small. This all comes from the Lord of hosts; he is wonderful in counsel and excellent in wisdom (Isa. 28:23, 29). One can say, therefore, that the world is pregnant with the causes of beings. "For as mothers are pregnant with unborn offspring, so the world itself is pregnant with the causes of unborn beings, which are not created in it except from that highest essence, where nothing is either born or dies, begins to be, or ceases to be."[121] This divine concurrence is rooted in God's active and immediate will that covers all creatures and all events. All things exist and live together in him (Acts 17:28; Col. 1:17; Heb. 1:3). God working through secondary causes does not mean they intrude between God and the effects with their consequences.

For that reason a miracle is not a violation of natural law, since God is no less involved with maintaining the ordinary order of the natural created world. In miracles God only puts into effect a special force that, like any other force, operates in accordance with its own nature and therefore also has an outcome of its own. At the creation God did build his laws into things, fashioning an order by which the things themselves are interconnected. Here we may speak of "causality," though never reduce it to mechanical causality only. There are laws and

---

121. Augustine, *The Trinity*, III, 9.

connections within creation in many spheres and we must honor their variation. Moral and intellectual relations have their own structure and law, as do various social institutions such as the family and civic life. In providence God respects and develops—and does not nullify—the things he called into being in creation. "It does not pertain to divine providence to corrupt the nature of things but to preserve [that nature]."[122] He thus governs angels in one way, humans another, and animals and plants in still different ways. In each case, then, he employs all sorts of creatures as means in his hand to fulfill his counsel and to reach his goal. By affirming the natural order of creation Christianity encouraged science and made it possible.[123] Deification and enchantment of nature hinders scientific progress; by ontologically separating the Creator and creature Christianity made it possible to see the study of nature as something other than a desecration of the sacred or a violation of deity. It also liberated human beings from all worship and dread of nature and gave them independent status vis-à-vis nature along with stewardly responsibility for it.[124] A believer bows down only before God; never any creature.

This is not fatalistic resignation. Nor may our legitimate responsibility become an excuse for overconfident arrogance about human ability. We are called to child-like submission to God and to exercising dominion over the earth as a service to God. There is, therefore, real piety in Cromwell's dictum: "Trust God and keep your powder dry." This honors God's sovereign providential rule *and* our human responsibility; it confesses *final* causality while respecting *secondary* or *efficient* causality. In pantheism there are no real causes; the immediate causes of things within the circle of created things are identified with the primary cause, which is God. Both materially and formally, God is the subject of all that happens, and hence also of sin. Accordingly, there are only phenomena, representations, and the only reality, power, and substance behind these phenomena is God himself.[125] Deism, on the other hand, has no real *secondary* causes because the primary cause is restricted to the original creation. In original Pelagianism God is included only in the original created possibility (*posse*) and excluded from the willing (*velle*) and doing (*facere*) of the human creature. In semi-Pelagianism (and synergism) the two causes are conceived as associated causes working with and alongside each other, like two draft horses pulling a wagon, though one may be stronger than the other.

---

122. T. Aquinas, *Summa Theol.*, II, 1, qu. 10, art. 4.

123. "Modern natural science, however paradoxical this may sound, owes its origin to Christianity" (E. H. DuBois-Reymond, *Culturgeschichte und Naturwissenschaft* [Leipzig: Veit, 1878], 28).

124. "The Hebrews faced the world and nature with sovereign self-awareness—being without fear of the world—but also with a sense of the utmost responsibility. As God's representative, humanity exercises dominion over the world but only as such. Human beings may not follow their arbitrary impulses but only the revealed will of God. Paganism, in contrast, alternates between presumptuous misuse of the world and childish dread before its powers" (R. Smend, *Lehrbuch der alttestamentlichen Religionsgeschichte* [Freiburg i.B.: Mohr, 1893], 453).

125. Cf. J. Kleutgen, *Die Philosophie der Vorzeit vertheidigt*, 2nd ed., 2 vols. (Münster: Theissing, 1878), II, 336–47; C. Hodge, *Systematic Theology*, I, 592.

Scripture, however, tells us both that God works all things so that the creature is only an instrument in his hand (Isa. 44:24; Pss. 29:3; 65:10; 147:15ff.; Matt. 5:45; Acts 17:25; etc.), *and* that providence is distinct from creation and presupposes the existence and self-activity of creatures (Gen. 1:11, 20, 22, 24, 28; etc.). Christian theology teaches that secondary causes are strictly subordinated to God as the primary cause, but nevertheless remain true causes. God makes possible every secondary cause and is present in it with his being at its beginning, progression, and end. He is "at work" [in us] "both to will and to do for his good pleasure" (Phil. 2:13). The primary and secondary causes remain distinct; the former does not destroy the latter and the second exists only as a result of the first. Secondary causes are genuine causes with a nature, vitality, spontaneity, manner of working, and law of their own. "Satan and evildoers are not so effectively the instruments of God that they do not also act in their own behalf. For we must not suppose that God works in an iniquitous man as if he were a stone or a piece of wood, but He uses him as a thinking creature, according to the quality of his nature, which He has given him. Thus, when we say that God works in evil doers, that does not prevent them from working also in their own behalf."[126] It is essential to keep this distinction clear if we are to speak faithfully about both God's sovereignty and human responsibility.

[306] Governance points to the final goal of providence: the perfection of God's kingly rule. It is not a third new element of providence, but implied in preservation and concurrence as the destiny of all creation in divine glory. God is King and his providence represents a kingly rule, a government. "King" is not to be set over against "Father," since the Old Testament and New Testament alike use both names for God (Ps. 103; Isa. 64:8; Mal. 2:10; Matt. 6:10, 13 [KJV], 33; 1 Tim. 1:17; 6:15; Rev. 19:6; etc.). All *patria* (lit., "fatherhood") in heaven and on earth derives its name from him who is the Father of our Lord Jesus Christ (Eph. 3:15). To speak of God as "king" is utterly fitting; the government of the universe is not democratic, nor aristocratic, nor republican, nor constitutional, but monarchical. To God belongs the one undivided legislative, judicial, and executive power. His sovereignty is original, eternal, unlimited, abundant in blessing. He is the King of kings and the Lord of lords (1 Tim. 6:15; Rev. 19:6). By his rule he upholds the world and establishes it so that it will not be moved (Ps. 93:1); he ordains the light and the darkness (Ps. 104:19–20), commands the rain and withholds it (Gen. 7:4; 8:2; Job 26:8; 38:22ff.), gives snow and hoarfrost and ice (Ps. 147:16), rebukes and stills the sea (Nah. 1:4; Pss. 65:7; 107:29), sends curses and destruction (Deut. 28:15ff.). This rule is comprehensive and definitive; no opposition stands a chance against him (Ps. 93:3–4); his kingdom *will* come (Matt. 6:10; 1 Cor. 15:24; Rev. 12:10); he *will* be king over the entire earth (Zech. 14:9); his kingdom is forever (Ps. 29:10; 1 Tim. 1:17; Rev. 5:13; 11:15).

126. J. Calvin, *Treatises against the Anabaptists and Libertines*, trans. B. W. Farley (Grand Rapids: Baker Academic, 1982), 245.

God's government over his rational creatures includes evil and those who love and do evil. Of course, God hates sin with his whole being, as all of Scripture testifies (Deut. 32:4; Ps. 5:4–6; Job 34:10; 1 John 5; etc.), and prohibits it in the law and judges it in time as well as eternity. At the same time the whole of Scripture also teaches that sin is subject to God's rule. God sometimes acts to stop it at its inception (Gen. 20:6; 31:7), destroys the counsel of the wicked (Ps. 33:10), gives strength to resist temptation (1 Cor. 10:13), and also inhibits the sinner through fear and trembling in his conscience. But God does not always prevent sin; he "permitted" Adam's fall and other human sins; he permits us to follow our own counsels (Ps. 81:12; Acts 14:16; 17:30) and gives people up to their own lusts (Rom. 1:24, 26, 28). He creates and arranges the opportunities and occasions for humans to be able to sin, to test them, strengthen and confirm their faith or to punish and to harden them (Gen. 27; Exod. 4:21; 7:3; etc.; 2 Chron. 32:31; Job 1; Matt. 4:1; 6:13; 1 Cor. 10:13). Evil acts that may at first appear to be arbitrary turn out later to have God's hand in them and be included in his counsel (Gen. 45:8; 2 Chron. 11:4; Luke 24:26; Acts 2:23; 3:17–18; 4:28). God is the potter and humans are the clay (Jer. 18:5ff.; Lam. 3:38; Isa. 45:7, 9; 64:7; Amos 3:6). God gives people over to their sins, allows them to fill the full measure of their iniquity (Gen. 15:16; Rom. 1:24), sends a strong spirit of delusion (2 Thess. 2:11), and sets Christ for the fall and rising of many (Luke 2:34; John 3:19; 9:39; 2 Cor. 2:16; 1 Pet. 2:8; etc.). Sin is never outside God's control; he restrains, restricts, or inhibits its momentum and even stops it with his judgment (Gen. 7:11; Exod. 15; Matt. 24:22; 2 Pet. 2:9). When he allows it to continue he directs it (Prov. 16:9; 21:1) and ultimately makes it subservient to the fulfillment of his counsel, the glorification of his name (Gen. 45:7–8; 50:20; Ps. 51:4; Isa. 10:5–7; Job 1:20–22; Prov. 16:4; Acts 3:13; Rom. 8:28; 11:36). While it is correct on occasion to speak of divine "permission," this must not be construed in such a way as to deny God's active sovereignty over sin and judgment.

Like sin (a culpable evil), so also suffering (a punitive evil) is subject to the dominion of God. Death, which was God's punishment and came at his command (Gen. 2:17), and all disasters and adversities, all sorrow and suffering, all afflictions and judgments, are imposed on humanity by God's omnipotent hand (Gen. 3:14ff.; Deut. 28:15ff.; etc.). Faith always wrestles with the dissonance that exists in this life between sin and punishment, holiness and blessedness (Ps. 73; Job; Ecclesiastes), and has no "solution" to it. What faith does is cling to the royal power and fatherly love of the Lord. The prosperity of the wicked is illusory while the righteous, even in their deepest suffering, still enjoy the love and grace of God (Ps. 73; Job). The suffering of the faithful is frequently rooted not in their personal sin but in the sin of humanity and has its goal in the salvation of humankind and the glory of God. Suffering serves different ends: retribution (Rom. 1:18, 27; 2:5–6; 2 Thess. 1–2); testing and chastisement (Deut. 8:5; Job 1:12; Ps. 118:5–18; Prov. 3:12; Jer. 10:24; 30:11; Heb. 12:5ff.; Rev. 3:19); reinforcement and confirmation (Ps. 119:67, 71; Rom. 5:3–5; Heb. 12:10–11; James

1:2–4); witness to the truth (Ps. 44:24; Acts 5:41; Phil. 1:29; 2 Tim. 4:6–8); and to glorify God (John 9:2). In Christ, suffering is the road to glory; all things are being led to the establishment of God's kingdom, the revelation of his attributes, the glory of his name (Rom. 11:32–36; 1 Cor. 15:18; Rev. 11:15; 12:10; etc.).

Many mysteries and riddles remain in our consideration of providence. But God shines the light of his Word over all these enigmas and mysteries, not to solve them but that "by steadfastness and by the encouragement of the Scriptures we might have hope" (Rom. 15:4). The doctrine of providence is not a philosophical system but a confession of faith that, notwithstanding appearances, only God—by his almighty and everywhere present power—preserves and governs all things. This conviction spares us from superficial optimism and presumptuous pessimism alike; we neither deny life's riddles nor wallow in despair. The providence of God encompasses all things, not only the good but also sin and suffering, sorrow and death; it would be an impoverished faith that only saw God's hand and counsel in momentous, miraculous, and good things but not in the ordinary, the seemingly insignificant, and painful. There is, furthermore, no power in a faith that recommends stoical indifference or fatalistic acquiescence as true godliness. Rather, the almighty and everywhere present power of God makes us grateful when things go well and patient when things go against us, prompts us to rest with childlike submission in the guidance of the Lord, and at the same time arouses us from our inertia to the highest levels of activity. In all circumstances of life, it gives us good confidence in our faithful God and Father that he will provide whatever we need for body and soul and that he will turn to our good whatever adversity he sends us in this sad world, since he is able to do this as almighty God and desires to do this as a faithful Father.[127]

127. Cf. Heidelberg Catechism, Lord's Days 9 and 10, Q&A 26–28.

PART III

HUMANITY AND SIN

11

THE IMAGE OF GOD

HUMAN ORIGINS

[279] Humanity, where the spiritual and material world are joined together, is the crowning culmination of creation. Created on the sixth day (Gen. 1:26ff.), following the creation of the land animals, human beings, male and female, share a kinship with animals.

There is also a major difference: animals were brought forth by the earth at God's command (Gen. 1:24); humanity, however, was created, after divine deliberation, in God's image, to be master over all things. This is confirmed by the two creation accounts in Genesis 1 and 2: chapter 1 offers a general history of creation, which has its goal and end in humanity; chapter 2 deals especially with the human creation and the relation of humans to other creatures. In the first report humanity is the crown of creation; in the second the beginning of history. Genesis 1 provides a more detailed report of creation in general and treats the creation of humanity succinctly; Genesis 2 presupposes the creation of heaven and earth, follows a topical order, and describes relationships of humans to other creatures. Genesis 2:4b–9 does not imply that the plants were formed after humans, but only that the Garden of Eden was planted after that event. Similarly, in Genesis 2:18ff., the intention is not to describe the objective course of creational events but only to show that a helper for man was not to be found among the animals and required a being like himself. The account of the creation of the woman does not conflict with that in Genesis 1 but is a further explication of it.

This divine origin of humankind has never been questioned in the Christian church and in Christian theology. But outside special revelation we find all sorts of conjectures like those of pagan sagas that attribute human creation to the gods or the demigods.[1] Others regard human beings as having emerged autochthonously from the earth, or evolved from some other animal, or as the fruit of some tree, and so forth. Of the many alternative conjectures about human origins that have been ventured outside of scriptural revelation, the hypothesis of Darwinian evolutionism through natural selection is dominant in our world. The Christian objection here is not to the idea of development as such, which goes back to Greek philosophy, but to the naturalism and materialism of the Darwinian hypothesis. Darwin's claim to fame is that he not only made numerous observations underscoring the kinship between humans and animals, but that he made them serviceable to a hypothesis that humans had descended from animal ancestors. Darwin's thesis, or rather, hypothesis, is this: species have no constant properties but are mutable; all higher organic beings including man have evolved from lower ones, from the higher apes; all organic matter, in turn, emerged from the inorganic under the sway of purely mechanical and chemical laws. The evolutionary mechanism by which this is accomplished is called "natural selection," the process by which nature selects the most fit species for survival and reproduction. None of this, of course, can be proved; instead we see assumptions and conjectures on the basis of kinship between organisms, the possibility of mutation and subsequent transmission of properties, and from embryology and the paleontological record.

[280] This theory has been seriously opposed, not only by Bible-believers but also by natural scientists and philosophers more broadly. At the end of the nineteenth century the intellectual life of people underwent a remarkable change. Although an array of brilliant results had been achieved in the natural sciences, in culture, and in technology, the human heart had been left unsatisfied, and so people turned from intellectualism to mysticism, from exact science to philosophy, from mechanism to dynamism, from dead matter to the vital force, from atheism back to pantheism. Monistic thought came to acknowledge that even materialism with its matter and force had not overcome dualism, and philosophical idealism yielded the insight that matter and all of nature are only given us in the form of an idea. As naturalism and materialism demonstrated spiritual bankruptcy, this new mystical and even pantheistic spirituality further discredited Darwinism. The critique of Darwinism includes at least the following four elements.

In the first place, the theory of descent has proved completely unable adequately to explain the origin of life. The explanation that an accidental combination of inorganic materials could produce organic entities (*generatio aequivoca*; "ambiguous generation") was proved untenable by Pasteur; subsequent explanations that "life seeds" (germs or protoplasm) had come from other planets by way of meteorites (Helmholtz, Thomson), or that life cells were eternal, all fail to satisfy the mind

1. Hesiod, *Works and Days*, I, 23–25; Ovid, *Metamorphoses*, I, 82ff., 363ff.

or heart and demonstrate a kind of desperation.[2] Consequently, many natural scientists have therefore returned to vitalism. Second, Darwinism is incapable of explaining the further development of organic entities. Whereas Scripture teaches that the essential diversity and dissimilarity of creatures is rooted in God's creative omnipotence, in Darwinism this diversity and dissimilarity of creatures, specifically of organic entities, remains a riddle. It is increasingly recognized that this diversity cannot be inferred from one single organism or even from four or five original organisms.[3] Both morphologically and physiologically the species are much too divergent. Transitions from one species into the other have never been observed, and natural and sexual selection are insufficient to make them possible, also because it is not sure that acquired traits are transmitted by heredity. Totally contrary to Darwin's theory, morphological properties are the most variable. If morphological changes proceed at a slow rate and were each time of little significance, they would be more of a handicap than an advantage in times of transition. For as long as breathing through gills changed into breathing by lungs, the process was more a hindrance than an advantage in the struggle for existence. For all these reasons, natural scientists would do well to refrain from making judgments too quickly and dogmatically. Darwinism is both historically and logically the result of philosophy, not of experimental science. Darwin himself even acknowledged that many of the views he presented were highly speculative.[4]

Darwinism is particularly problematic on the question of human origins. It has not provided conclusive positive proof of human descent from animal ancestry. Arguments from ontogeny[5] or the fossil record of human bones and skulls all flounder in the absence of transitional forms. There is an essential difference between humans and animals. Even more devastating is the failure of Darwinism to account for the psychic dimension of our humanity. Attempts to derive all human mental phenomena (consciousness, language, religion, morality, etc.) from those of animals have not been successful. Like the origin of movement, the origination of life, and teleology, so also human consciousness, language, freedom of the will, religion, and morality still belong to the enigmas of the world awaiting

2. In an essay ("Geist oder Instinkt," *Neue kirchliche Zeitschrift* [1907]: 39), Edmund Hoppe correctly comments: "Darwinism has ceased to produce an explanation of the theory of evolution; in its place has come the spiritualization of matter and voila! evolution has been rescued."

3. "There is no evidence at all in support of a monophyletic phylogeny" (Erich Wasmann, *Biology and the Theory of Evolution*, trans. A. M. Buchanan, 3rd ed. [St. Louis: B. Herder, 1923], 291).

4. Charles Darwin, *The Descent of Man* (New York: D. Appleton and Co., 1871), 620.

5. Ed. note: "Ontogeny recapitulates phylogeny." The theory that the embryonal development of an individual organism (its ontogeny) followed the same path as the evolutionary history of its species (its phylogeny) was proposed in 1866 by the German zoologist Ernst Haeckel (cf. *The History of Creation, or, The Development of the Earth and Its Inhabitants by the Action of Natural Causes* [*Natürliche Schöpfungsgeschichte*], trans. and rev. E. R. Lankester, 2 vols. [New York: D. Appleton, 1883]); idem, *The Riddle of the Universe at the Close of the Nineteenth Century*, trans. Joseph McCabe (New York: Harper & Brothers, 1900). Though discredited in its literal form, it continues to have advocates; see Stephen Jay Gould, *Phylogeny and Ontogeny* (Cambridge MA: Belknap Press, Harvard University Press, 1985).

resolution. The relation of the mind to our brain is quite unlike that of bile to the liver or urine to the kidneys. In the words of Max Müller, language is and remains the Rubicon between us and the animal world. The psychological explanation of religion is untenable and the derivation of morality from human social instincts alone fails to account for the imperatives of the good, for conscience, responsibility, the sense of sin, repentance, remorse, and punishment. Darwinism thus tends toward materialism, finds there its most significant support, and hence subverts religion and morality and destroys our humanness. If we are not *fallen* and *human* image bearers of God but only highly developed animals we are degraded as responsible, religious, moral beings. From the standpoint of evolution, humanity as the image of God cannot be maintained. The theory of evolution forces us to return to creation as Scripture presents it to us.

[281] The theory of evolution also clashes with Scripture on questions about the age, the unity, and the original abode of humanity. Many peoples of the world attribute great age to humanity; some speak of multiple world ages and of myriads and hundreds of thousands of years. Modern anthropology reintroduces these fabulous figures without much consistency; these numbers range between 10,000 and 500,000 years and even more.[6] Taking the theory of evolution seriously, calculations about how long it would take for the human eye to develop from a tiny spot of pigment and for the brains of mammals to develop from an original ganglion, and then multiplying these figures to account for all life on earth, the estimates become truly fantastic. Darwin himself in the first edition of his *Origin of Species* came to a figure of 300 million years for the age of life on earth, and others used even higher figures.[7] More recent figures narrow the range from 10 million to 100 million years—an uncertain figure subject to modification at a moment's notice[8]—and thus place the origin of life and of humanity much closer. Calculations based on geology are hypothetical and far from being certain. The data do not settle the matter.

We do, however, have some chronological data furnished by the history and monuments of different peoples, notably Egypt and Babylonia. Here, as Scripture itself teaches, we undoubtedly have ancient civilizations already existing as far as we can go back in history. But the chronology is nevertheless still so uncertain that one cannot base much on it. It is a labyrinth without a thread to guide the inquirer. Only in the case of the people of Israel can we actually speak of a history and a chronology. The chronology for the first thousand years before Christ is fairly well established, sometimes down to the details; in the second thousand years before Christ we seem to have been given only a few fixed reference points; and in the third thousand years, that is, before 2000 BC, everything is uncer-

6. A. R. Wallace, for example, speaks of a half million years, according to James Orr, *God's Image in Man and Its Defacement in the Light of Modern Denials* (London: Hodder & Stoughton, 1906), 166.

7. Hugo de Vries, *Species and Varieties*, ed. Daniel Trembly MacDougal, 2nd ed., corr. and rev. (Chicago: Open Court, 1906), 14; cf. J. Orr, *God's Image in Man*, 176.

8. J. Orr, *God's Image in Man*, 168.

tain.[9] We are thus led to a time that is not much beyond five thousand to seven thousand years before Christ, though we need to recognize that scholars are far from having reached agreement about the chronology of the Bible.

[282] There can be no doubt that Scripture teaches the unity of the human race (Gen. 1:26; 6:3; 7:21; 10:32; Matt. 19:4; Acts 17:26; Rom. 5:12ff.; 1 Cor. 15:21f., 45f.). Except for the Stoa which taught that all human beings formed one single inclusive body (*systeµma politikon*) and hence proclaimed universal justice and love,[10] this doctrine has almost never been acknowledged by those outside the circle of revelation. The Greeks proudly looked down on "barbarians," and the peoples of India created four castes of people, each of whom had a distinct origin. Following the Renaissance the idea of various origins of the human race again surfaced in the form of true *polygeneticism*, or *coadamitism*, that is, the descent of different races from different ancestors, or as *preadamitism*, that is, the descent of savage dark-skinned peoples from an ancestor before Adam, while Adam was considered the ancestor of the Jews or also of white humanity.[11] The notion of multiple origins became more plausible when in the eighteenth century knowledge of the peoples of the world gained currency and people began to realize the great diversity in color, hair, build, customs, etc. After 1860, Darwinism was added to these views, and many of its adherents became polygenetic even though the theory of variability in it could very well be used to defend monogeneticism. Darwinism cannot settle the question concerning the origin and age of humanity; the transition from animal to man occurred so slowly that there really was no first man.

Now the existence of various peoples and races within humanity is most certainly an important issue, whose solution we are not even close to finding. The differences in color, hair, skull, language, ideas, religion, mores, customs, and so on are so great and the expansion of the one human race over the globe—for example, to the South Sea islands and America—so unknown that the idea of the different origins of peoples can hardly surprise us. What Scripture teaches is that a single act of God in which he intervened in the development of humanity (Gen. 11) led to this variation. Most importantly, this scattering and diversification has a deep religious-ethical meaning. Isolation and intensification of language differences lead to intellectual and spiritual decline. The confusion of languages is the result of confusion in ideas, in the mind, and in life. Even then, with all that division and brokenness, unity has been preserved. As our knowledge of

9. According to F. Hommel, *Geschichte des alten Morgenlandes* (Leipzig: Göschen, 1895), 38.

10. E. Zeller, *Die Philosophie der Greichen*, 3 vols. (Leipzig: Fues [O. R. Reisland], 1879–1920), IV, 287ff.

11. The last of these views was promulgated by Isaac de la Peyrère, who in 1655 published (without indicating the name of the author, the printer, or the place) a small work titled *Praeadamitae* and subtitled *Systema theologiae ex praeadamitarum hypothesi.* Here he asserted that (with an appeal to Gen. 4:14, 16–17; 6:2–4) people had existed long before Adam and had not sinned positively against the law. His views were kept alive by Bayle, Arnold, and Swedenborg, and used to defend slavery against Wilberforce.

linguistics improves we increasingly find kinship and unity of origin in languages that in the past were not even remotely suspected of any; absolute classification remains elusive. Genesis 10, accordingly, maintains the unity of the race in the face of all diversity, and Johann von Müller with good reason said, "All history must start with this chapter."

Here Darwinism cannot raise objections against a common origin and even furnishes a conceptual framework for explaining the possibility of a wide assortment of changes within a given species as a result of various external influences. However great the difference between the races may be, the deeper unity and kinship is obvious. People of the most diverse races can mate and produce fertile children, share physiological and social attributes and practices, and have many intellectual, religious, moral, social, and political dimensions in common. The unity of the human race, as Scripture teaches, is powerfully confirmed by all this. This affirmation of unity is not a matter of indifference but of the utmost importance: it is the presupposition of religion and morality. The solidarity of the human race, original sin, the atonement in Christ, the universality of the kingdom of God, the catholicity of the church, and the love of neighbor—these all are grounded in the unity of humankind.

[283] Finally, there is the difference over the original abode of humankind. Genesis 2 relates that God, after he had created Adam, planted a garden in Eden (2:8). This *ʿēden* (delight, land of delight) is therefore not identical with paradise but a region in which the garden (LXX *paradeisos*) was planted. This paradise is then called "the garden of Eden" (Gen. 2:15; 3:23), "the garden of God" (Ezek. 31:8–9), "the garden of the LORD" (Isa. 51:3), and is sometimes equated with Eden (Isa. 51:3; Ezek. 28:13; 31:9). A river flows from the garden and divides into four heads or branches, which are named Pishon, Gihon, Hiddekel, and Phrath. The last two rivers are the Tigris and the Euphrates; but about the first two there has always been disagreement. Some interpreted this allegorically,[12] and most avoided trying to identify the geographic location of paradise until Augustine Steuchus of Gubbio, called Eugubinus (d. 1550), who in his work *Kosmopoiia* (Lyons, 1535) developed the hypothesis that the four rivers are the estuaries of one vast river, the so-called Tigris-Euphrates, and paradise is therefore situated near the present city of Corna. Roman Catholic and Protestant scholars alike warmly accepted this suggestion. Around the middle of the seventeenth century, another proposal, the so-called Armenia hypothesis, argued that the rivers could be located in a much more northern area, namely, Armenia. By contrast, Friedrich Delitzsch in his work, *Wo lag das Paradies?* (Leipzig: Hinrichs, 1881), looked for the location of paradise in a more southern direction: in the landscape of Babylon. Others treat the account as a saga in which Pishon and Gihon originally denote the Indus and the Oxus (J. D. Michaelis, Knobel, Bunsen, Ewald, and others), and still others regard

---

12. Augustine says there were three views on paradise; see his *Literal Meaning of Genesis*, VIII, 1.

it as a myth in which Havilah represents the golden land of the saga, and the Gihon is the Ganges or the Nile.[13]

Most anthropologists and linguists no longer take any account of Genesis 2 at all and mention a variety of countries as the original abode of humanity. But they are far from unanimous and have bestowed this honor on practically all countries. For that matter, many scholars assume not just a single original abode of man, but believe that the evolution from animal to man occurred in various parts of the earth, thus combining Darwinism with polygeneticism (e.g., Haeckel and others). These conjectures are an indication of science's inability to speak with certainty here. Ethnology, linguistics, history, and the natural sciences furnish us data that make plausible the choice of Asia as the original abode of man and that choice comports perfectly with biblical teaching. In Asia we find the most ancient peoples, the most ancient civilization, the most ancient languages; all of ancient history points us to this continent. From within this part of the earth Europe, Africa, Australia, and also America have been populated. Granted, in this connection many questions arise to which we do not yet know the answers. But this ignorance does not give us reason to overthrow the teaching of Scripture that Asia is the cradle of humanity. About the location of paradise and Eden, the different opinions suggest that the precise geography may no longer lie within our capacity to determine, but Scripture and science unite in the witness that it is in Asia that we must look for the original abode of man.

HUMAN NATURE

[284] To be human is to be an image bearer of God, created in his likeness and originally righteous and holy. The entire world reveals God's attributes and perfections, and every creature is in its own way the embodiment of God's thought. But only human beings are *images* of God, head and crown of the whole creation, both μικροθεος (microgod) and μικροκοσμος (microcosm). Even pagans recognized this and speak of humans as God's kin and offspring. In addition, virtually all peoples have traditions of a golden age of innocence and bliss, of full communion with the gods. These stories were celebrated in song by the poets Hesiod, Ovid, and Virgil, and acknowledged by philosophers. Only Scripture, however, sheds a full and true light on this doctrine of man's divine likeness. The first creation narrative tells us that God created humanity in his image and likeness (MT: בְּצַלְמֵנוּ כִּדְמוּתֵנוּ; LXX: κατ' εἰκονα ἡμετεραν και καθ' ὁμοιωσιν; Vulg.: *ad imaginem et similitudinem nostram,* Gen. 1:26–27). This is confirmed in Genesis 5:1 and 9:6 and celebrated in Psalm 8 as well as Ecclesiastes 7:29. For the rest, the Old Testament says little of the original state of integrity (*status*

13. See H. Zimmern, *Biblische und babylonische Urgeschichte,* 2nd ed., 2 vols. (Leipzig: J. C. Hinrichs, 1901), and his commentary on Genesis.

integratis). The New Testament directly speaks of it only in 1 Corinthians 11:7, where humans are called "the image and glory of God," and in James 3:9, that they "are made in the likeness of God." Luke 3:38 also calls Adam "the son of God," and Paul quotes a pagan poet to the effect that "we are indeed his offspring" (Acts 17:28). Indirectly, however, also Ephesians 4:24 and Colossians 3:10 are of great importance here in speaking of the "new man [self]" that must be "put on," "according to the likeness of God in true righteousness and holiness," and "renewed in knowledge according to the image of its creator." The new person in Christ is not created *ex nihilo* but *renewed*, as the word ἀνακαινοῦσθαι (Col. 3:10) clearly teaches. Underlying these two passages is the idea that humankind was originally created in God's image and in the re-creation is renewed on that model.

What does "image of God" mean? Although the two words "image" and "likeness" (צֶלֶם and דְּמוּת, εἰκών and ὁμοίωσις) are certainly not identical, they are used interchangeably and there is no essential material distinction between them. The concept of "image" is more rigid, that of "likeness" more fluid and more "spiritual," so to speak; in the former the idea of a prototype predominates, in the latter is the notion of an ideal.[14] The likeness is a further qualification, an intensification and complement of the image. "Likeness" as such is weaker and broader than "image"; an animal has some features in common with man (likeness) but is not the image of man. "Image" tells us that God is the archetype, humanity the ectype; "likeness" adds the notion that the image corresponds in all parts to the original. Nothing can be constructed on the basis of a variation in the prepositions "in" (בְּ) and "after" (כְּ) either; they are used indiscriminately. Furthermore, the words "image" and "likeness" do not suggest that we have been created after something in God that is called "image" or "likeness," but that we *are* his image and likeness. This does not refer to certain attributes, either on God's side or ours, such as the intellect or the soul, but rather that the *whole* human person is the image of the whole deity. Thus the meaning of God's image is given to us fully in the Son, who is the Word (λόγος); the Son *(υἱός);* the image (εἰκών), or imprint (χαρακτὴρ τοῦ θεοῦ), of God (John 1:1, 14; 2 Cor. 4:4; Col. 1:15; Heb. 1:3); the one to whom we must be conformed (Rom. 8:29; 1 Cor. 15:49; Phil. 3:21; Eph. 4:23f.; 1 John 3:2). Like the Son, so also humans as such *are* altogether the image of God. Only the Son, of course, is image in an absolute sense; he is the *eternal* only begotten Son while we are *created* "sons" of God. What this means is not fully stated, but it does include human dominion over all of the created world (Gen. 1:26; cf. Ps. 8; 1 Cor. 11:7) in conformity to God's will (Eccles. 7:29). And re-creation in conformity to the image of God or Christ primarily consists in putting on the new person in righteousness and holiness of truth.

14. F. Delitzsch, *A New Commentary on Genesis,* trans. Sophia Taylor (Edinburgh: T&T Clark, 1899), 98–100, on Gen. 1:26.

[285] The whole person is the image of the whole deity. The extensive debates about the image of God arose from partial definitions: human rationality, dominion over creation, freedom of the will, or moral qualities such as love or justice. But gradually two views came to the fore, both appealing to the distinction between image (צֶלֶם) and likeness (דְּמוּת). Some (Clement of Alexandria, Origen) restrict the original state to the "image," defined as *rationality*, with "likeness," as a potential *holiness* to be acquired in the way of obedience.[15] This "naturalist" view emphasized freedom of the will with holiness as a good to be achieved by moral effort.[16] Others believed that the likeness as a gift of positive holiness was also immediately received at creation but, lost in the fall, was regained only through Christ.[17] Pelagius later appealed to the first view when he identified the essence and original state of humanity with a formal freedom of moral choice. He believed that our natural God-given possibility of perfection cannot be lost and is therefore still intact; God bestows the ability (*posse*), but the will (*velle*) is up to us.[18] Later, this view found acceptance among the Socinians, the Anabaptists, Remonstrants, and numerous modern theologians, who locate the image of God solely in human free personality, in our rational or moral nature, our religious-ethical bent, our vocation to enter communion with God.[19] This opens the door to an evolutionary understanding that sees the essence of humanity in an endless process of self-willed improvement. Paradise lies before us, not behind us.

[286] This view is diametrically contrary to Scripture, which does not consider a primitive animal state as an early stage in human history. Science provides no evidence for this hypothesis either, and it faces numerous philosophical and theological objections. A prior philosophical definition of what it means to be human is determinative here, not historical evidence. On questions of life, consciousness, language, morality, religion, the difference between truth and untruth, and so forth, we find remarkable ambivalence among modernists. While affirming evolution and denying a state of integrity, they still want to affirm a uniqueness to the human religious and moral disposition and then seek refuge in a Pelagian notion of original innocence, moral indifference, and full potentiality. But this mediating "third way" beyond creation and evolution, which attempts to embrace both when it comes to the human person, is untenable.

15. Clement of Alexandria, *Stromateis*, II, 22; Origen, *On First Principles*, III, 6.

16. Adolf von Harnack, *History of Dogma*, trans. N. Buchanan, J. Millar, E. B. Speirs, and W. Mc-Gilchrist, ed. A. B. Bruce, 7 vols. (London: Williams & Norgate, 1896–99), II, 128–48.

17. Irenaeus, *Against Heresies*, V, 16, 2; Athanasius, *Against the Arians*, II, 59; idem, *Against the Pagans*, 2; idem, *On the Incarnation*, 3.

18. Augustine, *On the Grace of Christ*, I, 3ff.

19. I. Kant, *Religion within the Limits of Reason Alone*, trans. Theodore M. Greene and Hoyt H. Hudson (New York: Harper & Brothers, 1934), 21–23; J. G. Fichte, *The Vocation of Man*, trans. William Smith, 2nd ed. (Chicago: Open Court, 1910); F. Schleiermacher, *The Christian Faith*, ed. H. R. MacIntosh and J. S. Steward (Edinburgh: T&T Clark, 1928); Th. Häring, *The Christian Faith: A System of Dogmatics*, trans. John Dickie and George Ferries, 2 vols. (London: Hodder & Stoughton, 1913).

First, Scripture clearly teaches that both physically and psychically, humans were created as adults at "an age of vigor,"[20] as freely acting agents. From the divine approval given to them (Gen. 1:31), the probationary command (Gen. 2:16–17), the naming of the animals (Gen. 2:19–20), the pronouncement about Eve (Gen. 2:23–24), the manner of the temptation (Gen. 3:1ff.), and the attitude of Adam and Eve after the fall (Gen. 3:7ff.), it is clear that the first humans were created positively good, not morally indifferent. Second, this irresolution only compounds the problem; how does potentiality develop into actuality? In Fichte's words: "One wonders—if indeed it is necessary to assume an origin of the entire human race—who brought up the first human couple? They had to be brought up—a human being could not have educated them. Hence, they had to be brought up by another rational being, one who was not a human. . . . A spirit adopted them, quite in the manner pictured in a venerable ancient document, which generally speaking contains the profoundest and most sublime wisdom and posits results to which in the end all philosophy has to return."[21] Incredible! To avoid one miracle, many miracles are assumed. There remains no good reason to deny the creation of humanity in a state of integrity as Scripture teaches.

The view we are criticizing also holds that innate holiness is impossible; holiness, we are told, is always the product of struggle and effort. If Adam had been created a positively holy being, he was necessarily good and without freedom to be otherwise.[22] This requires an undifferentiated state anterior to the moral life from which humans then have to evolve by an act of free will in one direction or another and reduces the image of God to a purely naked, merely formal personality, an abstraction. No human reality corresponds to this; as creatures with concrete intellects and wills, our *doing* good depends on *being* good. Scripture, accordingly, teaches that both in creation and re-creation holiness is a gift from God; those who have it can further develop it in word and deed; those who don't are unable to acquire it on their own. Finally, truly problematic are the implications that God allowed his creatures to be tempted beyond their power to resist; the fall is then only a nonculpable misfortune, an almost unavoidable lot. This severs the boundary between the states of integrity and corruption; the purely formal image of God remains intact even after the fall.

[287] Over against this naturalist view of human nature the Roman Catholic tradition posits a supernatural one that sees infused grace as the means by which human beings achieve and merit their true and supernatural end, the vision of God. This view was derived from the idea of the state of glory (*status gloriae*) to which believers are elevated by Christ and his Spirit (John 1:12; Rom. 8:14–17;

20. Augustine, *Literal Meaning of Genesis*, VI, 13–14; Peter Lombard, *Sententiae in IV liberis distinctae*, 3rd ed., 2 vols. (Grottaferratta: Coleggi S. Bonaventurae et Claras Aquas, 1971–81), II, dist. 17.

21. J. G. Fichte, *Grundlage des Naturrechts nach Principien der Wissenschaftslehre* (Jena: Gabler, 1796). ET: *The Science of Rights*, trans. A. E. Kroeger (New York: Harper & Row, 1970 [1889]).

22. R. Rothe, *Theologische Ethik*, 2nd rev. ed., 5 vols. (Wittenberg: Zimmerman, 1867–71), §§480ff.

1 Cor. 2:7ff.; Eph. 1:15ff.; 2 Pet. 1:2ff.; 1 John 3:1–2; etc.).[23] Gradually, under Neoplatonic influence, this was viewed as a condition far transcending nature, a vision of God according to his essence, deiformity or deification, even a corporeal participation in the divine nature, a "melting union" with God. To this was added a doctrine of meritorious good works; though infused grace, granted in baptism, was definitely necessary, one was then able to do such good works as could *ex condigno* (by a full merit)[24] earn eternal blessedness. From this we get the Roman Catholic doctrine of the "superadded gift" (*donum superadditum*). Adam's earthly created righteousness was not sufficient to achieve his final destiny of glory; for that he needed a supernatural grace which is superadded to his creaturely human nature. Grace elevates and perfects nature. This supernaturalism constitutes one of the most important and characteristic loci of Roman Catholic theology and creates a dual conception of humanity: humanity without supernatural grace is sinless but its "natural" religion and virtue as well as its destiny are limited on earth; the superadded gift of God's image produces supernatural religion and virtue and a heavenly destiny.

Roman Catholic dualist theological anthropology does not stop here. If the superadded gift is necessary for a holy life that pleases God and earns eternal life, then its absence in the original state means Adam's susceptibility to death and suffering; death is then not the penalty for sin. Similarly, for sins such as lust (concupiscence), the conflict between flesh and spirit is natural to creatures. To sort this out, Rome inserted a third notion to *natural* gifts (given in creation) and *supernatural* gifts (superadded), namely *preternatural* gifts that kept Adam from being susceptible to suffering and death and restrained his concupiscence. These three gifts—natural, preternatural, and supernatural—have as parallel three kinds of justice. The Roman Catechism simply lists all these things without achieving a consistent view of the whole: thanks to a divine gift, Adam was not susceptible to death and suffering; his soul was created in God's image and likeness; furthermore, his concupiscence was restrained and made subject to reason; then to all this God added original righteousness and dominion. The Roman Catholic doctrine of the image of God is inherently incomplete and, in part for that reason, fails to satisfy the theological mind.

[288] This doctrine is inadequate because it is based on a mistaken view of our final destiny. The state of grace and glory, in which we participate both here and in the hereafter, is indeed described as participation in the divine nature, as the vision of God, as eternal life, as heavenly bliss, and so forth. What no eye has seen, nor ear heard, nor the heart of man conceived, that is what God, in the New Testament dispensation of the covenant of grace, has prepared for those who love him (1 Cor. 2:9). But Rome views this final human destiny as a Neoplatonic vision

23. M. J. Scheeben, *Handbuch der katholischen Dogmatik*, 4 vols. (Freiburg i.B.: Herder, 1933), II, 272–81.

24. Ed. note: Cf. Richard A. Muller, *Dictionary of Latin and Greek Theological Terms* (Grand Rapids: Baker Academic, 1985), s.v. "*meritum*," 190–92.

of God and a mystical fusion of the soul with God. In contrast, Scripture teaches that the benefits of Christ, including eternal life, are not just future but also present realities (1 Cor. 2:9–10; John 3:16, 36; 17:3; Rom. 8:14ff.; Gal. 4:6; 1 John 3:1–2); even participation in the divine nature is a promise already granted on earth (2 Pet. 1:4). Furthermore, the vision of God comes through ethical Christian living (Matt. 5:8; Heb. 12:10; 1 John 3:6), not through meritorious works, even those made possible only by grace. Our main objection is that Scripture does not speak of the state of glory as "supernatural" and "superadded" in the Roman Catholic sense. Although it is a gift of grace that far surpasses our thought and imagination (1 Cor. 2:9; 13:12; 1 John 3:2), and what Christ gained for us is so much more than what Adam lost, nothing in Scripture even hints at the notion that it is something "superadded" and not part of our original human nature. To construct a bridge of meritoriousness by which we in some sense deserve our final destiny (*ex condigno*: "by proportionate merit") fails to do justice to grace. Grace is then in physical opposition to nature, not to the ethical problem of sin; not God's response to sin and guilt but to the lower human nature. Original sin here loses its radicalness; it only refers to the lost supperadded gift. Even eternal life is no longer a truly gracious gift of God but a fitting, worthy, proportionate reward for work done.

Practically, this threefold understanding of human nature both ennobles sinful humanity beyond its proper place and creates an unwarranted hierarchy among believers. The end result is whole ranking and organization of those who are on the path to the *visio dei*—clergy and laypersons, monks and ordinary people—with the contemplative mystic on the highest level. In Catholicism there is a place for everyone; taking account of each person's capacity and fitness, it has varying ideals for different people and does not make the same moral and religious demands on everybody.

Rome shares with the Reformation the difficult task of explaining how Adam's original state of righteousness could be lost. Rome attempts to resolve it by dualistically positing spirit and matter as natural foes that require supernatural grace to avoid conflict. In the words of Trent's great apologist, Cardinal Bellarmine: ". . . from the beginning of creation divine providence, in order to apply a remedy *to this sickness or weakness of human nature that arises from its material condition*, added to man a certain noteworthy gift, namely, original righteousness, so as to hold, as though by a kind of golden bridle, the inferior part to the superior, and [to hold] the superior part, which is easily subjected, to God."[25] Flesh by its very nature is here opposed to the spirit. Hence, according to Rome, grace is a supernatural gift as such and not incidentally a divine response to sin. Sin does not in any way change the nature of grace; both before and after the fall it was an *elevation* of humanity *above nature*. As a religion of redemption, Christianity is not a *reparation* but an *elevation* of nature; it elevates nature above itself, it divinizes

---

25. Robert Bellarmine, *De gratia primi hominis* (Heidelberg: J. Lancellot, 1612), 5.

humanity. Speaking strictly and logically, the incarnation was necessary before the fall and apart from sin; in order that man might become like God, God had to become man. Atonement is subordinated to incarnation; the point of gravity does not lie in satisfaction for sin and the forgiveness of sin, but in the humanization of God and the divinization of humanity. The Reformation took its stand against this Neoplatonic Areopagite philosophy because Scripture knows no such contrast between the natural and the supernatural; it knows only one idea of humanness, one moral law, one final destiny, and one priesthood, which is the portion of all believers.

[289] Protestant theologians rejected this dualistic understanding, especially the meritorious character of natural elevation. They also judged that the Roman Catholic position weakened the doctrine of original sin. But the Reformers too had to distinguish what was left of the image from what was lost. To that end they used the words "substance," "essence," "attributes," "gifts," even "supernatural gifts." Even where Protestants retained the expression "supernatural gifts," they meant something else by rejecting any essential difference between being truly human and being Christian. Grace was not regarded as *elevating* and *perfecting* nature beyond its created character but as *restoring* and *healing* it from sin and its consequences. The Reformation opposed the Roman conception of nature and grace as a matter of fundamental principle. But there were differences: Lutherans tended to identify the image with the original gifts of righteousness, while the Reformed incorporated the whole human essence in the image, though they do speak of a narrow and broader sense of the image. This distinction preserves the scriptural teaching that on the one hand fallen humanity is still called the image of God and must be respected as such (Gen. 5:1; 9:6; Acts 17:28; 1 Cor. 11:7; James 3:9), and that on the other hand the primary content of the image of God (i.e., knowledge, righteousness, and holiness) was lost and regained only in Christ (Eph. 4:24; Col. 3:10). Reformed theologians thus avoided significant errors that set grace against nature rather than sin. The Reformed also added the important distinction between Adam as he was in the garden and what he had yet to become. It is only in these three areas, the image of God in the broad sense, the image of God in the narrow sense, and the development or destination of the image of God—that is, in the doctrine of the covenant of works—that the locus of the image of God can be treated adequately.

[290] These debates have a significance across the entire range of doctrine and theology. Was Adam's original righteousness *natural* or, at least in part, *supernatural*? Reformed theologians held the former to preserve the idea that the image of God—i.e., original righteousness—was inseparable from the very idea of being human. Losing the image is not accidental but fundamental. In Rome's view we can lose the "supernatural righteousness" and still be good, true, complete, sinless humans. Protestants categorically deny this. There is no intermediate state between being an image of God and a sinner; one is either a child of God, his off-spring, his image, *or* one is a child of wrath, dead in sins and trespasses. Receiving

Christ's perfect righteousness is indeed a supernatural gift, but it is "accidental," "incidental"; like a blind person who regains sight, we regain that which belongs to our very being; our true humanity is restored. The spiritual worship we offer to God, "living sacrifices, holy and pleasing" (Rom. 12:1), is simply what was originally and integrally human. God claims our whole person—mind, heart, soul, body, and all our energies—for his service and his love. The moral law is one for all humans in all times; there is no "lower" or "higher" righteousness, no double morality, no twofold set of duties.

Now this splendid view of the image of God and of original righteousness has come more clearly into its own in the Reformed church and Reformed theology than in the Lutheran. In Lutheran theology, the image of God is restricted to original righteousness and was therefore totally lost when the latter was lost. This results in too sharp a line of demarcation between the spiritual and the worldly, between the heavenly and the earthly; the connection between nature and grace, between creation and re-creation, is obscured. When we consider sinful people who are totally deaf and blind in spiritual matters but still able in earthly matters to do much good, we in a sense render them independent from God's grace in Christ. Reformed theology distinguishes a broader and a narrower sense of the image but insists that they are intimately connected and that together they make up the full image of God. The whole being, the whole human person and not just "something" in us is the image of God. Sin, which precipitated the loss of the image of God in the narrow sense and spoiled and ruined the image of God in the broader sense, profoundly affects the whole person, so that, consequently, the grace of God in Christ restores the whole person, and is of the greatest significance for his or her whole life and labor, also in the family, society, the state, art, science, and so forth.

[291] It is important to insist that the whole person is the image of the whole God, that is, the triune God. The human soul, all the human faculties, the virtues of knowledge, righteousness, and holiness, and even the human body, all of it images God. Thus, a human being does not *bear* or *have* the image of God but *is* the image of God. As human beings we are the likeness or offspring of God (Gen. 1:26; 9:6; Luke 3:38; Acts 17:28; 1 Cor. 11:7; James 3:9). Therefore, God himself, the entire deity, is the archetype of man. Scripture does not support the oft-proposed notion that humanity is specifically made in the image of the Son or of the incarnate Christ.[26] Scripture repeatedly tells us that humankind was made in the image of God, not that we have been modeled on Christ, but that he was made in our likeness (Rom. 8:3; Phil. 2:7–8; Heb. 2:14), and that we, having been conformed to the image of Christ, are now again becoming like God (Rom.

---

26. Clement of Alexandria, *Stromateis*, V, 14; Tertullian, *On the Resurrection of the Flesh*, c. 6; A. Osiander, according to J. Calvin, *Institutes of the Christian Religion*, I.xv.2; II.xii.6 (ed. John T. McNeill and trans. Ford Lewis Battles, 2 vols. [1559; Philadelphia: Westminster, 1960], 1:184–86, 470–71); Hans Martensen, *Christian Dogmatics: A Compendium of the Doctrines of Christianity*, trans. William Urwick (Edinburgh: T&T Clark, 1871), §§72, 136–37; F. Delitzsch, *A System of Biblical Psychology*, trans. Robert E. Wallis, 2nd ed. (Edinburgh: T&T Clark, 1875), 86–87; etc.

8:29; 1 Cor. 15:49; 2 Cor. 3:18; Phil. 3:21; Eph. 4:24; Col. 3:10; 1 John 3:2). It is therefore preferable to say that the triune God (not only Christ) is the archetype of humanity,[27] while at the same time exercising the greatest caution in exploring psychological trinitarian analogies in the human soul.[28] The image thus extends to the whole person; nothing is excluded, soul and body, all faculties and powers, in all conditions and relations. It is of course true that in the same way that God's attributes are more clearly revealed in some creatures than others, so also the image of God comes out more clearly in one part of the human organism than another, more in the soul than in the body, more in the ethical virtues than in the physical powers. This does not alter the truth that the whole person is the image of the triune God.

God is, first of all, demonstrable in the human soul. Scripture tells us that God formed man from the dust of the earth by breathing into his nostrils (נִשְׁמַת חַיִּים), whereby he became a living soul (נֶפֶשׁ חַיָּה, ψυχὴ ζῶσα). The breath of life is the principle of life; the living soul is the essence of humanity. With this combination Scripture accords humanity a unique and independent place and avoids both pantheism and materialism. The terms רוּחַ and נֶפֶשׁ (πνεῦμα and ψυχή), denoting the invisible component of man, simply reflect biblical parallelism. Since Scripture uses these anthropological terms interchangeably it is a mistake to attribute scientific precision to them; they do not denote two distinct substances and yield a trichotomy of body, soul, and spirit. Distinguishing "spirit" and "soul" does, however, remind us that humans are "spirit" in a way animals are not because of God's own breath of life (Gen. 2:7). In addition, our spirit is distinct from the Spirit of God (Gen. 41:8; 45:27; Exod. 35:21; Deut. 2:30; Judg. 15:19; Ezek. 3:14; Zech. 12:1; Matt. 26:41; Mark 2:8; Luke 1:47; 23:46; John 11:33; Acts 7:59; 17:16; Rom. 8:16; 1 Cor. 2:11; 5:3–5; 1 Thess. 5:23; Heb. 4:12; 12:23; etc.). Like the angels, we can also think about spiritual or heavenly things, and if necessary exist without a body. Unlike the angels, though, our spiritual component is adapted to and organized for a body and is tied, also for our intellectual and spiritual life, to the sensory world. As sentient and material beings we are related to the animals; as rational, spiritual beings we are akin to the angels. We exist between angels and animals; related to but distinct from both, we unite and reconcile within ourselves heaven and earth, things invisible and visible. In Christ, we must never forget, God assumed the nature of humanity, not that of angels. Precisely on that account human beings and not angels are the image, offspring, and children of God.

In the second place, the human faculties belong to God's image. While the spirit is the principle and the soul the subject of life in us, the heart, according to Scripture, is the *organ* of human life. It is, first, the center of physical life but then also, in a metaphorical sense, the seat and fountain of the entire psychic

---

27. Augustine, *The Trinity*, XII, 6; T. Aquinas, *Summa Theol.*, I, qu. 13, art. 5.
28. J. Calvin, *Institutes*, I.xv.4; idem, *Commentary*, on Gen. 1:26.

life, of emotions and passions, of desire and will, of thinking and knowing. From the heart flow "the springs of life" (Prov. 4:23). This life, which originates in the heart, then splits into two streams, the *mind* and the *will*. The "mind" embraces all impressions, awarenesses, perceptions, observations, thoughts, knowledge, and wisdom, and embodies itself in words and language. The heart is also the seat of all the emotions, passions, urges, inclinations, attachments, desires, and decisions of the *will*, which have to be led by the mind (νους) and express themselves in action. This rich diversity and abundance of these psychic capacities and activities of human beings reflect God; they make it possible for us to be conformed to and enjoy God in the fullest manner—from all sides, as it were, in all God's virtues and perfections. In the heart, mind, and will (*memoria, intellectus, voluntas*), Augustine even saw an analogy of the triune being of God. Just as the Father gives life to the Son and the Spirit, and the Spirit proceeds from the Father through the Son, so in human beings it is the heart (*memoria*), the deep, hidden life of the psyche, which gives birth and being to the intellect and the will, and specifically places the will second in order to the intellect. Thanks to Augustine's leadership, Western theology discovered the intimate connection between the doctrines of God and humanity; it taught that the deep, hidden life of the soul comes to expression through the cognitive and the conative capacities, and that the latter was led and guided by the former.[29]

[292] In the third place, the image of God manifests itself in the virtues of knowledge, righteousness, and holiness given with our original creation. We were not created as neutral beings with morally indifferent powers and potentialities, but immediately made physically and ethically mature, with knowledge in the mind, righteousness in the will, holiness in the heart. This original state of created goodness must not be conceived as childlike innocence, but it must not be exaggerated either, as though the original state of integrity (*status integratis*) were already equal to the state of glory (*status gloriae*). Adam's knowledge, though pure, was limited and capable of growth; he walked by faith, not by sight; he possessed not only intuitive knowledge but also discursive knowledge; he knew the future only by special revelation.[30] Similarly, his created righteousness and holiness still had to be preserved, developed, and converted into action. Adam's original righteousness (*justitia originalis*) was a free gift of God, and from moment to moment maintained by God's providence. It is inconceivable apart from communion with God. Just as the Son was already the mediator of union before the fall, so also the Holy Spirit was even then already the craftsman of all knowledge, righteousness, and holiness in humanity. In Adam's case this indwelling of the Holy Spirit was

29. Thus avoiding the error of Pelagians and rationalists, who detach the intellect and will from the heart; that of mysticism, which despises the conscious, active life of the will and retreats into the depths of the mind; and that of Greek Orthodox theology, which places head and heart immediately side by side. For further discussion on human psychology, see H. Bavinck, *Beginselen der Psychologie*, 2nd ed. (Kampen: Kok, 1923).

30. T. Aquinas, *Summa Theol.*, I, qu. 94, arts. 1–3.

entirely natural. No truly good and perfect human being is even conceivable apart from the fellowship of the Holy Spirit. Thus, also before the fall, a human being was the dwelling place of the entire holy Trinity, a most splendid temple of the Holy Spirit.

In the fourth place, the human body also belongs integrally to the image of God. Rejecting divine revelation always leads philosophers to lapse into empiricism or rationalism, materialism or spiritualism. But Scripture reconciles the two. A human person has a "spirit" (πνευμα), but that "spirit" is psychically organized and must, by virtue of its nature, inhabit a body. Human beings are by nature corporeal and sentient; first (logically, if not temporally) Adam's body was formed from the dust of the earth and then the breath of life is breathed into him. He is called "Adam" after the ground from which he was formed; he is "from the earth, a man of dust" (1 Cor. 15:47). The body is not a prison, but a marvelous piece of art from the hand of God Almighty, and just as constitutive for the essence of humanity as the soul (Job 10:8–12; Pss. 8; 139:13–17; Eccles. 12:2–7; Isa. 64:8). It is our earthly dwelling (2 Cor. 5:1) and so integral and essential to our humanity that, though violently torn from the soul by sin, it will be reunited with it in the resurrection of the dead. The nature of the union of the soul with the body is not ethical but physical. It is so intimate that one nature, one person, one self is the subject of both and of all their activities. It is one and the same life that flows throughout the body but operates and manifests itself in every organ in a manner peculiar to that organ. Now, this body, which is so intimately bound up with the soul, also belongs to the image of God. Of course, this does not mean that God himself also has a material body, as some have thought and taught.[31] God, after all, is "spirit" (πνευμα, John 4:24) and has no body. The human body is a part of the image of God in its organization as instrument of the soul, in its formal perfection, not in its material substance as flesh (σαρξ).[32]

God, though he is spirit, is nevertheless the Creator of a material world that may be termed his revelation and manifestation. This revelation comes to its climax in the incarnation and teaches us that the human spirit is designed for the body as its manifestation. The incarnation of God is proof that the human body is an essential component of that image. From the beginning, creation was so arranged and human nature immediately so created that it was amenable to and fit for the highest degree of conformity to God and for the most intimate indwelling of God. God could not have been able to become man if he had not first made man in his own image. From this we also conclude that the body originally participated in immortality. God is not a God of the dead, but of the living (Matt. 22:32). Death

31. E.g., the Lutheran Andreas Osiander (1498–1552).
32. Augustine, *Literal Meaning of Genesis*, VI, 12; Gregory of Nyssa, *On the Making of Man*, c. 8; T. Aquinas, *Summa Theol.*, I, qu. 93, art. 6; idem, *Summa contra gentiles*, IV, 26; J. Calvin, *Institutes*, I.xv.3; Johannes Polyander à Kerckhoven, André Rivet, Antonius Walaeus, and Antoine Thysius, *Synopsis purioris theologiae*, ed. H. Bavinck, 6th ed. (Leiden: Didericum Donner, 1881), XIII, 13; Peter van Mastricht, *Theoretico-practica theologia* (Utrecht: Appels, 1714), III, 9, 30.

is a consequence of sin (Gen. 2:7; 3:19; Rom. 5:12; 6:23; 1 Cor. 15:21, 56). In Adam's case this was conditional, only the possibility of not dying (*posse non mori*), rather than definite immortality (*non posse mori*) or eternal and imperishable life. The condition was obedience. Adam's human nature was created so that, in case of his violation of God's commandment, it could and had to die. Bound to the earth, Adam could still exercise dominion over it; dominion is an integral part of the image of God in humans (Gen. 1:26, 28; 2:19–20; 9:2–3; Ps. 8:7–9). As God's image bearers, humans are elevated above all other creatures and appointed lord and king over them all. Here, too, we acknowledge that habitation in paradise (Gen. 2:8–15) is part of the image of God. Holiness and blessedness, virtue and happiness, the ethical dimension and the physical dimension, the moral and the natural order in the world, being and appearance, spirit and matter, all belong together. Congruent with a fallen humanity, therefore, is an earth that lies under a curse; a place of darkness therefore awaits the wicked in the hereafter; the righteous will one day walk in the light of God's countenance; the not-yet-fallen but still earthly man makes his home in a paradise.

[293] So the whole human being is image and likeness of God, in soul and body, in all human faculties, powers, and gifts. Nothing in humanity is excluded from God's image; it stretches as far as and constitutes our humanity and humanness. All that is in God—his spiritual essence, his virtues and perfections, his immanent self-distinctions, his self-communication and self-revelation in creation—finds its admittedly finite and limited analogy and likeness in humanity. Among creatures, humans are the supreme and most perfect revelation of God. In the teaching of Scripture, God and the world, spirit and matter, are not opposites. The visible, material world is every bit as beautiful and lush a revelation of God as the spiritual. The whole world raises itself upward, culminates and completes itself, and achieves its unity, its goal, and its crown in humanity, the recapitulation of the whole of nature. As spirit, man is akin to the angels and soars to the invisible world; but he is at the same time a citizen of the visible world and connected with all physical creatures. Thus man forms a unity of the material and spiritual world, a mirror of the universe, a connecting link, compendium, the epitome of all of nature, a microcosm, and, as the image and likeness of God, a micro-divine-being (μικροθεος). As prophet, man explains God and proclaims his excellencies; as priest, he consecrates all that is created to God as a holy offering; as king, he guides and governs all things in justice and rectitude. In all this he points to One who in a still higher and richer sense is the revelation and image of God, to him who is the only begotten of the Father, and the firstborn of all creatures. Adam, the son of God, was a type of Christ.

HUMAN DESTINY

[294] The ultimate destiny of humanity, individually as well as corporately, was not given in Adam's creation; it was a goal. Christ, not Adam, is the first full, true,

spiritual man. In 1 Corinthians 15:45–49, Paul contrasts and compares Adam and Christ in terms of their nature and person rather than what they did (as in Rom. 5:12–21; 1 Cor. 15:22). The first man was created a "living being" (ψυχη ζωσα), "natural" (ψυχικος), "of the dust of the earth" (ἐκ γης χοϊκος); by his resurrection the second man became a "life-giving spirit" (πνευμα ζωοποιουν), "spiritual" (πνευματικος), "from heaven" (ἐξ οὐρανου). Since his body was not yet a glorified spiritual body, though created first, Adam is inferior to Christ. Even before the fall Adam was the type of Christ; in his creation Christ was already in view. Creation is properly infralapsarian; the natural precedes the spiritual; the spiritual builds on the natural. The apostle's case, set forth in great depth and breadth, is grounded in Genesis 1–2. There is a major difference between the natural and the pneumatic, between the state of integrity and the state of glory. After the resurrection both the stomach and food will be destroyed (1 Cor. 6:13) and God's children will no longer marry, but be like the angels (Matt. 22:30). Adam, however, needed food and the help of a wife.

THE COVENANT OF WORKS

Adam's state of integrity was provisional and temporary. Adam's conditional situation, tied as it was to obedience, along with the Christ/Adam parallel, prompted theologians to conceive the original state of integrity in terms of a covenant, a covenant of works. The only possible explicit scriptural reference to such a covenant is Hosea 6:7, which speaks of Israel and Judah transgressing the covenant, "like Adam" (MT: כְּאָדָם עָבְרוּ בְרִית; LXX: ὡς ἀνθρωπος; Vulg.: *sicut Adam*). The translations "like a man" or "at Adam" are possible but less likely. The parallel that Paul draws in Romans 5:12–21 between Adam and Christ is decisive here. We stand to Adam in the same relation as we stand to Christ; guilt and death accrue to us because of his transgression, and we are made righteous by the righteousness of Christ. Adam is thus a type of Christ; he is our representative, i.e., covenantal head.

[295] This richly valuable idea of Scripture was not honored by the naturalist or supernaturalist views discussed earlier in this chapter. Thinking of the image of God as something to be acquired by force of personality and will or denying original righteousness alike lead to distortions of biblical teaching. In the former death is considered natural; in the latter all susceptibility to suffering and pain was denied to Adam.[33] Others even went so far as to claim that before the fall, food was unnecessary or restricted to vegetation, that procreation occurred without any sensual pleasure or even apart from coitus.[34] Others believed that humanity

---

33. Augustine, *City of God*, XIV, 26; T. Aquinas, *Summa Theol.*, I, qu. 97, art. 2.
34. Augustine, *The Retractions*, I, 10; Gregory of Nyssa, *On the Making of Man*, 16–17; John of Damascus, *Exposition of the Orthodox Faith*, II, 30.

was created androgynous, that Eve's creation was proof of the fall,[35] and that women did not really participate in the divine image and in human nature.[36] In addition, paradise was often construed in very idealistic terms and interpreted allegorically: it was a place where animals did not die, no wild or unclean animals existed, roses blossomed without thorns, the air was cleaner, the water softer, and the light brighter.[37]

Still, everyone acknowledges that Adam did not yet possess the highest humanity, a truth implicit in the probationary command, the freedom of choice, the possibility of sin and death. Augustine clearly distinguished the ability not to sin (*posse non peccare*) and not to die (*posse non mori*), from the inability to sin (*non posse peccare*) and to die (*non posse mori*). The latter was not yet given to Adam but bestowed on condition of obedience. Even Augustine described this original stance of Adam vis-à-vis God as a covenant, a testament, a pact;[38] and the translation of the words כְּאָדָם by "like Adam" led many to a similar view.[39] Since the relation of believers to God in Christ is repeatedly described in Scripture as a covenant, Paul's parallel between Adam and Christ prompted theologians also to conceive the state of integrity as a covenant, a covenant they called the covenant of nature or of works (*foedus naturae* or *operum*). This language points to the foundation of the covenant on the moral law, known to humans by nature in the original state of righteousness.

Now this covenant, as parallel to the covenant of grace, was taught and developed with special predilection by Reformed theologians. Materially it is embodied in articles 14 and 15 of the Belgic Confession, in Lord's Days 3 and 4 of the Heidelberg Catechism (Q&A 6–11), and in chapter III/IV of the Canons of Dort. Formally, the covenant of works is incorporated in the Irish Articles (1615), the Westminster Confession (1647), the Helvetic Consensus Formula (1675), and the Walcheren Articles (1693). Although the doctrine of the covenant of works also found acceptance with some Roman Catholic and Lutheran theologians, it was vigorously opposed by Remonstrants and Rationalists. In recent years the doctrine of the covenant of works has been revived by a number of theologians.[40]

---

35. This was a feature of Jewish thought; cf. F. W. Weber, *System der altsynagogalen palästinischen Theologie* (Leipzig: Dörffling & Franke, 1880), 202ff.; Johannes Scotus Erigena, *On the Division of Nature*, trans. Myra L. Uhlfelder (Indianapolis: Bobbs-Merrill, 1976), II, 6, 10, 23; IV, 12; and many philosophers such as Böhme, Oetinger, Baader, and Schelling; J. P. Lange, *Christliche Dogmatik*, 3 vols. (Heidelberg: K. Winter, 1852), II, 324ff.; F. Delitzsch, *A System of Biblical Psychology* (Edinburgh: T&T Clark, 1899), 102ff.

36. Cf. Augustine, *The Trinity*, XII, 7; T. Aquinas, *Summa Theol.*, I, qu. 93, art. 4; I, qu. 99, art. 2.

37. Luther, on Gen. 3.

38. Augustine, *City of God*, XVI, 27.

39. J. Marck, *Historia Paradisi* (Amsterdam: Gerardus Borstius, 1705), II, 6–7.

40. Charles Hodge, *Systematic Theology*, 3 vols. (New York: Charles Scribner's Sons, 1888), II, 117; G. Vos, "The Doctrine of the Covenant in Reformed Theology," in *Redemptive History and Biblical Interpretation*, ed. Richard B. Gaffin Jr. (Phillipsburg: Presbyterian & Reformed, 1980), 234–70.

[296] The doctrine of the covenant of works has not always been articulated and defended as well as it should. It loses its vitality and significance when subjected to excessive Scholastic detail. Nonetheless, it is based on Scripture and is eminently valuable. Covenant is of the essence of true religion, making possible a relation between the Creator and the creature and underscoring the dependence of rational, moral human beings on God. Among rational and moral creatures all higher life takes the form of a covenant; it is a way of voluntarily obligating and binding people to each other. Love, friendship, marriage, as well as all social cooperation in business, industry, science, art, and so forth, is ultimately grounded in a covenant, that is, in reciprocal fidelity and an assortment of generally recognized moral obligations. It is therefore no surprise that Scripture uses it to characterize the highest and most richly textured life of human beings, namely, religion. This is so important that we must not yield to opposition to the doctrine, for example, opposition that points to the absence of the word בְּרִית in Genesis 1 and 2. Even if the term "covenant" never occurred in Scripture for the religious relation between Adam and God, not even in Hosea 6:7, still the religious life of man before the fall bears the character of a covenant. Reformed scholars were never so narrow as to insist on the word "covenant" since the matter itself was certain: one may doubt the word, provided the matter is safe (*de vocabulo dubitetur, re salva*). The matter in this case must never be surrendered inasmuch as covenant is the essence of true religion.

Why should this be? First of all, because there is an infinite distance between God the Creator and man the creature. If religion is to be more than the relation of a master and slave, if it is to be instead a communion, a fellowship with God, on the analogy of friendship and love among humans, then it must be in the character of a covenant. For then God must come down, condescend to his creatures, impart, reveal, and give himself away to them; then he who inhabits eternity and dwells in a high and holy place must also dwell with those who are of a humble spirit (Isa. 57:15). This is nothing other than the description of a covenant; over against religions that pantheistically pull God down into what is creaturely, or deistically elevate him endlessly above it, biblical religion speaks of a God who is both infinitely great and condescendingly good, sovereign but also Father. Only in this covenantal way are true fellowship and genuine religion possible. God is the God of the covenant. The second reason is that we cannot bring along or possess any rights before God; we cannot make claims on him. We are creatures, absolutely dependent and without any entitlements or merits on our own. When we have done everything we have been instructed to do, we are still unworthy servants (δοῦλοι ἀχρεῖοι, Luke 17:10). Yet, we do have the freedom to come to God with prayer and thanksgiving, to call him "Father," to appeal to his mercy, and expect salvation and life from him. All this is possible because God in his condescending goodness gives us these rights; all benefits are gifts of grace, undeserved and nonobligatory. True religion, therefore, must be covenantal, and it is now what it was in the garden. Finally, covenant honors the fact that God created men and women as rational and moral beings. He treats us as such by not coercing us but using persuasion; he wants us freely and willingly to serve him in love (Ps. 100:3f.). True religion is not a work we do to please God but a grace that privileges us to serve him in love and joy. On his part there is always the gift; on our part there is always and alone the gratitude. We must not assume that Adam's obedience would automatically yield eternal life as its reward. In the probationary command God showed humanity its true destiny and the only way to achieve it. Heavenly blessing and eternal life, however, remain God's gift; he is not obligated to grant it. There *is* no natural connection here between work and reward. The covenant of works does justice to both the sovereignty of God—which implies the dependency of creatures and the nonmeritoriousness of all their works—and to the grace and generosity of God, who nevertheless wants to give the creature a higher-than-earthly blessedness. It maintains both the dependence as well as the freedom of mankind. It is monopleuric (unilateral) in origin because it proceeds from a free, special, and gracious dispensation of God who decrees all the parts of it: condition and fulfillment, compliance and reward, transgression and punishment.

OTHER VIEWS OF HUMAN DESTINY

[297] The Roman Catholic doctrine of the *donum superadditum*, though it seeks to honor the conviction that eternal life is a gift of grace, in fact reintroduces meritorious good works. By contrast, Lutheran views exalt the original state of Adam as already a possession of highest possible blessing and thus tend to antinomianism—Adam was *ex lex*, outside the law. Lutheran theology frequently exaggerates the original state of humanity and fails to acknowledge the positive thrust of the probationary command. That is why the state of believers is essentially equated with that of Adam before the fall and salvation seen entirely in terms of forgiveness and justification. With that the Lutheran believer can be satisfied. No need is felt to connect it backward with eternal election and forward with the whole of the Christian life, good works, and eternal life. Neither predestination nor perseverance is needed here.[41]

But, before the fall, our first parents did not yet enjoy the eternal heavenly Sabbath; the state of integrity was not yet the state of glory. Reformed theology, by contrast, walked in the footsteps of Augustine in affirming that Adam did not yet possess the highest kind of life, namely the material freedom consisting of not being able to err, sin, or die, of being elevated absolutely above all fear and dread, above all possibility of falling. Christ does not merely restore us to Adam's prelapsarian state; he acquired and bestows that which Adam would have received

---

41. Luther, in J. Köstlin, *The Theology of Luther in Its Historical Development and Inner Harmony*, trans. Charles E. Hay (Philadelphia: Lutheran Publication Society, 1897), II, 361.

had he not fallen. Christ positions us not at the beginning but at the end of the journey set before Adam; he accomplished not only the passive but also the active obedience required; he not only delivers us from guilt and punishment, but out of grace immediately grants us the right to eternal life. Adam, however, did not yet have this high state of blessedness; he did not yet have eternal life. He still lived in the state of one who could sin and die, and was therefore still in some fear and dread. Reformed theologians rightly pointed out that this possibility, this being changeably good, this still being able to sin and die, was no part or component of the image of God, but was its boundary, its limitation, its circumference.[42] The image of God therefore had to be fully developed—thereby overcoming and nullifying this possibility of sin and death—and glitter in imperishable glory. Adam was not Christ. The natural was not the spiritual. Paradise was not heaven. Sin, according to Reformed theologians, spoiled and destroyed everything, but because it is not a substance it could not alter the essence or substance of the creation. The human being as sinner is still a human being, and all other creatures, despite sin's curse, essentially and substantially remained the same. As sin did not take away the substance of things, so grace therefore does not restore it. What is changed is not the stuff (*materia*) of creation but its *forma*; creation was *de*formed by sin in order to be entirely *re*formed again in the sphere of grace.[43]

The Reformed view has significant consequences. Against the Lutherans and Remonstrants it upholds the moral law for Adam as a positive good that he knew by nature. The probationary command was needed precisely to make clear to Adam's mind the possibility of sin; he needed to become aware of *pro*scription as well as *pre*scription. In the probationary command the entire moral law came to Adam at a single throw, confronting him with the dilemma: either God or self, God's authority or autonomy of insight, unconditional obedience or independent research, faith, or skepticism. It was a momentous test that opened the way to either eternal blessedness or eternal ruin. Reformed theologians also insisted that the Sabbath command belonged to the moral law; before the fall our first parents did not yet enjoy the eternal heavenly Sabbath but were subject to the rule of six days of labor and one of rest. This serves as a reminder that the religious life requires a form and service of its own alongside the life of culture. Reformed theologians also rejected magical theosophic notions that the two trees in the Garden of Eden in themselves possessed the power to kill or to make alive or that the eating of the fruit had an effect on human physical life. Reformed theologians regarded the tree of life as sign and seal of the covenant of works, which bestowed life in a sacramental manner. They also unanimously rejected,[44] as contrary to Scripture, all theosophic speculations concerning an androgynous maiden, the absence of the

---

42. H. Heppe, *Reformed Dogmatics*, rev. and ed. Ernst Bizer, trans. G. T. Thomson (London: Allen & Unwin, 1950; repr., Grand Rapids: Baker Academic, 1978), 249–50; W. G. T. Shedd, *Dogmatic Theology*, 2 vols. (New York: Charles Scribner's Sons, 1888–89), II, 104, 150.

43. Gisbert Voetius, *Selectae disputationes theologicae*, 5 vols. (Utrecht, 1648–69), I, 776.

44. Johannes à Marck, *Historia paradisi* (Amsterdam: Gerardus Borstius, 1705), 279ff.

sex drive, and magical generation. Finally, Calvin and most Reformed theologians[45] believed that there was no ground for assuming that prior to the permission given in Genesis 9:3 humans were forbidden to eat animal flesh. Genesis 9:1–5 is not a new commandment, but a renewal of creation's blessing; the only new feature is the prohibition against eating meat with its life, that is, its blood. There is no prohibition against shedding animal blood as there is for humans in Genesis 9:5–7. One might, in fact, expect that to counter lawlessness and degradation a requirement of vegetarianism would be more in accord with the postfall and postflood state of mankind. It is not present.

Reformed theology is deeply imbued with the idea that Adam did not yet enjoy the highest level of blessedness. Sin has profoundly affected everything in creation; the history of the earth and of humanity are unimaginable apart from it. Still, we cannot simply draw conclusions for the state of glory from the state of integrity. The diversity and differences of our present world may not be attributed simply to sin; many are rooted in the very creation order and good. Augustinian and Reformed theologians affirm that the stuff (*material*) of creation remains from the state of integrity; only the *forma* has been altered. Certain movements of socialism and communism, in rightly combating the appalling consequences of sin, forget this and launch assaults on nature and being itself. Christianity favors reformation, not revolution.

HUMAN ORIGINS IN UNITY: DESTINY IN COMMUNITY

[298] Covenant also reminds us that full and complete humanity is found in community; humanity as a whole is the image of God—in creation and in redemption. This underscores the notion of federal headship: Adam's over creation, Christ's over redeemed humanity. God said that it was not good for the man to be alone (Gen. 2:18); nor was it good that the two should be alone, and so he immediately pronounced on them the blessing of multiplication (Gen. 1:28). The image of God is much too rich for it to be fully realized in a single human being, however richly gifted, but can only be somewhat unfolded in its depth and riches in a humanity counting billions of members. This humanity is an organism; it is not a heap of souls on a tract of land, not a loose aggregate of individuals, but an organic unity created out of one blood; as one household and one family, humanity is the image and likeness of God. This image is not all given at the beginning but unfolds over time as both a gift (*Gabe*) of grace and a mandate (*Aufgabe*) to

---

45. John Calvin, *Commentary on Genesis*, trans. J. King (Grand Rapids; Baker, 1979), 98–100, 291–93 (on Gen. 1:29; 9:3); J. Heidegger, *De libertate christianorum a re cibaria* (1662); G. Voetius, *Select. disp.*, IV, 387; V, 194; Johannes Coccejus, *Summa theologiae ex Scripturis repetita* (Amsterdam: J. Ravenstein, 1665), XX, 17; J. Marck, *Historia paradisi*, 341; Bernhard de Moor, *Commentarius perpetuus in Johannis Marckii Compendium theologiae christianae didactico-elencticum*, 7 vol. in 6 (Leiden: J. Hasebroek, 1761–71), III, 35–38; etc.

be obeyed. Only humanity in its entirety—as one complete organism, summed up under a single head, spread out over the whole earth, as prophet proclaiming the truth of God, as priest dedicating itself to God, as ruler controlling the earth and the whole of creation—only it is the fully finished image, the most telling and striking likeness of God.

The same thing is in view with the biblical teaching that the church is the bride of Christ, the temple of the Holy Spirit, the dwelling of God, the new Jerusalem to which all the glory of the nations will be brought. While a picture of the state of glory that awaits us, it is also in veiled form given to us now. We have the down payment of this final state, and its rules do not change; true religion, the moral law, and our final destiny are essentially the same in both the covenant of works and the covenant of grace. In both the goal and end is a kingdom of God, a holy humanity, in which God is all in all. At this point we need to underscore an important truth about humanity as the image of God. For the image of God to be realized in the fullness of humanity redeemed, renewed, and glorifying God, it must be united and epitomized under one head. That is the crucial importance of the covenant of works doctrine. The human race was united in its origin in Adam; the redeemed and reconstituted humanity that is the church is united under its head, Jesus Christ. It is not enough that the human race be physically of one blood (Acts 17:26)—the same thing is true of each animal species—but what is needed is a moral and legal unity. Just as Christ is the cause of our righteousness and our life, so Adam is the cause of our sin and our death. God considers and judges the whole human race in one person. Only in Reformed understanding of the covenant of works does the ethical—not the physical—unity of mankind come into its own. The probationary command demonstrates that Adam was not only the ancestor but also the head and representative of the entire human race, and his conduct was decisive for all. Just as the fate of the whole body rests with the head, which thinks and judges and decides for all the organs, so also the fate of humanity was put in the hands of Adam. If we could not be subjected to condemnation in Adam without our knowledge, neither could we have been accepted unto grace in Christ without our participation. The covenant of works and the covenant of grace stand and fall together. As human beings we all stand together, tied not only by blood but also by common participation in blessing and curse, sin and righteousness, death and life.

[299] This emphasis on the organic unity of the human race also sheds light on its origins and propagation. The theory of the preexistence of human souls (Plato, Plotinus, Origen, Kant) is rooted in a pagan dualism between spirit and matter, destroys the unity of humanity, and erases the distinction between human beings and angels. Those who want to affirm a macro theory of evolution and still maintain a belief in the soul's immortality have little choice but to claim that souls always existed somehow and somewhere in the cosmos. But since the Christian religion arises from very different premises and is based on the confession of God's personal existence and creative activity; it has no room for this doctrine of the eternal preex-

istence of souls. The debate between creationism and traducianism is less fixed.[46] Although both face insoluble difficulties, Reformed along with Orthodox and Roman Catholic theologians, almost unanimously embraced creationism, while traducianism found acceptance mainly among Lutherans. The biblical case for either seems equally strong. Traducianism appeals to the creation of Eve "from" or "out of man" (*ex andros*; 1 Cor. 11:8; Gen. 2:23); to passages that speak of descendants being included in their father's loins (Gen. 46:26; Heb. 7:9–10); to the word יָדַע, to know, which includes a spiritual act; to creation's completion on the seventh day (Gen. 2:2); to animal reproduction after their own kind (Gen. 1:28; 5:3; 9:4; John 3:6); and especially to the hereditary transmission of sin and all sorts of psychological attributes. Creationism, on the other hand, appeals to the creation of Adam's soul (Gen. 2:7); to texts such as Ecclesiastes 12:7, Zechariah 12:1, and especially Hebrews 12:9 (cf. Num. 16:22), and above all from the simple, indivisible, immortal, spiritual nature of the soul.

Just as traducianism and creationism advance weighty arguments for their respective positions, so both are incapable of solving the difficulties. Traducianism neither explains the origin of the soul nor the hereditary transmission of sin. Attempting to solve these questions often ends in a restatement of the notion that the child's soul preexisted in the parents and ancestors or that the soul was materially present in the seed of the man or the woman or both. With respect to the transmission of sin, traducianism is of no help because sin is not material, not a substance, but a moral quality, moral guilt, and moral corruption.[47] Traducianism seems to be led either to the view that "somehow" the sperm and ovum carry their own animation or that God imparts life to them. In the former scenario we still do not know where this animation comes from; in the second we have a modified form of creationism. To incorporate this into an evolutionary notion of fetal development and conceive the union of sperm and egg as the initiating moment when the new being itself develops a soul only shifts the problem; it does not solve it. When traducianism pursues its own logic, it either lapses into materialism or again smuggles creationism into its tent under another label.

We face innumerable difficulties here. The moment an immortal spiritual soul dwells in an organism, there exists a human being, an individual, a personality, be it only germinally. *When* and *how* does the fetus become a human being; *when* and *how* does psychic life arise, and when does it become pneumatic life? To say that it occurs gradually, in keeping with the laws of evolution, eliminates the *essential* difference between the psychic and the pneumatic life, between the vital soul and the immortal spiritual soul, between animals and humans. There has to be a moment in which the fetus becomes a human being, an ensouled body, a self who will always exist. *When* this happens or *how* this happens is a mystery and neither

46. Ed. note: Traducianism holds that the soul is derived from the parents; creationism holds that God creates the soul at conception.

47. The objections to traducianism and the grounds for creationism are unfolded at length by A. G. Honig, *Creationisme of Traducianisme?* (Kampen: Bos, 1906).

theology nor science can provide an answer. Although neither creationism nor traducianism can explain this, the former has the advantage that it is prepared to leave this mystery alone and not attempt a spurious explanation. The latter is the danger to which traducianism exposes itself.

While traducianism does suggest an answer to what we observe about the hereditary transmission of many human physical, emotional, and spiritual character traits, we also know that heredity is immensely complex. We cannot account for genius, say that of Goethe, purely by genetic inheritance from his parents or ancestors. When we consider the uniqueness of each human soul and its frequently unique and outstanding gifts, we must acknowledge an important creationist component in the formation of the soul. God does not, however, first create a soul apart from the body in order then to introduce it into the body from without, but at the proper time and in a manner incomprehensible to us,[48] he elevates the existing psychic life to the level of a higher human spiritual life. Our sinful nature does not arise from our soul's contact with our body; sin is not something material. It is better to think of the soul, though called into being as a rational spiritual entity by a creative activity of God, as preformed in the psychic life of the fetus—that is, in the lives of parents and ancestors—and receives its being, not from above or outside but under the conditions of, and amid, the sin-nexus that oppresses the human race.[49]

[300] Although creationism and traducianism both face insoluble difficulties, it is nevertheless remarkable that Eastern Orthodox, Roman Catholic, and Reformed theologians almost unanimously embraced the former view, while the latter found acceptance only among the Lutherans. The reason lies in a different view of the nature and destiny of man. What is at stake here is the line of demarcation between humans and angels. When Lutherans locate the image of God solely in a number of moral qualities, notably original righteousness, then our embodiment is of negligible religious and theological significance. Hence, the boundaries between human beings and angels and between human beings and animals are no longer sharply drawn. But Roman Catholic and Reformed theologians, even if they sometimes still denominated the angels as "image of God," from the beginning sought the image of God in the total and entirely unique nature of human beings in its totality. It consists in the fact that the human spirit ($\pi\nu\epsilon\upsilon\mu\alpha$) was from the beginning adapted to union with a human body ($\sigma\omega\mu\alpha$), and that the body ($\sigma\omega\mu\alpha$) was from the beginning designed for the spirit ($\pi\nu\epsilon\upsilon\mu\alpha$). Before and after the fall, in the state of integrity and that of corruption, in the state of grace and that of glory—human beings always are and always remain essentially distinct from the angels and the animals. Thus the sinner who loses the image does not become an animal; redeemed people do not become angels; they forever are human and, as humans, God's image. This reality is sufficiently preserved only

---

48. T. Aquinas, *Summa Theol.*, I, qu. 118, art. 2; idem, *Summa contra gentiles*, 59, 68.

49. G. Voetius, *Select. disp.*, I, 1097; Francis Turretin, *Institutes of Elenctic Theology*, trans. George Musgrove Giger and ed. James T. Dennison, 3 vols. (Phillipsburg, NJ: Presbyterian and Reformed, 1992), IX, 12.

in creationism. Because human beings *exist* as wholly unique beings, they also *originate* in an entirely special way. Creationism alone sufficiently maintains the specific uniqueness of humanity since it fends off both pantheism and materialism and respects the boundaries between humanity and animals.

The Lutheran view of the image of God also makes the moral unity of the human race take a backseat to physical descent. When all spiritual and moral unity is lost in the fall, natural religion and natural morality are of almost no importance and only physical descent holds humanity together, including their unity in sin. Sin is not primarily ethical, and though it is not regarded as a substance, is still primarily a stain, a form of decay that affects the whole of a human being and above all kills the religious and ethical human faculties. Roman Catholic and Reformed theology insisted that the unity of the human race was not only of a physical but also of an ethical nature. Physical descent is not sufficient to explain original sin and risks materializing it. Realist approaches, e.g., that of Shedd,[50] fail adequately to explain either our solidarity in Adam's sin or our new righteousness in Christ. Only a notion of federal headship can do that. Furthermore, this moral unity of the human race can only be maintained on the basis of creationism, for it has a character of its own, is distinct from that of animals as well as that of the angels, and therefore also comes into being in its own way, both by physical descent and by a creative act of God.

Finally, Lutheran theology does not trouble itself much about human destiny. Adam had everything he needed; he only had to remain what he was. With no need to reach higher, there is no place for a covenant of works or for creationism. Traducianism is sufficient. Again, Roman Catholic and Reformed theology thought otherwise and affirmed a higher human destiny in heavenly blessedness, eternal life, the contemplation of God; all this to be reached in the way of obedience. Although Rome introduces the unbiblical notion of meritoriousness *ex condigno* at this point, both parties agree that the destiny of man lies in eternal blessedness, that this blessedness can only be reached in the way of moral obedience, and that on behalf of the whole human race God put the decision in this matter in the hands of Adam. For that reason these two parties also arrived at creationism. The two essential elements here are: (1) all humanity is included under one covenant head, Adam; (2) all human beings retain their full individual identity and moral agency. The traducianist position of physical descent alone would mean that our sin is a determinist fate, a process of nature, a sickness that incurs no guilt on our part. Neither sin nor righteousness are properly explained this way. Both our *sin* and our *righteousness* presuppose a federal relation between humanity as a whole and its heads.

Creationism alone sufficiently maintains the specific uniqueness of humanity, fends off pantheism and materialism alike, and respects both the organic unity of

50. Ed. note: See W. G. T. Shedd, *Dogmatic Theology*, 3rd ed., 3 vols. (New York: Scribner, 1891–94), II, chap. 1: "Anthropology."

the human race in its entirety and the independent value, worth, and mysterious individual personality of every single human being. We are living stones of the temple of God, each with an individual glorious destiny. Without our unity in Adam, our unity in Christ is jeopardized. If we could not have been condemned in Adam, neither can we be acquitted in Christ. The world, the earth, humanity are one organic whole; they stand, they fall, they are raised up together. The state of integrity—either through the fall or apart from the fall—is a preparation for the state of glory in which God will impart his glory to all his creatures and be "all in all" (1 Cor. 15:28).

12

The Fallen World

The Origin of Sin

[307] The fallen world in which we live rests on the foundations of a creation that was good. Yet, it had scarcely been created before sin crept into it. The origin of sin is a mystery; it is not from God, and at the same time it is not excluded from his counsel. God himself is holy (Deut. 32:4; Job 34:10; Ps. 92:15; Isa. 6:3; Hab. 1:13) and only good, the overflowing fountain of all good (Ps. 36:9; James 1:13, 17; 1 John 1:5). He hates sin, condemns, and judges it (Pss. 5:4; 45:7; Rom. 1:18), and prohibits it in his revealed law (Exod. 20; Deut. 5) and in the conscience of every human (Rom. 2:14–15). God also atones for sin in Christ (Rom. 3:24–26) and redeems his people by making them righteous and holy (1 Cor. 1:30). We are, however, left with inexplicable questions about the origin of sin and evil and its entry into God's good creation. Scripture does tell us that God decided to take humanity on the perilous path of covenantal freedom rather than elevating it by a single act of power above the possibility of sin and death. God created the sin's possibility by fashioning humanity as he did and giving Adam a probationary command that affected not only him but also his posterity. At the heart of the Genesis narrative is the tree of the knowledge of good and evil and the command not to eat of it. Superficial interpretations suggest that the story is about sexual awakening of the first parents from childlike innocence to adult maturity. Variants of this approach consider it in some sense as a story of "awakening," of gaining a knowledge that makes humans more god-like, a step of intellectual, moral, and spiritual "progress"—"a giant step for mankind." Others fragment the story by eliminating the tree altogether, not realizing the profound change that results.

340

Reading the narrative without bias, one gets an impression of profound unity and of its obvious aim to tell us not about the progress and development but about the fall of humankind. The context makes clear that it is a story about sin's origin, followed in Genesis by increasing human wickedness until the flood.

To what does "the knowledge of good and evil" refer? Proposals that the "knowledge" to be gained is cultural power, contrasting rural simplicity with a world-dominating culture, ignore the point of the story altogether. The Bible does not portray human cultural formation as an evil in itself; the point of the "fall" narrative in Genesis is the human desire for *autonomy* from God. To "know good and evil" is to determine good and evil, right and wrong, by oneself, and refuse to submit to any external law. It is, in short, to desire emancipation from God; it is to want to be "like God." The issue in Genesis is whether humanity will want to develop in dependence on God, whether it will want to have dominion over the earth and seek its salvation in submission to God's commandment; or whether, violating that commandment and withdrawing from God's authority and law, it will want to stand on its own feet, go its own way, and try its own "luck." When humanity fell, it got what it wanted; it made itself like God, "knowing good and evil" by its own insight and judgment (Gen. 3:22). This emancipation from God, however, did not and cannot lead to true happiness. That is why God in his probationary command forbade this drive to freedom, this thirst for independence. But humanity voluntarily and deliberately opted for its own way, thereby failing the test.

[308] Sin enters by way of the crafty serpent's lie. The serpent's speaking has often been mistakenly considered an allegory for lust, sexual desire, or errant reason. The various mythical interpretations, not to mention attempts to explain the narrative in terms of animal capacity for speech before the fall, all fail to meet the intent of the passage and the teaching of Scripture as a whole. The only appropriate explanation is to recognize, with ancient exegesis, the entrance of a spiritual superterrestrial power whose nature remains unknown to us. Genesis 3 simply sticks to the visible facts; it describes but does not explain. Furthermore, though its entire narrative rests on this spiritual conflict between the two kingdoms, the rest of the Bible is relatively silent about this. Sin did not start on earth but in heaven with a revolt of spiritual beings. In the case of humanity, the temptation by Satan resulted in the fall. Scripture looks for the origin of sin solely in the will of rational creatures. It is, nonetheless, understandable that Genesis 3 makes no mention of the spiritual background of the events in question. Sin's nature, power, and consequence only become apparent in the course of history; the depth of the darkness comes out as revelation progressively unfolds. The rest of Scripture is relatively silent about the fall into sin; the principal verses (Job 31:33; Ps. 90:3; Prov. 3:18; 13:12; Eccles. 12:7; Isa. 43:27; 51:3; 65:25; Joel 2:3; Hosea 6:7; Ezek. 28:13–15; John 8:44; Rom. 5:12ff.; 8:20; 1 Cor. 15:21–22, 42–49; 2 Cor. 11:3; 1 Tim. 2:14; Rev. 2:7; 22:2) are open to different interpretations and often contain little more than allusions.

Scripture's relative silence on the fall must not be misinterpreted, such as explaining it away as of "late" origin. The story of a "fall" from an original "golden age" can be found among all peoples, and Genesis is foundational to the entire biblical understanding of humanity from the Old Testament prophets to the apostle Paul's use of the First Adam/Second Adam parallel in Romans 5 and 1 Corinthians 15. Jesus tells us that the devil was a murderer from the beginning (ἀπ᾽ ἀρχης, *ap arches*; John 8:44; 1 John 3:8) and both Paul (1 Tim. 3:6) and Jude (v. 6) refer to the fall and condemnation of the devil and his angels. Scripture does not give us many details but is clear that sin did not start on earth but in heaven, at the feet of God's throne, in his immediate presence, and that the fall of angels preceded that of humans. How this is exactly connected to the original human sin is not explained but we do know that Satan is the adversary, the tempter, the slanderer of the human race, the murderer of mankind (Matt. 4:3; John 8:44; Eph. 6:11; 1 Thess. 3:5; 2 Tim. 2:26), the "great dragon," the "ancient serpent" (Rev. 12:9, 14–15; 20:2). For the rest, Scripture teaches us that even unclean spirits can do superhuman things and temporarily take possession of humans (Matt. 8:28ff.; Mark 5:7ff.; Luke 8:28ff.; Acts 19:15). Satan fell, tempted Adam and Eve, and they fell; the origin of sin lies solely in the will of rational creatures.

[309] The Christian church insists on a historical fall. This is challenged by historical criticism as well as evolutionary dogma. Geology, paleontology, and all prehistorical studies seem to exclude an original moral perfection and a subsequent fall of the first humans. Paradise supposedly lies ahead of rather than behind us as we emerge from darkness and progress in the direction of light and life, peace and happiness. Defenders of a notion of an original universal sin often accommodate themselves to this critique by arguing from experience as a way of validating Genesis 3. Bishop Charles Gore, for example, unwilling to acknowledge the historicity of Genesis 3 while at the same time not wishing to concede anything to critics of the Christian faith, writes: "the Christian doctrine of sin rests on a far broader and far surer foundation than the belief that the early chapters of Genesis belong to one form or stage of inspired literature rather than to another. It rests on the strong foundation of our Lord, *accepted and verified by man's moral consciousness*."[1] Replacing *faith* in Scripture's testimony with human experience of the world as the reason to accept Genesis 3 does not work. It falsely assumes that we are able to understand our world correctly without Scripture. While historical accounts are facts quite apart from our knowledge of them, it remains the case that all our knowledge of history depends on testimony, on reliable witnesses. That is why Genesis 3 is so important; it is the inspired testimony about our original and current state before God. Without it we would be ignorant of a truth that is essential to our well-being. The main critical objection, we must not forget, is directed not

---

1. C. Gore, *Lux mundi*, 13th ed. (London: Murray, 1892), 395; idem, *The New Theology and the Old Religion* (London: Murray, 1907), 233 (emphasis added, ed.); cf. also James Orr, *God's Image in Man and Its Defacement in the Light of Modern Denials* (London: Hodder & Stoughton, 1906), 298ff.

against the literary report in Genesis as such but against the event reported there. This event is of such great weight that the whole of Christian doctrine stands or falls with it. "All of faith consists in Jesus Christ and in Adam and all of morality in lust and in grace" (Pascal). The two truths or facts by which all of Christian dogmatics is governed are (1) the fall of Adam and (2) the resurrection of Christ.[2]

To this must be added that objections to the reality of the fall are themselves increasingly under review by recent trends in the biblical and archaeological/anthropological sciences. Proof of an evolution from animal existence to a primitive existence different from our human experience today is still wanting. The archaeological evidence suggests great *regression* over time from the heights of ancient Babylonian and Egyptian civilizations rather than unilinear *progress*. The Genesis account and the unity of the human race thus speaks positively to our conscience and our experience. All in all, the science of nature and history to this day lacks the right to pronounce on the truth of the state of integrity and the human fall. The Genesis testimony, confirmed by the later appeal made to it by prophets and apostles and Christ himself, and intertwined as a necessary constituent in the whole revelation of salvation, continues in people's conscience and meshes perfectly with the reality of our daily experience.

Although no true parallel to the biblical account has been found, it is clear from the myths of other ancients that underlying the religious and moral convictions of the human race are common beliefs in the divine origin and destiny of humanity, in a golden age and decline, in the conflict of good and evil, and in the wrath and appeasement of the deity. The origin and essence of sin, however, remain unknown to them. Pagans, though they gropingly searched for God, did not find him (Acts 17:27); they find sin's origin in nature itself rather than in the will of rational creatures. Confucianism is a shallow form of rationalism and moralism that considers humans naturally good and seeks salvation in virtuous lives that conform to the world order.[3] According to Buddhism, the divine substance—Atman or Brahman—is the only reality, all else is an illusion (*maya*) and in constant flux; suffering and sorrow are found in desire, including the desire for existence and will to live, while salvation consists of extinguishing consciousness and/or the annihilation of existence: nirvana.[4] Other religious directions such as Parsism are radically dualistic and trace evil to an equally ultimate and eternal evil principle.[5] Philosophers have treated sin as hubris that can be overcome by human will (Seneca), as ignorance to be overcome by education in virtue (Socrates), as inevitable and necessary (Stoics), or even as a fall of preexistent souls (Plato). However, outside of special revelation, sin is either treated deistically in terms

2. Jan Hendrik Gerretsen, *Rechtvaardigmaking bij Paulus in verband met de prediking van Christus in de synopticien de beginselen der Reformatie* (Nijmegen: Ten Hoet, 1905).

3. P. D. Chantepie de la Saussaye, *Lehrbuch der Religionsgeschichte*, 3rd ed., 2 vols. (Tübingen: Mohr [Siebeck], 1905), I, 249, A. I, 100ff.

4. Ibid., I, 411ff.; II, 89ff.

5. Ibid., II, 34ff., 199ff.

344   HUMANITY AND SIN

of human will alone or derived pantheistically from the very necessary nature of things.

[310] Both views found their way into Christianity. The British monk Pelagius rejected all notions of original sin and considered every person as having Adam's full moral choice of will. The fall did not happen at the beginning but is repeated in every human sin. Although the church rejected Pelagianism in its extreme form, Roman Catholicism lapsed into semi-Pelagianism, maintaining the notion of a less-than-completely fallen will and limiting the fall to the loss of the supernatural gifts which can only be restored by sacramental grace. When the Reformation rejected Roman Catholic dualism, streams within Protestantism, notably rationalist groups such as the Socinians as well as the Remonstrants, robbed Christianity by dispensing with the need for grace in some measure. They regard the image of God as a fully free will, which, like that of the pre-fall Adam, remains intact. We are born with an inclination to sin that is not culpable; atonement is needed only for actual sin. Suffering and death are not necessarily linked to sin; they are simply part of our human condition. Although this view is highly unsatisfying, it was revived in the late nineteenth century by, among others, Albrecht Ritschl.

Ritschl is noteworthy because he attempts the seemingly impossible: reconcile Pelagius with Augustine. Commendably, he begins with Christian revelation and faith but falsely concludes from this that our knowledge of sin does not come from the Old Testament—the fall, the law—but solely from the gospel, which for Ritschl is the person and teaching of Jesus. The gospel of forgiveness is the basis for the knowledge of our sinfulness. Ritschl agrees with Pelagius that human willing and actual sin precede the sinful state or condition of humanity but also that this precedence applies to the *collective* sin of all human beings, the sin of humanity as a whole, viewed as the sum of all individuals. He then resorts to Augustine by insisting that these singular sinful acts mutually reinforce each other and create a collective realm of sin that exerts influence on us, a reinforcing reciprocity that enslaves all people. In short: there is no original sin, but out of the sinful acts of all people collectively arises a collective unity, a realm of sin.[6]

When Ritschl's approach is combined with evolutionary theory—envisioned in strictly materialistic and mechanistic terms—all notions of good and evil, the possibility of a moral life, vanish behind physical and chemical processes. With ironic inconsistency, proponents of a mechanical evolution continue to speak of good and evil, of moral law and moral obligation, of a culture of the true, the good, and the beautiful. Because pure naturalism and mechanism are so dissatisfying to the human spirit, many accept the given theory of evolution with respect to our "animal ancestry" but object to construing the first human state in extremely primitive terms, creating a portrait of our ancestry that is "reprehensible . . . by

6. A. Ritschl, *Die christliche Lehre von der Rechtfertigung und Versöhnung*, 2nd ed., 3 vols. (Bonn: A. Marcus, 1880–83), II, 241–46; III, 304–57. Ed. note: The third volume of Ritschl's work is available in English: *The Christian Doctrine of Justification and Reconciliation* (Clifton, NJ: Reference Book Publishers, 1966); the section on sin is on 327–84.

the standards of contemporary ethics."⁷ As a solution, some envision a parallel "evolution of the spirit" in which we rise above our primitive animal nature to a more humanized, civilized plane. A sin is an act of reverting to the habits and tendencies "left over" from this state; sin is an anachronism—not living up to current standards—and "fallenness" merely states the threat, universally present in all of us, of those latent animal forces. Humanity did not fall once; it falls persistently when it violates, not perennial norms of right and wrong, but the social constraints and conventions of the day. These too, "evolve" as humans create new and more enlightened understandings of what is right and wrong. In other words, from an evolutionary viewpoint, "sin is not an innovation, but is the survival or misuse of habits and tendencies that were incidental to an earlier stage of development and whose sinfulness lies in their anachronism." Augustine was correct in insisting that this "fallenness" is universal; Pelagius was correct when he claimed that sin is always a willful act.⁸ We sin when we act contrary to our "better nature," against the way "civilized" people ought to act. Every human is "the Adam [or Eve] of his [or her] own soul."

[311] This attempt to reconcile Augustine and Pelagius fails at several levels. Apart from the lack of proof for materialistic evolution of humanity, it oscillates between Scripture and evolutionism, ignoring the troubling fact that these are two mutually exclusive views of human origins and original sin. Either there is or there is not a fundamental continuity between animals and humanity. One cannot have it both ways. If one affirms full continuity, then one is at a loss to explain the origin of a free human will in the evolutionary process. How does moral consciousness arise in primitive, animal-like man? If our natural instincts and desires are not evil in themselves, why try and whence the will to overcome them? Where could any notion of "our better selves" come from? It is much more than just "a stupendously difficult task"⁹; it is inconceivable and impossible. It is psychologically unthinkable to regard the will as somehow outside human nature. This theory of the origin of sin is diametrically opposed to the witness of Scripture and entails the modernization of the entire Christian confession concerning revelation, atonement, infant baptism, and so on.¹⁰ Even worse, with this understanding moral freedom not only becomes precarious, moral improvement becomes virtually impossible. Although it claims a Pelagian pedigree in affirming free will, in fact it provides a portrait of human enslavement to its animal nature. Sin's power increases, and explanations for its origin flounder. The hard choice

7. W. Ostwald, *Energetische Grundlagen der Kulturwissenschaft* (Leipzig: W. Klinkhardt, 1909), 120.

8. The following writers hold variations of this view: F. R. Tennant, *The Origin and Propagation of Sin*, 2nd ed. (Cambridge: Cambridge University Press, 1902); J. R. Illingworth, *Personality Human and Divine* (London: Macmillan, 1908); R. J. Campbell, *The New Theology*, popular ed. (New York: Macmillan, 1907); Sir Oliver Lodge, *The Substance of Faith Allied with Science: A Catechism for Parents and Teachers*, 3rd ed. (London: Methuen, 1907); W. E. Orchard, *Modern Theories of Sin* (London: Clark, 1909), 114ff.

9. F. R. Tennant, *Origin and Propagation of Sin*, 86, 92, 113, 118, 119.

10. Cf. ibid., xii, xxviii, 113, 119, 123ff., 144, 446.

between locating sin in humanity's sensual nature and thus calling into question human culpability and moral responsibility, or, in Pelagian fashion, attributing it all to rational acts of the human will and failing to do justice to sin's intractability—we are left here with an insoluble conundrum. Facing the riddle of sin, eventually, human speculation leads to finding the source of sin and evil in human nature itself, in the nature of the cosmos as a whole, or, even in God himself.

The first two postures are generally characterized by half-heartedness and inconsistency; advocates do not really want to attribute sin's impulses to human nature or to a sense of cosmic disorder or inadequacy. Notable is the "mixed" attitude toward human sexuality; on the one hand it is good; on the other it is the source of concupiscence and disordered affections. Inevitably, the third position returns: it is to God himself—his being or his acts—that we must turn to find answers to the "why" of sin and evil. Thus, the theosophical tradition represented by Böhme and Schelling locates evil in a tension of potencies within God himself. For Hegel the fall was the Ur-fact of history when the Absolute realized itself in the world as its own alternative existence. From here it is a small step to Buddhism, which considers existence itself as the greatest sin. Clearly, apart from Scripture's revelation, we are lost for answers; led astray into finally attributing sin and evil to either creation itself or to God. Undoubtedly, next to the question of existence itself, the origin of sin and evil is the greatest enigma of life and the heaviest cross for the intellect to bear. Where do we turn for answers?

[312] To begin, philosophy does provide evidence that this world is inexplicable without a fall but cannot tell us how or why. The sensual nature of humanity cannot be the source since the "spiritual" sins of the elderly—pride, envy, hatred, enmity against God—are often more appalling than the "fleshly" sins of youth. Asceticism solves nothing; monks take the sin in their hearts with them into the cloister. It is an error to appeal to Paul's understanding of "flesh" here. "Flesh" (בָּשָׂר and σαρξ) does point to the material substance of the human body (1 Cor. 15:39) in contrast to spirit (πνευμα), mind (νους), and heart (καρδια) (Rom. 2:28; 2 Cor. 7:5; Col. 2:5). It also points to humans as earthly, weak, fragile, and transient beings (Gen. 6:3; 18:27; Job 4:17–19; 15:14–15; 25:4–6; Pss. 78:39; 103:14; Isa. 40:6; Jer. 17:5; Rom. 3:20; 1 Cor. 1:29; Gal. 2:16). But its most profound use is to point out the sinful life orientation of humans as "carnal," "in the flesh," of "being, living, walking according to the flesh" (Rom. 3:7; 7:14; 8:3f.; 1 Cor. 3:3; 2 Cor. 10:2–3; etc.). "Flesh" is contrasted with "spirit," though not with the human πνευμα, which is also sinful and needs sanctification (Rom. 12:1–2; 1 Cor. 7:34; 2 Cor. 7:1; Eph. 4:23; 1 Thess. 5:23), but with the "Holy Spirit" (πνευμα άγιον) of God (Rom. 8:2, 9, 11), which renews the human spirit (Rom. 7:6; 8:14; Gal. 5:18) and consecrates the body (Rom. 6:13, 19; 12:1; 1 Cor. 6:13, 15, 19–20). "Flesh" describes the sinful heart's *direction* away from God's Holy Spirit and to the sinful self and its desires. Aptly, Paul describes hostility against God as the "mind of the flesh" (φρονημα της σαρκος; Rom. 8:7). Paul in no way suggests that the fleshly material body is the source of sin. This overlooks the spiritual-ethical

character of σαρξ, not to mention Paul's strong affirmation of *bodily* resurrection (1 Cor. 15) and repudiation of asceticism (Col. 2:16; 1 Thess. 4:4). σαρξ denotes the sinful life orientation of humans away from God and toward the creature.

This is not to deny or ignore the practical connection between human beings as σαρξ, now understood especially in that second sense of earthly weak, fragile, transient beings, and the reality of sin dwelling in us (Rom. 7:17–18). The "flesh" is the instrument of sin's dominion over us (Rom. 6:12). We are creatures of the earth and our sins are different from those of the angels. Temptations come to us from without via "the desire of the flesh, the desire of the eyes, and the pride in riches" (1 John 2:16). It is the sensual nature of human beings that leads to making a god of their belly, thinking the things that are below, being self-seeking, and honoring the creature above the Creator (Rom. 1:21ff.; Phil. 2:4, 21; 3:19; Col. 3:2; etc.). Explaining sins as arising from our sensual nature does not, however, stop here but has to move on to further explanation. Either one locates sin's cause in nature itself—physicality or finiteness—and is left with an eternal power independent of God, or one locates it in the dark nature or blind will within the divine being itself. This profound insight acknowledges the deep power and dominion of sin; if it is that serious it cannot have been an accident, outside God's will and counsel.

The move, therefore, to attribute all this to the Creator is a natural. Facing life's contradictions, some conclude that sin is the necessary obstacle we must overcome to develop morally and become perfect (Kant). We need sin to "grow." In Schelling's words: Without the ironclad law of contradiction as the principle of all being "there would be no movement, no life, no progress, but everlasting repose, the death slumber of all forces."[11] The law of contradiction is "the source of eternal life." For God to "become" God he must overcome the dark nature within himself. In himself he is an "unknown abyss" (βυθος ἀγνωστος), a dark nature, a blind will, and as such the creator of matter. "In order for there to be no evil, God himself would have to not be."[12] In support, proponents of this view appeal to those scriptural passages that speak of sins and disasters as "necessary" (Matt. 18:7; Luke 24:26; John 9:3; 1 Cor. 11:19; 2 Tim. 2:20) and to teachers such as Augustine and Calvin who include sin in God's counsel and providence.

There is a semblance of truth here; sin is not an accident or tragedy that surprises and distresses God. But this view makes sin eternal and God the eventual author of sin. There is in fact no real "sin" here; it is an illusion. If we must speak of "sin," it is the notion of sin itself that is wrong. Scripture and human moral consciousness rebel against these conclusions which lead naturally to pessimism and libertinism.

11. F. W. J. Schelling, *Ausgewählte Werke*, 4 vols. (Darmstadt: Wissenschaftliche Buchgesellschaft, 1968), V, 25, 127 ("Die Weltalter Erstes Buch" [1813]); *Sämmtliche Werke* (Stuttgart & Augsburg: J. G. Cotta'scher 1856–61), I/8, 219, 321; cf. also John Fiske, *Through Nature to God* (Boston and New York: Houghton Mifflin, 1899), first essay on "The Mystery of Evil."

12. F. W. J. Schelling, *Ausgewählte Werke*, IV, 347 ("Philosophische Untersuchungen über das Wesen der menschlichen Freiheit und die damit zusammenhängenden Gegenstände" [1809]; *Sämmtliche Werke*, I/7, 403).

Sin has an ethical character as an act of human willing and may not be reduced to something cosmically necessary or eternal. Evil has no ontological existence of its own and it is not merely a lower or lesser degree of the good; sin is parasitical and radically antithetical to God's good creation; it is that which must be overcome and defeated. Sin is neither rational nor lawful; it is lawlessness (ἀνομια); it is not necessary to the existence of either creatures or God. The good is necessary even for evil to exist, but the good does not need evil, nor does holiness need sin, nor truth falsehood, nor God Satan. Yes, human sin and evil sometimes serve to bring the good to fuller disclosure and to glorify God's attributes. But when this occurs—against sin's intent, not with its consent and cooperation—by the wisdom and omnipotence of God, sin is forced to serve the honor of God and the coming of his kingdom against its own genius. Sin has no power here; it is God's almighty power that brings good out of evil, light out of darkness, and life out of death. We may never seek out philosophical explanations that, in the name of human emancipation, rationalize and justify our sinful behavior by placing responsibility for it at God's feet.

[313] At the same time Scripture firmly announces that sin is not outside the counsel and government of the holy God in whom there is no sin.[13] The question of God's relation to sin is thus vexing. Those who rightly seek to absolve God for sin sometimes speak of "permission," but this always seems inadequate. Augustine understood this: "In a wondrous, indescribable way even that which is done against His will is not done without His will. It simply could not be done if He did not permit it, and of course He permits it not against His will, but with it; nor would He in His goodness permit evil unless in His omnipotence He could bring good even out of evil."[14] Reformed theology followed Augustine here and confronted the difficulty of Scripture's "hard sayings" about God, who not only *in some sense* willed the possibility of sin and created human creatures capable of sin but also hardens and softens hearts, commands sins, and loves and hates (e.g., Exod. 7:3; 2 Sam. 16:10; 24:1; Mal. 1:3; Luke 2:34; Rom. 9:17–18; 2 Thess. 2:11; etc.). The word "permission," conceived in a negative sense, offers no solution whatever to the problem of God's relation to sin, fails utterly to answer the objection that God is the author of sin, and in fact withdraws sin from God's providential government. All "permission" is an act of God's will; he *willed* to permit it. But God is never the *agent* of sin; only creatures are.

And though both good and evil are within God's providential governance of all things, he stands in a different relation to each. In the case of the good, this must be understood as God's Spirit working in a subject and positively enabling the good. We may never see sin this way; it is lawlessness and deformity, and does not have God as its efficient cause, but at most as its deficient cause. Light

13. See chapter 8, above; cf. H. Bavinck, *Reformed Dogmatics*, ed. John Bolt (Grand Rapids: Baker Academic, 2003–8), II, 345–47, 393–95, 615–19 (##233, 246, 306).

14. Augustine, *Enchiridion*, III, 95–100; idem, *The Trinity*, III, 4ff.; idem, *City of God*, XIV, 11; idem, *On Free Will*, 20–21.

cannot of itself produce darkness; the darkness only arises when the light is withdrawn. To say that sin is not outside God's providence means, in the first place, that God deals with sin in a way that corresponds to its nature. Like the natural laws governing gravity and celestial orbits, so sin too abides by God's ordinances. The parallel here is with illness, decomposition, and death, which are the antipodes of health, development, and life, but are still governed by laws. Thus the moral order follows its own order, and sin's consequences of death and destruction are played out in the course of human history. This normativity in sin demonstrates that God's kingdom governs over it as well. Sinners do not make themselves free and independent of God; on the contrary, though they were sons and daughters before, they are now slaves. Those who commit sin become the slaves of sin.[15]

[314] But why did God include sin in his decree and its execution? We know that God uses sin to punish the wicked (Deut. 2:30; Josh. 11:20; Judg. 9:23–24; John 12:40; Rom. 1:21–28; 2 Thess. 2:11–12), to save his people (Gen. 45:5; 50:20), to test and chastise them (Job 1:11–12; 2 Sam. 24:1; 1 Cor. 10:13; 11:19; 2 Cor. 12:7), and to glorify his name (Exod. 7:3; Prov. 16:4; Rom. 9:17; 11:33; etc.). Precisely because God is the absolutely Holy and Almighty One, he can do what we cannot: use sin as a means in his hand. God would never have tolerated sin had he not been able to govern it in an absolutely holy and sovereign manner. Being God, he did not fear its existence and its power. If he had not allowed it to exist, it might be said that he was not in all his attributes superior to a power whose possibility was inherent in creation itself. But God, because he is God, never feared the way of freedom, the reality of sin, the eruption of wickedness, or the power of Satan. Because he knew he was absolutely able to control sin, "he deemed it better to bring good out of evil than not to permit any evil to exist at all."[16] The many images that Augustine uses to assign sin a place in the order of the creation—shadows in a painting, contrasts in music, solecisms and barbarisms in language—all the antithetical elements that heighten the harmony and beauty of the whole,[17] contain some truth but also easily bring about misunderstanding. They

15. On God's relation to sin, see the church fathers Origen, Athanasius, Basil, and others in Wilhelm Münscher, *Lehrbuch der christlichen Dogmengeschichte*, ed. Daniel von Coelln, 3rd ed. (Cassel: J. C. Krieger, 1832–38), I, 157; and also T. Aquinas, *Summa Theol.*, I, qu. 49, art. 2; II, 1, qu. 79, art. 2; idem, *Summa contra gentiles*, III, 3, 71; John Calvin, *Institutes of the Christian Religion*, I.xviii; II.iv (ed. John T. McNeill and trans. Ford Lewis Battles, 2 vols. [1559; Philadelphia: Westminster, 1960], 1:228–37, 309–16); idem, *Concerning the Eternal Predestination of God*, trans. J. K. S. Reid (London: James Clarke, 1961), 162–82 (*Corpus reformatorum*, 36:347–66 and 37:262–318); Peter van Mastricht, *Theoretico-practica theologia* (Utrecht: Appels, 1714), III, 10, 19ff.; F. Turretin, *Institutes of Elenctic Theology*, trans. George Musgrove Giger and ed. James T. Dennison, 3 vols. (Phillipsburg, NJ: Presbyterian and Reformed, 1992), VI, qu. 8.

16. Augustine, *Enchiridion*, 112, 27; idem, *City of God*, XXII, 1; idem, *The Literal Meaning of Genesis*, trans. John Hammond Taylor (New York: Newman, 1982), II, 9; idem, *On Genesis, against the Manicheans*, II, 28.

17. Augustine, *City of God*, XI, 18; idem, *On Genesis, against the Manicheans*, I, 16; T. Aquinas, *Summa Theol.*, I, qu. 48, art. 2; idem, *Summa contra gentiles*, III, 61.

suggest that sin is somehow "fitting" in God's world, and fail to provide comfort and solace to those who wrestle with sin or are suffering. It is true that even in, and especially through, God's government over sin that we see a glorious display of his attributes, God's grace and compassion, his mercy and forebearance, his power to heal and save. When humanity broke the covenant of works, God gave us the covenant of grace, and his eternal Son for our salvation. The sin that is in the world, so far from being able to rob us of our faith in God, his love, and his power, rather confirms and strengthens us in that faith. *"If there is evil, there is a God.* For there would be no evil, if the order of good were removed, the privation of which is evil; and there would be no such order, if there were no God."[18] We do not doubt that God willed the possibility of sin and created angels and humans so that they could sin and fall.

[315] How that possibility became reality remains a mystery. Sin defies explanation; it is a folly that does not have an origin in the true sense of the word, only a beginning. It is helpful here to reflect on how our human faculties and our structured being as embodied souls make the path of sin possible and understandable. We must begin with the imagination. As Thomas à Kempis said: "At first it is a mere thought confronting the mind; then imagination paints it in stronger colours; only after that do we take pleasure in it, and the will makes a false move, and we give our assent."[19] The mind entertains the idea of sin, the imagination beautifies and converts it into a fascinating ideal, desire reaches out to it, and the will goes ahead and does it. Thus, in the case of both angels and humans, the imagination was the faculty that made the violation of the commandment appear as the road to equality with God. We must not, however, think of angelic and human sin and fall in parallel terms. What little we know about the fall of the angels (1 Tim. 3:6; 2 Pet. 2:4) suggests *pride*, the will to be equal to God in power and dominion, was the beginning and principle of their fall; temptation did not come from without; unlike humans, they were not *led* astray. As Jesus suggests when he notes that the devil speaks "according to his own nature" when he lies (John 8:44), they fell by their own agency. Human beings, however, are "from the earth, creatures of dust" who became living souls (1 Cor. 15:45ff.). As "earthly" embodied creatures, Genesis 3 indicates that Adam and Eve's temptation was less a matter of *pride* (though this is not excluded) than of yielding to Satan's external appeal to the lust of the eyes, the craving of the flesh, and the pride of life. For that reason Scripture so closely links the sensual nature of a human being and sin. Already from the first sin it was evident that human beings are ("flesh"); all subsequent sins highlight our human nature as temptable, weak, and unreliable. This is not the Greek dualism that separates the "material" and the "spiritual" but

---

18. T. Aquinas, *Summa contra gentiles*, III, 71.

19. Thomas à Kempis, *The Imitation of Christ*, trans. William C. Creasy (Macon, GA: Mercer University Press, 1989), I, 13, 5; Augustine (*On Genesis, against the Manicheans*, II, 21) therefore already pointed out that in the experience of everyone who falls into sin the same process occurs that is described for us in Gen. 3. See also James 1:13–15.

a reminder that all human sins, including intellectual and spiritual ones, bear a character that corresponds to our "psychic" (earthly) nature and thus differ from the sins of angels. The pre-fall human was not the image of God despite but *in* his or her peculiar "psychic" (earthly) nature which defined it.

We are, nonetheless, still left in the dark about the origin of sin. In fact, believing that sinful acts can be "explained" by tracing their "causes" is folly. Sin cannot be physically or logically deduced from antecedent circumstances, reasonings, or considerations. If sin were "understood," that is to say explained as a necessary consequence from antecedent factors, it would no longer be sin. Sinful acts are "caused" by sinful wills. Sin is a defect, a privation of good. "Trying to discover the causes of such deficiencies—causes which, as I have said, are not efficient but deficient—is like trying to see the darkness or hear the silence."[20] In its origin, therefore, sin was folly and an absurdity. Sin has no origin in the true sense of the word, only a beginning. Satan has, therefore, not incorrectly been called an "irony of all logic."[21] Here we arrive at the boundaries of our knowledge; sin *exists*, but it will never be able to justify its existence. It is unlawful and irrational.

[316] Attempting to locate the time of the fall, too, is impossible. Attempts to identify that time in the preformed chaos of Genesis 1:1 or in notions of preexistent souls are theologically and philosophically, as well as scripturally, without ground. The latter view is found in India, Persia, and Egypt; in various Greek philosophers such as Empedocles, Pythagoras, and Plato; in Rome; and in the Jewish Kabbalah, and the reason for its existence is easy to understand. When this life, beginning at conception and birth, frequently seems to be pure misery, preexistence points to a moral debt carried from a previous existence. The suffering and sorrow of this present life is a debt/penalty for evil done before; failure to pay this debt or even an increase in indebtedness consigns one to a future existence that justly rewards or punishes us for our conduct now. The ideas of the preexistence of souls and of the transmigration of souls, therefore, are correlative: both are controlled by the idea of retribution, of karma.[22] Even the church father Origen adopted the theory of the preexistence and fall of souls in order to explain the inequality of rational creatures in their lot in life.[23] Theosophists frequently combined notions of the soul's preexistence and fall with the idea that human beings were originally androgynous and that the creation of the woman was in fact proof of an antecedent fall.[24] In the nineteenth century, notions of preexistence were linked to the

20. Augustine, *City of God*, XII, 7.

21. A. Tholuck, *Die Lehre von der Sünde und vom Versöhner* (Gotha: F. A. Perthes, 1862), 15; W. G. T. Shedd, *Dogmatic Theology*, 3rd ed., 3 vols. (New York: Scribner, 1891–94), II, 156; J. Laidlaw, *The Bible Doctrine of Man* (Edinburgh: T&T Clark, 1895), 209.

22. P. Gennrich, *Die Lehre von der Wiedergeburt: Die christliche Zentrallehre in dogmengeschichtlicher und religionsgeschichtlicher Beleuchtung* (Leipzig: Deichert, 1907), 275ff.

23. Cf. H. Bavinck, *Reformed Dogmatics*, II, 460–63, 557–61 (##265, 292); J. Müller, *The Christian Doctrine of Sin*, trans. W. Urwick, 5th ed., 2 vols. (Edinburgh: T&T Clark, 1868), II, 76, 155.

24. Cf. H. Bavinck, *Reformed Dogmatics*, II, 565–68 (#295); Campegius Vitringa, *Doctrina christianae religionis*, ed. M. Vitringa, 8 vols. (Leiden: Joannis le Mair, 1761–86), II, 265.

theory of evolution in a curious way: If all higher forms of life have developed from lower forms, then the human soul too must have a preformation in the animal world, continuously develop in humans, and at death pass over into a higher form of existence. Here Darwinism and Spiritism are on the same wavelength. The preformation of humans downward is supplemented by their metamorphosis upward: the animal becomes a human and "man" becomes "Superman."[25]

Avoiding such speculation, we must be satisfied with the straightforward account of Scripture. The possibility of sin is given with creation but the fall is essentially distinct from it. Sin was brought into being by the will of the creature; it does not belong to the essential being of creation but came by way of disobedience. It is unlawfully there but its existence is no accident. To the extent that it clearly falls within God's purpose and will, we could say that up to a point and in some sense it *had* to be there. But then certainly it always *had to* be there as something that *ought not* to be there and has no right to exist.

THE UNIVERSAL SPREAD OF SIN

[317] The first sin of our original ancestors had calamitous consequences for them as well as their posterity and unleashed a flood of misery on creation. The entire human race bears the guilt, pollution, and consequence of sin. This universality of sin is also universally acknowledged—"To sin is common to all people"; "There will be faults as long as there are human beings"[26]—but most articulately voiced in Holy Scripture. After the story of the fall (Gen. 3) we are told how sin spread and expanded, finally reaching such a pitch that God sent the judgment of the flood. Of the generation before the flood, it is said that their wickedness was so great that "every inclination of the thoughts of their hearts was only evil continually," and that "the earth was corrupt in God's sight" and "filled with violence" (Gen. 6:5, 11–12). But the flood changed nothing. No one, laments Job, can bring a clean thing out of an unclean (14:4). When "the Lord looks down from heaven on humanity," "to see if there are any who are wise, who seek God" (Pss. 14; 53), he sees nothing but decline and iniquity: "They have all gone astray, they are all alike perverse; there is no one who does good, no, not one." No one, accordingly, can stand before the face of the Lord, for no human living is righteous before him (Ps. 130:3). The new covenant also leaves us in no doubt. John the Baptist came preaching repentance for the whole of God's people, and the apostles were clear in preaching that all people are sinners and need the forgiving love of the Father, redemption by Christ, the renewal of the Holy Spirit (Acts 2:38; 5:31; 10:43;

25. Cf. Herman Bavinck, *The Philosophy of Revelation* (Grand Rapids: Eerdmans, 1953), 293.

26. T.Pfanner, *Systema theologiae gentilis purioris* (Basel: Joh. Hermann Widerhold, 1679), IX, 7; K. G. Bretschneider, *Systematische Entwickelung*, 4th ed. (Leipzig: J. A. Barth, 1841), II, 16; F. R. de Lamennais, *Essay on Indifference in Matters of Religion*, trans. Henry Edward John Stanley (London: John Macqueen, 1895), III, 393–408.

etc.). Similarly, the apostle Paul in Romans argues at length that the whole world is damnable before God and therefore that no flesh will be justified by the works of the law (Rom. 3:19–20; cf. 5:12; 11:32; 2 Cor. 5:19; Gal. 3:22; 1 John 1:8; 5:19). Consequently, even the word "world" acquires the additional significance of a reality that was originally created by God (John 1:3; Col. 1:16; Heb. 1:2) but is now so corrupted by sin that it faces God as a hostile power. It does not know the Logos to whom it owes its existence (John 1:10), lies under the power of the evil one (1 John 5:19), is subject to Satan (John 14:30; 16:11), and will one day pass away (1 John 2:17).

Furthermore, sin characterizes us from our youth, our birth, even from our conception (Gen. 6:5; 8:21; Job 13:26; 14:4; Pss. 25:7; 51:5; 58:3; 103:14; Isa. 43:27; 48:8; 57:3; Ezek. 16:3; Hosea 5:7; John 3:6; Rom. 7:7ff.; Eph. 2:3). Scripture uses the language of "flesh" (σαρξ)—our earthly, sensual nature that is "from below"—to speak of this. "Flesh" is the obstacle to entering the kingdom of God, to pleasing God, to seeing God (John 3:6, 31; 8:23; Rom. 8:7–8; 1 Cor. 15:50). As σαρξ we are impure and corrupt from birth, "by nature (φυσει) children of wrath" (Eph. 2:3; cf. Rom. 2:14–15; 1 Cor. 2:14). Scripture simply assumes that sin and human depravity are universal and "natural"—not in the sense of "created that way" but as a given in our *fallen* world. The human heart, from which flow the springs of life (Prov. 4:23), is corrupt (Gen. 6:5; 8:21; Ps. 14:1; Jer. 17:9; Ezek. 36:26; Matt. 15:19), the source of all iniquities (Mark 7:21). The mind of humans is darkened (Job 21:14; Isa. 1:3; Jer. 4:22; John 1:5; Rom. 1:21–22; 1 Cor. 1:18–23; 2:14; Eph. 4:18; 5:8), proud, errant, polluted and needing to be broken, illumined, and cleansed (Ps. 51:19; Prov. 16:18, 32; Eccles. 7:9; Isa. 57:15; 66:2; 1 Cor. 7:34; 2 Cor. 7:1; 1 Thess. 5:23); the human soul is stained guilty and impure and needs atonement and repentance (Lev. 17:11; Pss. 19:7; 41:4; Prov. 19:3, 16; Matt. 16:26; Titus 1:15; Heb. 9:9, 14; 10:22; 1 Pet. 1:22). All the members of our bodies—the eyes (Deut. 29:4; Ps. 18:27; Isa. 35:5; 42:7; 2 Pet. 2:14; 1 John 2:16), the ears (Deut. 29:4; Pss. 115:6; 135:17; Isa. 6:10; Jer. 5:21; Zech. 7:11), the feet (Ps. 38:16; Prov. 1:16; 4:27; 6:18; Isa. 59:7; Rom. 3:15), the mouth and the tongue (Job 27:4; Pss. 12:3f.; 15:3; 17:10; Jer. 9:3, 5; Rom. 3:14; James 3:5–8)—are in the service of unrighteousness. Even the saints in Scripture have their sins, and Romans 7:10–25 is not a counterargument, since it too speaks of the struggle of the regenerate person.

Romans 7 does require some special attention on our part. Pelagians in all ages and most modern exegetes appeal to Romans 7 to prove that the human mind (νους) or the spirit (πνευμα) remains free from sin, which only resides in the flesh (σαρξ). The Augustinian exegesis—that Paul in using the present tense is speaking of the regenerate person's struggles with sin—is to be preferred for several reasons. According to Paul, the law that brought the believer to knowledge of sin and death (vv. 7–13) is not itself sinful and the consent given to it by the inner self is in tension with the opposition of one's own flesh (vv. 14–25). For the law to be considered "holy," more is required than approval by unregenerate persons; only the regenerate can make this judgment. Because the law is holy, the blame falls on sin, initially apart from the law (v. 9), but then through the law (vv. 8, 14). Sin thus revived and led Paul to despair of himself and his own righteousness; it led to his death (vv. 9ff.). But since this death was in communion with Christ (Gal. 2:19), Paul also arose to life and now discovers this conflict between his center and periphery. In his inner self he loves God's law, but in his members there is another power at work. When Paul says that he is "of the flesh," sold into slavery under sin (Rom 7:14), he does not mean that he is "in the flesh" (Rom. 8:8–9) or that he walks "according to the flesh" (8:4). In spite of this powerful pull, Paul gives thanks that he still "with the mind" (νοῦς) serves the law of God (Rom. 7:25). If Romans 7:14ff. spoke only of the unregenerate, rebirth would not be necessary; a helping, prevenient grace would be sufficient. Then the entire teaching of Scripture on sin and grace, justification and sanctification, faith and repentance would be toppled.

[318] According to Scripture, the universality of sin derives from the fall of our first parents, Adam and Eve. Although it is clearly implied in Genesis 3—the curse of Genesis 3:14ff. applies to Adam and Eve's posterity as well—and assumed in the rest of the Old Testament, it is especially the apostle Paul who spells this out in Romans 5 and 1 Corinthians 15. Post-lapsarian history offers plenty of proof for sin's universal spread and total scope, and Scripture regularly traces it to the perishable sensual nature of humanity (Job 4:17f.; 14:4; 15:14f.; 25:4f.; Pss. 78:38f.; 103:13f.; Mark 14:38; John 3:6; Rom. 6:7ff.; etc.). In Paul we must never overlook the strong emphasis on the superiority of Christ's gift when compared with the consequence of Adam's fall. The abundance of God's grace is in the foreground of his commentary in Romans 5. The phrase "inasmuch as all sinned" (ἐφ' ᾧ παντες ἥμαρτον; Rom. 5:12) does not mean that Paul locates the cause of every person's death in his or her actual sins, for in 1 Corinthians 15:22 he expressly states that all die in Adam. Nor does ἥμαρτον refer to a sinful state but to an act. The plain meaning is this: Adam sinned: consequently sin and death entered the world and reigned. It is of course true that we are also judged because of our own sin; however, Paul's point here is that our sinful condition is God's antecedent judgment on the entire human race thanks to the sin of the representative man, Adam. This is the doctrine of original sin. Because of one man's trespass, God pronounced a judgment of "guilty" accompanied by a death sentence on all human beings; because of this we are all personally sinners and die. God apprehends and regards, judges, and condemns all humans in one representative man; therefore they all descend from him as sinners and are all subject to death.

[319] Original sin was not a new teaching of Augustine,[27] though earlier theologians did tend to stress free will and actual sin more than the sin inherited from Adam. Still, when Pelagius appealed to earlier writers, he disguised the radical

27. Who said: "I did not dream up original sin, which the catholic faith believes from of old" (*On Marriage and Concupiscence*, II, 42).

novelty of his own anthropology. According to Pelagius, all persons are born with pure souls; sin and evil come into being only through imitation. On our own, without grace, we can will and do the good. Sin is always and only a *personal* matter. To charge us with the sins of others is contrary to God's justice. Pelagius's views had historical antecedents in Greek and Roman philosophy and in Jewish thought that considered created souls as pure. Pelagianism revived the doctrine of humanity's natural goodness. Even Roman Catholic thought sounds a semi-Pelagian note in its supernaturalist anthropology, where only the superadded gift of grace is lost in the fall and nature remains unblemished. Denial of original sin was the anthropological stock-in-trade of the Anabaptists, the Socinians, and all Rationalists. In the eighteenth century, Rousseau became the apostle of a "back to nature movement" that repudiated human culture as the source of all evil. If only, in education, religion, morality, society and the state, we would return to nature, to the idyllic circumstances of shepherds and farmers, the innocent and carefree lifestyle of natives, then humanity, virtue and happiness would instantly be restored.[28] The attempts to follow through on this vision—the French Revolution and all its stepchildren, a variety of utopian colonies—demonstrate the futile attempt to bring heaven to earth. Such efforts manufacture ideal "natural" societies on paper that inevitably fail in practice. Still, the dream lives on for many people as a guide for the upbringing of children and source of optimistic hopes for a better future world.[29]

Theologians have not been immune to this malady. Ritschl, for example, reduced sin to actual sins; "the law of sin" is only a sum of individual sins. The subject of sin is not humanity as a race—which is an abstraction and merely a mental picture—but humanity as the sum of all individuals. The reality of general sinfulness is the result of habitual sin giving rise to a habit or tendency with that sinful disposition "spilling over" to affect others. As social creatures we humans mutually reinforce our sinful habits. That, according to Ritschl, is the "law of sin reigning in our members," a common sinfulness arising from powerful "peer pressure." A sinless unfolding of life can therefore not be a priori ruled out; the will of children is not aimed at evil; rather, there is in them a general tendency toward the good.

History and experience are not strong allies of this view; rather, they suggest that the scriptural portrait is true. Even "innocent" children display that seeds of sin are sown in the soil of their hearts from the beginning. A claim of sinlessness is universally repudiated, and imitation cannot explain the universal power of sin. A people without sin has never existed. If anything is certain, it is that sin is not an accidental phenomenon in the life of individuals, but a state and manner of life involving the whole human race, a property of human nature. The sinful deeds, which occur not just now and then but characterize all persons of all ages

---

28. Jean-Jacques Rousseau, *Profession of Faith of the Vicar* (New York: P. Eckler, 1889).

29. Cf. H. Bavinck, *Paedagogische Beginselen* (Kampen: Kok, 1904), 82; idem, *Philosophy of Revelation*, 279.

and circumstances, point back to a sinful inner disposition, just as bad fruit pre-supposes a bad tree and muddied water an impure spring. We may speak of the "innocence of children" but it is only a relative innocence. The experience of all parents and teachers tells us that the seeds of all sorts of sins are present in chil-dren's hearts. Even less than the sensual sins, it is the spiritual sins of self-seeking, vanity, jealousy, lovelessness, pride, craftiness, deception, untruth, disobedience, stubbornness, and so on, that already surface in children at a young age and, if not checked by a wise upbringing, increase with the years. The conviction of universal sinfulness is so strong and widely held that anyone who claimed to be without sin would immediately be judged to lack self-knowledge or even be mentally ill.[30] Only nominalists who consider humanity only as the sum of its individuals, and sin not as a state but as acts of the will, could entertain the notion that sin is not universal.

The Pelagian view purports to be more humane, giving greater dignity and responsibility to the human person. In fact, however, it is the opposite; it is either a trivial doctrine or most cruel. The Pelagian faces a choice: If sin only comes by imitation then either outside influences have only incidental impact, in which case they explain nothing and the universality of sin is an enigma, or they do in fact *cause* this universal sinfulness in which case the human condition is far worse than the scriptural doctrine of original sin. Pelagianism seems led to a position of either irrelevance or cruel determinism.

[320] Pelagianism was condemned by the Christian church. Nonetheless, a semi-Pelagianism that taught a weakened but not totally corrupt will gained much headway in the church. This view holds that while Adam's fall had consequences also for his descendants, our moral condition is only sick and weak, prone to the desires of the flesh. The Council of Trent taught that the will's freedom had not been destroyed and that concupiscence as such was not sin. Anabaptists, Remon-strants, and many modern theologians agree. Adam's sin only weakens our will and does not plunge us into the total corruption of original sin. This semi-Pelagianism ignores the character and seriousness of sin as willful lawlessness, separates sin and guilt, and fails to resolve the question of human freedom. An intact but weakened will is no real improvement on a will bound by original sin. While imitation is a superficial explanation for the universality of sin, the semi-Pelagian rejection of imitation leaves it with no explanation at all. Acknowledging that the impure, sick state of all people without distinction leads to culpable, punishable deeds—rendering the weakened free will to virtual uselessness—they are simply unable to explain that appalling phenomenon. How can it be squared with God's justice that, aside now from the covenant of grace, he permits all humans to be born in such a state, a state that, in any case, for children dying in infancy entails death and exclusion from his fellowship, and for all others eternal ruin? The semi-Pelagian

---

30. J. Müller, *The Christian Doctrine of Sin*, trans. W. Urwick, 5th ed., 2 vols. (Edinburgh: T&T Clark, 1868), II, 261.

theory fails totally to enter into the problem and contents itself with a superficial and inconsequential doctrine of free will.[31]

[321] The apostle Paul and after him Augustine were instructed by the contrasting model of Christ as the second Adam and placed the blame for universal and original sin at the feet of the first Adam. The argument for original sin begins by explaining the appalling misery of the human race as a punishment upon sin. God, who certainly is good and just, could not condemn all humans to sin and death if they were completely innocent. There is no other way to understand the crushing yoke that weighs upon all the children of Adam. The miseries of human life, from the first cries of infants to the final groans of the dying, lead us to acknowledge, with Paul, the reality of original sin. "Inasmuch as God is not an unfair judge, we must acknowledge original sin in the misery of the human race, which begins with the tears of the little ones."[32] Adam's sin includes his posterity; he was not a private person, one individual alongside others, but all humans were included in him. "All were that one man; we all were in that one."[33] Augustine did not, however, adequately describe the transmission of guilt and pollution to Adam's posterity, and his understanding of concupiscence is too closely linked to spontaneous sexual desire. For Augustine, the depravity of nature comes out especially in the spontaneous motion of the genitals, which occurs independently of the will, and shame is there to prove it. By the sex drive, accordingly, sin propagates itself and turns all of humankind into a corrupt mass, subject to the wretched necessity of not being able not to sin.[34]

Roman Catholic Scholastic theology modified this view to understand original sin as the loss of a superadded gift of grace (original righteousness) to which was added the active element of concupiscence. The Council of Trent expressed itself very cautiously, saying that Adam not only lost righteousness but was also changed for the worse in soul and body. After being defiled, he transfused sin, death, and the punishments of the body into his descendants, and the sin of Adam is in each one as his own, not by imitation but by propagation, and can be removed only by Christ's merit in baptism.[35] But beyond that the council deliberately refrained from greater specifics.[36] The nature of sin was not further defined; the words "for the worse" say little. Concupiscence, which remains in the baptized, is not itself

31. Ibid., II, 388ff.

32. Augustine, *Against Julian, an Unfinished Book*, in *The Works of St. Augustine: A Translation for the 21st Century*, ed. J. E. Rotelle (New York: New City, 1999), II, 77 and passim; I, 25, 49; II, 107; III, 44, 202; VI, 17, 28.

33. Augustine, *On the Merits and Remission of Sins*, I, 10; idem, *City of God*, XIII, 14.

34. Thus, repeatedly in his *On Marriage and Concupiscence*; cf. Adolf von Harnack, *History of Dogma*, trans. N. Buchanan, J. Millar, E. B. Speirs, and W. McGilchrist, and ed. A. B. Bruce, 7 vols. (London: Williams & Norgate, 1896–99), V, 194ff.; Gustav Friedrich Wiggers, *Versuch einer pragmatischen Darstellung des Augustinismus und Pelagianismus*, 2 vols. (Hamburg: F. A. Perthes, 1830–31), I, 107ff.

35. Decrees of the Council of Trent, sessions V–VI.

36. J. A. Möhler, *Symbolik: Oder Darstellung der Dogmatischen Gegensätze der Katholiken und Protestanten nach ihren öffentlichen Bekenntnisschriften* (Mainz: F. Kupferberg, 1838), 57.

seen as sin but only arises from sin and inclines to sin. The free will is not lost but weakened and can also do good works before sin. In Roman Catholic theology, the center of gravity thus shifted from concupiscence to loss of original righteousness. When concupiscence is not itself seen as sinful, it is hard to see what concrete effects remain of original sin except for the imputation of Adam's trespass. The human state after Adam's fall differs little from the pre-fallen state. We are left in only a state of "naked naturalness," not a state of depravity.[37] There is not much left of original sin here; it consists in nothing but reduction to a merely natural state; the supernatural things having been lost, the natural nevertheless remains intact.

[322] The Reformation opposed this Roman Catholic weakening of original sin. It is not just a loss of something but a total corruption of our nature. If we call this "concupiscence," we must apply it to the totality of human appetites. As Calvin put it: "the whole man is of himself nothing but concupiscence."[38] In this sense, contrary to Augustine, concupiscence is itself sin, not merely the occasion for sin. This corruption of human nature is so total that humans are by nature incapable of any spiritual good, inclined to all evil, and on account of it alone deserving of eternal punishment. It cannot be denied that, out of reaction against Rome, especially among Lutherans, people sometimes expressed themselves too strongly and opened themselves up to serious misunderstanding. Examples include Luther calling original sin "essential sin" and "the essence of humans,"[39] and the Formula of Concord stating that in spiritual matters the mind, heart, and will were "altogether corrupt and dead," no more capable [of good] than "a stone, a trunk, or mud."[40]

The Reformed were more cautious and on guard against the strong expressions and vivid images used by the Lutherans. Still, they too taught that original sin consisted, negatively, in the loss of original righteousness and, positively, in the corruption of nature, and that it was rooted in the imputed trespass of Adam.[41]

---

37. "The state of man after Adam's fall does not differ much from his state in its natural purity, any more than a man stripped of his clothes differs from a nude; nor is human nature worse if you subtract original sin; neither does it labor more under infirmity and ignorance than it would have while established in its purely natural state. In like manner the corruption of nature did not flow from the lack of some natural gift nor from the accession of some bad quality but only from a loss of the supernatural gift occasioned by Adam's sin" (R. Bellarmine, "De gratia primi hominis," *De controversiis Christanae fidei, adversus huius temporis haereticos* [Cologne: gualtheri, 1617–20], 5).

38. J. Calvin, *Institutes*, II.i.8.

39. According to J. Köstlin, *Luthers Theologie in ihrer geschichtlichen Entwicklung und ihrem inneren Zusammenhange*, II, 366ff. Ed. note: ET: *Theology of Luther in Its Historical Development and Inner Harmony*, trans. Charles E. Hay, 2 vols. (Philadelphia: Lutheran Publication Society, 1897).

40. J. T. Müller, *Die symbolischen Bücher der evangelisch-lutherischen Kirche*, 8th ed. (Gütersloh: Bertelsmann, 1898), 589, 594; cf. F. H. Frank, *Theologie der Concordienformel*, 4 vols. in 2 (Erlangen: T. Blaesing, 1858–65), I, 138.

41. J. Calvin, *Institutes*, II.ii.5; idem, *Commentary on the Book of Psalms*, trans. James Anderson (Grand Rapids: Eerdmans, 1949), on Ps. 51:7; idem, *Commentary on the Epistle of Saint Paul to the Romans*, ed. and trans. John Owen (Grand Rapids: Eerdmans, 1948), on Rom. 5:12; H. Heppe, *Die Dogmatik der evangelisch-reformirten Kirche* (Elberseld: R. L. Friedrich, 1861), 245ff.

Opposition to this doctrine within the Reformed community arose in the school of Saumur (France) in the form of mediate imputation of sin. Instead of teaching that we are corrupt because of imputed guilt, Josua Placaeus (1596–1665) turned this around and said: "Original sin is imputed to us because we are born corrupt."[42] This view was also championed by Jonathan Edwards and the New England Theology. The classic Augustinian and Reformed view seemed to have had its time. Shallow views prevailed, like that of Gervinus who wrote in 1845: "We have lost the fear of hereditary sins which, like the fear of ghosts, was only the fear of a superstitious religious doctrine."[43] Today matters are different. Modern thought, including the philosophy of Kant, Schelling, Schopenhauer, and others; the theory of [human] heredity and [human] solidarity; a spectrum of historical and sociological studies—all have offered unexpected but significant support for the dogma of original sin. After theology rejected it, philosophy again took it up.

[323] The doctrine of original sin is one of the weightiest and most difficult subjects in Christian theology. Without it we cannot comprehend ourselves, and yet it remains an incomprehensible mystery to us. "Nothing is better known than original sin for preaching; for understanding, nothing is more mysterious."[44] "Original sin explains everything and without it one cannot explain anything" (de Maistre), and yet the doctrine itself needs explanation more than anything.[45] According to Scripture and for Christian thought, the cause can be no other than the first trespass of the first human, by which sin and death entered the world. Adam's disobedience is the originating sin. Scripture plainly teaches this (Rom. 5:12; 1 Cor. 15:22) and experience confirms it every minute. This is a shock to our reason. How can that not be seen as arbitrary? Without entirely removing all mystery from this most difficult of human questions, we can say a few things that will take away any appearance of arbitrariness on God's part. The key point is to remind ourselves that our organic unity and solidarity in Adam is more than physical but begins with his representative role. Here, too, we must begin with Christ, our representative mediator in redemption. If the strict parallel between Christ and Adam is not as representative of all humanity but is turned into something physical and realistic, theological error is the result. Then Christ, being truly human, Adam's son, cannot be without sin. Furthermore, representation is the only way to make sense of our redemption through Christ's righteousness. When we say Christ's obedience is imputed to us, *as though we ourselves had accomplished it*,[46] we do not mean that we personally and physically did it. Christ did it for us and in our place. So it is also with Adam: virtually, potentially, and seminally, we

42. Placaeus elaborated this in his "Two-Part Disputation concerning Adam's First Sin" (1655). His views were condemned by the Synod of Charenton in 1645.
43. F. Delitzsch, *System der christlichen Apologetik* (Leipzig: Dörffling & Franke, 1870), 119.
44. Augustine, *On the Catholic and Manichaean Ways of Life*, I, 22.
45. Even Rousseau acknowledges that original sin explained everything except itself.
46. Heidelberg Catechism, Q 60.

may have been comprehended in him; personally and actually, however, it was he who broke the probationary command, and not we.

REALISM AND FEDERALISM

Realistic views of the transmission of sin—accenting the physical link between humans—valiantly honor the unity of humanity in sin. It is true: Humanity is not an aggregate of individuals but an organic unity, one race, one family. Unlike the angels, God created all of us from one man (Acts 17:26); we are not a heap of souls piled on a piece of ground, but all blood relatives of one another, connected to one another by a host of ties, therefore conditioning one another and being conditioned by one another. But realism here also heaps on each of us the entirety of our ancestor's sins along with the imputed guilt of Adam and our own sin. In this way, the precious truth of individual personality is lost. Created in God's image, each individual person is uniquely gifted, called, and responsible to God. We are indeed members of the "human race" but also far more than ripples in the ocean, passing manifestations of humanity in general. We noted earlier that relations among human beings are different from those found among angels and animals. While related to both, humans are also different from both. They are creatures with a character of their own. For that reason, physical unity in their case is not enough; an ethical, federal unity is added as well.[47]

This is in keeping with what we know from human experience in community more broadly. Beyond communities based on physical descent there are "moral communities" of nations, churches, and states, all of which have a life of their own and are subject to their own particular laws. Even communities based on physical descent such as the family are not merely tied by blood but are chiefly moral communities as well. In such communities there is a bond that ties each member to another (1 Cor. 12:26) but also an order of representation in which fathers, mothers, guardians, caretakers, teachers, professors, patrons, guides, legislators, monarchs, and so on act in ways that are decisive for the whole community. The family of a drunkard is ruined, of a criminal disgraced, of a hero ennobled. Congregations languish under faithless pastors, nations decline and are eventually destroyed when ruled by fools. "In whatever thing the kings go crazy, the Achaeans [Homer's Greeks] are punished." Among people there is solidarity for good or ill: community in blessing and in judgment. We stand on the shoulders of earlier generations and inherit the things they have accumulated in the way of material and spiritual wealth. The good we reserve as a gift of grace, undeservedly bequeathed to us.

No one objects to receiving the blessings of earlier generations but when the consequences of sin are passed on, we consider it an injustice. The same son who

---

47. Cf. against realism, A. A. Hodge, *The Atonement* (Philadelphia: Presbyterian Board of Publication, 1867), 99ff.

blithely accepts his father's inheritance refuses to pay his father's debts. This is not a new lament; it was already voiced in the days of Ezekiel.[48] When Israel in its supposed righteousness complains about the Old Testament law of solidarity in sin (Gen. 9:25; Exod. 20:5; Num. 14:33; 16:32; Josh. 7:24–25; 1 Sam. 15:2–3; 2 Sam. 12:10; 21:1f.; 1 Kings 21:21, 23; Isa. 6:5; Jer. 32:18; Lam. 3:40f.; 5:7; Ezra 9:6; Matt. 23:35; 27:25), God does not respond by asserting his rights but by saying what he will do if Israel repents and turns to him. There is indeed a solidarity in sin and suffering, but God permits it and frequently gives people the power to break with it and become a new community that walks in the fear of the Lord and enjoys his favor. This is God's answer to solidarity in sin: Christ demonstrated the truth of the solidarity of the human race in another and better way than Adam. Solidarity is not destroyed—that would be the end of all love, compassion, friendship; in short, all that we consider "human." Rather, it is healed, made whole again in Christ.

The law of solidarity alone does not, however, account for original sin. We recognize that the blessings and curses left to us by parents and guardians, philosophers and artists, founders of religion and reformers, warriors, kings and conquerors, and so on, are significant but they are still limited. There are always "circumstances" of place, time, country, people, language, and so on that set limits to it. The circle within which their influence was exerted—for ill or good—was always enclosed within limited circles. For some—the giants of human civilization—that circle is very large but it can never be said to be universal, direct, and indelible. Only two persons have existed whose life and works extended to the boundaries of humanity itself, whose influence and dominion had effects to the ends of the earth and into eternity. We are, of course, referring to Adam and Christ. The former brought sin and death into the world, the latter righteousness and life. It follows from the totally exceptional position occupied by Adam and by Christ that they alone can be compared with each other, and that all other relations, which are derived from circles within humankind, though they can serve as illustrations and are of great value, merely offer analogies, not identity. They do not presuppose but constitute the organism of humanity. If Adam fell, humanity would fall; if Christ remained standing, humanity would be raised up in him. The covenant of works and the covenant of grace are the forms by which the organism of humanity is maintained also in a religious and an ethical sense. Because God is interested, not in a handful of individuals but in humanity as his image and likeness, it had to fall and be raised again in one person. So reads God's ordinance, so reads his judgment. In one person he declares all guilty, and so humankind is born—unclean and in the process of dying—from Adam; in one person he declares all righteous and consecrated to eternal life. "For God has imprisoned all in disobedience so that he may be merciful to all" (Rom. 11:32).

48. A. B. Davidson, *The Theology of the Old Testament*, ed. from the author's manuscripts by S. D. F. Salmond (New York: Charles Scribner's, 1904), 219ff., 283.

[324] Sin gives birth to sin. In the case of Adam and all his descendants, a sinful state followed a sinful deed. Original pollution is a punishment for original guilt. It is exactly this consequence that is denied by Pelagians who believe that the will that sins then remains fully free to sin or not to sin. Scripture, however, frequently regards consequent sins as punishment for previous sins (2 Sam. 12:11–12; 1 Kings 11:11–31; 22:30ff.; Isa. 6:9–10; 7:17; 10:5–7; 14:3; Jer. 50:6–8; Rom. 1:24–28; 2 Thess. 2:11–12; etc.). Experience also teaches us that every act of the will, arising from antecedent impulses and desires, has a retroactive impact on it and reinforces it. In this way sin becomes a habit and those who commit sins become servants of sin. Guilt and pollution go together. While sin, viewed by itself, can never be a punishment for sin since sin is an act of violating the law while punishment upholds the law, a subsequent sin may be called a punishment for a prior sin, since it distances the sinner even farther from God, makes him more wretched, and abandons him to all sorts of covetousness and passion, dread and remorse. In Adam's trespass an appalling degeneration of the human race had its inception. We are here confronting a horrible reality whose explanation escapes us. How can it be that one single sin had such dreadful consequences and brought about such a radical reversal in the nature of humans?

We know that frequently in human life the consequences of sin seem disproportionate to the sinful act. One thoughtless word can lead to a lifetime of tears; seemingly insignificant incidents have an aftermath that lasts for generations. Our happiness or unhappiness often hangs by the thread of a single "chance" event. Experience teaches us that all our acts to some degree boomerang on us and leave tracks on our character. Every act of the will, arising as it does from antecedent impulses and desires, has a retroactive impact on it and reinforces it. In that way every sin can become a habit, a tendentious pattern, a passion that controls a person like a tyrant. We humans are changeable, extraordinarily moldable, and pliable, adaptable to all occasions, circumstances, and environments. We can "get used to" anything. Those who commit sins become the servants of sin. Adam's sinful act was not spontaneous; anterior to the sinful deed, there were sinful considerations of the mind (doubt, unbelief) and sinful tendencies of the heart (covetousness, pride), prompted by the temptation of the serpent and fostered by his own will. Still, Adam's one trespass brought about an overall change in the thoughts, attitudes, and inclinations of his whole nature and left an indelible stain on all his posterity. Adam's sin involved a progressive detachment from God, his light, and his law; he set himself against God's fellowship and entered the sinful state of darkness, bringing all humanity with him. We are all born in the same moral state as that into which Adam fell by his trespass. Withdrawing from communion with God *is* to enter the state of sin, guilt, and death. In sin, guilt and pollution always go together.

[325] However we understand it—realistically or federally—Adam's trespass *is* the sin of all his descendants. We are comprehended in him and thus sinners, guilty before God; we share Adam's guilt and pollution, for these two always

go together. But how are we to think of this? As a divine ordinance. There is an antecedent judgment (κρίμα) of God as Judge on one human and one trespass, and this κρίμα contains the κατάκριμα (the sentence) that not only Adam but all his descendants were guilty, impure, and worthy of death (Rom. 5:16). The way in which this "originated sin" becomes the experience of all of us is not through imitation but through generation based on imputation. All people are born of Adam, guilty, impure, and in the process of dying. This Christian view has some interesting parallels with, but is not to be identified with, the notion of hereditary transmission of traits. The eighteenth century raved about the natural goodness of humans and held society responsible for imperfection; the nineteenth century saw an about-face. Influenced by a Darwinian, evolutionary mind-set, many now believed that the evil humans do arises from their animal nature. Concealed in every person is "the human beast" (*la bête humaine*). "Its [inherited] animal nature is humanity's defect." Here, human persons are nothing more than products of nature; this view risks becoming deterministic and fatalistic. If hereditary transmission of traits is an immutable law, then human dignity, independence, freedom, and moral responsibility is an illusion. We are only products and victims of "nature."

Explanations such as these attempt far too much. The notion of inherited traits is too complex to be summed up in a few laws; along with inherited continuities, there are also variations. Human beings are spiritual and moral beings who have the ability to rise above even strong negative inherited tendencies and traits. Physical heredity cannot explain original sin. It is not surprising that people rose in protest against such a materialist reduction. On the one hand, we know the truth of proverbial sayings such as: "like father like son" and "the apple never falls far from the tree." On the other hand, some traits are not transmissible, and we are not entirely certain which ones or why. Some traits—such as racial characteristics—have an uncertain pedigree and future because the human race was originally one and intermarriage across racial lines changes everything. Finding "laws" to cover all this is elusive because along with heredity we also observe significant variation. No two leaves on the same tree and branch are the same, and this is the case in all of organic creation. The children of the same parents sometimes differ a great deal, both physically and mentally. Our scientific work in this area is helpful but we must honor the significant mysteries that remain in our understanding of human behavior.

No traducionist explanation—seeing people totally from the perspective of their past—can succeed, for we are more than products of preexistent and external factors; we have an existence and life of our own; we are beings that know, and will, and can.[49] Human beings are capable of transcending the physical domain and entering another, a higher, moral world. That, too, is a world where law, rule,

49. The individual is not a mere manifestation of the race. God applies to the origination of every single man a special creative thought and act of will. John Cynddylan Jones, *Primeval Revelation: Studies in Genesis I–VIII* (London: Hodder & Stoughton, 1897), 263.

and order prevail. There is order and law here, cause and effect, but a different kind of order from that of nature's physical laws. Here, there is also great variation; all people are dissimilar, also in the degree of their self-reliance, freedom, responsibility, accountability, and guilt. To whom much is given, from him much will be required; and one to whom little has been given much less will be required. Humans act as *persons*; they are and remain the cause of their own actions. They act, not without reasons, but without compulsion. They are free and in proportion to their freedom remain responsible for their actions. We need to recognize both the moral freedom of individuals as well as the nomothetic regularity of the moral world order.

Christian theology has no desire to deny the facts of heredity or its extensive rule. God's laws in this domain must be recognized and respected in order to glorify the Creator who is not a God of confusion but of order. We must also acknowledge that we can never with complete accuracy indicate the boundaries that separate personal guilt from communal guilt. Original sin *is* the collective deed and collective guilt of the human race as a whole. The sins of generation after generation flow from previous generations' sons and condition the generations that follow. Sin is "in each the work of all and in all the work of each."[50] This gives us no right, however, to rob human beings of their independence and freedom and to picture them as passive instruments of evil powers. Such a destruction of all willpower wreaks incalculable devastation in the lives of people.

The scientific information about heredity should be gratefully acknowledged as support to the ecclesiastical doctrine of original sin. Nonetheless, it does not strengthen the doctrine any more than it would be weakened if tomorrow that same science might delight in pillorying it as foolish and nonsensical. Original sin cannot be equated with what is known today as heredity. It is not, after all, a generic trait that belongs to the human essence, inasmuch as it entered human nature by a violation of God's command and can be removed from it by regeneration and sanctification. Nor is it an individually acquired trait: it is so much a part of human nature that even the regenerate still produce children who are "by nature children of wrath." How original sin is propagated remains somewhat mysterious. It is not something physical—transmitted by propagation—but a moral quality of the person who lacks the communion with God that one should and does possess by virtue of one's original nature. Just as God withdrew his communion from Adam on account of Adam's trespass, so he withdraws it from all his descendants. Every human person, in virtue of the physical and ethical relation in which he or she stands to Adam, is born culpable and stained. "Each person, accordingly, is the proximate principle and subject and author of his or her own original sin."[51]

50. F. Schleiermacher, *The Christian Faith* (Edinburgh: T&T Clark, 1989), §71.1–2.
51. G. Voetius, *Selectae disputationes theologicae*, 5 vols. (Utrecht, 1648–49), I, 1104, 1078ff.; Francis Turretin, *Institutes of Elenctic Theology*, IX, 12; J. Edwards, *The Works of Jonathan Edwards*, ed. Paul Ramsey (New Haven, CT: Yale University Press, 1989), II, 478.

[326] There is no exception to the universal rule of sin except for our Lord Jesus Christ. "In Adam the person corrupts the [human] nature; in other humans the [human] nature corrupts the person."[52] Scripture gives no warrant to the Roman Catholic dogmas of Mary's immaculate conception and bodily assumption. The grounds given for Rome's declaration by Pius IX in the bull *Ineffabilis Deus* of December 8, 1854, "that the most Blessed Virgin Mary was preserved from all stain of original sin in the first instant of her Conception, by a singular grace and privilege of Almighty God, in consideration of the merits of Jesus Christ, Savior of the human race," are quite unconvincing. Appeal is made to the strangest texts and typologies: Genesis 3:15; Psalm 45:11f.; Song of Solomon 1:8–16; 2:2; 3:6; 4:1f.; 6:9; Wisdom 1:4; Luke 1:28, 41, 48; Revelation 12; and typologies such as Noah's ark, the dove with the olive branch, the burning bush, and so on.[53] These stretches reveal the dearth of arguments and require no further refutation. Scripture decisively teaches, rather, that all humans, Christ alone excepted, are sinners. No exception is ever made for Mary, who, though no specific sinful words or deeds are recorded of her (not in Mark 3:21; John 2:3–4 either), still rejoices in God her Savior (Luke 1:47) and is called blessed because of her motherhood of Christ but never because she is sinless (Luke 1:28, 48). Rome does not imply that Mary was not comprehended and fallen in Adam but only that she was preserved from all stain of original sin only by a special grace of God in consideration of the merits of Christ. Accordingly, she was preserved from original sin in the very first instant of her conception. There is, however, not the slightest ground for this dogma in Scripture, as Aquinas frankly admits: "nothing is handed down in the canonical Scriptures concerning the sanctification of the Blessed Mary as to her being sanctified in the womb."[54] Here is the only ground: Simply, like Mary's assumption, it is an inference from the mediatorship the Roman church gradually attributed to her. It is not fitting (*conveniens*) that Mary should be conceived in sin, should have committed sin, and died. She has to be sinless; therefore she *is* sinless, even though neither Scripture nor tradition teaches this.[55]

[327] If there are no individual human exceptions to the universality of sin, no aspect of human existence is free from the stain of sin either. Sin holds sway over the whole person, body and soul, mind and spirit, over all our human capacities and powers. A person's heart is evil from youth on and a source of all sorts

52. T. Aquinas, *Summa Theol.*, III, qu. 8, art. 5; qu. 69, art. 3.

53. Cf., e.g., Spencer Northcote, *Mary in the Gospels* (London: Burns & Oates, 1906); A. Schaefer, *The Mother of Jesus in Holy Scripture* (Ratisbon [Regensburg]: F. Pustet, 1913); Matthias Joseph Scheeben, *Handbuch der katholischen Dogmatik*, ed. Leonhard Atzberger, 4 vols. (1874–98; repr., Freiburg i.B.: Herder, 1933), III, 455–72.

54. T. Aquinas, *Summa Theol.*, III, qu. 27, art. 1.

55. Cf. E. Preuss, *The Romish Doctrine of the Immaculate Conception, Traced from Its Source*, trans. George Gladstone (Edinburgh: T&T Clark, 1867); O. Zöckler, "Maria," *PRE*³, XIII, 309–36; J. B. Mayor, "Mary," in *DB*, III, 286–93.

of evils (Gen. 6:5; 8:21; Ps. 51:5; Jer. 17:9; Ezek. 36:26; Mark 7:21). We are all
dead in our trespasses and sins (Eph. 2:1). Therefore, rebirth is a prerequisite to
entrance into the kingdom of God (John 3:3). The whole of salvation is objectively and subjectively a work of divine grace (John 6:44; 15:5; 1 Cor. 4:7; 15:10;
Phil. 2:13; etc.). Human persons are now under the hard necessity of not being
able not to sin. This doctrine of total human moral depravity is a hard one and
naturally evokes aversion and even incomprehension. Yet it is the clear teaching
of Scripture, which is confirmed by daily experience. If it is clearly elucidated, it
is daily confirmed by everyone's experience and vindicated by the witness of its
opponents themselves. Here are the main points.

1. The doctrine does not mean that people all maximize their evil inclinations; nor that they are incapable of accomplishing many "natural goods."
   It only refers to the deepest inclination, the innermost disposition, the
   fundamental directedness of human nature and confesses that it is not
   turned toward God but away from him. To or away from God: those are
   the only two options. The human being is at the center of his or her being
   either good or evil—there is no third option.
2. Although sin inhabits and infects all of us, it is not a substance; it is not
   and cannot be the essence of our humanity. We remain human after the fall.
   The doctrine of the total corruption of human nature by no means implies
   that the sinful disposition that lies at the bottom of the human heart always
   erupts in the kind of deeds that betray clear hostility and hatred toward
   God and one's neighbor. There are various circumstances that intervene and
   keep the disposition from fully expressing itself: restraint of sin by the sword
   of the government, public opinion, the fear of disgrace and punishment,
   and so on; as well as positive factors such as the natural love still inherent
   in every person, morality fostered by upbringing and struggle, favorable
   circumstances of constitution or environment, and so forth. All these may
   lead people to practice beautiful and praiseworthy virtues, though while
   they may for a time subdue the sinful disposition of the heart, they do not
   eradicate it.
3. Saying that humans are naturally incapable of any good does not refer to
   physical necessity or fatalistic coercion. Sin does not eradicate our will; it
   changed the inclination and direction of the will. We no longer want to
   do good; we now, voluntarily, do evil. "The will in us is always free but it
   is not always good."[56] In this sense the incapacity for good is not physical
   but ethical in nature: it is a kind of impotence of the will. The will, in its
   present fallen state, in virtue of its nature, cannot do other than to will

56. Augustine, *On Grace and Free Will*, 15; for the Reformed view, see H. Heppe, *Dogmatik*, 237,
264; W. Cunningham, *The Reformers and the Theology of the Reformation*, ed. James Buchanan and
James Bannerman (Edinburgh: T&T Clark, 1862), 471ff.; idem, *Historical Theology*, 3rd ed., 2 vols.
(Edinburgh: T&T Clark, 1870), I, 568ff.

freely; it cannot do other than what it wills, than that to which it is by nature inclined.[57]

4. Finally, one must bear in mind that Scripture and the church, in teaching the total depravity of humanity, apply the highest standard, namely, the law of God. The doctrine of the incapacity for good is a religious confession—before God we can do no good; we need to be renewed by God's Spirit. From this starting point, the follower of Augustine can be far more generous than the most confirmed Pelagian and wholeheartedly acknowledge that much of what people do is good and beautiful. The good of which we are speaking, however, is the highest good; the divine law with which we must comply. Virtues and good works are distinct. Good, true good—good in the eyes of a holy God—is only what is done out of faith, according to God's law and to God's glory. Weighed in the scales of God's sanctuary, all our works are found to be wanting. Given this standard, the only possible judgment is that of Scripture: "There is no one who does good, no, not one" (Pss. 14:3; 53:3).

Those for whom Scripture settles nothing may hear the same testimony from some of the great voices of our race: "Our virtues are often no more than vices in disguise" (Rochefoucauld). "Man is only a disguise, a lie and hypocrisy, both within himself and with respect to others" (Pascal). "Man to man is a wolf." Without the state, human society would degenerate into "a war of all against all" (Hobbes). According to Kant, that humans are by nature evil, possess a radical inborn evil, is amply borne out by the witness of history: "Every man has his price, for which he will sell himself." What Scripture says is a universal truth; there is no one who does good, not one.[58] Fichte, Hegel, Schelling, and Schopenhauer also bear witness: "Those who maintain the bondage of the will and characterize humans as stocks and blocks are completely correct."[59] "The natural heart in which a human is caught up is the enemy one must fight."[60] "Humans have from eternity entangled themselves in themselves and in self-seeking, and all who have been born were born with the attached dark principle of evil. This original evil in humans, which only those can dispute who have only a superficial acquaintance with people as they

57. Cf. T. Aquinas, *Summa contra gentiles*, IV, 52; idem, *Formula of Concord*, I, 12; J. Calvin, *Commentary*, on Eph. 2:3; Z. Ursinus, *The Commentary of Dr. Zacharius Ursinus on the Heidelberg Catechism*, trans. G. W. Willard (Grand Rapids: Eerdmans, 1954), qu. 5, 8; Helvetic Confession, §§21–22; F. Turretin, *Institutes of Elenctic Theology*, X, 4, 39; Charles Hodge, *Systematic Theology*, 3 vols. (New York: Charles Scribner Sons, 1888), II, 257–72; W. G. T. Shedd, *Dogmatic Theology*, II, 219–57; III, 364–74.

58. I. Kant, *Religion within the Limits of Reason Alone*, trans. Theodore M. Greene and Hoyt H. Hudson (New York: Harper & Row, 1960 [1934]), 34ff.

59. J. G. Fichte, *Das System der Sittenlehre nach den Prinzipien der Wissenschaftslehre* (Hamburg: Meiner, 1798), 265. Ed. note: ET: *The Science of Ethics as Based on the Science of Knowledge*, trans. William Torrey Harris (London: K. Paul, Trench, Trübner, 1897).

60. G. W. F. Hegel, *Sämtliche Werke*, 26 vols. (Stuttgart: F. Frommann, 1949–59), 16, 270 (*Werke*, XII, 270).

are in themselves and in their relation to others, in its origin is their own deed."[61] "The main and fundamental motive in people as in animals is egoism, that is, the drive to exist and to prosper. This egoism, in animals as it is in humans, is most intimately connected, yes, identical with their inner core and essence." When re- straints—decency, fear of punishment—are removed, "insatiable greed, despicable money-hunger, deeply concealed falseness, and spiteful evil again spring to the surface. . . . Thousands of people who before our eyes are peacefully commingling in public must be viewed as just so many tigers and wolves whose mouth has been secured by a strong muzzle." Even the composition of the human conscience is one-fifth fear of other humans, one-fifth superstition, one-fifth prejudice, one-fifth vanity, and one-fifth custom.[62]

It is truly not Scripture alone that judges humans harshly. It is human beings who have pronounced the harshest and most severe judgment on themselves. It is always better to fall into the hands of the Lord than into those of people, for his mercy is great. For when God condemns us, he at the same time offers his forgiving love in Christ, but when people condemn people, they frequently cast them out and make them the object of scorn. When God condemns us, he has this judg- ment brought to us by people—prophets and apostles and ministers—who do not elevate themselves to a level high above us but include themselves with us in a common confession of guilt. By contrast, philosophers and moralists, in despis- ing people, usually forget that they themselves are human. When God condemns, he speaks of sin and guilt that, though great and heavy, can be removed because they do not belong to the essence of humanity. But moralists frequently speak of egoistic animal tendencies that belong to humans by virtue of their origin and are part of their essence. They put people down but do not lift them up. If by origin we are animals, why then should we live as children of God?

We must never forget that as we are judged and condemned by God's stan- dard, he at the same time offers us his full love, mercy, and forgiveness in Christ. A lesser judgment on us would require a lesser grace and thus diminish the love of God to us.

---

61. F. W. J. Schelling, "Philosophische Untersuchungen über das Wesen der menschlichen Freiheit," in *Ausgewählte Werke*, IV, 332 (*Sämmtliche Werke*, I/7, 388).

62. A. Schopenhauer, *Die Beiden Grundprobleme der Ethik*, 3rd ed. (Leipzig: F. A. Brockhaus, 1881), 186ff.; idem, *Die Welt als Wille und Vorstellung*, 6th ed. (Leipzig: Brockhaus, 1887), I, 391ff.; idem, *Parerga and Paralipomena*, trans. E. F. J. Payne, 2 vols. (Oxford: Clarendon, 1974), II, 229ff.

13

SIN AND ITS CONSEQUENCES

THE RELIGIOUS CHARACTER OF SIN

[328] Original sin is not mere heredity; it is a universal reality in all people, everywhere. As we now go on to discuss the essential nature of sin we are limited in what we can learn from the original sin and its hereditary transmission because the fullness of sin's corruption becomes evident only upon a period of development. It is not surprising, therefore, that there is considerable disagreement about the character and nature of the first sin. For the angels, it is reasonable—in view of the nature of temptation in Genesis 3:5 and Matthew 4:3; 6:9, and the admonition in 1 Timothy 3:6 not "to be puffed up with conceit and fall into the condemnation of the devil"—to conclude that the first sin of the angels consisted in pride. Yet, we cannot claim certainty here; lying (John 8:44), or envy (Wis. 2:24) are also plausible candidates. Too little about this is revealed to us.

According to Roman Catholics, the first sin of humans also consisted in pride (from Sir. 10:13; Tob. 4:13; and Rom. 5:19; and on the testimony of Augustine, Aquinas, and others).[1] Protestants, however, in considering Eve's sin, usually begin with doubt and unbelief, followed by pride and covetousness.[2] But Tertullian and others correctly said that the original sin should not be reduced to

---

1. R. Bellarmine, "De gratia primi hominis," *Controversiis*, III, 4; Augustine, *The Literal Meaning of Genesis*, trans. John Hammond Taylor (New York: Newman, 1982), XI, 30; idem, *Enchiridion*, 45; idem, *City of God*, XIV, 13; T. Aquinas, *Summa Theol.*, II, 2, qu. 163ff.

2. Martin Luther, *Lectures on Genesis 1–3*, in vol. 1 of *Luther's Works*, ed. J. Pelikan and H. T. Lehman (St. Louis: Concordia, 1958); Johann Gerhard, *Loci theologici*, ed. E. Preuss, 9 vols. (G. Schlawitz, 1863–75), IX, 2; John Calvin, *Institutes of the Christian Religion*, II.i.4 (ed. John T. McNeill and trans. Ford

one kind of trespass; it was a conscious, willful disobedience that in principle transgressed all of God's commandments. It was disobedience to God, doubt, unbelief, self-elevation, pride, homicide, theft, covetousness, and so on. Adam's sin was a reversal of all created relationships and a rebellion against God decisive for the whole world. It involved the whole human person—intellect and will, soul and body, and triggered sinful thoughts, feelings, lusts, and movements.[3] It was a conscious and voluntary act—ἁμαρτια (sin), παραβασις (transgression), παραπτωμα (misstep), παρακοη (unwillingness to hear; disobedience), in the true sense of these words (Rom. 5:12ff.). The first humans did not sin as innocents who did not know better; as God's image bearers, they knowingly and willingly acted against God's express and clear command. This makes their disobedience all the more inexcusable. It was not a minor thing, a half-conscious, virtually innocent aberration, much less an instance of development and progress; it was a revolt against God, an uprising, a fall in the true sense, which was decisive for the whole world. The fall took the world on a road away from God, toward wickedness and corruption—it was an unspeakably great sin,[4] a fall in every sense of the word. The Christian church and Christian theology has always taken it with utmost seriousness.[5]

[329] Though sin is appallingly many-sided, with untold moral dimensions,[6] at its heart it is a religious revolt against God and thus appropriately summarized as lawlessness (ἀνομια, 1 John 3:4). It denotes a violation not of a human but of a divine law and situates us not in relation to fellow humans, society, and the state, but to God, the heavenly Judge. In different periods this law appeared in different forms. Adam's case was utterly unique; no one coming after him can commit sin in the way he did (Rom. 5:14). From Adam to Moses there was no positive, divinely proclaimed law. The objection could therefore be advanced that where there is no law, there can be no transgression, sin, and death either (Rom. 5:13; 4:15). But Paul's concern here is to say that Adam's trespass brought about sin's

---

Lewis Battles [1559; Philadelphia: Westminster, 1960], 1:244–46); H. Bavinck, ed., *Synopsis purioris theologiae* (Leiden: D. Donner, 1881), XIV, 9ff.

3. Tertullian, *An Answer to the Jews* 2 (*ANF*, III, 151–74); Augustine, *Enchiridion* 45; Johannes Marck, *Historia paradise* (Amsterdam: Gerardus Borstius, 1705), III, c. 2.

4. Augustine, *Against Julian*, trans. M. A. Schumacher, vol. 16 of *The Writings of Saint Augustine* (Washington, DC: Catholic University of America Press, 1984), I, 165.

5. Augustine, *City of God*, XIV, 11–15; XXI, 12; idem, *Enchiridion*, 26–27, 45; T. Aquinas, *Summa Theol.*, II, 2, qu. 163, art. 3; Decrees of the Council of Trent, V, 1; Belgic Confession, art. 14; Heidelberg Catechism, qu. 7, 9; P. van Mastricht, *Theoretico-practica theologia* (Utrecht: Appels, 1714), IV, 1, 15.

6. The key biblical words include חַטָּאת (missing the mark); עָוֹל or עָוֹן (injustice, twistedness, wrongness, deviation); פֶּשַׁע (crossing of set boundaries, breaking the covenant, apostasy and rebellion); שְׁגָגָה (unintentional wrong act); רֶשַׁע (godless, deviant, guilty conduct). Other descriptions include אָשָׁם (guilt or offense); מַעַל (unfaithfulness, infidelity, betrayal); נְבָלָה (folly); רַע (evil); and so on. The main Greek words are ἁμαρτια, ἁμαρτημα, ἀδικια, ἀπειθεια, ἀποστασια, παραβασις, παρακοη, παραπτωμα, ὀφειλημα, ἀνομια, παρανομια. They speak for themselves and describe sin as deviation, injustice, disobedience, violation, apostasy, lawlessness, guilt. The power of sin at work in humans is further denoted by such words as σαρξ, ψυχικος, and παλαιος ἀνθρωπος, and at work in the world as κοσμος.

dominance so that all people are also themselves personally sinners. This means that, since there was sin and death from Adam to Moses (Rom. 5:13–14), there must also have been a law—perhaps not a positive law such as given in paradise and on Mount Sinai, but still a law that obligated people personally and rendered them guilty. This is clearly the intent of Romans 2:12–26: The gentiles, who did not have the Mosaic law, nonetheless sinned and are lost apart from the law (ἀνόμως) because they are a law to themselves and their own consciences accuse them. There is a revelation of God in nature, a revelation both religious and intellectual in content, which is sufficient to strip them of all innocence (Rom. 2:18f.; 1 Cor. 1:21). But, unlike the gentiles whom God permitted to follow their own way, Israel was given the revelation of his law as a guide for all moral conduct. Sin involved moral misconduct.

In recent times this view has been sharply contested. Some argue that Israel's earliest notion of "sin" (as the reason for misery and misfortune) had nothing to do with moral conduct but was only a matter of "somehow" having offended an arbitrary and capricious deity. Originally, the word חטא meant nothing other than to be or to be put in the wrong over against a superior (Exod. 5:16; 1 Kings 1:21; 2 Kings 18:14). Only later, especially after the prophets had proclaimed ethical monotheism, did it come to mean a violation of God's law. The word therefore only gradually acquired ethical significance. This is not a new charge; it goes back to the gnostics and the Manicheans, who for that reason distinguished the God of the Old Testament from the Father of Christ,[7] and is a mixture of truth and falsehood. It is false to say that in ancient Israel the true concept of sin as an offense against God was lacking, as the following passages that speak of "sin against the Lord" clearly show: Genesis 13:13; 38:9–10; 39:9; 42:18; 1 Samuel 24:6; 25:39; 2 Samuel 1:14; 12:13; Psalm 51:4. All these testimonies together make abundantly plain that ancient Israel already knew very well that sin is an evil in the sight of God. And not only the sinful act but also the sinful disposition fell into the category of evil. God tests minds and hearts (Pss. 7:9; 17:3; 26:2; 139:23; Jer. 11:20; 17:10; 20:12), looks at the heart (1 Sam. 16:7), and demands a person's heart (1 Kings 11:4; 15:13; Isa. 29:13; Ezek. 33:31; Prov. 23:26), since from it flow the springs of life (Prov. 4:23), and he will give people a pure heart, a new heart, a heart of flesh (Ps. 51:12; Jer. 24:7; 31:33; 32:39; Ezek. 11:19; 36:26; etc.). The evil committed by human beings is discerned by the Lord not only in deeds but also in the inclinations of their hearts (Gen. 6:5).

Sin, therefore, is never an arbitrary matter, merely a whimsical displeasure of a jealous God. Sin is knowingly breaking God's command and flows from a heart that rebels against God. God's law, furthermore, is not arbitrary or mechanically imposed. When God gave his law to Israel, he did not abolish folk customs but instead recognized, incorporated, and modified them to fulfill his own purposes.

---

7. L. Diestel, *Geschichte des Alten Testament in der christlichen Kirche* (Jena: Mauka, 1869), 64ff., 114ff.

This includes circumcision, sacrifices, the priesthood, feast days, blood revenge, hospitality, and so on, customs existing among the nations and also in Israel. These were modified, incorporated, and made serviceable to a higher order of things in the covenant of grace. There is even more: with respect to divorce, Jesus says that Moses allowed it on account of the hardness of people's hearts (Matt. 19:8); this also is true of such matters as polygamy, slavery, blood revenge, corporate responsibility, and the like. We must not judge these by the standards of our own time but must take account of the peculiar circumstances of the Old Testament times and God's purposes for his people then. This includes realizing the *pedagogic* importance of the law as Israel in its state of spiritual immaturity is led to the full maturity of freedom in Christ (Rom. 4:15; 5:20; 7:4; Gal. 3:19, 23–24; 4:1f.). Thus, while God's law may incorporate human customs, it is always more than custom. The second table of the law especially is reflected in the laws of the nations, but for Israel all moral and ceremonial commands are framed by the command to serve the Lord God of Israel, the creator and redeemer of his people. The idea of sin is thereby expanded and broadened beyond external conformity to levitical purity to the inner righteousness of a heart inclined to obedience. Prophecy, therefore, at all times insisted on the Lord's assessment that obedience and mercy are better than sacrifices.

In keeping with this prophetic perspective, Jesus fulfills rather than repudiates Old Testament law. In Matthew 7:12 he does not propose any new ethical principle, but only offers a practical interpretation of the command to love one's neighbor. Nonetheless, Jesus does sharpen and deepen the concept of sin and the sense of sin. By moving away from human ordinances and going back to the law of God in the Old Testament, he again reveals the law's spiritual character (Matt. 5), reducing it to one spiritual principle, namely, love (Matt. 22:37–40), and communicates it to us as a single whole (cf. James 2:10). Judging by that law, he unmasks hypocrisy (Matt. 23), breaks the bond between the ethical and the physical (Mark 7:15), goes back to the heart as the source of all sin (Matt. 15:18–19), and even makes suffering independent of personal guilt (Luke 13:2–3; John 9:3). Against the backdrop of the revelation of God's grace in the gospel, sin stands out all the more darkly. The law remains the source of our knowledge of sin (Rom. 3:20; 7:7), but when read in light of the gospel, sin's hideousness becomes evident as a power that enslaves (John 8:34; Rom. 6:20), that finds its strength in the law (1 Cor. 15:56), is rooted in the flesh with its desires (Rom. 7:18; James 1:14), and can only be broken and overcome by Christ (John 8:36; Rom. 8:2). Because God's grace has fully appeared in Christ, unbelief is such a great sin (John 15:22, 24; 16:9), being offended at Christ is so serious (Matt. 11:6), falling away from grace is so frightful (Heb. 2:3; 4:1; 6:4–5; 10:26), and blaspheming the Holy Spirit is an unpardonable sin (Matt. 12:31).

Christ, who is the *end* of the law (Rom. 10:4; Gal. 3:24), frees us from the law's curse and yoke of servitude (Rom. 6:14; 7:4; 10:4; Gal. 2:19; 3:13; 5:18). This does not, however, cancel out the law's ethical content of that law, but rather confirms it (Rom. 3:31). The Spirit who renews the heart and teaches us to search out, know, and fulfill God's will (Rom. 12:2; Eph. 5:10; Phil. 1:10) also empowers us to walk according to the Spirit (Rom. 8:4). God's will, known and remaining knowable from the Old Testament (Rom. 13:8–10; 15:4; 1 Cor. 1:31; 10:11; 14:34; 2 Cor. 9:9; 10:17; Gal. 5:14), has been explained to us in Christ's words and life (1 Cor. 11:1; 2 Cor. 3:18; 8:9; 10:1; Phil. 2:5; 1 Thess. 1:6; 4:2), and resonates in our own consciences (1 Cor. 8:7; 10:25; 2 Cor. 1:12) because it is written in our hearts (Heb. 8:10; 10:16). Throughout Scripture, therefore, the essential character of sin consists in lawlessness (ἀνομια, 1 John 3:4), in violating the law that God has revealed in his Word.

Eꜱꜱᴇɴᴛɪᴀʟꜱ ᴏꜰ Sɪɴ

[330] On the basis of this biblical teaching, Christian theology has always rejected all substantive notions of sin. In this view the essence of sin is not found in any principle of wrath in God (Böhme), an evil power beside God (Mani), some kind of "stuff" such as matter (ὑλη) or flesh (σαρξ; Plato, the Jews, Flacius, and others). Also rejected are pantheistic notions of sin as pure negation, as a state of "not yet," as a necessary component in the development of being, or as an illusion of thought. All being is per se good. All that is natural, to the degree that it is natural, is good. Evil can therefore only be something about the good. Sin is a *no-thing*, can only be a *privation* or *corruption* of the good. Sin is a defect, a deprivation, an absence of the good, or a weakness, imbalance, just as blindness is a deprivation of sight.[8] The idea of sin as privation, however, is incomplete; sin is also an active, corrupting, destructive power. Sin is a privation of the moral perfection human persons ought to possess and includes active transgression; it is an active and corrupting principle, a dissolving, destructive power. Having no existence on its own, sin is ethical-spiritual in nature, though it always comes to expression in concrete terms. It is a deformity, a departure from God's perfect law by rational creatures who can know and do God's will. The characterization of sin as privation, accordingly, by no means excludes its being also—viewed from a different angle—an action. It is not a "substance" or thing, but in its being deprived of the good, it is an activity (ἐνεργεια), just as the hobbling of a crippled dog is still an activity, a defective "walking." Because in its existence it has no real right to exist, sin is a riddle, a mystery.

[331] On the basis of Holy Scripture, and in keeping with the confession of the Christian faith, therefore, the essential character of sin can be defined and explained as follows. It is, in the first place, not a physical or metaphysical but an ethical antithesis of the good and has no self-existent, independent being of its own.

---

8. Athanasius, *Against the Pagans*, 3ff.; Gregory of Nyssa, *The Catechetical Oration*, chap. 5; Pseudo-Dionysius, *The Divine Names*, chap. 5; John of Damascus, *Exposition of the Orthodox Faith*, 30.

The good, by a free choice, was the cause of evil and remains its substratum. Fallen angels and humans as creatures are and remain good and exist from moment to moment only by, and in, and for God. Sin has power to do anything only with and by means of the powers and gifts that are God-given. Satan has therefore correctly been called the ape of God. Even bands of robbers must respect rules if they are to exist. Liars always garb themselves in the guise of truth. Satan himself appears as an angel of light. In its operation and appearance, sin is always a parasite of the good. It cannot create; neither can it destroy. Accordingly, neither the essential character of the angels, nor that of humans, nor that of nature, has been changed as a result of sin. Substantially, sin has neither removed anything from humanity nor introduced anything into it. It is the same human person, but now walking, not toward God but away from him, to destruction. Human love, intellect, will, and freedom are not removed but redirected: from God to the creature; from seeking the true, the good, and the beautiful to considering lies as truth, pursuing evil as good, and accepting slavery as freedom. "Sin is not some positive essence but a defect, a corruptive tendency; that is, a force that contaminates mode, species, and order in the created will."[9] The image of God remains but has turned into its own caricature.

In the second place, the insistence on sin as privation, it must be remembered, is a repudiation of all Manichean notions that evil exists as an independent power over against God. However, because sin is always concrete and only occurs as the wrong "form" of an act that is essentially good, it may be hard to separate "matter" and "form," just as at any given time the heat of a stove cannot be separated from the stove. Yet, just as the stove is not identical with its heat, so the being or act to which sin is attached cannot be identified with sin. Even in the case of blasphemy, the power needed to express it and the language in which it is couched are themselves good; what makes it and all things wrong and sinful is the *deformity*, the departure from divine law. God's law alone is the standard of sin; he is the only Agent who has absolute authority over us and can bind and obligate us in our consciences. The violation of all other laws—aesthetic, social, political, ecclesiastical, and so on—is sinful only insofar as it directly or indirectly includes a violation of the moral law. It is this moral law—which was implanted in humans at their creation, had its post-fall effect in their consciences, was announced on Mount Sinai, and remains a binding rule of life for Christian believers as well—that is the source of the knowledge of sin (Rom. 3:20; 4:14; 5:20; 7:7).

In that sense, Schleiermacher, Ritschl, and others are correct when they insist that sin only comes to its most appalling manifestation *as sin* vis-à-vis the gospel of the grace of God in Christ.[10] However, from this it does not follow that all sins committed before or outside the knowledge of the gospel are merely sins

---

9. Bonaventure, *The Breviloquium*, vol. 2 of *The Works of Bonaventure*, trans. Jose De Vinck (Paterson, NJ: St. Anthony Guild Press, 1963), 109.

10. F. Schleiermacher, *The Christian Faith* (Edinburgh: T&T Clark, 1989), §112.5; A. Ritschl, *The Christian Doctrine of Justification and Reconciliation* (Clifton, NJ: Reference Book Publishers, 1966),

of ignorance and weakness, nor that the gospel rather than the law is the source of our knowledge of sin. Christian faith is needed to rightly know sin, but that faith also looks back toward the law, discovers its spiritual character, and thus receives insight into the true nature of sin. The gospel includes forgiveness of all those transgressions we have committed against the law of God. Just as grace presupposes sin, forgiveness, and guilt, so the gospel presupposes law. In that moral law, God comes to us not only as Father with fatherly admonitions and chastisements but, as the categorical imperative testifies to every human being, also as Lawgiver and Judge with commandments and punishments. Although it is not coercive like the laws of logic, or unbreakable as the laws of nature, the moral law surpasses all others in majesty. It addresses the will, breathes freedom, and desires fulfillment out of love. At the same time, it speaks to all humans without distinction, confronts them in all circumstances, extends not only to their words and acts but also to their moral condition, sticks relentlessly to its guns, speaks inexorably and categorically with sovereign authority, and avenges its violations with severe punishment. It is a divine decree, a revelation of the will of God, the expression of his being.

Third, the moral character of the law means that sin can only reside in a rational creature, a being endowed with intellect and will. More specifically, the will is the true subject, sin's showplace. What is morally good can only be realized by the will; what definitively passes by all influence of the will cannot be sin. Augustine was correct when he said: "In fact sin is so much a voluntary evil that it is not sin at all unless it is voluntary."[11] Care must be taken here to avoid the Pelagian notion that sin cannot consist in anything but an act of the will. Augustine and the medieval church wrestled with this matter by means of the notion of "concupiscence." The concern here was to acknowledge the weakened state of the human will after the original fall into sin. We, too, often "fall" into sin; thinking of sin as always a fully voluntary act fails to do justice to our experience of *knowing* that our overpowering desires are sinful and yet feeling that we lack the power to resist our desires. Aside from the vagueness of the term, Augustine and the Roman Catholic Church too easily accommodated human weakness by considering concupiscence to be sin only when one consents to it. Concupiscence does not injure those who do not consent to it and can be called sin only "because it is of sin, and inclines to sin."[12]

The Reformation strongly disagreed, insisting that the impure thoughts and desires that arose in us prior to and apart from our will are also sin. This did not mean that all desiring was sin in a psychological and philosophical sense, but that in a scriptural and theological sense concupiscence made us guilty before God. In this it was undoubtedly correct. For though sin certainly began with a conscious

---

407ff.; J. Kaftan, *The Truth of the Christian Religion*, trans. George Ferries, 2 vols. (Edinburgh: T&T Clark, 1894), 250.

11. Augustine, *True Religion*, 24.

12. *The Catechism of the Council of Trent*, trans. J. Donovan (New York: Catholic Publication Society, 1829), V, 5; *The Racovian Catechism*, trans. Thomas Rees (London, 1609; repr., London, 1818), II, 2, 7.

and voluntary act of the will, that first sinful act also corrupted human nature and left a condition that in all respects is contrary to the law of God. The sin that originated in the will now exists in us outside our will in all our other faculties and powers, in soul and body, in the lower and the higher cognitive and conative capacities (Gen. 6:3; 8:21; Exod. 20:17; Pss. 19:13; 51:5; Jer. 17:9; Matt. 5:28; Mark 7:21; Rom. 7:7, 15–17; 8:7; Gal. 5:7; etc.). Not all sin is therefore voluntary. This does not mean that some sin bypasses the will; the will is antecedent to all actual sins (James 1:15), but our sinful condition and our involuntary sins also do not occur totally apart from our wills. There is not only an antecedent but also a concomitant, a consequent, and an approving will. Later, to a greater or lesser degree, the will approves of the sinfulness of our nature and takes delight in it. Even when, illumined by reason, the will fights against sin, and the born-again person too can testify with Paul that he does not will the evil that he does (cf. Rom. 7:7–25), sin is not defined by our willing or lack of willing. Sin's only standard is the law of God. The same person, on the one hand, impurely pursues what is forbidden (concupiscence) and nevertheless in the deepest part of his will turns away from it and fights it. And since a human being, also the born-again person, for as long as he or she is in the flesh, always to some degree desires what is forbidden, even though he or she fights it in the restricted sense, it can be said that at the most fundamental level all sin is voluntary. There is nobody or nothing that compels the sinner to serve sin. Sin is enthroned not outside the sinner but in the sinner and guides the sinner's thinking and desiring in its own direction. It is the sinner's sin insofar as the sinner has made it his or her own by means of his or her various faculties and powers.[13]

When all is said and done, sin proves to be an incomprehensible mystery. It exists, but has no right to existence nor can anyone explain its origin. Having no independent existence of its own and wholly living off the good in creation, it is a powerful force of destruction and devastation. It is nothing, has nothing, and cannot do anything on its own, yet organizes the very God-created entities on which it depends into rebellion against him. It is dependence at war with the Independent One, and striving for its own independence. It is impermanent becoming in a struggle with him who exists eternally. It is the greatest contradiction tolerated by God in his creation, yet used by him in the way of justice and righteousness as an instrument for his glory.

VARIETIES AND DEGREES OF SIN

[332] There is variety and degree in sin, beginning with the distinction between human and diabolical sin. The Bible speaks of a kingdom (βασιλεια; Matt. 12:26;

---

13. Heidelberg Catechism, Q 113; Francis Turretin, *Institutes of Elenctic Theology*, trans. George Musgrove Giger and ed. James T. Dennison, 3 vols. (Phillipsburg, NJ: Presbyterian and Reformed, 1992), IX, 2; XI, 21.

Mark 3:24; Luke 11:17–18) of evil spirits,[14] of evil, a host of darkness ultimately opposed to Christ and his kingdom, the deceivers and accusers of God's children. At the head of it is Satan,[15] the archenemy of God and his people. Subordinate to him are numerous demons, evil spirits, unclean spirits, and spiritual hosts of wickedness, which are in turn subdivided into various classes and ranks (1 Cor. 15:24; Eph. 6:12; Col. 2:15; Jude 6), surpass each other in wickedness (Matt. 12:45; Luke 11:26), and together form Satan's messengers (Matt. 25:41; 2 Cor. 12:7; Rev. 12:7, 9). They live in sin as their natural element and never appear as the object of God's love, though they are his creatures. For them there is no hope of restoration and salvation. Always and everywhere they are the adversaries of God, the disturbers of his kingdom, the opponents of Christ, the deceivers of humans, the accusers of God's children.

Yet, even among devils, sin is form and not substance. They cannot be absolutely evil, for they are God's creatures and therefore good as such; yet they are only an object of God's hatred and eternal wrath. "We can only conceive of an absolutely evil being on condition that we either omit something from their absolute wickedness or from their true existence."[16] Belief in Satan is not an element of saving faith in Christ, but it is closely connected with it. There is truth in the saying "No devil, no redeemer!" If there were no sin, there would be no savior, and the seriousness of sin stands out most vividly in the doctrine of Satan.[17] There is no redemption for Satan and the devils. He was not "led" astray; the nature of his sin came completely from within himself. The angels are not constituted as a single race; they did not sin "in" Satan's sin but sinned individually; there is no covenant of works for them and hence no covenant of grace either. Satanic sin, therefore, for all its similarity to human sin, is nonetheless totally different in origin, character, and consequences. It bears an absolute character: Satan is the supreme revelation of evil. The comfort here is that Satan's victory is thus the complete triumph of sin. In Satan, God gave sin every opportunity to show what it is and what it can

14. Belief in evil spirits is found among all peoples. Just as, generally speaking, all natural phenomena are personified (animism), so especially disasters and accidents, earthquakes, storms, lightning, fire, misfortunes, and illnesses are attributed to evil spirits. This superstition in turn always led to magic, i.e., to the art of persuading supernatural personal spirits, by special words or actions, to effect something good or to avert some evil. Especially in Babylon this superstition flourished, which is then further traceable to ancient Sumerian culture (O. Weber). Although superstition and sorcery played a large role in Israel as well, the law and the prophets over and over again took a strong stand against them (Lev. 19:31; 20:6, 27; Deut. 18:10–11; Isa. 8:19–20; Jer. 27:9; 29:8–9; etc.).

15. A being given various names in Scripture: "devil," "Satan," "the enemy" (Matt. 13:39; Luke 10:19), "the accuser" (Rev. 12:10), "the evil one" (Matt. 13:19; Eph. 6:16; 2 Thess. 3:3; 1 John 2:13–14; 3:12; 5:18), "prince of demons" (Matt. 9:34), "the ruler of the kingdom of the air" (Eph. 2:2 NIV), "the ruler of this world" (John 12:31), "the god of this world" (2 Cor. 4:4), "the great dragon," "the ancient serpent" (Rev. 12:9; 20:2; etc.).

16. C. E. Nitzsch, *System of Christian Doctrines* (Edinburgh: T&T Clark, 1849), §116 (ed. note: Bavinck erroneously cites this as C. J. Nitzsch); F. A. B. Nitzsch, *Lehrbuch der Evangelischen Dogmatik*, prepared by Horst Stephan, 3rd ed. (Tübingen: Mohr, 1902), 337.

17. A. von Oettingen, *Lutherische Dogmatik*, 2 vols. (Munich: C. H. Beck, 1897–1902), II, 459.

do. And sin has made the highest and best, the most noble and greatest creature in God's creation, subservient to itself. And yet ... sin does not have the final victory. Sin is empty, hollow, weak and powerless—Sin *is* not; it *wants to be*; it neither has nor ever achieves true reality. "Lucifer—one can say—has learned from experience that nothing is true but God. Therefore Satan is as good a proof for God as an angel. Whereas goodness proves that God exists, evil proves that only God exists" (Baader).[18]

[333] There is also diversity in human sin. Human intention is very important in assessing degrees of culpability. Inadvertent sins done out of ignorance are not the same as those done consciously and intentionally (בְּיָד רָמָה—"with a high hand"). Sins against the first table of the law are more serious than those against the second. Circumstances and degree always need to be taken into account. Nonetheless, the character of sin is not defined by the subjective consciousness of guilt and even ignorance is not excuse, especially when consciousness of sin is weakened to the degree that sin has been pursued for a shorter or longer period (Amos 2:11f.; Hosea 4:6; Mic. 3:1; 6:8; Prov. 24:12; Eccles. 5:1). The standard of sin is not the consciousness of guilt but the law of God. Thus the sins of Jews and gentiles done in ignorance (Luke 23:34; Acts 3:17–19; 13:27; 17:30; Eph. 4:18; Heb. 5:2; 1 Pet. 1:14; 2:25) are not thereby stripped of their culpability (Rom. 1–3; 5:12f.; Eph. 4:17–19; Col. 3:5–7; 1 Cor. 15:9; 1 Tim. 1:13, 15). Schleiermacher spoke incorrectly when he claimed "that in general sin only exists insofar as there also exists an awareness of it."[19] Still, sins committed in ignorance are not the same as those coming from hard hearts; ignorance does constitute a ground for the plea for forgiveness.

Sin also develops in an order that is dynamic; there is a law of sin that proceeds from suggestion to enjoyment to consent to execution and involves both our sensuality and our self-seeking. No single human sin is exclusively either sensual or self-seeking. Neither sensuality nor self-seeking can be explained one from the other; both are involved in our sins as embodied spiritual persons. In humans every sin is a turning away from God, disobedience, rebellion, anarchy, lawlessness, and at the same time, since sin is never self-sufficient, a turning toward a creature, idolatry, pride, self-seeking, sensuality.[20] There are as many kinds of sin as there are different commandments, duties, virtues, and moral goods. In this variety we need to consider the traditional Roman Catholic distinction between

18. Augustine, *City of God*, XI, XII; Anselm, *The Fall of the Devil*, in *Anselm of Canterbury*, trans. and ed. Jasper Hopkins and Herbert Richardson, 4 vols. (Toronto and New York: Edwin Mellen, 1975), II, 127–77; T. Aquinas, *Summa Theol.*, I, qu. 63–64; Isaak August Dorner, *A System of Christian Doctrine*, trans. A. Cave and J. S. Banks, rev. ed., 4 vols. (T&T Clark, 1888), III, 85ff.; J. J. van Oosterzee, *Christian Dogmatics*, trans. J. Watson and M. Evans, 2 vols. (New York: Scribner, Armstrong, 1874), §76; A. Kuyper, *De Engelen Gods* (Amsterdam: Höveker & Wormser, 1900), 197ff.

19. F. Schleiermacher, *Christian Faith*, §68.2.

20. Bonaventure, *Disputata S. Bonaventurae in libros sententiarum* (Lugdini, 1510), II, dist. 42, art. 3, qu. 2.

mortal and venial sins. Rooted in the practice of penance, the distinction was intended to honor the diversity and degree of sin discussed above. However, the Reformers rejected the distinction. While not denying the variety and degree of sin, the Reformers insisted that sins must never be individualistically and atomistically abstracted from the person who commits the sin. It is the sinful person who needs forgiveness and liberation from all sin. If they did at times still use the words "mortal" and "venial" sins, they attached a different meaning to them; they meant by them that all sins, except the sin of blaspheming the Holy Spirit, can be forgiven and are actually forgiven to believers, but that they are all inherently deserving of death.[21]

The only passage offering any resemblance to the distinction between mortal and venial sins is Matthew 5:22 where our Lord teaches that when anger is accompanied by an insulting word, this sin is so great that at that very moment it deserves hellish punishment. But Jesus's intention here is not to distinguish lesser sins from greater ones but to observe that illegitimate anger, even if it does not result in homicide, is a grievous sin that under certain circumstances deserves hell's punishment. Properly understood, this text is an argument against rather than for the distinction between mortal and venial sins. Scripture teaches the organic unity of the law (James 2:10) and even the slightest violations of the law—an upsurge of anger, an impure desire, a redundant confirmation, an idle word (Matt. 5:22, 28, 37; 12:36; Eph. 5:4)—are sins equal, in principle, to sinful deeds and therefore to sin as lawlessness, hostility against God. The Reformed tradition rejects the abstract atomistic view that considers sin in quantitative terms that, isolated from sin's perpetrator, can be counted on one's fingers and weighed in a scale. The Roman Catholic approach all too often keeps souls in a perpetual state of fear about whether they have committed a mortal sin, or incites them to frivolousness and indifference, since the sins are usually of a very light kind and very easy to correct.

[334] Holy Scripture mentions only one sin that both in this life and in the life to come is "mortal" and unpardonable: blasphemy against the Holy Spirit. Although the Old Testament does speak of sins committed "high-handedly" (Num. 15:30), for which no sacrifice was instituted in the law because it set aside the law itself (cf. Heb. 10:28), Jesus is the first to speak of "blasphemy against the Holy Spirit" (Matt. 12:31; Mark 3:29; Luke 12:10). From the Gospels it is clear that Jesus is speaking of those who consciously, willingly, and deliberately blaspheme by rejecting the revelation of God's grace in Christ by the Holy Spirit. As the Pharisees who attribute Jesus's power to cast out demons to his being Satan's own agent (Mark 3:22; Matt.12:25–30), this is a willful blasphemy against the Holy Spirit because it puts God in Satan's place and Satan in God's place. This

21. J. Calvin, *Institutes*, II.viii.58; III.ii.11; III.iv.28; *The Catechism of the Council of Trent*, VI, 12; F. Turretin, *Institutes of Elenctic Theology*, IX, 4; P. van Mastricht, *Theologia*, IV, 3, 22; H. Heppe, *Die Dogmatik der evangelisch-reformirten Kirche* (Elberfeld: R. L. Friderichs, 1861), 257.

is a demonic posture; it is pure, conscious hatred of God and his work. For this there can be no forgiveness.

The blasphemy against the Holy Spirit, therefore, does not simply consist in unbelief, nor in resisting and grieving the Holy Spirit in general, nor in denying the personality or deity of the Holy Spirit, nor in sinning against better knowledge and to the very end without qualification. It is not a sin solely against the law but a sin specifically against the gospel, and that against the gospel in its clearest manifestation. There is, therefore, a context and a history to the sin. A revelation of God's grace in Christ has been given and even acknowledged. To repudiate the gospel after this is not simply doubting or denying truth but a denial that contradicts the conviction of the mind, the illumination of the conscience, and the intuitions of the heart. It is a conscious and intentional hatred against God; it is at this point no longer human but demonic. It is to repeat the sin of the fallen angels; it is blasphemy against the Holy Spirit. Specifically mentioned in the Gospels, it is also referred to indirectly in Hebrews 6:4–8 and 10:25–29 (cf. 2:3; 4:1; 12:15–17) and 1 John 5:16. In these passages we are dealing with sins that leave a person completely hardened and are therefore inherently unpardonable. Factually and materially, they coincide with the sin of blaspheming the Holy Spirit.

THE PUNISHMENT OF SIN

[335] The punishment of sin was not administered immediately after the fall; it does not even go into effect fully now but only after the final judgment. God delayed and moderated sin's punishment of death to make the continuation of human life and history possible. History continues after the fall thanks to God's grace which went into effect immediately. All the post-fall consequences and punishments of sin display a double character; they are appointed by God's justice but, also, without exception appointed means of grace, proofs of God's patience and compassion. God speaks truly in Genesis 2:17—"In the day that you eat of it you shall die"—because he announces there the true and full punishment that sin deserves: death, the broken communion with God that is death and deserves death. With death, after all, everything—life, joy, development, work, but also the possibility of repentance and forgiveness, the restoration of communion with God—ceases all at once. All other punishments that went into effect and were pronounced after the fall—such as shame, fear, concealment from God, the curse pronounced on the serpent and the earth, and so on—though indeed punishments, nevertheless also presuppose that God did not instantly and fully carry out his threat. God still has another plan for humankind and the world and therefore, in his patience and compassion, allows them to exist.

Punishment serves God's justice in a twofold way: it redresses past violations and seeks to prevent future ones. As among other peoples, especially the Egyptians, the law of retribution (*ius talionis*) was in force also in Israel. In practice the law of retribution was often abused, and Jesus spoke out against these abuses in the Sermon on the Mount (Matt. 5:38–42). Recognizing the human propensity to abuse the law of vengeance for self-interest, Jesus offered a higher principle: love and patience. His disciples must not resist one who is evil, that is, they must not (according to the rule "an eye for an eye and a tooth for a tooth") return evil for evil. In saying this, however, Christ is absolutely not condemning every instance of defending one's own rights, as he did before the high priest (John 18:22–23). The same is true for the apostle Paul (Acts 22:25; 23:3; 25:10). When we insist on rights, we must do so out of love for God and our neighbor. Vengeance and recompense, also according to the Old Testament, are the Lord's own cause (Deut. 32:35).

[336] Retribution, however, is Scripture's principle and standard of judgment. God is just and righteous; he never clears the guilty and is merciful to the poor and afflicted. Imposing judgment on another human being is permissible only to those who are legitimately clothed with authority; it is never the prerogative of the strong or the saintly. All authority is subject to God's justice and finally grounded in it. Efforts to establish justice, right and wrong, apart from God ultimately annihilate both justice and morality. "The doctrine of the divine justice of punishment is among the fundamental articles of the Christian faith. The fact that God punishes evil is the basis of all human punitive justice. Those who carry it out judicially act in the name of God as his servants, perform a sacred office on his orders. Punishment, therefore, is never a matter of expediency but rests in the inviolable ideas of good and evil that are rooted in the holy will of God."[22]

The history of the modern world is a case-study proof of this judgment. The decline of the ancient Christian worldview led to modifying and eventually abolishing and banishing the concepts of good and evil, responsibility and accountability, guilt and punishment. When belief in God's justice disappears, belief in justice on earth disappears as well. Atheism proved to be the annihilation of all justice and morality: no God, no master. Where vestiges of belief in good and evil, sin and virtue, still linger, explanations trace sins and crimes not to a sinful, evil human nature but to leftovers from our animal ancestry or to social environments. In this way human moral agency and responsibility are eliminated; society is the villain: "Societies have the criminals that they deserve" (Lacassagne).[23] Even guilt is attributed to society: "It is not [criminals] who must be nailed to a cross but those who have made them criminals."[24] The practical problem with this view, of course, is that it is difficult to throw the whole society into prison. This is not a coherent view. If society is to blame for crime—and modern criminologists, educationists, and sociologists vigorously propound this view—on what basis does one attribute

---

22. J. Kaftan, *Dogmatik* (Tübingen: Mohr, 1901), 339–40.

23. A. E. J. Modderman, *Straf geen kwaad* (Amsterdam: Muller, 1864); J. R. Brandes de Roos, *De strafmiddelen in de nieuwere strafrechtswetenschap* (Amsterdam: Scheltema, 1900).

24. Merkel, according to Dr. G. von Rohden, *Das Wesen der Strafe im ethischen und strafrechtlichen Sinne* (Tübingen, 1905), 53.

free will, moral responsibility, and culpability to society? Should society also not be given a break here? If society is to be blamed for the criminal's acts, then why should society too not be absolved? It too has a past to which it is bound, a past that may even be crippling. On what grounds do those who deny free will and moral agency to individuals then so cavalierly attribute them to society? Those who throw away ethical standards in the case of an individual's crime cannot again pick them up and apply them to society.

There remains an additional equally momentous inconsistency. Although criminals, in this view, are really innocent and more to be pitied than condemned, society does need to be protected from them. Modern criminology faces a real problem here. Having abolished clear, universal standards of justice, criminologists turn crime into a disease that needs to be "cured." Retribution is judged to be contrary to the "ethical" spirit of Jesus, ineffective as a deterrent to crime, and unusually harsh and cruel to the criminal. But, at what cost? Replacing retribution with cure does not solve the problem. Crimes are still punished when criminals are sent away to be "cured." If criminals are to be treated as sick people, the downside of this is that the sick must be "nursed" in the manner of criminals. If the state's only right to act against criminals is for self-protection and to improve them, how will we stop those who wish to deal with all kinds of sick people in similar manner, to view the religious and moral convictions that are judged to be contrary to the public good as so many diseases, remnants and aftereffects of an earlier state, and to take over the entire upbringing of its citizens and the whole culture of the society in question? When the boundaries between crime and disease are wiped out and justice declines into mere cultural preference, freedom itself is forfeited and citizens are handed over to an arbitrary and omnipotent state.

We must not overlook the positive elements in modern criminology. Over against an abstract view of crime and punishment, it correctly focuses attention on the connection between the act and the person of the criminal. Research into the causes, the treatment, and the means of diminishing crime is undoubtedly legitimate. In dealing with crime, we may and must take account of the person by whom and the circumstances under which the crime has been committed. The law of retribution does not demand the same thing from all but demands that to each be given his or her due; it does not demand a precise payment in kind but punishment proportionate to the seriousness of the offense. The interest of the state, self-defense, deterrence, amelioration are all components that can be incorporated into and be constituents of retributive justice. The state, however, cannot do without retribution and punishment. To reduce crime to disease and punishment to remediation is to enter a labyrinth. No earthly judge can know the human heart or decide a person's capacity for improvement. For modern criminology to eliminate notions of retribution and punishment in favor of moral improvement is to take away the norm of justice from the power of the state. Who determines whether a criminal has been "improved"? The purpose of punishment is justice; failure to serve that end results in mere coercion, an exercise of the will to power. Here the weak have no legal protection. Modern criminology, by calling the notions of retribution and punishment antiquated and adopting as its goal the moral improvement of the criminal, takes from the government's arm the power of justice and assigns to it a task for which it is utterly unqualified and unfit.

[337] For all these reasons, punitive justice cannot do without the element of retribution. Punishment is imposed, in the first place, not because it is useful, but because justice requires it, because the criminal has incurred a moral-judicial debt.[25] This justice is of such superlative value that it exacts the goods and lives of persons for its maintenance and restoration. It is moral world order not concocted by humans, not a state of affairs produced by men, but the revelation and operation of the justice of God in this world; it is rooted in the perfect, holy will of him who upholds and governs all things. "If justice should collapse, human life on earth would become worthless" (Kant). The purpose of punishment is the restoration of justice, the maintenance of divine justice. Failing to serve that end, it becomes coercion and a mere exercise of superior power.[26]

Punishment always consists in a kind of suffering, in the deprivation of a certain good, be it in property or in freedom, in body or in life. It is an "evil of suffering inflicted on account of an evil of action." Exactly why justice requires suffering from the guilty whereby the moral order is restored is hard to say, but it is certainly not caprice or accident. The moment the moral or judicial order has been violated, therefore, it rises up and demands restoration. It is the living, true, and holy God who stands behind the moral order and demands justice. If he did not punish sin, he would give to evil the same rights he accords to the good and so deny himself. The punishment of sin is necessary so that God may remain God. God cannot bear to let sinners, instead of submitting to his law and obeying it, defy it and in effect making themselves God's equals. Punishment is powerful proof that only justice has the right to exist, that only God is good and great.

In part, punishment flows from sin itself. To a degree, the history of the world is a judgment of the world if not *the* judgment of the world. God also visits this world with concrete and specific punishments in addition to "natural" punishments. We are warned in Scripture not to infer personal sin from a person's specific suffering (Luke 13:4; John 9:1) and reminded that God's fatherly power makes all things work together for our good (Rom. 8:28). At the same time, suffering does have a cause in the sin of a generation, a people, or humankind. Concrete punishments

25. "The principle aim of punishment is retribution. Not vengeful reprisal, nor coarse retaliation, or external repayment; it is rather the authoritative restoration of the broken judicial order, in accordance with the laws of a higher set of values, by a punishment that fits the measure of indebtedness. Other goals accompany this aim, such as the protection of society, deterrence, and improvement. For the administration of justice and expediency are not mutually exclusive. But these accompanying goals must be dovetailed with and subordinate to the fundamental idea of justice" (Kahl, "Die Reform des deutschen Strafrechts im Lichte evang. Sozialpolitik," in *Die verhandl. des vierzehnten Evang.-soz. Kongresses in Darmstadt am 3. und 4. Juni 1903* [Göttingen: Vandenhoeck & Ruprecht, 1903], 94–114).

26. Augustine, *City of God*, XIII; T. Aquinas, *Summa Theol.*, II, 2, qu. 164; idem, *Summa contra gentiles*, IV, 51.

are never arbitrary, even when we fail to see connections between them and our sin. It is indeed true that the sins of believers, those who have received forgiveness in full, in themselves always remain sins and therefore culpable. Therefore, the Reformed always insisted, against Antinomians, that believers must still pray for forgiveness of sins they commit. God has his own purposes in visiting us with guilt, pollution, suffering, death, and Satan's dominion. In God's providence and by his grace and wisdom, suffering serves not only as punishment but also as trial, as chastisement, and as nurture. The pious do not serve God for the sake of reward but neither are they indifferent to it, as the advocates of "disinterested love" say they are. Paul says that believers are of all people most to be pitied if for this life only they have hope in Christ (1 Cor. 15:19).

[338] The punishments that God has ordained for sin in this life are guilt, pollution, suffering, death, and the dominion of Satan. Sin always has guilt as its concomitant. Both Scripture and our consciences bear this witness of God to us. In Scripture sin, guilt, and punishment are so deeply interwoven that the words for sin (like עָוֹן and חַטָּאת) imperceptibly acquire the sense of guilt (Gen. 4:13; Exod. 34:7; Lev. 24:15; Num. 9:13; etc.). The word that actually denotes sin in the sense of guilt is אָשָׁם (Gen. 26:10; Lev. 4:13; 5:2; Num. 5:7; etc.) in the Old Testament and ὀφείλημα (Matt. 6:12; cf. 5:26; Luke 7:41–42; 13:4)[27] in the New Testament. Those who violate the law become more tightly bound to its demand. God never relinquishes his hold on the sinner; those who position themselves outside the law are struck with its curse (Deut. 27:26; Gal. 3:10). Curse (קְלָלָה, מְאֵרָה, אָלָה, κατάρα, ἀνάθεμα, maledictum) is the opposite of blessing (בְּרָכָה, εὐλογια, benedictio, Deut. 11:26; 30:19). Just as God's blessing bestows all kinds of well-being and life on a person, so a divine curse is the abandonment of a person to corruption, ruin, death, judgment, Satan. Human beings can only wish blessings or curses on another person, but God's blessing and cursing is always performative; it accomplishes what it wishes. After the fall, God in providential grace continues to bless the earth, but outside of God's own people this is not known; among pagans, awareness of curse and fear (δεισιδαιμονια, religio) dominate and outweigh trust in the gods. Not communion but separation prevails between God and humankind; the covenant has been broken; God has a quarrel with his creatures. All stand guilty and punishable before his face (Matt. 5:21–22; Mark 3:29; James 2:10); there is a divine curse resting on the world and humanity. The whole world is accountable to God (Rom. 3:19); it is subject to divine judgment and has no defense.[28]

This objective curse finds its reflection in human consciousness through the guilty conscience by which human beings condemn themselves as sinners. Guilt and the consciousness of guilt are not the same; there are sins that are hidden from ourselves and others (Ps. 19:12), and sins of ignorance are still culpable (Acts

---

27. H. Schultz, Alttestamentliche Theologie, 4th ed., 2 vols. (Göttingen: Vandenhoeck & Ruprecht, 1889), 684ff.

28. R. Kittel, "Segen und Fluch," PRE³, XVIII, 148–54; W. B. Stevenson, "Benediction," in DC, I, 189–91; James Denney, "Curse," in DB, I, 534–35; J. Heinrici, "ἀνάθεμα," PRE³, I, 493–95.

17:27–30; Rom. 1:19–21, 28; 1 Tim. 1:13–15). Yet, an objective guilt is more or less firmly reflected in the human consciousness and comes to expression in such universal phenomena as shame. Shame is the fear of disgrace, an unpleasant and painful sense of being involved in something wrong or improper. By the grace of God, humans still retain the consciousness that they ought to be different, that in all respects they must conform to God's law. But reality witnesses that they are not who they ought to be. And this witness is the conscience. The human conscience is the subjective proof of humanity's fall, a witness to human guilt before the face of God. God is not the only accuser of humankind; in their conscience humans condemn themselves and take God's side against themselves. The more precisely and meticulously the human conscience functions, the more it validates God's idea of humans in Scripture. The best and most noble members of our race, confirming God's truthfulness, have declared the race guilty at their very own expense.[29]

[339] Sin's punishment is also found in pollution, in the corruption of thought, desire, and inclination that is contrary to God's holiness. Whereas guilt obligates us to endure punishment, pollution renders us unclean. Sin is guilt inasmuch as it militates against God's righteousness; it is pollution inasmuch as it is contrary to his holiness. Guilt and pollution always go together as the two inseparable sides of sin; where the one is, there the other is also. Guilt applies to the objective brokenness of our relation to God; pollution describes the reality of our subjective communion with God. Human beings do not cease to be human, but our whole lives are disturbed and devoted to the service of sin. We are no longer God's covenant partners. Sin is simultaneously a violation of the covenant of works and the destruction of God's image. Paradise has been sealed shut to us; access to the tree of life has been denied. Reformed theology distinguishes here between a narrow sense of the image of God—the true righteousness and holiness lost in the fall—and the broader sense, which is retained though completely mutilated and corrupted.[30] Fallen humans are still image bearers of God. We are all part of a single corrupt race though we sin in a variety of ways. Individuals, families, generations, classes, peoples are utterly divergent also in sin. Sins in the East differ from those in the West, in tropical zones from temperate zones, in rural areas from cities, in civilized states from uncivilized ones, in the twentieth century from earlier centuries. There are family sins, societal sins, national sins. At certain times, situations, and distinct circles, there often appears a horrifying regularity in certain moral offenses such as homicide, suicide, illegitimacy, etc. Aside from what we call "original sin," there is also "corporate guilt and the corporate action of sin." As people are interconnected, so also are their sinful inclinations and deeds. We can even speak of a "realm of sin" that is driven by a single life principle but expresses itself in a diversity that is as rich as creation itself.[31]

29. Cf. also H. Bavinck, *Beginselen der Psychologie* (Kampen: Bos, 1897), 111, 303.

30. Belgic Confession, art. 14.

31. F. Schleiermacher, *Christian Faith*, §§71–72; A. Ritschl, *The Christian Doctrine of Justification and Reconciliation*, III, 334ff. (#41: "The Kingdom of Sin"); I. A. Dorner, *System of Christian Doctrine*, III, 54ff.

SUFFERING AND DEATH

[340] Thanks to the entry of sin to the world, humanity lost dominion and glory, and suffering is the result. Suffering is not always a consequence of personal sin, but it is nonetheless still a consequence of sin in general. Without sin there would be no suffering (Lev. 26:14f.; Deut. 28:15f.; Ezek. 4:17; Hosea 2:8f.; Rev. 18:8; 21:4). Even the irrational creation has been subjected to futility and decay and now collectively sighs, as though in labor pains, looking forward to the revelation of the glory of the children of God, in hope of being itself set free from bondage to decay (Rom. 8:19–22). Suffering is universal and often turns sensitive souls to pessimism and even despair. "To live in sorrow is the lot that the gods have decreed for mortals; only they themselves are free from cares" (Homer). Reason can neither explain nor ameliorate suffering. Even if all evil obviously caused by human sin were eliminated, disasters in nature would still cause suffering. While not directly traceable to a specific sin, there is a connection with sin; the world is under a curse. As in the case of human beings, a significant change has taken place in nature as a result of divine judgment. Scripture is not pessimistic in the usual sense of the word, but it knows and acknowledges suffering, interpreting it in the most moving laments (Gen. 47:9; Job 3; 6; 7; 9; 14; etc.; Pss. 22; 38; 39; 69; 73; 74; 79; 89; 90; etc.; Ecclesiastes; Lamentations; Matt. 6:34; Rom. 7:24; 8:19ff.; 1 Cor. 15:19; etc.).

The world's greatest minds have wrestled with the problem of human suffering. Modern thinkers increasingly turn to dialectic modes of thought that try to somehow incorporate suffering in the ontology of creation itself. For Schelling, all creation is brought out of primordial chaos: "Without this antecedent darkness, there is no creaturely reality; darkness is its necessary portion . . . all birth is birth out of darkness into light."[32] The entire world process is a *via dolorosa*. Similarly, Buddhism regards the will to live as the cause of all suffering. When philosophers attempt to account for suffering they often cast the blame, directly or indirectly, on God. Somehow, a world without suffering is unimaginable; we cannot picture a history without sin and misery; pain and death seem integral to all physical organisms. Modern science has everywhere made us see, in organic as well as in inorganic nature, an ongoing struggle for life in which all creatures are pitted against one another and aiming at one another's death. Yet, however natural pain and suffering may seem, one can on good grounds lodge the following objections against the above view.

1. If we could someday remove from the world and humankind all the suffering that has undoubtedly been directly and indirectly caused by sin, then in a flash, far and away the most painful suffering would have disappeared, and

---

32. F. W. J. Schelling, "Philosophische Untersuchungen über das Wesen der menschlichen Freiheit," in *Ausgewählte Werke*, 4 vols. (1809; repr., Darmstadt: Wissenschaftliche Buchgesellschaft, 1968), IV, 303ff. (*Sämmtliche Werke* [Stuttgart & Augsburg: J. G. Cotta'scher, 1856–61], I/7, 359ff.).

the problem of suffering would be reduced to very small dimensions. The close link between sin and misery is undeniable. A stream of spiritual and physical misery in individual persons, families, generations, and nations, in state, church, society, science, and art has its origin in sin. Remove it and—as everyone agrees—there is almost no suffering left. "The world is perfect everywhere—where humans have not trod with their troubles" (Schiller).

2. Yet, however much truth there is in Schiller's saying, it is not altogether correct. Even under the conditions described above—removal of all suffering caused directly or indirectly by sin—much suffering would remain: earthquakes, hurricanes, thunderstorms, floods, famines, plagues, train accidents, and so on. These cannot be ascribed as caused by personal sin (Luke 13:4; John 9:1) but still reflect a world under divine curse and subjected to futility. The forces of nature are no longer under human dominion but hostile and requiring great human effort to counter. In the struggle with nature, humanity as a whole has found a spur for its energy, material for its labor, a stimulus for its development. By God's grace the curse on the earth has been turned into a blessing for it.

3. All nature shares in humanity's fall; this is Scripture's clear teaching and also follows from the central place humans occupy in creation. Reformed theology has kept to a prudent sobriety here in speaking about the changes brought about in creation through the fall. The substance of things in creation was not changed; sin is not a substance that increases or decreases the substance of things. As humans remain human, so it is with nature as a whole. No new species were added in the world of plants and animals. Thorns and thistles were not created new by a word of God, like the vegetation, the herbs, and the fruit trees on the third day (Gen. 1:11). Creeping things and wild animals also existed prior to the fall (Gen. 1:24). Creation's functions, capacities, and forces—now corrupted by sin—began to function in another direction. Emancipated from the dominion and care of humans, and burdened by a divine curse, nature gradually became degraded and adulterated. Interesting questions remain for theologians such as whether animals that are now carnivorous were so before the fall. Fascinating for theologians is Charles Darwin's demonstration—in *The Variation of Animals and Plants under Domestication*—that animals can grow accustomed to a changed diet, citing various examples to this effect.[33] Similarly, as a result of degeneration, branches can change into thorns, and as a result of cultivation, thorns can change into branches.[34] We wonder: could human domestication of animals lead to the state described by Isaiah in chapters 11 and 65? It is not absurd to think that a significant change

---

33. C. Darwin, *The Variation of Animals and Plants under Domestication*, 2 vols. (New York: D. Appleton, 1896).

34. Ibid., 310.

took place in nature as it did in humans and that these will be reversed in the consummation.

4. We must not overlook the fact that, theologically speaking, the creation itself was in a sense infralapsarian.[35] For God the fall was neither a surprise nor a disappointment. He anticipated it, incorporated it into his counsel, and already took account of it in creating the world. Creation, therefore, took place in such a way that, in case Adam as its head fell, the whole world could become as it is now. Prior to the fall, the state of humanity and of the earth as a whole was a provisional one that could not remain as it was. It was such that it could be raised to a higher glory but in the event of human transgression could also be subjected to futility and decay. As a result of sin and the curse of God, there everywhere emerged from under and behind the primordial harmony, the "unruly," the chaotic, and the demonic, which confuses and frightens us. Spread over the whole creation there is now a veil of melancholy. "The whole creation has been groaning in labor pains" (Rom. 8:22).

[341] Suffering culminates in sin's other penalty, death. Many theologians today[36] are of the opinion that Scripture—aside from a few places—does not view death as a consequence and penalty of sin. Although there is some truth in the notion that the difference between the righteous and the wicked in the Old Testament rests not in death itself but in the meaning of suffering and death (Deut. 8:2f.; Hosea 2:5f.; Isa. 1:25f.; Jer. 5:3; 9:7; 31:18; Lam. 3:27f.; Ps. 119:67, 71, 75; Prov. 3:11f.; Job 1; etc.), and although death is naturally given with the material organism of a human being (Gen. 3:19; 18:27; Job 4:19; Pss. 89:48f.; 90:3; 103:14f.; 146:4; Eccles. 3:20; 12:7), Scripture does not consider death natural or necessary. The New Testament clearly teaches the bond between sin and death (John 8:21; Rom. 1:32; 5:12; 6:23; 1 Cor. 15:22, 55–56; Heb. 2:14; 1 Pet. 4:6; James 1:15; 5:20; Rev. 20:14; 21:4; etc.). The fear of death is innate in all things living; at bottom we do not believe we have to die. Death has always been for humans the last and greatest enemy. While it is true that some overcome this fear and die peacefully, and Romanticism even sentimentalized death, all recognize in death an unnatural power and flee from it as long as they can.[37] Natural science may call death natural,[38]

35. F. Delitzsch, *A New Commentary on Genesis*, trans. Sophia Taylor (Edinburgh: T&T Clark, 1899), 80.

36. F. Schleiermacher, *Christian Faith*, §59; A. Ritschl, *Christian Doctrine of Justification and Reconciliation*, III, 345ff.; J. Kaftan, *Dogmatik*, §29; K. Beth, "Über Ursache und Zweck des Todes," *Glauben und Wissen* (1909): 285–304, 335–48, demonstrates that science has not been able to explain the riddle of death but considers death to be natural to all earthly creatures and subordinates all exegesis of Scripture to this point of view.

37. For the people of nature (*natuurvolken*), cf. W. Schneider, *Die Naturvölker: Missverständnisse, Missdeutungen, und Misshandlungen*, 2 vols. (Paderborn: Schöning, 1885–86), II, 397ff.; C. P. Tiele, *Elements of the Science of Religion*, 2 vols. (Edinburgh and London: William Blackwood, 1899), II, 237.

38. Lauvergne, for example, said, "The death of humans is a logical and natural consequence of their existence. Everything has an end: it is a hard law but it is the law" (in F. Delitzsch, *System der christlichen*

but when it talks this way, science is saying more than it can account for. Death is a mystery in the full sense of the word. Many natural scientists claim that matter and energy, and even unicellular protozoa,[39] are immortal. Why then do organisms die? Add to this the fact that an organism's cells are constantly renewing, that cells also waste away, and that humans lose vitality as they age—all this remains a mystery. Science does not know why death is necessary. It remains a riddle, as much intact as that of life.[40]

[342] The full penalty of sin discussed in this chapter is the dominion of Satan in this world. Since Satan seduced humanity and brought about its fall (John 8:44; 2 Cor. 11:3; 1 Tim. 2:14; Rev. 12:9, 14–15; 20:2, 10), the world is in his power, lying as it does in the evil one (1 John 5:19). He is the "prince of this world" and the "god of this age" (John 12:31; 16:11; 2 Cor. 4:4). Although the devils have been thrown into hell till the judgment (2 Pet. 2:4; Jude 6), they still have great power, especially over the gentile nations (Acts 16:16; 26:18; Eph. 2:2; 6:12; Col. 1:13; 1 Cor. 10:20; 8:5; Rev. 9:20). Christ's ministry was open warfare against Satan and his hosts (Matt. 4:1–11; Luke 22:3; John 6:70; 8:44f.; 13:2, 27), and though it was Satan's hour (Luke 22:53; John 14:30), Christ prevailed in the battle (Luke 4:13; 10:18; 11:22; John 12:31; 14:30; 16:11; Col. 2:15; Heb. 2:14; 1 John 3:8) and in principle withdrew the domain of the church from his rule (Acts 26:18; Col. 1:13; 1 John 2:13; 4:4; Rev. 12:11). Nevertheless, Satan still engages in warfare against God's people (Luke 22:31; 1 Cor. 7:5; 2 Cor. 2:11; 11:3, 13–15; 12:7; 1 Thess. 2:18; 3:5; 1 Pet. 5:8; Rev. 12:10), so that the church is called to fight against him always (Matt. 6:13; Eph. 6:12f.; Rom. 16:20; 1 Pet. 5:9; James 4:7; Rev. 12:11). Although Satan will intensify his assault at the end times and rise up in all his power (Matt. 24; Mark 13; Luke 21; 2 Thess. 2:1–12; Rev. 12f.), he will also be overpowered by Christ and hurled with all his angels into the pool of fire (2 Thess. 2:8; 1 Cor. 15:24; Rev. 20:10). Belief in evil spirits occurs among all peoples and in all religions. Christians must clearly distance themselves from pagan superstitions that attribute all physical evil in the world—disease, crop failures, famine, plague, death—to Satan and the demonic. The church has not always been consistent in its opposition to this; some church fathers attributed personal demons along with guardian angels to each believer. Many medieval people believed that the devil could appear in all sorts of guises (cats, mice, goats, swine, werewolves), create all sorts of vermin, engage as incubus

Apologetik [Leipzig: Dörffling & Franke, 1870], 132). For similar expressions about the naturalness and necessity of death, see Rudolf Eisler, *Wörterbuch der Philosophischen Begriffe*, 3 vols., III: 1511–13 (Berlin: E. S. Mittler, 1910), s.v. "Tod."

39. Cf. W. von Schnehen, "Die Ewigkeit des Lebens?" *Glauben und Wissen* (March 1907): 91–99; Prof. Weismann calls the origin of death one of the most difficult questions in physiology; cf. James Orr, *God's Image in Man and Its Defacement in the Light of Modern Denials* (London: Hodder & Stoughton, 1906), 253ff.

40. N. Smyth, *The Place of Death in Evolution* (London: T. Fisher Unwin, 1897); C. T. Müller, *Das Rätsel des Todes* (Barmen: Wuppertaler Traktat-Gesellschaft, 1905); O. Bloch, *Vom Tode*, 2 vols. (Berlin: Juncker, 1909).

and succubus in fornication, seduce people into covenants sealed with blood, bewitch them, enter into them, ride with them through the air, change them into animals, and stir up all sorts of misfortune also in the natural environment. Even when Protestants repudiated elements of Roman Catholic superstition that saw Christians as threatened by devils everywhere, they were not entirely successful in eliminating such social evils as witches' trials. The Reformation, however, while acknowledging the reality of evil spirits, emphasized the sovereignty of God's providence and the victory of Christ and his kingdom. The church continues to struggle against the kingdom of darkness, but Jesus is Lord and Satan's power and influence are subject to God's providence. Our lives, and the ends of our lives, are not in Satan's hand but in God's.

Only by a faith that conscientiously follows Scripture can we overcome the superstition that has struck such deep roots in the human heart and, despite all so-called intellectual development, keeps on returning. The superstition that rationalism tried to root out reemerges in new guises—magnetism, hypnotism, telepathy, spiritism and other forms of occultism, astrology, and so on—especially in the circles of unbelief. Belief in the devil simultaneously upholds both the appalling seriousness of sin and the human capacity for redemption. Our choice here is between "a devil outside of humanity or thousands of devils in human form."[41] The spiritual struggle of our age and others is real. There is a sinful power at work in the world that forms its own kingdom, a kingdom that, in its opposition to God and his kingdom, operates systematically. There is a deliberate methodical opposition to God and all that is his. And the leadership of this opposition is in the hands of him who is called in Scripture "the prince of this world" and "the god of this age." He made his appearance in the Garden of Eden, concentrated his power against the incarnate Christ (Matt. 4:24; 8:16, 29, 31; 10:1; Mark 1:26, 32, 34; 3:11, 15; Luke 4:34, 41; 8:2, 30; 13:32; Acts 16:17–18; 19:15), and will once again, toward the end of history, be exposed and vanquished (1 Thess. 2:18; 2 Thess. 2:8–11; Rev. 9:1–11; 13:13–15; 19:20).

41. Albert Maria Weiss, *Apologie des Christentums*, 5 vols. in 7 (Freiburg i.B.: Herder, 1904–8), II, 519.

PART IV

CHRIST THE REDEEMER

14

The Only Begotten Son of the Father

The Covenant of Grace

[343] The universal reality of misery evokes in all people a need for deliverance, a deliverance from above. "All humans have need of the gods" (Homer, *Odyssey* III, 48). But to the degree that the misery is construed differently, to that degree the salvation people look for also changes. Pagans who construe misery as basically physical—misfortune, disaster, sickness, death—know neither the essential character of sin nor the deliverance of grace. Scripture, however, sees our misery as sin, as an ethical violation of communion with God, who alone can restore fellowship. This requires grace, which in biblical revelation assumes the form of a covenant, a covenant that arises, not by a natural process, but by a historical act and hence gives rise to a rich history of grace that begins immediately after the fall when the punishment threatened in Genesis 2:17 is obviously not fully carried out. Had it been, the whole human race would have been annihilated, the earth laid waste, and the cosmos would have returned to chaos or to nothingness, and Satan would have been victorious. Instead, aware they were naked, Adam and Eve demonstrated the end of their innocence, and a sense of guilt first became manifest in their sense of shame. Their conscience had awakened—the realization that they had sinned and deserved punishment—which shows that unlike the fallen angels they had not been hardened, they had not become devils but remained human and redeemable. God did not withdraw himself after the fall, nor does he even for a moment abandon the transgressors. Their sense of guilt, shame, and fear is

already an operation of God's Spirit in them, indeed a revelation of his wrath but also of his grace, a revelation that is the foundation of all the religious and ethical life that persists in humans after the fall. God's grace is shown especially when God comes to Adam and Eve and seeks them out. He does not abandon them to their own folly but calls them back to himself. Then, in his punishment on the serpent and on humanity, God's mercy triumphs over judgment as he annuls the covenant made with evil and puts enmity between the seed of the serpent and the seed of the woman. Now the path of glory must pass through suffering for man and woman.

A dual principle of wrath and grace, justice and mercy takes effect: the penalty for the original transgression strikes the woman (Gen. 3:16) both as mother and as wife: suffering and pain in bringing forth children, desire for and submission to her husband. Yet, she will also be the mother of all living and blessed in bearing children (1 Tim. 2:15). For the man the ground is cursed, he toils in sweat, and after a life of toil and trouble returns to the dust (Gen. 3:17–19). Driven from paradise and sent into the wide world (Gen. 3:22–24), he is still blessed with a nobility in his labor; though it is burdensome and exhausting, human labor still reflects the dominion given him as the image of God. After the fall a dual principle immediately takes effect: wrath and grace, justice and mercy. This is a world full of humor, laughter mixed with tears, existing in the sign of the cross, and given immediately after the fall to Christ, the Man of Sorrows, that he might save and subdue it. Thus, after hearing God pronounce his verdict, Adam and Eve humbly bow their heads. They have nothing left to say; in silence they accept the divine verdict without objection. Nonetheless, leaning on God's promise, Adam calls his wife Eve: life, source of life, mother of the living. In the promise of Genesis 3, we find the gospel in a nutshell and, in principle, the entire history of the human race.

[344] The word "covenant" is not found in Genesis 3, but the reality is. Modern critics judge that covenant ideas arose late in Israel's history (and are first found in the book of Deuteronomy) and are properly a postexilic phenomenon projected back on to the history of the patriarchs.[1] The case depends on circular reasoning; Israel's history is reconstructed by alleging that certain biblical sources are inauthentic, which history is then used to invalidate the documents that witness against it.[2] It is better scholarship to see the latter prophets as standing on the foundation of a real covenant made with the patriarchs (Gen. 15:18; 17:2, 7, 9–14; and so on). For all the prophets proceed from the idea that there exists a special relationship between Yahweh and the people of Israel. Amos insists that God will not spare Israel precisely because she alone he has known of all the families of the earth (3:2). Hosea pictures the relation between God and his people as a marriage, and in 6:7 and 8:1 speaks of the covenant that Israel has broken. The prophets

1. J. Wellhausen, *Geschichte Israels*, 2 vols. (Berlin: Reimer, 1878), I, 434ff.; R. Smend, *Lehrbuch der alttestamentlichen Religionsgeschichte* (Freiburg i.B.: Mohr, 1893), 116ff.
2. Cf. G. Vos, "Recent Criticism of the Early Prophets," *Presbyterian and Reformed Review* 9 (April 1898): 214–18.

are not the founders of a new religion but, jointly with the people, stand on the foundation of the same covenant, therefore calling the people to repentance and conversion. Israel always traces its history to the patriarchs (Deut. 26:5; Hosea 12:13), but the covenant established at Sinai is above all the basis on which Israel's whole religion rests.

The derivation of the word "covenant" (בְּרִית) is not entirely helpful in determining its meaning. It likely comes from the verb ברה, "to cut," and refers to the ancient Eastern custom of passing between the parts of slain animals laid out on opposite sides from each other, to symbolize that the violator of the covenant will suffer the same fate as that of the animals, hence the expression "to cut a covenant" (כָּרַת בְּרִית, ὅρκια τεμνειν, foedus ferire; cf. Gen. 15:8f.; Jer. 34:19ff.). It is clear from Genesis 21:22f.; 26:26.; and 31:44f. that a בְּרִית is characterized by three factors: an oath or promise including stipulations, a curse for violation, and a cultic ceremony symbolically representing the curse. Because it was used in the profane everyday world of contracts and treaties בְּרִית must have been a familiar term to Noah and Abraham and later Israel so that it could be appropriated as the framework for understanding the religious as well as social character of God's relation with his people. Whether a biblical covenant is unilateral (royal grant) or bilateral cannot be determined from the word itself; it is determined by the nature of the two parties involved. In God's covenant with humans the unilateral dimension comes to the fore; there is, after all, not parity between the parties; God is the sovereign who imposes his ordinances on his creatures. When God makes a covenant with Abraham (Gen. 15:8f.), it is not really a compact but a pledge. God's promise obligates him to fulfill it, and he passes between the pieces of the sacrificial animal. Elsewhere he swears by himself (Gen. 22:16), by his life (Deut. 32:40), by his "soul" (nephesh; Amos 6:8; Jer. 51:14) to show to people "the unchangeable character of his purpose" (Heb. 6:17). The bilateral dimensions of God's covenant—the obligations on those with whom it is made—are never *conditions for entering the covenant*, but understood as the rules of conduct for those who by grace had been incorporated into it (Gen. 17:1–2; Exod. 19:5–6, 8; 24:3, 7; Lev. 26:14f.; Deut. 5:29; 27:10f.; 28:1f.; 30:1f.; etc.). The covenant of grace is unilateral, indissolubly grounded in the merciful promises of the sovereign God. God cannot break his promise; he has sworn himself to uphold it. This indissolubility, which was inferred with increasing clarity from the covenant idea by Old Testament prophecy, is probably also the reason why the word is translated in the Septuagint, not by συνθήκη (covenant) but by διαθήκη (testament).

In this firmness and steadiness of the covenant of grace lies the glory of the religion we as Christians confess. If religion is to be a true fellowship between God and humanity, fellowship in which not only God but also the human partner preserves his or her independence as a rational and moral being and along with his or her duties also receives rights, this can only come into being by God's coming down to humans and entering into a covenant with them. In this action God obligates himself with an oath to grant the human partner eternal salvation despite his apostasy and unfaithfulness; but by the same token, the human partner on his or her part is admonished and obligated to a new obedience, yet in such a way that "if we sometimes through weakness fall into sins we must not despair of God's mercy, nor continue in sin," since we have an everlasting covenant of grace with God.[3] The covenant of grace is unalterably grounded, not in our virtues and works, but in God's mercies.

[345] The doctrine of the covenant achieved dogmatic significance in the Christian church because the Christian religion had to understand its relation to and distinction from Judaism. Over against gnosticism and Marcion, the church had to maintain the unity of and, over against Judaism, the distinction between the two covenants. The Judaizers of Paul's day demanded the keeping of the Mosaic law—specifically the law of circumcision—also by Christians from among the gentiles (Acts 15; Rom. 16:17f.; 1 Cor. 7:18; Gal. 5:3; 6:13; Phil. 1:15f.; 3:2f.; Col. 2:16, 21; 1 Tim. 1:7f.; Titus 1:10, 14; 3:9). The church broke with Judaism, and when Temple Judaism was itself destroyed (AD 70 and AD 135), the Judaizing party became a sect within the Christian church (Nazarenes and Ebionites) that denied the deity of Christ. On the other side, dualistic gnosticism, in the person of Marcion, attacked the Old Testament as the religion of an inferior God. In Christ a totally different god—all grace and love—revealed himself. The church never accepted Marcion's dualism. Instead, she confessed that nature and grace, law and gospel, Old and New Testaments, are to be distinguished but never separated. During the Reformation this issue became crucial as Anabaptists and others (Arminians, Socinians) again devalued the Old Testament. Key differences also arose between the Lutheran and Reformed traditions. It is in the latter, beginning with Zwingli and Calvin, that the doctrine of the covenant is most fully developed, notably in the German Reformed theology of Olevianus and Ursinus, English Puritanism, and the Westminster Confession. At the heart of this covenantal theology is the doctrine about the old and the new "covenant" (διαθηκη, 2 Cor. 3; Latin *testamentum* or *instrumentum*, words first applied to the economies, then to the Scriptures, of the Old Testament and the New Testament). The two are one in origin and content. God, or the Logos, is the author of both, and in both we are presented one faith, one covenant, one way of salvation. The only difference is that the Messiah promised in the Old has now come.

The doctrine of the covenant was most fully developed in Reformed theology. Covenant theology goes back to Zwingli and his polemic against the Anabaptists for the essential unity of the Old and New Testaments. It passed from Zwingli to Bullinger and Calvin and through them to the theologians of the German Palatinate (Olevianus, Ursinus, Hyperius) and the English Puritans (Rollock, Perkins, Ames, the Westminster Confession [ch. 7], Francis Thomas Boston, and others). Among the Dutch Reformed, Cloppenburg and Cocceius made

---

3. Ed. note: Much of this sentence is quoted from the Form for Infant Baptism used from the sixteenth century onward in the Reformed Churches of the Netherlands.

THE ONLY BEGOTTEN SON OF THE FATHER

the covenant the fundamental premise and controlling principle of dogmatics as a whole. Cocceius had an eccentric view of the covenant, notably the notion of successive covenantal abrogations, which in fact undermined the key element of grace, making it uncertain. The polemic against Cocceius was directed against his view of the Sabbath, his understanding of the church in the two economies, and forgiveness (πάρεσις, a casting aside) in the Old Testament. What was objectionable was not Cocceius's concept of the covenant but his biblical theology and historical method. He rejected "Scholastic" theology for a more "biblical" theology which turned out to be a historicized dogmatics that effectively destroyed the unity of the covenants. By construing the covenant of grace exclusively in negative terms, as a gradual, historical, and successively unfolding abolition of the covenant of works, nothing of covenant was left; it was merely a temporary, human, and ever-changing form of religion.[4] After Cocceius, a more general disparagement of the Old Testament took place among modern thinkers such as Spinoza, Kant, Hegel, and Schleiermacher. Judaism was then seen as no better than paganism as preparation for Christianity.[5]

The old covenant with Israel is the necessary preparation for the new covenant in Christ. Although the covenant is one, there are two dispensations. In God's own time, the promise of the old covenant was fulfilled in the new. The shadow and particularity of the letter became the substance, universality, and freedom of the Spirit. The church fathers taught that just as fruit is separated from seed even though it comes out of seed, so also the gospel is separated from the law, inasmuch as it proceeds from the law; the one comes from the other but is not alien to it, different though not opposed to it.[6] Nothing of the Old Testament is lost in the New, but everything is fulfilled, matured, has reached its full growth, and now, out of the temporary husk, produces the eternal core.

THE COVENANT OF REDEMPTION, OF NATURE, AND ELECTION

[346] In the Reformed church and theology, covenant became a very important practical encouragement for Christian living. Here the basis of all covenants was found in the eternal counsel of God, in a covenant between the very persons of the Trinity, the *pactum salutis* (counsel of peace; covenant of redemption). The

4. Cf. H. Bavinck, *Reformed Dogmatics*, ed. John Bolt (Grand Rapids: Baker Academic, 2003–8), I, 603–7 (#156); G. F. Karl Muller, "Coccejus," *PRE³*, IV, 186–94; Heinrich Heppe, *Geschichte des Pietismus und der Mystik in der reformirten Kirche: Namentlich der Niederlande* (Leiden: Brill, 1879), 217ff.; W. Geesink, *De Ethiek in de Gereformeerde Theologie* (Amsterdam: Kirchner, 1897), 49ff. Ed. note: For recent scholarship on Cocceius that is more sympathetic, see W. J. Van Asselt, *The Federal Theology of Johannes Cocceius: (1603–1669)*, trans. Raymond Andrew Blacketer (Leiden: Brill, 2001).

5. Friedrich Schleiermacher, *The Christian Faith* (Edinburgh: T&T Clark, 1989), §8.4, §12, §132.

6. Tertullian, *Against Marcion*, V, 11.

work of salvation is an undertaking of the one God in three persons in which all cooperate and each one performs a special task. It is the triune God—Father, Son, and Spirit—who together conceive, determine, carry out, and complete the entire work of salvation. The benefit to the believer is in knowing that the covenant of grace executed and revealed in time and history nevertheless rests on an eternal, unchanging foundation, the counsel of the triune God. The Father is the eternal Father, the Son the eternal Mediator, the Holy Spirit the eternal Paraclete.

The classic text (Zech. 6:13) cited in support of this doctrine does not prove anything, but from Job 17:3; Isaiah 38:14; and Psalm 119:122 (none of which refer to the Messiah), and from Hebrews 7:22 (where we are told only that Christ, because he lives forever, is the guarantee that the new covenant will continue forever), it was inferred that in the pact of salvation Christ had from all eternity become our guarantor before God. Scholastic subtlety aside, this doctrine of the pact of salvation is rooted in a scriptural idea. For as Mediator, the Son is subordinate to the Father, calls him his God (Ps. 22:2; John 20:17), is his servant (Isa. 49f.) who has been assigned a task (Isa. 53:10; John 6:38–40; 10:18; 12:49; 14:31; 17:4) and who receives a reward (Ps. 2:8; Isa. 53:10; John 17:4, 11, 17, 24; Eph. 1:20f.; Phil. 2:9f.) for the obedience accomplished (Matt. 26:42; John 4:34; 15:10; 17:4–5; 19:30). The incarnation does not initiate this, since the mediating work of Christ is present in Israel in the leadership of the Angel of Yahweh (Exod. 3:2f.; 13:21; 14:19; 23:20–23; 32:34; 33:2; Num. 20:16; Isa. 63:8–9), as passages in the New Testament also suggest (John 8:56; 1 Cor. 10:4, 9; 1 Pet. 1:11; 3:19). Since there is but one mediator between God and humankind (John 14:6; Acts 4:12; 1 Tim. 2:5), who is the same yesterday and today and forever (Heb. 13:8), who was chosen as Mediator from eternity (Isa. 42:1; 43:10; Matt. 12:18; Luke 24:26; Acts 2:23; 4:28; 1 Pet. 1:20; Rev. 13:8) and as Logos existed from eternity as well (John 1:1, 3; 8:58; Rom. 8:3; 2 Cor. 8:9; Gal. 4:4; Phil. 2:6; etc.), it seems appropriate to think of the work of redemption effected by Father, Son, and Holy Spirit in covenantal terms and of the life of the three persons in the Divine Being as a covenantal life, a life of consummate self-consciousness, freedom and communion. The character of this covenant life is a pact (συνθήκη) in the full sense of the word. The work of salvation is an undertaking of three persons in which all cooperate and each performs a special task.

This pact of salvation, however, is inextricably linked to the salvation history effected in time; the covenant of grace revealed in time does not hang in the air but rests on an eternal, unchanging foundation, the counsel and covenant of the triune God infallibly applied and executed. Christ does not begin to work only with and after his incarnation, and the Holy Spirit does not first begin his work with the outpouring on the day of Pentecost. Just as creation is a trinitarian work, so too re-creation was from the start a triune project. All grace extended to the creation after the fall comes to it from the Father, through the Son, in the Holy Spirit. Although we see change, development, and progress in salvation history, from God's side there is no variation or shadow due to change (James 1:17). The

Father is the eternal Father, the Son the eternal Mediator, the Holy Spirit the eternal Paraclete. The sun only gradually illumines the earth, but itself remains the same, morning and evening, during the day and at night. Although Christ completed his work on earth only in the midst of history and although the Holy Spirit was not poured out till the day of Pentecost, God nevertheless was able, already in the days of the Old Testament, to fully distribute the benefits to be acquired and applied by the Son and the Spirit. Old Testament believers were saved in no other way than we. There is one faith, one Mediator, one way of salvation, and one covenant of grace.[7]

[347] Care must be taken in considering the execution of the pact of salvation in time and history. Although God elects Abraham and Israel as his chosen people, his salvific purpose is universal, with all peoples. In the fullness of time, humanity as a whole, Jew and gentile, is reconciled in the one man, Jesus Christ, at the cross. After the fall, the first promises of grace that are addressed by God to Adam and Eve concern the whole human race. Religion, too, survived the fall and acquired fixed forms in sacrifice (Gen. 4:3), prayer, and preaching (Gen. 4:26). Culture got started with agriculture, cattle breeding, and the construction of cities (Gen. 4:17); the arts and sciences began to flourish (Gen. 4:20ff.). In the beginnings of human history, we see great blessing in remarkable longevity but also great wickedness in fratricide, in domination and exertion of power by the sword (Gen. 4:20ff.) until God judges that the imagination of the thoughts of human hearts were continually only evil (Gen. 6:5). The great blessing yields to the great judgment of the flood. After the flood (Gen. 8–11), God makes a covenant with nature not to destroy the world with water again, reduces human life span, and spreads humanity across the world, preventing humans from reaching heaven itself with their ambition. Despite letting the gentiles walk in their own ways, God providentially grants them significant cultural and social development. He did not leave them without witnesses to himself through the works of his hands (Acts 14:16–17; 17:27–28; Rom. 1:19; James 1:17). The Holy Spirit is the author of all life, power, and virtue, also among the gentiles (Gen. 6:17; 7:15; Job 32:8; Pss. 33:6; 104:30; 139:2; Eccles. 3:19). In this way God is present to all people, and they are in some sense "prepared" for the message of salvation.

[348] The universal scope of God's intention for all peoples—Jew and gentile—must never obscure the special favor of God to Israel. While Israel is drawn from the nations and there are analogies between Israel's religious practices and those of the nations—circumcision, sacrifice, prayer, priesthood, temple, altar, ceremonies, feast days, mores, customs, political and social codes; even theophany, prophecy, and miracle—the essential difference is that special grace is reserved for Israel and is not known among the pagans. Pagan religion is self-willed and legalistic. The covenant made with Abraham is new and comes from God alone.

7. G. Vos, "The Doctrine of the Covenant in Reformed Theology," in *Redemptive History and Biblical Interpretation*, ed. Richard B. Gaffin Jr. (Phillipsburg: Presbyterian & Reformed, 1980).

Through his covenant with Abraham and Israel, the Creator proves himself to be also the Re-creator and Savior. Elohim, Creator of heaven and earth, is Yahweh, the God of the covenant (Gen. 2:4; Exod. 20:11). In Israel the God-world relation is never conceived other than as that between the Creator and the creature. With this one dogma alone, all paganism is in principle rejected; it is the foundation of true and pure religion. This Creator of heaven and earth, moreover, is also he who maintains and governs the world and who freely and graciously entered into a special relationship with Israel. By the miraculous birth of Isaac, God proves himself both the Creator and the Re-creator of Israel. In the religion of Israel it is not humans who search for God but God who seeks out humans. This covenant with the ancestors continues at Sinai, albeit in another form. The covenant with Israel was essentially no other than that with Abraham. The covenant on Mount Sinai is and remains a covenant of grace. "I am the LORD your God, who brought you out of the land of Egypt, out of the house of slavery" (Exod. 20:2) is the opening statement and foundation of the law, the essence of the covenant of grace. It is an everlasting covenant that cannot be broken even by any sins and iniquities on the part of Israel (Deut. 4:31; 32:26f.; Judg. 2:1; Pss. 89:1–5; 105:8; 111:5; Isa. 54:10; Rom. 11:1–2; 2 Cor. 1:20).

The covenantal benefits given to Israel are the same as those given to Abraham. The one great promise to Abraham is "I will be your God, and you and your descendants will be my people" (Gen. 17:8, paraphrase). In the same way, God is Israel's God, and Israel is his people (Exod. 19:6; 29:46; etc.). Israel, accordingly, receives a wide assortment of blessings, not only temporal blessings such as the land of Canaan, fruitfulness in marriage, long life, prosperity, plus victory over its enemies, but also spiritual and eternal blessings such as God's dwelling among them (Exod. 29:45; Lev. 26:12), the forgiveness of sins (Exod. 20:6; 34:7; Num. 14:18; Deut. 4:31; Pss. 32; 103; etc.), sonship (Exod. 4:22; 19:5–6; 20:2; Deut. 14:1; Isa. 63:16; Amos 3:1–2; etc.), sanctification (Exod. 19:6; Lev. 11:44; 19:2), and so on. Clothed in sensory forms in the Old Testament, their full spiritual significance is made clear in the New Testament. Yet, all the covenant expectation is summed up in the words to Abraham: "Walk before me, and be blameless" (Gen. 17:1). Kept under the tutelage of the law like a minor (Rom. 10:4; Gal. 3:23f.; 4:1f.), Israel in its history prepared the way for the fullness of time and the coming of Christ. Israel's experience of consciousness of sin, failure and coming under judgment, intensely longing for the richer revelation of God's grace and the day of salvation—all this led to Christ and to a readiness for him. There was need for preparation and nurture. "It was not fitting for God to become incarnate at the beginning of the human race before sin. For medicine is given only to the sick. Nor was it fitting that God should become incarnate immediately after sin that man, having been humbled by sin, might see his own need of a deliverer. But what had been decreed from eternity occurred in the fullness of time."[8]

8. T. Aquinas, *Summa Theol.*, III, qu. 1, art. 5.

This time of upbringing and preparation is not necessary for God or Christ as if there was variability in God, nor is it waiting for the spiritual benefits as though they did not yet exist. Rather, the need is subjective, in the condition of the human race, which, precisely as a race, had to be saved and hence had to be gradually prepared and educated for salvation in Christ.[9] Christ and his cross are the turning point of world history; everything leads up to them and everything follows from them. The old covenant with Israel is the necessary preparation for the new covenant in Christ. Although the covenant is one (Luke 1:68–79; Acts 2:39; 3:25), there are two dispensations related as promise and fulfillment (Acts 13:32; Rom. 1:2), as shadow and substance (Col. 2:17), as the letter that kills and the Spirit that makes alive (2 Cor. 3:6ff.), as servitude and freedom (Rom. 8:15; Gal. 4:1ff., 22ff.; Col. 2:20; Heb. 12:18f.), as particular and universal (John 4:21; Acts 10:35; 14:16; Gal. 4:4–5; 6:15; Eph. 2:14; 3:6). In God's own time, the promise of the old covenant was fulfilled in the new. The shadow and particularity of the letter became the substance, universality, and freedom of the Spirit. Nothing of the Old Testament is lost in the New, but everything is fulfilled, matured, has reached its full growth, and now, out of the temporary husk, produces the eternal core. The road was the same on which believers in the Old and the New Testaments walked, but the light in which they walked was different.[10] The old covenant people have moved out of the shadows into the light of the new. The sun of righteousness rose to its zenith in the heavens and shone out over all peoples. The law and the prophets have been fulfilled and, in Christ as their end and goal, reached their destiny.

[349] The covenant of grace, fulfilled in the New Testament, was and is surrounded and sustained by God's covenant with nature, with all creatures. Unlike what Cocceius taught, the covenant of grace is not the successive abolition of the covenant of works but its fulfillment and restoration. "Grace repairs and perfects nature." God's demand of obedience remains the only way to eternal life. The difference between the covenant of works and that of grace is that God now approaches us not in Adam but in Christ, who fulfilled all of Adam's obedience. Christ is the second and last Adam who restores what the first Adam had corrupted; the head of a new humanity. Grace and grace alone is the essential character and content of this new covenant in Christ. The covenant of grace is the divine work par excellence; it is everlasting and cannot be broken; it rests solely in the good pleasure of God, in the work of the Mediator, in the Holy Spirit, who remains forever. It is God's work alone and his work totally—all human boasting is excluded; all glory is due to the Father, Son, and Holy Spirit.

The covenant of grace is also integrally united with the counsel of peace, though it should be distinguished from it. In the counsel of peace, Christ is the guarantor

9. John Calvin, *Institutes of the Christian Religion*, II.xi, xiii, xiv (ed. John T. McNeill and trans. Ford Lewis Battles, 2 vols. [1559; Philadelphia: Westminster, 1960], 1:449–64, 474–93).

10. J. Calvin, *Commentary on the Epistles of Paul the Apostle to the Galatians, Ephesians, Philippians and Colossians*, trans. T. H. L. Parker (Grand Rapids: Eerdmans, 1965), on Gal. 3:23.

and head; in the covenant of grace, he is the mediator. In this way the doctrine of the covenant maintains God's sovereignty in the entire work of salvation. It is the Father who conceives, plans, and wills the work of salvation; it is the Son who guarantees it and effectively acquires it; it is the Spirit who implements and applies it. Since it is apparent from 1 Corinthians 15:45ff. that Adam was a type of Christ even before the fall, so the covenant of grace was prepared, not first by Noah and Abraham nor first by the covenant of grace with Adam, but already in and by the covenant of works, and all points back to the eternal counsel of God. God, who knows and determines all things and included the breach of the covenant of works in his counsel when creating Adam and instituting the covenant of works, already counted on the Christ and his covenant of grace.[11]

[350] Thus in a marvelous way the doctrine of the covenant maintains God's sovereignty in the entire work of salvation. It far surpasses the covenant of works to the degree that Christ exceeds Adam. God's threefold being is manifest much more clearly in re-creation than in creation. It is the Father who conceives, plans, and wills the work of salvation; it is the Son who guarantees it and effectively acquires it; it is the Spirit who implements and applies it. This entire work of salvation is God's work exclusively; nothing derives from humans—it is all pure grace and undeserved favor. At the same time, the covenant of grace also allows the rational and moral nature of human beings to come into their own. Here it differs from election, in which humans are strictly passive. The covenant of grace describes the road by which elect people attain their destiny; it is the channel by which the stream of election flows toward eternity. Christ sends his Spirit to instruct and enable his own so that they consciously and voluntarily consent to this covenant. The covenant of grace comes with the demand of faith and repentance, which may in some sense be said to be its "conditions." Yet, this must not be misunderstood. God himself supplies what he demands; the covenant of grace is thus truly unilateral—it comes from God, who designed, defines, maintains, and implements it. It is, however, designed to become bilateral, to be consciously and voluntarily accepted by believers in the power of God. In the covenant of grace, God's honor is not at the expense of but for the benefit of human persons by renewing the whole person and restoring personal freedom and dignity.

The covenant of grace, with Christ as the new head of humanity, reminds us of the organic unity of the church. The covenant of grace reminds us that election is about not only individual persons but also organic wholes, including families and generations. The covenant of grace does not leap from individual to individual but perpetuates itself organically and historically. It passes through a history and through different dispensations. It accommodates itself to times and occasions appointed by the Father as Creator and Sustainer. It is never made with a solitary individual but always also with his or her descendants. It is a covenant from generation to generation. The covenant of grace is the organization of the

11. Cf. H. Bavinck, *Reformed Dogmatics*, II, 561–62 (#293).

new humanity under Christ as its head, as it links up with the creation order and, reaching back to it, qualitatively and intensively incorporates the whole of creation into itself. Therefore, some who remain inwardly unbelieving will for a time, in the earthly administration and dispensation of the covenant of grace, be part of the covenant people. They will be *in* the covenant but not *of* the covenant. The final judgment belongs to God alone, and in this life the church must regard such with the judgment of charity (Matt. 3:12; 13:29; John 15:2; 2 Tim. 2:20).

THE PERSON OF CHRIST THE MEDIATOR

[351] The covenant of grace also differs from the covenant of works in that it has a mediator who not only unites God and humanity but prior to this reconciles the two, so restoring the broken fellowship between them. The necessity of a mediator between humanity and the divine is universally found in all religions. Heroic figures abound whose extraordinary words and deeds profoundly affect the life and development of nations by transcending their times and changing history. This phenomenon is not accidental but rooted in human nature and religion itself. Belief in mediators is universal[12] and includes medicine men among aboriginal peoples, soothsayers, priests, and kings among the religions of the more developed peoples.

Many historical religions, moreover, are linked to the names of certain founders who were later elevated above the rank of ordinary people and to some extent deified. The ideas of incarnation and apotheosis occur in virtually all religions. In many religions there is even an anticipation that good will eventually overcome evil through the ministrations of a specific person—Krishna, Osiris, Balder. Like the gods, kings—Cyrus, Philip of Macedon, Caesar Augustus—were often addressed and greeted as σωτηρ (savior). Myths such as that of Hercules, Plato's familiar statement about the just man in book VII of his *Republic*, and especially the fourth eclogue of Virgil and the Sibylline books,[13] all allow us to speak with some justification of "unconscious prophetic tendency" in paganism.

[352] This has led many to treat Israel's messianic expectations as simply borrowed from the nations surrounding it. There is something salutary about this development in Old Testament scholarship. Formerly, the critical historical and literary approach treated all the messianic prophecies as *vaticinia ex eventu* (prophecies made after and on the basis of the event) and removed them as later interpolations wherever they occurred in preexilic writings. Prophetic messianic expectation is now acknowledged as authentic to the preexilic era with parallels

12. C. P. Tiele, *Elements of the Science of Religion*, 2 vols. (Edinburgh and London: William Blackwood, 1899), I, 130, 167; II, 119ff.

13. A. Deissmann, *Light from The Ancient East: The New Testament Illustrated by Recently Discovered Texts of the Graeco-Roman World*, trans. Lionel R. M. Strachan, new and rev. ed. (Grand Rapids: Baker Academic, 1965), 362–3; W. O. E. Oesterley, *The Evolution of the Messianic Idea* (London: Pitman, 1908).

in the religions of the surrounding peoples. Scholarship now acknowledges the antiquity of eschatological ideas concerning the day of the Lord, the destruction of Israel's enemies, the salvation of the people, the appearance of the Messiah, the completion of the kingdom of God, and so on. Thus, the Old Testament image of the Messiah is able to come into its own, including such supernatural traits as the miraculous birth (Isa. 7:14; Mic. 5:2), the divine names (Isa. 9:6), and so on.

The history-of-religions school, however, takes this insight and pushes it to the opposite extreme by claiming that the Israelite prophets, in their description of the Messiah and his kingdom and in their eschatological expectations in general, employed notions and expressions, similes and imagery that had existed for a long time, and date back to a remote past in Babylonia, Assyria, Persia, and Egypt. There is an element of truth here since the messianic promises given to the people of Israel are broadly based in the promises that God gave to humanity as a whole and, after the flood, specifically to the Semitic peoples. Similar "borrowing" occurred in the giving of the law, for temples, altars, priesthood, sacrifices, circumcision, and so on among many peoples, and prophecy is similarly rooted in the history of Israel and that of the surrounding nations. There is a "symbolism in creation," a typology in nature that, as evident from Jesus's parables, finds its realization in him and his kingdom. There is an unconscious expectation and hope in the religion and history of the nations, which is realized in Christianity. But the history-of-religions school mistakes analogy for identity and overlooks key differences. To begin with, after God's election of Abraham the human race is split up, and Israel is separated from the other nations. As a result, prophecy in Israel includes divine judgment on God's own people, and the Savior delivers them from sin and death rather than provide social and political deliverance. In the nations around Israel we find expectation of kingly figures who will deliver the people from their distress; the name σωτηρ (savior) is even accorded to kings and emperors. But in the New Testament the term is used for a savior who delivers people from sin and death and grants them righteousness and life. And Israel's vision is universal: Old Testament prophecy does not limit its field of vision to the people of Israel and the land of Canaan but extends it to the whole earth and promises the blessing of Abraham to all of humankind; and the central content of that blessing is that God will be his God and the God of his children. It is a universal spiritual kingdom that God promises to his people at the end of human history.

[353] Prophecy, charting a new course in Israel's history, includes divine promise and typological messianic fulfillment. A promise is given to King David that the kingship will remain in his house (2 Sam. 7:8–16; cf. Amos 9:11; Hosea 1:11; 3:5; Mic. 5:1–2; Isa. 9:6–7; 11:1–2, 10; Jer. 23:5; 30:9; 33:17, 20–22, 26; Ezek. 34:23–24; 37:22–24); it is fulfilled in David's great Son who founds a kingdom that includes the gentiles. He is an eternal king who bears the name Wonderful, Counselor, mighty God (cf. Isa. 10:21; Deut. 10:17; Jer. 32:18), everlasting Father (for his people), Prince of Peace (Isa. 9:6–7). He will reign forever; found a kingdom of righteousness, peace, and prosperity; and also extend his domain

over the gentiles to the ends of the earth (Pss. 2; 45; 72; Ezek. 37:25; Zech. 6:13; 9:10; etc.). He is the Lord's anointed on whom the Spirit of God rests (Deut. 18:15; Isa. 11:2; 40–60; Mal. 4:5); he is prophet and priest as well as king (Ps. 110; Jer. 30:21; Zech. 3; 6:13).

[354] Messianic expectation lived on in the hearts of the people of Israel after the demise of prophecy. In (Jewish) apocryphal literature, we encounter the expectation of Israel's future deliverance and rule, but only a few references to the Messiah (1 Macc. 2:57; 4:46; 9:27; 14:41). Generally speaking, the self-righteousness of Judaism was not favorable to messianic expectation. Israel, after all, had the law; it was righteous by its observance of the law and needed no Savior. At most there was room for an earthly king/messiah who could deliver the Jews and restore their political fortunes. A current of expectation was maintained and fed by the reading of the Old Testament as Jews interpreted the Old Testament messianically, finding as many as 456 messianic promises in it. Messianic expectation was highlighted and elaborated in the apocalyptic literature of *1 Enoch*, the *Psalms of Solomon*, *2 (Apocalypse of) Baruch*, the *Sibylline Oracles*, and *4 Ezra* [2 Esdras]. He was usually described as the Messiah, the Son of Man, the Chosen One, or the Son of David and a few times as the Son of God and was viewed as a preexistent human being, coming forth from Bethlehem. He was righteous, holy, and endowed with many gifts and would establish God's kingdom on earth. According to the New Testament witness, this corresponds in good measure to the expectation found among the poor and lowly (Luke 1:48, 74; 2:25; etc.).

In the context of these expectations, Christ himself appeared, preaching the gospel of the kingdom of God and saying: "The time is fulfilled, and the kingdom of God has come near; repent and believe in the gospel" (Mark 1:15). Jesus introduces a new understanding of the kingdom: it is religious-ethical and not political; it is present in repentance, faith, and rebirth, and it is yet to come as a full eschatological reality. The God of Israel (Matt. 15:31), whom Jesus recognizes and confesses as his God, is above all king (Matt. 5:35; 18:23; 22:2), the Lord of heaven and earth (Matt. 11:25). But he is also the Father in heaven, whose kingly rule is a Father over his children; his kingdom is simultaneously a family, a community (Matt. 6:4, 6, 9; 7:11; Mark 3:34–35). Kingship and the fatherhood of God do not compete with but reinforce each other. The kingdom must both be sought (Matt. 5:20; 6:33; 13:44–46) and received as a gift (Matt. 19:29; 23:12; 24:47; 25:21, 34; Luke 6:32f.; 12:32, 37; 17:10; 22:29) that has as its content forgiveness of sins (Matt. 9:2; 26:28; Luke 1:77; 24:47), righteousness (Matt. 6:33), and eternal life (Matt. 19:16; 25:46; Mark 9:43). Scholars such as Schmoller and Weiss were mistaken in attributing an exclusively eschatological meaning to the kingdom of God in Jesus's teaching.[14] Jesus does take over the eschatological idea

---

14. O. Schmoller, *Die Lehre vom Reiche Gottes in den Schriften des Neuen Testaments* (Leiden: Brill, 1891); J. Weiss, *Die Predigt Jesu vom Reiche Gottes* (Göttingen: Vandenhoeck & Ruprecht, 1892); in the second, revised edition (1900), the eschatological perspective is maintained though slightly softened;

of the kingdom of God, developed in Scripture and especially later in apocalyptic literature. But, for Jesus, the one idea of the kingdom of God—God's intervention in judgment and deliverance—is realized in two sweeping moments. The Old Testament prophets only saw a single coming of the Messiah; the coming of Jesus divides this into two: one for the purpose of salvation, the other for judgment; one for preparation, the other for completion.

[355] Jesus did not arrive at this distinction because his work, begun with hope in Galilee, later seemed to have failed. From the very beginning, starting with John's designation of Jesus in his baptism (Matt. 3:11ff.; John 1:26ff.), Jesus was completely clear about his role in that kingdom whose gospel he preached. Jesus's realization that he was the Messiah flowed from the knowledge that he enjoyed an utterly unique relationship to God. He, accordingly, called himself the Son of Man but also "the Son of God." The term "Son of Man" was unusual; it was reminiscent of Daniel 7:13, and understood in the apocalyptic literature of that time (*1 Enoch* and *4 Ezra* [2 Esdras]) as a reference to the Messiah. In using this name, Jesus intends to distinguish himself from and position himself above all other humans while at the same time implying that he was truly human, akin not only to Israel but to all human beings. Jesus knows himself to be both the apocalyptic Son of Man from Daniel 7 and the royal Son of God, the one whom the Father loved and sent as his emissary. It is as the Son who alone knows the Father and is known by the Father that Jesus exercises his special authority to forgive sins, to reveal the Father's will. The kingdom is indeed still in the future (Matt. 5:3f., 20; 6:10, 33; 7:21; 18:3; 19:23–24; 25:34; 26:29; etc.), but is also a present reality (Matt. 11:11–12; 12:28; 13:11, 19, 24, 31, 52; Mark 4:26–29; 9:1; Luke 10:9; 17:21); believers are already citizens of and participants in it (Matt. 7:13–14; 13:23, 30; 28:18, 20; Mark 10:15; Luke 7:28). Christ is king now and makes his own into kings and priests as well (Rev. 1:6, 18; 3:21; 5:10). Yet the kingdom of God is only made complete at his return (Rev. 19–21).

The name "Son of Man" also afforded Jesus an opportunity to cut off in advance all misunderstanding about his person and work, and to gradually inject into it the true meaning of his messiahship. This meaning comes down to the fact that the Christ, who came from above, had to suffer many things and after that enter his glory. Jesus thus reveals (1) that he is not just the Son of David and King of Israel but the Son of Man, connected with all humans and giving his life as a ransom for many; (2) that he occupies an utterly unique place among all humans, because as the one who descended from above, lived in constant communion with the Father, and had power to forgive sins, to bestow eternal life; (3) that he could not grasp this power by violence, as the Jews expected their Messiah to do, but that as the Servant of the Lord, he had to suffer and die for his people; and (4) that precisely by taking this road he would attain to the glory

---

ET, *Jesus's Proclamation of the Kingdom of God*, trans., ed., and with an introd. by Richard Hyde Hiers and David Larrimore Holland (Philadelphia: Fortress, 1971).

of the resurrection and the ascension, the elevation to God's right hand, and the coming again for judgment.

Jesus also called himself "Son of God." In the Old Testament this name was applied to the people of Israel, then to the king, and especially to the Messiah,[15] and likely had this theocratic meaning when used by the demoniacs (Matt. 8:29), the Jews (Matt. 27:40), the high priest (Matt. 26:63), and even the disciples in the early period (John 1:49; 11:27; Matt. 16:16). But Jesus invests it with another and deeper meaning; he is king because he is the Messiah, because he is the Son of the Father. God is his Father (Luke 2:49); he is the only Son, whom the Father loved and whom he sent as his last emissary (Mark 12:6). God calls him his "beloved son with whom he is well pleased" (Matt. 3:17; 17:5). This sonship is the source of his whole life, all his thinking and acting; he pronounced people blessed (Matt. 5:3ff.; Luke 10:23), forgave sins (Mark 2:10), demanded that his disciples leave everything for his sake (Matt. 5:11; 10:18, 22; etc.), and linked with it entrance into eternal life.

All the things that the apostles and the Christian church later taught about the person of Christ are already contained in principle in the Synoptic Gospels. The resurrection illumined, clarified, and confirmed what the Synoptics teach: Jesus is the unique Son of God, God himself in the flesh. The apostles only expanded and developed what the gospels teach: Jesus became human—"flesh" (John 1:14; 1 John 4:2–3); he is Abraham's offspring (Gal. 3:16), from the tribe of Judah (Heb. 7:14), a descendant of David (Rom. 1:3), born of a woman (Gal. 4:4; Heb. 2:14); a human in the full and true sense of the word (Rom. 5:15; 1 Cor. 15:45; 1 Tim. 2:15) who was tired, thirsty, sad, happy as we are (John 4:6ff.; 11:33, 38; 12:27; 13:21; Heb. 4:15); he was under the law (Gal. 4:4), learned obedience unto death (Phil. 2:8; Heb. 5:8; 10:7, 9). He was also free from sin (Matt. 7:11; 11:29; John 4:34; 8:29, 46; 15:10; Acts 3:14; 2 Cor. 5:21; Heb. 4:15; 7:26; 1 Pet. 1:19; 2:22; 1 John 2:1; 3:5); he also rose again, was glorified, and is seated at God's right hand (Acts 2:34; 5:31; 7:55; etc.). He existed before his incarnation (John 1:1; 17:5; 1 Cor. 10:4, 9; Heb. 11:26) and was then "in the form of God" (Phil. 2:6), the firstborn of all creation (Col. 1:15), the one by whom God created all things and in whom all things hold together (John 1:3; 1 Cor. 8:6; Eph. 3:9; Col. 1:16), the Son of God in an utterly unique sense (John 1:14; 5:18; Rom. 8:3, 32; Gal. 4:4), and himself God (John 1:1; 20:28; Rom. 9:5; 1 Thess. 1:1; Titus 2:13; Heb. 1:8–9; 2 Pet. 1:1; 1 John 5:20).

[356] This glorious truth was too rich and too deep to be immediately absorbed into the Christian consciousness and reproduced in a clear formula to provide proof against all error. Ebionitism regarded Jesus as only a superior man; gnosticism sharply divided the material from the divine. In neither case did the full union of the human and divine receive proper treatment. Irenaeus, though he

---

15. Cf. H. Bavinck, *Reformed Dogmatics*, II, 264–68 (#214); W. Sanday, "Son of God," in *DB*, IV, 568ff.; J. Stalker, "Son of God," in *DC*, II, 654ff.

does not yet have the two-natures formula, clearly teaches that Christ is truly the Son, the Logos, and himself God; that as such he became a human; and that this incarnate Logos constitutes an unbreakable unity. He is truly man and truly God (*Adv. haer.* IV, 6, 7); it is one and the same Christ who created the world and who was born and died (*Adv. haer.* III, 9, 3, 16, 6, 19, 1, etc.). Tertullian speaks even more forcefully of two substances in Christ, a fleshly and a spiritual substance; of two conditions, a divine and a human (*De carne chr.* 5); and assumed there was in him a double state, not confused but conjoined in one person, truly God and truly human (*Adv. Pr.* 27). Not until Chalcedon did the Nestorian tendency to separate the divine and the human and the Eutychian tendency to commingle them get definite formulation: "One person in two natures, without confusion, without change, without division, without separation." The formula did not, however, prevent the East from tending toward Monophysitism and erroneous notions of divinization (θέωσις),[16] nor was the West free from mysticism and deification of the human.

THE TWO NATURES OF CHRIST

[357] The two natures of Christ, according to Roman and Scholastic theology, remained distinct though there was communication of properties from the divine to the human nature. This led to the idea that Jesus was never really a child; in him, from the beginning, the human nature was divinized as heat permeates and sets an iron aglow. The human nature thus becomes participatory in the divine glory, wisdom, and power (περιχώρησις, θέωσις), and therefore is to be worshiped. Lutheran theology, though it regarded the communication of properties as taking place from the divine nature to the person rather than the human nature, also considered the divine and the human natures as "united and commingled" with their attributes, thus elevating the human nature above the boundaries set for it.[17] There is therefore kinship between Roman Catholic and Lutheran thought in Christology as well as the Lord's Supper.

In the course of the development of Lutheran theology, a logical distinction was made between the incarnation (the assumption of flesh) and the exinanition (self-emptying: conception in the womb). Only the Logos is the subject of the former; the "God-man" was the subject of the latter. This not only called into question the distinction between the divine and the human natures but also that between the state of humiliation and that of exaltation. A great debate arose about the nature of this "exinanition" between the schools of Giessen and Tübingen (1607–24). According to the Tübingers, Christ only refrained from the *public* use of these

16. Cf. H. Bavinck, *Reformed Dogmatics*, I, 134n51 (#42).
17. See "Formula of Concord," in *The Book of Concord: The Confessions of the Evangelical Lutheran Church*, ed. Robert Kolb and Timothy J. Wengert (Minneapolis: Fortress, 2000); discussion of the person of Christ can be found in article 8 of both the "Epitome" and "Solid Declaration" (508–14, 616–34).

attributes; he retained them and only used them in a latent or hidden manner; the state of exaltation is thus nothing other than a visible display of what existed invisibly already from the hour of his conception. Jesus's whole human development became mere appearance. For that reason the Giessen theologians, as well as the later Lutherans, preferred to say that in the moment of exinanition Christ totally ceased to use the attributes communicated to him. Though he retained them, he retained them only as a capacity but did not use them. Only after his exaltation did he also exercise them.[18]

In contrast, Reformed theology, insisting that "the finite is not capable of [containing] the infinite," clearly distinguished without separation the human and divine natures and applied the *finitum non capax infiniti* rule to the state of exaltation as well as humiliation. Reformed theology thus secured space for a purely human development of Christ, for a successive communication of gifts, and for a real distinction between humiliation and exaltation while avoiding the Nestorianism of which it was always accused. Whereas in Greek, Roman, and Lutheran theology the emphasis always fell on the incarnation of the divine being, the divine *nature* as the necessary means to achieve salvation as communion with God, Reformed theology stressed that it was the *person* of the Son who became flesh. It was not the *substance* (the underlying reality) but the *subsistence* (the particular being) of the Son that assumed our nature. The unity of the two natures is unalterably anchored in the person. As it does in the doctrine of the Trinity, of humanity in the image of God, and of the covenants, so here in the doctrine of Christ as well, the Reformed idea of conscious personal life as the fullest and highest life comes dramatically to the fore.[19]

[358] Many modern thinkers are no longer satisfied with Chalcedon's boundaries. They consider Chalcedon a fruit of Greek rationalism and seek to redefine the person of Christ in a new religious-ethical direction.[20] For Immanuel Kant, since the moral imperative "you shall" necessarily implies "you can," Jesus can only be a moral model, a teacher of virtue. The historical Jesus and his ministry, death, and resurrection are unimportant; it is the ideal Christ that counts.[21] In different ways, the same basic approach is taken by Fichte, Schelling, and Hegel. Fichte

18. F. A. Philippi, *Kirchliche Glaubenslehre*, 3rd ed., 7 vols. in 10 (Gütersloh: Bertelsmann, 1870–90), IV, 1, 243ff.; E. Güder, "Stand Christi, Doppelter," *PRE¹*, XV, 784–99; J. Wagenmann, "Kenotiker und Kryptiker," *PRE²*, VII, 640–46; R. Seeberg, "Communicatio idiomatum," in *PRE³*, IV, 254–61.

19. See also J. Owen, "Declaration of the Glorious Mystery of the Person of Christ, God and Man," in vol. 1 of *The Works of John Owen*, ed. William H. Goold (Edinburgh: T&T Clark, 1862).

20. D. F. Strauss, *Die christliche Glaubenslehre in ihrer Geschichtlichen Entwicklung*, 2 vols. (Tübingen: C. F. Osiander, 1840–41), II, 153ff.; A. von Harnack, *History of Dogma*, trans. N. Buchanan, J. Millar, E. B. Speirs, and W. McGilchrist, and ed. A. B. Bruce, 7 vols. (London: Williams & Norgate, 1896–99), I, 1ff.; VII, 118ff., 168ff.

21. I. Kant, *Religion within the Limits of Reason Alone*, trans. Theodore M. Greene and Hoyt H. Hudson (New York: Harper & Brothers, 1934), 115ff.; cf. Isaak August Dorner, *History of the Development of the Doctrine of the Person of Christ*, trans. W. L. Alexander, 5 vols. (Edinburgh: T&T Clark, 1863–78), V, 35; J. W. Chapman, *Die Teleologie Kant's* (Halle: C. A. Kaemmerer, 1905).

proceeded from the idea that God and humanity are absolutely one; Christ's great historical significance is that we were the first to recognize this truth and clearly articulate it in him. The historical Jesus is unimportant; what counts is the eternal, metaphysical truth of our oneness with God.[22] For the early Schelling, the absolute is an eternal becoming that comes to manifestation in the world as its Logos and Son. As historical fact, Christianity is of passing significance. The idea, however, endures forever: the world is the Son of God; it is God himself in the process of becoming. The incarnation of God is the first principle of all life and history. All things must be understood in terms of the idea of incarnation. This is the esoteric truth of Christianity as well: the outward historical expression is but the form for this eternal idea.[23] Hegel, too, said that what theology conveys symbolically in graphic representation, philosophy converts into concepts. Christ is not the only divine-human figure; humans are basically one with God and, at the apex of their development, also become conscious of this fact.[24] Taking the next logical step, Strauss in his *Life of Jesus*[25] states that humanity itself is the incarnate God who was conceived by the Holy Spirit, lives a sinless life, rises from the dead, ascends to heaven, and so on. In the modern theology that flows from these philosophical constructs, the historical Jesus disappears behind the veil of an idea of the unity between God and humanity; he is only a religious genius, a teacher of enlightenment. The person of Christ himself, however, is actually not a part of basic Christianity.[26]

Schleiermacher, on the other hand, rejected this speculative philosophical approach and sought Jesus's significance for the church in his powerfully developed God-consciousness, which is what was divine in Jesus. He is the religious archetype of humanity who passed on his God-consciousness to his followers. It is the person of Jesus and his religious life rather than his teaching or moral example that are essential for Christianity.[27] Schleiermacher's relocation of the realization

22. J. G. Fichte, *Die Anweisung um seligen Leben oder auch die Religionslehre* (Berlin: Verlag der Realschulbuchhandlung, 1806); cf. I. A. Dorner, *Person of Christ*, V, 95ff.

23. F. W. J. Schelling, "Vorlesungen über die Methode des akad. Studiums [1803]," in *Ausgewählte Werke*, 4 vols. (Darmstadt: Wissenschaftliche Buchgesellschaft, 1968), II, 520ff. (*Sämmtliche Werke* [Stuttgart & Augsburg: J. G. Cotta'scher, 1856–61], I/5, 286ff.); ed. note: Bavinck is referencing the eighth lecture, "Über die historische Construktion des Christenthums." Cf. I. A. Dorner, *Person of Christ*, V, 100.

24. G. W. F. Hegel, "Religionsphilosophie," in *Sämtliche Werke*, 26 vols. (Stuttgart: F. Frommann, 1949–59), XVI, 235ff. (*Werke* XII, 235ff.); ed. note: Bavinck is referring to the third part of Hegel's philosophy of religion (1831 lectures), "The Consummate (Absolute) Religion," specifically the section "The Kingdom of the Father." An abbreviated form of this can be found in *Hegel: Lectures on the Philosophy of Religion*, vol. 3, *The Consummate Religion*, ed. Peter C. Hodgson (Berkeley: University of California Press, 1985), 363–64. Cf. I. A. Dorner, *Person of Christ*, V, 131ff.

25. D. F. Strauss, *The Life of Jesus: Critically Examined*, trans. Marian Evans, 2 vols. (New York: Calvin Blanchard, 1860; repr., St. Clair Shores, MI: Scholarly Press, 1970), sect. 144–52, pp. 867–901.

26. D. F. Strauss, *The Old Faith and the New*, trans. Mathilde Blind (New York: Hold, 1873), 26ff.

27. F. Schleiermacher, *The Christian Faith* (Edinburgh: T&T Clark, 1989), §§91ff.; I. A. Dorner, *Person of Christ*, V, 98ff.

of the religious idea in the person of Christ rather than in his humanity exerted enormous influence and again secured for Christology a place in dogmatics as theologians tried to come to terms with Jesus Christ as a most extraordinary and wholly unique revelation of God.[28] The newer Christology also developed a new interest in the historical human development of the person of Jesus and attempted to hold on to the Chalcedonian confession of a "God-man" by improving on it. Thus, the idea of *becoming* was applied to the God-man as God. Initiated by the later Schelling,[29] the idea of the "God-man's" becoming exerted great influence in theosophic circles and on theologians.[30]

While theology after Schleiermacher did place a great deal of emphasis on the historical personality of Jesus and stimulated a great deal of creative christological reflection in the nineteenth century, the results did not satisfy many, and, following the lead of Albrecht Ritschl, theologians turned back to ethical concerns as Kant had done. Ritschl rejects all metaphysics and everything that is condemned by natural science and historical criticism, such as the preexistence of Christ, his supernatural conception, resurrection, ascension, and second coming. Jesus was an ordinary man with extraordinary ethical sensitivity and awareness whose will was completely in tune with God's plan and purpose for the world and humanity. In him God himself, his grace and faithfulness, his will and purpose for humankind have become manifest so that he was able to found the kingdom of God on earth. His death confirms that the kingdom of God is the destiny of all humans. Christ is not God in a metaphysical sense; rather, in his case the name "God" denotes his rank and status in the kingdom of God. It is not a reference to his being, but to his office. Christ may be called "God" because in his relation to us he occupies the place and value of God.[31]

[359–61] In this approach, Ritschl was followed by others such as Herrmann and Harnack, all of whom sought the "Jesus of history." All followers of Ritschl have in common the motto "From Paul and John we have to go back to the Jesus of the Synoptics, especially to the Jesus of the Sermon on the Mount." Thus, for example, Harnack can define the essence of the Christian faith as the assurance

28. E.g., among others, R. Rothe, Hofstede de Groot, C. E. Nitzsch, F. A. Kahnis, G. Thomasius, J. P. Lange.

29. Cf. H. Bavinck, *Reformed Dogmatics*, II, 322–29 (#230); F. W. J. Schelling, *Sämmtliche Werke*, II, 3, 317ff.

30. Gottfried Thomasius, *Christi Person und Werk*, 3rd ed., 2 vols. (Erlangen: A. Deichert, 1886–88), I, 409–45; H. L. Martensen, *Christian Dogmatics*, trans. W. Urwick (Edinburgh: T&T Clark, 1871), §133; F. Delitzsch, *A System of Biblical Psychology*, trans. Robert E. Wallis (Edinburgh: T&T Clark, 1899), 384ff.; F. L. Godet, *Commentary on John's Gospel* (Grand Rapids: Kregel, 1978), on John 1:14; J. J. van Oosterzee, *Christian Dogmatics*, trans. J. Watson and M. Evans, 2 vols. (New York: Scribner, Armstrong, 1874), II, 752. This hypothesis was also received favorably by many English and Americans; see B. B. Warfield, "Recent Theological Literature," *Presbyterian and Reformed Review* 10 (1899): 701–25; W. Lock, "Kenosis," in *DB*, II, 835; Alfred E. Garvie, "Kenosis," in *DC*, I, 927–28.

31. A. Ritschl, *The Christian Doctrine of Justification and Reconciliation* (Clifton, NJ: Reference Book Publishers, 1966), III, 379ff.

that, by the appearance, the doctrine, and the life of Jesus, people can incur the experience that God is their Father and that they are his children.[32]

The Ritschlian project was not a success. Not only were the Ritschlians divided among themselves, even radical critical New Testament scholarship did not permit theologians to assert the simple, ethical Jesus portrayed by the Ritschlians. Johannine and Pauline ideas are found *in nuce* in the Synoptics themselves with Jesus highly self-conscious of his messianic role, speaking as an apocalyptic figure, doing miracles, and taking on divine prerogatives such as forgiving sins. The real historical Jesus proved to be elusive and, contrary to the manner in which the Bible's critics had separated the historical Jesus from the apostolic Christ, it became clearer that they were the same.[33] One cannot honor Jesus without accepting him as the Christ, the Son of the living God. Furthermore, it became clearer that the revisionist portraits of Jesus were woefully inadequate in explaining the rise of the Christian church and the strength of its confession about Jesus the Christ, the Son of God. To suggest all this as the fantastic creation of the church herself stretches credulity. The conclusion of the matter: the historical Jesus of the Gospels is one and the same as the confessed Christ of Paul, John, and the early church.

THE CENTRALITY OF THE INCARNATION

[362] The doctrine of Christ is not the starting point but it certainly is the central point of the whole system of dogmatic theology. Here, too, pulses the whole of the religious-ethical life of Christianity. Christ, the incarnate Word, is thus the central fact of the entire history of the world. The incarnation has its presupposition and foundation in the trinitarian being of God. The Trinity makes possible the existence of a mediator who participates in both the divine and human natures and thus unites God and humanity. For here God remains who he is and can yet communicate himself to others. The incarnation is the work of the entire Trinity; Christ was sent by the Father and conceived by the Holy Spirit. It is also important, therefore, to maintain that not the divine nature as such but specifically the person of the Son became a human. The church has at all times condemned patripassianism. Although in its older forms—Praxeas, Hermogenes, Noetus, Beron, Beryll, and Sabellius—it no longer occurs, in its basic idea it is inherent in the pantheistic systems of Hegel, Schelling, Hartmann, and others, who conceive the absolute not as *being* but as *becoming* and who allow the divine to pour itself out in the world and to finitize itself. The world and humanity with all its sorrow and misery is then a moment in the life of God, and the history of revelation is

---

32. Adolf von Harnack, *What Is Christianity?* trans. Thomas Bailey Saunders (New York: Harper, 1957), 148; idem, *History of Dogma*, I, 17; cf. H. Bavinck, *Reformed Dogmatics*, I, 117 (#36).

33. A large body of literature has appeared in recent years on the relation between Jesus and Paul; important works include W. Bousset, *What Is Religion?* trans. Florence B. Low (New York: Putnam, 1907); J. Weiss, *Paul and Jesus*, trans. H. J. Chaytor (New York: Harper, 1909).

the history of God's suffering. But Holy Scripture ascribes the incarnation to the Son (John 1:14; Phil. 2:6; Heb. 2:14–15). The Reformed even preferred to say that the *person* of the Son, rather than the *divine nature* in the Son, as the Lutherans said, had become human. The difference is certainly not very important, yet—against every tendency to mix the two natures—the Reformed emphasized that the person of the Son, in whom the divine nature existed in a manner of its own, had assumed human nature

[363] Incarnation is also related to creation. The incarnation was not necessary, but the creation of human beings in God's image is a supposition and preparation for the incarnation of God. Given with and in creation is the possibility of revelation and also incarnation. In fact, creation itself must be conceived in infralapsarian fashion and Adam seen as a type of Christ. The world was so created that when it fell, it could again be restored. While the notion that the incarnation could have taken place apart from sin's entry has much about it that is attractive—sin cannot be accidental; true religion needs a mediator; Christ precedes the church—there is no need for the hypothesis. The scriptural teaching of God's decree and counsel is sufficient. The incarnation was prepared from eternity; it does not rest in the essence of God but in the person. It is not a necessity as in pantheism, but neither is it arbitrary or accidental as in Pelagianism.

[364] The incarnation did not take place immediately after the fall but was prepared for by a long history of divine revelation. Revelation, like the eternal generation of the Son and the creation of man, is another presupposition and preparation for the incarnation. In speaking of the fullness of time (Eph. 1:10; Gal. 4:4), Scripture shows that this delay was not an accident or an arbitrary thing, but thus determined by God in his wisdom. It is especially John in his prologue who brings out this historical preparation for the incarnation. The Logos, who was with God and by whom all things were made, is the One who became flesh. Revelation and incarnation are both based on the communicability of God. The history of revelation as preparation for the incarnation is concentrated and comes to completion in the election and favoring of Mary the mother of Jesus, the blessed one among women. Mary is thus held in high esteem by all Christians, although the veneration paid to her by Rome, including the doctrines of her immaculate conception, sinlessness, and assumption into heaven are excessive and unscriptural, tied more to tradition and the Roman hierarchical system. In Rome, Mariolatry increasingly crowds out the true Christian worship of God. It is against this idolization of the human that the Reformation rose up in protest. Though they are cautious, all Protestants who confess the incarnation of the Word hold Mary in high esteem as the favored one among women, chosen and prepared by God to be the mother of his Son.

[365] Although in his incarnation Christ connected with preceding revelation and prepared his own coming by way of nature and history, he is not a product of the past nor the fruit of Israel or humanity. If it is true of all human beings that they cannot be explained simply in terms of their parents and environment, it

is especially true of the Christ. For, according to Scripture, it was in Christ that God's Word became flesh—the One who was in the beginning with God and himself God. The doctrine of the incarnation has often met with fierce resistance, usually beginning with an illusory appeal to Scripture. But this will not do; it is Jesus himself who is the obstacle. An honest assessment of what he says about himself and what he does, what his followers ascribe to him, how they venerate him; all this forces us to choose between Jesus as a mad fanatic, a horrendous blasphemer, or the true Son of God. Scripture attributes deity to Christ—not in few rare instances but repeatedly—that he exists personally from eternity (John 1:1; 8:58; 17:5; Rom. 8:3; 2 Cor. 8:9; Gal. 4:4; Phil. 2:6), he is God's Son in a supernatural sense (Matt. 3:17; 11:27; 28:19; John 1:14; 5:18; Rom. 8:32), the creator and sustainer of all things (John 1:3; 1 Cor. 8:6; Eph. 3:9; Col. 1:16–17; Heb. 1:3; Rev. 3:14), Lord of the church (Matt. 3:2; 5:11; 10:32, 37; John 18:37; 1 Cor. 11:3; Eph. 1:22; Col. 1:18), King over all creation (Matt. 11:27; 28:18; John 3:35; 17:2; Acts 2:33; 1 Cor. 15:27; Eph. 1:20–22; Phil. 2:9; Col. 2:10; Heb. 2:8), who will come to judge the living and dead (John 5:27; Acts 10:42; 17:31; Rom. 14:10; 2 Cor. 5:10). The seeds of later church doctrine are truly present in the New Testament. Finally, the Christian religion itself, that is, true communion between God and humans, can be maintained in no way other than by confessing the deity of Christ. Christ occupies a very different place than Buddha, Zarathustra, and Muhammad do in their respective religions. Christ is not the teacher, not the founder, but the content of Christianity. Modern attempts to permit the name "God" for Jesus while denying the incarnation are in the final analysis a pantheistic mixing of Creator and creature and a return to pagan idolatry. The irony here is that, like Roman notions of divinization, modern theology denies the deity of Christ while positing the possibility of human apotheosis as a reasonable conclusion to the process of evolution.

[366–67] According to the Scriptures, the incarnation takes place through a virgin birth. This doctrine, too, has been attacked throughout the history of the church and again in the late nineteenth century by textual critics who claim, from the evidence of a Syrian text, that the reference to virgin birth in Matthew 1 was not original. The textual evidence does not warrant this conclusion, and though it is found in only the two Gospels of Matthew and Luke, we can be certain that Jesus's supernatural conception was part of the original message of the Gospel. The doctrine has been part of Christian confession from the time of the earliest symbols of the faith. All Gospels consistently portray Jesus as the eternal Son of God who is also the Son of David. For this to be possible, that the eternal Son of God could simultaneously be human, descended from other human beings, it was necessary for him to be supernaturally conceived by the Holy Spirit. Our Lord was not born by the will of man. Some critics point to pagan fables about the sons of the gods as evidence for "borrowing" on the part of the Gospel writers. The likelihood runs the opposite direction: because such pagan fables would certainly have frightened Christians away from a teaching that seemed so closely akin to them, the authenticity of the apostolic testimony to the virgin birth is highly probable. For that matter, there is only superficial external similarity and profound essential difference between evangelical teaching and pagan mythology. The shameless glorification of sensual lust attributed to the gods in the teaching of the fables is a million miles removed from the simplicity, the delicacy, and the sanctity one marvels at in the Gospel stories.[34]

It needs to be said that the importance of the virgin birth does not depend on the theological construct that Mary during and after the birth remained a virgin. Questions here center around the Gospel reference to Jesus's "brothers" and "sisters" (Matt. 12:46–47; 13:55; Mark 3:21, 31; 6:3–4; Luke 2:7; 8:19; John 2:12; 7:3, 5; Acts 1:14; 1 Cor. 9:5; and Gal. 1:19). Some (following Jerome) consider these as references to his cousins; others believe they refer to the sons of Joseph from a previous marriage and were therefore his stepbrothers; a third view holds that they were truly the children of Joseph and Mary. The perpetual virginity of Mary is a later notion, and debates about whether Mary had more children, though interesting and contentious, are dogmatically of secondary importance. The supernatural conception by the Holy Spirit is crucial, however, and it does not stand alone. Conceived by the power of the Holy Spirit (or "the power of the Most High" [Luke 1:35]), Christ was anointed in a special way with the Holy Spirit which he received without measure (John 3:34), an anointing that continued throughout his entire life, even into the state of exaltation. As Scripture prophesied, the Messiah would be anointed. The exclusion of a man from his conception meant that Jesus was not included in the covenant of works and thus, in the judgment of God, remained exempt from human sin. By the Holy Spirit's power, he remained free from sin. From this it is evident that the activity of the Holy Spirit with respect to this conception did not consist in the infusion of any heavenly or divine substance in Mary but in a demonstration of power that made her womb fertile in the act of overshadowing her as with a cloud (cf. Exod. 40:34; Num. 9:15; Luke 9:34; Acts 1:8).

CHRIST'S HUMANITY AND DIVINITY

[368] In this way the Son of God became truly and completely human. In the history of the church, there have been any number of strange attempts to deny the full and true humanity of Jesus. Gnostics had philosophical objections to it; others (Valentinus) believed that Jesus brought a glorious spiritual body from heaven which only passed through Mary like water through a conduit, or even that he had assumed a phantom body that was abandoned when he returned to heaven (Apelles). Similar notions were present in the medieval sects and flour-

34. G. H. Box, "The Gospel Narratives," *Zeitschrift für neutestamentliche Wissenschaft* (1905): 80ff.; L. M. Sweet, "Heathen Wonderbirths and the Birth of Christ," *Princeton Theological Review* 6 (1908): 83–117.

ished among the Anabaptists who could not reconcile the assumption of Christ's body from Mary with his sinlessness. Although these ideas strike us as bizarre, in other forms they express nothing but what modern philosophy since Kant and Hegel has proposed with its split between the ideal Christ and the historical Jesus. Scripture, however, clearly portrays his full humanity, growing up and developing, experiencing hunger and thirst, anger and grief, and then suffering and dying (Matt. 4:2; 26:38; Luke 2:40, 52; 18:41; 19:41; John 2:17; 11:35; 12:27; 19:28; Acts 2:30; Rom. 1:3; 5:15; 9:5; 1 Cor. 15:21; 1 Tim. 2:5; Heb. 2:14, 17–18; 4:15; 5:1). For Scripture it is so much an established fact that Christ came in the flesh that it calls the denial of it anti-Christian (1 John 2:22). Denials of Christ's humanity were rightly opposed by the early church for pastoral and soteriological reasons with the formula "What is not assumed is not saved." Objections are for the most part rooted in a dualism that is antithetical to the Christian religion. Whether it is found in ancient or modern gnosticism, in Reformation-era Anabaptism, or in nineteenth-century speculative philosophy, the dualist conviction that the finite and the infinite are mutually exclusive must be repudiated. If even one essential constituent in the human nature of Christ is excluded from true union and communion with God, there remains an element in creation dualistically alongside and opposed to God. Then God is not the Almighty, Creator of heaven and earth. Then the Christian religion is not truly catholic. Over against all such dualisms, the Christian faith asserts that there is one mediator between God and humanity, the true God-man Jesus Christ (1 Tim. 2:5). This is the heart of the gospel.

[369] The scriptural teaching that God and man are united in Christ was drawn together in the church's language of the "two natures." In Scripture, both divine and human predicates are attributed to the same personal subject, the one person, Jesus Christ. For according to Scripture, the Word that was with God and was himself God became flesh (John 1:14). He who was the reflection of God's glory and the exact imprint of God's very being has become partaker in our flesh and blood and like us in all things (Heb. 1:3; 2:14). God sent into the world his own Son, who was born of a woman (Gal. 4:4). Although existing in "the form of God," he "emptied himself, taking the form of a slave" (Phil. 2:7). From the fathers, according to the flesh (κατα σαρκα) comes the Messiah, who is over all, God blessed forever (Rom. 9:5). In him the fullness of deity dwells bodily (σωματικος, Col. 2:9). Modern attempts to reduce the divinity to a mere moral unity with God revive the ancient heresy of Nestorius and utterly fail to do justice to biblical givens. Nestorius believed that the eternal and natural Son of God was distinct from and other than the son of David who was born of Mary. Mary, therefore, cannot be called "mother of God" (θεοτοκος), and the human being born of her is not the eternal Son of God but his adopted Son. The union between God and man in Christ is not a natural but a moral union; not a union (ενωσις) but a conjunction (συναφεια) of two natures. The indwelling of God in Christ does not differ in kind but only in degree from that in believers. In response,

Chalcedon correctly pronounced that the union of the two natures was without division or separation and without confusion or change. Both Monophysitism and Kenoticism in all their varieties are unacceptable because they are at odds with the immutability of God and with the nature of a finite being. Although it is true, especially in Paul, that only through his resurrection did Christ enter into full sonship (Rom. 1:4; cf. Acts 2:36; 5:30), become Lord from heaven and life-giving Spirit (1 Cor. 15:45; 2 Cor. 3:17), and receive a name above every name (Phil. 2:9), Paul does not for that reason in any way deny that also before his incarnation Christ already possessed a personal divine existence (2 Cor. 8:9; Phil. 2:6; Col. 1:15–17) and was God's own Son (Rom. 1:3; 8:32; Gal. 4:4). Therefore, a deity or divine attribute that is purely a "potentiality" is inconceivable, and a human being who by development appropriates the divine nature ceases to be a creature. Such a being cannot be the mediator between God and man since he is neither.

It was to do justice to all the scriptural data concerning the person of Christ that Christian theology arrived gradually at the two-natures doctrine. It did not put this doctrine forward as a hypothesis, nor did it intend it as an explanation of the mystery of Christ's person. It only summed up, without mutilation and diminution, the whole scriptural doctrine of Christ and thereby maintained it against the numerous errors that cropped up both to the left and to the right: those that devalued the divinity and those that devalued the humanity of Christ. Chalcedon, accordingly, correctly pronounced that the union of the divine and the human nature in Christ was without division (ἀδιαιρετος) and without separation (ἀχωριστος). But over against the opposing school, it maintained with equal firmness that the union was without change (ἀτρεπτος) and without confusion (ἀσυγχυτος). Mary is thus properly called "mother of God" (θεοτοκος).

[370] Theology, if it truly wants to be scriptural and Christian, cannot do better for now than to maintain the two-natures doctrine. The language of Chalcedon is not sacrosanct and is open to reformulation. However, up to now all efforts to improve on it have failed. Since the essence of religion is communion with God, the two-natures doctrine is integrally connected to the heart of religion. If the incarnation is impossible, then religion cannot consist in communion between God and human creatures. But since religion in this sense has been disturbed by sin, there is no true, blessed communion between God and humanity. For that reason the union forged in Christ between the divine and the human natures had to be of a very special kind. It could not be identical with the existing religious relation between God and humanity but had to represent a new beginning, a realization of a restored, true religion. In short, it had to be covenantal in nature; Christ is not an individual beside other individuals, but the head and representative of humanity, the second and last Adam, the mediator between God and humanity. Hence the union of the divine and the human natures in Christ is not a union of *persons*; Christ assumed our human *nature*. The result is not a moral union of *persons* but a union of *natures* in the person of the Son, not a *natural* but

a *personal union*.[35] The result of that union is not a new nature, nor even a new personality, but only the person of Christ as Christ. He who existed in the form of God from that time on existed also in the form of a man. In virtue of its wholly unique nature, this union can only be conceived as a union of the person of the Son with an impersonal human nature. That is why the distinction between "nature" and "person" is so important. Ancient and modern thinkers—from Nestorius and Eutyches to Hegel and Dorner—fail to grasp this. How utterly this mystery of the union of the divine and human natures in Christ exceeds all our speaking and thinking of it. All comparison breaks down, for it is without equal. But it is, accordingly, the mystery of godliness, which angels desire to look into and the church worshipfully adores.

[371] Yet, as a serious objection to the two-natures doctrine, it is forever being advanced that it fails to do justice to the human nature of Christ and makes any human development in him an impossibility. This does carry some credibility in some versions of Roman Catholic and Lutheran theology where the communication of properties of the divine to the human nature seems to overwhelm the latter. The Lutherans took the communication of proper qualities to mean that not only the attributes of the two natures were communicated to the one [divine] person but that those of the divine nature were also communicated to the human nature. By its union with the divine nature, the human nature was elevated to a position of divine omnipotence and omnipresence.[36] Catholic scholars, on the other hand, while indeed teaching a communication of gifts and opposing the Lutheran doctrine of the communication of proper qualities, say that in virtue of the hypostatic union, the human nature of Christ, at the first moment of its conception, received a "copious supply of the Spirit of God and an abundance of spiritual gifts."[37] Here the doctrine of communication of properties is itself destroyed; why should such gifts be needed when they are already shared? Both Lutheran and Catholic Christology, consequently, contain within them a docetic element. The purely human development does not come into its own in them. In reaction, theologians in the nineteenth century swung over to the other extreme and denied the deity of the Lord.

Reformed theologians, however, have so construed the communication of the gifts as to make possible a human development in Jesus. Reformed theology insisted that Christ as the second Adam was nonetheless different from Adam, particularly in the fact that Adam was an adult while Christ came as an infant, not to a paradise but to a sinful world where he faced its temptation and evil in every way. Unlike Adam, Christ came in the form of sinful flesh, susceptible to suffering and death. God sent his Son in the likeness of sinful flesh, that is, in flesh

---

35. Francis Turretin, *Institutes of Elenctic Theology*, trans. George Musgrove Giger and ed. James T. Dennison, 3 vols. (Phillipsburg, NJ: Presbyterian and Reformed, 1992), XIII, 6, 3.

36. J. T. Müller, *Die symbolischen Bücher der evangelisch-lutherischen Kirche*, 8th ed. (Gütersloh: Bertelsmann, 1898), 679–80.

37. Roman Catechism, I, 4, 4.

that was the same in form and appearance as sinful flesh (Rom. 8:3). In virtue of this splendid doctrine of the communication of proper qualities, Reformed theology was able, better than any other, to maintain in addition to Christ's deity also his true and genuine humanity. In this regard it renders excellent service.

Reformed theologians disagreed over the question whether the incarnation as such, aside from the condition of sin in which it occurred, was already an act of humiliation. On the one hand, the distance between God and humanity is so enormous that the incarnation as such is an act of humiliation. On the other, one could say in that case Christ would even now, glorified at the Father's right hand, be in a state of humiliation.[38] The controversy can best be settled by saying that the incarnation as such, without any further qualification, always was and remains an act of condescending goodness but not, strictly speaking, a step in the state of humiliation. It became this as a result of the fact that it was an incarnation, the assumption of a weak human nature. Christ grew in wisdom and knowledge; on earth he too was a pilgrim. By nature, faith for Adam and Christ was nothing other than the act of clinging to the word and promises of God, a holding on to the Invisible One. That is what Jesus did as well (Matt. 27:46; Heb. 2:17–18; 3:2). His divine and human consciousness were united in that he knew the Father's will perfectly but not exhaustively. Just as behind our limited consciousness there also lies within us a world of being, so behind the human consciousness of Christ there lay the depths of God, which could only very gradually and to a limited degree shine through that human consciousness.[39] Jesus also grew morally. Although he was not able to sin, his sinlessness had become manifest through response to temptation and struggle. In this, too, Christ's humanity was more fully developed than Adam's; in the state of integrity there was simply no occasion for many emotions, such as anger, sadness, pity, compassion, and so on. But Christ did not just visit us with the inner movements of God's mercy; rather, in his human nature he opened for us the abounding world of the mind and the heart that did not and could not yet exist in Adam.

[372–73] In addition, there was in Christ a human faculty of knowing, intellectual development, an increase in wisdom and knowledge. Because Arians and Apollinarians, according to whom the Logos occupies the place of the spirit (πνεῦμα) in Christ, along with Monophysites, could not accept the presence of such human knowledge in Christ, the church fathers tended increasingly to present the human knowledge of Christ as perfect from the first moment on and insusceptible to increase. Failing to find adequate scriptural grounds for this—appeals to John 1:14; 2:24–25; 6:64; 13:3; and Col. 2:3, 9 speak of the whole Christ and not his

---

38. A. Kuyper, *De vleeschwording des Woords* (Amsterdam: Wormser, 1887), 38ff., 180ff.

39. F. Turretin, *Institutes of Elenctic Theology*, XIII, 12–13; W. G. T. Shedd, *Dogmatic Theology*, 3rd ed., 3 vols. (New York: Scribner, 1891–94), II, 281, 307, 329; A. Kuyper, *De vleeschwording des Woords*, 152; idem, *The Work of the Holy Spirit*, trans. Henri de Vries (Grand Rapids: Eerdmans, 1941), I, chaps. 5 and 6 (ed note: Originally published in 3 volumes by Funk & Wagnalls, New York, 1900; also published by AMG Publishers, Chattanooga, TN, 2001).

human development!—they found it in the "fittingness" that requires that God in fact *had* to give the human nature, which was so closely united with him, this gift of knowledge.[40] Reformed theologians responded by teaching that Christ's infused and acquired knowledge was not immediately complete but gradually increased; and, second, that Christ on earth was a pilgrim, not a comprehensive knower, that he walked by faith and hope, not by sight, that he did not yet share the "beatific knowledge" (*scientia beata*) here on earth. Naturally, "faith" for Christ was not a trust in the divine grace of mercy, which gift is given by faith only to sinners. Faith for Christ (and for Adam before the fall) was nothing other than the act of clinging to the word and promises of God; this is exactly what Jesus did (Matt. 27:46; Heb. 2:17–18; 3:2). In the case of Christ, that faith and that hope were not wavering and hesitant but firm and strong. They kept him, the pioneer and perfecter of our faith, standing in the midst of temptation, enabling him, for the joy awaiting him as the reward for this labor, to endure the cross and to despise its shame (Heb. 12:2). Christ's human consciousness was limited and it grew as he did.

From this, one may not infer, however, that in various domains Jesus could err. It is spurious to argue, for example, that Jesus's views on demon possession, botany, his relation to the Old Testament, or predictions about the future, were mistaken. Such objections sidestep the reason for his coming. Granted, Jesus did not give instruction in any human science; he did not come on earth for that purpose but to make known to us the Father and to carry out his work. But to that end he also needed to know the Father in his revelation and works, and hence whether the Old Testament was, or was not, the Word of God. This was knowledge not of a purely scientific but of a religious nature, one that was of the greatest importance for the faith of the church. One who in this respect charges Jesus with error comes into conflict not only with his divine nature but also with his prophetic office and with all the testimonies in which he ascribes his teaching to the Father (John 7:16; 8:26, 28, 38; 12:49–50).[41]

When it comes to Jesus's moral development, the challenge to Jesus's sinlessness is rooted in a failure to take account of the deity of Christ. It proceeds from the mistaken idea that there is no virtue other than what is acquired by struggle, and at most achieves a factual, historical sinlessness, which is insufficient for Jesus as Mediator.[42] In Christ there is moral development but not as construed

40. Joseph Kleutgen, *Die Theologie der Vorzeit vertheidigt*, 2nd ed., 5 vols. (Münster: Theissing, 1867–74), III, 251.

41. Cf. H. Bavinck, *Reformed Dogmatics*, I, 394–402 (##107–8); W. Caven, "The Testimony of Christ to the Old Testament," *Presbyterian and Reformed Review* 3 (1892): 401–20; J. Denney, "Authority of Christ," in *DC*, I, 146–53; D. W. Forrest, *The Authority of Christ* (Edinburgh: T&T Clark, 1906).

42. Objections to Jesus's sinlessness found in the early church return later in the rationalism of Kant, Fichte, Strauss, and others. Additional arguments are advanced, such as the claim that Jesus's temptations necessarily imply fallibility; that certain givens from his life present him as less than perfect, such as his baptism by John (Matt. 3:13), his relationship to his parents (Luke 2:49; John 2:4; Mark 3:33), his appearance in the temple (John 2:15; Matt. 21:12), his sharp rebukes of the Pharisees (Matt. 23:13), his

by Theodore of Mopsuestia, Nestorius, and others, for whom Jesus brought with him the possibility of sinning, but by moral exertion and struggle actually kept himself free from all sins, developed himself ethically to the highest level, and made himself worthy of union with God. Although Jesus "learned obedience" (Heb. 5:8ff.), Christian theology affirms a necessary sinlessness as well. He is the Son of God, the Logos, who was in the beginning with God and himself God. He is one with the Father and always carries out his Father's will and work. For those who confess this of Christ, the possibility of him sinning and falling is unthinkable.

Still, this is not to cancel the essential distinction between the holiness of God and the holiness of Christ as a human being. Jesus said that no one is good, no one is goodness itself but God alone (Matt. 19:16–17; Mark 10:17–18; Luke 18:18–19). The goodness or holiness of Christ according to his human nature is not a divine and original goodness but one that has been given, infused, and for that reason must also—in the way of struggle and temptation—reveal, maintain, and confirm itself. Infused goodness does not rule out acquired goodness. The latter presupposes the former; good fruit grows only on a good tree, but the soundness of the tree still has to be shown in the soundness of the fruit. Thus, Christ had to manifest his innate holiness through temptation and struggle, a struggle that is not made redundant or vain by virtue of the inability to sin (*non posse peccare*). Jesus's temptations came from without rather than within, but he possessed a real human nature which dreaded suffering and death.[43] Thus, his temptations—by Satan, his enemies, and even his disciples (Matt. 4:1–11; Mark 1:13; Luke 4:1–13; Matt. 12:29; Luke 11:22; Matt. 16:23; Mark 8:33)—were also real. In those temptations he was bound, fighting as he went, to remain faithful, but this inability to sin (*non posse peccare*) was not a matter of coercion but ethical in nature and manifested ethically.

Although as the Son of God he was omnipotent, he was nevertheless limited as it concerns the power of his human nature. We must—with Scripture and the church—distinguish the two natures of Christ and view the two natures as being united in such a way that in the one divine-human work each nature does the thing that belongs to it. For that reason the performance of miracles, the forgiving of sins, the granting of eternal life, and all that belongs to the work of the mediator is attributable not only to his deity but also to his humanity. Christ as Son of

---

sending demons into the swine (Matt. 8:31), his curse of the fig tree (Matt. 21:19)—especially noted by F. Pécaut, *Le Christ et la conscience* (Paris: Cherbuliez, 1859), and E. Renan, *The Life of Jesus* (Buffalo: Prometheus Books, 1991)—and, finally, arguments that seek to prove that Christ, in order to be our mediator, had to be born under the curse of original sin and take on sinful flesh.

43. The temptation to which Jesus was exposed according to Hebrews (2:18; 4:15) did not lie, strictly speaking, in the realm of morality and was not a temptation to sin, but consisted in the fact that the manifold and heavy suffering he had to endure tested him on the point of whether he would persevere to the end in his messiahship, in his calling as Redeemer, in his office of Savior. But Jesus was and remained Christ. He *learned* obedience, not in the sense that he gradually changed from disobedience to obedience but in the sense that, in and through suffering, he increasingly proved his perfect obedience by his deeds. Cf. Karl Bornhauser, *Die Versuchung Jesu nach dem Hebräerbrief* (Leipzig: Deichert, 1905).

Man, as Messiah, therefore, ascribes to him this power to forgive and to come in judgment (Matt. 9:2–8; John 5:27). Upon his being touched, power comes forth from him (Luke 6:19). His flesh is the bread that gives life to the world (John 6:51). The Father has given all things into his hand (John 3:35; 13:3; 17:2). No one can snatch the sheep out of his hand or his Father's hand (John 10:28–30). Like the Father, he answers prayer (John 14:13; cf. 16:23), sends the Spirit (John 15:26; cf. 14:26), and gives eternal life (John 10:28; 17:2). Still, all this does not rule out that his power, as human power, is susceptible to increase. He was born as a tiny child, weak and helpless; he needed food and drink; he was exhausted by travel and sat down by the well (John 4:6). Even in the performance of miracles, he was dependent on the faith of people (Matt. 13:58). In the garden he was strengthened by an angel (Luke 22:43). Only after the resurrection does he say that all power in heaven and on earth has been given him (Matt. 28:8; Mark 16:20; Luke 24:19). Then as mediator he receives the glory he had beforehand with the Father as the Son (John 17:5) and causes his human nature to share in it. By his resurrection Christ—also as a human being—became Lord over the living and the dead, received a name that is above every name and power over all creatures (Matt. 28:18; Phil. 2:9; Col. 2:3, 9; Heb. 2:7–8).

It is for that reason alone that Christ is worshiped and adored. Scripture leaves no doubt about whether Christ, who may be the object of our faith and trust (John 14:1; 17:3; Rom. 14:9; 2 Cor. 5:15; Eph. 3:12; 5:23; Col. 1:27; 1 Tim. 1:1; etc.), may also be the object of our religious veneration and worship (John 5:23; 14:13; Acts 7:59; 9:13; 22:16; Rom. 10:12–13; 1 Cor. 1:2; 2 Cor. 12:8; Phil. 2:9–11; Heb. 1:6; Rev. 5:12; 12[:10–11]; 22:17, 20). The ground for this worship, according to the Scriptures, can be derived only from his deity. The word of Scripture is firm: "Worship the Lord your God, and serve only him." In principle this condemns all pagan and Roman Catholic creature deification. The dignity and the works of the mediator can and may be motives for worship and adoration, just as all sorts of benefits prompt us to worship God. They may also be called "grounds" for worship insofar as the divine being works and reveals himself in them. But the foundation of worship is the mediator's being God alone.

15

THE SERVANT SAVIOR: CHRIST'S HUMILIATION

RELIGION, CULTURE, REDEMPTION, AND SACRIFICE

[374] The universal sense of sin and misery among the peoples of the world is accompanied by the felt need and hope for salvation, bound up in many religions with a coming person and specifically built on the appearance of a king.[1] Here we may add that the idea of redemption is almost always coupled with that of reconciliation.[2] In the struggle for existence and as protection against the forces of disorder and violence in nature and other humans, people form communities and create cultures. Culture, creating civilizations, satisfies many needs, but—often in its very successes—creates other needs and shows itself inadequate for quenching the thirst for eternity, for redemption. "The more abundantly the benefits of civilization come streaming our way, the emptier our life becomes."[3] This longing can only be met by religion, the basis of all culture. For the redemption that humans seek and need is one in which they are lifted above the whole world into communion with God.

People take various roads toward redemption—magic, mysticism and ecstasy, naturalism, legalism and moralism—but the virtual universality of sacrifice re-

---

1. Cf. H. Bavinck, *Reformed Dogmatics*, ed. John Bolt (Grand Rapids: Baker Academic, 2003–8), III, 238–40 (#351).

2. Ed. note: In this chapter, the Dutch word *verlossing* will be translated as "redemption"; *verzoening* will be translated as "reconciliation," when used in a general sense, and as "atonement," when used in a more specific sense as the doctrine of Christ's saving work on the cross.

3. G. Heymans, *Der Toekomstige Eeuw der Psychologie* (Groningen: Wolters, 1909), 9.

quires explanation. By sacrifice we understand the religious act in which a person voluntarily offers a material gift to the deity and destroys it (זֶבַח, עֹלָה, מִנְחָה, אִשֶּׁה; δωρον, ἱερειον, προσφορα, θυσια, τελετη; *oblatio, sacrificium*) in the service of that deity in order to secure the deity's favor. The Vedic religion, for example, speaks of sacrifice as the navel of the world. A multitude of hypotheses have arisen to explain the origin and nature of sacrifice: expiation of guilt, expression of gratitude or token of devotion, an exchange of favors with the deity (*do-ut-des*; "I give that you may give"), or even communion with the deity (shared meal). Others consider sacrifice a form of totemism: an attempt to gain the powers of the animal by drinking its blood and eating its flesh. Explanations of the origin, nature, and purpose of sacrifices vary widely, and it is unlikely that a satisfactory single explanation of sacrifice will ever be found.[4] Nonetheless, the universal, profound, and powerful urge that at all times and places drives people to offer sacrifices is truly remarkable; human beings possess an ineradicable sense that they are related to an invisible divine power, whether reconciled or unreconciled, and that by their sacrifice they can exert some influence on the deity. Likely, a notion of sacrifice as a gift of communion to God existed before the fall. As Augustine put it, sacrifice is "every work that unites us in a holy communion with God."[5] Sin's entrance did not introduce sacrifice as something new, added to human life, but changed its nature into an expiatory act arising out of awareness of sin and guilt. Fear and guilt now impel humans to sacrifice (as well as to pray) rather than reverence and gratitude. Therefore, the idea of redemption is wedded to that of reconciliation, and the two are so closely coupled that we cannot draw a sharp distinction between ordinary and expiatory sacrifices. In all sacrifices there is a certain acknowledged expiatory power.[6] To the degree that a sense of guilt and misery increases, the actual expiatory sacrifice increasingly becomes the center of the liturgy.

A special class of priests—holy persons who effect and maintain communion with God—also gradually arose in all religions to offer sacrifices and serve as mediators. Magicians and fortune-tellers, and especially kings, prophets, and priests, act as such mediators. The origin of priesthood is unknown but it is reasonable to assume that as the sense of sin among people grows, so does the idea of mediatorship. Having lost their own priestly roles, human beings felt a need for special persons to take their place and plead their case before God. In that way, all human priesthood and sacrifice points—directly in Israel, indirectly also among other peoples—to the one perfect sacrifice that was brought in the fullness of time by Christ, the mediator between God and humankind, on Golgotha.

4. Ed. note: The two primary sources Bavinck uses for his data about sacrifice in the world's religions are P. D. Ch. de la Saussaye, *Lehrbuch der Religionsgeschichte*, 3rd ed., 2 vols. (Tübingen: Mohr [Siebeck], 1905); and C. P. Tiele, *Elements of the Science of Religion*, 2 vols. (Edinburgh and London: William Blackwood, 1899).

5. Augustine, *City of God*, X, 6.

6. W. Robertson Smith, *Die Religion der Semiten* (Freiburg i.B.: Mohr, 1899), 305, 309.

[375] Israel's priests instructed the people in God's law (Exod. 28:30; Deut. 17:9; 33:8–10; Jer. 18:8; Ezek. 7:26; 44:23–24; Hag. 2:12; Mal. 2:7), performed the sacrifices (Lev. 21:8; Num. 16:5; etc.), and blessed Israel on Yahweh's behalf (Lev. 9:23; Num. 6:23). The offerings Israel had to bring were of different kinds: paschal offering (Exod. 12), covenant offering (Exod. 24:3–11), burnt offering and thank offering (Lev. 1; 3), sin (חַטָּאת) and guilt (אָשָׁם) offerings (Lev. 4–6). The last-mentioned presupposes a break in communion with God because of inadvertent sin and, by the sprinkling of the blood of the slain animal, offered a cover for sin and restoration of communion. Atonement occurs when one transfers to the animal by the laying on of hands. It is the blood that effects atonement; this was God's design because the blood is the bearer of the soul, the carrier of a life that had again been made free from sin after and by the slaying (Lev. 17:11). Now when this blood on the altar or on the mercy seat came into God's presence, the offerer or his sin was thereby covered before the holy face of God; or rather, it was God himself (Deut. 21:8; Jer. 18:23; Mic. 7:19) and the priest as his deputy (Lev. 5:13; 10:17; 15:15) who by the sacrifice—conceived as a ransom (כֹּפֶר, λυτρον)—covered the persons of the offerers from their sins or even covered those sins themselves before his face (כִּפֶּר with the preposition עַל or בְּעַד). It is important to stress that the sacrifices for atonement are not universal but apply restrictively to specific unintentional sins. The penalty for sins committed "high-handedly" (sins of defiance) was death (Num. 15:30). Furthermore, the covenant of grace that God made with Israel was not based on the sacrifices for atonement but preceded them and had its basis exclusively in the promise: "I am the Lord your God." In addition, countless sins remained for which the law did not indicate any atonement by sacrifices; for a wide range of spiritual and carnal sins, sins by thoughts and words, sins of pride and self-seeking, no prescribed sacrifices existed. The key to Old Testament sacrifice is atonement, covering for sin by means of shed blood, but the sacrificial cult itself served primarily to point God's people to his mercy for their appeal. Old Testament sacrifices were incomplete and insufficient; the priests themselves were sinners; the blood of bulls and goats could not take away sins; the sacrifices had to be endlessly repeated. The ceremonial dispensation of the Old Testament had a passing, symbolic, and typological significance.

All this anticipated the coming Suffering Servant, who would make himself an offering for the sins of the people (Isa. 53:10). In the Old Testament, the promises of the Suffering Servant and the anointed king run parallel. It is thus clear that God's righteousness will be obtained only in the way of suffering. It is the necessity of the sacrifice of atonement that is symbolized by the sacrificial cult. Many Old Testament examples—Moses, David, Job, the prophets, the small group of the faithful who did not bow their knees before Baal—show that the righteous suffer most, that they who represent God's cause must pass through suffering to glory. In the exile and thereafter as a religious community, Israel became the servant of the Lord who in distress and misery, and oppressed on every side, would still be redeemed by the Holy One of Israel (Isa. 41:8f.). Yet Israel is not the true servant of the Lord either; Israel herself needs redemption (Isa. 41:14; 42:19f.). Thus the way is prepared for the coming of Him who is the prophet of the new covenant (Deut. 18:15; Isa. 11:2; Jer. 31:31; Mal. 4:5), the new royal high priest after the order of Melchizedek (Ps. 110; Jer. 30:21; Zech. 6:13; Heb. 4–8), the humble anointed king who will execute righteousness (Isa. 11:1–2; Mic. 5:1–2; Ezek. 17:22; Jer. 23:6) and make all sacrifices obsolete (Isa. 60:21; 61:6; Jer. 24:7; 31:34; Ezek. 36:25, 27). But the expectation of a suffering Messiah was not the content of popular belief at the time of Jesus's coming; his disciples show themselves to be unreceptive to it (Matt. 16:22; Luke 18:34; 24:21; John 12:34).

[376] According to the New Testament, Christ fulfills the Old Testament law and prophets with their sacrificial system. In him all the promises of God are yes and amen (Rom. 15:8; 2 Cor. 1:20). He is the true Messiah, the king of David's house (Matt. 2:2; 21:5; 27:11, 37; Luke 1:32; etc.), the prophet who proclaims good news to the poor (Luke 4:17f.), the true covenant sacrifice, the Lamb of God who takes away the sins of the world (John 1:29, 36) by being obedient to death on the cross (Rom. 5:19; Phil. 2:8; Heb. 5:8). By his sacrifice he acquired his own exaltation and, for his own people, the blessings of salvation, notably the forgiveness and removal of our sins, peace with God. Christ's work in the state of humiliation is a work that the Father gave him to do (John 4:34; 5:36; 17:4); it consisted in doing God's will (Matt. 26:42; John 4:34; 5:30; 6:38). This one work (ἔργον) is differentiated in many works (ἔργα, John 5:36), which are the works of his Father (John 5:20; 9:3; 10:32, 37; 14:10), and include his miracles which prove that the Father loves him, dwells in him (John 5:20; 10:38; 14:10), and has sent him (John 5:36; 10:25); they manifest his divine glory (John 2:11; 11:4, 40). As the incarnate, Spirit-conceived, risen and glorified Son of God, he is himself the greatest miracle, the center of all miracles, the author of the re-creation of all things, the firstborn of the dead, preeminent in everything (Col. 1:18).

It was also the will of God that the only Son of the Father should lay down his life for his own (John 10:18). The New Testament views Christ's death as a sacrifice and the fulfillment of the Old Testament sacrificial cult. His blood is the blood of the new covenant (Matt. 26:28; Mark 14:24; Heb. 9:13f.); a sacrifice (θυσια, זֶבַח); an offering (προσφορα, δωρον; מִנְחָה, קָרְבָּן; Eph. 5:2; etc.); a ransom (λυτρον, ἀντιλυτρον; Matt. 20:28; Mark 10:45; 1 Tim. 2:6; a translation of the Hebrew words כֹּפֶר, פְּדוּים, גְאֻלָה) and therefore denoting the price of release, a ransom to purchase someone's freedom from prison, and hence a means of atonement, a sacrifice by which to cover other people's sin and so to save them from death. He is a payment (τιμη, 1 Cor. 6:20; 7:23; 1 Pet. 1:18–19), an expiation (ἱλαστηριον, Rom. 3:25); a sacrifice of atonement (θυμα), and a curse (καταρα, Gal. 3:13) who took over from us the curse of the law. He did this on our behalf (ὑπερ σου, Philem. 13) and obtained for us all the benefits of salvation (σωτηρια, Matt. 1:21; Luke 2:11; John 3:17; 12:47), and more specifically the forgiveness of sins (Matt. 26:28; Eph. 1:7); the removal of our sins (John 1:29; 1 John 3:5); the cleansing or deliverance of a bad conscience (Heb. 10:22); justification (Rom.

4:25); righteousness (1 Cor. 1:30); sonship (Gal. 3:26; 4:5–6; Eph. 1:5); confident access to God (Eph. 2:18; 3:12). He is the light of the world (John 8:12); the way, the truth, the resurrection, and the life (11:25; 14:6); our wisdom, our righteousness, holiness, and redemption (1 Cor. 1:30); our peace (Eph. 2:14); the second and last Adam (1 Cor. 15:45); the head of the church (Eph. 1:22); the cornerstone of the temple of God (Eph. 2:20), and for that reason there is no participation in his benefits except by communion with his person. The gift of the Holy Spirit (John 15:26; Acts 2; Gal. 4:6) unites us with Christ in his death, resurrection, and ascension (Rom. 6:3f; Gal. 2:20; 6:14; Eph. 2:6; Phil. 3:20) so that we are cleansed (Eph. 5:26; 1 John 1:7, 9), washed from our sins (1 Cor. 6:11; Rev. 1:5; 7:14), and reborn as children of God (John 1:12–13). Free from the law's curse, we stand victorious in Christ over Satan (Luke 11:22; John 14:30; Col. 1:13; 2:15; 1 John 3:8), the world (John 16:33; 1 John 4:4, 5:4), death, the fear of death, and judgment (John 11:25; Rom. 5:12f.; 1 Cor. 15:21, 55f.; Heb. 2:15; 10:27–28). As we await our heavenly inheritance (John 14:2; 1 Pet. 1:4), we enjoy the beginning of eternal life with the inception of faith (John 3:15, 36) until it manifests itself fully in glory (Mark 10:30; Rom. 6:22) with the new heaven and new earth (2 Pet. 3:13; Rev. 21:1, 5) and the restoration of all things (Acts 3:21; 1 Cor. 15:24–28).

[377] The history of the doctrine of Christ's work lacks the sharp controversy and clear-cut formulation that characterize the trinitarian and christological dogmas. The rich diversity of Scripture's teaching yields an array of views, all of which contain a core of truth. Christ is prophet, priest, and king; his death is ransom, sacrifice, satisfaction, payment, healing, and reconciliation. One-sided views did arise and were connected to divergent understandings of sin. When sin is viewed as lack of knowledge, Christ is seen as the Logos who reveals full truth and provides an example of virtue. When sin is perceived more as a power than as guilt, deliverance or redemption is accented above reconciliation. Another widely held view—repudiated by Gregory of Nazianzus[7]—was that Christ had delivered himself up to Satan as a ransom, bait, or snare (Job 40:24), and thus conquered him by cunning and snatched people from his control.[8] Views that consider Christ's work as primarily exemplary or as a mystical reality in believers, are inadequate and to be rejected. The best articulations—Justin Martyr, the *Letter to Diognetus*, Irenaeus—regarded the sacrifice of Christ on our behalf as a complete reconciliation with God, securing a full salvation, forgiveness, and eternal life. In the writings of Tertullian and Augustine we find a strong emphasis on the juridical or satisfaction element in sacrifice, an emphasis that is crowned in the Middle Ages with Anselm of Canterbury's great work *Cur Deus homo* (Why God Became Man). Anselm's contribution—against Duns Scotus who saw it as an

---

7. Gregory of Nazianzus, *Theological Orations*, 45, 22.
8. Origen, on Matt. 20:28; Gregory of Nyssa, *The Catechetical Oration*, trans. J. H. Srawley (Cambridge: Cambridge University Press, 1903), orat. 22–26; John of Damascus, *The Orthodox Faith*, III, 1, 27.

arbitrary act of God's power and Abelard who found only exemplary significance in it—was his emphasis on the fitting necessity of the atoning death of Christ. In its essential constituents, Anselm's teaching achieved permanent significance in later theology. He was the first to understand, and to understand most clearly, that the redemption accomplished by Christ was a deliverance, not primarily from the consequences of sin, from death and Satan's power, but above all from sin itself and sin's guilt. Christ's redemption, thus, consists mainly in reconciliation between God and humanity.

The Reformation placed this doctrine in a new perspective and within another context. For the Reformation, atonement from sin—understood primarily as guilt—became central in the work of Christ. Sin was of such a nature that it aroused God's wrath, and only the atoning death of the God-man could satisfy God's justice and still that wrath. He put himself in our place as the guarantor of the covenant, taking on himself the full guilt and punishment of sin, and submitting to the total demand of God's law. Hence the work of Christ consists not so much in his humility, nor only in his death, but in his total—active as well as passive—obedience as prophet, priest, and king. Calvin, in his Genevan Catechism and in the 1539 edition of the *Institutes*,[9] treated the work of Christ under the rubric of the threefold office and was, in time, followed in this by numerous Reformed, Lutheran, and Roman Catholic theologians. In this way the objective and subjective sides of reconciliation are clearly distinguished. Since by his sacrifice Christ met the requirements of God's justice, he objectively changed the relation between God and humankind and, consequently, all other creaturely relations. The primary benefit of forgiveness of sin is accompanied by deliverance from pollution, death, law, and Satan. Christ is the only mediator between God and humankind, the all-sufficient Savior, the highest prophet, the only priest, the true king.

[378] This understanding was not shared by all. In the early church the Ebionites regarded Christ only as a prophet who by his teaching and example gave people power for the struggle against sin. To gnostics, Christ was an aeon of divine wisdom, appearing on earth in phantom human form to enlighten us, free us from the bonds of matter, and make us πνευματικοι (spirituals). Similarly, in the dualistic, pantheistic, apocalyptic, and libertinistic sects of the Middle Ages, Christ's only significance was to reveal to humans their true nature and destiny and, in the age of the Spirit, realize their full potential to become what Christ was. The true death and resurrection of Christ takes place in the rebirth of every person. These ideas—the essence of Christianity is found in the *spirit* of Jesus *in us* (*in nobis*)—were still fermenting in the time of the Reformation and triggered opposition to the emphasis in Luther and Calvin on the proclaimed Word of the Christ *for us* (*pro nobis*). Carlstadt, Franck, Schwenckfeld, Weigel, and others

---

9. John Calvin, *Institutes of the Christian Religion*, II.xv–xvii (ed. John T. McNeill and trans. Ford Lewis Battles, 2 vols. [1559; Philadelphia: Westminster, 1960], 1:494–534).

regarded trust in Christ's imputed righteousness a dangerous error; our salvation, they said, lies not in what Christ does outside us and for us but in what he does in and through us, in mystical communion with God.[10] Similar views can be found in Jacob Böhme[11] and in the Quaker doctrine of the inner light.[12] The church's doctrine concerning the work of Christ came under attack not only from the side of mysticism but also from that of rationalism. Examples include Stancarus's teaching that Christ is our mediator only in his human nature[13] and Johannes Piscator's denial of Christ's active obedience.[14] Church teaching rejects views that consider Christ's work as primarily exemplary or only as a mystical reality in believers.

The most serious challenge to the doctrine of vicarious satisfaction came from the rationalist Socinians, who also denied the doctrines of the Trinity and the deity of Christ. In their view satisfaction is unbiblical, unnecessary, and impossible—an innocent cannot die for the guilty. The words "redemption," "reconciliation," and so on only indicate that Christ has shown us the way in which we may be freed from the service and punishment of sin, but definitely not that God had to be reconciled by a sacrifice, for God was graciously disposed toward us and has made this known to us by Christ. Christ's death is needed to confirm God's love to us with unmistakable clarity;[15] the purpose of his resurrection was to show by his example that those who obey God are freed from all death and to give to Christ himself the power to bestow eternal life on all who obey him.[16] According to the Socinians, the traditional doctrine of substitutionary atonement opens the door to carelessness and ungodliness; after all, if all sins have been atoned for, we are free to sin as much as we please. Hugo Grotius attempted to justify the doctrine of Christ's satisfaction[17] by deriving it from God's "governmental" justice, a justice outside God to which God is bound. Christ's satisfaction was thus turned into exemplary undeserved suffering designed to deter others. Grotius's governmental theory influenced the New England theology of Jonathan Edwards and Timothy Dwight as well as British thinkers such as Hobbes, Locke, Coleridge, John Taylor, Priestley, and others who argued that Christ was a revelation of God's love more

---

10. H. W. Erbkam, *Geschichte der protestantischen Sekten im Zeitalter der Reformation* (Hamburg and Gotha: Perthes, 1848), 247ff., 340ff., 441ff.

11. Joh. Claassen und J. Böhme, *Jakob Böhme: Sein Leben und seine theosophischen Werke*, 3 vols. (Stuttgart: J. F. Steinkopf, 1885), III, 31–76.

12. R. Barclay, *Verantwoording van de ware Christ* (Godgel, Amsterdam, 1757), 154; ed. note: ET: *Barclay's Apology in Modern English*, ed. Dean Freiday (Alburtis, PA: Hemlock, 1967).

13. D. H. Benroth (Schmidt), "Stancarus," *PRE*[3], XVIII, 752–54.

14. J. Piscator, *Epist. praest. virorum*, 156; cf. also Piscator, *Theses theol.*, XV, 18–19. Ed. note: cf. recent work on Piscator by Heber Carlos de Campos Jr., *Johannes Piscator (1546–1625) and the Consequent Development of the Doctrine of the Imputation of Christ's Active Obedience* (Lewiston, NY, and Lampeter, Wales: Edwin Mellen, forthcoming).

15. *Racovian Catechism*, trans. Thomas Rees (London, 1818), qu. 380, 383.

16. Ibid., qu. 384.

17. In his *Defensio fidei catholicae de satisfactione Christi* (1617).

than his justice and punishes sin only with pedagogically useful "natural" (consequential) punishments. The death of Christ has to do with how it changes us, not how it satisfies the wrath of God. The criticism by Faustus Socinus was so sharp and complete that later dissenters could do little other than repeat his arguments. The Remonstrants still tried to maintain the doctrine of Christ's satisfaction, but in fact adopted all the objections lodged against it.

[379] Although orthodox theologians raised serious objections against such views, the Socinian turn greatly influenced modern theology in its revisioning of the doctrine of Christ's office and work. Modern atonement theories replace the juridical doctrine of satisfaction—Christ fulfilling God's righteousness in our place—with an emphasis on Christ acting in a personal ethical manner so as to effect a moral change in us—be it more in our mind, or in our heart, or in our will. In the idealist thought of Schelling and Hegel, the historical Jesus is of little importance; it is the *idea* of the world departing from and returning to God that is central. The world and humanity, subject as they are to time and finiteness, are the suffering and dying God.[18] The reconciliation of God is a necessary objective moment in the cosmic process: God reconciles himself to himself and returns to himself from a state of estrangement.[19] Actual existence is the incarnation of the deity; the cosmic process is the story of God's passion and at the same time the way to the redemption of the One crucified in the flesh.[20] According to A. Drews, a mediator of redemption is not even a possibility, for all redemption is self-redemption by God in us, for God is the essence of a human being, and in humans he himself achieves self-consciousness and spiritual freedom.[21] We are saved by an immanent deity who indwells all humans and brings them to salvation through suffering and death. Here, forgiveness of sins cannot precede moral renewal or sanctification but rather follows them; we become children of God after we are renewed.[22] The subjective and ethical side of religion dominates the objective; religion becomes a matter of morality and self-salvation.

There was no lack of rescue efforts to secure the person and work of Christ after the attacks by Drews and others, notably by Schleiermacher and Ritschl.

18. F. W. J. Schelling, *Ausgewählte Werke*, 4 vols. (Darmstadt: Wissenschaftliche Buchgesellschaft, 1968), I/5, 386–400.

19. G. W. F. Hegel, *Philosophie der Religion* (2), in *Sämtliche Werke*, 26 vols. (Zürich: J. H. Bodmer, 1700), XVI, 249–56 (*Werke*, XII, 249–56); ed. note: The section Bavinck cites here is from "The Absolute Religion," and the section referred to can be found in P. Hodgson, ed., *Hegel: Lectures on the Philosophy of Religion*, vol. 3, "The Consummate Religion" (Berkeley: University of California Press, 1988), 201–11.

20. E. von Hartmann, *Das sittliche Bewusstsein* (Leipzig: W. Friedrich, 1886), 688.

21. A. Drews, *Die Religion als Selbst-Bewusstsein Gottes* (Jena and Leipzig: E. Diederichs, 1906), 238ff.; ed. note: Drews was part of a group of "Jesus-myth" scholars who questioned the existence of the historical Jesus; see Arthur Drews, *The Christ Myth*, trans. from the 3rd ed. (rev. and enlarged) by C. Delisle Burns (Chicago: Open Court, 1910; repr., [Westminster College-Oxford Classics in the Study of Religion] Amherst, NY: Prometheus, 1998).

22. Cf., e.g., J. A. L. Wegscheider, *Institutiones theologiae christianae dogmaticae* (Halle: Gebauer, 1819), §§140–42; T. Hobbes, *Leviathan* (London: J. M. Dent, 1924), chap. 41.

Schleiermacher posited a mystical reconciliation effected by Christ in us, while Ritschl made of Christ the perfect man who brings the moral kingdom of God to humanity. Although Schleiermacher used the language of the church—even taking over the language of the three offices—his notion of mystical communion with Christ failed to do justice to the reality of sin and guilt and viewed redemption too one-sidedly from the aesthetic perspective as harmony with the world. Ritschl attempted to refocus attention on the historical Jesus and his perfect obedience and vocational faithfulness to the point of death but rejected all notions of divine judgment and wrath in favor of a God understood only as love. With Ritschl, and those who succeeded him—Kaftan, Herrmann, Harnack—Christianity is only an ethical matter of living in accord with the divine will and the death of Christ a *pedagogical* means to that end. Jesus is not the constituent *content* of the gospel; he is only a *guide* to the Father, one who personally realized its power in love.[23]

[380] Similar attempts at mystically or ethically reconstructing the doctrine of the work of Christ were made in other countries as well.[24] At first, modern theology had little interest in the doctrine of the atonement (*verzoening*).[25] The problem here was sin: modern theology had a high view of human moral capability and was content with Jesus as prophet, example, and moral ideal. Sin is a defect, a lag in human development that will be overcome when more and more people travel the path trod by Christ. No atonement is really needed; a call to follow Jesus and persevere in moral goodness is needed. Where dissatisfaction with modern theology arose, notably in the English-speaking world,[26] and the atonement was reemphasized, the vicarious substitutionary understanding of Christ's death was still rejected. Gradually the center of gravity shifted from the objective work of Christ to the subjective change in us. Horace Bushnell saw Christ's suffering as a species of the substitutionary character of all suffering love, and John McCleod Campbell likewise inferred Christ's suffering from God's love, not from his justice. Christ offered to the Father a *vicarious repentance* on our behalf; the atonement is not legal but moral and spiritual and is not imputed to us juridically but mystically and ethically. A similar path of thought was followed by Thomas Erskine, R. C. Moberly, F. D. Maurice, R. J. Campbell, and others,[27] and theology in France and

23. Adolf von Harnack, *What Is Christianity?* trans. Thomas Bailey Saunders (New York: Harper, 1957), 51–56, 63–70, 77, 125ff.

24. In the Netherlands by the Groningen School and the "ethical" theology of Daniel Chantepie de la Saussaye; cf. H. Bavinck, "Recent Dogmatic Thought in the Netherlands," *The Presbyterian and Reformed Review* 3/10 (1892): 209–28.

25. See note 2 above.

26. R. W. Dale, *The Atonement*, 18th ed. (London: Congregational Union of England and Wales, 1896).

27. Horace Bushnell, *The Vicarious Sacrifice, Grounded in Principles of Universal Obligation* (New York: C. Scribner's Sons, 1866); John McLeod Campbell, *The Nature of the Atonement and Its Relation to Remission of Sins and Eternal Life*, 6th ed. (London: Macmillan, 1886); cf. H. F. Henderson, "The Row Heresy," in *The Religious Controversies of Scotland* (Edinburgh: T&T Clark, 1905), 147–81; R. C. Moberly, *Atonement and Personality*, 6th ed. (London: Murray, 1907); Thomas Erskine, *The Uncondi-*

Switzerland followed suit: the doctrine of vicarious satisfaction gradually made way for the mystical, ethical, or moral view of the work of Christ.[28] Common to all these efforts is a rejection of all notions of penal substitution accompanied by a strong desire to maintain the belief that the death of Christ has and remains a source of rich blessings for the human race. Furthermore, it is possible to share in those blessings by in some way uniting ourselves with Christ. Despite all these modern reconstructions, the confession of Jesus's vicarious suffering and death remains alive in the church and is still frequently and more or less decisively advocated in theology as well.[29]

JESUS THE MEDIATOR

[381] From the beginning, the belief that Jesus is the Christ has been the heart and core of the Christian confession. In the biblical view, Jesus is the anointed mediator, who fulfills the office of prophet, priest, and king. He is the perfect mediator between God and man because he is himself true God and true man. All who are in communion with Christ are named "Christian" (Acts 11:26) and anointed to be prophets, priests, and kings in him. In the apostolic writings, the names "Jesus" and "Christ" were very soon linked in the closest possible way and were mutually explanatory, just as the person of Christ is known from his work and the work of Christ is known from his person. The name, which is reproduced in Greek by Ἰησους and in Latin by *Jesus, Jhesus,* or *Hiesus,* was common among Israelites and is spelled out as יְהוֹשׁוּעַ (Deut. 3:21; Judg. 2:7) or written as יְהֹשֻׁעַ

---

tional Freeness of the Gospel: In Three Essays (Boston: Crocker & Brewster, 1828); F. D. Maurice, *The Doctrine of Sacrifice Deduced from Scriptures* (Cambridge: Macmillan, 1854); R. J. Campbell, *The New Theology* (New York: Macmillan, 1907); cf. further F. L. Godet, *The Atonement in Modern Religious Thought: A Theological Symposium* (London: Clarke, 1900); A. C. Lyttelton, "The Atonement," in *Lux Mundi,* ed. C. Gore (London: J. Murray, 1892), 201–29; G. B. Stevens, *The Christian Doctrine of Salvation* (Edinburgh: T&T Clark, 1905); W. Porcher Dubose, *The Soteriology of the New Testament* (New York: Longmans, Green, 1906); H. C. Beeching and A. Nairne, *The Bible Doctrine of Atonement* (London: Murray, 1906).

28. A. Sabatier, *The Doctrine of the Atonement and Its Historical Evolution,* trans. Victor Leulitte (New York: Putnam, 1904); E. Ménégoz, *La mort de Jésus et le dogme de l'expiation* (Paris: Fischbacher, 1905).

29. In addition to the works already cited, cf. also C. Hodge, *Systematic Theology,* 3 vols. (New York: Charles Scribner's Sons, 1888), II, 480ff.; W. G. T. Shedd, *Dogmatic Theology,* 3rd ed., 3 vols. (New York: Scribner, 1891–94), II, 378ff.; A. A. Hodge, *The Atonement* (1907; repr., Grand Rapids: Baker Academic, 1974); B. B. Warfield, "Modern Theories of the Atonement," *Princeton Theological Review* 1 (1903): 81–92; R. S. Candlish, *The Atonement: Its Reality, Completeness, and Extent* (London: T. Nelson & Sons, 1861); H. Martin, *The Atonement in Its Relations to the Covenant, the Priesthood, the Intercession of Our Lord* (London: James Nisbet, 1870; Edinburgh: Knox, 1976); J. S. Lidgett, *The Spiritual Principle of the Atonement as a Satisfaction Made to God for the Sins of the World,* 2nd ed. (London: Charles H. Kelley, 1898); J. Denney, *The Death of Christ: Its Place and Interpretation in the New Testament* (London: Hodder & Stoughton, 1909); idem, *The Atonement and the Modern Mind,* 2nd ed. (London: Hodder & Stoughton, 1908); J. Stalker, *The Atonement* (London: Hodder & Stoughton, 1908); J. J. van Oosterzee, *Christian Dogmatics,* trans. J. Watson and M. Evans, 2 vols. (New York: Scribner, Armstrong, 1874), §§108ff.

(Exod. 17:9; Num. 13:16; Josh. 1:1; Judg. 2:6; 1 Sam. 6:14, 18; 2 Kings 23:8; Hag. 1:1; Zech. 3:1); sometimes it occurs in the abbreviated form הוֹשֵׁעַ (Num. 13:8; 2 Kings 15:30; Neh. 10:23; Hosea 1:1) or יֵשׁוּעַ (Ezra 2:2, 6; Neh. 7:7, 11, 39; etc.). Whatever the form or its derivation, nowadays many scholars view the name as composed of יהו and שׁוּעַ, so that its meaning is "Yahweh is help or salvation" (cf. approximately the same combination, in the reverse order, in the name יְשַׁעְיָהוּ, Isa. 1:1).[30] Moses intentionally gave to Hoshea the son of Nun the name Joshua (Num. 13:8, 16), and in Matthew 1:21, Joseph, at the express command of the angel, gave to his son the name Jesus, because he would save his people from their sins. Although occasionally the name was give to other persons (Acts 7:45; Col. 4:11; Heb. 4:8 KJV), it belongs to Jesus in an utterly unique sense. Believers, therefore, call themselves by the name of Christ, since this is not the personal and historical name but the official one, and in communion with this Christ they are themselves anointed as prophets, priests, and kings.

In addition to this historical and official name, Christ is given many other names in Scripture. He is called the Son of God, the only begotten, beloved Son of God, the Word, the image of God, the reflection of God's glory and the exact imprint of God's very being, the firstborn of all creation, the true God and eternal life, God to be praised above all (or perhaps more correctly: God overall, to be praised forever [Rom. 9:5]), Immanuel. He is also called the Son of Man, the son of Joseph and David, the Nazarene (Matt. 2:23), the Galilean, the second Adam, the firstborn of all creatures, and the firstborn of the dead. Finally, in terms of his office and work, he is called Prophet, Master, Teacher, Priest, the Great Priest, the High Priest, the Servant of the Lord, the Lamb of God, the King, the King of kings, the Lord, the Lord of glory, the Lord of lords, the head of the church, the bridegroom of the church, the shepherd and guardian of souls, the pioneer and perfecter of the faith, the pioneer of salvation, the way, the truth, and the life, the bread of life, the prince of life, the resurrection and the life, the shepherd of the sheep, the door of the sheepfold, the light of the world, the shining morning star, the lion of the tribe of Judah, the Amen, the faithful and true witness, the Alpha and the Omega, the first and the last, the beginning and the end, the judge of the living and the dead, the heir of all things by whom, in whom, and for whom all things have been created. All these names sufficiently prove the incomparable dignity and entirely unique place that belong to Christ.[31] He is the mediator of both creation and re-creation.

The word μεσίτης occurs in the Septuagint, Job 9:33. It denotes the rescuer or helper (umpire, arbitrator) whom Job wished would stand between God and himself. In the New Testament the name is given only to Moses (Gal. 3:19–20) and to Christ (1 Tim. 2:5; Heb. 8:6; 9:15; 12:24) while the verb μεσιτεύειν (to act

---

30. Cf. E. Nestle, "Jesus," in *DC*, I, 860.

31. For the meaning of all these names, cf. B. B. Warfield, *The Lord of Glory* (New York: American Tract Society, 1907).

as go-between, intervene) is once used of God (Heb. 6:17). Denoting someone who takes a position between two parties in order to reconcile them (Deut. 5:5), the word "mediator" is eminently suited to describe the place of Jesus's person and the character of his work. Although the idea is integral to all religions, it is realized only in Jesus Christ. He is not a third party between God and us but is himself the Son of God and at the same time the Son of Man, head of all humanity, Lord of the church. He does not stand between two parties: he *is* those two parties in his own person.

Even within this framework, Reformation theologians debated questions such as whether Christ was the mediator in both natures or only in his human nature (Stancarus). Lutherans and Reformed theologians insisted that Christ was a mediator in both natures, that he had been appointed as such from eternity, and that he had fulfilled the office of mediator already in the days of the Old Testament.[32] For though it is true that Christ became flesh only in the fullness of time, he was chosen and appointed as the mediator from eternity. Because the Son was in the beginning with God and himself God, his election as the mediator did not occur apart from him but bears the character of a "pact of salvation" (*pactum salutis*). Redemption is a joint work of the Father, Son, and Spirit. In the same sense in which the Father was Father of his children from eternity and the Holy Spirit was the comforter of believers from eternity, the Son was appointed the mediator from eternity and began his work immediately after the fall. Already under the Old Testament [dispensation], he was active as prophet, priest, and king.[33] Because, immediately after the fall, the world was handed over to the Son as the mediator for the purpose of atonement and redemption, the royal office stands out in the work of Christ, especially in the Old Testament. The kingship of Christ, however, is very different from that of earthly rulers. Prefigured in the theocratic Davidic kingship, it is a kingship in God's name, subject to God's will, designed to direct all things to God's honor. It is not a kingship of violence and weapons; it rules by Word and Spirit, by grace and truth, by justice and righteousness. This king, accordingly, is at the same time a prophet and priest. His power is designed to be used in the service of truth and righteousness.

For this reason there are those who object to the notion of a kingly office or, in the case of Christ, use the royal title metaphorically.[34] Others rejected the distinction between the three offices or acknowledged only one at the expense of the others. In fact, many deem it better, in the case of Christ, to speak not of office but of a personal calling, for [the idea of] office belongs in a juridical com-

32. J. T. Müller, *Die symbolischen Bücher der evangelisch-lutherischen Kirche*, 8th ed. (Gütersloh: Bertelsmann, 1898), 622, 684; K. Benrath, "Stancarus," *PRE*³, XVIII, 753; Francis Turretin, *Institutes of Elenctic Theology*, trans. George Musgrove Giger and ed. James T. Dennison, 3 vols. (Phillipsburg, NJ: Presbyterian and Reformed, 1992), XIV, qu. 2.

33. Augustine, in H. Reuter, *Augustinische Studien* (Gotha: Perthes, 1887), 93.

34. J. A. L. Wegscheider, *Inst. theol.*, §144; J. H. Scholten, *De Leer der Hervormde Kerk in Hare Grondbeginselen*, 2nd ed., 2 vols. (Leyden: P. Engels, 1850–51), I, 369ff.

munity, whereas Christ's kingdom is a realm of love, not of justice.[35] "Office" is distinct from "calling" in that it involves appointment by a government and that is precisely why "office" is the word that must be used with respect to Christ. For he did not assume the dignity of the mediator himself: God chose, called, and appointed him (Pss. 2:7; 89:19–21; 110:1–4; 132:17; Isa. 42:1; Heb. 5:4–6). The name "Christ" is not a professional name but the name of an office, a title, a dignity Jesus can claim because he has been chosen by God himself. Under the old covenant especially, kings were anointed (Judg. 9:8, 15; 1 Sam. 9:16; 10:1; 16:13; 2 Sam. 2:4; 5:3; 19:10; 1 Kings 1:34, 39; 2 Kings 9:1–3; 11:12; 23:30), probably with holy oil (1 Kings 1:39; Ps. 89:20). "Anointed one" was the title of the theocratic king (Pss. 20:6; 28:8; 84:9; 89:38; etc.). The anointing with oil was a symbol of divine consecration, of being equipped with the Spirit of God (1 Sam. 10:1, 9–10). Thus, Christ was anointed—by the Holy Spirit (Isa. 11:2; 42:1; 61:1; Pss. 2:6; 45:7; 89:20; Luke 4:18; John 3:34; Acts 4:27; 10:38; Heb. 1:9), on the occasion of his conception by the Holy Spirit (Luke 1:35) and at his baptism by John (Matt. 3:16; Mark 1:10; Luke 3:22; John 1:32). It is as the anointed, righteous king, the servant of the Lord, that he begins his public ministry and founds a kingdom of God that, though now it exists only spiritually and morally, is destined one day to manifest itself also externally and bodily in the city of God, from which all the ungodly are banished and in which God will be all in all. Because he is such a king, a king in the true and full sense, his kingship includes the prophetic and priestly offices.

[382] Many theologians, however, object to the threefold office of Christ on the ground that one office cannot be distinguished from the others.[36] It is true that no single activity of Christ can be exclusively restricted to one office, and it is an atomistic approach to detach certain specific activities from the life of Jesus and assign some to his prophetic and others to his priestly or royal office. Christ is the same yesterday, today, and forever; he is himself, in his whole person, prophet, priest, and king. Everything he is, says, and does manifests that threefold dignity. To take just two examples: His miracles are signs of his teaching (John 2:11; 10:37; etc.), but also a revelation of his priestly compassion (Matt. 8:17) and his royal power (Matt. 9:6, 8; 21:23). In his intercessory prayer, not only his high priestly but also his prophetic and royal offices are evidenced (John 17:2, 9–10, 24). Granted, in his activities as our mediator, one or more of the offices may come to the fore: the prophetic office in the days of the Old Testament and his ministry on earth; the priestly office more in his suffering and death; his kingly office more in his state of exaltation. But he actually bears all three offices at the

---

35. A. Ritschl, *The Christian Doctrine of Justification and Reconciliation* (Clifton, NJ: Reference Book Publishers, 1966), III, 425.

36. In the past already among Socinians, Ernesti, Doederlein, and others, and in modern times in A. Ritschl, *Die christliche Lehre von der Rechtfertigung und Versöhnung*, 2nd ed., 3 vols. (Bonn: A. Marcus, 1880–83), I, 520ff.; idem, *Justification and Reconciliation*, III, 408ff.; Theodor Häring, *The Christian Faith*, trans. John Dickie and George Ferries (London: Hodder & Stoughton, 1913), II, 493ff.

same time and consistently exercises all three at once both before and after his incarnation, in both the state of humiliation and that of exaltation. Christ, both as the Son and as the image of God, for himself and also as our mediator and savior, had to bear all three offices. He had to be a prophet to know and to disclose the truth of God; a priest, to devote himself to God and, in our place, to offer himself up to God; a king, to govern and protect us according to God's will. To teach, to reconcile, and to lead; to instruct, to acquire, and to apply salvation; wisdom, righteousness, and redemption; truth, love, and power—all three are essential to the completeness of our salvation. In Christ's God-to-humanity relation, he is a prophet; in his humanity-to-God relation he is a priest; in his headship over all humanity he is a king. While rationalists acknowledge only Christ's prophetic office, mystics only his priestly, millennialists only his royal office, Scripture, consistently and simultaneously attributing all three offices to him, describes him as our chief prophet, our only [high] priest, and our eternal king. He is always all these things in conjunction, never the one without the other: mighty in speech and action as a king and full of grace and truth in his royal rule.

[383–84] In the entirety of his person and work, this Christ is a revelation of God's love. This means, on the one hand, that it is a mistake to regard Christ's work solely as a revelation of God's punitive justice. This would turn God the Father of our Lord Jesus Christ into a pagan deity whose wrath must be averted by sacrifice. Yet it is also a mistake to see Christ's death as solely a demonstration of God's love, at least not love as we frequently conceive it;[37] it is also an act of God's justice. The gnostic and Marcionite disjunction between the Old Testament God of wrath and vengeance and the New Testament God of love and mercy is unknown to Scripture. Yahweh Elohim in the Old Testament, though just, holy, zealous for his honor, and full of ire against sin, is also gracious, merciful, eager to forgive, and abounding in steadfast love (Exod. 20:5–6; 34:6–7; Deut. 4:31; Ps. 86:15; etc.). There is no antithesis between the Father and Christ; the Father is himself the Savior (σωτηρ; Luke 1:47; 1 Tim. 1:1; Titus 3:4–5), the One who in Christ reconciles the world to himself, not counting its trespasses against it (2 Cor. 5:18–19). Christ, therefore, did not first by his work move the Father to love and grace, for the love of the Father is antecedent and comes to manifestation in Christ, who is himself a gift of God's love (John 3:16; Rom. 5:8; 8:32; 1 John

37. P. Schwartzkopff, "Gottes Liebe und Heiligkeit," *Theologische Studien und Kritiken* (1910): 300–313, recognizes that the love of God must be a holy love that reacts against sin and that righteousness, wrath, vengeance, and so on cannot simply be denied to God as anthropomorphisms, for then, and for the same reason, there could be no love in God either. But he tries, further, to combine love and holiness so that the latter is subordinate and serviceable to the former. God is the Father and attempts to lead all his children to salvation. But if these children resist it to the end, God's holy love drives them away and abandons them to ruin. Wrath, judgment, and punishment, accordingly, are the expression and consequence of love. In that way, however, God's righteousness retains only an eschatological character, is dependent in its manifestation on the human will, and no justice is done to the Pauline idea that God, by openly putting Christ forward as an expiation by faith in his blood, revealed his righteousness in that he could justify those who believed in Jesus.

4:9–10). There is no conflict between God's justice and his love. God's justice and wrath are not opposed to grace but in a sense included in it; in the expiatory sacrifice of Christ, by faith, a way was opened to justify the ungodly out of grace; and the grace by which we are justified realized itself in the way of justice and righteousness. "Hidden behind the wrath, as final agent, is love, just as the sun is hidden behind thunder clouds" (Delitzsch).

This leads us to ask: Was Christ's death necessary? Was it arbitrary (Duns Scotus)? The incarnation as well as the satisfaction of Christ's death are not necessary in any absolute sense; they are not a necessity imposed on God from without or from which he cannot except, but they are necessary as actions that are in agreement with his attributes and display them most splendidly to his glory. A number of reasons lead us to this conclusion. First, Scripture teaches that God does all things for his own sake (Prov. 16:4; Rom. 11:36). The final ground and ultimate purpose, also of Christ's incarnation and satisfaction, has to lie in God himself. For his own sake, he sent his Son into the world as an expiation for our sins that his attributes and perfections might thus be manifested. In his omnipotence he knows how to utilize [even] sin as a means of self-glorification. Second, it is the teaching of Scripture that God as the absolutely righteous and holy one hates sin with divine hatred (Gen. 18:25; Exod. 20:5; 23:7; Ps. 5:6–7; Nah. 1:2; Rom. 1:18, 32). Sin cannot exist without eliciting God's hatred and punishment. If God recognized the validity of sin and accorded equal rights to Satan, he would deny himself. Third, God is most certainly the Father of humankind, but it is one-sided and conducive to error if one takes only this name—disregarding others such as Creator, Ruler, Sovereign, Lawgiver, and Judge—to be the full revelation of God. God is not just an aggrieved party who can cancel debts and forgive insults, but is himself the giver, protector, and avenger of the law. He is righteousness in person and as such cannot forgive sin without atonement (Heb. 9.22). God does not need to restore justice or nullify it by grace, but lets both justice and grace come to expression in the cross of Christ. Fourth, the moral law as such is not an arbitrary positive law but law grounded in the nature of God himself. It is therefore unbreakable and inviolable. Christ, accordingly, came not to abolish the law but to fulfill it (Matt. 5:17–18; Rom. 10:4). He upheld its majesty and glory; and faith, accordingly, does not nullify the law but upholds it (Rom. 3:31). Fifth, among the many characteristics of sin portrayed in Scripture, it is a crime against the holy majesty of God and appropriately deserves the judgment of death (Rom. 1:32; 3:19). Finally, sin is so enormous "that God, rather than . . . leave it unpunished, punished it in his beloved Son, Jesus Christ, with the bitter and shameful death on the cross."[38] If righteousness could have been obtained in any other way, Christ would have died to no purpose (Gal. 2:21; 3:21; Heb. 2:10). In sum, Christ's incarnation and satisfaction occurred to the end that God would

---

38. Ed. note: Quoted by Bavinck, without reference, from the Form for Communion used for centuries in Reformed churches.

again be recognized and honored as God by his creatures. In Christ, God again revealed himself, restored his sovereignty, vindicated all his perfections, glorified his name, and maintained his deity.

[385] The belief that Christ's death as an atonement (satisfaction) for sin was necessary has met and continues to meet with fierce resistance. A long-standing position in broader Christian circles sets justice and love, gospel and law, Old Testament and New Testament, over against each other. God, in this view, is only a loving Father, never a judge who punishes sin. The Christian religion has nothing to do with law and satisfaction or justice; it is a spiritual-moral program of salvation. Only the state is the sphere of law and punishment, and this is separated entirely from the gospel of grace. This Marcionite juxtaposition of opposites has always been rejected by Christianity. As we saw in the previous section, it is false to posit a sharp contrast in God between justice and love. If sin does not deserve punishment, there is no grace either. Those who deny justice thereby also deny grace. Nor is it proper to set justice over against religion (conceived as morality). Both are rooted in God's divine right and just claim on his creatures. Service to God in love agrees with God's law and reflects God's own nature. True religion does not seek to abolish law; all religion and morality presuppose a law. God wills that we love him and his law, even apart from sin, as the norm for our lives. To set this aside in the name of love robs the gospel of its core. Then, forgiveness has no objective reality, it is only a subjective realization that sins are not culpable and do not deserve punishment. There is, in fact, no need for forgiveness at all. Sanctification is autonomous self-development. With tragic irony, the burden of self-salvation by doing good returns under the guise of rejecting legalism. Could God voluntarily relinquish the right of satisfaction—at least theoretically? In a sense, this is a minor question, but the more important issue here is to insist that we may not use forgiveness in opposition to satisfaction as though they were mutually exclusive. Scripture not only connects them (Lev. 4:31; Rom. 3:24–26; Heb. 9:22), but in such a way that it is exactly satisfaction that opens the way to forgiveness. Unlike financial debts, where satisfaction cancels the obligation, personal moral debts must be paid by the person. Permitting a substitute in exchange for the guilty person is always an act of grace. Satisfaction is something Christ gives to God, but forgiveness is something God gives to us. For God, Christ's satisfaction opens the way—without violating his rights—to forgive sins out of grace and so to justify the ungodly. This is of enormous consolation to believers when their consciences accuse them; Christ's perfect satisfaction (atonement) is the guarantee of our absolute, irrevocable, and eternal forgiveness.

CHRIST'S OBEDIENT DEATH FOR US

[386] The work Christ accomplished for his own consisted in general in his absolute and total obedience to the will of God (Matt. 3:15; 20:28; 26:42; John 4:34;

5:30; 6:38; Rom. 5:19; Gal. 4:4; Phil. 2:7–8; Heb. 5:8; 10:5–10; etc.). In theology this rich idea has frequently not come into its own. Christ's suffering has often been separated from its act of obedience and made into an object of pious reflection for imitation by martyrs and monks, ascetics, beggars and flagellants. In this way Christ's active obedience becomes ambiguous or, as in the case of Piscator, even denied.[39] Reformed theologians considered Christ's entire life and work, from his conception to his death, as substitutionary in nature, a totally voluntary act of self-denial, an offering presented to the Father as head of the new humanity. It is one single work that the Father assigned to him and that he finished in his death (John 4:34; 17:4; 19:30). Born under the law (Gal. 4:4), in the likeness of sinful flesh (Rom. 8:3), at his incarnation he already emptied himself and assumed the form of a servant; he continually humbled himself and became obedient even to death (Phil. 2:7–8; 2 Cor. 8:9). So it is one single ministry and one obedience, which gives "life-giving justification" (δικαιωσις ζωης) to many (Rom. 5:18–19). It is totally contrary to Scripture, therefore, to restrict the "satisfactory" (atoning) work of Christ to his suffering. The redemption he obtained for us is also complete redemption of the whole person, body and soul. The whole renewal of all things is the fruit of his obedience, though we now experience it only in part, particularly as deliverance from sin's guilt and power. The whole person of Christ, in both his active and his passive obedience, is the complete guarantee for the entire redemption that God in his grace grants to individual persons, to humanity, and to the world.[40]

[387] Whereas in earlier centuries Piscator and many others excluded Christ's active obedience from his mediatorial work, in modern theology his passive obedience is very frequently misjudged or totally denied and opposed. Modern theology tends to reject all notions of satisfying God's righteousness and prefers seeing his life merely as an exemplary instance of holy, moral obedience. His redemptive significance comes from in some way transferring that vocational faithfulness to his followers. Under Hegel's influence, the ancient idea resurfaced that God became human so that we might become his children, which redirected attention to the incarnation itself as the salvific act. For Schleiermacher and others, it was Jesus's highly developed God-consciousness that is the path to our salvation. Others took their position in the *work* of Christ and reframed it in terms of building the kingdom of God on earth through solidarity with human suffering. As the Son of Man he entered into the human fellowship of suffering and death, took on himself its sorrows and diseases, and in his life and death showed what love is and is capable of doing. Some even push this toward a universal atonement, one that covers the sins of the entire human race.

39. See H. Bavinck, *Reformed Dogmatics*, III, 345–47 (#378).
40. On Christ's active obedience, see further: J. Calvin, *Institutes*, II.xvi.5; III.xiv.12; idem, *Commentaries*, on Romans 5:19 and Galatians 4:4; F. Turretin, *Institutes of Elenctic Theology*, XI, 22; A. Ritschl, *Rechtfertigung und Versöhnung*, I, 271ff.; A. A. Hodge, *Atonement*, 248–71; J. Scott Lidgett, *Spiritual Principle of the Atonement*, 139ff.

This variety of views on Christ's death is sometimes justified by the claim that Scripture itself has no one definitive understanding and thus legitimates different theories of the atonement. It is better to acknowledge that while there is indeed a rich variety of images in the New Testament to explain Christ's death and no one single formula suffices, there is a consistent explanation. Theories of the atonement need to be put in their proper perspective. Against those who make too much of them we need to remind ourselves that it is the death of Christ that saves us, not a doctrine or theory about it. The power of the death of Christ is independent of the more or less clear interpretation we can give of it. At the same time, this does not mean that views of the atonement can be treated as so many hypotheses all with an equal right to exist. The question is what in all these ideas agrees with Scripture and what Scripture itself teaches concerning the significance and power of the death of Christ. For this, the general picture is quite clear. Christ Jesus was sent by the Father, entered our existence, took on himself the guilt of our sins, gave his life as the Lamb of God for the sins of the world, as a ransom, and having completed his priestly work continues to intercede for us. Within this frame, Scripture illumines numerous aspects. Like the person, the mediatorial work of Christ is so multifaceted and rich that it cannot be captured in a single word nor summarized in a single formula.

In the Synoptics, Christ appears on the scene as a preacher and founder of the kingdom of God. That kingdom includes within itself the love of the Father, the forgiveness of sins, righteousness, and eternal life; and Jesus, in his capacity as Messiah, ascribes to himself the power to grant all these benefits to his disciples. He gives his life as a ransom for many, breaks his body and sheds his blood to inaugurate and confirm the new covenant with all its blessings (Matt. 20:28; 26:28). In the Acts of the Apostles, the death of Christ is especially presented as an appalling crime inflicted on Christ by lawless men but nevertheless from eternity included in the counsel of God (Acts 2:23; 4:28; 5:30). Raised from the dead and exalted as Lord, he gives repentance and forgiveness of sins (Acts 2:36; 4:12; 5:31). For Paul, the cross was the great offense by which it pleased God to save us and grant us in him wisdom and righteousness, sanctification and redemption, salvation and eternal life (Rom. 3:24; 1 Cor. 1:30; 2 Cor. 5:21; Gal. 3:13). The Letter to the Hebrews describes Christ especially as the perfect and eternal high priest who, perfected through suffering (2:10; 5:9), by his one perfect sacrifice put away the sins of his people (7:27; 9:26; 10:12) and continues as high priest in heaven on our behalf (7:3, 25; 8:1; 9:14; 10:12ff.). Peter pictures Christ's suffering as that of a lamb who bore our sins, redeemed us from our futile way of life, and left us an example to follow in his steps (1 Pet. 1:18f.; 2:21f.). And John makes Christ known to us both as the lamb and the lion, as the life and the light, as the bread and the water of life, as the grain of wheat that, dying, bears fruit, and as the good Shepherd who gives his life for the sheep, as the Savior who gives life to the world, and as the alpha and the omega, the beginning and the end, the first

THE SERVANT SAVIOR: CHRIST'S HUMILIATION

and the last, and so on. These all do not exclude but supplement each other and enrich our knowledge of the work of Christ.

The many diverse theories are thus not untrue as such; only when they become exclusive and particularly when they are used to deny the propitiatory character of Christ's death are they incomplete and in error. Even the mystical and ethical views discussed above legitimately appeal to key scriptural data. Christ, by his incarnation, in his person indeed brought about the union of God and humanity and is, as such, God's representative to us and our representative to God: the Immanuel who as prophet makes God known to us and as priest consecrates himself on our behalf to the Father. He came on earth to fulfill a vocation, to found the kingdom of heaven, to confirm the new covenant in his blood; and in order to do that, he submitted to the will of the Father, became obedient unto death, and pronounced the "Amen" on the righteous judgment that God executed upon death in his suffering and dying. His suffering was not only an atonement for our sins and a ransom for our redemption, but in his death the believing community was crucified with him, and in his resurrection this community itself arose from the grave. Christ was never alone; always he stood in fellowship with the humanity whose nature he had assumed. We must not neglect any of these emphases but unite them into a more unified whole, tracing the unity that underlies them in Scripture.

[388] Still, though the mystical and ethical ideas concerning the death of Christ are not incorrect as such, by themselves they are incomplete and insufficient. The irony here is that they cannot even be maintained if they are not linked with the substitutionary-expiation view of Christ's suffering and death, a view that is systematically removed and opposed by these theories. What is common in modern mystical and ethical views of the death of Christ, in spite of considerable diversity among them, is a transmutation of objective satisfaction into subjective reconciliation and a replacement of the substitutionary-expiatory view of Christ's suffering by a solidaristic-reparatory one. Christ saves us not, so it is said, by taking the guilt of our sin and bearing our punishment but by his holy and exemplary life, which left a permanent influence on the world and created a new religious-moral situation in which people are deterred from sin and attracted by God's love to become better people. Christ did not actually secure these benefits but only created the potential or possibility of our redemption by the spiritual and moral influence he exerts through his powerful example.

It is in this connection that some theologians refuse to speak about an "office" for Christ and speak only of a "vocation" or calling. There is a vast difference between these terms. The latter does not acknowledge the divinely appointed character of Christ's mission and reduces him to a mere human person of great gift or genius who senses a duty to God and humanity. He does not then have a special revelation and unique mission from God himself. This view, however, does not adequately explain the death of Christ or do justice to the biblical givens concerning our Lord's own consciousness of his office. That Jesus was aware of his mission from the beginning, and not only after Peter's confession that he was the Christ (Matt. 16:20ff.), is clear from his baptism by John (esp. in John 1), his application of Isaiah's prophecy to himself (Luke 4:21), the prediction that as the bridegroom he would be taken away from his disciples (Mark 2:20); and, finally, the comparison of himself to Jonah (Matt. 12:40) and to the bronze serpent in the wilderness (John 3:14). According to the apostle Peter at Pentecost, Jesus was handed over to those who killed him "by God's set purpose and foreknowledge" (Acts 2:23). Jesus's death was not an accident; it had to happen. Neither Matthew 26:39, 42 nor Hebrews 5:7 contradict this when they point to Christ's prayer(s) for deliverance. The suffering and death of Christ bear an exceptional character. Though fully aware of God's will and submissive to it, Jesus agonizes over his coming death; he did not go rejoicing to his death but was disturbed, sad, astonished, fearful unto death, and intensely conflicted, so that his sweat became like drops of blood (Matt. 26:37–38; Mark 14:33; Luke 22:44; John 12:27). His cry of dereliction points to an objective and awful forsakenness by God; this was not the death of a sage, stoic, or martyr. "If the life and death of Socrates are those of a sage, the life and death of Jesus are those of a God" (Rousseau). At the same time, seeing the death of Christ as satisfaction for sin, as divine punishment, does not mean that there is a rift in the Godhead between an angry Father and the loving Son he punishes.[41] Through Christ's death, expiation of sins, righteousness, and eternal life are secured for believers. God's grace does not nullify the satisfaction and merit of Christ but is the ultimate ground for that merit. It is the love of God that sent the Son into the world (John 3:16), and on the cross Jesus remained the beloved Son. Mystical and moral theories of the atonement, though they contain elements of scriptural truth, cannot stand detached from this foundation.

[389] The full scriptural teaching concerning the connection between Christ's death and our salvation comes into its own only when his full and complete obedience is viewed as vicarious satisfaction. This is clearly taught in Romans 3:26. One can distinguish in Christ's perfect obedience (Ps. 4:8; Matt. 26:39; Heb. 10:5–7) an active and a passive side. The demand posed by God to fallen humanity was twofold: one, that humans would keep the law perfectly, and two, that they would redress the violation of it by punishment.[42] The benefits Christ obtained for us are twofold: to bear our punishment and to obtain for us the righteousness and life Adam had to secure by his obedience. Christ's obedience returns us not to the beginning but to the end of the road Adam had to walk. Those who believe in him are not condemned and have eternal life (John 3:16, 18), two benefits that are inseparable but still distinguishable (Dan. 9:24; John 3:36; Acts 26:18;

41. Calvin puts it correctly: "Yet we do not suggest that God was ever inimical or angry toward him. How could he be angry toward his beloved Son, 'in whom his heart reposed' [cf. Matt. 3:17]? How could Christ by his intercession appease the Father toward others, if he were himself hateful to God? This is what we are saying: he bore the weight of divine severity, since he was 'stricken and afflicted' [cf. Isa. 53:5] by God's hand, and experienced all the signs of a wrathful and avenging God" (*Institutes*, II.xvi.11).

42. Cf. H. Bavinck, *Reformed Dogmatics*, III, 348–49, 377–80 (##378, 386).

Rom. 5:17–18; Gal. 4:5; Rev. 1:5–6). Christ's active and passive obedience stand side by side. Although distinguishable, concretely they always coincide in the life and death of Christ. His activity was suffering and his suffering an action. It was one single work that Christ accomplished, but one so rich, so valuable in the eyes of God, that the righteousness of God was completely satisfied by it, all the demands of the law were fully met by it, and the whole of (our) eternal salvation was secured by it.

Christ's satisfaction was a vicarious satisfaction, an expiation, a substitutionary atonement. Prefigured in the ram substitute for Isaac in Genesis 22 and ritually performed in the Old Testament cult of transferring the sins of the offerer to the sacrificial animal by the laying on of hands (Lev. 16:21), the portrait of the Suffering Servant of Isaiah 53 provides the most powerful portrait in Scripture of our Lord's mediatorial suffering. The New Testament brings this to light clearly with words such as λυτρον (Matt. 20:28; Mark 10:45; 1 Tim. 2:6), derived from λυειν, "to release," and denoting the means by which someone is released from bonds or prison; hence in general a ransom or sum of money paid to have someone discharged. In the Septuagint it is the translation of גְּאֻלָּה (Lev. 25:51–52) or of פְּדוּיִם (Num. 3:46) or of כֹּפֶר (Exod. 21:30; 30:12; Num. 35:31–32; Prov. 6:35; 13:8), though this last word also has other translations. The word λυτρον (Mark 10:45) is further illumined by all those places in the New Testament where the suffering and death of Christ is presented as a τιμη, a costly price (1 Cor. 6:20; 7:23; 1 Pet. 1:18–19), by which believers have been redeemed or ransomed (ἀντιλυτρον, 1 Tim. 2:6; λυτρουσθαι, Luke 24:21; Titus 2:14; 1 Pet. 1:18; ἀπολυτρωσις, Rom. 3:24; 1 Cor. 1:30; etc.; ἀγοραζεσθαι, 1 Cor. 6:20; 7:23; etc.; or ἐξαγοραζεσθαι, Gal. 3:13; 4:5). The idea here is that humans naturally find themselves in the bondage or slavery of sin and are released from it by the costly ransom of the blood of Christ.

In considering the full teaching of the New Testament, we must also consider the prepositions that connect Christ's sacrifice to us and our sins: ὑπερ, περι, δια, which by themselves mean not "in the place of" but "for the benefit of," "for the sake of," "on account of," "by reason of." Yet they forge such a link between Christ's sacrifice and our sins that the idea of substitution cannot be dispensed with or removed from it. Even the mystical and moral interpretation of Jesus's suffering and death cannot even be maintained if it is not acknowledged beforehand that in a legal sense he suffered and died *in our place*. Now this is what Scripture teaches in the clearest terms when it says that Christ, though personally without sin, has been put forward as an expiation to show God's righteousness (Rom. 3:25), has been made to be sin for us (2 Cor. 5:21), became a curse for us (Gal. 3:13), bore our sins in his body on the tree (1 Pet. 2:24); that God condemned sin in his flesh (Rom. 8:3) and punished him with the accursed death on the cross and that through him we now receive reconciliation and forgiveness, righteousness and life. We can construe the interconnection between all these scriptural pronouncements in no other way than that Christ put himself in our place, has borne the punishment of our sin, satisfied God's justice, and so secured salvation for us.[43]

[390] Serious objections have been raised against the doctrine of vicarious substitution. The Socinians deemed it to be immoral to judge another for sins committed by someone else. They also denied the possibility of God's wrath against a Christ who was without sin. Much of the objection to vicarious substitution arises from serious misunderstanding. This substitution must not be understood in a pantheistic-physical or mystical sense; it bears a legal character. The understanding of Christ's paying for human sin must never be taken in a purely quantitative sense; the sin for which Christ atones is not something that can be weighed and measured, though it was not completely without justification that Aquinas called Christ's passion not only a sufficient "but a superabundant satisfaction for the sins of the human race."[44] Reformers broke with quantification altogether and spoke simply of Christ's death as completely sufficient for the atonement of the sins of the whole world. The Reformation also included the active obedience of Christ in this satisfaction, thus breaking with the Roman pattern of insisting that faith needed to be augmented with good works. The important point to keep in mind here is that vicarious satisfaction is a matter of God's accepting Christ's obedience *on behalf of the whole human race*. The world that fell under the representative head Adam, and under divine curse and judgment, is restored unto favor with God by the death of Christ, the second Adam, who fulfilled all righteousness and bore the punishment of God on our behalf and in our place.

[391] The moral objection that one cannot suffer and die for another is contradicted by the human reality of loving sympathy and "suffering with." The idea of substitution is thus deeply grounded, also morally, in human nature and embodied in priesthood and sacrifices and expressed in various ways in poetry and mythology. The literature of "tragedies," where heroes die and bring atonement or deliverance, points to a great truth: all human greatness walks past abysses of guilt, and satisfaction occurs only when what is noble and great, which for some reason has gone astray, perishes in death. The downfall of Orestes, Oedipus, Antigone, Romeo and Juliet, Max and Thekla, Iphigenia, and others reconciles us with them and their generation. "Pure humanity atones for all human weaknesses" (Goethe). Real history also affords many examples. We live and benefit from the suffering and even death of others. In the saying, "Say nothing of the dead but what is good," we all honor the atoning power of suffering and death. It is particularly in suffering love—sympathy—that substitutionary atoning power is demonstrated. Those who love most suffer most. All human analogies, however, pale in significance before the great love of Christ for us in his obedience and death. Christ took on himself the unimaginable burden of all human sin and guilt under God's punishment.

43. Plantz, "Vicarious Sacrifice," in *DC*, II, 793–800; A. A. Hodge, *Atonement*, 161ff.; H. Martin, *Atonement*, 198ff.; Scott Lidgett, *Spiritual Principle of the Atonement*, 286ff.
44. T. Aquinas, *Summa Theol.*, III, qu. 48, art. 2; cf. Roman Catechism, I/4, qu. 13, 2.

The sacrifice of Christ does not come into its own, however, when we see it *only* as the greatest demonstration of sympathy in human history. As our holy and merciful high priest his sympathy undoubtedly caused him deep and painful suffering (Matt. 8:17; 9:36; 14:14; etc.), but Christ himself considered his suffering a punishment laid on him by God on account of our sins (Matt. 20:28; 26:28; 27:46), and Scripture testifies that he was made to be sin for us and became a curse (2 Cor. 5:21; Gal. 3:13). A realistic-mystical understanding of Christ's substitution—our participation in his death through mystical union—is fully scriptural (Rom. 6–8; Gal. 2:20; Eph. 2:6; Col. 2:11; 3:3; etc.), but not the only and first relation between Christ and his own. In Scripture this relation is built on the federal relation: Romans 6–8 follows Romans 3–5 and loses its foundation when separated from it. The mystical union in the scriptural sense can only be maintained in conjunction with the *objective* atonement of Christ's sacrifice, when Christ is first of all viewed as the head of the covenant, who took the place of his own in a federalistic legal sense. The covenant of grace, in fact, is anterior to the person and sacrifice of Christ. Christ himself is the guarantor and mediator of the new covenant (Heb. 7:22; 8:6; 12:24); his blood is blood of the covenant and therefore atoning (Matt. 26:28). This covenant was not first established in time, but has its foundation in eternity. Vicarious satisfaction has its foundation in the counsel of the Triune God, in the life of supreme, perfect, and eternal love, in the unshakable covenant of redemption. Based on the ordinances of that covenant, Christ takes the place of his own and exchanges their sin for his righteousness, their death for his life. "Oh, the sweet exchange! Oh, the unfathomable accomplishment! Oh, the unexpected benefits!—that the wickedness of the many should be hidden in the One who is just; and that the righteousness of the One should justify the wicked many!"[45]

[392] Christ accomplished this obedience throughout the entire state of his humiliation. In order to link the teaching about Christ's human and divine natures with his humiliation, theologians began to speak of the two states—humiliation and exaltation. These must always be seen together; Christ's whole life was in the service of his office as mediator. The life of Jesus, beginning with the incarnation, begins his suffering, which culminates on the cross. The incarnation itself was already a self-emptying (κενωσις; Phil. 2:7–8; 2 Cor. 8:9; Rom. 8:3; Gal. 4:4; John 1:14), an exchange of the divine mode of existence (μορφη θεου) for the human (μορφη δουλου). The moment this had taken place, his humiliation (ταπεινωσις) began and consisted in being and remaining obedient to God until death served as proof that he was truly human and the offspring of Abraham, that as such he was a member of the community of our sin and had to receive the sign signifying the cutting off of our sin; and at the same time, that God was his God and that he was the Son of God. His circumcision (Luke 2:21), a sign that he was a member of our community of sin, pointed to and was completed in his death

---

45. *Diogn.* 9; cited from *The Faith of the Early Fathers* (Collegeville, MN: Liturgical Press, 1970), 42.

(Col. 2:11–12). His baptism—which he needed for himself no more than he did circumcision (Matt.3:14)—took place because it was fitting for him to fulfill all the righteousness of the mediator, receive the sign and seal of his communion with God, and be anointed with the Holy Spirit. As the second Adam he was tempted by Satan but did not break covenant with God and did the will of his heavenly Father (John 5:19f.; 6:38); showed his priestly mercy to the poor, the sick, and the lost (Matt. 8:17; 11:5); and demonstrated his royal power over Satan, the world, sin, and all their operations (Luke 10:18; John 12:31; 14:30; 16:33; 18:37). The suffering of Christ, which begins with his incarnation and is completed in his "great passion," is the will and command of the Father (Matt. 26:39, 42; John 10:17–18), proof of his absolute obedience (Phil. 2:8; Heb. 5:8), an example to be followed by his disciples (1 Pet. 2:21), a ransom for their sins (Matt. 20:28; 26:28), a victory over the world (John 16:33; Col. 2:15). Tried before Pilate, a legal judge, and declared innocent before the world, he was condemned because he confessed that he was the Son of God and Israel's Messiah (Matt. 26:63; 27:11). In this way the character of his death as a dying for others (Matt. 20:28) would be clearly and incontrovertibly made manifest before the eyes of all. The savage and cruel death satisfied the most rigorous demand of the law and made him accursed before God so that he might remove the curse of the law from us (Deut. 21:23; Gal. 3:13) and completely deliver us from all the evil to which the law condemns us on account of our sins. The cross, therefore, stands at the center of the gospel (1 Cor. 1:23; 2:2; Gal. 6:14). The blood that Christ shed demonstrates that he voluntarily consecrated his life to God,[46] that he gave it as an offering and by it brought about atonement and peace (Matt. 26:27; Acts 20:28; Rom. 3:25; 5:9; Eph. 1:7; Col. 1:20; Heb. 9:12, 22). His burial proved that he really died and reminds us that he spent three days in the state of death bearing sin's punishment (Gen. 3:19).

[393] The creedal statements about his burial and descent into hell have elicited much discussion. Does this refer to a stay in the abode of the dead? This idea surfaced rather early in the Christian church as a comfort to believers concerning those who had already died, including Old Testament saints. The only biblical passage that merits serious attention here is 1 Peter 3:18–22, and its interpretation is difficult and varied. Augustine, and the Reformed tradition later, took it to refer to the pre-incarnate Christ speaking in the Spirit through Noah; another takes a literal view and thinks of Christ leaving the grace, entering hades, and preaching to the spirits of Noah's contemporaries; a third associates "spirits in prison" with fallen angels. There are two seemingly insurmountable problems for those who find in this passage the meaning of the creedal "descent into hell." First, Peter is clearly speaking, not of what Christ did between his death and resurrection, but of what he did either before his incarnation or after having revived his body. Second, the word "hades" gradually changed its meaning. The statement that

---

46. "He died, not on account of weakness, but strength" (Augustine, *On Nature and Grace*, 26).

Christ had descended into hades could emerge only at a time when this word still denoted the "world after death" in general and had not yet acquired the meaning of "hell." The idea that Christ had descended to the place of torment, the actual hell, is nowhere to be found in Scripture, nor does it occur in the most ancient Christian writers. Since the biblical passages adduced as warrant for this view are not very convincing, Reformation theologians, even when they disagreed with Rome, also disagreed among themselves.

The case with this article of the creed, briefly put, is as follows:

1. The phrase "descended into hell," to the extent that it may have been derived from texts such as Acts 2:27; Romans 10:7; Ephesians 4:9, has historically acquired a very different meaning from what is contained in these texts.

2. The Greek (Orthodox) and Roman Catholic explanation of this article, to the effect that Christ went to hades to conduct the devout of the Old Testament from the limbo of the fathers to heaven, lacks all support in Scripture, even in John 8:56; Hebrews 10:20; 11:40; 12:22f.

3. The Lutheran view, according to which Christ went down into hades to make his victory and power known to Satan, even though, as we will see later, it was based on firm pronouncements in Scripture, cannot be considered a correct explanation of the words "descended into hell," since these words do not—scripturally and historically—permit such an explanation and can evidently not describe a step in the state of exaltation but only a step in the state of humiliation.

4. For the same reason the modern idea that Christ descended into hell to preach the gospel to everyone who did not hear it on earth cannot be viewed as a correct explanation of this article of the faith either.

5. First Peter 3:19–22 at most says (though it will be shown later that this is not the correct understanding) that Christ preached the gospel to Noah's contemporaries *after* his resurrection, but there is absolutely no ground in this passage for an expansion of this preaching to all or many of the lost.

6. The exegesis that associates "the spirits in prison" (1 Pet. 3:19) with fallen angels is refuted by the further description and the contrast with the eight souls in verse 20.

7. The article concerning the descent into hell is interpreted most congruently with related expressions in Scripture (Acts 2:27, 31; Rom. 10:7; Eph. 4:9), with the probable origin and sense of the words, and with its place between the other articles, when it is understood as referring to the state of death in which Christ existed between his dying and rising again to bear the punishment of sin to the end and to redeem us from it. "Christ descended into hell so that we would not have to go there."

This interpretation, as has consistently been recognized by all Reformed theologians, is not a contradiction or antithesis, but rather an augmentation and extension of the idea expressed in their explanation of this article by Calvin and the Heidelberg Catechism. For Christ in truth bore unspeakable distress, sorrows, horror, and hellish torment on the cross in order that he might redeem us from them. The state of death in which Christ entered when he died was as essentially a part of his humiliation as his spiritual suffering on the cross. In both together he completed his perfect obedience. He drank the cup of suffering to the last drop and tasted death in all its bitterness in order to completely deliver us from the fear of death and death itself. Thus he destroyed him who had the power of death and by a single offering perfected for all time those who are sanctified (Heb. 10:14).

16

THE EXALTED LORD CHRIST

THROUGH DEATH AND HUMILIATION TO LIFE AND EXALTATION

[395] For Christ, his death was the end of his humiliation and, at the same time, the road to his exaltation. In all religions, and for Israel too, death is seen as the road to life. The mythology of pagan religions with its deification of the annual cycle of nature, however, offers no real hope of life, only a general sense of alternation between death and life in endless struggle. All that is provided is some vague sense that struggle and suffering are often the prelude to victory and freedom, and the human soul can gain independence by self-denial and abstinence. At the time Christianity made its appearance, the nature religions of Greece and Rome had been influenced by Eastern mystery religions and transformed into mystical religions of release from the natural world. The natural vegetative processes of life were given a spiritual and moral interpretation; liberation was sought from the visible, corrupt, and polluted world into a purified, invisible world of the spirit. Superstition and magic joined knowledge (γνωσις)[1] and frequently led to excesses of asceticism, on the one hand, and libertinism, on the other.

We enter a very different world when in antiquity we turn to Israel. We also encounter here, from the outset (Gen. 3:14ff.), suffering, conflict, and the idea that death is the road to life. The history of the whole human race, confirmed in bold relief in the history of God's people, is a constant struggle between sin and righteousness, darkness and light, death and life, between the things that are above

---

1. Ed. note: The specific reference to γνωσις here is from the editor, not Bavinck.

and the things that are below. In the midst of this history of suffering, oppression, and death, Israel's hope, based on prophetic promise, came to rest on the Suffering Servant of the Lord (Isa. 53:10f.), the Old Testament figure with whom Jesus was already identified at the beginning of his ministry (Luke 4:16ff.). In his teaching, he said that the blessedness of the kingdom of heaven was for the poor in spirit, the pure of heart, the meek, and so on (Matt. 5:3–12), and that one entered it by suffering, self-denial, cross-bearing, abandoning all for his sake (Matt. 10:37–38; 16:24). The law of the kingdom is that we are saved by losing ourselves (Matt. 10:39; 16:25; 19:29). Jesus himself lived by that law and for that reason calls his followers to do so (Matt. 10:24). However, this self-denial must not be equated with self-torture, self-destruction, the stupefaction of one's consciousness, or the extinction of one's personality, but is exactly the way to save oneself, to share in eternal life, and to regain all that was left behind.

This close connection between humiliation and exaltation is made even clearer in the Gospel of John than in the Synoptics. The Word became flesh, yet in his servant form he still manifested the glory he shared with the Father (1:14; 2:11; 11:4, 40), even and especially in his suffering and death (12:23; 13:31). Unless the grain of wheat falls into the earth and dies it cannot bear fruit (12:24). His exaltation, thus, begins not at his resurrection and ascension but already at his crucifixion (3:14; 8:28; 12:32). Lifted up on the cross by human hands (8:28), it is Jesus who by that event elevates himself above the earth and draws people to himself (12:32). Cross and crown, death and resurrection, humiliation and exaltation lie on the same line. As Jesus put it after his resurrection: It was *necessary* that the Christ should suffer these things and so enter his glory (Luke 24:26).

The sum and substance of the original gospel, therefore, was the Christ who died and rose again. The offense of the cross—also for the disciples (Matt. 26:31)—was removed by the resurrection. Then they perceived that Jesus had to die and did die in accordance with the counsel of the Father (Acts 2:23; 3:18; 4:28), and that by his resurrection God had made him Lord and Christ (Acts 2:36), in order by him to give repentance, forgiveness of sins, the Holy Spirit, and eternal life (Acts 2:38; 3:19; 5:31; 10:43; 1 Pet. 1:3ff., 21). Now taken up into heaven, he remains there until he comes again for judgment (Acts 1:11; 3:21), for he is the one ordained by God to be judge of the living and the dead (Acts 10:42; 17:31), and then all things will be restored of which God spoke by the mouth of his holy prophets of old (Acts 3:21). Similarly, Paul teaches that precisely because of his deep humiliation, God highly exalted him, giving him the name that is above every other name, that is, the name "Lord" (1 Cor. 12:3; Phil. 2:11), granting him dominion over the living and the dead (Rom. 14:9), and subjecting all things under his feet (1 Cor. 15:25, 27). As such he is the Lord of glory (1 Cor. 2:8), seated at God's right hand (Rom. 8:34; 1 Cor. 2:8), in whom the fullness of the deity dwells bodily (Col. 1:19; 2:9), who is the head of the church, prays for it, and fills it with all the fullness of God (Rom. 8:34; Eph. 1:23; 3:19; 4:16). Hebrews adds to this profile the unique idea that Christ, the Son, who with the Father was the Creator of all things, was also appointed "the heir of all things" (Heb. 1:2; 2:8) by the Father and designated eternal high priest (5:6; 7:17). For a while he became lower than the angels (2:7, 9), assumed our flesh and blood (2:14), became like us in all respects except sin (2:17; 4:15), and learned obedience from the things he suffered (5:8). But thereby he also sanctified, that is, perfected himself (2:10; 5:9; 7:28), and was designated by God a high priest according to the order of Melchizedek (5:10), a high priest who is seated at the right hand of the throne of the Majesty in heaven (1:13; 8:1; 10:12). The Apocalypse, finally, loves to picture Christ as the Lamb who purchased us and washed us by his blood (5:9; 7:14), but also as the firstborn of the dead, the ruler of the kings of the earth (1:5), the King of kings and the Lord of lords, who with the Father sits on the throne, has power and honor and glory, even the keys of hades and death (1:18; 3:21; 5:12–13; 19:16). Clothed with such power, he rules and protects his church (2:1, 18; etc.) and will one day triumph over all his enemies (19:12f.).

[396] All this is neatly summarized in Philippians 2:6–11, which teaches that because Jesus humbled himself unto death, God has exalted him and given him a name above all names. This passage is as foundational as any for the doctrine of the two states of humiliation and exaltation, but the rest of Scripture affirms the same. In the Old Testament, we encounter traces of it in the figure of the Servant of the Lord, and the whole of the New Testament, not only Philippians 2, teaches the humiliated and exalted, crucified and resurrected Christ as the core of the gospel. The resurrection decisively uncovered the meaning of Jesus's suffering and death for the disciples, so that they looked back on his earthly life from the vantage point of belief in his exaltation. Paul, for example, testifies to Jesus's Davidic origin, his birth from the fathers, his perfect obedience, his institution of the Lord's Supper, his suffering and death on the cross (Rom. 1:3; 9:5; Phil. 2:8; 1 Cor. 11:23; etc.), but the direct object of his and the church's faith was the exalted and glorified Christ, who, however, is the same as the one who descended. Although it does not explicitly speak of two states, the Apostles' Creed nonetheless does sketch the order in which Christians of all ages have understood the facts of redemptive history and confessed their faith: Christ Jesus is the only begotten Son of God, who was conceived by the Holy Spirit, born of the Virgin Mary, crucified, died, and was buried; the third day he arose from the dead, ascended to heaven, is seated at the right hand of God, whence he will come to judge the living and the dead.

The history of the church, however, is filled with dogmatic disputes about the person and the work of Christ. Drawing a sharp distinction between the historical Jesus and the heavenly Christ who had existed from eternity and revealed himself only for a short while in a phantom body, gnostics denied Christ's real suffering and had no room in their system for either Christ's humiliation or his exaltation.[2] Others also had difficulties with Christ's full humanity and by implication shifted

2. Isaak August Dorner, *History of the Development of the Doctrine of the Person of Christ*, trans. William Lindsay Alexander, 5 vols. (Edinburgh: T&T Clark, 1863–78), III, 310ff.

the incarnation into eternity and volatized the historical appearance of Christ as a symbol of an eternal idea. But the theologians who took their position in the Chalcedonian confession also faced serious difficulties. On the one hand the intimate union of Christ's human nature with the Logos meant that it had to be conceived of as endowed with various extraordinary gifts and powers and seen with highest dignity and honor. At the same time, in order to save fallen humanity, that same human nature had to be conceived as being so weak and lowly that it not only remained purely human but could even suffer and die. Maintaining both the historical reality of incarnation and humiliation and the glory of the exalted Christ as the God-man has proved difficult for theology.

[397] The two successive states, humiliation and exaltation, were sometimes too closely linked with the two-natures doctrine—human and divine—thus creating confusion. This is particularly true in the case of Lutheran Christology. For whereas the Scholastics spoke only of a communication of extraordinary divine gifts to the human nature of Christ, the Lutherans, as a result of their doctrine of the Lord's Supper, arrived at the confession that certain divine attributes were given to the human nature. Furthermore, since the God-man then put these attributes aside in respect to their use or at least to their public use, he nevertheless kept them. Thus, among the Lutherans, the state of exaltation cannot be anything other than a resumption of the use or the public use of the divine attributes laid aside earlier. Hence at his exaltation, Christ received nothing he did not have already; strictly speaking, nothing new is communicated to Christ in the state of exaltation that was not his from the time of conception.[3] Furthermore, since from the moment of vivification the human nature of Christ, by its union with the Logos, was immediately omnipotent, omniscient, and omnipresent, there is no real succession in the degrees of exaltation. To complete the picture, in radical Anabaptism and Socinianism, a dualism between eternity and time makes both incarnation and exaltation impossible, reducing them to ideas. The resurrection and ascension, the seat at the right hand of God, and the coming again for judgment are not facts but merely graphic representations of the idea that the moral ideal that Christ pursued corresponds to the will of God and will be realized by him.[4]

[398–99] The Reformed view is that Christ is the mediator in accordance with both natures. The office and work of the mediator could only be accomplished by one who was both true God and true man. The divine and human participate in both states in the one person. Difficult questions remained, however, such as the issue of kenosis: Did the Son of God set aside his divine attributes in the incarnation? Reformed theology rejected the Lutheran logical distinction between

3. "In his exaltation Christ was not given a new power, virtue, or majesty, which he did not have before, but only the full faculty of administering his kingdom, which he received through that union itself" (J. A. Quenstedt, *Theologia didactico-polemica sive systema theologicum* [1685], III, 368).

4. F. Schleiermacher, *The Christian Faith* (Edinburgh: T&T Clark, 1989), §§99, 105; A. Schweizer, *Christliche Glaubenslehre* (Leipzig: S. Hirzel, 1863–72), §123; D. F. Strauss, *Die christliche Glaubenslehre*, 2 vols. (Tübingen: C. F. Osiander, 1840–41), §§63–66.

incarnation (the assumption of flesh) and exinanition (the conception in the womb) along with the communication of divine attributes to the human nature. This led to the Lutheran debate between those who argued that Christ laid aside the *use* of these attributes during his earthly life, either by concealment [κρυψις], according to the Tübingen position, or by self-emptying [κενωσις], according to the Giessen position.[5] Reformed theologians always construed the human nature of Christ as weak, susceptible to suffering and death, like us in every respect barring sin, and not glorified until the resurrection. In this way they honored a purely human and genuine development in Jesus, as Luke 2:40, 52 indisputably teaches. Treating the kenosis question with great caution—not for a moment wanting to grant that the κενωσις (self-emptying) consisted in putting aside some or all of the divine attributes—Reformed theologians claimed that Christ had voluntarily from all eternity taken on the form of a servant and in his incarnation laid aside or concealed the divine glory of his divinity and never used it during his humiliation to defeat his enemies or please himself. He fought and won the battle with his self-denying sacrificial love, culminating in death on the cross. His exaltation is thus a real change, a state gained as a reward of his obedience. The preposition διο ("therefore") in Philippians 2 as well as the Letter to the Hebrews points to Christ earning his exaltation through obedience. This is consistent with the overall teaching of Scripture that Christ could only attain his exaltation by way of his humiliation (Isa. 53:10–12; Matt. 23:12; Luke 24:26; John 10:17; 17:4–5; Phil. 2:9; Heb. 1:3; 2:9–10; 5:7–10; 10:12; 12:2).

What Christ "earned" by his humiliation was not participation in divinity nor his office as prophet, priest, and king. Scripture states repeatedly that in the beginning he was with God and himself God (John 1:1ff.; 17:5; Rom. 8:3; 2 Cor. 8:9; Gal. 4:4; Col. 2:9; Heb. 1:3; etc.), and that from eternity he had been anointed prophet, priest, and king by the Father and was active as such already in the days of the Old Testament and further again during his sojourn on earth (2 Tim. 1:9; Titus 3:4; Heb. 13:8; 1 Pet. 1:11, 20). By his birth Christ became the offspring of David (Rom. 9:5), assumed "the likeness of sinful flesh" (Rom. 8:3), became weak (2 Cor. 13:4); but by the resurrection he was openly designated Son of God (Rom. 1:4; cf. Acts 17:31). Whereas at his incarnation he exchanged "the form of God" (μορφη θεου; Phil. 2:6) for the "form of a servant" (μορφη δουλου; Phil. 2:7), at the resurrection he received the glory that according to his Godhead he already had before (John 17:2, 24), became the Lord of glory (1 Cor. 2:8), the power of God (1 Cor. 1:24), obtained a name above every name, that is, the name of "Lord" (κυριος; John 20:28; Acts 2:36; 1 Cor. 12:3; Phil. 2:9–10). He thereby received the κυριοτης, the authority and power to exercise lordship over all creatures as mediator, prophet, priest, and king, to subdue his enemies, to gather his people, and to regain the fallen creation of God (Pss. 2; 7; 110; Matt.

5. Cf. H. Bavinck, *Reformed Dogmatics*, ed. John Bolt (Grand Rapids: Baker Academic, 2003–8), III, 257–58 (#357).

28:18; 1 Cor. 15:21ff.; Eph. 1:20–23; Phil. 2:9–11; Heb. 1:3f.; 1 Pet. 3:22; Rev. 1:5; etc.). In the resurrection God openly appointed him Son of God, Lord, King, and Mediator, saying to him: "You are my Son; today I have begotten you" (Acts 2:33, 36; 3:15; 5:31; 13:33; 17:31; Heb. 1:5).

Because the Socinians were prepared to grant royal dignity and the rank of deity only in Christ's state of exaltation, many theologians understandably objected to speaking of merit in reference to Christ. We must be clear: The state of exaltation refers not to the person of Christ and his nature(s) but to the glory of his mediatorial work. By his resurrection and ascension, Christ enters a new state; as the mediator he is now at the right hand of glory. Although he was truly God in his state of humiliation, the glory was hidden. In the state of exaltation, the divine glory radiates outward for all to see, and all who see must confess Jesus as Lord to the glory of God the Father. He who was made alive by the Spirit of God (1 Pet. 3:18) is now himself the life-giving Spirit (πνευμα ζωοποιουν; 1 Cor. 15:45). He whose own body was transformed from a σωμα ψυχικον into a σωμα πνευματικον now has the power to transform our bodies in a similar manner. That is why Paul can say, "The Lord is the Spirit" (2 Cor. 3:17). He is not here describing Christ's substantial being but underscoring his argument that Christians are free from the law, for where the Spirit of the Lord is, there is freedom. Christ, in whom all the "fullness of deity dwells bodily" (Col. 2:9; 1:19), is the visible image of the invisible God (Col. 1:15). The divine glory is now manifest in his human nature and radiates from his face (2 Cor. 3:18; 4:4, 6).

THE STEPS OF CHRIST'S EXALTATION: RESURRECTION, ASCENSION, SESSION, AND RETURN

[400] If, in keeping with the Reformed confession, the descent into hell belongs to the state of humiliation, we may distinguish in the exaltation four so-called steps: the resurrection, the ascension, the seating at God's right hand, and the return for judgment. Resurrection is the first step in Christ's exaltation. Raised by the power of God, he is the firstborn of all creation, the one who has the keys of death and hades, the one who has power to give eternal life. The historical reality of the resurrection is clearly attested by Jesus's appearances and the apostolic witness to them. Jesus foretold his own resurrection (Matt. 16:21; 20:19) and said that he would raise up the temple of his body in three days (John 2:19–21), that he had power to lay down his life and to take it up again (John 10:18), and that he himself was the resurrection and the life (John 11:25). He truly is "the first to rise from the dead" (Acts 26:23), "the firstfruits of those who have fallen asleep" (1 Cor. 15:20), "the firstborn from the dead" (Col. 1:18; Rev. 1:5), the firstborn among many brethren (Rom. 8:29). In the counsel of God, it was not possible for Christ to be held by death, and therefore God raised him up, having freed him from the pangs of death (Acts 2:24). Death, as it were, ensnared Christ with

its pangs (ὠδῖνες, following the Septuagint translation of the Hebrew "bands" or "cords"; Ps. 18:5), but those pangs were the labor pains of the resurrection, which would be undone by God in the moment of resurrection. He can never die again because death no longer has dominion over him (Rom. 6:9, 10). He died, but now he lives forevermore and has the keys of death and hades (Rev. 1:18). His resurrection was a birth from death and hence a victory over death and over him who had the power of death, the devil (1 Cor. 15:21f.; Heb. 2:14; 2 Tim. 1:10).

From the beginning, the resurrection of Christ was an enormously important constituent of the faith of the church: without that faith it would never have started. All the disciples had been offended by the cross; when Jesus was taken prisoner and killed, they had fled (Mark 14:50) and gone into hiding. But their faith revived when they learned that Jesus had risen; they were now able to reconsider his whole life in the light of the resurrection. They now understood how he had been anointed with the Holy Spirit and power (Acts 4:27; 10:38), how his works and wonders bore witness to his messiahship (Acts 2:22; 10:38), how he had to die according to God's counsel (Acts 2:23; 4:28), and how by his resurrection Jesus had been appointed Lord and Christ, Leader and Judge (Acts 2:20, 25, 36; 3:15; 4:26; 5:31; 10:42; cf. 1 Cor. 15:3–4). Belief in the resurrection belonged to the confession of the very earliest church; an important mark of the apostolic office was to have been a witness of Jesus's resurrection (Luke 24:48; Acts 1:22; 2:32; 3:15; etc.). The appearances of Jesus to his disciples after his resurrection were the crucial foundation for this faith. Certainty about the resurrection rested on appearances that the disciples/apostles themselves had received or the testimony of others in whom they had complete trust (Luke 24:34; 1 Cor. 15:5ff.). These appearances probably took place in Jerusalem because the disciples refused to believe the report of the women (Luke 24:11, 24–25; Mark 16:11, 13–14) and in this state of mind were certainly not inclined to go to Galilee with the expectation of seeing him there. But then followed the appearances in Galilee, with Jesus going there before his disciples (Matt. 28:16ff.; Mark 16:7; John 21), though Luke makes no reference to the Galilean appearances and records Jesus's instruction to his disciples to wait in Jerusalem until they were clothed from on high (Luke 24:19; Acts 1:4); it was in the vicinity of Jerusalem that the resurrection took place.

According to the unanimous witness of all concerned, the resurrection occurred on the third day. The formula "the third day" (Matt. 16:21; 20:19; etc.) alternates with "after three days" (Mark 8:31; 10:34; etc.) without implying any difference in duration (Gen. 42:17–18). But the expression "three days and three nights" (Matt. 12:40; 16:4) has to be understood figuratively and was chosen in these texts on account of the comparison with Jonah or as a general description of a very short period. How the disciples came unanimously to put the resurrection on the third day if it did not really take place is hard to say. Merely attributing this to Old Testament predictions or to mythology fails the test of plausibility. Something must have happened on that third day for the disciples to situate it unanimously on that day. Add to this the difficulty of explaining the empty tomb if

Christ did not actually arise with the same body he left behind in death. Although the empty tomb is not itself proof or a ground for belief in the resurrection, it is nevertheless of great significance. For some time people attempted to "explain" the resurrection by assuming that Jesus only *appeared* to be dead (rationalists, Schleiermacher) or by having Jesus's body stolen. When these failed to convince, they were abandoned and replaced with theories of *subjective* visions on the part of the disciples. The problem with this is that such a subjective vision *presupposes* faith rather than produces it, and the disciples' state of mind was far from believing: they were despondent, dejected, in great doubt, and initially unwilling to believe the report of the resurrection. Visions, furthermore, are often accompanied by psychological abnormalities that taint their credibility; the New Testament provides no evidence of such among the apostles. Furthermore, the appearances of which the New Testament speaks are all specific—place, time, person—and form a series that begins on the third day and ends with the appearance to Paul and must, therefore—as opposed to possible visions—have had a distinct and identifiable character. All spiritualizing and subjectivizing interpretations of the resurrection must, therefore, be rejected. Only the bodily resurrection can explain the empty tomb and the firm faith of the disciples; nothing else does justice to the biblical witness. It should be noted that a visionary explanation of the appearances as a "telegram from heaven"[6] is no less miraculous than the straightforward account of the bodily resurrection, but it does add elements of deceit and trickery to the apostolic message of the gospel. The bodily resurrection, after three days, is proof of Christ's divine sonship (Acts 13:33; Rom. 1:3), his messiahship (Acts 2:36; 3:13–15; 5:31; 10:42; etc.), the Father's endorsement of his work as mediator (Acts 2:23–24; 4:11; 5:31; Rom. 6:4, 10; etc.), the inauguration of the exaltation he accomplished by his suffering (Luke 24:26; Acts 2:33; Rom. 6:4; Phil. 2:9; etc.), the guarantee of our forgiveness and justification (Acts 5:31; Rom. 4:25), the gift of the Spirit (Acts 2:33), eternal life (Rom. 6:4f.), the ground and pledge of our salvation (Acts 4:2; Rom. 8:11; 1 Cor. 6:14; etc.), and the foundation of apostolic Christianity (1 Cor. 15:12ff.).

[401] After the important period of forty days (Acts 1:3) when Jesus instructed his disciples, he ascended into heaven and was exalted at the Father's right hand. These forty days constitute a very peculiar period in the life of Jesus. On the one hand, he is bodily the same: he shows his hands and his side (John 20:20; cf. Matt. 28:9; Luke 24:39); he is touched (John 20:27), eats food (Luke 24:43; John 21:12f.), and is taken up visibly (Acts 1:9), the same way he will return

---

6. C. H. Weisse, *Die evangelische Geschichte*, 2 vols. (Leipzig: Breitkopf & Hartel, 1838), II, 432; T. Keim, *Geschichte Jesu von Nazara in ihrer Verkettung mit dem Gesamtleben seines Volkes*, 3 vols. (Zürich: Orelli, Füssli, 1867–72), III, 605; A. Schweizer, *Christliche Glaubenslehre*, II, 216ff.; H. Lotze, *Microcosmus*, trans. Elizabeth Hamilton and E. E. Constance Jones (New York: Scribner & Welford, 1866), III, 365ff.; Adolf von Harnack, *What Is Christianity?* trans. Thomas Bailey Saunders (New York: Harper, 1957), 124ff.; Kirsopp Lake, *The Historical Evidence for the Resurrection of Jesus Christ* (London and New York: Williams & Norgate, 1907), 265–79.

(Acts 1:11; Rev. 1:7). At the same time he may not be touched (John 20:17), is not recognized (Luke 24:16; John 20:14), appears and disappears in a mysterious manner (Luke 24:36; John 20:19), and startles the disciples at his coming (Luke 24:37; John 21:12). It is the same Jesus but now appearing in another form (Mark 16:12) with a body (σωμα) that has been sown in dishonor and weakness but raised in glory and power, and changed into a spiritual body (σωμα πνευματικος; 1 Cor. 15:42ff.; 2 Cor. 13:4; Phil. 3:21). By the resurrection he has become a life-giving spirit (πνευμα ζωοποιουν; 1 Cor. 15:45; 2 Cor. 3:17). The forty days are a period of transition, for Jesus and for his disciples. Jesus is still on earth, appears from time to time to his disciples, but things are not the same as they were before; Jesus is not the same as he was before; he is leaving his disciples and moving in the direction of his Father's home (John 20:17; cf. 14:2–4; 16:5–10; 17:13). The disciples are being prepared for a new relationship with the exalted Christ, a communion in the Holy Spirit. Jesus would remain with them and work with them and through them, but in another mode and different form (μορφη). For that time they are instructed during the forty days by Jesus himself (Acts 1:3; 10:40–42; 13:31). Only then did they for the first time understand the words he had spoken to them earlier, words about the necessity and significance of his suffering (Luke 24:26–27), the explanation of the prophecies of the Old Testament in light of their fulfillment (Luke 24:27; 44–46), the glory and power to which he was now being raised (Matt. 28:18).

On the fortieth day, after Jesus had thus instructed and equipped his disciples, he ascended to heaven. The event is recorded only in the Gospel of Luke (24:50–51) though the New Testament makes much of its significance. Jesus himself predicted it (Matt. 26:64) and repeatedly alluded to it (John 6:62; 13:3, 33; 14:28; 16:5, 10, 17, 28; 17:24). Peter, in his public ministry in Jerusalem, mentions it over and over (Acts 2:33–34; 3:21; 5:31; cf. 1 Pet. 3:21). Paul refers to it repeatedly (Acts 13:30–37; Eph. 4:8–10; Phil. 1:23; 2:9; 3:20; Col. 3:1; 1 Thess. 1:10; 4:14–16; 1 Tim. 3:16), as does the Letter to the Hebrews (2:9; 4:14; 6:19–20; 7:26; 9:24; 10:12–13; 12:2) and John's Revelation (1:13; 5:6; 14:14; 19:11–16; 22:1). The ascension was a constituent of the faith of the church from the beginning, as much as the resurrection. Its meaning consists in the fact that Jesus Christ has been exalted by the Father and received in heaven until the time of the restitution of all things (Acts 3:21). While the ascension must be considered in close connection with the resurrection, it is a mistake to equate the two; that would be to deny the scriptural teaching about the appearances. The ascension is the entry into the state of glory that Christ obtains in heaven that is described with the term "sitting at the right hand of God" (Rom. 8:34; Eph. 1:20; Col. 3:1; Heb. 1:3, 13; 8:1; 10:12; 12:2; 1 Pet. 3:22; Rev. 3:21). The session is closely linked with the resurrection and ascension but is distinct from both events (Acts 2:32–34; 1 Pet. 3:21–22; Rom. 8:34). This seat at the right hand of God had already been predicted by Christ (Matt. 19:28; 22:44; 25:31; 26:64), and after the resurrection and ascension had taken place, the disciples immediately knew that he was seated at the right hand of God (Acts 2:34; 7:56). Caution must be observed when speaking specifically about the "place" of God's right hand. We must never forget that we are expressing ourselves here, not incorrectly, but still in a human manner and in imagery (1 Kings 2:19; Pss. 45:9; 110:1; Matt. 20:21). The Christian church thus refrains from any further specification of the place of Christ's exaltation. What is clearly meant by the phrase is that Christ has been exalted to the highest power, dignity, and honor conceivable and possible under that of God himself; he received a dignity that prompts every knee in heaven, on earth, and under the earth to bow itself and every tongue to confess that he is Lord to the glory of God the Father. He must reign as king "until he has put all his enemies under his feet" (1 Cor. 15:25; Heb. 2:8–9). This is great comfort to believers: our Priest-King pleads on our behalf and is coming to judge the living and the dead at the time of his great and final exaltation.

RECONCILIATION (ATONEMENT)

[402] As our mediator, Christ has obtained the full benefits of our whole salvation, beginning with an objective atonement for our sin, reconciliation (καταλλαγη). According to Scripture, Christ's sacrifice has objective significance, also valid to God. In the Old Testament, the sacrifices were intended to cover the sins of the offerer before the face of God (כפר, LXX ἐξιλασκεσθαι). Atonement takes place in relation to God and occurs before his face (Lev. 1:3; 6:7; 10:17; 15:15, 30; 19:22; Num. 15:28; 31:50); it aims, by covering the sin, to avert his wrath (Num. 8:19; 16:46) and to propitiate him (ἱλασκεσθαι). Similarly, in the New Testament, Christ is an expiation (ἱλαστηριον; Rom. 3:25), the atonement for our sins (ἱλασμος; 1 John 2:2; 4:10), a merciful and faithful high priest in the service of God "to make atonement for the sins of the people" (Heb. 2:17). Reconciliation, therefore, is not unilateral but bilateral: not only must we be reconciled with God, but God, too, must be reconciled with us in the sense that, by giving Christ as expiation (ἱλασμος; Rom. 3:25; Heb. 2:17; 1 John 2:2; 4:10), he puts aside his wrath and establishes a relation of peace between himself and us (Rom. 5:9–10; 2 Cor. 5:18–19; Gal. 3:13). Refusals to acknowledge propitiation as the heart of his death and resurrection result from a misunderstanding of God's love. For the wrath of God is no evil passion or malice, and his righteousness is not thirst for vengeance. On account of our sins, we are indeed objects of God's wrath, writes Calvin, "but because the Lord wills not to lose what is his in us, out of his own kindness he still finds something to love."[7] Thus, God's wrath and his righteousness are consistent with the highest love since it is his love that provides Christ as the means of propitiation. It is God himself who brings about reconciliation in Christ

---

7. John Calvin, *Institutes of the Christian Religion*, II.xvi.3 (ed. John T. McNeill and trans. Ford Lewis Battles [1559; Philadelphia: Westminster, 1960], 1:505–6).

(2 Cor. 5:19). "Already loving us he reconciled us to himself. Because he first loved us he afterward reconciled us to himself."[8] By Christ's sacrifice a new relation of reconciliation and peace has been accomplished between God and humanity. The benefit of this work of Christ is unrestricted; it covers every dimension of experience; it extends to all creation. Καταλλαγη, accordingly, is the reconciliation effected by expiation and propitiation. This καταλλαγη is the content of the gospel: everything is done, God is reconciled. On our part there is nothing left to do, and the entire ministry of reconciliation consists in an invitation to people: Be reconciled to God! Believe the gospel (Rom. 5:9–10; 2 Cor. 5:18–21; cf. Eph. 2:16; Col. 1:20–22).

The grace of God and the free gift through grace are superabundant (Rom. 5:15), and the benefits that accrue to us too numerous to mention. A summary list follows:

The *juridical*, that is, forgiveness (Mark 14:24; Heb. 9:22); justification (Rom. 3:24; 4:25; 5:9; 8:34; 1 Cor. 1:30; 2 Cor. 5:21); adoption (Gal. 3:26; 4:5–6); heavenly inheritance (Rom. 8:17; 1 Pet. 1:4); redemption (ἀπολυτρωσις;[9] Eph. 1:7; Col. 1:14; Heb. 9:15);[10]

The *mystical*, consisting in being crucified, buried, raised, and seated with Christ in heaven (Rom. 6–8; Gal. 2:20; Col. 3:1–13);

The *ethical*, that is, regeneration (John 1:12–13), being made alive (Eph. 2:1, 5); sanctification (1 Cor. 1:30; 6:11); being washed (1 Cor. 6:11), cleansed (1 John 1:9), and sprinkled (1 Pet. 1:2) in body, soul, and spirit (2 Cor. 5:17; 1 Thess. 5:23);

The *moral*, consisting in the imitation of Christ, who has left us his example (Matt. 10:38; 16:24; Luke 9:23; John 8:12; 12:26; 2 Cor. 8:9; Phil. 2:5; Eph. 2:10; 1 Pet. 2:21; 4:1);

The *economic*, that is, the fulfillment of the Old Testament covenant and inauguration of the new (Mark 14:24; Heb. 7:22; 9:15; 12:24), freedom from the law (Rom. 7:1ff.; Gal. 2:19; 3:13, 25; 4:5; 5:1; etc.), cancellation of

8. Augustine, *The Trinity*, V, 16; idem, *Enchiridion*, 33; T. Aquinas, *Summa Theol.*, III, qu. 49, art. 4; J. Calvin, *Institutes*, II.xvi.2–4; F. Turretin, "De satisf.," in *Institutes of Elenctic Theology*, trans. George Musgrove Giger and ed. James T. Dennison, 3 vols. (Phillipsburg, NJ: Presbyterian and Reformed, 1992), 49, 86, 87; W. G. T. Shedd, *Dogmatic Theology*, 3rd ed., 3 vols. (New York: Scribner, 1891–94), II, 401; A. A. Hodge, *The Atonement* (Philadelphia: Presbyterian Board of Publication, 1867), chap. 9; J. Scott Lidgett, *The Spiritual Principle of the Atonement as a Satisfaction Made to God for the Sins of the World*, 2nd ed. (London: Charles H. Kelley, 1898), chap. 5.

9. The ἀπολυτρωσις of believers by Christ is strikingly illustrated by the then-current custom of ransoming or buying of slaves: G. A. Deissmann, *Licht vom Osten* (Tübingen: Mohr, 1908), 234ff.; E. Schürer, *Geschichte des judischen Volkes im Zeitalter Jesu Christi*, 4th ed., 3 vols. (Leipzig: J. C. Hinrichs, 1901–9), III, 18, 53.

10. Ἀπολυτρωσις sometimes has a broader meaning as well (Rom. 3:24; 8:21, 23; 1 Cor. 1:30; Eph. 1:14; 4:30; 1 Pet. 1:18–19).

the bond with its legal demands, the breaking down of the dividing wall, and reconciliation of Jew and gentile and all binary opposites into unity in Christ (Gal. 3:28; Eph. 2:11–22; Col. 2:14);

The *physical*, that is, victory over the world (John 16:33), over death (2 Tim. 1:10; Heb. 2:15), over hell (1 Cor. 15:15; Rev. 1:18; 20:14), and over Satan (Luke 10:18; 11:22; John 14:30; Heb. 2:14; 1 Cor. 15:55–56; Col. 2:15; 1 Pet. 3:22; 1 John 3:8; Rev. 12:10; 20:2; etc.).

The whole enterprise of re-creation, the complete restoration of a world and humanity which, as a result of sin, is burdened with guilt, corrupted, and fragmented, is the fruit of Christ's work. Objectively, in the cross, καταλλαγη was established between God and the world. In due time, Christ will present the church without spot or wrinkle to the Father and deliver the kingdom to God, and God will be all in all (1 Cor. 15:22–28).

[403] In modern times, to describe the fruit of Christ's work, words such as "redemption" (*Erlösung*) and "reconciliation" (*Versöhnung*) have come to replace those of the early church—θεοποιησις (making divine), θειωσις (becoming divine, deification)—as well as post-Anselmian terms such as "satisfaction" and "merit." Schleiermacher brought the former term into vogue; he understands redemption to consist of the *mystical* communication of Jesus's God-consciousness to the fellowship of believers resulting in a subjective change in them. By contrast, Ritschl focuses on the *ethical* dimension of this change; Jesus by his life assures us that God does not hate us but loves us and inspires us to follow his teaching and example. In this way it is the *consciousness* of sin and guilt that is removed, and we are reconciled. There are differences between Schleiermacher and Ritschl; the former places the person of Christ in the foreground, the latter the work of Christ. What they have in common is that they shift the redemptive work of Christ away from Christ's objective obedient sacrifice of propitiation on our behalf and in our place to the subjective mystical and moral influence on us and in us. Christ here is only a divinely inspired human being (ἀνθρωπος ἐνθεος) and not the eternal and only begotten Son of God. This is not only a misconstrual of the person of Christ but also a diminution of his work and robs us of the assurance that in Christ all things will be renewed; it leaves the matter up to us. Because the work of re-creation is so enormous, bigger even than that of creation and providence, he to whom this task was assigned had to be not only a true and righteous human being, but also stronger than all creatures, that is, truly God. Only the same being by whom God created the world could be the mediator of re-creation also.[11]

[404] Christ's redemptive work is of infinite value and extends to the whole world. Christ came not to condemn but to save the world (John 3:17; 4:42; 6:33, 51; 12:47), to reconcile all things in heaven and earth to God (John 1:29;

11. Bonaventure, *The Breviloquium*, vol. 2 of *The Works of Bonaventure*, trans. Jose De Vinck (Paterson, NJ: St. Anthony Guild Press, 1963), IV, chap. 1.

2 Cor. 5:19; Col. 1:20). This universal scope, also found in passages such as Isaiah 53:6; Romans 5:18, 8:32; 1 Corinthians 15:22; 2 Corinthians 5:15; Hebrews 2:9; 1 Timothy 2:4, 6; 2 Peter 3:9; 1 John 2:2, has sometimes been misunderstood as a promise of salvation to all discrete individual persons, in short, as universal salvation. Over against such—e.g., Origen, Pelagius, and Arminius—the mainstream of the Christian church has been true to the particularist teaching of Augustine that not all are saved. Augustine took passages such as 1 Timothy 2:4 ("God wants all men to be saved") to refer to the wide diversity of peoples, classes, and ranks, and continued to insist on a restricted scope of salvation to the predestined.[12] By his resurrection Christ has called "us who are predestined" to a new life; by his blood he purchased into freedom "sinners who are going to be justified"; "everyone who has been redeemed by the blood of Christ is a human; yet not everyone who is a human has been actually redeemed by the blood of Christ."[13] Scholasticism, too, remained largely faithful to Augustine: 1 Timothy 2:4 must not be understood as if God in fact wanted to happen what does not happen, as though he wanted those to be saved who in fact are not saved. Wide acceptance of the Augustinian consensus did not stop theologians and churchmen from intensely debating the issue with such distinctions as God's antecedent will and consequent will and, above all, "sufficient but not efficacious."[14] Semi-Pelagianism triumphed with the former distinction[15]: by an antecedent will, God wills the salvation of all, but by his consequent will, he wills that salvation only for those whose faith and perseverance he foresaw. This view held sway in Roman Catholicism and eventually also found acceptance in Lutheran theology.[16] In both, however, a clear and firm confession of the Trinity, deity of Christ, and satisfaction prevented the Pelagian principle from fully triumphing. With the Socinians and Remonstrants this changed; the former rejected all objective Christian doctrine and, though the Arminians attempted to hold fast to the great Christian truths, they too succumbed with their belief that Christ's death was made for all people, even those who will never believe. In that case the death of Christ is only exemplary; it appropriates nothing for anyone but the "possibility" for God to deal again with man and to prescribe new conditions, such as he might desire, obedience to which, however, depended on the free will of man."[17] Once again, it was all up to man. The Canons of Dort explicitly

---

12. Augustine, *Enchiridion*, 103.

13. Augustine, *Confessions*, IX, 1; idem, *The Trinity*, IV, 13.

14. E.g., Peter Lombard, *Sententiae in IV liberis discinctae*, 3rd ed., 2 vols. (Grottaferrata: Colleggi S. Bonaventurae et Claras Aquas, 1971–81), III, 20, 3: "Christ offered himself to the Trinity, a ransom sufficient for all, but only efficacious for the elect, because he effected salvation only for the predestined."

15. From ancient times, this had already been the confession of the Greek [Orthodox] Church; see John of Damascus, *The Orthodox Faith*, II, chap. 29; *Orthodox Confession*, 34, 47.

16. Cf. H. Bavinck, *Reformed Dogmatics*, II, 351–58 (##235–36); Council of Trent, VI, chaps. 2–3; Roman Catechism, I, 3, 7; J. T. Müller, *Die symbolischen Bücher der evangelisch-lutherischen Kirche*, 8th ed. (Gütersloh: Bertelsmann, 1898), 781.

17. Canons of Dort, II; Apol. conf., VIII, 10; J. Arminius, *Opera theologica* (Lugduni Batavorum [Leiden]: Godefridum Basson, 1629), 153.

teach particular atonement, though they also declare Christ's sacrifice "of infinite worth and value, abundantly sufficient to expiate the sins of the whole world." The Arminians were condemned but not defeated. Their ideas made inroads into the Lutheran and the Anglican [Episcopal] Church and were taken over by an assortment of Protestant religious modalities that separated themselves from the official churches (Baptists, Wesleyan Methodists, Quakers, deists, and others) and also exerted a powerful influence within the Reformed churches.

[405] It is in England and in Scotland especially that the doctrine of limited atonement was challenged within the Reformed camp itself. Already in the early eighteenth century, a "moderate" group of English theologians, represented especially by Richard Baxter,[18] agreed with the French theologians Cameron, Testard, Amyraut, and others in distinguishing an antecedent decree by which Christ had conditionally satisfied for all, on condition of faith, from another subsequent particular decree by which he had so made satisfaction for the elect that he would in time also grant them faith and infallibly lead them to salvation.[19] In Scotland, the so-called "Marrow Men" (James Hog, Thomas Boston, Ralph and Ebenezer Erskine, Alexander Moncrieff, and others)[20] taught that Christ's sacrifice possessed a "legal, federal sufficiency" for all humans and served as the basis for a universal offer of grace. Everyone may be told that there is good news for them, that "Christ is dead" for them, that is, that a Savior has been provided for them; there is a crucified Christ for them (though not that "Christ died for them" because one does not know if it is true). The scope of the atonement returned as a matter of debate in the 1820s when McLeod Campbell began to teach that Christ died for all men; he had been perfectly obedient to God's law and therefore also to the commandment to love one's neighbor. Since Christ himself taught universal neighbor love, his death had to be for all men. Though McLeod Campbell was deposed in 1831, his views were very influential and contributed significantly to the virtually universal abandonment of the doctrine of limited atonement after several centuries of debate.[21]

---

18. Richard Baxter (1615–91) published his *Universal Redemption of Mankind by the Lord Jesus Christ* and thereby contributed substantially to the introduction of Amyraldism in England. His contemporary, Isaac Barrow (1630–77), author of *The Doctrine of Universal Redemption Asserted and Explained*, had committed to Arminianism (see W. Cunningham, *Historical Theology*, 3rd ed., 2 vols. [Edinburgh: T&T Clark, 1870], II, 328). Against their hypothetical universalism it was objected that if Christ died for all on condition of faith, he cannot have died for the children who can never actually believe. Cf. B. B. Warfield, "The Making of the Westminster Confession, and Especially of Its Chapter on the Decree of God," *Presbyterian and Reformed Review* 12 (1901): 226–83.

19. Cf. H. Bavinck, *Reformed Dogmatics*, II, 368–72 (#239).

20. Cf. H. Bavinck, *Reformed Dogmatics*, I, 191–92 (#57); and, further, an article on the Marrow controversy in *Princeton Theological Review* (1906): 331–35.

21. Cf. W. Cunningham, *Hist. Theol.*, II, 323ff.; J. Walker, *The Theology and Theologians of Scotland*, 2nd ed. (Edinburgh: T&T Clark, 1888), 79ff.; A. Robertson, *History of the Atonement Controversy in Connexion with the Secession Church from Its Origin to the Present Time* (Edinburgh: Oliphant, 1846); H. F. Henderson, *The Religious Controversies of Scotland* (Edinburgh: T&T Clark, 1905).

[406] It is important to get the terms of this debate straight. The issue is not about whether the death of Christ has infinite value or worth, nor is it about whether in fact some are not saved. The question is whether it was God's will and intent that Christ made his sacrifice for the sins of all people without exception or only for the sins of the elect.[22] When framed thus, the teaching of Scripture is not really in doubt. Scripture consistently links the sacrifice of Christ only to the church, whether it is described by the word "many" (Isa. 53:11–12; Matt. 20:28; 26:28; Rom. 5:15, 19; Heb. 2:10; 9:28), by "his people" (Matt. 1:21; Titus 2:14; Heb. 2:17; 7:27; 13:12), by "his sheep" (John 10:11, 15, 26f.; Heb. 13:20), by "his brothers" (Heb. 2:11), by "the children of God" (John 11:52; Heb. 2:13–15), by "those whom the Father has given him" (John 6:37, 39, 44; 17:2, 9, 24), by "his church" (Acts 20:28; Eph. 5:25), by "his body" (Eph. 5:23), or also by "us" as believers (Rom. 5:9; 8:32; 1 Cor. 5:7; Eph. 1:7; 2:18; 3:12; Col. 1:14; Titus 2:14; Heb. 4:14–16; 7:26; 8:1; 9:14; 10:15; 1 John 4:10; 1 Pet. 3:18; 2 Pet. 1:3; Rev. 1:5–6; 5:9–10; etc.). Texts such as Ezekiel 18:23; 33:11; John 1:29; 3:16; 4:42; 1 Timothy 2:4, 6; Titus 2:11; Hebrews 2:9; 2 Peter 3:9; 1 John 2:2; 4:14; are not incompatible with this since the New Testament is distinguished from the Old Testament precisely in the expansion of gospel proclamation to all creatures (Matt. 28:19). There is no respect of persons with God and no longer any distinction between gentile and Jew (Acts 10:34–35; Rom. 3:29; 10:11–13). Furthermore, references to "many" or "all"—as in "God has no pleasure in the death of the wicked" (Ezek. 18:23) and "wants all humans to repent and be saved" (1 Tim. 2:4, 6)—do not point to universal intent for the atonement but to Christ's death being for *many*, for a large multitude, and not just for a few. Scripture is not afraid that *too* many people will be saved. But when universalists deduce from this that the atonement is completely universal, they run afoul of both Scripture and reality, for both show clearly that not all hear the gospel. We are dealing here with God's *revealed* will that indicates the standard for human response to God. Beyond that, to "the will of God's good pleasure," we are not permitted to go; we do not need to know specifically for whom Christ died, only that the gospel call comes to all.

Scripture also implies that the sacrifice and intercession of Christ, hence also the acquisition and application of salvation, are inseparably connected. The sacrifice is the basis for Christ's intercession; the scope of the latter, accordingly, is as extensive as that of the former. If then the intercession is particular, as it is (John 17:9, 24; Rom. 8:34; Heb. 7:25; 1 John 2:1–2), so is the sacrifice. The acquisition and application of salvation are thus inseparably linked (Rom. 8:28–34) and grounded in Christ's death (Rom. 5:8–11). The application of salvation must therefore extend just as far as its acquisition; the former is comprehended in the latter and is its necessary development. Those whom God loves and for whom Christ made satisfaction are saved without fail. We have to make a choice: either

22. W. Cunningham, *Hist. Theol.*, II, 334.

God loved all people and Christ made satisfaction for all—and then they will all, without fail, be saved—or Scripture and experience testify that this is not the case.[23]

The key point here concerns assurance to believers: Did Christ in his death and resurrection really procure the salvation of his own, or was this only a potentiality, mere possibility? The Reformed tradition took a clear stance in favor of the former view—only this truth could maintain the unity of the work of the Triune God: Father, Son, and Holy Spirit. The advocates of a universal scope for the atonement, ironically, diminish the value and power of Christ's work. The center of gravity shifts from Christ to the Christian; salvation comes to depend on our faith. The Reformed, however, were of a different mind; rather than opening up the mere *possibility* of salvation, Christ truly effects the salvation of his own. "In and with Christ, God gives to believers all they need (Rom. 8:32f.; Eph. 1:3–4; 2 Pet. 1:3). Election in Christ carries all blessings with it: adoption as children, redemption by his blood (Eph. 1:3ff.), the gift of the Holy Spirit (1 Cor. 12:3), faith (Phil. 1:29), repentance (Acts 5:31; 11:18; 2 Tim. 2:25), a new heart and a new spirit (Jer. 31:33–34; Ezek. 36:25–27; Heb. 8:8–12; 10:16).

One final matter here: universalism[24] leads to all sorts of false positions. It introduces separation between the three persons of the Divine Being, for the Father wills the salvation of all, Christ makes satisfaction for all, but the Holy Spirit restricts the gift of faith and of salvation to a few. It introduces conflict between the purpose of God, who desires the salvation of all, and the will or power of God, who either will not or cannot grant salvation to all. It gives precedence to the person and work of Christ over election and the covenant, so that Christ is isolated from these contexts and cannot vicariously atone for his people, since there is no fellowship between him and us. It also denigrates God's justice and elevates human free will to god-like status to affirm or undo the work of Christ. Finally, in clear conflict with all of Scripture, it suggests that the only sin leading to perdition is the sin of unbelief; all other sins have been atoned for, including even those of the "man of sin," the Antichrist.

[407] The atonement is thus particular: it is restricted *in its intent* for the elect. Nonetheless, we must not overlook the fact that this particular atonement still has universal significance. Church and world are to be considered separate and distinct, yet it is an error to deny the common favor of God to all people

---

23. "For this was the sovereign counsel and most gracious will and purpose of God the Father that the quickening and saving efficacy of the most precious death of His Son should extend to all the elect, for bestowing upon them alone the gift of justifying faith, thereby to bring them *infallibly* to salvation; in other words, it was the will of God that Christ by the blood of the cross, whereby he confirmed the new covenant, should *effectually* redeem out of every people, tribe, nation, and language, all those, and those only who were from eternity chosen to salvation and given to Him by the Father" (Canons of Dort, II, 8); also, cf. Westminster Confession, VIII, 8; III, 6.

24. Ed. note: For clarity's sake, it is important to point out that the term "universalism/universalist" here refers not to universal salvation (ἀποκατάστασις, *apokatastasis*, "restoration"; on which see *Reformed Dogmatics*, IV, 720–27 [##578–79]) but only to the scope of the atonement, which in the Reformed tradition is *particular*.

by virtue of creation, a favor the elect also share. Strictly speaking, that the elect are born and live, that they receive food, shelter, clothing, and an assortment of natural benefits, is not to be included as part of the benefits of Christ's sacrifice. It is true that God providentially permits the world to continue because of his higher purposes for his elect. It is also a mistake, with Herrnhutters and Pietists, to erase the boundaries between nature and grace, creation and redemption, and to put Christ in the Father's place on the throne of the universe. Even election and the covenant of grace, presupposing as they do the objects of the one and the participants of the other, were not acquired by Christ but precede his merits. In creation, the Father lays the groundwork for the work of re-creation; with his work the Son goes back deeply—as far as sin reaches—into the work of creation. Still the two works are distinct and must not be confused since Christ did not, for each of his own, acquire the same thing. There is great diversity among believers before they come to the faith—gender, age, class, rank, character, gifts, and so on—and in the measure of grace and gifts bestowed on them (Rom. 12:3; 1 Cor. 12:11; Eph. 3:7; 4:7). Grace does not abolish these natural endowments but heals and perfects them. That is why the church is *in* the world though not *of* the world. Christ assumed the flesh and blood that is common to all people and thus honored the whole human race; according to the flesh, he is the brother of all the members of the human family. His work has value for all, even for those who have not believed and will never believe in him since it is for his sake that the entire world was spared. "Without Jesus Christ the world would not exist, for it would necessarily either be destroyed or be a hell" (Pascal). Although Christ is only head of the church as prophet, priest, and king, all human beings benefit from the light that the gospel shines into the world. The liberation of the created world from the bondage of decay, the glorification of creation, the renewal of heaven and earth—all this is the fruit of the cross of Christ (Rom. 8:19ff.). All creation, even the angels,[25] are enfolded into the glorious redemption of all things (Eph. 1:10; Col. 1:20). The whole creation as one day it will stand perfect—without spot or wrinkle—in God's presence is the work of Christ, the Lord of lords and the King of kings (Heb. 12:22–28).

[408] For Christ to carry out this grand project assigned by the Father to bring the lost and fallen creation to its consummated fullness, one immediately senses that the state of exaltation is as necessary as the state of humiliation. We cannot be satisfied with historical Jesus who was holy, pious, and good and influenced history by his wonderful example. In his exaltation he continues his work as mediator; in other words, Christ's threefold office continues into his state of exaltation. He

25. Angels, of course, do not need Christ for themselves as Reconciler and Savior; only humans are God's image bearers. Nonetheless, the only way to honor the τα παντα of Eph. 1:10 and Col. 1:20 is to take Paul as teaching that the demons along with the wicked will be sent to hell and in this way the organic wholeness of creation, including the angelic realm, will be restored. Sin disturbed all; Christ's atoning death restores all. The whole creation (organically rather than in particular) will be made new (Rom. 8; Rev. 21–22).

not only was but still is our chief prophet, our only high priest, and our eternal king. He is the same yesterday, today, and forever.

There is of course an important difference between Christ's humiliation and his exaltation. He who was the servant is now Lord and Ruler; his work is now no longer a sacrifice of obedience, but the conduct of royal dominion until he has gathered all his own and put all his enemies under his feet. He went to heaven to prepare a place for his own there and to fill them here on earth with the fullness that he acquired by his perfect obedience. It is to perfect the church that he is exalted to the Father's right hand. The work of the Mediator is one grand, mighty, divine work that began and will only be completed in eternity. But in the moment of the resurrection, it was divided into two parts: suffering and glory. Then it was a descent to the nethermost parts of the earth; now it is an ascent on high. But the two are equally necessary to the work of salvation. In both states it is the same Christ, the same Mediator, the same Prophet, Priest, and King.

[409] As Prophet, Christ teaches his disciples in the forty days, and by the Holy Spirit sent at Pentecost, he makes known to the world all the treasures of wisdom and knowledge hidden in him. The promised Holy Spirit (John 14:26; 16:13), given to the apostles (John 20:22) and to all believers (Acts 2), makes known and confirms the truth of the gospel (Mark 16:17; Acts 5:15; 8:6–7, 13; Rom. 15:18; etc.), bringing people into faith and fellowship with him and with the Father (John 17:20; 1 John 1:3). By the ordinary office of pastors and teachers (Rom. 12:7; 1 Cor. 12:28; Eph. 4:11; 1 Tim. 5:17), he builds up his church in the grace and knowledge of its Lord and Savior, and by the working of the Holy Spirit, he shines on it the light of the gospel of his glory (2 Cor. 4:4, 6). Christ himself teaches them by his Word and Spirit, so that, being taught by God, they would all be prophets and proclaim the marvelous works of God (Num. 11:29; Jer. 31:33–34; Matt. 11:25–27; John 6:45; Heb. 8:10; 1 John 2:20). He continues this instruction until they have all attained to the unity of the faith and the knowledge of the Son of God (Eph. 4:13; 3:18f.). All these ministries and workings proceed from the exalted Christ, who is the one Lord of the church (1 Cor. 8:6), in whom all the treasures of wisdom and knowledge are hidden (Col. 2:3; 1 Cor. 1:30). He is the truth who has made known the Father, leads us to the Father, and, in the knowledge of God, grants eternal life (John 1:17–18; 14:6; 17:3). His followers have and need no other teacher (Matt. 23:8, 10).

In the same manner, as the Epistle to the Hebrews points out, Christ continues to intercede for us as our high priest. To carry out this high-priestly office, he had to be the Son who, as "the reflection of God's glory and the exact imprint of God's very being," creates, upholds, and inherits all things (Heb. 1:1–3; 4:14; 5:5; 9:14). He also needed through suffering and trials to learn obedience and so be "perfected," be fully prepared, for his high-priestly ministry in heaven (2:10f.; 4:15; 5:7–10; 7:28). With his perfect sacrifice he effected purification for our sins (1:3; 7:27; 9:12; etc.), and as high priest entered the heavenly sanctuary foreshadowed in the Old Testament holy of holies (6:20; 9:12, 24)—not with the blood of goats and calves but by the power of his own blood (9:12–14), through the tent of his body (9:11), the curtain of his flesh (10:20)—in order to appear there on our behalf in the presence of God and to pray for those who through him draw near to God (7:25; 9:24). His unique and perfect sacrifice (7:27; 9:12, 26, 28; 10:10, 12, 14; 13:12) established the new covenant (8:8f.; 9:15f.) and secured the forgiveness of sins (8:12; 10:18) and full and free access to God (4:16; 10:19). This is once and for all; it need not and cannot be repeated (9:12, 26–28). We now have a high priest seated at the right hand of the throne of majesty on high (1:3; 3:1; 4:14; 6:20; 8:1), a perfect high priest who secured the right to sit at the right hand of God. Like Melchizedek, he is at the same time king of righteousness and king of peace, an eternal, spiritual, and heavenly king who acquired, possesses, and distributes the heavenly goods to come; one who can appear in heaven before the face of God for our benefit, pray for us, and save us completely (7:25; 9:24). Even more vividly than Paul (e.g., in Phil. 2:6–11), the Letter to the Hebrews views Christ's state of humiliation from the vantage point of his exaltation and regards the former as preparation and practice for the latter. Having offered himself up for his own, he now continues his priestly role "since he always lives to make intercession for them" (7:25). So, since Christ is an eternal priest-king, the church on earth no longer needs a priest. All believers are priests (Rom. 12:1; 1 Pet. 2:5; Rev. 1:6). Thus Christ is our only priest who, according to the order of Melchizedek, remains forever, continually covers our sins with his sacrifice, and always acts as our Paraclete with the Father pleading our cause against all the accusations of Satan, the world, and our own hearts. He also makes our prayers and thanksgivings pleasing to the Father, consistently assures us of free and confident access to the throne of grace, and out of his fullness sends to us all the blessings of grace (Luke 22:32; John 14:16; 17:9f.; Rom. 1:7; 8:32f.; 1 Cor. 1:3; 2 Cor. 1:2; Eph. 1:3; 1 Tim. 4:8; Heb. 7:25; 9:24; 1 John 2:2).

In this way Christ is and always remains our eternal king as well who rules us by his Word and Spirit and equips us to be victorious over sin and Satan. Christ began to act as king only upon his exaltation when he received the name "Lord," was designated Son of God (Rom. 1:4), and received all power in heaven and on earth (Matt. 28:18–20). Christ is first of all king over his people in the kingdom of grace (Ps. 2:6; Isa. 9:6; 11:1–5; Luke 1:33; 19:21–23; 23:42–43; John 18:33; 19:19; etc.). He demonstrates his kingship in gathering, protecting, and ruling his church, leading it to eternal blessedness (Matt. 16:18; 28:20; John 10:28). In the New Testament, because his kingship bears a very different character from that of the rulers of the earth, he is much more often called the head of the church (1 Cor. 11:3; Eph. 1:22; 4:15; 5:23; Col. 1:18; 2:19) who gathers, protects, and leads his church to eternal salvation. As Mediator, he has power over all creatures (Pss. 2:8; 72:8; 110:1–3; Matt. 28:18; 1 Cor. 15:24, 27; Eph. 1:22; Phil. 2:9–11; 1 Pet. 3:22; Rev. 1:5; 17:14); those who do not yet bow the knee, eventually will (Phil. 2:10). Here it is important to underscore Christ's power over Satan and the realm of evil. He came to earth to destroy the works of the devil (1 John 3:8) and battled against him all his life (Luke 4:13). Especially by the cross he triumphed over authorities and powers (Col. 2:15), took from Satan the weapons of sin, death, and the world (John 16:33; 1 John 4:4; 1 Cor. 15:55–56; Heb. 2:14), and cast him out of the territory of his kingship (John 12:31). In his ascension especially, he triumphed over the evil spirits as Paul observes in Ephesians 4:8: "When he ascended on high, he led captives in his train." In other words, he overcame all the hostile powers who resisted and opposed him and, as it were, captured them as prisoners of war (cf. Col. 2:15).[26]

We probably find the same idea expressed in the difficult text 1 Peter 3:19–22, which certainly does not speak of a descent into hell to proclaim the gospel to the lost. The phrase "in which" (ἐν ᾧ) clearly refers to the Christ who had been made alive; the words "having gone" (πορευθείς; cf. v. 22) permit no other interpretation than that Peter is not speaking about Christ's preaching in the Spirit to Noah's contemporaries. The pericope is about something very different. The case is this: Peter is admonishing believers to suffer while doing good and to follow Christ's example in this regard. The Christ who suffered and died, was resurrected in the Spirit and went to heaven (not hell; cf. v. 22), and it is this victory of the Spirit of Life over all suffering and death that is the message (κηρυγμα) to the spirits in prison. The reference to Noah and his contemporaries is an appropriate reminder that ungodly enemies of God's people suffer judgment while Noah and his family were saved; in the same way, as a result of *the resurrection of Christ*, the water of baptism is the ruin of the ungodly and salvation for believers. For Christ, who arose from the dead and instituted baptism and gives power to it, after subduing all angels, authorities, and powers by his ascension, now sits at God's right hand. Christ suffered doing good and overcame; now let believers follow in his footsteps! And just as he has power over all fallen spirits, so, as Mediator, Christ also has power (in his kingdom of power) over all his enemies. He will not rest until he has put all his enemies under his feet.

Christ's mediatorial office ceases at the consummation when he delivers the βασιλεία, the kingship, the royal office, to the Father. Some (e.g., Marcellus of Ancyra) took this to mean that the kingdom of Christ and also the union of his human nature with the Logos would end.[27] To the confession that Christ would come again to judge the living and the dead, the Niceno-Constantinopolitan Creed added the words "of whose kingdom there will be no end."[28] Among the Reformed there was also disagreement on this point. The differences can be easily resolved by saying that the *mediatorship of reconciliation* ends, and to that extent also the prophetic, priestly, and royal office of Christ. God will be king and [thus] all in all.

---

26. The link between the victory over his enemies and his ascension, therefore, has been repeatedly noticed and expressed. The Larger Catechism of Westminster, Q 53, for example, says that Christ, "triumphing over enemies, visibly went up into the highest heavens."

27. Joseph Schwane, *Dogmengeschichte*, 2nd ed., 4 vols. (Freiburg i.B.: Herder, 1882–95), II, 136, 148.

28. A. Hahn, *Bibliothek der Symbole und Glaubensregeln der alten Kirche*, 3rd ed. (Breslau: E. Morgenstern, 1897), 146–66.

But what remains is the *mediatorship of union*. Christ remains Prophet, Priest, and King as this triple office is automatically given with his human nature, included in the image of God, and realized supremely and most magnificently in Christ as the Image of God. Christ is and remains the head of the church, from whom all life and blessedness flow to it throughout all eternity.[29] Those who would deny this must also arrive at the doctrine that the Son will at some point in the future shed and destroy his human nature; and for this there is no scriptural ground whatever.

29. A. Kuyper, *Principles of Sacred Theology*, trans. J. Hendrik De Vries (Grand Rapids: Eerdmans, 1954 [1898]), 372; idem, *De vleeschwording des Woords* (Amsterdam: Wormser, 1887), 31, 195.

PART V

THE HOLY SPIRIT AND SALVATION IN CHRIST

17

THE ORDER OF SALVATION

THE WAY OF SALVATION

[410] The application of Christ's work to the salvation of his own by the Holy Spirit must be viewed theologically, that is, from God's point of view. All religions seek a way of salvation; all human beings long for happiness because the human heart is created for God and restless until it finds him (Augustine). However, in the darkness of our understanding and the evil thoughts of our hearts, we seek him not in the right way and not where he may be found. Pagan religions have no concept of the holiness of God; they do not understand sin aright and know nothing of grace. Not knowing Christ, they seek salvation by way of works.[1] "Be

1. From a speech that Max Müller delivered before the British and Foreign Bible Society about the sublime nature of the Bible, the publication *Der Beweis des Glaubens* (April 1901): 159, cites the following remarkable words: "I may say that for 40 years, as at the University of Oxford I carried out my duties as professor of Sanskrit, I devoted as much time to the study of the holy books of the East as any other human being in the world. And I venture to tell this gathering what I have found to be the basic note, the one single chord, of all these holy books—be it the Veda of the Brahmans, the Purana of Siwa and Vishnu, the Qur'an of the Muslims, the Sendavesta of the Parsis, etc.—the one basic note or chord that runs through all of them is salvation by works. They all teach that salvation must be bought and that your own works and merits must be the purchase price. Our own Bible, *our* sacred book from the East, is from start to finish a protest against this doctrine. True, good works are also required in this holy book ... but the works referred to are the outflow of a grateful heart. They are only the thank offerings, only the fruits of our faith. They are never the ransom of the true disciples of Christ. [We must not overlook what is good and noble in these (other) books but there is only one that provides true comfort]; the message which is surely true and worthy of full acceptance, and concerns all humans, men, women, and children—that Christ Jesus came into the world to save sinners."

your own light!" Buddha told his pupils. "Be your own refuge. Do not take refuge in anything else. Hold onto the truth as to a lamp. Do not look for a refuge in anyone other than yourself."[2] Islam finds redemption in liberation from hellish punishment, automatically received when one believes in the oneness of God and in Muhammad as his prophet and in addition performs the duties of religion (prayer, alms, fasts, pilgrimage). Here too, redemption is not a gift of God but a person's own act.[3] Unique to the Christian religion is the reality of Jesus Christ and the redemption he brings as fully God's initiative; all other religions seek redemption through human action. Because they do not know the person of Christ, however the human problem is conceived, all pagan religions require human beings to satisfy the demands of the law. Whether the works to be done are magical actions and ritual ceremonies or rigorous moral conduct, all religions or philosophies other than the Christian faith are autosoteric.

The biblical viewpoint is radically different; salvation is solely a gift of grace. God puts enmity between the seed of the woman and the serpent (Gen. 3:15), elects his people (Gen. 12:1; Exod. 15:13, 16; 19:4; 20:2; Deut. 7:6f.), makes a covenant with them and gives them his laws (Gen. 15:1; 17:2; Exod. 2:24–25; Deut. 4:5–13). This covenant also demanded reciprocal duties of love and obedience (Gen. 17:1; Exod. 20; Deut. 10:15–16; etc.), though observance of the law was not an antecedent condition for the covenant; it rested solely in God's electing love. The Old Testament does speak of "righteous" people—in contrast to the "ungodly" (Pss. 7:8; 17:1ff.; 18:21; 26:1ff.; 35:24; 41:12; 44:18, 21; 71:2; 119:121; 2 Kings 20:3; Job 16:17; Neh. 5:19; 13:14; etc.)—who frequently cry out to God for deliverance, appealing to their righteousness as ground. The righteousness of these godly people, however, is not a personal quality but a characteristic of the cause they represent. They have right on their side because they abandon themselves to God. They believe in God (הֶאֱמִין, Gen. 15:6; Exod. 14:31; 2 Chron. 20:20; Isa. 28:16; Hab. 2:4), trust in him (בטח, Pss. 4:5; 9:10), take refuge in him (חסה, Pss. 7:1; 18:2), fear him (ירא, Pss. 22:23; 25:12), hope in him (הוֹחִיל, יחל, Pss. 31:25; 33:18), expect things from him (קוה, Ps. 25:21), wait for him (חִכָּה, Ps. 33:20), lean on him (סמוך, Ps. 112:8; נכון, Ps. 57:7), and remain faithful to him (דבק, חשׁק, Ps. 91:14; 2 Kings 18:6; etc.). This faith is counted as righteousness (Gen. 15:6), just as elsewhere the keeping of God's commandments is called righteousness (Deut. 6:25; 24:13).

The fact that this subjective righteousness, which basically consists in trust in God, is also the fruit of God's grace and a working of his Spirit is the nature of the case in the Old Testament. The prophets proclaimed that God on his part will never break his covenant with his people nor abandon them (Num. 14:16; Deut. 32:26–27; 1 Sam. 12:22; Joel 2:17–19; Isa. 43:21, 25; 48:8–11; Jer. 14:7, 20–21; Ezek. 20:43–44; 36:32). It is an eternal covenant that cannot fail because

---

2. Oldenberg, cited in H. Bouwman, *Boeddhisme en Christendom* (Kampen: Bos, 1906), 62.

3. W. Knieschke, *Die Erlösungslehre des Qoran* (Berlin: Runge, 1910), 34ff.

it is anchored in the grace of God (2 Kings 13:23; 1 Chron. 16:17; Pss. 89:1–5; 105:10; 106:45; 111:5; Isa. 54:10). Furthermore, he will establish a new covenant, not let his Word and Spirit depart from them, but forgive their sins for his name's sake, pour out his Spirit on all, give them a heart of flesh, write his law in their inmost being, and cause them to walk in his statutes (Deut. 30:6; Isa. 44:3; 59:21; Jer. 24:7; 31:31f.; Ezek. 11:19; 16:60; 18:31; 36:26; 39:29; Joel 2:28; Mic. 7:19; etc.). Trusting this covenant God is essentially what makes one righteous in the Old Testament. Pious Israelites meditated on God's law, found their righteousness not in their own works but in God's grace, sought forgiveness, and abandoned their own cause in hope to a righteous God. Israel, too, lived in faith, resting in the eternal faithfulness of her covenant God.

[411–12] However, after the exile, Judaism drifted into greater and greater nomism and prepared itself for the coming Messiah by scrupulous attention to the law's demands. Reinforced by the oppression and persecution she endured, Israel experienced God as distant and turned to the law of God itself more than to the true and living God, who had revealed himself throughout the centuries. The messianic expectation that continued to be alive in Israel, and frequently awakened with fanatic strength in time of oppression, did not include an expectation of atonement for sin and the establishment of a new covenant but a hope for justice to Israel, deliverance from all oppression, and restoration of her dominion over all the people of the earth. Israel, accordingly, had to prepare for the coming of the Davidic king by rigorously observing the law. The result was Pharisaic pride, on the one hand (Matt. 19:20; Luke 18:11), and despair for the sinner, on the other. The law enslaved because of the fear of death (Heb. 2:15); it was a yoke impossible to bear (Acts 15:10). No assurance of salvation, no delight in God or comfort and peace in his fellowship was experienced by those under this yoke. In the words of *4 Ezra*, "We who have received the law must nevertheless perish on account of our sins."[4]

In this context, Jesus announced the good news of God's reign: forgiveness of sins by the gift of grace. The kingdom was for all who were poor in spirit, not just for Jews who kept the law. It is a treasure kept in heaven and distributed as a reward to the righteous (Matt. 6:20, 33; 13:43–46; 19:21; 25:46; Mark 9:43–47; 10:28–29), but it is also a very different kingdom from what the Jews envisioned at that time. It is spiritual, not political, in nature (Matt. 4:1–10), is characterized by purity of heart, meekness, mercy, humility, and so on (Matt. 5:3ff.; 18:4; 20:26–27), and is universal, not only for the Jews (Matt. 8:11; 21:43). Also, it is present now and not just in the future (Matt. 11:12; 12:28; Luke 17:21), grows and expands like the seed and the leaven (Matt. 13:24ff.), and is entered into by faith as a child would receive it (Mark 10:15). Although in an eschatological sense it is a reward, the work and the reward are in no way proportionate, and reward virtually vanishes (Matt. 19:29; 20:13–15; 25:21; Mark 10:30; esp. Luke

4. Ed. note: The reference is to 2 Esd. 9:36.

17:10). The righteousness required to enter the kingdom is itself a gift of God (Matt. 6:33) along with forgiveness of sins (Matt. 26:28; Luke 1:77; 24:47; etc.) and eternal life (Mark 10:30; Luke 18:30). It is given, not to the righteous, but to publicans and sinners (Matt. 9:13), to the lost (Matt. 18:11), to the poor (Matt. 5), to children (Matt. 18:3; Mark 10:15). One's own righteousness is useless; what is needed are repentance (μετανοια) and faith (πιστις), the acceptance of and trust in the gospel of the kingdom as God's gift to the lost.

The application of salvation is both distinct from and inseparable from the acquisition of salvation. The apostolic preaching was directed to the accomplished work of Christ as the mediator empowered by the Holy Spirit. In his exaltation Christ becomes the life-giving Spirit equipping his disciples for the work of ministry and convicting the world of sin and judgment. This is the same Spirit by whom he was conceived in Mary's womb (Luke 1:35), anointed at his baptism (Matt. 3:11), guided in the wilderness (Matt. 4:1), preached the gospel (Luke 4:18ff.), healed the sick and cast out unclean spirits (Matt. 12:28). He was always full of the Holy Spirit (Luke 4:1) by whose power he accomplished all his work (Acts 10:38), offered himself up in death (Heb. 9:14), and was declared to be the Son of God with power when he was raised from the dead (Rom. 1:3–4). At the ascension, the Holy Spirit became Christ's possession to such a high degree that he can be referred to as the Spirit (2 Cor. 3:17); in his exaltation he made all angels, authorities, and powers subject to him (Eph. 4:8–10; 1 Pet. 3:22), and became a life-giving Spirit (1 Cor. 15:45) who gives the Holy Spirit and his gifts to his followers.

The Holy Spirit, who existed before the day of Pentecost and did great works, now, after Christ's ascension, began to dwell in the church as his temple. The outpouring of the Holy Spirit, promised by Old Testament prophets (Isa. 44:3; Ezek. 39:29; Joel 2:28ff.), is the third great work of God after the creation and the incarnation. There are two kinds of activity associated with the Holy Spirit in Jesus's own teaching. For the disciples of Jesus only (John 14:17), the Holy Spirit will comfort them, lead them into the truth, and stay with them forever (John 14:16; 15:26; 16:7). From within the church, the Holy Spirit convicts the world of sin and righteousness and judgment, proving it wrong on all three points (John 16:8–11). On the day of Pentecost Christ made the church into his temple, a temple he perpetually sanctifies, builds up, and never again abandons; this indwelling of the Holy Spirit confers on the church of Christ an independent existence beyond the narrow bounds of ethnic Israel. The Spirit must now consecrate and perfect the body of Christ—as it did Jesus in his earthly ministry—until she achieves her full maturity and becomes the fullness (*pleroma*) of him who fills all in all (Eph. 1:23).

The outpouring of the Holy Spirit on the apostles was accompanied by extraordinary forces and works, including the miracle of languages on Pentecost (Acts 2:4). The phenomenon on the day of Pentecost was undoubtedly related to glossolalia (see Acts 10:47; cf. 11:17; 15:8, where Peter says that others received the Holy Spirit, for otherwise Peter could not have said that Cornelius and his household had received the Holy Spirit "just as we have") but there was a difference. Acts 2:4 does not describe a "hearing miracle"; people heard the apostles speaking in their own native languages and not in an unintelligible tongue that required the *spiritual* gift of interpretation (Acts 2:6, 8). One might say that the speaking of languages in Jerusalem was a combination of glossolalia and prophecy, an intelligible proclamation of God's mighty deeds in the native languages of the peoples [represented there]. Later instances of the different gift of glossolalia were weaker and diminished instances of this Pentecost miracle (see Acts 10:46–47; 11:17; 15:8; 19:6). The purpose of this miracle of speech was not to equip the disciples permanently with the knowledge of foreign languages, but in an extraordinary way to produce a powerful impression of the great fact of salvation history that had now taken place. At the creation the morning stars sang, and all the children of God shouted with joy. At the birth of Christ a multitude of heavenly hosts raised a song of jubilation to God's good pleasure. On the birthday of the church, the church itself acclaims in many languages the great works of God.[5]

[413–16] These and other extraordinary workings of the Holy Spirit continued throughout the apostolic period, when they were necessary to effect in the world the acceptance and permanence of the confession that Jesus is Lord. We read, for example, that by the Spirit the disciples were given "boldness" in speaking the word (Acts 4:8, 31), an unusual measure of faith (6:5; 11:24), comfort and joy (9:31; 13:52), wisdom (6:3, 10), glossolalia (10:46; 15:8; 19:6), prophecy (11:28; 20:23; 21:11), appearances and revelations (7:55; 8:39; 10:19; 13:2; 15:28; 16:6; 20:22), miraculous healings (3:6; 5:12, 15–16; 8:7, 13). As did Jesus's own works, so also these extraordinary feats of power manifested in the church provoked fear and amazement (2:7, 37, 43; 3:10; 4:13; 5:5, 11, 13, 24); they provoked hearts of enemies to hatred and persecution but also prepared the soil for the reception of the seed of the gospel. The gifts listed in 1 Corinthians 12:8–10 and Romans 12:6–8 are said by Paul to have been distributed by one and the same Spirit, apportioned to each one individually as he wills (1 Cor. 12:11), and are a fulfillment of the promise made in the Old Testament (Gal. 3:14). They are the firstfruits that guarantee a great harvest and serve as an advance on the future heavenly inheritance (Rom. 8:23; 2 Cor. 1:22; 5:5; Eph. 1:14; 4:30). These gifts

5. W. van Hengel, *De Gave van Talen: Pinksterstudie* (Leiden: D. Noothoven van Goor, 1864); commentary of H. Meyer et al. on Acts 2 and 1 Cor. 14 in *Critical and Exegetical Hand-Book to the New Testament*, 9 vols. (New York: Funk & Wagnalls, 1884); H. Cremer, "Geistesgaben," *PRE*[3], VI, 460–63. In recent years, glossolalia gained renewed attention through the phenomena that accompanied the revivals in Wales, Los Angeles, Christiania, Hamburg, Kassel, and other places. Compare, among others, Sir Robert Anderson, *Spirit Manifestations and the Gift of Tongues* (London: Evangelical Alliance, 1900). D. Walker, *The Gift of Tongues and Other Essays* (Edinburgh: T&T Clark, 1906), sees glossolalia as actually speaking in foreign languages and points out several related phenomena among the Montanists, Camisards, Irvingites, and others; for more on the latter, see F. Hencke, "The Gift of Tongues and Related Phenomena at the Present Day," *American Journal of Theology* 13 (1909): 193–206.

and their use must agree with the confession of Jesus as Lord (1 Cor. 12:3) and
be sincerely and readily used for the benefit of one's neighbor and fellow body
member (1 Cor. 12:12–30); the key question is whether or not they serve to
edify the church (1 Cor. 12:7; 14:12). Love is the most excellent gift; without
it all other gifts are worthless (1 Cor. 12:31–13:13). The apostle thus shifts the
center of gravity from the temporary and passing manifestations of the Spirit
to those regular activities of a spiritual and moral nature that the Holy Spirit
continually brings to bear in the church. The great sign of the Spirit's presence is
the creation of an independent holy community that persevered in the apostles'
teaching and fellowship, in the breaking of bread and the prayers (Acts 2:42). As
Luke testifies in Acts, they were of one heart and soul, and no one said that any of
the things he possessed was his own, but they had everything in common (Acts
4:32). By that Spirit they gained the freedom and boldness to speak the word,
were strengthened in their faith, comforted, and given joy in oppression (Acts
4:8, 31; 6:5; 9:31; 11:24; 13:52; etc.). The Holy Spirit does not only confirm the
gospel proclamation of forgiveness in the hearts of believers (John 15:26–27; Acts
5:32; 1 Cor. 2:4; 2 Cor. 4:13; 1 Thess. 1:5–6; 1 Pet. 1:12) and assure them that
they are children of God (Rom. 8:15–16)—i.e., justification—but also follows
through with the ethical and mystical benefit of sanctification; Romans 3–5 is
followed by Romans 6–8. The Holy Spirit creates new life in believers (2 Cor.
5:17; Eph. 2:10; 4:24; Col. 3:9–10) so that they exist, live, think, and act in Christ
(John 17:21; Rom. 8:1, 9–10; 12:5; 1 Cor. 1:30; 2 Cor. 5:17; Gal. 3:28; 5:25;
Eph. 1:13; Col. 2:6, 10). Christ is all and in all (Col. 3:11). By his Spirit Christ
comes to take up residence in his own and fill them with his fullness (John 14:23;
1 Cor. 3:16–17; 6:19; 15:28; 2 Cor. 6:16; Eph. 2:22). Believers thus participate
in all Christ's benefits, his wisdom (1 Cor. 2:6–10), righteousness (1 Cor. 6:11),
holiness (1 Cor. 6:11; Rom. 15:16; 2 Thess. 2:13), redemption (Rom. 8:2, 23).
In the Spirit they grow up together to maturity in Christ (1 Cor. 3:10–15; Eph.
4:1–16; Gal. 2:19), are sealed and glorified (Rom. 8:11, 23; 2 Cor. 1:22; 5:5;
Eph. 1:13–14; 4:30).

AUGUSTINE AND THE PELAGIAN THREAT; THE REFORMATION

Early church theologians such as Irenaeus intimately linked salvation to the applied
work of Christ by the Holy Spirit, but for many others the gospel increasingly
became construed as a new law, a work that involved human willing and acting.
Repentance degenerated into penance, and salvation was externalized as a copy-
ing of Christ's life and especially his suffering. Martyrs, ascetics, and monks were
often seen as the best Christians. This trend culminated in the teaching of Pelagius,
who did not deny grace but understood it as a universal gift to all people, enabling
them to choose the good and refuse evil. Grace, then, is emptied of its real meaning since our appropriation of grace depends on our own will; God helps those

who help themselves. When he severed all connections between Adam's sin and ours, Pelagius also robbed Christianity of its absolute significance. Since *creating* grace—the natural ability of being able to will was given to all—and *illuminating* grace, which comes from gospel proclamation or the example of Christ, were not strictly necessary for salvation, grace is neither efficacious nor irresistible; it is only a form of assistance to people. In the Pelagian view, many good works are performed by humans without any grace.[6]

The great gift of Augustine to the church was his definitive repudiation of all forms of Pelagianism. According to Augustine, our wills are bound, from beginning to end, being redirected to God's good and persevering in it; it is a matter of gift not of merit, of grace not of works. The Holy Spirit blows where he wills, "not following merits but producing them."[7] Grace is anterior to all merits; it is prevenient, preparatory, antecedent, and efficacious. It "is prevenient to the unwilling to make him will."[8] God's grace, furthermore, is irresistible; it inexorably and insuperably has its way with the human will.[9] Objectively and subjectively, from beginning to end, the work of salvation is a work of God's grace and of his grace alone. This does not mean that God's grace suppresses or destroys the free will of humans; on the contrary, grace liberates the will from the slavery of sin. "Do we then by grace make void free will? God forbid! No, rather we establish free will. For even as the law is established by faith, so free will is not made void by grace but established, for grace restores the health of the will."[10] Like the beginning, so also the progress of faith and love is due solely to God's grace. Without Christ we can do nothing. Therefore, "as we begin, it is said: 'his mercy shall go before me'; as we finish, it is said: 'his mercy shall follow me.'"[11] It is God "who prepares the will and perfects in us by his cooperation what he initiates by his operation."[12] God's mercy "follows the willing that he may not will in vain."[13] "The human will must be assisted by the grace of God to every good movement of action, speech, or thought."[14] Objectively and subjectively, from beginning to end, the work of salvation is a work of God's grace and of his grace alone. Augustine's viewpoint became the dogma of the church and remains the teaching of all orthodox, evangelical Christianity.

Pelagianism was condemned at the Synod of Carthage (418); again at the Council of Ephesus (431) and the Synod of Orange (529), which also rejected

6. B. B. Warfield, *Two Studies in the History of Doctrine: Augustine and the Pelagian Controversy* (New York: Christian Literature, 1897), 7ff.

7. Augustine, *On the Grace of Christ and Original Sin*, 24.

8. Augustine, *Enchiridion*, 32.

9. Augustine, *On Admonition and Grace*, 12.

10. Augustine, *On the Spirit and the Letter*, 30, cf. 33–34; see also Augustine, *On Grace and Free Will*; idem, *City of God*, XIV, 11; idem, *Against Two Epistles of the Pelagians*, I, 2.

11. Augustine, *Against Two Epistles of the Pelagians*, II, 9.

12. Augustine, *On Grace and Free Will*, chap. 33.

13. Augustine, *Enchiridion*, 32.

14. Augustine, *Against Two Epistles of the Pelagians*, II, 5.

semi-Pelagianism; its canons were confirmed by Boniface II.[15] Pelagianism and semi-Pelagianism are thus condemned by official Roman Catholic teaching and by the great Roman theologians such as Aquinas and Bonaventure. However, it is fair to ask whether, in a roundabout way, Rome has not smuggled semi-Pelagianism back in again. Does Rome, in speaking of prevenient grace, have in mind anything more than the external call of the gospel, which exerts moral impact on the intellect and will, and which was also recognized by Pelagius and his followers? Among theologians there was much disagreement also about the characteristic nature of that preparatory grace, but some lines are clear. In the first place, Rome taught that the freedom of the will, though weakened by sin, is not lost;[16] the "natural man" as such is a complete human.[17] Second, Rome views "prevenient grace" as a grace that confers the *capacity* (*posse*) to believe but not the act of believing itself. Instead, prevenient (actual) grace is granted to all adults within hearing of the gospel, but it lies in their power to accept or reject it. According to the Second Council of Orange, "The Catholic faith believes this also, that after grace has been received through baptism, all the baptized with the help and cooperation of Christ can and ought to fulfill what pertains to the salvation of the soul, if they will labor faithfully."[18] Trent also declared that humans can consent to prevenient grace and cooperate with it but also reject it.[19] Faith here too is not seen as central to justifying faith; it is only assent to the truth of Christianity. Taken by itself it does not justify; it is only preparatory to the infusion of sacramental grace. By the merit of condignity, this grace enables human beings to do good and to merit heavenly beatitude. By grace the Roman Catholic Church does not, at least not primarily, mean the free favor of God by which he forgives sins. Rather, grace is a quality or supernatural power infused in human beings, lifting them into a supernatural order and enabling them to do good works and to merit heavenly blessedness by the merit of condignity.

[417–18] It was the Roman Catholic penitential system in general and the sale of indulgences in particular that prompted Luther's reformational activity. Luther reemphasized God's righteousness not as his own attribute but as the righteousness of faith granted by God in grace, through faith alone.[20] This led to conflict with Roman church authorities over the abuse of indulgences, though this practice is

15. H. Denzinger, *Enchiridion symbolorum* (Wirceburgi, 1856), #200; ed. note: ET: *The Sources of Catholic Dogma* (London and St. Louis: Herder, 1955), 81–82.

16. Synod of Orange (529), in H. Denzinger, *Enchiridion*, #144; Council of Trent, session VI, canon 1 and canon 5.

17. Cf. H. Bavinck, *Reformed Dogmatics*, ed. John Bolt (Grand Rapids: Baker Academic, 2003–8), II, 539–42 (#287).

18. H. Denzinger, *Enchiridion*, #169.

19. Council of Trent, session VI, canon 5 and canon 4.

20. This new understanding is already reflected in Luther's Psalms Commentary (1513–15), was deepened by Luther's growing acquaintance with a body of mystical writings, especially the *Deutsche Theologie* (*Theologia germanica*) and by his continued study of Paul and Augustine, and came to clarity in his Lectures on the Letter to the Romans (1515).

itself a direct consequence of Rome's nomist degradation of the gospel.[21] Luther learned from Romans 1:17 and Matthew 4:17 that the meaning of "righteousness of God" (δικαιοσυνη θεου) and repentance (μετανοειν) had nothing to do with the Roman institution of confession but involved a change of heart characterized by true sorrow for sin and in the word of absolution proclaimed in the gospel of grace. It is not the sacrament but faith that justifies.

The Reformation was thus religious in origin and evangelical in character; Luther helped people once again understand the original and true meaning of the gospel of Christ. Luther again put sin and grace in the center of the Christian doctrine of salvation. The forgiveness of sins, that is, justification, does not depend on repentance, which always remains incomplete, but rests in God's promise and becomes ours by faith alone.

How Luther construed the relation between repentance and faith, however, is much disputed. The three components in Luther's understanding are contrition, faith, and then good works. Luther always taught absolute predestination, though in his later period, to offset misuse of the doctrine, he accented the revelation of God in Christ and the universal offer of salvation in the world of the gospel. Melanchthon, however, with increasing firmness, adopted a synergistic position. As a result, a covert or overt synergism can be found in Lutheranism. Grace is always resistible and therefore amissible, that is, losable, and can be lost and regained over and over again.[22] In the order of salvation, therefore, the center of gravity lies with the human person. Human resistance can nullify the entire work of God the Father, Son, and Spirit. The center is in faith and justification; calling, contrition, and regeneration have only a preparatory function. Everything depends on faith, specifically on the act of believing. Failing to understand the work of God's grace as proceeding from his eternal decree and covenant, Lutherans also fail to relate it back to nature, the world, and humanity. It is sufficient for them to live in communion with Christ, and they feel no urge to fight under Christ as king.

[419] Although the Reformed view shares much with the Lutheran, the order of salvation in Reformed theology presupposes communion with Christ, a bond between the mediator and the elect forged in eternity, in the counsel of peace (*pactum salutis*) between Father and Son. Atonement and justification are already objectively, actively present in Christ as the fruit of his work and are appropriated by the believer by the Spirit of Christ. All is finished: God has been reconciled; nothing remains to be added from the side of humans. The application of salvation, too, is Christ's work, not ours; soteriology must be viewed theologically, as a work of God the Father, Son, and Holy Spirit. Just as surely as the re-creation took place objectively in Christ, so surely it must also be carried out subjectively by the Holy

---

21. Most striking are the points of resemblance between Roman Catholic and Jewish nomism mentioned in H. Bavinck, *Reformed Dogmatics*, III, 495 (#410).

22. Formula of Concord, "Solid Declaration," article II, 58–60, 69–73, 85, in vol. 3 of *Creeds of Christendom*, ed. Philip Schaff and rev. David S. Schaff, 6th ed. (New York: Harper & Row, 1931; repr. Grand Rapids: Baker, 1983).

Spirit in the church. The covenant of grace precedes and is the foundation and starting point for the work of salvation. While it is true that the believer first, by faith, becomes aware that he or she belongs to the covenant of grace and to the number of the elect, the epistemological ground is distinct from the ontological ground. In the same way that the acquisition of salvation took place in the way of a covenant, the application is also covenantal. Regeneration, faith, and conversion are not preparations for but the benefits of covenantal fellowship of believers with God in Christ imparted to us by the Holy Spirit. Therefore, the ingathering of the elect must not be conceived individualistically and atomistically.

Lutherans and Reformed people, as a result, view penitence in somewhat different ways. The difference in Luther's and Calvin's experiences plays some role here. Luther lived for a long time under a heavy sense of guilt and in anguish of conscience, feeling the curse of the law and the wrath of God on him. In the end he found peace in the gracious forgiveness of sins by faith alone. Calvin's conversion involved gradual acceptance of the truth of the Reformation while holding back from public affirmation until, finally, he overcame all doubt and hesitation and surrendered himself unconditionally and completely to the will of God. For Calvin the newness consisted not so much in a sudden experience of grace and salvation as in a firm decision and the decisive act of obedience to God's will. Calvin, especially noting the practice of some Anabaptists to force new converts to first practice penitence for a few days in order thereafter to be admitted into the communion of grace, resisted all legalistic forms of penitence and insisted on a different kind of penitence, namely, that which proceeds from faith, which is possible only in communion with Christ, continues throughout life, and consists in mortification and vivification, "both of which happen to us by participation in Christ."[23] Here the Lutheran understanding of conversion, differentiated—in the Lutheran confession and Lutheran theology[24]—into two parts: *contrition* and *faith*, corresponding to the contrast between law and gospel, gave way to Calvin's insistence that "repentance and faith, although held together by a permanent bond, require to be joined rather than confused."[25] Faith and repentance, therefore, each obtained a more or less independent meaning in the order of salvation. The advantage of this approach is that justification is now seen more purely as an act of juridical acquittal, and faith gains in surety and assurance. Lutheran theology on this point, as we will see later in the locus on justification, is far from clear. The Christian life now also gains a greater ethical significance and the law a greater role as a rule and motivator of the human will *as a rule of gratitude*. The Reformed

---

23. John Calvin, *Institutes of the Christian Religion*, III.iii.2, 9 (ed. John T. McNeill and trans. Ford Lewis Battles, 2 vols. [1559; Philadelphia: Westminster, 1960], 1:593–95, 600–602).

24. Cf. Joseph T. Müller, *Die symbolischen Bücher der evangelisch-lutherischen Kirche*, 8th ed. (Gütersloh: Bertelsmann, 1898), 41, 167, 171, 174, 312, 634; Heinrich Friedrich Ferdinand Schmid, *The Doctrinal Theology of the Evangelical Lutheran Church*, trans. Charles A. Hay and Henry Jacobs, 5th ed. (Philadelphia: United Lutheran Publication House, 1899), 339ff.

25. J. Calvin, *Institutes*, III.iii.5.

Christian is called actively to fight against sin. The Christians' moral life has faith as its root, the law as its rule, and the honor of God as its goal. This theme is not entirely absent in Luther, Melanchthon, and the later Lutherans, but in Bucer, Calvin, and the later Reformed, this idea acquired a much deeper and broader meaning. Obedience to God's will in the interest of advancing his glory—*that*, in Reformed circles, became the task of the Christian life.[26]

[420] Other prominent understandings of the way of salvation include the diametrically opposed approaches of mysticism and rationalism. Mysticism is a phenomenon that appears in all the higher religions and seeks to deepen the religious life, usually out of reaction to faith in external authority. It seeks by extraordinary practices, disciplines, and powers—*via negativa, purgativa*—to achieve a higher knowledge or a more intimate communion with the divine than can be attained via the reigning orthodoxy. Mysticism frequently lapses into a pantheistic mingling of the divine and the human (not only in Brahmanism, Neoplatonism, Sufism, and others but also in Christianity, in the case of John Scotus Erigena, the Brothers of the Free Spirit, Böhme, and others).[27] In the footsteps of Plato, Philo, and Plotinus, and following Pseudo-Dionysius, mainly three stages are distinguished in the mystical life: κάθαρσις (the *via purgativa*, asceticism), φωτισμος (the *via illuminativa*, meditation), and ἐποπτεια (the *via unitiva, contemplativa*, ecstasy). At the stage of purgation the soul cleanses itself from sin and withdraws from all that is earthly; in illumination, the soul concentrates on one specific thing (the suffering of Christ, his wounds, the love or the holiness of God); and in the final stage, the soul is most intimately united and, as it were, identified with the object to which it fully surrendered by meditation. It then falls into a state that, according to all mystics, is practically indescribable and is therefore denoted by various terms: seraphic contemplation, the mystical union, a betrothal, the mystical kiss, a passive transformation, a mystical sleep, death, or annihilation, the tomb of the soul, and others.[28]

Rationalism, on the other hand, only sees Jesus as a teacher to be followed and imitated as best we can. Following him, humans—weakened by sin but not powerless—obtain salvation. The call that comes to them from the gospel therefore only exerts a moral influence on their intellect and will.

Related to these two are those one-sided conceptions of the order of salvation known as antinomianism and neonomianism. The former reduces the application of salvation to and virtually equates it with its acquisition, thereby eschewing all works; the latter reinstitutes law. In antinomianism Christ has accomplished everything, removing not only the guilt of our sin but also its pollution. Sanctification is already ours, there is nothing left for humans to do. Any talk of "doing" is

---

26. Ed. note: This is eloquently summarized in the first answer of the Westminster Shorter Catechism: "Man's chief end is to glorify God and to enjoy him forever."

27. Cf. E. Lehmann, *Mystiek heidensche en christelijke*, trans. from the Danish by J. E. van der Waals (Utrecht: Honig, 1908).

28. Cf. H. Bavinck, *Reformed Dogmatics*, I, 146–49 (#46).

legalism; all we have to "do" is believe, i.e., come to the insight that we are already perfect in Christ or set aside the illusion that God is angry with us. Here sin is an illusion and leads to anarchy. In ancient times such sentiments were propagated by the gnostics and Manicheans, in the Middle Ages by numerous libertinistic sects, and during and after the Reformation they revived among the Anabaptists, in the sect of the Libertines,[29] in the independentistic disturbances in England around the middle of the seventeenth century.[30] Antinomianism is a phenomenon that occurs not only in religion but also in morality and politics. In modern times it found an interpreter in Friedrich Nietzsche and in the spokesmen for anarchism. All the Reformers rejected all antinomianism as resolutely as possible.

[421] In nomism and neonomianism, by contrast, keeping the law becomes the unevangelical way of salvation. Under Socinian and Remonstrant influence, nomism penetrated Protestantism. Here, too, we need to differentiate a rationalist school from a Pietist one. The rationalistic school is rooted basically in Piscator's teaching, according to which the righteousness we need is accomplished not by the active but solely by the passive obedience of Christ![31] Although this view was rejected by the Reformed churches in France at their synods of Gap (1603) and Rochelle (1607), it nevertheless found much acceptance, especially in the school of Saumur (John Cameron and Moïse Amyraut). In England, Amyraldism and Arminianism became allies and shaped the features of that conception of the order of salvation that is known as neonomianism, which posits the ground for the believer's justification not in the imputed righteousness of Christ, but in the believer's own, sincere, though imperfect, righteousness. According to this view, Christ's satisfaction made salvation possible for all humans, bringing them all into a "salvable state." Having fulfilled the law of the covenant of works, Christ introduced a new law," a law of grace, which is content with faith and repentance, with sincere, albeit imperfect, obedience of the contrite sinner. Debates and controversies about the law between neonomians and anti-neonomians raged in England and Scotland[32] throughout the seventeenth and eighteenth

29. Against whom Calvin battled. On the linkage between the opposition in Geneva and the sect of the Libertines, see F. Kampschulte and W. Goetz, *Johann Calvin: Seine Kirche und sein Staat in Genf*, 2 vols. (Leipzig: Duncker & Humblot, 1869–99), II, 13. Ed. note: See John Calvin, *Treatises against the Anabaptists and against the Libertines*, trans. and ed. Benjamin Wirt Farley (Grand Rapids: Baker Academic, 1982).

30. H. Weingarten, *Die Revolutionskirchen Englands* (Leipzig: Breitköpf & Hartel, 1868), 72ff.

31. Cf. H. Bavinck, *Reformed Dogmatics*, III, 347–51, 377–80 (##378, 386).

32. The debate in Scotland, known as the "marrow controversy," was initiated by the 1718 publication of a new edition of Edward Fisher's *Marrow of Modern Divinity* (1647). Prominent antineonomians were John Eaton, *The Honey-Combe of Free Justification by Christ Alone* (London: Robert Lancaster, 1642); William Eyre, *Vindiciae justificationis gratuitae* (London: Edward Forrest, 1654); Tobias Crisp, *Christ Alone Exalted, in the Perfection and Encouragements of the Saints, Notwithstanding Sins and Trials* (London: R. Noble, 1643); John Saltmarsh, *Free Grace, or, The Flowings of Christs Blood Free to Sinners* (London: Giles Calvert, 1647); Samuel Crisp, *Christ Made Sin, Evinced from Scripture (2 Cor. v.21)* (London: J. A., 1691); Thomas Tully, *Justificatio Paulina sine operibus ex mente Ecclesiae Anglicanae, omniumque reliquarum quae reformatae audiunt, asserta & illustrata* (Oxford: Hall, 1674); Isaac

centuries; the end result there, as well as in the Netherlands, was a weakening of the principles of the Reformation. In the same way, the denial by Jonathan Edwards of immediate imputation in the case of Adam and Christ had the effect of increasingly leading New England theology along the lines of Placaeus.[33]

[422] Neonomianism also took a different shape in Pietism and Methodism, where faith and experience, rather than faith and obedience, became the condition for justification. From the beginning in the Reformed church and Reformed theology, there was a practical school of thought that was averse to all Scholasticism and put all emphasis on *life*. It was supported and promoted especially by strongly anti-Aristotelian philosopher Peter Ramus, who wanted more simplicity in philosophy and described theology as the "doctrine of living well" whose purpose is not the "knowledge of things but practice and consistent application."[34] This view gained acceptance with many Reformed theologians, including Sturm (Strasbourg), Tremellius (Heidelberg), Piscator (Herborn), and Perkins (Cambridge), whose pupil Ames—later professor in Franeker alongside Maccovius—described theology as "the doctrine of living for God, the pursuit of piety," rooted in the will.[35] Consequently, a practical form of Pietism arose, represented by men such as Richard Baxter, Herman Witsius, Willem á Brakel, and Willem Schortinghuis.[36] Parallel movements took place within the orbit of Lutheranism (Philipp J. Spener, 1635–1705) and led to the Pietism in which Zinzendorf (1700–1760) was brought up.

Mention must also be made here of the Methodism of John Wesley (1703–91) and George Whitefield (1714–71). Whereas continental Pietism was inordinately introspective, emphasizing long-lasting "penitential struggle" (*Busskampf*) and arduous self-examination that often crippled any assurance of faith, Methodism betrayed its English and Reformed roots by having nothing to do with preparation and gradual progression of conversion, with penitential struggle, "breakthough" conversion, followed by Holy Spirit "sealing," and instead concentrated on a single point, keeping conversion in the full light of a person's consciousness, and keeping a record of "saved" souls. Then, having converted people, it thrusts them straightway into active Christian service, organizes them into an army that goes to work by way of attack under the motto "blood and fire" (redemption and sanctification), marches into the world, and takes it by storm for Christ. Although

---

Chauncy, *Neonomianism Unmask'd, or, The Ancient Gospel Pleaded against the Other, Called a New Law or Gospel* (London: J. Harris, 1692–93); idem, *Alexipharmacon, or, A Fresh Antidote against Neonomian Bane and Poyson to the Protestant Religion* (London: W. Marshall, 1700). For further information on the neonomian and antineonomian debate, see James Buchanan, *Doctrine of Justification: An Outline of Its History in the Church and of Its Exposition from Scripture* (Edinburgh: T&T Clark, 1867), lectures 6 and 7.

33. Cf. H. Bavinck, *Reformed Dogmatics*, III, 100 (#322).

34. On Ramus, see P. Lobstein, *Petrus Ramus als Theologe: Ein Beitrag zur Geschichte der protestantischen Theologie* (Strassburg: C. F. Schmidt, 1878); F. Cuno, "Ramus," *PRE*[3], XVI, 426–28.

35. H. Visscher, *Guilielmus Amesius: Zijn leven en werken* (Haarlem: J. M. Stap, 1894).

36. Cf. H. Heppe, *Geschichte des Pietismus und der Mystik in der reformierten Kirche* (Leiden: Brill, 1879); A. Ritschl, *Geschichte des Pietismus in der reformierten Kirche* (Bonn: A. Marcus, 1880).

properly reacting to dead orthodoxy in the church, and rightly calling for genuine conversion and true faith, this emphasis on living faith as a practical reality led to a new form of legalism dividing believers into "weak" and "strong," "carnal" and "spiritual." Although in its revivalist, Methodist form this type of Christianity has borne much fruit for renewing people and society, the weakness remains that the human subject and *present* experience or obedience takes center stage rather than the grace of God and the work of Christ. Methodism, for example, typically attaches but little value to doctrine, largely turns its back on the old organized churches, and directs its vision outward on the world. Although one-sided, this form of Christianity has borne abundant good fruit.[37]

THE MODERN TURN TO THE SUBJECT

[423] Modern thought similarly turns away from God and the objective factors of salvation (Christ, church, word, sacrament) and places the religious subject in the center. Descartes found the foundation and starting point of all knowledge in the certainty of the existence that is locked in thought, and further made the clarity and distinctness of knowledge the standard of its truth.[38] For Spinoza, good and evil do not exist objectively but are nothing but "modes of thinking, that is, notions," and "the knowledge of good and evil is nothing but an affect of joy or sadness insofar as we are conscious of it."[39] The rule that clarity is the standard of truth subsequently achieved dominance in the Enlightenment. Consistent rationalism also rejected all external authority, all special notions of revelation and grace that made individual persons dependent both in intellect and will. People must follow their own insight as free rational beings; enlightenment of the intellect and moral improvement were seen as the road to blessedness.[40]

Kant subjected this rationalism to sharp critique and restricted (pure) reason to the world of sense perception. Kant, however, retained room for faith in practical reason. After concluding that human nature is not intrinsically good but flawed and evil, requiring rebirth and renewal, Kant followed the Pelagian route and inferred an ultimate human freedom and moral capacity from the existence of the moral imperative: "Thou shalt" necessarily implies "thou can." Human beings simply suf-

---

37. P. Schaff, ed., *The Creeds of Christendom*, I, 882; III, 807; F. Loofs, "Methodismus," *PRE*³, XII, 747–801; John L. Nuelsen, "Methodismus in Amerika," *PRE*³, XIII, 1–25; T. Kolde, *Der Methodismus und seine Bekämpfung* (Erlangen: Deichert, 1886); idem, *Die Heilsarmee: Ihre Geschichte und ihr Wesen* (Erlangen: Deichert, 1885); E. Kalb, *Kirchen und Sekten der Gegenwart* (Stuttgart: Verlag der Buchhandlung der Evangelischen Gesellschaft, 1907), 310ff.; W. J. Townsend, H. B. Workman, and George Eayrs, *A New History of Methodism*, 2 vols. (London: Hodder & Stoughton, 1909).

38. "Consequently I now seem to be able to establish as a general rule that everything that I clearly and distinctly perceive is true" (Descartes, *Discourse on Method*, chap. 4).

39. Baruch Spinoza, *Ethics*, ed. and trans. James Gutman (New York: Hafner, 1949), IV, pref. and prop. 8; ed. note; see *Spinoza Reader* (Princeton: Princeton University Press, 1994), 199, 204.

40. J. A. L. Wegscheider, *Institutiones theologiae christianae dogmaticae* (Halle: Gebauer, 1819), §152.

fer from a conflict of two predispositions—one toward evil and the other toward good—and must by an intelligible act of freedom redeem themselves. In that effort we can hope for but never be sure of "cooperation from above." Remarkably, Kant here also teaches a form of assurance of faith in perseverance; those who increase in moral betterment may conclude divine favor and the hope of reaching moral perfection. Moral improvement is an endless process, but "those who consistently work at self-improvement, those we can redeem" (Goethe).

Other thinkers such as Schopenhauer and especially Eduard von Hartmann used the language of faith to point to the reality of human evil and the need of grace, but meant something quite different from Christian orthodoxy. For them, grace still includes human moral effort; faith is a totally human act by which we gain grace. The human subject remains at the center.

[424] By another route, philosophy after Kant developed into the idealistic systems of Fichte, Schelling, and Hegel. In philosophical idealism, too, self-determination, the ego, is the essence of human freedom. The historical work of Christ is slighted; it becomes only a metaphysical and moral ideal to be achieved by human willing. Fichte, Schelling, and Hegel, each in his own way, sought to unify philosophic thought with Christian truth, but they so subordinated faith to intellectual constructs such as the Absolute that historical Christianity with the person and work of Christ at the center became unrecognizable. Fichte shifted the center of gravity from theoretical to practical reason, from the intellect to the will, from knowledge to moral conduct, and completely subordinated knowledge to action. In the beginning was the deed, not the word. The "I" (or self-consciousness) is its own product even, and the "non-I" (the world as idea) is posited by the "I." Nothing exists but the I: "The I is everything." Human redemption is a matter of striving for self-improvement: "posit yourself, become conscious of yourself, strive to be independent, make yourself free."[41] Later in life Fichte became more "religious." Not activity and action, not independence and freedom, but life in God, resting and delighting in his fellowship, intellectual love (*amor intellectualis*), as Spinoza called it, is the destiny of humankind. That is the supreme, the blessed and eternal life. Fichte believed he had found this idea in Christianity, more specifically in the Gospel of John. Jesus is the instantiation of the innermost essence of religion: the eternal oneness of the divine and the human; his historical appearance is an eternally valid historical truth. Now we know God's will for it was realized in history; we are saved, we find eternal life, when we also make this will our own.

Schelling and Hegel, each in his own way, came to similar conclusions: Christ represents the unity of subject and object, of spirit and nature, of finite and infinite, of God and man. Hegel especially strove mightily to secure a place in his philosophical system for Christianity and the redemption that constitutes its core. He therefore laid the foundation for reconciliation in the movement of the

41. K. Fischer, *J. G. Fichte und seine Vorgänger*, 2nd ed. (Munich: Basserman, 1884), 432.

Absolute itself from mere potentiality, by way of an eternal process of becoming, to actuality of redemption where all the conflicting opposites are reconciled into the essential oneness of God. In the idea of God in Christ, the divine-human person, the infinite and the finite, God and humanity, are eternally one. Christ is the "God-man," his death the center of reconciliation, for his death was the death of death, the negation of negations, and so led to resurrection and ascension. In Christ, God assumed finiteness, along with evil as its extremity, in order to kill it by his death. "It is infinite love for God to identify himself with what is foreign to him in order to destroy it." With that death, accordingly, begins the reversal of consciousness. With it begins "a new world, a new religion, a new reality, another cosmic condition." The church has been built on this foundation. Although faith may start on the sensible (and historical) side, it nevertheless penetrates to the idea and has to become totally "spiritual." "The true content of the Christian faith has to be vindicated by philosophy, not by history." It is the task of the institutional church to nurture its members and introduce them to this truth. In baptism it declares the truth that children are born not in misery, but in the fellowship of the church, and that, though first receiving the truth on authority, they must gradually appropriate it for themselves. They are born in and for freedom. They do not have to experience regeneration and conversion like others who come to the church from the outside, but may proceed from the thought that God has been reconciled, that evil has been overcome, and that the Spirit of God, who by faith is also their Spirit, fights against sin in and through them. In the Lord's Supper, which is the center of Christian doctrine and therefore viewed so variously, believers see exhibited, in a sensory, graphic way, the reconciliation with God and the indwelling of the Spirit in their hearts.[42]

[425–26] It is remarkable that the philosophy that emerged after the Enlightenment and started with Kant did seek to link itself with Christianity and to incorporate its religious truths in its philosophical system. Although modern thought after Kant attempted to overcome rationalism and develop a "philosophy of redemption," it achieved this only in form and not in substance. It is still human thought that brings about true redemption; Christianity's doctrine of reconciliation is only brought to light by philosophy. Stripped of all the speculative wording and reduced to simple words, idealistic philosophy still advocates salvation by human effort of intellect and will. Conversion, for example, is really a human act of penitence viewed from God's perspective. It is philosophy and not religion that saves. "Philosophy is theology insofar as it represents the reconciliation of God with himself and with nature; it affirms that nature, that otherness as such, as divine; it affirms that the finite Spirit characteristically elevates itself

---

42. See esp. G. W. F. Hegel, *Philosophie der Religion*, in *Sämtliche Werke*, 26 vols. (Stuttgart: F. Frommann, 1949–59), XVI, 204–28 (*Werke*, XII, 204–29). Ed. note: Hegel discusses communion as a sacrament in *Lectures on the Philosophy of Religion*, vol. 3, *The Consummate Religion*, ed. Hodgson et al. (Berkeley: University of California Press, 1985), 23, 152–56, 235–36, 337–39, 372–73.

toward reconciliation and in part comes to it in the history of the world."[43] This could not last; post-Hegelian history clearly demonstrated that the baby had been thrown out with the bathwater and that with the form also the content itself had gone down the drain. People had simply been left to save themselves by acts of their intellect or will.

Although modern theology, beginning with Schleiermacher, took the historical person of Jesus more seriously, the human subject remained at the center of its Christian understanding. Furthermore, though it frequently uses traditional Christian terms, it fills them with quite different meaning. Since grace actually coincides with divine providence, conversion is simultaneously and totally the work of both God and man. For Schleiermacher, after Christ entered into our communion of sin and misery, he possessed the power and the calling to incorporate us into his communion of holiness and blessedness. We enter this communion by sharing the God-consciousness of Jesus in absolute dependence. Justification is not a transcendent act of God but the removal of the *consciousness* of guilt, a change in the consciousness of one's relation to God, the cancellation of the split between the natural "I" and its destiny.[44]

For Ritschl, justification is synthetic judgment—pronounced not on the basis of good works but prior to good works—valid for the community;[45] he is to be praised for placing this once again in the center of the redemptive order and for his emphasis on the church and not just individuals being the object of election.[46] It is to Ritschl's credit that, in a time when the Reformation doctrine of justification was misconstrued and confused with that of sanctification, he again called attention to its significance for the religious life. Yet, to be faulted is Ritschl's one-sided focus on God's love and his denial of God's wrath on sin as well as his seeming indifference to personal justification and assurance in his desire to motivate Christians to action in the world of culture. Ritschl tragically separated theology from metaphysics, gave free reign to the sciences, and was content to give religion, both objectively and subjectively, a small place. This in effect made religion subservient to culture and gave rise among the Ritschlians to a cultural optimism (*Kulturseligkeit*) with the belief that the kingdom of God entailed world improvement. This confidence in human progress gradually yielded to the insight that science and technology, intellectual knowledge and material prosperity cannot produce peace of heart; material improvement was accompanied by spiritual poverty. Longing for a more mystical and spiritual Christianity grew; tired of *doing,* people again thirsted for *being.* Ritschl's dogmatic theology gradually became a part of the history of dogma followed by a new mysticism and a new

---

43. G. W. F. Hegel, *Philosophie der Religion,* in *Sämtliche Werke,* XVI, 287–88 (*Werke,* XII, 287–88); ed. note: this passage is in *The Consummate Religion,* ed. Hodgson et al., 370–73.

44. F. Schleiermacher, *The Christian Faith* (Edinburgh: T&T Clark, 1989), §§106–12.

45. Albrecht Ritschl, *The Christian Doctrine of Justification and Reconciliation* (Clifton, NJ: Reference Book Publishers, 1966), 27–130.

46. Ibid., 118–19.

philosophy; his theological method made way, on the one hand, for the school of
the history of religion and, on the other, for that of the psychology of religion.[47]

[427a] The psychological study of religion is a relatively new science with
roots in movements such as Pietism in Germany and Methodism in England
and America that had in common a shift in the center of gravity from the object
of religion to the subject. Psychology of religion takes its departure from subjective religious experience and seeks to infer from it a law governing all religious
development. Parallel to the evolutionary notion that ontogeny recapitulates
phylogeny, the development of religious sensibility is seen to move from childlike
obedience to rules and dogmas, through the labor pains of adolescent conflict
into individuality and capacity for reflection, to adult maturity, in a manner following the development of civilized society from stages of primitivism through
atavism to a higher level. The stages of development observed in individuals are
characteristic of humanity as a whole; humanity's development is recapitulated
in the individual person. Human beings emerged from the animal world into
their infancy, evolved into social creatures in their adolescence, and enter the
new world of universal humanity. A child enters life with basically the same instincts as animals and is by nature self-seeking, self-willed, and combative, carry-
ing with it the elementary instinct of self-preservation, which manifests itself in
anger, touchiness, jealousy, and the like. Here psychology of religion affirms the
doctrine of original sin. For a child, all religion is external; "God is a being above
and beyond him." The period of adolescence that follows is a time of storm and
stress; bodily changes explode and the young man and woman enter a world of
new sensations, new feelings of pleasure and displeasure, sympathy and aversion,
new desires, wishes and ideals. Sexual life is awakened and they become capable
of reproductive life and the possibility of contributing to and integrating with the
larger society of the human race. The capacity for abstract thought and reasoning
becomes possible as well as spiritual openness to high and noble ideals. Those who
grow into healthy adults need to experience a "double conversion," a "second birth"
in which they overcome their animal natures, their childish self-centeredness
and reliance on external rules and control and, through the labor pains of crises
in which they struggle to find their identity, become free personalities who are
capable of self-sacrifice and responsible membership in the human community.
If puberty is a second birth, a rebirth, the birth of a new personality, one's own

47. Cf. H. Bavinck, *Reformed Dogmatics*, I, 70–76 (##17–18), 170–74 (#53), 542–48 (##142–43);
ed. note: also see Herman Bavinck, *Essays in Religion, Science and Society*, ed. John Bolt, trans. Harry
Bonstra and Gerrit Sheeres (Grand Rapids: Baker Academic, 2008), esp. chaps. 1, 3, 4, 9, 11, 12. Ed. note:
The first part of the section that follows (#427a in the full volume) is entirely new in the Dutch second
edition and represents Bavinck's serious interest, during the last decade of his life, in the psychology of
religion. The material was adapted from Bavinck's lecture on the psychology of religion given at the Royal
Academy of the Sciences in 1907 and published in H. Bavinck, *Verzamelde Opstellen* (Kampen: Kok, 1921),
55–77; ET: *Essays in Religion, Science and Society*, chap. 4. For Bavinck's interest in and further explora-
tion of the topic, see H. Bavinck, *The Philosophy of Revelation* (Grand Rapids: Eerdmans, 1953), chap. 8,
"Revelation and Religious Experience"; idem, *Bijbelsche en Religieuze Psychologie* (Kampen: Kok, 1920).

and simultaneously a social personality, this second birth brings with it its own pathologies and risks, its own aberrations and sins. During these years, while the soul is torn by continual unrest and disturbance, we must take into account the interesting parallel between sexual awakening and religious conversion, while never simply explaining the latter by the former.

When people use religious language to describe the turn from a stormy, confused, and anxious situation of crisis to one of inner peace and rest, being relatively carefree and happy, confident and secure, they speak of "conversion," and Christianity views it as the fruit of a supernatural operation of God the Holy Spirit. But according to the psychology of religion, there is no necessity, scientifically speaking, to resort to any supernatural factor for an explanation of this religious crisis. However strange and abnormal it may seem, this is a completely natural process that can be adequately explained by psychology as part of ordinary human development that occurs in all religions in formally similar patterns. While it is true that individual differences remain among people in their development—depending, among other things, on upbringing and environment, character and temperament, gender and age—and there are different types of religious experience, it is also true that religious and sexual awakening consistently appear at roughly the same time in a young person's life and follow certain patterns. Religious experiences during this time typically include a sense of sin, feelings of guilt, fear of punishment, dejection, melancholy, repentance, dread, and a sense that two powers—again pictured differently as the old and the new person, darkness and light, sin and virtue, Satan and Christ—wrestle with each other. "Conversion" takes place when, after struggle, finally, the experiences of sin, misery, and calamity make way for those of peace and joy, of forgiveness and reconciliation, of the favor of God and communion with him. These religious experiences are qualitatively the same as those that are typical of puberty in general and different only in that, being transferred to the religious sphere, they are naturally religiously colored and interpreted.

According to the psychology of religion, we also need to bear in mind that the religious experiences of "conversion," "awakening," "realization," and so on, occur in all religions and peoples. Buddha, Muhammad, and others experienced religious crises as much as Paul, Augustine, and Luther. Beyond Christianity, all religions can speak of revivals both in the lives of individuals and in that of masses of people. In addition to sharing objective religious phenomena—dogma, cult, church—as well as subjective experience—mysticism, asceticism, ecstasy, revelation, inspiration—all religions, either consciously or unconsciously, agree in accepting a connection between religious development and puberty. All religions, at this age, have rituals of passage into full religious communion: first communion among Roman Catholics, confirmation among Lutherans, public profession of faith among the Reformed.

Now, psychology of religion believes that all this can be explained by the phenomenon of ongoing change in human consciousness, including the "subconscious" or "subliminal." Bombarded as we constantly are with new perceptions, the unconscious material of the impressions is continually kept in motion and may be "aroused" and altered at any time by new perceptions. What may seem on the face of it to be a significant and sudden "conversion" may in fact simply be a coming to consciousness of perceptions and impressions that have been "under the surface" all along and are now simply brought out into the open and made conscious. "Spontaneous awakenings are the fructification of that which has been ripening within the subliminal consciousness." Such transformations take place in human consciousness all the time; they are a normal part of our human experience. Conversion, in this view, is not a *sui generis* experience of some but the common experience of all: an expression of the awakening of one's religious personality during the years of puberty, a natural, necessary, and normal psychological process in adolescence. The sudden character of a given religious awakening, therefore, is not proof for its miraculous supernatural origin. This psychological explanation of conversion finds support in the religious development that manifests itself at a later age and can in general be described with the term "sanctification." As a rule when humans reach maturity, they get past their doubts and begin to reconstruct their faith and life. According to the psychology of religion, mature adults seem to "settle down" religiously, and the importance of dogmas and beliefs recedes while religious experience and good conduct increases in importance. Egocentric tendencies begin to yield to other tendencies of which society, the world, and God constitute the center.

To sum this all up—according to the psychology of religion, there is both idea and law, dynamic and design, in religious development, in humanity as well as in the individual person. The former recapitulates itself in the latter. One must discern in it three components: first, the evolution of the human being into an independent personality of its own, corresponding to the centuries-long birth of humans from the animal world; then, the evolution of the individual person into a social entity, corresponding to the slow genesis of society with its infinite forms and complex relations; finally, the evolution of the social person into a part of humanity, of the world as a whole, of the deity, "the Power that makes for righteousness." According to Stanley Hall,[48] right now we are in the middle of this period. The evolution of humans has an infinite number of centuries behind it, also countless centuries ahead of it. Right now we are in the world's adolescence. The twilight we observe is not that of the evening but that of the dawn. The soul *is* not, but is still in the process of *becoming*—"the soul is still in the making"; there are forces in it that are now still slumbering like sleepers in the forest but which

---

48. Ed. note: Much of Bavinck's discussion in this section is a direct engagement with G. Stanley Hall, *Adolescence: Its Psychology and Its Relations to Physiology, Anthropology, Sociology, Sex, Crime, Religion and Education*, 2 vols. (New York and London: D. Appleton, 1904); the expression "storm and stress" (from German *Sturm und Drang*) is Hall's signature term for the period of adolescence. The other psychologist Bavinck mentions is Edwin Diler Starbuck, *The Psychology of Religion: An Empirical Study of the Growth of Religious Consciousness* (London: W. Scott; New York: Scribner, 1901). Cf. Bavinck, *Essays on Religion, Science and Society*, 63n2; and "Editor's Introduction," in Bavinck, *Reformed Dogmatics*, III, 19.

will one day awaken. More than is now possible, they will then more forcefully promote the coming reign of "the kingdom of man."

These psychological studies and observed parallels cannot be overlooked by theology as it explores the meaning of such events as conversion. We reject all materialist explanations and theories that *reduce* spiritual changes such as conversion to mere biological or psychological causes; we insist on the independent value of the life of the soul and its religious content. At the same time we also affirm the psychosomatic unity of the human person and recognize the mutual interdependence of soul and body. Furthermore, it is indisputable that the adolescent period of life with its storms and stresses contains important parallels in a young person's religious and sexual development alike; this is the period in which the independent personality, including spiritual maturity as well as sexual and social identity and maturity, is born in people. The psychological study of religious experience has been profitable in bringing this to light.

[427b] Since God has put eternity in the human heart we can never escape the need to—in some way—formulate the question: How do I find the supreme good and lasting happiness?[49] How can I be reconciled to God and incorporated in his fellowship? How do I find a gracious God? (Luther) What is the road that leads to eternal life? Theologically, these questions belong to the category of the order or *way of salvation* (*ordo* or *via salutis*). Initially, Reformed theology usually treated the order of salvation under three headings: repentance, faith, and good works. But this series was soon expanded to include, among other topics, calling, illumination, regeneration, conversion, faith, justification, sanctification, and more. As we have seen,[50] Reformed theology was characterized by great diversity in treatments of this order though the emphasis consistently was on the beneficial *application* of Christ's work to the believer by the Holy Spirit. Calvin, thus, gave to the third book of his *Institutes* the title: "The way in which we receive the grace of Christ: what benefits come to us from it and what effects follow."

When we return to the starting point of Scripture for our understanding of the order of salvation, we encounter an immediate difficulty. Although Christ's death has accomplished everything for our salvation, we are not immediately completely delivered from sin, suffering, and death and given full holiness and blessedness. On the contrary, we are exhorted, in time, to faith and repentance; have to be regenerated, justified, sanctified, and glorified; remain subject in this life to sin, suffering, and death; and only enter the kingdom of heaven through much affliction. Scripture seems to tell us two apparently contradictory truths: on the one hand, everything has been accomplished, so that there is nothing left

---

49. Ed. note: The transition here from the previous discussion is abrupt; Bavinck does not continue the discussion of religious psychology and, somewhat uncharacteristically, does not provide a substantive critical response but is content with description. It is very apparent that this new field of study was very important to him.

50. Cf. H. Bavinck, *Reformed Dogmatics*, III, 520–22 (#418).

for us humans to do; on the other hand, the most important things still have to happen in the life of humans if they are to obtain the salvation acquired.

For that reason, we run the risk of Pelagian nomism on the one hand, and antinomianism, on the other. These are the twin submerged rocks on which the ship of the Christian order of salvation is always in danger of suffering shipwreck. Nomism (Pelagianism in its various forms and degrees) not only collides with the decrees of God,[51] but also fails to do justice to the person and work of Christ. If so much is left for us to do because Christ at most acquired the *possibility* of our being saved and leaves the decision in our hands, then what is decisive in salvation is up to us. Christ is reduced to a position of exemplary teacher and is not the all-sufficient savior. Pelagianism, in effect, blurs the boundary between Christianity and the pagan religions and has people gain salvation by their own wisdom and strength. Thus, it removes certainty and brings people back to a situation in which they are without God and without hope in the world (Eph. 2:12). The very outcome of world history becomes unclear; with respect to the most important question of all—the world's eternal destiny—the management of the world rests in human hands.[52] While Pietism and Methodism were right in their opposition to dead orthodoxy and desire to stir Christians up to greater spirituality and good works, applying Christianity to life, they frequently swung to the other extreme and shifted the emphasis from the objective to the subjective. They did not deny the acquisition of salvation by Christ, but directed their energy and effort to themselves and the experience of faith (Pietism) or the obedience of good works (Methodism). Whether in Pietistic fashion it withdraws from the world or in Methodist style acts aggressively in the world, this Christianity remains separate, stands dualistically alongside the natural life, and therefore does not have an organic impact on the family, society, and the state, on science and art. Sanctification is more negative than positive; it consists primarily in abstaining from ordinary things.

On the other side of the spectrum stands antinomianism. It does stand for an important truth that we must acknowledge: Christ has accomplished everything and we have not, cannot, and need not add anything to his sacrifice for our salvation. But antinomians employ this truth to proclaim a quite different doctrine,

51. Cf. H. Bavinck, *Reformed Dogmatics*, II, 347–51 (#234), 377–82 (##242–43).

52. Ed. note: It is therefore quite consistent for Arminian theologians to also become advocates of so-called "open theism," the conviction that God does not know future contingent events; see David Basinger, *The Case for Freewill Theism: A Philosophical Assessment* (Downers Grove, IL: InterVarsity, 1996); Gregory A. Boyd, *God of the Possible: A Biblical Introduction to the Open View of God* (Grand Rapids: Baker Books, 2000); Christopher A. Hall and John Sanders, *Does God Have a Future? A Debate on Divine Providence* (Grand Rapids: Baker Academic, 2003); William Hasker, *Providence, Evil and the Openness of God* (London and New York: Routledge, 2004); Clark H. Pinnock, *Most Moved Mover: A Theology of God's Openness* (Grand Rapids: Baker Academic; Carlisle, Cumbria, UK: Paternoster, 2000); Pinnock et. al., *The Openness of God: A Biblical Challenge to the Traditional Understanding of God* (Downers Grove, IL: InterVarsity, 1994); John Sanders, *The God Who Risks: A Theology of Providence* (Downers Grove, IL: InterVarsity, 1998).

namely that Christ too has nothing left to do after his resurrection and glorification. But, in the state of exaltation, there remains much for Christ to do. He must
also apply and distribute to his church the salvation he acquired. Antinomianism
thus ignores the application of the work of salvation and, in principle, denies the
personality and activity of the Holy Spirit. Antinomianism is inwardly motivated
by a pantheistic impulse; God and humanity are essentially one and therefore
reconciled from eternity. The whole of redemption is that we be better informed
and enlightened about our true state; abandon the illusion that God is angry
with us and acknowledge that he loves us as our Father. There is no repentance
needed, no contrition, no regret over sin, no fear of hell, no dread of judgment,
no prayer for forgiveness, no sanctification: those are all Pelagian errors, which
fail to do justice to the objective facts of God's grace and atonement. Here too,
Jesus is only a prophet, a teacher who enlightens us about God's love and ways;
we simply need to be relieved of our wrong views. Like nomism, so also antinomianism ends with a total rejection of the essence of Christianity, sinks back into
paganism, and locates salvation from sin in the rationalistic enlightenment or
moralistic improvement of humans. Both, either in an Arian or a Sabellian sense,
reject the confession of the Trinity.

THE TRINITARIAN WAY OF SALVATION AND TRUTH

[428] The biblical view of salvation must be fully trinitarian, acknowledging the
distinct work of the Holy Spirit. What Christ gained for us is complete but must
be applied to and in us in justification and sanctification, freedom from the guilt,
pollution, and power of sin. Just as a child, even before birth, has a claim on all the
goods of his or her father but only at a much later age enters into possession of it,
so also all those who will later believe have—long before they believe—owner-
ship rights in Christ to all the benefits he has acquired but only enter into the
possession of them by faith. The acquisition of salvation therefore calls for the
application of these benefits. That application is twofold: because Christ redeems
us from sin and its consequences—taking over our guilt and punishment he also
fulfilled the law in our stead—in the Spirit's power we acquire justification (i.e.,
the assurance of the forgiveness of sins and the right to eternal life). We are also
given the Spirit's power unto sanctification (i.e., the renewal in us of the image
of Christ); the Holy Spirit "bears witness with our spirit that we are children of
God" (Rom. 8:16) and regenerates us and refashions us after the image of God.
This work of application is just as much a divine work as the creation by the Father and the redemption by the Son; and the Holy Spirit who brings it about is
therefore, together with the Father and the Son, the one, sole God, to be praised
and blessed forever.

Here the Reformation principle becomes clear: nature is a creation of God and
subject to his providence and thus of no less value than grace. The Holy Spirit's

work in redemption is thus also linked to creation. Natural life itself is renewed. The Reformation taught that grace is opposed only to sin, not to nature; in principle there is only one antithesis, namely that of sin and grace. For this reason the Reformation could accord to God's guidance in the life of nature, both in that of peoples and that of special persons, a pedagogical role and significance. It is God himself who prepares the gracious working of the Holy Spirit in the line of generations; and the Holy Spirit in his activities links up with the guidance of God in the natural life and attempts by his grace to restore the natural life, to free it from the power of sin and consecrate it to God. At the same time, the work of the Holy Spirit does not override human willing and acting; grace opposes not our nature but our sin. From the essential unity of Father, Son, and Spirit, it also follows that the Holy Spirit is connected with the work of the Son. One in essence, the three Persons, in their varying activities, work together.

Having been equipped by the Spirit for his work on earth and anointed without measure with him, Christ has fully acquired that Spirit and received all the gifts of that Spirit and now lives, rules, and governs by that Spirit. The Spirit of the Father and the Son has become *his* Spirit, the Spirit of Christ. Before Christ was glorified, he was not yet that Spirit, but now he is the Spirit of Christ, his rightful property, his possession. So, on the day of Pentecost, he sends that Spirit in order by the Spirit to apply all his benefits to his church. The Holy Spirit takes everything from Christ: as the Son came to glorify the Father, so the Holy Spirit in turn came down to glorify the Son. He applies all Christ's benefits, to each in his measure, at his time, according to his order, until the fullness of Christ dwells in his church and she has reached maturity, "the measure of the full stature of Christ" (Eph. 4:13). The order of redemption is the application of salvation (*applicatio salutis*) and the relevant question is not, first of all, "What must one do to be saved?" but "What is God doing in his grace to make the church participate in the complete salvation acquired by Christ?" The "application of salvation" is a work of God that must be viewed theologically, not anthropologically, which has the Holy Spirit as its author and may be called his special work. The whole "way of salvation" is the "applicatory grace of the Holy Spirit."

Against this view of the order of salvation and from the side of Pelagianism, however, the objection is always raised that the rights of humanity are denied, human self-activity is suppressed, and an ungodly life is fostered. This objection is fundamentally calculated to overturn the scriptural testimony that by the works of the law no human being will be justified (Rom. 3:20) and thus it is inadmissible. It is also based on a serious misunderstanding. Believing that the "application of salvation" is God's work does not exclude but includes the full recognition of all those moral factors that, under the guidance of God's providence, affect the intellect and heart of the unconverted person. It is God himself, after all, who thus leads his human children, witnesses to them, and showers benefits down on them from heaven (cf. Acts 14:17) that they should seek God in hope of finding him (cf. Acts 17:27). The application of salvation is and remains a work of the

Spirit, the Holy Spirit, the Spirit of Christ, and is therefore never coercive and violent but always spiritual, lovely, and gentle, treating humans not as blocks of wood but as rational beings, illuminating, persuading, drawing, and bending them. The Spirit causes the darkness of human sin to yield to the light of God's grace and replaces spiritual powerlessness with spiritual power. It is God's Spirit who "bears witness with our spirit that we are children of God" (cf. Rom. 8:16). "I no longer live, but Christ lives in me; the life I now live in the body, I live by faith in the Son of God" (cf. Gal. 2:20). "It is God who is at work in you, enabling you both to will and to work for his good pleasure," who himself wants us to work out our salvation "with fear and trembling" (cf. Phil. 2:12–13). This theological view alone gives assurance and guarantees the reality of a new Christian life; the Pelagian view, by contrast, makes everything wobbly and uncertain—even the victory of the good and the triumph of the kingdom of God—because it hangs everything on the incalculable arbitrariness of humans. Standing up for the rights of humankind, it tramples on the rights of God, and for humans ends up with no more than the right to be fickle. The theological view of the order of salvation gathers up all the good that is concealed in the anthropological view and does justice to humans as God's rational and moral creatures, but the reverse does not happen. Those who start with humans and first of all seek to secure their rights and liberties always end up limiting the power and grace of God.

[429] All this is summed up in the word "grace," which denotes the unmerited favor of God and the many benefits flowing from it, the gifts of grace (Rom. 5:20; Eph. 1:7; 2:5, 8; Phil. 1:2; Col. 1:2; Titus 2:11; 3:7; etc.). Here we discuss only those gifts of grace that the Holy Spirit communicates subjectively—internally—to humans and that are most intimately related to their salvation: those gifts of God's special grace which in the preaching of the gospel are offered to all hearers and are effectively granted to the elect. Rome and the Reformation differ here; Rome sees a supernatural power that illumines the intellect and inspires the will, the Reformation thinks of the gracious invitation and call of the gospel. For Rome, habitual or infused grace is a gift of God by which humanity "is elevated to the supernatural order and in some manner made a participant of the divine nature."[53] Grace, in the thinking of Rome, is, in the first place, a supernatural quality added to human beings by which they are in principle taken up into a supernatural order, become partakers of the divine nature, of the vision of God, and are able to perform supernatural acts such as by a condign merit deserve eternal life. In this substantial view of grace, the forgiveness of sins is secondary to elevation and divinization, "both becoming like God and union with him."[54]

For the Reformation, grace, like sin, is never a substance and does not elevate us beyond nature but rather frees us from the enslavement of sin within our natural

53. Christian Pesch, *Praelectiones dogmaticae*, 9 vols. (Freiburg: Herder, 1902–10), V, 172, 188.
54. Dionysius, in Joann Baptist Heinrich and Constantin Gutberlet, *Dogmatische Theologie*, 2nd ed., 10 vols. (Mainz: Kirchheim, 1881–1900), VIII, 595.

order; the "physical" opposition between the natural and the supernatural yields
to the ethical opposition between sin and grace. Christ does not bring us back
to the point on the road where Adam stood but has covered the whole journey
for us to the very end. He not only accomplished the passive but also the active
obedience. He acquired an inamissible salvation, eternal life, which for Adam still
lay in the future. Yet grace does not give us any more than what, if Adam had not
fallen, would have been acquired by him in the way of obedience. The covenant
of grace differs from the covenant of works in method, not in its ultimate goal. It
is the same treasure that was promised in the covenant of works and is granted in
the covenant of grace. Grace restores nature and takes it to its highest pinnacle,
but it does not add to it any new and heterogeneous constituents. The re-creation
is not a second, new creation. It does not add to existence any new creatures or
introduce any new substance into it, but it is truly "re-formation." In this process
the working of grace extends as far as the power of sin. Sin has infected everything;
it has corrupted the organism of the creation, the very nature of creatures. Grace,
accordingly, is the power of God that also frees humankind inwardly, in the core
of its being, from sin and presents it before God without spot or wrinkle. Grace is
the beginning, the middle, and the end of the entire work of salvation; it is totally
devoid of human merit. Like creation and redemption, so also sanctification is a
work of God. It is of him, and through him, and therefore also leads to him and
serves to glorify him.

[430] The special benefits of grace are manifold and inexhaustible. Theologians
have labored mightily to treat them in an orderly and comprehensive manner.
Roman Catholic theology treated them from the point of view of the church
and ordered them hierarchically: actual grace, habitual grace, the fruits of grace.
The priest, by means of the sacraments, infuses, restores, and increases grace in
the hearts of believers. Grace follows the track of the sacraments. The Reformation, however, focused more on believers and on the way they were brought to
salvation than on the church and sacraments. When, in the order of salvation,
the Reformation thus again placed the work of the Holy Spirit in the foreground,
it initially simply discussed it under the three headings of repentance, faith, and
good works. But soon it saw itself compelled to give a fuller treatment. Over
against Anabaptists, who detached Spirit and Word, and the Remonstrants who
accused the Reformed, with their doctrine of an "immediate" operation of the
Holy Spirit, of neglecting and disdaining the preaching of the Word, Reformed
theologians assigned the first place in the order to "calling." As in creation and
providence, so in re-creation God also brought all things into being by means of
the Word. Calling, furthermore, was divided into an external and internal call[55]
when regeneration was understood in a restricted sense and assigned to a place
before faith. Over against the Remonstrants and the Amyraldians, the Reformed
insisted on regeneration as prior, acknowledging the Holy Spirit as the agent

55. Canons of Dort, III–IV, 6–10.

moving the human will before any act of its own. Theologians also felt compelled to distinguish between the working of the Holy Spirit and the fruit of that operation; in other words, between the faculty and the act of faith, between conversion in a passive and in an active sense; or also between regeneration in a restricted sense and faith (with conversion in the active sense). In regeneration the Holy Spirit does not merely by the Word illumine the intellect but also directly and immediately infuses new affections into the will.[56] Faith and repentance are the fruits of an omnipotent operation of the Holy Spirit, the fruits of a seed planted in the heart by the Holy Spirit.

Further nuances were made in response to challenges, especially by the revivalism of Pietism and Methodism. The Reformed did not deny that many of those who are saved are only born again and converted at a later age. However, since they believed that regeneration (in the restricted sense) in covenant children preceded faith and conversion in the active sense, it did not always have to be accompanied, as Pietism and Methodism later demanded, by a "noteworthy impact and strong attraction" but could also occur "in time, in stages, and gracefully." It was also not necessary that people knew exactly and could give a clear account of the manner and time of their conversions, as John Wesley, for example, knew that for him it occurred at a quarter to nine in the evening on the twenty-fourth of May 1738. Regeneration was not concentrated then at a single point in time but extended over the whole of the Christian life. As such it is best described as a continuing mortification of the old and an ongoing resurrection of the new person.[57]

Also with respect to the doctrine of justification, finally, some Reformed theologians arrived at a somewhat different view than was generally assumed earlier. In order to address the errors of the neonomians—faith as condition for forgiveness—and the over correction of the antineonomians—justification only forensic as a consequence of Christ's passive obedience—Reformed theology affirmed both the doctrine of free justification and the imputation of Christ's person and the benefits of his active obedience. Justification, in other words, did not occur as a result of or by faith, but *with a view* to faith. Before the elect receive faith, they have already been justified. Indeed, they receive this faith precisely because they have already been justified beforehand. This objective and active justification was made known in the gospel from Genesis 3:15 on and in the resurrection of Christ (Rom. 4:25), but had actually already occurred in the decree of election when they were given to Christ and Christ was given to them, when their sin was imputed to Christ and his righteousness was imputed to them. Some Reformed theologians spoke of *eternal* justification, but fear of the antinomianism that, on the basis of an eternal justification, opposed the satisfaction of Christ, changed the nature of faith, and rejected the normative use of the law, kept Reformed

---

56. See H. Bavinck, *Saved by Grace*, ed. J. Mark Beach, trans. Nelson D. Kloosterman (Grand Rapids: Reformation Heritage Books, 2008), 41–64.

57. Heidelberg Catechism, Lord's Day 23; Zacharias Ursinus, *The Commentary of Dr. Zacharius Ursinus on the Heidelberg Catechism*, trans. G. W. Willard (Grand Rapids: Eerdmans, 1954), qu. 59–61.

theology from shifting the doctrine of justification back to that of the decrees. Furthermore, for those who did use the language of eternal justification, this had little or no influence on the treatment of the order of salvation. Even Maccovius expressly rejected and opposed it, treating the benefits in the following order: active justification, regeneration, faith, passive justification, good works; he nevertheless continued to distinguish justification from its decree in eternity.[58] The conditions that gradually began to prevail in the churches during the eighteenth and nineteenth centuries made it difficult to maintain the Reformed scheme of the order of salvation. When worldliness penetrates the church, the pattern of covenant youth coming to faith and conversion "in stages and gracefully" is less apparent, and many people grow up and live for years without showing any fruits worthy of faith and repentance. At such times, serious-minded believers feel called to warn against trusting in one's childhood regeneration and one's historical faith in Christian doctrine and to insist on true conversion, conversion of the heart, an experiential knowledge of the truths of salvation. Against a dead orthodoxy, Pietism and Methodism, with their conventicles and revivals, always have a right and reason to exist.

[431] As we noted,[59] the revivals triggered the rise of the new science we know as the psychology of religion. Reformed people should have no difficulty with the possibility and legitimacy of examining religious phenomena from a psychological perspective, provided this is done with appropriate sensitivity and respect. Because the world exists for us humans solely in and through our consciousnesses, the content of the consciousness can therefore be considered and studied objectively, in itself and for its own sake, but also subjectively, from a psychological angle. The distinctive features in the religious life of a child, a young man or woman, the adult, or the elderly; the links between religious development and physical, psychological, and moral development; the connection between religious awakening and puberty; the clarification of conversion through recurring transformations of one's consciousness; and the operation of subliminal forces in the religious process—all that and much more broadens one's vision, deepens one's insight into the religious life, and produces valuable results for the theologian, pastor, preacher, missionary, teacher, and nurturer. But the psychology of religion is still a young science and therefore at times bent on picking fruit before it is ripe. Whatever difficulties Reformed people have with aspects of revivalism, and though they acknowledge the legitimacy of a psychological study of religion, they also insist that religious phenomena cannot be exhaustively explained in psychological terms. The psychology of religion can up to a point teach us what conversion often means in the practice of life, but by itself it cannot possibly tell us what the difference is between a true conversion and a pseudoconversion, between worldly grief and

58. Johannes Maccovius, *Loci communes theologici* (Amsterdam: n.p., 1658), 676. Cf. what will be said later about justification.
59. See H. Bavinck, *Reformed Dogmatics*, III, 556 (#426).

godly grief; why conversion takes place in the life of one person and not in the life of another, or why it occurs in one person's life in this period, and in another person's life in a much earlier or later period. The psychology of religion has no criteria of its own, and of itself it does not know what conversion is—and has to be; only God in his revelation can do that. It is, therefore, arrogant for some psychologists of religion to tell us that only psychological factors are operative in conversion and that there is no room for a supernatural factor. The point where the finite touches the infinite and rests in the infinite is everywhere undemonstrable; what happens in the depths of a human soul, behind one's consciousness and will, is a mystery even for the person in question, and all the more so for those who are on the outside and have to rely on phenomena. Just as the idealism that is grounded in theoretical knowledge, by removing from observation the implied belief in the reality of the outside world, undermines human knowledge, so the psychology of religion, which denies to metaphysics its right to exist, dissolves religious phenomena into delusions.

Particularly, this study can say nothing about the truth of a religion. William James attempted to draw the norm for making judgments about religious experience from the religious phenomena themselves. They are to be judged, says the pragmatist James, on the basis of their social utility; what matters in religion is not so much what God is as how he is used by us. "Not God, but life, more life . . . is the end of religion. God is not known, he is used" (James). Still, even with this utilitarian norm, James fails to surmount the difficulty, for if "life force" is the sole criterion for deciding the truth and validity of religion, it remains a question—one that can never be answered by historical research—which religion, or pagan superstition for that matter, produces that "value." In other words, how do we come to agreement about "value"? Pragmatism, to be consistent, would now have to say that "value" can only be argued by its "value" and so on ad infinitum. Since this is impossible, pragmatism dead-ends unless it turns around and argues the truth and validity of religion by a route other than "value." For that reason, James had to admit failure and finally turn to mysticism: "The heart has its reasons which reason does not know." Concluding that God's grace works its way through "the subliminal door," James, not without reason, calls himself a "supernaturalist," be it in a highly modified sense. The knowledge obtained in this manner is minimal: an awareness that there is "something more," a higher power. From this it is clear that the psychology of religion, although it can make important contributions to a better understanding of the religious life, can never, not any more than can the history of religions, replace or make up for dogmatics, philosophy, or metaphysics. It is restricted to affirming that religious phenomena (ideas, sensations) do have a psychological value, and seeking the reality of religion in a vague and undefinable "essence" of religion. It should be clear by now: Religion can only be maintained as real or true when it rests on revelation.

[432] In distinction from the psychology of religion, a science that can give only an inadequate account of subjective piety, the task of dogmatics is to set forth

what the order of salvation is according to the word and thought of God. Now Scripture is very rich and effusive in summing up and describing the benefits of salvation in Christ. Caution must be observed here; the words that dogmatics employs do not always have precisely the same content they have in Holy Scripture. "Its expressions are, so to speak, collective concepts, which do not denote either the individual stages, levels, degrees, or phases of development, but rather the completed fact itself."[60] We cannot use Scripture alone to create a scientific lexicon of words for salvation; they are used there to describe various aspects of the one work of transformation brought about by the Holy Spirit. This, however, should not prevent theologians from attempting to derive from the variety of terms and images in Scripture an orderly account of the Holy Spirit's work in us. As in the doctrine of the Trinity and the person of Christ, theologians will indeed be compelled sometimes to use words that do not occur in Scripture or to assign to them a broader or narrower meaning than they possess in some places there. But their duty is not to repeat Scripture literally word for word but to discover the ideas that are concealed in the words of Scripture and to explicate the relationships between them. The various words and images that the authors of the books of the Old and the New Testament employ all contribute to the disclosure of the pivotal issue from a variety of perspectives and in all its riches and fullness.

Keeping this in mind, the following is suggested as a framework or a set of parameters within which a Reformed treatment of the order of salvation ought to work: All the benefits that Christ acquired and distributes to his church are benefits of the covenant of grace. This covenant has its foundation in eternity; it is grounded in the good pleasure or counsel of God. It is God's electing love, the Father's good pleasure, out of which all these benefits flow to the church. These benefits are acquired first by Christ in all fullness in an objectively real way. Then they are applied by the Holy Spirit to believers. The Holy Spirit on the one hand takes everything from Christ and freely binds himself to his Word but, on the other hand, since the day of Pentecost, also dwells personally in the church and in each of its members and fills them with all the fullness of God. All the benefits of salvation that the Father has awarded to the church from eternity and the Son acquired in time are at the same time gifts of the Holy Spirit. Thus Christ by the Spirit, and the Father himself by Christ, incorporates all his children into most intimate fellowship with himself.

The benefits of the salvation acquired by Christ and applied by the Holy Spirit are not an accidental aggregate but organically connected. Those who believe will be saved. Regeneration is necessary for us to enter the kingdom of God. Without faith it is impossible to please God. Without holiness no one will see God. Those who persevere to the end will be saved. One cannot obtain the ensuing benefits without having received the preceding ones. Calling, the preaching of the gospel, therefore, precedes all other benefits, for as a rule the Holy Spirit binds himself

---

60. W. Schmidt, *Christliche Dogmatik*, 4 vols. (Bonn: E. Weber, 1895–98), II, 432.

to the Word. Word proclamation continues in the church even for those who already believe. Although it is legitimate to distinguish mission preaching from established church-oriented preaching, pastoral sensitivity to the congregation's spiritual health demands that sometimes the staff of consolation is needed while at other times the rod of chastisement is called for. Sometimes one must build; at other times one must break down. From this, however, it is clear that calling (external and internal), with the corresponding acts of faith and repentance (arising from regeneration in the restricted sense), are, as it were, the initiatory benefits by which one obtains those that follow.

To summarize: justification based on Christ's objective atonement precedes the acts of repentance of believers and their lives of sanctification in which they grow in grace. For this reason the immediate work of the Holy Spirit in regeneration precedes faith, and since only those who are holy will gain eternal life, sanctification precedes perseverance in order. Another way of stating this is to say that Christ first restores our relationship to God, then renews us after God's image, and finally preserves for us our heavenly inheritance. Another way is to say that we are called as prophets, justified as priests, sanctified and glorified as kings. There are, thus, four groups of benefits in the order of salvation: calling (with regeneration in a restricted sense, faith, and repentance); justification; sanctification; and glorification[61] All this is from God, in Christ, through the power and working of the Holy Spirit.

61. Although glorification is usually treated at the conclusion of dogmatics, in the doctrine of the last things (eschatology), it nevertheless actually belongs to the way of salvation (*via salutis*) and is inseparably bound up with justification and sanctification. A pattern of order like this can be found, among other places, in Rom. 8:30 and 1 Cor. 1:30.

18

Calling and Regeneration

The Call of God

[433–34] The Triune God produces all things in creation and new creation by his Word and Spirit (Gen. 1; Ps. 33:6; John 1:3; Heb. 1:3; 11:3); all things speak to us of God. God's external call as law comes to all people in nature, in history, and in a variety of experiences. While insufficient unto salvation, this call upholds human existence in society and culture, despite the ubiquity of sin, and prepares the way for the gospel call. Although the restricted call unto salvation comes through the word of the gospel, it may not be separated from nature and history. The covenant of grace is sustained by the cosmic covenant of nature. The Logos who created all things and as light shines into the darkness enlightening every human coming into the world (John 1:14) leaves no one without a witness, but does good from heaven and fills also the hearts of gentiles with food and good cheer (Ps. 19:2–4; Matt. 5:45; John 1:5, 9–10; Acts 14:16–17; 17:27; Rom. 1:19–21; 2:14–15). All things hold together in Christ, who upholds all things by the word of his power (Col. 1:16; Heb. 1:3). Just as the Father created all things through the Christ, and he is the one who obtains our salvation, he is also the one who calls (Matt. 11:28; Mark 1:15; 2:17; Luke 5:32; 19:10), sends laborers into his vineyard (Matt. 20:1–7), invites guests to the wedding feast (Matt. 22:2), gathers children as a hen gathers her chicks (Matt. 23:37), appoints apostles and teachers (Matt. 10; 28:19; Luke 10; Eph. 4:11), whose voice has gone out to all the earth (Rom. 10:18). The Logos who became incarnate is the One by whom all things were made. Grace does not abolish nature but restores it. Still, the special call of the gospel does not proceed from law—not even revealed law—and invite us to obedience, but is a proclamation that flows forth from grace and invites us to faith. Further, it is always accompanied by a certain working and witness of the Spirit, whom Christ poured out as his Spirit upon the church (John 16:8–11; Matt. 12:31; Acts 5:3; 7:51; Heb. 6:4).

The call to faith must be universally preached; this is Christ's command (Matt. 28:19), and the Bible tells us that many who do not come are nevertheless called (Matt. 22:14; Luke 14:16–18). The outcome must be left in God's hands; we are simply to obey.

Those who reject the gospel (John 3:36; Acts 13:46; 2 Thess. 1:8) are therefore guilty of the appalling sin of unbelief (Matt. 10:15; 11:22, 24; John 3:36; 16:8–9; 2 Thess. 1:8; 1 John 5:10). Critics of the Reformed faith, such as universalists, charge that the doctrines of election and limited atonement imply a denial of the universal call of the gospel. In response, we need to say that the gospel is to be preached to human beings, not as elect or reprobate, but as sinners, all of whom need redemption. To them, Reformed preachers, no less than Arminian or universalist ones, proclaim as the content of the gospel the message: "Believe in the Lord Jesus and you will receive the forgiveness of sins and eternal life." Of course, not to each individual person can it be said, "Christ died in your place." But neither do those who deny limited atonement and preach a hypothetical universalism do that since they only believe in the possibility of universal salvation, conditional upon human acceptance. This no one knows for sure; God has kept to himself whether or not he will bestow that faith. He only tells us what he wants us to do: that we humble ourselves and seek our salvation in Christ alone. Since it is clear from history that the outcome of God's call does not universally lead to faith, we cannot avoid the intellectual problem. With all due respect, it is not our task but God's responsibility to square this outcome with the universal offer of salvation. The intellectual problem is not solved through weakening the call by expanding it for the purpose of greater inclusiveness. We must avoid the human temptation to want to be sure of the outcome before using the means, and in order to be exempt from using the means. Our Lord's command settles the matter; we must proclaim the gospel, along with the command to repent and believe, to all people "promiscuously and indiscriminately."[1]

Acknowledging in humility the mystery of God's will, we recognize that God's own glory is its final purpose and believe that his Word never returns to him empty. What God does is never futile. Even those who reject the call of God cannot escape the significant demonstration in the proclamation itself that God's love is infinite and that he has no pleasure in the death of sinners but rather that they should turn and live (Ezek. 18:23, 32). God never releases his grip on us and never abandons his claims on us, on our service, and on our complete consecration. For that reason, by nature and history, heart and conscience, blessings

---

1. Ed. note: Language taken from the Canons of Dort, second head, art. 5: "*Quae promissio omnibus populis et hominibus . . . promiscue et indiscriminatim et proponi debet cum resipiscentiae et fidei mandato.*"

and judgments, law and gospel, he summons us to return to him. The call, in its broadest sense, is the preaching of God's claims upon his fallen creatures. As such it maintains in each person and in the whole human race the religious and moral awareness of dependence, awe, respect, duty, and responsibility, without which humanity cannot exist. Religion, morality, law, art, science, family, society, the state—they all have their root and foundation in the call that comes from God to all people. The call is "repressive grace" and proof that God is God, that he is indifferent toward nothing, and that not only the world beyond but also this world has value to him. The call of law also prepares the way for the gospel, not in the Arminian sense[2] of an evolution from preparatory grace[3] to saving grace through human willing, but as the created natural foundation for salvation. The spiritual life that is implanted in regeneration differs essentially from the natural and moral life that precedes it.

Nonetheless, God who is the creator, sustainer, and ruler of all things also orders the lives of those on whom he will, in his time, bestow the gift of faith, and in many different ways prepares for his gracious work in human hearts. All things, accordingly, are connected by divine prearrangement to their subsequent "enlistment" and calling in the church. Thus the "natural" circumstances of a person's life—place of birth, family, nation, upbringing, and education; experiences of suffering and blessing; the preaching of law and gospel; development of conscience—are providential and gracious ways God prepares people for rebirth by the Holy Spirit and for the roles that they as believers will later play in the church. To speak of "preparatory grace" in such a sound sense is a valuable reminder that God links his work of grace to our natural lives; creation, redemption, and sanctification are the work of the Triune God in the divine economy of Father, Son, and Holy Spirit. God is sovereign, his leadings diverse, and the grace of the Holy Spirit is rich, abundant, and free. We are brought into the kingdom in different ways and called to perform different tasks in God's service. Unlike those who seek to convert and mold everyone according to a single model of calling, Reformed theology respects the free sovereignty of God and marvels at the riches of his grace.

[435] Following Augustine, Reformed theology distinguishes an external or revealed call from the savingly efficacious internal call of the Holy Spirit.[4] This distinction honors Scripture's testimony concerning the universality of sin. All

---

2. Canons of Dort, first head, Rejection of Errors IV: "Who teach, that in election to faith a prerequisite condition is that man should rightly use the light of nature, be upright, unassuming, humble, and disposed to eternal life, as though election depended to some extent on these factors." H. Witsius, *The Oeconomy of Covenants between God and Man*, 3 vols. (New York: Lee & Stokes, 1798), III, 6, 9: "Hence it appears, there are no preparations antecedent to the first beginning of regeneration." Cf. Remonstrant Confession and *Apologia pro confessione*, XI, 4; Peter van Mastricht, *Theoretico-practica theologia* (Utrecht: Appels, 1714), VI, 3, 19–28.

3. Reformed theologians preferred to speak of "antecedent grace" rather than "preparatory grace."

4. Cf. Augustine, *Predestination of the Saints*, chap. 8; Calvin, on Romans 10:16; idem, *Institutes of the Christian Religion*, ed. John T. McNeill and trans. Ford Lewis Battles (Philadelphia: Westminster, 1960), III.xxiv.8.

humans stand condemned before God (Rom. 3:9–19; 5:12; 9:21; 11:32), are dead in their sins and trespasses (Eph. 2:2–3), and darkened in their understanding (1 Cor. 2:14; Eph. 4:18; 5:8). Why some believe and others do not cannot be explained in terms of human capacities. God and his grace alone make the difference (1 Cor. 4:7). The preaching of the Word by itself is not sufficient (Isa. 6:9–10; 53:1; Matt. 13:13ff.; Mark 4:12; John 12:38–40; etc.). The Holy Spirit, promised in the Old Testament (Isa. 32:15; Jer. 31:33; 32:39; Ezek. 11:19; 36:26; Joel 2:28), was poured out at Pentecost to regenerate people (John 3:5ff.; 6:63; 16:13), lead them to confess Jesus as Lord (1 Cor. 12:3), and bear witness to Christ (John 15:26–27). So it depends not on human will or exertion but on God who shows mercy (Rom. 9:16). The calling is the implementation of divine election (Rom. 8:28; 11:29). It is God who is at work in us, enabling us both to will and to work according to his good pleasure (Phil. 2:13), and to that end uses a power like the power by which he raised Christ from the dead and made him sit at his right hand (Eph. 1:18–20). The work of redemption, therefore, is ascribed completely to God, both subjectively and objectively.

Rebirth

The very act by which God accomplishes this change in humans is often called "rebirth" (John 1:13; 3:3ff.; Titus 3:5; etc.), and the fruit of it is called a new heart (Jer. 31:33), a new creation (2 Cor. 5:17), the work of God (Rom. 14:20), his workmanship created in Christ Jesus (Eph. 2:10), and his building (1 Cor. 3:9; Eph. 2:21; etc.). Scripture, thus, speaks of calling in a dual sense. Repeatedly it refers to a calling and invitation to which there was no positive response (Isa. 65:12; Matt. 22:3, 14; 23:37; Mark 16:15–16; etc.); people remain obstinate, refuse to believe, and resist God's call (Matt. 11:20ff.; 23:37; Luke 7:30; Acts 7:51). To them the gospel is foolishness (1 Cor. 1:18, 23) because they do not understand (1 Cor. 2:14); it becomes to them a word of judgment (2 Cor. 2:15–16). But Scripture also knows a calling from God—a realization of election—that is always efficacious (Rom. 4:17; 8:30; 9:11, 24; 1 Cor. 1:9; 7:15ff.; Gal. 1:6, 15; 5:8; Eph. 4:1, 4; 1 Thess. 2:12; 2 Tim. 1:9; also cf. 1 Pet. 1:15; 2:9; 5:10; 2 Pet. 1:3). Believers are therefore repeatedly described simply as "those who are called" (Rom. 1:7; 1 Cor. 1:2, 24), and "those who are called in Christ" or "in the Lord" (1 Cor. 7:22); that is, those who are called by God belong to Christ and live in communion with him. As a power of God (1 Cor. 1:18, 24), the gospel proves itself to those who are called by God according to his purpose (Rom. 8:28; 9:11; 11:28; Eph. 1:4–5).

[436] The efficacious call of God is comprehensive and thus calls to mind all the work of God by his Word and Spirit—internally and externally, mediately and immediately—that brings to birth a new, spiritually alive being, in communion with Christ from a formerly spiritually dead person. The Greek word

παλιγγενεσια does not occur for the first time in the New Testament but is also found in other literature, and the notion of rebirth is found in other religions of the Ancient East, notably in mystery religions such as Mithraism. Attempts to explain the Christian understanding of regeneration by means of the dying and rising gods of the mystery religions are not very persuasive. Even considering the paucity of our knowledge about the mystery religions, their ideas and practices come from an entirely different religious environment and worldview. The faith of the early Christian church was centered in the person of Christ and from the beginning took an antithetic position to all pagan religions. Even when the New Testament employs the same words that were current in the common Greek of that time—the only way the gospel could have found a hearing and acceptance—it often attributes to those words another, deeper sense and gradually makes that meaning the content of human consciousness. That is the case with words such as σωτηρια (salvation), ζωη (life), ἀπολυτρωσις (redemption) as well as with the idea of rebirth, which in Scripture is only twice rendered by παλιγγενεσια (Matt. 19:28; Titus 3:5) and for the rest by many other terms.

[437–38] The New Testament here rather builds on the Old Testament. At the time of the giving of the law and later in prophecy the Word is first of all addressed to all the people God has included in his covenant, and on the basis of that covenant the people are confronted with the demand that they serve the Lord with all their hearts and souls (Deut. 11:13; Josh. 22:5). But as apostasy, unfaithfulness, and the hardness of people's hearts became more and more evident in history, the prophets stressed with increasing forcefulness that an inner change had to come, not only among the people as a whole, but also in the heart of every member of that people. Of themselves, human beings are unable to bring about this change (Gen. 6:5; 8:21; Job 14:4; 15:16; Ps. 51:5). No more than anyone can change his/her skin color or the leopard his spots can Israel do good, for it has learned to do evil (Jer. 13:23). The heart is deceitful above all things and lethally corrupt (17:9). Only God can accomplish this new birth (Ps. 51:10–12). Then Israel will be his people, a shoot of his planting, a work of his hands, that he may be glorified (Deut. 10:16; 30:1–6; Isa. 54:13; 60:21; Jer. 24:7; 31:18, 31ff.; 32:8ff.; Ezek. 11:19; 36:25ff.).

From the baptism of John through the preaching of Jesus and into the apostolic proclamation, the one consistent message is the need for μετανοια, for a radical turnabout, if one wishes to enter the kingdom of heaven. As Jesus taught Nicodemus, one must be "born from above," that is to say, from *the* Spirit, who is God himself (John 3:6–8). By faith, Christ or his Spirit is the author and origin of a new life in those who are called (Gal. 3:2; 4:6) so that they are now a "new creation" (2 Cor. 5:17). While there is a difference between the Old Testament and New Testament in language and manner of presentation, the basic truth is the same. Whether rebirth is called "circumcision of the heart," the giving of a new heart and a new spirit, or a birth from God, it is always in the strict sense a work of God by which a person is inwardly changed and renewed. This change is signified and sealed in baptism. According to the apostle Peter, the content of the new life is hope. The lives of believers are totally sustained and guided by hope. Hope characterizes their whole lifestyle. In any case it is not a static possession but living, active, and strong. It reaches out and binds believers to the heavenly inheritance (1 Pet. 1:4–13). It also enables them to live a holy life in accordance with Christ's example (1 Pet. 1:14ff.). In the writings of Paul, what he experienced on the way to Damascus—having been taken hold of by Christ (Phil. 3:12)—is claimed for all believers: at that very moment they obtain faith and by that faith they receive justification and the adoption as children (Rom. 3:22, 24; 4:5; 5:1; Gal. 3:26; 4:5; etc.), with the assurance of sonship by the witness of the Holy Spirit (Rom. 8:15–16; Gal. 4:6; 2 Cor. 1:22; Eph. 1:13; 4:30). Those who are efficaciously called are also immediately, by faith, included in fellowship with Christ. They are buried, raised (Rom. 6:3ff.), and made alive with him (Eph. 2:1, 5), and conformed to his image (Rom. 8:29–30; 1 Cor. 4:15–16; 2 Cor. 3:18; Gal. 4:19). Christ lives in them and they live in Christ (Gal. 2:20). They have been crucified to the flesh and to the world (Gal. 5:24; 6:14), passed from death into life (Eph. 2:5; 5:14; Col. 3:1); they are new creations (2 Cor. 5:17), God's workmanship (Eph. 2:10). They walk in newness of life, are now temples of the Holy Spirit, and are led by the Holy Spirit (Rom. 6:4; 8:14; 1 Cor. 6:19; Gal. 5:25; etc.). This entire transformation takes concrete form for them in baptism, the great turning point in their lives, the break with all their previous conduct, the complete surrender to Christ and his service. But from God's side, baptism is also the seal showing that they are taken up into communion with Christ and participate in all his benefits (Rom. 6:3ff.; Gal. 6:17). Even more than in Paul, rebirth or regeneration occupies a central place in John where rebirth and regeneration are described as a γεννηθηναι ἀνωθεν ("being born from above": John 3:3; cf. 3:31; 8:23; 19:11; of God: 1:13; 1 John 3:9; etc.), of water and Spirit (John 3:5), that is, of the Spirit (3:6, 8), whose cleansing activity is symbolized by water (cf. Ezek. 36:25–27; Matt. 3:11). God sent his Son into the world, so that whoever believes in him should not perish but have eternal life (John 3:16, 36; 6:47; 20:31). Although sin continues to cling to believers throughout their lives (1 John 1:8), the seed of God remains in them (1 John 3:9), and they are still admonished to remain in Christ and in his Word (John 15:4–10; 1 John 2:24) and to manifest the love of God in their lives (1 John 3:11–24; 4:7–12). In both the Old Testament and New Testament, rebirth to a living hope is simultaneously a rebirth to a new and holy life. Rebirth encompasses the entire scope of re-creation from its very first beginning in the hearts of people to its ultimate completion in the new heaven and new earth. The goal of this regenerative process is that Christians should be the firstfruits of God's creation, as the true Israel, the special possession of God, like the people of Israel who existed in the days of the Old Testament (Exod. 19:5; Deut. 7:6; 14:2; 26:18; Ps. 135:4; Isa. 43:21; Mal. 3:17; cf. 1 Pet. 1:23; 2:9) and as such the firstfruits of the kingdom that God will establish throughout his creation (cf. Rom. 8:19–23; Heb. 12:23). Thus, Scripture speaks of rebirth mainly in three ways: (1) as the principle of new life planted by the Spirit of God in humans before they believe, (2) as the moral renewal of humans manifesting itself in a holy walk of life, and finally (3) as the restoration of the whole world to its original completeness.

[439] In the missionary context of the early church, the rebirth signified by baptism was a momentous and life-changing event for the believer. It required a complete break with either Judaism or paganism and was an act of joining a poor, marginalized, and unsophisticated church of Christ. Christians felt themselves to be a unique, chosen people, a new kind of people, new creatures, who in Christ had obtained communion with God and a new and authentic life.[5] The work of salvation was confined on God's part to his calling, and when people on their part listened to that call, repented, and believed, they received in baptism the forgiveness of all their past sins. Baptism was the great turning point, the radical change, the decisive passage from a sinful past into the holy present.

Moving beyond this context, as the church gained its members more from its own children than by conversion and baptized infants and children, she had to modify her understanding of the connection between baptism and regeneration. In Western Catholicism, children were baptized not on the basis of their personal faith but the faith of the church in whose fellowship they were born. Baptism no longer signaled a break with the old and the principle of a new life but an infusion of supernatural power, and regeneration then was increasingly understood in terms of the infusion of sacramental grace at the time of baptism. Baptism is therefore strictly necessary for salvation and people, consequently, are absolutely dependent on the church and its priest not only at the beginning but throughout life. In the Eastern Church, a similar result was achieved but baptism was thought of in terms of implanting a new seed of immortality. A new quality was infused into the soul, and baptism itself became essential for salvation. In the West, regeneration lost its real meaning and changed into justification with the mediation of the church and her sacraments being necessary for remaining in the state of grace. Here regeneration is not an enduring good but is continually dependent on human effort, both for its existence and development.[6]

[440–41] It is this sacramental system that the Reformation protested, restoring a direct relationship between God and the soul through the Holy Spirit. This gave Scripture priority over the church, and the Word priority over the sacrament. This principle brought its own dangers and difficulties as the Anabaptists rejected church and sacraments as means of grace and made personal faith and confession the condition for baptism. In response, Lutherans again made regeneration dependent on baptism and, by implication, on the church,

---

5. See, e.g., *Barn.* 6, 11; Ign. *Eph.* 19–20; Ign. *Magn.* 1, 9; Ign. *Smyrn.* 4; *1 Clem.* 29, 58.

6. The Council of Trent, sess. VI, 4ff.; Roman Catechism, II, chap. 2, qu. 25ff. Ed. note: The post–Vatican II edition titled *The Roman Catechism*, trans. Robert I. Bradley, SJ, and Eugene Kevane (Boston: Daughters of St. Paul, 1985), drops the enumeration of the introduction so that chapter 1 begins the section on baptism. In this annotation, the proper reference would be II, chap. 3, qu. 26ff.; cf. H. Bavinck, *Reformed Dogmatics*, ed. John Bolt (Grand Rapids: Baker Academic, 2003–8), III, 514–17 (#416).

thus creating a dualism between primary regeneration, which precedes faith, and subsequent secondary renewal, which arises from faith. Reformed theologians wrestled mightily with this issue but found no solution satisfactory to everyone when it came to grounds for baptizing the children of believers. The attempt to ground it in a notion of prebaptismal regeneration satisfied some but ran aground on the reality that some who are baptized do not come to full faith as adults. While it is necessary *logically* to distinguish regeneration and repentance or conversion and insist that the former precedes the latter, caution must be observed when it comes to the *temporal* order. Reformed theology confined itself to the general statement that regeneration could take place before, during, or at some time after, baptism.[7]

During the time when the church increasingly fell into decline and conformity to the world,[8] solutions to the problem of "easy faith" and "cheap discipleship" were found in reversing the regeneration/repentance relationship. The sacraments were seen only as indicators of a general assurance of God's universal love and goodwill, and the church invited people to accept the gospel and turn to God in repentance. Having the moral strength to believe and repent, one was obligated to believe ("you can" [*du kannst*] and therefore "you must!" [*du sollst!*]). By that faith a person was then regenerated and amended his or her life. In the Enlightenment, finally, people got to the point where they preferred to avoid the term "rebirth" altogether. "Enlightenment," "culture," "development," "moral nurture," and "amendment of life," it was said, were greatly superior terms and also materially much more apt.

But after the Enlightenment had exchanged the term "rebirth" for that of moral amendment, it was picked up again by idealistic philosophy. Of course, as they had done with words such as "Trinity," "incarnation," "atonement," and

---

7. Reformed theologians unanimously agreed on the following points: (1) that the benefits of the covenant of grace were usually distributed by God in connection with the means of grace; hence regeneration is in connection with the Word; (2) that God, however, is not bound to these means, and hence he could also take an unusual route and regenerate and save especially young children without the Word; (3) that he, as a rule, worked that way in the case of children of believers who were taken by death before reaching the age of discretion; (4) that the baptized children of believers who were part of the life of the congregation had to be considered elect and regenerate until the contrary was evident from what they said and did; and (5) that this, however, was a judgment of charity, which must indeed be the rule for our attitude toward these children but cannot claim to be infallible. On the other hand, from the very beginning there was disagreement over whether the children of believers, to the extent that they were elect, were regenerated already before, or in, or only after baptism. Some—like Martyr, à Lasco, Dathenus, Alting, Witsius, Voetius, Mastricht—tended to favor the first view. But the majority—Calvin, Beza, Musculus, Ursinus, de Brès, Acronius, Cloppenburg, Walaeus, Maccovius, Bucanus, Turretin, Heidegger, and others—left the question undecided.

8. Ed. note: Bavinck does not specify the period, but he is undoubtedly referring to the seventeenth and eighteenth centuries when the so-called Dutch Further Reformation, paralleling the English Puritans, sought to revitalize the churches with passionate calls for deeper piety and holy living. See, e.g., Willem Teellinck, *The Path of True Godliness*, ed. Joel R. Beeke, trans. Annemie Godbehere (Grand Rapids: Baker Academic, 2003).

"redemption," philosophers such as Kant, Fichte, Schelling, Hegel, Schopenhauer, and von Hartmann filled "regeneration" or "rebirth" with meaning that was far removed from what the Christian church meant by them. At the same time, it is noteworthy that much of the discussion in idealistic philosophy, at least in its early stages, came with a tie-in to the Christian doctrine of total depravity: A deep moral corruption is present in human beings, "a bent toward evil" that no enlightenment and gradual self-improvement can remove. What is needed is nothing less than a radical reformation, a revolution of the minds, a total reversal in the maxims of one's life and conduct. As idealistic philosophy developed in a pantheistic direction, such a rebirth of humans was viewed simultaneously as their own deed and a work of God: it was a "divine transmutation."[9] Thus, these currents do not entirely break with the modern faith in human self-achievement,[10] but they are sufficiently uncomfortable with it that they posit a "life of the spirit" which is free and independent from the mechanisms of nature. Human beings need to rise above what they are and become what they ought to be. This is possible only when there is some kind of "divine intervention": "In spiritual things every pathway of man leads to a Yea through a Nay, and all toil is in vain without an inner elevation through the energy of an Absolute Life."[11] The content is quite different, but the language itself sounds Christian.

It was Schleiermacher who restored the idea of regeneration to theology by making it the center of his understanding of the Christian faith. For him, regeneration is the new consciousness of God's grace and human dependence on God gained by sharing in the consciousness of Christ. It is Schleiermacher's virtue that he again included regeneration in dogmatic theology, understood it as a religious-ethical process, and also related it to the person of Christ. But in the process he was not able to disentangle himself completely from the influence of pantheistic philosophy. In his doctrine there is no room for an objective justification that precedes conversion, is based on the righteousness of Christ, and is accepted and enjoyed by faith alone.[12]

9. F. W. J. Schelling, *Ausgewählte Werke*, 4 vols. (Darmstadt: Wissenschaftliche Buchgesellschaft, 1968), IV, 332; idem, "Philosophische Untersuchungen über das Wesen der menschlichen Freiheit und die damit zusammenhängenden Gegenstände" (*Sämmtliche Werke* [Stuttgart & Augsburg: J. G. Cotta'scher, 1856–61], I/7, 388). Profound also is Goethe's saying in the poem "A Holy Longing": "And as long as you do not possess it / this: die and be reborn / You are only a troubled guest on the dark earth" (translation of Henry Hatfield, *Goethe, a Critical Introduction* [Cambridge, MA: Harvard University Press, 1963], 118).

10. Consider, for example, the following from Rudolf Eucken: "Religion rests on the presence of a Divine Life in man; it unfolds itself through the seizure of this Life as one's own nature. Religion, too, subsists in the fact that man in the inmost foundation of his own being is raised into the Divine Life, and participates in the Divine Nature" (*The Truth of Religion*, trans. W. T. Jones [New York: G. P. Putnam's Sons, 1911], 206).

11. R. Eucken, *Truth of Religion*, 240; cf. also, idem, *Hauptprobleme der Religionsphilosophie der Gegenwart*, 2nd ed. (Berlin: Reuther & Reichard, 1907), 83ff.; 95ff.

12. F. Schleiermacher, *The Christian Faith*, ed. H. R. MacIntosh and J. S. Steward (Edinburgh: T&T Clark, 1928), §§106–9.

In Mediating Theology (*Vermittelungstheologie*),[13] sin played a more significant role, but at bottom the new life in Christ was a participation in a new personality; there was no objective atonement for sin or justification, only a subjective appropriation of new consciousness. Faith's content is here reduced to mystical experience. These ideas, which lived on in pietistic circles, again came to the fore in the theosophical speculations of Schelling, von Baader, and others. Regeneration consists in a person's becoming spirit: achieving an absolute union between thought and existence, idea and nature. Human beings enter into a process of spiritualization—a new human in process of becoming—until Christ or the Spirit completely indwells him or her.[14] This view of a substantial restoration of human beings[15] as such already strikes us as strange, and the Reformation of doctrine fails to receive its due. In response, Ritschl again put justification into the limelight, conceived it as a synthetic judgment, and regarded it as a possession of the church.[16] His critics, however, argued that Ritschl's system failed to address individual justification and regeneration. The same could be said of Herrmann who equated regeneration with the experience of faith; by looking to Jesus we are freed from feelings of guilt, fear, and dread, are assured of God's love, and calmly and courageously proceed to do our moral work. Rebirth in the sense of new spiritual power does not exist according to Herrmann; regeneration, in fact, is nothing other than faith, which of course carries with it rebirth, a new mind-set, and new courage.[17]

[442] The relation to justification, though very important, is definitely not the only issue that presents itself in connection with regeneration. This locus of theology, namely, soteriology, is as beset with difficulties as are the doctrines of the Trinity and of the two natures of Christ. While it is understandable that missionary proclamation begins with repentance and faith and only after that speaks of regeneration, upon reflection on Scripture and experience we come to realize that, properly speaking, regeneration must precede faith. Questions about the destiny of the children of believers who die in infancy are troubling if repentance must precede regeneration—being as yet unconverted, they would then be lost. By contrast, it is not only Christian sentiment but the scriptural doctrine of the covenant of grace that includes these children. Furthermore, if salvation truly rests in God's will and not in the human will, the order of regeneration preceding repentance is inviolable. Augustine must be chosen over Pelagius. However, there are ethical/practical considerations too. Is it possible that an overemphasis on regeneration could lead some to become indifferent about their need to repent

---

13. Ed. note: Mediating theology, inspired by Schleiermacher, proceeded from the subjectivity of faith and attempted to join Christian faith with the modern scientific worldview of its "cultured despisers." Cf. H. Bavinck, *Reformed Dogmatics*, I, 49 (#9), 127 (#39), 166 (#51), 519–20 (#135), 522–24 (#136).

14. R. Rothe, *Theologische Ethik*, 2nd rev. ed., 5 vols. (Wittenberg: Zimmermann, 1867–71), 742–76.

15. F. Delitzsch, *A System of Biblical Psychology*, trans. R. E. Wallis, 2nd ed. (Edinburgh: T&T Clark, 1875), 381–417.

16. Cf. H. Bavinck, *Reformed Dogmatics*, III, 590 (#432).

17. J. Kaftan, *Dogmatik* (Tübingen: Mohr, 1901), 54–55.

and believe while others become uncertain about their regeneration and are paralyzed in their response to the gospel call—waiting for God to regenerate them? Similarly, what about children of believers? Does the church baptize children of believers on the ground of presumed regeneration? Or, as in Roman Catholicism and Lutheranism, does baptism somehow impart a seed of regeneration? The Reformed tradition distinguishes regeneration and faith, baptizes infants on the basis of covenant promises, but also acknowledges that the Holy Spirit could work sovereignly in the hearts of children apart from the preaching of the Word. Therefore, in general the children of believers should, in accordance with the judgment of charity, be regarded as elect and regenerate until from their "talk" or their "walk" the contrary is evident. Hence both in the case of adults and children, regeneration in the restricted sense preceded—if not *temporally* then certainly always *logically*—faith and repentance.

THE NATURE AND EXTENT OF REGENERATION

[443] Because notions of rebirth are found outside Scripture in the world's religions, it is important to be clear about the distinguishing features of the biblical view. Unlike Oriental theosophical wisdom like Buddhism or Hinduism, which began to exert strong influence on Western thought from the end of the eighteenth century to the present, rebirth does not mean reincarnation.[18] Unlike Christian eschatology which produces hope and eager expectation, Buddhist notions of reincarnation—innumerable and cyclical incorporations of souls in a series of different bodies without it effecting any change in the soul—produce only anxiety and dread and call for suppression of consciousness and will.[19] While rebirth does apply to the Christian understanding of conversion, it is not sufficient to compare the biblical view with initiation into Greek mystery religions or even with Jewish proselytism. Regeneration is more than a change of consciousness, an enlightenment of the mind, or even a reformation of conduct, though it does include all of these. Nor should we be satisfied with the gnostic notion of redemption as the deliverance of the inner self from the "flesh" or matter. Neither rationalism nor mysticism, such as that inspired by Pseudo-Dionysius, provides us with a correct view of regeneration. These insist on claiming a higher knowledge of God and a more intimate fellowship with God than those that are attainable by the ordinary believer. According to mysticism, regeneration becomes an essential participation in the divine nature, a substantial union of the soul with the deity. When the soul frees itself from all earthly ties, suppresses all its conceptual images, kills

---

18. The doctrine of reincarnation (metempsychosis) will be treated later, in the doctrine of the last things, as will the notion of world renewal associated, among other things, with the word "rebirth" (παλιγγενεσια) in Matt. 19:28 (see H. Bavinck, *Reformed Dogmatics*, IV, 702–7 [#575]).

19. Paul Gennrich, *Die Lehre von der Wiedergeburt* (Leipzig: Deichert, 1907), 275–355; J. S. Speyer, *De Indische Theosophie en hare Beteekenis voor Ons* (Leiden: Van Doesburgh, 1910), 86–93.

consciousness and will, and turns inward to its own deepest being, it finds God himself there and enters into full communion with him; on this sublime level God and the soul are one.[20] Others reduce "rebirth" to a figurative way of speaking about the reformation of life—to living more and more in accord with the teaching and example of Jesus. Here, regeneration and conversion are one and the same thing, viewed in the former case from God's perspective and in the latter from the human side.[21] By contrast, Reformed theologians stressed even more vigorously that not just the actions and not even the faculties alone but also the whole person with all one's capacities, soul and body, heart, intellect, and will, is the subject of regeneration. Regeneration, therefore, consists in dying to the "old man" that must not only be suppressed but also killed, and in the rising of a totally new person created in the likeness of God in true righteousness and holiness.[22]

When regeneration is thus traced back from the actions to the faculties, and from the faculties to the soul itself, and from the soul to its essence and substance, it naturally and necessarily has to take place in the unconscious. Now in the past, in psychology and hence also in the locus on regeneration, little notice was taken of the unconscious. Over against the Anabaptists, the Reformed did not want to exclude children from the benefit of regeneration even before they became self-conscious, nor did they agree that believers always had to know the time of their regeneration.[23] Rebirth as such, it was said, was not a matter of experience but of faith. "This birth is neither seen nor apprehended but only believed."[24] But ever since Leibniz, "the unconscious" has become of great significance both in philosophy and in psychology. The term, however, is unclear and can be taken to mean very different things. For our purposes there are essentially two areas that may be treated under the heading of the unconscious. In the first place, one can list under this heading all those impressions, ideas, passions, desires, and so forth, that at any given moment are not present in our consciousness but may be aroused on some occasion or other by recollection, association, and so forth. Included here are childhood memories as well as skills and abilities acquired by long practice and training. In the second place, the unconscious may also be associated with all those intuitions that strike the consciousness like lightning, have such weighty significance in the lives of geniuses, heroes, prophets, and seers, and also assert themselves in clairvoyance, somnambulism, telepathy, and a wide range of occult phenomena. In the opinion of many people, these phenomena

20. Cf. H. Bavinck, *Reformed Dogmatics*, III, 528–31 (#420).

21. This was the view of the Socinians and Remonstrants and, according to Hodge, also the theologians of the New Divinity School in America (i.e., Emmons, Finney, and Taylor). See Charles Hodge, *Systematic Theology*, 3 vols. (New York: Charles Scribner's Sons, 1888), III, 7–15.

22. J. Calvin, *Institutes*, III.iii.5; P. van Mastricht, *Theologia*, VI, 3, 6–18; H. Bavinck, ed., *Synopsis purioris theologiae*, 6th ed. (Leiden: Donner, 1881), disp. 32, 13, 18–19; H. Witsius, *Oeconomy of the Covenants*, III, 6, 4; cf. also Canons of Dort, III–IV, 11.

23. J. Calvin, *Institutes*, III.iii.2.

24. Luther in W. Herrmann, *Der Verkehr des Christen mit Gott*, 6th ed. (Stuttgart; Cotta, 1908), 278.

point back to mysterious forces hidden in the human mind or to another spiritual world with which humans are, or can be, in touch. Depending on whether the unconscious was viewed in the former or the latter sense, modern psychologists of religion presented a different version of regeneration or conversion. In the first case, regeneration was said to occur when our consciousness is disturbed by some trauma or other and radically transformed. Since this deprived *religious* phenomena of their unique value and validity, others who found this explanation unsatisfactory posited some objective supernatural factor—which we generally call "God"—that provides people with a new energy, a new, broader and richer life. These people feel united with that Being, who works throughout the universe and saves both them and all the world.

Although these explanations of regeneration (conversion) sound new and original, they are reminiscent of those given through the ages by rationalism and mysticism respectively. The former is more deistic, the latter more pantheistic. The former explains everything in terms of the working of the Word; the latter goes back behind the Word and speaks of the Spirit. In the former, regeneration has a purely moral character; in the latter, it is the revelation of a supernatural power. Both interpretations, however, bring out the serious weaknesses inherent in the psychology of religion. No matter how hard it tries to be objective and unbiased, psychology of religion is able to describe but not to penetrate the inner nature of religious phenomena and must remain embarrassed and powerless as it faces the question of truth. The explanations given inevitably reflect the bias of the psychologist and turn out to be free, subjective, and arbitrary. Conversion then becomes a phenomenon that is on a level with various other alterations of human consciousness, or, equally arbitrarily, is explained in terms of the unconscious inward operation of some supernatural factor. But what conversion really is and, similarly, what faith, prayer, justification, religion, and so forth really are, neither the psychology nor the philosophy of religion can tell us. Only Scripture can.

[444] It is helpful to recognize a broader and more narrow use of the term "regeneration." In the broadest and fullest sense, regeneration refers to the total transformation of a person; in the restricted sense, it has in view the implantation of new life that precedes faith and repentance and further sanctification.[25] The active Word of God here—calling—must also be differentiated from the passive reception or fruit of God's initiating work. God's call has both an external and internal component. The external proclaimed Word addresses human consciousness convincingly; human response requires an inner work of the Holy Spirit. In Reformed thought, calling and regeneration are never separated and God's inner call is always seen as logically preceding the outward call. The Reformed tradition also acknowledges the reality of the faith community's involvement in

---

25. When Reformed theology restricts the term "regeneration" to the implantation of the spiritual life, it is giving it a more restricted sense than the way in which Scripture usually speaks of "regeneration" (or "birth from above" or "birth from God") and must therefore be on its guard not to cite it by its sound alone.

the external call on its own children as a gracious work of God the Holy Spirit. In their polemics with the Anabaptists they consistently tried to maintain the connection between calling and regeneration; in their confessions, catechisms, and dogmatic manuals, they remained steadfastly faithful to the order of calling and regeneration. Against the Anabaptists on the one hand, so against Pelagians of all sorts they took the position that the external call and moral suasion by the Word is insufficient for salvation and has to be followed by a special operation of the Holy Spirit in the human heart.

[445] This operation of the Holy Spirit is both immediate and irresistible. The point made by Reformed theology here against the Pelagians, Arminians, and the theologians of Saumur is that God's operation on the human person is independent of the will as well as the intellect. There is no room here to speak of cooperation or of God merely enlightening the mind, which then informs and changes the will. Rather, God's Spirit itself directly enters the human heart and with infallible certainty brings about regeneration without in any way being dependent on the human will. Furthermore, if the operation of God's Spirit in regeneration is absolutely independent of the human will, it may be called "irresistible." Augustine already stated: "Aid must be given to the weakness of the human will in order that divine grace may be inexorably and invincibly effective."[26] Although the term "irresistible" was used by opponents of the Reformed faith and does not sufficiently capture the Reformed view,[27] its meaning is clear: When God freely chooses to renew a person's will, no one can withstand God. God's inner call is efficacious. That Rome does not agree is clear from declarations of both Trent and the [First] Vatican Council. Trent stated that when the human heart has been touched by the illumination of the Holy Spirit, "neither is man himself utterly without doing anything while he receives that inspiration, forasmuch as he is also able to reject it; yet he is not able, by his own free will, without the grace of God, to move himself unto justice in his sight."[28] Vatican I declared: "Faith in itself is a gift of God, even if it does not work through love; and an act of faith is a work pertaining to salvation. Through this act man freely renders obedience to God Himself by consenting to and by cooperating with His grace, when he could resist it."[29] Here the teaching of Pelagians and semi-Pelagians won out over Augustine and Thomas and found acceptance also among the Anabaptists, Socinians, the later Lutherans (et al.), and in the Netherlands by the Remonstrants. The point of the disagreement was not about unregenerate people resisting God's general external call but whether they could ultimately—at the specific moment

---

26. Augustine, *On Admonition and Grace*, XII, 30.

27. Reformed theologians had some objections to the term "irresistible grace" because they did not in any way wish to deny that grace is often and indeed always resisted by the unregenerate person. They therefore preferred to speak of the efficacy or of the insuperability of grace, or interpreted the term "irresistible" in the sense that grace is ultimately irresistible.

28. Decree of the Council of Trent, VI, 5.

29. Documents of the Vatican Council I, III, 3.

in which God wanted to regenerate them and work with his efficacious grace in their heart—still reject that grace. Blurring the distinction between the will of God's good pleasure and his revealed will as well as that between the (sufficient) external and (efficacious) internal call, the Remonstrants answered in the affirmative while the Reformed said "no!" All the important doctrines affirmed by the Synod of Dort are wrapped up in this answer: the corruption of human nature; election (based or not based on foreseen faith); the universality and particularity of Christ's atonement; perseverance of the saints. Reformed theologians took their cue from Scripture's picture of fallen humanity as blind, powerless, natural, dead in sins and trespasses (Jer. 13:23; Matt. 6:23; 7:18; John 8:34; Rom. 6:17; 8:7; 1 Cor. 2:14; 2 Cor. 3:5; Eph. 2:1; etc.), along with the forceful words and images with which the work of grace in the human soul is described (Deut. 30:6; Jer. 31:31; Ezek. 36:26; John 3:3, 5; 6:44; Eph. 2:1, 6; Phil. 2:13; 1 Pet. 1:3; etc.), and spoke of the efficacy and invincibility of God's grace in regeneration.

[446] Against this confession of God's omnipotent and infallibly effective grace in regeneration, the Remonstrants cite a series of Scripture verses that contain all sorts of admonitions and threats and are addressed to the heart and conscience, the mind and the will, of humans. The Pelagian and Arminian desire is to honor human freedom and responsibility and not reduce humans to marionettes controlled by God. Upon reflection, however, the reality is the opposite of what objectors to the notion of God's sovereign, and finally irresistible grace, believe. If one proceeds from human free will as the important matter to maintain above all, one cannot possibly do justice to all those texts that unmistakably teach God's efficacious and insuperable grace. On the other hand, if one proceeds along theological lines and seeks above all to secure the rights of God, one will still always have room left for the content of the Scripture verses that consistently address and treat humans as rational, moral beings. While the Augustinian and Reformed view can and does make room for human beings as created, rational, moral agents, the Pelagian and Remonstrant view cannot account for Scripture's teaching about the radical need for grace. If grace is resistible, God is deprived of his sovereignty; if the human will is capable on its own of assenting to God, then regeneration is unnecessary; and if, as the Pelagian and Remonstrant position teaches, some prevenient grace is necessary to prompt human willing, then the notion of an indifferent will remains a fiction. The only gain here is an apparent but not real one, as becomes apparent with the case of children who die in infancy. Either they are saved by sovereign grace alone without any choosing on their part, or such grace is insufficient and all infants who die before choosing are lost. The Pelagian and Arminian position is not at all merciful.

In the final analysis, it remains a riddle what Pelagianism can have against God glorifying his efficacious grace in the lives of sinners. If it is to ask why God does not grant his grace to all, it would find a well-disposed response everywhere. Who has not felt that question rising in his or her own mind and has not been profoundly moved by it? But that is a question that neither Pelagius nor Augustine can answer; all of us must rest in the good pleasure of God. Those who confess God's sovereignty insist with equal measure that the gospel must be preached to all creatures and that the external call of God is a blessing to humanity. However, they also insist that no one is sufficient on his or her own to opt for the gospel; a supernatural rebirth is needed. In any case the Reformed have the advantage over the proponents of free will in knowing that God's counsel will stand, that his covenant of grace will not waver, that Christ is the true and perfect Savior, and that goodness will one day triumph infallibly over evil. What serious objections could possibly be raised against that position? If, without our knowledge, we can share in Adam's condemnation—a fact that nobody can deny—why could we not much more, without our knowledge, be received into God's favor in Christ? The objection is made that such an understanding of grace is coercive. Speaking bluntly, suppose this was the case; God is God and who would have the right to complain if he or she were forcefully snatched out of eternal perdition and transferred into eternal life? Who would agree with the man who complained that someone had rescued him from mortal danger without respecting his freedom of choice? But it is not so: in the internal calling and regeneration, there is no coercion on the part of God. Not a single godly person, even if one had been snatched like a piece of kindling from the fire, has ever spoken of coercion in connection with the work of grace. Still, coercion is alien to the essence of God; God does not coerce but persuades. There is, we all know, an unequal apportionment in both the natural and spiritual realms; not all are born in the same healthy manner and circumstance; not all receive the same gifts and advantages; not all people are saved. Attempts to explain this in terms of some theory of karma or just reward based on performance fail the test of the gospel message. Jesus did not pronounce the self-righteous blessed but the poor in spirit and the meek. He came not to call the righteous but publicans and sinners to repentance, to seek and to save what is lost. The grace of God in Christ, grace that is full, abundant, free, omnipotent, and insuperable, is the heart of the gospel.

[447] The purpose of regeneration is to make us spiritual people, those who live and walk by the Spirit. This life is one of intimate communion with God in Christ. Scripture describes it as a circumcised heart (Deut. 30:6; Rom. 2:29), a pure heart and a firm spirit (Ps. 51:17), a heart of flesh instead of a heart of stone (Jer. 31:33ff.; Ezek. 11:19; 36:25), a new creation (2 Cor. 5:17), God's workmanship (Rom. 14:20; Eph. 2:10), a new self (Eph. 4:24; Col. 3:10 NRSV), a new life (Rom. 6:11; Eph. 2:5; Col. 3:3), and so forth. Noteworthy also is that Scripture pictures regeneration as transforming humans into *spiritual* persons (John 3:6; 1 Cor. 4:1; Gal. 6:1), with spiritual understanding (Col. 1:9) to discern all things without being subject to anyone else's scrutiny (1 Cor. 2:15) and to offer spiritual sacrifices (1 Pet. 2:5). They bear the image of the second Adam who became a life-giving spirit and is the Lord from heaven (1 Cor. 15:45–49) and will one day receive a spiritual body (1 Cor. 15:44) that will be like the glorious body of Christ (Phil. 3:21). This Spirit is the Spirit of God, by whom he created and upholds

the world (Gen. 1:2; Pss. 33:6; 104:30), distributes gifts and powers (Exod. 31:3; Judg. 6:34; 14:6), sends and anoints the prophets (Isa. 48:16; 59:21; Ezek. 37:1) and renews and sanctifies his people (Pss. 51:10; 143:10; Isa. 11:2; 28:6; 32:15ff.; Ezek. 36:27; 39:29; Zech. 12:10). Conceived and anointed by the Holy Spirit, Christ accomplished his work in the Spirit's power and so completely acquired that Spirit that he himself can be called the Spirit, the life-giving Spirit (2 Cor. 3:17; 1 Cor. 15:45), that henceforth the Spirit of God is the Spirit of his Father, the Spirit of the Son, the Spirit of Christ, the Spirit of the Lord Jesus (Matt. 10:20; Rom. 8:2, 9; 2 Cor. 3:17–18; Gal. 3:2; 4:6; Phil. 1:19; 1 Pet. 1:11; Rev. 3:13), and that he can be fully imparted by Christ to his church (John 15:26; 16:7; Acts 2:4, 33; etc.).

Immediately after being poured out on the day of Pentecost, the Spirit became the giver of boldness in public speech (Acts 4:8, 31), of the power of faith (6:5; 11:24), of consolation and joy (9:31; 13:52). Later, when the extraordinary gifts decreased, his presence and working were especially perceived in that he brought people to confess Jesus as Lord (1 Cor. 12:3), assured believers of their status as children of God, guided all believers (Rom. 8:14–16; Gal. 4:6), poured the love of God into their hearts (Rom. 5:5), and renewed and sanctified them (1 Cor. 6:11; Titus 3:5; 1 Pet. 1:2). He caused them to bear spiritual fruits (Gal. 5:22–23), faith, hope, and above all love (1 Cor. 13). He sealed them for the day of promise (Rom. 8:23; 2 Cor. 1:22; 5:5; Eph. 1:13; 4:30), indwelled their bodies so that the parts of their bodies became instruments of righteousness (Rom. 6:13; 1 Cor. 3:16; 6:19) and therefore also made their bodies share in the life that was already granted to them by Christ in the present and would one day be fully manifested in the resurrection (Rom. 8:11; Col. 3:4; 1 Cor. 15:42ff.). The life that originates in rebirth can, from the human perspective, be called a life of faith (Gal. 2:20), but objectively it is the life of the Spirit, the life of Christ, the life of God in the believer, and therefore supernatural and miraculous in its origin and essence. Just as the wind blows where it chooses, without letting any human prescribe its course, and just as its sound is heard, but no one can tell where it comes from or where it is headed, so it is with everyone who is born of the Spirit (John 3:8). To those who believe, God now further grants the Spirit of consolation, the Spirit of adoption as children, of sanctification (John 14:16–17; Gal. 3:14). We must add to this that though the life of the Spirit is most certainly a gift to each believer in particular, at the same time it is from the very beginning a life of intimate communion, with God and with all who share communion in Christ. Believers are all baptized into one body by one Spirit (1 Cor. 12:13), have access to the Father by one Spirit (Eph. 2:18), are together in one body and one Spirit (Eph. 4:4), are built together on one foundation into a spiritual house, a dwelling place of God in the Spirit (1 Cor. 3:9; Eph. 2:22; 1 Pet. 2:5), and enjoy the same fellowship of the Spirit (2 Cor. 13:13; Phil. 2:1).

[448] Surveying this work of the Spirit from Genesis 1 to Revelation 22 and specifically focusing on his regenerative activity, we need not refute the opinion that

regeneration is totally or in part a human achievement and exists solely in the moral improvement of one's life and conduct. The rebirth Scripture speaks of is not merely a psychic phenomenon that could be explained as the product or concomitant of physiological changes. No more than being the makers of life itself are humans the sole or partial creators of their regeneration. Like all life, so a fortiori the new life of regeneration is not a chemical article, a product of human labor, a fruit of slow and long evolution, but a product only of a creative act of God, a special supernatural operation of God's Spirit. Originally created good, humans sinned and became wholly corrupt, incapable of fellowship with God. On our own we are radically evil; for our redemption a rebirth is needed that affects our entire being.

At the same time, according to Scripture, regeneration does not exist in a totally new second creation. Although believers are made new creatures in Christ, this does not mean that their created nature is qualitatively transformed. Believers remain fully human, fully created image-bearers of God as in the beginning. The continuity of their selfhood is retained in redemption just as the re-creation that will take place in the renewal of heaven and earth (Matt. 19:28) is not the destruction of this world and the subsequent creation out of nothing of another world or the introduction of some new substance but the liberation of the creature that is now subject to futility. Sin is not of the essence of creation but its deformity; Christ is not a second Creator but creation's Redeemer. Salvation is the restoration of creation and the reformation of life. Redemption is not coercive; it delivers people from the compulsion and power of sin. The new life comes from God and is born in his love. Nor could this be otherwise, for God's honor as Savior hinges precisely on his reconquest from the power of Satan of *this* human race and *this* world. Regeneration does not remove anything from us other than what, if all were well, we should do without, and it restores to us what we, in keeping with the design of our being, should have but lost as a result of sin. In principle it restores us to the likeness and image of God.

If regeneration is neither mere reformation of life and conduct nor an infusion of some new substance, then what is it concretely? Here, too, as with any other dogma, it is easier to reject an error than constructively to unfold the truth, for in all that God reveals, we finally encounter an impenetrable mystery at the point where the eternal touches the temporal, the infinite the finite, the Creator the creature. On earth that which lies behind the phenomena remains, for others and for ourselves, an object of faith; the spiritual life is hidden with Christ in God (Col. 3:3). Now if regeneration is neither an actual creation (an infusion of substance) nor a merely external moral amendment of life, it can only consist in a spiritual renewal of those inner dispositions of humans that from ancient times were called "habits" or "qualities."[30] Guided by the testimonies of Scripture, we can

---

30. Jonathan Edwards, *Religious Affections*, ed. J. E. Smith (1746; repr., New Haven: Yale University Press, 1959), 206 (part III, 1), spoke of "principles of nature," but added "for want of a word of more determinate signification."

nevertheless say, with an appropriate degree of modesty, that whole persons are the subject of regeneration and that not only their deeds and conduct, their lives' purpose and direction, their ideas and activities changed, but humans themselves are transformed and renewed in the core of their being. To describe this process Scripture refers to the heart "from which flow the springs of life" (Prov. 4:23), in one's consciousness as well as in the emotions and will. If, as Jesus says (Matt. 15:19), it is from the heart that all evil and incomprehension flow, then that is the center where the change called regeneration must occur, a change that affects the whole person including the body. Paul expressly states that the Holy Spirit also dwells in the body as his temple (1 Cor. 6:19), that the resurrection of the body has to follow because of the Spirit who dwells in it (Rom. 8:11), that spiritual persons make the body parts into instruments of righteousness (6:13), that the life of Jesus also becomes visible in our mortal flesh (2 Cor. 4:11). In short, the "newness" brought about in regeneration is a restoration of our human nature to a state of health. The confession of Dort states this in wonderful language: "When God carries out his good pleasure in his chosen ones, he, by the effective operation of the same regenerating Spirit, also penetrates into the inmost being of man, opens the closed heart, softens the hard heart, and circumcises the heart that is uncircumcised. He infuses new qualities into the will, making the dead will alive, the evil one good, the unwilling one willing, and the stubborn one compliant; he activates and strengthens the will so that, like a good tree, it may be enabled to produce the fruits of good deeds."[31] This has nothing to do with coercion; it is deliverance from the coercive bondage and compulsive power of sin. From its earliest beginnings the spiritual life is eternal life, and the seed that remains in the regenerate is imperishable. It is born of God, flows down to us from the resurrection of Christ, and is from the beginning effected, maintained, and confirmed in the fellowship of the Holy Spirit. For that reason it cannot sin or die, but lives, works, and grows, and in due time manifests itself in deeds of faith and conversion.

31. Canons of Dort, III–IV, art. 12.

19

FAITH AND CONVERSION

THE KNOWLEDGE OF FAITH

[449] New life in Christ, just like all natural life, must be nourished and strengthened. Regenerate persons continually need to be "strengthened in their inner being with power through God's Spirit" (cf. Eph. 3:16). Believers only become strong in the Lord and in the strength of his might (Eph. 6:10) by the Spirit of Christ and in communion with him (Rom. 8:13, 26; 2 Cor. 13:13; Eph. 3:16). In regeneration the whole person is, in principle, re-created. A person's self dies and lives again in and by the power of Christ (Gal. 2:20). Working from the center of their being to the circumference, the Spirit creates a new person (καινος ἀνθρωπος, *kainos anthrōpos*) in Christ (Eph. 4:24; Col. 3:10), a creation that, though small and delicate, is nevertheless complete in all its parts. The spiritual life, though mysteriously and untraceably implanted in humans by the Spirit (John 3:8), is from the beginning bound to the Word of God. The inexpressible Word that was written in the human heart learns to know itself by the Word that Christ speaks in Scripture.

Now in Scripture the act by which the Holy Spirit causes us to understand the Word of Christ in its spiritual sense and content and opens our consciousness to the truth is called "enlightenment." Since sin has darkened the mind (Rom. 1:21; 1 Cor. 1:21; 2:14; Eph. 4:18; 5:8), what is needed is a renewal of the mind (Rom. 12:2; Eph. 4:23) by the Holy Spirit—the spirit of wisdom and revelation (Eph. 1:17)—who leads in all truth (John 16:13), teaches all things (John 14:26; 1 John 2:20), and enables us to understand the things of God (1 Cor. 2:10–16). Just as at the creation, God, by his word of power, caused light to shine out of darkness, so by his Son (Matt. 11:27) and by the Spirit he shines in the hearts of people (2 Cor. 4:6) and enlightens the eyes of the heart (Eph. 1:18). As a result they are children of light (Luke 16:8; Eph. 5:8; 1 Thess. 5:5), citizens of the kingdom of light (Col. 2:12; 1 Pet. 2:9), and they walk in the light (Eph. 5:8; 1 John 1:7; 2:9–11). In God's light they now see light (Ps. 36:9).[1]

Enlightened by the Spirit, believers gain a new knowledge of faith. Salvation that is not known and enjoyed is no salvation. God saves by causing himself to be known and enjoyed in Christ. The knowledge of God in the face of Jesus Christ saves, justifies, and bestows on us the forgiveness of sins and eternal life (1 Kings 8:43; 1 Chron. 28:9; Ps. 89:15; Isa. 1:3; 11:9; 53:11; Jer. 4:22; 31:34; Hosea 2:19; 4:1, 6; Matt. 11:27; Luke 1:77; John 8:32; 10:4, 14; 17:3; Rom. 10:3; 2 Cor. 2:14; Gal. 4:9; Eph. 4:13; Heb. 8:11; 2 Pet. 1:2; 3:18; 1 John 5:20). This knowledge of faith is not a supernatural addition to human nature since believing in general is something every person does, always and in all areas of life. Faith is a universal, created human capacity; there is no knowledge at all without some belief. Re-creation never introduces a new substance into the world, and faith does not bestow on humans a new capacity, function, or activity that human nature finds foreign to God's original creation of humans in his image. It is proper to speak of the "restoration of faith" only in the sense that in regeneration all of a person's abilities and powers are renewed including faith, hope, and love. To the regenerate person, believing in God or in Christ as such is just as natural as it is for everyone to believe in the world of the senses. Just as seeds require good soil, moisture, and sun—so the capacity to believe implanted by regeneration only becomes an act of faith in response to the ongoing internal calling. In regeneration, God restores the vital rapport that originally existed between him and humanity; created in God's image, humans are again related to God himself and to all that is his: Crucified to the world and to sin, the regenerate live to God. Having been enlightened by the Holy Spirit, they know God and are saved through that knowledge (John 17:3).

It is also important to emphasize that this argument does not agree with the attempts by mystics to draw the knowledge of Christ from their own hearts and thus pit Word and Spirit against each other, despise the letter, highlight the internal Word at the expense of the external Word, and even appeal for this position to Holy Scripture (Isa. 54:13; Jer. 31:34; Matt. 11:25, 27; 16:17; John 6:45; 1 Cor. 2:10; 2 Cor. 3:6; Heb. 8:10; 1 John 2:20, 27). Against this we want to affirm the following:

1. All knowledge presupposes a relationship between the object and the subject. For us to see, we need eyes to see; for us to know, we need an intellect to know. Such kinship between the seer and the seen, the knower and the known, requires that they be created for each other.[2] So also in the spiritual

1. Cf. H. Bavinck, *Reformed Dogmatics*, ed. John Bolt (Grand Rapids: Baker Academic, 2003–8), I, 347–48 (#96); R. Seeberg, "Erleuchtung," in *PRE*[3], V, 457–59.

2. I.e., by the same Logos; cf. H. Bavinck, *Reformed Dogmatics*, I, 78–81 (#20), 217–19 (#65), 301–12 (##85–86), 356–59 (#98), 380–85 (##104–5), 586–90 (#152), 605–13 (##156–58).

realm, for us to know God in the face of Christ, the Spirit has to be added to the Word, the internal calling to the external calling, and illumination to revelation.

2. When Scripture states that in God's light alone we see light it is not saying that we draw the material content of this knowledge from within ourselves; instead it refers us away from ourselves and to the revelation of God in nature, the law, and the gospel (Deut. 4:1; Isa. 8:20; John 5:39; Rom. 1:20; 15:4; 2 Tim. 3:15; 1 Pet. 1:25; 2 Pet. 1:19; 1 John 2:20–27; etc.).

3. In the natural world the *content* of our knowledge—even though we bring our own consciousness, intellect, and reason—always comes from without.[3] This is intensified in matters spiritual where we need an objective, external revelation serving as a rule for doctrine and life. Left to ourselves we lapse into error and lies.

4. Furthermore, the object of this religious knowledge is not visible but invisible, spiritual, and eternal. What no eye has seen nor ear heard nor the human heart conceived, *that* God has prepared in the gospel for those who love him (1 Cor. 2:9). To know these things we need a faithful image, pure and unalloyed. We do not walk here by sight, so we must behold the glory of the Lord in a mirror that we may be changed into his likeness (cf. 2 Cor. 3:18).

5. Finally, the new life in the believer is always drawn toward the gospel, the Word of Christ, the Scriptures, as the basis of its support, as the food by which faith is strengthened. The witness of the Holy Spirit binds them to Scripture to the same degree and with the same force as to the person of Christ himself.

The expression "the knowledge of faith" should not be taken to mean that we are saved, properly speaking, by faith or knowledge instead of by God in Christ by the Holy Spirit.[4] Unlike in Buddhism, where "unconscious" salvation may be the pinnacle of being, Christian salvation fully benefits us only if we know about it; for Christians the highest state of being is to *know* God and by that knowledge to have eternal life. Knowledge, therefore, is not an accidental and externally added component of salvation but integral to it. Salvation that is not known and enjoyed is no salvation. Nonetheless, since our communion with God in Christ in this life is not complete and our knowledge imperfect, our knowledge of God on earth is "a knowledge of faith." Faith is the only way to appropriate the knowledge of God. All benefits (forgiveness, regeneration, sanctification, perseverance, the blessedness of heaven) exist for us only by faith. We enjoy them only by faith. We are saved only through hope (cf. Rom. 8:24).

3. Cf. H. Bavinck, *Reformed Dogmatics*, I, 78–81 (#20), 217–19 (#65); II, 68–70 (#170).
4. B. B. Warfield, "Faith," in *DB*, I, 837: "The saving power of faith resides thus not in itself, but in the Almighty Saviour, on whom it rests."

[450] Biblically speaking, *faith* is trust-filled surrender to God and his word of promise. Assuming the form of a covenant that rests in the electing love of God, salvation appears in the form of a promise that can only be accepted by faith (Gen. 3:15; 6:22; 7:5; 8:22; 12:4; 15:6; 17:21ff.; 22:2; Exod. 20:2; Deut. 7:8; 14:1; etc.). This religious relationship between humans and God is usually expressed by other words such as fearing, serving, loving, adhering to, trusting God, relying on him, and so forth.[5]

Although the Old Testament does not contain a technical word for faith, the closest word, related to our word for "believing," is the verb הֶאֱמִן (Hiphil of אָמַן), meaning "to make firm, attach oneself to something, lean on, trust." In the Old Testament, to believe is to trust in God fully. God is the faithful one (Deut. 7:9; Pss. 33:4; 89:37; Isa. 49:7; 65:16), and those who—despite conflict and opposition—continue to believe in him are the faithful (2 Sam. 20:19; Pss. 12:1; 31:23; 101:6).

In the New Testament, the word faith (πιστις) is given its full religious significance. The noun for faith (πιστις) and the verb "to believe" (πιστευειν) occur frequently in the New Testament and acquired the technical meaning: to believe is to become a Christian (Acts 2:44; 4:4; 13:48; etc.); "believers" is another word for Christians (Acts 10:43; 1 Tim. 4:3, 12). Furthermore, "faith" is frequently synonymous with the Christian religion, which has now become an objective power in the church (Acts 6:7; Gal. 3:23, 25; 6:10; etc.).[6] In the Gospels, salvation is bound to faith (Luke 7:50; Mark 5:34). As soon as Jesus arose from the dead, ascended into heaven, and sent the Holy Spirit, the apostles began to proclaim him as the one whom God had made both Lord and Messiah (Acts 2:36) that he might give repentance to Israel and forgiveness of sins (2:38; 5:31). Before long a church originated that was marked by its belief in the Lord (5:14; 9:42; 11:17; 14:23).

From the very beginning this faith included two elements: (1) acceptance of the apostolic message concerning the Christ and (2) personal trust in that Christ as now living in heaven and mighty to forgive sins and to bestow complete salvation. The first emphasis is especially found in John's writings (John 2:22; 4:50; 5:47; 6:69; 8:24; 11:42; 13:19; 17:8, 21; 1 John 5:1, 5), the second in Paul (Rom. 3:22; Gal. 2:16, 20; 3:22; Eph. 3:12; Phil. 3:9). The apostles' individuality comes out in their descriptions of faith. James, opposing a one-sided intellectualistic view of faith, emphasizes genuine faith in Jesus Christ (James 2:1), which must prove itself as a living faith in the performance of good works (James 2:17ff.). Peter, the apostle of hope, relates faith, which makes us partakers in the righteousness of Christ (2 Pet. 1:1) and is the principle of good works (1 Pet. 1:7, 21; 5:9), to obtaining the outcome of faith: salvation. Paul focuses especially on faith's object, Jesus Christ, whom God made our wisdom, righteousness, sanctification, and

---

5. Cf. H. Bavinck, *Reformed Dogmatics*, III, 491–95 (#410).
6. B. B. Warfield, "Faith," in *DB*, I, 828–31; also in 1 Tim. 1:19; 3:9; 4:1; etc.; the verb πιστευειν [or the noun πιστις], in his view, does not refer to the doctrine of the faith but to "subjective faith conceived of objectively as a power" (831).

redemption (1 Cor. 1:30), and in whose person and benefits we can participate only by faith apart from the works of the law (Rom. 3:21–28). The author of the Letter to the Hebrews, though recognizing that Jesus Christ is the object (Heb. 3:14; 10:22; 13:7–8) as well as "the pioneer and perfecter of our faith" (12:2), looks at faith from its subjective rather than from its objective side. He was concerned to remind his readers that faith—the assurance of things unseen, eternal, and still coming (11:1)—must prove its genuineness by clinging to God's faithfulness (11:11), power (11:18–19), and promises (4:1–2; 6:12; 10:36; 11:6, 9, 26), and calls for boldness (3:6; 4:16; 10:19, 35), firmness (3:14; 11:1), endurance (10:36; 12:1), and hope (3:6; 6:11, 18; 10:23). Finally, John mainly presents faith from the perspective of its present reality to those who believe that Jesus Christ came in the flesh (1 John 4:2), and grants us eternal life (John 3:16; 5:24; 6:47, 54; 20:31; 1 John 3:14–15; 5:11). He who has the Son has life (1 John 5:12).

Nevertheless, in all this colorful diversity, the unity remains perfectly intact. Believing always includes accepting the witness God has given of his Son through the apostles as well as unlimited trust in the person of Christ. The two are inseparable. Those who truly accept the apostolic witness trust in Christ alone for their salvation; those who put their trust in Christ as the Son of God also freely and readily accept the apostolic witness concerning that Christ. Christ is both a historical person, the Christ of the Scriptures, and at the same time the glorified Lord in heaven who lives and reigns as the head of his church. He secured salvation in the past but personally applies it in the present. Faith as Scripture speaks of it excludes both a faith of the heart that does not confess what it knows and a confession that is not rooted in the faith of the heart. It is simultaneously mystical and noetic, an unlimited and unwavering trust in Christ as he who, as Scripture says, has accomplished everything for me and on that basis is now and forever my Lord and my God.

[451] In church history, however, this multifaceted scriptural doctrine of faith did not come into its own, and its rich and full religious significance was lost.[7] In the case of Rome, faith was reduced to intellectual assent to all that God has revealed. A distinction was then made between "uninformed faith"[8] and faith informed by love; only the latter justifies and saves. This means that faith's object is not the special grace of God in Christ and does not consist in the confidence that Christ is *my* Lord and *my* Savior, and that *my* sins are forgiven *me*. After all, faith is seen as a matter of the intellect and trust as a matter of human willing;

---

7. Cf. H. Bavinck, *Reformed Dogmatics*, I, 571 (#148).

8. Ed. note: Uninformed faith (*fides informis*) does not mean "ignorant faith" or "faith without knowledge" as the term suggests in ordinary English usage. Rather, it is contrasted in medieval Scholastic theology with *fides caritate formata* ("faith informed by love"), which is "faith that is animated and instructed by love (*caritas*) and is therefore active in producing good works. . . . This conception of faith is denied by the Reformers and the Protestant orthodox insofar as it implies the necessity of works for justification" (Richard A. Muller, *Dictionary of Latin and Greek Theological Terms* [Grand Rapids: Baker Academic, 1985], s.v. *fides caritate formata*; *fides informis*).

trust is a consequence of faith and not part of it. This trust, we should also note, is not absolute but only a moral and conjectural certitude that does not exclude the possibility of error and loss of grace.[9]

Unlike Rome's position in which personal assurance was decidedly secondary and often lost altogether, for the Reformation and Calvin, faith was personal confidence in God's benevolence toward us "revealed to our minds and *sealed on our hearts* by the Holy Spirit."[10] This includes knowledge of the content of the gospel—the history of God's saving deeds—but emphasizes trust in the promises of God to us, promises that find their very being in Christ himself. In Calvin the "assent" of faith is more of the heart than of the brain, more affect than understanding.[11] Furthermore, faith in the case of the Reformers, whether it is described as knowledge (*cognitio*) or as confident trust (*fiducia*), is always a *certain* knowledge, a *firm* confidence. Faith is the opposite of doubt and includes the certainty of personal salvation. This is not to say that believers have a kind of absolute certainty or to deny that believers struggle with various kinds of uncertainty, but it is to say that faith as such is always a matter of certainty.[12]

[452] The view of faith presented by the Reformation did not, however, settle all questions. While it made clear that knowledge was not to be set aside in faith but that knowledge and trust, intellect and will, were both included, Reformation Christians still struggled with how to relate them and with the problem of assurance. The churches were often torn between those who emphasized the mind and those who sought assurance in the mysticism of the heart or in the good works of practical Christianity. The Heidelberg Catechism simply put the two side by side, connecting them only by a both/and formula: "not only but also."[13] This was not entirely satisfying since it raised further questions about how two different faculties could produce the one fruit of faith. While different theologians attempted to solve this with varying sets of distinctions beyond the three classic ones of knowledge (*notitia*), assent (*assensus*), and trust (*fiducia*), multiplying categories led to the danger that faith would no longer be seen as the appropriating organ in justification. In response, Alexander Comrie and his followers tried to work back from the *act* of faith to the *disposition* (*habitus*) by which a believer is ingrafted into Christ, which is then followed by acts of faith. This does not seem to do justice to Q&A 21 of the Heidelberg Catechism and failed to resolve matters because the disposition of faith (seed, root, faculty or principle of faith) cannot be formally

9. T. Aquinas, *Summa Theol.*, II, 1, qu. 112, art. 5; Council of Trent, VI, c. 9, can. 13–15; cf. H. Bavinck, *Reformed Dogmatics*, I, 571 (#148); III, 514–17 (#416).

10. J. Calvin, *Institutes of the Christian Religion*, III.ii.7 (ed. John T. McNeill and trans. Ford Lewis Battles [Philadelphia: Westminster, 1960], 1:549–51); cf. idem, *Commentary*, on Rom. 10:10.

11. J. Calvin, *Institutes*, III.ii.8.

12. J. Calvin, *Institutes*, III.ii.17ff.

13. Lord's Day 7, Q&A 21: Q. What is true faith? A. True faith is not only a knowledge and conviction that everything God reveals in his Word is true. It is also a deep-rooted assurance, created in me by the Holy Spirit through the gospel, that, out of sheer grace, earned for us by Christ, not only others, but I too have had my sins forgiven, have been made forever right with God, and have been granted salvation.

called faith. As Voetius noted, "This [principle] cannot be called faith except by analogy and improperly by metonymy of the cause or of principle; formally this is no more faith than a seed is a tree, or an egg a chicken, or a bulb a flower."[14]

[453] Problems also arose when some theologians objected to regarding trust or confidence (*fiducia*) as the true, formal act of faith because this confidence could not be identical to the faith by which one accepts Christ. This objection, made by Robert Bellarmine and others, was acknowledged by Reformed theologians[15] and led them to distinguish the faith *through* which we are justified (*fides, per quam justificamur*) from the faith *by which* we believe that through Christ our sins have been forgiven (*fides, qua credimus nobis per Christum remissa esse peccata*). The former precedes justification, the latter follows it. This distinction was intended more in a logical than in a temporal sense yet was complicated because of the doctrine of particular atonement. According to the Reformed confession, Christ obtained salvation only for the elect. Because we do not know the elect by name, the gospel is preached without distinction to all; all are called and obligated to believe. A general faith that believes the gospel proclamation and takes refuge in Christ precedes the reflexive act of faith whereby one becomes aware of one's salvation. Between that initial direct act of faith and conscious reflection, a serious question intervenes: Is my faith genuine? Could it be only a temporal or historical faith? The question was less pressing for that first generation of Reformers whose joyful experience of liberation by grace led to glad and full assurance of faith. Assured Christians in subsequent generations became rarer as far too many church members became indifferent, content with their orthodoxy, or seekers and doubters who could not find peace of mind and heart. In addition, Christian living left much to be desired.

Under the influence of English and Scottish practitioners, preachers arose who lamented the decay of the church and the doctrine of morals, announced the judgments of God, and expected salvation only from a reformation of human hearts and lives.[16] They summoned governments and church ministers to do their

14. Gisbert Voetius, *Selectae disputations theologicae*, 5 vols. (Utrecht, 1648–69), II, 499; V, 288.

15. W. Ames, *The Marrow of Theology*, trans. J. D. Eusden (1968; repr., Grand Rapids: Baker Academic, 1997), I.27.16 (p. 162); Peter van Mastricht, *Theoretico-practica theologia* (Utrecht: Appels, 1714), I, 1, 25; Francis Turretin, *Institutes of Elenctic Theology*, trans. George Musgrove Giger and ed. James T. Dennison, 3 vols. (Phillipsburg, NJ: Presbyterian & Reformed, 1992), XV, qu. 8, 7, 11; qu. 10, 3; qu. 12, 6; W. à Brakel, *The Christian's Reasonable Service*, trans. Bartel Elshout, 4 vols. (Ligonier, PA: Soli Deo Gloria, 1992–95), III, 357ff. (Dutch: XXXIV, 27). Cf. also Westminster Confession, c. 18, 3; Rev. D. Beaton, "'The Marrow of Modern Divinity' and the Marrow Controversy," *Princeton Theological Review* 4 (July 1906): 327–31.

16. Great influence was exerted mainly by W. Teellinck, H. Witsius, and J. van Lodenstein. Ed. note: See Willem Teellinck, *The Path of True Godliness*, ed. Joel Beeke, trans. Annemie Godbeheere, in *Classics of Reformed Spirituality* (Grand Rapids: Baker Academic, 2003); Carl J. Schroeder, *In Quest of Pentecost: Jodocus van Lodenstein and the Dutch Second Reformation* (Lanham, MD: University Press of America, 2001). Ed. note: Bavinck refers here to the so-called Dutch "Further Reformation" (*Nadere Reformatie*), which parallels the English Puritan movement of the seventeenth and eighteenth centuries. Dutch scholars who have a periodical devoted to this movement define it as follows: "The Dutch Second (or 'Further') Reformation is that movement within the Dutch Reformed Church during the

duty and urged self-examination. Some even vigorously took up arms against mere knowledge of the letter and fought fervently for a practical, kindhearted, and experiential Christianity.[17] Others, with little confidence in a so-called "evangelical conversion," insisted on the contrition of the heart, conviction of sin, and a sense of misery as conditions for obtaining Christ and his benefits; and in the order of salvation accorded a place to justification and rebirth *after* faith.[18]

Viewing this dejected and indecisive state of people's spiritual life, still others sought to take a safer route and again included the certainty of salvation in the essence of faith, but they usually erred as far left as their adversaries erred right regarding deep-seated confidence as the full substance, the formal act (*actus formalis*), of the faith.[19] This easily led to the antinomian view that faith consists in the intellectual acceptance of the sentence "Your sins are forgiven," a sentence not first uttered in the gospel by God himself but contained from all eternity in the decree of election, and finally only revealed by the person and work of Christ.

---

seventeenth and eighteenth centuries, which, as a reaction to the declension or absence of a living faith made both the personal experience of faith and godliness matters of central importance. From that perspective the movement formulated substantial and procedural reformation initiatives, submitting them to the proper ecclesiastical, political, and social agencies, and pursued those initiatives through a further reformation of the church, society, and state in both word and deed" (*Documentatieblad Nadere Reformatie* 19 [1995]: 108; cited in *The Path of True Godliness*, 7–8, the series preface of the Classics of Reformed Spirituality series).

17. Ed. note: Bavinck cites the following: J. Eswijler, *Ziels-eenzame meditatiën* (Rotterdam: 1685; 1739); J. Verschuir, *Waarheid in het binnenste, of bevindelyke Godtgeleertheit*, 5th ed. ('s Gravenhage: J. Thierry, 1776);. W. Schortinghuis, *Het innige Christendom* (1710; 2nd ed., 1740); Dr. J. C. Kromsigt, *Wilhelmus Schortinghuis* (Groningen: J. B. Wolters, 1904), 141ff.

18. Cf. Jac. Koelman, *De natuur en gronden des geloofs*, 4th ed. (Utrecht: Willem David Gromme, 1700); T. van der Groe, *Toetssteen der waare en valsche genade*, 8th ed., 2 vols. (Rotterdam: H. van Pelt & A. Douci Pietersz, 1752–53), I, 151, 251; II, 743ff., 951ff.; Adriaan van der Willegen, and Theodorus van der Groe, *Beschrijvinge van het oprecht en zielzaligend geloove* (Rotterdam: R. C. Huge, 1742). According to Lampe, faith precedes regeneration (F. A. Lampe, *De verborgenheit van het genaade-verbondt*, 4 vols. [Amsterdam: Antony Schoonenburg, 1726–39], 254–69, 287). Faith as refuge-taking trust in Christ is distinguished from deep-rooted, assured trust and can only arise if by self-examination one has become convinced of the genuineness of one's faith. Later he became more moderate and acknowledged that the hungering and thirsting to some extent implied the eating and being satisfied. Those who truly seek Jesus enjoy him as well; those who seek have found. Deep-rooted assurance, accordingly, does not arise from refuge-taking trust as the root grows from the seed. The latter is itself a kind of implicit trust. Cf. J. C. Kromsigt, *Wilhelmus Schortinghuis*, 82ff.; 96ff.

19. Some (e.g., Jac. Schuts, *Beschrijving van het Zaligmahend Geloof* [Rotterdam: R. van Doesburgh, 1692]) held that the acts of faith—knowing, assenting, trusting, and so forth—already presuppose faith, and that faith essentially consists in holding as true God's witness concerning Christ, hence in assent. Others (especially Theod. van Thuynen, *Korte uitlegginge van het gereformeerde geloof* [Leeuwarden: Henrick Halma, 1722]) insisted that faith itself essentially consists in the deep-rooted confidence that we are reconciled to God and have received the forgiveness of sins. In his opinion, the precisionists, whom he combats, turn the order around and think that God is only reconciled by our faith (religious experience, good works). They—like Roman Catholics and Remonstrants—have justification follow faith, whereas, according to the Reformed confession, it precedes it. Cf. A. Ritschl, *Geschichte des Pietismus in der reformierten Kirche* (Bonn: A. Marcus, 1880), 321ff.; J. C. Kromsigt, *Wilhelmus Schortinghuis*, 74ff.

[454] In this manner the ground was prepared for the rationalistic and moralistic approach to the order of redemption followed by nearly all theologians in the eighteenth century. Abandoning Reformed principles, this school of thought aligned itself with Socinians and Arminians and taught that faith—conceived only as assent or to some extent also as trust (*fiducia*)—could itself justify a person only insofar as it contained within itself the new obedience and was a source of virtue.[20] Schleiermacher validly argued against this by teaching that in the Christian religion everything is related to the redemption brought about by Jesus of Nazareth; however, in the resulting "mysticism of the heart," faith consisted only in "the appropriation of the perfection and blessedness of Christ."[21] Unsatisfied by Schleiermacher, Ritschl focused on the "historical" Jesus as depicted in the Synoptic Gospels and to his work of establishing a spiritual kingdom among humans.[22]

These new views of faith tried to transcend the opposition between Pelagianism and Augustinianism and let faith arise by way of paths God follows with all human beings, i.e., with an ongoing interaction with humanity. Faith is not a matter of doctrine but a personal relationship of trust in God through Christ. But if faith, however inwardly conceived, is to remain Christian, it will always presuppose or include a certain "knowledge" and "assent."[23] Finally, the newer descriptions of faith show great convergence in that they powerfully underscore the ethical nature of faith. For Ritschl, for example, faith consists especially in working for the kingdom of God and essentially coincides with love.[24] Yet, others rightly maintain the religious nature of faith and regard justification and the mystical union as benefits granted to every individual believer, but they too do their best to hold on to the inner connectedness between faith and love, between justification and sanctification, and to bring to the fore the morally renewing powers of the Christian religion.

REGENERATION, FAITH, AND KNOWLEDGE

[455] The descriptions that have been given of faith since the Reformation are so numerous and divergent as to make a person almost despair of the possibility of

20. On neonomism, see H. Bavinck, *Reformed Dogmatics*, III, 531–35 (#421).

21. F. Schleiermacher, *The Christian Faith*, ed. H. R. MacIntosh and J. S. Steward (Edinburgh: T&T Clark, 1928), §108; cf. H. Bavinck, *Reformed Dogmatics*, III, 550–54 (#425).

22. A. Ritschl, *The Christian Doctrine of Justification and Reconciliation*, trans. H. R. Mackintosh and A. B. Macauley (Edinburgh: T&T Clark, 1900; repr., Clifton, NJ: Reference Book Publishers, 1966), 98ff., 568ff., 582ff.; cf. also H. Bavinck, *Reformed Dogmatics*, III, 550–54 (#425).

23. W. Herrmann, *Der Verkehr des Christen mit Gott*, 6th ed. (Stuttgart: Cotta, 1908), 180: "The Christian faith is not, first of all, concerned generally about doctrine, but rather about an encounter that firmly impacts the life of people who are called to faith. Nonetheless, knowledge is indeed a precondition of faith."

24. A. Ritschl, *Justification and Reconciliation*, 584: "The belief in Christ and God falls under the scope of . . . the concept of love. It is the continuous direction of the will to God and Christ, which is part of the content of faith itself."

correctly and clearly defining the nature of faith. Roman Catholic theology has the advantage of a very simple and understandable definition when it describes faith solely as assent. In Scripture, however, faith is not merely an intellectual act, but also a personal relation, a spiritual bond, with Christ who is now seated at the right hand of the power of God. Faith is the principle of the Christian life as a whole, the means by which we obtain Christ and all his benefits, the subjective source of all salvation and blessing. Wherever faith may be rooted in human beings, it affects all our capacities and powers; gives us direction and guidance; and controls our intellect and heart, our thinking and activity, our life and conduct. Not surprisingly, theology has had to struggle to give a somewhat correct definition of this rich notion of faith. Life is always more mysterious and complex than definitions allow. Still, it is not impossible, in the order of redemption, to give faith the place and the significance that is due it according to Scripture.

We can make headway here only when we acknowledge that neither faith nor conversion is the condition that acquires salvation for us. Reconciliation (καταλλαγη) is not distinguished from expiation (ἱλασμος) by the fact that while the latter is objective the former is subjective and objective. The content of the gospel message is this: God *has been* reconciled; accept this reconciliation and believe the gospel. Objectively realized in Christ, salvation is individually applied and distributed in the internal calling and passively accepted on the human side in regeneration. Whenever regeneration takes place, before or during the hearing of the Word, logically it always precedes the act of really believing. "For no one can hear the word of God salvifically unless he is regenerate."[25] No one can come to Christ unless the Father draws him (John 6:44; also cf. Rom. 8:7; 1 Cor. 2:14; 12:3; etc.). Emphasizing divine initiative, Reformed theology came to consider the strict sense of regeneration to be the first logical step in the order of salvation. Reformed churches do not baptize children of believers on the basis of a presumed regeneration but do hold a judgment of charity with respect to them. The objection against this view that freedom and independence are lost applies equally to all unless one takes the Pelagian route and makes regeneration completely dependent on a person's religious free choice. This is a great consolation to believers that their children are received by God without their knowing and acting, especially when children die in infancy. That this gift is miraculously given even to infants is fitting for the God to whom no door is locked, no creature unapproachable, no heart inaccessible. With his Spirit he can enter the innermost being of every human, with or without the Word, by way of or apart from all consciousness, in old age or from the moment of conception. Christ's own conception by the Holy Spirit in Mary's womb is proof that the Holy Spirit can, from that moment on and continually, be active in a human being with his sanctifying presence. A person's spiritual life from the very earliest beginning is a divine gift of grace; its continuation toward the full regeneration of the whole person is the same gift of life, and

---

25. Johannes Maccovius, *Loci communes theologici* (Amsterdam: n.p., 1658), 710.

it continues until the consummation in eternity. This doctrine of regeneration in a restrictive sense is a precious part of our Reformed confession.

The confession of regeneration as the implantation of the new life principle is of inestimable *pedagogical* value. Reformed theologians have never held as an incontrovertible dogma that *all* covenant children or even all *elect* covenant children have already been regenerated in their infancy before or in baptism, but they firmly maintain that such a rebirth in early childhood before the years of discretion *could* take place. Therefore, they held firmly to the rule that we must regard and treat all covenant children born and baptized in the fellowship of the church in accordance with the judgment of charity, as true children of the covenant, until from their "talk" and "walk" the contrary is evident. This approach produces a very different view of education and upbringing in family, school, and church settings.[26] It also maintains the bond between nature and grace; proceeds from the reality of the covenant of grace and baptism; believes in the unity and organic development of the spiritual life; and fully recognizes that God does not always work faith and repentance in the human heart suddenly, but often causes them to proceed and develop from the implanted life gradually, by a psychological and pedagogical process.

This view is consistent with Scripture's description of faith as a gift of God (Matt. 11:25–27; 16:17; John 1:12–13; 6:44; 1 Cor. 12:3; Gal. 1:16; Eph. 1:11; 2:8; Phil. 1:29; 2:13). The means by which God carries out his counsel is included in that counsel. Whether he does so suddenly or gradually it is the same gracious omnipotent God, who works both the willing and the working according to his good pleasure. The God who makes us new is the same God who brought the world into being. By his Spirit he indwells the entire created world, and by that same Spirit, as the Spirit of Christ, he is present in the entire church and in each of its members. He strengthens and nourishes the spiritual life [of his children] from moment to moment by the power of his grace and the blessing of his Word. The means God uses include the reading of Scripture, the advice to and admonition of parents, the instruction of teachers, and public preaching. Faith and the Word of God belong together. Faith comes from what is heard, and what is heard comes through the Word of Christ (Rom. 10:17).

[456–57] Since there is no active faith apart from the Word of God, there must be a connection between knowledge (assent) and faith. Discerning the proper relation between them is a challenge. Too often, out of reaction to intellectualism, people put all the emphasis on the element of feeling and trust present in saving faith, only to have the opposite reaction take place. The close connection between faith and knowledge is apparent from our ordinary use of the word "faith" in our daily lives, which shares features with its religious sense as Scripture itself demonstrates when it uses the Hebrew word הֶאֱמִן and the Greek word πιστευειν in both senses. The relationship between knowledge and faith is complex and varies from person

---

26. H. Bavinck, *Paedegogischen beginselen* (Kampen: Kok, 1904), 90–92.

to person; there are those who are brought to Christ by the Scriptures and also those who are brought to the Scriptures by Christ.[27] *Logically speaking*, historical knowledge precedes faith, though it can never on its own produce faith as saving faith is a sure knowledge that produces assurance and certainty, and knowledge and trust go together. Pietism correctly insisted on an experiential knowledge that was differentiated from a formal knowledge of Christianity; it erred when it spoke of a different, higher spiritual truth that it separated from historical truth. From the very beginning, the Reformation held to the necessity of a personal, saving faith which included historical truth. Calvin refered to this as "a firm and certain knowledge of God's benevolence toward us, founded upon the truth of the freely given promise in Christ, both revealed to our minds and sealed upon our hearts—not in our heads!—by the Holy Spirit."[28] While historical faith, therefore, may often precede saving faith in time and as such have undeniable pedagogical value, the "firm and certain knowledge," as Calvin put and meant it, of God's grace in Christ plus all the truths of salvation are the fruit, or rather the content, of true saving faith and can be considered complete. Not only does Scripture alternate "believing" with "knowing" (John 6:69; 7:3–4; 1 Cor. 1:21; 2 Cor. 4:6; etc.), but in Calvin's definition *general* faith (the central promise of salvation in Christ) and *special* faith (*fides specialis*, faith in God's benevolence toward us) are organically interrelated; saving faith is a single act that knows and accepts Christ in the garment of Scripture, "clothed with his gospel,"[29] and this avoids both an arid rationalism and a false mysticism. Christian faith is nothing else but the assurance that "the eternal Faith of our Lord Jesus Christ, who out of nothing created heaven and earth and still upholds and governs them by his eternal counsel and providence, is our God and Father because of Christ his Son" (Heidelberg Catechism, answer 26).

Having accepted Calvin's definition, theology did not stop there, for in practice it proved inadequate. In order not to confuse the "knowledge" (*cognitio*) of saving faith with the "knowledge" (*notitia*) and "assent" (*assensus*) of historical faith and risk returning to the Roman Catholic view of faith,[30] it became necessary to make a clear distinction between the knowledge (*cognitio*) of saving faith and the knowledge (*notitia*) of historical faith. But this in turn set up the old polarity of heart versus head and made assurance of faith problematic by speaking of faith as only knowledge (*cognitio*) but also (and hence especially) assurance (*fiducia*). In this way knowledge was pushed into the background and led to a multitude of further distinctions in the area of assurance itself.

27. Cf. H. Bavinck, *Reformed Dogmatics*, I, 569–70 (#148).

28. J. Calvin, *Institutes*, III.ii.6–8.

29. Ibid., III.ii.6.

30. Roman Catholics expressly reject the distinction between historical faith and saving faith, as does Robert Bellarmine, "De justif.," in *De controversiis christianae fidei adversus huius temporis haereticos* (Cologne: G. Gualtheri, 1617–20), I, chap. 4, but sharply separate faith and love, ibid., chap. 15. The Remonstrants, on the other hand, deny the distinction between temporary and saving faith and include obedience in faith, and so forth. Remonstrant Confession of Faith, X; Apologia pro confessione, XVIII.

Although making distinctions was not wrong as such, it soon led people to view these two acts of faith as temporally consecutive, to insert the practice of self-examination between taking refuge and an assured confidence, and to view the different activities of faith as so many stages in believing. In keeping with these stages [there came a tendency] to divide believers into groups, each of which—in the application of sermons and in devotional literature—was then addressed separately. In short, the Reformation's restoration of the religious nature of faith brought the discovery that faith is something quite different from assent to religious truths. The profound insight that true faith is a special faith—with the person of Christ and God's benevolence to us as its object—made it progressively more clear that faith was not one simple thing but a vastly complex phenomenon. It included intellect and will, and was rooted in two faculties and included many properties. It was knowledge in the intellect, agreement in the will, love, desire, joy.[31] Any number of activities converge in it, even if people limit them in the main to knowing, assenting, and trusting, or even if one accords the central place to the reception of Christ.[32] Saving faith is not "one simple disposition but a composite one, one that cannot be comprehended under a single heading."[33]

We are led, therefore, to follow Comrie in speaking first of the habit or disposition of faith (*habitus fidei*) by which we are incorporated into Christ; the churches of the Reformation, following Scripture, increasingly spoke of faith as that new, normative, spiritual, and comprehensive relationship in which God first of all (in regeneration or habitual faith) directs us to himself, and we, with all our capacities and powers (in actual faith), direct ourselves to God. Our relationship to God—believing, trusting, loving, thanking, and serving the God and Father of our Lord Jesus Christ, who is eternal, omnipotent, gracious and merciful—is not a matter of *sight* but of *faith*, a faith that will one day become sight when we shall see God face to face.

Now if this is the nature of saving faith, it does not much matter whether one describes it as knowledge or trust or as both in conjunction; knowledge (*cognitio*) as Calvin views it includes trust (*fiducia*), and trust in turn is not possible without knowledge. Mere juxtaposition or linkage by the words "not only but also" (Heidelberg Catechism, Q&A 21) does not suffice to describe the organic interconnection between them. What counts is the reception of Christ, a personal acceptance, not of a doctrine but of the person of Christ, as he is presented to us in the gospel. True faith, in short, is the great benefit of the covenant of grace by which we are incorporated into Christ and accept him with all his benefits. Faith is nothing other than the subjective, personal (passive in habitual faith, active in actual faith) acceptance of Christ along with all his benefits and brings with it its own certainty. It is the opposite of anxiety (Matt. 6:31; 8:26; 10:31),

---

31. P. van Mastricht, *Theologia*, II, 1, 8–10.

32. Ibid., II, 1, 11; A. Comrie, *The ABC of Faith*, trans. J. Marcus Banfield (Ossett: Zoar, 1978).

33. F. Turretin, *Institutes of Elenctic Theology*, XV, 8, 13.

of fear (Mark 4:40; 5:36), of doubt (Matt. 14:31; 21:21; Rom. 4:20; James 1:6), and of being troubled (John 14:1). It is unlimited confidence (Matt. 17:20), the assurance (ὑπόστασις) and conviction (ἔλεγχος) of unseen things (Heb. 11:1). To deny the possibility of certainty as Rome does[34] is as much an error as that of nomistic pietism which sought assurance in the way of continual introspection and prolonged and anxious self-examination, relieved only by occasional extraordinary revelations. Faith, we must insist, is more than "naked assent" and includes certainty; certainty is not an external additive to faith but is in principle integral to it from the start. It is not obtained by looking at ourselves but by looking away from ourselves to Christ and is grounded in the promises of God, not in changing experiences or imperfect good works.

Doubts and fears do certainly arise from time to time in the believer's heart (Matt. 8:25; 14:30; Mark 9:24), and these remain a struggle in a believer's life, a struggle in which victory comes only by holding on to the certain promises of God.[35] Therefore, the various acts of faith, such as knowing, assenting, trusting, and so forth, acts that in turn must be distinguished from the fruits of faith or good works, are not the steps or stages of faith that succeed each other in time but activities that themselves, and in connection with each other, can be either weak or strong depending on whether we are babes in Christ or more mature saints. So then faith is and remains by its very nature essentially the same as it was in the days of the Old and New Testaments: an unlimited and unconditional trust of the heart in the riches of God's grace in Christ, a believing against hope (Rom. 4:18), the assurance of things hoped for and the conviction of things unseen (Heb. 11:1), a deep-seated confidence that with God all things are possible (Mark 10:27; 11:23–24), that he who raised Christ from the dead (Rom. 4:24; 10:9) still raises the dead, still saves sinners, and forever calls into existence the things that do not exist (4:17).

CONVERSION AND REPENTANCE

[458] The new life implanted in regeneration yields, in relation to the intellect, faith and knowledge and wisdom; in relation to the will, conversion and repentance. In a broad sense conversion includes all religious changes by which someone breaks from sinful habits and practices and enters upon a path of virtue. God has not left himself without a witness to anyone, but through nature and history, heart and conscience, effects a "real" [mediated through things] call that keeps alive religious and moral consciousness among all peoples. Even though they suppress God's truth by their wickedness and thereby become inexcusable (Rom. 1:18ff.), all humans have a more or less acute consciousness of sin, guilt, and punishment

34. Council of Trent, VI, c. 9, can. 13–15.
35. J. Calvin, *Institutes*, III.ii.17ff.

and the moral law they are obligated to follow (Rom. 2:14–15). Such awareness among gentiles has led to profound insights into the human soul. In his graphic personification of the Furies, for example, Aeschylus captured well the repentance, regret, and remorse that follows a sinful deed: "It is their own evil deed, their own terror that torments them more than anything else; each of them is harassed and driven to madness by his own crime; his own evil thoughts and the stings of conscience terrify him."[36] There is also awareness that the key to conversion and a virtuous life is self-knowledge as well as a realization that self-knowledge is incredibly elusive and hard to achieve. Self-knowledge, therefore, along with remorse and confession, is the first step on the road to self-improvement, but "penitence is never too late."[37]

Not only Christianity but all religions and systems gain influence by the conversions they bring about, the changes they produce in the ideas, dispositions, and actions of people. Some conversions are more religious, others more ethical, still others more intellectual or aesthetic, but all agree that the lives of people are organized around a new center of ideas, and that souls begin to take an interest in things they did not know before, neglected, or despised. Because changes such as this are found in all religions and in people who find "spiritual new birth" in adopting new philosophies or discovering new literature,[38] the psychology of religion included religious conversion in a longer list of "personality changes." As an antidote against this leveling of all differences, however, one needs to consider that conversion has a specific meaning and belongs in the sphere of religion. Psychology of religion cannot penetrate to the essential nature of conversion, and its commitment to "presuppositionlessness" gives it no criteria by which it can discern and distinguish the psychological phenomena that it categorizes as conversion. Here Scripture, importantly, provides a very specific and clear concept of conversion.[39]

We can begin with the words that have been translated in our own language as "repentance" or "conversion," but we must also look at Scripture's instructive examples. The most frequent words used in the Old Testament are נָחַם (*nāḥam*) and שׁוּב (*šûb*). The first (נָחַם) means to be sorry, to suffer grief, to repent, and is used with reference to persons (Judg. 21:6, 15; Job 42:6; Jer. 8:6; 31:19) but especially of God (Gen. 6:6–7; Exod. 32:12, 14; Deut. 32:36; Judg. 2:18; etc.). The other word (שׁוּב) means to turn, to turn around, to turn back, and is used metaphorically to mean to turn away from some activity such as sin (1 Kings

36. M. T. Cicero, *Pro sexto Rosico Amerino*, in *The Speeches*, trans. John Henry Freese (London: W. Heinemann; New York: G. P. Putnam's Sons, 1930), c. 24; F. F. K. Fischer, *De deo Aeschyleo* (Amsterdam: J. A. Wormser, 1892), 62ff.; R. Mulder, *De conscientiae notione* (Leiden: Brill, 1908).

37. For a great many similar statements (from antiquity), see R. Schneider, *Christliche Klänge* (Leipzig: Siegismund & Volkening, 1877), 272ff.

38. For example, John Stuart Mill in 1826 was rescued from depression and lethargy by reading, among other things, the poetry of William Wordsworth; see G. Jackson, *The Fact of Conversion* (New York and Chicago: Revell, 1908), 140.

39. Cf. H. Bavinck, *Reformed Dogmatics*, III, 584–88 (#431).

8:35), iniquity (Job 36:10), transgression (Isa. 59:20), wickedness (Ezek. 3:19), or wicked works (Neh. 9:35; etc.). The direction to which a person then turns is indicated by the preposition אֶל (*'el*, toward). Yet, the word שׁוּב is not restricted to what dogmatics call "conversion"; it applies to God turning away from his wrath (Exod. 32:12) and to Israel turning away from the Lord and toward idols (Josh. 22:16, 18, 23; Judg. 2:19). It is in the prophetic literature that the word שׁוּב increasingly acquired a religious-ethical meaning. The return promised by the prophets, however, was not merely local and temporal but had to and would be accompanied by, and as it were coincide with, a conversion in a religious-ethical sense, a change of heart and life. Both senses can be found in passages such as Isaiah 10:21; Jeremiah 31:21; 46:27; Hosea 6:1; 14:7; and Zechariah 9:12, and it is often hard to tell whether the first or second meaning is denoted. This much is certain: a total, not just an external but also an internal change is needed for the people. What God requires is a broken and contrite heart (Ps. 51:17); a conversion of the whole heart (Joel 2:12). He not only demands this but also promises it and will some day grant it in the days of the new covenant (Jer. 31:31ff.; Ezek. 36:25ff.; Zech. 13:1; Mal. 4:6). After the exile, a nomistic trend arose that abandoned this prophetic line of thought and increasingly viewed conversion as a work that had to compensate and be atoned for by acts of penitence for the sins committed earlier. Upon restoration through completion of penitence, people could again accumulate merits that gave them a claim to reward here or in the hereafter.[40]

[459–61] Against the externalization of conversion, John the Baptist and Jesus came and demanded μετανοια (*metanoia*, repentance). Like נָחַם and שׁוּב, μετανοια denotes something beyond religious-ethical conversion, and in ordinary Greek it already had the sense of being sorry and of breaking with one's past and turning to a better life. In the Septuagint, שׁוּב was usually translated by ἐπιστρεφειν (*epistrephein*), which also occurs in ordinary and New Testament Greek in a (metaphorical) moral sense. Between μετανοια and ἐπιστροφη there is indeed a distinction: the first word accentuates the internal change of mind that moves a person to turn away from one's sinful past, while the second focuses on the new relation in which, as a result of that change of mind, that person manifests him or herself outwardly. The verb μεταμελεσθαι (*metamelesthai*, to repent) occurs a few times in the New Testament (Matt. 21:29, 32; 27:3; 2 Cor. 7:8; Heb. 7:21). We must remember that these biblical terms for what we call repentance or conversion are not defined logically or dogmatically but are used variously in a broader or more restricted sense. The doctrine of conversion is certainly not based exclusively on those texts in which these words occur, but is rooted in everything Scripture portrays to us with respect to the natural state of humankind and the necessity, character, manner, and fruit of the religious and moral turnabout of humans. Jesus tells Nicodemus that he must be "born again" (John 3:3, 5, 8) and Paul implies the same when he tells us that we must

40. Cf. ibid., III, 495–99 (#411).

be crucified, buried, and, above all, resurrected to a new life in Christ (Rom. 6:3ff.; Gal. 2:19–20); put off the old self and put on the new (Eph. 4:22–24; Col. 3:9–10); put to death our earthly nature (Col. 3:5); walk by the Spirit (Rom. 8:4); be alive to God in Christ Jesus (6:11); and offer the parts of our body to God as instruments of righteousness (6:13; etc.).

Scripture also distinguishes between varying kinds of repentance. In 2 Corinthians 7:10 Paul refers to a godly sorrow that brings repentance leading to salvation and leaves no regrets, and a worldly sorrow that is superficial, characterized by short-term regret, not deeply rooted in the heart, and produces death. It may even bring about guilty remorse that is overwhelming but not at all godly. Some people are temporarily halted in their sinful careers by adversity, disaster, or a death, and even affected by preaching of the law or gospel (Matt. 13:20–21), join the church and participate in its means of grace, but they quickly return to a life that is hostile to God. Scripture also provides us with many such examples (1 Kings 21:27; Acts 8:9ff.; 1 Tim. 1:19–20; 2 Tim. 2:17; 4:10); and the many who, even in the apostolic period, "went out from us because they were not of us" (1 John 2:19) and denied the Master, who had bought them (2 Pet. 2:1).

All these are far short of true conversion, which arises from godly sorrow and includes profound antipathy toward one's own sin, which is accompanied by open turning away from sin and positively toward God and his law (2 Cor. 7:10). It is demanded by God but, as importantly, freely given by him and leads infallibly to salvation. Of such genuine repentance Scripture also offers many examples and testimonies (2 Kings 5:15; 2 Chron. 33:12–13; Matt. 3:6; 9:9 [Mark 2:14]; Luke 19:8; 23:42; John 1:46ff.; 4:29, 39; 9:38; Acts 2:37ff.; 8:37; 9:6ff.; 10:44ff.; 16:14, 30ff.; and so forth). The commonality in all these stories is an internal change of mind that prompts reflection on one's sinful past in the light of God's face; leads to sorrow, regret, humiliation, and confession of sin; and is, both inwardly and outwardly, the beginning of a new religious-moral life. But there is also diversity in the circumstances and means by which conversion takes place. For Jews, who knew the Old Testament, lengthy demonstrations from Scripture (Acts 8:35; 17:3; 18:28) serve as the means to point them to the Christ. The Jews did not have to learn to serve another God but to recognize Jesus as the Messiah; gentiles, however, had to turn away from vain things to the living God (Acts 14:15; 15:19; 26:20; 1 Thess. 1:9) and totally break with their previous religious and moral lives.

Yet, believers are not perfect or sinless (James 3:2; 1 John 1:8) and still need to "turn back" when they fall into sin. So should we speak of the "conversion" of believers? In the New Testament, conversion always applies to those who, having been raised as Jews or gentiles, were incorporated into the church by baptism as the sign and seal of conversion. The New Testament does not contain the history of the established church but tells the story of the founding of the church in the then-known world. In some cases, it became necessary in the course of the church's history to speak of the conversion of believers when they fell into gross sin. Initially, the preaching of the gospel brought about such a striking change that even the pagan unbelievers attested to it. Catechumens were instructed in the content of the Christian faith and lifestyle. As baptism became the recognized sign of forgiveness and a belief arose that the sacrament only retroactively forgave sins committed before baptism, many people postponed baptism as long as possible. With the establishment of the church and most of its increase coming from within, such postponement became practically impossible and child baptism became the rule. Thus, sins committed after baptism became an issue and caused much consternation. Attempts were made to distinguish major sins—from which Christians were supposed to be free—from minor ones which were more easily forgivable. At times perfectionist movements attempted to impose rigorous moralism on church members by refusing those who lapsed into sin to return to church. A more gentle view prevailed and led to a judgment that at least one additional conversion was possible.[41]

Over time, having to come to terms with lapses during times of persecution and difficulties in separating major and minor sins, excessive rigor was replaced by a more humane system of penance, stressed especially by monks such as Cassian and popes such as Gregory. This began as confession of sin before God in solitude, but as the idea prevailed that one had also to *do* penance, distinctions were multiplied,[42] and the church through its priests and bishops was sacramentally the means by which Christ issued the grace of forgiveness. The priest now heard the voluntary confession and imposed the penance that could cover the offense of venial sins. While the priest could pronounce absolution, sinners remained obligated to perform the penance the priest simultaneously imposed on them. This development was aided by the translation of the Greek words μετανοια and μετανοειν by "penitence" and "doing penance." Inasmuch as penance could not be completely carried out in this life, the deficit had to be made up in the hereafter by suffering in purgatory. Eventually, this approach led to the corrupt practice of indulgences whereby an imposed penance could be decreased or shortened through the intercession and merits of another. From the eleventh century on, indulgences multiplied and became a business by which the papacy enriched its coffers. At Trent, the Roman Catholic Church condemned the abuses that crept into the sale of indulgences but firmly maintained the use of indulgences as being "most salutary for Christian people."[43]

With respect to this Roman Catholic sacrament of penance, one must bear in mind that indulgences as a "work of satisfaction" (*satisfactio operis*) do not grant absolution from eternal punishment; this has already been secured by Christ and is granted the penitent after "the contrition of the heart" (*contritio cordis*) and "confession of the mouth" (*confessio oris*). The "work of satisfaction" consists

---

41. Herm. *Vis.* 2; Herm. *Mand.* 3; Herm. *Sim.* 8.11; but elsewhere he expresses himself less generously.

42. Among others, between venial and mortal sins; a liability to guilt (*reatus culpae*) and the liability to punishment (*reatus poenae*).

43. Council of Trent, sess. 25 cont., "Decretum de indulgentiis."

only in bearing the *temporal punishment* merited by sin, which could be reduced by means of an indulgence.[44] However, these fine distinctions were usually lost on ordinary believers and the practice of indulgences, along with the elaborate casuistry brought about by the distinction between contrition and attrition (imperfect contrition) in the Roman Catholic sacramental system,[45] tended to create the impression of being saved by doing penance.

Even apart from popular piety, however, penance is regarded in Roman Catholic theology to be an essential part of the church's sacramental *power*; the priest is not just the witness to a believer's confession before God, he is the authorized dispenser of the benefits of forgiveness acquired by Christ in the declaratory formula, *Absolvo te* ("I absolve you").[46] The absolution pronounced in the sacrament of penance is absolute though it is made on the assumption of "the temporal satisfaction that must still be made."[47] For that reason the "work of satisfaction" does not belong to the essence of the sacrament but to its wholeness.

The Roman Catholic penitential system culminated when penance was included among the seven sacraments. The holy sacrament of penance is a second baptism but a "laborious baptism," the only remedy for those who by a mortal sin have lost the sanctifying grace received in baptism. It is also beneficial for those who have committed venial sins and hence to be used at least once a year by every believer, according to the canon of the Fourth Lateran Council.[48] Penance is also distinguished from baptism in that in the former the priest also functions as judge. He hears confession, takes note of sins committed, and then, with the aid of penitential books, he assesses the appropriate penance and, in the expectation that the penitent will bear these penalties willingly and completely, pronounces a

44. The definition of an indulgence, accordingly, is usually the following: "Indulgence is the remission, in the divine court (*in foro Dei*), of the temporal penalty owed for sin, as validated by application [of merit] from the treasury of the church." Cf. J. H. Oswald, *Die dogmatische Lehre von den heiligen Sakramenten der katholischen Kirche*, 2nd ed., 2 vols. in 1 (Münster: Aschendorff, 1864), II, 201.

45. Thomas clarifies the terms "contrition" and "attrition" as follows: "In corporeal matters, those things are said to be attrite, which in some way are diminished, but not perfectly; whereas contrition is identified, when all parts are removed at the same time by division to the least; and for that reason attrition in spiritual matters signifies some dissatisfaction with sins committed, but not perfectly, but contrition perfectly [signifies dissatisfaction]" (*Summa Theol.*, III, supplement, q. 1, art. 2); cf. Council of Trent, sess. XIV, c. 4.

46. "Those words (*Illa*) 'I absolve you' manifest the effective remission of sins by the administration of this sacrament" (Roman Catechism, II, chap. 5, qu. 14; ed. note: The post–Vatican II edition titled *The Roman Catechism*, trans. Robert I. Bradley, SJ, and Eugene Kevane (Boston: Daughters of St. Paul, 1985) = Bradley and Kevane below, drops the enumeration of the introduction so that chapter 1 begins the section on baptism. In this annotation, the proper reference would be II, chap. 4, qu. 14.

47. J. H. Oswald, *Die dogmatische Lehre*, II, 102; cf. Council of Trent, XIV, c. 5: "If a sick person is ashamed to reveal his wound to the physician, the medicine does not heal it."

48. This council, held under Pope Innocent III in 1215, declared in canon 21: "All faithful persons of both sexes, after they have reached an age of discretion, ought faithfully to confess all of their own sins, at least once a year, to their own priest." Cf. Council of Trent, XIV, c. 5, can. 6; Roman Catechism, II, chap. 5, qu. 32ff. Ed. note: in Bradley and Kevane, II, chap. 4, qu. 32ff., the Greek church refers to penance four times a year; see the Orthodox Confession, 164.

formally absolute pardon. Thus in Roman Catholicism the sacrament of penance is a spiritual court and the action of the priest is a judicial act.[49]

[462] In practice, the consequences of this judicial-sacramental system are that laypersons are permanently—at least to their dying hour—kept dependent for their salvation on the priest. Two personal-practical results are then possible: *Either*, believers resign themselves to a superficial assessment of their sins and cherish a false sense of security by performing their penitential duties for absolution, *or*, they torment themselves in dread and uncertainty about their salvation. By contrast, the Reformation rejected the complicated Roman sacramental system and understood conversion to be a twofold action of dying to self and rising to Christ in a life of obedience.[50] Luther rediscovered the scriptural meaning of μετανοια as repentance and forgiveness of sins. All of this was a gift of grace, the application of Christ's finished work to the believer. True conversion is a religious-ethical matter that involves the whole person in a turn from sin and to God. It is helpful to note that in Scripture, conversion sometimes has a broader meaning, at other times a more restricted sense. Sometimes it includes regeneration, faith, and the total renewal of a person, and sometimes faith is clearly distinguished from it. Conversion sometimes occurs at the beginning of the new life, but also in the progression and restoration of the new life. Sometimes the internal change of mind and outlook is in the foreground (as in the word μετανοια); at other times, the accent lies on the external turnabout that is its outcome and manifestation (as in the word ἐπιστροφη). Early on, Reformed theology made a distinction between μεταμελεια (*metameleia*) and μετανοια (*metanoia*), between penitence and conversion, not only in degree but also in principle and essence. In that way, the concept of conversion was at least defined in one direction: it occurs not before and apart from but within the new life, proceeds from faith, and arises from regeneration (in the more restricted sense). In time, the conflict with the Anabaptists and Remonstrants raised questions about faith and conversion.

To address these concerns Reformed theologians made a distinction between the disposition (*habitus*) of faith and the act (*actus*) of faith, and similarly between the disposition to conversion and actual conversion. "For the grace of conversion is twofold: habitual and actual. The former is that by which a human is regenerated by the power of the Holy Spirit or is given the powers of faith and love. The latter is that by which the already-regenerate person, with the aid of God's Word and Spirit, exercises these powers in the activity of believing and loving."[51] The Reformed considered habitual conversion (*conversio habitualis*) as an infused (not

---

49. Of the wealth of literature on penance (penitence), see the book that probably dates from the eleventh century and is mistakenly credited to Augustine: *On True and False Penitence*. T. Aquinas, *Summa Theol.*, III, qu. 84–90; suppl., qu. 1–28; idem, *Summa contra gentiles*, IV, c. 70–72; Council of Trent, XIV; Roman Catechism, II, chap. 5. Ed. note: in Bradley and Kevane, II, chap. 4.

50. H. Bavinck, *Reformed Dogmatics*, III, 517–19 (#417).

51. Ed. note: Bavinck fails to annotate this lengthy Latin citation. It is from the Leiden *Synopsis purioris theologiae*, disp. 32, 2. The author is Antonius Walaeus.

an acquired) disposition, attributed solely to the regenerating grace of God; the Remonstrants reversed the order and regarded actual conversion as a synergistic product of cooperating grace and human free will. For this reason, conversion gradually acquired a definite place in the Reformed understanding of the *ordo salutis*. It is more than a law-driven repentance and also distinct from regeneration in the restricted sense. At the same time, as the "first actual conversion" (*conversio actualis prima*) it was also distinguished from the "continual conversion" (*conversio continua*) that goes on throughout the Christian life, as well as from the "second actual conversion" (*conversio actualis secunda*) that again is necessary in the case of believers after a period of aberrancy and a lapse from faith or following a slump in one's spiritual life.

MORTIFICATION AND VIVIFICATION

The Reformed also distinguished themselves from Lutheran understandings of conversion. In Lutheran theology, conversion is said to consist of three parts: contrition, faith, and good works; by contrition is meant the terrors of conscience induced by the law which faith, as the assurance of God's grace in Christ, quiets and produces peace of mind and rest of soul. The difficulty here is that an organic connection between the three seems lost; contrition does not always lead to faith and it is not clear how new obedience proceeds from faith.[52] Following Calvin, Reformed theology placed penitence (*poenitentia*) outside Christian experience and full conversion (*resipiscentia*) within it. Faith was not included in conversion but distinct, and both were seen as the fruit of regeneration. Consequently faith was especially related to justification and conversion to sanctification, and so conversion (*resipiscentia*) acquired, besides a religious sense, an eminently ethical meaning as well.[53] To define conversion, Calvin, following Romans 6, did not use the language of contrition and faith (with or without good works) but spoke of putting to death the old self (mortification) and bringing to life the new self (vivification); he was followed in this by countless Reformed theologians—among others, by Ursinus in his catechism and commentary (*Explications*). As terms became more refined, it was necessary to distinguish more clearly mortification and vivification as parts of regeneration and as aspects of conversion. In the former they are exclusively acts of God in which a human is passive; but if the putting to death and the bringing to life are aspects of actual conversion (*resipiscentia*), they are activities of the person who has been regenerated by the Spirit of God and endowed with the virtues of faith and love.[54]

In this understanding, conversion as the "first actual conversion" (as it is considered here [in order] after regeneration in a restricted sense, alongside and in

52. H. Bavinck, *Reformed Dogmatics*, III, 520–22 (#418).
53. Ibid., III, 522–28 (#419).
54. A. Polanus, *Syntagma theologiae christianae* (Hanover, 1609; Geneva, 1617), 469.

connection with faith, and [in order] before justification), is the activity of the regenerate person by which one learns to know, hate, and flee sin in its true nature, returns with a humble confession of sin to God as Father in Christ, and proceeds with a joyful heart to walk in his ways. Included are illumination of the intellect by which one learns to know sin in its true character, grief, sorrow, regret, and shame, humble confession, hatred of sin and a conscious and firm decision to flee it, a heartfelt joy in God through Christ, a sincere desire and love to live in keeping with the will of God, in all good works. True conversion, therefore, does not consist in an incidental act of moral self-improvement, in breaking with some gross sin and adapting oneself to virtue. It is a complete reversal in one's way of life, a fundamental break with sin. True conversion encompasses the whole person: faith and repentance both arise from regeneration; both are rooted in the heart. But whereas faith tends to work from there to the side of consciousness and appropriates the forgiving grace of God in Christ, conversion exercises its activity more in the sphere of the will and turns it away from evil and toward the good. However, just as the intellect and the will share a common root in the heart of a person so also it is with faith and conversion. They are consistently interconnected and reciprocally support and promote each other.

[463] Although true conversion is always the same in essence, yet, in the manner and the time when it occurs, there are all sorts of differences. When Christianity first makes its appearance in a place, making major changes from the religion and custom of one's past requires great sacrifice and commitment. Since there is usually no honor or advantage connected with this transition, there is little danger that people would have themselves baptized and incorporated in the church for their own secret reasons. Although from the beginning there was also chaff amid the wheat, conversion (ἐπιστροφη) was generally a clear sign and proof of an inner change of mind (μετανοια). However, when the church acquires status, privilege, and power, motives to convert may include other human considerations that are less honorable. Whether one considers the new coming to faith on a mission field or the coming to awareness in children of the church, it is a mistake to prescribe only one normative pattern. It is a mistake to force people into a single mode or to hurry the work of the Spirit in a person's life. The Bible only requires that sorrow for sin be genuine and that a person wholeheartedly seek God's favor. One does not need to know the exact hour of one's conversion; one must seek genuine amendment of life. As for the children of believers, we must be aware of the temptation to take faith for granted; for that reason the revivalist and pietist protests of the seventeenth through nineteenth centuries legitimately reacted against the indifference of the established churches. To turn this protest into a system, however, and demand from everyone a "penitential struggle" and "breakthrough," a period of dread and despair and a sudden subsequent surge of peace and joy, is to call into question God's covenant promise and weaken the meaning of baptism; it is to close one's eyes to the power of tradition, to the constant quiet work of the Christian family, to the mysterious inner working of God's Spirit in the heart. It

robs the school and education in general of their significance and, by focusing on a sudden crisis, an intense emotion or conscious turnaround, gives an unnatural character to Christian nurture, making children anxious, fearful, and nervously introspective. The children of believers are to be regarded and treated as heirs of the promise until the contrary is clearly demonstrated by their "talk" and "walk."

Aware that during puberty children go through a crisis that is of greatest importance for their physical, mental, and spiritual development as they pass from dependence to independence and freedom,[55] we should not consider the "conversion" of the children of believers as unnecessary, redundant, or useless. When children who were born and baptized into the covenant of grace enter the years of discretion, they have to answer for their baptism and the new obedience to which it obliges and admonishes them. That this happens during years of a general crisis in their development should lead us to greater appreciation of rituals and ceremonies that celebrate "coming of age." Even pagans recognize the significance by subjecting boys and girls to tests that induct them by means of solemn ceremonies into the next phase of life.[56] Christian churches have generally fixed the first communion or confirmation, public confession, admission to the Lord's Supper, or the reception into full membership in this period. It is a mistake to attempt this with artificial efforts to provoke such a crisis with religious activities at too young an age. We need to follow and stimulate with great sensitivity the religious development of children, to reckon with the nature of childhood and not demand from it what can only develop in later years—to leave much to the hidden and quiet guidance of the Holy Spirit. The kingdom of heaven does not come with outward show but is like a seed that sprouts and grows (Mark 4:27). Adolescence is the time when this usually happens; to that extent one can say that "conversion is a distinctively adolescent phenomenon."[57] Respecting diversity in conversion comes from respecting the varied hidden and amazing leadings of the Holy Spirit. We may not infer the authenticity or inauthenticity of conversion from a variety of intense feelings and odd incidents or from their absence. Much of this depends on upbringing and environment, nature and disposition, life and work. Sin is so multiform that everyone has a pet sin from which he or she needs deliverance; the gospel is so full of riches that one moment it can enlighten and comfort a seeker of salvation with one truth and the next moment with another. All we can say is that the substance of true conversion always consists both in hating and fleeing from sin, and in a sincere love for God and his service.

[464] Of these two aspects of conversion, sometimes the one or the other gets emphasized. There are Christians who reject the universal offer of grace and want nothing to do with preaching the gospel to the unconverted. They confront them with nothing but the demands and penalties of the law and depict the hellish,

---

55. H. Bavinck, *Reformed Dogmatics*, III, 556–64 (#427a).

56. G. S. Hall, *Adolescence*, 2 vols. (New York: D. Appleton, 1904), II, 232–80.

57. Edwin Diler Starbuck, *The Psychology of Religion: An Empirical Study of the Growth of Religious Consciousness* (London: W. Scott; New York: Scribner, 1901), 28.

eternal damnation awaiting them in their unconverted state. When Protestant churches fell into decline, Pietism and Methodism seized on the proclamation of judgment to wake up the sleeping souls and to make them cry out for salvation and mercy. Sadly, from this some concluded that misery *had* to precede the state of grace, resulting in many Christians who habitually complain about their sins but almost never experience heartfelt joy in God through Christ nor ever arrive at a life of gratitude. In other instances, the desire to replace the chronic illness of indifference with an acute crisis led to intensity of emotions and gave rise to convulsions and hysteria, loud screams and cries, wailing exclamations and unintelligible sounds, a flood of tears alternating with dancing and a leaping with joy. While this greatly pleased some—Wesley and Whitefield, for example—Jonathan Edwards carefully distinguished affects that proceeded from spiritual workings on the heart and those that arose as a result of impressions made on the imagination.[58] Similar phenomena in other revivals also elicited a variety of verdicts. Frequently, the "one-sidednesses" that often marked revivals elicited strong reactions and repulsions which lead to church splits or alternative theological ideals such as strands of liberal theology.[59]

American revivalism underwent an important change from the time of Jonathan Edwards to that of Charles Finney (1792–1875). When Edwards preached to the unconverted he spoke of God's wrath and the torments of hell; conversion moved the sinner from dread and fear to comfort and peace. Finney proceeded from the assumption that human beings are sinners voluntarily and urged them to make a decision to give their heart to God now, in this very moment. In this he was followed by Moody and other evangelistic preachers, though, whereas Finney tended to be the preacher of duty, as Edwards was of fear, Moody highlighted the love and gift of God in Christ. Taking the reaction against remorse and grief for sin to the full opposite extreme, Christian Science in a pantheistic manner considers sin as it does sickness and death; they are errors of the mind that can be completely overcome by "mind cure": "thoughts are things, thoughts are forces, and therefore as a man thinks, so is he."[60]

These and similar reactions against a plaintive Christianity are understandable, and to a degree warranted, but they are also marked by gross exaggeration. Since all of us have consciences that regularly accuse and judge us, we also have some sense that contrition and confession are the first step on the road to conversion.[61]

---

58. In his *Treatise concerning Religious Affections* (1746), in *The Works of Jonathan Edwards*, vol. 2, *Religious Affections*, ed. J. E. Smith (New Haven: Yale University Press, 1959); cf. J. Ridderbos, *De Theologie van Jonathan Edwards* ('s Gravenhage: J. A. Nederbragt, 1907), 246ff.

59. In 1741, when Gilbert Tennent preached a sermon before the synod at Philadelphia on "The Danger of an Unconverted Ministry," it resulted in a divison of the Presbyterian church into "new lights" or "new side" and "old side."

60. Cf. H. Bavinck, *Reformed Dogmatics*, III, 569n212 (#427b); W. James, *The Varieties of Religious Experience* (New York: Modern Library, 1902), 96ff.; Samuel McComb, "The Christian Religion as a Healing Power," *Hibbert Journal* 8 (October 1909): 10–27.

61. Cf. H. Bavinck, *Reformed Dogmatics*, III, 129–36 (#329).

A Christian knows from experience that sin evokes a correspondingly stronger feeling of grief and regret. True inward confession of sin is heard not from the lips of the ungodly but from those of the devout (Pss. 6; 25; 32; 51; 130; 143; Ezra 9:6; Neh. 9:33; Isa. 53:4ff.; 59:12; Jer. 3:25; 14:20; Lam. 3:39; Dan. 9:5ff.; Matt. 26:75; Rom. 7:14ff.; 1 John 1:8–9). Sorrow for sin is an integral part of conversion and constitutes the other side of the renewal of life (Luke 15:18; 18:13; Acts 2:37; 9:6ff.; 16:30; 2 Cor. 7:10). Great care must be taken not to specify exactly how or how long or what form such grief must take; in some pious circles too much is often made of the importance of knowing the exact time of one's conversion, that one must spend a period of time in great dread and fear, and be saved from it in a special or miraculous manner.

Scripture only requires that there be uprightness and truth in the hearts of people; that grief over sin must be genuine. Conversion is a matter of the heart (Jer. 3:10; Luke 1:17; Acts 16:14; Rom. 2:29; 10:10). There have been times when deep spiritual practices occupied a greater place in the Christian life of discipleship than they do today. Even then, the wise among them urged moderation.[62] Genuine and heartfelt grief over sin is neither unprofitable nor a waste of time, but is the way God works with us to free us inwardly from sin. In recent years the psychology of religion has proposed that repentance is proof that a person is still capable of righteousness. For in repentance a person condemns himself, dissociates himself from sin, sides with righteousness, and paves for himself the way to forgiveness.[63] This is true, but repentance must not be confused with mere regret; true repentance is not possible for the "natural man" but requires the regenerating power of the Holy Spirit. True conversion, true grief over sin, and genuine restoration to God and his service, therefore, are brought about not just by the law but even to a much higher degree by the gospel. The knowledge of sin is most assuredly derived from the law inasmuch as all sin has its standard in the law and is therefore lawlessness (ἀνομια, *anomia*); but the fact that humans learn to see and acknowledge sin in its true nature is because of the gospel and is to be viewed as the fruit of faith. Law and gospel, accordingly, work together in human conversion. The law points pedagogically to Christ, but the gospel also sheds its light on the law.[64]

CONFESSION OF SIN, PENANCE, AND PUNISHMENT

[465] Since, then, conversion is a matter of the heart, the Reformers rejected the Roman idea of "attrition" as being insufficient; penitence involving all sorts of

62. G. Voetius, *Exercitia pietatis* (Gorinchem: Paul Vink, 1664), 228; Roman Catechism, II, chap. 5, qu. 23, 27 (ed. note: in Bradley and Kevane, II, chap. 4, qu. 23, 27).

63. R. C. Moberly, *Atonement and Personality* (London: John Murray, 1901), 19ff.; cf. H. Bavinck, *Reformed Dogmatics*, III, 295–98 (#368), 370–73 (#384), 380–85 (#387), 399–402 (#390).

64. Cf. H. Bavinck, *Reformed Dogmatics*, III, 520–28 (##418–19).

terror and dread may precede conversion but differs from true repentance (*resipiscentia*), is not even a part of it, and does not infallibly lead to it. Rome's careful distinction between "contrition" and "attrition" led to interminable debates and failed to settle practical issues. When contrition is specified so carefully to become valid only in cases of vigorous, keen, and ardent penitence, only a small number obtain it. Then, "attrition" as "imperfect contrition" that arises only out of fear of hell's punishments can still be regarded, under certain circumstances, as "a gift of God and an impulse of the Holy Spirit." According to Trent, although this attrition cannot by itself effect justification, it "disposes the sinner to obtain the grace of God in the sacrament of penance."[65] Despite this Tridentine pronouncement many Roman Catholic theologians continue to plead for the necessity of uniting with attrition at least an act of charity. But the attritionism that considered fear of hellish, or even of temporal, punishments prior to the reception of absolution in the sacrament to be sufficient gained the upper hand. The decree of Pope Alexander VII prohibited the sharply contending parties from condemning each other as heretics but left the issue unresolved. While theologians argue, the faithful suffer under the uncertainty of fear. When is fear sufficient for receiving the sacrament and the absolution granted in it? When both confessors and penitents remain in doubt about these matters, imagine what happens in popular practice with attrition! Casuistic inquiry into how little can suffice for someone to obtain absolution is diametrically opposed to the spirit of the gospel.

Likewise, according to the Fourth Lateran Council (1215), believers must confess all their sins in secret at least once a year before their own priests as soon as they have reached the years of discretion (as a rule, their seventh year).[66] Technically, confession is necessary only after the commission of a mortal sin and the loss of God's sanctifying grace. Yet, it would be imprudent for a Roman Catholic believer not to make use of the sacrament of penance; the boundary line between mortal and venial sins is difficult to determine and, with only a few exceptions, all believers do commit mortal sins after baptism and repeatedly fall from the state of grace. So confession is practically necessary for all believers, not just once a year but preferably as often as possible.[67] This confession must be both comprehensive and absolute.[68] Catholic theologians themselves recognize that private confession before a priest does not directly and literally occur in Scripture.[69] In the Old and New Testaments there is repeated mention of the confession of sin (Lev. 5:5; 16:21;

---

65. The Council of Trent, sess. XIV, c. 4.

66. Reiterated at the Council of Florence, 1439; Council of Trent, sess. XIV, cap. 5; Roman Catechism, II, chap. 5, qu. 38 (ed. note: in Bradley and Kevane, II, chap. 4, qu. 38).

67. Roman Catechism, II, chap. 5, qu. 39, 46 (ed. note: in Bradley and Kevane, II, chap. 4, qu. 39, 46).

68. Council of Trent, sess. XIV, c. 5; Roman Catechism, II, chap. 5, qu. 40–41 (ed. note: in Bradley and Kevane, II, chap. 4, qu. 40–41).

69. According to J. Pohle, *Lehrbuch der Dogmatik*, III, 484: "There are hardly any direct and explicit references to the sacrament of penance in the New Testament. Even though that is the case, this fact does not provide strong proof." For similar statements from Duns Scotus and others, see C. Pesch, *Praelectiones dogmaticae*, 9 vols. (Freiburg: Herder, 1902–10), VII, 155ff., 161ff.

Num. 5:7; Josh. 7:19; Ezra 10:1, 11; Neh. 1:6; 9:2–3; Ps. 32:5; Dan. 6:11; 9:4, 20; Matt. 3:6; Acts 19:18; James 5:16; 1 John 1:9). However, following the Council of Trent, theologians infer its warrant from reasoning based on the promise of Christ to Peter in Matthew 16:19 and to all the apostles in Matthew 18:18, giving them the power of the keys, and from the fulfillment of that promise in John 20:22–23. With these words, then, Christ appointed the apostles—and further the bishops and priests—to be rulers and judges "to whom all the mortal sins into which the faithful of Christ may have fallen should be brought in order that, by virtue of the power of the keys, they may pronounce the sentence of remission and retention of sins."[70] In Rome, accordingly, confession is a consequence of the judicial character of the church's remission of sins, just as this judicial character of the church's remission of sins is "to a certain extent the pivotal point of the entire Catholic view of the sacrament of penance."[71]

Considering the confession's occasional practical utility, one can understand that in some countries the Lutheran Church still for a time wanted to retain it,[72] and that some Protestants either want to restore it or at least want something to take its place.[73] But those who understand the link between confession and the falsification of the gospel, the grace of forgiveness, and the office and power of the church never want it back. When the Roman Catholic Church authorizes its bishops and priests to be judges of the deepest motives of the human heart, placing a person's trust for all eternity into the judgment of other humans, it is arrogating to itself a right and power that in the nature of the case can only belong to God as the infallible knower of human hearts. Who can forgive sins but God alone? (Isa. 43:25; Mark 2:7).[74]

[466] To this it must be added that the priest—since perfect contrition is usually lacking and only a kind of attrition is present—as a rule may only give absolution along with the imposition of a number of good works to be performed. It is true that Scripture includes examples of believers, who, despite the forgiveness they received, were still subject to various kinds of punishment:[75] Adam and Eve (Gen. 3:16ff.), Miriam (Num. 12:14), Moses and Aaron (Num. 20:12; 27:13–14; Deut. 34:4), David (2 Sam. 12:13–14), and the believers in Corinth (1 Cor. 11:30). The forgiveness of sins is a benefit of grace of which nature is ignorant, and the righ-

---

70. Council of Trent, sess. XIV, chap. 5.

71. J. Wilhelm and T. B. Scannell, *A Manual of Catholic Theology*, 4th ed., 2 vols. (London: Kegan Paul, Trench, Trübner; New York: Benziger Brothers, 1909), IV, 3, 681. J. Pohle, *Lehrbuch der Dogmatik*, III, 416.

72. Augsburg Confession, arts. 11–12, in *The Book of Concord*, ed. Robert Kolb and Timothy J. Wengert (Minneapolis: Fortress, 2000), 45; Apology of the Augsburg Confession, art. 11 (Kolb and Wengert), 185ff.; Smalcald Articles, part III, art. 8 (Kolb and Wengert), 321–23; "The Sacrament of Holy Baptism," art. 4 of The Small Catechism (Kolb and Wengert), 360–62; "A Brief Exhortation to Confession" (Kolb and Wengert), 476–80.

73. W. Caspari, "Beichte," in *PRE*[3], II, 540ff.

74. J. Calvin, *Institutes*, III.iv.4–24.

75. Council of Trent, sess. XIV, c. 12–15; cf. VI, can. 30.

teous must enter the kingdom of God through many tribulations (Acts 14:22). *But* Scripture teaches that all the suffering that comes to believers on account of their own sins or those of others has lost for them the character of punishment and is only a useful chastisement in order that they may share in God's holiness (Job 5:17; Prov. 3:11; 1 Cor. 11:32; Heb. 12:5–11; Rev. 3:19).[76] Rome's problem is that even the most saintly people in the Roman Catholic Church have not been able to deliver themselves from the suffering of this present age or from death. The "satisfactions of work" (*satisfactiones operis*), accordingly, have little or no significance for this life; their entire value, both theoretically and practically, consists in the diminution or mitigation of these punishments in purgatory. Furthermore, there are many sins that God does not punish in this life at all. Here it is necessary for Rome to develop an additional casuistry concerning the works necessary to remove the punishments of purgatory. There are three kinds of goods that humans can offer to God in compensation for the sins they have committed: goods of the spirit (*boni anima*), which they offer in prayer; goods of the body (*boni corporis*), which they surrender in fasting; goods of fortune (*boni fortunae*), which they offer up in the giving of alms.[77] Since they are performed by believers and in their case flow from a supernatural principle, they have a "satisfactory" value, or a meritorious value "of condignity." They secure heavenly blessedness for believers such as delivering them from temporal punishments in purgatory.

Rome knows how to accommodate itself to circumstances and has done so also by weakening contrition and then greatly reducing the severity of the penitential "satisfactions" that the priest imposes on the sinner, and then assuring believers that "the payment of the punishment of sin is assured in purgatory." At the same time, it robs people of assurance when it teaches that the grace granted in the sacrament of penance can be lost at any moment by a mortal sin, that penitential good works and indulgences only deliver from temporal punishment when they meet the demands of God's righteousness and are performed with absolute precision. Inasmuch as the priest is not a "supreme master" but a "lower judge," he is never certain whether the punishment imposed is not perhaps less than God's justice requires, and therefore "only God knows how great a punishment is remitted by a given satisfaction."[78]

This entire penitential system was therefore rejected by the Reformation as absolutely incompatible with the spirit of the gospel. For the church's entire power of the keys consists in administering the Word of God. It is not a "power

76. J. Calvin, *Institutes*, III.iv.31ff.

77. Council of Trent, sess. VI, c. 14 puts it this way: Penance for Christians after falling must include "satisfaction by fasting, almsgiving, prayers, and other devout exercises of the spiritual life, not indeed for the eternal punishment . . . but for temporal punishment" (H. Denzinger, ed., *The Sources of Catholic Dogma*, trans. from 30th ed. by R. J. Deferrari [London and St. Louis: Herder, 1955], #806); cf. T. Aquinas, *Summa Theol.*, qu. 15, art. 3.

78. On the uncertainty brought about by the Roman Catholic doctrine of penance, see J. Calvin, *Institutes*, III.iv.17, 22.

separate from the gospel,"[79] but coincides with it. When we look at the people who proclaim that gospel, such proclamation is not a power but a ministry, for Christ did not actually give that power to people but to his Word, "of which he made humans ministers."[80] Luther in his Ninety-five Theses emphasized that Christ wants the whole life of a Christian to be penitential and the fight against sin lifelong. In Calvin's words: "And indeed, this restoration is not accomplished in a moment or in a day or a year; but through continual and sometimes even slow advances, God wipes out in his elect the corruptions of the flesh, consecrates them to himself as temples, renewing all their minds to true purity that they may practice repentance throughout their lives and know that this warfare will end only at death."[81]

In the Reformation, therefore, and particularly in Calvin, conversion acquired profound ethical significance. Because Christ completed everything and atoned for all sins (Rom. 3:25; Heb. 10:14; 1 Pet. 2:24; 1 John 1:7; 2:1), God does not count our trespasses against us (2 Cor. 5:19). Good works, accordingly, are not the cause but the fruit of the forgiveness of sins, and repentance is not "a second plank after shipwreck" but a return to one's baptism: an independent, personal, and lifelong appropriation of the treasures of grace that are present in Christ, the progressive dying away of the old self and the coming to life of the new. Only in that way does Christ preserve his honor, but also in only that way can the human conscience obtain peace and rest.[82] If assurance must be earned by our works, we will be continually in fear and dread over whether in all these matters we have done what we ought, and do not even arrive at doing good works out of childlike love and obedience. But if by faith in the forgiveness of our sins we have been given assurance beforehand, we are also heartily willing to walk as children according to all God's commandments. The first and continuing conversion, therefore, consists in walking in God's commandments and doing everywhere and always what is pleasing to him.

Similarly, the coming to life of the new self, the second part of true repentance, is not limited to "the happiness that the mind receives after its disturbance and fear have been quieted," but rather means "the desire to live in a holy and devoted manner, a desire arising from rebirth; as if it were said that humans die to themselves that they may begin to live to God."[83] If believers sometimes through weakness fall into sins, they must not for that reason despair of God's mercy, nor continue in sin, since baptism is a seal and indubitable testimony that they have an eternal covenant with God.[84] This repentance of the fallen and

79. Ibid., III.iv.14.
80. Ibid., IV.xi.1.
81. Ibid., III.iii.9.
82. Ibid., III.iv.27; cf. III.iv.2.
83. Ibid., III.iii.3.
84. Bavinck here cites lines from the classic liturgy for infant baptism used in Reformed churches for centuries. See *Psalter Hymnal* (Grand Rapids: CRC Publications, 1987), p. 957.

turning around of life does not, like the first conversion, relate to the entire state of sin, but is especially focused on the specific grave sin into which the believer has fallen and from which, in the power of God, the believer now turns away. As a particular conversion, therefore, it is distinct from the former, which is an all-encompassing conversion.

20

JUSTIFICATION, SANCTIFICATION, AND PERSEVERANCE

FORGIVENESS

[467] Rebirth, faith, and conversion are the conditions for human beings receiving and enjoying the benefits of the covenant of grace. Of all God's benefits given in the covenant of grace, first place belongs to justification, to forgiveness of sins. All joy and peace, all certainty of communion with God, rest on this forgiveness, a benefit no mind can fully comprehend or believe. Paganism could never grasp this; picturing the gods as human with passions meant that when insulted, the gods needed to be appeased by human gifts and prayers. This at least takes sin more seriously than the shallow idea that forgiving is natural for God, just as sinning is normal for humans.[1] Opposition to the expiatory sacrifice of Christ,[2] accordingly, arises from a total denial of the value of justice as well as of the idea of forgiveness. Forgiveness in the true sense of the word is not easy and often conflicts with our sense of justice, but it precisely presupposes justice and stands or falls with it. Christianity distinguishes itself by tying justice and love together at the cross. In traditional Eastern religions and Western thought, the ironclad law

---

1. According to Wernle, "If sin is fitting to humanity, then forgiveness is appropriate to God." Cited by W. Walther, *Rechtfertigung oder religiöses Erlebnis*, 2nd ed. (Leipzig: A. Deichert, 1917), 33.
2. A. von Harnack, *What Is Christianity?* trans. Thomas Bailey Saunders, 2nd rev. ed. (New York and Evanston, IL: Harper & Row, 1957), 142ff.

of causal necessity (karma) reigns. There is no forgiveness, only retribution;[3] the idea of eternal punishment is completely natural. Nature knows no forgiveness.

We find a different circle of ideas in Scripture because the covenant of God is based on the gracious disposition of God and, by implication, on a historical act. The sin offerings, which presuppose the covenant of grace, opened a way of atoning for sins occurring "unwittingly" (Lev. 4:2ff.); these, in turn, are distinguished from all sins that were committed "with a high hand" and not covered by the sin offerings (Num. 15:30 RSV). Because Israel did not adhere to the rule of the covenant and repeatedly committed such sins as idolatry, image worship, Sabbath desecration, and so forth—sins that broke the covenant itself and that by implication could not be atoned for by covenant sacrifices—the prophets, speaking in the name of the Lord, announced to an apostate people the coming day of judgment and the punishment of the exile. Israel is punished precisely *because* she is the people of God (Amos 3:2). Because God is just, he will be exalted in justice and show himself holy in righteousness (Isa. 5:16); because of his covenantal love he cannot forget Israel (Hosea 11:8); because he has bound his own name and honor to them in pledge he cannot abandon them but will save a part of his people, the remnant that repents (Isa. 4:3; 6:13; 7:3ff.; etc.). With them he will make a new covenant, forgive them all their sins, give them a new heart and spirit, and cause them to walk in his statutes (Jer. 24:7; 31:31ff.; 32:37ff.; Ezek. 11:19ff.; 36:24ff.). For them he will prepare salvation, through the Messiah who will also bring forth justice to the gentiles (Isa. 42:1). From him, accordingly, is their righteousness (54:17); only in him are righteousness and strength (45:24). He is the Lord, their righteousness (Jer. 23:6; 33:16).[4]

The Old Testament uses many varied metaphors and images to depict God as gracious. Some examples are נָשָׂא (*nāśā'*, suspend, accept, pardon; 1 Sam. 15:25; Job 7:21; Pss. 32:1; 85:2; Isa. 33:24), סָלַח (*sālaḥ*, forgive; Exod. 34:9; Lev. 4:20; Pss. 25:11; 103:3), עָבַר (*'ābar*, pass over, through; hiph.: let pass by, put away; 2 Sam. 12:13; 24:10; Job 7:21), כִּפֶּר (*kipper*; pi.: cover, make atonement [Lev. 16:17; etc.], and, hence, forgive; Pss. 65:3; 78:38; 79:9; Isa. 6:7; Jer. 18:23; Dan. 9:24), מָחָה (*māḥâ*, wipe, wipe out, eradicate; Ps. 51:1; Isa. 43:25; 44:22; Jer. 18:23), and כָּבַס (*kābas*, wash, make clean; Ps. 51:2), סוּר (*sûr*, depart, cease; Isa. 6:7), and many others and further expressions such as "not seeing" (Num. 23:21), "not imputing" (Ps. 32:2), "not entering into judgment" (Ps. 143:2), "not remembering" (Isa. 43:25), "hiding one's face" (Ps. 51:9), "casting behind one's back" (Isa. 38:17), and "casting into the depths of the sea" (Mic. 7:19). In these connections, God's divine nature shines out in forgiving the iniquity of his people (Mic. 7:18), for he forgives only for his name's sake and his fame and honor among the gentiles (Pss. 25:11; 79:9; Isa. 43:25; Ezek. 36:11, 23; Exod. 32:12; Num. 14:13, 16;

---

3. J. S. Speyer, *De Indische theosophie en hare beteekenis voor ons* (Leiden: Van Doesburgh, 1910), 83ff.

4. Cf. H. Bavinck, *Reformed Dogmatics*, ed. John Bolt (Grand Rapids: Baker Academic, 2003–8), II, 223–24 (#206); III, 491–95 (#410).

Deut. 9:28; 32:27). He acts out of sheer compassion (Ps. 78:38), for the sake of his covenant with Abraham and David, for the sake of the oath he swore to them (Pss. 89:3ff.; 105:8–9; 111:5; Jer. 11:5; Ezek. 16:60; Mic. 7:20). It must never be forgotten that it is always God and he alone who grants forgiveness (Isa. 43:25; 45:21–25; 48:9–12); it cannot be earned.

[468] After the exile, instead of expecting their righteousness and salvation from God, the Jews increasingly sought to construct a righteousness of their own out of works (nomism).[5] Both John the Baptist (Matt. 3:2–10) and Jesus brought the message that circumcision was not enough, that a baptism of repentance for the forgiveness of sins and accepting God's righteousness as a gift (Matt. 6:33) was needed. Furthermore, God grants this benefit to publicans and sinners, to the lost, to the heavy laden, to children who fully expect all their well-being from God. It is as the Messiah of the kingdom that Jesus distributes the benefit of forgiveness (Matt. 9:2ff.; Luke 7:48ff.), gives his life as a ransom for many (Matt. 20:28), creates the new covenant in his blood, allows his body to be broken and his blood to be shed for the forgiveness of sins (26:26ff.), and promises eternal life to all who become his disciples (10:37ff.; 16:24ff.). In all the diversity of the apostolic preaching, forgiveness of sins as the great benefit that Christ has won and that is received by faith is the constant (John 3:36; Heb. 8:12; 10:17, 22; James 2:1; 1 Pet. 1:2, 19; 2:24; 3:18; 1 John 1:9; 2:1–2, 12; 3:5). While the Old Testament, particularly the Psalms, portrays God's nature as merciful, the New Testament proclaims the One who came to seek and save the lost, to lift the burdens of the heavy hearted. Proclaimed throughout the New Testament in various ways, forgiveness is underscored in its forensic dimension as justification, especially by the apostle Paul. Reflecting on his life experience as a Pharisee under the law, Paul accents the righteousness (or justice; Gk.: δικαιοσυνη, *dikaiosynē*) of Christ imputed to believers by faith alone. This justification produces liberty, frees believers for service, and assures them of eternal life (Rom. 1:17; 3:5, 21–22, 25–26; 10:3; 2 Cor. 5:21; cf. Phil. 3:9; James 1:20; 2 Pet. 1:1).

Paul combats nomism and rules out all human boasting by insisting that no flesh can be justified by the works of the law (Rom. 3:20; 4:2, 5; 8:3; Gal. 2:16; 3:24–26; 4:1–7; cf. 1 Cor. 1:29; 4:7); however, even as a Christian, Paul remains faithful to the forensic scheme and agrees that salvation can be obtained only through righteousness (or justice; Gk.: δικαιοσυνη). The law as such is holy, just, and good (Rom. 7:12, 14; 1 Tim. 1:8; cf. also Rom. 3:31; 8:4; 13:8, 10; Gal. 5:14). God was pleased to manifest (and maintain!) his *righteousness* in another way, that is, apart from the law (Rom. 3:21). Paul's theocentric position retains the forensic, juridical dimension that is exaggerated in nomism. The law and the expectation of obedience are not set aside. The issue is not whether there will or will not be righteousness or justice with respect to the law of God, but whether we earn that righteousness or receive it as a gift of grace; is it law or gospel, work

5. Ibid., III, 495–99 (#411).

or faith, merit or grace? Everything rests on how we answer this. If communion with God, life, and salvation are to remain gifts of God, they must precede all our works and be their basis and starting point. In that case religion is the basis of morality. We love God because he first loved us (1 John 4:19), and in his love offered Christ for us as a sacrifice of atonement for sin. God preserved his justice and also justified those who have faith in Jesus (Rom. 3:25–26). This righteousness is not external to a believer nor infused into us but conferred on us through God's just act of acquittal. It was necessary for God to put Christ forward as a sacrifice of atonement and to bring about in him a righteousness (1 Cor. 1:30; 2 Cor. 5:21; Phil. 3:9) that is the diametrical opposite of a righteousness we accomplish by our own law-keeping (Rom. 10:3; Phil. 3:9). God justifies us on the basis of Christ's righteousness, which is ours through faith (Rom. 1:17; 3:22; 25, 28, 30; 10:6; Gal. 2:16; 3:8, 24, 26; Eph. 2:8; Phil. 3:9; 2 Tim. 3:15). This faith is reckoned to us as righteousness (Rom. 4:3, 5, 9, 11, 22; Gal. 3:6) and consists in heartfelt trust in God's grace in Christ, a personal relationship and communion with Christ (Rom. 10:9; 1 Cor. 6:17; 2 Cor. 13:5; Gal. 2:20; Eph. 3:17). Justification frees believers from all dread and fear; and grants the assurance that they are adopted children and heirs (Rom. 8:15–17, 23; Gal. 4:5–7), the hope of righteousness (Gal. 5:5). After all, if God justifies, who is to condemn?

[469] Already in Paul's own day, this doctrine was misunderstood as being antinomian (Rom. 3:8, 31; 6:1, 15; etc.). Some clearly needed James's warning that a dead, inactive faith is insufficient for justification (James 2:14ff.). Others, acting out of reaction, began to cultivate a nomistic and ascetic lifestyle (Rom. 14:1ff.; Gal. 4:10; Col. 2:16; 1 Tim. 4:3–4). Living with this tension, the church often oscillated between extremes and increasingly moved toward seeing the Christian life in terms of obeying God's commandments with penance, and good works becoming the way of dealing with sins committed after baptism. Although absolved from the guilt of sin and eternal punishment, believers remained obligated to bear temporal punishments and to perform the good works imposed on them (the work of satisfaction). Grace here is understood as a divine infusion into the believer via the sacraments.

In the development of Roman Catholic doctrine, the benefits of forgiveness and removal of sin's pollution (justification and sanctification) are intimately connected but not identical. The Council of Trent stated that justification is "not only the remission of sins but also the sanctification and renewal of the inward man through the voluntary reception of grace and the gifts."[6] Nonetheless, the distinction was better in the abstract than in concrete practice. Justification, in the thinking of Rome, is therefore that act of God by which he forgives the guilt of sin and absolves persons from eternal punishment *and* internally regenerates

---

6. Council of Trent, sess. VI, c. 7. According to M. J. Scheeben and L. Atzberger, *Handbuch der Katholischen Dogmatik*, 4 vols. (orig. pub. 1874–98; Freiburg i.B.: Herder, 1933), IV, 60, there is a real difference between the two.

and renews them; the latter results in the former. Habitual grace is the formal cause both of the remission of sins and of sanctification. God forgives people their sins because, logically speaking, he first makes them holy.[7] Rome fails clearly to distinguish between justification and sanctification. In fairness, Rome does attribute this whole splendid benefit solely to the mercy of God, who purifies, sanctifies, and anoints people with the Holy Spirit of promise solely on the basis of Christ's meritorious work. Rome also assigns an important place to faith—"the beginning of human salvation, the foundation of our justification"—yet, because faith is understood as only an assent to the truths of revelation and we cannot be united to Christ without hope and love,[8] believers cannot *by faith alone* have the assurance that they belong to Christ.[9] Rome does not deny that the righteousness of Christ is imputed to believers but maintains that justification also includes the ethical infusion of Christ's righteousness.[10]

The Reformation was triggered by Luther's opposition to the entire Roman penitential system, particularly the trade in indulgences. Luther developed this opposition over a longer period as he wrestled with the meaning of "righteousness of God." Luther's great discovery was that this did not mean "the righteousness by which God is righteous in himself but the righteousness by which we are justified from within himself, which happens through faith in the gospel."[11] The seeds of Luther's mature convictions are already present in his lectures on the Letter to the Romans in 1515 and 1516.[12] The original material is especially oriented to the contrast between sin and grace, law and gospel, works and faith, one's own righteousness and God's. "To justify," in Scripture, means "to regard as just, to treat a person as accepted, not to impute sin, to remit impiety, to grant righ-

---

7. This underevaluation of the benefit of sanctification is closely tied to the weakening of a sense of sin as guilt. Cf. H. Bavinck, *Reformed Dogmatics*, III, 93–97 (#321).

8. Council of Trent, sess. VI, c. 7–8.

9. Ibid., c. 9, can. 13–16. Ed. note: Evidence for the inherent tension between the Roman Catholic and Protestant views on this very point can be found in John Calvin's published debate with Cardinal Jacopo Sadoleto: *A Reformation Debate: Sadoleto's Letter to the Genevans and Calvin's Reply*, ed. John Olin (New York: Harper & Row, 1966; repr., Grand Rapids: Baker, 1976).

10. C. Pesch, *Praelectiones dogmaticae*, 9 vols. (Freiburg i.B.: Herder, 1902–10), V, 186.

11. This new understanding comes to expression in a marginal note on the *Sentences* of Peter Lombard, dating from 1509/1510; cf. H. Bavinck, *Reformed Dogmatics*, III, 517–19 (#417).

12. Johannes Ficker, ed., *Luthers Vorlesung über den Römerbrief 1515/1516*, 2 vols. (Leipzig: Dieterich, 1908). Ed. note: The preceding edition of Luther's lectures on Romans that Bavinck cites was a preliminary one; the definitive edition was published as vol. 56, *Die Brief an die Römer*, in the Weimar edition of *D. Martin Luthers Werke* (Weimar: Böhlau, 1938). The initial two volumes containing Luther's "Glosses" on the text (vol. 1) and his "Scholia" (vol. 2) were joined in the one Weimar volume. One year later (1939), Ficker also published extant student notebook manuscripts; these appeared as vol. 57 of the Weimar edition. English translation of the Romans commentary (glosses and scholia only) and information concerning the manuscript history can be found in vol. 25 of *Luther's Works*, ed. H. C. Oswald (St. Louis: Concordia, 1972). Although the translations of the Luther passages are our own, we will provide the corresponding reference in *Luther's Works* (English ed.). This will be followed by parenthetical references to *Luthers Werke* in the Weimarer Ausgabe edition (e.g., WA 56:35) as well as Bavinck's original reference to Ficker's preliminary two-volume text (e.g., Ficker, I, 32).

teousness through reconsideration without works, to impute righteousness." Furthermore, believers are to take God at his word, recognizing that healing is a lifelong process and that we are justified for good works. "We are not made just by doing right things but by being just do we do right things. Therefore only grace justifies us."[13] "For the fact that a person is just is not the reason why God regards him as just, but he is just because he is so regarded by God"; "first the person, then the works."[14] The Christian life is a life of faith; trusting in God's promises, we may neither despair nor be falsely secure.

Faith includes (1) believing that we are sinners and (2) believing that out of grace God justifies us for Christ's sake. We have to accept that we are sinners but because God says so.

> Even if we do not recognize any sin in ourselves, we must nevertheless believe that we are sinners. . . . For just as the righteousness of God is alive in me by faith, so by the same faith sin is alive in me; i.e., by faith alone we must believe that we are sinners, because it is not obvious to us. . . . Therefore we must stand by God's judgment and believe the words by which he tells us that we are unjust, because he cannot tell a falsehood.[15]

Luther distinguishes passive justification—taking God at his word that his judgment of us is true—from active justification where we in faith believe that he justifies us.[16] But because "God regards as righteousness the faith that justifies his words," passive and active justification coincide. "When he is justified he justifies, and when he justifies he is justified." Indeed: "God's passive and active justification and faith or belief in him are the same. The fact that we justify his speech is his own gift, and on account of that very gift he regards us as just, that is, justifies us."[17]

By intimately connecting faith and justification, Luther avoids reducing justification to a mere sentence that God pronounces to himself and that has no further consequences. Thus, God "is effectively justified in us and praiseworthy inasmuch as he makes us like himself."[18] We are regarded as righteous and made righteous. By Christ's death he made satisfaction for sin and by his resurrection he brought about righteousness for us. Luther did not, however, locate the righteousness that is the basis for justification in believers. Instead, believers throughout their lives confess to God, "We have not done, and cannot do, what you command, but give what you command; give us both the will and the ability to do what you ask! The self-righteous person trusts in a righteousness he achieved; the believer aspires to

13. *Luther's Works*, 25:19n13 (WA 56:22n4; Ficker, I, 20); 25:35–36 (WA 56:40–41; Ficker, I, 38); 25:261–62, 277 (WA 56:274–75, 290; Ficker, II, 113, 119).
14. *Luther's Works*, 25:19 (WA 56:22; Ficker, I, 20); 25:256 (WA 56:268; Ficker, II, 103–4).
15. *Luther's Works*, 25:215 (WA 56:231; Ficker, I, 69); cf. 25:239 (WA 56:252; Ficker, II, 89).
16. *Luther's Works*, 25:210 (WA 56:226; Ficker, II, 64).
17. *Luther's Works*, 25:211–12 (WA 56:226–27; Ficker, II, 65–66).
18. *Luther's Works*, 25:205–7 (WA 56:220–22; Ficker, II, 59–61).

a righteousness to be acquired."[19] While believers may in principle be righteous, the righteousness they possess is solely because of God's grace. Throughout their lives believers continue to believe that they are sinners and that their righteousness is grounded solely in the righteousness of God. While on earth, believers are and remain sick as well as healthy, sinners as well as righteous, guilty and innocent. "Intrinsically the saints are always sinners; extrinsically, therefore, they are always justified." Our righteousness is "only by virtue of God's imputation. For justification is neither in us nor in our power. Intrinsically and from within ourselves we are and will always remain impious."[20] Justification, accordingly, is always a work in progress. In their case it is better to speak of "the justified" (*justificati*) than of "the just" (*justi*), for Christ alone "is just, and we are still always being justified and in the process of justification."[21]

Guided by this view of justification, Luther was led to warn against both false security and despair. Our entire life on earth, he said, is "a time of desiring righteousness, yet in no way of fully attaining it; it is fully attained only in a future life." Yet, we should not despair because we cannot radically remove internal sin from us, for it is impossible in this life, and God forgives and does not impute sin to those who invoke his mercy. The Christian life remains a life of faith. God does not forsake the work of his hands but accomplishes what he has promised.[22] Christians exhibit that faith in their obedience to God's Word. Obedience does not consist of book learning nor in the accumulation of many good and great works but is frequently manifest in fidelity to what is small,[23] in free acts of loving obedience empowered by the Holy Spirit and measured by the standard of God's Word.[24]

[470] From the start, the Reformation was both a religious and an ethical movement, although time and polemics brought about changes in emphases as well as greater clarity. This puts the lie to claims that Luther's doctrine of justification came from his conviction that original sin—which Luther is said to have equated with sensual desire—was insurmountable in believers and that, therefore, a mere trust in God's mercy and an externally imputed righteousness of Christ was sufficient for salvation.[25] Luther nowhere makes a sharp distinction between justification (in a forensic sense) and sanctification; for Luther, declar-

19. *Luther's Works*, 25:251 (WA 56:264; Ficker, II, 99).

20. *Luther's Works*, 25:257 (WA 56:269; Ficker, II, 104–5).

21. *Luther's Works*, 25:43n2 (WA 56:265n2; Ficker, I, 45).

22. *Luther's Works*, 25:41–42n27 (WA 56:48n2; Ficker, I, 44); cf. 25:267 (WA 56:279; II, 128).

23. *Luther's Works*, 25:420 (WA 56:427; Ficker, II, 253).

24. *Luther's Works*, 25:359 (WA 56:368–70; Ficker, II, 203); cf. 25:407–10 (WA 56:415–18; Ficker, II, 242–43).

25. That the new ideas in Luther's thinking sprang not from a moral bankruptcy but from a profound sense of sin has been documented with strong evidence by W. Braun, *Die Bedeutung der Concupiscenz in Luthers Leben und Lehre* (Berlin: Trowitzsch, 1908). Nor, in Luther's thinking, is concupiscence the same as sexual lust but refers to the root of a whole range of sins, including spiritual ones. Cf. F. Loofs, *Leitfaden zum Studium der Dogmengeschichte*, 4th ed. (Halle a.S.: M. Niemeyer, 1906), 696; K. Holl,

ing righteous and making righteous are under the single heading of justification. Even though articulated differently by the various Refomers, the combined religious and ethical concern of the Reformation was to insist that salvation is from beginning to end a divine and not a human work.[26] The contrast between law and gospel, the opposition to all the merits of congruity and condignity, the emphasis on justification apart from merits, the glorification of God's grace and the merits of Christ, were all part of the Lutheran polemic against Rome[27] and led Lutherans increasingly to follow Melanchthon and ascribe to justification an exclusively juridical meaning. The Formula of Concord[28] confessed: (1) Faith alone, which, however, "is not a mere knowledge of the stories about Christ," but "a gift of God and a true and living faith," is the means and instrument through which we lay hold of Christ as our Savior and thus, in Christ, lay hold of "this righteousness that avails before God"; (2) God forgives us our sins by sheer grace, without any works, merit, or worthiness of our own in the past, at present, or in the future; that he gives us and reckons to us the righteousness of Christ's obedience; and that because of this righteousness, we are accepted by God into grace and regarded as righteous; (3) "Although the contrition that precedes justification and the good works that follow it do not belong in the article on justification before God, nevertheless a person should not concoct a kind of faith that can exist and remain with and alongside an evil intention to sin and to act against conscience. . . . Good works always follow justifying faith and are certainly found with it, when it is a true and living faith. For faith is never alone but is always accompanied by love and hope."

During the seventeenth century, under the pressure of rationalism and Pietism, the Lutheran church and its theology underwent a shift away from predestina-

---

"Luthers Rechtfertigungslehre 1516," *Zeitschrift für Theologie und Kirche* 20 (1910): 265; H. Bavinck, *Reformed Dogmatics*, III, 98–100 (#322).

26. E.g., it "means that out of unrighteous people righteous people are made or regenerated," but "it also means that they are pronounced or regarded as righteous. [For Scripture speaks both ways]" (Apology of the Augsburg Confession, art. 4, pars. 79–120, in *The Book of Concord*, ed. Robert Kolb and Timothy J. Wengert [Minneapolis: Fortress, 2000], 133–40); the citation is from art. 4, par. 72 (Kolb and Wengert, 132). Attempts to reconcile these two definitions of justification have not been lacking in recent years: J. Kunze, *Die Rechtfertigungslehre in der Apologie* (Gütersloh: C. Bertelsmann, 1908). However, O. Ritschl ("Der doppelte Rechtfertigungsbegriff in der Apologie der [Augsburg] Konfession," *Zeitschrift für Theologie und Kirche* 20 [1910]: 292–338), calls this a desperate tour de force. Melanchthon originally understood *justificatio* to refer not only to forgiveness of sins but also to regeneration. Gradually, from 1529 to 1532, he came to realize that this word really included only the first benefit. . . . [Consequently] justification in the sense of "being made a righteous person from an unrighteous one or as regeneration, accepting the forgiveness of sins," is called, "justification in consciousness" (later, passive justification). Justification in the sense of "being pronounced righteous or reckoned righteous" should be understood by what is later called "active justification," that is to say, the justification that takes place in God's judgment.

27. Also in Lutheran circles in the conflicts with Osiander, Stancarus, Major, and Amsdorf.

28. Citations that follow are from Formula of Concord, "Epitome," art. 3, "Righteousness," in Kolb and Wengert, 495–96.

tion, and human achievement and good works began to have a role in faith, the order of grace gave way to the order of reward, the gospel to law, faith to works. Justification increasingly became a subjective matter, an experience of forgiveness and renewal. Schleiermacher viewed justification as the reverse side of conversion and as part of regeneration, actually making it dependent on the new life in communion with Christ. Ritschl, however, again fixed attention on the objective significance of justification and therefore viewed it as a synthetic judgment that preceded good works. But, by understanding it as a possession of the church's faith in Jesus's message of the love of God which the individual gains by joining the church, he severed it from the satisfaction of Christ's atoning death and reduced justification to religious experience.[29]

[471] Although there is no material difference between Lutheran and Reformed theology with respect to the doctrine of justification, in the latter it occupies a different place and acquires a different accent. Calvin made predestination the center of his theology and viewed justification in its light. It is the elect who are justified. "When the Lord calls, justifies, and glorifies us, he declares nothing other than his eternal election."[30] As a result, the righteousness of Christ is presented more as a gift granted to us by God than as a benefit we accept by faith.[31] Additionally, Calvin maintains our "being justified apart from our own merits" on account of Christ's merits being sufficient, believers' need for assurance, and the glory of God. All boasting is stopped; the elect are justified by God so that they would glory in him and in nothing else.[32] Especially in his opposition to Osiander, Calvin distinguishes justification and sanctification but never separates them. Christ cannot be divided any more than the light and the warmth of the sun, though the two certainly produce distinct effects.[33] Christ does not justify anyone whom he does not also at the same time sanctify. We, accordingly, are not justified by works, but neither are we justified without works.[34] "Indeed, we do not contemplate Christ from afar in order that his righteousness might be imputed to us, but because we put on Christ and are ingrafted into his body—in short because he deigns to make us one with him. For this reason we glory that we have fellowship of righteousness with him."[35] In Calvin's thinking, therefore, while justification was truly important it did not become the one thing that overshadowed everything else in the order of salvation. It was given a place between election and the gift of Christ on the one hand, and salvation

29. H. Bavinck, *Reformed Dogmatics*, III, 550–53 (#425).

30. John Calvin, *Institutes of the Christian Religion*, III.xiii.2 (ed. John T. McNeill and trans. Ford Lewis Battles [1559; Philadelphia: Westminster, 1960], 1:764–65); Cf. H. Bavinck, *Reformed Dogmatics*, III, 522–28 (#419).

31. J. Calvin, *Institutes*, III.xi.1, 7, 17–18; etc.

32. Ibid., III.xii. Cf. Willy Lüttge, *Die Rechtfertigungslehre Calvins und ihre Bedeutung für seine Frömmigkeit* (Berlin: Reuther & Reichard, 1909), 76–82.

33. J. Calvin, *Institutes*, III.xi.6, 11, 24; III.xiv.9.

34. Ibid., III.xvi.1.

35. Ibid., III.xi.10; cf. H. Bavinck, *Reformed Dogmatics*, III, 522–28 (#419).

and glorification on the other. It was "something in the middle of the transition from eternal predestination to future glory."[36]

Although Calvin kept justification closely connected to election and satisfaction on the one hand, and sanctification and glorification on the other, those who followed him did not, to some degree because he failed to resolve all the theological difficulties in this article of faith—particularly the relationship of justification to election and satisfaction and to sanctification and glorification. Overemphasizing the objective, forensic character of justification and tying it to election and satisfaction, opens the door to reducing faith to a passive vessel of the eternally imputed righteousness of Christ. It is difficult to derive the new life of sanctification from such a notion, yet emphasizing communion with the righteousness of Christ runs the risk of undermining the objective grounds of our forgiveness. What Calvin held together, those who succeeded him often rent asunder.

Rationalism emphasized the human subject's faith and obedience, creating a new form of nomism or legalism; Pietism and Methodism, for all their differences with the preceding, also represented a turn toward human subjectivity and the experience of faith, insisting either on a lengthy period of religious experience or a sudden conversion as the condition for the acquisition of salvation. In reaction, some Reformed theologians overemphasized the objectivity of justification and encouraged antinomianism by downplaying the importance of human response; again, in reaction, an antineonomianism arose in which justification preceded faith. Reformed theologians tried to avoid both extremes and began to carefully distinguish active and passive justification. This was intended as logical, not temporal distinction. Some objected to it because the gospel never says to anyone personally, "your sins have been forgiven." Because preachers do not know who is elect, they cannot give anyone the assurance that his/her sins are forgiven; persons who hear the gospel can and may not believe this either, since before and without faith they cannot be conscious of their election. Practically, individuals are encouraged to penitentially humble themselves, seek refuge in Christ, and gradually surrender to him more and more. Then, convinced by self-examination, individuals receive the boldness to consider themselves assured of the forgiveness of their sins and future salvation. However, when this process is pushed to the limit, the focus turns again to a person's faith and a "decision" to surrender to Christ; the attention is directed away from the God of grace to the human subject, away from God's act to human action. Because of these complexities, Reformed theology no less that Lutheran failed to achieve complete agreement. To this day, the two different emphases—the objectivity of divine promise and the subjectivity of faith's response—remain in the Reformed churches.

---

36. Lüttge, *Die Rechtfertigungslehre Calvins*, 102. Lüttge persuasively refutes the invalid ethical and eschatological interpretation of Calvin's doctrine of justification advocated by Schneckenburger and M. Schulze (36, 56, 70, 85, 89) and properly restores the correct role of Bucer on Calvin (83).

JUSTIFICATION IS FORENSIC AND IMPUTED

[472–73] Justification is the doctrine on which the church stands or falls. Either we must do something to be saved, or our salvation is purely a gift of grace. If our work, our virtue, our sanctification is primary, then we remain in doubt and uncertainty to our last breath; Christ's unique, all-encompassing, and all-sufficient mediatorial office is set aside and God is robbed of his honor. Driven by a motive to preserve these three, the Reformation took up cudgels against Rome, declared that the Triune God's grace alone is the impelling and efficient cause of our entire salvation and that grace was not some metaphysical quality that was infused into humans and elevated them to a supernatural state (*gratia elevans*), but rather the forgiving mercy and favor of God that precedes all human effort and again receives them, freely, into his fellowship. The Father justifies effectively; the Son, meritoriously; the Holy Spirit, applicationally. To complete the picture at once: faith apprehends, the sacraments seal, and works declare.[37]

Justification is not an ethical but a forensic act. Rome reverses the true order of things when it incorporates good works into the understanding of justification itself, which Scripture contradicts. The Hebrew הִצְדִּיק (*hiṣdîq*) denotes the act of a judge whereby he declares a person innocent and is the antonym of הִרְשִׁיעַ (*hiršiaʿ*), to condemn (Deut. 25:1–2; Job 32:2; 33:32). It is so used of God (Exod. 23:7; 1 Kings 8:32; 2 Chron. 6:23; Isa. 50:8). In the Old Testament the word does not yet serve to express the forgiveness of sins as is indicated by the following words: to deliver (Pss. 39:8; 51:14), not to impute (Ps. 32:2), to forget and not remember (Isa. 43:25; Jer. 31:34), to cast behind one's back (Isa. 38:17), to blot out (Ps. 51:1, 9; Isa. 43:25), to forgive (Exod. 34:9; Ps. 32:1). In the New Testament, under the influence of the Old, the Greek word δικαιουν (*dikaioun*, "to deem right and fair") acquired a consistently juridical, as opposed to ethical, sense (Matt. 11:19; 12:37; Luke 7:29; 10:29; 16:15; 18:14), and the forensic meaning is certain in Paul. The word cannot have an ethical meaning because the subject is God, who is justified in his words (Rom. 3:4). It alternates, moreover, with "to be reckoned as righteousness" (4:3, 5), and is opposed to the words "to judge" (κρινειν, *krinein*), "to bring a charge against" (ἐγκαλειν, *enkalein*), and "to condemn" (κατακρινειν, *katakrinein*; 8:33–34), just as δικαιωμα (*dikaiōma*, justification) is the opposite of κατακριμα (*katakrima*, condemnation, 5:16). Δικαιουν means to acquit someone, to declare someone righteous (δικαιον καθισταναι, *dikaion kathistanai*; 5:19). While the word הִצְדִּיק (*hiṣdîq*), δικαιουν (*dikaioun*), "to justify," can have an ethical meaning, we need to remember that the opposition between Rome and the Reformation in the locus of justification was not formulated in terms of "ethical" versus "juridical," but in terms of justification by works (love) versus justification by faith on the basis of Christ's righteousness. It was sometimes stated that the

---

37. B. de Moor, *Commentarius perpetuus in Joh. Marckii Compendium theologiae christianae didactico-elencticum*, 6 vols. (Leiden: J. Hasebroek, 1761–71), IV, 562.

word "justification" could have a broader sense and an appeal made to passages such as Isaiah 53:11; Daniel 12:3; 1 Corinthians 6:11; Titus 3:7; and Revelation 22:11.[38] A closer look at all these passages makes it clear that what is *possible* is still not probable. In each instance the juridical reading is most likely or even definitive. Thus any stringent evidence that the word δικαιουν is ever used in an ethical sense in Scripture is lacking.

The law of God is clear (Deut. 25:1): the righteous must be acquitted and the unrighteous condemned. Even God acts according to this rule: he by no means clears the guilty, nor does he condemn the innocent (Exod. 20:5ff.; 34:7; Num. 14:18). "One who justifies the wicked and one who condemns the righteous are both alike an abomination to the Lord" (Prov. 17:15; cf. Exod. 23:7; Prov. 24:24; Isa. 5:23). Yet, seemingly in flat opposition to this and contrary to what God himself has said (Rom. 1:18; 2:13), Paul says that God justifies the ungodly (4:5). It is not entirely surprising, therefore, that Pelagians find the ground for acquittal in faith, that is, in the good disposition, virtues, and good works of humans, and mark them as perfect since they carry the warrant of perfection in themselves, or are counted as perfect by God for Christ's sake. Scripture, however, sets our righteousness and the righteousness of faith in contrast with each other (Rom. 10:3; Phil. 3:9); they are mutually exclusive as "works" and "faith" (Rom. 3:28; Gal. 2:16), as "reward" and "grace" (Rom. 4:4; 11:6). God who is holy did not give up the demands of the law but put forward Christ as a means or sacrifice of atonement, thus showing himself to be righteous and at the same time able to justify or acquit those who have faith in Jesus (3:21–26).[39] Christ's righteousness is inseparable from faith in his name; the righteousness of God has been revealed in Christ by his being put forward as a sacrifice of atonement by his blood, but he is that δια πιστεως (*dia pisteōs*, through faith; 3:25), and people are justified freely, out of grace, through the redemption that is in Christ Jesus (3:24). The righteousness of God is the righteousness of God through faith in Jesus Christ (3:22). But, does this mean that faith becomes the ground of a believer's justification? This is, in different ways, the position of Roman Catholics, Remonstrants, rationalists, mystics, and numerous modern Protestants. Notwithstanding divergences among them, they all locate righteousness, on the basis of which God acquits the sinner, in whole or in part in the human subject. Even if our righteousness is imperfect, God nevertheless counts it as perfect, either for Christ's sake or because it is a form of obedience to God's will expressed in the gospel and thus makes the human agent acceptable to God, or because it is perfect in principle and carries within itself the warrant of future perfection.

This does not hold up under Scripture's scrutiny. First, the righteousness of God in terms of which he acquits believers is objectively revealed in the gospel,

---

38. A. Thysius, in H. Bavinck, ed., *Synopsis purioris theologiae*, 6th ed. (Leiden: Donner, 1881), disp. 33, 3. Curaeus regarded sanctification as the other part of justification; see H. Heppe, *Dogmatik des deutschen Protestantismus im sechzehnten Jahrhundert*, 3 vols. (Gotha: F. A. Perthes, 1857), II, 312.

39. See H. Bavinck, *Reformed Dogmatics*, IV, 185 (#468).

apart from the works of the law and before faith (Rom. 1:17; 2 Cor. 5:19). God put Christ forward as a propitiatory sacrifice (ἱλαστηριον, *hilastērion*; Rom. 3:25) for our trespasses (4:25a), and Christ was raised for our justification (4:25b), because we were or had to be justified in him. This is a gift of his grace (Rom. 3:24; 5:15–17). The parallelism between Adam and Christ (Rom. 5), which points to death for all along with the gift of God, that is, righteousness in Christ, speaks of δικαιωμα, that is, a verdict of acquittal, for many (5:16). By the obedience of one person the many are treated as righteous (5:19). Second, faith is never presented as the ground for justification. Righteousness, or justification, is ἐκ πιστεως (*ek pisteōs*, through faith), δια πιστεως (*dia pisteōs*, through faith), or πιστει (*pistei*, by faith; Rom. 1:17; 3:22, 26, 28, 30; Gal. 2:16; 3:8, 24; Phil. 3:9; and so forth), but never δια πιστιν (*dia pistin*, on account of faith). Faith does not justify by its own essence or act because it itself is righteousness, but by its content, because it is faith in Christ, who is our righteousness; the faith that justifies is precisely the faith that has Christ as its object and content. In justification faith is so far from being regarded as a ground that Paul can say that God justifies the ungodly (Rom. 4:5). Third, the expression that "faith was accounted as righteousness" cannot mean that faith itself was accepted by God as a work of righteousness in place of or alongside "the righteousness of God in Christ." The word λογιζεσθαι (*logizesthai*) can certainly mean "to hold or consider a person for what he or she is" (1 Cor. 4:1; 2 Cor. 12:6), but here it has the sense of "to credit to a person something one does not personally possess." Thus the sins of those who believe are not counted against them although they do have them (Rom. 4:8; 2 Cor. 5:19; cf. 2 Tim. 4:16), and they are counted against Christ, although he was without sin (Isa. 53:4–6; Matt. 20:28; Rom. 3:25; 8:3; 2 Cor. 5:21; Gal. 3:13; 1 Tim. 2:6). To those who believe, a righteousness is imputed that they do not have (Rom. 4:5), and for that reason that act of imputation is a gift (κατα χαριν, *kata charin*, according to grace; 4:4). Those who believe have the righteousness of God (δικαιοσυνη θεου, *dikaiosynē theou*), which God grants them in Christ. Finally, if faith itself is the ground of justification, God accepts a lesser righteousness than he demands in his law, and gospel nullifies law rather than confirms it (Rom. 3:31). God then relinquishes his own righteousness and denies himself, or he accounts faith as something it is not, as sufficient righteousness, and so fails to do justice to his truthfulness. Here believers are robbed of all consolation; if our weak faith is the ground of our justification, the Christian life is a life of continual fear and uncertainty; we look to ourselves rather than being fixed on Christ. A truly Christian life lived in the service of God becomes impossible, for one's dread before God as Judge has to be transmuted into the consciousness of his fatherly love before one can speak of good works.

[474] Significant objections have been raised against the notion of imputed righteousness. It is argued, for example, that if Christ's righteousness is *only* imputed to us and remains outside us, it cannot be the essential form in which we are justified before God. God, whose judgment is true, cannot pronounce a

person righteous who in fact is not. In justification, it is said, the righteousness that is imputed cannot be our true form; we can only be justified on the basis of an indwelling righteousness. This is the objection to the Reformation doctrine that recurs in its critics.

In response, it must be noted that the objection is really against the apostle Paul, who says in Romans 4:5 and 5:16 that God justifies the ungodly. The best human analogy here is adoption; an adopted child is truly a member of the family, entitled to all its benefits. This is a judicial change in status.[40] God declares sinners righteous, adopts them as children, promises them Christ and all his benefits; for that reason they are called righteous and will one day gain possession of all the treasures of grace. Critics misconstrue imputation when they describe it as a product of the imagination, while infused grace is "real" grace, but justification is as real and necessary as sanctification, and imputation is no less real and necessary than infusion. The only difference is this: in justification, righteousness is granted to us in a *juridical* sense, while in sanctification, it becomes ours in an *ethical* sense. The judicial act is not fiction even if the owner has not yet taken possession. If this is true for earthly judges, how much more so for the Heavenly Judge? "It is God who justifies. Who is he that condemns?" (Rom. 8:33–34).

The righteousness legally imputed to us must still become ethically effective in sanctification. Our being made righteous rests in God's decree and in the *pactum salutis*. The covenant of grace precedes both our birth and our coming to believe. Our righteousness is "alien" in only a certain sense; it is the righteousness of the "head," which is therefore also that of the members. When God justifies the ungodly, he does it on the basis of a righteousness that he has effected in Christ.

[475] Scripture posits the closest relation between faith and justification. It is faith that is counted as righteousness (Gen. 15:6; Rom. 4:3; Gal. 3:6). The righteous live by faith (Hab. 2:4; Rom. 1:17; Gal. 3:11). The righteousness of God is manifested through faith (Rom. 3:22), and we are justified by faith (3:26; 5:1; 10:4, 10; Gal. 2:16). It is even written that we have believed in Christ Jesus so that we might be justified (Gal. 3:6–18, 22–24; also cf. Acts 10:43; 13:39; Heb. 10:38; and so forth). Does justification occur in eternity or in time and, if the latter, does it occur in the death or the resurrection of Christ, in the preaching of the gospel, or before or at the same time as, along with or after faith? Antinomians as well as antineonomians hold to an eternal justification; for the former our faith only involves acknowledging what God has done in eternity; the latter, urgently seeking to keep the pure gospel of grace from being mixed with law, saw eternal justification as the beginning and foundation of justification in time. Although it is important to insist that God's decree of election is eternal, speaking of justification as taking place in eternity is not advisable or scriptural and does not eliminate the problem of needing to explain its execution and outward

---

40. Ed. note: The adoption metaphor is Bavinck's, but the extrapolation of the adoption metaphor is the editor's.

realization in time. Reformed theology wisely distinguishes between the eternal decree and its execution in time.

When justification is tied to the death and resurrection of Christ (Rom. 4:25), we are on firm scriptural ground. Our justification has been obtained by Christ; it is objectively accomplished. Since 2 Corinthians 5:19 connects reconciliation in Christ with the nonimputation of the sins of the world, Reformed theologians wrestled with how precisely to tie the death and resurrection of Christ to justification. The gospel does not read: God will reconcile himself with you if you, humans, believe, repent, and fulfill his commandments; rather it says this: God is reconciled; he has forgiven the world its trespasses. Now believe this gospel, people; enter into this reconciliation; put aside your hostility; be reconciled to God.[41] The forgiveness of sins does not come into being by faith and is not acquired by our activities, but it is completely stored up, so to speak, in Christ, precedes faith, and is received and apprehended by faith alone. As the Apostles' Creed articulates: I believe in . . . the forgiveness of sins.

To clarify matters, Reformed theologians distinguished an active justification from a passive justification; justification is acquired and applied. As Savior, Christ not only aims at objective satisfaction but also at the subjective redemption of his own from sin. Again, this is not a temporal but logical distinction; concretely, the two coincide and always go together; acquisition and application are so tightly connected that neither the former nor the latter can be conceived of or exist apart from the other; acquisition necessarily entails the application. Active justification already in a sense occurred in the proclamation of the gospel, in the external calling, but it occurs especially in the internal calling when God by his Word and Spirit effectually calls sinners, convicts them of sin, drives them out toward Christ, and prompts them to find forgiveness and life in him. The distinction seeks to preserve the dual conviction that faith is both necessary for justification and that such a faith is itself the fruit of God's regenerating work through the Holy Spirit. This distinction helps us to avoid nomism, to strengthen believers' assurance by turning them away from introspective self-examination and toward Christ himself, and to recognize that faith is simultaneously a receptive organ and an active power. Faith is not the material or formal cause of justification; it is the very act of accepting Christ and all his benefits. Faith therefore is not an instrument in the true sense but is a sure knowledge and firm confidence that the Holy Spirit works in one's heart and by which he [the Spirit] convinces and assures people that, despite all their sins, they share in Christ and all his benefits.[42] This faith is active along with works and "is brought to completion by the works" (James 2:22).[43] In this sense, faith itself is a work (John 6:29), the best work, and the principle of all good

41. Cf. H. Bavinck, *Reformed Dogmatics*, III, 447–52 (#402).
42. J. Calvin, *Institutes*, III.xi.5; Heidelberg Catechism, Q 61; Belgic Confession, art. 22; Westminster Confession, art. 14.
43. On Paul and James, see J. Calvin, *Institutes*, III.xvii.11; idem, *Commentary*, on James 2.

works. Calvin put it this way: "It is faith alone that justifies; nevertheless the faith that justifies is not alone."[44] Paul and James are not at odds.

[476] Reformed theologians have not always agreed on the various elements of justification and how they are related to each other. It is best to define justification as the imputation of Christ's obedience as a whole to the believer, and to consider its two parts to consist in forgiveness of sins and the right to eternal life.[45] Sometimes adoption as children was mentioned as the second part of justification, but others preferred to consider this a fruit of justification.[46] The forgiveness that is a part of justification is nothing less than the complete acquittal of all the guilt and punishment of sin, not only of past and present but also of future sins. The fear of antinomianism must not hinder us from making this claim but does call us to be vigilant in continuing to pray for forgiveness daily. Reformed theologians maintained that while forgiveness removes the "actual liability" of sin, it does not remove its "potential liability." Sin's consequences remain, even those of forgiven sins. For believers especially, sin brings with it a sense of guilt, pain, regret, alienation from God, and remorse, and takes away one's tranquility of conscience and the boldness and assurance of faith. Even when believers, having long before received forgiveness, take a deeper look at the corruption of their own hearts, they feel a need even to confess their past sins (Pss. 25:7; 51:4–5). Therefore, for believers to remain assured, confession and prayer are the means by which God the Holy Spirit arouses and reinforces our consciousness of forgiveness. When our faith is weak, when we lapse into sin, believers always have the right and the freedom to go with confidence to the throne of grace and plead on the basis of the faithfulness of him whose gift of grace and calling are irrevocable (Rom. 11:29; Heb. 4:12; 1 John 1:9). Believers do not pray out of doubt and despair; they do not pray as though they are no longer children of God and again face eternal damnation; they pray from within the faith as children to the Father who is in heaven, and says Amen to their prayer.

Although understanding of justification is sometimes limited to forgiveness, what must not be overlooked is our adoption as children and the right to eternal

---

44. J. Calvin, "Acta Synodi Tridentinae cum Antidoto," in *Calvini opera* (CR XXXV), VII, 477; idem, *Institutes*, III.xi.20.

45. Gisbert Voetius, *Selectae disputationes theologicae*, 5 vols. (Utrecht, 1648–69), V, 279ff.; Francis Turretin, *Institutes of Elenctic Theology*, trans. George Musgrove Giger, ed. James T. Dennison, 3 vols. (Phillipsburg, NJ: Presbyterian & Reformed, 1992), XVI, 4.

46. F. Turretin, *Institutes of Elenctic Theology*, XVI, 6; A. Ritschl, *The Christian Doctrine of Justification and Reconciliation*, trans. H. R. Mackintosh and A. B. Macauley (Edinburgh: T&T Clark, 1900; repr., Clifton, NJ: Reference Book Publishers, 1966), 93; Otto Pfleiderer, *Der Paulinismus: Ein Beitrag zur Geschichte der urchristlichen Theologie*, 2nd ed. (Leipzig: O. R. Reisland, 1890), 189; H. J. Holtzmann, *Lehrbuch der neutestamentlichen Theologie*, 2 vols. (Freiburg i.B. and Leipzig: Mohr, 1897), II, 124. P. Martyr Vermigli, *Loci communes*, ed. R. Massonius (London, 1576), 354; Campegius Vitringa, *Doctrina christianae religionis, per aphorismos summatim descripta*, 6th ed., 8 vols. (Leiden: Joannis le Mair; Arnheim: J. H. Möelemanni, 1761–86), III, 324; cf. also J. Orr, *Sidelights on Christian Doctrine* (London: Marshall Bros., 1909), 157; R. S. Candlish, "Adoption," in *DB*, I, 41.

life (Gal. 4:5; cf. Dan. 9:24; Acts 26:18; Rev. 1:5–6). This adoption υἱοθεσια (*huiothesia*, adoption) is both juridical (Paul) and ethical (John); the latter will be discussed in the following section on sanctification. Just as on the basis of Christ's righteousness believers receive the forgiveness of sins, so they are also adopted as children (υἱοι θεου, *huioi theou*; not τεκνα θεου, *tekna theou*). This adoption, which therefore rests on a declaration of God, has been procured by Christ (Gal. 4:5) and becomes ours by faith (3:26). Those who have been pronounced free from the guilt and punishment of sin are thereby simultaneously adopted as children and counted as objects of God's fatherly love. Believers are thereby put in the same position as Christ, who is the firstborn among many brothers (Rom. 8:29). He was the Son of God by nature (8:32) and was so designated at his resurrection (1:3); believers become the "children of God" by adoption. Just as at his resurrection Christ was declared to be Son of God according to the Spirit of holiness (1:3), believers are justified in the Spirit of our God (1 Cor. 6:11) and are assured of their sonship by the same Spirit (Gal. 4:6). As children, then, they are also heirs according to the promise (Gal. 3:29; 4:7; Rom. 8:17), and since this inheritance still awaits them in the future, their adoption, in its fullness, is still an object of hope (Rom. 8:23).

Already in the Old Testament, God is called the Father of his people and Israel his Son, but in the New Testament this fatherhood and sonship acquire a much deeper meaning. God is now the Father of believers, not in a theocratic but in an ethical sense; and believers are his children, born of him, and by faith in Christ obtain the power to become his children (John 1:12) until one day, when they see him as he is, they will be perfected as his children (1 John 3:2). We are God's children; our legal status is provided in Christ and guaranteed by the Holy Spirit as a pledge until the day of full redemption. The Spirit is given to believers as pledge and guarantee that their adoption is sealed for the day of their redemption (2 Cor. 1:22; 5:5; Eph. 1:13–14; 4:30) and kept for their heavenly inheritance (1 Pet. 1:4–5). By that Spirit, they are continually led (ἀγονται, *agontai*, as in Rom. 8:14; not φερονται, *pherontai*, as in 2 Pet. 1:21), assured of the love that God has for them (Rom. 5:5; cf. 5:8) and of their adoption (8:15–16; Gal. 4:6), and are now already the beneficiaries of peace (Rom. 5:1; Phil. 4:7, 9; 1 Thess. 5:23), joy (Rom. 14:17; 15:13; 1 Thess. 1:6), and eternal life (John 3:16). Justification, which has its origin in eternity, is realized in the resurrection of Christ and the calling of believers, and is only fully completed when God in the last judgment repeats his sentence of acquittal in the hearing of the whole world, and every tongue will have to confess that Christ is Lord, to the glory of God the Father. Justification is able to produce all of these splendid fruits because along with active justification it includes passive justification, and by the testimony of the Holy Spirit gives believers the consciousness and assurance that their sins are personally forgiven them (*fides specialis*).

This doctrine should provide the greatest comfort and assurance to believers, and it equips them for great works, for faith, by its very nature, is opposed to all doubt. Certainty is not added to faith; it is from the beginning implicit in faith and in due time produced by it, for it is a gift of God, a working of the Holy Spirit who bears witness with our spirits that we are children of God (Rom. 8:16; Gal. 4:6) and assures us that nothing can separate us from the love of God in Christ (Rom. 8:38–39). If in justification we have been granted peace with God, sonship, free and certain access to the throne of grace, freedom from the law, and independence from the world,[47] then from that faith will naturally flow a stream of good works. They do not serve to acquire eternal life but are the revelation, seal, and proof of the eternal life that every believer already possesses. Faith includes the assurance that with God all things are possible, that he gives life to the dead, calls into existence the things that do not exist (Rom. 4:17), and always enables people to do great things. This faith says to a mountain: "Be lifted up and thrown into the sea," and it will be done (Matt. 21:21).[48]

SANCTIFICATION: HOLINESS AS GIFT AND REWARD

[477] From the beginning, God's plan of redemption included sanctification and glorification. Israel was called to be a holy people (Gen. 17:7; Exod. 19:6; Lev. 11:44; 19:2; 20:7, 26); purity of heart and act was the goal. This sanctification extended to the people as a whole and applied to all aspects of life—religious and moral, civil and social—and under the Old Testament dispensation bore a specifically ceremonial character.[49] When Israel failed to meet this requirement of the covenant and was deserving of judgment, the prophets announced that God would not break his covenant and forget his people but establish a new covenant in which he would forgive all their iniquities and give them new hearts (Jer. 31:31–34; Ezek. 11:19). Just as in the case of the forgiveness of sins, sanctification would be his work and his gift.[50]

After the exile, Israel increasingly opted for the way of self-righteousness and regarded its relationship with God in a consistently nomistic way, treating the whole of life by the scheme of work and reward.[51] Here Jesus returned to the spiritual sense of the law, distinguishing himself and the righteousness of the kingdom from the Pharisees (Matt. 5:20; Luke 18:10–14). God desires mercy, not sacrifice (Matt. 9:13). This love for God with all one's heart, mind, soul, and strength and love for one's neighbor as for oneself (Mark 12:33) is obtained only by conversion, faith, regeneration (Mark 1:15; John 3:3). By laying down his life

47. On the freedom of the law, see the discussion in H. Bavinck, *Reformed Dogmatics*, IV, 443–60 (##519–22).

48. On the certainty of faith, see J. Calvin, *Institutes*, III.ii.14ff.; L. Ihmels, "Rechtfertigung," in *PRE*³, XVI, 482–83.

49. H. Bavinck, *Reformed Dogmatics*, II, 218–21 (#205).

50. Ibid., III, 493–95 (#410).

51. Ibid., III, 495–99 (#411).

for his friends (John 15:10ff.) in death (Matt. 20:28; 26:26, 28), Jesus gives us an example to follow in our own pilgrimage of bearing our cross and following him (Matt. 5:10ff.; 7:13; 10:32–39; 16:24–26). Although he departs to go to the Father, he continues to live among them (Matt. 18:20; 28:20), remains in them (John 14:16–17), incorporates them into himself as branches in the vine (John 15:1–10), so that they can bear God-glorifying fruit (15:8), do the works he did (14:12), obey his commandments and remain in his love (14:15, 24; 15:5, 10).

Having been forgiven, the disciple of Jesus is called to follow him, deny self, and take up a cross. Those who follow Jesus must be prepared to give up everything (Matt. 19:10–12; 10:35–36; 19:21), even their lives (10:39; 16:25). But Jesus was not an ascetic; he participated in feasts (Matt. 11:19; John 2:2), did not require his disciples to abstain from marriage, food, or drink (Matt. 6:16; 9:14), but viewed love as the fulfillment of the law (5:43–48; 22:37–40), called for conscientious stewardship (25:15–30), and as the one who would one day be judge of all insisted on faithfulness and caution (wisdom, prudence) in life (7:24; 10:16; 24:15–18). Jesus even uses the idea of reward for works done—for enduring persecution (Matt. 5:10–12), loving one's enemies (5:46), giving alms (6:4), confessing Jesus's name (10:32), service to his disciples (10:41–42), faithfulness in one's vocation (24:45–47), careful management of the goods entrusted to us (25:14–30), mercy toward the disciples of Jesus (25:32–46), and so forth—as an incentive to spur us on to faithfulness. But Jesus also reminded his hearers that those who show off their works lose their reward from God (6:2, 5, 16), and that the reward of the kingdom of God is disproportionately far greater than all the labor and toil we have given it (5:46; 19:29; 20:1ff.; 25:21–23; Luke 12:33). It is a *gift* of God (Matt. 6:33; 20:14–15; 26:28; Mark 10:30; Luke 1:77; 24:47). Furthermore, the blessings of the kingdom are not first of all happiness consisting in external blessings but being a child of God and having purity of heart (Matt. 5:8, 9, 45, 48, and so forth).

After Christ completed his work on earth, he was glorified at the right hand of God and by the Spirit communicated himself to his church on the day of Pentecost. The Spirit initially gave extraordinary gifts and powers but also established and maintained communion between Christ and his church.[52] Believers are people who by the grace of God have not only received the forgiveness of sins but also, having been brought into fellowship with Christ (Rom. 6:3–11) by their baptism, were transferred out of darkness into the light (Col. 1:13) and now constitute an elect race, a royal priesthood, a holy nation (1 Pet. 2:9). They have received Christ not only as righteousness but also as ἁγιασμος (*hagiasmos*)—not holiness, as ἁγιοτης (*hagiotēs*) or ἁγιωσυνη (*hagiōsynē*), but sanctification—so that what is in view here is not the result but the progression of sanctification or consecration to God (cf. Rom. 6:22; 1 Thess. 4:4; 1 Tim. 2:15; Heb. 12:14). Believers are washed and sanctified in Christ (1 Cor. 6:11), are temples of the Holy Spirit

52. Ibid., III, 499–506 (##412–13).

(1 Cor. 3:16; 6:19; 2 Cor. 6:16), and made new creatures (2 Cor. 5:17; Eph. 2:10). Sanctification, accordingly, is in the first place a work of God (John 17:17; Phil. 1:6; 1 Thess. 5:23), more specifically of Christ and his Spirit (Rom. 8:4, 9–11; 1 Cor. 1:30; 6:11; Eph. 5:27; Col. 1:22; 2 Thess. 2:13; Heb. 2:11; 9:14; 10:10, 14, 29; 13:12; 1 Pet. 1:2).

Nonetheless, since God enables them both to will and to work, believers must work out their own salvation with fear and trembling (Phil. 2:12–13; 2 Pet. 1:10) by keeping their entire spirit, soul, and body blameless in sanctification until the day of the Lord Jesus Christ (Eph. 1:4; Phil. 2:15; 1 Thess. 3:13; 5:23). They continually have to battle against the flesh (1 Cor. 3:1; Gal. 5:17) and are called to purify themselves, crucify the flesh with all its passions and desires, and present their bodies as a living sacrifice, holy and acceptable to God (Rom. 6:13; 12:1; 2 Cor. 7:1; Gal. 5:24), to overcome the world, to keep God's commandments, to purify themselves, and to walk in the light (1 John 1:7; 2:1; 3:6, 9; 5:4; etc.). All this is summed up in the practice of love (Rom. 12:10; 13:8–10; 1 Cor. 13; Eph. 1:4; 5:2; Col. 3:14; 1 Thess. 4:9; 1 John 3:11ff.; 4:8; etc.). While certain forms of abstinence may at times be advisable—e.g., from marriage (1 Cor. 7:8, 20ff.)—the prohibition to marry and the injunction to abstain from foods is a teaching of those who have departed from the faith (1 Tim. 4:3). For nothing is unclean of itself (Matt. 15:11; Rom. 14:14); every creature of God is good; grace does not suspend nature (1 Cor. 7:20–23).

Christians are called to follow a simple lifestyle (1 Tim. 2:9; Titus 2:3; 1 Pet. 3:3) and to flee wordly desires (1 John 2:15–17). Christians are compelled to holy living out of gratitude (Rom. 12:1; 2 Cor. 8:9; 1 John 4:19), because they have died to sin and been raised to new life (Rom. 6:3–14; 7:4; Gal. 2:19; Col. 3:1–2), they do not walk according to the flesh but according to the Spirit, they are temples of the Holy Spirit (Rom. 8:5; 1 Cor. 6:15ff.), and because they are children of light and must walk in the light (Rom. 13:12; Eph. 5:8; 1 John 1:6; etc.). God's children in Christ are commanded to become holy. As believers we also anticipate the joys of future glory which are a gift of grace (Rom. 6:23; 2 Cor. 8:9; Eph. 2:8; etc.) but still are also a spur to patience and perseverance (Rom. 8:18; 1 Cor. 15:19; 2 Cor. 4:10, 17; Rev. 2:7, 10–11, 17; etc.). God does reward those who seek him (Heb. 11:6, 26), are generous (1 Tim. 6:19), confident in their faith (Heb. 10:35), and faithful in their labor (1 Cor. 3:8, 14; 9:18; Col. 3:24; 2 Tim. 4:8; etc.). There is even mention of a special reward for those who build on the foundation of Christ (1 Cor. 3:12–15; cf. Paul in 1 Cor. 9:16–17). Although salvation is granted to all believers, there will be differences in glory among them, depending on their works (Matt. 10:41; 18:4; 20:16; 25:14ff.). The connection in Scripture is between sanctification and glorification; what is sown here is harvested in eternity (Matt. 25:24, 26; 1 Cor. 15:42ff.; 2 Cor. 9:6; Gal. 6:7–8). Without sanctification no one will see God (Matt. 5:8; Heb. 12:14). Sanctification is not nullified by grace but made serviceable to it. Believers are God's workmanship, created in Christ Jesus for good works, which God prepared beforehand to be our way of life (Eph. 2:10). As children we are also heirs of God and fellow heirs of Christ (Rom. 8:17). Precisely because they work with enthusiasm, they also know that they will receive from the Lord the reward of their inheritance, for they serve the Lord Christ (Col. 3:23–24).

[478] The post-apostolic church, following the admonitions of the New Testament, continued to insist on holiness of life as Christians distinguished themselves from the world as a new race, the new people of God. In time, however, the church's cultural context affected her conduct and she had to contend with the reality of postbaptismal sin. Since it was believed that baptism only covered sins committed in the past and the rigorous practice of permanently excommunicating sinners seemed harsh, the church began to make distinctions between serious and less serious sins. Influenced by Jewish and Stoic beliefs, the church became committed to the notion that the gospel of grace only had effect until baptism; after baptism a sinner had to secure forgiveness by doing good works, repentance, confession (private or public), prayer, patience, fasting, alms, and so forth.[53] Those who sinned after receiving baptism fell under the law and had to work out their own salvation. This nomistic tendency, which construed the gospel as a new law, was significantly reinforced by the development of an increasingly authoritarian and hierarchical church. Obedience to the church became the one all-inclusive virtue, and religion as well as morality was increasingly seen as the observance of church-imposed duties.

Naturally linking up with this nomism was the emergence of a twofold morality—one for ordinary believers and the other for "saints"—that contributed to the growth of the eremitic and monastic life. Regular precepts were supplemented by "counsels of perfection," namely, the negative virtues of chastity, poverty, and obedience. In the Greco-Roman context of polytheism, emperor worship, theaters, etc., many Christians were intent on fleeing from the world instead of winning it. While this could have been coupled with principle-based opposition to asceticism, the practice of life led in another direction. The rigorism that was observed in countless circles outside the Christian church—among gnostics, Marcionites, Montanists, and Jewish and pagan sects—was imitated by many Christians who envied them. Men and women who had demonstrated greatness in self-denial and self-sacrifice—not only the apostles but also martyrs and confessors—became admired models. People began to venerate them and set them apart as "saints," a term that in earlier times referred to all believers. The observance of certain days of fasting and of set times for prayer, abstinence from luxury, abstinence especially from marriage, and avoidance of the world in general, accordingly, from ancient times—as witnessed to in early Christian writings—were glorified as special Christian virtues. When in the second and third centuries the secularization of the church increased, many of its members fled and practiced their beliefs outside the church and initiated first the eremitic and later the monastic life.

Now the distinction between two kinds of morality acquired its fixed terminology—"precepts" and "counsels of perfection"—from Origen who wrote

---

53. Cf. H. Bavinck, *Reformed Dogmatics*, IV, 142 (#460).

that what Paul recommends in 1 Corinthians 7:25 is "a work surpassing the precept," and Tertullian who translated 1 Corinthians 7:25 into Latin with the words: "I do not have a precept [*praeceptum*] of the Lord, but I offer [this] advice [*consilium*]." Although never formally enacted by the church,[54] the distinction nevertheless constitutes an indispensable element and occupies a supremely important place in Catholic doctrine and practice. Gradually, the "counsels" (*consilia*), which surpass the "precepts" (*praecepta*), were construed as the three virtues of chastity (abstention from marriage; Matt. 19:11–12; 1 Cor. 7:7ff.), poverty (Matt. 19:21; 1 Cor. 9:14), and obedience (Matt. 16:24; Luke 14:26ff.).[55] In this way the Roman Catholic Church, besides upholding the duties that apply to everyone, keeps open a place for the free practice of virtue, an area for things that are desirable and praiseworthy. Over and above the practical life, it ascribes great value to the ascetic and contemplative life. While the precepts are necessary for people to obtain eternal life, the counsels are free and optional but have the advantage that they enable people to reach this goal "better and more expeditiously."[56]

This nomistic (and semi-Pelagian) trend led naturally to the doctrine of the meritoriousness of good works. The whole relationship between God and humanity is cast in the scheme of *do ut des* (I give that you may give). Those who serve God and keep his commandments can justly claim a reward.[57] This Jewish viewpoint exerted great influence in Christian circles, especially as a result of the apocryphal books included in the Septuagint. For Rome, the meritoriousness of good works is an article of faith that includes the following:

1. The will, weakened by sin, is not deprived of all liberty and can under God's providence still naturally do good works.[58]
2. Those who make good use of these natural powers cannot make themselves worthy of infused grace but can, negatively, prepare themselves for grace by removing obstacles to it.[59]
3. Positive preparation requires prevenient (actual) grace, but those who do prepare are worthy of a merit of congruity.[60]
4. Baptism confers infused grace, that is, "a quality inhering in the soul," deliverance from all the guilt and pollution of sin and inner renewal. It

54. The "counsels of perfection" received only incidental support at the Council of Trent (sess. XXIV, can. 10), where celibacy and virginity are pronounced better and more blessed than marriage (H. Denzinger, ed., *The Sources of Catholic Dogma*, trans. from the 30th ed. by R. J. Deferrari [London and St. Louis: Herder, 1955], #980).

55. Although frequently this trio was expanded and augmented with counsels derived from the Sermon on the Mount (Matt. 5:16, 29–30, 34–37, 39–41, 44; 6:31; 7:1; etc.).

56. T. Aquinas, *Summa Theol.*, II, 1, qu. 106–8.

57. H. Bavinck, *Reformed Dogmatics*, III, 496 (#411).

58. T. Aquinas, *Summa Theol.*, II, 1, qu. 109, art. 2–5; Council of Trent, sess. VI, c. 1, can. 5–7.

59. Cf. H. Bavinck, *Reformed Dogmatics*, III, 514–17 (#416).

60. T. Aquinas, *Summa Theol.*, II, 1 qu. 109, art. 6; Council of Trent, sess. VI, c. 5–6.

heals and elevates the baptized to the supernatural order, the superadded gift granted to Adam.[61]

5. Added to this infused grace are the three theological virtues—faith, hope, and love[62]—which are not human but superhuman, or divine, virtues and therefore differentiated from human virtues which are divided into intellectual virtues (wisdom, science, understanding, prudence, art) and moral or cardinal virtues (prudence, justice, fortitude, temperance). All have as their object the final and supreme goal, a supernatural end.[63]

6. By this grace, humans are enabled to do supernaturally good works and by it to merit an increase of grace, eternal life in the vision of God, and within that setting a lower or higher degree of glory (crown or nimbus).[64] According to Trent this does nullify grace because it all rests on God's decree and presupposes the merits of Christ and the gift of grace.[65]

7. The good works that merit a great reward are especially those that are not strictly commanded and go beyond the exact letter of the law, such as prayer and fasting, renunciation of worldly goods, celibacy, the monastic life, self-flagellation, martyrdom. Those who do these things are "saints," "religious" par excellence;[66] their deeds of supererogation[67] add to the "treasury of merit" that the church, through indulgences, can dispense to the faithful as needed.

SANCTIFICATION AND THE CRITIQUE OF JUSTIFICATION

[479] The Reformation repudiated this entire scheme and took its position on the doctrine of justification by faith alone. This faith is a personal heartfelt trust in the grace of God in Christ Jesus. Communion with God comes about not by

61. H. Bavinck, *Reformed Dogmatics*, III, 515–17 (#416).

62. According to the catechism of the Council of Trent, "This grace is accompanied by a most splendid train of all the virtues, which are divinely infused into the soul along with grace" (Roman Catechism, II, chap. 2, qu. 50). The post–Vatican II edition titled *The Roman Catechism*, trans. Robert I. Bradley, SJ, and Eugene Kevane (Boston: Daughters of St. Paul, 1985) drops the enumeration of the introduction so that chapter 1 begins the section on baptism. In this annotation, the proper reference would be II, chap. 1, qu. 51.

63. On the doctrine of the virtues in Roman Catholic theology, see T. Aquinas, *Summa Theol.*, II, 2.

64. The Council of Trent, accordingly, states that the one justified "by the good works he performs truly merits an increase of grace, eternal life, and in case he dies in grace, the attainment of eternal life itself and also an increase in glory" (sess. VI, can. 32).

65. Council of Trent, sess. VI, can. 16; T. Aquinas, *Summa Theol.*, qu. 114. In Roman Catholic theology, the doctrine of grace is usually discussed in three parts: actual grace (*gratia actuali*) is considered first; then habitual, or justifying, grace (*gratia habituali [justificante]*); finally, the fruit of grace or concerning merits (*fructu gratiae seu de merito* [*Theologia Wirceburgensis*, VII, 467ff.]).

66. T. Aquinas, *Summa Theol.*, II, 2 qu. 81, art. 1, ad 1; and qu. 180ff., where Thomas discusses the contemplative life.

67. The term "supererogation" is derived from Luke 10:35, where the word προσδαπανήσῃς has been translated into Latin by *supererogaveris*.

human exertion, but solely on the part of God, by a gift of his grace. Religion was again placed before morality. It is best to think of justification in receptive terms: to say that it is through faith that the believer receives Christ the Savior. It must also be said that this is a living, active, and forceful faith that renews people and produces heartfelt joy. From its beginning, faith was two things at once: a receptive organ and an active force; a hand that accepts the gift offered but also works outwardly in the service of the will; a bond to invisible things and a victory over the visible world; at once religious and ethical.

Especially in Reformed theology, faith was seen to arise from regeneration and accompanied by constant repentance. This is not a matter of extraordinary obedience in order to increase merit or reward but a childlike obedience, an obedience of faith that consists in doing the will of our heavenly Father as it is concisely laid down in the Ten Commandments. Alongside the commandments, prayer also occupies a prominent place in the Christian's life of gratitude. Religion and morality, accordingly, remain distinct. In Protestant theology, the discipline of ascetics emerged alongside ethics;[68] theology and ethics were united. Calvin, for example, does not lose himself in a wide-ranging exposition of all sorts of virtues and duties but conceives all of life as a unity controlled by one universal rule[69] derived from Romans 12:1.[70] The entire life of the Christian is dedicated to the worship of God—we are not our own; we are God's. We belong to God completely and always, in life and in death. Starting from this principle, Calvin then pictures the Christian life as expanding in three directions as described in Titus 2:12: Christians renouncing irreligion and worldly passions have to live sober, upright, and godly lives—soberly in relation to ourselves, justly in relation to others, and devoutly in relation to God.

This Reformation understanding of faith as living faith rooted in the regenerating work of the Holy Spirit experience opposition from two sides. Humanist rationalists sought to emancipate the various areas of life from the dominion of theology and the influence of Christianity. From the other side, Reformation sectarians and mystics were dissatisfied with the doctrine of justification by faith alone and insisted on a vigorous augmentation of justification with sanctification. When Protestant churches lapsed into doctrinalism, mystical Anabaptist ideas in particular, which sharply contrasted flesh and spirit, the church and the world, resonated with many hearts. Among Pietists and Methodists, justification had to be followed by sanctification unto perfection, a constant communion with God in love and obedience. Pietism prescribed a specific method of conversion and then gathered the devout in small sealed-off circles [conventicles] that were "extra-

---

68. G. Voetius, *Exercitia pietatis* (Gorichem: Paul Vink, 1664); H. Heppe, *Geschichte des Pietismus und der Mystik in der reformirten Kirche* (Leiden: Brill, 1879), 23ff, names other works as well.

69. J. Calvin, *Institutes*, III.vi–x.

70. By contrast, when Melanchthon gradually returned to philosophy, he began to treat ethics and politics under the guidance of Aristotle and restricted Christianity to the interior life of the soul, the exterior life of the Christian governed by natural law.

mundane" and marked by a rigorous yet narrowly defined moral life.[71] Methodism not only advanced a specific method of conversion but also gradually arrived at a special doctrine of sanctification. Humans can no more do any good works after justification than before. But, if after God justifies, he then proclaims: "Be pure!" and regenerates and sanctifies, the root of evil is removed from our hearts, and sin no longer exists. Holy perfection is "a real change"—and justification only "a relative change"[72]—a second blessing. It is the second of sin's "double cures."[73] Notwithstanding some later qualifications, Wesley's deepest conviction was that, after justification, complete holiness was at once obtainable by faith, for God wanted it, and Christ was mighty and ready to grant it in an instant.[74]

This doctrine of Christian perfection, alongside that of conversion, is so prominent that it can be called the great, all-controlling idea of Methodism. It mainly comes down to the following:

1. Justification or the forgiveness of sins, which is received by faith, must be followed by sanctification because Christ is a complete Savior, who not only delivers us from the guilt and punishment of sin but also from its pollution and power.
2. Although there are disagreements about the details, this sanctification consists in complete deliverance from the pollution and power of sin.
3. This perfection is obtained by faith but this faith is the conviction that God is mighty and willing to grant this complete holiness *now* at this very moment to *me* personally. When we totally and unconditionally yield ourselves to God, he says: "Let it be according to your faith!" and cleanses us from all iniquity. Whatever we ask for in prayer, believing that we have received it (in an alternative reading), will become ours (Mark 11:24). "Faith is not *only* expectation; there is a faith *that counts the thing that it asks as having been given.*"[75]
4. The reception of the Spirit is often accompanied by deep emotions and strong physical tremblings. Methodism also envisions this "second bestowal" of the Spirit as the beginning of a new age on earth in which Christ's return—inaugurating the glorious age of the kingdom of peace on earth—is imminent. Although this emphasis can lead to eccentricities—disdain for earthly callings, devaluation of church, confession, offices, and sacra-

---

71. H. Bavinck, *Reformed Dogmatics*, III, 535–40 (#422).

72. Ed. note: "Real change" and "relative change," in English, are Bavinck's own terms, though he provides no direct quotation or source.

73. Ed. note: The reference is to Augustus Toplady's hymn text, "Rock of Ages": "Be of sin the double cure: Save from guilt and make me pure." The reference is the editor's addition.

74. H. Bavinck, *Reformed Dogmatics*, III, 536–40 (#422); R. Southey, *The Life of John Wesley* (London: Hutchinson, 1903), 234–64; F. Loofs, "Methodismus," in *PRE*³, XII, 799.

75. R. A. Torrey, *The Holy Spirit: How to Obtain Him in Personal Experience, How to Retain Him* (Chicago: Bible Institute Colportage Association, 1900–1928), 23.

ments—as well as ascetic legalism, it has also produced great works of mission and philanthropy. Active Christianity, in the church and in society, in philanthropy and missions, can be directly or indirectly attributed to Methodism.[76]

[480] A proper understanding of sanctification begins with the conviction that Christ is our holiness in the same sense in which he is our righteousness. He is a complete, all-sufficient Savior who saves us really and completely. He does not rest until, after pronouncing his acquittal in our conscience, he has also imparted full holiness and glory to us. Christ does not just restore us to the state of the just who will escape the judgment of God in order then to leave us to reform ourselves after God's image and to merit eternal life. Christ *is* "our righteousness, holiness, and redemption" (1 Cor. 1:30). The holiness that must completely become ours therefore fully awaits us in Christ. In Christ God grants us, along with righteousness, also complete holiness, and does not just impute it but also inwardly imparts it by the regenerating and renewing working of the Holy Spirit until we have been fully conformed to the image of his Son.

Logically, justification, which clears our guilt, precedes sanctification (Rom. 8:30; 1 Cor. 1:30), which cleanses us from our pollution. Furthermore, while justification is a juridical act, completed in an instant, sanctification is an ethical process that continues throughout our lives. Although justification and sanctification are distinct,[77] they must never be separated. Christ's obedience to the point of death was aimed at redemption in its entire scope (ἀπολύτρωσις, *apolytrōsis*), not only as redemption from the legal power of sin (Rom. 3:24; Eph. 1:7; Col. 1:14) but also as deliverance from its moral domination (Rom. 8:23; 1 Cor. 1:30; Eph. 1:14; 4:30). The distinction rests on the fact that God is both righteous and holy. As the Righteous One, he wants all his creatures to stand before him free from guilt and punishment; as the Holy One, he demands that they appear before him pure and unpolluted by sin. Furthermore, justification and sanctification are united in the power and work of the Holy Spirit. This Spirit equipped Christ himself for his work, leading him from his conception to his ascension, and by this same Spirit he now also shapes and equips his church. The Spirit whom Jesus promised to his disciples and poured out in the church is not only a Spirit of adoption, who provides assurance, but also the Spirit of renewal and sanctification. The Holy

76. J. L. Nuelsen, "Methodismus in Amerika," in *PRE*[3], XIII, 14; all these points on Methodism are based on J. Wesley, *A Plain Account of Christian Perfection* (New York: Methodist Book Concern, 1925). In Germany, this doctrine gained significant entry thanks to the work of Theodor Jellinhaus, *Das völlige gegenwärtigen Heil durch Christum*, 5th ed. (Berlin: Thormann & Goetsch, 1903). Cf. M. Schian, *Die moderne Gemeinschaftsbewegung* (Stuttgart: Greiner & Pfeiffer, 1909); idem, "Die moderne deutsche Erweckungspredigt," *Zeitschrift für Religionspsychologie* 10 (1908): 11.

77. Those who mix them undermine the religious life, take away the comfort of believers, and subordinate God to humanity. Those who separate them undermine the moral life and make grace subservient to sin.

Spirit dwells in believers and they live and walk in the Holy Spirit (Rom. 8:1, 4, 9–11; 1 Cor. 6:19; Gal. 4:6; etc.). To that end Christ gives himself to them, not only objectively in redemption, but also imparts himself subjectively in sanctification and unites himself with them in a spiritual and mystical manner. Christ thus lives and dwells in believers (John 14:23; 17:23, 26; Rom. 8:10; 2 Cor. 13:5; Gal. 2:20; Eph. 3:17), and they are united to him as branch and vine (John 15), as head and members (Rom. 12:4; 1 Cor. 12:12; Eph. 1:23; 4:15), husband and wife (1 Cor. 6:16–17; Eph. 5:32), cornerstone and building (1 Cor. 3:11, 16; 6:19; Eph. 2:21; 1 Pet. 2:4–5).

[481] Sanctification as well as justification is a gift, purely of grace. In both, the benefit given to us is Christ himself; by justification we become the righteousness of God in him; by sanctification he himself comes to dwell in us by his Spirit and renews us after his image. Here, as in our discussion of justification,[78] we need to distinguish a passive from an active sanctification. When in Scripture sanctification is attributed to the Father (John 17:17; 1 Thess. 5:23; Heb. 13:20–21), to the Son as life-giving Spirit (1 Cor. 15:45; Eph. 5:26; Titus 2:14) and particularly to the Holy Spirit (Titus 3:5; 1 Pet. 1:2), believers are passive; they are sanctified in Christ (John 17:19; 1 Cor. 1:2; 6:11), they are God's workmanship (Eph. 2:10)—all this is from God (2 Cor. 5:18). God's people are called "saints" (Rom. 1:7; 1 Cor. 1:2); they are holy and called to be holy, "a chosen race, a royal priesthood, a holy nation, God's own people" (1 Pet. 2:9). Believers are "sanctified in Christ Jesus" (1 Cor. 1:2), regenerated, purified, renewed by the Holy Spirit (John 3:3; 1 Cor. 6:11; Titus 3:5). They are new persons (2 Cor. 5:17; Gal. 6:15; Eph. 2:10; 4:24; Col. 3:10) whose walk of life contrasts with their old life in sin (1 Cor. 6:10; Eph. 2:1) and increasingly conforms to the image of Christ (Rom. 8:29; Gal. 4:19). Here sanctification coincides with glorification: "Those whom he called he also justified, and those whom he justified he also glorified" (Rom. 8:30). This glorification is continued throughout the Christian life (2 Cor. 3:18) until it is completed in Christ's return (1 Cor. 15:49, 51ff.; Phil. 3:21; Col. 3:4).

Sanctification is also a call to active continued repentance on the part of the Christian. Sanctification is both gift and task. We are to die to sin and "present our members as instruments of righteousness" and give ourselves wholly to God (Rom. 12:1; 2 Cor. 7:1; 1 Thess. 4:3; Heb. 12:14; etc.). We are grafted into Christ the vine and also implored to bear fruit (John 15). Scripture always holds on to both facets: God's all-encompassing activity and our responsibility (see Phil. 2:12–13). Active sanctification coincides with what is called "continued repentance," which, according to the Heidelberg Catechism, consists in the dying away of the old self and the coming to life of the new self.[79] This duality has been misunderstood by nomists and antinomians. The former insist that good works are necessary conditions for salvation; the latter are indifferent to repentance, prayer for forgiveness,

---

78. See H. Bavinck, *Reformed Dogmatics*, IV, 186–95 (#469).
79. Heidelberg Catechism, Q&A 88.

and good works, since Christ's perfect sacrifice made them superfluous. Lutherans had special difficulty with this tension, which caused bitter debates.[80] Reformed theologians had less difficulty, speaking of good works as necessary in the sense of presence rather than in the sense of merit. The presence of good works is a sign of God's work of grace in a believer. This is the teaching of Scripture which definitely insists on sanctification, both its passive and active aspects, and proclaims both the one and the other with equal emphasis and posits no contradiction or conflict between them. God and humanity, religion and morality, faith and love, the spiritual and the moral life, praying and working are not opposites. Our dependence on God is precisely what grounds our freedom. We are not under law but grace, and therefore sin may not have dominion over us (Rom. 6:14); we are dead to sin and alive to God in Christ (Rom. 6:11). Believers stand in the freedom with which Christ has made them free; in Christ, nothing has any power, except faith working through love (Gal. 5:1, 6). The bodies of believers are members of Christ and temples of the Holy Spirit; they have been bought at a high price and must glorify God in their bodies and spirits, which belong to God (1 Cor. 6:15, 20).

GOOD WORKS, PERFECTIONISM, AND PERSEVERANCE

[482] Good works in the strict sense are those done out of true faith, in conformity with God's law, and to his glory.[81] The virtues of the pagans are not good works though the Reformed have always fully acknowledged and valued them[82] as a fruit of God's common grace.[83] The truly spiritually good, in the highest sense as it can only exist in the eyes of God, can only be accomplished by those who

---

80. Some defended good works, but others considered them detrimental and went so far as to say that good works are harmful to and pernicious for salvation. The Formula of Concord condemned both positions and stated only that good works are "signs of eternal salvation," inasmuch as it is God's will and express command that believers should do good works, which the Spirit works in their hearts and which God accepts and rewards for Christ's sake in this life and the life to come (Formula of Concord, "Solid Declaration," art. 4, "Concerning Good Works," in *The Book of Concord*, ed. Robert Kolb and Timothy J. Wengert [Minneapolis: Fortress, 2000], 574ff.).

81. Heidelberg Catechism, Q&A 91.

82. The Pelagians obliterated the distinction between virtues and good works, between pagan religions and the Christian faith. They believed that the law of nature, the Mosaic law, and the law of Christ were essentially the same. The Romans distinguished natural good works and supernatural good works and judged even fallen humanity capable of the former. But Tertullian (*The Apology*, c. 45–46) and Augustine (*Against Julian*, trans. M. A. Schumacher, vol. 16 of *Writings of St. Augustine* [Washington, DC: Catholic University of America Press, 1984], IV, c. 3, §§17, 25, 33) judged otherwise. Reformed thinkers readily acknowledged the virtues of the pagans and considered them for the most part an example that should shame believers. However, they did not lose sight of the fundamental difference between these virtues and the good works of believers. See J. Calvin, *Institutes*, II.ii.12ff.; II.iii.3ff.

83. Even after the fall, people remained human and continue inwardly to possess many virtues and outwardly to do many good deeds that, viewed through human eyes and measured by human standards, are greatly to be appreciated and of great value for human life.

know and love God and, moved by that love, keep his commandments. As long as we are on earth and cannot see God face-to-face, faith is the only means of accepting his revelation and of knowing him as he truly is; faith is needed not only at the beginning in justification but must accompany the Christian throughout one's entire life and play a permanent and irreplaceable role in sanctification. In sanctification, too, it is exclusively faith that saves us and it is the one great work Christians have to do in sanctification. Faith breaks all self-reliance and fastens on to God's promise. Having first received, faith can now give; having opened our hearts to the grace of God and experiencing the joy of communion with Christ in the power of the Holy Spirit, faith awakens our gratitude and enables us to do great things. Faith prompts the believer to say: "I can do all things through Christ who strengthens me" (Phil. 4:13). Faith allows the law to stand and refuses to lower the moral ideal, but also refrains from all attempts to find salvation, life, and peace through its observance. It is out of faith working through love that believers seek to do God's will as expressed in the Ten Commandments. Both nomists and antinomians forget that the law of God is rich and full and cannot be reduced to "precept upon precept, line upon line." The commandments must be understood in their augmentation and application by the prophets and by our Lord. In our time antinomianism achieved its greatest triumph in Friedrich Nietzsche, who called good evil and evil good, and enthroned moral anarchism. This anarchism in morality, preceded by anarchy of thought, and followed by anarchy of action, produces another "double morality" and is a particular temptation for those who are really "in the know" (γνωστικοι, *gnōstikoi*)—intellectuals and artists, geniuses and heroes—and who claim to be above the "common morality" of "horde." Even Nietzsche considered his morality to be fit only for "supermen." Moral anarchism, however, bore such pernicious fruit in practice that it could not be recommended as a universal rule of life.

Although nomism is diametrically opposed to this antinomianism, it nevertheless shows some kinship with it, particularly as it too has led to a similar, though differently articulated, dualism in morality. Rome's distinction between "precepts" of the law which are valid for all and "evangelical counsels" which are not binding for all Christians but may be followed by those who wish to merit "sainthood," and similar distinctions in Pietism, Methodism, and related religious movements, all start out with a desire to reform the church and elevate its morality, but end up creating a small church (*ecclesiola*) of elite Christians in the broader church (*ecclesia*). The life of Christian holiness is only for some.

There is a truth in this double morality with which Protestantism has not sufficiently dealt. However many theoretical reservations we may have about the men and women who with total self-denial and extraordinary dedication devote themselves to the cause of Christ, practically and spontaneously we deeply admire them. It is too easy for us to say that the renunciation of all earthly goods, abstention from marriage, avoidance of the world, and enduring all sorts of misery and pain all arise from a desire for merit and reward; it is hard to prove and thereby also too easy to dismiss our Lord's instruction in the Sermon on the Mount along with similar injunctions in the New Testament. Individual believers do possess the Christian liberty to apply the deeper life of love to their own circumstances and contexts, but there are also cases in which what is in itself permissible becomes impermissible (Rom. 14:21, 23; 1 Cor. 8:13; 10:23); and there also are circumstances in which abstention from marriage (Matt. 19:11; 1 Cor. 7:7), giving up remuneration (1 Cor. 9:14–19), the renunciation of all earthly goods (Matt. 19:21), or the like, is a duty. Both the realm of Christian liberty (adiaphora) and the "counsels of perfection" must be seen within the unity and universality of the moral law. When a double morality becomes legalistic, it usually leads to perfectionism and works righteousness.

[483] Advocates of a double morality eventually all arrive at the doctrine of the perfectibility of the saints, the meritoriousness of good works, and the transferability of merits. Nomism leads naturally to perfectionism,[84] which is a heresy that has again arisen in our day. Ritschl and others claim that Paul himself, after being converted, had no consciousness of being imperfect and failed to reflect on such consciousness in believers in general;[85] he was an impractical idealist who, under the impression of Christ's imminent return, completely overlooked the presence of sin in the lives of believers.[86] The element of truth in this assertion is that Scripture can scarcely find words enough to describe the glory of the people of God: In the Old Testament Israel is called a priestly kingdom, chosen and loved by God, his very own possession and inheritance, his son and servant, made perfect in beauty by the glory of God (Exod. 19:5–6; Deut. 7:7ff.; 32:6, 8–9, 18; Isa. 41:8; Ezek. 16:14; etc.); the New Testament uses language such as salt of the earth (Matt. 5:13), light of the world (v. 14), born of God and his children (John 1:12–13), his elect race and royal priesthood (1 Pet. 2:9–10), sharing in the divine nature (2 Pet. 1:4), anointed with the Holy Spirit (1 John 2:20), made kings and priests by Christ (Rev. 1:5), unable to sin (1 John 3:9; 5:18ff.), and so forth. Scripture assigns a high position to the church, calls it by splendid names, and ascribes to it a holiness and glory that render it godlike. This is not hyperbole but the description that comes from faith. Yet, Paul does know his sin; in spite of his intentions, evil lies close at hand (Rom. 7:21); he lives in the flesh (Gal. 2:20), the flesh's desires are opposed to the Spirit (Gal. 5:17), nothing good dwells in his flesh (Rom. 7:18), and he has not attained perfection (Phil. 3:12).

84. Cf. H. Bavinck, *Reformed Dogmatics*, IV, 237–48 (##478–79); L. Lemme, "Vollkommenheit," in *PRE*³, XX, 733; O. Zöckler, "Perfectionisten of Oneida-Kommunisten in Amerika," in *PRE*³, XV, 130. Ed. note: Remarkably, Bavinck fails to mention the important and thorough work of Benjamin B. Warfield, *Perfectionism*, in *The Works of Benjamin B. Warfield*, 10 vols. (New York: Oxford University Press, 1929–1932; repr., Grand Rapids: Baker Academic, 1991), vols. VII and VIII.

85. A. Ritschl, *Die christliche Lehre von der Rechtfertigung und Versöhnung*, 4th ed., 3 vols. (Bonn: A. Marcus, 1895–1903), II, 365.

86. H. Scholz, "Zur Lehre vom 'Armen Sünder,'" *Zeitschrift für Theologie und Kirche* 6 (1896): 463ff.

Romans 7:7–25 is especially important for rejecting perfectionism and for maintaining the Reformational understanding that the tension of sin and grace continues in the regenerate's life. The strongest reason for maintaining the Reformation interpretation of Romans 7 lies in the text itself, where the present tense that Paul uses can only be understood of the present. "In reality one turns the Apostle into a comedian if one believes he could only speak as he does here in the recollection of a state he left behind years before," says Clemen.[87] Scripture everywhere proceeds from the assumption that sin remains a reality in believers throughout their lives. They are in permanent need of the prayer for forgiveness (Matt. 6:12–13) and confession of sins (1 John 1:9). All the admonitions and warnings in Scripture presuppose that believers have only a small beginning of perfect obedience. They all make many mistakes every day (James 3:2). If they say they have no sin, they deceive themselves (1 John 1:8). Still, Scripture never weakens the demands of the law or tailors it to accommodate the weakness of believers. This is something that nomistic perfectionists do; they degrade the moral law and make a distinction between mortal and venial sins, or between committing and harboring sin, and similarly between earthly and heavenly, relative and absolute perfection. But Scripture demands: "Be holy as I am holy" (1 Pet. 1:16); "Be perfect as your heavenly Father is perfect" (Matt. 5:48; James 1:4). We face a clear choice: If our works are imperfect and incomplete, all meritoriousness of our works disappears. This is the Reformation's answer to Rome. Furthermore, all notions of possible perfection in this life require a weakening of the law's demands and adaptation to existing practice. In both cases the organic unity of God's moral law is lost and therefore also the unity of the work of Christ. The Methodist separation of sanctification from justification as an isolated benefit obtained by a special act of faith (the "double cure") misconstrues the life of faith. Faith in Christ is a unitary act that actively appropriates the whole Christ and his benefits. In Christ, we are forgiven and holy; we grow more and more into Christ our head until we reach the fullness of our life in him and see him face to face. Now we are able to understand Scripture's language of "reward." Our works are not something offered to God for which we receive the "wage" of eternal life. God speaks to us in the language of "reward" to give us eschatological incentives.[88] God on his part pictures the salvation and glory he desires to give to his children using the imagery of wages and reward. He does that to spur on, to encourage, and to comfort his children, who being his children, are also already his heirs. We must avoid all literalism here; the economic realm fails us completely. A better earthly analogy is found in human relations when acts of service and love—a son helping a father, a physician healing a sick person, artists who create beauty for others, inventors who benefit the human race—receive recognition, honor, and

87. Carl Clemen, *Die christliche Lehre von der Sünde* (Göttingen: Vandenhoek & Ruprecht, 1897), I, 112, who also refers to W. C. van Manen, *De brief aan de Romeinen* (Leiden: Brill, 1891), 71.

88. Ed. note: The expression "eschatological incentive" is not Bavinck's but the editor's; it does, however, accurately capture his thought.

even tangible rewards. But, the activity is not understood correctly when viewed in strict economic terms as a "work for hire." What child of God would have the nerve to let such an idea arise in one's mind and express it before the judgment seat of God? The "works" we offer to God, when done from true faith, conform to God's law, and are done for his glory, to delight our God. That is also our reward and is itself a gift of grace.

[484] Scripture speaks of the perseverance of the saints as it does of sanctification—as both gift and task. The New Testament repeatedly admonishes believers to remain faithful, to stay true to their Savior and Lord (Matt. 24:13; John 15:1–10; Rom. 2:7–8; Col. 1:23; Heb. 2:1; 3:14; 6:11; 1 John 2:6, 24, 27; 3:6, 24; 4:12ff), even unto death (Rev. 2:10, 26). Sometimes it speaks as if apostasy is a possibility: "If you think you are standing, watch out that you do not fall" (1 Cor. 10:12); it threatens heavy punishment for unfaithfulness (Ezek. 18:24; Matt. 13:20–21; John 15:2; Rom. 11:20, 22; 2 Tim. 2:12; Heb. 4:1; 6:4–8; 10:26–31; 2 Pet. 2:18–22). On the basis of some texts that describe falling away (Gal. 5:4; 1 Tim. 1:19–20; 4:1; 2 Tim. 2:17–18; 4:10), many traditions have taught the possibility of a complete loss of the grace received. Augustine, on the other hand, arrived at the confession of the perseverance of the saints; the Reformed alone maintained this doctrine and linked it with the assurance of faith.[89] The question is not whether believers on their own can maintain or lose their faith; the question is whether God upholds, continues, and completes the work of grace he has begun, or whether he sometimes permits it to be totally ruined by the power of sin. Perseverance is not an activity of the human person but a gift from God. Among the Reformed the doctrine of perseverance is seen as a gift of God who assures that the work of grace is continued and completed, which he does through believers. In regeneration and faith, he grants a grace that as such bears an inadmissible character; he grants a life that is by nature eternal; he bestows the benefits of calling, justification, and glorification that are mutually and unbreakably interconnected.

In the case of those Scriptures that seem to point to true believers falling away (1 Tim. 4:1; Heb. 6:4–8; 10:26–31; 2 Pet. 2:1, 18–22), we must plead ignorance; we do not know, either whether they had truly received the grace of regeneration, *or* whether they really lost it. It is therefore completely mistaken to reason from the admonitions of Holy Scripture to the possibility of a total loss of grace. The certainty of the outcome does not render the means superfluous but is inseparably connected with them in the decree of God. Paul knew with certainty that in the case of shipwreck no one would lose one's life, yet he declares, "Unless these men stay in the ship, you cannot be saved" (Acts 27:22, 31). When Scripture expressly states that it is *impossible* to restore to repentance those who are in view in these

---

89. Heidelberg Catechism, Q 1, 53–54; Canons of Dort, V; F. Schleiermacher, *The Christian Faith*, ed. H. R. MacIntosh and J. S. Steward (Edinburgh: T&T Clark, 1928), §111; J. J. van Oosterzee, *Christian Dogmatics*, trans. J. Watson and M. Evans, 2 vols. (New York: Scribner, Armstrong, 1874), §121.

texts (Heb. 6:4; 10:26; 2 Pet. 2:20; 1 John 5:16), it cannot be denied that the reference is to a sin that carries with it a judgment of hardening and that makes repentance impossible. There is only one such sin, namely, the sin of blasphemy against the Holy Spirit.[90]

Those who deny perseverance of the saints have their own theological and pastoral problems. They are forced to multiply distinctions such as the one between the sins by which the grace of regeneration is lost and other sins by which it is not lost; for example, the Roman Catholic distinction between mortal and venial sins. Elaborate and oppressive casuistries then need to be invented so that the believer can test whether grace has been irrevocably lost or not. How can a believer find assurance and work in the joy and peace of salvation for greater sanctification? If apostasy of the saints is possible, furthermore, the difficulties are not removed but multiplied. If one holds on to God's immutable decrees then all human willing cannot undo the outcome; if one denies predestination and foreknowledge in any sense, everything becomes uncertain and unstable, including the love of the Father, the grace of the Son, and the communion of the Holy Spirit. Ultimately, right up until the hour of one's death—indeed, why not also on the other side of the grave?—the human will remains the decisive and all-controlling power. Everything will be as that will determines it will be.

Scripture, however, teaches a very different doctrine: In the Old Testament, while the covenant of grace carries with it the obligation to walk in the way of the covenant, the covenant of grace does not depend on the obedience of human beings. It depends solely on God's faithfulness. When Israel becomes unfaithful and adulterous, the prophets do not conclude from this that God changes, that his covenant wavers, and that his promises fail; on the contrary: God cannot and may not break his covenant because he has voluntarily—with a solemn oath—bound himself by it to Israel. When Paul confronts the same fact of Israel's unfaithfulness, his heart filled with grief, he does not conclude that the word of God has failed, but continues to believe in God's compassion, is sure that God's gifts and calling are irrevocable, and that not all who are descended from Israel belong to Israel (Rom. 9–11). Similarly, John testifies of those who fell away: they were not of us or else they would have continued with us (1 John 2:19). The covenant of grace is firm and confirmed with an oath (Heb. 6:16–18; 13:20), unbreakable like a marriage (Eph. 5:31–32), like a testament (Heb. 9:17), and by virtue of that covenant, God calls his elect. He inscribes the law on their inmost being, puts his fear in their hearts (Heb. 8:10; 10:14ff.), will not let them be tempted beyond their strength (1 Cor. 10:13), confirms and completes the good work he has begun in them (1 Cor. 1:9; Phil. 1:6), and keeps them for the return of Christ to receive the heavenly inheritance (1 Thess. 5:23; 2 Thess. 3:3; 1 Pet. 1:4–5). Those who are called are also glorified (Rom. 8:30). Those who are adopted as children are heirs of eternal life (8:17; Gal. 4:7). Those who believe have eternal

90. Cf. H. Bavinck, *Reformed Dogmatics*, III, 155–57 (#334).

life already here and now (John 3:16). That life itself, being eternal, cannot be lost. It cannot die since it cannot sin (1 John 3:9). Faith is a firm ground (Heb. 11:1), hope is an anchor (6:19) and does not disappoint us (Rom. 5:5), and love never ends (1 Cor. 13:8). God cannot and will not abandon his people. Faith will never disappoint us.

PART VI

THE SPIRIT CREATES
A NEW COMMUNITY

21

THE CHURCH
AS A SPIRITUAL REALITY

THE CHURCH'S SPIRITUAL ESSENCE

[485] Although the term "church" is restricted to Christianity, there are analogies to the Christian church in other religions. We are by nature social beings, "political animals" (ζῷον πολιτικον, *zōon politikon*);[1] we are born out of, in, and for community and cannot for a moment exist apart from it. Because we are all image bearers of God and our relationship with God flows out to other human beings, religion includes a powerful social element.[2] The religious bond is the strongest form of all human community; religion cannot be purely individual and private. Since a person's very soul and salvation are at stake in religion, every religion seeks to propagate itself and engages in mission. Religion always produces a common dogma and a common form of worship, sustained as it were by the consciousness that humanity as a whole is the completed image of God, his temple and body. Apart from special revelation, however, the sense of the oneness of God and of humanity has been universally lost; unity is limited to the members of one's own tribe or people in which civil and religious com-

---

1. Ed. note: Without attribution, Bavinck here directly cites Aristotle, "Man is a political animal" (from *Politica*, 1253a2, 1253a3; ET: *Politics*, trans. C. Lord (Chicago: University of Chicago Press, 1984), 37.
2. F. Schleiermacher, *The Christian Faith*, ed. H. R. MacIntosh and J. S. Steward (Edinburgh: T&T Clark, 1928), §6; C. P. Tiele, *Elements of the Science of Religion*, 2 vols. (Edinburgh and London: W. Blackwood & Sons, 1897–99), II, 155–58.

munity coincide. The state itself is also a cultic community. Although there have arisen some independent forms of priesthood, sacrifices, ceremonies, and secret societies, none of the pagan religions produced an independent organization like the church in Christianity. Islam only founded a kind of theocratic state, while Buddhism only formed societies of world-avoiding monks who exerted paralyzing pressure on civil society and never achieved independence from the state.[3]

The foundations of the Christian church were laid in the Old Testament where the covenant community of Israel was both a national and religious community, governed by a single divine law. Although there was no regulated common cult—families of believers were religious communities, fathers serving as priests—Genesis 4:26 implies that the Sethites—not the Cainites—began to call on and proclaim the name of YHWH, and after the flood a split occurred among the Shemites, the Japhethites, and the Hamites. When God established a covenant with Abraham and his offspring, he externally separated the church from the world by the sign of circumcision. At the foot of Mount Sinai, it was confirmed and elevated to a national covenant. Although the church and state were not identical in Israel where priest and king, temple and palace, religious and civil laws remained differentiated,[4] the two were so closely united that citizens and believers, the nation and the people of God, coincided, and it was a single divine law that controlled the entire life of Israel. Israel as a people was an עֵדָה יהוה (ʿēdâ YHWH) or a קְהַל יהוה (qāhāl YHWH). Both words are used in the Old Testament for the assembly or congregation of Israel without any distinction in meaning.

However, after the exile, Judaism became a religious community only, gathered for worship in the temple and, more importantly, during the Diaspora, in the synagogue where assemblies of believers came together on the Sabbath (Ps. 74:8; Acts 15:21) to read the Torah and be instructed in it. The primary component of the synagogue worship service was teaching (Mark 1:21; 6:2). These meetings (συναγωγη, synagōgē) increasingly became the center of Jewish religious life; the temple at Jerusalem continued to exist and was still honored as the location of God's special presence, yet the Jews of the Diaspora found their worship in preaching and prayer apart from the temple and the altar, the priesthood and sacrifices. The Greek words συναγωγη (synagōgē) and ἐκκλησια (ekklēsia) were originally used interchangeably for these religious assemblies of the Jews, but a distinction gradually arose such that συναγωγη tended to denote the empirical assembly (congregation, meeting) and ἐκκλησια became the word for the ideal

---

3. P. D. Chantepie de la Saussaye, *Lehrbuch der Religionsgeschichte*, 2 vols. (Freiburg i.B.: Mohr [Siebeck], 1887–89), I, 132; C. P. Tiele, *Elements of the Science of Religion*, II, 155–81; R. Falke, *Buddha, Mohammed, Christus*, 2nd ed., 2 vols. (Gütersloh: C. Bertelsmann, 1900), II, 155ff.

4. Ed. note: What Bavinck takes note of here is the basis for the modern democratic conviction that church and state must be *institutionally* separate. This is not to be confused with the *removal* of all religious commitment from the public square.

community defined as those whom God had called to his salvation (convocation, community).⁵

[486] The Christian church, initially often gathered in synagogues, soon became designated by the word ἐκκλησια (*ekklēsia*). Christ himself first applied the word קָהָל, ἐκκλησια to the church community he gathered around himself (Matt. 16:18; 18:17). The conjectures of modern critics that this word was later put in Jesus's mouth⁶ are groundless. There is nothing unusual about Jesus employing this word in a general sense and calling the group of disciples gathered around him קָהָל (ἐκκλησια). When Jesus uses this word in Matthew 16:18 and 18:17 with reference to his "church," he is therefore still employing it in a very general sense. There is more at stake here, however: was Jesus conscious from the beginning of his Sonship, messiahship, and future suffering,⁷ and did he intend to form a new Israel by restoring the true קָהָל?⁸ The full awareness of this was not known to the disciples before the ascension and Pentecost, for as yet the Spirit had not been given (John 7:39). After the ascension, the community of Christ believers became the church, an independent religious assembly acting in the place of Israel as the new people of God. In Acts 5:11; 11:26; 1 Corinthians 11:18; 14:19, 28, 35 the word ἐκκλησια clearly refers to the gathering or assembly of the congregation; but elsewhere it refers repeatedly to the church itself, even when it is not gathered, and one can therefore speak of ἐκκλησιαι (*ekklēsiai*) in the plural (Rom. 16:4; 1 Cor. 16:1; Gal. 1:2; 1 Thess. 2:14; etc.). Begun in Jerusalem, the church spread into Asia Minor, yet even as the church grew, many passages conceive all the churches as one ἐκκλησια and described as the body, the bride, or the fullness (πληρωμα, *plērōma*) of Christ (Rom. 12:5; 1 Cor. 12:12–28; 15:9; Gal. 1:13; Eph. 1:22; 5:32; Phil. 3:6; and Col. 1:18, 24–25). The word underscores the basic organic unity of individual congregations and local gatherings of believers in the one universal body of Christ. The ἐκκλησια is the elect people of God. The church's unity does not come into being a posteriori by the establishment of a creed, a church order, and a synodical system, and she is not an association of individual persons who first became believers apart from the church and subsequently united themselves. The church is an organism in which the whole exists prior to the parts; its unity precedes the plurality of local churches and rests in Christ her head (Eph. 1:23; 4:16; 5:23; Col. 1:18; 2:19), who gathers and governs it (John 10:16; 11:52; 17:20–21; Acts 2:33, 47; 9:3ff.), always remains with it (Matt. 18:20), is most

5. E. Schürer, *The History of the Jewish People in the Age of Jesus Christ* (*175 B.C.–A.D. 135*), rev. and ed. Géza Vermès and Fergus Millar (Edinburgh: T&T Clark, 1979), II, 423–53 (German reference: *Die Geschichte des jüdischen Volkes im zeitalter Jesu Christi*, 4th ed. [Leipzig: Hinrichs, 1907], II, 497ff.); H. L. Strack, "Synagogen," in *PRE*³, XIX, 223.

6. A. von Harnack, *The Constitution and Law of the Church in the First Two Centuries* (London: Williams & Norgate; New York: Putnam & Sons, 1910), 15.

7. Cf. H. Bavinck, *Reformed Dogmatics*, ed. John Bolt (Grand Rapids: Baker Academic, 2003–8), III, 248–53 (#355).

8. Cf. T. Zahn, *Das Evangelium des Matthäus*, 4th ed. (Leipzig: A. Deichert, 1922), 540.

intimately connected with it (John 15:1ff.; 17:21, 23; 1 Cor. 6:15; 12:12–27; Gal. 2:20), and dwells in it by his Holy Spirit (Rom 6:5; 8:9–11; 1 Cor. 6:15ff.; Eph. 3:17; etc.). Every local church is the people of God, the body of Christ, built on the foundation of Christ (1 Cor. 3:11, 16; 12:27), because in that location it is the same as what the church is in its entirety, and Christ is for that local church what he is for the universal church.[9] In its broadest sense the ἐκκλησια is the gathering of all the people of God, not only on earth but also in heaven (Heb. 12:23), not only in the past and present but also in the future (John 10:16; 17:20).

UNITY AND CATHOLICITY

[487] This spiritual unity of the church of Christ continually comes to the fore also in the postapostolic period. Christians are the saints, the elect; they have one God, one Christ, one Spirit of grace, one calling.[10] Christians are the soul of the world,[11] the true Israel, the blessed people of God;[12] they are all priests[13] and have all received the Holy Spirit,[14] and their common unity is proved "by fellowship in communion, by the name of brother, and the mutual pledge of hospitality,"[15] and so forth. In the face of challenges to the apostolic faith, the natural question arose: "Which is the true church?" Increasingly the answer given was: "The church that remains with the body as a whole; i.e, maintains fellowship with the Catholic Church." The true Catholic Church embraces all believers on earth at all times and places, and outside it there is no salvation.[16] Thus the unity and catholicity of the church was increasingly externalized and embodied in institutional form. The development of this "catholic" view of the church was fostered by opposition from heretical sects such as the Novatianists and Donatists. Responding to claims of the sects that they had the Holy Spirit, Irenaeus wrote: "For where the church is, there is the Spirit of God, and where the Spirit of God is, there is the church and every kind of grace, but the Spirit is truth."[17] According to Cyprian, just as there is only one God and one Lord, so there is also but one church, one flock, one mother out of which all believers are born and outside of which there is no salvation.[18]

Augustine, too, thanks especially to his controversy with the Donatists (AD 393–411), was forced to reflect more intentionally on the church's nature. Still,

---

9. T. Zahn, *Introduction to the New Testament*, 3 vols. (Edinburgh: T&T Clark, 1909), I, 509.

10. *1 Clem.* 46.

11. *Diogn.* 6.

12. Justin Martyr, *Dialogue with Trypho*, 116, 123, 135.

13. Irenaeus, *Against Heresies*, IV, 8.3; Tertullian, *Exhortation to Chastity*, 7.

14. Irenaeus, *Against Heresies*, IV, 36.2.

15. Tertullian, *Prescription against Heretics*, 20.

16. *1 Clem.* 57; Ign. *Eph.* 16; Ign. *Trall.* 7; Ign. *Phld.* 3; Herm. *Sim.* 9.16.

17. Irenaeus, *Against Heresies*, III, 24, 1; Tertullian, *On Prayer*, 2; Clement of Alexandria, *Paedagogus*, I, 6; idem, *Stromateis*, VIII, 17.

18. Cyprian, *De unitate ecclesiae* (New York and Toronto: Macmillan, 1928), 5, 7.

grace and not the doctrine of the church became the central focus of his thinking and life. For Augustine, while the church is not the dispenser of grace, he defends her as the "mother" of believers, the circle within which God as a rule grants grace, the place where the Spirit, love, and perseverance are present and outside which there is no salvation. Thus, he is not a perfectionist about the church and distinguishes between the church as "the true body" and the church as "the mixed body" [of Christ].[19] "There is chaff among the wheat; there are bad fish among the good; there are many sheep outside and many wolves inside."[20] "Many who are in the fellowship of the sacraments *with* the church are nevertheless not *in* the church."[21] The church is the "devoted mother," "the bride without spot or wrinkle," "the precious dove," "the holy church" and remains so even if the ungodly are in the majority, since to Augustine all its holiness is to be found much more in the objective institution with its doctrine, means of grace, and cult than in its members. Those who do not have the church as their mother do not have God as their Father.[22] The net effect of all this is that the universal church increases in importance; the local churches no longer have historical priority for they are only parts of the whole and are true churches only for as long as they remain with that body as a whole and submit to its episcopate.

The climax of this doctrine of the church was reached in the medieval notion of the "teaching church" (*ecclesia docens*) with its hierarchical structures and grace-imparting sacraments, which is anterior to the listening church (*ecclesia audiens*) and highly elevated above it. The latter is passively subservient to the former and its highest virtue—necessary to salvation—is belief in what the church believes, obedience to the hierarchy, and submission to the pope. "Where the pope is, there is the church" (*ubi papa, ibi ecclesia*). The nature of the church therefore does not depend on the quality of this "listening church" since the objective "teaching church" would remain the true church even if all its members were unbelievers and ungodly people. The hierarchical, institutional church is all-important, as necessary as the body is to the human soul. External participation in its sacraments is essential for salvation. For the church is as "visible and palpable as the assembly of the people of Rome or the kingdom of Gaul or the republic of the Venetians. It is a gathering of humans bound together by profession of the same Christian faith and participation in the same sacraments under the control of legitimate pastors and particularly of Christ's vicar on earth, the pope of Rome."[23]

19. Augustine, *On Christian Doctrine*, III, 32.

20. Chrysostom, *Homilie in Joannem*, 45; Augustine, *Against the Letters of Petilianus*, III, 3; idem, *On Baptism*, I, 10.

21. Augustine, *De unitate ecclesiae liber*, I, 74; ed. note: This work is also known as *Ad catholicos fratres* and is not available in English translation; Latin text is in PL 43:391–446; and in *Corpus scriptorum ecclesiasticorum latinorum* (Vienna: Tempsky, 1909), 52:231–322.

22. Augustine, *On Baptism*, VII, 44; idem, *De unitate ecclesiae liber*, I; idem, *Answer to Letters of Petilian*, III, 9 (*NPNF¹*, IV).

23. R. Bellarmine, "De eccl. mil.," in *De controversiis christianae fidei adversus huius temporis haereticos* (Cologne: G. Gualtheri, 1617–20), III, 1.

[488] It was this vision of the church that was resisted by sectarian movements such as the Albigensians and Waldensians, by John Wycliffe and John Huss. In their case the criterion for identifying the true church was not found in the objective ministry of Word and sacrament but in holy living, in life lived according to the law of Christ in love, poverty, and so forth. Hence the transition from the idea of the church to the reality of the world was lacking; attempts at reformation could not carry over into other areas or they ended in disappointment.[24] Not until the sixteenth-century Reformation was a fundamentally different view of the church posited as an alternative to Rome. Luther found peace for his soul, not in the sacrament, which worked *ex opere operato*, nor in good works, but in the forgiveness of sins by faith alone. Rejecting the importance of externals such as priesthood, sacrifices, monasticism, and the sacramental efficacy of the institutional church, he proclaimed the freedom of the Christian and viewed the church as a gathering of believers, a "communion of saints." A distinction was made between the visible and invisible church, the latter being an object of faith. The true visible church is marked by pure administration of the Word and sacraments; the church is the communion of saints, the congregation of the faithful. Where the Word is preached and sacraments administered according to the Word, one can be certain a church is present even if only among infants in the cradle. "God's Word cannot be without God's people." Over against Rome, the distinction between a visible and an invisible church asserted that the essence of the church consists in that which is invisible, in faith, in communion with Christ and his benefits by the Holy Spirit. It was also used to acknowledge that "in this life many evil persons and hypocrites are mixed in with the church, who, though in the matter of the rites of the church they are members of the true church, nevertheless do not form the church and belong rather to the kingdom of the devil."[25]

For Reformed theology the invisible church was characterized especially as the elect, known only to God.[26] While God ordinarily grants the benefits of Christ by means of Word and sacraments, he is not bound to this method and very rarely also grants salvation outside the institution of the church.[27] In addition, the

24. A. von Harnack, *History of Dogma*, trans. N. Buchanan, J. Millar, E. B. Speirs, and W. McGilchrist, and ed. A. B. Bruce, 7 vols. (London: Williams & Norgate, 1896–99), VI, 118–49.

25. Joseph T. Müller, *Die symbolischen Bücher der evangelisch-lutherischen Kirche*, 8th ed. (Gütersloh: Bertelsmann, 1898), 153–55; ed. note: This specific reference is to the Apology of the Augsburg Confession, art. 7, pars. 9–16, in *The Book of Concord*, ed. Robert Kolb and Timothy J. Wengert (Minneapolis: Fortress, 2000), 174–77.

26. Genevan Catechism, in *Calvin: Theological Treatises*, ed. J. K. S. Reid, Library of Christian Classics (Philadephia: Westminster, 1954), 103; also in E. F. K. Müller, *Die Bekenntnisschriften der reformierten Kirche* (Leipzig: Deichert, 1903), 126; First Scotch Confession, art. 16; Westminster Confession, art. 25; J. H. Alsted, *Theologica didactica* (Hanau: C. Eifrid, 1618), 590, etc.

27. John Calvin, *Institutes of the Christian Religion*, IV.xvi.19 (ed. John T. McNeill and trans. Ford Lewis Battles [1559; Philadelphia: Westminster, 1960], 2:1341–42); Z. Ursinus, *The Commentary of Dr. Zacharius Ursinus on the Heidelberg Catechism*, trans. G. W. Williard (Grand Rapids: Eerdmans, 1954), qu. 21.

Reformed churches also placed holy living and church discipline as a key mark. While election is the foundation of the church, it only manifests itself in faith and good works. Reformed theologians used the visible/invisible distinction in various ways as they wrestled with realities such as the presence of brokenness and hypocrites within the church while trying to avoid spiritual elitism, judgmentalism, or a split between doctrine and life.

Reformation Tangents; the People of God

[489] The Reformation brought a multiformity into the church. Taking advantage of this, Remonstrants, Socinians, and Rationalists in turn made of the church a limited religious society dedicated to bringing the kingdom of God on earth;[28] there was little room for the church as instituted by Christ. In response, mystical and pietist sectarian movements sought unity in religious experience and separatism but achieved the same result: a dualistic separation of grace from the created, natural world. Whether one considers the excesses of the Münsterites; the gentler Anabaptism of Menno Simons; the sectarian impulses of Jean de Labadie, Nicholas von Zinzendorf, and the English Independentists; or the Quakers, the church is seen as a fellowship of the spiritual who are separated from the world by voluntary actions of renunciation involving swearing oaths, civil service, and certain foods, clothing, and social contact. Similar views were found among the Methodists and later in the Salvation Army. In this world of religious imagination it is no wonder that John Darby, the founder of modern dispensational premillennialism, proceeded, openly and decisively, to reject every church and all ecclesiastical forms which he regarded as Babel, preparations for the coming of the antichrist, totally corrupt, and to be completely repudiated by true believers. Now these believers' only task is to withdraw from the world, edify each other with their respective gifts at their meetings, and quietly await the return of Christ.[29]

Although these trends seem to point in the direction of the dissolution of the church and to a radical modification of the idea of the church, there are also counter indicators. The Russian church, whose supreme government rests with the Holy Synod and is bound to the emperor [czar] by way of a procurator, maintains its claim to being the only true Orthodox church and strives, through the suppression of sects, for unity of belief throughout the empire.[30] The Roman

---

28. Apology of the Remonstrants, 21–22; ed. note: This work is found in Simon Episcopius, *Apologia pro confessione sive declaratione sententiae eorum* (n.p., 1629); ET: *The Confession or Declaration of the Ministers or Pastors Which in the United Provinces Are Called Remonstrants, concerning the Chief Points of the Christian Religion*, trans. T. Taylor (London: Francis Smith, 1676). P. van Limborch, *Theologia christiana* (Amsterdam: Arnhold, 1735), VII; I. Kant, *Religion within the Limits of Reason Alone*, trans. T. M. Greene and H. H. Hudson (New York: Harper & Brothers, 1934), 92ff., 109ff.

29. F. Kattenbusch, *Die Kirchen und Sekten des Christentums in der Gegenwart* (Tübingen: Mohr [Siebeck], 1909).

30. See K. P. Pobedonoszew, *Streitfragen der Gegenwart* (Berlin: Deubner, 1897).

Catholic Church still in principle cannot recognize and tolerate churches besides itself.[31] In spite of attempts to impose unity, the church is increasingly losing its uniform character in the modern world. The Protestant world fares no better. "The same motives of distinctive piety which lead in Catholicism to the creation of new orders tend in Protestantism to produce new sects."[32] When Protestantism understands the church as Schleiermacher did—"The Christian church takes shape through the coming together of regenerate individuals to form a system of mutual interaction and cooperation."[33]—it, too, for the sake of history, has lost sight of the church as a divine institution. Taking refuge in the terms "visible" and "invisible" church as essence and appearance, as idea and reality,[34] or speaking instead of the kingdom of God and the church,[35] or of believing community and church,[36] as ways of separating the visible, human church community from its invisible, "spiritual," and "divine" core, solves nothing. In all cases, the reality of the church as a body of Christ *on earth* is sacrificed for a nonhistorical idea or ideal. It is no surprise that many modern theologians view the church as an institution that Christ neither wanted nor intended and is in fact the reason for Christianity's corruption.[37]

[490] Scripture provides us with a rich language about the church. The word קָהָל (*qāhāl*), ἐκκλησια (*ekklēsia*), by virtue of its derivation from verbs that mean "to call together," already denotes a gathering of people who come together for some purpose and are mutually united for such a purpose. In the New Testament, God's people of Israel have been replaced by the church of Christ, which is now the "holy nation, the chosen race, the royal priesthood" of God. The word "church" (*kirk, kerk, kirche, chiesa*), used to translate ἐκκλησια, does not express as clearly as the original this character of the church of Christ. It is probably derived from κυριακη (*kyriakē*; completed by οἰκια [*oikia*, house] being understood) or κυριακον (*kyriakon*; completed by οἰκον [*oikon*, house] being understood) and hence originally meant not the congregation itself but its place of assembly, the

---

31. Ed. note: For an important updating of Bavinck's comments here, it is necessary to consult the Second Vatican Council's "Decree on Ecumenism" (*Unitatis redintegratio*) of November 21, 1964, as well as Pope John Paul II's encyclical, *Ut unum sint* (1995).

32. Albrecht Ritschl, *Geschichte des Pietismus in der reformierten Kirche*, 3 vols. (Bonn: A. Marcus, 1880), III, 303.

33. F. Schleiermacher, *The Christian Faith*, §115.

34. C. E. Nitzsch, *System of Christian Doctrine* (Edinburgh: T&T Clark, 1849), 186–88; J. P. Lange, *Christliche Dogmatik*, 3 vols. (Heidelberg: K. Winter, 1852), II, 1090ff.; H. Martensen, *Christian Dogmatics*, trans. W. Urwick (Edinburgh: T&T Clark, 1871), §191.

35. August Johannes Dorner, *Kirche und Reich Gottes* (Gotha: F. A. Perthes, 1883); Alfred Krauss, *Das protestantische Dogma von der unsichtbaren Kirche* (Gotha: F. A. Perthes, 1876).

36. Ferdinand Julius Stahl, *Die Kirchenverfassung nach Lehre und Recht der Protestanten*, 2nd ed. (Erlangen: T. Bläsing, 1862), 67; H. Bavinck, *De theologie van Daniel Chantepie de la Saussaye* (Leiden: Donner, 1884), 66ff.; J. J. van Oosterzee, *Christian Dogmatics*, trans. J. Watson and M. Evans, 2 vols. (New York: Scribner, Armstrong, 1874), §129.

37. H. Faber, *Das Christenthum der Zukunft* (Zürich: Schulthess, 1904).

church building.[38] In the word "church" the meaning of the New Testament word ἐκκλησια has been obscured and the sense that "church" is the name for "the people of God" has almost totally eroded.

Observations on translating ἐκκλησια:[39] This is also the reason why ἐκκλησια is often translated in the Dutch (and German) language by *gemeente* (*Gemeinde*) instead of *kerk* (*Kirche*). As with the English word "community," this communicates more effectively the church as a *fellowship* of believers, a communion of saints. However, since *gemeente* also serves as a civic term to denote local government entities (*gemeentehuis* = city hall; *gemeenteraad* = city council; English language parallel: "community center"), the word *kerk* has become the preferred translation and standard usage. Dutch law, in a deliberate effort to disestablish the national Dutch Reformed Church in the nineteenth century, began to use the term *kerkgenootschap* or "church society." This underscores the voluntary character of the church and its role as a social institution, but does so at the expense of its identity and its unity as the body of Christ created by the Holy Spirit.

Perhaps even more importantly, "church," as the people of God, must not be confused or identified with the eschatological notion of the kingdom of God. The kingdom is not organized on earth as the church—properly!—is; the kingdom is the special possession of the poor in spirit, the pure in heart, the "children," and consists in peace, joy, and delight engendered by the Holy Spirit. "Church" is a this-worldly term and its characteristic essence is that it is the people of God, the realization of God's own electing love. The blessings granted to the church are primarily internal and spiritual in character and consist in calling and regeneration, in faith and justification, in sanctification and glorification. They are the goods of the kingdom of heaven, benefits of the covenant of grace, promises for this life and, above all, for the life to come. Nonetheless, it is true that the benefits of the kingdom, notably the gifts of the Holy Spirit, are given to the church on earth for the mission of God's people. The gifts of the Holy Spirit are distributed to believers to benefit others, to call men and women to faith in Christ. These gifts include both supernatural and natural gifts, natural gifts that have been heightened and sanctified by the Holy Spirit. The kingdom and the church are inseparable; Christ has been given to be the head of the church

38. J. C. Suicerus, *Thesaurus ecclesiasticus* (Amsterdam: J. H. Wetsten, 1682), s.v. ἐκκλησια; J. Köstlin, "Kirche," in *PRE*[3], X, 316. Some scholars still dispute this derivation and consider *circus* to be the source (ibid., 317). Also, according to E. Glaser (*Woher kommt das Wort "Kirche"?* [Munich: H. Lukaschik, 1901]), the word is derived from the root *krk* or *krkh* (from the Syriac *karkha* = a specific place) so that the word refers to the church building as a fortress or castle of God.

39. Ed. note: This paragraph is a highly condensed adaptation of more than a page of text in the Dutch original, where Bavinck provides a detailed discussion of the complications in translating ἐκκλησια into the Dutch language. His chief concern is to remind his Dutch readers not to forget that though the word *kerk* includes the building, the institution, and the civil/societal dimension of the fellowship of Christian believers in a specific time and place, the church is first and above all the body of Christ, the fellowship of the Holy Spirit, the communion of the saints, those who have been *called out*.

precisely in order that in the end God might publicly appear as king of his people and be all things in all people.[40]

On these grounds, the church is the body of Christ (1 Cor. 12:27; Eph. 5:23; Col. 1:18), the bride of Christ (2 Cor. 11:2; Eph. 5:32; Rev. 19:7; 21:2), the sheepfold of Christ who gives his life for the sheep and is known by them (John 10), the building, the temple, the house of God (Matt. 16:18; Eph. 2:20; 1 Pet. 2:5), built up out of living stones (1 Pet. 2:5) on Christ as the cornerstone, and on the foundation of apostles and prophets (1 Cor. 3:17; 2 Cor. 6:16–17; Eph. 2:20–22; Rev. 21:2–4), the people, the possession, the Israel of God (Rom. 9:25; 2 Cor. 6:16; Heb. 8:10; 1 Pet. 2:9–10). Organic images such as vine and branches (John 15) are used to contrast believers from those who are chaff (Matt. 3:12), bad branches in the vine (John 15:2), called but not chosen (Matt. 22:14). In its *essence* the church is a gathering of true believers. Those who do not have an authentic faith may externally belong to the church but do not make up its essential character; in the church, they are not the church.

This is confirmed by the manner in which Scripture speaks of the communion of saints. Believers have one Lord, one baptism, one God and Father of all, and similarly they have one Spirit (Eph. 4:4–6), in whose fellowship they live, by whom they are regenerated, baptized into one body, and united with Christ (John 3:5; 14:17; Rom. 8:9, 14, 16; 1 Cor. 12:3, 13; 2 Cor. 1:22; 5:5; Eph. 1:13; 4:30; 1 John 2:20). In this oneness the Spirit does not undo but rather maintains and confirms the diversity that exists among believers. The charismata include the benefits of grace imparted to all believers (Rom. 5:15–16; 6:23), but in a more restricted sense denote those special gifts that are granted to believers in variable measure and degree for each other's benefit (Rom. 1:11; 1 Cor. 1:7; 2 Cor. 1:11; 1 Tim. 4:14; 2 Tim. 1:6; and particularly Rom. 12:6–9 and 1 Cor. 12:12ff.). The Holy Spirit, who takes them all from Christ (John 16:13–14; Eph. 4:7), is the distributor of all these gifts. It is hard to classify the lists of gifts in the New Testament. Some clearly bear a supernatural character while others tend to be more like natural gifts that have been heightened and sanctified by the Holy Spirit. The former were more prominent in the early days of the church; the latter are more characteristic of the church in its normal historical development. They are to be shared[41] and used "readily and cheerfully for the benefit and enrichment of the other members,"[42] for the upbuilding of the church (1 Cor. 14:12; Eph. 4:12). The gifts are subordinate to love, which is the most excellent gift (1 Cor. 13). This love, greater than the universal love of one's neighbor, is love for the brothers and sisters, the members of the household of faith. Jesus calls this love a new commandment (John 13:34–35; 15:12; 17:26) because, unlike the love among

---

40. F. A. Philippi, *Kirchliche Glaubenslehre*, 3rd ed., 7 vols. (Gütersloh: Bertelsmann, 1883–1902), V, 3, 203; F. H. R. Frank, *System der christlichen Wahrheit*, II, 375; Julius Kaftan, *Dogmatik* (Tübingen: Mohr, 1901), 584.

41. J. Calvin, *Institutes*, IV.i.3.

42. Heidelberg Catechism, A. 55.

those who are intertwined with ties of blood as Israel was, Jesus calls his disciples to practice a pure love, unmixed with other things, free from all earthly attachments. In Christ we are brothers and sisters (Matt. 12:48; 18:15; 23:8; 25:40; 28:10; John 15:14–15; 20:17; Rom. 8:29; Heb. 2:11; and so forth), children of one family, with God as our Father (Eph. 4:6) and Jesus as our eldest brother (Rom. 8:29). The church is a fellowship or communion of saints.[43]

[491] In its broadest sense, then, the church embraces all who have been saved by faith in Christ or will be saved thus. When defined in this manner, Adam and Eve *before* the fall do not yet belong to the church, for they did not yet need a Savior. Neither can angels be counted as members of it, as many theologians have done; for while Christ is indeed the Lord of angels and has by his cross reconciled all things, including angels and humans, to God and to each other, angels were not created in God's image, did not fall, and have not been redeemed by Christ, and so are not members of the church that Christ gathers to eternal life.[44] The members of the church are only people who have been saved by faith in Christ. All the believers who lived on earth from the time of the paradisal promise to this very moment are members as well as those who will later, even to the end of the ages, believe in Christ. Thus, the church as the gathering of believers who at a given time live on earth (the church militant) is only a small part of the church taken in its broadest sense. Still it is one single gathering, one ἐκκλησια (*ekklēsia*), composed of those who are enrolled in heaven and who will one day stand before God as a bride without spot or wrinkle. Our sense of that unity gives courage to the church militant; we are part of an enormous company of witnesses (Heb. 12:1) that began in Paradise (Gen. 3:15)—or, as it concerns the time of the New Testament, in Jerusalem (Acts 1:8)—and remains until our Lord's return. In this sense, the universal church is antecedent to the particular or local church; she is an organism in which the whole is prior to the parts.

From the earliest times, the church has wrestled with the problem of unbelievers in her midst. In the Old Testament, the entire nation was called the people of God, although far from everything that was called Israel was of Israel. In the churches of the New Testament, though to a much lesser extent, there was also chaff amid the grain and weeds among the wheat. Theology, like Scripture, acknowledges this fact and consistently states that the basic nature of the church is determined by believers, not unbelievers.[45] Even though the churches after the apostolic period repeatedly became worldly, corrupt, and divided, we still call all of them churches. From Augustine to the Roman Catechism the church has recognized that according to Scripture there are weeds in the field and chaff on the

43. Cf. H. Bavinck, *Reformed Dogmatics*, III, 499–506 (##412–13); W. Ames, *The Marrow of Theology*, trans. J. D. Eusden (1968; repr., Grand Rapids: Baker Academic, 1997), I, 31–32 (pp. 175–81); A. Neander, *History of the Planting and Training of the Christian Church by the Apostles*, 2 vols. (London: Bell & Daly, 1864); Cremer, "Geistesgaben," in *PRE*³, VI, 460.
44. Cf. H. Bavinck, *Reformed Dogmatics*, II, 461–63 (#265); III, 470–75 (##407–8).
45. See H. Bavinck, *Reformed Dogmatics*, IV, 279–81 (#486).

threshing floor, foolish virgins among the wise and unclean animals in the ark.[46] Rome's problem here is that she also consistently fosters the idea that external membership, a historical faith, observance of the commandments of the church, and submission to the pope constitute the essence of the church. Over against this the Reformation posited the distinction between the visible and invisible church. This distinction can only be applied to the church militant, and then means the church is invisible with respect to its spiritual dimension and its true members. We do not call it "invisible" because we are unable to see all its members, because it goes into hiding at times of persecution, or is sometimes deprived of the ministry of the Word and sacraments. No human being has received from God the infallible standard by which one can judge another's spiritual life. "The church makes no judgment concerning the most private things."[47] The Lord alone knows those who are his. The fact is that the church is and remains an object of faith. The word "church" is applied to the people of God in terms of the believers who constitute its essential element and determine its nature. There is something metaphorical about the word "church"; the whole is called after the part; a church is and remains the gathered company of true Christ believers.

[492] Another conceptual difficulty is that the church is both a living organism, gathered by the Holy Spirit and charismatically led, and at the same time an institution structured by a specific polity. Two errors can be noted here: (1) indifference to the earthly institution in favor of a purely spiritual membership in the body of Christ, the error of enthusiasm; and (2) an identification of the church with its institutional, hierarchical structure, the error of Rome. In the former the church on earth is defined in terms of an idea or ideal, its election or its perfection; the difficulty is that election, as it exists in the mind and decree of God, is an abstraction and does not correspond to people who are actual members of a church on earth, and perfection describes no real gathering on earth. The church becomes totally invisible. The latter, where the church's essence is defined in terms of the hierarchical institution, the "teaching church" (*ecclesia docens*) rather than in the "listening church" (*ecclesia audiens*), fails to acknowledge that external membership, calling, and baptism are no proof of genuine faith; many are called who are not chosen; many baptized who do not believe. Not all are Israel who are of Israel. So, whereas the former group fails to arrive at a visible church, the latter neglects the invisible church. These errors are not addressed by identifying the visible church with the institution and the invisible church with the organism. Institution and organism are aspects of the visible church on earth, and both have an invisible spiritual background. The only resolution is to acknowledge that the old Adam that continues to exist in believers also does not belong to the church, and that the church is in a process of becoming. The true and full measure of the church's identity is not achieved until the consummation. The invisible and the

46. Roman Catechism, I, 10, qu. 6–7.
47. *De intimis non judicat ecclesia* (F. L. Rutgers, *Die kerkrecht* [Amsterdam: Wormser, 1894], art. 61).

visible are not two churches—the elect and hypocrites—but two sides of one and the same church. The same believers are viewed in the one case from the perspective of the faith that dwells in their heart and is only known with certainty to God; and in the other case they are viewed from the perspective of their witness and life, the side that is turned toward and can be observed by us. Because the church on earth is in the process of becoming, these two sides are never—not even in the purest church—identical. Although there are always unbelievers within and believers—who for one reason or another live outside the fellowship of the organized ("instituted") churches and yet have true faith—outside the church, the essence of the church consists in believers alone. The church is and always remains—until the consummation—an article of faith.

THE MARKS OF THE CHURCH

[493] Although the church's true membership is known only to God, we are not without guidance by which to discern the true church. Rome states more than it can deliver when it asks for absolute certainty on this question. The external "proofs" it proclaims such as its antiquity, the succession of its bishops, miracles, unity of its members, and the earthly prosperity of the church,[48] are every bit as subjective as the Protestant appeal to the pure administration of the Word. Even with its nuanced understanding of "credible evidences," Rome still insists that there has to be "the effective help of power from on high."[49] The deepest ground for faith, also in the case of Rome, is not Scripture or the church but the "interior light." It is God's Spirit alone that can convince a person inwardly and with full assurance of the truth of divine revelation. Rome, with its infallible church and infallible pope, fundamentally has no advantage over the churches of the Reformation, for the church and the pope, however visible, remain "articles of faith."[50] The only standard by which the church can be judged is Scripture itself. The true church really has only one mark: the Word of God, which is variously administered and confessed in preaching, instruction, confession, sacrament, and life. The Word and the Word alone is truly the soul of the church.

Rome celebrates its unity and catholicity and expresses some self-satisfaction at the divisions present in Protestantism, yet for this she pays a heavy price. Because Rome defines the essence of the church in terms of the hierarchy and papacy—"Where the pope is, there is the church" (*ubi papa, ibi ecclesia*)—it is easy to overlook the fact that there are as many divisions in the Roman Catholic Church as there are in Protestantism. Within the Roman Church these are often expressed in the formation of religious orders that are permitted to exist side by

---

48. R. Bellarmine, "De eccl. Mil.," in *Controversiis*, III, 10–12; IV, c. 4–18.
49. H. Denzinger, ed., *The Sources of Catholic Dogma*, trans. from the 30th ed. by Roy J. Deferrari (London and St. Louis: Herder, 1955), #1794.
50. Cf. H. Bavinck, *Reformed Dogmatics*, I, 510–12 (#133), 578–82 (#150).

side. Furthermore, Rome pays the heavy price of holding that outside the church there is no salvation (*extra ecclesiam nulla salus*). The Fourth Lateran Council (1215) declared in its opening chapter that there is one catholic church of believers "outside which no one at all is saved."[51] Trent confirmed this in its fifth session [June 17, 1546], claiming that without the catholic faith it is impossible to please God,[52] and Pius IX, in his allocution of December 9, 1854, declared that "we must maintain on the basis of faith that outside of the apostolic Roman church no person can be saved."[53] By its very nature, therefore, Rome has to be intolerant. Yet here too, the fact of millions of Christians outside the Roman Catholic Church has proved to be too powerful to ignore; even for Roman Catholics themselves it is hard to remain true to this doctrine, and many are inclined to make concessions. Rome repudiated the thesis of Michael Baius (1513–89) that, "Purely negative infidelity in those among whom Christ has not been preached, is a sin,"[54] and in his allocution Pius IX immediately added this to the *nulla salus* claim: "It must be considered certain that those who labor in ignorance of true religion, even if this ignorance is invincible, cannot be faulted on this account."

[494] For Protestantism, the doctrine concerning the marks of the true church functioned differently. To justify the act of Reformation, the Reformers had to argue that the church of Rome was not the true church and that the churches of the Reformation were true to Scripture's teaching. Their withdrawal from Rome presupposed that the church was not trustworthy in and of itself (αὐτόπιστος, *autopistos*), that it could depart from the truth, and that above it was a higher authority which could only be Holy Scripture. In keeping with Scripture's own standards—and allowing for great variety of expression among them—it finally came down to the Word of God as the key mark of the church. Christ gathers his church (Matt. 28:19), which is built on the teaching of the apostles and prophets, by Word and sacrament (Matt. 16:18; Eph. 2:20). The Word is truly the soul of the church;[55] all ministry in the church is a ministry of the Word. The various objections raised against the Protestant understanding of the marks failed to hit the mark because they claimed more for the marks than is warranted. For example, the criteria are not absolute or infallible; they do not set up completely false churches over against completely true churches, but give us criteria by which we can make informed judgments. Even though there are unbelievers within a body of believers and there remain impure elements in doctrine or practice, this does not disqualify a church body altogether. The pure administration of the Word is not a mark for determining the sincere faith of individual members but [a mark] of the church as the gathering of believers. The Reformed also emphasized that the church as gathering of believers is manifest not only in the institution but also in

---

51. Ed. note: H. Denzinger, *Sources of Catholic Dogma*, #430.
52. Ed. note: Ibid., #787.
53. Ed. note: Ibid., #1647; the reference is to the allocution, "Singulari quadem," December 9, 1854.
54. Ed. note: H. Denzinger, *Sources of Catholic Dogma*, #1068.
55. J. Calvin, *Institutes*, IV.xii.1.

faith, the avoidance of sin, the pursuit of righteousness, love for God and neighbor, and the crucifixion of the flesh.[56] The pure administration of the Word also includes the application of ecclesiastical discipline. A true church in an absolute sense is impossible on earth. For that matter, neither can a wholly false church exist; to qualify for that description, it would no longer be a church at all. The Protestants, though firmly rejecting the church hierarchy of Rome, continued to fully recognize the Christian elements in the church of Rome. However corrupted Rome might be, there were still left in it "vestiges of the church," "ruins of a disordered church"; there was still "some kind of church, be it half-demolished," left in papacy.[57] That is why the Reformers warned against absolutism and arbitrary separation: According to Calvin, one has the duty to leave only when the "high points of necessary doctrine" or "the foremost doctrines of religion" have been exchanged for a lie.[58] Later, facing the degeneration of the state churches and the pressure to leave, the majority of ministers were led to oppose separatism on the same grounds.[59] Consequently, an important distinction arose between a "true" and a "pure" church,[60] with the former not understood in any exclusive sense but as a description of an array of churches that upheld the fundamental articles of Christian faith[61] while differing from each other in degrees of purity. "False church" became the term for the hierarchical power of superstition or unbelief that set itself up in local churches and accorded itself and its ordinances more authority than the Word of God.[62]

[495] The "real" church in history is not perfect but, rather, has an undeniably dark side to it. The church is rent asunder by schisms and divisions, some going back to the apostolic era. These offer the world an occasion for pleasure and scorn, give it a reason for its nonbelief, and are a sin against God, in conflict with Christ's [high-priestly] prayer [for unity], and caused by the darkness of our minds and

56. Belgic Confession, art. 29.

57. J. Calvin, *Institutes*, IV.ii.11. Ed. note: Bavinck refers here to a passage in Calvin's "Reply to Sadoleto": "But what arrogance, you will say, to boast that the Church is with you alone, and to deny it to all the world besides! We indeed, Sadoleto, deny not that those over which you preside are Churches of Christ" (John Calvin and Jacopo Sadoleto, *A Reformation Debate*, ed. J. C. Olin [New York: Harper & Row, 1966; repr., Grand Rapids: Baker, 1976], 75).

58. J. Calvin, *Institutes*, IV.i.12–20; idem, *Commentary*, on Matt. 13:40–41; idem, *Commentary*, on 2 Thess. 3:6.

59. Gisbert Voetius, *Politicae ecclesiasticae*, 3 vols. (Amsterdam: Joannis a Waesberge, 1663–76), IV, 488; W. à Brakel, *The Christian's Reasonable Service*, trans. B. Elshout, 4 vols. (Ligonier, PA: Soli Deo Gloria, 1992–95), II, chap. 25.

60. A. Polanus, *Syntagma theologiae christianae*, 532; Johann Heinrich Alsted, *Theologica didactica, exhibens locos communes theologicos method scholastic* (Hanau: C. Eifrid, 1618), 601ff.; A. Walaeus, in H. Bavinck, ed., *Synopsis purioris theologiae*, 6th ed. (Leiden: Donner, 1881), disp. 40, 37; Samuel Maresius, *Systema theologicum* (Groningen: Aemilium Spinneker, 1673), XVI, 20; Campegius Vitringa, *Doctrina christianae religionis, per aphorismos summatim descripta*, 6th ed., 8 vols. (Leiden: Joannis le Mair; Arnheim: J. H. Möelemanni, 1761–86), IX, 79.

61. Cf. H. Bavinck, *Reformed Dogmatics*, I, 612–13 (#158).

62. Belgic Confession, art. 29.

the lovelessness of our hearts.[63] As Christians we cannot humble ourselves deeply enough over the schisms and discord that have existed throughout the centuries in the church of Christ. Tragically, Christians have also allowed themselves to be led astray by the attempt to bring about or to maintain this fervently desired unity of the church of Christ by violent means—using the state—or artificially by syncretism and fusion.[64] Still, because history, like nature, is a work of God and does not take shape apart from his providence which governs also the divisions and schisms of his church on earth, we can learn from it. Christ's prayer for unity was not born of unfamiliarity with the history of God's people nor from his inability to govern it. His prayer is the guarantee that unity already exists in him and that in due time, accomplished by him, it will also be manifest in all believers.

With that in mind, we consider the following for a correct understanding of the divisions in the church of Christ.

1. All the divisions and schisms that exist in the church of Christ basically have their roots in the apostolic age. The apostles in Jerusalem and Paul, Jewish-Christian and gentile-Christian churches, parted company over many and even important issues (Acts 15:39; Gal. 2:11); heresies and schisms of various kinds already occurred then as well (1 Cor. 1:10; 11:18–19; etc.).

2. These divisions and schisms in the apostolic age do not leave such a deep impression because in the New Testament we always have to deal primarily with local churches. When the churches moved from a purely spiritual bond of union to a hierarchical, institutional body that viewed itself as "the essence" of the church, it was this development that alienated many true believers and provoked heresies and schisms. Protestantism denies its own first principle if it seeks to maintain the unity of Christianity by any form of hierarchical coercion.

3. Precisely because the Word [Scripture] is the mark of the church and there exists no infallible interpretation of that Word, Christ gave to everyone the freedom to understand that Word personally as he or she interprets it and to separate from bodies deemed unfaithful. Even though horrendous misuse can and has been made of this right of interpretation, we must respect it, and avoid the temptation to abolish that freedom.

4. Undoubtedly the divisions of the church of Christ are caused by sin; at the same time because God loves diversity in unity, it is a mistake to reject all

---

63. J. H. Gunning, *De eenheid der kerk* (Nijmegen: Ten Hoet, 1896); idem, *Hooger dan de kerk!* (Nijmegen: Ten Hoet, 1897); idem, *Rekenschap* (Nijmegen: Ten Hoet, 1898).

64. In England, Scotland, America, and Australia there exists a powerful drive toward unity; the Edinburgh Missionary Conference strongly emphasized unity, and many strive for it in order to bring about what Principal Forsyth calls "the United States of the Church." In Germany, home of confessional strife, there are repeated pleas for confessional peace, e.g., L. K. Goetz, *Ein Wort zum konfessionellen Frieden* (Bonn: Carl Georgi, 1906); P. Tschackert, *Modus vivendi* (Munich: Beck, 1908); R. Schmölder, *Zum Frieden unter den Konfessionen* (Bonn, 1910), 168.

diversity in the church. As a parallel we believe that though the division of humanity into peoples and languages was occasioned by sin, it also has something good in it. From many races and languages and peoples and nations Christ gathers his church on earth.

5. If therefore we again understand by churches the local churches spread out over the globe wherever Christianity has gained a foothold, then there are no true and false churches in an absolute sense. While there are great differences in the purity of confessions and churches, and we must aim and strive for the purest, we must distinguish fundamental and non-fundamental articles of faith. With this we do not intend to foster indifferentism and syncretism; nothing is indifferent in connection with "the truth which leads to godliness" (Titus 1:1).

6. One must therefore be cautious with the terms "heresy" and "schism." The former breaks the unity of the church on matters of doctrine, the latter in fellowship of communion. Undoubtedly both of these are great sins. At the same time, in practice, there is for us an inevitable elasticity thanks to the church's de facto pluriformity which forces us to look for its unity in the spiritual bond of faith rather than in the external form of its government.[65]

THE ATTRIBUTES OF THE CHURCH

[496] We are obligated to first of all bind ourselves in spiritual bonds of unity rather than external, institutional ones. It is here, as we seek to understand the key church attributes of unity, holiness, catholicity, and apostolicity, that Protestantism finds itself with a different view from Rome. Protestants do not seek these attributes first of all, as Rome does, in a specific, hierarchically ordered institution. *Unity* is not found in the hierarchy and the papacy but in the *spiritual* unity of the church with its head (Eph. 1:10; 5:23); and further, with the unity of faith, hope, and love, and of baptism, and so forth (Eph. 4:3–5). This spiritual unity is not simply invisible, it comes to expression in that which all Christians have in common in spite of their divisions. *Holiness* does not consist primarily in liturgical, ceremonial holiness achieved by the salvific use of the sacraments, and, only secondarily in the personal holiness of some of its members,[66] but because of the *spiritual* communion of the *saints*—those who, being born again of water and

65. W. E. Gladstone, "The Place of Heresy and Schism in the Modern Christian Church," *Nineteenth Century* 36 (August 1894): 157–94; P. Hinschius, "Häresie," in *PRE*³, VII, 319–21; E. Sehling, "Schisma," in *PRE*³, XVII, 575–80. Concerning pluriformity in the church, see A. Kuyper, *Encyclopedia of Sacred Theology* (New York: C. Scribner's Sons, 1898), 658ff.; Th. F. Bensdorp, *Pluriformiteit: Een fundamenteele misvatting van Dr. A. Kuyper of een hopeloos pleidooi* (Amsterdam: G. Borg, 1901).

66. Roman Catechism, I, art. 10, qu. 13; ed. note: Bavinck erroneously cites qu. 12; the post–Vatican II edition titled *The Roman Catechism*, trans. Robert I. Bradley, SJ, and Eugene Kevane (Boston: Daughters of St. Paul, 1985), drops the enumeration of the introduction so that chap. 1 begins the first article of the creed. In this annotation, the proper reference would be II, chap. 9, qu. 15.

spirit in the inner self, desire, with all seriousness of purpose, to live not only according to some but according to all the commandments of God[67] (John 17:19; Eph. 5:25–27; 1 Thess. 4:3; Titus 2:14; Heb. 12:14; 1 Pet. 2:9). *Catholicity* is not just a geographical, spatial, and temporal matter—spread over the whole earth and existing in an unbroken line from the apostles—but also a pointer to the fullness of the grace and truth intended by God for all people. In catholicity, Roman Catholic Christians look for an essential mark of the true church, and their appeal to the church fathers for support has merit. However, like them, Rome also tends to exaggerate the growth of its own fellowship and underestimate that of Protestants. Statistics do not say everything; there is a fundamental contradiction between the terms "Roman" and "catholic." The name "Roman" or "papal church" therefore expresses its nature much more accurately than "Catholic." All Protestants confess "I believe the . . . catholic church" in the Apostles' Creed.[68] Here they simply follow Old and New Testament teaching that God intends his salvation for all peoples (Gen. 12:3; Ps. 2:8; Isa. 2:2; Jer. 3:17; Mal. 1:11; Matt. 8:11; 28:19; John 10:16; Rom. 1:8; 10:18; Eph. 2:14; Col. 1:6; Rev. 7:9; and so forth). Christianity is a world religion and that church is most catholic that most clearly expresses in its confession and applies in its practice the international and cosmopolitan character of a faith suited and intended for every people and age, for every class and rank, for every time and place. The Reformed had an eye for it when they confessed their faith in various countries, and at the Synod of Dort invited delegates from all over Reformed Christianity.[69]

Catholicity is closely linked to the fourth attribute of apostolicity in Roman Catholic thought. Rome claims this attribute because it was founded by the apostles and agrees in its doctrine, organization, and ministry with those of the apostles, but especially because its office-bearers [officeholders] are the successors, in an unbroken line, of the apostles and received their power and authority from those who themselves in turn received it in lawful succession from the apostles. Scripture, however, says nothing about such an apostolic succession, and succession in itself is no guarantee of purity of doctrine. Protestants, therefore, turned away from "succession of places and persons" (*successio locorum et personarum*) to "the succession of doctrine" (*successio doctrinae*) as a distinguishing feature of the true church.

Finally, the attributes of indefectibility and infallibility follow from our Lord's promise that the gates of hell would not prevail against the church, and that he would preserve her to the end of the world (Matt. 16:18; 28:20; Eph. 4:11–13; 1 Tim. 3:15). It does not lead to the claim of papal infallibility pronounced by the [First] Vatican Council,[70] nor does it promise the church earthly success and

67. Ed. note: Here Bavinck cites, without attribution, Heidelberg Catechism, Lord's Day 44, Q&A 114.
68. Belgic Confession, art. 27; Apology of the Augsburg Confession, arts. 7–8.
69. H. Bavinck, "The Catholicity of Christianity and the Church," trans. John Bolt, *Calvin Theological Journal* 27 (1992): 220–51.
70. H. Denzinger, *Sources of Catholic Dogma*, ##1832–40.

safety. Rather, the New Testament points to suffering and persecution, especially in the "last days" (Matt. 24:21–22; Luke 18:8; 2 Tim. 3:1). Jesus's promise is simply a guarantee that there will always be a gathering of believers on earth. Christ, as king of his church, will see to it that on earth there will always be a gathering of believers, however small and unimpressive it may be, that confesses his name and finds all its salvation in him. All the attributes are eschatological dimensions of the church; they are ours in Christ, true now but only fully realized in eternity. The attributes are thus callings to be pursued in the power of the Holy Spirit.

THE CHURCH AS ORGANISM AND INSTITUTION

[497] The church cannot do without government; like other entities she is unthinkable without an authority that sustains, guides, cares for, and protects her. Although all final authority rests in God, he appoints Christ as mediator from eternity, and Christ carried out his prophetic, priestly, and kingly office from the time of paradise, continued it in the days of the Old Testament and during his sojourn on earth, and now fulfills it in heaven, where he is seated at the Father's right hand.[71] It was, however, Christ's pleasure, without in any way transferring his sovereignty to people, to nevertheless use them in the exercise of his sovereignty. As the gathering of believers, the church is used by Christ as an instrument to bring others to his fold, in part because the church is in process of becoming and is thus both passively a gathered community or organism, and actively the mother of all believers, an institution. This is a distinction within the visible church that reminds us of the church's duality in the present age: we see the church in the offices and means of grace (institution) and in a community of faith and life (organism). Although theologians have made claims and counterclaims about which has the priority, neither must be played against the other; both are the work of Christ. The efforts of some—Schleiermacher, J. Möhler—to use this distinction as a way to distinguish Protestant (the individual precedes the invisible organism) from Roman Catholic (the visible, institutional church precedes the individual) ecclesiology, misrepresents the church's history for a number of reasons.

The Reformation quarreled with Rome not on the importance of the institutional church but on the way Rome bound salvation to priests and sacraments, as the means of grace. Protestants, including Calvin,[72] agree with Roman Catholics that the church is both a gathered community (*coetus*) and the mother of believers (*mater fidelium*), simply because Christ arranged it in this way. The community did not produce the church; Christ did through gathering the community. The church does not come into being as the gathering of believers "through the coming together of regenerate individuals."[73] From whence would they come? The

---

71. H. Bavinck, *Reformed Dogmatics*, III, 475–82 (#409).
72. J. Calvin, *Institutes*, IV.i.4.
73. F. Schleiermacher, *The Christian Faith*, §115.

real issue between Rome and the Reformation is whether Christ is bound to the administration of sacramental grace by priests or graciously gathers his people through his proclaimed Word and his Spirit. The Reformers insisted that God's people are where God's Word is, but the church may be present even where there is no priest or pope, no pastor or presbyter. Nevertheless, the church as the gathering of believers does not take shape without the use of means; fellowship with Christ is bound to fellowship with the Word of the apostles (John 17:3; 1 John 1:3). As in the natural world, every human being is a product of communion, and the individual believer is born from the womb of the believing community. The universal church is anterior to the particular church and to individual believers just as in every organism the whole precedes the parts. Believers are simultaneously producer and product. In other words, Christ gathers his church through the church. In understanding the church this way the Reformation avoided both the hierarchy of Rome and the enthusiasm of the Anabaptists while still doing justice to the truth in both. The distinguishing mark of the church is the pure administration of the Word and the confession and conduct of believers. Offices and gifts, governance and the people, institution and organism—all these belong together. They are inseparable.

[498] Holy Scripture makes this point very clear. The church is God's creation, from the beginning of human sinful history—Adam, Abram, Israel, the early church—all are religiously as well as civilly organized by tabernacle and altar, sacrifice, priesthood. Abraham, and his immediate descendents, were given the sign of circumcision and served their families as priests who passed on the promises to their children and offered sacrifices of worship and thanksgiving to God. At Sinai the people of Israel received both a civil and a religious organization and became manifest—in the priesthood and sacrifices, in the tabernacle and the altar, in a wide array of laws and ordinances—as the people of God. John the Baptist preached a baptism of repentance for the forgiveness of sins and called the people of God to be apart from sinful Israel. Jesus took over this message and this baptism from John, added the Lord's Supper, gathered around him an ἐκκλησια (*ekklēsia*),[74] directly governed it himself while on earth, and appointed twelve apostles to be his witnesses. The entity known as "the twelve apostles" was established long before Paul joined them (Matt. 26:33; 28:18–20; Luke 24:47; John 20:19, 21; 1 Cor. 15:5, 7; Rev. 21:14); it had been assigned by Jesus himself (Luke 6:13; cf. 11:49; Matt. 10:2; 23:34; Mark 3:14; 6:30; Luke 9:10; 17:5; 22:14; 24:10). The word "apostle"[75] was an office-related name from the beginning, even to the extent that the term "false apostle" (ψευδοαποστολος,

74. The manner in which Jesus speaks of his church (Matt. 16:18; 18:17) already in principle includes its organization. Cf. P. A. E. Sillevis Smitt, *De organisatie van de Christelijke kerk in den apostolischen tijd* (Rotterdam: T. de Vries, 1910), 36.
75. It is not impossible that the term "apostles" had already been in vogue among the Jews for those men who were sent out by the Sanhedrin to carry out certain mandates with respect to Jewish customs outside Judah. See A. von Harnack, *The Mission and Expansion of Christianity*, trans. J. Moffatt (New

pseudoapostolos) could be formed (2 Cor. 11:13). Still, it is not exactly certain who must be counted as belonging to this group of twelve as the variations in lists attest (Matt. 10:2–4; Mark 3:16–19; Luke 6:14–16; Acts 1:13). We know that Matthias replaced Judas (Acts 1:15–26), but Paul's relation to the Twelve is far from clear. He is the apostle to the gentiles (Acts 9:15; 13:47; 22:21; Rom. 11:13; Gal. 1:16; 2:7–9; Eph. 3:8; 1 Tim. 2:7; 2 Tim. 1:11), though in his preaching of the gospel he always turned first to the Jews (Acts 13:5, 14, 46; etc.), and after the resurrection the Twelve were commissioned to preach the gospel to all peoples (Matt. 28:19; Acts 10:42). Paul's apostolate, however, is unique; he vigorously maintains the divine origin, the independence, and the authenticity of his apostolic office (Gal. 1–2; 1 Cor. 1:10–4:21; 2 Cor. 10:13), yet his apostolic "witness" to the risen Christ is not like those who were with him during his sojourn of earth. Nonetheless, his contribution was to confirm and expand the apostolate by moving it into the world of the gentiles so that it could become the permanent grounding of the church. His ministry helped the church divest itself of Jewish exclusivism and graft the gentiles as wild branches into the cultivated olive tree of Israel (Rom. 11:24). Jew and gentile came together and built a new people of God, with Christ as the cornerstone and the apostles as the foundation.

The role of Paul as an "apostle" and the broader sense of the term in the New Testament (Acts 13:2–3; 14:4, 14; Rom. 16:7; 1 Cor. 4:6, 9; 9:5; 15:7; 2 Cor. 8:23; 11:3, 5, 13; 12:11; Gal. 1:19; 1 Thess. 2:7; Rev. 2:2), and in the postapostolic period (as in the *Didache*), which includes apostolic helpers called "evangelists" or "prophets," teaches us important things about church structure. Evangelists are servants (1 Thess. 3:2; 1 Tim. 4:6; 6:11; 2 Tim. 2:24); in addition to their charisma (1 Tim. 4:14; 2 Tim. 1:6), they are called and appointed to an *office*, with a name (Acts 21:8), rank of their own (Eph. 4:11), and a special task (2 Tim. 4:5). Their office is not restricted to a local church but extends to all the churches, the church universal (Acts 13:4ff.), with power and authority in all the churches (Titus 1:5). They are "fellow workers" (1 Thess. 3:2), "traveling companions" (Acts 19:29), "fellow soldiers" (Phil. 2:25), "fellow servants" (Col. 1:7; 4:7) of the apostles *and* subject to them (Acts 19:22; 1 Cor. 4:17; 1 Tim. 1:3; Titus 1:5; etc.). In the postapostolic period, the office disappears, and the name "evangelist" is used for the authors of the four Gospels, rendering, as it were, the persons of the evangelists superfluous.[76]

We also encounter "prophets" alongside evangelists (Rom. 12:6; 1 Cor. 12:28–29; Eph. 2:20; 3:5; 4:11). Promised by Jesus (Matt. 23:34; Luke 11:49), raised up by the Holy Spirit (Acts 2:17–18; 1 Cor. 12:11; Rev. 1:10), prophets occur in large numbers in almost all the churches (Acts 6:5, 8; 11:27; 13:1; 21:9–10; Rom. 12:6; 1 Cor. 12; Eph. 2:20; 3:5; 4:1–11; 1 Thess. 5:20). The last of them is John

---

York: Harper, 1908), I, 458ff.; W. Staerk, *Neutestamentliche Zeitgeschichte*, 2 vols. (Berlin: G. J. Göschen, 1907), II, 43.

76. On the evangelists, see Suicerus, *Thesaurus ecclesiasticus*, s.v. εὐαγγέλιον; V. H. Stanton, "Gospels," in *DB*, II, 234–49; N. J. D. White, "Gospels," in *DC*, I, 663–71.

the apostle (Rev. 1:1), and then as a class they disappear from the church, though Montanism and other enthusiastic movements of earlier or later date tried to revive prophecy and even Zwingli and many after him introduced so-called "prophecies" that served to explain Scripture to the people.[77] The latter does not correspond to what the New Testament calls "prophecy." Prophets may be regarded as office bearers but they are not immediately called and appointed by Christ or by his church; instead, they receive a special charisma from the Holy Spirit and their task is ad hoc in nature. Unlike the evangelists who help the apostles in their mission work, prophets assist them in edification and instruction. Although it is rated higher than glossolalia (1 Cor. 14:5, 32), prophecy is nevertheless momentary and extraordinary, the fruit of revelation (14:30). Whatever similarities exist between the New Testament apostles and later offices, there is something distinct and unique about the original apostles, however; the universal church of all ages is bound to their witness; they shared the Holy Spirit in extraordinary measure; their witness was sealed by God the Holy Spirit with signs and wonders and rich spiritual blessings. Apostolicity is undoubtedly an attribute and distinguishing mark of the church of Christ.[78]

Peter is foremost among the apostles, the first among equals. Already at his first encounter with Jesus, he received the commitment that he would later be called Κηφας (Kēphas, Cephas; the Greek form of the Hebrew כֵּף [kēp], with the Aramaic article [appended to the end of the word, כֵּיפָא, kêpā᾿]), the rock, ἡ πετρα (hē petra), as a masculine proper name Πετρος (Petros; John 1:44). His bold confession of Jesus as Messiah (Matt. 16:13–20) led to Jesus calling him and his confession the "rock" on which Christ would build his church so solidly that the gates of hades would not prevail against it. Peter is the principal founder of the church, the example and leader of all the confessors of Christ throughout the centuries. Contrary to Rome, the apostolic foundation of the church and its government does not mean a continuing apostolate. For us it survives, not as an institution but only in the apostolic Word, which remains as the foundation of the church. When the apostles founded churches in various places, they instituted offices that differed essentially from their own, offices that came into being also through the cooperation of the churches. There is a difference between the extraordinary apostolic office (as well as evangelists and prophets) and the ordinary offices of presbyters and deacons instituted within and by the churches.

[499–500] Christ himself appointed the apostles; those who followed them were appointed in and by the congregations that arose after the apostles' successful preaching. As the church spread and believers gathered in homes, arrangements for the community were made by designated people, perhaps on the model of the Jewish synagogue. While the apostolate was an extraordinary and temporary of-

77. Güder, "Prophezei," in PRE[3], XVI, 108–10.

78. Cf. H. Bavinck, Reformed Dogmatics, I, 397–402 (#108); A. von Harnack, The Mission and Expansion of Christianity, I, 458ff.; W. Patrick, "Apostles," in DC, I, 101ff.

fice, a founding office even preceding the existence of the church as a gathering of believers, the offices of teacher, elder/overseer, and deacon presuppose the existence of the church, a church that as a local body has the right to designate and elect the bearers of these offices. From a situation where tasks and offices were quite fluid, over time they were differentiated and the distinct office of deacon was added (Acts 6). This office of mercy administration arose out of need; διακονια (*diakonia*) is the New Testament word for every office and gift that, having been given by the Lord, is used in the service of and for the benefit of the church community. Every member of the church is a δουλος (*doulos*, slave) of Christ and a διακονος (*diakonos*, servant) of fellow believers. The office of deacon was regularized so that in addition to the ministry of the Word (Acts 6:4; 20:24; 1 Tim. 1:12), the church would always maintain the ministry of mercy to the poor, the sick, the stranger, and so forth (Rom. 12:7; 1 Cor. 12:28; 1 Pet. 4:11). The term "elder" (πρεσβυτερος, *presbyteros*), used to describe the office of overseer, was later more precisely described and replaced by that of "overseer" (ἐπισκοπος, *episkopos*; Acts 20:28; Phil. 1:1; 1 Tim. 3:2; Titus 1:7; 1 Pet. 2:25). Paul, after speaking about the offices in 1 Timothy 3, nevertheless describes in 1 Timothy 5 the attitude that Timothy must adopt toward various church members, both older and younger ones, both men and women (cf. 1 Pet. 5:5), and the Apostolic Fathers speak clearly of a class of elders apart from the church's actual office-bearers.[79] Distinguishing ἐπισκοπος from πρεσβυτερος is the only way to make sense of 1 Timothy 5:17 ("Let the elders who rule well be considered worthy of double honor."); not all πρεσβυτεροι serve as ἐπισκοποι but those who do deserve double respect. The elders or presbyters constituted a class or group in the church, while overseers were office-bearers who ruled. According to this text, there is a clear distinction between overseers charged with governing and others charged with teaching and preaching and consequently with the administration of the sacraments. Of course, as it often happens, elders and overseers may be the same persons and bearers of the same office (Acts 20:17, 28; 1 Tim. 3:1; 4:14; 5:17, 19; Titus 1:5, 7; 1 Pet. 5:1–2). The name "presbyters" sheds no light on their office and for that reason made way for other names, especially "overseers" (Acts 20:28; Phil. 1:1; 1 Tim. 3:2; Titus 1:7); "those who are over you" (Rom. 12:8; 1 Thess. 5:12); "those with gifts of administration" (1 Cor. 12:28); "leaders" (Heb. 13:7, 17, 24); "pastors" (Eph. 4:11). Keeping in mind the requirement that they rule their own households well (Acts 20:28; 1 Tim. 3:1–7; Titus 1:5–9; 1 Pet. 5:1–3), it is evident that the office of elder was charged primarily with the oversight, government, and guidance of the church. The responsibility of elders at the Council of Jerusalem (Acts 15:4, 22–23) also shows that it is essential that they have some knowledge of the truth. Yet originally the office of overseer was not one of teaching but of ruling the church. In the early years of the church there was as yet no pressing need for a separate teaching office; the apostles, evangelists, and prophets served as teachers

79. *1 Clem.* 1:3; 3:3; 21:6; 47:6; 57:1; 63:3–4; Herm. *Vis.* 2.4; 3.1.

(Acts 13:1; 1 Cor. 14:3; 1 Tim. 1:11), and the activity of teaching (διδασκαλια, *didaskalia*), just as in the synagogue (Luke 4:16), was freely given to many who had no special office (Rom. 12:7; 1 Cor. 12:8, 28–29; 14:26).

The organization described in the preceding paragraph, an organization that can be called aristocratic-presbyterial, soon developed into a monarchical-episcopal arrangement. This started early in the East; the West soon followed suit. Much of this is understandable; as the church expanded and the period of the apostles passed, the extraordinary gifts ceased, errors and heresies surfaced inside and outside the church, and competent teachers were needed not only to instruct and admonish but also to refute those who rejected the truth (1 Tim. 3:16; Titus 1:9). Schooling and a more permanent ecclesiastical structure were needed. Following the pattern of the Jewish scribes and Jesus himself, reliable people were entrusted with the message of the gospel who in turn would be qualified to teach others (2 Tim. 2:2). These laborers are worth their wages, according to Jesus (Matt. 10:10; Luke 10:7), a rule also observed by Paul (Rom. 15:27; 1 Cor. 9:6, 11, 14; 2 Cor. 11:7–9; Gal. 6:6; 1 Thess. 2:5; 1 Tim. 5:17–18; 2 Tim. 2:6). The necessity of schooling and the provision of a living were the reasons that the ministry of the Word was assigned not to all the overseers but to only a few. Selection to specific tasks and offices initially involved the congregations as well (Acts 13:1–3; 1 Cor. 2:15; 12:10; 14:29; 2 Cor. 8:19, cf. v. 23; 1 Thess. 5:19–21; 1 Tim. 1:18; 4:14; 6:12; 2 Tim. 1:6; 2:2; 1 John 2:20, 27; Rev. 2:2, 6, 14–15, 20; 3:1ff.).[80] However, in the course of time, in the interests of stabilizing the institutional character of the church, her evangelistic, prophetic, and didactic activities were attached to the office of the bishops: *they* became the true evangelists, prophets, and teachers.[81] In the face of heresies and sectarian movements, the important question became: "Where is the true church?" The answer: The true church is the church that adheres to the body as a whole, the catholic church, and this church is where the bishop is.[82] Here the bishop is no longer regarded as the first among equals but as one with definite priority and authority. The pattern in which the overseers and deacons were chosen by and with the consent of the community was reversed; the bishops came to be seen as the successors of the apostolate and thus vested with special authority as the bearers of the tradition. Central to this episcopal system is the distinction between the teaching church, or clergy, and the laity, or listening church.

This change in government did not come about in all the churches at the same time, at least in the West. It is not found in the *Didache*,[83] the Shepherd of Hermas,[84] or *1 Clement*.[85] It is in the East that the monarchical episcopate developed very

---

80. *Did.* 15; *1 Clem.* 44; Pol. *Phil.* 11 (*ANF*, I, 135–46); cf. Ign. *Phld.* 10 (*ANF*, I, 113–17); *Apostolic Constitutions* VIII, 4.

81. *Did.* 15.

82. Ign. *Smyrn.* 8.

83. *Did.* 15.

84. Herm. *Vis.* 3.5; 2.4.

85. *1 Clem.* 42, 44, 47.

early; Ignatius provides incontrovertible evidence for this when he speaks repeatedly—as much as thirteen times—of overseers (*episcopoi*), presbyters, and deacons as three distinct kinds of office-bearers. Nevertheless, the episcopal idea is still at the beginning of its development in the writings of Ignatius. The *episcopus* is a man sent from Christ, a gift of God (χαρις θεου, *charis theou*), a likeness of God or Christ,[86] and it is important to maintain unity with him, avoiding all heresy and schism. But he is not the bearer of the tradition, nor a New Testament priest, nor an apostolic successor; he is always surrounded by the council of presbyters and deacons, as Christ was by his apostles. He is an office-bearer in a local church and has no authority outside that local church. Ignatius still consistently connects this *episcopus* to the presbyters and deacons, but he also elevates him far above them in status; he regularly compares him with God or with Christ and demands almost unlimited obedience to him from church members. Here, Rev. 1:20–3:22 is important because it describes the bishop in such a prominent role that he could be described as a messenger (ἀγγελος, *angelos*) and regarded as the representative of the whole congregation.[87] It is likely that the development of the monarchical episcopate has its roots there. Eventually, in communities with several congregations, the church with which the bishop was associated acquired a certain priority. This helps explain how the bishop alone was authorized to conduct certain ecclesiastical rites such as the Eucharist, the ordination of office-bearers, and absolution.

[501] In this development, we witness a reversal of the entire earlier relationship. Moving away from congregational involvement in the setting aside for office we come, in the second half of the second century, to the distinction between the clergy (κληρος, *klēros, clerus*) and the laity (λαος, *laos*), contrasted as "the teaching church," and "the listening church," which no longer had anything to say and whose only role was to listen and obey.[88] The episcopal system of church government with the bishop as the legitimate successor of the apostles and the spiritual ruler of the believers now functioned as the manner and means of church governance. This is the system by which various Christian churches have been organized—the Greek Orthodox and many other Eastern churches and sects.[89] In Roman Catholicism the episcopacy also developed into a papal system, with the bishop of Rome having preeminent authority. It was in Rome, in the middle of the second century, that the first list of bishops was drawn up; it was there that the idea of episcopal

86. Ign. *Eph.* 6; Ign. *Magn.* 2, 7; Ign., *Trall.* 2–3; Ign. *Smyrn.* 8.

87. Cf. the position of honor held by James, the Lord's brother, in the church of Jerusalem (Acts 12:17; 15:13; 21:18; Gal. 1:19; 2:9).

88. H. Cremer, *Biblical-Theological Lexicon of New Testament Greek*, trans. D. W. Simon and W. Urwick (Edinburgh: T&T Clark; New York: Charles Scribner's Sons, 1895), s.v. κληρος; A. von Harnack, *History of Dogma*, trans. N. Buchanan et al., ed. A. B. Bruce, 7 vols. (London: Williams & Norgate, 1896–99), II, 87–88; W. Caspari, "Geistliche," in *PRE*[3], VI, 463; H. Achelis, "Laien," in *PRE*[3], XI, 218.

89. R. H. Hofmann, *Symboliek of stelselmatige uiteenzetting van het onderscheidene Christelijke kerkgenootschappen en voornaamste sekten* (Utrecht: Kemink en Zoon, 1861), §§44, 55, 62ff.

succession and the bishops' apostolic dignity was raised. In the early period, however, this primacy of the church at Rome had only a moral-religious character; Rome was first among equals with the other Christian churches.[90] Cyprian, too, still has the same view: all bishops are equal, maintain a certain independence, share in the same episcopal dignity, are as it were one bishop, are jointly the head of the church, and must preserve "the love of [our] heart, the honor of [our] colleagues, the bond of faith and the concord of the priesthood."[91] The new view of the episcopate, however, in the nature of the case, had to be to the advantage of Rome; the prestige and eminence of the Roman church and its bishop seemed to make primacy a natural outcome. Thus, the terms "Roman" and "Catholic" were linked from the start and evolved together.[92] The church of the cosmopolis became the center of the Christian church. The central significance that Rome had in the pagan empire was transferred to the church and made it the head of all Christendom. It was Leo I (440–461) who clearly and with all deliberateness in several letters developed this primacy of the Roman See and elevated it to the rank and value of a religious dogma, one that has its basis in Matthew 16:18.[93]

The East, however, continued steadfastly to resist the aggressive dominance of the primacy of the bishop of Rome and asserted the rights of the See of Constantinople. Thus the Canons of the Council of Nicea (canons 2 and 3) restricted the power of the bishop of Alexandria to Egypt and added: "the bishop of Constantinople shall have the primacy of honor after the bishop of Rome, because the same is the new Rome." The Council of Chalcedon (451), canon 28, acknowledged the priority (τα πρεσβεια) of the older Rome because it was the imperial city ("because that city was imperial") but assigned equal priority (τα ισα πρεσβεια, *ta isa presbeia*) to "the most holy See of New Rome." The bishop of Rome, accordingly, has never been the shepherd of all Christendom. He only became the head of Western (Latin) Christendom. Papal power also increased politically, particularly during the conciliar movement of the ninth through fifteenth centuries. Prior to this time councils were imperial synods, convened and officially or unofficially guided and validated by the emperor. As the pope's power expanded, he moved beyond convening and leading provincial and national synods—just as other bishops did—to convening ecumenical synods of the entire Western church, just as the bishop of Constantinople had done for the Greek church with his regional synods. The ecumenical councils of Western Christianity, accordingly, evolved from Roman synods and were therefore convened, led, and validated by the popes. In addition to the power of primacy, indefectability was attributed to

90. Irenaeus wrote that every church and all believers should agree with the church of Rome "on account of its preeminent authority," since in it the apostolic tradition has been kept pure (Irenaeus, *Against Heresies*, III, 3).

91. Cyprian, *Epistles*, 43.5; 49.2; 55.24; 72.3; 73.26.

92. A. von Harnack, *History of Dogma*, II, 105.

93. J. B. Heinrich and K. Gutberlet, *Dogmatische Theologie*, 2nd ed., 10 vols. (Mainz: Kirchheim, 1881–1900), II, 325ff.

Rome. Gregory VII in his Papal Dictate declared that "the church of Rome has never erred; neither, as Scripture testifies, will it ever err." Boniface VIII in his bull *Unam Sanctam* of 1302 decreed: "We declare, we define, we proclaim, that it is absolutely necessary for salvation that every human creature be subject to the Roman Pontiff."[94] The final, full statement of Petrine supremacy was declared by the First Vatican Council on July 18, 1870. The council declared that this primacy of jurisdiction over the whole church was immediately and directly promised to Peter and conferred on him by Christ; continues in the bishop of Rome as his successor; and consists in the "full and supreme power of jurisdiction over the whole church, and this not only in matters of faith and morals, but also in those which concern the discipline and government of the church dispersed throughout the whole world," so that he is "the supreme judge of the faithful," has the final decision in all matters pertaining to the churches, is above the judgment of all and subject to no council.[95]

[502] The Reformation set itself in full opposition to the very notion of a hierarchical church and the disjunction between clergy and laity. While Scripture does distinguish between shepherds and flock, builders and temple, planters and fieldwork, teachers and disciples, leaders and followers (and so forth), it knows nothing of a special class of ecclesiastical persons who constitute a unique group of "clerics" who serve the laity as necessary, even indispensable, mediators of salvation.[96] Even in the Old Testament the people as a whole were the κλῆρος (*klēros*), the possession and inheritance of the Lord, a priestly kingdom, a holy nation (Exod. 19:5–6; Deut. 7:6; 14:2; 26:18–19; 32:9; 1 Kings 8:51, 53; Ps. 135:4; Isa. 19:25; 41:8; Jer. 12:7–8; Joel 2:17; etc.). The New Testament teaches that the Holy Spirit is poured out on all believers and calls all to service (*diakonia*). Office in the church of Christ is not a *magisterium* but a *ministerium*, not a hierarchy but a *hierodulia*, a ministry (διακονια, *diakonia*) or stewardship (οἰκονομια, *oikonomia*), which utterly rules out any domination over the inheritance of the Lord (των κλήρων, *tōn klērōn*; 1 Pet. 5:3; i.e., the churches entrusted to the care of the presbyters: Matt. 20:25–26; 1 Cor. 3:5; 4:1; 2 Cor. 4:1–2; Eph. 4:12).[97]

From a scriptural perspective, the presbyter and bishop/overseer are practically identical; there is no ground for hierarchical ordering of the offices. The Reformers categorically rejected the papal system, particularly the notion of apostolic succession, and separate themselves from the Greek Orthodox and Anglicans as well as Roman Catholics. The New Testament does not know of any official distinction

94. Ibid., II, 357ff.

95. H. Denzinger, ed., *The Sources of Catholic Dogma*, ##1822–40.

96. Roman Catechism, II, chap. 6, qu. 13; ed. note: This enumeration follows the post–Vatican II edition; trans. R. I. Bradley, SJ, and E. Kevane.

97. Cf. Luther's doctrine of the universal priesthood of all believers, in J. Köstlin, *The Theology of Luther in Its Historical Development and Inner Harmony*, trans. Charles E. Hay, 2 vols. (Philadelphia: Lutheran Publication Society, 1897), I, 361, 371; II, 538ff.; J. Calvin, *Institutes*, IV.iv.9; IV.xii.1; idem, *Commentary*, on 1 Pet. 5:3; W. Caspari, "Geistliche," in *PRE*[3], VI, 463.

between overseer (ἐπίσκοπος, *episkopos*) and elder (πρεσβύτερος, *presbyteros*); it does not recognize a special institution of the episcopate alongside the presbyterate. Aside from the extraordinary offices of apostle, prophet, and evangelist, there are only two ordinary offices, that of deacons and that of πρεσβύτεροι (Phil. 1:1; 1 Tim. 3:1, 8): pastors and teachers (Eph. 4:11; 1 Tim. 5:17), those with gifts of administration (1 Cor. 12:28), those in positions of authority (Rom. 12:8; 1 Thess. 5:12), and leaders (Heb. 13:7, 17). There is no hierarchy in the church of Christ (Luke 22:25–26; 2 Cor. 1:24; 1 Pet. 5:3). For that reason, the Reformers followed many church fathers such as Theodoret, Chrysostom, Epiphanius, and others, along with the Waldensians, and Wycliffe, who acknowledged that in the New Testament the terms "presbyter" and "episcopus" are used interchangeably. Even where the term "bishop" was sometimes kept and transferred to the civil governor, or one member of the circle of ministers was given the title "bishop" or "superintendent" and charged with the supervision of a group of local churches,[98] this is something essentially different from the episcopal office in the Roman Catholic Church. According to Scripture, the apostolate was an exceptional, temporary, and nonrenewable office in the New Testament church. The apostles had been the ear- and eyewitnesses of Jesus's words and deeds. Directly called by Christ to their office, they received a special measure of the Holy Spirit, and were called to a unique task to lay the foundation of the church and to offer in their message the permanent medium of fellowship between Christ and his church. Their office extended to the entire church, indeed, to the entire world (Matt. 28:20). Even Roman Catholic theologians recognize that nothing Scripture tells us about Peter's primacy over the other apostles (Matt. 16:18; Luke 22:32; and John 21:15–17) proves his primacy of jurisdiction over them.[99] Peter's confession is the rock on which Christ builds his church; more to the point, Christ himself is the rock that the apostles by their preaching laid as the foundation of the church (Acts 4:11; Rom. 9:33; 1 Cor. 3:10–11; Eph. 2:20; 1 Pet. 2:5–6; Rev. 21:14). The power of the keys given to Peter (Matt. 16:19) was extended to all the apostles in 18:18 and John 20:23. The special enablement and guidance of the Holy Spirit was the privilege equally of all the apostles (Matt. 10:20; John 14:26; 15:26; 16:13; 20:22; Acts 1:8; Eph. 3:5).

Finally, even if we were to grant Peter a jurisdictional primacy, it is not clear how this transfers to the bishop of Rome. The historical reasons usually adduced for Petrine and Roman primacy are spurious. Proving (1) that Peter was in Rome; (2) that he held the office of bishop and primate there; and (3) that he consciously and intentionally transferred these two offices to one specific successor, is more than one can demonstrate with any degree of historical confidence. At very best,

---

98. E. Sehling, "Episkopalsystem in der evangelischer Kirche," in *PRE*[3], V, 425; Calvin, for one, had no objection to this practice (J. Calvin, *Institutes*, IV.iii.8; IV.iv.2ff.; IV.v.1ff.).

99. Joseph Wilhelm and Thomas Bartholomew Scannell, *A Manual of Catholic Theology: Based on Scheeben's "Dogmatik,"* 4th ed., 2 vols. (London: Kegan Paul, Trench, Trübner; New York: Benziger Brothers, 1909), II, 313ff.

the data link Peter and Paul in Rome; the most ancient tradition consistently mentions Peter and Paul in the same breath and tells us that *together* they started and built up the church at Rome. Here it is worth noting that Peter not only had no jurisdiction over Paul, but was actually rebuked by him! (Gal. 2:6, 9, 11). It is clear from the bishops' lists in Hegesippus, Irenaeus, the Muratorian Fragment, Hippolytus, Tertullian, and Epiphanius that at the end of the second century and even in the beginning of the third, Peter was not yet considered a bishop of Rome, and the common view was that Peter and Paul founded the church and charged Linus with the ministry of the episcopacy.[100] It was not until the time of Victor I or Zephyrinus (180–217) that this ancient tradition was modified so that Paul increasingly lost his share in the founding and establishment of the church at Rome, and Peter was exclusively pictured as the initiator of the episcopate and subsequently also as the first bishop of Rome.[101] At this time the legend of Peter's twenty- to twenty-five-year ministry as bishop began to circulate. The whole edifice of Rome's primacy, of papal authority, and hence the truth of the Roman Catholic Church and the salvation of its members are all based on a historical probability that can at any moment be nullified by new witnesses. Eternity, here, hangs on a cobweb. The so-called Catholic Church is, in truth, the Roman church: that is its name and its essence.

CHRIST IS KING OF THE CHURCH

[503–4] We must never forget: The apostles were and remain the founders of the church. Through their witness they are the foundation of the church. There is no communion with Christ except by communion with their witness! That is why the opposition and resistance to the Roman hierarchy of the Middle Ages, which increased proportionately as the hierarchy expanded, must not be followed in its repudiation of all ecclesiastical institutions, or view of them as merely a free and arbitrary creation of the believing community. Because Luther largely regarded church polity as an external and indifferent matter, the tradition that followed him tacitly assigned all church government to Christian civil authorities.[102] The Reformed regarded this as problematic for a number of reasons. The New Testament people of God are different from Old Testament Israel which intertwined civil and religious life. Pentecost separated the church from all tribal identities and gave it an independent status. The church's origin is a miraculous gift of the Holy Spirit; it cannot be a creation of human willings. For that reason, it must have a government of its own; polity is not a matter of complete adiaphora. While Scripture is not a book of church order, it does provide important principles

---

100. Irenaeus, *Against Heresies*, I, 27, 1; III, 1, 1.

101. Tertullian, *On Modesty*, 21; Cyprian, *Epistles*, 55.8; 59.14; 71.3; 75.17; Eusebius, *Ecclesiastical History*, III, 2; III, 4, 9; II, 14, 6.

102. See H. Bavinck, *Reformed Dogmatics*, IV, 291–96 (#489).

that cannot be ignored without spiritual injury. Although circumstances affect particulars of church order, the churches are not at liberty to abolish offices or give their task to civil authority. Although a Christian society will find itself in greater agreement with a Christian magistrate than one who is not, the tasks of church and state are distinct. The same sin will be differently punished in the church than in the state; the discipline that the former practices differs vastly from the punishment the latter imposes. The care of the poor, the oversight of the flock, the administration of Word and sacrament, the calling and election of ministers—these all remain the inalienable right and solemn duty of the local congregation. All this the Reformed understood thanks to their deep sense of the sovereignty of God. Those who proceed unilaterally from the goodness or the love or the fatherhood of God do not grasp this.

God is sovereign always and everywhere, in nature and grace, in creation and re-creation, in the world and in the church. His statutes and laws are the rule of our lives, for humans are his creatures, subject to him, and obligated to respond in total obedience. In the church this view naturally led to the confession of the kingship of Christ. Although Christ was from eternity anointed king, on account of his humiliation God highly exalted him and gave him a name above every name. By his resurrection he was declared with power to be the Son of God, became Lord, received all power in heaven and on earth, and now reigns until he has completed the kingdom and put all his enemies under his feet.[103] This kingship of Christ is twofold: a kingship of power (Pss. 2:8–9; 72:8; 110:1–3; Matt. 28:18; 1 Cor. 15:27; Eph. 1:21–22; Phil. 2:9–11; Heb. 1:6; 1 Pet. 3:22; Rev. 17:14) and a kingship of grace (Ps. 2:6; Isa. 9:5–6; Jer. 30:9; Ezek. 37:24; Luke 1:33; John 18:33ff.; Eph. 1:22; 4:15; 5:23; Col. 1:18; 2:19). The former is subordinate to and in service of the latter; the Father has given to Christ the right to rule all things for the sake of his own (Ps. 2:8; Heb. 1:2). Christ's kingship over his church—as its "head" (Eph. 4:16; Col. 2:19)—is radically different from the kings of the earth; it is a rule by Word and Spirit. As our Mediator, he is still always active in heaven and present by his Spirit on earth in church and in the offices, in Word and sacrament. All these are instruments in his hand as he *applies* the work of salvation. This kingship of Christ was the material principle of Reformed church government, is included in its confessions, and, since the sixteenth century, has been the driving force in combating all human dominance in the church of Christ and in regaining and preserving its freedom and independence.[104]

Christ's kingly rule over his church begins with his building the church on the rock of the confessing apostles (Matt. 16:18), who as his instruments build the church on him as the foundation (1 Cor. 3:11). He equips and nourishes them as the vine sustains the branches (John 15). Inasmuch as the church is an organism,

---

103. H. Bavinck, *Reformed Dogmatics*, III, 475–82 (#409).

104. First Helvetic Confession, art. 18; Second Helvetic Confession, art. 17; Gallic Confession, art. 30; Belgic Confession, art. 31; Scots Confession, art. 16; Westminster Confession, arts. 25, 30; J. Calvin, *Institutes*, II.xv.3–5.

the head is antecedent to the members and the universal church antecedent to the particular [local] church. While every particular [local] church is a manifestation of the universal church, of the people of God, at the place where it manifests itself in action, each church possesses its own fullness and is independent. There are no mother churches—including Jerusalem and Rome—in the sense that the one church might be free to lord it over other churches. All churches are equal because they are all—even if one has been planted by another—dependent in the same way, that is, directly and absolutely, on Christ and bound to his Word. For this reason the Reformed also abolished the diocese and parish, structures where local churches are linked to and controlled by the cathedral church and its bishop. In Scripture every church is independent, completely equal in rights to all the other churches. Yet Reformed ecclesiology is not independentist; because local churches are spiritually one and historically connected, they have an obligation from the Lord to maintain fellowship with all who share the same faith. Every local church is therefore simultaneously an independent manifestation of the body of Christ *and* part of a larger whole. Facing hardship and persecution from authorities, including religious authorities, Reformed believers do not arbitrarily split up into conventicles and congregations, nor decide on their own with whom they want to meet for worship and fellowship. Christ constitutes his church and, just as God determines allotted periods and the boundaries of everyone's habitation (Acts 17:26), so too Christ gathers believers locally and causes them to act as an independent *ecclesia*. Here grace and nature are not antithetic to each other; rather, grace restores nature, and the gospel is the fulfillment of the law.

In these local churches Christ pours out a wide assortment of gifts, not only the saving gifts of rebirth, conversion, faith, and so forth but also the spiritual gifts known as charismata. But partly changed in nature and operation since the apostolic era, the Holy Spirit still imparts them to believers today so that by them they can serve each other and manifest themselves as a single body. The congregation has "an anointing from the Holy One" (1 John 2:20), consists of many members who all need one another, and may not neglect the gifts given them. Every local church is and has to be a salvation army that under Christ's leadership fights the devil, the world, and the flesh and knows no retired or deactivated soldiers. It is a communion of saints in which all suffer and rejoice with each other and use their special gifts "readily and cheerfully for the service and enrichment of the other members" [Heidelberg Catechism, Q&A 55]. Just as all believers have a gift, so also they all hold an office. Not only in the church as organism but also in the church as institution, they have a calling and a task laid on them by the Lord. Antecedent to all special offices in the church is the universal office of believer. Christ is present where two or three come together in his name (Matt. 18:19–20); he acquired for everyone the Holy Spirit, who dwells in all believers as his temple (Acts 22:17; 1 Cor. 6:19; Eph. 2:22; etc.), so that they, being anointed with that Spirit, are [made] a holy, royal priesthood (1 Pet. 2:5, 9). They are prophets who declare the excellencies of God, confess his name, and know all things (Matt.

10:32; 1 John 2:20, 27); priests who offer up their bodies as living sacrifices, holy and pleasing to God (Rom. 12:1; Heb. 13:16; 1 Pet. 2:5, 9; Rev. 1:6; 5:10); kings who fight the good fight, overcome sin, the world, and death, and will someday reign with Christ (Rom. 6:12–13; 1 Tim. 1:18–19; 2 Tim. 2:12; 4:7; 1 John 2:13–14; Rev. 1:6; 2:26; 3:21; 20:6); and therefore they bear the name Christians, "anointed ones" (Acts 11:26; 26:28; 1 Pet. 4:16).

This prophetic, priestly, and royal activity of believers may properly be called the exercise of an office. God created us after his image for himself, in order that we might know, love, and glorify him and serve him as prophets, priests, and kings. We follow Christ who was specifically appointed by the Father as media- tor, servant of the Lord, prophet, priest, and king, to fulfill our office, and it is to this task that believers are called as well. As anointed people we are called to the same work, ministry, and struggle (John 12:26; 14:12); from then on we belong to Christ. We are the salt of the earth, the light of the world; and in and with respect to the church, are given a threefold task. Believers are obligated to join the church and maintain fellowship with it. They are also called to use their gifts for the sake of the body, to suffer and rejoice with their fellow church members, to attend the gathering of believers, to proclaim the Lord's death, to exercise oversight over each other, to engage in the ministry of mercy (and so forth). Finally, they are obligated, each in one's own way and extent, to be active in the formation and reformation of the church.

[505] On the basis of these gifts and this office of all believers, Christ has also instituted special offices in the church. The apostles indeed performed a ministe- rial service in this connection, but it is Christ nevertheless who gives these offices and equips and elects persons to them. Reformed authors sometimes voice the view that the power of the ministers actually belongs to the congregation but is exercised by them in its name.[105] In modern times there is the common view that the office is an organ of the church. All this is only partly correct. In Matthew 18:17–18 Jesus indeed grants the power of the keys to the entire church but still uses this word in a very general sense, without mentioning the organization that was to be introduced later. As soon as this organization exists, we note that the power of the keys rests with the apostles and then with the overseers. The power of the keys can in general be said to have been given to the church; it is "indeed intended for the edification of the whole church but must properly be handled by its ministers alone."[106] The offices in the church of Christ are not a ruling but a serving power. They exist for the sake of the church (1 Cor. 3:22; 2 Cor. 4:5; Eph. 4:12). Though in that sense offices exist *for the sake of the church*, offices are not functions of the church and the authority of an office is not given by the church. Old Testament priests and prophets were called by God (Isa. 6:8; Jer.

105. W. Ames, *Marrow of Theology*, I, 35, 6; F. Turretin, *Institutes of Elenctic Theology*, trans. G. M. Giger, ed. J. T. Dennison, 3 vols. (Phillipsburg, NJ: Presbyterian & Reformed, 1992), XVIII, qu. 24, 7, 8, 19, 26.

106. Samuel Maresius, *Systema theologicum* (Groningen: Aemilium Spinneker, 1673), XVI, 70.

1:4–5; Hosea 1:1); New Testament apostles were chosen and equipped by Christ (Rom. 1:1; Gal. 1:1; and so forth). False prophets and apostles, by contrast, come only in their own name (Jer. 23:21, 32; John 5:43). True servants are "ministers of Christ" (διακονοι Χριστου, *diakonoi Christou*; Acts 20:24; Col. 1:7; 1 Tim. 1:12), "servants of Christ" (δουλοι Χριστου, *douloi Christou*; Rom. 1:1; Gal. 1:10; 2 Pet. 1:1; ὑπηρεται Χριστου, *hypēretai Christou*; Acts 26:16; 1 Cor. 4:1), "servants of God" (δουλοι θεου, *douloi theou*; Acts 16:17), and "fellow workers with God" (συνεργοι θεου, *synergoi theou*; 1 Cor. 3:9). For that reason they have been placed as overseers (ἐπισκοποι, *episkopoi*) and caretakers (προισταμενοι, *proistamenoi*) over the church. They are its overseers (*episkopoi*), those in charge (*proistamenoi*), its leaders (ἡγουμενοι, *hēgoumenoi*), responsible for its spiritual well-being, and can claim its esteem and obedience. No one may take that honor upon himself except those who are called by God (John 10:1–2; Heb. 5:4). Although all believers are called to proclaim the gospel (Acts 8:4; 13:15; 1 Cor. 14:26), to do this with power and authority in the Lord's name, "to one a fragrance from death to death, to the other a fragrance from life to life" (2 Cor. 2:16), demands a special mission and mandate.

Church office includes teaching and ruling but is always about service and never about power. Office-bearers are ministers of Christ who serve his church. The route by which Christ puts his servants into office runs through three stages: vocation, examination, and ordination. Internal calling, involving assessment of personal gifts and desire, must be confirmed by the external call of the church done on Christ's behalf. In the examination of teaching elders or ministers, though the church's own teaching doctors (professors of theology) may be deputized by the church and could certainly assist the church in its examination, yet the right and responsibility finally belongs to the church (Acts 1:23–26; 6:2–6; 2 Cor. 8:19).[107] When a congregation makes a choice, that choice is made under the leadership of those who are already in office, apostles, evangelists, and so forth (Acts 1:15; 6:2; 14:23; Titus 1:5), and later of neighboring bishops. That choice, moreover, is not absolutely free but bound to conditions and criteria laid down by Christ for the office in question (Acts 1:21; 6:3; 1 Tim. 3). The final step of ordination, involving the laying on of hands (Acts 6:6; 13:3; 1 Tim. 1:18; 4:14; 5:22; 2 Tim. 1:6; and so forth), is not a sacrament and does not bestow but presupposes the charismata required for office. Scripture indicates other instances of laying on hands that have nothing to do with ordination: Old Testament blessings (Gen. 48:14; Lev. 9:22), and sacrifices (Exod. 29:10; Lev. 1:4), an indictment (Lev. 24:14), and Jesus's healing people (Matt. 8:15; 9:18; Mark 5:23, cf. 2 Kings 4:34; 5:11), and blessing them (Matt. 19:15; Luke 24:50). The appointments of Matthias, Paul, Barnabas, Silas, Luke, and so forth, do not mention any laying on of hands. Laying on hands is appropriate but not an essential element in ordination. Furthermore, ordination does not constitute the office; it is rather the solemn public declaration before

---

107. Cf. H. Bavinck, *Reformed Dogmatics*, IV, 345–46 (#499).

God and his congregation that the person is indeed called by God and ought to be received, recognized, and honored as an office-bearer.

[506] In the Christian church, there is little agreement concerning the number of offices that Christ has instituted. In the apostolic period, the boundaries between extraordinary and ordinary offices and hence between offices and gifts were, in the nature of the case, fluid, but the hierarchical development that began with the rise of the episcopacy deprived the local church of all freedom and independence and separated the offices from it by a huge gap. The laity became dependent on the clergy, who constitute a distinct class, propagate themselves by succession, and include those who belong to the clerical class even without having a specific ministry in the local church. A distinction was made between "minor orders" (unconsecrated) and the "major orders" (consecrated), the latter including the episcopal and diaconal office. The diaconate was totally changed in character to levitical service of assisting the priest-bishop who holds the one true office in the church. Where the bishop is; there the church is. Only the bishop may ordain other priests; the bishop is the propagator of the priesthood, and by implication, the church. In the face of this hierarchy, Luther contented himself with the restoration of the original office of preacher. Admittedly, for the purpose of discipline, he acknowledged the need for a council of elders and, for the care of the poor, a council of deacons, but he did not restore their office.

It is to Calvin that we owe the restoration of a biblically based presbyterial form of church government. Recognizing the need for elders to carry out church discipline, Calvin made the office of elder a distinguishing mark of Reformed church government.[108] The presbyterial system of church government was not derived from some abstract principle but from the Word of God and introduced to the church on its authority. By restoring the office of elder and deacon alongside that of the minister of the Word, the Reformed tradition most accurately grasped the idea of Scripture and most firmly recognized the rights of the local church. In modern times theologians have indeed spoken of "the principle of the local congregation" (*Gemeindeprinzip*) and on that basis constructed all sorts of presbyterial and diaconal offices. Calvin and the Reformed tradition, of course, also recognized the need for any people or society to have orderly government,[109] but their passion was for the church to be faithful to Christ's own institution. Church order must be governed by Scripture. To be sure, Scripture is Scripture and not a book of statutes, does not deal in detail with a host of particulars, and leaves a great deal to the discretion of the churches.[110] Disagreement remained among the

108. E. C. Achelis, "Presbyter in der alten Kirche," in *PRE*³, XVI, 5–9; E. F. K. Müller, "Presbyter, Presbyterialverfassung seit der Reformation," in *PRE*³, XVI, 9–16.

109. J. Calvin, *Institutes*, IV.xi.1; J. à Lasco, *Opera tam edita quam inedita*, ed. Abraham Kuyper, 2 vols. (Amsterdam: F. Muller, 1866), II, 45.

110. Synod of Wezel (1568), I, 9–10; Westminster Assembly (1648), "Form of Government," chap. 1, art. 6: "That though the character, qualifications, and authority of church officers are laid down in the Holy Scriptures, as well as the proper method of their investiture and institution, yet the election of the

Reformed about the number of offices. What the Reformed did, in restoring the office of elder and deacon alongside the minister of the Word, is grasp Scripture's own idea of office and recognize the rights of the local church.

Christ alone is the king of the church. He continues to care for his church through his own threefold office of prophet, priest, and king, not exclusively, but also through the three offices he instituted for his church. In that care he uses people, all believers as well as office-bearers. From the standpoint of its invisible side, the church's government is strictly monarchical. On the visible side of the church, his government is not democratic, nor monarchical, nor oligarchic, but aristocratic and presbyterial. Office-bearers are the ἄριστοι, the best, not in money and possessions but in spiritual gifts, whom Christ himself equips and allows the church to set apart for his service. By them he takes care of the spiritual and material interests of his church. By the teaching office he instructs, by the office of elder he leads, and by the diaconal office he takes care of his flock. By all three of them in conjunction he proves himself to be our chief prophet, our eternal king, and our merciful high priest. We follow the servant Lord in faithful, loving service.

THE CHURCH'S SPIRITUAL POWER

[507] The church no more belongs to the original institutions of the human race than the state. The family is the basic form of human community, combining civil and religious life under the leadership of a single patriarchal prophet, priest, and king. After sin, God basically instituted government when he enjoined the death penalty for homicide (Gen. 9:6); consequently, after the building of the Tower of Babel and under God's providence, government soon appeared in all the nations in which humanity was divided. Sin also created institutional social divisions, though in Israel all spheres were under God's theocratic rule. The split between civilian and religious life creates a dual situation and the ever-present possibility of a clash; alongside the civil rulers we see priests in public life, and the boundaries between the civil and religious authorities are redrawn differently in every nation. Generally, in the East, the power of rulers was subject to the priesthood; in the West, among Greeks and Romans, religion was a political matter and priests were functionaries of the state. A complete separation between the two was not to be found anywhere in antiquity; a neutral state was simply unknown

Originally designed as a patriarchal society, and divided into households, extended families, clans, and tribes, under the monarchy the genealogical division continued to exist with the heads of the tribes (etc.) settling important issues in tribal meetings. This provided a certain democratic cast to Israel's governance. It is incorrect to say that in Israel church and state were identical. From the beginning,

persons to the exercise of this authority, in any particular society, is in that society" (*Constitution of the Presbyterian Church in the United States of America* [Philadelphia: Office of General Assembly, 1955], 240).

there was a difference between civil and religious interests, between Moses and Aaron, between scribes and judges, on the one hand, and priests and Levites, on the other. The laws, institutions, offices, and office-bearers of the religious realm were different from the civil, in part even in their membership.[111] The priests' role was to serve in the temple, draw near to God with the sacrifices of the people, distribute God's grace and blessing to the people, and instruct them in the Torah (Lev. 9:22; 10:11; 21:8; Num. 6:22ff.; 16:5; Ezek. 44:23), but they also had to offer sacrifices for themselves (Lev. 9:7; 16:6), were bound to the law (Deut. 33:10; Jer. 18:18), and were dependent for their livelihood on the people (Lev. 23:10; Num. 18:8–32; etc.). The priests exercised no independent civil power; Israel was never a hierocracy. The freedom of the people was secured against the priestly class by the freedom of the prophets to speak God's word to the people; strangers could become citizens of Israel by the rite of circumcision (Exod. 12:48), and the impure and the leprous remained citizens even if they were temporarily segregated.

Israel was a theocracy: God was its lawgiver, judge, and king (Isa. 33:22). Not even the king could be a despot, but he had to be chosen by God, taken from among his brothers, and bound by God's law (Deut. 17:14–20; 1 Sam. 10:25). The law of God was supreme over all offices, institutions, and persons, and it regulated Israel's entire life and had to be observed by everyone without distinction. Israel had to be a holy people and a priestly kingdom (Exod. 19:6; Deut. 7:6). Without erasing the difference between civil and religious life, the government nevertheless had to enforce the law of God in its own sphere. Idolatry, image worship, sorcery, blasphemy, Sabbath desecration, all of them violations of the first table of the law, were therefore often punished with death (Exod. 22:18, 20; Lev. 20:2, 6, 27; 24:11–16; Num. 25:5, 7; Deut. 13:1–5; 17:2–7; 18:9–12; and so forth). Religion was a national matter; sin was a crime; a violation of the first table of the law was a breach of the covenant. In this connection it must be remembered, however, that the law furnished only a very few general rules and in many cases left the execution of punishment to God himself; the destruction of the Canaanites, the execution of Agag and of Ahab's "house" are isolated cases; the reformation undertaken by the kings was mostly restricted to the destruction of idols and the restoration of the public worship of YHWH; unbelief and heresy, though a frequent occurrence, were not tracked down by an inquisition, and coercion of conscience was entirely unknown. As Israel lost its political independence, especially after the exile, religious institutions became increasingly independent from the civil. The power of priests and the high priest gradually increased but had to contend with the dangerous competition of Pharisees and scribes. In the synagogue, religious life became independent, not only vis-à-vis the state but also vis-à-vis the temple and the priesthood. Life in its entirety was increasingly focused on the Torah, the teaching of which was the principal purpose of the synagogue (Matt. 4:23; Mark 1:21; Acts 15:21; 2 Tim. 3:15).

111. Ph. J. Hoedemaker, "Kerk en staat in Israël," *Troffel en Zwaard* 1 (1898): 208–37.

[508] Jesus organized his disciples into an ἐκκλησια with specific offices and endowed them with special spiritual power while at the same time recognizing the legitimacy of all other authority. The power of the keys entrusted to Peter on account of his confession (Matt. 16:19) was our Lord's way of appointing him as a house steward (οἰκονομος, *oikonomos*) of the kingdom of heaven. Keys are a sign of control or mastery (Isa. 22:22; Luke 11:52; Rev. 1:18; 3:7; 9:1; 20:1) and here denote the "binding" (δεειν; *deein*) and "loosing" (λυειν; *lyein*) of *actions*—not persons!—and signify "declaring something to be either permitted or prohibited."[112] As a rule this refers not to past but to future matters. Peter, accordingly, here receives from Jesus the power to determine—on the basis of or in agreement with his confession of Jesus as the Christ—what will or will not be allowed in the kingdom of heaven that has been established here on earth and has its center in the church. Matthew 16:19, therefore, not only accords to Peter and the apostles the right to exercise discipline but also the entire range of power that will soon also be entrusted to them. To their word, the church of all ages will be bound (John 17:20; 1 John 1:3); there is no gospel other than that which was proclaimed by them (Gal. 1:8). This power of the apostles does include the right to judge persons, as John 20:23 makes clear. Elsewhere the whole believing community receives the right to regard an impenitent brother, after repeated and failed attempts at reconciliation, as "a Gentile and a tax collector" (Matt. 18:17). The power that Christ here gave to Peter, to the apostles, and also to the church in its entirety, is further defined in many places in the New Testament. From this we see that this power is not an authoritarian, independent, sovereign rule (Matt. 20:25–26; 23:8, 10; 2 Cor. 10:4–5; 1 Pet. 5:3), but a ministry (διακονια, *diakonia*; λειτουργια, *leitourgia*; Acts 4:29; 20:24; Rom. 1:1; etc.), bound to Christ, to whom all power has been given in heaven and on earth (Matt. 28:18), who is the only head of the church (Eph. 1:22), and who as such distributes all the gifts and offices (Eph. 4:11). It is bound to his Word and Spirit, by which Christ himself governs his church (Rom. 10:14–15; Eph. 5:26), and exercised in his name and power (1 Cor. 5:4). Accordingly, it is indeed a power, a real and comprehensive power, a spiritual and moral power consisting in the ministry of Word and sacrament (Matt. 28:19).

All this power is essentially distinct from all other power that God has bestowed on persons over people or other creatures in the family, society, state, art, and science. For Jesus acted in no way other than as the Christ—as prophet, priest, and king; he had no other office. He recognized the authority of the high priest, the Sanhedrin, Herod, Pilate, and so forth: he pays the tax (Matt. 17:24–27); refuses to be an arbitrator between two brothers who fought over an inheritance (Luke 12:14); tells his disciples to give Caesar his due (Matt. 22:21); rebukes James and John for wanting fire to come down from heaven (Luke 9:54–55) and Peter for cutting off Malchus's ear (John 18:10–11); and forbids his disciples to

112. T. Zahn, *Das Evangelium des Matthäus*, 2nd ed. (Leipzig: A. Deichert, 1905), 544ff.

fight with the sword for his name and cause (Matt. 26:52). The gospel of Christ never opposes nature as such. It did not come into the world to condemn but to save (John 3:16–17), and it leaves the family, marriage, and the relationships between parents and children, masters and servants, and government and people intact. The gospel is not a revolutionary force but a spiritual and reforming one; it acknowledges and honors all legitimate authority rooted in creation's institutions and opposes only the sin and deception found in all areas of life. The pervasive reform it seeks comes through the power of the proclaimed and lived gospel. In this manner, in keeping with Jesus's command that the gospel must be preached to all creatures (Mark 16:15), it is "a power of God for salvation to everyone who believes" (Rom. 1:16), a two-edged sword that "pierces down to the division of soul and spirit" (Heb. 4:12), a leaven that leavens everything (Matt. 13:33), a principle that re-creates everything, and a power that overcomes the world (1 John 5:4).

[509] The power of the early church came through its testimony and proclamation, and the quiet, peaceable, godly, and respectful lives of believers (1 Tim. 2:2). As the church gained prominence and cultural power, over time it also increasingly accented *sacramental* and *juridical* power in the episcopacy, in the teaching and ruling church. Belonging to the power of jurisdiction is the power or right to teach (*potestas docendi*); the power of holy orders (*potestas ordinis*), which is the power to administer the sacraments and can only be obtained through the sacrament of orders, which is administered by the bishop. In keeping with this view, the forgiveness of sins is not granted in the preaching of the Word, which has only preparatory significance, but in the sacrament, which contains and infuses grace *ex opere operato* (by the act performed) in the recipient. It is specifically communicated in baptism, and for sins committed after baptism in the sacrament of penance. Sacraments are a judicial act. The priesthood, in the thought of Rome, can also exist apart from the preaching of the gospel.[113]

[510] To its credit, in contrast to the Caesaropapist East, the Western church retained its independence from the power of the state. Nonetheless, the church's independence was severely compromised by the increasing secular power the church arrogated to itself, a power that culminated in the full power of the infallible papacy as claimed by the First Vatican Council in 1870.[114] Although the papal claim is politically and juridically impressive, it is exactly to that same degree that it is religiously and ethically weak. In the Roman Catholic Church, the pope, through his infallibility, is the only absolute sovereign, the source of all ecclesiastical authority and power. "Where the pope is, there the church is." According to the council the pope's power is immediate, conferred by Christ, as

---

113. "If any one says that there is no . . . priesthood or . . . not any power of consecrating and offering the true body and blood of the Lord, and of forgiving and retaining sins, but only an office and bare ministry of preaching the gospel; or that those who do not preach are not priests at all—let him be anathema" (Council of Trent, sess. 23, "Canons on the Sacrament of Order," canon 1, in H. Denzinger, *Sources of Catholic Dogma*, #961).

114. First Vatican Council, IV, c. 3–4, in H. Denzinger, *Sources of Catholic Dogma*, ##1826–40.

well as full and supreme, absolute and subject to no laity, bishop, or council, but only to God. All the members of the church, whether individually or all together, and all bishops, whether individually or assembled in synods, owe absolute obedience to the pope, not only in matters of faith and morals, but also in matters of the discipline and government of the church. "This is the teaching of Catholic truth, from which no one can deviate without danger to faith and salvation." One part of this power is the teaching office concerning which it is determined that when the pope speaks ex cathedra, he is, by virtue of divine assistance, infallible.

After all that has been said earlier about the doctrine of Scripture and the most ancient ecclesiastical witnesses, we no longer need to argue that this papal system rests on an unscriptural foundation. However powerfully this papal edifice, thanks to its rigorous unity, often appeals to many Protestants, it is religiously and ethically weak to the degree that it is politically and juridically impressive. The reasons are, first, the nature and character of this infallibility remain insufficiently defined. Although it would be consistent with its position, Rome has not gone so far as to ascribe to the pope the same infallibility it recognizes in the apostles. The pope is infallible, not by inspiration but by the assistance of the Holy Spirit, by a special provision of God by which the church is kept from error and preserved in the truth. His infallibility consists only in the fact that he can faithfully preserve and explain the tradition handed down by the apostles. Although this infallibility is a special gift, it is not always a peculiar characteristic of the pope, nor of his person, but only as pope, as the head of the whole church. Second, to say that the pope is infallible when he speaks *ex cathedra* is practically useless as a standard since no one can tell whether a pope has spoken *ex cathedra* except the pope himself. A pope is always free to reject his own pronouncements or those of other popes by saying that they were not spoken *ex cathedra*, or to declare them binding by saying that they were. Since the infallible teaching office is a part of the "full and supreme power of jurisdiction in the universal church," whether the pope is fallible or infallible, all persons without distinction and any right of criticism ("nor may anyone examine judicially its decision") must unconditionally obey the pope, and that on peril of losing salvation. In session IV, canon 4, of the [First] Vatican Council, infallibility is expressly assigned only to the pope when he speaks *ex cathedra* and, as shepherd and teacher of all Christians, defines a "doctrine concerning faith or morals which must be held by the whole church."[115] But from this statement we have absolutely no right to infer that at other times he is not infallible. The term *ex cathedra* in fact draws no boundaries whatsoever. In fact, there is a vicious circle involved in the council's own declaration that the pope is infallible for the council itself is not infallible in making this declaration. Accordingly, for the Roman Catholic Christian, where is this highly acclaimed certainty? The [First] Vatican Council has put in place a result manufactured from a long historical process which includes the idea that the pope, in order to

115. First Vatican Council, sess. IV, c. 4.

be independent in the spiritual sphere, also had to be sovereign in secular matters. After the abolition of the ecclesiastical state in 1870, this idea gained increased prominence and was expressed with even stronger emphasis. Pius IX and Leo XIII have not neglected to repeat over and over that, as the universal bishop, the popes could not be the subject of any particular ruler nor bear a specific nationality,[116] and their pronouncements are binding for Catholic believers. Not only is such an idea of an ecclesiastical or sacerdotal state completely obsolete, violating the unity of Italy, it would be harmful to both church and state.

From all this, one senses the all-determining place the pope has in the life of Catholic Christians. The Roman Catholic Church is a monarchy, a kingdom, a state headed by a spiritual ruler. "Where the pope is, there the church is" (*ubi papa, ibi ecclesia*). The primacy of the pope is "the quintessence of the Christian religion" (*summa rei Christiane*).[117] Without the pope there is no church, no Christianity.[118] Submission to the pope is for all people a condition for salvation (Boniface VIII, *Unam Sanctam*). The pope is the mediator of salvation, the way, the truth, and the life. The only thing still lacking is that he is worshiped, but that too is only a matter of time.[119] Indeed, Scheeben and Atzberger are correct in saying that if the primacy of the pope is not the work of God, it is "a blasphemous and diabolical usurpation."[120]

[511] The Reformation rebelled against this degeneration of ecclesiastical power and sought to restore the understanding of spiritual power in the proclaimed Word. [In Luther's words:] "The kingdom of Christ is not a physical, worldly or earthly regime, like the way lords and kings govern on earth, but a spiritual and heavenly regime, in which one deals not with temporal goods, nor with the things that concern this life, but with hearts and consciences, how one must live before God and obtain his grace."[121] Since Christ is the only head of the church, only the Word of God can and may rule in the church, not by coercion, but only by love and free obedience.[122]

Calvin similarly differentiated between church and state as between soul and body, the future and the present life, and ascribed to the church its own offices,

---

116. Gerardus Martinus Jansen, *Praelectiones theologiae dogmaticae*, 3 vols. in 2 (Utrecht: Van Rossum, 1875–79), I, 657; K. von Hase, *Handbuch der protestantischen Polemik gegen die römisch-katholische Kirche*, 6th ed. (Leipzig: Breitkopf & Härtel, 1894), 254.

117. R. Bellarmine, "De rom. pontif," in *Controversiis*, in the foreword.

118. Veuillot, according to K. von Hase, *Handbuch der protestantischen Polemik*, 187.

119. A. von Harnack, *History of Dogma*, VII, 116–17.

120. Matthias Joseph Scheeben and Leonhard Atzberger, *Handbuch der katholischen Dogmatik*, 4 vols. (1874–98; repr., Freiburg i.B.: Herder, 1933), IV, 427.

121. Ed. note: The citation here is clearly from Luther, though Bavinck cites only secondary literature. [Cited by] R. Sohm, *Kirchenrecht*, 2 vols. (Leipzig and Munich: Duncker & Humblot, 1892–1923), 464, 488; cf. also J. Köstlin, *Theology of Luther*, II, 521ff., 541ff.; P. Drews, *Entsprach das Staatskirchentum dem Ideale Luthers?* (Tübingen: Mohr [Siebeck], 1908); K. Müller, *Kirche, Gemeinde und weltliche Obrigkeit nach Luther* (Tübingen: Mohr [Siebeck], 1910).

122. Luther, according to R. Sohm, *Kirchenrecht*, 464, 468.

power, and jurisdiction.[123] The administration of Word and sacrament is the only form of church government, the sum of all ecclesiastical power, the totality of the power of the keys. Christ's authority as given in the word of the proclaimed gospel is the church's only proper power. Either directly or indirectly, all power in the church is administration of the Word. Reformed people began with the conviction that Christ, whom God anointed king over Zion, exercises his spiritual authority through instruments that are not autonomous, independent, sovereign, but bound to him, that is, to his Word. Every office in the church of Christ is a ministry (διακονια, *diakonia*). For the Reformed churches this meant that for confession as an institution of the church, they only retained the regular or occasional confession of sins customary in preparing for the celebration of the Lord's Supper, and for the rest replaced private confession with the practice of Word-directed discipline in personal home visitation.[124] What marks the Reformed tradition's polity is the conviction that, while church and state are distinct from each other, the church also distributes its spiritual goods for the benefit of the whole of humanity and for every aspect of human life. This is Christianity's true catholicity. The magistrate, appointed by God, is also bound to God's law and Word; the Bible that sheds light on the human condition as a whole is also accessible to governments. In practice, however, this theory was not sustained and, out of concern for freedom of conscience and religion, yielded to absolute separation of church and state.

There were, however, some differences between the Lutheran and Reformed traditions. Luther, though he rejected the Roman Catholic ban and removed all civil penalties from ecclesiastical discipline, definitely desired the application of discipline in the church of Christ to remove, after repeated admonition, the evildoer from its midst.[125] But the absence of the office of presbyter and the exercise of ecclesiastical discipline by the pastor alone led to such abuses that it soon disappeared and, to the extent that it remained, was left to mixed consistories (consisting of both ecclesiastical and civil members).[126] For Calvin, ecclesiastical discipline was a matter of life and death, and he fought for twenty years in Geneva for the church's right to remove the evil person from its midst, acquiring it only in 1555. Although discipline could not be the soul of the church, it nevertheless has to serve as its sinews. Thinking of church discipline as obligatory, necessity, and useful discipline distinguished the Reformed on the one hand from Roman

---

123. J. Calvin, *Institutes*, IV.i–xi.

124. Thus Zwingli, according to E. Zeller, *Das theologische System Zwingli's* (Tübingen: L. F. Fues, 1853), 153; cf. P. Biesterveld, *Het huisbezoek* (Kampen: Bos, 1900).

125. J. Köstlin, *Theology of Luther*, II, 526ff., 533ff.; the Lutheran Confessions in Joseph T. Müller, *Die symbolischen Bücher der evangelisch-lutherischen Kirche*, 75, 152, 165, 288, 329, 342; ed. note: These specific references are to the following Lutheran documents: Apology of the Augsburg Confession, "Preface" (Kolb and Wengert, 110); ibid., arts. 7–8 (Kolb and Wengert, 174ff.); ibid., art. 11, pars. 60–62 (Kolb and Wengert, 290–91); Treatise on the Power and Primacy of the Pope, pars. 7–11, 70–73 (Kolb and Wengert, 331, 341–42).

126. Ed. note: Bavinck's expression is simply "mixed consistories" (*gemengde consistoriën*); from the context it is apparent that he is referring to a "mixture" of ecclesiastical and civil authorities.

Catholics and Lutherans, and on the other from Anabaptists and Mennonites, who as a result of their nature-grace antithesis sometimes applied excommunication with excessive severity and deprived it of its spiritual character.[127] Reflected here is a different understanding of the relationship of Christianity to the natural life. All the Reformers united in liberating the natural life from the pressure and power of the church, confessing that though the world is under the control of the evil one (1 John 5:19), it remains in itself holy and good, a work of God the Almighty, Creator of heaven and earth. The quantitative antithesis of the natural and the supernatural is here traded for the qualitative, ethical antithesis of sin and grace.

Nonetheless, differences among the Reformers remained. Zwingli never quite transcended the medieval dualism between "flesh" and "spirit," between human and divine justice, and Luther frequently so limited the work of Christ to the religious and ethical that the natural came to stand independently alongside that area. While the gospel only changed the internal, the mind, the heart, it had no transforming effect on the natural life as a whole. This explains the disdain with which Luther often spoke of reason, philosophy, and jurisprudence. As long as Lutherans had the pure administration of Word and sacrament, other matters—ceremonies, external government of the church—could be treated as adiaphora or left to the jurisdiction of the civil authorities. The Reformed churches, however, were opposed to this arrangement because they regarded Christ alone as king of his church. To be sure, civil authority was also appointed by God, but it was distinct from the church in origin, nature, and government, and to transfer the church's power to the state was a violation of the kingship of Christ. But this distinction was never meant to be a separation, and the Reformed called on the government in a Christian country to protect the true church, to support its expansion and extension, to resist all idolatry and false religion, and to destroy the kingdom of the antichrist (Belgic Confession, art. 36). The magistrate too is bound by God's Word; the content of the Bible is not exclusively religious and ethical and only valid for the church, but a word from God that goes out to the whole of humanity and sheds light on every creature and all of life; Christian truth was universal and catholic, plain and clear, and therefore accessible also to the government.[128]

127. J. Calvin, *Institutes*, IV.xii; P. van Mastricht, *Theoretico-practica theologia* (Utrecht: Appels, 1714), VII, 6; H. Bavinck, *Synopsis purioris theologiae*, disp. 48; F. Turretin, *Institutes of Elenctic Theology*, XVIII, qu. 32; S. Gallic Confession, art. 27; Belgic Confession, art. 29; Heidelberg Catechism, Q&A 83–85; Helvetic Confession, II, 18.

128. Cf. H. A. Niemeyer, *Collectio confessionum in ecclesiis reformatis publicatarum*, 2 vols. (Leipzig: Iulii Klinkhardti, 1840), 9, 32, 54, 55, 82, 98, 114, 122, 326, 355, 387, 534, 610, 765, 810; ed. note: These specific references are to the following reformational documents: U. Zwingli, The Sixty-seven Articles (##29–41); 11th article on the magistrate; idem, Exposition of the Christian Faith, art. 87, "Magistratus"; First Confession of Basle (1534), art. 8; ibid., art. 8, disp. 221; Second Helvetic Confession, chap. XXX; Catechism of Geneva, art. 21; Gallican Confession, art. 24; First Scotch Confession, art. 24; Belgic Confession, art. 36; Thirty-nine Articles of the Church of England, art. 36 (art. 37); Tetrapolitan Confession (Strasburg Confession, 1530), art. 23; Bohemian Confession (1535), art. 16; J. Calvin, *Institutes*, IV.xx.

But life proved stronger than doctrine, and gradually this absolute position weakened. Already in the sixteenth century some Anabaptists and Socinians insisted that the government should abstain from all intervention in matters of religion and specifically from the punishment of heretics. Reformed teaching concerning the state, accordingly, encountered numerous practical difficulties. In theory church and state were indeed distinct, but in fact the state was frequently subject to the pronouncements of the church and bound to its confession. By virtue of its close connection with the church and the obligation it had assumed, the government engaged in acts of violence and coercion that were repugnant to the government itself, acts that gave the government a bad name among numerous noble-minded people, invited the appearance of Roman Catholic tyranny, and were inconsistent with Protestant demands for freedom of conscience and religion. When in Protestantism a wide diversity of churches and creeds arose whose Christian character could not be denied, it became impossible even for the most rigorous Christians to maintain the confessional character of the state and to insist that heretics should be punished. Thus, guided by the facts, people gradually moved from a confessional to a generally Christian view, and from there to a deistic view of the state, and "tolerance" and "moderation" became the rallying cries of the eighteenth century. Beginning with Roger Williams (ca. 1603–83) the modern world has heard repeated calls for the absolute freedom of religion, which he applied to Rhode Island, the colony he founded. This theory increasingly met with approval both among Christians and within the revolutionary camp. While some American states adopted it after 1776, and the French Revolution made it mandatory in many countries, it exists nowhere in a pure and consistent form, and in practice everyone shrinks from its consequences.

THE OFFICES AND ASSEMBLIES OF THE CHURCH

[512] The church cannot live without order, regulation, structure, and exercise of power. Generally speaking, it is an undeniable truth that nothing can exist without order and regulation, and that a true formless substance (ὕλη, *hylē*) is nothing more than a philosophical abstraction. This is generally acknowledged whether one considers families, businesses, armies, societies, or society at large. Anarchy does not work. In the church the debate is not about *whether* there should be rules and order but about the *how* and *what* of that order; about the exact *form* and *nature* of the church's polity. Christ did indeed say that his kingdom is not of this world, but he is not a spiritual king in the sense that he has absolutely no interest in external and earthly things. The reality of the incarnation reminds us that Christ came not to remove us *from* the realities of this world but to save us *in* them. He came to destroy the works of the devil everywhere and to spark the acknowledgment of the rights and honor of God; his reconciling and renewing activity extends as far as sin has destroyed and corrupted everything. Christ

planted his kingdom in that world and made sure that it could exist in it and, like a leaven, have a transforming impact in all areas of life.

To the offices he instituted in his church, Christ linked a special power (ἐξουσια, *exousia*), consisting in the proclamation of the gospel (Matt. 10:7; Mark 3:14; 16:15; Luke 9:2; etc.), the administration of the sacraments (Matt. 28:19; Mark 16:15; Luke 22:19; 1 Cor. 11:24–26), performing different kinds of miracles (Matt. 10:1, 8; Mark 3:15; 16:18; Luke 9:1; 10:9, 19; etc.), retaining or forgiving sins (Matt. 16:19; 18:18; John 20:23), feeding the flock (John 21:15–17; Acts 20:28), exercising discipline (Matt. 18:17; 1 Cor. 5:4), serving tables (Acts 6:2), and the right to earn a living from the gospel (Matt. 10:10; 1 Cor. 9:4ff.; 2 Thess. 3:9; 1 Tim. 5:18). The power Christ gives to the offices and office-bearers in his church is unique, differing in kind from all political power with respect to its origin, operation, nature, purpose, and means. Power and authority in other areas—family, business, school, society, state—comes from God as the creator of heaven and earth (Rom. 13:1), but ecclesiastical power comes directly from God as the Father of our Lord Jesus Christ (1 Cor. 12:28; Eph. 4:11; Acts 20:28) and is therefore completely free and independent from all other earthly powers. It is, in short, a *spiritual* power.

To say it is a "spiritual" power does not mean it is invisible and completely internal, for though Christ is a spiritual king, he rules over both body and soul. Word and sacrament are directed toward the whole person; the ministry of mercy must even alleviate primarily the physical needs of humans. "Spiritual" means the following: the church's power is given by the Holy Spirit of God (Acts 20:28); can only be exercised in the name of Christ and in the power of the Holy Spirit (John 20:22–23; 1 Cor. 5:4); only applies to humans as believers (1 Cor. 5:12); works and can only work in a spiritual and moral manner, not with coercion and penalties in money, goods, or life, but by conviction, faith, good will, freedom, and love, and hence only with spiritual weapons (Mark 16:16; John 8:32; 2 Cor. 3:17; 10:4; Eph. 6:7; etc.). It also has the spiritual *purpose* of salvation, for building up, not for destruction, for the perfection of the saints and the upbuilding of the body of Christ (Matt. 10:13; Mark 16:16; Luke 2:34; 2 Cor. 2:16; 10:4, 8; 13:10; Eph. 4:12; 6:11–18; etc.).[129] Ecclesiastical power, thus, differs in kind from all political power, as Jesus himself indicated, prohibiting his disciples from "worldly" exercises of power (Matt. 20:25–26; 22:21; Luke 12:13–14; John 6:15; 18:36; 1 Pet. 5:3). The church eschews all forms of coercion, violence, and sword power and refuses to accept the secular power that properly belongs to the state. It is sinful confusion to assign ecclesiastical power to the state as well as it is to change ecclesiastical power into political power. Both extremes are rooted in an excessive antithesis between nature and grace. Anabaptism tends to abolish nature by thinking of the church as a political entity; Rome suppresses nature by subordinating it to the realm of the sacerdotal church. The latter also robs ecclesiastical power

129. G. Voetius, *Pol. eccl.*, IV, 783.

of its spiritual character by turning it into something political. Traditionally, this meant an unwillingness to distinguish ecclesiastical power from civil power and punishment. In its turn Reformation ecclesiology insisted on a purely spiritual power exercised in ministry of the Word and sacraments and through discipline. Accordingly, in connection with the offices of pastor, presbyter, and deacon and further in connection with the threefold office of Christ—the prophetic, the royal, and the priestly office—we must distinguish three kinds of power in Christ's church: power to teach (prophetic office), power to govern (kingly office), and the power or ministry of mercy (priestly office).

[513] The power to teach (*potestas docendi*) has its roots in the prophetic office for which Christ has been anointed and which he still exercises by his Word and Spirit. The church itself is a prophetess, and all Christians share in Christ's anointing and are called to confess his name. Christ is the Chief Prophet, but he regularly employs people as his organs, not only office-bearers in the strict sense, but all believers, every one of them according to the grace given to them. There are many charismata that belong to the church's teaching power: wisdom, knowledge, prophecy, and so forth (1 Cor. 12:8ff.). The responsibility of teaching the truth of the gospel is given to all believers in their various places and callings, but in an official way through the teaching of the minister of the Word. The office does not suppress the gifts but, rather, only guides them. This teaching power of proclamation must not—as Roman Catholics do—be subordinated to the sacraments since, according to Scripture, the Word has precedence over the sacraments. There is no sacrament without the Word, but there is a Word without the sacrament, and those who administer the Word do not therefore always have to administer the sacrament (1 Cor. 1:14–17). The sacrament follows the Word. Official administration of the Word may not be leveled to all teaching of the Word undertaken by believers among themselves. It is also distinct from evangelistic words addressed to "outsiders" and to application of Scripture by elders to church members. Official proclamation is properly said to be an independent task.

All Word application—official or otherwise—is a feeding of the flock of Christ the Good Shepherd (Pss. 23:1; 80:1; Isa. 40:11; 49:10; Jer. 31:10; Ezek. 34:15; 23; John 10:11, 14; Heb. 13:20; 1 Pet. 2:25; 5:4; Rev. 7:17); ministers too, under Christ, bear the name of shepherds or pastors (Isa. 44:28; Jer. 2:8; 3:15, 23:1ff.; Ezek. 34:2ff.; John 10:2; 21:15–17; Acts 20:28; 1 Cor. 9:7; Eph. 4:11; 1 Pet. 5:2).[130] At the same time, however, since the two activities of pastoring and teaching, of ruling and laboring in the Word and in doctrine, have been separated, and each of them has obtained its own organ (Eph. 4:11; 1 Tim. 5:17), the name "teacher" has become the characteristic title of the minister of the Word. By his preparation and training, by his total devotion to laboring in the Word, by his right to live

---

130. Cf. *Formulier om te bevestingen de dienaren des Goddelicken Woorts* (Amsterdam and Haarlem: J. Brandt and Johannes Enschede, 1870); ed. note: ET: *Form of Ordination of the Ministers of God's Word*, in *The Psalter with the Doctrinal Standards and Liturgy of the Christian Reformed Church*, 2 vols. in 1 (Grand Rapids: Eerdmans-Sevensma, 1914), II, 70–72.

from the gospel, by his official administration of the Word and sacrament in the gathering of believers, he has been distinguished from the ruling elder, who is especially charged with feeding the flock (Acts 20:28; 1 Pet. 5:2). Official teaching is never to be taken as something primarily intellectual. Ministers require thorough training and supervision so that the church may maintain the truth of God's Word at all times, but ministers must preach appropriately to the various levels of their congregation. The church, it must be said, does possess the authority to confess the truth it believes, to maintain it as confession in its midst, and to ask its office-bearers to subscribe to its rule of faith. Objections that such a subscription is inconsistent with the all-sufficiency of Scripture, destroys Christian liberty, introduces intolerable tyranny, and cuts off further investigation and development ignore the responsibility Scripture itself places on the church to be a "pillar and foundation of the truth," confess it before all people, avoid those who deviate from the doctrine of the truth, and maintain the Word of God against all its adversaries. In a world immersed in lies and deception, a church cannot exist without a rule of faith; it falls prey—as especially the history of the nineteenth century teaches—to all sorts of error and confusion without a fixed confession, and becomes subject to the tyranny of prevailing schools of thought and opinions. Almost from the outset (that is, from the beginning of the second century), the church has been a confessional church that found its unity in the rule of faith, in baptismal formularies and symbols, and eventually in the apostolic symbol. The rule of faith is not a standard of coercion but of persuasion and voluntary submission. Furthermore, Scripture alone is trustworthy in and of itself (αὐτόπιστος, *autopistos*), unconditionally binding us to faith and obedience, unchanging; a confession, on the other hand, always remains examinable and revisable by the standard of Scripture.

[514] Christ is not only a prophet but also a king who still continually rules his church personally from heaven (*potestas gubernationis*). In a broad sense, we mean by this power all the leadership and care that believers exert and bestow on one another (Rom. 15:14; Col. 3:16; 1 Thess. 5:11), for which the Spirit bestows gifts (Rom. 12:8; 1 Cor. 12:28), the greatest of which, the one that must govern them all, is love (Rom. 12:10; 1 Cor. 13:13; Phil. 2:3; 1 Pet. 5:5). Inasmuch as Christ is king in the realm of grace, this governance is spiritual and characterized by loving service; in Scripture it is called "taking care of the flock" (John 21:15–17; Acts 20:28; 1 Pet. 5:2), and all that suggests earthly power and political dominion is excluded from it (2 Cor. 1:24; 1 Pet. 5:2–3). As king of the church Christ has also instituted a specific office, the office of the presbyter (elder), by which he governs his church. While in a broad sense this "taking care of the flock" also includes the work of the minister of the Word, there is nevertheless a big distinction between the public proclamation of the Word and the personal and individual application of it, between shepherding the flock in general and caring for each of the sheep in particular. Discipling does involve discipline and chastisement, even excommunication in extreme cases. Scripture sets forth a clear

pattern for church discipline, characterized by patience, love, and other spiritual means. The goal is always the restoration of the sinner. While the Roman Catholic practice of confession has something good in it (James 5:16),[131] it cannot make up for the well-regulated ministry of the presbyterate. Compulsory confession violates the liberty of the human conscience, makes grace and one's salvation at every moment uncertain and unsettled, and forces the church's ministers into a casuistic and quantitative treatment of sin and punishment, thereby occasioning all sorts of immoral practices.[132] Scripture, by example and precept, points us to Nathan going to David, Elijah to Ahab, and Isaiah to Hezekiah, to remonstrate with them personally over their sins. The condition of the church of Christ in this dispensation requires ongoing spiritual care; a planted church is not immediately perfect. On the contrary, it is a field that needs to be constantly weeded, a tree that must be pruned at the proper time, a flock that must also be led and pastured, a house that requires constant renovation, a bride who must be prepared to be presented as a pure virgin to her husband. In addition to the sick, the dying, the tested, the grieving; those who are under attack, conflicted, in doubt, fallen, imprisoned, and so forth who need teaching and instruction, admonition and consolation, the church must increase in the knowledge and grace of the Lord Jesus Christ. Ministers are also weak and sinful people who need supervision. Failure to supervise them may lead to ministers abusing their office. In a word, the preachers sow the Word, the elders look for the fruit.[133]

[515] The work of church discipline (*potestas disciplinae*) belongs particularly to the task of the overseer. The Hebrew word for it is מוּסָר (*mûsār*), which really means "discipline by chastisement" and has been translated into Greek by νουθετημα (*nouthetēma*, admonition), διδασκαλια (*didaskalia*, instruction), νομος (*nomos*, custom, law), and σοφια (*sophia*, wisdom) and is rendered in the New Testament especially by παιδεια (*paideia*, training, education, mental culture). Both words indicate in general that something young, tender, small, and weak be brought up with care. Because bringing up children involves countering abnormal development, the word "discipline" acquired the connotation of correction, chastisement, and punishment and is also so used in the New Testament (2 Tim. 3:16; Heb. 12:5–11; Rev. 3:19). An exclusively ecclesiastical penalty for sins in Israel, including the expulsion from the community of believers (Ezra 10:8), arose only when she became a synagogue-based community. Jesus giving the keys of the kingdom to Peter (Matt.16:19), to the church (Matt. 18:18), to the apostles (John 20:23), is perhaps in line with this synagogue-based discipline. Matthew 18:15–17 shows us how this discipline must be exercised: first a personal rebuke to win a brother over; then in the presence of witnesses; finally before the whole church. If all this fails, the rebuked one may be treated as a pagan or tax

---

131. J. Calvin, *Institutes*, III.i.13.

132. See H. Bavinck, *Reformed Dogmatics*, IV, 147–49 (#462).

133. Concerning the office of the presbytery: J. Calvin, *Institutes*, IV.i.22; A. Kuyper, *Encyclopaedie der heilige godgeleerdherd*, 2nd ed., 3 vols. (Kampen: Kok, 1908–9), III, 524; P. Biesterveld, *Het huisbezoek*.

collector. Beyond this is God's own discipline, sometimes exercised in his name by the apostles. Included are: the death of Ananias and Sapphira (Acts 5:1–11); Elymas struck with blindness (Acts 13:11); judgment upon an incestuous person in the church (1 Cor. 5); sickness and death because of unworthy participation in the Lord's Supper (1 Cor. 11:30). In the case of 1 Corinthians 5 and 1 Timothy 1:20 and 2 Timothy 2:17, we have here a special apostolic act of power and not an ordinary act of excommunication, as for example in Matthew 18:17. In such case we are not called to break off contact with all sinful people—that would be impossible—but to avoid close fellowship with unrepentant former believers (Rom. 16:17; 2 Cor. 2:5–10; 2 Thess. 3:6, 14; Titus 3:10; Rev. 2:2, 14, 20, 24).

Reformed churches have been the most conscientious in applying this scriptural teaching on discipline. They always regard specific individual persons who are members of the church, either by baptism or by profession of faith, as the proper objects for discipline; address only sins that cause offense among the members of the congregation; clearly distinguish hidden or private sins—to be dealt with according to Matthew 18—and public sins; follow clear procedure in the case of public sins; apply only spiritual punishment such as barring from the table of the Lord; and use excommunication only as an extreme remedy of last resort with readmission to the church upon confession of sin always a possibility (Matt. 16:19; 18:18; John 20:23; 2 Cor. 2:5–10).

[516] In the third place, Christ is also a priest who from heaven still consistently exercises this office in his church, an office characterized by the power of mercy. Our Lord healed people, sent out his disciples to preach, cast out evil spirits, and healed every disease and sickness (Matt. 10:1, 8; Mark 3:15; Luke 9:1–2; 10:9, 17), and calls his church to a robust diaconal ministry of mercy in his name. In keeping with Jesus's own promise (Mark 16:17–18), many extraordinary gifts of healing and manifestations of power were granted to his disciples (Acts 2:44–45; 4:35; Rom. 12:7–8; 1 Cor. 12:28). As things went with the gifts of teaching and government, however, so they went with the works of mercy. Increasingly they were linked with the offices: doctrine was assigned to the teacher (διδασκαλος, *didaskalos*), government to the presbyter, and similarly the ministry of mercy to the deacon (Acts 6). The gifts themselves became more simple and ordinary; the treasures of love and mercy that Christ poured out in his church richly manifested themselves in private benevolence. Rome, though its organization of the ministry of mercy leaves much to be desired, outshines other churches. For while the Reformed churches did restore the office of deacon, they did not properly define and regulate its role and ministry nor develop its outreach. Reformed churches need to honor the diaconal office more than it has been up until now as an independent organ of the priestly mercy of Christ.[134] Love and mercy need to be recognized

---

134. Ed. note: The sentences that follow, which are a summary of eleven substantive points in the full text of the *Reformed Dogmatics*, are remarkable because Bavinck here goes beyond dogmatic exposition to definite programmatic recommendations for the church's ministry.

and practiced as the most outstanding Christian virtues, and deacons instructed to teach all members, especially the wealthier, to be on guard against the sin of covetousness and to practice mercy. The diaconate should stimulate, regulate, and guide—not kill—the practice of private benevolence, and in large churches avail themselves, if necessary, of the assistance of deaconesses in the same way the two other offices employ catechists and pastoral visitors of the sick. Deacons should extend their help to all the poor, the sick, the strangers, the prisoners, the mentally retarded, the mentally ill, the widows and orphans, to all the wretched and needy in the church who are either completely or partly deprived of help from other sources, and that by word and deed they seek to relieve their suffering. The ministry of mercy should be given a much larger place on the agenda of all ecclesiastical assemblies than has been the case up until now, and deacons delegated to major assemblies and be given a vote in all matters pertaining to the ministry of mercy. At these assemblies the ministry of mercy should be organized in terms of general principles, bearing in mind the difference in congregational circumstances; for broader needs it should be undertaken communally and expanded by asking the local churches to assist other churches by aiding poor and oppressed fellow believers abroad. The gifts of God's people must be distributed in Christ's name, as taken from the tables of the Lord on which they have been deposited by the congregation and given to Christ himself (Matt. 25:40). This ministry of mercy done by the church institution should never be absorbed in, fused with, or confused with state welfare. The church's diaconal ministry must remain independent.

[517] Christ rules his church through the offices and councils of local congregations. According to the New Testament, every local church is independent, a "complete church" (*ecclesia completa*), and therefore, like the church in its entirety, bears the name "temple of God" (1 Cor. 3:16–17; 2 Cor. 6:16), "bride" (2 Cor. 11:2), or "body of Christ" (1 Cor. 12:27). However, believers do not stand apart in isolation from each other, and from the beginning local churches gathered together to address common concerns. Traces of this occur already in the New Testament, in practice in Jerusalem (Acts 1:14; 2:41ff.; 5:12; 6:2; 15:2, 6, 22), and by apostolic example and injunction elsewhere (1 Cor. 11:4–6, 34; 14:27ff.; 16:1; 1 Tim. 3; 4:14). In the Book of Acts the disciples come together for the election of an apostle (chap. 1) and the church chooses deacons (chap. 6). Paul speaks of a body of elders as a *presbyterium* in 1 Timothy 4:14, and in 1 Corinthians 5 he calls them to exercise discipline. And also the local churches together form a unity. Collectively they too are called an ἐκκλησια (*ekklēsia* [sing.]) and subject to the apostles, to whom has been given the task of leading and governing the whole church. Such a larger assembly is described in Acts 15 when the churches of Antioch and Jerusalem, along with others, gathered to address the circumcision of gentiles.

All these meetings reported in the New Testament were assemblies of the local church, attended only in Acts 15 by representatives from other places. At the synods of the first three centuries, presbyters and deacons as well as bishops were in attendance. Even the Council of Nicea was attended, aside from bishops, also by presbyters, deacons, and members who took part in the debates. In the second and third centuries, moreover, all congregational meetings, attended by delegates from neighboring churches, were equal in rank. There was not yet hierarchy of ecclesiastical assemblies; there were as yet no provincial, metropolitan, or ecumenical councils. Increasingly, however, more hierarchical patterns were established, and gradually there emerged a ranking of provincial, national, patriarchal, and ecumenical councils.[135] The result of the development of the hierarchical idea was that the consent of the congregation was increasingly less frequently requested, the presbyters and deacons were detached from the congregation and changed into counselors and helpers of the bishop, and the synods were gradually held only by bishops. All this makes it hard to designate the characteristic feature of an ecumenical council. The Roman Catholic Church, however, designates ecumenical councils as such: To Rome a council is ecumenical only when its decrees have been endorsed by the pope and have thereby acquired an infallible, universally binding character.[136]

In Protestant churches, synodical forms of church government developed gradually, especially in Reformed churches, and though their history is not always glorious, they are both necessary and useful. In 1528 at Zurich, Zwingli instituted synods convoked by the [city] council—consisting of preachers from the city and the country and a few members of the [city] council—which mainly had to weigh complaints against the teaching and conduct of the preachers.[137] Calvin similarly laid down in the *Ecclesiastical Ordinances* that the preachers had to assemble every three months to supervise each other's teaching and conduct and, additionally, introduced an annual visitation in 1546.[138] A synodical church order first came into being in France, where the churches were fast expanding and, out of a need for unity, first came together in synod at Paris on May 26, 1559, and united in adopting a common confession and church order.[139] Remarkable here is that the general synod originated first, that this synod introduced the provincial synods, and that later, in 1572, a classis was inserted between the provincial synods and local church councils.[140] Later such a synodical form of church government was

---

135. R. Sohm, *Kirchenrecht*, 247–344; A. Hauck, "Synoden," in *PRE*[3], XIX, 262ff.; A von Harnack, *The Mission and Expansion of Christianity*, II, 172; O. Berzl, *Ursprung, Aufgabe, und Wesen der christlichen Synoden* (Würzburg: Stadenraus, 1908); ed. note: Bavinck erroneously cites the author of this latter work as G. Osten.

136. R. Bellarmine, "De conciliis et ecclesia lib.," in *Controversiis*, bks. I and II.

137. J. K. Mörikofer, *Ulrich Zwingli, nach den urkundlichen Quellen*, 2 vols. (Leipzig: Hirzel, 1867–69), II, 118ff.

138. F. W. Kampschulte and W. Goetz, *Johann Calvin: Seine Kirche und sein Staat in Genf*, 2 vols. (Leipzig: Duncker & Humblot, 1869–99), I, 408.

139. G. V. Lechler, *Geschichte der Presbyterial- und Synodalverfassung seit der Reformation* (Leiden: Noothoven van Goor, 1854), 69.

140. Ibid., 81; cf. for Scotland, 97; H. E. von Hoffmann, *Das Kirchenverfassungsrecht der niederländischen Reformierten bis zum Beginne der Dordrechter Nationalsynode von 1618/19* (Leipzig: Hirschfeld, 1902).

also introduced in other Reformed churches: in Poland, Bohemia, Hungary, Germany, the Netherlands, Scotland, England, America, and so forth. Opposition, however, arose from two quarters: (1) Those who regarded them as permissible but unnecessary and believed that they were under the authority of the state (Remonstrants); (2) those who considered every group of believers independent, and rejected every binding classical or synodical linkage (Anabaptists, Independents). The objectors raise valid points. In the New Testament, congregations *are* independent under Christ. Additionally, the history of synods does not always speak well of their usefulness and frequently makes them appear to be the cause of all sorts of dissension and division, so that Gregory of Nazianzus could already say, "I saw the end of not even one synod as being useful," and there is some truth in the proverb that "every council gives birth to [further] battles."

Other considerations, however, clearly bring out the necessity and usefulness of synods. The absence of any classical or synodical connection among the churches in the New Testament is easily accounted for by the role the apostles played in the early church. There is evidence of at least a *permission* to assemble, deliberate with other churches and even request adjudication in certain disputes (Acts 1; 6; 15; 21). In a very general sense "synods" are "permitted by divine law." Although synods are not strictly necessary for the "being" of the church, and are not specifically mandated by the Word of God, they are permitted and necessary to the "well-being" (*bene esse*) of the church. This necessity arises from the fact that the unity of doctrine, discipline, and worship to which the church is called, the order and peace and love it has to preserve, and the common interests assigned to it (such as the training, calling, and sending out of ministers; evangelism; the support of needy churches; and so forth) can only come into their own by means of synods. Synods subvert hierarchies by maintaining the independence of the local congregation, protecting them from pastoral and other forms of domination, and giving them a right of appeal. Synods can carefully investigate, allow for ample discussion, and peacefully settle the disputes that invariably arise in the church on earth over doctrine, discipline, and ministry. In order that they may serve their purpose, synods ought always to be assemblies of churches whose members (pastors, presbyters, deacons, or ordinary members) are the delegates of churches and bound to the credentialed letters of instruction from churches. Assemblies should not be ranked in a hierarchical order of higher to lower for all are equally bound to the Word and share equally in the promise of the Spirit. Assemblies are not representative bodies from church but gatherings of office-bearers who are called, in Christ's name, to govern his church. The authority of all churches and church assemblies comes from Christ, the Lord of the church. His Word alone is decisive. Only that which the Holy Spirit approves in and through the members is binding in the church of Christ.

[518] Thus the church exists in the midst of the world with an origin, essence, activity, and purpose of its own. While in every respect it is distinct from that world, it never stands apart from or alongside the world, but relates to it organi-

cally, spiritually, and morally. The various postures taken by Christian groups to understand the relation between the church and the world can be reduced to three basic ones: Anabaptist *avoidance*; Roman Catholic supernatural elevation of the natural and perfection through *ascesis*; Protestant, and especially Reformed *renewal* and *sanctification*. The last two are the two major options. Rome does not view the natural as sinful in the manner of Anabaptism and thus does not advocate avoidance and separation, but it does teach that the natural is of a lower order, easily becomes the cause of sin, and therefore needs the restraint of the supernatural. Grace is mechanically "added on" to the natural, and those who want to live according to the ideal of Rome have to become ascetics, suppress the natural, and devote themselves totally to religion. Those unable to do this obtain the necessary space for the natural and find in the supernatural the boundary that marks the limits of this space.

The Protestant (Reformed) view begins with the conviction that there is only one God in creation and in re-creation and that the God of creation and of the Old Testament is not lower than the God of the re-creation, than the Father of Christ, than the God of the new covenant. Christ, the mediator of the new covenant, is also he by whom God created all things. And the Holy Spirit, who is the author of regeneration and sanctification, is the same as he who in the beginning hovered over the waters and adorned the heavens. Creation and re-creation, therefore, cannot be contrasted in terms of being lower and higher. They are both good and pure—splendid works of the one Triune God. The grace that comes after the fall into sin is not a substance or matter, enclosed in Word or sacrament and distributed by the priest, but a renewing and transforming force *in creation*. This grace is distributed in a twofold form: as common grace with a view toward restraining [evil] and as special grace with a view to renewing [the world]. Both have their unity in Christ, the king of the realm of power and grace. Both are directed against sin; both ensure the connectedness between creation and re-creation. Neither has the world been left to itself after the fall, nor deprived of all grace, but it is sustained and spared by common grace, guided and preserved for special grace in Christ. Separation and suppression, accordingly, are impermissible and impossible. The world after the fall is not "godless" nor deprived of all grace; avoidance, separation, and suppression are impermissible and impossible. We are human before we are Christian; becoming a Christian does not take us out of our humanity or elevate us above it: the Christian is nothing other than a reborn, renewed, and hence a truly human person. The incarnation of Christ involved the taking on of our full humanity, and he did not regard anything human and natural as strange or alien. Accordingly, the relationship that has to exist between the church and the world is in the first place organic, moral, and spiritual in character. Christ is prophet, priest, and king, and by his Word and Spirit he persuasively impacts the entire world. The spiritual life is meant to refashion the natural and moral life in its full depth and scope according to the laws of God. Through renewed people all the circles of the natural life are changed; the family is restored to honor, the wife (woman) is again viewed as the equal of the husband (man), the sciences and arts are Christianized, the level of the moral life is elevated, society and state are reformed, laws and institutions, morals and customs, are made Christian.

The greatest difficulty here—theoretically and practically—concerns the relation between the church and the state. Christ rules his church also by the offices and institutions. The question is whether the church's relation to the various areas of the natural life can also be regulated officially and institutionally. Caesaropapism regulates the relationship so that the church is subject to the Christian state and must conduct itself in accordance with its laws. We can appreciate the gains when the civil authority considers Christian morality to be an important guide for public life. However, the loss in independence for the church is too steep a price to pay, even though the church's real power—the ministry of Word and sacraments—essentially remains the same, however significantly its exercise has been modified. On the other side is the papal system, which indeed deserves praise insofar as it maintains the independence and freedom of the church, but for the rest seeks to subject, if not the whole world, then surely all of baptized Christianity in all its spheres and relations, judicially and legally, to the pope. In the view of Rome, the family, society, the state, art, science, and so forth have to be ecclesiastical, for to be ecclesiastical is identical with being Christian, Roman Catholic, papal.

Luther and Calvin's mighty act of reformation consisted in the fact that they restored the religious-ethical significance of Christianity as the religion of grace and delivered the realm of the natural, not from this Christianity but from the jurisdiction of the Roman Catholic Church. Calvin sharply and clearly drew a boundary line between church and state but did so differently than we do. The area in which both church and state had authority was much larger than we today define it as being. Also in its domain and in its measure, the government as Christian government had to guard the honor of God, the vitality of his church, and the expansion of his kingdom. Nevertheless, the relationship between church and state, Calvin said, is contractual and free. The church has no choice but to preach the Word of God, to witness to his commandments in his name; but if the government or anyone else refused to listen, then the church, then Calvin himself, then any Christian whatever, no longer had any power or right to resort to coercion. Persuasion is the church's only public weapon. Here, all right to practice coercion and inflict punishment is taken from the church, and Christianity is restored and respected as a purely spiritual power.

The church must continue to exercise this spiritual power in a comprehensive manner. Although its witness has been weakened by its multiformity, the church calls all creatures, arts, sciences, family, society, state, and so forth to submit to the Word of the Lord. This demand is only a message, a moral witness; it is persuasion, never coercion. Christian civil authorities are called to promote God's honor, protect his church, and destroy the works of the antichrist, but they must do it in ways that are compatible with the gospel and their particular scope of authority; individual liberties and those of other spheres must be fiercely protected even when they act contrary to God's law. Clear lines between sin and crime must be established and honored. Care must be taken to not designate boundaries in the abstract for they vary with different peoples and in different ages and can only be somewhat determined in their basic direction by the witness of the popular conscience. In short: Its influence in the world is not political, and it seeks the reformation of society only through proclamation, persuasion, and witness.

22

THE SPIRIT'S MEANS OF GRACE

THE MEANS OF GRACE

[519] All salvation and blessedness comes to fallen people via God's gracious character.[1] Objectively, that grace with all its benefits appeared in Christ, who acquired and distributes them in the way of the covenant. The fellowship of those who have received Christ with all his benefits is called "the church" or "the Christian community." *How does Christ communicate his benefits to his people, to the church? Does he use means? Mystics deny this.* As dualists they cannot conceive of grace as being dependent on or bound to external signs and actions and consider God alone, or the Christ in us, the Spirit, or the inner word or light to be what works grace in humans. The Word and sacrament can do no more than point to or depict that internal grace. The written Word only expresses and the sacraments only show visibly what is already internally in our hearts. Mysticism here joins the rationalism of Socinians[2] and Remonstrants[3] who see in the sacraments only ceremonial precepts, memorial signs, and acts of confession. By contrast, Rome insists that means are essential and tied to the sacramental power of the institutional church's priesthood. Romanism conceives of grace as absolutely bound to means. According to Rome, after all, the Spirit-sustained visible church *is* the

---

1. Ed. note: Bavinck speaks here of "grace as a virtue of God" (*als deugd Gods*). To translate this as "attribute" would be too strong and not consistent with Bavinck's own usage of *eigenschappen* for "attributes" in volume 2. Hence the translation "God's gracious character."

2. O. Fock, *Der Socinianismus* (Kiel: C. Schröder, 1847), 559ff.

3. *Apologia pro confessione Remonstrantium* (1629); Apology of the Augsburg Confession, c. 23; P. van Limborch, *Theologia christiana* (Amsterdam: Arnhold, 1735), V, c. 66.

actual, authentic, perfect means of grace, the sacrament par excellence. The church is Christ on earth, especially in his priestly office, and communicates the fullness of his grace and truth which serves above all to elevate humans from the natural to the supernatural order. It is elevating grace, a supernatural physical power that in the sacrament is infused *ex opere operato*[4] into "the natural man" by the priest.[5] Apart from Christ, apart from the church, apart from the priest, and apart from the sacrament, accordingly, there is no salvation. Proclamation is only preparatory and pedagogical and serves to arouse faith, that is, assent; even belief is only one of the seven preparations for grace,[6] and the discipline maintained in the church serves only to foster obedience to the moral law. The sacrament administered by the priest is the real means of grace.

The Reformation adopted a position between this mystical undervaluation and magical overvaluation of the means of grace. According to the Reformers, Christ is the complete Savior, the only mediator between God and humanity, and the church is first of all the communion of saints, but Christ also instituted an official body of ministers (not priests!) to proclaim the Word of God. Changed also was the medieval Roman understanding of grace as a sacerdotal power to a spiritual power of the Word. Scripture and not the church was regarded as the means of grace. The sacrament was subordinated to the Word and had neither meaning nor power apart from that Word. Thus the relationship between Scripture and the church was also changed;[7] instead of thinking of the church as anterior to Scripture, the Reformation again put the church on the foundation of Scripture and elevated Scripture high above the church. Scripture, the Word of God, and not the church became the means of grace par excellence. Furthermore, the Word was put into everyone's hands, considered plain to everyone who studied it with a desire for salvation, and regarded as powerful and gracious not only in public proclamation but also when it was studied and read at home. Thus Christians, who accepted that Word with a believing heart, were liberated from sacerdotalism.

Yet against mysticism, which denied the necessity of the means of grace in Word and sacraments, the Reformation understood the Word and sacraments to be God's ordinary means of imparting grace. The church is the mother of believers, and the offices are instituted for the administration of the Word and sacraments. And grace consists primarily in being restored to God's favor, in the forgiveness of sins, in the spiritual renewal after his image. Means of grace may never be detached from

---

4. Ed. note: *Ex opera operato*, "by the work performed"; this refers to "the assumption of medieval Scholasticism and Roman Catholicism that the correct and churchly performance of the rite conveys grace to the recipient, unless the recipient places a spiritual impediment (*obex*) in the way. Sacraments themselves, therefore, have a *virtus operativa*, or operative power" (Richard A. Muller, *Dictionary of Latin and Greek Theological Terms* [Grand Rapids: Baker Academic, 1985], s.v. *ex opera operato*).

5. Cf. H. Bavinck, *Reformed Dogmatics*, ed. John Bolt (Grand Rapids: Baker Academic, 2003–8), III, 516–17 (#416).

6. Cf. H. Bavinck, *Reformed Dogmatics*, III, 515 (#416); IV, 108–10 (#451), 188–89 (#469).

7. Cf. H. Bavinck, *Reformed Dogmatics*, I, 452–59 (##118–19).

the person and work of Christ who continues to exercise his prophetic, priestly, and royal office nor from the church he instituted on earth and those in office to whom he entrusts his signs of Word and sacrament. Of course, God is above all else sovereign, and as the Reformed faced pastoral questions such as comforting believing parents of covenant children who died in infancy, they acknowledged that God could also regenerate and save people without the Word and the sacrament, that is, by the Holy Spirit alone.[8] Nevertheless, they presented these cases as exceptions and maintained as the rule that for those who reached adulthood the Word and sacraments were the ordinary means by which God gave his Spirit and imparted his grace. None of this should lead to speculation about regeneration lest we forget to rest in God's good pleasure, which distributes salvation in no way other than in and through Christ. God freely binds the distribution of his grace to the church of Christ which is the communion, and hence also the mother, of believers. God establishes his covenant with the parents and in them with their children. He distributes his benefits in the way of the covenant. The church exists on earth to be the holy circle within which Christ communicates all his benefits, also the benefit of regeneration, and to enable her to be that he equipped her with the Holy Spirit, poured out in it a wide assortment of gifts, instituted in it the church's offices, and entrusted to it the administration of the Word and sacraments. All this is included in the term "means of grace," which can even be stretched to include all the things that are needed on our part to enjoy, for the first time or continually, the benefits of the covenant, such as faith, conversion, the struggle against sin, and prayer,[9] though care must be taken here with this usage. Strictly speaking, the Word and the sacraments alone can be viewed as means of grace, that is, as external, humanly perceptible actions and signs that Christ has given his church and with which he has linked the communication of his grace. These means may not even for a second be detached from the person and work of Christ, nor from the church as organism and as institution.

PROCLAMATION OF THE WORD

[520] The most important means of grace is the Word of God. Since the Word contains both the law and the gospel, the covenant of works and the covenant of grace, it has a universal significance even beyond its public proclamation in church as a means of grace. In a Christian society, the Word of God comes to

---

8. Luther, according to R. H. Grützmacher, *Wort und Geist: Eine historische und dogmatische Untersuchung zum Gnadenmittel des Wortes* (Leipzig: Deichert, 1902), 9ff.; J. Calvin, *Institutes of the Christian Religion*, IV.xvi.17–18 (ed. John T. McNeill and trans. Ford Lewis Battles [Philadelphia: Westminster, 1960], 2:1339–41).

9. J. Calvin, *Institutes*, IV; Second Helvetic Confession, #16; Westminster Confession, chap. 14.1; F. Schleiermacher, *The Christian Faith*, ed. H. R. MacIntosh and J. S. Steward (Edinburgh: T&T Clark, 1928), §127.

people in all sorts of ways, in all kinds of forms, from all directions, and it comes to them from their earliest childhood onward. Indeed, in the internal calling, God frequently introduces that Word, even before the consciousness has awakened, to the hearts of children to regenerate and to sanctify them, just as in every person from one's earliest existence God inscribes the work of the law in their hearts and plants in them the seed of religion. For this reason, we must distinguish between the "Word of God" and Scripture. The "Word of God" does not come only in the form of Scripture and its public proclamation; it also comes to us indirectly, secondarily, having been absorbed from Scripture into the consciousness of the church or a society of people. Above all, it is not merely a sound but also a power and the accomplishment of God's will (Isa. 55:11). By his Word, God creates and maintains the world (Gen. 1:3; Pss. 33:6; 148:5; Isa. 48:13; Rom. 4:17; 2 Cor. 4:6; Heb. 1:3; 11:3), and Jesus stilled the sea (Mark 4:39), healed the sick (Matt. 8:16), cast out demons (9:6), and raised the dead (Luke 7:14; 8:54; John 5:25, 28; 11:43; etc.). By his Word, he also works in the area of morality and spirituality.

God uses his Word to make his will known in the areas of morality and spirituality, and it must be differentiated as law and gospel. When Jesus brought the gospel of forgiveness and salvation to publicans and sinners, the poor and the imprisoned (Matt. 5:1ff.; 11:5, 28–30; Luke 4:18–19; 19:10; etc.), he automatically clashed with the Pharisaic and nomistic view of religion, which prevailed in his day. Still, though he rejected the human ordinances of past teachers of the law (Matt. 5:21ff.; 15:9), and had a different view of murder (5:21–22), adultery (5:27–28), oaths (5:33–37), fasting (6:16–18), divorce (19:9), and the Sabbath (Mark 2:27–28), he does uphold the whole law, also its ceremonial elements (Matt. 5:23–24; 17:24–27; 23:2–3, 23; Mark 1:44; 11:16). He also explains it in its spiritual sense (Matt. 5–7), stresses its ethical content, considers love to God and one's neighbor its sum (7:12; 9:13; 12:7; Mark 7:15; 12:28–34), and desires a righteousness different from and more abundant than the righteousness of the Pharisees (Matt. 5:20). He came to fulfill the law and the prophets and does not abolish it (5:17). Although the new wine of the kingdom calls for new wineskins (9:17), and the days of the temple and people and law have been numbered (Mark 13:2), Jesus's agenda is not a revolutionary overthrow of the old covenant, but the reformation and renewal that is naturally born from its complete fulfillment.[10] That is why the early church at Jerusalem still stuck to the temple and the law (Acts 2:46; 3:1; 10:14; 21:26; 22:12).

With the conversion of the gentiles, the question arose about the meaning of the Mosaic law. Paul was the first to understand fully that in the death of Christ the written code of the law had been canceled (Col. 2:14). By "law" (νομος, *nomos*) Paul always understands—unless a further stipulation indicates otherwise (e.g., Rom. 3:27; Gal. 6:2)—the Mosaic law, the entire Torah, including the ceremonial commandments (Rom. 9:4; Gal. 2:12; 4:10; 5:3; Phil. 3:5–6). Still, Paul consid-

10. Cf. H. Bavinck, *Reformed Dogmatics*, III, 222 (#348).

ers that law as the revelation of God's will, as a religious/ethical requirement and demand, as the God-willed regulation of the revelation between him and human beings. While it cannot, as the Pharisees asserted, produce righteousness, but is made powerless by the flesh (Rom. 8:3), served for a time as pedagogy (Rom. 5:20; Gal. 3:19, 24; 4:2–3), increases trespasses (Rom. 5:20; Gal. 3:19), produces wrath, a curse, and death (Rom. 4:15; 2 Cor. 3:6; Gal. 3:10), it is nonetheless God-given, holy, and good (Rom. 2:18; 7:22, 25; 9:4; 2 Cor. 3:3, 7). In Christ the law has attained its end [τελος, *telos*] (Rom. 10:4) and believers are free from the law (Gal. 4:26–5:1), delivered from the curse of the law (3:13; 4:5), and have received the spirit of adoption, the spirit of freedom (Rom. 8:15; 2 Cor. 3:16–17; Gal. 5:18). This freedom of faith, however, does not cancel out the law but confirms it (Rom. 3:31); its just requirement is fulfilled precisely in the lives of those who walk according to the Spirit (8:4) as Spirit-renewed believers delight in God's law in their inner selves and try to find out what God's holy will is (Rom. 7:22; 12:2; Eph. 5:10; Phil. 1:10).

[521] The Word is differentiated into law and gospel. Antinomianism in its various forms—gnosticism, Manichaeism, Anabaptism, and so forth—exacerbates the antithesis between law and gospel, while nomism in its varieties—Pelagianism, semi-Pelagianism, Romanism, Socinianism, rationalism, and so forth—weakens or cancels the antithesis. Rome equated the old and new covenants with law and gospel respectively—not just Moses but also Christ was a legislator—and denied the presence of the gospel in the Old Testament and that of the law in the New Testament, but by accepting its laws and threats turned the gospel into a new law, thereby erasing the Pauline antithesis of law and gospel. It was granted that law and gospel do not differ in the sense that the former only demands and the latter only promises, for both contain commandments, threats, and promises; mysteries, promises, and precepts; things to be believed, things to be hoped for, and things to be done. In all these, moreover, the gospel of the New Testament, the new law, far surpasses the law of the Old Testament, the old law. The law is the incomplete gospel; the gospel the complete law. The gospel was contained in the law as a tree in a seed, a grain in an ear of corn.[11]

Now, this "law" and "gospel" distinction can for the most part, but not completely, be endorsed. The Reformation held to the unity of the covenant of grace in its two dispensations while at the same time sharply contrasting law and gospel. While, on the one hand, the Reformers held on to the unity of the covenant of grace in its two dispensations against the Anabaptists, on the other hand, they also

---

11. Cf. H. Bavinck, *Reformed Dogmatics*, III, 206–12 (#345); J. C. Suicerus, *Thesaurus ecclesiasticus* (Amsterdam: J. H. Wetsten, 1682), s.v. νομος and εὐαγγελιον; Augustine, *City of God*, VIII, 11; idem, *Sermon 30 on the Gospel of John*; idem, *On the Spirit and the Letter*, 19–20; P. Lombard, *Sententiae in IV libris distinctae*, 3rd ed., 2 vols. (Grottaferrata: Colleggi S. Bonaventurae ad Claras Aquas, 1971–81), III, dist. 25, 40; T. Aquinas, *Summa Theol.*, III, qu. 106–8; Council of Trent, VI, can. 19–21; Robert Bellarmine, "De justif.," in *De controversiis christianae fidei adversus huius temporis haereticos* (Cologne: G. Gualtheri, 1617–20), IV, c. 2ff.

perceived the sharp contrast between law and gospel as two essentially different revelations of divine will and thereby again restored the peculiar character of the Christian religion as a religion of grace. There was a promise given to Abraham (Gal. 3:17, 21), that the gospel was preached in the old covenant (Gal. 3:8), and righteousness was obtained from and by faith (Rom. 4:11–12; 11:32; Gal. 3:6–7). Law and gospel do not cancel each other out, the law/gospel distinction is not identical to that between the old and new covenants; there is law *and* gospel in *both* covenants. The law too is the will of God (Rom. 2:18, 20), holy, wise, good, and spiritual (7:12, 14; 12:10), giving life to those who maintain it (2:13; 3:2); it is sin that caused it to stimulate covetousness, increase sin, arouse wrath, kill, curse, and condemn (Rom. 3:20; 4:15; 5:20; 7:5, 8–9, 13; 2 Cor. 3:6ff.; Gal. 3:10, 13, 19). Over against it stands the gospel of Christ, the εὐαγγελιον, which only contains the fulfillment of the Old Testament promise (Mark 1:15; Acts 13:32; Eph. 3:6), comes to us from God (Rom. 1:1–2; 2 Cor. 11:7), and has Christ as its content (Rom. 1:3; Eph. 3:6); and conveys nothing other than grace (Acts 20:24), reconciliation (2 Cor. 5:18), forgiveness (Rom. 4:3–8), righteousness (Rom. 3:21–22), peace (Eph. 6:15), freedom (Gal. 5:13), life (Rom. 1:17; Phil. 2:16), and so forth. In these texts law and gospel are contrasted as demand and gift, as command and promise, as sin and grace, as sickness and healing, as death and life. The law proceeds from God's holiness, is known from nature, addresses all people, demands perfect righteousness, gives eternal life by works, and condemns. By contrast, the gospel proceeds from God's grace, is known only from special revelation, addresses only those who hear, grants perfect righteousness, produces good works in faith, and acquits.

This understanding of law and gospel gives rise to the question whether the preaching of faith and repentance, which seemed after all to be a condition and a demand, really belonged to the gospel and should not rather be counted as law. Indeed, strictly speaking, there are no demands and conditions in the gospel but only promises and gifts. Faith and repentance are as much benefits of the covenant of grace as is justification. But, concretely, the gospel is always united with law and is therefore always interwoven with the law throughout Scripture. The gospel always presupposes the law because it comes to human beings who are created in God's image, who stand before God as rational creatures and know his law through external testimony and the inner call of their conscience. God is not absent from people until the gospel comes to them; the gospel call does not come as the first call from God. Every person is obligated not first of all by the gospel but by nature, the law, to take God at his word, and by implication to accept the gospel in which he speaks to us humans. The demanding and summoning form in which the gospel is cast is derived from the law. Faith and repentance are therefore demanded of people in the name of God's law, by virtue of their relation to God as his image bearers, and that demand is addressed not only to the elect and regenerate but to all humans without distinction. Nonetheless, faith and repentance are always components of gospel, not of law. The gospel, therefore, always presupposes the law and differs from it especially in content. For while the law demands faith in God in general, it does not demand the special faith that directs itself toward Christ, and while the law can produce penitence (μεταμελεια, *metameleia*), it cannot produce conversion (μετανοια, *metanoia*), which is rather the fruit of faith. That is why we can speak of a law of faith, of a commandment of faith, of the obedience of faith (Rom. 1:5; 3:27; 1 John 3:23), of being disobedient to and judged according to the gospel (Rom. 2:16; 10:16; and so forth). Law and gospel both command and make promises; the difference is that the law demands that humans work out their own righteousness while the gospel invites them to renounce all self-righteousness and to accept the righteousness of Christ and even offers the gift of faith to that end.

Yet on this point the Reformed held a different view than the Lutherans. Lutherans almost exclusively have an eye for the accusing and condemning function of the law and therefore know no higher bliss than deliverance from the law. Law is necessary only because of sin. Lutherans do speak of a threefold use of the law, not only of a political, that is, civil, use for the purpose of restraining sin, and of a pedagogical use to arouse the knowledge of sin, but also of a didactic use of the law to be a rule of life for believers. This last use, however, is solely necessary since and insofar as believers continue to be sinners and have to be restrained by the law and led to a continuing knowledge of sin. By itself, when faith and grace come on the scene, the law expires and loses all its meaning. It is because of sin that law and gospel remain a part of Christian experience from the time of conversion until death. According to the Reformed, since the law is an expression of God's being, humans are naturally subject to it. The law is everlasting; it was inscribed on Adam's heart and is again engraved on the heart of the believer by the Holy Spirit; in heaven all believers will live according to it. Freedom from the law, therefore, does not mean that Christians no longer have anything to do with that law, but that the law can no longer demand anything from them as a condition for salvation and can no longer judge and condemn them. For the rest they delight in the law in their inmost being (Rom. 7:22) and meditate on it day and night (Ps. 1:2). The gospel is temporary; the law is everlasting and precisely that which is restored by the gospel. Accordingly, the law, which among the Reformed occupies a much larger role in the doctrine of gratitude than in that of misery, must always be proclaimed in the church alongside the gospel.

The Spirit, the Word, and Power

[522] Besides the relationship between law and gospel, there is often disagreement over the power and efficacy of the Word, as well as the relationship between Word and Spirit. Nomism (Judaism, Pelagianism, rationalism, Romanism) considers the special supernatural power of the Holy Spirit superfluous, while antinomianism (Anabaptism, mysticism) expects everything from the inner light of the

Holy Spirit and finds in the Word only a sign and shadow. In the latter, the opposition initially is to the law and the Old Testament, but soon moves on to dissent from every external word and the entire objective historical mediation of salvation, and expects everything from the operation of the Holy Spirit, from the Christ in us, from the internal word and inner light. Knowledge of the word as such, accordingly, affords us nothing and leaves us cold and dead. The word is no more than a sign, a shadow, an image, and a symbol expressing what is already internally written on our hearts. The internal word, therefore, precedes and is superior to Scripture, which is only a paper word and, additionally, obscure and full of contradictions. That internal word is nothing other than God or Christ or the Holy Spirit, who is one and the same in all people from the moment of their rebirth, or sometimes also dwells in them by nature as internal light and is the fullness of truth in its entirety. Accordingly, to find God and know the truth, we need not go outside ourselves to Scripture or the historical Christ; but going down into ourselves, withdrawing from the world, killing the intellect and the will, and passively awaiting an internal and immediate revelation, we find God, live in communion with him, and are saved in contemplating him. This Anabaptism was in fact a revival of the pantheistic mysticism that regards the finite as an eternally changing manifestation of the infinite and seeks communion with God in the intimate depths of feeling, where God and humans are one.

By contrast, both Lutherans and Reformed, against nomism and antinomianism alike, taught that though the Holy Spirit can work apart from the Word, ordinarily Word and Spirit go together. Lutherans, however, prefer to speak of the Spirit working *per verbum* (through the Word), while the Reformed prefer *cum verbo* (with the Word). We must never forget that the Word of God, also through law, always comes with power. Since it is not a human word but God's (Acts 4:29; 1 Thess. 2:13), it is living and lasting (1 Pet. 1:25), living and active (Heb. 4:12), a lamp shining in a dark place (2 Pet. 1:19); a seed sown in the human heart (Matt. 13:3), growing and multiplying (Acts 12:24), of great value even if those who planted and watered it are nothing (1 Cor. 3:7). It is, in sum, the "power of God for salvation" (Rom. 1:16; 1 Cor. 1:18; 2:4–5; 15:2; Eph. 1:13). The truth of this must be maintained in all its fullness and richness of meaning over against every form of spiritualism. Here we must also reject all dualisms that set in opposition the internal versus external, the spiritual versus the material, eternity against time, essence against form, and so forth. God is creator of heaven and earth, soul and body, matter and spirit. The Word that proceeds from God creates and maintains, judges and kills, re-creates and renews, and always accomplishes what it is meant to accomplish and never returns empty. Unlike human words, whose power depends on the extent to which a person puts one's heart and soul into it, God is always fully present in his powerful Word. The freely proclaimed word rooted in Scripture, even if not identical with Scripture's own words, is still a word from God, a word that comes to human beings but is originally from God, is spoken in the power of the Holy Spirit and therefore always effective. The Word of God is never separate

from God, from Christ, from the Holy Spirit; it has no permanence or existence
in itself and cannot be deistically separated from its creator and author. "The Holy
Spirit is always present with that word." The Holy Spirit is not an unconscious
power but a person who is always present with that word, always sustains it and
makes it active, though not always in the same manner.

This fact, that the word does not always produce the same effect, reminds us
that the regenerating, renewing effect of the word cannot be understood without
acknowledging the work of the Holy Spirit as a distinct work. The Spirit who
renews is always and only the Spirit of Christ, who works through the means
appointed by Christ. The Word is always efficacious, never powerless. The gospel
exerts its effect even in those who are lost; to them it is a reason for their falling,
an offense and foolishness, a stone over which they stumble, a fragrance from
death to death (Luke 2:34; Rom. 9:32; 1 Cor. 1:23; 2 Cor. 2:16; 1 Pet. 2:8). In
accordance with the unsearchable good pleasure of God, he uses that word for
bringing people to repentance but also for hardening; for the rising but also for
the falling of many. He always works through the word but not always in the same
way. When he wants to work through it so that it leads to faith and repentance,
he does not objectively have to add anything to the word. That word is good
and wise and holy, a Word of God, a Word of Christ, and the Holy Spirit takes
everything from Christ.

Nonetheless, for the seed of the word to bear good fruit, it has to fall in soil that
has been well prepared; the field has to be made ready for the reception of the seed.
Hence the subjective activity of the Holy Spirit has to be added to the objective
word. This opening of the heart (Acts 16:14) or enlightenment of the mind (Eph.
1:18; Col. 1:9–11) is a distinct but not a wholly separate work of the Holy Spirit.
For the Spirit who regenerates is not the Spirit of God in general, but the Spirit
of Christ, the Holy Spirit, the Spirit acquired by Christ, through whom Christ
governs, who takes all things only from Christ, and whom Christ has poured out
in the church and is therefore the Spirit of the believing community. Although
there are extraordinary exceptions, the Spirit usually works through human means
such as the covenant community to bring people to faith. The Holy Spirit follows
Christ in his journey through history. The Holy Spirit, who in regeneraration applies nothing other than the word, power, and merit of Christ, also automatically
leads the conscious life of the person toward the word that he took from Christ
and caused to be recorded by the prophets and apostles.

THE SACRAMENTS

[523] In addition to the Word, the sacraments are a second means of grace. Scripture
does not have the word "sacrament," nor does it have a doctrine of the sacraments in
general; it speaks of circumcision and Passover, of baptism and the Lord's Supper,
but does not sum up these ordinances under a single term. We know little about

the way in which the gatherings of the Jerusalem church were arranged apart from reading that they "devoted themselves to the apostles' teaching and fellowship, to the breaking of bread and the prayers" (Acts 2:42). Acts 6:4 also refers to "a ministry of the Word." From 1 Corinthians 11:1–14:40 we learn a little more. After admission to the church on the basis of a personal profession of faith ("into one body"—Rom. 6:3–5; 1 Cor. 12:13; Gal. 3:27), by baptism, and in the name of Christ, they met regularly on the Lord's Day (Acts 20:7; 1 Cor. 16:2; Rev. 1:10).

There appear to have been two meetings, one for the ministry of the Word, to which also nonmembers were admitted (1 Cor. 14:23), where Scripture was read and there was prayer and song (Acts 2:42; Rom. 12:12; 1 Cor. 14:14–15, 26), and another for the celebration of the Lord's Supper ("for the purpose of eating," 1 Cor. 11:33), in which only believers were permitted to take part (10:16ff.; 11:20ff.). Here there was first prayer and thanksgiving, then a common meal (ἀγαπη, *agapē*; Jude 12; 2 Pet. 2:13) composed of gifts presented by the believers themselves was held, again followed by prayers and thanksgiving (εὐχαριστια, *eucharistia*), and the Lord's Supper was celebrated. Although some scholars aver that in the apostolic era the Lord's Supper was not separated from the common meal but that the entire love feast (ἀγαπη) was a thanksgiving (εὐχαριστια), a "Lord's Supper," Paul makes a distinction between the two in 1 Cor. 11:20–21 and suggests that the two be totally separated by eating the regular meal at home beforehand (1 Cor. 11:22).[12]

In the second century, however, these two ministries were united and the Lord's Supper was integrated into the regular worship service.[13] Since the second part of the worship service, the Lord's Supper, was exclusively for baptized members, it gradually acquired a mysterious character. The influence of Greek mystery religions on the Christian religion led to a change in understanding the New Testament's use of the word μυστηριον (*mystērion*). Properly understood, the word refers to the mighty and marvelous acts of God that were formerly hidden but have now been revealed.[14] It came to be understood by the church as synonymous with the incomprehensible and was translated by the Latin word *sacramentum*, with the result that any content of revelation could be referred to as a "sacrament," as well as all sacred actions, the consecration of a priest, marriage, exorcism, the celebration of the Sabbath, circumcision, and all ceremonies.[15] Augustine employed this broad sense of the term and was followed by Pseudo-Dionysius and Scholasticism. Although baptism and the Lord's Supper remained prominent in the designation

12. T. Zahn, "Agapen," in *PRE*[3], I, 234–37; P. Drews, "Eucharistie," in *PRE*[3], V, 560–72.
13. Cf. P. Drews, "Eucharistie," in *PRE*[3], V, 562.
14. Cf. H. Bavinck, *Reformed Dogmatics*, I, 619–21 (#160).
15. Edwin Hatch, *The Influence of Greek Ideas on Christianity* (1890; repr., New York: Harper, 1957); the history-of-religions attempt to understand the Christian sacraments as coming completely or at least for the most part from the pagan mystery religions has not been at all successful. F. Kattenbusch, "Sakrament," in *PRE*[3], XVII, 349–81, says that although there is undoubtedly some influence, "the genre shows that there is little likelihood that such an influence had a major impact on Christianity."

of sacred actions as "sacraments," the vagueness of the term was the reason the number of sacraments for a long time remained indefinite.

While the church fathers did not develop a clear doctrine of the sacraments, medieval Scholasticism elaborated on the sacraments in great detail. Lombard is the first to list the familiar seven,[16] but after him theologians and synods (e.g., the [Third] Lateran Council of 1179) still speak of sacraments in a broad sense. This continues until Lombard's *Sentences* became the general handbook for the study of theology and the Council of Florence (1439) established the number at seven.[17] The definition of the term went hand in hand with this restriction of the number, and Roman Catholic doctrine was established at the Council of Trent.[18] Included in this medieval consensus is the claim that Christ instituted seven sacraments in the new covenant—baptism, confirmation, the Eucharist, penance, extreme unction, holy orders, and marriage—and that they supply special grace, differ in value, are necessary for salvation, communicate grace "through the act performed" (*ex opere operato*), are lawfully administered only by ordained priests who act according to the true intention of the church, and are truly received when the recipients intended to receive what the church bestowed. Every sacrament supplies a special grace; and baptism, confirmation, and holy orders supply an "indelible character" (*character indelebilis*).

[524] The development of this doctrine of the sacraments shows a movement progressively farther from Scripture. In saying that the sacrament only imparts sanctifying grace, Rome removes grace almost completely from guilt and the forgiveness of sins and transforms it into a supernatural gift coming down to people from without. Rome almost completely severs the bond between the sacrament and the Word, giving the latter only a provisional and preparatory meaning. Sacramental grace thus becomes independent of the Word and even exceeds it in value. Faith is no longer a requirement for the recipient of the sacrament; grace as sanctifying grace is imparted by the sacrament *ex opera operato*, and at most presupposes that the recipient will refrain from putting an insurmountable obstacle in its way. The sacrament, accordingly, works physically and magically by virtue of a power granted to the priest by God, as an instrument in his hand.

The Reformation modified the Roman Catholic doctrine according to Scripture. Zwingli, Luther, and Calvin all taught that the sacrament imparted forgiving grace, that it was valueless without the Word, and its operation presupposed faith

---

16. P. Lombard, *Sent.*, IV, dist. 2.

17. J. Schwane, *Dogmengeschichte*, 4 vols. (Freiburg i.B.: Herder, 1882–95), III, 584ff.; F. Loofs, *Leitfaden zum Studium der Dogmengeschichte*, 4th ed. (Halle a.S.: M. Niemeyer, 1906), 568ff.

18. Council of Trent, sess. VII; Roman Catechism, II, chap. 1. Ed. note: The post–Vatican II edition titled *The Roman Catechism*, trans. Robert I. Bradley, SJ, and Eugene Kevane (Boston: Daughters of St. Paul, 1985), drops the enumeration of the introduction so that chap. 1 begins the section on baptism. In this annotation, the proper reference would be II, "Introduction." On sacramental theology in the Greek church, see F. Kattenbusch, *Lehrbuch der vergleichenden Confessionskunde* (Freiburg i.B.: Mohr [Siebeck], 1892), I, 393ff.

in the recipient. Yet the Reformers also differed on the doctrine of the sacraments since the sacraments embodied in practice their theological teaching. Luther emphasized their objective character against the Anabaptists, Zwingli taught that they were signs of faith, and Calvin taught that they were signs and seals of God's promises in the covenant of grace. In Lutheran understanding, the "heavenly substance" is concealed *in, with,* and *under* the elements, just as the power of the Holy Spirit entered the Word, and grace works through the sacraments as through its instruments, media, helps, vehicles, and organs.[19] For Zwingli, since the sacraments are administered only to those who have faith, and through that faith share in Christ and all his benefits, they are in the first place signs and proofs of faith, acts of confession. Only secondarily are they means of strengthening faith, inasmuch as they remind us of the benefits toward which our faith is directed; they increasingly direct our faith away from ourselves to God's grace in Christ and so exercise and strengthen that faith.[20] Calvin indeed also views the sacraments as acts of confession: "the mutual attestation of our piety toward God." But this is secondary to their being "a testimony of divine grace toward us confirmed by an outward sign," signs and seals of the promises of God in his Word, mirrors in which we contemplate the riches of his grace. Sacraments have no intrinsic power of their own; they are God's chosen instruments to impart grace to those who believe. In this way God strengthens and nourishes their faith; unbelievers only receive the sign, not the thing signified. Yet neither Calvin nor the later Reformed tradition were clear as to how God distributes grace in the sacraments. Zwingli's doctrine was increasingly accepted outside the Lutheran and Reformed churches, including among the Anabaptists, Socinians, Remonstrants, Rationalists, and Quakers. The sacraments became mere memorials and confessional signs whose purpose was the promotion of virtue and which could therefore easily be supplanted with other solemn ceremonies. Although Schleiermacher attempted to maintain the objective character of the sacraments and to combine all the various views into a higher unity, his description failed to satisfy and achieve reconciliation in the church because it left undecided what is primary and most important in the sacraments.[21]

19. J. Köstlin, *The Theology of Luther in Its Historical Development and Inner Harmony*, trans. Charles E. Hay, 2 vols. (Philadelphia: Lutheran Publication Society, 1897), II, 511; Joseph T. Müller, *Die symbolischen Bücher der evangelisch-lutherischen Kirche*, 8th ed. (Gütersloh: Bertelsmann, 1898), 39, 41, 202, 264, 321; ed. note: These specific references are to the following Lutheran documents: Augsburg Confession, art. 5, in *The Book of Concord*, ed. R. Kolb and T. J. Wengert (Minneapolis: Fortress, 2000), 40; ibid., art. 13 (Kolb and Wengert), 46; Apology of the Augsburg Confession, art. 13, pars. 1–5 (Kolb and Wengert), 219–20; ibid., art. 24, pars. 69–70, 270–71; Smalcald Articles, part III, art. 7 (Kolb and Wengert), 321.

20. U. Zwingli, *An Account of the Faith of Huldreich Zwingli* (*Fidei ratio*, 1530), in *On Providence and Other Essays*, ed. S. M. Jackson and W. J. Hinke (1922; repr., Durham, NC: Labyrinth, 1983), 7th article on the sacraments; idem, *Exposition of the Christian Faith*, "Sacraments."

21. Schleiermacher described the sacraments as "continued activities of Christ, enshrined in church actions and bound up therewith in the closest way. By their instrumentality he exerts his priestly activity

[525] From this it is understandable that a great many people objected to the word "sacrament" and would rather replace it with those of signs, seals, code language, mysteries, and the like. After all, the term does not occur in Scripture and objections are even intensified by the fact that the Greek meaning of the word μυστηριον (*mystērion*), translated in Latin by *sacramentum*, exerted influence on the understanding of the church rites described by that term. Still, all this is no reason to reject the word, and it remains useful for summarizing what the special ordinances in Scripture have in common. Theology, we know, employs many terms that do not occur in Scripture and that have acquired technical meaning in their own sphere. If theology had to refrain from using such terms, it would have to cease all scientific labor and all preaching and exegesis of God's Word, and indeed even the translation of Scripture would be impermissible. Nor, for the same reason, should we hesitate in treating the [general] doctrine of the sacraments prior to that of baptism and the Lord's Supper. There are no "sacraments as such" described in Scripture, only the concrete special ordinances of circumcision and the Passover, baptism, and the Lord's Supper. Still, a prior chapter on the sacraments in general specifically enables us to sum up what these special ordinances have in common in Scripture, and to posit this correct scriptural understanding against the unsound doctrine that has gradually penetrated the Christian church with respect to the sacraments.

In the definition of the sacraments the Reformed aligned themselves as closely as possible with Scripture. While Roman Catholic theology understands the sacrament as a "sacred, secret, and hidden thing," Scripture speaks of it as a sign and seal of the covenant (Gen. 9:12–13, 17; 17:11; Rom. 4:11). In keeping with this, Reformed theology described the sacraments as visible, holy signs and seals instituted by God so that he might make believers understand more clearly and reassure them of the promises and benefits of the covenant of grace, and believers on their part might confess and confirm their faith and love before God, angels, and humankind. Noteworthy here is that God is said to be the one who instituted the sacraments. "It is not for humans to institute and shape the worship of God; their task, rather, is to receive and preserve that which has been handed down by God."[22] Generally speaking, we can say that on this point there is no disagreement in the Christian churches. Here Rome has a problem because Christ only instituted the sacraments of baptism and the Lord's Supper. Before the Council of Trent many theologians asserted that the sacraments—say, confirmation and confession—were not directly instituted by Christ but by the apostles.[23] The Council

---

on individuals, and sustains and propagates that living fellowship between him and us by virtue of which alone God sees individuals in Christ" (F. Schleiermacher, *The Christian Faith*, §143).

22. Second Helvetic Confession, 19.

23. P. Lombard, *Sent.*, IV, dist. 3; Hugh of St. Victor, *On the Sacraments of the Christian Faith*, trans. R. J. Deferrari (Cambridge, MA: Mediaeval Academy of America, 1951), II, 15, 2. See also Hales, Bonaventure; J. Schwane, *Dogmengeschichte*, III, 597.

of Trent expressly declared,[24] however, that all seven sacraments were instituted by Jesus Christ our Lord himself, not mediately—for this was acknowledged by all; in that case no council decree would have been necessary—but immediately,[25] and in so declaring imposed on theology an obligation it could not fulfill. Yet the council was correct insofar as it recognized that the right to institute sacraments could not be transferred to creatures even by God. Human beings can only make the sacrament known (Exod. 12:1ff.; Mark 1:4; 11:30; 1 Cor. 11:23) and announce the grace of God bestowed by it. What they cannot do, in the nature of the case, is to actually grant this grace, because the favor and fellowship of God is inseparable from God and therefore cannot be imparted by a creature, either a human or an angel. Christ, through the Holy Spirit, is the only "institutor" but also the only "distributor" of the sacrament; it is Christ himself who baptizes and celebrates the Lord's Supper in his church, though he does, of course, employ humans as his instruments.[26]

Noteworthy in the Reformed definition of the sacraments, in the second place, is that they are described as signs, connected to the generic concept of signs, seals, images, symbols, types, or antitypes. Lutherans, by contrast, regard the sacrament first of all as an action consisting in the communication of grace in, with, and under the sign. Now the Reformed did believe that there is an action occurring in the sacraments; but this is the hidden invisible action of Christ, who inwardly confers grace in the hearts of believers through the Holy Spirit. The main thing is not the action of the minister, as if that action were so freighted with meaning as even to bring about a consubstantiation or transubstantiation, but in the sacrament's being a sign that images and assures us of the action of Christ. The Reformed definition of the sacraments is special, in the third place, in that it unites the action of God with the confession of believers taking place in them. In that way Calvin reconciled Luther and Zwingli.[27] Calvin agreed with Luther in saying that God's action in the sacrament is primary, but Calvin with Zwingli judged that in the sacrament believers made confession of their faith and love before God, angels, and humans. In the sacrament God first comes to believers to signify and seal his benefits. He assures them with visible pledges that he is their God and the God of their children. He attaches seals to *his* Word to strengthen *their* faith in that Word (Gen. 9:11–15; 17:11; Exod. 12:13; Mark 1:4; 16:16; Luke 22:19; Rom. 4:11; and so forth). On the other hand, the sacraments are also acts of confession in which believers confess their conversion, their faith, their obedience, their communion with Christ and with each other. Every observance of the sacrament is an act of

24. Council of Trent, sess. VII, can. 1.

25. R. Bellarmine, "De sacr.," in *Controversiis*, I, c. 23.

26. Second Helvetic Confession, 19; A. Rivetus, in H. Bavink, ed., *Synopsis purioris theologiae*, 6th ed. (Leiden: Donner, 1881), disp. 43, 8; F. Turretin, *Institutes of Elenctic Theology*, trans. G. M. Giger, ed. J. T. Dennison (Phillipsburg, NJ: Presbyterian & Reformed, 1992), XIX, 1, 14.

27. J. Calvin, *Institutes*, IV.xiv.1.

covenant renewal, a vow of faithfulness, an oath that obligates those who take it to engage in the service of Christ (Mark 1:5; 16:16; Acts 2:41; 8:37; Rom. 6:3ff.; 1 Cor. 10:16ff.).[28]

[526] The terms sign and seal imply that the sacrament consists of two parts distinguished as "word" and "element." Signs may be either natural (e.g., smoke, footprints) or instituted (e.g., alphabet, slogans, flags). Instituted signs are further distinguished as either ordinary or extraordinary (e.g., miracles), regarding things past, present, or future. In Scripture the latter are frequently described as σημεῖα, because they are proofs and signs of God's presence, of his grace or power, of his truth or righteousness. Signs are further subdivided in terms of whether, like memorial signs, they refer to something in the past (Josh. 4:6), or like predictive signs, to something in the future (Gen. 4:15), or also, like so many signs, to something present and permanent (Deut. 6:8). Sacraments are extraordinary signs taken, according to a preformed analogy, from visible things to designate invisible and eternal goods. They are seals since they confirm God's trustworthiness and strengthen for us the "element" of the covenant of grace that is summed up in Christ the Mediator, with all his benefits and blessings. In addition to being signs, the sacraments are also seals that serve to confirm and strengthen. Seals serve to authenticate, to validate and confirm; like trademark and documentary seals, they serve to distinguish the true from the false, the genuine from the spurious. In Scripture, too, there are references to seals when something has to be marked as genuine and protected from falsification or from being violated and desecrated (1 Kings 21:8; Neh. 9:38; Esther 3:12; Isa. 8:16; Jer. 32:10; Dan. 6:17; 12:4; Matt. 27:66; Rev. 7:2; 22:10). God seals all believers with the Holy Spirit in order that, as heirs, they may be kept for future salvation (2 Cor. 1:22; Eph. 1:13; 4:30). In blessing Paul's labors, God gave him a seal, a confirmation of his apostleship (1 Cor. 9:2). He presses his seal on the building of the church as a pledge that it is his possession (2 Tim. 2:19). God seals the pit in which Satan has been confined so that he can no longer deceive the nations (Rev. 20:3). He seals his servants in the final tribulation so they can no longer be harmed (7:3; 9:4). Seals, accordingly, are always means for the purpose of guaranteeing the genuineness of persons and things or protecting them from violation. Aside from being signs, therefore, sacraments are also seals that God attaches to his word in order to highlight its trustworthiness for our benefit and to our mind. Both the elements—water, bread, and wine—and the various ceremonial actions accompanying them—sprinkling or immersion, blessing, breaking, distribution, and reception of bread—have significative and sealing power. They are not arbitrary and indifferent customs, but combine to form the constituents of the sacraments, enable us to better understand the promises and benefits of the covenant, and together with the

---

28. Cf. Belgic Confession, art. 36; Ed. note: Bavinck also refers to the liturgical forms of the Dutch Reformed Church for baptism and the Lord's Supper.

elements form the sacraments into signs and seals of the invisible benefits of redemption.[29]

The "internal matter" in the sacrament, the invisible substance depicted and sealed in it, is the covenant of grace (Gen. 9:12–13; 17:11); the righteousness of faith (Rom. 4:11); the forgiveness of sins (Mark 1:4; Matt. 26:28); faith and repentance (Mark 1:4; 16:16); communion with Christ, with his death and resurrection (Rom. 6:3ff.), with his flesh and blood (1 Cor. 10:16); and so forth. In other words, Christ is the "internal matter," the "heavenly substance," the thing signified in the sacrament. In the early period [of the Reformation] Lutheran dogmaticians called the two components of the sacrament "the word" and "the element," and so understood the sacrament to impart the same grace as that imparted by the Word. Gradually, however, the doctrine of consubstantiation led to the view that, in addition to the Word, a "heavenly substance" or divine power was imparted through the sacrament. The Word and sacrament were thus viewed as imparting different benefits. Modern theology repeatedly set forth such a view of the sacrament and so differentiated between the Word and the sacrament that the former exerted a person-centered effect and the latter a natural effect; the former a means of the "metanoetic" working of the Holy Spirit and the latter a means of the "anagennetic" working of the Spirit; that the Word changes the consciousness, but the sacrament the mind, the self, the psychophysical nature of a person.[30]

This view is an importation of Roman Catholicism and conflicts with Scripture. For those who believe are born again (John 1:12–13), have eternal life (John 3:36), are justified (Rom. 3:28; 5:1), are sanctified (John 15:3; Acts 15:9), are glorified (Rom. 8:30), have fellowship with Christ (Eph. 3:17), with his flesh and blood (John 6:47–51), with his Father (1 John 1:3), with the Holy Spirit (John 7:39; Gal. 3:2, 5), and so forth. The Word contains all the promises of God, and faith appropriates them all. The content of the Word is Christ, the whole Christ, who is also the content of the sacrament. There is not a single benefit of grace that, withheld from us in the Word, is now imparted to believers in a special way by the sacrament. There is neither a separate baptismal grace nor a separate communion grace. The content of Word and sacrament is identical. While differing in external form and manner, they nonetheless contain the same Mediator, covenant, benefits, salvation, and fellowship with God. From the difference in the *manner* in which they offer Christ and all his benefits to us, we may further infer that the sacrament is subordinate to the Word. It is a sign of the content of the Word; a seal that God has attached to his witness; a pillar, as Calvin puts it, which has been erected on the foundation of the Word; an appendix that comes with the Word and has been added to it. The Word, accordingly, is something, even much, without the sacrament, but the sacrament is nothing without the Word

29. Campegius Vitringa, *Doctrina christianae religionis, per aphorismos summatim descripta*, 6th ed., 8 vols. (Leiden: Joannis le Mair; Arnheim: J. H. Möelemanni, 1761–86), VI, 352.

30. Cf. H. Bavinck, *Reformed Dogmatics*, IV, 62–63, 67–68, 73–75 (##441–43).

and in that case has neither value nor power. It is nothing less but also nothing more than the Word made visible. All the benefits of salvation can be obtained from the Word and by faith alone, while there is not a single benefit that could be obtained without the Word and without faith from the sacrament alone. Those who define the Word and sacraments differently, and ascribe to them distinct operations of grace, separate Christ from his benefits; break the unity of the covenant of grace; materialize grace; make the sacrament something independent of, contrary to, and above the Word; reverse the relationship between Scripture and the church; and make the sacrament necessary for salvation and the people dependent on the priest. For that reason the Reformed, as well as the Lutherans in that early period, never tired of stating over and over again that the sacrament is subordinate to the Word, and that they both serve to direct our faith toward Christ's sacrifice on the cross as the sole ground of our salvation.[31]

[527] The relationship between the sign and thing signified is not a physical, local, corporeal, or substantial connection. The expression "sacramental union" does not express properly the connection between "the internal and external matter," *signa* ("sign") and *res* ("thing signified"); no one would call the connection existing between a word and the thing it signifies, between an image and the person it represents, between a pledge and that of which it is a pledge, a union. It is, rather, an ethical connection identical with that between Christ and the gospel. A special word from God was needed for us to see in the natural signs a depiction of the spiritual goods of salvation. This does not make them arbitrary. On the contrary, now that God has informed us of it in his Word, we can see the most striking correspondence between the sign and the thing signified. For that matter, it is the same God and Father who rules both in the realm of nature and in that of grace. He so created the visible world that we can understand from it the things that are invisible. The natural is an image of the spiritual. The "form of the sacrament" therefore includes the relationship between sign and thing signified, and the divine institution that establishes the connection between sign and thing signified. In Roman Catholic and Lutheran theology, the words of institution either change or incorporate the sign into the thing signified, and consequently the words are directed more to the element than to the listeners. For the Reformed,

---

31. Cf. J. Köstlin, *The Theology of Luther*, II, 511; J. T. Müller, *Die symbolischen Bucher*, 202, 320, 487, 500; ed. note: These specific references are to the following Lutheran documents: Apology of the Augsburg Confession, art. 13, pars. 1–5 (Kolb and Wengert), 219–20; Smalcald Articles, part III, arts. 5–6 (Kolb and Wengert), 319–21; The Larger Catechism, part IV, "Concerning Baptism" (Kolb and Wengert), 458; ibid., part V, "The Sacrament of the Altar" (Kolb and Wengert), 467–68. Heinrich Heppe, *Dogmatik des deutschen Protestantismus im sechzehnten Jahrhundert*, 3 vols. (Gotha: F. A. Perthes, 1857), II, 36; J. Calvin, *Institutes*, IV.xiv.3, 5, 6, 14; Consensus Tigurinus (1549), in H. A. Niemeyer, *Collectio confessionum in ecclesiis reformatis publicatarum*, 2 vols. (Leipzig: Iulii Klinkhardti, 1840), 204, 206 (ed. note: ET in J. Calvin, *Selected Works of John Calvin: Tracts and Letters* [Grand Rapids: Baker Academic, 1983], II, 223–27); Gallican Confession, art. 34; Belgic Confession, art. 33; Heidelberg Catechism, Q 66; Second Helvetic Confession, chap. XIX; P. van Mastricht, *Theologia*, VII, 3, 11; F. Turretin, *Institutes of Elenctic Theology*, XIX, 3, 6.

by contrast, the public word has no hidden, mysterious, and magical power, does not change the sign, but only sets it apart from common usage for the listeners. Without the Word, water, bread, and wine are just ordinary daily fare. "Take away the word, and water is nothing more and nothing less than water; add the word to the element, and it becomes a sacrament" (Augustine). Accordingly, while the Reformed teach that God alone, rather than the minister, is the distributor of grace in the sacrament, Roman Catholics and Lutherans make the grace of the sacrament dependent on the minister.

Even though the connection between the sign and the thing signified does not consist in a corporeal or local union of the two, it can nevertheless very well be objective, real, and essential. Roman Catholics and Lutherans, however, differ from the Reformed in their understanding of reality. When the thing signified is not physically united with the sign, they believe the connection between the two is not real or essential and that Christ along with his benefits is therefore not imparted and enjoyed in the sacrament. The difference in the doctrine of the sacraments, however, does not concern the question whether God really imparts his grace but in what way he does this. Roman Catholics view the visible sign as absorbing the invisible grace so that the sacrament works "by the act performed" (*ex opere operato*) and only requires negatively that the recipient does not pose an obstacle to its operation. The Reformed hold to a spiritual communication since the essence of grace is spiritual, and consider the sacraments are signs and seals of the covenant of grace; therefore grace is only imparted where faith is present. In this respect the sacrament is identical to the Word; Christ is truly and essentially offered and granted to everyone who believes. The sacrament grants the same full Christ as the Word and in the same manner, that is, a spiritual manner by faith, even though the means differ, one being audible and the other visible. Although the Reformed reject the doctrine that grace comes to us through the sign as its channel, in so doing they have in no way detracted from the authenticity of the sacrament. Indeed, by taking this position they have much more effectively maintained the spiritual nature of grace than Rome or Luther. For the rest, the manner in which God uses the Word and the sacraments in distributing his grace remains a mystery. Scripture also says of the Word of God that it creates and re-creates, regenerates and renews, justifies and sanctifies. But who can describe the manner in which God uses the Word in this connection and, similarly, the sacraments?

[528] Despite the objections of Lutherans and Roman Catholics to the contrary, Reformed theology preserves the reality and objectivity of the sacrament. Both Lutheran and Reformed theology rejected Roman Catholic notions that sacramental grace is dispositional, infused, sanctifying grace with its further designation of three sacraments—baptism, confirmation, and holy orders—that impress upon the soul of the recipient an indelible mark (*character indelibis*). Further, they insisted that sacraments are meant only for believers and therefore always presuppose faith (Mark 16:16; Acts 8:37–38; 9:11, 17–18; 10:34–35;

Rom. 4:11; etc.). Lutherans seem to be on firmer ground when they fail to extricate themselves entirely from Rome and maintain some sense of efficacious grace in the Word and sacrament by themselves. But this advantage is only a matter of appearance. The connection between the sign and thing signified in the sacraments is the same as that between the word of the gospel and the person of Christ. The spiritual reality of the sacrament is no less real than physical reality. Roman Catholics and Lutherans alike require faith in adults for the reception of the sacrament and even Roman Catholics demand that the recipient of the sacrament refrain from placing an obstacle in the way of grace. According to both Lutherans and Roman Catholics, therefore, the sacrament does not *absolutely* work *ex opere operato*. Cases exist in which the sacrament does not work, that is, yields no grace, and nevertheless retains its objective character. Roman Catholics and Lutherans no less than Reformed face the difficulty of the question of when the sacraments impart grace to the recipients. The Reformed taught that though Christ is offered to participants in the sacrament, as he is in the Word to all who hear it, still, subjectively, a working of the Holy Spirit is needed for them to enjoy the true power of the sacrament. "The signs are of benefit, not to all promiscuously but only to the elect of God to whom the inner and efficacious operation of the Spirit has already come."[32]

To believers, those who receive and enjoy the sacraments in faith, they are signs and seals of the covenant of grace. With an eye to the many people who, though receiving the sacrament, do not believe, Gomarus and others already made a distinction between an internal [covenant] and an external covenant.[33] This is not entirely helpful; the internal and external covenant are two covenants no more than the invisible and visible church are two churches. Sacraments do not guarantee general truths but are seals of covenantal promise: "I am your God and the God of your children." They "present to our senses both that which he declares to us by his Word and that which he works inwardly in our hearts, thereby confirming in us the salvation he imparts to us." They are designed to help us understand more clearly and certify to us that, on account of Christ's one sacrifice finished on the cross, God grants to us, by grace alone, the forgiveness of sins and eternal life.[34] Those who receive the sacrament without faith may enjoy some temporary benefit from it, for God is rich in mercy, but the full and true benefit of the sacraments, like that of the Word, is only for believers. Believers are assured by them of their salvation.

Sacraments are, therefore, of great value. They are not inherently necessary, for God did not have to ordain them and they are not absolutely necessary for

---

32. Consensus Tigurinus (1549), in Niemeyer, *Collectio confessionum*, 209. Ed. note: ET in J. Calvin, *Selected Works of John Calvin: Tracts and Letters*, II, 231.

33. Franciscus Gomarus, "Disp. de sacr.," in *Opera theologica Omnia* (Amsterdam: J. Jansson, 1644), disp. 31; A. Essenius, *Compendium theologiae dogmaticum* (Utrecht: Meinhard à Dreunen, 1669), VI, 6 (commentary on 1 Cor. 7:14).

34. Belgic Confession, art. 33; Heidelberg Catechism, Q 66ff.

salvation, since Scripture binds salvation only to faith (John 3:16). It is not deprivation of, but contempt for, the sacrament that makes a person guilty before
God. Because we are not [disembodied] spirits but sensuous earthly creatures
who understand spiritual things in humanly perceptible forms, God instituted the
sacraments in order that by seeing those signs we might gain a better insight into
his benefits, receive a stronger confirmation of his promises, and thus be supported
and strengthened in our faith. The sacraments do not work faith but reinforce it,
as a wedding ring reinforces love. They confer the whole Christ, whom believers
already possess by the Word, in a different way, renew the believers' covenant with
God, strengthen them in the communion of Christ, join them more closely to
each other, set them apart from the world, and witness to angels and their fellow
human beings, [showing] that they are the people of God, the church of Christ,
the communion of the saints.[35]

[529] The number of sacraments depends on whether the term "sacrament" is
understood in a more restricted or a broader sense. Thus the Reformed counted
a great many sacraments in Scripture both in the covenant of works (Sabbath,
paradise, tree of knowledge, tree of life) and the various dispensations of the
covenant of grace in the Old Testament (circumcision, Passover, expulsion from
paradise, skin garments, Abel's sacrifice, Noah's rainbow, passage through the Red
Sea, manna, water from the rock, bronze serpent, Aaron's rod, Gideon's fleece,
Hezekiah's sundial, and so forth). When it came to the New Testament sacraments, however, the Reformed used a more restricted definition of "sacrament."
Over against Rome, Protestants insist that scriptural evidence is lacking for the
five sacraments added to baptism and the Lord's Supper. On occasion Protestants have envied the greater number of sacraments and ceremonies in Roman
Catholicism. This is unnecessary. When one bears in mind the lack of assurance
that one finds in popular Roman Catholicism because one cannot be sure one
is in a state of grace, there is no advantage to having more sacraments than two.
For Protestants, the two sacraments instituted by Christ and accepted in faith are
enough to possess the whole Christ, with his perfect righteousness and holiness.
Finally, it is not the number of sacraments that is decisive but Christ's institution
and the fullness of grace he imparts in a sacrament.

BAPTISM

[530] In the New Testament, baptism has its foundation in the circumcision of the
Old Testament (Gen. 17:10ff.). Just as God utilized practices existing among other
peoples in the institution of the temple and the priesthood, of sacrifice and altar,
of laws and ordinances in Israel, he also did so in the case of circumcision. Among
other peoples it may have had religious as well as hygienic reasons, in the Old Testa-

---

35. C. Vitringa, *Doctr. christ.*, VI, 422–37.

ment it was a sacramental sign and seal of the forgiveness of sins and sanctification in the covenant of grace, whose one great and all-embracing promise is: "I will be your God and the God of your descendants after you" (Gen. 17:7). When God initiated circumcision in the life of Abraham he ordered that every male should be circumcised, the slave as well as the son of the house; that this circumcision must be administered on the eighth day; and that it should serve as a sign of the covenant, so that he who did not receive this sign was a covenant breaker and had to be "cut off" from his people. It seals the two benefits of the covenant—of the righteousness of faith (Rom. 4:11) and the circumcision of the heart (Deut. 10:16; 30:6; Jer. 4:4; Rom. 2:28–29; Col. 2:11); that is, of righteousness or the forgiveness of sins, and of regeneration or sanctification. External circumcision without the circumcision of the heart is of no value (Acts 7:51; Rom. 2:28–29; 3:21, 30; 1 Cor. 7:19); as a seal of the righteousness of faith, it presupposes faith.

For that reason God, through John [the Baptist], instituted water baptism even before Jesus started his public ministry. This baptism, too, was not something absolutely new. All of antiquity attributed a religious-symbolic significance to water; the rivers of the Euphrates, the Indus, and the Ganges, among others, were considered to have healing, atoning, and sanctifying power. Greek and Roman mystery religions initiated people through prescribed washings,[36] and even in Israel proselytes were required to be baptized and present a sacrifice as well as be circumcised to be admitted to the believing community.[37] Baptism, however, only becomes a sacrament, a sign and seal of grace, as a result of being instituted by God. The New Testament expressly teaches that "a word of God" came to John to baptize (Luke 3:2–3), that God sent him for this purpose (John 1:33), that his baptism was not "from men" but "from heaven" (Matt. 21:25), and that the publicans who had themselves baptized "justified God," while the Pharisees and scribes, having refused to be baptized by John, "rejected God's purpose for themselves" (Luke 7:29–30). Despite objections to the contrary, John's baptism is identical to that of Jesus's disciples; it is a baptism "for the forgiveness of sins" (Acts 2:38). Jesus himself was baptized with John's baptism and made no distinction between the baptism administered by his disciples and that of John (John 3:22–23; 4:1ff.), but simply adopted the disciples baptized by John without baptizing them again (John 1:37; Acts 18:25). Some raise the objection—from Matthew 3:11; Mark 1:8; and Luke 3:16—that John's baptism and Christian baptism are opposed to each other as water baptism is to Spirit baptism or baptism by fire. However, Acts 1:5 clearly teaches that John here does not contrast his baptism with Christian baptism but with the—figuratively so-called—"baptism" of the Holy Spirit on the day of Pentecost. Christian baptism is a baptism with water, signifying the washing away of sins. John's baptism was similarly a baptism with water, but one that at

36. T. Pfanner, *Systema theologiae gentilis purioris* (Basel: Joh. Hermann Widerhold, 1679), 346.
37. Emil Schürer, *The History of the Jewish People in the Age of Jesus Christ (175 B.C.–A.D. 135)*, rev. and ed. Géza Vermès and Fergus Millar (1885; Edinburgh: T&T Clark, 1979), III, 165.

the same time sealed repentance and forgiveness. The two baptisms, accordingly, completely agree both in the sign and in the thing signified. Both John's baptism and that of his disciples *before* Pentecost are to be distinguished from all Christian baptisms after the Holy Spirit is poured out. The same is true of the baptisms done by Jesus and his disciples before Pentecost! Believers are baptized "into the name of Jesus" just as the Israelites were baptized "into Moses" (1 Cor. 10:2) and the disciples at Ephesus "into John's baptism" (Acts 19:3), because believers are adopted by Jesus and put their trust in him alone. The distinction in Acts 19 also does not contradict the identity of the two baptisms pre-Pentecost; Paul apparently did not regard the baptism they had received [earlier] as true and genuine. We do not know the precise reasons but we do know that all sorts of error, also regarding baptism, had crept into the circle of John's disciples who had not switched over to Jesus. Consequently, the disciples in Ephesus did not have to be baptized in Jesus's name again but *for the first time*, for their baptism into John's name was not a true baptism, not a truly Christian baptism, nor the true, original Johannine baptism.[38] The institution by God of baptism, accordingly, already occurs in the ministry of John, but Jesus, after undergoing it himself, adopted it from him and had it administered by his disciples (John 3:22; 4:1–2). In Matthew 28:19 Jesus does not institute another or a new baptism but expands it to include all the nations. The formula "into the name of the Father and the Son and the Holy Spirit" does not prescribe what the apostles are to say but what they have to do. The name here indicates that the baptized person is placed in relationship with the Father, Son, and Holy Spirit.

John and Jesus both contrasted "water baptism" and "Spirit baptism"; what is now their relation after Pentecost? The two are clearly linked in the New Testament but not inseparably. In Acts 2:33 all the disciples received that Spirit without [water] baptism, and in Acts 9:17 and 10:44 the gifts of the Spirit are given to Paul, Cornelius, and others even before baptism (cf. 11:15–17). Furthermore, in Acts 8:15–17; 9:17; and 19:6 glossolalia and the gift of prophecy are not bestowed through baptism but through the laying on of hands. Still for those who were "outside," the baptism of repentance was the ordinary way by which they could also receive the gifts of the Spirit (Acts 2:38; 19:5–6). This connection, however, was temporary. Glossolalia and prophecy were not the true benefits of baptism. Christian baptism essentially remained a baptism of repentance and of faith in Christ for the forgiveness of sins. Throughout the New Testament baptism is thus described as salvation from sin (Rom. 4:25; 6:3–6, 11, 13; 12:5; 1 Cor. 3:1, 13; 6:11; 12:13; 10:1–12; Gal. 2:20; 3:27–29; Col. 2:12; Eph. 5:26; Heb. 6:2; 9:10; 10:22–23; 1 Pet. 3:20–22). In Paul's view, water baptism is simultaneously a Spirit baptism, not a baptism with the spiritual gifts of glossolalia and prophecy, but with the Spirit as the principle of a new life. This renewal of human beings

38. W. Baldensperger, *Das Prolog des vierten Evangeliums* (Freiburg i.B.: Mohr, 1898), believes that the entire prologue of John 1 is written to oppose these baptists or followers of John the Baptist.

by the Holy Spirit in baptism is not something detached from and alongside, nor an accidental addition to, justification by faith. Baptized people are new, spiritual people (πνευματικοι) who are simultaneously washed, sanctified, and justified (1 Cor. 6:11).

[532] The ancient Christian church did not have a universally practiced rite of baptism, though the Teaching of the Apostles (*Didache*) already has the trinitarian formula. However, when from the second century onward worship services were split into a public and a private part, the administration of baptism and the Lord's Supper increasingly assumed a more mysterious character, was surrounded by many rituals,[39] and changed into a magically operative means of grace. Although it is clearly stated that the water in baptism retains its ordinary nature, the linking of the sign and the thing signified is frequently expressed in a mystical manner: "If there is any grace in the water, it is not because of the nature of the water but because of the presence of the Spirit."[40] "Through that water divine grace bestows eternal life."[41] Baptism, accordingly, is described by various names derived from the mysteries: illumination, mystery, completion, fulfillment, initiation, induction into the mysteries, and regarded as "a vehicle toward heaven," "a vehicle toward God," or "a key of the kingdom of heaven."[42] Simplicity was no longer the watchword. Augustine contributed to this trend by teaching that baptism worked *ex opere operato* for infants, and was later followed by the Scholastics who deemphasized the importance of the subjective demands of baptism. This formed the basis for the Roman Catholic view, which understands baptism to be the entry into the church and strictly necessary for salvation.

[533] The battle that was waged by the Reformation against Rome's doctrine of the sacraments was concentrated, not around baptism, but around the Lord's Supper. The German Reformers even believed that baptism had been kept almost intact under papacy and therefore adopted it with only a few minor changes. The Lutherans departed but little from Rome's teaching and retained many of its

---

39. Such as the presentation of the child or person receiving baptism by sponsors, making profession of faith, blowing on the face of the candidate for baptism and making the sign of the cross, putting consecrated salt into the mouth of the candidate for baptism, exorcism, the thrice-repeated immersion or sprinkling, the anointing with chrism, the giving of a new name, the putting on of a white garment, the handing over of a lighted candle, the admission to the church, the fraternal kiss. See J. C. Suicerus, *Thesaurus ecclesiasticus*, s.v. βαπτισμα; *The Roman Catechism*, trans. Bradley and Kevane, II, chap. 1, qu. 46; P. Drews, "Taufe, Liturg. Vollzug," in *PRE*[3], XIX, 424–50.

40. Basil, *On the Holy Spirit*, c. 15.

41. Theodoret, *Questions on Genesis*, qu. 26 (ed. note: PG, vol. 80; cf. also *Theodoreti cyrensis quaestiones in octateuchum*, ed. Natalio Fernández Marcos and Angel Sáenz-Badillos [Madrid: Biblia Poliglota Matritense, 1979]); J. C. Suicerus, *Thesaurus ecclesiasticus*, s.v. βαπτισμα; cf. Tertullian, *On Baptism*, 4.

42. J. Schwane, *Dogmengeschichte*, II, 735; E. Hatch, *Griechentum und Christentum* (Freiburg i.B.: Mohr, 1892), 219; J. C. Suicerus, *Thesaurus ecclesiasticus*, s.v. βαπτισμα. F. Kattenbusch ("Taufe, Kirchenlehre," in *PRE*[3], XIX, 403) correctly observes, "Obviously this does not mean that the particular ideas by which people consider initiation rituals in the mystery religions as confirmation-seal or enlightenment were simply carried over into the εκκλησια by the action of name-giving in baptism." The term "seal," for example, was already used by the Jews with respect to circumcision (cf. Rom. 4:11).

ceremonies—such as the giving of a name, the sign of the cross, exorcism, spon-sorship, the laying on of hands, the white garment, the blessing, and so forth—in part because Luther insisted on an objective realistic union of the Word with the water. Baptism is "a word of God joined with immersion in water included in the divine command and sealed with the word of God." The water in baptism, as Luther put it elsewhere in his *Sermon on Baptism*, "is permeated by the divine majesty and presence," as iron glows with the heat of fire.

The Reformed tradition, however, rejected most of the ceremonies that had gradually become associated with baptism and returned to the simplicity of Scrip-ture. They also proceeded from, and attempted to hold on to, the idea that baptism had been instituted for believers and therefore did not effect but strengthened faith. Consequently they faced a twofold difficulty in connection with infant baptism. In the first place, they had to demonstrate—primarily against the Ana-baptists but also against Roman Catholics and Lutherans—that the children of believers were to be regarded as believers even before baptism and as such ought to be baptized. And in the second place, they were obligated to answer the ques-tion of what the gracious operation of baptism consisted in the case of small children, since, if they had not yet reached the age of discretion and hence did not yet possess "actual faith," they could hardly be strengthened and confirmed in that faith. The second question received less attention than the first. Children, but also adults, had to be judged in light of the rule of that covenant. A person is entitled to baptism not by faith and repentance but only because of the covenant. The children born of believing parents were not pagan children, not subject to the wrath of God, nor under the power of Satan, so that in their case an exor-cism had to be conducted first. On the contrary: even before baptism they were children of the covenant. Baptism, accordingly, was not even absolutely necessary to salvation; neither was there any need for emergency baptisms administered by laypeople. The implications of this led to further debates about the relation between election and covenant and regeneration as the presumed condition for baptizing. While many of the Reformed initially maintained the unity of election and covenant, on account of decay in the church, baptism gradually was totally separated from regeneration and deprived of its value. Remonstrants, Rationalists, Quakers, and modernist Protestants likewise see in the sacrament a *human* act of confession rather than a divine seal. The nineteenth century saw a number of attempts to restore the objective character of baptism. Schleiermacher first of all regarded baptism as an action of the church by which it receives the individual believer into its fellowship, but then, implied in this, is the simultaneous incorpo-ration of that believer into full-life communion with Christ.[43] Other theologians, highlighting the gracious act of God implicit in the sacrament, taught that, while baptism does not presuppose regeneration, it nevertheless imparts the power of regeneration or regeneration itself, is the point of initial contact established by

43. F. Schleiermacher, *The Christian Faith*, §§136–38.

Christ for the love bond between him and the believer and lays a foundation for all later benefits, benefits that from then on can only be obtained in the way of faith.[44] In the Netherlands Dr. A. Kuyper attempted to maintain the objective character of baptism by ascribing to it a special grace. This grace consists, not in regeneration—which is presupposed in baptism and therefore no longer needs to be conferred—but in a special and otherwise unobtainable benefit, namely, in incorporation into the body of Christ, or rather, in the implantation in our faith of the disposition or tendency not to exist by oneself but in our feeling one with the entire body of Christ.[45]

THE MODE AND MANNER OF BAPTISM; INFANT BAPTISM

[534] Apart from Baptist churches and mission fields, most now know baptism almost exclusively as infant baptism.[46] Yet Scripture nowhere speaks of infant baptism and always assumes the baptism of adults. Even the Old Testament prophets proclaimed that God would in the future grant to Israel repentance and life, a new heart and a new spirit, forgive all their sins, pour out his Spirit on them, sprinkle clean water on them, and cleanse them from all their impurities (Hosea 6:2; Joel 2:28–29; Mic. 7:18–20; Isa. 1:16; 40:1ff.; Jer. 31:31–34; 33:8; Ezek. 11:17–20; 36:25–28; 37:1–14; 39:29; Zech. 13:1; etc.). Regeneration, repentance, and faith were necessary, for Israel as well as for the gentiles, to enter into the kingdom of heaven and partake of its benefits. This was the message with which John and Jesus confronted Israel, and those who accepted it were baptized. Accordingly, the presentation and acceptance of the word of the gospel preceded baptism, and there is no disagreement among Christian churches over the necessity of a confession of faith prior to the baptism of adults. Even Rome recognizes that in the case of adults seven preparations have to precede baptism, and Rome makes not the objective validity of the sacrament but its subjective operation dependent on a "virtual intention" as a *conditio sine qua non* in the recipient of the sacrament.[47] Still for Rome, preaching and faith have only preparatory significance while the real, sanctifying, supernatural grace is imparted only by the sacrament of baptism, which is strictly necessary for salvation for all people, adults as well as children. The sacrament as such provides benefits, even apart from faith. The Reforma-

44. I. A. Dorner, *A System of Christian Doctrine*, trans. A. Cave and J. S. Banks, 4 vols. (Edinburgh: T&T Clark, 1882), IV, 290; cf. H. Bavinck, *Reformed Dogmatics*, IV, 67–71, 190 (##442–43, 469).

45. A. Kuyper, "Van de genademiddelen," *De Heraut*, 646ff. (11 May–July 1890). Ed. note: For Bavinck's thoughtful dissent from Kuyper's notion of "presumed regeneration," see Herman Bavinck, *Saved by Grace: The Holy Spirit's Work in Calling and Regeneration*, ed. J. Mark Beach, trans. Nelson D. Kloosterman (Grand Rapids: Reformation Heritage Books, 2008).

46. Ed. note: While this *may* have been true in Bavinck's day, it clearly is not true in the third millennium thanks to the explosive growth around the world of evangelical Pentecostalism.

47. Council of Trent, sess. VI, can. 5, 7; Roman Catechism (Bradley and Kevane), II, chap. 2, qu. 31, 45.

tion, by contrast, posited the scriptural principle that the sacrament imparts no other benefit than that which believers already possess by trusting in the Word of God. Faith alone apart from any sacrament communicates, and causes believers to enjoy, all the benefits of salvation. Involved here is a Protestant principle: those who attribute to baptism a communication of grace that cannot be obtained through the Word and by faith open the door to the Roman Catholic doctrine of the sacrament.

The "form" of baptism is the deliberately chosen sign of the washing away of pollution in the soul, just as dirt is washed away by water. The sign, therefore, is not arbitrary or accidental. Just as water washes away the dirt from the body, so the blood of Christ cleanses us from all sins. Water has a richly symbolic meaning among virtually all peoples and in all religions and serving in all sorts of ceremonial washings, and foreshadowing the spiritual cleansing that all persons need to enter into communion with God. This was the case even in Old Testament worship (Exod. 30:18–20; 40:30; Lev. 6:28; 8:6; 11:32; 15:12; Num. 8:7; 19:7ff.; etc.; cf. Ezek. 36:25; 37:23; Zech. 13:1). In the first period of the church, baptism consisted in immersion, as already indicated by the Greek βαπτιζειν (*baptizein*) and the scriptural reports of baptism. Accordingly, baptism by immersion was the standard practice in the West, while sprinkling was less common. After the thirteenth century, however, sprinkling became more common. Yet while immersion illustrates the meaning of baptism more clearly, the issue itself is a matter of adiaphora.

[535] The water of baptism becomes a sacrament through the words of institution. In Scripture, baptism is sometimes called a baptism "in the name of Christ" (Acts 2:38; 8:16; 10:48; 19:5; cf. Rom. 6:3; 1 Cor. 1:13–15; 6:11; Gal. 3:27) and at other times a baptism "in the name of the Father, the Son, and the Holy Spirit" (Matt. 28:19). These expressions are not intended to furnish a formula that has to be voiced in baptism—evident from the fact that no such formula is mentioned on the occasion of circumcision and Passover or at John's baptism and the Lord's Supper—but describe the essence of Christian baptism: this must be a baptism into the name of Christ and hence into the name of the Triune God. It was by natural processes that there emerged for public use on this occasion a fixed formula that was derived from the words of institution in Matthew 28:19; the *Didache* speaks of Christians as "those who have been baptized into the name of the Lord," but it does already know the trinitarian formula.[48] In the face of heresies, in order to defend the Christian character of baptism, to guarantee that the baptism administered was the true Christian baptism, and to introduce the desired consistency and stability into liturgical practice, the trinitarian formula must increasingly have been viewed as necessary.[49] But this trinitarian formula is not couched in the same words in the different churches; the Greek church uses

---

48. *Did.* 9.5; 7.1, 3; cf. Justin Martyr, *1 Apology*, 61.
49. Cyprian, *Epistles* 73.16–18; Suicerus, *Thesaurus ecclesiasticus*, s.v. βαπτισμος.

its own distinct formula, and though Latin churches recognize the validity of those baptisms, it uses the simple "I baptize you in the name of the Father, and the Son, and the Holy Spirit." This is also the formula that Protestants took over.

The trinitarian baptismal formula does not magically turn the water into the blood of Christ. The work of the Holy Spirit in the sacrament, like that in the case of the Word, is not physical but spiritual. Whereas Roman Catholics, and to a lesser degree Lutherans, localize the Spirit's work in baptism as going through the water, the Reformed reject the idea of a local and physical union and instead assume the presence of a union like that in the case of the Word. Just as the Holy Spirit indeed works with the Word but does not confine his power and operation within that Word, so it is also with the water of baptism. In Ephesians 5:26 Paul deliberately distinguishes the working of Christ by the Word from that by the water, as is also done in Hebrews 10:22 and 1 Peter 3:21. It is not the minister nor the water but Christ who makes the church holy and gives the thing signified (Matt. 3:11; 1 Cor. 6:11; Heb. 9:14; 1 John 1:7). If the water of baptism effected regeneration, Paul would not have been able to say in 1 Corinthians 1:14 that "Christ did not send me to baptize but to proclaim the gospel." Nonetheless, Reformed churches also confess that in baptism Christ promises and assures everyone who receives it that "as surely as water washes away the dirt from the body, so certainly his blood and his Spirit wash away the impurity of the soul."[50] There is also substantial agreement with respect to the benefits that in baptism are granted to adult believers. They are: Justification or the forgiveness of sins (Mark 1:4; Acts 2:38; 22:16; Heb. 10:22; 1 Pet. 3:21); regeneration, repentance, the dying away of the old self, and the coming to life of the new self through fellowship with the death and resurrection of Christ (Mark 1:4; Rom. 6:2–10; 1 Cor. 6:11; Eph. 5:26; Col. 2:12); fellowship, not only with Christ but also with the church, which is his body (Matt. 28:19; John 4:1; Acts 2:40–41; Rom. 6; 1 Cor. 12:13). These benefits come from the Word of promise, received in faith, and signed and sealed in baptism. All God's promises taken together are conveyed in Word and baptism alike; nothing that is given in the one is not given in the other. In baptism the Father witnesses to us that he makes an eternal covenant of grace with us and adopts us as his children and heirs (Gen. 17:7, 10; Acts 2:39). The Son assures us that he washes us in his blood and incorporates us into the fellowship of his death and resurrection (Rom. 6:3; Gal. 3:27). The Holy Spirit assures us that he lives in us and sanctifies us to be members of Christ (1 Cor. 6:11; 12:13; Titus 3:5).

[536] The big divide in Christendom concerning baptism, of course, has to do with infant baptism. From its introduction until now, this baptism is rejected by a considerable part of Christianity. Until the present day infant baptism has been rejected for two chief reasons: it does not occur in Scripture, and it presupposes faith and repentance, which do not occur or are not recognized in small children. Because of the rapid expansion and ordinary occurrence of adult baptism in the

---

50. Heidelberg Catechism, Q 69.

first and second centuries of the church, direct witness to infant baptism is lacking until the time of Tertullian.[51] Not too much should be made of this silence, however. When Tertullian for the first time makes mention of infant baptism, he opposes it, to be sure, but not on the ground that it is an innovation and not customary in apostolic times, but because it is his general conviction that "deferment of baptism is more profitable. . . . All who understand what a burden baptism is will have more fear of obtaining it than of its postponement."[52] Tertullian was not alone in holding this conviction, and Origen testifies that in his days infant baptism was in general use and of apostolic pedigree. Cyprian for his part, agreeing with the Council of Carthage held in 256, defended the view that infant baptism should not be delayed till the eighth day but already administered on the second or third day after the birth.[53] When infant baptism became the rule rather than the exception, it became necessary to defend its legitimacy. Arguing against the Pelagians, Augustine defended infant baptism as necessary to remove original sin, and appealed to the faith of the parents of the child. "About this there is a good pious belief that the child is benefited by the faith of those who present it for baptism."[54] Indeed, the faith of the whole church is to their advantage: "Little ones are, of course, presented to receive spiritual grace, not so much from those in whose hands they are carried—though they do receive it from them if they are good believing people—as from the universal society of the saints and believers."[55] On this basis, says Augustine, the children of believers have a right to baptism, and in this baptism they themselves obtain the forgiveness of sins and regeneration, with the understanding, however, that "if baptized infants upon coming to the age of reason do not believe and do not refrain from illicit desires, they derive no benefit from what they received as children."[56]

Such dependence on the faith of another (*fides aliena*), however, cannot compensate for the lack of personal faith in the child and therefore leads imperceptibly to the doctrine of regeneration by baptism. The Council of Trent decreed that the New Testament sacraments contain grace in themselves and impart it to all who place no obstacle in its path, so that in baptism also the children receive grace and

---

51. Ed. note: This judgment may be in error thanks to new historical evidence. See J. Jeremias, *Infant Baptism in the First Four Centuries*, trans. David Cairns (London: SCM, 1960).

52. Tertullian, *On Baptism*, 18; cf. also Irenaeus, *Against Heresies*, II, 22, 4.

53. J. W. F. Höfling, *Das Sakrament der Taufe* (Erlangen: Deichert, 1859), I, 104ff.

54. Augustine, *On Free Will*, III, 23.

55. Augustine, *Letter to Boniface (Letter 98)*, in *The Works of St. Augustine: A Translation for the 21st Century*, ed. John E. Rotelle, OSA., trans. Roland J. Teske, SJ, vol. II/1 (Hyde Park, NY: New City, 2001), 429.

56. Augustine, *The Punishment and Forgiveness of Sins and the Baptism of Little Ones*, I.xxv, in *The Works of St. Augustine*, vol. I/23 (1997), 47–48; cf., T. Aquinas, *Summa Theol.*, III, qu. 68, art. 9; Bonaventure, *The Breviloquium*, vol. 2 of *The Works of Bonaventure*, trans. Jose DeVinck (Paterson, NJ: St. Anthony Guild Press, 1963), VI, 7; Roman Catechism, II, (Bradley and Kevane): II, chap. 1, qu. 28, 31; J. Köstlin, *The Theology of Luther*, I, 399; II, 45, 510; J. Calvin, *Defensio orthodoxae fidei* (1554), in *Calvini opera* (CR XXXV), VIII, 483, 493.

the virtues *ex opere operato*, and though they are not believers beforehand, they become believers by baptism.[57] The Lutherans opposed the idea that children had faith before baptism and also that they were baptized "upon the faith of another" (*in aliena fide*); instead they taught that children received the faith in baptism and not just the disposition or power but even the act. "A true, saving, vivifying and *actual* faith arises in infants through baptism and in the baptism of the Holy Spirit, whence it is that baptized infants truly believe."[58] Corresponding to this is the doctrine of the High Churchmen [in the Anglican Church] who believe in baptismal regeneration. The problems with this view are numerous. The "faith of another" (*fides aliena*) becomes totally superfluous if baptism imparts grace *ex opere operato* and presupposes nothing other than a "passive capacity" in the child, and would seem to call for mass baptism of all children. Baptism is robbed of its scriptural character when it is detached from faith and the Word, ceases to be a sign and seal of God's promises, becomes an independent self-operative means of grace, and even takes first place among the means of grace. The benefits imparted by baptism are exaggerated on one hand and weakened on the other. Scripture and experience make it clear that not all baptized children later prove to be believers and are saved. This would mean that baptism's benefits are admissible until accepted in faith. They are sufficient for salvation in the case of children who die in infancy, but insufficient for growing children and put the latter in a dubious category between believers and unbelievers. In response, the Reformed in defending infant baptism took their position in the covenant of grace, which, according to God's promise, embraces not only believers but also their descendants. Not regeneration, faith, or repentance, much less our assumptions pertaining to them, but only the covenant of grace gave people, both adults and children, the right to baptism.[59] No deeper or more solid ground was possible or necessary.

[537] The validity of infant baptism depends exclusively on how Scripture regards the children of believers and hence wants us to regard them. If Scripture speaks about such children in the same way it does about adult believers, the right and hence the duty to practice infant baptism has been established. For we may not withhold from the children what we grant to adults. In the case of infant baptism, therefore, we are permitted to require neither less nor more than in the case of adult baptism. When the Anabaptists argued against infant baptism, that children could not experience faith and repentance, the Reformed replied that although children did not possess the acts of faith, they still could possess the disposition (*habitus*) of faith. Since absolute certainty about the internal state of the recipient is never certain in the case of either adults or children, the question is whether we have the same certainty in either case. Those who want absolute certainty can never dispense any sacrament. It is not surprising that the

57. Council of Trent, sess. VII, can. 6–8; "De bapt.," chaps. 13–14.
58. J. Quenstedt, *Theologia didactico-polemica sive systema theologicum* (1685), IV, 147.
59. J. Calvin, *Institutes*, IV.xvi.23–24.

New Testament does not mention infant baptism since adult baptism was the rule, and infant baptism would have been the exception. Yet this does not exclude infant baptism since it may be derived from original baptism by legitimate inference. According to Colossians 2:11–12, baptism replaced Old Testament circumcision. Baptism, therefore, is more than circumcision, not in essence but in degree. Circumcision pointed forward to the death of Christ; baptism points back to it. The former ends, the latter begins, with that death. If, however, that circumcision as the sign of the covenant could and must be administered to the children, the same applies a fortiori to baptism, which is not poorer but much richer in grace. This is made manifest in part by the fact that the sacrament of the old covenant was only administered to male persons, but the new covenant is also administered to female persons.

Circumcision is far from being the only proof that the Old Testament regards the children as partakers of the covenant. After all, the covenant is distinct from election in that it shows how election is realized in an organic and historical way. It is never established only with an individual person, but in that person also immediately with that person's descendants. There is a kind of communion of parents and children in sin and misery, over against which God has established a communion of parents and children in grace and blessing. The covenant of God with its benefits and blessings perpetuates itself from child to child and from generation to generation (Gen. 9:12; 17:7, 9; Exod. 3:15; 12:17; 16:32; Deut. 7:9; Ps. 105:8; etc.). While grace is not automatically inherited, as a rule it is bestowed along the line of generations. "For the infants of believers their first and foremost access of salvation is the very fact of their being born of believing parents."[60] This view is continued in the New Testament where despite the Jews' rejection of Jesus he continues to regard their children as children of the covenant (Matt. 18:2ff.; 19:13ff.; 21:15–16.; Mark 10:13ff.; Luke 9:48; 18:15ff.). He calls them to himself, embraces them, lays hands on them, blesses them, tells them that theirs is the kingdom of heaven. Furthermore, the church (ἐκκλησια, *ekklēsia*) has replaced the Israel of the Old Testament as the people of God who is their Father (Matt. 1:21; Luke 1:17; Acts 3:25; Rom. 9:25–26; 11:16–21; 2 Cor. 6:16–18; Gal. 3:14–29; Eph. 2:12–13; Titus 2:14; Heb. 8:8–10; 1 Pet. 2:9; Rev. 21:3), and children of believers are included among the people of God as "households" come to faith and are baptized (Luke 10:5; 19:19; Acts 5:42; 11:14; 16:15, 31, 34; 18:18; 20:20; 1 Cor. 1:16). According to Paul (1 Cor. 7:14), even the children from a household of which only one of the parents has become a believer are holy. Paul's sole interest here is to show that the Christian faith does not cancel out the natural ordinances of life, but rather confirms and sanctifies them (cf. 1 Cor. 7:18–24); the whole family is regarded in light of the confession of the believing spouse. Scripture knows nothing of a

---

60. T. Beza, *Resp. ad coll. Mompelg*, 103, according to J. Gerhard, *Loci theologici*, ed. E. Preuss, 9 vols. (Berlin: G. Schlawitz, 1863–75), XX, 211.

neutral upbringing that seeks to have the children make a completely free and independent choice at a more advanced age.[61] The children of believers are not pagans or children of the devil who still—as Roman Catholics and Lutherans hold—have to be exorcized at their baptism,[62] but children of the covenant, for whom the promise is meant as much as for adults. They are included in the covenant and are holy, not by nature (Job 14:4; Ps. 51:5; John 3:6; Eph. 2:3) but by virtue of the covenant.[63] All this is the more compelling because grace—especially in the New Testament dispensation—is much more abundant than sin (Rom. 5:12–21). Anabaptism sets a limit to the operation of grace—in the child's age, in the child's not yet having attained the age of discretion, that is, in law and ordinances that have been established by God at the time of creation in nature—while grace knows no such boundaries. In the New Testament all boundaries of people, country, sex, and age have been erased. Anabaptism fails to appreciate the catholicity of Christianity. Just as with adults, the hearts of infants should be judged according to charity. Baptism—whether as an infant or an adult—does not establish a person's salvation; the basis for baptism is not the assumption that someone is regenerate, nor even that [there is] regeneration itself, but only the covenant of God.

The essence of baptism may not in any way be made dependent on its effect in life. Just as a sincere faith is what it is according to the description of the Heidelberg Catechism [Lord's Day 7, Q&A 21], even though the reality of life shows deviations from and malformations of it, so also baptism is and may not be other than what Scripture teaches concerning it. Ultimately the fruit of baptism is enjoyed only by those who are elect and therefore come to faith in God's time. Everyone must acquiesce in that outcome, whether they are Catholic or Protestant, Lutheran or Reformed. "The sacraments effect what they depict only in the elect," said Augustine. The elect have laid hold of it; the rest were hardened. "It is the children of the promise who are regarded as Abraham's offspring" (Rom. 9:8 NIV). The benefits of baptism are the same for children as for adults: the forgiveness of sins, regeneration, and incorporation into the church of Christ.

Baptism confers the same benefits as the Word, it confers them in a different manner and form so that faith is confirmed and strengthened by it in the measure that God has given to each. This rule applies equally to children, to new adult believers, to Christians who are at varying stages of maturity in their faith and walk of life. At work here, as in so many areas, there is a mysterious reciprocal activity. Just as light and the human eye presuppose and support each other, so faith enjoys the sacrament more to the degree that it is stronger, and faith is sealed and reinforced by the sacrament to the same degree as well. For maturing

61. Council of Trent, sess. VII, "De bapt.," chap. 14.
62. Cf. G. Kawerau, "Exorcismus bei der Taufe," in *PRE*³, V, 695–700; F. J. Dölger, *Der Exorcismus in der altchristlichen Taufritual* (Paderborn: Schöningh, 1909).
63. Heidelberg Catechism, Q 74; Canons of Dort, I, 17.

believers, therefore, the sacraments do not gradually decrease in importance but continually gain in value. To the eye of faith they ever more beautifully and gloriously display the riches of God's grace. For every believer and for the whole church, they are proof of grace received, a sign of God's faithfulness, a basis for pleading one's case in prayer, a supporting pillar for one's faith, and an exhortation to new obedience.[64]

[538] The one who administers this baptism is Christ, and only when he baptizes a person, and along with the sign also grants the thing signified, is that person truly baptized. But in administering baptism Christ employs people—ordained people—showing that the sacraments are subordinate to the preaching of the Word. This was different in the Old Testament where circumcision was not limited to any particular office. In the New Testament, however, this changes and administration of baptism is restricted to those who held an office: John (Mark 1:4); Jesus's disciples (John 4:2); the apostles (Acts 2:38), who were specifically charged by Christ to do this (Matt. 28:19); Philip (Acts 8:38; 21:8); Ananias (9:17–18); Paul, who sometimes baptized but for the rest left this rite to be administered by his fellow workers since as apostle to the gentiles he was first of all called to preach the gospel (1 Cor. 1:14–17; cf. Acts 10:48). The administration of the sacraments, though subordinate to the preaching of the Word, was at all times bound up with it. The sacrament follows the Word, and so the right to administer it passed automatically from the apostles and evangelists to the ministers, those presbyters who labored in the Word and in teaching. Baptism is therefore not the cause but rather the sign and seal of regeneration, which is bestowed before and apart from the sacrament. This means that baptism is not strictly necessary for salvation. The sacrament must always be closely joined with the Word. It is not the fact of being deprived of baptism, but contempt for baptism, that renders a person guilty before God.

There is therefore no reason to depart from apostolic usage and in cases of emergency to permit people other than the ministers of the church to administer baptism.[65] In this connection the Reformed also favored having baptism consistently take place in the midst of the congregation. Although cases are conceivable in which the administration of baptism could be allowed to take place in private homes, they can and must be of a highly exceptional nature. Such cases are not to be judged by the minister of the Word alone but by the entire church council and even then require that the baptism take place only in the presence of the council. For what matters in the distribution of the sacrament is not the building but the gathering of the church. The sacrament is a constituent of a public worship service, a good that Christ granted to his church, and therefore it must be openly administered, together with the Word, in the midst of the congregation.

64. Concerning infant baptism, cf. J. Calvin, *Institutes*, IV.xvi; F. Turretin, *Institutes of Elenctic Theology*, XIX, qu. 20; J. J. van Oosterzee, *Christian Dogmatics*, trans. J. Watson and M. Evans, 2 vols. (New York: Scribner, Armstrong, 1874), §138.
65. J. Calvin, *Institutes*, IV.xv.20.

With respect to time of the administration of baptism, the Greek Orthodox, Roman Catholic, Lutheran, and Reformed all agree that it should be soon after birth. The system of "baptismal witnesses," "sureties," "sponsors," "guarantors," "receivers," "spiritual fathers and mothers," or "godparents" came up when infant baptism became the general custom and is already mentioned by Tertullian.[66] Needed at this time were persons who professed faith in the place of the child and answered the usual questions; who acted, as it were, as bondspersons and sponsors for the child and promised, on the basis of the child's baptism, to give the child a Christian upbringing. Lutheran and Reformed theologians *consider this* to be *a matter of adiaphora*, yet the Reformed especially stressed that in the first place it was the *parents* who should answer the baptismal questions and act as receivers and sponsors for their children, and they demanded that if sponsors were invited to play a role, they should be sound in their confession and walk of life.[67] The Reformed churches, at the suggestion of Calvin, also replaced the obligation of godparents to bring up their godchildren in the faith with the catechetical instruction of their baptized youth and assigned this task to their ministers.

The entire doctrine of baptism, as it has been developed by the Reformed, shows how closely they aligned themselves with Scripture. To avoid all sectarianism and to preserve a genuinely Christian magnanimity and breadth of vision, in accord with the Catholic Church in its struggle with the North African churches, the Reformed unanimously taught that the baptism of heretics, provided it was administered in the name of the Triune God, had to be recognized. But since they did not have a magical view of the baptismal formula and did not detach baptism from the church and its offices, they added the further qualification that it had to be administered by a minister who was officially recognized as such in a Christian church. They also admitted to baptism all children who after the death of their parents, or as foundlings, had been adopted into Christian families, who were born from illegitimate unions or from excommunicate, schismatic, or heretical parents as long as there was some ground for the assumption that the lineage of the covenant was not completely broken. The Reformed have maintained, in eminent fashion, the unity and catholicity of the church of Christ on earth. All Christian churches still recognize each other's baptisms and thereby say that in all these churches there is still so much truth that the possibility of salvation is not ruled out. There is one confession on the foundation of which they have all been built, one faith in which they all share. Despite all the differences and controversy, all of them nevertheless recognize *one* Lord, *one* faith, and *one* baptism.

66. A. Drews, "Taufe: Liturgischer Vollzug," in *PRE*[3], XIX, 447ff.

67. J. Calvin, "Letter to Caspar Olevianus, November 1560," in *Op. ed. Amsterdam* (Schippers), IX, 142. Ed. note: The letter concerns the polity of the church in Geneva and can be found in *Calvini opera* (CR XLVI), XVIII, cols. 235–37. C. Hooijer, *Oude kerkenordeningen der Nederlandsche Hervormde gemeenten, 1563–1638* (Zalt-Bommel: Noman, 1865), 7, 11, 17, 46, 69, 105, 153, 205, 265, 314, 344, 456.

THE LORD'S SUPPER

A Shared Sacrificial Meal

[539–40] As the second sacrament, after baptism, comes the Lord's Supper, whose Old Testament model is the Passover feast. Just as among the gentiles (Num. 25:2), so also in Israel meals were frequently combined with sacrifices as acts of atonement. Like the Passover, the Lord's Supper is a meal where God meets with his people and, on the basis of the sacrifice made and accepted, unites himself with them, and meets his people in joyful celebration. God himself as the host shares the fruit of the supper with his people. Levitical purity was required since God only comes to the children of Israel and dwells among them in a clean place (Exod. 20:24; 29:42–46; 33:7; Num. 11:25; 12:5; 17:4; Deut. 31:15). Those who participated entered into a covenant with him. Participation in the sacrificial meals of the gentiles, accordingly, was forbidden to Israel (Exod. 34:15); it was an act of attaching themselves to and joining themselves with false gods (Num. 25:3, 5; Ps. 106:28). The apostles later prohibited Christians from participation in them (Acts 15:29; 21:25) or warned against them for the sake of weak believers (1 Cor. 8:1ff.; 10:18ff.).

The feast of Passover occupied an entirely unique place in the cultic life of Israel; it was instituted by God on a special occasion prior to all the other sacrifices and therefore has a nature of its own. Although first of all a sacrifice (and sacrament) the Passover must also be seen as a meal. After the lamb had been slaughtered at twilight on the fourteenth of Abib and its blood dabbed on the doorframes of the house, or in a later period sprinkled on the altar, it—without a bone being broken in its body—had to be roasted as a whole, head, legs and inner parts, over a fire. Then, in the same night of the fourteenth of Abib, it had to be eaten with unleavened bread and bitter herbs by everyone in the house. It had to be eaten in haste, with loins girded, feet shod, and a staff in one's hand, in the house or later at the sanctuary, and what remained was to be burned (Exod. 12:1–28, 43–49; 13:3–9; 23:15; Lev. 23:5–14; Num. 9:10–14; 28:16–25; Deut. 16:1ff.). It is a sacrifice of atonement and meal of communion with God and one another. It is simultaneously a sacrifice and a sacrament.[68] The New Testament ascribes to this Passover a typological significance, so that it is not only an act of remembering the liberation from Egypt, but also a sign and pledge of liberation from the bondage of sin and of communion with God in the person of the promised Messiah. When Jesus instituted the Lord's Supper he deliberately associated it with the celebration of the Passover. The Lord's Supper, however, is only a meal. Its sacrificial character is fulfilled once and for all by the sacrifice of Christ. Although modern scholars debate whether Jesus himself instituted the Lord's Supper, none of the arguments against it are very compelling. To doubt this is to doubt Jesus's own self-consciousness of his death and its saving significance. The variant Gospel

---

68. C. Orelli, "Passah," in *PRE³*, XIV, 750–57; W. J. Moulton, "Passover," in *DB*, III, 684–92.

readings of Jesus's Last Supper with his disciples confirm this, and Paul's description of the institution (1 Cor. 10:16; 11:24–25) confirms the close tie between the Passover and the Lord's Supper. That Jesus died as the true Passover lamb is indicated by John's Gospel (19:33, 36) and also by Paul, who expressly states in 1 Cor. 5:7 that our paschal lamb, Christ, has been slain, and that believers must therefore cleanse out the old leaven of sin and walk as "unleavened" persons, new creatures, unmixed with any unrighteousness. To this we may add that the lamb led to the slaughter (Isa. 53:7) probably contains an allusion to the Passover lamb and is thus applied in the New Testament to Christ (John 1:29, 36; Acts 8:32; 1 Pet. 1:19; Rev. 5:6). Just as circumcision was a model for baptism, and as a result of Christ's death passed into that baptism, so the Passover feast pointed forward to the Lord's Supper and was, in keeping with Christ's command, replaced by it. However, whereas Passover was still primarily a sacrifice, the Lord's Supper has entirely lost this character. The reason is that the sacrifice offered in the Passover found its fulfillment in the death of Christ. It is on the basis of that once-for-all, completed, and perfect sacrifice that Christ founded the new dispensation of the covenant of grace and invited his disciples to, and strengthened them at, his holy table.

Although we need not doubt that our Lord himself instituted the Lord's Supper—even Paul indicating (1 Cor. 11:23) that he received his instruction (not παρα [para, with] but άπο του κυριου [apo tou kyriou, from the Lord])—we still need to ask how Christ instituted this Supper and what he intended to accomplish by it. We must first of all note that Jesus instituted his Supper on the occasion of the Passover meal, probably after the Passover lamb had been eaten—"after the supper" (Luke 22:20)—in connection with the third cup, the cup of thanksgiving.[69] He took the ordinary bread and the ordinary wine used at the Passover and, according to all four reports (Matt. 26:26–29; Mark 14:22–25; Luke 22:19–20; 1 Cor. 11:23–25), related them directly to his death. In Jesus's time the celebration of the Passover had been expanded and included the important slaughtering of the Passover lambs in the temple court by the Levites the afternoon of the fourteenth of Nisan. There is not a single reason for doubting that Jesus knew of and anticipated his death, and specifically construed it as a sacrifice: that way alone can we explain the words and actions that accompany the institution of the Supper. Just moments before, the Passover meal had been consumed; that Passover had been the start and foundation of the covenant that God had established with Israel in the wilderness. For since the lamb had been slaughtered and its blood

69. The Passover itself began with a cup of wine circulating around the room and with thanksgiving; the bitter herbs were eaten, the lamb was put with the unleavened cakes, the exodus story related, the first part of the Hallel (Pss. 113–14) sung, the second cup was passed; then the actual meal began and was followed by the third cup, blessed by the father and emptied by him and all the participants. The whole event was then concluded with the pouring of the fourth cup, the singing of the second part of the Hallel (Pss. 115–18), the blessing of the fourth cup by the father with the words of Ps. 118:26, and the cup's emptying by the guests sitting around the table.

shed and sprinkled on the altar, the rite of Passover first served as an offering of atonement and was then used as a sacrificial meal to signify God's communion with his people. All this Christ transfers to himself. He is the true Passover lamb, who by his death, by the breaking of his body and the shedding of his blood, effects atonement with God and lays the foundation for a new covenant. While breaking and distributing the bread, he said: "This is my body" (Matthew and Mark), "This is my body given for you" (Luke), or "This is my body which is for you" (Paul). "Broken" (κλωμενον, *klōmenon*) is lacking in the most important manuscripts (of 1 Cor. 11:24) and alternates in others with "broken in pieces" (θρυπτομενον, *thryptomenon*) and "given" (διδομενον, *didomenon*). When he offered the cup, he said; "Drink from it, all of you. This is my blood of the covenant, which is poured out for many for the forgiveness of sins" (Matthew); "This is my blood of the covenant, which is poured out for many" (Mark); "This cup is the new covenant in my blood, which is poured out for you" (Luke); "This cup is the new covenant in my blood" (Paul). The variant readings sufficiently demonstrate that Jesus no more prescribed a fixed, unchangeable formula at the Supper than he did in connection with baptism. The exact words are not as important as the clear sense that Jesus made the bread and wine of the Passover meal into signs of his body and blood, and indeed of the body and blood as they would before long be given up in death as a sacrifice of atonement. Jesus proceeds here from the Passover meal and the Old Testament sacrifices, adopts the action and terminology customary in that connection, and applies them to his death. Since in a sacrifice the shedding of blood is the main component (Heb. 9:22), the blood of Christ, of which the wine is the sign, is sacrificial blood, the blood of atonement that has been shed for many and is therefore the beginning and initiation of a new covenant. Just as Passover and the old covenant are connected, so also the Supper and the new covenant belong together. The cup, therefore, is "my blood of the covenant" or "the new covenant in my blood," that is, covenant blood (Exod. 24:8). For the disciples, saddened and dreading the death of Christ which they did not understand, Jesus explains to them that his death is to their advantage. It is by that death that the very forgiveness and the very covenant come about that were foreshadowed and foretold in the Old Testament. The time of promise is past; the time of fulfillment is dawning. The old is over; behold, all things are new.

But Jesus does not stop here. He not only offered an explanation of his death in the signs of bread and wine but also gave them to his disciples: "Take, eat" and "Drink from it, all of you." Jesus did not just change bread and wine into signs of his body and blood, but as such he also handed them to his disciples for their consumption. After the Passover meal had been eaten, Jesus instituted a new meal whose components were bread and wine, not of and by themselves, but as signs of his broken body and shed blood. There are differences between the Passover and the Lord's Supper; the eating of the Passover lamb was not the same as eating Christ's broken body, as the eating of the bread in the Supper is now. And though in the sacrifices of the old covenant the blood was shed and sprinkled, it was never drunk. The idea that Jesus's flesh had to be eaten and his blood drunk, accordingly, was so alien to the Jews that they were offended by it and left Jesus (John 6:52, 60, 66). Although the institution of the Supper indeed occurred in connection with Old Testament ideas of covenant and sacrifice, it nevertheless far surpasses them. The Lord's Supper is akin to but not identical with Passover. Because Christ has offered the true and complete sacrifice, the communion with God in the Lord's Supper is much richer and fuller than it could be in the days of the Old Testament. The Lord's Supper is a meal, the essential meal of God and his people; it is a sacrificial meal par excellence at which believers receive Christ himself as he gave his life for them. Jesus expresses this reality by the action of giving his disciples bread and wine as signs of his broken body and shed blood for them to "enjoy."[70] He not only gave himself *for* his own; he also gives himself *to* his own. The cup and the bread in the Lord's Supper is "a participation in the blood and in the body of Christ" (1 Cor. 10:16). The Lord's Supper, which Christ himself instituted at the Passover table, is the same meal as that which since his death has been celebrated in the Christian church up until the present. In it he depicts his sacrifice before our eyes but also has us enjoy it. And that enjoyment is definitely what the Lord's Supper is about. Jesus *gave* us the signs of bread and wine. He did not keep them in his hands but distributed them and told his disciples to take and eat them, adding according to Luke (only with the distribution of the bread) and Paul (also in passing the cup) the words: "Do this in remembrance of me." These words do not mean that the Lord's Supper is only a memorial meal but indicate that the entire Supper, which is in essence a sacrificial meal and an exercise of communion with Christ, must be done in remembrance of him as a continual proclamation of his death (1 Cor. 11:26). For that reason we find in Paul the additional words: "as often as you eat this bread and drink this cup" (1 Cor. 11:25–26).

Christ instituted the Supper as a permanent "good" for his church to endure until he returns. His death must be proclaimed until he comes again. It is the cross that is and remains the source and cause of all blessings, the center of the church's remembrance. Jesus said that from that time of the institution and observance of the Supper, he would never drink of the fruit of the vine until he would drink it anew with his disciples in his Father's kingdom (Matt. 26:29; Mark 14:25; cf. Luke 22:16, 18). He, we know, was going to heaven to prepare a place for his disciples. Only when he returns and has taken his disciples to himself will he sit down with them at the wedding supper of the Lamb and drink with them the new wine that his Father's kingdom will yield in the new heaven and on the new earth. For that intermediate period Christ instituted the Supper as an act of remembering his suffering, as a proclamation of his death, as a means of his abundant grace.

[541] The Lord's Supper has played an important part in the church's life from its beginning. It was usually celebrated in a special gathering of the church in the

---

70. Ed. note: Here and below, "enjoy" is the translation of Bavinck's Dutch word *geniet, genieten*.

evening of the Lord's Day in combination with a regular meal or *agapē* feast, which must be distinguished from the "Eucharist." The one worship service was soon split into two parts: the first, the administration of the Word, was also open to catechumens, penitents, and unbelievers; the second, the celebration of the Lord's Supper, was open only to those who had been baptized. The latter increasingly acquired a mysterious character, and baptism and the Lord's Supper both became mysteries (μυστηριον, *mystērion*) or sacraments.[71] In the early years of the church there was no controversy about the sacraments, and the question concerning the nature of the union between the sign and the thing signified did not arise. Over time, the sacrament became more and more mysterious and was seen as a sacrifice. In the New Testament, to be sure, the sanctification of the body (Rom. 12:1), prayer (Heb. 13:15; cf. Rev. 5:8; 8:3), and doing good and sharing one's possessions (Phil. 4:18; Heb. 13:16) are called "sacrifices," but never the Lord's Supper. This development came about because the connection of the Lord's Supper with an ordinary meal had "offerings" brought for it—especially by the more affluent members—which were received with prayers of thanksgiving, set on tables, and designated for the maintenance of the ministers and the support of the poor. In time the Lord's Supper itself as well as the two elements were called "thanksgiving" (εὐχαριστια), and the Supper was viewed as an offering brought to God by the congregation as a "pure sacrifice," as the *Didache*, appealing to Malachi 1:11, already calls it.[72]

This was innocent as long as the Lord's Supper was really regarded as a meal and a thanksgiving prayer was offered on behalf of the entire congregation. The content of the sacrifice was not the body and blood of Christ, but the gifts assembled by the congregation, so that in the early period people thought in this connection only of a thank offering and not an expiatory offering. However, the Lord's Supper and the love feasts separated, and the Supper increasingly acquired the character of a sacrifice offered not by the congregation but by the bishop, consisting not in its presentation by the congregation but in its character of thanksgiving and consecration by the bishop, and relating not to the gifts but to the elements of the Lord's Supper.[73] This view of the Lord's Supper as a sacrifice in turn influenced the idea people had of the sacramental union and vice versa. To the extent that the bishop was viewed as a priest, the thanksgiving as a consecration, and the Lord's Supper as a sacrifice, the realistic union of bread and wine with the body and blood of Christ also had to become more appealing. The symbolic and spiritualistic view of Origen, also found in other Eastern fathers,[74] gave way for the realistic doctrine of transformation (μεταποιησις, *metapoiēsis*), which later passed

71. Tertullian, *Against Marcion*, 4, 34.

72. *Did.* 14.3; cf. F. A. Loofs, "Abendmahl, Kirchenlehre," in *PRE*³, I, 44; P. Drews, "Eucharistie," in *PRE*³, V, 560ff.

73. Justin Martyr, *Dialogue with Trypho*, 41, 70; Irenaeus, *Against Heresies*, IV, 18, 5.

74. Eusebius of Caesarea, Cyril, Basil, and Gregory of Nazianzus, Gregory of Nyssa, Chrysostom, and John of Damascus.

over into the doctrine of transubstantiation (μετουσιωσις, *metousiōsis*).[75] This development also took place in the West where it was reinforced by a sacerdotal, clerical church structure, with the bread and wine believed to be converted by a mysterious power of the ordained priest into the real body and blood of Christ. Augustine, in using biblical terms, calls the bread "the body of Christ" and the wine "the blood of Christ," but he has nothing of the future transubstantiation theory.[76] Bread and wine, says Augustine, are similitudes, signs, reminders of the body and blood of Christ. "The Lord did not hesitate to say: 'This is my body.' With the sign he gives of his body."[77] Christ is no longer physically with us but has ascended to heaven. "We always have Christ in respect to the presence of his majesty, but in regard to the presence of his flesh he directly told his disciples: 'You will not always have me.'"[78] He never tires of assuring us that the use of the Lord's Supper is not sufficient by itself; that it is only a blessing for believers, but for others it is to their ruin; that truly eating of Christ's body consists in believing: Believe and eat![79]

For a long time Augustine's teaching by its powerful influence held back the full development of a realist theory and was still dominant under the Carolingian theologians. Over time his views were increasingly suppressed and finally replaced by the metabolic theory. The word "transubstantiation" occurred for the first time in the twelfth century, and the Fourth Lateran Council (1215) decreed that the body and blood of Christ "are truly contained in the sacrament of the altar under the appearance of bread and wine, the bread being transubstantiated into the body and the wine into blood by divine power."[80] In time this led to such traditional Roman Catholic practices as the elevation, adoration, and [p]reservation of the host. In this view, when the Savior at the Last Supper spoke the words, "This is my body, this is my blood," he did not just change bread and wine into his body and blood on that occasion alone, but in pronouncing these words simultaneously appointed his disciples as priests and injected into the words he spoke a power to change the substance of bread and wine. The administration of the Eucharist, therefore, is above all priestly work and may never be performed by anyone other than an ordained priest. When the priest pronounces the words of consecration, the substance of bread and wine changes into the substance of the body and blood of Christ. The accidents of bread and wine, that is, the form, taste, smell, color, and even the nutritive power, while they remain after the consecration, no

---

75. John of Damascus, *Exposition of the Orthodox Faith*, IV, 14; Orthodox Confession, qu. 107; F. A. Loofs, "Abendmahl, Kirchenlehre," in *PRE*³, I, 44–57.

76. Cyprian, *Epistles*, 63.2, 14.

77. Augustine, *Against Adimantus*, chap. 12.

78. Augustine, *Homilies on the Gospel of John*, tract. 1.

79. Augustine, *Homilies on the Gospel of John*, tract. 25; F. A. Loofs, "Abendmahl, Kirchenlehre," in *PRE*³, I, 61ff.

80. H. Denzinger, ed., *The Sources of Catholic Dogma*, trans. from the 30th ed. by R. J. Deferrari (London and St. Louis: Herder, 1955), 298, 357.

longer inhere in a subject. The substance of which they are the properties has been removed and replaced by a totally different substance of which they are not the properties, but which they only conceal from the eye by their appearance.

The Eucharist, accordingly, is distinct from all the other sacraments. The role of the recipient is absent; the formula uttered on this occasion is directed not to the recipient but to the element and serves to change this element into the body and blood of Christ. The sacrament of the Eucharist essentially consists in the consecration itself, in the transubstantiation effected by it, in the action of the priest, that is, in the sacrifice. The Eucharist is not only a sacrament; it is also primarily a sacrifice. When Christ spoke the words, "This is my body," he at that very moment offered himself up to God. When he said, "Do this in remembrance of me," by that token he ordained that his priests would repeat that sacrifice daily (Mal. 1:11). The sacrifice that the priest effects in the Mass is the same as that accomplished on the cross. It is not just an image, symbol, or reminder of it; it is identical with it. It is entirely the same sacrifice, the only difference being that the one on the cross was a bloody sacrifice, and the one that occurs in the Mass is unbloody. It is Christ himself who, through the priest, offers himself up to God and therefore through the priest's mouth speaks the words "This is *my* body." The Mass is the center of Roman Catholic worship, the awe-inspiring mystery, the *mysterium tremendum*. Because the whole Christ is physically present in the elements of bread and wine, they must be carefully preserved, held out in a monstrance (receptacle) for the people to worship, to be carried around in solemn procession on the feast of Corpus Christi; and can be served to the sick in their homes and given to the dying as a *viaticum* [lit. "traveling provision"].[81]

[542] The Reformation unanimously rejected the Roman Catholic doctrine of transubstantiation and the sacrifice of the Mass. Differences remained, however, among the followers of Luther, those who accepted Zwingli's notion of a memorial, and Calvin's doctrine of the presence through the Holy Spirit. Luther maintained—especially from 1524 onward against Carlstadt and Zwingli, on the basis of a synecdochic interpretation of the words of institution, that the body of Christ, in keeping with the will and omnipotence of God and its own ubiquity, is realistically and substantially present in, with, and under the [elements of the] Lord's Supper. He saw this as being analogous to the presence of Christ's divine nature in his human nature and as heat is or can be present in iron. Zwingli rejected the physical presence of Christ in the Lord's Supper, interpreted the words of institution figuratively, and explained the vocable "is" by the word "means," a recurrent practice elsewhere in Scripture: Genesis 41:26; John 10:9; 15:1, for example. The bread and wine in the Lord's Supper, therefore, are the signs and reminders of Christ's death, and believers, trusting in that reality, partake of the body and blood of Christ in these signs. This was not to deny the spiritual presence of Christ in the Supper. In the Lord's Supper, accordingly, we confess

81. Council of Trent, sess. XIII, XXI–XXII; Roman Catechism, II, chap. 4 (Bradley and Kevane).

our faith and express what Christ continually means to us by faith and what we enjoy of him. We do this in remembrance of Christ, to proclaim and give thanks for his benefits.[82] Between the German and Swiss Reformations it was not long, however, before schism and controversy broke out—a dispute that was settled neither by the Marburg conference on religion nor by the mediating attempts of Bucer on the Reformed side and Melanchthon on the Lutheran side. People just did not understand one another when it came to the "true presence."

When Calvin appeared on the scene, there was no longer any hope of reconciliation, although with his doctrine of the Lord's Supper he took a position between and above the two parties. With Zwingli, Calvin firmly rejected any kind of physical, local, and substantial presence of Christ in the signs of bread and wine because it was inconsistent with the nature of a body, with the true humanity of Christ, with Christ's ascension, with the nature of the communion that exists between Christ and his own. Calvin objected to Zwingli's doctrine of the Lord's Supper that it allowed the gift of God to recede behind what believers do in it and hence one-sidedly views the Lord's Supper as an act of confession. Zwingli sees nothing other and higher than believing in Christ's name, the act of trusting in his death. On this point Calvin put himself on Luther's side and said that Christ is present in the Supper and is received there—not physically and locally, to be sure, but certainly truly and essentially, with his whole person, including his body and blood. Between him and Luther there was disagreement not over the fact but only over the manner of that presence. Eating Christ's body in the Supper is not exhausted by believing in him, by relying on his death; eating is the fruit of believing, just as in Ephesians 3:17 Christ's indwelling in us, though it happens by faith, is nevertheless distinct from that faith. Calvin's concern evidently was the mystical union, the communion of believers with the whole person of Christ. This communion is not created by the Supper, for Christ is the bread of our soul already in the Word, but it is granted "more distinctly" in the Lord's Supper and sealed and confirmed in the signs of bread and wine. It is a communion with the person of Christ that does not consist in a physical descent of Christ from heaven, nor even in a mixture or transfusion of the flesh of Christ with our souls, but in the elevation of our hearts heavenward, in a union with Christ by the Holy Spirit, in communion with his body as a result of which "Christ, from the substance of his flesh, breathes life into our souls—indeed, pours forth his very life into us."[83] Calvin's representation is not clear in every respect, especially not as it concerns communion with the true flesh and blood of Christ and the life that flows from them, and the confessions and doctrines of Reformed churches and theologians express the truth about the Lord's Supper in a variety of ways. But Calvin's main idea—that in the Lord's Supper, by the Holy Spirit, believers experience spiritual

82. U. Zwingli, *Opera*, ed. Schuler and Schulthess, 8 vols. in 7 (Zurich: Schulthessiana, 1828–42), II, 1, 426; II, 2, 1ff.; III, 239–326, 459; IV, 51, 68.

83. J. Calvin, *Institutes*, IV.xvii; cf. H. Bavinck, "Calvijns leer over het Avondmaal," *De Vrije Kerk* 13 (1887): 459–87; ed note: Also published in *Kennis en leven* (Kampen: Kok, 1922), 165–83.

fellowship with the person of Christ and hence also with the body and blood of Christ and are thereby nourished and refreshed unto eternal life—has been taken over in the various Reformed confessions[84] and become the common property of Reformed theology.

It was not long, however, before opposition to this Calvinistic doctrine of the Lord's Supper asserted itself. Little by little the Zwinglian view again gained ground, according to which the eating is nothing other than believing, and fellowship with Christ no more than the acceptance of his benefits. Relaxation of discipline further contributed to this externalization of the Lord's Supper and prompted people to view the sacraments as being merely signs of an external covenant, to which everyone who lived a decent life was entitled. Viewing sacraments as mere signs led to the rationalism of the Socinians, the Remonstrants, and the Mennonites, who saw in the Supper only a memorial, a confession of believers, and not a means of grace. Some Protestant churches, notably the Church of England, even drifted back toward Rome, as in the Oxford movement.

THE PURPOSE OF THE SUPPER

[543] In Scripture and the Reformed tradition, the Lord's Supper is first of all a meal, food for the Christian pilgrimage. The Lord's Supper is described by the terms "the Lord's supper" (1 Cor. 11:20), "the table of the Lord" (10:21), "the breaking of bread" (Acts 2:42; 20:7), "the cup of the Lord" (1 Cor. 11:27), and "the cup of blessing" (10:16). Although Luther continued to speak of "the sacrament of the altar,"[85] Protestants in general favored the term "holy Supper" or "the Lord's Supper" and in so doing also held on to the principle that the Supper is a true meal. But it is a meal of the Lord (δειπνον κυριακον, *deipnon kyriakon*). Jesus was the inaugurator of it, and in this regard also fulfilled his Father's will, which it was his food to do (John 4:34). The Lord's Supper, like baptism, is and has to be of divine origin to be a sacrament, for God alone is the distributor of grace, and he alone can bind its distribution to the means ordained by him. Jesus specifically instituted this Supper in his capacity as mediator. In it he acts as prophet, who proclaims and interprets his death; as priest, who gave himself up to the cross on behalf of his own; as king, who freely makes available the grace secured and gives it to his disciples to enjoy under the signs of bread and wine. He is also host and administrator of the Supper; he takes the bread and wine, blesses them, and distributes them to his disciples—at the meal of the Last supper but always and wherever *his* meal is celebrated. Every Supper, administered according to his institution, is a Supper of the Lord, by example and by precept. It is a meal in remembrance of

84. Gallican Confession, art. 36; Belgic Confession, art. 35; Heidelberg Catechism, Q 75–80; Scots Confession, art. 21; Second Helvetic Confession, ch. XXI; Westminster Confession, chap. 29.
85. Smalcald Articles, part III, art. 6 (Kolb and Wengert), 320–21; The Larger Catechism, part V, "The Sacrament of the Altar" (Kolb and Wengert), 467ff.

him (1 Cor. 11:24); a proclamation of his death (11:26); a participation in his body and blood (10:16, 21; 11:27). In the Lord's Supper Christ comes together with his church, and the church comes together with Christ, thereby testifying to their spiritual communion (cf. Rev. 3:20).

Presiding ministers do so in the name of Christ; they are his instruments (1 Cor. 10:16). In Matthew 28:19 the administration of baptism along with that of the Word has been entrusted to the apostles. They, along with the ministers, are the distributors of the mysteries of God, proclaimers of the "secrets" that God has revealed in the gospel of Christ (1 Cor. 4:1), stewards of God whose task is to distribute his grace (9:17; Titus 1:7–9). With reference to these mysteries, one must undoubtedly first of all think of the word of the gospel. The sacrament follows the Word and is always connected with it. In Jerusalem the apostles devoted themselves to the ministry of prayer and the Word (Acts 6:4). Both baptism and the Lord's Supper are thus uniquely linked to the Word and to those who have been given the office to proclaim it. The minister acts in the name of Christ and functions as the steward and distributor of his mysteries. The Lord's Supper is a meal whose host is Christ.

And it is a meal! Jesus, after all, instituted the Supper on an occasion when he along with his disciples reclined at the Passover table. The signs of bread and wine in the Lord's Supper have no more been arbitrarily or accidentally chosen than the water in baptism. The signs of bread and wine are eminently suited since in the East they were the regular constituents of a meal. Everywhere and at all times even now they are easy to obtain. They are the chief means for strengthening and rejoicing the human heart (Ps. 104:15) and a graphic symbol of the communion of believers with Christ and one another. It is not helpful to create controversy about the matter of the elements—whether the bread is made of wheat, rye, or barley and whether the wine is white or red; whether the bread is leavened (the practice of the Greek Orthodox Church) or unleavened (the practice of the Roman Catholic Church); and whether the wine (in keeping with the doctrine of Armenian Christians) is unmixed, or mixed with water. In none of these points has Christ prescribed anything. The Reformed did not even hesitate to say that in the event bread or wine were definitely lacking, another food and drink, say rice or nutritious food, could be used as sign in the Lord's Supper.[86] This is not to say, however, that any arbitrary departure from the institution of Christ is permissible, particularly when because of, let us say, ascetic principles, water is substituted for wine at the Lord's Supper. We must not be wiser than Christ, who expressly designated wine as the sign of his blood and whose command in this matter has at all times been followed by the Christian church.[87]

---

86. G. Voetius, *Politicae ecclesiasticae*, 3 vols. (Amsterdam: Joannis a Waesberge, 1663–76), I, 732, 738; B. de Moor, *Commentarius perpetuus in Joh. Marckii Compendium theologiae christianae didactico-elencticum*, 6 vols. (Leiden: J Hasebroek, 1761–71), V, 575; C. Vitringa, *Doctr. christ.*, VIII, 1, 46.

87. C. Vitringa, *Doctr. christ.*, VII, 1, 71–78.

As a meal, the bread and wine can be seen as something to be enjoyed, and enjoyed in fellowship with other Christians. Only gradually was the Lord's Supper detached from the love feasts (ἀγάπαι), shifted from the evening to the morning service, and administered also to the sick and dying in their homes totally outside and apart from a meeting of the congregation; and the frequency of celebration was set for believers at three times or at least once a year as a minimum.[88] While the Reformed acknowledged that in very special cases the Lord's Supper might be administered to the sick in their homes, they generally maintained that as part of public worship it belonged in the gathering of the congregation and should not be celebrated privately. If baptism as incorporation into the Christian church ought to take place in the public gathering of believers, this certainly applies much more to the Lord's Supper, which is essentially a meal, a coming together (συναξις, *synaxis*), and a banquet (*convivium*), and includes not only an exercise of communion with Christ but also such an exercise with one's fellow believers. Although practice proved stronger than theory and the celebration of the Lord's Supper was usually restricted to six or four times a year,[89] originally it was nevertheless Calvin's wish to celebrate it at least once a month.[90]

The Lord's Supper is best served around a table, not an altar of sacrifice. Jesus and his disciples sat at a table when they celebrated the Supper, and the early Christians knew nothing of an altar. But gradually the difference between the Old and the New Testament dispensation was lost; when the Lord's Supper turned into a sacrifice, the minister became a priest, and the table an altar.[91] In the Roman Catholic and the Greek Orthodox Churches, worship was controlled by this view. The Anglican (Episcopal) Church largely took it over and tends increasingly in that direction. The Lutheran Church kept the altar, regarding the matter an adiaphoron [a matter of no spiritual consequence]. But the Reformed restored the scriptural idea of the Lord's meal, also in having a table for the Supper. The only altar Christians have is the cross on which Christ brought his sacrifice (Heb. 13:10; cf. 7:27; 10:10). Believers need bring no sacrifice other than the sacrifice of praise, the fruit of lips that praise his name (13:15). The Lord's Supper is a sacrificial meal, a meal of believers with Christ on the basis of his sacrifice and therefore one that must be served on a table, not an altar. "This is indeed very certain: that the cross of Christ is overthrown, as soon as the altar is set up."[92]

88. Council of Trent, sess. XIII, can. 9.

89. Ed. note: For the church order articles of the early Reformed churches on this point, see Bavinck, *Reformed Dogmatics*, IV, 565n67 (#543).

90. F. W. Kampschulte and W. Goetz, *Johann Calvin: Seine Kirche und sein Staat in Genf.*, 2 vols. (Leipzig: Duncker & Humblot, 1869–99), I, 460.

91. Ed. note: Pope Paul VI's Apostolic Constitution, *Missionale Romanun* (1969), effectively restored the table character of the altar in Roman Catholic churches by encouraging priests to face the congregation rather than to stand facing the altar with their backs to the people.

92. J. Calvin, *Institutes*, IV.xviii.3; Müller, "Altar," in *PRE*³, I, 391–404.

[544–46] So then, though the Lord's Supper is a real meal, as such it has a spiritual significance and purpose of its own. The "matter" of the sacrament, the thing signified in the meal, is the body and blood of Christ broken and shed for our sins, Christ and all his benefits. In a moral and rationalistic view of the Lord's Supper—only a memorial meal and an act of confession—this meaning does not come into its own. The Lord's Supper is above all a gift of God, not our memorial and confession. In the Lord's Supper we indeed do not receive any other or any more benefits than we do in the Word, but also no fewer. The Lord's Supper is on the same level as the Word and baptism and therefore must, like them, be regarded first of all as a message and assurance to us of divine grace signifying the mystical union of the believer with Jesus Christ. On the point of this reality of communion with our Lord there is no disagreement among Roman Catholics, Lutherans, and Reformed Christians. However, practices such as Masses without communicants, the use of a single element (bread) alone, and withholding the cup diminish the significance of the Lord's Supper as a meal of communion. The mystical union is always a union of persons, believers joined to Christ through the Holy Spirit. Although the truth of the sacrament does not depend on faith, it is the indispensable requisite for the reception of the sacrament. For just as in the case of the Word, so in the case of the Supper, God has obligated himself truly to bestow Christ and all his benefits on everyone who believes. Needed—to receive the promises and benefits of Word and sacrament—therefore, is a working of the Holy Spirit in the heart of a person, and it is precisely this working of the Spirit that effects and maintains this communion with Christ, both apart from and in the Lord's Supper.

From this perspective it is not hard to infer the benefits enjoyed in the Lord's Supper. Foremost is the strengthening of the believer's communion with Christ. Believers already enjoy this communion by faith, and in the Supper they receive no other communion than that which they already enjoy by faith. But when Christ himself, acting through the minister, gives them, with the signs of bread and wine, his body to eat and his blood to drink, they are strengthened and confirmed in that communion by the Holy Spirit and ever more intimately united in soul and body with the whole Christ, both in his divine and in his human natures. For "the eating of the body of Christ is nothing other than the closest union with Christ."[93] In this connection, the Lord's Supper is distinguished from baptism by the fact that baptism is the sacrament of incorporation, while the Lord's Supper is the sacrament of maturation in communion with Christ. By baptism we are buried with Christ in his death and raised in his resurrection, and are therefore passive, but in the Lord's Supper we go into action, eating the body and drinking the blood of Christ, and are thus fed by communion with him unto eternal life.[94]

93. Franciscus Junius, *Theses theol.*, in vol. 1 of *Opuscula theological selecta*, ed. Abraham Kuyper (Amsterdam: F. Muller, 1882), 52, 7.

94. H. Weber, "Taufe und Abendmahl als Symbole unserer doppelten Stellung zum Heilsgut," *Zeitschrift für Theologie und Kirche* 19 (1909): 249–79.

But if we share in the person of Christ, we naturally also share in his benefits. Among these benefits, the forgiveness of sins is mentioned first and with the most emphasis in Scripture. In the Lord's Supper, Christ gives his body and blood as food for our souls, and they are depicted separately, each by a sign of its own. To that end Christ expressly states that his body was given and his blood shed for the forgiveness of sins. It is the blood that makes atonement for sins on the altar, and the communion realized through faith and strengthened in the Supper remains a communion with his crucified body and with his shed blood. Added to the benefit of forgiveness is that of eternal life. The Lord's Supper is a spiritual meal at which Christ feeds our souls with his crucified body and shed blood. Eating and drinking them serves to strengthen our spiritual, that is, our eternal life, for those who eat the flesh of the Son of Man and drink his blood have eternal life and are raised up on the last day (John 6:54). It is, of course, not by a literal eating but by faith that humans become partakers of eternal life and receive the hope of the resurrection. The Holy Spirit, who dwells in believers, is the surest pledge of the resurrection of the body and the day of redemption (Rom. 8:11; Eph. 1:13–14; 4:30). Still, the Spirit of Christ does indeed use the Supper to strengthen believers in the hope of eternal life and of a blessed resurrection on the last day. "For where the soul is healed, the body is helped as well."[95] In this sense the Lord's Supper may be called "the medicine of immortality."[96] Finally, the Lord's Supper also serves as the confession of our faith before the world and strengthens the communion of believers among themselves. Believers are one in Christ and therefore also one among themselves. "For as out of many grains one meal is ground and one bread baked, and out of many berries, pressed together, one wine flows and is mixed together, so shall we all who by true faith are incorporated in Christ be altogether one body."[97] This they confess at the Lord's Supper in the face of a world that does not know their unity.

[547] Like baptism, the Lord's Supper was instituted only for believers. Jesus observed it only with his disciples. Whether Judas was still present at that time or whether he left the room before the institution of the Lord's Supper cannot be said with certainty. In the New Testament the Lord's Supper was exclusively celebrated by believers in the circle of the congregation (Acts 2:42; 20:7); unbelievers had access to the gathering of the congregation where the Word was administered (1 Cor. 14:22–24) but were excluded from gatherings in which the love feasts were held and the communion celebrated (11:18, 20, 33). This is how it remained also when in the second century the Lord's Supper was gradually separated from the love feasts and took place in the morning in the same gathering where the administration of the Word occurred. The first part of the service was accessible to all, but the second only started after unbelievers, catechumens,

---

95. Julius Müller, *Dogmatische Abhandlungen* (Bremen: C. E. Müller, 1870), 419.

96. Ign. *Eph.* 20.

97. Ed. note: These words are taken from the traditional Dutch Reformed Church's liturgy for the Lord's Supper.

excommunicates, and so forth had been dismissed. In this second part of the service, the sacraments were administered, and it was an ancient and general custom that those who upon completion of their catechumenate were baptized received the Lord's Supper immediately thereafter.

The history of the church bears witness to numerous abuses and corruptions of the Lord's Supper that made reformation necessary. From ancient times already there was the custom of bringing offerings for deceased relatives on the anniversaries of their deaths and of praying for their souls; over time the working of the sacrament not only extended to the living but was seen to benefit the dead. When the doctrine of purgatory had been fixed by Gregory the Great, the Lord's Supper was viewed as an offering up of Christ's own body and blood, and the participation of the congregation increasingly diminished. It soon became a fixed doctrine that the Mass could bring about a lessening of penances and temporal punishments, not only for the living—whether present or absent—but also for the dead in purgatory.[98] All these corruptions made necessary a return to Scripture, according to which the Lord's Supper is a meal that is inconceivable without guests in attendance and exclusively intended for believers. The Reformed posed two questions: (1) Who have a right as well as an obligation to come to the Supper? (2) Who must be admitted to or barred from the Supper by the church?[99] The first question deals with the duty of communicants, and the second with the duty of the church and its ministers. To the latter question the answer given was—and according to Scripture could not be other than—that the church had to bar all those who by their talk and walk presented themselves as unbelieving and ungodly people. The Lord's Supper is a good of the church given by Christ to his people and is therefore to be enjoyed only by the members of the household of faith. This meant an end to all Masses for the dead. It also restricted the private administration of the Supper to the sick and to children. In support of the latter restriction we need to note that there is a great difference between circumcision and Passover; the former is prescribed for all male children, the latter is celebrated, not immediately at its institution but later in Palestine, near the temple at Jerusalem and thus automatically excluded very young children. The difference between baptism and the Lord's Supper is great; in the former a human is passive, but the Lord's Supper is the sacrament of maturation in communion with Christ, the formation of the spiritual life, and presupposes conscious and active conduct on the part of those who receive it. In 1 Corinthians 11:26–29 Paul insists that people should examine themselves before celebrating the Lord's Supper in order to be able to discern the body of the Lord and not eat and drink unworthily, a demand that automatically excludes children. Withholding the Lord's Supper from children does not deprive them of any benefit of the covenant of grace. Those who administer baptism to

98. C. Vitringa, *Doctr. christ.*, VIII, 733; P. Drews, "Messe, liturgisch," in *PRE*[3], XII, 722ff.; H. A. Köstlin, "Requiem," in *PRE*[3], XVI, 665–69.
99. Heidelberg Catechism, Q 81–82.

children but not the Lord's Supper acknowledge that they are in the covenant and share in all its benefits. They merely withhold from them a particular manner in which the same benefits are signed and sealed, since this manner is not suited to their age. The Lord's Supper, after all, does not confer a single benefit that is not by faith granted through the Word and through baptism. For this reason and also to avoid all notions of magic concerning the sacrament, communicants must be properly prepared and required to examine themselves before they partake.

The Reformation rejected a sacrament of confirmation, since it had no foundation in Scripture, and replaced it with catechesis and public profession of faith. By this process the transition was made from baptism to the Lord's Supper, at the same time preserving the church from corruption. It was Calvin's wish that, after a child had been sufficiently instructed in the catechism, the child would make public profession of one's own faith. The orders of the Dutch Reformed churches similarly prescribed a profession before the church council or in the midst of the congregation and sometimes still speak of a preceding examination before the church council.[100] This theory is sound enough: the children of believers are baptized as believers, then instructed in the truth; upon sufficient instruction and after public profession of faith, they are admitted to the Lord's Supper, or, in case of unchristian views or irregular conduct, they are, after repeated admonition, removed from the church. The practice of these good principles is not always easy; Pietism and rationalism are ever prone to separate what God has joined together, and either with disdain for the sacrament stress personal conversion or emphasize the practice of ecclesiastical confirmation. But the rule of the covenant is that the church must nurture its youthful members, who were born as children of the covenant and incorporated as members by baptism, to where they can make an independent personal profession of faith and on that basis admit them to the Lord's Supper. It does not and cannot judge the heart. Accordingly, while on the one hand it bars from the Lord's Supper all those who by their talk or walk manifest themselves as unbelieving and ungodly people, it never, on the other hand, desists from seriously preaching that the Lord's Supper is instituted only for those who are displeased with themselves because of their sins but who nevertheless trust that their sins have been forgiven for Christ's sake and who also desire more and more to strengthen their faith and lead a better life.[101]

100. W. Caspari, "Konfirmation," in *PRE*³, X, 676–80; E. Sachsse, "Katechese, Katechetik," in *PRE*³, X, 121–29; F. Cohrs, "Katechismen und Katechismusunterricht," in *PRE*³, X, 135–64.

101. Ed. note: This is a clear allusion to Heidelberg Catechism Q 81, though Bavinck does not cite this specific reference.

PART VII

THE SPIRIT MAKES ALL THINGS NEW

23

THE INTERMEDIATE STATE

THE QUESTION OF IMMORTALITY

[548] The end of things, like their origin and essence, is unknown to us. To the question of their destiny, science no more furnishes a satisfying answer than it does to that of their origin. Still, religion has an urgent need to know something of the destiny of the individual, of humanity, and of the world. The desire to know what happens to us after death is a universal human desire. In spite of claims made that such beliefs as the immortality of the soul are not universal,[1] and evolutionary thought attributing them to external and accidental circumstances and forces, the most respected historians of religion tell us that belief in the immortality of the soul occurs among all peoples and is a component even of the most primitive religions.[2] The eschatologies of the world's religions all point to the longing to overcome the finality of death. It is found everywhere and at every stage of human development, wherever it has not as yet been undermined by philosophical doubts or thrust into the background by other causes; and in every case it is bound up with religion. It may even be said to be a natural belief. Like the author of the Garden of Eden narrative in Genesis, says Tiele, all peoples take for granted that humans are by nature immortal and that it

---

1. E. Haeckel, *The Riddle of the Universe at the Close of the Nineteenth Century*, trans. J. McCabe (New York: Harper & Brothers, 1900), 192; L. Büchner, *Kraft und Stoff* (Leipzig: T. Thomas, 1902), 156–77. ET: *Force and Matter; or Principles of the Natural Order of the Universe*, 4th ed., translated from the 15th German ed. (New York: P. Eckler, 1891).

2. C. P. Tiele, *Elements of the Science of Religion*, 2 vols. (Edinburgh and London: W. Blackwood & Sons, 1899), II, 113–14.

is death, not immortality, that requires explanation; it is death that seems to be unnatural. The sagas of many peoples, differing in origin and development, express the same idea: there was a time when neither sickness nor death was known on earth. The forms in which the afterlife of the soul were presented were very diverse and often variously combined: belief that souls after death lived near their graves and needed to be fed; souls experiencing numerous metamorphoses and spending time in other bodies (reincarnation) before being purified or attaining the perfection of nirvana.

This teaching of personal immortality passed from religion into philosophy. Following the example of Pythagoras, Heraclitus, and Empedocles, especially Plato (in his *Phaedo*) sought to undergird his religious belief in immortality by philosophical argumentation. His proofs come down to the view that the soul, which draws its knowledge of ideas from memory, existed already before dwelling in a body and will therefore continue to exist after leaving it. Furthermore, by its contemplation of the eternal ideas, the soul is akin to the divine being, and as an independent and simple entity, by its control over the body and its desires, is on a level far above that of the body. With this theory of the immortality of the soul, Plato then combined a variety of notions about the soul's preexistence, fall, union with the body, judgment, and transmigration that in large part bear a mythical character and are certainly not all intended, even by Plato himself, in a purely scientific sense. Plato's doctrine exerted immense influence in both theology and philosophy. The mythical components of preexistence, metempsychosis, and the like, often found acceptance in sectarian circles. Thanks to Plato's influence, theology went beyond Scripture in its attention to the immortality of the soul; it became an *articulus mixtus*, whose truth was argued more on the basis of reason than revelation.[3] Still, some awareness of the difference between the two persisted because Scripture consistently attaches a religious-ethical meaning to life and death; life is never merely ongoing existence, and death is never extinction. On the contrary, life includes communion with God, and death means the loss of his grace and blessing. For that reason, even those Christians who used the notion of the soul's immortality clearly saw it as a divine bestowal rather than an immortality inherent in the soul itself. God alone was in himself immortal, and the soul could only be immortal by his will; this also meant that Plato's notion of the soul's preexistence had to be rejected.

The immortality of the soul has had mixed reception in the modern world. Descartes conceived spirit and matter, soul and body, as two separate substances, each with its own attribute, thought, and extension, each capable of existing by itself and therefore capable only of being united mechanically. The deistic philosophy of the eighteenth century kept faith with the trilogy of God, virtue, and immortality, and of the three it most esteemed the third. Following Leibniz, Wolff, Mendelssohn,

3. Tertullian, *A Treatise on the Soul*, 22; Origen, *On First Principles*, VI, 36; Irenaeus, *Against Heresies*, II, 34.

and others, its truth was argued by means of a wide assortment of metaphysical, theological, cosmic, moral, and historical proofs, and it urged on readers by means of sentimental observations on the blissful recognition and reunions of souls on the other side of the grave. All these, along with the sophisticated arguments for the immortality of the human soul developed in classic philosophy, were effectively challenged by Kant, who demonstrated the inadequacy of all proofs advanced for the immortality of the soul and maintained it as acceptable only as a postulate of practical reason. Similarly, the idealistic philosophy of Fichte, Schelling, and Hegel left no room for the immortality of the soul. The materialistic arguments of Vogt, Moleschott, Büchner, Haeckel, and others so strongly impressed many people that they have abandoned the immortality of the soul or at most assert its possibility and merely speak of a hope of immortality. Theologians, too, often attach little or no value to the proofs for the immortality of the soul.

[549] The arguments for the immortality of the soul derived from history and reason; though they fail to furnish adequate certainty, they are nevertheless not without value. It is significant that consensus of the nations (*consensus gentium*) is as strong about belief in immortality as in the case of belief in God.[4] In the case of the belief in the immortality of the soul, as in that of the existence of God, we are dealing rather with a conviction that was not gained by reflection and reasoning but precedes all reflection and springs spontaneously from human nature as such. It is self-evident and natural, found wherever no philosophical doubts have undermined it. Along with the consciousness of having an independent, individual existence of one's own, there also arises an awareness of the continuation of the self after death. Genuine self-consciousness—not the abstract self-consciousness with which psychology occupies itself—the self-consciousness of humans as personal, independent, rational, moral, religious beings always and everywhere includes belief in immortality. The so-called arguments for immortality amount to nothing more than an attempt of this belief to give some account of itself, without ever really depending on them; their power as well as their weakness is that they are witnesses *of*, not grounds *for*, the belief in immortality. Just as God does not leave himself without a witness but speaks to us from all the works of his hands, so the conviction that a person does not perish like the beasts of the field is thrust upon a person from within one's own being. This is exactly what the *ontological* argument for God's existence does; it articulates the sense that belief in immortality is not arbitrary or accidental but a fact of human nature and morally necessary to human beings. All *metaphysical* arguments, which deduce the soul's immortality from its very nature, have some value in directing us to a "life force," an autonomous spiritual principle that seems independent of our physical existence and may even sustain it, but fails at a number of levels. Even though the soul is an active vital principle, it is nevertheless never identical with life itself. God alone is life itself; he alone is immortal (1 Tim. 6:16). If the soul continues to exist, this can only occur by

---

4. Cicero, *Tusculan Disputations*, I, 3.

696   THE SPIRIT MAKES ALL THINGS NEW

virtue of God's omnipresent and omnipotent power. The most serious objection here is that one can pursue the same line of reasoning in the case of plants or at least animals, and still not make their immortality plausible.

The most helpful argument from reason alone is the *anthropological* argument, which, starting from the uniqueness of the psychic life of human beings, comes to the conclusion that there is a spiritual existence distinct from animals and plants. Humans not only possess perception and observation but also intellect and reason by which they are able to transcend the sensible, material, finite world. A person rises up toward the ideal, the logical, the true, the good, and the beautiful that eye has not seen and cannot be touched with hands and seeks a lasting, an *ever*lasting, happiness, a highest good that this world cannot give. Human beings are citizens and inhabitants of another, a higher kingdom than that of nature. The rational, moral, religious consciousness of humans points to a psychic existence that reaches beyond the visible world. That which by virtue of its nature seeks the eternal must be destined for eternity. To this, finally, must be added the *moral* argument and the argument of *retribution*, which demonstrates the disharmony existing between morality (*ethos*) and nature (*physis*) and infers from it another kind of existence in which the two are reconciled. Of course, the devout of all ages are profoundly aware that God must be served for his own sake and not for the sake of any reward.[5] At the same time they also know that if for this life only they had hoped in Christ, they would be of all people most to be pitied (1 Cor. 15:17, 19, 30, 32). At stake here is the rule and triumph of justice; In the end, is it good or evil, God or Satan, Christ or the antichrist who will win? History fails to furnish an adequate answer. From the viewpoint of the present world (*Diesseits*), no satisfying explanation of the world is possible; our sense of justice, which a righteous God has planted deep in the human heart, therefore demands that at the end of time the balance of justice be redressed. If justice does not prevail in the end, there is no justice. If in the end God does not prove to be the conqueror of Satan, life is not worth living. What comes to expression in the moral argument is not an egoistic desire but a profound sense of justice, the thirst for harmony, a yearning for the total glorification of God in whom holiness and bliss are one. Even art, when it exhibits ideal reality visibly before our eyes, prophesies such a future. All these arguments or proofs—especially those derived from human perfectibility, from the moral personality of humans, from the numerous uninhabited stars, from spiritistic experiences, and so on—are not proofs in the sense that they silence all contradiction. Rather, they are witnesses and indications that belief in immortality arises with complete naturalness and spontaneity from human nature. Whoever denies and combats it violates his own nature. "The idea of immortality is already the first act of immortality."[6]

5. J. Calvin, *Institutes of the Christian Religion*, III.ii.26; III.xvi.2 (ed. John T. McNeill and trans. Ford Lewis Battles [Philadelphia: Westminster, 1960], 1:572–73, 798–800).
6. Von Baer, cited by F. J. Splittgerber, *Tod, Fortleben und Auferstehung*, 3rd ed. (Halle: Fricke, 1879), 93.

[550] While Christian theology may find some of the traditional arguments for the immortality of the soul useful at points, Scripture is more restrained. In fact, while the immortality of the soul may seem to be of the greatest importance for religion and life, Scripture never explicitly mentions it. In the face of death the immortality of the soul is no real comfort. While death is not the end, the shadowy afterlife of Sheol is seen as a diminished existence. The Bible affirms and celebrates God's gift of life as a blessing; death is punishment for sin. The victory of Christ over sin and death means that believers enjoy the firstfruits of Christ's kingly reign now and, immediately after death, a provisional bliss with Christ in heaven, while unbelievers enter a state of torment.

In revealing himself to Israel, God accommodated himself to the historical circumstances under which it lived; grace did not undo nature but renewed and consecrated it. This is also what happened with the popular belief in the afterlife. The custom of burial and the great importance attached to it was as such already proof for that belief. Cremation was not indigenous in Israel; it occurred only after an execution (Gen. 38:24; Lev. 20:14; 21:9; Josh. 7:15). Burial, however, was highly valued in the Old Testament; to remain unburied was a terrible disgrace (1 Sam. 17:44, 46; 1 Kings 14:11, 13; 16:4; 2 Kings 9:10; Ps. 79:3; Eccles. 6:3; Isa. 14:19–20; Jer. 7:33; 8:1–2; 9:22; 16:6; 25:33; Ezek. 29:5). A dead person no longer belongs in the land of the living; his unburied body arouses loathing. Shed blood calls for vengeance (Gen. 4:10; 37:26; Job 16:18; Isa. 26:21; Ezek. 24:7) because blood is the basis of the soul (Lev. 17:11), and the deceased must therefore be covered, concealed, withdrawn from view. Through death all souls enter the abode of the dead, Sheol (שְׁאוֹל, šĕ'ôl). Sheol is located in the depths of the earth so that one goes down into it (Num. 16:30; Pss. 30:3, 9; 55:15; Isa. 38:18); it belongs to the lowest places of the earth (Ps. 63:9; Ezek. 26:20; 31:14; 32:18), lying even below the waters and the foundations of the mountains (Deut. 32:22; Job 26:5; Isa. 14:15). For that reason Sheol is linked closely with the grave (קֶבֶר, qeber) or the pit (בּוֹר, bôr). While the two are not identical—the unburied dead are nevertheless in Sheol (Gen. 37:35; Num. 16:32–33)—yet, just as soul and body together form one human and are thought to be in some kind of reciprocal relationship also after death, so also the grave and Sheol cannot be pictured in isolation from each other. Sheol is the place where all the dead without exception congregate (1 Kings 2:2; Job 3:13ff.; 30:23; Ps. 89:48; Isa. 14:9ff.; Ezek. 32:18; Hab. 2:5), and from which no one returns except by a miracle (1 Kings 17:22; 2 Kings 4:34; 13:21); those who go down to Sheol do not come up again (Job 7:9–10; 14:7–12; 16:22). This realm of the dead is therefore squarely opposed to the land of the living (Prov. 15:24; Ezek. 26:20; 32:23ff.). It is the place where the dead know nothing, no longer work, no longer calculate their chances, no longer possess wisdom and knowledge, and have no share whatever in all that happens under the sun (Eccles. 9:5–6, 10). The dead are רְפָאִים (rĕpā'îm), from the adjective רָפֶה (rāpeh, feeble; Job 26:5; Ps. 88:10; Prov. 2:18; 9:18; 21:6; Isa. 14:9), weak (Isa. 14:10), without strength (Ps. 88:4 KJV). This entire representation of Sheol is formed from the perspective of this earthly existence and is valid only by contrast with the riches of life enjoyed by people on earth. The state of Sheol, though not an annihilation of one's existence, is still a dreadful diminution of life, a deprivation of everything in this life that makes for its enjoyment.

In the Old Testament, there is no room for a view that permits only the body to die and comforts itself with the immortality of the soul. The whole person dies when at death the spirit, or "breath" (Ps. 146:4; Eccles. 12:7), or the soul (Gen. 35:18; 2 Sam. 1:9; 1 Kings 17:21; Jon. 4:3) departs from him. Just as the whole person was destined for life through obedience, so the whole person also by his transgression succumbs body and soul to death (Gen. 2:17). This idea had to be deeply impressed on the consciousness of humankind; and in antiquity it was also realized by all peoples that death is a punishment, that it is something unnatural, something inimical to the essence and destiny of human beings. The revelation God gave to Israel is therefore bound up with this realization. In the same way that Old Testament revelation took over so many customs and ceremonies (sacrifice, priesthood, circumcision, and so forth) while purging them of impure accretions such as self-mutilation (Lev. 19:28; 21:5; Deut. 14:1) or consulting the dead (Lev. 19:31; 20:6, 27; Deut. 18:10–11), so the idea of the unnaturalness of death was also allowed to continue and take over.

But revelation does something else, and more as well. It not only maintains and reinforces the antithesis between life and death but also introduces into this life an even sharper contrast. This life, after all, is not the true life, inasmuch as it is a sinful, impure life plagued by suffering and destined for death. It only becomes real life and only achieves real content through the service of YHWH and in fellowship with God. The Old Testament conceives the connection between godliness and life in a way that regards godliness as receiving its benefits and reward in a long life on earth (Exod. 20:12; Deut. 5:16, 29; 6:2; 11:9; 22:7; 30:16; 32:47; etc.). Into the fabric of the universally known natural antithesis between life and death, there is also woven a moral and spiritual contrast—that between a life in the service of sin and a life in the fear of the Lord. Death is bound up with evil; life is bound up with good (Deut. 30:15). The God of Israel is not a God of the dead but of the living. For that reason the eschatological hope of Israel's pious was almost exclusively directed toward the earthly future of the nation, the realization of the kingdom of God. The question concerning the future of individuals in Sheol remained totally in the background. God, nation, and land were inseparably bound up with each other, and individuals were incorporated in that "covenant" and viewed accordingly. Only after the exile, when Israel became a religious community and religion was individualized, did the question of each person's future fate force itself into the foreground. The basic elements for this development were already present in the revelation of the past. The person who serves God continues to live (Gen. 2:17); life is bound up with the keeping of his commandments (Lev. 18:5; Deut. 30:20); his word is life (Deut. 8:3; 32:47). In Proverbs it is remarkable that as a rule this book associates death and Sheol only with the wicked and, by contrast, attributes life almost exclusively to the righteous (2:18; 5:5; 7:27; 9:18). Wisdom, righteousness, and the fear of the Lord are the way to life (8:35–36; 11:19; 12:28; 13:14; 14:27; 19:23). One is blessed whose God is YHWH (Deut. 33:29; Pss. 1:1; 2:12; 32:1–2; 33:12; 34:8; etc.); the wicked perish and come to an end no matter how much they prosper for a time (Ps. 73:18–20). From within this perspective the pious not only expect deliverance from oppression and adversity in time, but also looking at things through the eyes of faith frequently penetrates the world beyond the grave and anticipates a blessed life in fellowship with God.

[551] This teaching of the Old Testament, though not entirely absent from later Jewish literature, was nevertheless modified and expanded by various nonindigenous elements during the Intertestamentary Period. A more individualistic view of religion is present and, under the influence of the idea of retribution, it teaches a provisional separation immediately at death between the righteous and the wicked, and offers a more elaborate account of the different places they inhabit. Some of the books of the period—the apocryphal writings of the Maccabees, Baruch, *4 Ezra* [in the Vulgate appendix; 2 Esdras in NRSV], *Enoch*, the *Testaments of the Twelve Patriarchs*—attribute only a provisional character to the intermediate state. The *Apocalypse of Enoch*, for example, locates Sheol in the west, describes it as being transected and surrounded by streams of water, and distinguishes four sections in it, two for the good and two for the wicked (*1 Enoch* 17.5–6; 22.2ff.). The point of emphasis in these books lies in their universal eschatology, in the coming of the Messiah, and in the establishment of the kingdom of God at the end of time. Until then the souls of the dead are kept in hades as in a ταμιεια (*tamieia*, storehouse), *promptuaria animarum* (a repository of souls; *2 Bar.* 21.23; *4 Ezra* 4:35; 5:37). Resting and sleeping, they await the final judgment (*4 Ezra* 7:32–35; *2 Bar.* 21.23–24; 23.4; 30.2). Another set of writings—such as Sirach, Wisdom of Solomon, Philo, Josephus, and so on—particularly stress individual eschatology, allowing the coming of the Messiah, the resurrection, final judgment, and the kingdom of God on earth either to recede into the background or to be kept out of the picture. The principal dogma is that of the immortality of the soul, which according to Philo was preexistent. On account of its fall it was temporarily locked up in the prison house of the body and, depending on its conduct, moves into other bodies after death, or in any case receives the definite settlement of its fate immediately after death (Sir. 1:13; 7:17; 18:24; 41:12; Wis. 1:8–9; 3:1–10). In the end it goes either to a holy heaven or to a dark hades.[7]

At the time of Christ, accordingly, a wide range of sometimes overlapping eschatological images whirled about the people of Israel. The Pharisees believed in a continued existence and a provisional retribution after death, but alongside these held to the expectation of the Messiah, of the resurrection of the dead—if not of all people, then certainly of the righteous—and of the establishment of

7. Fl. Josephus, *Jewish War* III, 8, 5.

God's kingdom on earth. The Sadducees denied the resurrection (Matt. 22:23; Mark 12:18; Luke 20:27; Acts 23:8) and, according to Josephus,[8] retribution after death and immortality as well. The Essenes believed that the body was mortal but that the soul was immortal. Originally the souls dwelt in the finest ether but, being caught up in sensual lust, were placed in bodies, from which they are again liberated by death. Good souls are given a blessed life on the other side of the ocean in a place untouched by rain, snow, or heat, but the bad must suffer everlasting pains in a place of darkness and cold.[9]

Consistent with the Law and the Prophets, the New Testament devotes much more attention to universal than to particular eschatology. Still it is incorrect to contend that Scripture says virtually nothing about the intermediate state or at least contains no teaching that is valid for us. Scripture is not lacking in statements that spread as much light as we need in and for this life. The New Testament brings out—even more forcefully than the Old—that death is a consequence of sin and punishment for sin (Rom. 5:12; 6:23; 8:10; 1 Cor. 15:21) and that death extends to all people (1 Cor. 15:22; Heb. 9:27). Only a rare individual, such as Enoch, is taken so that he would not see death (Heb. 11:5). And those who experience the parousia of Christ are changed in a twinkling of an eye without the intervention of death (1 Cor. 15:51–53; 1 Thess. 4:14–17; cf. John 21:22–23), so that Christ will not only judge the dead but also the living (Acts 10:42; 2 Tim. 4:1; 1 Pet. 4:5). But death is not the end of a person; the soul cannot be killed (Matt. 10:28), the body will one day be raised (John 5:28–29; Acts 23:6; Rev. 20:12–13), and believers even take part in an eternal life that cannot be destroyed (John 3:36; 11:25).

According to the New Testament, all the dead will be in hades, the realm of the dead, until the resurrection. In Matthew 11:23 and Luke 10:15 the expression "be brought down to hades" (καταβιβασθηση ἑως ᾁδου, *katabibasthēsē heōs hadou*) signifies that haughty Capernaum will be profoundly humbled. In Matthew 16:18, Jesus promises his church that "the gates of hades" (πυλαι ᾁδου, *pylai hadou*) will have no power over it, that death will not triumph over it. According to Luke 16:23, the wretched Lazarus will be carried by angels to Abraham's bosom, and the rich man, upon his death and burial, immediately arrives in hades, where hades is not yet the same as a place of torment since this is indicated only by the addition of "being in torment" (ὑπαρχων ἐν βασανοις, *hyparchōn en basanois*). Jesus, too, as long as he was in the state of death, dwelt in hades, even though it could not hold him there (Acts 2:27, 31). He, after all, descended to the "lower parts of the earth" (εἰς τα κατωτερα της γης, *eis ta katōtera tēs gēs*; Eph. 4:9). So all the dead are "under the earth" (καταχθονιοι, *katachthonioi*; Phil. 2:10). Not only the wicked but also believers find themselves in hades after death. They are the dead in Christ (1 Thess. 4:16; cf. 1 Cor. 15:18, 23). At the time of the resurrection the sea, death, and hades give up all the dead who are in them, in order that they may

8. Fl. Josephus, *Jewish War* II, 8, 14; *Jewish Antiquities* XVIII, 1, 4.
9. Fl. Josephus, *Jewish War* II, 8, 11.

be judged by their works (Rev. 20:13). Hades follows with and after death, so that death always brings about a relocation [of souls] into hades (Rev. 6:8). This view—from death until the resurrection believers too, according to Scripture, are in hades—is reinforced by the expression "resurrection from the dead" (ἀναστασις ἐκ [των] νεκρων, *anastasis ek [tōn] nekrōn*; Matt. 17:9; Mark 6:14; Luke 16:30; John 20:9; Eph. 5:14; etc.), which means not "from death" but "from the dead," that is, from the realm of the dead.

However, this common situatedness in the state of death does not exclude the fact that the lot of believers and unbelievers in it is very diverse. Jesus promises one of the men crucified alongside him, "Today you will be with me in Paradise" (Luke 23:43). The word "paradise" is of Persian origin and in general refers to a garden (for pleasure; Neh. 2:8; Eccles. 2:5; cf. Song 4:12). The Septuagint used it as the word for the Garden of Eden in Genesis 2:8–15, and the Jews used the word to describe the place where God grants his fellowship to the righteous after their death.[10] In 2 Corinthians 12:2, 4, "paradise" is used interchangeably with "the third heaven"; in Revelation 2:7 and 22:2 it refers to the place where in the future God will dwell among his people. In keeping with this, the Gospel of John teaches that believers who here on earth already possess the beginning of eternal life and have escaped the judgment of God (3:15–21; 5:24) share in a communion with Christ that is broken neither by his going away (12:32; 14:23) nor by death (11:25–26), and which will someday be completed in being together with him eternally (6:39; 14:3, 19; 16:16; 17:24). At the time of his death, Stephen prayed that the Lord Jesus would take his spirit to him in heaven (Acts 7:59). Paul knew that the believer shares in a life that is far superior to death (Rom. 8:10) and that nothing, not even death, could separate him from the love of God in Christ (8:38–39; 14:8; 1 Thess. 5:10). Although he must for a time remain in the flesh for the sake of the churches, he nevertheless desires to depart and to be with Christ (2 Cor. 5:8; Phil. 1:23). According to Revelation 6:9 and 7:9, the souls of the martyrs are with Christ beneath the altar that stands before the throne of God in the temple of heaven (cf. 2:7, 10, 17, 26; 3:4–5, 12, 21; 8:3; 9:13; 14:13; 15:2; 16:17; see also Heb. 11:10, 16; 12:23).

Just as immediately after death believers enjoy a provisional state of bliss with Christ in heaven, so unbelievers from the moment of their death enter a place of torment. The rich man was in torment when he opened his eyes in hades (Luke 16:23). Unbelievers who reject Christ remain under the wrath of God and are condemned already on earth (John 3:18, 36) and must—along with all others—expect judgment immediately after death (Heb. 9:27). Still, this place of torment is not yet identical with Gehenna (γεεννα, *geenna*) or the lake of fire (λιμνη του πυρος, *limnē tou pyros*), for Gehenna is the place of inextinguishable and eternal fire prepared for the devil and his messengers (Matt. 18:8; 25:41, 46; Mark 9:43,

10. F. W. Weber, *System der altsynagogalen palästinischen Theologie* (Leipzig: Dörffling & Franke, 1880), 330; S. D. F. Salmond, "Paradise," in *DB*, III, 668–772.

47–48), and the pool of fire is not the present but the future place of punishment for the kingdom of the world and the false prophet (Rev. 19:20), Satan (20:10), and all the wicked (21:8; cf. 2 Pet. 2:17; Jude 13). The case is rather that now they are all kept in a prison (φυλακη, *phylakē*; 1 Pet. 3:19) or in the abyss (ἀβυσσος, *abyssos*; Luke 8:31; cf. Matt. 8:29–32; Rom. 10:7; Rev. 9:1–2, 11; 11:7; 17:8; 20:1, 3). This difference in the intermediate state between the good and the evil does not conflict with the fact that they are all together in hades, for all the dead are as such καταχθονιοι (*katachthonioi*, inhabitants of the lower regions); before the resurrection they belong to the realm of the dead and only by that resurrection are completely liberated in soul and body from the rule of death (1 Cor. 15:52–55; Rev. 20:13).

AFTER DEATH, THEN WHAT?

[552] Early Christian theology honored the scriptural reserve concerning the intermediate state. The Apostolic Fathers still had no doctrine concerning the intermediate state and in general believed that at death the devout immediately experience the blessedness of heaven and the wicked the punishment of hell. Only when the parousia of Christ did not come as soon as almost all believers initially expected and various heretical thinkers distorted or opposed the doctrine of the last things did the church's thinkers begin to reflect more intentionally on the intermediate state. Ebionitism tried to hold on to the national privileges of Israel at the expense of Christian universalism and was therefore generally disposed to millenarianism. Gnosticism, by virtue of its basic dualism, rejected Christian eschatology altogether and held to no other expectation than that of the liberation of the spirit from matter and its assumption into the divine *plērōma* immediately after death. As a result, Christian theology was compelled to seek a clearer understanding of the character of the intermediate state and of its connections both with this life and with the final state following the last judgment. The initial understanding of a more-or-less neutral abode of all the dead became increasingly differentiated into immediate bliss for believers and punishment for unbelievers. Justin already stated that after death the souls of the devout were in a better place and the souls of the unrighteous in a worse one as they awaited the judgment. According to Irenaeus, the souls of the devout at death do not immediately enter heaven, paradise, or the city of God—which following the last judgment will be three distinct dwelling places of the righteous—but an invisible place determined by God, where they await the resurrection and the subsequent vision of God. We encounter the same view of the various "receptacles" in hades, where the dead await the last day, in other thinkers,[11] but to the degree that the parousia of Christ receded into the distance,

11. Hippolytus, Tertullian, Novatian, Commodian, Victorinus, Hilary, Ambrose, Cyril, and also still in Augustine.

it became increasingly harder to maintain the old representation of hades and to regard the stay in it as a brief, provisional, more-or-less neutral experience. Already at an early date an exception was made for the martyrs who were said to enter heaven immediately after death and be admitted to the vision of God.

In this connection Christ's descent into hades was understood as the means by which Old Testament saints were released from the limbo of the fathers (*limbus patrum*) and transferred to heaven. As the teaching of the necessity and meritoriousness of good works made increasing inroads in the church it led to the idea that extraordinarily devoted believers too were now also, immediately at death, worthy of heavenly bliss. Thus hades was gradually depopulated. Only those Christians who until then had not made enough progress in sanctification to be able, immediately at death, to enter the glory of heaven would have to spend time in hades. Gradually linked with this development was the idea of purification by fire, first uttered by Origen, who regarded all punishments as medicines (φαρμακα, *pharmaka*), and all of hades, Gehenna included, as a place of purification.[12] Sins were specifically consumed and people cleansed by purifying fire (πυρ καθαρσιον, *pyr katharsion*), which at the end of this dispensation would set the world aflame.[13] Following Origen, Greek theologians adopted the idea that the souls of many of the dead would have to suffer sorrows until released from them by the intercessions and sacrifices of the living; they nevertheless objected to a special fire of purification as the Western church taught it.[14] In the West, on the other hand, the fire of purification of which Origen spoke was moved from the last judgment to the intermediate state. Augustine occasionally said that following the general resurrection or at the last judgment, certain additional purgatorial pains would be imposed,[15] though he does not regard it as impossible that "some of the faithful are saved by a sort of purgatorial fire, and this sooner or later according as they have loved more or less the goods that perish."[16] Others developed the idea that specifically venial sins could be expiated here or in the hereafter, which when combined with the church practice of making intercessions and sacrifices for the dead, made the dogma of purgatory complete, and the Councils of Florence (1439) and Trent (1545–63)[17] made it a church doctrine. All this furthered discrimination among levels of merit and perfection in believers, and theology attached to it ever-increasing importance for the life of religion and the church.

According to Catholic doctrine, the souls of the damned immediately enter hell (Gehenna, the abyss, the inferno) and are tormented in everlasting and inextinguishable fire. The souls of those who after receiving baptism are not again tainted by sin

12. Origen, *Against Celsus*, III, 75; VI, 25–26.

13. Ibid., VI, 12–13, 21, 64; V, 15–16; cf. R. Hofmann, "Fegfeuer," in *PRE*[3], V, 788–92.

14. The Orthodox Confession of the Eastern Church, arts. 64–68, in *Creeds of Christendom*, ed. Philip Schaff (New York: Harper & Brothers, 1877), II, 342–48.

15. Augustine, *City of God*, XX, 25; XXI, 24.

16. Augustine, *Enchiridion*, 69.

17. Canons and Decrees of the Council of Trent, VI, canon 30; XXII, c. 2, canon 3; XXV.

or are purified from it here or hereafter are immediately taken up into heaven to behold the face of God, be it in various degrees of perfection, depending on their merits.[18] By Christ's descent into hell also the souls of the saints who died before that time are transferred from the limbo of the fathers (Abraham's bosom) to heaven. Infants who die before being baptized, according to the most common view, go to a special division (*limbus infantum*) to suffer only an "eternal punishment of condemnation" (*aeterna poena damni*) but no "physical punishment" (*poena sensa*).[19] But those who commit venial sins after baptism and have not been able to "pay" the appropriate temporal punishments in this life are not immediately admitted to the beatific vision of God in heaven but go to "purgatory"[20] to clear up the hindrances that stand in the way of their entry into heaven. There they have to bear the temporal punishments that remain the set penalty for those sins even after forgiveness and serve ideally to have a purifying impact on "poor souls." By virtue of the communion of saints, the church can come to the aid of these suffering souls for the purpose of softening and shortening their punishment by intercessions, sacrifices of the Mass, good works, and indulgences. While no one knows for certain which souls have to go to purgatory or for how long and under what conditions on their part the prayers and sacrifices of the living are to their benefit, increasingly the rule is that, barring a few exceptions, such as martyrs or particular saints, the great majority of believers first go to purgatory. They are, nonetheless far ahead of the living, who still face purgatory. Although on the one hand they are "poor souls," viewed from another angle they are "blessed" souls who along with the angels and those in a state of beatitude are invoked for help by those living in distress.[21]

[553] The Reformation saw in this notion of purgatory a limitation on the merits of Christ and taught—by virtue of its principle of justification by faith alone—that a human, immediately after a particular judgment undergone in the death struggle, entered into the blessedness of heaven or the perdition of hell. Reformed theology in particular also emphasized the difference between the state of the dead before and after the last day. In his writing on "the sleep of the soul," Calvin states that "Abraham's bosom" only means that after death the souls of the faithful will enjoy full peace, but that up until the day of resurrection something will still be lacking, namely, the full and perfect glory of God to which they always aspire, and that therefore our salvation always remains in progress until the day that concludes and terminates all progress.[22]

18. H. Denzinger, ed., *Sources of Catholic Dogma*, trans. from the 30th ed. by R. J. Deferrari (London and St. Louis: Herder, 1955), ##870, 875.

19. Peter Lombard, *Sententiae in IV libris distinctae*, 3rd ed., 2 vols. (Grottaferrata: Colleggi S. Bonaventurae ad Claras Aquas, 1971–81), II, dist. 33; T. Aquinas, *Summa Theol.*, suppl., qu. 69, art. 4.

20. Ed. note: Bavinck here in parentheses notes that the Dutch term for "purgatory," *vagevuur*, is etymologically derived from *vagen, vegen*, which means "purify" or "cleanse."

21. Roman Catechism, I, c. 6, qu. 3.

22. J. Calvin, *Institutes*, III.xxv.6: "The fact that the blessed gathering of saintly spirits is called 'Abraham's bosom' [Luke 16:22] is enough to assure us of being received after this pilgrimage by the common Father of the faithful, that he may share the fruit of his faith with us. Meanwhile, since Scripture every-

After the Reformation, however, other ideas, including soul sleep, annihilation, reincarnation, and varieties of universalism sprang up. In Protestant theology following the eighteenth century, all the ideas expressed earlier by pagans and Christians, philosophers and theologians, returned. The Catholic doctrine of purgatory was again taken up by many mystics and pietists such as Böhme, and further by Leibniz, Lessing, J. F. von Meyer, and many others.[23] The Socinians, following certain ancient Christian writers, taught that just as bodies returned to earth, so souls returned to God and there, until the resurrection, led an existence without perception or thought, pleasure or discomfort.[24] Closely connected with this view was the doctrine of soul sleep, which had already been advocated by certain heretics, later by the Anabaptists, and found acceptance again in the eighteenth century. Not a few thinkers have even returned to the ancient doctrine of the transmigration of souls or metempsychosis, commending a form of it that says that, by a process of repeated passages from one human body into another, souls may eventually arrive at perfection.[25] Nowadays, the idea of development is so strong that it is being applied even to the state after death. The doctrine of the limbo of the fathers (*limbus patrum*) has again been taken over by Martensen, Delitzsch, Vilmar, and the like,[26] and the view that in the intermediate state there will still be gospel preaching and the possibility of conversion is a favorite notion of the new theology.[27] Many even view the whole of the beyond (*Jenseits*) as an ongoing purgation. The result of this is that some

---

where bids us wait in expectation for Christ's coming, and defers until then the crown of glory, let us be content with the limits divinely set for us: namely, that the souls of the pious, having ended the toil of their warfare, enter into blessed rest, where in glad expectation they await the enjoyment of promised glory, and so all things are held in suspense until Christ the Redeemer appear" (ed. John T. McNeill and trans. Ford Lewis Battles [Philadelphia: Westminster, 1960], 2:998). Cf. Calvin, "Psychopannychia," in *Tracts and Treatises*, trans. Henry Beveridge, 3 vols. (Grand Rapids: Eerdmans, 1958), 3:413–90.

23. G. W. von Leibniz, *System der Theologie* (Mainz: Müller, 1820), 345; G. E. Lessing, *Erziehung des Menschengeschlechts*, ed. Louis Ferdinand Helbig (Bern and Las Vegas: Peter Lang, 1980); J. F. von Meyer, *Blätter für höhere Wahrheit*, 11 vols. (Frankfurt a.M.: H. L. Brönner, 1818–32), VI, 233; J. H. Jung-Stilling, *Theorie der Geister-Kunde* (Leipzig: Dieter, ca. 1890), §211; H. Martensen, *Christian Dogmatics*, trans. W. Urwick (Edinburgh: T&T Clark, 1871), §§276–77; I. A. Dorner, *A System of Christian Doctrine*, trans. A. Cave and J. S. Banks, 4 vols. (Edinburgh: T&T Clark, 1882), IV, §153; J. J. van Oosterzee, *Christian Dogmatics*, trans. J. Watson and M. Evans, 2 vols. (New York: Scribner, Armstrong, 1874), §142. Especially Anglican theologians had much sympathy for the doctrine of purgatory; cf. W. Walsh, *The Secret History of the Oxford Movement*, 6th ed. (London: Church Association, 1899), 281ff.

24. O. Fock, *Der Socinianismus* (Kiel: C. Schröder, 1847), 714ff.

25. The doctrine of the transmigration of souls, reincarnation, or metempsychosis was traditionally one of the most fundamental tenets of Hinduism (J. S. Speyer, *De Indische theosophie en hare beteekenis voor ons* [Leiden: S. C. van Doesburgh, 1910], 86f.), and, according to Herodotus, was embraced also by the Egyptians and found acceptance later in the case of Pythagoras, Empedocles, Plato, the Stoics, Neoplatonists, Pharisees, Kabbalists, gnostics, and Manichaeans; in later years again in Lessing, Schlosser, Ungern-Sternberg, Schopenhauer.

26. H. Martensen, *Christian Dogmatics*, §277; Franz Delitzsch, *A System of Biblical Psychology*, trans. Robert E. Wallis, 2nd ed. (Edinburgh: T&T Clark, 1875), 477ff.

27. J. J. van Oosterzee, *Christian Dogmatics*, §142.

may be lost forever (hypothetical universalism), or that those who persist in the wrong will be annihilated (conditional immortality), or that in the end all will be saved (ἀποκαταστασις, *apokatastasis*).[28]

[554] The history of the doctrine of the intermediate state shows that it is hard for theologians and people in general to stay within the limits of Scripture and not attempt to be wiser than they can be. This preoccupation with the intermediate state is neither scriptural nor healthy. The biblical data about the intermediate state are sufficient for our needs in this life. If we persist and try to solve the many unanswered questions that may arise in the inquisitive mind we can only take the course of speculation and conjecture and run the risk of negating the divine witness by the inventions of human wisdom. Philosophy, for example, deals with death and immortality by viewing death as something natural, and thinks that the idea of immortality, that is, the continued existence of the soul, is enough for it. But Scripture teaches that death is not natural but arises from the violation of the divine commandment (Gen. 2:17); from the devil (John 8:44); from sin (James 1:15); and from the judgment of God (Rom. 6:23). In Scripture this death is never identical with annihilation, with nonbeing, but always consists in the destruction of harmony, in being cut off from the various life settings in which a creature has been placed in keeping with one's nature.

By virtue of their creation, humans are linked with nature and the human world, visible and invisible things, heaven and earth, God and angels. The fullness of their life is to stand in the right, that is, in the God-willed relation to the whole of their surroundings. Thus, in its essence and entire scope, death is disturbance, the breakup of all these relations in which humans stood originally and still ought to stand.[29] Death's cause, therefore, is and can be none other than the sin that disturbs the right relation to God and breaks up life-embracing fellowship with God. In this sense sin not only results in death but also coincides with it; sin is death, death in a spiritual sense. Those who sin, by that token and at the same moment, put themselves in an adversarial relationship toward God, are dead to God and the things of God, have no pleasure in the knowledge of his ways, and in hostility and hatred turn away from him. Since this relation to God, this being created in his image and likeness, belongs to the essence of being human, the disturbance of this relationship will inevitably have a devastating impact on all the other relationships in which human beings stand—to themselves, to their fellow humans, to nature, to the angels, to the whole creation. Actually, in terms of its nature, at the very moment it was committed, sin should have resulted in a full, across-the-board death (Gen. 2:17), a return of the entire cosmos to its primeval chaotic condition. By nature, all that is inside and outside humanity is torn up into mutually hostile segments, but God in his mercy has intervened, first with his common grace to curb the power of sin and death, then with his special grace to

---

28. For further discussion, see chapter 25 of this volume, "The Consummation."
29. Henry Drummond, *Natural Law in the Spiritual World* (New York: J. Pott, 1887), 149ff.

break down and conquer that power. Not only is physical death postponed, and not only did God by various measures make human existence and development possible; but also Christ by his cross fundamentally achieved a victory over sin and death and brought life and immortality to light (Rom. 5:12ff.; 1 Cor. 15:45; 2 Tim. 1:10; Heb. 2:14; Rev. 1:18; 20:14), so that everyone who believes in him has eternal life and will never die (John 3:36; 5:24; 8:51–52; 11:25). Now it is this life and this immortality that in Holy Scripture stand in the foreground.

Immortality in a philosophical sense—the continuation of the soul after death—is of subordinate value in the Bible. What we learn from Scripture is that naked existence, mere unenhanced being—on this side of the grave and even more on the other side—is not yet life as it befits and behooves human beings. On earth human life stands in a web of varied relationships and from it receives a measure of content and value. Death breaks the varied and wonderful bonds of life relations in this world. In comparison with life on this side of the grave, death results in nonbeing, the disturbing negation of the rich and joyful experience of life on earth. Never again will the dead have any share in all that happens under the sun (Eccles. 9:6). Death is the fruit of sin; sin is death. Only when Christ died and rose again did imperishable life come to light. Christ's death and resurrection are thus the restoration of life. Christ did not gain or disclose immortality in the philosophical sense, the sense of the continued existence of souls after death, but again filled the life of humans, exhausted and emptied by sin, with the positive content of God's fellowship, with peace and joy and blessedness. For those who are in Christ Jesus, death is no longer death but a passage into eternal life, and the grave is a place of sanctified rest until the day of resurrection. This rich biblical perspective rules out other attempts to reduce the sting of death.

[555] Those who lose sight of this scriptural teaching on immortality fall into various errors. It is simply a fact that we cannot picture a pure [disembodied] spirit—its existence, life, and activity. About God, who is pure Spirit, we can only speak in an anthropomorphic manner, a procedure modeled to us by Scripture itself. Angels are spiritual beings but are presented in human form; when they appear on earth, they often assume human bodies. Although human persons are not merely physical beings, all their activities are bound to the body and dependent on it, not just the vegetative and animal functions but also the intellectual ones of thinking and willing. Inasmuch as the body is not the prison house of the soul but belongs integrally to the essence of our humanity, we cannot form any mental picture of the life and activity of a soul that is separated from the body, and we are therefore readily inclined to conjectures and guessing. In the main, accordingly, three hypotheses have been conceived to make the existence of souls after death somewhat intelligible: soul sleep, intermediate corporeality, and some form of contact between the living and the dead.

Many pagan thinkers and also some Christians have believed that souls, after being separated from the body, are capable only of leading a dormant life. The change that begins at death is indeed of extraordinary significance. The entire content of our psychic life is after all derived from the external world; all knowledge begins with sense perception; the entire form of our thought is material; we even speak of spiritual things in words that originally had a sensory meaning. If then, as Scripture teaches, death is a sudden, violent, total, and absolute break with the present world, there is ostensibly no other possibility than that the soul is completely closed to the external world, loses all its content, and sinks back as it were into itself. In sleep as well, the soul withdraws from the outside world and breaks off its interaction with it, although only in a relative way since our dreams remain connected with it. It is understandable, therefore, that a notion of "soul sleep," where after death souls are in a dormant, unconscious state, should gain currency. Scripture even seems to commend the idea by referring to death as sleep (Deut. 31:16 KJV; Jer. 51:39, 57; Dan. 12:2; Matt. 9:24; John 11:11; 1 Cor. 7:39 in Greek; in KJV: 1 Cor. 11:30; 15:6, 18, 20, 51; 1 Thess. 4:13–15; 2 Pet. 3:4; etc.). Still, psychopannychism does face objections.

In the first place, it is clear that the soul's dependence on the body does not necessarily exclude its independence. The external world may prompt the awakening of our self-consciousness and be the initial source of our knowledge; thinking may be bound to our brains and have its seat and organ there; yet it has not been and cannot be proved that the psychic life of humanity has its source and origin in physical phenomena. Thinking and knowing are activities of the soul; it is not the ear that hears and the eye that sees but the psychic "I" of a human being that hears through the ear and sees through the eye. The body is the instrument of mind, or spirit. Why could the soul not continue its activities without the body? To deny conscious life to spirit as such would logically lead one to deny consciousness and will to God and the angels who are spiritual, noncorporeal beings and nevertheless possess consciousness and will. Furthermore, though Scripture teaches with the greatest possible clarity that death is a total break with all this earthly life, and to that extent it is sleeping, resting, or being silent, it nowhere says that the soul of the deceased sleeps. On the contrary, Scripture always represents the person after death as being more or less conscious with another set of relations with another world. Whereas immediately after his death the rich man is in torment, the wretched Lazarus is carried to Abraham's bosom (Luke 16:23). And all believers who on earth already participated in eternal life, so far from losing it by dying (John 11:25–26), after death enjoy it all the more intensely and blessedly in fellowship with Christ (Luke 23:43; Acts 7:59; 2 Cor. 5:8; Phil. 1:23; Rev. 6:9; 7:9–10). Being at home in the body is being away from the Lord; therefore, to die is the way to a closer, more intimate fellowship with Christ (Phil. 1:23). Finally, it need not surprise us that those who rose again and returned to this life tell us nothing about what they saw and heard on the other side. Most likely they have not been permitted, or are unable, to convey their experiences on the other side of the grave. Moses and the prophets are enough for us (Luke 16:29). After being caught up into the third heaven, Paul could say only that he had heard things that are not to be told and that no mortal is permitted to repeat (2 Cor. 12:4).[30]

[556] Others believe that after death, souls receive a new corporeality and are on that account able again to enter into contact with the external world. They base this opinion on the fact that we cannot visualize the life and activity of the soul aside from the body and, further, on those passages in Scripture that seem to accord a kind of corporeality to the souls of the dead. The denizens of the realm of the dead are described precisely as they appeared on earth. Samuel is pictured as an old man clothed with a mantle (1 Sam. 28:14); the kings of the nations sit on thrones and go out to meet the king of Babylon (Isa. 14:9); the gentiles lie down to rest with the uncircumcised (Ezek. 31:18; 32:19ff.). In speaking of the dead, Jesus still refers to their eyes, fingers, and tongues (Luke 16:23–24). Paul expects that if the earthly tent is destroyed, he will have a building from God and not be unclothed but further clothed (2 Cor. 5:1–4). And John saw a great multitude, standing before the throne and the Lamb, robed in white, with palm branches in their hands (Rev. 6:11; 7:9). However, this anthropomorphic mode of speech in Scripture tells us no more about the corporeality of souls after death than a reference to the "eyes of God" (2 Chron. 16:19) tell us about God having a corporeal body. Those who attribute to souls a kind of body must, to be consistent, follow through and, along with theosophists, represent God and the angels as in some sense physical as well. The corporeality ascribed to souls after death is a concept without any specifiable content; for this very reason, opinions on it tend to be very diverse. No matter how it is presented, it does not become any clearer. We know only of spirit and matter. An "immaterial corporeality" is a contradiction that was inauspiciously taken from theosophy into Christian theology and seeks in vain to reconcile the false dualism of spirit and matter, of thesis and antithesis.

[557] In the third place, there are many who believe that souls after death still maintain some kind of relationship with life on earth. Prevalent among many peoples is the idea that souls after death remain near the gravesite, leading to the widespread practice of providing the deceased in their graves with food, weapons, possessions, and sometimes even wives and slaves. Usually this veneration of the dead was not restricted to the day of the burial or the time of mourning but continued afterward as well and was incorporated into ordinary private or public cultic practice. The purpose of this veneration by the people was in part to come to the aid of the dead but especially to avert the evil the dead could do and to ensure themselves, whether in ordinary or extraordinary ways, by oracles and miracles, of their blessing and assistance.[31] From as early as the second century, all of these elements penetrated Christian worship as well. Just as monks in Buddhism and mystics in Islam, so the martyrs in the Christian church soon became the objects

---

30. For opposition to the idea of soul sleep, see Tertullian, *A Treatise on the Soul* 58; J. Calvin, "Psychopannychia."

31. P. D. Chantepie de la Saussaye, *Lehrbuch der Religionsgeschichte*, 2 vols. (Freiburg i.B.: Mohr [Siebeck], 1887–89), I, 79–87.

of religious veneration. Altars, chapels, and churches were built at sites where they had died or their relics were interred. After the fourth century this veneration of the virgin Mary, angels, patriarchs, prophets, and martyrs was extended to include bishops, monks, hermits, confessors, and virgins, as well as a variety of saints, their relics, and their images.[32] In this cult the Roman Catholic Church in a practical way celebrates the communion of the saints. The one Christian church has three divisions: the triumphant church (*ecclesia triumphans*) in heaven, the suffering church (*ecclesia patiens*) in purgatory, and the militant church (*ecclesia militans*) on earth. The souls in heaven intercede for those in purgatory; those on earth seek, by their good works, to soften and shorten their punishment; those in purgatory may be invoked so that their intercessions help and strengthen believers on earth. There are variations in veneration: Adoration (*latria*) is due only to God. Mary is entitled to *hyperdulia*, the saints to *dulia* (veneration), their relics to relative religious devotion, and so on; there are as many kinds of adoration as there are kinds of excellence; adoration is varied according to the diversity of excellence.[33]

Many of these notions—that after death there continues to be a certain connection between the soul and the body, that souls maintain some kind of relationship with the earth, know about the most important events, pray for us, look down upon us, and bless us—returned from time to time in Protestant theology.[34] Many eighteenth-century thinkers like Swedenborg, Jung-Stilling, and Oberlin believed they were in direct contact with the spirits of the dead.[35] The possibility of such apparitions was acknowledged as well by men such as Kant, Lessing, Jung-Stilling, J. H. Fichte, and others; and spiritism, which arose after 1848, seeks intentionally to put itself in touch with the spirit world, and believes it can by this route receive all kinds of revelations.[36]

[558] To start with this latter issue, we need to note that superstitious practices occur among all peoples, also those with whom Israel came in contact, such as the Egyptians (Gen. 41:8; Exod. 7:11), the Canaanites (Deut. 18:9, 14), the Babylonians (Dan. 1:20; 2:2), and so on. These practices penetrated Israel as well and often flourished there (1 Sam. 28:9; 2 Kings 21:6; Isa. 2:6). Among these practices was that of consulting the dead; those who practiced it were called אֹבוֹת (*'ōbôt*, mediums) or יִדְּעֹנִים (*yiddĕ'ōnîm*, wizards). Soothsaying might occur in many ways, among others by consulting the dead (Deut. 18:11).[37] But the Law

---

32. Joseph Schwane, *Dogmengeschichte*, 4 vols. (Freiburg i.B.: Herder, 1882–95), I, 389ff.; II, 620ff.

33. See further H. Bavinck, *Reformed Dogmatics*, ed. John Bolt (Grand Rapids: Baker Academic, 2003–8), II, 468–72 (#267; *In the Beginning*, ed. John Bolt [Grand Rapids: Baker Academic, 1999], 88ff.); III, 281–82 (#364).

34. J. T. Beck, *Umriss der biblischen Seelenlehre*, 3rd ed. (Stuttgart: Steinkopf, 1871), 40ff. (ed. note: ET: *Outlines of Biblical Psychology* [Edinburgh: T&T Clark, 1877]); F. Delitzsch, *Biblical Psychology*, 444f.

35. See especially J. C. Wötzel, *Meiner Gattin wirkliche Erscheinung nach ihrem Tode* (Chemnitz: Jacobäer, 1804).

36. O. Zöckler, "Spiritismus," in *PRE*[3], XVIII, 654–66.

37. B. Stade, *Geschichte des Volkes Israel*, 2 vols. (Berlin: G. Grote, 1887–88), I, 443f.; F. Schwally, *Das Leben nach dem Tode: Nach den Vorstellungen des Alten Israel* (Giessen: J. Ricker, 1892), 69f.

and the Prophets were firmly opposed to the practice and called the people back
to the Lord, his revelation, and his testimony (Exod. 22:18; Lev. 19:26, 31; 20:6,
27; Deut. 18:11; 1 Sam. 28:9; Isa. 8:19; 47:9–15; Jer. 27:9; 29:8; Mic. 3:7; 5:12;
Nah. 3:4; Mal. 3:5); the New Testament puts its seal on this witness (Luke 16:29;
Acts 8:9ff.; 19:13–20; Gal. 5:20; Eph. 5:11; Rev. 9:21; 21:8; 22:15).

One cannot even prove that Holy Scripture accepts the possibility of calling
up the dead and having them appear. Admittedly, by God's miraculous power
the dead have sometimes been raised, and Scripture acknowledges the demonic
powers and workings that surpass the capacity of humans (Deut. 13:1–2; Matt.
24:24; 2 Thess. 2:9; Rev. 13:13–15). But nowhere does it teach the possibility
or reality of the dead appearing. The only passage that can be cited for this view
is 1 Sam. 28, where Saul seeks out the medium at Endor. But though we must
reject the rationalistic explanation that only sees in this story the account of an
intentional deception by the woman, neither can we accept the idea of a real,
objective appearance of Samuel. There is nothing in 1 Samuel 28 that goes beyond the familiar phenomena of hypnotism and somnambulism and cannot be
explained in the same way.

There are many people, however, who believe that precisely from these phenomena of hypnotism, somnambulism, spiritism, and the like they must deduce
the operation of spirits. But as yet this hypothesis seems completely unwarranted.
Aside from the many hoaxes that have been perpetrated in this domain, the things
that have been said of the appearance and operation of spirits are so puerile and
insignificant that we certainly do not have to assume the involvement of the spirit
world to explain them. This is not to deny that a wide range of phenomena occur
that have not yet been explained; but these are all of such a nature (e.g., the sudden onset of the ability to understand and speak foreign languages, clairvoyance,
hypnosis, suggestion, second sight, premonition, synchronic telecognition, telepathy, and so forth) that they are by no means made any clearer by the hypothesis
of spirit apparitions.

Further, the whole of Scripture proceeds from the idea that death is a total
break with life on this side of the grave. True, the dead continue to remember the
things that happened to them on earth; their deeds follow those who died in the
Lord (Rev. 14:13). The things we have done on earth become our moral possession and accompany us in death. There is no doubt either that the dead recognize
those whom they have known on earth. The rich man knows Lazarus (Luke 16).
The friends we make on earth by the good we do will one day receive us with joy
in the eternal homes (Luke 16:9). But for the rest, Scripture consistently tells us
that at death all fellowship with this earth ends. The dead no longer have a share
in anything that happens under the sun (Eccles. 9:5–6, 10). Nowhere is there any
sign that the dead are in contact with the living: they belong to another realm,
one that is totally separate from the earth.

For that reason there is no room for the invocation and veneration of saints.
Holy Scripture does say that believers on earth may appeal to each other for

intercession (Num. 21:7; Jer. 42:2; 1 Thess. 5:25), but never mentions asking the dead for their intercession; and both angels and human beings expressly refuse to accept the religious veneration that is due only to God (Deut. 6:13; 10:20; Matt. 4:10; Acts 14:10ff.; Col. 2:18–19; Rev. 19:10; 22:9). Nor is there any reference to the veneration of relics. Even though God sometimes performs miracles through them (2 Kings 13:21; Matt. 9:21; Luke 6:19; Acts 5:15; 19:12), they must not be the objects of veneration (Deut. 34:6; 2 Kings 18:4; 2 Cor. 5:16). In the practices of Roman Catholicism the communion of saints degenerates into mutual veneration that crowds the Mediator of God and humanity into the background.

BETWEEN DEATH AND RESURRECTION

[559] Until now we have discussed only whether the dead still have any kind of contact with life on earth. Now what about the new relations and conditions in which the dead find themselves on the other side of the grave? Scripture clearly teaches a distinction between the destiny of the righteous and the unrighteous after death but not a great deal about their exact condition. Already in the Old Testament we see the lines, when extended, lead to a difference in the state of the righteous and the unrighteous after death. The fear of the Lord leads to life, but the ungodly perish and are ruined. Scripture uses language of heaven "above" and Sheol, hades, Gehenna, and the abyss as "below" but this cannot and must not be understood topographically. The concepts taken in a local sense are very relative and, in this context, have only ethical significance. We locate the kingdom of darkness directly across from the kingdom of light, and in accordance with a natural symbolism we look for the first below us and for the second above us. All fixation of the place of punishment for the dead—in the earth, under the earth, in the sea, in the sun, in the air, or on one of the planets—is mere conjecture. What *can* be stated is that the beyond is not only a state but also a place. For the rest it is more in keeping with the sparse data Scripture offers us to abstain from any attempt to determine the place of punishment for the dead. "Do not ask where it is but how you may escape it" (Chrysostom). Nor do we know anything more about the state of unbelievers and the ungodly after death up until the last judgment.

The question has been raised, however, whether on the other side of the grave, for those who have not heard the gospel here on earth or only very dimly, there will not be another opportunity to repent and to believe in Christ. On the basis of 1 Peter 3:18–19, Clement and Origen gave an affirmative answer, inferring from that passage that Christ and also the apostles had proclaimed the gospel to the dead in hades who were susceptible to it. Although Augustine and others refuted this sentiment, and though Christ's descent into hell is usually interpreted differently, the idea kept coming back and, in the case of many people, found acceptance in the nineteenth century when the huge number and rapid increase of non-Christians began to dawn on them. We must not dismiss the burden of our realization that there have been and still are millions of people who have never had any knowledge of the way of salvation in Christ and therefore never were in a position to embrace him with a believing heart or decisively to reject him. These people cannot be numbered among the unbelievers in a strict sense, and Scripture itself says that they must be judged by a different standard than Jews and Christians (Matt. 10:15; 11:20–24; Luke 10:12–24; 12:47–48; John 15:22; Rom. 2:12; 2 Pet. 2:20–22). From this it does not follow, however, that there is or has to be preaching of the gospel on the other side of the grave. Scripture never speaks a single word about it.

The only texts to which one can appeal for a preaching of the gospel in hades with some semblance of justification are 1 Peter 3:19–21 and 4:6. But these texts do not contain what people wish to read in them. Even if they speak of a proclamation by Christ after his resurrection to the contemporaries of Noah in hades, this would only establish the fact that it occurred, but by no means would it warrant the teaching that there is ongoing preaching of the gospel in hades to all who have not heard it on earth. The truth, after all, is that Noah's contemporaries were precisely not the kind of people who had never during their lifetime heard the Word of God on earth. Whatever we may do with this text, we are dealing here with a very special case that provides no warrant for any further conclusions. Also, the aorist ἐκήρυξεν (ekēryxen; 1 Pet. 3:19) indicates that this preaching by Christ occurred only once and it cannot have been a proclamation of the gospel unto salvation. Other difficulties abound. According to 1 Peter 3:18–19, Christ delivered that preaching specifically after he had been made alive and was risen. Did he at that time go physically to hades? When did he do that? How long did he stay there? And suppose all this were possible—however unlikely it is as such—who then is conducting this preaching in hades on an ongoing basis after this time? Is there a church in the underworld? Is there an ongoing mission, a calling and ordination to ministry? Are they humans or angels, apostles or other ministers of the Word, who after their deaths are proclaiming the gospel there? The theory of a mission center in hades is, in a variety of ways, in conflict with Scripture. The best we can make of this passage is to relate it to 1 Peter 4:6 where the aorist εὐηγγελίσθη (euēngelisthē) by its very form also refers not to ongoing preaching but to a specific event. That proclamation of the gospel occurred once, and with the intent that those who heard it would be judged like everyone else, "in the flesh," that is, they would die, but might live, as God does, "in the spirit." The preaching of the gospel, therefore, preceded their death; the νεκροι are those who are now dead but who heard the gospel during their lifetime. From the previous verse (5) we see why Peter calls these people νεκροι (nekroi, dead [ones]); there we read that Christ "stands ready to judge the living and the dead." Now then, just as the gospel is preached to the living today, so it was in the past preached to those who are now dead, so that, while they would indeed still die in the flesh [as everyone else does], they would nevertheless even now already live in the spirit in God's presence.

Given these objections, which are derived from Scripture, the entire theory of gospel preaching in the intermediate state collapses. We could add questions such as to whom is such preaching directed, and if not to all, why not? Does this not make life on earth and the choices we make completely without value or meaning? The set of assumptions behind this entire way of thinking center on the belief that it is God's intent to save all humans, that the preaching of the gospel has to be absolutely universal, that all humans must be personally and individually confronted by the choice for or against the gospel, that in making that choice the decision lies within human power, that original and actual sins are insufficient to condemn anyone, and that only deliberate unbelief toward the gospel makes a person worthy of eternal ruin. All these assumptions are in conflict with firm scriptural statements and make the theory of gospel preaching in the intermediate state unacceptable. Is this not a hard conclusion? How can we accept the eternally lost condition of many, who through no fault of their own, have not heard the gospel? Here, in this most solemn matter, not our feeling but the Word of God decides. The theory of a preaching of the gospel to the dead in no way relieves the problem, inasmuch as it only helps those who had already prepared themselves for the faith here on earth. It even aggravates the problem because it pays no attention to the interest of the millions of children who die in infancy and in fact excludes them from the possibility of being saved. Finally, it takes no account of the sovereign freedom and omnipotence of God, which can save also without the external preaching of the Word, solely by the internal calling and regeneration of the Holy Spirit.

[560] Similarly, the initially attractive notion of postdeath purification, including the Roman Catholic doctrine of purgatory, also has no basis in Scripture. The idea of such a state of purification is of pagan origin and occurred especially in two forms. The theory of the transmigration of souls, found among the people of India, Egyptians, Greeks, Jews, and the like, holds that before entering the human body the soul has already lived in other bodies; after it has left the human body, it also enters new organisms—all with a view toward self-purification and ultimately reaching perfection. This theory is too contrary to Scripture for it ever to have found acceptance, aside from a few sects and individual persons within the bounds of Christianity. It proceeds, after all, from the idea that souls are preexistent, and is in conflict with the doctrine of redemption accomplished by Christ because it views purification and perfection as the work of humans themselves. Finally, it entirely fails to make clear how souls, by repeatedly passing into other bodies, could be freed from sins and trained toward holiness.

Another idea—found in Parsism[38] and Judaism[39]—and one that had greater influence on Christian theology, is that souls after death still need to be purified for a time by an assortment of punishments before they can attain the highest

---

38. P. D. Chantepie de la Saussaye, *Lehrbuch der Religionsgeschichte*, II, 51.
39. F. W. Weber, *System der altsynagogalen palästinischen Theologie*, 327.

level of blessedness. Since Origen, this conception also spread among Christians, leading to the Catholic doctrine of purgatory, or a period of purification, which is accepted by many Protestants. At first blush, this idea is quite appealing. Believers, after all, at the moment of their deaths are all still saddled with sin; even the most saintly still possess only a small beginning of perfect obedience. How does death suddenly remove all the pollution of sin in the soul? Our experience teaches us that in this life all changes are slow; gradual growth and development are everywhere. Hence everything favors the idea that after death the souls of believers need to undergo a purification before being taken up into heaven and admitted to the vision of God.

However, no matter what human argumentation would favor such a purgatory, the primary and conclusive objection is that Scripture nowhere speaks of it. The texts advanced in favor of the idea (Matt. 5:22–25; 12:32; 1 Cor. 3:12–15) do not explicitly refer to a purgation of souls; only creative exegetical stretching yields anything close to it. Only one passage in the Old Testament Apocrypha, 2 Maccabees 12:41–45, shows that the Jews at that time considered offerings and prayers for the dead who had died in their sins to be a good and necessary thing—something we know from other sources as well. It is therefore all the more noteworthy that this folk belief existing among the Jews is never reported, much less sanctioned, in either the Old or the New Testament.

The doctrine of purgatory is most closely bound up with justification. By justification, the church of Rome understands the infusion of supernatural sanctifying grace that in turn enables humans to do good works and thereby earn eternal life. Since this sanctifying grace is subject to being increased and decreased, one who loses it as a result of mortal sin and then dies is lost; one who by keeping the precepts and counsels achieves perfection in the hour of death immediately enters heaven. However, one who still has to pay the debt and bear the temporal punishment because of a venial sin or who in the sacrament of penance has received back the infused grace lost as a result of a mortal sin and is at his death still in arrears in "paying off" the temporal punishments—such a person is consigned to purgatory and remains there until he has paid the last penny. In the church of Rome, justification, sanctification, and glorification are the work of humans, be it on the basis of the supernatural grace infused into them. After receiving it, they have to make themselves worthy of eternal life and the beatific vision of God in heaven by a condign or full merit;[40] if they fail to achieve this on earth, they must—just as the pagans pictured it—continue the work on earth in the hereafter until they have attained perfection.

But from Scripture the Reformation again came to know the justification of sinners by faith and therefore had to come to a rejection of the fire of purification. Christ accomplished everything; not only did he bear the punishment, but he also

---

40. Ed. note: Cf. Richard Muller, *Dictionary of Latin and Greek Theological Terms* (Grand Rapids: Baker Academic, 1985), s.v. *meritum de condigno* and *meritum de congruo*, 191f.

won eternal life for us by his keeping the law. All the benefits that Christ gained by his suffering and death and that are present and available in him in perfection are immediately conferred on those who believe in truth. He who believes *has* eternal life. In justification, not only the merit of Christ's passive obedience is imputed but also that of his active obedience. In that benefaction, believers receive forgiveness, exemption from punishment. Sanctification here is not self-preparation for heaven, or self-perfection, but solely the unfolding in believers of what they already possess in Christ, a walking in the good works that God in Christ prepared [for them] (Eph. 2:10). Those who believe have forgiveness and eternal life; they are ready and fit for heaven and need not go through a purgatory either here or hereafter. Even the suffering they often still—even as a result of sin—have to bear on earth is not a punishment, a penalty, a required late payment of the demands of the law, but a fatherly chastisement that serves their maturation.

On a Reformational basis, then, the only question is this: When do believers enter into full possession of the benefits that Christ has granted them? Those who believe receive them at once in a juridical sense; in Christ they are entitled to all the benefits of the covenant, the whole of salvation. But on earth they do not yet enter into full possession of them. When, then, does this occur? When do believers cease to be pilgrims and arrive in their homeland? To this question Scripture has but one answer: at death, when they enter their homeland (Ps. 73:24–25; Luke 23:43; Acts 7:59; 2 Cor. 5:1; Phil. 1:23; 2 Tim. 4:7). Of course, the manner in which the state of holiness commences immediately at the death of believers cannot be understood or clearly described. Regeneration and sanctification effected here on earth by the Holy Spirit is a mystery as well. This does not imply Platonic dualism as though the soul's mere liberation from the body would already constitute its sanctification, for sin is rooted precisely in the soul. Nor is this in the sense of sentimental rationalism, which has death, as a messenger of peace, turn people into angels, for death as such is a revelation of God's wrath and the wages of sin. But death does serve to sanctify us; it is for the believer a dying to sin. The consequence of ethical death, that is, dying to sin in communion with Christ, is that a person is freed from and dead to sin and henceforth lives for God in Christ (Rom. 6:6–11; 8:10; 1 Pet. 2:24). This ethical death culminates in physical death (Rom. 7:24; 2 Cor. 5:1; Phil. 1:21, 23). It is not at all strange that, as he does with all suffering, God should employ death as a means of sanctifying the soul of the believer and cleansing it from all the stains of sin.[41] In fact, the doctrine of purgatory is no help here. Purgatory is not a mission center, an institution for conversion, or a school of sanctification, but a place where only temporal punishment can be "paid off." Since purgatory is not the place where sins are forgiven but only debts accrued for venial sins are "paid off," how does purgatory bring about the sanctification of souls? If the souls in purgatory are still more or less stained by sin, how can we be sure they will not continue to sin and

41. Westminster Larger Catechism, qu. 85.

completely suffer the loss of grace? If, on the other hand, the souls are inherently pure and holy and have only to bear certain temporal punishments they could not bear on earth, it is again incomprehensible that the perfectly righteous could still be temporarily excluded from heaven and subjected to the torments of purgatory. In both cases it remains puzzling how purgatory can be a "purifying fire" (*ignis purgatorius*); it is nothing but a fire of retribution (*ignis vindicativus*). Oswald correctly points out that the purifying character of purgatory belongs among the more difficult questions![42]

Veneration of the dead by sacrifices and prayers was common among pagans. Intercession for the dead became a practice among the Jews later (2 Macc. 12:40–45) and remains to the present.[43] In the Christian church there soon arose the custom of wishing for the dead to receive peace, light, and refreshment (*refrigerium*) and remembering them in prayers and at the celebration of the Lord's Supper. Initially, these offerings and sacrifices were solely memorial in nature, but gradually a distinction was made between the souls who were immediately taken up into heaven and others who still had to spend time in purgatory. Communion with the first then gradually began to be practiced by invocation and veneration, and with the second by intercessions, good works, indulgences, and Masses for the soul.[44] The Reformed rejected this intercession for the dead on the ground that their lot was unalterably decided at death.[45] The fact is that neither the Old nor the New Testament breathes a word about such intercession. The only passage to which appeal can be made is 1 Corinthians 15:29, where Paul mentions those who had themselves baptized ὑπὲρ νεκρῶν (*hyper nekrōn*). However, from this it cannot be inferred that such a baptism was received by the living for the benefit of the dead. The apostle here is only expressing the thought that baptism presupposes belief in the resurrection of Christ and of believers. Take away the resurrection, and baptism becomes an empty ceremony. There is no evidence that such a practice existed in Paul's time or later.

[561] All offerings and intercessions for the dead are useless and weaken confidence in the sufficiency of Christ's sacrifice and his effectual intercession. Nonetheless, there still is and remains a communion between the church militant on earth and the church triumphant in heaven that cannot be broken. Believers on earth, when they became Christians, came to the heavenly Jerusalem above, which is the mother of us all; to the innumerable angels who serve and praise God there; to the assembly of the firstborn, that is, the devout of the Old Testament who are enrolled in heaven and have their citizenship there; to the spirits of the just, that is, the Christians who have already died and reached perfection, the consummation;

42. J. H. Oswald, *Eschatologie* (Paderborn: F. Schöningh, 1869), 116.
43. F. Schwally, *Das Leben nach dem Tode*, 188–90.
44. Canons and Decrees of the Council of Trent, XXII, 2, 3; XXV.
45. J. C. Suicerus, *Thesaurus ecclesiasticus* (Amsterdam: H. H. Wetsten, 1682), s.v. ταφη; B. de Moor, *Commentarius perpetuus in Joh. Marckii Compendium theologiae christianae didactico-elencticum*, 6 vols. (Leiden: J. Hasebroek, 1761–71), V, 30–32.

to Christ the mediator of the New Testament and to God the judge of all (Heb. 12:22–24). Although the souls of believers in heaven experience no change of status, they are confirmed and grow in their knowledge and love of God. Communion between the church in heaven and the church on earth does not imply direct interaction any more than lack of personal contact destroys the solidarity of the human race or the unity of believers in one holy, catholic, Christian church. The unity that binds all believers together, the dead as well as the living, is anchored in Christ, and through him in fellowship with the same Father, in the possession of the same Spirit, and in joint participation in the same treasures of salvation. The love we share in Christ leads to deep respect for the saints who preceded us, striving to follow their good example, and living in anticipation of going to them, that together with them and all created beings we may magnify the Lord.

Included in our communion is hope of reunion on the other side of the grave. This is completely natural, genuinely human, and also in keeping with Scripture. For Scripture teaches us not a naked immortality of spectral souls but the eternal life of individual persons. The joy of heaven, to be sure, first of all consists in communion with Christ but, further, in the fellowship of the blessed among themselves as well. Similarly, it is not absurd to think that the blessed in heaven yearn for the believers who are on earth. After all, they have a store of memories of the persons and conditions they knew on earth (Luke 16:27–31). The souls under the altar cry out for vengeance on account of the blood that had been shed (Rev. 6:10). The bride, that is, the entire community of believers both in heaven and on earth, prays for the coming of the Lord Jesus (22:17). Although Scripture gives us no warrant for believing that the blessed in heaven know everything that happens here on earth, still it is likely that they know as much about the church militant on earth as the latter does about them. The state of the blessed in heaven, therefore, does bear a provisional character; there is still room for faith and hope, for longing and prayer (Rev. 6:10; 22:17). Like believers on earth, they eagerly await the return of Christ, the resurrection of the dead, and the restoration of all things. Only then has the end been reached (1 Cor. 15:24). The souls in heaven, thus, cannot be conceived of as inactive. Although their work on earth is finished, they have other works to do in heaven. Scripture teaches this plainly. Those who have died in the Lord are with Jesus (Phil. 1:23), stand before the throne of God and of the Lamb (Rev. 7:9, 15), cry out and pray, praise and serve him (6:10; 7:10, 15; 22:17).

We do not need any doctrine of "receptacles," either for the Old Testament saints (*limbus patrum*) or for children who die in infancy (*limbus infantum*). According to the Reformed, the children of the covenant, whether baptized or unbaptized, go to heaven when they die; and so little has been disclosed to us about the fate of those outside the covenant that we had best abstain from any definite judgment.[46]

---

46. B. B. Warfield, "The Development of the Doctrine of Infant Salvation," in his *Two Studies in the History of Doctrine* (New York: Christian Literature, 1897).

What is right about the Roman Catholic doctrine here is the idea that there are varying degrees both in the punishment of the ungodly and in the blessedness of the devout. There is distinction of rank and activity in the world of angels, created beings, and most abundantly among humans. There is distinction of place and task in the church of Christ. On earth every believer is given one's own gifts and charged with one's own task. In death the works of each follow the person who dies in the Lord. Undoubtedly this diversity is not destroyed in heaven but, on the contrary, is purified of all that is sinful and multiplied abundantly (Luke 19:17–19). Still this difference in degree detracts nothing from the blessedness each enjoys in keeping with one's own capacity. For all will be at home with the same Lord (2 Cor. 5:8), are taken up into the same heaven (Rev. 7:9), enjoy the same rest (Heb. 4:9), and find joy in the same service of God (Rev. 7:15).

24

THE RETURN OF CHRIST

VISIONS OF THE END

[562] Just as it is appointed for humans to die once, so also there must come an end to the history of the world. Science as well as religion has always been convinced of this. The universe is finite, and its history will come to an end. Beliefs that the world was eternal and had neither beginning nor end seem even more untenable with today's knowledge of the cosmos. The rotational speed of the earth decreases by at least one second every 600,000 years and those who think this seems infinitessimally small, after billions of years, it nevertheless brings about on earth a reversal in the relationship between day and night, which brings all life to an end. Further, since the rotation of the earth is continually being slowed by the alternation of high and low tides, the earth therefore moves ever closer to the sun and must ultimately disappear in it. Neither will the sun last forever. The question is simply whether the sun or the earth will last longer. If it is the sun, the earth will ultimately be swallowed up by it, and everything will end in conflagration. If it is the earth, the heat supply will one day be exhausted, and life will expire in a death of extreme cold.[1] There is also a limit to the world's resources; growing populations and greater consumption will eventually exhaust it. Accordingly,

1. The law of entropy—according to which work can be completely converted into heat but heat can never be totally converted back to work, and which, applied to the universe by Clausius, leads to a state in which the temperature difference necessary for the conversion of heat into work has disappeared—has been used repeatedly as an argument for the end, hence also for the beginning of the world; and further, even as proof for the existence of God. C. Isenkrahe, *Energie, Entropie, Weltanfang, Weltende* (Trier: Lintz, 1910). But H. Bavinck, "Das Entropiegesetz und die Endlichkeit der Welt," *Der Geisteskampf der*

from the viewpoint of science, there is absolutely no room for an optimistic outlook on the future. Nonetheless, this has not prevented people from dreaming of steady progress and a future paradise of mankind in the present world (*Diesseits*). Humanists and materialists vie with each other in fostering such illusions. On the basis of the principle of cosmic evolution, they believe that their professional prophecies cannot go wrong. In their opinion, by the increase of ideal goods such as science, art, and morality, or by progress in material prosperity, that is, by an abundance of food, shelter, and clothing, the happiness of humanity will one day be fully realized. Kant, Lessing, Herder, Fichte, Schelling, and the like envision a future in which the ethical kingdom of God will embrace all human beings. All will participate in the Enlightenment, and full humanity will be the principle of the life of everyone. Even Darwin, at the end of his book on *The Origin of Species* and in the final chapter of his *Descent of Man*, expresses the hope that humanity, which has already risen so far above its animal origins, is moving toward a still higher destiny in the distant future. Even more extravagant are the expectations of the Socialists, these millennialists of unbelief, who think that in the future state of their dreams all sin and struggle will have vanished, and a carefree life of contentment will be the privilege of everyone.

Others are more gloomy. After all, even culture cannot be conceived as endless. One may arbitrarily assume the passage of billions of years in the past or future of the world but cannot picture it concretely as being filled with history. Humanity is finite, and therefore human civilization cannot be conceived as endless either. Both for the earth and for our race, an infinite period of time is an absurdity, even more palpably so than the foolishness of the millions of years known to us from pagan mythologies. From the perspective of science, there is much more reason to accept the pessimism of Schopenhauer and Eduard von Hartmann, which stakes the salvation of the world on the absolute negation of will, that is, on the annihilation of the world itself. But even then there is not the slightest guarantee that the absolute will's negation will succeed and not pass over into another world process and ever and again start over ad infinitum. Thus, Otto Henne Am Rhyn ends his history of culture with the prediction that one day the whole of humankind along with its culture will disappear without a trace. "One day everything we have accomplished will be nowhere to be found." And in the face of that prospect, he can only console himself with the thought that it will be a long time before we will get there.[2] Those who live without God and without hope and have to expect everything from the present world (*Diesseits*), from immanent cosmic forces, find it hard to accept the finiteness of this world and often turn to illusory dreams of progress or give up in despair. Finally, there are those who follow some of the Greek philosophers in positing multiple worlds prior to this one; Windelband

---

Gegenwart 45 (1909): 260–67, questions the validity of that argument. Cf. also the article "Entropie" in *Meyers kleines Konversations-Lexikon*.

    2. Th. Ziegler, in his *Sittliches Sein und sittliches Werden* (Strassburg: K. J. Trübner, 1890), states: "What the final end, the goal of history itself is, I do not know, and none of us knows" (141).

rightly calls it a painful idea that "in the periodic return of all things the human personality, with all its activities and suffering, will return as well."[3]

[563] Religion has never been at peace with philosophical theories that posit endless development or the total ruination of the world. All such theories fail to do justice to the value of personhood and tend to sacrifice it to the world as a whole. They further fail to appreciate the significance of the life of religion and morality and assign to it a position far below that of culture; they build only on immanent forces in the cosmos and fail to take into account divine reality or power. All religions, therefore, have another outlook on the future. They more or less clearly know of a struggle between good and evil; cherish the hope of the victory of the good, in which the virtuous are rewarded and the wicked are punished; and as a rule consider that future attainable in no other way than by a manifestation of supernatural forces.[4] Persian religion even expected the appearance, at the end of the third world period, of the third son of Zarathushtra, Saoshyant, who would introduce a thousand-year kingdom of peace and complete the redemptive work of his father.[5] Among the Muslims, along with belief in the return of Jesus, there gradually arose the expectation of a Mahdi who would take believers back to the golden age of the "four righteous Khalifs."[6] In Israel, future hopes were based on the foundation of the covenant God had established with Abraham and his seed. For this covenant is everlasting and is not nullified by human unfaithfulness.

The Old Testament hope is based on an anticipated restoration of the earth as the kingdom of God. All the prophets proclaim to Israel and Judah *a day of judgment and punishment*. The יוֹם יהוה (*yôm YHWH*), the time in which the Lord will have compassion on his people and inflict vengeance on their enemies, was viewed very differently by the prophets than by the people. The people misused this expectation and thought that—quite apart from their own spiritual state—YHWH would protect them from all danger (Jer. 28–29; Ezek. 33:23ff.; Amos 5:18; 6:13). But the prophets said that the day of the Lord would be a day of judgment for Israel as well. The people would be exiled and their land devastated (Isa. 2:11ff.; 5:5ff.; 7:18; Jer. 1:11–16; Hosea 1:6; 2:11; 3:4; 8:13; 9:3, 6; 10:6; 11:5; 13:12; 13:16; Joel 2:1ff.; Amos 2:4ff.; 5:16, 18, 27; 6:14; etc.; Mic. 3:12; 4:10; 7:13; Hab. 1:5–11; Zeph. 1:1–18; etc.). But this punishment is temporary. God's chastisement of his people is measured (Isa. 27:7ff.; Jer. 30:11). He leaves them only for a short while; his wrath is for a moment, but his loving-kindness is forever (Isa. 54:7–8). Prophetically prefigured in the return from Babylonian captivity,

3. W. Windelband, *Geschichte und Wissenschaft*, 3rd ed. (Strassburg: Heitz, 1904), 22; cf., H. Bavinck, *The Philosophy of Revelation* (New York: Longmans, Green, 1909), 242–315.

4. See H. Bavinck, *Reformed Dogmatics*, ed. John Bolt (Grand Rapids: Baker Academic, 2003–8), III, 238–40 (#351); A. Kuyper, *Van de voleinding* (Kampen: Kok, 1928–31), I, 64–127.

5. E. Lehmann, in P. D. Chantepie de la Saussaye, *Lehrbuch der Religionsgeschichte*, 2 vols. (Freiburg i.B.: Mohr [Siebeck], 1887–89), II, 225.

6. C. Snouck Hurgronje, *Der Mahdi* (Amsterdam, 1885; extract from the *Revue Coloniale Internationale*, 1 [1885]).

the conversion of Israel, and renewal of temple worship, the final expression of Israel's hope is cosmic—the gentiles share in the full blessing of a cleansed and transformed earth. While the Old Testament regards the messianic kingdom as the full establishment of the kingdom of God, and God sends the *Messiah* from the house of David, it also gives hints of a greater reality breaking through—the eternal, spiritual reign of God. It is important here to note that the prophets at the same time view Israel's return from exile as an ethical return, that is, as a *conversion*. Gathering together from among the nations and circumcision of the heart go together (Deut. 30:3–6). Not all return (Ezek. 20:34ff.; Hosea 2:13; Amos 9:8–10) but only a remnant (Isa. 4:3; 6:13; 7:3–25; 10:21; 11:11). The Lord will destroy the proud but rescue a poor and wretched people (Zeph. 3:12), and keep alive his work (Hab. 3:2). One from a city and two from a family will be brought back (Jer. 3:14); two-thirds will be cut off, but one-third will be purified (Zech. 13:8–9). Those who remain, however, will be a holy people to the Lord, a people to whom he betroths himself forever (Isa. 4:3–4; 11:9; Hosea 1:10–11; 2:15, 18, 22). He will forgive them, cleanse them, give them new hearts, pour out his Spirit on them, and make a new covenant with them (Isa. 43:25; 44:21–23; Jer. 31:31; Ezek. 11:19; 36:25–28; 37:14; Joel 2:28; Mic. 5:11–14; Zech. 13:2; etc.). Everything will be holy, even the bells of the horses (Zech. 14:20–21). For the glory of the Lord has risen over them (Isa. 60:1; Zech. 2:5), and God himself dwells among them (Hosea 2:22; Joel 3:17; Obad. 21; Zech. 2:10; 8:8; etc.).

In addition to a return from exile, the prophets point to the restoration of the *temple* and *the temple worship services*. Mount Zion will be a refuge (Obad. 17, 21); the Lord will dwell there and sanctify Jerusalem (Joel 3:17, 20); though Zion will be plowed as a field and Jerusalem reduced to a heap of ruins, still the mountain of the house of the Lord will be established as the highest of the mountains; out of Zion the law will go forth and the word of the Lord from Jerusalem, and the Lord will dwell in Zion (Mic. 3:12; 4:1–2; 7:11). Isaiah speaks in the same manner (2:2; 3:16–17; 28:16; 30:18, 19; 31:38; 33:18, 21; 33:5; 35:10; 52:1; 56:6–7; 60:7; 61:6; 66:20–23). Haggai predicts that the splendor of the second temple will be greater than that of the first (2:6–10), and Zechariah announces that Jerusalem will be rebuilt and expanded, that the priesthood and temple will be renewed, and that God will dwell in Jerusalem in the midst of his people (1:17; 2:1–5; 3:1–8; 6:9–15; 8:3ff.). But none of the prophets develops this vision of the future in such meticulous detail as Ezekiel (34–37; 40–48). Leaving aside the details for now, the point is that if Israel lives in accordance with God's ordinances, it will enjoy immense blessing. From under the threshold of the temple door flows a stream that becomes ever deeper, makes the land fertile, and even makes fresh the stagnant waters of the Dead Sea. On its banks on both sides of the river are trees whose fruit is for food and whose leaves are for healing.[7]

7. For a correct understanding of this vision, see A. B. Davidson, *The Theology of the Old Testament* (New York: Charles Scribner's Sons, 1914), 343ff.

The concrete, earthly, material blessings must not be overlooked. Under the Prince of Peace of the house of David, Israel will live securely. There will no longer be war: bow and sword will be abolished (Hosea 2:18); horses will be cut off, chariots destroyed, strongholds thrown down (Mic. 5:10–11); and swords will be beaten into plowshares and spears into pruning hooks. All will sit down under their vines and their fig trees (Isa. 2:4; Mic. 4:3–4), for the kingdom is the Lord's and he is their stronghold (Joel 3:16–17; Obad. 21). The land will become extraordinarily fertile, so that the mountains will drip sweet wine and the hills will flow with milk. A fountain issuing from the house of the Lord will irrigate the dry land and turn the desert into a Garden of Eden. Wild beasts will be driven away, enemies will no longer rob the harvest, and all the trees, seasonally refreshed by gentle rains, will bear abundant fruit (Isa. 32:15–20; 51:3; 60:17–18; 62:8–9; 65:9, 22; Jer. 31:6, 12–14; Ezek. 34:14, 25–26, 29; 36:29; 47:1–12; Hosea 2:15, 18–19; 14:5–7; Joel 3:18; Amos 9:13–14; Zech. 8:12; 14:8, 10). An enormous reversal will occur, even in nature: animals will receive a different nature (Isa. 11:6–8; 65:25), heaven and earth will be renewed, and the former things will no longer be remembered (34:4; 51:6; 65:17; 66:22). Sun and moon will be altered: the light of the moon will be like the sun, and the light of the sun will be seven times its normal strength (30:26). Indeed, the sun and moon will be no more: there will be continuous day, for the Lord will be the people's everlasting light (60:19–20; Zech. 14:6–7).

In the human world as well the change will be enormous. Once Israel is gathered, Palestine will resound with people (Mic. 2:12–13). The descendants of the children of Israel will be like the sand of the sea, and especially the progeny of the house of David and of the Levites will be multiplied (Isa. 9:3; Jer. 3:16; 33:22; Hosea 1:10). On account of the multitude of people and animals, Jerusalem will become immeasurable and will have to be inhabited like villages (Zech. 2:1–4). Many Israelites—after a number of them have been returned—will come to Jerusalem and share in the blessing of Israel (Jer. 3:14, 16, 18; Zech. 2:4–9; 8:7–8). Also the Israelites who have died will share in those blessings. All of Israel can then be said to have been brought back to life (Isa. 25:8; Ezek. 37:1–14; Hosea 6:2). Isaiah (26:19) and Daniel (12:2) announce that the defeated Israelites will arise from the sleep of death and at least in part awaken to everlasting life. Finally, all the citizens of the kingdom will reach a very advanced age. There will no longer be in it "an infant that lives but a few days, or an old person who does not live out a lifetime; for one who dies at a hundred years will be considered a youth, and one who falls short of a hundred will be considered accursed" (Isa. 65:20; cf. Zech. 8:4–5). There will no longer be sickness, nor mourning, nor crying (Isa. 25:8; 30:19; 65:19); the Lord will even destroy death, swallowing it up in victory (25:7).

Finally, the *gentiles* will share in that blessing of the kingdom of God. Woven throughout Old Testament prophecy is the thought that God will avenge the blood of his servants on his enemies. The prophets of God, therefore, announce God's judgments over several peoples: Philistia, Tyre, Moab, Ammon, Edom, Asshur, and Babel. But the final effect of these judgments is not the destruction but the salvation of the gentiles: in Abraham's seed all the nations of the earth will be blessed (Gen. 12:3). Granted, in one prophet it is more the political side of this subjection of the gentiles under Israel that comes to the fore, while in another it is the religious, spiritual side. All of them nevertheless expect that the rule of the Messiah will be extended to all peoples (cf. Pss. 2; 21; 24; 45; 46; 47; 48; 68; 72; 86; 89; 96; 98; etc.). Israel will, by hereditary right, possess the gentiles (Amos 9:12; Rev. 17–21). While they will be judged (Joel 3:2–15), everyone who calls on the name of the Lord will be saved, for in Mount Zion is deliverance (Joel 2:32 KJV). The Ruler from Bethlehem will be great to the ends of the earth and protect Israel from its enemies (Mic. 5:3ff.). Still, the gentiles will go to Mount Zion to discover the ways of the Lord (Mic. 4:1–2). Ethiopia will bring gifts to the Lord in Zion (Isa. 18:7). Egyptians and Assyrians will serve him (19:18–25). Tyre will hand over its profits to the Lord (23:15–18), and on Mount Zion he will prepare for all peoples a feast of rich food (25:6–10). Indeed, the servant of the Lord will be a light also to the gentiles. His messengers will make known the Lord among the nations of the earth, and he will be served by them. The Lord's house will be a house of prayer for all peoples. All will bring their sacrifices there, worship the Lord, and call themselves after his name. They will pasture Israel's flocks and cultivate its fields, so that the Israelites can completely devote themselves as priests to the service of the Lord (Isa. 40–66, passim). When Israel has been restored and Jerusalem is the throne of the Lord, all the gentiles will be gathered there around the name of the Lord, bless themselves, and boast in the Lord (Jer. 3:17; 4:2; 16:19–21; 33:9). In the end all peoples will acknowledge that the Lord is God (Ezek. 16:62; 17:24; 25:5ff.; 26:6; 28:22; 29:6; 30:8–26). All the gentiles will bring their treasures to Jerusalem and fill the house of the Lord with splendor (Hag. 2:7–10). Peoples will come and say to one another, "Let us go to entreat the favor of the LORD." "Ten men . . . will take hold of a Jew, grasping his garment and saying, 'Let us go with you, for we have heard that God is with you'" (Zech. 8:21–23; cf. 2:11; 14:16–19). The people of the holy ones will receive dominion over all the nations of the earth (Dan. 7:14, 27).

[564] These messianic expectations of the Old Testament, as any reader can see at once, are of a unique kind: they limit themselves to a future blessed state *on earth*. While in the Old Testament it may sometimes happen that a believer will express the hope that after death he will be taken up in eternal glory, this expectation is individual and stands by itself. As a rule, the eye of prophecy is directed toward that future in which the people of Israel will live securely under a king of David's dynasty in Palestine and will rule over all the nations of the earth. An assumption of believers into the heaven of glory at the end of time is not part of the Old Testament outlook. Salvation is expected on earth, not in heaven. In this connection Old Testament prophecy knows only of one coming of the Messiah. He will be a totally different king from the rulers of the earth; he will be humble, gentle, doing justice, and protecting his people; a prophet and priest as well as a

king. But Old Testament prophecy never clearly separates the Messiah's state of humiliation from the state of exaltation. It gathers up both in a single image and does not distinguish first coming for salvation from a second for judgment, a long time after the former. It is one single coming in which the Messiah bestows righteousness and blessedness on his people and brings it to dominion over all the peoples of the earth. The kingdom he is coming to establish, therefore, is the completed kingdom of God. He will govern his people as king, but in that capacity he is still no more than a theocratic king who does not rule in accordance with his own powers but in an absolute sense realizes the rule of God. Old Testament prophecy also does not make a temporal distinction between the rule of Christ and the rule of God. It does not view the future, which it depicts as being in the messianic kingdom, as an intermediate state that in the end must yield to a divine government in heaven. It regards the messianic kingdom as the final state and clearly views God's judgment over enemies, the repulsion of the final attack, the transformation of nature, and the resurrection from the dead as events that precede the initial and full establishment of this kingdom. And this kingdom is sketched by the prophets in hues and colors, under figures and forms, which have all been derived from the historical circumstances in which they lived; it is all described in terms of Israel's own history and nation. In that shell is an imperishable core that, sometimes even in the Old Testament itself, breaks through. Return from exile coincides with true conversion; the religious and political sides of Israel's victory over its enemies are most intimately bound up with each other; the Messiah is an earthly ruler but also an everlasting king, a king of righteousness, an eternal father to his people, a prince of peace, a priest-king. The enemies of Israel are subjected to Israel, but in the process acknowledge that the Lord is God and serve him in his temple. This temple with its priesthood and sacrificial worship are visible proof that all the citizens of the kingdom serve the Lord with a new heart and a new spirit and walk in his ways. And the extraordinary fertility of the land presupposes a total transformation of nature, the creation of a new heaven and a new earth, the home of righteousness.

CHILIASM

The major objection to chiliasm is that it overlooks the New Testament's own spiritual application of Old Testament prophecy. It is the old rather than the new covenant that is the real intermezzo in salvation history. Later Judaism introduced an assortment of changes in these Old Testament expectations. Robbed of political sovereignty and scattered among the nations, it began increasingly to take account of the future destiny of individuals and broadened its horizon to include humanity and the world as a whole. Someday—it was believed—on the basis of its own strictly law-abiding righteousness, Israel, led by the Messiah, would achieve political dominion over all nations. But this messianic kingdom was of a provisional and temporary kind. In the end it would make way for a kingdom of God, for a blessedness of the righteous in heaven, which would be introduced by the resurrection of all human beings and universal judgment. In that way the political and religious sides, which in the prophetic vision of the future were most intimately united, were torn apart. In Jesus's day Israel expected a tangible, earthly, messianic kingdom whose conditions were depicted in the forms and images of Old Testament prophecy. But when these forms and images were taken literally, the way was paved for chiliasm.

This is how the doctrine of chiliasm arose where frequently, especially in the *Apocalypse of Baruch* and *4 Ezra*, we find the view that the glory of the messianic kingdom is not the last and the highest. On the contrary, after a specific period of time, often calculated—for example, in the Talmud—at four hundred or one thousand years, this kingdom has to make room for the heavenly blessedness of the kingdom of God. Accordingly, chiliasm is not of Christian but of Jewish and Persian origin.[8] It is always based on a compromise between the expectations of an earthly salvation and those of a heavenly state of blessedness. It attempts to do justice to Old Testament prophecy in the sense that it accepts the earthly messianic kingdom predicted by it but claims that this kingdom will be replaced after a time by the kingdom of God. In Christian terms, chiliasm posits a twofold return of Christ and a double resurrection. The first establishes an earthly millennial kingdom, the second the final consummation.

Although the Old Testament is decidedly not chiliastic because its depiction of the messianic kingdom is one that lasts forever (Dan. 2:44), preceded by judgment, resurrection, and world renewal, chiliasm nevertheless found credence among the Jews and also with many Christians. It surfaced over and over when the world developed its power in opposition to God and brought suffering on the church by persecution and oppression. In the earliest period we encounter it in Cerinthus, in the *Testaments of the Twelve Patriarchs*, in the thought of the Ebionites in the *Epistle of Barnabas*, and in Papias, Irenaeus, Hippolytus, Apollinaris, Commodian, Lactantius, and Victorinus. Augustine resisted it most vigorously, while the changed situation of the church, which had overcome the world power of the day and increasingly viewed itself as the kingdom of God on earth, gradually prompted it to die out completely. It came up again before and during the Reformation, when many began to view Rome as the harlot of Revelation and the pope as the antichrist. It revived among the Anabaptists, the David-Jorists, and the Socinians and since then has not died out again although the official churches rejected it. Over and over political disturbances, the wars of religion, persecutions, and sectarian movements breathed new life into it. Even some Reformed theologians—Piscator, Alsted, Cocceius, Brakel, and others—tended toward a moderate form of chiliasm.

8. Cf. for the history of chiliasm, K. G. Semisch (rev. and enl. by E. Bratke), "Chiliasmus," in *PRE*³, III, 805–17; and G. E. Post, "Millennium," in *DB*, III, 370–73, and the literature cited there.

In the eighteenth and nineteenth centuries, under the pressure of societal and political upheavals, it found acceptance not only among Swedenborgians, Darbyists, Irwingians, Mormons, Adventists, and others, but was also embraced by many theologians in the churches of the Reformation.[9] The basic ideas of chiliasm are virtually the same in all its forms. They come down to the assertion that we must distinguish between a twofold return of Christ and a double resurrection. They go on to say that at his first return Christ will overcome the forces of the antichrist, bind Satan, raise the believers who have died, and gather the church around himself, in particular the community of Israel, now repentant and brought back to Palestine. From within that community he will rule over the world and usher in a period of spiritual florescence and material prosperity. At the end of that time he will return once more to raise all humans from the dead, judge them before his throne of judgment, and decide their eternal destiny.

Still, these basic thoughts allow for a multitude of incompatible variations all of which constitute as many objections against chiliasm. It cannot even stand before the tribunal of Old Testament prophecy, a court to which it loves to appeal. Chiliasm is guilty of the greatest arbitrariness in interpreting prophecy; it is devoid of all rule and method and arbitrarily calls a halt, depending on the subjective opinion of the interpreter. It is capricious to take one feature of the prophetic picture literally and another "spiritually." Prophecy pictures for us but one single image of the future. And either this image is to be taken literally as it presents itself—but then one breaks with Christianity and lapses back into Judaism—or this image calls for a very different interpretation than that attempted by chiliasm. Such an interpretation is furnished by Scripture itself, and we must take it from Scripture.

[565] In the Old Testament already there are numerous pointers to a new and better interpretation of the prophetic expectations than chiliasm offers. Even the modern view of the history of Israel recognizes that the Yahwism of the prophets distinguishes itself from the nature religions by its moral character and gradually gave a spiritual meaning to the religious laws and customs in use in Israel. True circumcision is that of the heart (Deut. 10:16; 30:6; Jer. 4:4). The sacrifices pleasing to God are a broken heart and a contrite spirit (1 Sam. 15:22; Pss. 40:6; 50:8ff.; 51:17; Isa. 1:11ff.; Jer. 6:20; 7:21ff.; Hosea 6:6; Amos 5:21ff.; Mic. 6:6ff.). The true fast is to loose the bonds of injustice (Isa. 58:3–6; Jer. 14:12). In large part the struggle of the prophets is directed against the external, self-righteous worship of the people. Accordingly, the essence of the future dispensation is that the Lord will make a new covenant with his people. He will give them new hearts and write his law on them. He will pour out his Spirit on all so that they will love him with their whole hearts and walk in his ways (Deut. 30:6; Jer. 31:32–34; 32:38f.; Ezek.

9. E.g., H. Martensen, *Christian Dogmatics*, trans. W. Urwick (Edinburgh: T&T Clark, 1871), §280; J. J. van Oosterzee, *Christian Dogmatics*, trans. J. Watson and M. Evans, 2 vols. (New York: Scribner, Armstrong, 1874), §146.

11:19; 36:26; Joel 2:28; Zech. 12:10). While it is true that this future is depicted in images derived from the historical circumstances of the prophet's own time, all of us do the same when speaking of God and his acts. The New Testament takes over this language and, in speaking about the future kingdom of God, refers to Zion and Jerusalem, to temple and altar, to prophets and priests. Literalistic realism also violates the character of prophetic language as poetry. Thinking of the future messianic king as a "shoot to come forth from the stump of Jesse" in a strictly literal manner makes Isaiah's wonderful image incomprehensible. Excessively realistic interpretations become self-contradictory, misjudge the nature of prophecy, and lead to faulty interpretation of the text.

The prophets themselves were aware of this. They knew the distinction between the thing [they asserted] and the image [in which they clothed it]. In the names for Sodom, Gomorrah, Edom, Moab, Philistia, Egypt, Asshur, and Babel they repeatedly refer to the power of the gentile world that will someday be subject to Israel and share in its blessings (Isa. 34:5; Ezek. 16:46ff.; Dan. 2:17ff.; Obad. 16–17; Zech. 14:12–21). Zion often serves as the name for the people, the believing community of God (Isa. 49:14; 51:3; 52:1). And although it is true that Old Testament prophecy cannot conceive of the future kingdom of God without a temple and sacrifice, over and over it *transcends* all national and earthly conditions. It proclaims, for example, that there will no longer be an ark of the covenant, since all Jerusalem will be God's throne (Jer. 3:16–17); that the kingdom of the Messiah will be everlasting and encompass the whole world (Pss. 2:8; 72:8, 17; Dan. 2:44); that the inhabitants will be prophets and priests (Isa. 54:13; 61:6; Jer. 31:31); that all impurity and sin, all sickness and death, will be banished from it (Ps. 104:35; Isa. 25:8; 33:24; 52:1, 11; Zech. 14:20–21); and that it will be established in a new heaven and on a new earth and will no longer need the sun or the moon (Isa. 60:19–20; 65:17; 66:22). Even Ezekiel's realistic picture of the future contains elements that require a symbolic interpretation such as the equal shares assigned to all the tribes, though in numbers [of tribal members] they vary widely. However, the question is not whether the prophets were totally or partly conscious of the symbolic nature of their predictions, for even in the words of classic authors there is more than they thought or intended. It is a question, rather, what the Spirit of Christ who was in them wished to declare and reveal by them. And *that* is decided by the New Testament, which is the completion, fulfillment, and therefore interpretation of the Old. The nature of a tree is revealed by its fruit. Even modern criticism recognizes that not Judaism but Christianity is the full realization of the religion of the prophets.

The New Testament views itself—and there can certainly be no doubt about this—as the spiritual and therefore complete and authentic fulfillment of the Old Testament. The spiritualization of the Old Testament, rightly understood, is not an invention of Christian theology but has its beginning in the New Testament. The Old Testament in spiritualized form, that is, the Old Testament stripped of its temporal and sensuous form, is the New Testament. The peculiar nature of the old dispensation consisted precisely in the fact that the covenant of grace was presented in graphic images and clothed in national and sensuous forms. Sin was symbolized by levitical impurity. Atonement was effected by the sacrifice of a slain animal. Purification was adumbrated by physical washings. Communion with God was connected with the journey to Jerusalem. The desire for God's favor and closeness was expressed in the longing for his courts. Eternal life was conceived as a long life on earth, and so forth. In keeping with Israel's level of understanding, placed as Israel was under the tutelage of the law, all that is spiritual, heavenly, and eternal was veiled in earthly shadows. Even though the great majority of the people frequently fixated on the external forms—just as many Christians in participating in the sacraments continue to cling to the external signs—and while devout Israelites with their hearts indeed penetrated to the spiritual core that was hidden in the shell, they nevertheless saw that spiritual core in no other way than in shadows and images.

For that reason the New Testament says that the Old was "a shadow of the things to come, but the substance belongs to Christ" (σκια των μελλοντων, το δε σωμα του Χριστου, *skia tōn mellontōn, to de sōma tou Christou*; Col. 2:17), "a model and shadow of the heavenly sanctuary" (ὑποδειγμα και σκια των ἐπουρανιων, *hypodeigma kai skia tōn epouraniōn*; Heb. 8:5). The shadow, while not itself the body, does point to the body but vanishes when the body itself appears. The New Testament is the truth, the essence, the core, and the actual content of the Old Testament. The Old Testament is revealed in the New, while the New Testament is concealed in the Old (*Vetus Testamentum in Novo patet, Novum Testamentum in Vetere latet*). For that reason the New Testament frequently refers to "the truth." Over against the law given by Moses stands the truth that came through Jesus Christ (John 1:14, 17). Jesus Christ is the truth (14:6), and the Spirit sent out by him is the Spirit of truth (16:13; 1 John 5:6). The Word of God he preached is the word of truth (John 17:17). The benefits of salvation promised and foreshadowed under the Old Testament have become manifest in Christ as eternal and authentic reality. All the promises of God are "yes" and "amen" in him (2 Cor. 1:20). The Old Testament was not abolished but fulfilled in the new dispensation, is still consistently being fulfilled, and will be fulfilled, until the parousia of Christ. All Old Testament concepts shed their external, national-Israelitish meanings and become manifest in their spiritual and eternal sense. Christ is, therefore, the true prophet, priest, and king; the true servant of the Lord, the true atonement (Rom. 3:25), the true circumcision (Col. 2:11), the true Passover (1 Cor. 5:7), the true sacrifice (Eph. 5:2), and his body of believers the true offspring of Abraham, the true Israel, the true people of God (Matt. 1:21; Luke 1:17; Rom. 9:25–26; 2 Cor. 6:16–18; Gal. 3:29; Titus 2:14; Heb. 8:8–10; James 1:1, 18; 1 Pet. 2:9; Rev. 21:3, 12). The New Testament gave to the particularistic ideas of the Old Testament a universal and cosmic meaning.

Totally wrong, therefore, is the chiliastic view according to which the New Testament, along with the church composed of gentiles, is an intermezzo, a detour taken by God because Israel rejected its Messiah, so that the continuation and fulfillment of the Old Testament can begin only with Christ's second coming. The opposite, rather, is true. Not the New Testament but the Old is an intermezzo. The covenant with Israel is temporary; the law has been inserted between the promise to Abraham and its fulfillment in Christ, that it might increase the trespass and be a disciplinarian leading to Christ (Rom. 5:20; Gal. 3:24ff.). For that reason Paul always goes back to Abraham (Rom. 4:11ff.; Gal. 3:6ff.) and links his gospel to the promise made to him. Abraham is the father of believers, of *all* believers, not only believers from among the Jews, but also from among the gentiles (Rom. 4:11). The children of the promise are his offspring (9:6–8). In Christ the blessing of Abraham comes to the gentiles (Gal. 3:14). Those who belong to Christ are Abraham's offspring and heirs according to the promise (3:29).

Israel was chosen, not to the detriment of but for the benefit of the nations. From its earliest beginning the promise to Adam and Noah had a universal thrust. In Christ, the curtain has been torn, the dividing wall has fallen, the handwriting of the law has been nailed to the cross. Now gentile believers, along with Jews, as fellow heirs, fellow citizens, fellow saints, fellow members of the household of God, have been brought near in Christ and are built upon the same foundation of apostles and prophets (Eph. 1:9–11; 2:11–22).

Therefore the New Testament is not an intermezzo or interlude, neither a detour nor a departure from the line of the old covenant, but the long-aimed-for goal, the direct continuation and the genuine fulfillment of the Old Testament. Chiliasm, judging otherwise, comes in conflict with Christianity itself. In principle it is one with Judaism and must get to where it attributes a temporary, passing value to Christianity, the historical person of Christ, and his suffering and death, and it only first expects real salvation from Christ's second coming, his appearance in glory. Chiliasm reinforces the veil that lies over the minds of the Jewish people when they hear the reading of the Old Testament, and promotes the illusion that the physical descendants of Abraham will as such still enjoy an advantage in the kingdom of heaven. Scripture, on the other hand, tells us that the true reading and interpretation of the Old Testament is to be found with those who have turned in repentance to the Lord Christ (2 Cor. 3:14–16). It tells us that a person is a Jew who is one inwardly, and that circumcision is a matter of the heart (Rom. 2:29). It teaches that in Christ there is neither man nor woman, neither Jew nor Greek, but that they are all one in Christ Jesus (1 Cor. 12:13; Gal. 3:28; Col. 3:11). The Jewish person who becomes a Christian was not a child of Abraham but becomes such by faith (Gal. 3:29).[10]

10. Against chiliasm, cf. also Augustine, *City of God*, XX, chaps. 6–9; Luther in Julius Köstlin, *The Theology of Luther*, trans. Charles E. Hay, 2 vols. (Philadelphia: Lutheran Publication Society, 1897), II, 575; J. Gerhard, *Loci theologici*, ed. E. Preuss, 9 vols. (Berlin: G. Schlawitz, 1863–75), XXIX, chap. 7; Johann Andreas Quenstedt, *Theologia didactico-polemica sive systema theologicum* (1685), IV, 649; J. Calvin, *Institutes of the Christian Religion*, III.xxv.5 (ed. John T. McNeill and trans. Ford Lewis Battles [Philadelphia: Westminster, 1960], 2:994–96); A. Walaeus, *Opera omnia* (Leiden, 1643), I, 537–54;

ISRAEL, THE MILLENNIUM, AND CHRIST'S RETURN

[566] Although in the previous section we generally established that the New Testament is antichiliastic,[11] we do need to demonstrate this in greater detail. The chiliast expectation that a converted nation of Israel, restored to the land of Palestine, under Christ will rule over the nations is without biblical foundation. There are variations among chiliasts about such questions whether the conversion will precede the return or vice versa,[12] but all the scenarios involving Zionism and a possible return of Jews to Palestine have nothing to do with New Testament eschatology. When the fullness of time had come, the Jews, considered as a nation, were on the same level as the gentiles, worthy of condemnation. For that reason, God sent John to them with the baptism of repentance, and Jesus followed in his tracks. He took over John's baptism and had it administered by his disciples. Like John he publicly proclaimed that the kingdom was drawing near, but he understood very differently from his contemporaries; for him it was not a political but a religious-ethical dominion in which rebirth from water and Spirit gave a person access to the kingdom of heaven rather than physical descent from Abraham. As a result he gradually gathered around him a group of disciples that distinguished and separated itself from the Jewish people. These were the true ἐκκλησια (*ekklēsia*, church), the real people of God, as Israel should have been but now in its rejection of the Messiah proved itself not to be. Whatever the political future of Israel as a nation, the real *ekklēsia*, the people of God, transcends ethnic boundaries.

This separation between the Jews and the New Testament *ekklēsia* became increasingly sharper. As a whole the people rejected him. Although a rising for some, for many he was to be a falling and a sign that was opposed (Luke 2:34). He came to his own people, but they did not accept him (John 1:11). Jesus himself says that "prophets are not without honor except in their own country" (Matt. 13:57). Over and over he experienced that the Jews did not wish to come to him (John 5:37–47; 6:64); he testified that they would die in their sin (8:21), that

---

Gisbert Voetius, *Selectae disputations theologicae*, 5 vols. (Utrecht, 1648–69), II, 1248–72; F. Turretin, *Institutes of Elenctic Theology*, trans. G. M. Giger, ed. J. T. Dennison, 3 vols. (Phillipsburg, NJ: Presbyterian & Reformed, 1992), XX, q. 3; B. de Moor, *Comm. theol.*, VI, 149–62; E. W. Hengstenberg, *Openbaring van Johannes* ('s Hertogenbosch: Muller, 1852); C. F. Keil, *Biblical Commentary on the Prophecies of Ezekiel*, trans. J. Martin (repr., Grand Rapids: Eerdmans, 1970), II, 382–434; Th. Kliefoth, *Christliche Eschatologie* (Leipzig: Dörffling & Franke, 1886), 147ff.; F. A. Philippi, *Kirchliche Glaubenslehre*, 3rd ed., 7 vols. (Gütersloh: Bertelsmann, 1883–1902), VI, 214ff.; C. Hodge, *Systematic Theology* (New York: Charles Scribner's Sons, 1888), III, 805; B. B. Warfield, "The Millennium and the Apocalypse," *Princeton Theological Review* 2 (October 1904): 599–617; G. Vos, "The Pauline Eschatology and Chiliasm," *Princeton Theological Review* 9 (January 1911): 26–60; H. Hoekstra, *Het chiliasme* (Kampen: Kok, 1903); A. Kuyper, *Van de voleinding*, IV, 254–62, 318–48.

11. According to A. Kuenen, *The Prophets and Prophecy in Israel*, trans. Adam Milroy (London: Longmans, Green, 1877; repr., Amsterdam: Philo, 1969).

12. É. Guers, *Israel in the Last Days*, trans. Aubrey Price (London: Wertheim, MacIntosh, & Hunt, 1862), 155–57.

they were children of their father the devil (8:44), plants not planted by the Father (Matt. 15:13–14); and he regarded their unbelief not as an accidental, unforeseen circumstance but as the fulfillment of prophecy (Matt. 13:13–15; John 12:37ff.). Not only did Jesus not expect anything *from* the Jews in the present; in the future also he expected nothing *for* them. On the contrary, he announced the total destruction of the city and the temple so that not one stone would be left upon another (Matt. 22:7; 23:37–39; 24:1ff.; Mark 13; Luke 21:6ff.; John 2:18–21). During his entry into Jerusalem he wept over the city (Luke 19:41–44). On the occasion of his going to the cross, he commanded the women not to weep over him but to weep over [the people of] Jerusalem (Luke 23:28). He even proclaimed that the salvation rejected by Israel would be shared by the gentiles. The kingdom of God would be taken from Israel and given to a people who would produce the fruits of that kingdom (Matt. 21:43). The vineyard would be rented out to other tenants (21:41). Invited to the wedding are the people from the main streets (22:9). The lost son takes precedence over the older son (Luke 15). Similarly, Jesus states that many would come from the east and the west and sit down in the kingdom of heaven with Abraham, Isaac, and Jacob (Matt. 8:10–12), and that he has other sheep not of this sheepfold (John 10:16). He rejoices that, as certain Greeks desire to see him, he will soon, like a grain of wheat, fall into the earth and die and so bear much fruit (John 12:24). Accordingly, after his resurrection he instructs his disciples to preach the gospel to all nations (Matt. 28:18–20).

In the case of the apostles we encounter the same judgment concerning Israel. As Jesus's witnesses they must indeed begin their work in Jerusalem but then continue to the ends of the earth (Acts 1:8). Peter therefore immediately brings the gospel to the Jews (2:14; 3:19; 5:31) but then learns in a vision that from then on no one is unclean but that anyone who fears God, no matter in what nation he has been born, is acceptable to him (10:35, 43). Paul always begins his preaching among the Jews, but when they reject it, he turns to the gentiles (13:46; 18:6; 28:25–28). "First to the Jew but then also to the Greek" is the rule he observes on his missionary journeys (Rom. 1:16; 1 Cor. 1:21–24). For both Jews and gentiles are worthy of condemnation before God and need the same gospel (Rom. 3:19ff.). There is but one way to salvation for all, faith—the faith as it was practiced by Abraham even before the law came, and was reckoned to him as righteousness (Rom. 4:22; Gal. 3). Those of the Jews who reject Christ are not really true Jews (Rom. 2:28–29). The Jews who slander the church of Smyrna, though they say they are Jews, are not; rather they are a synagogue of Satan (Rev. 2:9; 3:9). Real Jews, the true children of Abraham, are those who believe in Christ (Rom. 9:8; Gal. 3:29; etc.). This is the New Testament's judgment concerning the Jews. The community of believers has in all respects replaced carnal, national Israel. The Old Testament is fulfilled in the New.[13]

13. Cf. A. Harnack, *The Mission and Expansion of Christianity*, trans. J. Moffatt (New York: Harper, 1908), 53ff.

[567] There are a few passages that seem to be at variance with this consistent teaching of Scripture and to mean something different. The first is Matthew 23:37–39 (Luke 13:34–35), where Jesus tells the inhabitants of Jerusalem that their house will be left to them desolate and that they will not see him again until they say, "Blessed is the one who comes in the name of the Lord." Here Jesus in fact expresses the expectation that one day, namely, at his return, the Jews will recognize him as the Messiah. But there is nothing here about a mass conversion or a rebuilding of the city and the temple prior to his return; in fact, Jesus here expressly states that Jerusalem will be left desolate until then. Jesus is not saying that the trampling of Jerusalem will end before his parousia, for after having pronounced judgment over Jerusalem, he immediately proceeds to discuss the signs that will occur before and at his return (Luke 21:25ff.). The times of the gentiles continue until his return. Again, if the New Testament taught a twofold return of Christ, this passage could be interpreted in terms of it, but it will become evident in a moment that there is no ground in the New Testament for this position. A second passage to be considered is Luke 21:24, where Jesus says that Jerusalem will be trampled on by the gentiles until the times of the gentiles are fulfilled. The conjunction "until" (ἄχρι, *achri*) does not suggest or imply that, with the onset of the period described in the following clause, the opposite will occur (the Jews will rebuild and inhabit Jerusalem). But even if this were the case, Jesus does not say that this trampling of Jerusalem will cease prior to his return; he immediately follows this text with a discussion of the signs that will occur prior to and at his return.

The third text that comes up in this connection is Acts 3:19–21, where Peter calls the Jews to repentance that their sins may be wiped out, times of refreshing (καιροι ἀναψυξεως, *kairoi anapsyxeōs*) may come from the presence of the Lord, and he, that is, God, may send the Messiah appointed for the Jews, that is, Jesus, who must remain in heaven until the time of the restoration of all things. It is difficult to consider "times of refreshing" to begin when the Jewish people are converted and all things are again restored in the millennium in keeping with their original destiny, and that these "times" will then last until the second return of Christ. The times of universal restoration (χρονοι ἀποκαταστασεως παντων, *chronoi apokatastaseōs pantōn*) can hardly be understood as the restoration of natural and moral relations expected by chiliasts in the millennium. We are clearly told that these times occur at the end of Jesus's stay in heaven. Until that time, then, Jesus will be at his Father's right hand and, since Scripture knows of only one return of Christ, the times of the restoration of all things will coincide with the consummation of the world. In addition, the expression "the restoration of all things" (ἀποκαταστασις παντων, *apokatastasis pantōn*) is much too strong for the restoration of the Jewish kingdom expected by chiliasm. Accordingly, the times of refreshing are not identical with but precede the times of the restoration of all things. The most probable interpretation of "times of refreshing" is that they take place at certain future times of divine blessing and favor. Then what Peter says here is this: "Repent, O Jews, that your sins may be wiped out, so that for you too, as a people who have handed over, rejected, and killed Christ (Acts 3:13–15), times of refreshing may come from the presence of the Lord, and God may afterward send the Christ who was appointed for you in the first place (Acts 3:26) in order, also for your salvation, to restore all things." Whether such times will ever come for the Jews, Peter does not say. That depends on their conversion, a conversion of which nothing is said to suggest that it is to be expected.

The most challenging passage is Romans 11:11–32, particularly the phrase in verse 26: ". . . in this way all Israel will be saved." In Romans 9–11 Paul deals with the awesome problem of how God's promise to Israel can be squared with the rejection of the gospel by the greater majority of the people of Israel. In response, the apostle replies in the first place that the promise of God concerns not the carnal but the spiritual offspring of Abraham, and he works this out in great detail in chapters 9 and 10. In the second place he remarks that God still has his elect also in Israel and therefore has not rejected that people. Paul himself is proof of this, and many others with him. Although many have become hard and blind, the elect have received salvation; there has consistently been a remnant chosen by grace (Rom. 11:1–10). But this hardening that has come over the great majority of the people of Israel is not God's final goal. In his hand it is rather a means to bring salvation to the gentiles in order that they, accepting that salvation in faith, may in turn arouse Israel to jealousy (11:11–15). After admonishing believers from the gentiles not to boast of their advantage (11:16–24), Paul further develops this thought, saying that a hardening has come over a part of Israel until the πληρωμα (*plērōma*) of the gentiles, the full number of those from their midst who were destined for salvation, has come in (11:25). In that way, in keeping with God's promise, all Israel will be saved. Hence, though now the unbelieving Jews are enemies of God as regards the gospel in order that the salvation they have rejected should come to the gentiles, as regards election they are beloved for the sake of their ancestors, for God's promises are irrevocable. Therefore, just as things were with the gentiles, so will they go with the Jews who are hardened. First the gentiles were disobedient and now they receive mercy, so now the Jews too are disobedient that through the mercy shown to the gentiles, they may receive mercy as well. For God has imprisoned all, gentiles and Jews, in disobedience so that he may be merciful to all (11:25–32).

Most interpreters think that the question of whether God has rejected his people (Rom. 11:1) has not been fully answered by the assertion that in Israel God always has his elect, the people who, in the course of centuries, are successively brought in (11:1–10). By "all Israel" (πας Ἰσραηλ, *pas Israēl*) they therefore understand that in the last days the whole of the people of Israel will repent and turn to the Lord. But no matter how commonly this explanation is held, there are weighty objections to it. The most obvious is that it places Paul at odds with himself. In 9:6ff., he stated that the promises of God have not failed because they concern the spiritual offspring of Abraham and will still consistently find their fulfillment in this spiritual offspring (11:1–10). To then say that it is Paul's intent in Romans 11:25–32 to give a new, supplementary answer, involving the salvation of physical Israel, his reasoning at the end would contradict his beginning and starting point. It is a priori very unlikely that Paul later reconsidered this reasoning, supplementing and improving it in the sense that the promises of God are not fully realized in the salvation of spiritual Israel, but will be fully realized only when in the last days a national conversion of Israel takes place. Furthermore, Paul does not breathe a word about such an expectation for the people of Israel in Romans 9:1–11:10. There is nothing that prepares or intimates it, and even 11:11–24 as yet contains nothing that points to it. But even if these words were to be understood as the description of a fact, they convey no more than the idea that Israel's rejection of Christ was a great gain for the gentiles for by it the reconciliation effected by Christ's death fell to the gentiles. If that was the case, how much more will the gentiles be blessed when Israel has reached its πληρωμα (*plērōma*), because then, when the plērōma of the gentiles has entered in, the resurrection from the dead will take place. The gentile world owes its reconciliation, mediately speaking, to Israel's failure; to Israel's fullness (*plērōma*) it will someday owe its life from the dead.

In Romans 11:26 Paul is not seeking to convey a new fact for he does not say *and then*, or *thereupon*, that is, after the fullness of the gentiles has come in, all Israel will, but "and in *that way* all Israel will be saved" (και ούτως πας Ἰσραηλ σωθησεται, *kai houtōs pas Israēl sōthēsetai*). That can only point back to the preceding verses. Just prior to this, in verse 25, Paul stated that a hardening has come over only a part (ἀπο μερους, *apo merous*) of Israel. Lest believers among the gentiles begin to think—as Israel used to think—that they alone were the elect people of God and that Israel was totally rejected, Paul says No! Israel as such has not been rejected; the hardening that has come *upon a part* of Israel is a mystery (μυστηριον, *mystērion*; 11:25); among them there has always been a remnant chosen by grace. True enough, some branches have been broken off, and in their place a wild olive shoot has been grafted in, but the stem of the tame olive tree has been preserved. When the *plērōma* (fullness) of the gentiles comes in, also the *plērōma* of Israel is brought in, and *in that way* all Israel is saved. Paul is simply saying here what he does elsewhere: gentiles are now fellow heirs and fellow citizens with the saints, fellow members of the household of God. Never, until the end of the ages, will God totally reject his ancient people; alongside a part from the gentile world, he will always bring to faith in Christ a part from Israel as well. The gentiles, but also the Jews, had deserved a very different fate. But this is the great mystery: that God is rich in mercy; that he gathers his elect from every nation, also that of the Jews who rejected him; that he imprisoned all in disobedience that he might be merciful to all. That mystery sends the apostle into ecstasy and causes him to marvel at and adore the depth of God's wisdom and knowledge (11:33–36). "All Israel" (πας Ἰσραηλ, *pas Israēl*) in 11:26 is not, therefore, the people of Israel that at the end of time will be converted en masse. Nor is it the church of the Jews and the gentiles together. But it is the *plērōma* that in the course of centuries will be brought in from Israel. A full *plērōma* will come from the gentile world, as well as from Israel, and that *plērōma* will be all Israel (*pas Israēl*). In that *plērōma* all Israel is saved, just as in the church as a whole the whole of humanity is being saved.

In conclusion, it should be noted that even if Paul expected a national conversion of Israel at the end, he does not say a word about the return of the Jews to Palestine, about a rebuilding of the city and a temple, about a visible rule of Christ. In his picture of the future there simply is no room for all of this.

[568] In our discussion of the expectations that the New Testament fosters with regard to the future of the people of Israel, we left undecided the question whether the New Testament, in passages other than the ones cited in this connection so far, perhaps taught the existence of an interim state between this dispensation and the consummation of the ages. We acknowledged that if this were the case, Matthew 23:37–39; Luke 21:24; and Acts 3:19–21, although by themselves giving us no reason whatever for the acceptance of a transitional period, could nevertheless be understood and explained along those lines. We now face the question, therefore, whether according to Jesus and the apostles there awaits the church a period of power and glory that precedes the general resurrection of the dead and the event of world judgment. If this were so, we would expect clear mention of it in the eschatological discourse that Jesus gave his disciples in the final days of his life (Matt. 24; Mark 13; Luke 21). But in this discourse not a word is said, not even an allusion is made, about such a kingdom. The New Testament nowhere suggests that the church of Christ will ever achieve earthly power and dominion such as that of Old Testament Israel. Instead, like its Master, the pilgrim church can expect a cross of persecution and suffering. The New Testament does not recommend virtues that lead believers to conquer the world but rather patiently to endure its enmity.

In his eschatological discourse Jesus responds to two questions put to him by his disciples: one about the fall of Jerusalem and the other about his parousia. Jesus answers the first by pointing to the early signs (Mark 13:1–8; cf. Matt. 24:1–8; Luke 21:5–11), then with the fate of the disciples (Mark 13:9–13; cf. Matt. 24:9–14; Luke 21:12–19), and finally with the catastrophe in Judea (Mark 13:14–23; cf. Matt. 24:15–28; Luke 21:20–24). The second question, the one concerning the parousia of Jesus and the consummation of the world, is answered in Mark 13:24–31 (cf. Matt. 24:29–35; Luke 21:25–33). In this connection Jesus links his parousia immediately with the destruction of Jerusalem. In the fall of this city he sees the announcement and preparation of the consummation of the world (Matt. 24:29, "immediately," εὐθέως, *eutheōs*; Mark 13:24, "in those days," ἐν ἐκείναις ταῖς ἡμέραις, *en ekeinais tais hēmerais*). He even states that "this generation will certainly not pass away until all these things have taken place" (Matt. 24:34; Mark 13:30; Luke 21:32). However we understand this expectation of Jesus, in any case it is clearly evident that in this discourse there is no room for a thousand-year glorious kingdom on earth. Jesus only knows of two aeons: the present and the future aeons, and in the former good and evil, the wheat and the tares, remain together side by side (Matt. 13:37–43, 47–50). In the present aeon [age] his disciples cannot expect anything other than oppression and persecution and must forsake all things for his sake. Jesus nowhere predicts a glorious future on earth before the end of the world. A disciple is not above his teacher, nor a slave above the master; his disciples will suffer as he did. Only in the age to come will his disciples receive everything back along with eternal life (Matt. 19:27–30; cf. Matt. 5:3–12; 8:19–20; 10:16–42; 16:24–27; John 16:2, 33; 17:14–15; etc.). Accordingly, when the disciples in Acts 1:6 ask Jesus whether this is the time he will restore the kingdom to Israel, he does not deny it but tacitly admits that this will happen someday. But he says that the Father has set the times or seasons for this by his own authority, and that in this period the disciples have the calling to act as his witnesses from Jerusalem to the ends of the earth.

The whole New Testament, which was written from the viewpoint of the "church under the cross," speaks the same language. Believers, not many of whom are wise, powerful, or of noble birth (1 Cor. 1:26), should not expect anything on earth other than suffering and oppression (Rom. 8:36; Phil. 1:29). They are sojourners and foreigners (Heb. 11:13); their citizenship is in the heavens (Phil. 3:20); they do not look at the things that can be seen (2 Cor. 4:18), but mind the things that are above (Col. 3:2). Here they have no lasting city but are looking for the city that is to come (Heb. 13:14). They are saved in hope (Rom. 8:24) and know that if they suffer with Christ they will also be glorified with him (Rom. 6:8; 8:17; Col. 3:4). Therefore, along with the entire groaning creation, they wait with eager longing for the future of Christ and for the revelation of the glory of the children of God (Rom. 8:19, 21; 1 Cor. 15:48ff.), a glory with which the sufferings of the present time are not worth comparing (Rom. 8:18; 2 Cor. 4:17). Nowhere in the New Testament is there a ray of hope that the church of Christ will again come to power and dominion on earth. The most it may look for is that, under kings and all who are in high positions, it may lead a quiet and peaceable life in all godliness and dignity (Rom. 13:1; 1 Tim. 2:2). Therefore, the New Testament does not first of all recommend the virtues that enable believers to conquer the world but, while it bids them avoid all false as-ceticism (Rom. 14:14; 1 Tim. 4:4–5; Titus 1:15), lists as fruits of the Spirit the virtues of "love, joy, peace, patience, kindness, generosity, faithfulness, gentleness, and self-control" (Gal. 5:22–23; Eph. 4:32; 1 Thess. 5:14ff.; 1 Pet. 3:8ff.; 2 Pet. 1:5–7; 1 John 2:15; etc.).

It is a constant New Testament expectation that to the extent to which the gospel of the cross is spread abroad, to that extent the hostility of the world will be manifested as well. Christ is destined to be a rising for many but also to be a falling for many, and to bring out into the open the hostile thoughts of many. He has come into the world for judgment (κρίσις, *krisis*) so that those who do not see may see and that those who see may become blind (Matt. 21:44; Luke 2:34; John 3:19–21; 8:39; Rom. 9:32–33; 1 Cor. 1:23; 2 Cor. 2:16; Heb. 4:12; 1 Pet. 2:7–8). In the last days, the days that precede the return of Christ, the wickedness of human beings will rise to a fearful level. The days of Noah will return. Lust, sensual pleasures, lawlessness, greed, unbelief, pride, mockery, and slander will erupt in fearful ways (Matt. 24:37ff.; Luke 17:26ff.; 2 Tim. 3:1ff.; 2 Pet. 3:3; Jude 18). Among believers as well there will be extensive apostasy. Temptations will be so powerful that, if it were possible, even the elect would be caused to fall. The love of many will grow cold, and vigilance will diminish to the extent that the wise will fall asleep along with the foolish virgins. Apostasy will be so general that Jesus can ask whether at his coming the Son of Man will still find faith on earth (Matt. 24:24, 44ff.; 25:1ff.; Luke 18:8; 1 Tim. 4:1).

The book of Revelation, which John wrote, is in agreement with this. The letters to the seven churches deal with concrete conditions prevailing in those churches at the time and are first of all addressed to those churches to incite them to watchfulness and to prepare them for the coming persecutions and the return of Christ. Still, their intent and import are clearly much broader. The number seven, which in Revelation is consistently charged with symbolic meaning, already points in that direction. It is the number of completeness and makes the seven churches, which have here been selected from among the many churches in Asia Minor, appear as types of the Christian church as a whole. The letters addressed by John to the churches did not first have a separate existence but belong together, were composed together and joined to each other, and are addressed to the whole church: "Let anyone who has an ear listen to what the Spirit is saying to all the churches." But this broader significance is not that they describe successive periods in the history of Jesus's church and together make up a little compendium of the whole history of the church. Instead, they depict church conditions that were then present and are at the same time typical for the church of Christ as a whole, conditions that may recur over and over in the church and will recur especially at the end of history. For it is clear that they were all written under the impression of approaching persecution and the speedy return of Christ. They all contain a reference to the parousia, and with a view to it they exhort the churches to be watchful and faithful. They serve to call an increasingly worldly Christianity back to its first love, to arouse it from apathy, and, with an eye toward the crown awaiting it, to equip it for battle and to prompt it to persevere, with unyielding loyalty, even unto death.

John alternately positions the reader on earth and in heaven. In heaven, for there everything has already been settled and determined; there honor is already being brought to God and to the Lamb; there the battle has, as it were, already been fought and won (Rev. 4 and 5). There the souls of the martyrs are already clothed in long white garments and await the fulfillment of their number (6:9–11). There John proleptically sees the whole multitude of the redeemed standing before the throne (7:9–17). There the prayers of the saints have already been heard by God (8:1–4). There, proleptically as well, the 144,000 who were sealed (7:1–8) have been taken up; as firstfruits they precede the rest (14:1–5) and have gained victory over the beast and his image (15:1–4). There the whole multitude of the redeemed are already bringing glory and honor to God since the marriage of the Lamb has come (19:1–8).

The church on earth therefore does not need to be afraid of the judgments with which God in the end visits the world. The 144,000 servants of God out of every tribe of the sons of Israel are sealed in advance (Rev. 7:1–8). The Christian church, though persecuted by Satan for Christ's sake, finds a place of refuge in the wilderness (12:1–14). In principle, the battle has been decided and Satan has been defeated (12:5, 7–11) and has but little time left on earth (12:12). He effects the rise of the beast (11:7; 13:1; 17:8) and gives it power and glory. This beast (the Roman Empire; 13:1–10) is supported by the beast of the earth—the false prophet, false religion, the antichrist (13:11–18)—who comes to full development in a single person (13:3, 12, 18; 17:8, 10–11) and has his center "Babylon" (Rome), the great harlot, who rules over all the nations (Rev. 17–18). But this massive development of power is futile. By opening the seven seals, by blowing the seven trumpets, by emptying the seven bowls, God displays his wrath, visits nature and humanity with his judgments, and makes preparations for the final judgment. First "Babylon" falls (Rev. 18). Then Christ appears (19:11–16) and conquers the beast from the sea and the beast of the earth (19:19–21), and soon Satan as well (20:1–3).

[569] Now it is very peculiar that this last victory over Satan occurs in two phases. First he is bound for a thousand years and thrown into the bottomless pit; then he again deceives the nations and makes war against the church. But finally he is overcome for good and thrown into the lake of fire and brimstone (Rev. 20:1–10). Proponents of chiliasm find in this pericope—aside from the Old Testament—their most powerful support, while opponents are not a little perplexed at this passage and have tested all their exegetical skills on it. The idea that, following the conquest of the world empire, a final attack from the side of the nations still has to be repulsed is one that John undoubtedly borrowed from Ezekiel. The latter expects that Israel, having returned to its own land and living there in security, will once more be attacked by Gog of the land of Magog, the chief prince of Meshech and Tubal, that is, the nation of the Scythians allied with a variety of other nations from the north, east, and south. The attack ends, however, when God himself in his wrath destroys these nations on the mountains of Israel (Ezek. 38–39). Now the Old Testament prophets who proclaimed the day of the Lord did indicate that God would judge not only those historical nations in the midst of whom Israel lived and with whom it came in contact, but all the pagans living far off as well (Isa. 25:5–8; 26:21; Jer. 12:14–16; 30:23–24; Dan. 11:40–45; Joel 2:32; 3:2, 11ff.; Mic. 4:5, 11–13; 5:7–9; Zech. 12–14). The expectation of prophecy was twofold: it envisioned first a victory of the people of God over the nations in whose midst it lived and then a victory over the nations that up until then had not yet appeared on the stage of world history. This

double expectation passed into the apocryphal literature[14] and also into the New Testament. The first expectation is, of course, in the foreground. The appearance of Christ arouses and activates the anti-Christian principle. Jesus speaks of false prophets (ψευδοπροφηται, *pseudoprophētai*) and false Christs (ψευδοχριστοι, *pseudochristoi*), who position themselves against him and his kingdom (Matt. 7:15; 24:5, 24; Mark 13:21–22; Luke 17:23). In 2 Thessalonians 2, Paul points out that the day of Christ will not come unless the apostasy and the man of sin come first. There is now something restraining him; what is at work already is the mystery of lawlessness (το μυστηριον της ἀνομιας, *to mystērion tēs anomias*). The Apocalypse sees anti-Christian power embodied in the beast from the sea (the Roman Empire), whose head is a specific emperor, and parallel to this, in the beast of the earth, false prophecy that seduces people into worshiping the world empire and its emperor. In his letters, John first calls this adversary of Christ by the name of antichrist (ἀντιχριστος, *antichristos*), and he sees his essence realized in those who in principle deny the coming of Christ in the flesh (1 John 2:22; 4:2–3; 2 John 7).

Since Scripture's portrait of the antichrist is diverse, it is evident that in seeing the word "antichrist," we must think not exclusively of one person or of a group of persons—the Roman Empire, Nero, the Jews, Muhammad, the pope, Napoleon, and the like—but of a power that has its own history, manifests itself at different times and in different ways and finally evolves into a general apostasy, embodies itself in a world empire that utilizes the false church, and apotheosizes itself by deifying the head of that empire. Christ himself, by his appearing, then destroys this anti-Christian power in its highest and latest manifestation.[15] But with this, complete victory has not yet been achieved. In the nature of the case the anti-Christian principle can only become active in those nations that have known the gospel and have finally, in conscious and deliberate hostility, rejected it. That is why Jesus says (Matt. 24:14) that the end will not come until the gospel has been preached throughout the entire inhabited world as a testimony to all nations. This certainly does not imply that someday Christianity will be the dominant religion in all nations, or that it will be known to all people individually, but that preaching of the gospel will eventually get through to all nations. It by no means defines the measure in which, or the limits to which, this will happen.

It is this reality that is reflected in the twentieth chapter of John's Revelation. Because we read there of a thousand-year binding of Satan and of martyrs living and ruling with Christ in that time, many have believed that here, in clear, undeniable language, a thousand-year reign is being taught. In fact, however, this interpretation of Revelation 20, though it is in accord with the analogy of apocryphal literature,

---

14. Emil Schürer, *The History of the Jewish People in the Age of Jesus Christ (175 B.C.–A.D. 135)*, rev. and ed. G. Vermès and F. Millar (Edinburgh: T&T Clark, 1979), II, 525–26.

15. Cf. F. A. E. Sieffert, "Antichrist," in *PRE*[3], I, 577–84; M. R. James, "Man of Sin and Antichrist," in *DB*, III, 226–28, and the literature cited here.

is not in accord with the analogy of Scripture.[16] Revelation 20 as such contains nothing of all the things that belong to the essence of chiliastic belief. Why? The chapter says nothing about a conversion and return of the Jews, of the rebuilding of Jerusalem, of a restoration of the temple and temple worship, or of an initial renewal of the earth. Nowhere does it say that dead Christians will arise and live in Jerusalem. Although the earthly Jerusalem is occasionally called the holy city, and the temple in Jerusalem is called the temple of God (Rev. 11:1–2), still that Jerusalem is allegorically called "Sodom" and "Egypt" (11:8). The true Jerusalem is above (3:12; 21:2, 10), and there too is the temple of God (3:12; 7:15; 11:19; etc.), the ark (11:19), and the altar (6:9; 8:3, 5; 9:13; 14:18; 16:7). That Jerusalem does not come down from heaven in Revelation 20 but only in Revelation 21.

The most telling objection is that the life and rule of the believers who remained faithful in the great tribulation take place in heaven, not on earth. Not a word is said about the earth. John saw the angel who binds Satan come down from heaven (20:1); the thrones he saw (20:4) are located in heaven (4:4; 11:16), and the souls of the martyrs are seen here (20:4), as in every other passage, in heaven (6:9; 7:9, 14–15; 11:12; 14:1–5; 18:20; 19:1–8). Christ already on earth made believers kings and priests to God (1:6). That is what they *are* in heaven (5:10), and they expect that one day they will be that on earth as well (5:10), but this expectation is only fulfilled in the new Jerusalem that comes down from above. Then they will be kings forever (22:5). But now, in heaven, this kingship is temporary: it lasts a thousand years.

Finally, the notion of two resurrections—a physical resurrection that precedes the millennium and a second that follows it—is foreign to John and to Scripture. There is indeed mention of a spiritual resurrection from sin (John 5:25–26; Rom. 6:4; etc.). There is also a resurrection from the dead (ἀναστασις ἐκ νεκρων, *anastasis ek nekrōn*) that refers to individual cases, such as the resurrection of Christ (1 Pet. 1:3; cf. Acts 26:23; 1 Cor. 15:23), or only to believers (Luke 20:35–36; Acts 4:2), but in that case it is absolutely not distinguished temporally by a thousand-year reign from the universal resurrection from the dead (ἀναστασις νεκρων, *anastasis nekrōn*; Matt. 22:31; John 5:28–29; Acts 24:15; 1 Cor. 15:13, 42). The resurrection of believers will occur at the time of Christ's parousia, and it will be immediately followed by the end and the delivering up of the kingdom, because all [God's] enemies have been vanquished and the last enemy, death, has been destroyed (1 Cor. 15:20–28). Even Revelation 20 does not teach a twofold resurrection. The souls (τας ψυχας, *tas psychas*) of the martyrs (20:4) that John mentions are clearly the same as those in Revelation 6:9 where there is no mention of bodily resurrection. However, he further says that the souls lived and reigned immediately as kings with Christ a thousand years—not that they arose or were resurrected or

---

16. Ed. note: Bavinck here refers to the hermeneutical principle of *analogia Scripturae*, the analogy of Scripture, in which unclear, difficult, or ambiguous passages are interpreted by comparing them with clear and unambiguous passages on the same topic. See Richard A. Muller, *Dictionary of Latin and Greek Theological Terms* (Grand Rapids: Baker Academic, 1985), s.v. "*analogia Scripturae*."

entered into life—and also the rest of the dead (οἱ λοιποι των νεκρων, *hoi loipoi tōn nekrōn*). All this assumes that the believers whose souls he saw in heaven still in a sense belong to the dead but nevertheless lived and reigned. One can, as it were, feel the contrast: the first resurrection here is not a physical resurrection prior to a thousand-year reign but consists in the "living" and "reigning" in heaven with Christ of the believers who remained faithful. The believers to whom John is writing and who are soon going to encounter the tribulation must not think that they will only experience salvation at the end of time. No: "Blessed are the dead who die in the Lord *from now on*" (ἀπ᾽ ἀρτι, *ap᾽ arti*; Rev. 14:13). They immediately gain rest from their labors. Upon their death they immediately receive a crown. They live and reign in heaven with Christ from the moment after their death, and they can therefore face the coming tribulation with confidence. The crown of life awaits them (2:10). Here, in Revelation 20:4–5, John is repeating, in brief, what he wrote earlier to the seven churches (2:7, 17, 26, 28; 3:5, 12, 20, 21). What John saw earlier in the form of a promise he now sees in the form of fulfillment in chapter 20: those who remain faithful until death immediately live and reign with Christ on his throne in heaven. They already have the crown of life and already eat the manna of life and therefore need not fear the judgment to come. *That* is the *first* resurrection. This is confirmed by what John says about the "second death," which refers to the reality of being thrown into the lake of fire (20:14). "Whoever conquers will not be harmed by the second death" (2:11), which goes into effect at the final judgment. To those who have persevered to the end, they will be immediately crowned, and though the *first* death still reigns over their bodies, they cannot be hurt by the *second* death.

[570] It is important to note that the location of the vision in Revelation 20 following that of chapter 19 has no bearing on the chronological sequence of events. Generally speaking, the art of writing, in distinction, say, from the art of painting, can only narrate consecutively events that are actually simultaneous. Scripture is no exception. It frequently relates successively things that in reality occurred side by side. In the prophets it often happens that they see and describe consecutively things that happen or will happen simultaneously or even in a totally different order. This is especially the case, as it is increasingly being recognized, in the book of Revelation. The letters to the seven churches do not furnish a description of ecclesiastical conditions succeeding each other in that same order. The seven seals, the seven trumpets, and the seven bowls do not constitute a chronological series but run parallel and in each case take us to the end, the final struggle of the anti-Christian power. So in itself there is no objection to the assumption that what is narrated in Revelation 20 runs parallel to the events of the previous chapters. It needs to be recognized that in reference to the world empire that he depicts, John is thinking of the Roman Empire. In the same way that the book of Daniel leads up to Antiochus Epiphanes and regards him as the personification of hostility against God and his people, John derives from the Roman Empire of his day the features he needs for his world empire. Although everything that has

been written beforehand has been written for our instruction, the Revelation of John is nevertheless primarily a book of consolation for "the church under the cross" of his own time, to urge it to persevere in the struggle and to encourage it by picturing the crown awaiting it.

If John really believed privately that in a few years the Roman Empire would be destroyed by the appearing of Christ, and that Christ would come in just a few years to put an end to it, that would not in any way be unusual or something at variance with the spirit of prophecy. We are not bound by John's personal opinion but by the word of his prophecy. And the prophecy that throws its light on history is in turn interpreted and unveiled by history.

However, just as the letters to the seven churches and similarly the seven seals, trumpets, and bowls first of all relate to conditions and events in John's day but then have further implications for the church of all times and for the history of the world as a whole, so it is true of the world empire depicted in Revelation: it is modeled on the Roman Empire of the first centuries but does not achieve its full realization in that empire. It keeps rising again and again and must always succumb to the appearance of Christ until it finally exerts its utmost powers, exhausts itself in a final gargantuan struggle, and is then forever annihilated by the coming of Christ. If this view is correct, the vision of Revelation 20 is not intended to relate to us the things that will occur in chronological order after the events of Revelation 19, but has a place of its own and reports to us things that run parallel with the preceding. The ultimate ending of the history of the world to be narrated, it turns out, is twofold: one is the ending of the historical nations in which Christianity is openly active, and another is the ending of the barbaric nations that—as Revelation 20:8 clearly tells us—are "at the four corners of the earth," and have therefore lived away from the center of history and outside the circle of mankind's culture. As Satan assaults the church, over and over again, and is rebuffed, he forges new instruments for other places. First he is thrown from heaven; then he works on earth and raises up a world empire against Christ; and finally he summons up the barbaric nations from around the world to fight the final battle against Christ. But all this occurs, not in chronological sequence, but in a logical and spiritual sense. The thousand years, as is generally recognized today, are symbolic. They contrast with the few days during which the believers who remain faithful are oppressed and persecuted here on earth (Rev. 12:17), but also with the completed glory that is eternal (22:5). They denote the holy, blessed rest of believers who have died and are in heaven with Christ as well as the longing with which they look for the day when their blood will be avenged (6:10), while on earth the struggle of world empire and the international world against Christ continues. In 19:21 people are slain by the sword of Christ; in 20:9 they are consumed by fire from heaven. But after the world empire, the false prophet, and Satan have been condemned and thrown into the lake of fire (19:20; 20:10), all the dead arise and are judged according to their works (20:11–15).

The teaching of Scripture unfolded up to this point makes clear that the course and outcome of world history are very different from the way people usually imagine them. It is most certainly true of the end of things, if anywhere, that God's ways are higher than our ways and his thoughts higher than our thoughts. The kingdom of God, although analogous to a mustard seed and leaven and a seed that sprouts and grows aside from any knowledge and involvement of human beings (Matt. 13:31, 33; Mark 4:27), nevertheless does not reach its completion by way of gradual development or an ethical process. According to the incontrovertible testimony of Scripture, the history of humankind, both in the case of culture-producing and of uncultured nations, rather ends in a general apostasy and an appalling final struggle of a coalition of all satanic forces against God and his kingdom.

But then, in any case, the end is there. The world and its power and powers is ripe for judgment and suddenly collapses at the appearance of Christ. In the end a catastrophe, a divine act of intervention, terminates the rule of Satan here on earth and brings about the completion of the unshakable kingdom of heaven. Just as in the case of a believer, perfection is not the fruit of a slowly progressing process of sanctification but sets in immediately after death, so also the perfection of humanity and the world comes about, not gradually, but suddenly by the appearance of Christ. It is specifically Christ who is appointed by the Father to bring about the end of the history of humankind and the world. He is appointed to this role because he is the Savior, the perfect Savior. The return of Christ unto judgment is not an arbitrary addition that can be isolated from his preceding work and viewed by itself. It is a necessary and indispensable component of that work. It brings that work to completion and crowns it, the last and highest step in the state of his exaltation. Because Christ is the savior of the world, he will someday return as its judge. The crisis, or judgment (κρισις, *krisis*), that he precipitated by his first coming he consummates at his second coming. The Father gave him authority to execute judgment (κρισιν ποιειν, *krisin poiein*) because he is the Son of Man (John 5:27). This judgment is the completion of Christ's mediatorial work as Prophet, Priest, and King. In accord with Scripture, we can go back even farther. The Son is not only the mediator of reconciliation (*mediator reconciliationis*) on account of sin, but even apart from sin he is the mediator of union (*mediator unionis*) between God and his creation. In the Son the world has its foundation, example, and goal; it is created through him and for him as well (Col. 1:16). Because the creation is *his* work, it cannot and may not remain the booty of Satan. The second coming is therefore required by his first coming. It is implied in the first; in time, by inner necessity, it will proceed from the first. The second coming brings the first coming to its full effect and completion and was therefore comprehended in a single image with the first coming by Old Testament prophecy. There is a real bond between the first and second comings. Just as the Old Testament was a continual coming of God to his people until in Christ he came to live bodily among them, so the dispensation of the New Testament is a continued coming of Christ to his inheritance in order in the end to take possession of it forever. Christ is not only he who was to come in the days of the Old Testament and actually came in the fullness of time. He is also the Coming One (ὁ ἐρχόμενος, *ho erchomenos*) and the one who will come (ὁ ἐρχόμενος ἥξει, *ho erchomenos hēxei*; Heb. 10:37; cf. Rev. 1:4, 8; etc.).[17] Christ's second coming is the complement of the first.

[571] This ideal and real connection between the first and second comings of Christ also explains the manner in which the New Testament speaks of the time of his parousia. An entire series of texts posits this parousia as being very close at hand. Jesus links the prophecy of the consummation immediately to that concerning the destruction of Jerusalem (Matt. 24:29ff. and parallels). Paul considers it possible that he and his fellow believers will still experience the parousia of Christ (1 Cor. 15:51; 1 Thess. 4:15). And all the apostles assert that they are in the last days, that the future of the Lord is at hand, and derive from this expectation a motive for vigilance (Rom. 13:11; 1 Cor. 10:11; Heb. 3:14; 6:11; 10:25, 37; James 5:7–9; 1 Pet. 1:6, 20; 4:17; 5:10; 1 John 2:18; Rev. 1:3; 3:11, 20; 22:7, 10, 12, 20).

Errors have been made in both directions in the interpretation of this New Testament expectation of the early return of Christ. The New Testament contains no doctrine concerning the time of Christ's return. It by no means establishes as a fact that Christ's return will occur before or immediately after the destruction of Jerusalem. Jesus spoke of his coming in various senses. In John 14:18–24 (cf. 10:16–18) he speaks to his disciples of his coming in the Spirit after Pentecost or, according to other interpreters, of his coming after the resurrection, when he will again appear to his disciples for a little while. In Matthew 26:64, before the [Jewish] council, Jesus not only confirmed his messiahship under oath but also stated that he would convince them of it because they would from that time on (ἀπ᾽ ἄρτι, *ap᾽ arti*) see him sitting at the right hand of God's power and coming on the clouds of heaven. Elsewhere also there is mention of such a coming in glory. Matthew 16:28 (cf. Mark 9:1; Luke 9:27) leaves no room for doubt about this. Jesus says here that some of his bystanders will not taste death before they see the Son of Man coming in his kingdom.

Since by his resurrection and ascension Christ was appointed by the Father to be head, king, and Lord (Acts 2:33; 5:31); and from that time onward, in the measure in which his kingdom is founded and extended on earth, he is continually coming in his royal dignity, the phrases in Matthew 10:23; Mark 9:1; and Luke 9:27 can be explained by saying that many will not taste death before they have seen the kingdom of God, or have seen it come with power. This is confirmed by Matthew 24:34 (cf. Mark 13:30; Luke 21:32), where Jesus says that "this generation will not pass away until all these things take place." The

17. Ed. note: For a contemporary development of this christological/eschatological idea of Christ as the Coming One, see Adrio Konig, *The Eclipse of Christ in Eschatology: Toward a Christ-Centered Approach* (Grand Rapids: Eerdmans, 1989).

words "this generation" (ἡ γενεα αὐτη, *hē genea hautē*) cannot be understood to mean the Jewish people, but undoubtedly refer to the generation then living. On the other hand, it is clear that the words "all these things" (παντα ταυτα, *panta tauta*) do not include the parousia itself but only refer to the signs that precede and announce it. Jesus therefore does not say that his parousia will still occur within the time of the generation then living. What he says is that the signs and portents of it, as they would be visible in the destruction of Jerusalem and concomitant events, would begin to occur in the time of the generation then living. Of this Jesus is so sure that he says that while heaven and earth will pass away, his words will by no means pass away. For the rest, however, Jesus abstains from all attempts at further specifying the time. His intent is not to inform his disciples of the precise moment of his parousia, but to urge them to be watchful. Taking notice of the signs of the times is a duty for Jesus's disciples; the calculation of the precise time of his coming is forbidden to them and also impossible. The former demands that Jesus shed his light on the events that will occur, and so he does, as did all the prophets before him, and as after him all his apostles have done. This responsibility of discipleship knows not the time line; Jesus does not say how long the span of time will be between the destruction of Jerusalem and his parousia. That would have immediately rendered powerless the admonition to be watchful. As prophecy has at all times done, so Jesus announces the approach of the end *in* the events of his time. The apostles follow his example when, in heresy and deception, in ordeals and judgments, in Jerusalem's fall and Rome's empire, they depict for us the early messengers of Christ's return and the initial fulfillment of his prophecy. For all believers ought at all times to live as though the coming of Christ is at the door. "The proximity of the parousia is, so to speak, only another way of expressing its absolute certainty."[18] But for the same reason, the calculation of the precise moment of the parousia is also inappropriate for Christians. After all, Jesus deliberately left this completely uncertain. His coming will be sudden, unexpected, surprising, like that of a thief in the night (Matt. 24:43; Luke 12:39; cf. "like a trap," Luke 21:35).

Many things have to happen before the end comes (Matt. 24:6). The gospel must be preached throughout the whole world (24:14); weeds and wheat must grow together until the harvest (13:30); the mustard seed must grow into a tree, and the yeast must leaven the whole batch of dough (13:32–33). Jesus expressly stated that the day and the hour of his coming are not known to anyone (Mark 13:32). All the apostles echo this language: Christ comes like a thief in the night (1 Thess. 5:1–2; 2 Pet. 3:10; Rev. 3:3; 16:15), not until after the antichrist has come (2 Thess. 2:2ff.). The resurrection is scheduled to occur in a fixed sequence, first that of Christ, then that of believers at his coming (1 Cor. 15:23). That future

---

18. "Die Nähe der Parusie ist gewissermassen nur ein anderer Ausdruck für die absolute Gewissheit derselben" (Baldensperger in H. J. Holtzmann, *Lehrbuch der neutestamentlichen Theologie* [Freiburg i.B. and Leipzig: Mohr, 1897], I, 312).

is delayed inasmuch as the Lord uses another standard for measuring time than we and wishes in his patience that all should come to repentance (2 Pet. 3:8–9).

About the *manner* of Jesus's return, Holy Scripture speaks as soberly as it does about its timing. In the New Testament, Christ's second coming is frequently referred to with the name παρουσια (*parousia*, coming), either absolutely (Matt. 24:3) or further described as "the coming of the Son of Man" or as "the coming of our Lord Jesus Christ" (Matt. 24:27, 37, 39; 1 Thess. 3:13; 4:15; 5:23; etc.) or as "the coming of the day of God" (2 Pet. 3:12). The word *parousia* as such does not include the idea of return but indicates that Jesus, after having been absent and hidden for a time (Acts 3:21; Col. 3:3–4) and having then come back (Matt. 16:27; 24:30; etc.; cf. Luke 19:12, 15), will again be and remain present. For that reason *parousia* alternates with ἐπιφανεια (*epiphaneia*, manifestation; 1 Tim. 6:14; Titus 2:13), ἀποκαλυψις (*apokalypsis*, revelation [or with the cognate verb]; Luke 17:30; 1 Cor. 1:7; 2 Thess. 1:7; 1 Pet. 1:7, 13), and φανερωσις (*phanerōsis*, appearance [or with the cognate verb]; Col. 3:4; 1 Pet. 5:4; 1 John 2:28); in 2 Thessalonians 2:8 we even read of "the manifestation of his coming" (ἡ ἐπιφανεια της παρουσιας αὐτου, *hē epiphaneia tēs parousias autou*). This parousia is a work of God insofar as God will send his Anointed and to that end fixes the times and seasons (Acts 1:7; 3:20–21; 1 Tim. 6:14–16). But it is also an act of Christ himself as Son of Man, to whom the Father has given authority to execute judgment, and who must rule as king until all his enemies have been put under his feet (John 5:17; 1 Cor. 15:25). Since upon his departure from earth he was taken up into heaven, at his parousia he will return from heaven (Phil. 3:20; 1 Thess. 1:10; 2 Thess. 1:7; Rev. 19:11). As at his ascension a cloud enclosed him and hid him from the eyes of his disciples (Acts 1:9), so, in the language of the Old Testament, he is also described as returning on the clouds of heaven, which like a triumphal chariot will carry him down to earth (Matt. 24:30; 26:64; Mark 13:26; 14:62; Luke 21:27; Rev. 1:7; 14:14). For he returns not in the form of a servant but with great power and with his own and the Father's glory (Matt. 16:27; 24:30; Mark 8:38; 13:26; Luke 21:27; Col. 3:3–4; 2 Thess. 1:9–10; Titus 2:13), as "King of kings and Lord of lords" (Rev. 17:14; 19:11–16), surrounded by his angels (Matt. 16:27; 25:31; Mark 8:38; Luke 9:26; 2 Thess. 1:7; Rev. 19:14) and by his saints, among whom the blessed in heaven are perhaps included (1 Thess. 3:13; 2 Thess. 1:10; Jude 14). Although on account of its unexpected character, his parousia is comparable with the breaking into a house by a thief in the night, it will nevertheless be visible for all human beings on earth, be like the lightning that flashes from one side of the sky to the other (Matt. 24:27; Luke 17:24; Rev. 1:7), and be announced by the voice of an archangel and the trumpet of angels (Matt. 24:31; 1 Cor. 15:52; 1 Thess. 4:16).

In short, Jesus's disciples are to be watchful of the signs but they are also forbidden to calculate. All believers ought at all times to live as though the coming of Christ is at hand.

25

The Consummation

THE DAY OF THE LORD

[572] The day of the Lord (יוֹם יהוה, *yôm YHWH*) or the day of our Lord Jesus Christ (ἡ ἡμερα του κυριου ἡμων Ἰησου Χριστου, *hē hēmera tou kyriou hēmōn Iēsou Christou*; Matt. 24:36ff.; Luke 17:24ff.; 21:34; Acts 17:31; 1 Cor. 1:8; 5:5; etc.) begins with the appearance of Christ on the clouds. "Day" must not be taken in an excessively literal manner as twelve or twenty-four hours. In Old Testament times the day of the Lord was the time in which God, in a marvelously glorious way, would come to his people as king to redeem them from all their enemies and to settle them with him in Jerusalem in peace and security. It was a great turning point in which the old aeon passed into the new, and all conditions and connections in the natural and human world changed totally. According to the New Testament, the last part of the present aeon (αἰων οὑτος, *aiōn houtos*) began with the first coming of Christ, so that now we live in the last days or the last hour (1 Cor. 10:11; Heb. 1:2; 9:26; 1 John 2:18), and the aeon to come (αἰων μελλων, *aiōn mellōn*) starts with his second coming (Matt. 19:28–29; Mark 10:30; Luke 18:30; 20:35; 1 Cor. 15:23; Heb. 2:5; etc.). This age to come (*aiōn mellōn*) begins with the day of the Lord (ἡμερα του κυριου, *hēmera tou kyriou*), that is, the time in which Christ appears, raises the dead, executes judgment, and renews the world. In the New Testament this period is never represented as lasting long. Paul says in 1 Corinthians 15:52, for example, that the transformation of believers still living and the resurrection of believers who have died will occur in a moment, "in the twinkling of an eye" (cf. 1 Thess. 4:15–17). The resurrection and the last judgment are intimately associated as in a single act (Luke 14:14; 2 Cor. 4:14;

Rev. 20:11–13). Judgment is fixed on a day (Matt. 10:15; 11:22; etc.) and even on an hour (Rev. 14:7). But this last term is proof that Scripture is in no way minded to fit all the events associated with Christ's parousia precisely into a time frame of twenty-four hours or sixty minutes: the word "hour" (ὥρα, *hōra*, originally "season") often refers to a much longer period of time than an hour of sixty minutes (Matt. 26:45; John 4:21; 5:25; 16:2, 32; Rom. 13:11; 1 John 2:18). The events that are destined to occur in the parousia of Christ are so comprehensive in scope that they are bound to take considerable time. The inventions of the past century—for the purpose of mutual contact, the exercise of community, hearing and seeing things at a great distance—have shrunk distances to a minimum; and it is likely that they are a mere beginning and prophecy of what will be discovered in the centuries ahead. The doctrine of the last things certainly has to reckon with all these things. Still, such events as the appearance of Christ so that all will see him, the resurrection of all the dead and the transformation of those still living, the rendering of judgment on all people according to their deeds, and the burning and renewal of the world—these are such immense occurrences that they can only take place over a certain period of time.

The first event that follows the appearance of Christ is the resurrection of the dead by an omnipotent, creative act of God (Matt. 22:29; 1 Cor. 6:14; 15:38; 2 Cor. 1:9). The Father specifically carries out this work by the Son, who is the resurrection and the life, the firstborn of the dead (John 11:25; Acts 26:23; 1 Cor. 15:20; Col. 1:18; Rev. 1:5), and will bring about the resurrection of his own (John 6:39–40; 1 Cor. 15:20–23, 47–49). Undoubtedly Scripture teaches a general resurrection, a resurrection not only of believers but also of unbelievers and of all human beings (Dan. 12:2; Matt. 5:29–30; 10:28; John 5:29; Acts 24:15; Rev. 20:12–13), and attributes this resurrection to Christ as well (John 5:29).

The resurrection of the dead in general, therefore, is primarily a judicial act of God. But for believers this act is filled with abundant consolation. In Scripture, the resurrection of the believing community is everywhere in the foreground, so much so that sometimes the resurrection of all human beings is even left out of consideration or deliberately omitted (Job 19:25–27; Ps. 73:23–26; Isa. 26:19–20; Ezek. 37; Hosea 6:2; 13:14; Mark 12:25; 2 Cor. 5; Phil. 3:11; 1 Thess. 4:16). This is the real, the true resurrection, an event in which believers, united in soul and body, enter into communion with Christ and are being re-created after God's image (Rom. 8:11, 29; Phil. 3:21). For that reason Paul has the resurrection of believers coincide with the transformation of those who are left alive. The latter will have no advantage over the former, for the resurrection will take place prior to the transformation, and together they will go forth to meet the Lord in the air (1 Cor. 15:51–52; 2 Cor. 5:2, 4; 1 Thess. 4:15–17). In this resurrection the identity of the resurrection body with the body that has died will be preserved. Jesus arose with the same body in which he suffered on the cross and which was laid in the tomb of Joseph of Arimathea. At the time of Jesus's death many bodies of the saints were raised and came forth from their tombs (Matt. 27:52). In the resurrection of the last day, all who are in the tombs will hear Jesus's voice and come forth (John 5:28–29; Rev. 20:13). Paul teaches that the resurrection body proceeds from the body that has died, just as from the grain that has been sown God raises up new grain (1 Cor. 15:36ff.).

In the Christian religion this identity of the resurrection body with the body that was laid aside at death is of such great significance that it is diametrically opposed to all dualistic theories in which the body is merely an incidental dwelling place or prison of the soul. The essence of a human being consists above all in the most intimate union of soul and body in a single personality; they belong together. The continuity of an individual human being is maintained as much in the identity of the body as in the identity of the soul. Christ's redemption, therefore, is not a second, new creation but a re-creation. It was God's good pleasure to raise the fallen world up again and to free from sin the same humanity that sinned. This deliverance consists in the forgiveness of sin from all the consequences of sin,[1] including the complete triumph over death as well. Death is the last enemy to be annihilated. And the power of Christ is revealed in the fact that he not only gives eternal life to his own but in consequence also raises them on the last day. Christ is a complete Savior: The rebirth by water and Spirit finds its completion in the rebirth of all things (Matt. 19:28). Spiritual redemption from sin is only fully completed in bodily redemption at the end of time. The Christian church and Christian theology, accordingly, vigorously maintained the identity of the resurrection body with the body that had died.

This has implications for the care of the dead. Cremation is not to be rejected because it is assumed to limit the omnipotence of God and make the resurrection an impossibility. Nevertheless, it is of pagan origin; it was never a custom in Israel or in Christian nations, and it militates against Christian mores. Burial, on the other hand, is much more nearly in harmony with Scripture, creed, history, and liturgy; with the doctrine of the image of God that is also manifest in the body; with the doctrine of death as a punishment for sin; and with the respect that is due to the dead and the resurrection on the last day. Christians do not, like the Egyptians, artificially preserve corpses; nor do they mechanically destroy them, as many people desire today. But they entrust them to the earth's bosom and let them rest until the day of the resurrection.

[573] As our Lord's own resurrection shows, the final resurrection maintains continuity between the earthly body and the glorified resurrection body. Persons retain their individual identities. Precisely how this happens we do not know and should not speculate; what is important is the substantial unity as well as qualitative distinction between what the apostle calls the "natural body" and the "spiritual body" (1 Cor. 15). For strictly speaking, Scripture does not teach the resurrection of the *flesh*, but of the *body*. While in the case of resurrections in Scripture, including the resurrection of our Lord, we have examples of bodies that

1. Ed. note: Bavinck is speaking eschatologically here, that is, about the final judgment.

were still whole and, in the case of Christ's body, had not even been given over to corruption (Acts 2:31). But the bodies of those who rise in the parousia are totally decomposed and scattered in all sorts of ways and have passed into other creatures. In this case we can hardly speak of flesh in a literal sense, for flesh is always animated. That which is no longer alive and animated therefore also ceases to be flesh and returns to dust (Gen. 3:19). This neither proves the resurrection of the *flesh* in a strict sense—actual recomposition of a person's very atoms and molecules—nor the evasive exegetical move that thinks of the deceased body not rising at all but that the resurrection occurs right at the time of a person's death.

However, this is still not sufficient to prove the resurrection of the *flesh* in the strict sense of this word. For though the flesh of which Job's body consisted was indeed the substratum for the resurrection body, it did not for that reason form the substance of it. And Jesus arose with the same body in which he died and which had not even seen corruption, and he remained moreover in a transitional state up until his ascension, so that he could still eat food as well. Paul teaches very clearly that flesh and blood, being perishable, cannot inherit the kingdom of God, which is imperishable (1 Cor. 15:50). Holsten, Holtzmann, and others have mistakenly inferred from this that, according to Paul, the deceased body does not rise at all. The apostle expressly attests to his faith in the bodily resurrection and defends it against those in the church of Corinth who denied it, and he is also thoroughly convinced that the same body that is laid in the grave is raised again in the resurrection. At the same time he asserts that the resurrection is not a rehabilitation but a re-formation from one that is weak, perishable, and mortal to one clothed in imperishability and glory (1 Cor. 15:35–54).[2] There are, therefore, important differences between the present body and the future body, as is evident from the contrast between Adam and Christ (1 Cor. 15:42–49). The first is a natural body (σωμα ψυχικον, *sōma psychikon*) composed of flesh and blood, a body that is subject to change and animated by a soul (ψυχη, *psychē*), but the latter is a spiritual body (σωμα πνευματικον, *sōma pneumatikon*). Although it is a true body, it is no longer controlled by a soul but by the spirit (πνευμα, *pneuma*). It is no longer composed of flesh and blood; it is above the sex life (Matt. 22:30) and the need for food and drink (1 Cor. 6:13). In these respects it is distinguished even from the body that humans possessed before the fall; it is immortal, imperishable, spiritualized, and glorified (1 Cor. 15:42ff.; Phil. 3:21). In short, according to Paul, the identity

---

2. Ed. note: Bavinck draws a distinction here between *restauratie* (translated "rehabilitation") and *reformatie*. This distinction, for which he more frequently uses the contrast between *restauratie* and *herstel* (re-creation), is used repeatedly by Bavinck to make the important point that the fullness of redemption in Christ is more than a mere repristination of the original created and prefallen status of Adam. Although grace restores rather than abolishes nature, the *status gloriae* is more excellent than the *status integratis*. Cf. H. Bavinck, *Our Reasonable Faith*, trans. H. Zylstra (Grand Rapids: Eerdmans, 1956), 218–20. For a helpful discussion of Bavinck's understanding of grace's relation to nature, see Jan Veenhof, *Revelatie en Inspiratie* (Amsterdam: Buijten & Schipperheijn, 1968), 345–65. This section of Veenhof's work has been translated into English by Albert Wolters and published by the Institute for Christian Studies, Toronto, and reprinted as *Nature and Grace in Herman Bavinck* (Sioux Center, IA: Dordt College Press, 2006).

of the resurrection body with the body entrusted to the earth is independent of body mass and its constant change. All organisms, including human bodies, are composed of the same materials in kind, not in number. Therefore it is not necessary for the resurrection body to consist of the same atoms in terms of number as those of which it consisted when it was laid in the grave. But for the resurrection body's identity with the flesh-and-blood body laid in the grave, it *is* required that it have the same organization and shape, the same basic configuration and type, which marked it here as the body of a specific person. In all the metamorphoses to which all creatures are subject, their identity and continuity are preserved. While after death the bodies of humans may disintegrate and, in terms of their material mass, pass into all sorts of other organisms, on earth something remains of them that constitutes the substratum of the resurrection body. Just what that is we do not know and will never be able to discover. But the oddness of this fact vanishes the moment we consider that the ultimate components of all things—including the most minute components of atoms—are totally unknown to us. Still, in the case of all organisms and therefore also in the case of the human body, there has to be something that keeps its identity in the ever-ongoing process of metamorphosis. Then what is so absurd about believing that such an "organic mold" or "pattern of individuality" of the body remains even after death to serve as "seed" for the resurrection body? The resurrection body does not come from heaven but from the earth. It is not a self-generated product of the spirit (*pneuma*) or the soul (*psychē*) but arises from the body that was laid in the grave at death. Accordingly, it is not spiritual in the sense that its substance is spirit (*pneuma*), but it is and remains material. That matter, however, is no longer organized into perishable flesh and blood but into a glorified body.

[574] After the resurrection comes the judgment. While there is already an immanent judgment on sin in our world and history, it is a pantheistic error to reduce world judgment to world history. The final judgment will be a global and public vindication of the gospel and Christ's rule. The objections to eternal punishment of the wicked and the various alternatives to it, such as hypothetical and unconditional universalism as well as conditional immortality, appeal naturally to human sentiment but finally have no ground in Scripture. The clear teaching of Scripture, along with firm conviction about the integrity of God's justice, should be sufficient and deter us from undue speculation. God will be God and will be glorified.

After the resurrection comes the judgment, an event pictured in the Old Testament as a victory of the Messiah over all Israel's enemies but described in the New Testament more spiritually as a judicial work of Christ in which he judges and sentences all people in accordance with the law God gave them. The first time, to be sure, Jesus came on earth not to judge the world but to save it (John 3:17; 12:47). Still, immediately at his appearance he produced a judgment (κρισις, *krisis*) whose purpose and result is that those who do not see can see, and that those who see may become blind (3:19–20; 9:39). As Son of Man, Jesus continually exercises judgment when, to those who believe already, he grants eternal life here on earth and allows the wrath of God to continue to rest on those who do not believe (3:36; 5:32–38). We can speak, therefore, properly of an internal spiritual judgment at work, an immanent judgment this side of the beyond that takes place in the consciences of human beings, and that is realized from generation to generation. Here on earth faith and unbelief already bear their fruit and bring their reward. Scripture and history vie with each other in teaching that blessing and curse, compassion and anger, signs of favor and judgment alternate in the lives of people and nations. There is great truth in the poet Schiller's saying that "the history of the world is the judgment of the world" (*die Weltgeschichte ist das Weltgericht*).

Still, though in part this saying is true, it is also false. In origin it is pantheistic, not theistic, and undermines all judgment instead of confirming and honoring it. For *if* the history of the world is *the* judgment of the world, it totally ceases to be a judgment and becomes a natural process. This natural process is not at all concerned about the awesome contrast between good and evil and forces it back, and that only for a time, into the hidden recesses of the conscience. In that case, all that remains is the power of nature; there is no independent power of moral good; there is no God who can make the natural order subservient to the moral order. According to pantheists, this should not be a problem because we ought to do good for its own sake and not from a hope of reward or fear of punishment. But the desire of the soul for the triumph of the good, the victory of justice, has nothing at all in common with the self-centered wish for earthly happiness and the satisfaction of the senses. Scripture holds before our eyes a reward that is "great in heaven" (Matt. 5:12), though that reward is always subordinate to the honor of God's name and is secured by Christ along with the good works in which believers walk (Eph. 2:10). The glory of God's name is tied to the triumph of his cause (and ours).[3] All of history cries out for world judgment. The whole creation longs for it. All people witness to it. The martyrs in heaven cry out for it with a loud voice. The believing community prays for the coming of Christ. And Christ himself, the Alpha and the Omega, says: "See, I am coming soon; my reward is with me, to repay according to everyone's work" (Rev. 22:12). So, however firmly Scripture—especially in the Gospel of John—recognizes spiritual judgment that is operative throughout history, it nevertheless speaks of a final judgment as well, the judgment that brings about the triumph of the kingdom of Christ over all unrighteousness. The history of the world may be *a* judgment of the world, but *the* judgment of the world will take place at the end of time, when Christ comes to judge the living and the dead.

In this connection, Scripture repeatedly attributes this judgment to the Father (Matt. 18:35; 2 Thess. 1:5; Heb. 11:6; James 4:12; 1 Pet. 1:17; 2:23; Rev.

---

3. Ed. note. The parenthetical ("and ours") was added by the editor and refers to Belgic Confession, art. 37.

20:11–12). Still he accomplishes this work through Christ, to whom all judgment has been given, whom he has appointed as judge (John 5:22, 27; Acts 10:42; 17:31; Rom. 14:9), and who will therefore summon all human beings before his judgment seat and judge them according to what they have done (Matt. 25:32; Rom. 14:9–13 KJV; 2 Cor. 5:10; 2 Tim. 4:1, 8; 1 Pet. 4:5; Rev. 19:11–21). This is vitally important since it is a person's relationship to Christ that determines his or her eternal weal or woe. In his judgment of the living and the dead, he celebrates his highest triumph and realizes the consummation of his kingdom and the total subjection of all his enemies. For that reason the main issue in the final judgment is that of faith or unbelief. For faith in Christ is the work of God par excellence (John 6:29; 1 John 3:23). Those who believe do not come into judgment (John 5:24); those who do not believe are already condemned and remain under God's wrath (John 3:18, 36). Therefore, the standard in the final judgment will in the first place be the gospel (John 12:48); but that gospel is not opposed to, and cannot even be conceived apart from, the law. The requirement to believe, after all, is itself grounded in the law, and the gospel is the restoration and fulfillment of the law. In the final judgment, therefore, all the works performed by people and recorded in the books before God are considered as well (Eccles. 12:14; 2 Cor. 5:10; Eph. 6:8; 1 Pet. 1:17; Rev. 20:12; 22:12). Those works, after all, are expressions and products of the principle of life that lives in the heart (Matt. 7:17; 12:33; Luke 6:44) and encompass everything effected by humans, not in the intermediate state but in their bodies, not the deeds alone (Matt. 25:35ff.; Mark 9:41–42; Luke 6:35; 14:13–14; 1 Cor. 3:8; 1 Thess. 4:6; etc.) but also the words (Matt. 12:36) and the secret purposes of the heart (Rom. 2:16; 1 Cor. 4:5). For nothing remains hidden and everything will be revealed (Matt. 6:4, 6, 18; 10:26; Eph. 5:11–14; 1 Tim. 5:24–25). In the final judgment, therefore, the norm will be the entire Word of God in both its parts: law and gospel.

Nonetheless, Scripture also clearly states that consideration will be given to the measure of revelation that any given person has received. Those who knew the will of the Lord and did not do it will be given "a more severe beating" (Luke 12:47). It will be more tolerable for Tyre and Sidon in the day of judgment than for Jerusalem and Capernaum (Matt. 10:15; 11:22, 24; Mark 6:11; Luke 10:12, 14; Heb. 2:3). Those who did not hear the gospel are not judged by it but by the law. The gentiles who did not know the Mosaic law but sinned against the law known to them by nature perish apart from the Mosaic law, whereas Jews are judged above all by this law (Rom. 2:12). Although Scripture views the judgment as extending to all humans without exception (Matt. 25:32; Acts 17:31; Rom. 2:6; 14:10; 2 Cor. 5:10; 2 Tim. 4:1; Rev. 20:12), it nevertheless makes a distinction between the nations that knew the gospel and finally produced anti-Christianity, and the other nations that never heard of Christ and therefore first learn of him at his parousia. It further speaks in particular of the judgment of evil angels, and of the role the good angels and believers play in the final judgment.

It is not at all easy to gain a clear picture of that judgment. There is certainly not exclusively an internal and spiritual event occurring solely in the human conscience. It is definitely a judgment that is realized externally as well and is visible to all creatures. The appearance of Christ, the resurrection, and everything associated with the judgment are drawn too realistically to give us the freedom to spiritualize everything. That being the case, the execution of this judgment also requires a place and a space of time, for Scripture prompts us to think of it as occurring successively. The angels gather the righteous, separate the evil from the righteous, and drive them away (Matt. 13:30, 49; 24:31). Following the resurrection of the believers who died and the transformation of those who remain alive, they are together caught up in the clouds to meet the Lord in the air (1 Thess. 4:17). Just as Christ's resurrection and ascension were disjoined and even separated by a period of forty days, so it is not impossible that the resurrection and transformation of believers at the end of time will not yet, at one stroke, confer on them the full glory that they will receive after the renewal of the world in a new heaven and a new earth. However this will be, the resurrection and transformation of believers includes, as it did for Christ, their justification.

Scripture does indeed say that all humans without distinction, hence also believers, must appear before the judgment seat of Christ. But it also attests that believers are not condemned and do not come into judgment, for they already have eternal life (John 3:18; 5:24); that those who have died are already with him and are clothed in long white garments (2 Cor. 5:8; Phil. 1:23; Rev. 6:11; 7:9, 14); and that Christ is coming to be glorified in his saints and to be marveled at among all who believe (2 Thess. 1:10). Believers even participate in pronouncing his verdict on the evil angels, on the anti-Christian world, and on barbaric peoples (1 Cor. 6:2–3; Matt. 19:28; Luke 22:30, Rev. 4:4; 11:16; 20:4, 6). The angels too, therefore, will receive a place in the future kingdom of God in accordance with the service they have rendered in relation to Christ and his church. Accordingly, in John's vision Christ, surrounded by his armies, goes out to meet the anti-Christian forces (Rev. 19:11–21). The church triumphant takes part in the royal reign of Christ (20:4–6). Christ finally annihilates all opposition when he judges the nations who are at the four corners of the earth (20:7–10).

[575] In the New Testament the place to which the wicked are consigned is called Gehenna. The Hebrew גֵּי הִנֹּם (gê hinnōm) was originally the name for the valley of Hinnom, which was located southwest of Jerusalem and, according to Joshua 15:8 and 18:16, served as the boundary line between two tribes. Under Ahaz and Manasseh this valley became a site for the worship of Molech, in whose honor children were slain and burned (2 Kings 16:3; 21:6; 2 Chron. 28:3; 33:6; Jer. 32:34–35). Under Josiah this place was destroyed, therefore, and declared unclean by the priests (2 Kings 23:10). Jeremiah prophesied that here a terrible bloodbath would be inflicted on the Israelites, and the Topheth valley would be called the Valley of Slaughter (Jer. 7:32; 19:6). The pseudepigraphic book of *1 Enoch* predicted that in this valley the wicked would be gathered up for judg-

ment. For this reason the name "Gehinnom" was later transferred to the place of punishment for the wicked after death. This transfer has been explained differently. According to later Jews, after the valley of Hinnom had been destroyed by Josiah, it was used for dumping and burning all kinds of trash. Just as Gan [Hebrew for "garden"] Eden referred to the place where the righteous lived after death, Gehinnom became the name of the place to which the unclean and the ungodly were consigned to suffer punishment in the everlasting fire.

Fire, for that matter, was from ancient times the revelation and symbol of the anger and wrath of the Lord. Israel's God is a consuming fire, an eternal flame (Deut. 4:24; 9:3; Isa. 33:14). He spoke to the children of Israel from the midst of the fire (Deut. 4:12, 33; 5:4, 22–26; 9:10; 10:4; cf. Exod. 3:2, 4). His wrath is a red-hot fire flaming forth from his nostrils (Pss. 18:8; 79:5; 89:46; Jer. 4:4). Fire coming forth from the presence of the Lord consumes the offering (Lev. 9:24). By fire he destroyed Nadab and Abihu (10:2), complainers from among his people (Num. 11:1; Ps. 106:18), the descendants of Korah (Num. 16:35), and the regiments of fifty sent out against Elijah (2 Kings 1:10ff.). One day he will come in a blaze of fire to do justice on earth and to punish the wicked (Deut. 32:22; Pss. 11:6; 83:14–15; 97:3; 140:10; Isa. 30:33; 31:9; 66:15–16, 24; Jer. 4:4; 15:14; 17:4; Joel 2:30; Amos 1:4ff.)—a fire burning to the depths of Sheol (Deut. 32:22), a fire that will never be quenched (Isa. 66:24) and that burns forever (Jer. 17:4). This representation [of judgment] then passed into the New Testament. Gehenna, the place of punishment after the day of judgment, is distinct from hades (ἄδης, hadēs), the underworld (φυλακη, phylakē), and the pit (ἄβυσσος, abyssos) but identical with the furnace of fire (καμινος του πυρος, kaminos tou pyros; Matt. 13:42, 50) and the lake of fire (λιμνη του πυρος, limnē tou pyros; Rev. 19:20; 20:10, 14–15; 21:8). It is a place destined for the beast from the pit and for the false prophet (19:20), for Satan and his angels (20:10), for death and hades (20:14), and for all the wicked (20:15; 21:8). These are all hurled into it *after* the resurrection (Matt. 5:29–30; 10:28), and *after* the final judgment (Rev. 19:20; 20:10, 14–15; 21:8). Before that time hades, the prison house (φυλακη, phylakē; 1 Pet. 3:19; Rev. 20:7), or the pit (ἄβυσσος, abyssos) were their abode, and the punishment of everlasting fire or the dimness of the outer darkness was still reserved for them (Matt. 8:29–32; 25:41, 46; 2 Pet. 2:17; Jude 13). Burning in that Gehenna is everlasting, unquenchable *fire* (Matt. 18:8; Mark 9:43–44, 48). This is where the *worm* that does not die keeps gnawing (Mark 9:44, 46, 48 KJV) and the *torment* never ends (Matt. 25:46; 2 Thess. 1:9; Rev. 14:11). It is a Gehenna or *furnace of fire* (Matt. 5:22; 13:42, 50; 18:9) and at the same time a place of extreme, outer *darkness* (Matt. 8:12; 22:13; 25:30; 2 Pet. 2:17; Jude 13; cf. Deut. 5:22; Ps. 97:2–3). It is located "outside" (Rev. 22:15), in the *depths*, so that one is thrown down into it (Matt. 5:29–30; Rev. 19:20; 20:10, 14–15).

This place is far from the marriage table of the Lamb (Matt. 8:11–12; 22:13), far from fellowship with God and with Christ (7:23; 25:41; Luke 13:27–28;

2 Thess. 1:9); it is rather in the company of Satan and his angels (Matt. 25:41; Rev. 20:10, 15). The *wrath of God* in all its terror is manifested there (Rom. 2:5–8; 9:22; 1 Thess. 1:10; Heb. 10:31; Rev. 6:16–17). Consequently, Gehenna is not only a place of privation but also of sorrow and pain, in both soul and body; a place of *punishment* (κολασις, *kolasis*; Matt. 25:46; Rev. 14:10–11), of *weeping* (κλαυθμος, *klauthmos*) and *gnashing of teeth* (βρυγμος των ὀδοντων, *brygmos tōn odontōn*; Matt. 8:12; 13:42; etc.), of *anguish* and *distress* (θλιψις, *thlipsis*; and στενοχωρια, *stenochōria*; Rom. 2:9; 2 Thess. 1:6), of *destruction* (ἀπωλεια, *apōleia*; Matt. 7:13; Rom. 9:22; Phil. 1:28; 3:19; 2 Pet. 3:7; Rev. 17:8, 11), of *corruption* (φθορα, *phthora*; Gal. 6:8), and of *ruin* (ὀλεθρος, *olethros*; 1 Thess. 5:3; 2 Thess. 1:9; 1 Tim. 6:9). Gehenna is the realm of the second death (Rev. 2:11; 20:6, 14–15; 21:8).

ALTERNATIVES TO ETERNAL PUNISHMENT

On this firm scriptural basis, the Christian church built a doctrine of the eternity of hellish punishment. Accordingly, in theology as well as in the pulpit, in poetry as well as in the graphic arts, people frequently vied with each other in offering graphic descriptions and realistic portrayals of the pains experienced in the eternal fire in both soul and body. Nevertheless, from time to time objections were raised against this doctrine. After the Enlightenment of the eighteenth century introduced a milder assessment of sin and crime, abolished instruments of torture, moderated punishments, and aroused a sense of humaneness everywhere, there arose a very different view of the punishments of hell. Many people either altered their idea of them or rejected them altogether. The grounds on which people argue against the eternity of hellish punishment always remain the same:

a. Eternal punishment is incompatible with the goodness, love, and compassion of God and makes him a tyrant who takes pleasure in inflicting pain and torment and who prepares praise for himself out of the everlasting moans of millions of unfortunate creatures.
b. Eternal punishment is incompatible with the justice of God, since it is unrelated and in no way proportionate to the sin in question.
c. Such eternal punishment is also unimaginable and inconceivable. The images of fire, a worm, and darkness, taken literally, are mutually exclusive. And, what's the point?
d. Scripture, accordingly, does not teach an eternal and endless punishment in hell. The word "eternal" does not mean "endless" but refers to a period of time the limit of which eludes our perception or calculation: a thing is eternal (αἰωνιος, *aiōnios*) if it exceeds a longer or shorter age (αἰων, *aiōn*). Instead, the condition of the lost is described in terms of "destruction" (ἀπωλεια, *apōleia*), "corruption" (φθορα, *phthora*), "ruin" (ὀλεθρος, *olethros*),

and "death" (θανατος, *thanatos*), which suggests either complete annihilation or total restoration.

e. Scripture offers hope for restoration when it teaches that Christ is the propitiation for the sins of the whole world (Col. 1:19–20; 1 John 2:2), and that God desires all humans to be saved that way (1 Tim. 2:4; 4:10). "For as all die in Adam, so all will be made alive in Christ" (Rom. 5:18; 1 Cor. 15:22). Now God gathers up all things under Christ as head (Eph. 1:10), so that someday every knee will bow before Christ (Phil. 2:10) and God may be all in all (1 Cor. 15:28). "God has imprisoned all in disobedience so that he may be merciful to all" (Rom. 11:32).

From this there are three hypotheses that have been constructed to address the question of the final end of unbelievers.

1. Hypothetical universalism: Hell and eternal punishment depend entirely on human decision. Here a possibility of repentance is said to be open, not only in the intermediate state right up until the final judgment,[4] but also thereafter and for all eternity. The preaching of faith and repentance never stops and the human will continues to be free. Here people flatter themselves with the hope that in the end all will repent and enter into eternal life. What this hypothetical universalism comes down to, therefore, is a theory of ongoing purgation and a renewal of the doctrine of the migration of the soul. Whereas, metempsychosis has this purgation occur in the present world (*Diesseits*), hypothetical universalism situates it in the next (*Jenseits*).

2. Unconditional Universalism: A belief that in the end all creatures will participate in eternal salvation and glory. That which is desired and hoped for in the former is expected as certain and proclaimed as dogma by the latter. The doctrine of the return of all things into God already occurs in Indian and Greek philosophy; from there it passed into gnosticism and Neoplatonism and was for the first time represented in Christian theology by Origen. The problem is that because the free will ever remains the same, it can equally well return from the evil to the good as from the good to the evil, and so there is a continual alternation between apostasy and the restoration of all things, an endless creation and annihilation of the material world.[5] Among those who held this position are: In antiquity: Gregory of Nazianzus, Gregory of Nyssa, Didymus, Diodorus of Tarsus, Theodore of Mopsuestia; in the Middle Ages, Scotus Erigena, the Brothers and Sisters of the Free Spirit; after the Reformation, Denck and numerous Anabaptists,

---

4. Cf. H. Bavinck, *Reformed Dogmatics*, ed. John Bolt (Grand Rapids: Baker Academic, 2003–8), IV, 629–32 (#559).

5. L. Atzberger, *Geschichte der christlichen Eschatologie* (Freiburg i.B. and St. Louis: Herder, 1896), 366–456.

Jung-Stilling, Swedenborg, and so on; and in modern times by Schleiermacher and many others.[6]

3. Conditional Immortality: We are created mortal; immortality of the soul
is a gift of God in case of obedience, a gift not granted to the disobedient. This was taught by the Socinians, picked up by Locke and others, but
caught on and gained adherents after it was advocated by Edward White
in his *Life in Christ*.[7]

[576] If human sentiment had the final say about the doctrine of eternal punishment, it would certainly be hard to maintain and even today finds few defenders.
First, it needs to be gratefully acknowledged that since the eighteenth century
the idea of humaneness and the sense of human sympathy have had a powerful
awakening and have put an end to the cruelty that used to prevail, especially in
the field of criminal justice. No one, however, can be blind to the reality that this
humanitarian viewpoint also brings its own imbalances and dangers. The mighty
turnabout that has occurred can be described in a single sentence: whereas before
the mentally ill were treated as criminals, now criminals are regarded as mentally
ill. Before that time, every abnormality was viewed in terms of sin and guilt; now
all ideas of guilt, crime, responsibility, culpability, and the like are robbed of their
reality.[8] The sense of right and justice, of the violation of law and of guilt, are
seriously weakened to the extent that the norm of all these things is not found in
God but shifted to the opinions of human beings and society. In the process all
certainty and safety is gradually lost. For when the interest of society becomes the
deciding factor, not only is every boundary between good and evil wiped out, but
also justice runs the danger of being sacrificed to power. "It is better for you to
have one man die for the people than to have the whole nation destroyed" (John
11:50) then becomes the language of the administration of justice. And the same
human sentiment that first pleaded for the humane treatment of a criminal does
not shrink, a moment later, from demanding death by torture of the innocent.
Hosannas make way for a cross. The voice of the people (*vox populi*), which is
often wrongly revered as the voice of God (*vox Dei*), recoils from no horrors
whatever. Whereas the righteous person still takes account of the needs of his
animals, even the soft interior of the wicked, their hearts and minds, is still cruel
(Prov. 12:10). Human feeling is no foundation for anything important, therefore,
and neither may nor can it be decisive in the determination of law and justice. All

6. Friedrich Schleiermacher, *The Christian Faith*, ed. H. R. MacIntosh and J. S. Stewart (Edinburgh: T&T Clark, 1928), §§117–20, 163, 720–22, appendix on eternal damnation; cf. J. Köstlin,
"Apokatastasis," in *PRE*³, I, 616–22.

7. E. White, *Life in Christ: A Study of the Scripture Doctrine on the Nature of Man, the Object of the
Divine Incarnation and the Conditions of Human Immortality*, 3rd, rev. and enlarged ed. (London: Elliot
Stock, 1878). Ed. note: This is also the view of Adventists such as the Seventh-Day Adventists and the
Jehovah's Witnesses.

8. See H. Bavinck, *Reformed Dogmatics*, III, 163–64 (#336).

appearances notwithstanding, it is infinitely better to fall into the hands of the Lord than into human hands (1 Chron. 21:13). The same applies with respect to eternal punishment in hell.

It must be noted that this doctrine, though it is often depicted in too much realistic detail in the church and in theology, is nevertheless grounded in Scripture. And no one in Scripture speaks of it more often and at greater length than our Lord Jesus Christ, whose depth of human feeling and compassion no one can deny and who was the meekest and most humble of human beings. It is the greatest love that threatens the most severe punishments. Over against the blessedness of eternal life that he acquired for his own stands the disaster of eternal ruin that he announces to the wicked. In the Old Testament both were veiled in shadows and presented in imagery. But in the New Testament it is Christ who opens a vista both into the depths of outer darkness and into the dwellings of eternal light.

That the punishment in this place of outer darkness is eternal is not something one can doubt on the basis of Scripture. It is indeed true that the adjective αἰώνιος, aiōnios (from αἰών, aiōn; Heb. עוֹלָם, 'ōlām), the present world age (αἰὼν οὗτος, aiōn houtos; the age to come, αἰὼν μελλων, aiōn mellōn), very often refers to a period of time that is beyond human calculation but certainly not endless or everlasting. But in the New Testament the word αἰώνιος (aiōnios) functions especially to describe the imperishable nature—a nature not subject to any corruption or decay—of the salvific benefits gained by Christ, often linked with the word "life" (ζωή, zōē)—the eternal life that Christ imparts to everyone who believes. It has its beginning here on earth but will only be fully revealed in the future. It essentially belongs to the age to come (αἰὼν μελλων, aiōn mellōn; Luke 18:30), is indestructible (John 11:25–26), and is called "eternal," just as God, Christ, and the Holy Spirit are also called "eternal" (Rom. 16:26; Heb. 9:14; 13:8; etc.). Over against this it is stated that the punishment of the wicked will consist in eternal fire (το πυρ το αἰώνιον, to pyr to aiōnion; Matt. 18:8; 25:41; Jude 7), eternal punishment (κολασις αἰώνιος, kolasis aiōnios; Matt. 25:46), eternal destruction (ὄλεθρος αἰώνιος, olethros aiōnios; 2 Thess. 1:9), and eternal judgment (κρισις αἰώνιος, krisis aiōnios; Mark 3:29 KJV). Like eternal life, so by this description also eternal punishment is presented as belonging to the coming age (αἰὼν μελλων, aiōn mellōn) in which a change of state is no longer possible. Scripture nowhere with a single word indicates or even leaves open the possibility that the state that begins there can still come to an end. And positively it says that the fire there is unquenchable (Matt. 3:12), that the worm does not die (Mark 9:48), that the smoke of torment goes up forever (Rev. 14:11) and continues day and night for all eternity (20:10), and that as eternal pain it contrasts with the eternal life of the righteous (Matt. 25:46). Unbiased exegesis will not find anything here other than eternal, never-ending punishment.

The state of the lost is described as destruction (ἀπωλεια, apōleia; Matt. 7:13), corruption (φθορα, phthora; Gal. 6:8), ruin (ὄλεθρος, olethros; 2 Thess. 1:9), and death (θανατος, thanatos; Rev. 2:11; etc.), which agrees with the fact that, according to the Old and New Testaments, the wicked will be destroyed, eradicated, ruined, put away, cast out, cut off, burned as chaff, and so on. While this is understood by the proponents of conditional immortality in terms of complete annihilation,[9] life, in Scripture, is never mere existence, and death is never the same as annihilation. For sin is not a substance and does not destroy the existent but steers it in a wrong direction, a direction away from God. Physical death is not merely a natural consequence, but a positive—divinely threatened and executed—punishment of sin. In the event of that death, God does not annihilate human beings but temporarily separates soul and body in order to maintain both and to reunite them at the resurrection. When conditionalism views the destruction (ἀπωλεια, *apōleia*) that is the punishment of sin as an annihilation of the human substance, it is confusing the ethical with the physical. Just as God does not annihilate human beings in the first death, so neither does he annihilate them in the second. The state of the wicked can be called destruction (ἀπωλεια, *apōleia*), corruption (φθορα, *phthora*), ruin (ὀλεθρος, *olethros*), and death (θανατος, *thanatos*) because in a moral and spiritual sense they have become total wrecks, and in an absolute sense they lack the fullness of life granted by Christ to believers. Thus the prodigal son is called "dead" (νεκρος, *nekros*) and "lost" (ἀπολωλως, *apolōlōs*; Luke 15:24, 32), the Ephesians in their earlier state are described as "dead" (νεκροι, *nekroi*) through their trespasses and sins (Eph. 2:1; 4:18), and the people of the church of Sardis are called "dead" (νεκροι, *nekroi*; Rev. 3:1; etc.), but no one ever thinks of these three parties as being nonexistent.

The same failure to recognize the ethical character of sin marks the proponents of ἀποκαταστασις (*apokatastasis*, restoration of all things). Scripture nowhere teaches that one day all humans and even all devils will be saved. Often it indeed uses very universalistic language, but that is because, intensively, Christ's work is of infinite value and benefits the whole world and all of humanity in its organic form of existence. But it unambiguously excludes the idea that all human individuals or even the devils will at some time become citizens in the kingdom of God. The doctrine of the restoration of all things, accordingly, has at all times been taught by only a handful of persons. Even today the theory of conditional immortality has more support among theologians than that of the *apokatastasis*. In any case, this doctrine is of pagan—not Christian—origin; it is philosophical, not scriptural, in character. Underlying the theory is pantheism, which views all things as proceeding from God and, similarly, of successively returning to him. In this view God is not the lawgiver and judge who will one day judge the world with equity (Ps. 9:8) but an unconscious immanent force that propels all things to the end and will one day recapture all things into himself. Sin, in this view, is not lawlessness (ἀνομια, *anomia*) but a necessary moment in the evolution of the world. And redemption in Christ is not juridical restoration and ethical renewal but a physical process that controls everything.

9. E. White, *Life in Christ*, 358–90.

In order to appreciate the fact of eternal punishment, it is above all necessary, therefore, to recognize along with Scripture the integrity of the justice of God and the deeply sinful character of sin. Sin is not a weakness, a lack, a temporary and gradually vanishing imperfection, but in origin and essence it is lawlessness (*anomia*), a violation of the law, rebellion and hostility against God, and the negation of his justice, his authority, even his existence. On earth, not all sins (and crimes) are punished the same way. One person who commits a misdemeanor may be given a fine while a murderer is given the death penalty and thereby transferred into an irremediable state by an earthly government. God acts the same way: what the death penalty is on earth, the punishment of hell is in the final judgment. He judges and punishes sin in accordance with its intrinsic quality. That sin is infinite in the sense that it is committed against the Highest Majesty, who is absolutely entitled to our love and worship. God is absolutely and infinitely worthy of our obedience and dedication. He who commits the sin is a slave to sin: he will not and cannot do otherwise than sin. It is truly not his own doing when he is denied the opportunity to continue his sinful life. In terms of his interior desire, he would not want anything other than to live forever so that he could sin forever. Who then, looking at the sinful nature of sin, would have the nerve to say that God is unjust if he visits the sin not only with temporal but also with eternal punishments?

The argument against eternal punishment is often passionately rendered out of conviction that it is inconsistent with the goodness and love of God. However, if it is not inconsistent with the justice of God, it is not and cannot be inconsistent with his goodness either. We have no choice at this point. If eternal punishment is unjust, then that condemns it, and one need no longer appeal to God's goodness. If, however, it is consistent with God's justice, then God's goodness remains unscathed: if a thing is just, it is also good. The argument against eternal punishment derived from God's goodness, therefore, in the manner of Marcion, secretly introduces a conflict between God's justice and his goodness and offers up the former to the latter. But goodness that nullifies justice is no longer true and real goodness. It is mere human weakness and wimpiness and, when projected onto God, an invention of the human brain, one that in no way corresponds to the true and living God who has revealed himself in Scripture as well as in nature. For if eternal punishment is inconsistent with God's goodness, then temporal punishment is inconsistent with it as well. But the latter is a fact no one can deny. Humankind is consumed by God's anger and terrified by his wrath (cf. Ps. 90:7). Who can square this world's suffering with God's goodness and love? Still it must be possible, for it exists. Now if the existence of immense suffering in this world may not lead us to question God's goodness, then neither may eternal punishment prompt us to deny it. If this world is consistent with God's love, as it is and has to be, then hell is too. For aside from Scripture there is no stronger proof for the existence of hell than the existence of this world, the world from whose misery the features of the [biblical] picture of hell are derived.[10]

Furthermore, for the person who disputes [the reality of] eternal punishment, there is enormous danger of playing the hypocrite before God. Such a person presents himself as extremely loving, one who in goodness and compassion far outstrips our Lord Jesus Christ. This does not stop the same person, the moment one's own honor is violated, from erupting in fury and calling down on the violator every evil in this life and the life to come. Resentment, hatred, wrath, and vindictiveness arise in the hearts of all human beings against anyone standing in their way. We promote our own honor, but the honor of God is of no concern to us. We stand up for our own rights but let others trample the rights of God into the dirt. Surely this is sufficient evidence that we humans are not suitable judges of the words and actions of God. Nevertheless, in that act of standing up for our own rights and reputation, there is something good. However wrongly applied, there is implicit in it the fact that our rights and reputation are more precious than our goods and life. Slumbering even in the sinner, there is still a deep sense of justice and honor. When that sense is violated, it is aroused and suppresses all pity. When, in a given conflict between two people or two nations, the issue is one of justice, each party passionately prays that God may bring about the triumph of the right and strike its violators with his judgment. In the day of judgment, too, the issue is one of justice, not some private right or other, but *justice* par excellence, justice in its full import and scope, the justice of God—that God himself may be honored as God in all eternity.

There is, therefore, no doubt that in the day of judgment God will fully vindicate himself in the presence of all his creatures even when he pronounces eternal punishment upon sinners. In Christ he has fully revealed his love, a love that is so great precisely because it saves us from the wrath to come and from eternal destruction. Critics of eternal punishment not only fail to do justice to the doomworthiness of sin, the rigorousness of divine justice; they also infringe on the greatness of God's love and the salvation that is in Christ. If the object had not been salvation from eternal destruction, the price of the blood of God's own Son would have been much too high. The heaven that he won for us by his atoning death presupposes a hell from which he delivered us. The eternal life he imparted to us presupposes an eternal death from which he saved us. The grace and good pleasure of God in which he makes us participants forever presuppose a wrath into which we would otherwise have had to be plunged forever. For that reason it is this Christ who will one day execute judgment and pronounce his sentence. A human being, a true and complete human being who knows what is in human beings, who is the meekest of human beings, will be the judge of human beings, a

---

10. Cf. A. Strindberg, *The Dance of Death*, trans. A. Paulsen (New York: W. W. Norton, 1976), 41 (act 1, scene 1): "Don't you [believe in hell]—you who are living in one?" (German: Glaubst du nicht daran [an die Hölle], wo du mitten in ihr bist?).

judge so just that all will acknowledge his justice, and every knee will bow before him, and every tongue confess that Christ is Lord to the glory of God the Father (Phil. 2:10–11). In the end God will be recognized as God by all creatures, if not willingly then unwillingly.

This should be enough for us. Inquiries into the location and size of hell, the nature of the fire and the worm, the psychic and physical state of the lost—these lead nowhere because Scripture is silent on these topics. All we know besides the things we have discussed so far is that the punishment of hell does not begin until after the day of judgment; that such punishment is consistently threatened against those who stubbornly resist the truth of God; and that even so, this punishment differs in the measure of each person's unrighteousness. Scripture nowhere teaches that there will still be room in hell for repentance and forgiveness. In its essence punishment consists in the maintenance of justice and, after the judgment, serves specifically to requite all persons according to their work, not to purify them. Scripture nevertheless teaches very clearly that there are degrees of punishment. All will receive according to their works (Matt. 10:15; 11:24; 23:14; 24:51; Luke 10:12, 14; 12:46–47; 2 Cor. 5:10; etc.). This fact as such still demonstrates something of God's mercy.[11] All sin is absolutely opposed to the justice of God, but in punishing it God nevertheless takes account of the relative difference existing between sins. There is infinite diversity also on the other side of the grave. For in eternal punishment God's justice always manifests itself in such a way that his goodness and love remain inviolate and can never be justly faulted. The saying that he does not willingly afflict or grieve anyone (Lam. 3:33) applies also in hell. The pain he inflicts is not an object of pleasure, either for him or for the blessed in heaven, but a means of glorifying his virtues, and hence [the punishment is] determined in severity and measure by this ultimate goal.[12]

11. Cf. H. Bavinck, *Reformed Dogmatics*, II, 386, 388–89 (##244–45).

12. See further Augustine, *Enchiridion*, 110–13; *City of God*, XXI; Peter Lombard, *Sententiae in IV libris distinctae*, 3rd ed., 2 vols. (Grotta ferrata: Colleggi S. Bonaventurae ad Claras Aquas, 1971–81), IV, dist. 46–50; T. Aquinas, *Summa Theol.*, suppl., qu. 97–99; A. Dante, "Inferno"; D. Petavius (Petau), "De angelis," III, c. 4–8, in *Opus de theologicus dogmatibus* (Antwerp: Gallet, 1700), IV; Josef Sachs, *Die ewige Dauer der Höllenstrafen* (Paderborn: Schöningh, 1900); J. Bautz, *Die Hölle in Anschluss an die Scholastiek dargestellt* (Mainz: Kirchheim, 1905); J. Stufler, *Die Heiligkeit Gottes und die ewige Tod* (Innsbruck: Rauch, 1903), opposes H. Schell, who assumes the possibility of an *apokatastasis*. F. X. Kiefl undertook to defend him in "Herman Schell und die Ewigkeit der Hölle," *Theologisch-praktischen Monatsschrift* 14 (1904): 685–709, and received a reply from Stufler, *Die Verteidigung Schells durch Prof. Kiefl* (Innsbruck: Rauch, 1904); A. M. Weiss, *Die religiose Gefahr* (Freiburg i.B.: Herder, 1904), 277, 353. Protestantism was consistent in its view of eternal punishment; see, briefly, B. de Moor, *Commentarius perpetuus in Joh. Marckii Compendium theologiae christianae didactico-elencticum*, 6 vols. (Leiden: J. Hasebroek, 1761–71), III, 354–58; Campegius Vitringa, *Doctrina christianae religionis, per aphorismos summatim descripta*, 6th ed., 8 vols. (Leiden: Joannis le Mair; Arnheim: J. H. Möelemanni, 1761–86), IV, 175; II, 305, 320. In modern times, the idea that the hereafter does not bring a state of bliss for everyone sometimes encounters greater appreciation on the basis of the absolute character of the moral law or on the basis of the law of retribution (karma) that makes the consequences of sin inevitable; cf. Bavinck, *Philosophy of Revelation* (New York: Longmans, Green, 1909), 295, 314. On the ideas of pagans relative

THE RENEWAL OF CREATION

[577] Following the final judgment comes the renewal of the world. In the Old Testament, the day of the Lord is indeed preceded by a range of fearful signs, and judgment on the nations takes place amid appalling events of different kinds. However, the new earth, with its extraordinary fruitfulness, comes into being only when victory over Israel's enemies has been achieved and the people have returned to their land and been restored in it. According to the New Testament as well, the day of judgment is preceded by many signs, such as the darkening of sun and moon and stars, the shaking of the powers of heaven, and so on (Matt. 24:29). The burning of the earth, though, does not occur until the day of the Lord (2 Pet. 3:10), and then follows the coming of the new heaven and new earth in which righteousness dwells (3:13). Once judgment has been executed, John sees the new Jerusalem coming down out of heaven from God (Rev. 21:1f.). In this expectation of world renewal, Scripture assumes a position between two extremes. On the one hand, many thinkers have asserted that this world is destined to continue in its present form forever. On the other hand, there are those who believed that the world would not only be changed in form but also destroyed in substance and replaced by a totally new world.[13]

According to Scripture, however, the present world will neither continue forever nor will it be destroyed and replaced by a totally new one. Old Testament passages that are assumed to teach the total destruction (Ps. 102:26; Isa. 34:4; 51:6, 16; 65:17; 66:22) do indeed describe in very graphic terms the change that will set in after the day of the Lord, but they do not imply the destruction of the substance of the world. In the first place, the description given in these passages is much too rich in imagery for us to infer from them a reduction to nothing (*reductio ad nihilum*) of the entire world. Further, the perishing (אָבַד, *'ābad*) of heaven and earth (Ps. 102:26), which by itself never conveys an absolute destruction of substance, is explained by the fact that it will wear out like a garment, be changed like clothing, wither like a leaf on a vine, or vanish like smoke (Ps. 102:26; Isa. 34:4; 51:6). Finally, the Hebrew word "create" (בָּרָא, *bārā'*) used with reference to the new heaven and the new earth (Isa. 65:17) does not always mean creating something out of nothing but frequently denotes a divine activity by which God brings forth something new from the old (Isa. 41:20; 43:7; 54:16; 57:18). For that reason it also frequently alternates with planting, laying the foundations of, and making (Isa. 51:16; 66:22).

In the same way, the New Testament proclaims that heaven and earth will pass away (Matt. 5:18; 24:35; 2 Pet. 3:10; 1 John 2:17; Rev. 21:1), that they will perish and wear out like clothing (Heb. 1:11), dissolve (2 Pet. 3:10), be burned with fire (3:10), and be changed (Heb. 1:12). But none of these expressions implies a

---

to reward and punishment on the other side of the grave, cf. F. Hettinger, *Apologie du Christianisme*, 5 vols. (Bar-le-Duc: L. Guérin, 1869–70), IV, 320.

13. C. Vitringa, *Doctr. christ.*, IV, 194–200.

destruction of substance. Peter, for example, expressly teaches that the old earth, which originated as a result of the separation of waters, was deluged with water and so perished (2 Pet. 3:6), and that the present world would also perish, not—thanks to the divine promise—by water but by fire. The world was not totally destroyed in the flood, and so we must no more think of a destruction of substance with fire than we would do with water: fire burns, cleanses, purifies but does not destroy. The contrast in 1 John 2:17 ("the world and its desire are passing away, but those who do the will of God live forever") teaches us that the first statement does not imply a destruction of the substance of the world but a vanishing of the world in its present, sin-damaged form. Paul also states very clearly that the present form (το σχημα, *to schēma*) of this world passes away (1 Cor. 7:31). Only such a renewal of the world, for that matter, accords with what Scripture teaches about redemption which is never a second, brand-new creation but a re-creation of the existing world. God's honor consists precisely in the fact that he redeems and renews the same humanity, the same world, the same heaven, and the same earth that have been corrupted and polluted by sin. Just as anyone in Christ is a new creation in whom the old has passed away and everything has become new (2 Cor. 5:17), so also this world passes away in its present form, in order out of its womb, at God's word of power, to give birth and being to a new world. Just as in the case of an individual human being, so at the end of time a rebirth of the world will take place as well (Matt. 19:28). This constitutes a spiritual renewal, not a physical creation.

This renewal of the visible world highlights the one-sidedness of the spiritualism that limits future blessedness to heaven. While the kingdom of God is first planted spiritually in human hearts, the future blessedness of biblical hope, rooted in incarnation and resurrection, is creational, this-worldly, visible, physical, bodily hope. In the case of Old Testament prophecy, one cannot doubt that it describes earthly blessedness. Its expectation is that following the great day, the people of God will live in security and peace in Palestine under the anointed king of the dynasty of David, surrounded and served by the gentile nations. There is some truth in Delitzsch's comments on Isaiah 66:24 when he describes the Old Testament as "bringing down the life to come to the level of this life, whilst the New Testament lifts up this life to the level of the life to come."[14] There is a process of spiritualization that takes place as we move from the Old Testament to the New Testament.

Since Jesus's advent breaks up into a first and a second coming, the kingdom of God is first planted in human hearts spiritually, and the benefits of that kingdom are all internal and invisible: forgiveness, peace, righteousness, and eternal life. The essence of future blessedness, accordingly, is also construed more spiritually, especially by Paul and John, as being always with the Lord (John 12:26; 14:3;

14. F. Delitzsch, *Biblical Commentary on the Prophecies of Isaiah*, trans. J. Martin, 2 vols. (Edinburgh: T&T Clark, 1869–80; repr., Grand Rapids: Eerdmans, 1954), II, 517.

17:24; 2 Cor. 5:8; Phil. 1:23; 1 Thess. 4:17; 5:10; 1 John 3:2). But this does not confine this blessedness to heaven. This cannot be the case as is basically evident from the fact that the New Testament teaches the incarnation of the Word and the physical resurrection of Christ; it further expects his physical return at the end of time, and immediately thereafter has in view the physical resurrection of all human beings, especially that of believers. All this spells the collapse of spiritualism, which if it remains true to its principle—as in Origen—has nothing left after the day of judgment other than spirits in an uncreated heaven.

But the teaching of Scripture is very different. The world, according to it, consists of heaven and earth; humans consist of soul and body; and the kingdom of God, accordingly, has a hidden spiritual dimension and an external, visible side. Whereas Jesus came the first time to establish that kingdom in a spiritual sense, he returns at the end of history to give visible shape to it. Reformation proceeds from the inside to the outside. The rebirth of humans is completed in the rebirth of creation. The kingdom of God is fully realized only when it is visibly extended over the earth as well. This is how also the disciples understood it when, after Jesus's resurrection, they asked him whether this was the time he would restore the kingdom to Israel. In his reply, Jesus does not deny that one day he will establish such a kingdom but says only that the times for it have been set by the Father and that now his disciples are called, in the power of the Holy Spirit, to be his witnesses to the ends of the earth (Acts 1:6–8). Elsewhere he expressly states that the meek will inherit the earth (Matt. 5:5). He pictures future blessedness as a meal at which the guests sit down with Abraham, Isaac, and Jacob (8:11), enjoy food and drink (Luke 22:30), eat of the new and perfect Passover (Luke 22:16), and drink of the fruit of the new vine (Matt. 26:29). In this dispensation and right up until the parousia, the eyes of believers are directed toward heaven, where their treasure is (6:20; 19:21), where Jesus, who is their life, sits at the right hand of God (John 14:3; 17:24; Col. 3:1–3). While they are aliens here, their citizenship is there (Phil. 3:20; Heb. 11:13–16).

But this inheritance is destined to be revealed. Someday Christ will return visibly and then cause the whole believing community—indeed, the whole world—to participate in his glory. Not only are believers changed after his likeness (John 17:24; Rom. 8:17–18, 28; Phil. 3:21; Col. 3:4; 1 John 3:2), but also "the whole creation itself will be set free from its bondage to decay and obtain the freedom of the glory of the children of God" (Rom. 8:21). Earth and heaven will be renewed so that justice will be at home in them (2 Pet. 3:13; Rev. 21:1). The heavenly Jerusalem, which is now above and was the model for the earthly Jerusalem, then comes down to earth (Gal. 4:26; Heb. 11:10, 13–16; 12:22; 13:14; Rev. 3:12; 21:2ff.). The heavenly Jerusalem is a city built by God (Heb. 11:10). It is the city of the living God, inasmuch as God is not just its architect but also makes it his home (Rev. 21:3). In it the angels are the servants and constitute the royal entourage of the great king (Heb. 12:22), while the blessed are its citizens (Rev. 21:27; 22:3–4).

The description John gives of that Jerusalem (Rev. 21–22) should certainly not be taken literally any more than his preceding visions. The details provided are not intended to give a sketch of the city; rather, they are grand images used—since he cannot do it any other way—to bring the glory of the divine kingdom home to us. So he draws his material from paradise, with its river and tree of life (21:6; 22:1–2); Jerusalem, with its gates and streets (21:12ff.); the temple, with its holy of holies in which God himself dwelt (21:3, 22); and the entire realm of nature, with all its treasures of gold and precious stones (21:11, 18–21). These images are not illusions or fabrications, but this-worldly depictions of otherworldly realities. All that is true, honorable, just, pure, pleasing, and commendable in the whole of creation, in heaven and on earth, is gathered up in the future city of God—renewed, re-created, boosted to its highest glory.

The substance [of the city of God] is present in this creation. Just as the caterpillar becomes a butterfly, as carbon is converted into diamond, as the grain of wheat upon dying in the ground produces other grains of wheat, as all of nature revives in the spring and dresses up in celebrative clothing, as the believing community is formed out of Adam's fallen race, as the resurrection body is raised from the body that is dead and buried in the earth, so too, by the re-creating power of Christ, the new heaven and the new earth will one day emerge from the fire-purged elements of this world, radiant in enduring glory and forever set free from the "bondage to decay" (δουλειας της φθορας, *douleias tēs phthoras*; Rom. 8:21). More glorious than this beautiful earth, more glorious than the earthly Jerusalem, more glorious even than paradise will be the glory of the new Jerusalem, whose architect and builder is God himself. The state of glory (*status gloriae*) will be no mere restoration (*restauratie*) of the state of nature (*status naturae*) but a re-formation[15] that, thanks to the power of Christ, transforms all matter (ὑλη, *hylē*) into form (εἰδος, *eidos*), all potency into actuality (*potentia, actus*), and presents the entire creation before the face of God, brilliant in unfading splendor and blossoming in a springtime of eternal youth. *Substantially* nothing is lost. Outside, indeed, are the dogs and sorcerers and fornicators and murderers and idolaters and everyone who loves and practices falsehood (Rev. 22:15). But in the new heaven and new earth, the world as such is restored; in the believing community the human race is saved. In that community, which Christ has purchased and gathered from all nations, languages, and tongues (Rev. 5:9; etc.), all the nations, Israel included, maintain their distinct places and calling (Matt. 8:11; Rom. 11:25; Rev. 21:24; 22:2). All those nations—each in accordance with its own distinct national character—bring into the new Jerusalem all they have received from God in the way of glory and honor (Rev. 21:24, 26).

[578] The salvation of the kingdom of God, including communion with God as well as the communion of the saints, is both a present blessing and a future, consummated, rich glory. The kingdom of God has come and is coming. The scope

---

15. Ed. note: See note 2 above or H. Bavinck, *Reformed Dogmatics*, IV, 697n5 (#573).

of God's mercy is wide. While we should abstain from a firm judgment concerning the salvation of pagans or children who die in infancy, the Reformed confessions are magnanimous in their outlook. Although many fall away, in Christ the human race, the world, is saved. The final rest of God's children is not to be conceived as inaction; his children remain his servants, who joyfully and in diverse ways serve him night and day. What we sow on earth is harvested in eternity; diversity is not destroyed in eternity but cleansed from sin and made serviceable to fellowship with God and others. Scripture even teaches degrees of glory in the future kingdom, commensurate with one's works. The blessedness of salvation is the same for all, but there are distinctions in glory. This distinction is not merited by good works but [comes through] a sovereign, free, and gracious covenantal disposition of God—a given right to believers merited by Christ. God thus crowns his own work in order that in such active diversity the glory of his own attributes shines out. All creatures will then live and move and have their being in God, who is all in all, who reflects all of his attributes in the mirror of his works and glorifies himself in them.

The blessings in which the blessed participate are also material and physical in nature. As misguided as it is—along with pagan peoples and some chiliasts—to make the material into the chief component of future blessedness, so it is also one-sided and stoic to regard the physical indifferently or to exclude it totally from the state of blessedness. Scripture consistently maintains the intimate connectedness of the spiritual and the natural. Inasmuch as the world consists of heaven and earth and humans consist of soul and body, so also sanctity and glory, virtue and happiness, the moral and the natural world order ought finally to be harmoniously united. The blessed will therefore not only be free from sin but also from all the consequences of sin, from ignorance and error (John 6:45), from death (Luke 20:36; 1 Cor. 15:26; Rev. 2:11; 20:6, 14), from poverty and disease, from pain and fear, hunger and thirst, cold and heat (Matt. 5:4; Luke 6:21; Rev. 7:16–17; 21:4), and from all weakness, dishonor, and corruption (1 Cor. 15:42; etc.).

Still the spiritual blessings are the more important and innumerably abundant: holiness (Rev. 3:4–5; 7:14; 19:8; 21:27); salvation (Rom. 13:11; 1 Thess. 5:9; Heb. 1:14; 5:9); glory (Luke 24:26; Rom. 2:10; 8:18, 21); adoption (Rom. 8:23); eternal life (Matt. 19:16–17, 29; etc.); the vision of, and conformity to, God and Christ (Matt. 5:18; John 17:24; Rom. 8:29; 1 Cor. 13:12; 2 Cor. 3:18; Phil. 3:21; 1 John 3:2; Rev. 22:4); and fellowship with, and the service and praise of, God and Christ (John 17:24; 2 Cor. 5:8; Phil. 1:23; Rev. 4:10; 5:9–13; 7:10, 15–17; 21:3; 22:3; etc.). Against the abstract supernaturalism of the Greek Orthodox and Roman Catholic Churches—which see salvation as exclusively transcendent and therefore, as it concerns the earth, consider the Christian life embodied ideally in monasticism—this [present-worldly] view stands for an important truth. The Reformation, going back to Scripture, in principle overcame this supernaturalistic and ascetic view of life. Those who believe, at the very moment of believing, receive the forgiveness of sins and eternal life. They are children of God, who serve the

Father not as hired employees in hope of compensation, but as children who do the will of the Father out of love and gratitude. They carry out this will not by fleeing from the world, but by being faithful in the calling entrusted to them on earth. Living for heaven, therefore, does not compete with life in the midst of the world: it is precisely in the world that Christ keeps his disciples from the evil one.

The new heaven and earth, as we indicated earlier, is composed of the elements of the world that exists now, and the believing community is humanity restored under Christ as head. Yet our enjoyment of salvation is not yet full; we are saved in hope (Rom. 8:24). Believers are children of God but still await the full realization of their "sonship" (Matt. 5:9; Rom. 8:23). They have eternal life but must still receive it at the resurrection (John 5:20–29; 6:40, 44–45). Both are therefore true: the kingdom of heaven has come and it is still coming. And this twofold truth conditions the entire character of the state of glory. As the new heaven and earth are formed out of the elements of this world, and the believing community is a re-creation of the human race that fell in Adam, so the life of the redeemed in the hereafter is to be conceived as analogous with the life of believers here on earth. It is neither an ethereal contemplation of God (*visio Dei*) done by those whose human nature has been elevated by a superadded gift (*donum superadditum*), nor is it simply an extension of the present life of sanctification on earth. In that life, religion—fellowship with God—is primary and central. But that fellowship will be richer, deeper, and more blessed than it ever was or could be on earth, since it will not be disturbed by any sin, or interrupted by any distance, or mediated by either Scripture or nature. Then they will receive and possess everything they expected here only in hope.

[579] The blessedness of communion with God is enjoyed in and heightened by the communion of saints. On earth already this communion is a wonderful benefit of faith. Those who for Jesus's sake have left behind house or brothers or sisters or father or mother or wife or children or fields already in this life receive houses, brothers, sisters, mothers, children, and fields—along with persecutions—(Mark 10:29–30), for all who do the will of the Father are Jesus's brother and sister and mother (Matt. 12:50). Through the mediator of the New Testament, believers enter into fellowship, not only with the militant church on earth, but also with the triumphant church in heaven, the assembly of the firstborn, the spirits of the righteous made perfect, even with innumerable angels (Heb. 12:22–24). But this fellowship, though in principle it already exists on earth, will nevertheless be incomparably richer and more glorious when all dividing walls of descent and language, of time and space, have been leveled, all sin and error have been banished, and all the elect have been assembled in the new Jerusalem. Then will be fully answered the prayer of Jesus that all his sheep may be one flock under one Shepherd (John 10:16; 17:21). All the saints together will then fully comprehend the breadth and length and height and depth of the love of Christ (Eph. 3:18–19). And sitting down at one table with Abraham, Isaac, and Jacob (Matt. 8:11), they will, united, lift up a song of praise to the glory of God and of the Lamb (Rev. 4:11;

5:12; etc.). Speaking of the believing community on earth, Scripture frequently says that it is a "little flock" (Matt. 7:14; 22:14; Luke 12:32; 13:23), a statement confirmed by history right up until the present. Old Testament prophecy already announced that only a remnant of Israel would repent and be saved. The New Testament likewise expects that those who persevere to the end will be few (Matt. 24:13; 25:1ff.; Luke 18:8).

On the other hand, however, Scripture often uses very universalistic language. In Adam the covenant of grace is made known to humanity as a whole (Gen. 3:15). The covenant of nature concluded after the flood embraces all creatures (9:9–10). In Abraham all generations of the earth are blessed (12:3). The salvation that will one day be granted to Israel profits all the gentiles. Jesus says that he will give his life as a ransom for *many* (Matt. 20:28) and that *many* will come from east and west to sit down with Abraham, Isaac, and Jacob in the kingdom of heaven (8:11). The grace that appeared in Christ is much more abundant than the trespass of Adam: it comes to all people for justification and life (Rom. 5:12–20; 1 Cor. 15:22). In this dispensation all things in heaven and on earth will be gathered up under Christ (Eph. 1:10). One day at the end every knee will bow before Christ and every tongue will confess him as Lord (Phil. 2:10–11). Then a great multitude that no one can number will stand before the throne and the Lamb (Rev. 7:9; 19:1, 6). *Nations* will be saved and walk in the light of the new Jerusalem (21:24, 26; 22:2). And God will then be all in all (1 Cor. 15:28).

THE WIDENESS OF GOD'S MERCY

Because of this last series of texts, many people have cherished the hope that in the end, if not all creatures, then surely all humans—or if this should fail, then far and away the majority of humans—will be saved. Hell will either be totally nonexistent or only a small and remote corner of the universe. Even among those who adhere to the confession that no one comes to the Father except by Christ, and that only one name has been given under heaven for salvation (John 14:6; Acts 4:12), there have always been a few people who believed in the possibility of salvation in this life aside from the preaching of the gospel. They taught this view with respect to children of the covenant, to all children who die in infancy within or outside the bounds of Christianity, to the developmentally or emotionally handicapped, and to the hearing- and speech-impaired, who are practically shut off from the preaching of the gospel. The same applies to some or many pagans who in terms of their clear insights and virtuous lives gave evidence of true piety. Some of the church fathers assumed that the Logos was active in the pagan world.[16] Augustine believed that from the beginning there have always been

16. Cf. H. Bavinck, *Reformed Dogmatics*, I, 229–30 (#68); II, 565–68 (#295); IV, 33–35, 51, 61 (##433, 438, 441).

a few persons, in Israel but in other nations as well, who believed in the Logos and lived faithfully and righteously in accordance with his commandments.[17] Abelard asserted that pagans too could inherit salvation. Zwingli believed that God had his elect also among pagans.[18] But others left open only the possibility and did not venture to go beyond hoping and wishing. This opinion, however, was never held by more than a handful.

In their confessions the churches made no pronouncements on this issue, and most theologians opposed the idea.[19] Somewhat more favorable were their views on the salvation of children who died in infancy. Catholics teach that all children of Christian parents who died, having been baptized through express intention (*voto*) or in reality (*re*), were saved and that all other children who died young suffered a penalty of damnation but not of sensation (*poene damni*, not *sensus*) in the limbo of children (*limbus infantum*).[20] With respect to children of Christian parents, Lutherans hold the same view as Catholics and leave the others to the judgment of God.[21] The Reformed were inclined to believe that all children who were born in the covenant of grace and died before reaching the age of discretion attained to blessedness in heaven,[22] though in this connection as well many of them made a distinction between elect and reprobate children and did not dare to attribute salvation with certainty to each of these children individually.[23] As for children outside the covenant who died in infancy, the judgment of some was quite magnanimous. Junius, for example, would rather surmise out of love that they were saved than that they were lost.[24] Voetius said, as to whether they are lost or some among them are elect and were regenerated before they died, "I would not wish to deny, nor am I able to affirm" (*nolim negare, affirmare non possum*).[25]

In light of Scripture, both with regard to the salvation of pagans and that of children who die in infancy, we cannot get beyond abstaining from a firm judgment, in either a positive or a negative sense. Deserving of note, however, is that in the face of these serious questions Reformed theology is in a much more favorable position than any other. For in this connection, all other churches can

17. Augustine, *Letters*, 102; *City of God*, XVIII, 47; and other places. Cf. H. Reuter, *Augustinische Studien* (Gotha: Perthes, 1887), 90ff.

18. U. Zwingli, *Exposition of the Christian Faith*, chap. x, "Everlasting Life," in *On Providence and Other Essays*, ed. S. M. Jackson and W. J. Hinke (1922; repr., Durham, NC: Labyrinth, 1983), 272.

19. Cf. the literature in C. Vitringa, *Doctr. christ.*, I, 29.

20. P. Lombard, *Sent.*, II, dist. 33.

21. J. Gerhard, *Loci theologici*, ed. E. Preuss, 9 vols. (Berlin: G. Schlawitz, 1863–75), XVI, §169; J. F. Buddeus, *Institutiones theologiae dogmaticae* (Frankfurt and Leipzig, 1741), V, 1, 6.

22. Canons of Dort, I, 17; Gisbert Voetius, *Selectae disputationes theologicae*, 5 vols. (Utrecht, 1648–69), II, 417.

23. P. Martyr Vermigli, *Loci communes*, ed. R. Massonius (London, 1576), 76, 436; and similarly Beza, Pareus, Zanchius, Perkins, and others.

24. F. Junius, *Opuscula theologica selecta*, ed. A. Kuyper (Amsterdam: F. Muller, 1882), II, 333.

25. G. Voetius, *Select. disp.*, II, 413; further: C. Vitringa, *Doctr. christ.*, II, 51–52. Cf. esp. B. B. Warfield, "The Development of the Doctrine of Infant Salvation," in *Two Studies in the History of Doctrine* (New York: Christian Literature, 1897), 143–299.

entertain a more temperate judgment only if they reconsider their doctrine of the absolute necessity of the means of grace or infringe upon that of the accursedness of sin. But the Reformed refused to establish the measure of grace needed for a human being still to be united with God, though subject to many errors and sins, or to determine the extent of the knowledge indispensably necessary to salvation. Furthermore, they maintained that the means of grace are not absolutely necessary for salvation and that also apart from the Word and sacraments God can regenerate persons for eternal life.

Thus, in the Second Helvetic Confession, article 1, we read: "At the same time we recognize that God can illuminate whom and when he will, even without the external ministry, for that is in his power" (*agnoscimus Deum illuminare posse homines, etiam sine externo ministerio, quos et quando velit; id quod ejus potentiae est*). And the Westminster Confession states (in ch. X, §3) that "elect infants, dying in infancy, are regenerated and saved by Christ through the Spirit, who works when, and where, and how he pleases" (*Christus, qui quando et ubi et quo sibi placuerit modo operatur*), and that this applies also to "all other elect persons who are incapable of being outwardly called by the ministry of the Word" (*quotquot externae vocationis per ministerium verbi sunt incapaces*). Reuter, accordingly, after explaining Augustine's teaching on this point, correctly states: "One could in fact defend the paradox that it is precisely the *particularistic* doctrine of predestination that makes possible those *universalistic*-sounding phrases."[26] Even the universalistic passages of Scripture cited above come most nearly and most beautifully into their own in Reformed theology. For these texts are certainly not intended universalistically in the sense that all humans or even all creatures are saved, nor are they so understood by any Christian church. All churches without exception confess that there is not only a heaven but also a hell. At most, therefore, there is a difference of opinion about the number of those who are saved and of those who are lost. But that is not something one can argue about inasmuch as that number is known only to God. When Jesus was asked: "Lord, will only a few be saved?" he only replied: "Strive to enter through the narrow door; for many . . . will try to enter but will not be able" (Luke 13:24).

Directly important to us is only that we have no need to know the number of the elect. In any case, it is a fact that in Reformed theology the number of the elect need not, for any reason or in any respect, be deemed smaller than in any other theology. In fact, at bottom the Reformed confessions are more magnanimous and broader in outlook than any other Christian confession. It locates the ultimate and most profound source of salvation solely in God's good pleasure, in his eternal compassion, in his unfathomable mercy, in the unsearchable riches of his grace, grace that is both omnipotent and free. Aside from it, where could we find a firmer and broader foundation for the salvation of a sinful and lost human

26. Hermann Reuter, *Augustinische Studien* (Gotha: Perthes, 1887; repr., Aalen: Scientia-Verlag, 1967), 92.

race? However troubling it may be that many fall away, still in Christ the believing community, the human race, the world, is saved. The organism of creation is restored. The wicked perish from the earth (Ps. 104:35); they are cast out (John 12:31; 15:6; Rev. 22:15). Still, all things in heaven and earth are gathered up in Christ (Eph. 1:10). All things are created through him and for him (Col. 1:16).

[580] The communion with God that is enjoyed in the communion of saints no more excludes all action and activity in the age to come than it does in the present dispensation. As a rule Christian theology indeed paid little attention to this fact and primarily spoke of heavenly blessedness as a matter of knowing and enjoying God. And this, undoubtedly, is the core and center, the source and power, of eternal life. Also, Scripture offers but little information enabling us to form a clear picture of the activity of the blessed. It describes this blessedness more in terms of resting from our earthly labors than of engaging in new activities (Heb. 4:9; Rev. 14:13). Still, the rest enjoyed in the new Jerusalem is not to be conceived, either in the case of God (John 5:17) or in the case of his children, as blessed inaction. Scripture itself tells us that eternal life consists in knowing and serving God, in glorifying and praising him (John 17:3; Rev. 4:11; 5:8–10; etc.). His children remain his servants, who serve him night and day (Rev. 22:3). They are prophets, priests, and kings who reign on earth forever (1:6; 5:10; 22:5). Inasmuch as they have been faithful over little on earth, they will be put in charge of many things in the kingdom of God (Matt. 24:47; 25:21, 23). All will retain their own personalities, for the names of all who enter the new Jerusalem have been written in the Lamb's book of life (Rev. 20:15; 21:27), and all will receive a new name of their own (Isa. 62:2; 65:15; Rev. 2:17; 3:12; cf. 21:12, 14). The dead who die in the Lord rest from their labors but each is followed by one's own works (Rev. 14:13). Tribes, peoples, and nations all make their own particular contributions to the enrichment of life in the new Jerusalem (5:9; 7:9; 21:24, 26). What we have sown here is harvested in eternity (Matt. 25:24, 26; 1 Cor. 15:42ff.; 2 Cor. 9:6; Gal. 6:7–9). The great diversity that exists among people in all sorts of ways is not destroyed in eternity but is cleansed from all that is sinful and made serviceable to fellowship with God and each other. And just as the natural diversity present in the believing community on earth is augmented with spiritual diversity (1 Cor. 12:7ff.), so also this natural and spiritual diversity is in turn augmented in heaven by the diversity of degrees of glory present there.

Moved by their opposition to the meritoriousness of good works, some Reformed scholars[27] have denied—as did Jovian in the fourth century, and later certain Socinians, and Gerlach even today—that there is any distinction in glory. It is true that all believers have been promised the same benefits in Christ's future: they all receive the same eternal life, the same abode in the new Jerusalem, the same fellowship with God, the same blessedness, and so on. Nevertheless, Scripture

27. Examples: P. Martyr Vermigli, *Loci comm.*, III, 17, 8; similarly Cameron, Tilenus, Spanheim, and others.

leaves no doubt whatever that in all that oneness and sameness there is enormous variation and diversity. Even the parable frequently cited to prove the opposite (Matt. 20:1–16) argues for such distinction. By this parable, Jesus makes the point that many who in their own opinion and that of others have worked long and hard will certainly not be behind in the messianic kingdom of the future by comparison with those who worked in the vineyard a much shorter period. The latter catch up with the former for, though many have been called and labor in the service of the kingdom of God, in the hereafter few will on that account enjoy special status and receive a position of distinction.

Such degrees of distinction in glory are taught much more clearly in other passages in Scripture, especially in those stating that all will receive a reward commensurate with their works. That reward is now kept in heaven (Matt. 5:12; 6:1ff.; Luke 6:23; 1 Tim. 6:19; Heb. 10:34–37) and will be publicly distributed only at the parousia (Matt. 6:4, 6, 18; 24:47; 2 Thess. 1:7; 1 Pet. 4:13). It is then given as compensation for that which the disciples of Jesus have given up and suffered on his account on earth (Matt. 5:10ff.; 19:29; Luke 6:21ff.; Rom. 8:17–18; 2 Cor. 4:17; 2 Thess. 1:7; Heb. 10:34; 1 Pet. 4:13) and also as a reward for the good works they have done; for example, the good use they made of their talents (Matt. 25:14ff.; Luke 19:13ff.), the love of one's enemies and the practice of selfless generosity (Luke 6:35), the care of the poor (Matt. 6:1), prayer and fasting (6:6, 18), ministering to the saints (10:40–42), and faithful service in the kingdom of God (24:44–47; 1 Cor. 3:8; etc.). That reward will be linked with and proportionate to the works performed (Matt. 16:27; 19:29; 25:21, 23; Luke 6:38; 19:17, 19; Rom. 2:6; 1 Cor. 3:8; 2 Cor. 4:17; 5:10; 9:6; Gal. 6:8–9; Heb. 11:26; Rev. 2:23; 11:18; 20:12; 22:12). Blessedness is indeed the same for all, but there are distinctions in "brightness" and glory (Dan. 12:3; 1 Cor. 15:41). In the Father's house, in which all God's children are welcomed, there are many dwelling places (John 14:2); the churches all receive from the King of the church a precious token and crown of their own in accordance with their faithfulness and dedication (Rev. 1–3).

Misuse of the notion of reward[28] does not alter the truth that there is disparity in glory depending on the works done by believers on earth. There is no reward to which humans are by nature entitled, inasmuch as the law of God is absolutely binding and does not let the demand of fulfillment depend on the free choice of people. Therefore, even if they have fulfilled the whole law, it only behooves them to say: "We are worthless slaves; we have done only what we ought to have done!" (Luke 17:10). All claims to reward can therefore flow only from a covenant, a sovereignly free and gracious disposition of God, and hence [reward] is a *given* right. Christ has fulfilled all the requirements; he not only suffered the penalty but also, by fulfilling the law, won eternal life. The eternal blessedness and glory he received was, for him, the reward for his perfect obedience. But when he confers this righteousness of his on his own people through faith and unites eternal life

---

28. For example, Roman Catholic notions of the meritoriousness of good works.

with it, then the two, both the righteousness conferred and future blessedness, are the gifts of his grace, a reality that utterly excludes all merit on the part of believers. For believers are what God has made them, created in Christ Jesus for good works, which God prepared beforehand to be their way of life (Eph. 2:10). In the cause of Christ it is graciously given them not only to believe in him, but also to suffer for him (Acts 5:41; Phil. 1:29). God crowns his own work, not only in conferring eternal life on everyone who believes but also in distributing different degrees of glory to those who, motivated by that faith, have produced good works.

His purpose in doing this, however, is that on earth as in heaven, there would be profuse diversity in the believing community, and that in such diversity the glory of his attributes would be manifest. Indeed, as a result of this diversity, the life of fellowship with God and with the angels, and of the blessed among themselves, gains in depth and intimacy. In that fellowship everyone has a place and task of one's own, based on personality and character, just as this is the case in the believing community on earth (Rom. 12:4–8; 1 Cor. 12). While we may not be able to form a clear picture of the activity of the blessed, Scripture does teach that the prophetic, priestly, and royal office, which was humanity's original possession, is fully restored in them by Christ. The service of God, mutual communion, and inhabiting the new heaven and the new earth undoubtedly offer abundant opportunity for the exercise of these offices, even though the form and manner of this exercise are unknown to us. That activity, however, coincides with resting and enjoying. The difference between day and night, between the Sabbath and the workdays, has been suspended. Time is charged with the eternity of God. Space is full of his presence. Eternal becoming is wedded to immutable being. Even the contrast between heaven and earth is gone. For all the things that are in heaven and on earth have been gathered up in Christ as head (Eph. 1:10). All creatures will then live and move and have their being in God (Acts 17:28), who is all in all (1 Cor. 15:28), who reflects all his attributes in the mirror of his works, and glorifies himself in them.

Scripture Index

11:19 742
12 77, 365, 389, 422
12:1–14 740
12:5 740
12:7 278, 282, 377
12:7–11 740
12:9 342, 377, 377n15, 389
12:10 221, 305, 307, 377n15,
389, 460
12:10–11 422
12:11 389
12:12 740
12:14–15 342, 389
12:17 744
13:1 740
13:1–10 740
13:3 740
13:8 247, 261, 267, 271, 398
13:11–18 740
13:12 740
13:13–15 75, 390, 711
13:18 740
14:1 77
14:1–5 739, 742
14:2 77
14:7 263
14:10 207, 281
14:10–11 758
14:11 757, 761
14:13 223, 701, 711, 743, 775
14:14 457, 748
14:18 742
15:1 278
15:1–4 739
15:2 701
15:3 185
15:4 307
15:7 189, 196
16:7 185, 742
16:15 747
16:17 701
16:19 207
17–18 740
17–21 725
17:5 143n59
17:7 143n59
17:8 267, 702, 740, 758
17:10–11 740

17:11 758
17:14 467, 618
18 740
18:1 283
18:8 386
18:20 742
19 743, 744
19–21 406
19:1 77, 213, 772
19:1–8 740, 742
19:5 185
19:6 305, 772
19:7 598
19:8 770
19:10 79, 284, 712
19:11 748
19:11–16 457, 740
19:11–21 755, 756
19:12 451
19:14 278, 748
19:15 207
19:16 213, 451
19:19–21 740
19:20 390, 702, 744, 757
19:21 744
20 741, 742, 743, 744
20:1 625, 702, 742
20:1–3 740
20:1–10 740
20:2 342, 377n15, 389, 460
20:3 657, 702
20:4 742, 756
20:4–5 743
20:4–6 756
20:6 620, 756, 758, 770
20:7 757
20:7–10 756
20:8 744
20:9 744
20:10 389, 702, 744, 757, 758,
761
20:11–12 754–55
20:11–13 750
20:11–15 744
20:12 247, 755, 776
20:12–13 700, 750
20:13 701, 702, 751

20:14 388, 460, 707, 743, 757,
770
20:14–15 757, 758
20:15 757, 758, 775
21 742
21–22 78, 465n25, 769
21:1 427, 766, 768
21:2 598, 742
21:2–4 598, 768
21:3 76, 77, 185, 192, 672, 730,
768, 769, 770
21:4 386, 388, 770
21:5 427
21:6 185, 269, 769
21:8 75, 702, 711, 757, 758
21:10 77, 191, 742
21:11 769
21:12 730, 769, 775
21:14 608, 616, 775
21:18–21 769
21:22 169, 185, 769
21:23 169, 190, 216
21:24 769, 772, 775
21:26 769, 772, 775
21:27 77, 247, 768, 770, 775
22 520
22:1 457
22:1–2 769
22:2 341, 701, 769, 772
22:3 770, 775
22:3–4 768
22:4 76, 77, 168, 770
22:5 185, 213, 216, 742, 744,
775
22:6 75n36, 269
22:7 746
22:8 77
22:9 284, 712
22:10 657, 746
22:11 564
22:12 746, 754, 755, 776
22:13 149, 185
22:15 75, 77, 711, 757, 769, 775
22:16 75n36, 169
22:17 223, 422, 718
22:18–19 94
22:19 247
22:20 422, 746

Name Index

Innocent III (pope) 151, 541n48
Irenaeus 11n19, 33n9, 33n10, 34, 57n18, 94, 95n6,
    96n7, 96n8, 97, 173n1, 199n67, 224, 236n34,
    240n50, 268n20, 269n23, 273n42, 284n71,
    319n17, 427, 592n13, 592n14, 592n17,
    614n90, 617, 617n100, 670n52, 680n73, 727
Isenkrahe, C. 720n1
Isidore of Seville 39, 96n7, 196n58

Jackson, G. 537n38
Jacobi, Friedrich H. 42, 43, 64, 172, 174
James, M. R. 741n15
James, William 501, 546n60
Jansen, Cornelius 41
Jansen, G. M. 151n9, 628n116
Jellinhaus, Theodor 578n76
Jeremias, A. 71n25
Jeremias, J. 670n51
Jerome 36, 37, 39, 96, 97, 197n58
Joachim of Fiore 240, 264
John of Damascus 35, 138n48, 177, 178n16,
    186, 235n30, 235n33, 236n35, 237n38, 239,
    239n48, 279n60, 289n78, 329n34, 373n8,
    427n8, 461n15, 680n74, 681n75
John Paul II (pope) 42n21, 596n31
Jones, John Cynddylan 363n49
Josephus 699n7, 700n8, 700n9
Jovian 775
Julian (the Apostate; Roman emperor) 31n5, 99
Julian of Eclanum 38n19
Julius Caesar 403
Jung-Stilling, J. H. 705n23, 710, 759–60
Junius, Franciscus 99n18, 687n93, 773, 773n24
Justin Martyr 11n18, 68, 68n15, 72, 94n3, 113n2,
    120n15, 149, 149n3, 241, 427, 511n7, 592n12,
    668n48, 680n73

Kaftan, Julius 8, 43, 100–101, 101n24, 101n25,
    138n50, 138n51, 252n92, 375n10, 381n22,
    431, 513n17
Kahl, W. 383n25
Kähler, M. 215n99
Kahnis, F. A. 411n28
Kalb, E. 486n37
Kampschulte, F. W. 484n29, 638n138, 686n90
Kant, Immanuel 25, 43, 43n22, 50, 64, 69, 83n49,
    115, 118, 120–22, 121n16, 121n19, 122n21,
    122n23, 130–31, 130n37, 152–53, 152n13,
    154, 160, 163, 164, 164n43, 178, 190, 190n37,
    192, 230, 242, 271, 275, 319n19, 335, 347, 359,
    367n58, 383, 409n21, 416, 420n42, 486, 487,
    488, 512, 6, 12, 710, 721
Kattenbusch, F. 595n29, 652n15, 653n18, 665n42

Kawerau, G. 673n62
Keerl, P. F. 292
Keil, C. F. 732n10
Keim, T. 456n6
Kellner, K. A. 31n4
Kiefl, F. X. 765n12
Kittel, R. 384n28
Kleutgen, Joseph 159n33, 271n29, 304n125, 420n40
Kliefoth, Th. 732n10
Kluge, F. 181n23
Klutgen, Joseph 195n50
Knieschke, W. 474n3
Knox, John 45
Koelman, Jac. 530n18
Koeppel, W. 95n5
Kolde, T. 486n37
Kölling, Wilhelm 97n11
Konig, Adrio 746n17
Köstlin, Julius 98n14, 128n30, 138n49, 151n9,
    159n35, 181n23, 207n83, 243n67, 284n74,
    332n41, 358n39, 615n97, 628n121, 629n125,
    654n19, 659n31, 670n56, 689n98, 731n10
Kromsigt, J. C. 530n19
Krug, Heinrich 216n103
Kuenen, A. 91n1, 732n11
Kuyper, Abraham 20n27, 99n18, 171n51, 195n47,
    218n4, 223n8, 243n67, 266n14, 269n25,
    419n38, 419n39, 469n29, 622n109, 635n133,
    667, 667n45, 722n4, 732n10
Kuyper, Herman H. 264n2

Labadie, Jean de 595
Lacassagne, Alexandre 381
Lactantius, Lucius C. 3n1, 33, 35, 53, 53n12, 59,
    59n21, 149n4, 207n82, 275, 275n51, 727
Ladd, G. T. 71n26
Laidlaw, J. 351n21
Lake, Kirsopp 456n6
Lamennais, F. R. de 352n26
Lampe, F. A. 530n18
Lange, F. A. 265n12, 290n85
Lange, Johann Peter 241n59, 243n67, 330n35
La Peyrère, Isaac de 315n11
La Rochefoucauld, François de 367
Lasco, John à 511n7
Lauvergne 388n38
Lechler, G. V. 638n139
Lehmann, E. 483n27, 722n5
Leibniz, Gottfried Wilhelm 41, 50, 83n49, 160,
    243n67, 705n23
Lemme, L. 582n84
Leo I (pope) 614

Subject Index

Abraham, offspring of 731, 735
absolute power 213
absolute rule 260
absolutism 603
accommodation 83, 167–72
acquired theology 140
active obedience 716
actual faith 535, 542
ad extra works 26, 79, 223, 239–40, 245–46, 253, 299
adiaphora 668, 675
ad intra works 246, 253, 299
adoption 136, 185, 566, 568–69
adoptionism 39, 228
adoration 147
Adventists 728, 760n7
affections 58–59
age to come 737–38, 749, 761, 770, 775
agnosticism 18, 43, 108, 152, 153, 154–55, 156
Albigensians 594
alcohol 47
Alexandrian theologians 34
allegorical exegesis 32, 34, 36
allegory 83, 292
"all Israel" 735–37
Alpha and Omega 186
Amyraldianism 45, 498
Anabaptists
  on baptism 510, 666, 671
  chiliasm of 727
  Christology of 270, 415–16, 452
  on church discipline 630
  on civil government 631, 632

and covenant theology 396
dualism of 595
on free will 319
on order of salvation 498
on original sin 355, 356
and pantheism 264, 650
on penitence 482
on Reformed faith 45
on regeneration 515
on revelation 88
and sanctification 576
on soul sleep 705
on synods 639
on theology 138
analogical knowledge 171, 172, 179, 180
analogy 161, 178, 196–97, 236
angel of the Lord 218
angels 75, 184, 380, 599, 756
  fall of 342, 350, 377, 393
  and image of God 337
  ministry of 281–85
  in Scripture 277–81
  and spiritual world 275–77
  veneration of 284–85
Anglicans 615–16
  on baptism 671
  on Lord's Supper 686
animals 696
animism 71
annihilation 209, 705, 706, 759
anonymous 179
anthropological argument (immortality) 696
anthropology 66, 117, 314

831

teaching 633
teaching church 593, 600, 612, 613
teleological argument 163, 164–65
telepathy 74, 85
temple, restoration of 723
tetragrammaton 182–83
theism 167, 179, 212, 252, 265
theistic worldview 84–85
theocracy 185
  Israel as 624
theogony 240, 244, 264, 265, 270
theologia symbolica 171
theological ethics 10–11
theology 19
  and faith 13, 137–43
  foundations of 50
  organization of 20–28
  and philosophy 140
  as science 8–13, 14
theophany 74, 75–76, 81, 218
theosophy 74, 153, 196, 230, 243, 264, 292, 351, 709
Third Lateran Council (1179) 653
Thirty-nine Articles 47
Thomism 42
thousand years 740–41, 744
threefold use of the law 649
time 188–91, 253, 271–72, 291
  in age to come 777
  of creation 287
  fullness of 746
times of refreshing 734–35
tobacco 47
Torah 91, 96
totemism 424
tradition 15, 87
  and Scripture 12
traducianism 336–38, 363
transcendence 192
transformation, doctrine of 680–81
transmigration of souls 714
transubstantiation 680–82
tribulation 742
trinitarian dogma 33
Trinity 61, 101, 116, 142, 181, 186, 197
  analogies for 241–44
  confession of 232
  and covenant of redemption 397–99
  and creation 267–71
  distinction within 225, 234–39
  dogma of 223, 224–27
  economic 239–41, 269

and incarnation 412
language of 230–34
ontological 225, 230, 239, 240
relation among 220
in Scripture 217–23
and simplicity 195
speculation on 244–45
unity in 225
and way of salvation 495–503
triplicity 242
tritheism 155, 232
true religion 400
trust 127
truth 7, 133, 194, 202–4, 730
Tübingen 408–9, 453
two aeons 737–38
typology 404–5

Unam Sanctum 615
unbelief 84, 156, 275, 362, 369, 380, 505, 624
unbelievers and the church 599–600
ungodly, punishment of 719
unilateral 395
uninformed faith 527
union with Christ 683, 687, 745
union with God 82
Unitarianism 35, 229
universal atonement 439, 463
universal consent, argument from 166
universalism 45, 461, 464, 505, 705, 762, 772
  hypothetical 706, 759
  unconditional 759–60
universality of religion 156–57
universals and realism 51–53
unknowability. *See* God: incomprehensibility of
utopianism 355

Vatican I. *See* First Vatican Council
Vedic religion 424
veneration
  of angels 284–85
  of the dead 709–10, 717
venial sins versus mortal 378–79
verbal inspiration 97
vicarious atonement 101, 142, 429, 442–43, 444
virgin birth 414–15
visible church 594–95, 600–601
visio dei 82
vivification 543–47
vocation 441, 621
volition 208
voodoo 74